MISCELLANIES

BY

WILLIAM M. THACKERAY.

IV.

THE FOUR GEORGES, THE ENGLISH HUMORISTS, ROUNDABOUT PAPERS, ETC., ETC.

HOUSEHOLD EDITION.

Illustrated.

NEW YORK:
HARPER & BROTHERS, PUBLISHERS,
FRANKLIN SQUARE.
1877.

CONTENTS.

THE FOUR GEORGES: SKETCHES OF MANNERS, MORALS, COURT, AND TOWN LIFE.

THE ENGLISH HUMORISTS OF THE EIGHTEENTH CENTURY.

ROUNDABOUT PAPERS.

THE SECOND FUNERAL OF NAPOLEON.

LITTLE TRAVELS AND ROADSIDE SKETCHES.

THE FITZ-BOODLE PAPERS.

CRITICAL REVIEWS.

LIST OF ILLUSTRATIONS.

THE FOUR GEORGES.

THE ENGLISH HUMORISTS.

ROUNDABOUT PAPERS.

THE FOUR GEORGES:

SKETCHES OF MANNERS, MORALS, COURT, AND TOWN LIFE.

George the First.

GEORGE THE FIRST.

A VERY few years since, I knew familiarly a lady, who had been asked in marriage by Horace Walpole, who had been patted on the head by George I. This lady had knocked at Dr. Johnson's door; had been intimate with Fox, the beautiful Georgina of Devonshire, and that brilliant Whig society of the reign of George III.; had known the Duchess of Queensberry, the patroness of Gay and Prior, the admired young beauty of the court of Queen Anne. I often thought as I took my kind old friend's hand, how with it I held on to the old society of wits and men of the world. I could travel back for seven score years of time — have glimpses of Brummell, Selwyn, Chesterfield, and the men of pleasure; of Walpole and Conway; of Johnson, Reynolds, Goldsmith; of North, Chatham, Newcastle; of the fair maids of honor of George II.'s court; of the German retainers of George I.'s; where Addison was secretary of state; where Dick Steele held a place; whither the great Marlborough came with his fiery spouse; when Pope, and Swift, and Bolingbroke yet lived and wrote. Of a society so vast, busy, brilliant, it is impossible in four brief chapters to give a complete notion; but we may peep here and there into that bygone world of the Georges, see what they and their courts were like; glance at the people round about them; look at past manners, fashions, pleasures, and contrast them with our own. I have to say thus much by way of preface, because the subject of these lectures has been misunderstood, and I have been taken to task for not having given grave historical treatises, which it never was my intention to attempt. Not about battles, about politics, about statesmen and measures of state, did I ever think to lecture you: but to sketch the manners and life of the old world; to amuse for a few hours with talk about the old society; and, with the result of many a day's and night's pleasant reading, to try and while away a few winter evenings for my hearers.

Among the German princes who sat under Luther at Wittenberg, was Duke Ernest of Celle, whose younger son, William of Lüneburg, was the progenitor of the illustrious Hanoverian house at present reigning in Great Britain. Duke William held his court at Celle, a little town of ten thousand people that lies on the railway line between Hamburg and Hanover, in the midst of great plains of sand, upon the river Aller. When Duke William had it, it was a very humble wood-built place, with a great brick church, which he sedulously frequented, and in which he and others of his house lie buried. He was a very religious lord, and was called William the Pious by his small circle of subjects, over whom he ruled till fate deprived him both of sight and reason. Sometimes, in his latter days, the good Duke had glimpses of mental light, when he would bid his musicians play the psalm-tunes which he loved. One thinks of a descendant of his, two hundred years afterwards, blind, old, and lost of wits, singing Handel in Windsor Tower.

William the Pious had fifteen children, eight daughters and seven sons, who, as the property left among them was small, drew lots to determine which one of them should marry, and continue the stout race of the Guelphs. The lot fell on Duke George, the sixth brother. The others remained single, or contracted left-handed marriages after the princely fashion of those days. It is a queer picture — that of the old Prince dying in his little wood-built capital, and his seven sons tossing up which should inherit and transmit the crown of Brentford. Duke George, the lucky prizeman, made the tour of Europe, during which he visited the court of Queen Elizabeth; and in the year 1617, came back and settled at Zell, with a wife out of Darmstadt. His remaining brothers all kept their house at Zell, for economy's sake. And presently, in due course, they all died — all the honest Dukes; Ernest, and Christian, and Augustus, and Magnus, and George, and John — and they are buried in the brick church of Brentford yonder, by the sandy banks of the Aller.

Dr. Vehse gives a pleasant glimpse of the way of life of our Dukes in Zell. "When the trumpeter on the tower has blown," Duke Christian orders — viz. at nine o'clock in the morning, and four in the evening — every one must be present at meals, and those who are not must go without. None of the servants, unless it be a knave who has been ordered to ride out, shall eat or drink in the kitchen or cellar; or, without special leave, fodder his horses at the Prince's cost. When the meal is served in the court-room, a page shall go round and bid every one be quiet and orderly, forbidding all cursing, swearing, and rudeness; all throwing about of bread, bones, or roast, or pocketing of the same. Every morning, at seven, the squires shall have their morning soup, along with which, and dinner, they shall be served with their under-drink — every morning, except Friday morning, when there was sermon, and no drink. Every evening they shall have their beer, and at night their sleep-drink. The butler is especially warned not to allow noble or simple to go into the cellar: wine shall only be served at the Prince's or councillors' table; and every Monday, the honest old Duke Christian ordains the accounts shall be ready, and the expenses in the kitchen, the wine and beer cellar, the bakehouse and stable, made out.

Duke George, the marrying Duke, did not stop at home to partake of the beer and wine, and the sermons. He went about fighting wherever there was profit to be had. He served as general in the army of the circle of Lower Saxony, the Protestant army; then he went over to the Emperor, and fought in his armies in Germany and Italy; and when Gustavus Adolphus appeared in Germany, George took service as a Swedish general, and seized the Abbey of Hildesheim, as his share of the plunder. Here, in the year 1641, Duke George died, leaving four sons behind him, from the youngest of whom descend our royal Georges.

Under these children of Duke George, the old God-fearing, simple ways of Zell appear to have gone out of mode. The second brother was constantly visiting Venice, and leading a jolly, wicked life there. It was the most jovial of all places at the end of the seventeenth century; and military men, after a campaign, rushed thither, as the warriors of the Allies rushed to Paris in 1814, to gamble, and rejoice, and partake of all sorts of godless delights. This Prince, then, loving Venice and its pleasures, brought Italian singers and dancers back with him to quiet old Zell; and, worse still, demeaned himself by marrying a French lady of birth quite inferior to his own — Eleanor d'Olbreuse, from whom our Queen is descended. Eleanor had a pretty daughter, who inherited a great fortune, which inflamed her cousin, George Louis of Hanover, with a desire to marry her; and so, with her beauty and her riches, she came to a sad end.

It is too long to tell how the four sons of Duke George divided his territories amongst them, and how, finally, they came into possession of the son of the youngest of the four. In this generation the Protestant faith was very nearly extinguished in the family: and then where should we in England have gone for a king? The third brother also took delight in Italy, where the priests converted him and his Protestant chaplain too. Mass was said in Hanover once more; and Italian soprani piped their Latin rhymes in place of the hymns which William the Pious and Dr. Luther sang. Louis XIV. gave this and other converts a splendid pension. Crowds of Frenchmen and brilliant French fashions came into his court. It is incalculable how much that royal bigwig cost Germany. Every prince imitated the French King, and had his Versailles, his Wilhelmshöhe or Ludwigslust; his court and its splendors; his gardens laid out with statues; his fountains, and water-works, and Tritons; his actors, and dancers, and singers, and fiddlers; his harem, with its inhabitants; his diamonds and duchies for these latter; his enormous festivities, his gaming-tables, tournaments, masquerades, and banquets lasting a week long, for which the people paid with their money, when the poor wretches had it; with their bodies and very blood when they had none; being sold in thousands by their lords and masters, who gayly dealt in soldiers, staked a regiment upon the red at the gambling-table; swapped a battalion against a dancing-girl's diamond necklace; and, as it were, pocketed their people.

As one views Europe, through contemporary books of travel in the early part of the last century, the landscape is awful — wretched wastes, beggarly and plundered; half-burned cottages and trembling peasants gathering piteous harvests; gangs of such tramping along with bayonets behind them, and corporals with canes and cats-of-nine-tails to flog them to barracks. By these passes my lord's gilt carriage floundering through the ruts, as he swears at the postilions, and toils on to the Residenz. Hard by, but away from the noise and brawling of the citizens and buyers, is Wilhelmslust or Ludwigsruhe, or Monbijou, or Versailles — it scarcely matters which, — near to the city, shut out by woods from the beggared country, the enormous, hideous, gilded, monstrous marble palace, where the Prince is, and the Court, and the trim gardens, and huge fountains, and the forest where the ragged peasants are beating the game in (it is death to them to touch a feather); and the jolly hunt sweeps by with its uniform of crimson and gold; and the Prince gallops ahead puffing his royal horn; and his lords and mistresses ride after him; and the stag is pulled down; and the grand huntsman gives the knife in the midst of a chorus of bugles; and 'tis time the Court go home to dinner; and our noble traveller, it may be the Baron of Pöllnitz, or the Count de Königsmarck, or the excellent Chevalier de Seingalt, sees the procession gleaming through the trim avenues of the wood, and hastens to the inn, and sends his noble name to the marshal of the Court. Then our nobleman arrays himself in green and gold, or pink and silver, in the richest Paris mode, and is introduced by the chamberlain, and makes his bow to the jolly Prince, and the gracious Princess; and is presented to the chief lords and ladies, and then comes supper and a bank at Faro, where he loses or wins a thousand pieces by daylight. If it is a German court, you may add not a little drunkenness to this picture of high life; but German, or French, or Spanish, if you can see out of your palace-windows beyond the trim-cut forest vistas, misery is lying outside; hunger is stalking about the bare villages, listlessly following precarious husbandry; ploughing stony fields with starved cattle; or fearfully taking in scanty harvests. Augustus is fat and jolly on his throne; he can knock down an ox, and eat one almost; his mistress, Aurora von Königsmarck, is the loveliest, the wittiest creature; his diamonds are the biggest and most brilliant in the world, and his feasts as splendid as those of Versailles. As for Louis the Great, he is more than mortal. Lift up your glances respectfully, and mark him eying Madame de Fontanges or Madame de Montespan from under his sublime periwig, as he passes through the great gallery where Villars and Vendôme, and Berwick, and Bossuet, and Massillon are waiting. Can Court be more splendid; nobles and knights more gallant and superb; ladies more lovely? A grander monarch, or a more miserable starved wretch than the peasant his subject, you cannot look on. Let us bear both these types in mind, if we wish to estimate the old society properly. Remember the glory and the chivalry? Yes! Remember the grace and beauty, the splendor and lofty politeness; the gallant courtesy of Fontenoy, where the French line bids the gentlemen of the English guard to fire first; the noble constancy of the old King and Villars his general, who fits out the last army with the last crown-piece from the treasury, and goes to meet the enemy and die or conquer for France at Denain. But round all that royal splendor lies a nation enslaved and ruined: there are people robbed of their rights — communities laid waste — faith, justice, commerce trampled upon, and well-nigh destroyed — nay, in the very centre of royalty itself, what horrible stains and meanness, crime and shame! It is but to a silly harlot that some of the noblest gentlemen, and some of the proudest women in the world, are bowing down; it is the price of a miserable province that the King ties in diamonds round his mistress's white neck. In the first half of the last century, I say, this is going on all Europe over. Saxony is a waste as well as Picardy or Artois; and Versailles is only larger and not worse than Herrenhausen.

It was the first Elector of Hanover who made the fortunate match which bestowed the race of Hanoverian Sovereigns upon us Britons. Nine years after Charles Stuart lost his head, his niece Sophia, one of many children of another luckless dethroned sovereign, the Elector Palatine, married Ernest Augustus of Brunswick, and brought the reversion to the crown of the three kingdoms in her scanty trousseau.

One of the handsomest, the most cheerful, sensible, shrewd, accomplished of women, was Sophia, daughter of poor Frederick, the winter king of Bohemia. The other daughters of lovely, unhappy Elizabeth Stuart went off into the Catholic Church; this one, luckily for her family, remained, I cannot say faithful to the Reformed Religion, but at least she adopted no other. An agent of the French King's, Gourville, a convert himself, strove to bring her and her husband to a sense of the truth; and tells us that he one day asked Madame the Duchess of Hanover, of what religion her daughter was, then a pretty girl of thirteen years old. The duchess replied that the princess *was of no religion as yet*. They were waiting to know of what religion her husband would be, Protestant or Catholic, before instructing her! And the Duke of Hanover having heard all

Gourville's proposal, said that a change would be advantageous to his house, but that he himself was too old to change.

This shrewd woman had such keen eyes that she knew how to shut them upon occasion, and was blind to many faults which it appeared that her husband the Bishop of Osnaburg and Duke of Hanover committed. He loved to take his pleasure like other sovereigns — was a merry prince, fond of dinner and the bottle; liked to go to Italy, as his brothers had done before him; and we read how he jovially sold 6,700 of his Hanoverians to the seigniory of Venice. They went bravely off to the Morea, under command of Ernest's son, Prince Max, and only 1,400 of them ever came home again. The German princes sold a good deal of this kind of stock. You may remember how George III.'s Government purchased Hessians, and the use we made of them during the War of Independence.

The ducats Duke Ernest got for his soldiers he spent in a series of the most brilliant entertainments. Nevertheless, the jovial Prince was economical, and kept a steady eye upon his own interests. He achieved the electoral dignity for himself: he married his eldest son George to his beautiful cousin of Zell; and sending his sons out in command of armies to fight — now on this side, now on that — he lived on, taking his pleasure, and scheming his schemes, a merry, wise prince enough, not, I fear, a moral prince, of which kind we shall have but very few specimens in the course of these lectures.

Ernest Augustus had seven children in all, some of whom were scapegraces, and rebelled against the parental system of primogeniture and non-division of property which the Elector ordained. "Gustchen," the Electress writes about her second son: — "Poor Gus is thrust out, and his father will give him no more keep. I laugh in the day and cry all night about it; for I am a fool with my children." Three of the six died fighting against Turks, Tartars, Frenchmen. One of them conspired, revolted, fled to Rome, leaving an agent behind him, whose head was taken off. The daughter, of whose early education we have made mention, was married to the Elector of Brandenburg, and so her religion settled finally on the Protestant side.

A niece of the Electress Sophia — who had been made to change her religion, and marry the Duke of Orleans, brother of the French King; a woman whose honest heart was always with her friends and dear old Deutschland, though her fat little body was confined at Paris, or Marly, or Versailles — has left us, in her enormous correspondence (part of which has been printed in German and French), recollections of the Electress, and of George her son. Elizabeth Charlotte was at Osnaburg when George was born (1660). She narrowly escaped a whipping for being in the way on that auspicious day. She seems not to have liked little George, nor George grown up; and represents him as odiously hard, cold, and silent. Silent he may have been; not a jolly prince like his father before him, but a prudent, quiet, selfish potentate, going his own way, managing his own affairs, and understanding his own interests remarkably well.

In his father's lifetime, and at the head of the Hanover forces of 8,000 or 10,000 men, George served the Emperor, on the Danube against Turks, at the siege of Vienna, in Italy, and on the Rhine. When he succeeded to the Electorate, he handled its affairs with great prudence and dexterity. He was very much liked by his people of Hanover. He did not show his feelings much, but he cried heartily on leaving them; as they used for joy when he came back. He showed an uncommon prudence and coolness of behavior when he came into his kingdom; exhibiting no elation; reasonably doubtful whether he should not be turned out some day; looking upon himself only as a lodger, and making the most of his brief tenure of St. James's and Hampton Court; plundering, it is true, somewhat, and dividing amongst his German followers; but what could be expected of a sovereign who at home could sell his subjects at so many ducats per head, and make no scruple in so disposing of them? I fancy a considerable shrewdness, prudence, and even moderation in his ways. The German Protestant was a cheaper, and better, and kinder king than the Catholic Stuart in whose chair he sat, and so far loyal to England, that he let England govern herself.

Having these lectures in view, I made it my business to visit that ugly cradle in which our Georges were nursed. The old town of Hanover must look still pretty much as in the time when George Louis left it. The gardens and pavilions of Herrenhausen are scarce changed since the day when the stout old Electress Sophia fell down in her last walk there, preceding but by a few weeks to the tomb James II.'s daughter, whose death made way for the Brunswick Stuarts in England.

The two first royal Georges, and their father, Ernest Augustus, had quite royal notions regarding marriage; and Louis XIV. and Charles II. scarce distinguished themselves more at Versailles or St. James's, than these German sultans in their little city on the banks of the Leine. You may see at Herrenhausen the very rustic theatre in which the Platens danced and performed masques, and sang before the Elector and his sons. There are the very fauns and dryads of stone still glimmering through the branches, still grinning and piping their ditties of no tone, as in the days when painted nymphs hung garlands round them; appeared under their leafy arcades with gilt crooks, guiding rams with gilt horns; descended from "machines" in the guise of Diana or Minerva; and delivered immense allegorical compliments to the princes returned home from the campaign.

That was a curious state of morals and politics in Europe; a queer consequence of the triumph of the monarchical principle. Feudalism was beaten down. The nobility, in its quarrels with the crown, had pretty well succumbed, and the monarch was all in all. He became almost divine: the proudest and most ancient gentry of the land did menial service for him. Who should carry Louis XIV.'s candle when he went to bed? what prince of the blood should hold the king's shirt when his Most Christian Majesty changed that garment? — the French memoirs of the seventeenth century are full of such details and squabbles. The tradition is not yet extinct in Europe. Any of you who were present, as myriads were, at that splendid pageant, the opening of our Crystal Palace in London, must have seen two noble lords, great officers of the household, with ancient pedigrees, with embroidered coats, and stars on their breasts and wands in their hands, walking backwards for near the space of a mile, while the royal procession made its progress. Shall we wonder — shall we be angry — shall we laugh at these old-world ceremonies? View them as you will, according to your mood; and with scorn or with respect, or with anger and sorrow, as your temper leads you. Up goes Gesler's hat upon the pole. Salute that symbol of sovereignty with heartfelt awe; or with a sulky shrug of acquiescence, or with a grinning obeisance; or with a stout rebellious No — clap your own beaver down on your pate, and refuse to doff it to that spangled velvet and flaunting feather. I make no comment upon the spectators' behavior; all I say is, that Gesler's cap is still up in the market-place of Europe, and not a few folks are still kneeling to it.

Put clumsy, high Dutch statues in place of the marbles of Versailles:

fancy Herrenhausen waterworks in place of those of Marly: spread the tables with Schweinskopf, Specksuppe, Leberkuchen, and the like delicacies, in place of the French *cuisine;* and fancy Frau von Kielmansegge dancing with Count Kammerjunker Quirini, or singing French songs with the most awful German accent: imagine a coarse Versailles, and we have a Hanover before us. "I am now got into the region of beauty," writes Mary Wortley, from Hanover in 1716; "all the women have literally rosy cheeks, snowy foreheads and necks, jet eye-brows, to which may generally be added coal-black hair. These perfections never leave them to the day of their death, and have a very fine effect by candle-light; but I could wish they were handsome with a little variety. They resemble one another as Mrs. Salmon's Court of Great Britain, and are in as much danger of melting away by too nearly approaching the fire." The sly Mary Wortley saw this painted seraglio of the first George at Hanover, the year after his accession to the British throne. There were great doings and feasts there. Here Lady Mary saw George II. too. "I can tell you, without flattery or partiality," she says, "that our young prince has all the accomplishments that it is possible to have at his age, with an air of sprightliness and understanding, and a something so very engaging in his behavior that needs not the advantage of his rank to appear charming." I find elsewhere similar panegyrics upon Frederick Prince of Wales, George II.'s son; and upon George III., of course, and upon George IV. in an eminent degree. It was the rule to be dazzled by princes, and people's eyes winked quite honestly at that royal radiance.

The Electoral Court of Hanover was numerous — pretty well paid, as times went; above all, paid with a regularity which few other European courts could boast of. Perhaps you will be amused to know how the Electoral Court was composed. There were the princes of the house in the first class; in the second, the single field-marshal of the army (the contingent was 18,000, Pöllnitz says, and the Elector had other 14,000 troops in his pay). Then follow, in due order, the authorities civil and military, the working privy councillors, the generals of cavalry and infantry, in the third class; the high chamberlain, high marshals of the court, high masters of the horse, the major-generals of cavalry and infantry, in the fourth class; down to the majors, the hofjunkers or pages, the secretaries or assessors, of the tenth class, of whom all were noble.

We find the master of the horse had 1,090 thalers of pay; the high chamberlain, 2,000 — a thaler being about three shillings of our money. There were two chamberlains, and one for the Princess; five gentlemen of the chamber, and five gentlemen ushers; eleven pages and personages to educate these young noblemen — such as a governor, a preceptor, a fecht-meister, or fencing master, and a dancing ditto, this latter with a handsome salary of 400 thalers. There were three body and court physicians, with 800 and 500 thalers; a court barber, 600 thalers; a court organist; two musikanten; four French fiddlers; twelve trumpeters, and a bugler; so that there was plenty of music, profane and pious, in Hanover. There were ten chamber waiters, and twenty-four lackeys in livery; a maïtre-d'hôtel, and attendants of the kitchen; a French cook; a body cook; ten cooks; six cooks' assistants; two Braten masters, or masters of the roast — (one fancies enormous spits turning slowly, and the honest masters of the roast beladling the dripping); a pastry-baker; a pie-baker; and finally, three scullions, at the modest remuneration of eleven thalers. In the sugar-chamber there were four pastry-cooks (for the ladies, no doubt); seven officers in the wine and beer cellars; four bread-bakers;

and five men in the plate-room. There were 600 horses in the Serene stables — no less than twenty teams of princely carriage horses, eight to a team; sixteen coachmen; fourteen postilions; nineteen ostlers; thirteen helps, besides smiths, carriage-masters, horse-doctors, and other attendants of the stable. The female attendants were not so numerous: I grieve to find but a dozen or fourteen of them about the Electoral premises, and only two washerwomen for all the Court. These functionaries had not so much to do as in the present age. I own to finding a pleasure in these small-beer chronicles. I like to people the old world, with its every-day figures and inhabitants — not so much with heroes fighting immense battles and inspiring repulsed battalions to engage; or statesmen locked up in darkling cabinets and meditating ponderous laws or dire conspiracies — as with people occupied with their every-day work or pleasure: my lord and lady hunting in the forest, or dancing in the Court, or bowing to their Serene Highnesses as they pass in to dinner; John Cook and his procession bringing the meal from the kitchen; the jolly butlers bearing in the flagons from the cellar; the stout coachman driving the ponderous gilt wagon, with eight cream-colored horses in housings of scarlet velvet and morocco leather; a postilion on the leaders, and a pair or a half-dozen of running footmen scudding along by the side of the vehicle, with conical caps, long silver-headed maces, which they poised as they ran, and splendid jackets laced all over with silver and gold. I fancy the citizens' wives and their daughters looking out from the balconies; and the burghers over their beer and mumm, rising up, cap in hand, as the cavalcade passes through the town with torch-bearers, trumpeters blowing their lusty cheeks out, and squadrons of jack-booted lifeguardsmen, girt with shining cuirasses, and bestriding thundering chargers, escorting his Highness's coach from Hanover to Herrenhausen; or halting, mayhap, at Madame Platen's country house of Monplaisir, which lies half-way between the summer-palace and the Residenz.

In the good old times of which I am treating, whilst common men were driven off by herds, and sold to fight the Emperor's enemies on the Danube, or to bayonet King Louis's troops of common men on the Rhine, noblemen passed from court to court, seeking service from one prince or the other, and naturally taking command of the ignoble vulgar of soldiery which battled and died almost without hope of promotion. Noble adventurers travelled from court to court in search of employment; not merely noble males, but noble females too; and if these latter were beauties, and obtained the favorable notice of the princes, they stopped in the courts, became the favorites of their Serene or Royal Highnesses; and received great sums of money and splendid diamonds; and were promoted to be duchesses, marchionesses, and the like; and did not fall much in public esteem for the manner in which they won their advancement. In this way Mdlle. de Querouailles, a beautiful French lady, came to London on a special mission of Louis XIV., and was adopted by our grateful country and sovereign, and figured as Duchess of Portsmouth. In this way the beautiful Aurora of Königsmarck travelling about found favor in the eyes of Augustus of Saxony, and became the mother of Marshal Saxe, who gave us a beating at Fontenoy; and in this manner the lovely sisters Elizabeth and Melusina of Meissenbach (who had actually been driven out of Paris, whither they had travelled on a like errand, by the wise jealousy of the female favorite there in possession) journeyed to Hanover, and became favorites of the serene house there reigning.

That beautiful Aurora von Königsmarck and her brother are wonderful as types of bygone manners, and strange illustrations of the morals of old days. The Königsmarcks were descended from an ancient noble family of Brandenburg, a branch of which passed into Sweden, where it enriched itself and produced several mighty men of valor.

The founder of the race was Hans Christof, a famous warrior and plunderer of the Thirty Years' war. One of Hans's sons, Otto, appeared as ambassador at the court of Louis XIV., and had to make a Swedish speech at his reception before the Most Christian King. Otto was a famous dandy and warrior, but he forgot the speech, and what do you think he did? Far from being disconcerted, he recited a portion of the Swedish Catechism to his Most Christian Majesty and his court, not one of whom understood his lingo with the exception of his own suite, who had to keep their gravity as best they might.

Otto's nephew, Aurora's elder brother, Carl Johann of Königsmarck, a favorite of Charles II., a beauty, a dandy, a warrior, a rascal of more than ordinary mark, escaped but deserved being hanged in England, for the murder of Tom Thynne of Longleat. He had a little brother in London with him at this time: — as great a beauty, as great a dandy, as great a villain as his elder. This lad, Philip of Königsmarck, also was implicated in the affair; and perhaps it is a pity he ever brought his pretty neck out of it. He went over to Hanover, and was soon appointed colonel of a regiment of H. E. Highness's dragoons. In early life he had been page in the court of Celle; and it was said that he and the pretty Princess Sophia Dorothea, who by this time was married to her cousin George the Electoral Prince, had been in love with each other as children. Their loves were now to be renewed, not innocently, and to come to a fearful end.

A biography of the wife of George I., by Dr. Doran, has lately appeared, and I confess I am astounded at the verdict which that writer has delivered, and at his acquittal of this most unfortunate lady. That she had a cold selfish libertine of a husband no one can doubt; but that the bad husband had a bad wife is equally clear. She was married to her cousin for money or convenience, as all princesses were married. She was most beautiful, lively, witty, accomplished: his brutality outraged her: his silence and coldness chilled her: his cruelty insulted her. No wonder she did not love him. How could love be a part of the compact in such a marriage as that? With this unlucky heart to dispose of, the poor creature bestowed it on Philip of Königsmarck, than whom a greater scamp does not walk the history of the seventeenth century. A hundred and eighty years after the fellow was thrust into his unknown grave, a Swedish professor lights upon a box of letters in the University Library at Upsala, written by Philip and Dorothea to each other, and telling their miserable story.

The bewitching Königsmarck had conquered two female hearts in Hanover. Besides the Electoral Prince's lovely young wife Sophia Dorothea, Philip had inspired a passion in a hideous old court lady, the Countess of Platen. The princess seems to have pursued him with the fidelity of many years. Heaps of letters followed him on his campaigns, and were answered by the daring adventurer. The princess wanted to fly with him; to quit her odious husband at any rate. She besought her parents to receive her back; had a notion of taking refuge in France and going over to the Catholic religion; had absolutely packed her jewels for flight, and very likely arranged its details with her lover, in that last long night's interview, after which Philip of Königsmarck was seen no more.

Königsmarck, inflamed with drink

—there is scarcely any vice of which, according to his own showing, this gentleman was not a practitioner—had boasted at a supper at Dresden of his intimacy with the two Hanoverian ladies, not only with the princess, but with another lady powerful in Hanover. The Countess Platen, the old favorite of the Elector, hated the young Electoral Princess. The young lady had a lively wit, and constantly made fun of the old one. The Princess's jokes were conveyed to the old Platen just as our idle words are carried about at this present day: and so they both hated each other.

The characters in the tragedy, of which the curtain was now about to fall, are about as dark a set as eye ever rested on. There is the jolly Prince, shrewd, selfish, scheming, loving his cups and his ease (I think his good-humor makes the tragedy but darker); his Princess, who speaks little but observes all; his old painted Jezebel of a mistress; his son, the Electoral Prince, shrewd too, quiet, selfish, not ill-humored, and generally silent, except when goaded into fury by the intolerable tongue of his lovely wife; there is poor Sophia Dorothea, with her coquetry and her wrongs, and her passionate attachment to her scamp of a lover, and her wild imprudences, and her mad artifices, and her insane fidelity, and her furious jealousy regarding her husband (though she loathed and cheated him), and her prodigious falsehoods; and the confidante, of course, into whose hands the letters are slipped; and there is Lothario, finally, than whom, as I have said, one can't imagine a more handsome, wicked, worthless reprobate.

How that perverse fidelity of passion pursues the villain! How madly true the woman is, and how astoundingly she lies! She has bewitched two or three persons who have taken her up, and they won't believe in her wrong. Like Mary of Scotland, she finds adherents ready to conspire for her even in history, and people who have to deal with her are charmed, and fascinated, and bedevilled. How devotedly Miss Strickland has stood by Mary's innocence! Are there not scores of ladies in this audience who persist in it too? Innocent! I remember as a boy how a great party persisted in declaring Caroline of Brunswick was a martyred angel. So was Helen of Greece innocent. She never ran away with Paris, the dangerous young Trojan. Menelaus, her husband, ill-used her; and there never was any siege of Troy at all. So was Bluebeard's wife innocent. She never peeped into the closet where the other wives were with their heads off. She never dropped the key, or stained it with blood; and her brothers were quite right in finishing Bluebeard, the cowardly brute! Yes, Caroline of Brunswick was innocent; and Madame Laffarge never poisoned her husband; and Mary of Scotland never blew up hers; and poor Sophia Dorothea was never unfaithful; and Eve never took the apple—it was a cowardly fabrication of the serpent's.

George Louis has been held up to execration as a murderous Bluebeard, whereas the Electoral Prince had no share in the transaction in which Philip of Königsmarck was scuffled out of this mortal scene. The Prince was absent when the catastrophe came. The Princess had had a hundred warnings; mild hints from her husband's parents; grim remonstrances from himself—but took no more heed of this advice than such besotted poor wretches do. On the night of Sunday, the 1st of July, 1694, Königsmarck paid a long visit to the Princess, and left her to get ready for flight. Her husband was away at Berlin; her carriages and horses were prepared and ready for the elopement. Meanwhile, the spies of Countess Platen had brought the news to their mistress. She went to Ernest Augustus, and procured from the Elector an order for the arrest of the Swede. On the way by which he was to come, four guards were commissioned to take him. He strove to cut his way through the four men, and wounded more than one of them. They fell upon him; cut him down; and, as he was lying wounded on the ground, the Countess, his enemy, whom he had betrayed and insulted, came out and beheld him prostrate. He cursed her with his dying lips, and the furious woman stamped upon his mouth with her heel. He was despatched presently; his body burnt the next day; and all traces of the man disappeared. The guards who killed him were enjoined silence under severe penalties. The princess was reported to be ill in her apartments, from which she was taken in October of the same year, being then eight-and-twenty years old, and consigned to the castle of Ahlden, where she remained a prisoner for no less than thirty-two years. A separation had been pronounced previously between her and her husband. She was called henceforth the "Princess of Ahlden," and her silent husband no more uttered her name.

Four years after the Königsmarck catastrophe, Ernest Augustus, the first Elector of Hanover, died, and George Louis, his son, reigned in his stead. Sixteen years he reigned in Hanover, after which he became, as we know, King of Great Britain, France, and Ireland, Defender of the Faith. The wicked old Countess Platen died in the year 1706. She had lost her sight, but nevertheless the legend says that she constantly saw Königsmarck's ghost by her wicked old bed. And so there was an end of her.

In the year 1700, the little Duke of Gloucester, the last of poor Queen Anne's children, died, and the folks of Hanover straightway became of prodigious importance in England. The Electress Sophia was declared the next in succession to the English throne. George Louis was created Duke of Cambridge; grand deputations were sent over from our country to Deutschland; but Queen Anne, whose weak heart hankered after her relatives at St. Germains, never could be got to allow her cousin, the Elector Duke of Cambridge, to come and pay his respects to her Majesty, and take his seat in her House of Peers. Had the Queen lasted a month longer; had the English Tories been as bold and resolute as they were clever and crafty; had the Prince whom the nation loved and pitied been equal to his fortune, George Louis had never talked German in St. James's Chapel Royal.

When the crown did come to George Louis he was in no hurry about putting it on. He waited at home for awhile; took an affecting farewell of his dear Hanover and Herrenhausen; and set out in the most leisurely manner to ascend "the throne of his ancestors," as he called it in his first speech to Parliament. He brought with him a compact body of Germans, whose society he loved, and whom he kept round the royal person. He had his faithful German chamberlains; his German secretaries; his negroes, captives of his bow and spear in Turkish wars; his two ugly, elderly German favorites, Mesdames of Kielmansegge and Schulenberg, whom he created respectively Countess of Darlington and Duchess of Kendal. The Duchess was tall, and lean of stature, and hence was irreverently nicknamed the Maypole. The Countess was a large-sized noblewoman, and this elevated personage was denominated the Elephant. Both of these ladies loved Hanover and its delights; clung round the linden-trees of the great Herrenhausen avenue, and at first would not quit the place. Schulenberg, in fact, could not come on account of her debts; but finding the Maypole would not come, the Elephant packed up her trunk and slipped out of Hanover, unwieldy as she was. On this the Maypole straightway put herself in motion, and followed her beloved George Louis. One seems to be speaking of Captain Macheath, and Polly, and

Lucy. The king we had selected; the courtiers who came in his train; the English nobles who came to welcome him, and on many of whom the shrewd old cynic turned his back — I protest it is a wonderful satirical picture. I am a citizen waiting at Greenwich pier, say, and crying hurrah for King George; and yet I can scarcely keep my countenance, and help laughing at the enormous absurdity of this advent!

Here we are, all on our knees. Here is the Archbishop of Canterbury prostrating himself to the head of his church, with Kielmansegge and Schulenberg with their ruddled cheeks grinning behind the defender of the faith. Here is my Lord Duke of Marlborough kneeling too, the greatest warrior of all times; he who betrayed King William — betrayed King James II. — betrayed Queen Anne — betrayed England to the French, the Elector to the Pretender, the Pretender to the Elector; and here are my Lords Oxford and Bolingbroke, the latter of whom has just tripped up the heels of the former; and if a month's more time had been allowed him, would have had King James at Westminster. The great Whig gentlemen made their bows and congées with proper decorum and ceremony; but yonder keen old schemer knows the value of their loyalty. "Loyalty," he must think, "as applied to me — it is absurd! There are fifty nearer heirs to the throne than I am. I am but an accident, and you fine Whig gentlemen take me for your own sake, not for mine. You Tories hate me; you archbishop, smirking on your knees, and prating about Heaven, you know I don't care a fig for your Thirty-nine Articles, and can't understand a word of your stupid sermons. You, my Lords Bolingbroke and Oxford — you know you were conspiring against me a month ago; and you, my Lord Duke of Marlborough — you would sell me or any man else, if you found your advantage in it. Come, my good Melusina, come, my honest Sophia, let us go into my private room, and have some oysters and some Rhine wine, and some pipes afterwards: let us make the best of our situation; let us take what we can get, and leave these bawling, brawling, lying English to shout, and fight, and cheat, in their own way!"

If Swift had not been committed to the statesmen of the losing side, what a fine satirical picture we might have had of that general *sauve qui peut* amongst the Tory party! How mum the Tories became; how the House of Lords and House of Commons chopped round; and how decorously the majorities welcomed King George!

Bolingbroke, making his last speech in the House of Lords, pointed out the shame of the peerage, where several lords concurred to condemn in one general vote all that they had approved in former parliaments by many particular resolutions. And so their conduct was shameful. St. John had the best of the argument, but the worst of the vote. Bad times were come for him. He talked philosophy, and professed innocence. He courted retirement, and was ready to meet persecution; but, hearing that honest Mat Prior, who had been recalled from Paris, was about to preach regarding the past transactions, the philosopher bolted, and took that magnificent head of his out of the ugly reach of the axe. Oxford, the lazy and good-humored, had more courage, and awaited the storm at home. He and Mat Prior both had lodgings in the Tower, and both brought their heads safe out of that dangerous menagerie. When Atterbury was carried off to the same den a few years afterwards, and it was asked, what next should be done with him? "Done with him? Fling him to the lions," Cadogan said, Marlborough's lieutenant. But the British lion of those days did not care much for drinking the blood of peaceful peers and poets, or crunching the bones of bishops. Only four men were executed in London for the rebellion of 1715; and twenty-two in Lancashire. Above a thousand taken in arms, submitted to the King's mercy, and petitioned to be transported to his Majesty's colonies in America. I have heard that their descendants took the loyalist side in the disputes which arose sixty years after. It is pleasant to find that a friend of ours, worthy Dick Steele, was for letting off the rebels with their lives.

As one thinks of what might have been, how amusing the speculation is! We know how the doomed Scottish gentlemen came out at Lord Mar's summons, mounted the white cockade, that has been a flower of sad poetry ever since, and rallied round the ill-omened Stuart standard at Braemar. Mar, with 8,000 men, and but 1,500 opposed to him, might have driven the enemy over the Tweed, and taken possession of the whole of Scotland; but that the Pretender's Duke did not venture to move when the day was his own. Edinburgh Castle might have been in King James's hands; but that the men who were to escalade it staid to drink his health at the tavern, and arrived two hours too late at the rendezvous under the castle wall. There was sympathy enough in the town — the projected attack seems to have been known there — Lord Mahon quotes Sinclair's account of a gentleman not concerned, who told Sinclair, that he was in a house that evening where eighteen of them were drinking, as the facetious landlady said, "powdering their hair," for the attack on the castle. Suppose they had not stopped to powder their hair? Edinburgh Castle, and town, and all Scotland were King James's. The north of England rises, and marches over Barnet Heath upon London. Wyndham is up in Somersetshire; Packington in Worcestershire; and Vivian in Cornwall. The Elector of Hanover, and his hideous mistresses, pack up the plate, and perhaps the crown jewels in London, and are off *viâ* Harwich and Helvoetsluys, for dear old Deutschland. The King — God save him! — lands at Dover, with tumultuous applause; shouting multitudes, roaring cannon, the Duke of Marlborough weeping tears of joy, and all the bishops kneeling in the mud. In a few years, mass is said in St. Paul's; matins and vespers are sung in York Minster; and Dr. Swift is turned out of his stall and deanery house at St. Patrick's, to give place to Father Dominic, from Salamanca. All these changes were possible then, and once thirty years afterwards — all this we might have had, but for the *pulveris exigui jactu*, that little toss of powder for the hair which the Scotch conspirators stopped to take at the tavern.

You understand the distinction I would draw between history — of which I do not aspire to be an expounder — and manners and life such as these sketches would describe. The rebellion breaks out in the north; its story is before you in a hundred volumes, in none more fairly than in the excellent narrative of Lord Mahon. The clans are up in Scotland; Derwentwater, Nithsdale and Forster are in arms in Northumberland — these are matters of history, for which you are referred to the due chroniclers. The Guards are set to watch the streets, and prevent the people wearing white roses. I read presently of a couple of soldiers almost flogged to death for wearing oakboughs in their hats on the 29th of May — another badge of the beloved Stuarts. It is with these we have to do, rather than the marches and battles of the armies to which the poor fellows belonged — with statesmen, and how they looked, and how they lived, rather than with measures of State, which belong to history alone. For example, at the close of the old Queen's reign, it is known the Duke of Marlborough left the kingdom — after what menaces, after what prayers, lies, bribes offered, taken, refused, accepted; after what dark doubling and tacking, let history, if she can or dare, say. The Queen dead; who so eager to return as my lord duke? Who shouts God save the King! so lustily as the great conqueror of Blenheim and Malplaquet? (By the way, he will send over some more money for the Pretender yet, on the sly.) Who lays his hand on his blue ribbon, and lifts his eyes more gracefully to heaven than this hero? He makes a quasi-triumphal entrance into London, by Temple Bar, in his enormous gilt coach — and the enormous gilt coach breaks down somewhere by Chancery Lane, and his highness is obliged to get another. There it is we have him. We are with the mob in the crowd, not with the great folks in the procession. We are not the Historic Muse, but her ladyship's attendant, tale-bearer — *valet de chambre* — for whom no man is a hero; and, as yonder one steps from his carriage to the next handy conveyance, we take the number of the hack; we look all over at his stars, ribbons, embroidery; we think within ourselves, O you unfathomable schemer! O you warrior invincible! O you beautiful smiling Judas! What master would you not kiss or betray? What traitor's head, blackening on the spikes on yonder gate, ever hatched a tithe of the treason which has worked under your periwig?

We have brought our Georges to London city, and if we would behold its aspect, may see it in Hogarth's lively perspective of Cheapside, or read of it in a hundred contemporary books which paint the manners of that age. Our dear old "Spectator" looks smiling upon the streets, with their innumerable signs, and describes them with his charming humor. "Our streets are filled with Blue Boars, Black Swans, and Red Lions, not to mention Flying Pigs and Hogs in Armor, with other creatures more extraordinary than any in the deserts of Africa." A few of these quaint old figures still remain in London town. You may still see there, and over its old hostel in Ludgate Hill, the "Belle Sauvage" to whom the "Spectator" so pleasantly alludes in that paper; and who was, probably, no other than the sweet American Pocahontas, who rescued from death the daring Captain Smith. There is the "Lion's Head," down whose jaws the "Spectator's" own letters were passed; and over a great banker's in Fleet Street, the effigy of the wallet, which the founder of the firm bore when he came into London a country boy. People this street, so ornamented, with crowds of swinging chairmen, with servants bawling to clear the way, Mr. Dean in his cassock, his lackey marching before him; or Mrs. Dinah in her sack, tripping to chapel, her footboy carrying her ladyship's great prayer-book; with itinerant tradesmen, singing their hundred cries (I remember forty years ago, as boy in London city, a score of cheery, familiar cries that are silent now). Fancy the beaux thronging to the chocolate-houses, tapping their snuff-boxes as they issue thence, their periwigs appearing over the red curtains. Fancy Saccharissa, beckoning and smiling from the upper windows, and a crowd of soldiers brawling and bustling at the door — gentlemen of the Life Guards, clad in scarlet, with blue facings, and laced with gold at the seams; gentlemen of the Horse Grenadiers, in their caps of sky-blue cloth, with the garter embroidered on the front in gold and silver; men of the Halberdiers, in their long red coats, as bluff Harry left them, with their ruff and velvet flat caps. Perhaps the King's Majesty himself is going to St. James's as we pass. If he is going to Parliament, he is in his coach-and-eight, surrounded by his guards and the high officers of his crown. Otherwise his Majesty only uses a chair, with six footmen walking before, and six yeomen of the guard at the sides of the sedan. The officers in waiting follow the King in coaches. It must be rather slow work.

Our "Spectator" and "Tatler"

are full of delightful glimpses of the town life of those days. In the company of that charming guide, we may go to the opera, the comedy, the puppet-show, the auction, even the cock-pit: we can take boat at Temple Stairs, and accompany Sir Roger de Coverley and Mr. Spectator to Spring Garden — it will be called Vauxhall a few years hence, when Hogarth will paint for it. Would you not like to step back into the past, and be introduced to Mr. Addison? — not the Right Honorable Joseph Addison, Esq., George I.'s Secretary of State, but to the delightful painter of contemporary manners; the man who, when in good-humor himself, was the pleasantest companion in all England. I should like to go into Lockit's with him, and drink a bowl along with Sir R. Steele (who has just been knighted by King George, and who does not happen to have any money to pay his share of the reckoning). I should not care to follow Mr. Addison to his secretary's office in Whitehall. There we get into politics. Our business is pleasure, and the town, and the coffee-house, and the theatre, and the Mall. Delightful Spectator! kind friend of leisure hours! happy companion! true Christian gentleman! How much greater, better, you are than the King Mr. Secretary kneels to!

You can have foreign testimony about old-world London, if you like; and my before-quoted friend, Charles Louis, Baron de Pöllnitz, will conduct us to it. "A man of sense," says he, "or a fine gentleman, is never at a loss for company in London, and this is the way the latter passes his time. He rises late, puts on a frock, and, leaving his sword at home, takes his cane, and goes where he pleases. The park is commonly the place where he walks, because 'tis the Exchange for men of quality. 'Tis the same thing as the Tuileries at Paris, only the park has a certain beauty of simplicity which cannot be described. The grand walk is called the Mall; is full of people at every hour of the day, but especially at morning and evening, when their Majesties often walk with the royal family, who are attended only by a half-dozen yeomen of the guard, and permit all persons to walk at the same time with them. The ladies and gentlemen always appear in rich dresses, for the English, who, twenty years ago, did not wear gold lace but in their army, are now embroidered and bedaubed as much as the French. I speak of persons of quality; for the citizen still contents himself with a suit of fine cloth, a good hat and wig, and fine linen. Everybody is well clothed here, and even the beggars don't make so ragged an appearance as they do elsewhere." After our friend, the man of quality, has had his morning or undress walk in the Mall, he goes home to dress, and then saunters to some coffee-house or chocolate-house frequented by the persons he would see. "For 'tis a rule with the English to go once a day at least to houses of this sort, where they talk of business and news, read the papers, and often look at one another without opening their lips. And 'tis very well they are so mute: for were they all as talkative as people of other nations, the coffee-houses would be intolerable, and there would be no hearing what one man said where they are so many. The chocolate-house in St. James's Street, where I go every morning to pass away the time, is always so full that a man can scarce turn about in it."

Delightful as London city was, King George I. liked to be out of it as much as ever he could; and when there, passed all his time with his Germans. It was with them as with Blucher, 100 years afterwards, when the bold old Reiter looked down from St. Paul's, and sighed out, "Was für Plunder!" The German women plundered; the German secretaries plundered; the German cooks and intendants plundered; even Mustapha and Mahomet, the German negroes, had a share of the booty. Take what you can get, was the old monarch's maxim. He was not a lofty monarch, certainly: he was not a patron of the fine arts: but he was not a hypocrite, he was not revengeful, he was not extravagant. Though a despot in Hanover, he was a moderate ruler in England. His aim was to leave it to itself as much as possible, and to live out of it as much as he could. His heart was in Hanover. When taken ill on his last journey, as he was passing through Holland, he thrust his livid head out of the coach-window, and gasped out, "Osnaburg, Osnaburg!" He was more than fifty years of age when he came amongst us: we took him because we wanted him, because he served our turn; we laughed at his uncouth German ways, and sneered at him. He took our loyalty for what it was worth; laid hands on what money he could; kept us assuredly from Popery and wooden shoes. I, for one, would have been on his side in those days. Cynical, and selfish, as he was, he was better than a king out of St. Germains with the French King's orders in his pocket, and a swarm of Jesuits in his train.

The Fates are supposed to interest themselves about royal personages; and so this one had omens and prophecies specially regarding him. He was said to be much disturbed at a prophecy that he should die very soon after his wife; and sure enough, pallid Death, having seized upon the luckless Princess in her castle of Ahlden, presently pounced upon H. M. King George I., in his travelling chariot, on the Hanover road. What postilion can outride that pale horseman? It is said, George promised one of his left-handed widows to come to her after death, if leave were granted to him to revisit the glimpses of the moon; and soon after his demise, a great raven actually flying or hopping in at the Duchess of Kendal's window at Twickenham, she chose to imagine the king's spirit inhabited these plumes, and took special care of her sable visitor. Affecting metempsychosis — funereal royal bird! How pathetic is the idea of the Duchess weeping over it! When this chaste addition to our English aristocracy died, all her jewels, her plate, her plunder went over to her relations in Hanover. I wonder whether her heirs took the bird, and whether it is still flapping its wings over Herrenhausen?

The days are over in England of that strange religion of king-worship, when priests flattered princes in the Temple of God; when servility was held to be ennobling duty; when beauty and youth tried eagerly for royal favor; and woman's shame was held to be no dishonor. Mended morals and mended manners in courts and people, are among the priceless consequences of the freedom which George I. came to rescue and secure. He kept his compact with his English subjects; and if he escaped no more than other men and monarchs from the vices of his age, at least we may thank him for preserving and transmitting the liberties of ours. In our free air, royal and humble homes have alike been purified; and Truth, the birthright of high and low among us, which quite fearlessly judges our greatest personages, can only speak of them now in words of respect and regard. There are stains in the portrait of the first George, and traits in it which none of us need admire; but, among the nobler features, are justice, courage, moderation — and these we may recognize ere we turn the picture to the wall.

George the Second.

GEORGE THE SECOND.

On the afternoon of the 14th of June, 1727, two horsemen might have been perceived galloping along the road from Chelsea to Richmond. The foremost, cased in the jackboots of the period, was a broadfaced, jolly-looking, and very corpulent cavalier; but, by the manner in which he urged his horse, you might see that he was a bold as well as a skilful rider. Indeed, no man loved sport better; and in the hunting-fields of Norfolk, no squire rode more boldly after the fox, or cheered Ringwood and Sweettips more lustily, than he who now thundered over the Richmond road.

He speedily reached Richmond Lodge, and asked to see the owner of the mansion. The mistress of the house and her ladies, to whom our friend was admitted, said he could not be introduced to the master, however pressing the business might be. The master was asleep after his dinner; he always slept after his dinner: and woe be to the person who interrupted him! Nevertheless, our stout friend of the jackboots put the affrighted ladies aside, opened the forbidden door of the bedroom, wherein upon the bed lay a little gentleman; and here the eager messenger knelt down in his jackboots.

He on the bed started up, and with many oaths and a strong German accent asked who was there, and who dared to disturb him?

"I am Sir Robert Walpole," said the messenger. The awakened sleeper hated Sir Robert Walpole. "I have the honor to announce to your Majesty that your royal father, King George I., died at Osnaburg, on Saturday last, the 10th inst."

"*Dat is one big lie!*" roared out his sacred Majesty King George II.: but Sir Robert Walpole stated the fact, and from that day until three and thirty years after, George, the second of the name, ruled over England.

How the King made away with his father's will under the astonished nose of the Archbishop of Canterbury; how he was a choleric little sovereign; how he shook his fist in the face of his father's courtiers; how he kicked his coat and wig about in his rages, and called everybody thief, liar, rascal, with whom he differed: you will read in all the history books; and how he speedily and shrewdly reconciled himself with the bold minister, whom he had hated during his father's life, and by whom he was served during fifteen years of his own with admirable prudence, fidelity, and success. But for Sir Robert Walpole, we should have had the Pretender back again. But for his obstinate love of peace, we should have had wars, which the nation was not strong enough nor united enough to endure. But for his resolute counsels and good-humored resistance we might have had German despots attempting a Hanoverian regimen over us: we should have had revolt, commotion, want, and tyrannous misrule, in place of a quarter of a century of peace, freedom, and material prosperity, such as the country never enjoyed, until that corrupter of parliaments, that dissolute tipsy cynic, that courageous lover of peace and liberty, that great citizen, patriot, and statesman governed it. In religion he was little better than a heathen; cracked ribald jokes at bigwigs and bishops, and laughed at High Church and Low. In private life the old pagan revelled in the lowest pleasures: he passed his Sundays tippling at Richmond; and his holydays bawling after dogs, or boozing at Houghton with boors over beef and punch. He cared for letters no more than his master did: he judged human nature so meanly that one is ashamed to have to own that he was right, and that men could be corrupted by means so base. But, with his hireling House of Commons, he defended liberty for us; with his incredulity he kept Church-craft down. There were parsons at Oxford as double-dealing and dangerous as any priest out of Rome, and he routed them both. He gave Englishmen no conquests, but he gave them peace, and ease, and freedom; the three-per-cents. nearly at par; and wheat at five and six and twenty shillings a quarter.

It was lucky for us that our first Georges were not more highminded men; especially fortunate that they loved Hanover so much as to leave England to have her own way. Our chief troubles began when we got a king who gloried in the name of Briton, and, being born in the country, proposed to rule it. He was no more fit to govern England than his grandfather and great-grandfather, who did not try. It was righting itself during their occupation. The dangerous, noble old spirit of cavalier loyalty was dying out; the stately old English High Church was emptying itself: the questions dropping which, on one side and the other; — the side of loyalty, prerogative, church, and king; — the side of right, truth, civil and religious freedom — had set generations of brave men in arms. By the time when George III. came to the throne, the combat between loyalty and liberty was come to an end; and Charles Edward, old, tipsy, and childless, was dying in Italy.

Those who are curious about European Court history of the last age know the memoirs of the Margravine of Bayreuth, and what a Court was that of Berlin, where George II.'s cousins ruled sovereign. Frederick the Great's father knocked down his sons, daughters, officers of state; he kidnapped big men all Europe over to make grenadiers of: his feasts, his parades, his wine-parties, his tobacco-parties, are all described. Jonathan Wild the Great in language, pleasures, and behavior, is scarcely more delicate than this German sovereign. Louis XV., his life, and reign, and doings, are told in a thousand French memoirs. Our George II., at least, was not a worse king than his neighbors. He claimed and took the royal exemption from doing right which sovereigns assumed. A dull little man of low tastes he appears to us in England; yet Hervey tells us that this choleric prince was a great sentimentalist, and that his letters — of which he wrote prodigious quantities — were quite dangerous in their powers of fascination. He kept his sentimentalities for his Germans and his queen. With us English, he never chose to be familiar. He has been accused of avarice, yet he did not give much money, and did not leave much behind him. He did not love the fine arts, but he did not pretend to love them. He was no more a hypocrite about religion than his father. He judged men by a low standard; yet, with such men as were near him, was he wrong in judging as he did? He readily detected lying and flattery, and liars and flatterers were perforce his companions. Had he been more of a dupe he might have been more amiable. A dismal experience made him cynical. No boon was it to him to be clear-sighted, and see only selfishness and flattery round about him. What could Walpole tell him about his Lords and Commons, but that they were all venal? Did not his clergy, his courtiers, bring him the same story? Dealing with men and women in his rude, sceptical way, he came to doubt about honor, male and female, about patriotism, about religion. "He is wild, but he fights like a man," George I., the taciturn, said of his son and successor. Courage George II. certainly had. The Electoral Prince, at the head of his father's contingent, had approved himself a good and brave soldier under Eugene and Marlborough. At Oudenarde he specially distinguished himself. At Malplaquet the other claimant to the English throne won but little honor. There was always a question about James's courage. Neither then in Flanders, nor afterwards in his own ancient kingdom of Scotland, did the luckless Pretender show much resolution. But dapper little George had a famous tough spirit of his own, and fought like a Trojan. He called out his brother of Prussia, with sword and pistol; and I wish, for the interest of romancers in general, that that famous duel could have taken place. The two sovereigns hated each other with all their might; their seconds were appointed; the place of meeting was settled; and the duel was only prevented by strong representations made to the two, of the European laughter which would have been caused by such a transaction.

Whenever we hear of dapper George at war, it is certain that he demeaned himself like a little man of valor. At Dettingen his horse ran away with him, and with difficulty was stopped from carrying him into the enemy's lines. The King, dismounting from the fiery quadruped, said bravely, "Now I know I shall not run away;" and placed himself at the head of the foot, drew his sword, brandishing it at the whole of the French army, and calling out to his own men to come on, in bad English, but with the most famous pluck and spirit. In '45, when the Pretender was at Derby, and many people began to look pale, the King never lost his courage — not he. "Pooh! don't talk to me that stuff!" he said, like a gallant little prince as he was, and never for one moment allowed his equanimity, or his business, or his pleasures, or his travels, to be disturbed. On public festivals he always appeared in the hat and coat he wore on the famous day of Oudenarde; and the people laughed, but kindly, at the odd old garment, for bravery never goes out of fashion.

In private life the Prince showed himself a worthy descendant of his father. In this respect, so much has been said about the first George's manners, that we need not enter into a description of the son's German harem. In 1705 he married a princess remarkable for beauty, for cleverness, for learning, for good temper — one of the truest and fondest wives ever prince was blessed with, and who loved him and was faithful to him, and he, in his coarse fashion, loved her to the last. It must be told to the honor of Caroline of Anspach, that, at the time when German princes thought no more of changing their religion than you of altering your cap, she refused to give up Protestantism for the other creed, although an archduke, afterwards to be an emperor, was offered to her for a bridegroom. Her Protestant relations in Berlin were angry at her rebellious spirit; it was they who tried to convert her (it is droll to think that Frederick the Great, who had no religion at all, was known for a long time in England as the Protestant hero), and these good Protestants set upon Caroline a certain Father Urban, a very skilful Jesuit, and famous winner of souls. But she routed the Jesuit; and she refused Charles VI.; and she married the little Electoral Prince of Hanover, whom she tended with love, and with every manner of sacrifice, with artful kindness, with tender flattery, with entire self-devotion, thenceforward until her life's end.

When George I. made his first visit to Hanover, his son was appointed regent during the royal absence. But this honor was never again conferred on the Prince of Wales; he and his father fell out presently. On the occasion of the christening of his second son, a royal row took place, and the Prince, shaking his fist in the Duke of Newcastle's face, called him a rogue, and provoked his august father.

He and his wife were turned out of St. James's, and their princely children taken from them, by order of the royal head of the family. Father and mother wept piteously at parting from their little ones. The young ones sent some cherries, with their love, to papa and mamma; the parents watered the fruit with tears. They had no tears thirty-five years afterwards, when Prince Frederick died — their eldest son, their heir, their enemy.

The King called his daughter-in-law "*cette diablesse madame la princesse.*" The frequenters of the latter's court were forbidden to appear at the King's: their Royal Highnesses going to Bath, we read how the courtiers followed them thither, and paid that homage in Somersetshire which was forbidden in London. That phrase of "*cette diablesse madame la princesse,*" explains one cause of the wrath of her royal papa. She was a very clever woman: she had a keen sense of humor: she had a dreadful tongue: she turned into ridicule the antiquated sultan and his hideous harem. She wrote savage letters about him home to members of her family. So, driven out from the royal presence, the Prince and Princess set up for themselves in Leicester Fields, "where," says Walpole, "the most promising of the young gentlemen of the next party, and the prettiest and liveliest of the young ladies, formed the new court." Besides Leicester House, they had their lodge at Richmond, frequented by some of the pleasantest company of those days. There were the Herveys, and Chesterfield, and little Mr. Pope from Twickenham, and with him, sometimes, the savage Dean of St. Patrick's, and quite a bevy of young ladies, whose pretty faces smile on us out of history. There was Lepell, famous in ballad song; and the saucy, charming Mary Bellenden, who would have none of the Prince of Wales's fine compliments, who folded her arms across her breast, and bade H. R. H. keep off; and knocked his purse of guineas into his face, and told him she was tired of seeing him count them. He was not an august monarch, this Augustus. Walpole tells how, one night at the royal card-table, the playful princesses pulled a chair away from under Lady Deloraine, who, in revenge, pulled the King's from under him, so that his Majesty fell on the carpet. In whatever posture one sees this royal George, he is ludicrous somehow; even at Dettingen, where he fought so bravely, his figure is absurd — calling out in his broken English, and lunging with his rapier, like a fencing-master. In contemporary caricatures, George's son, "the Hero of Culloden," is also made an object of considerable fun.

I refrain to quote from Walpole regarding George — for those charming volumes are in the hands of all who love the gossip of the last century. Nothing can be more cheery than Horace's letters. Fiddles sing all through them: wax-lights, fine dresses, fine jokes, fine plate, fine equipages, glitter and sparkle there: never was such a brilliant, jigging, smirking Vanity Fair as that through which he leads us. Hervey, the next great authority, is a darker spirit. About him there is something frightful: a few years since his heirs opened the lid of the Ickworth box; it was as if a Pompeii was opened to us — the last century dug up, with its temples and its games, its chariots, its public places — lupanaria. Wandering through that city of the dead, that dreadfully selfish time, through those godless intrigues and feasts, through those crowds, pushing and eager, and struggling — rouged, and lying, and fawning — I have wanted some one to be friends with. I have said to friends conversant with that history, "Show me some good person about that Court; find me, among those selfish courtiers, those dissolute, gay people, some one being that I can love and regard." There is that strutting little sultan George

II.; there is that hunchbacked, beetle-browed Lord Chesterfield; there is John Hervey, with his deadly smile, and ghastly, painted face — I hate them. There is Hoadly, cringing from one bishopric to another: yonder comes little Mr. Pope, from Twickenham, with his friend, the Irish dean, in his new cassock, bowing too, but with rage flashing from under his bushy eyebrows, and scorn and hate quivering in his smile. Can you be fond of these? Of Pope I might; at least I might love his genius, his wit, his greatness, his sensibility — with a certain conviction that at some fancied slight, some sneer which he imagined, he would turn upon me and stab me. Can you trust the Queen? She is not of our order: their very position makes kings and queens lonely. One inscrutable attachment that inscrutable woman has. To that she is faithful, through all trial, neglect, pain, and time. Save her husband, she really cares for no created being. She is good enough to her children, and even fond enough of them: but she would chop them all up into little pieces to please him. In her intercourse with all around her, she was perfectly kind, gracious, and natural: but friends may die, daughters may depart, she will be as perfectly kind and gracious to the next set. If the King wants her, she will smile upon him, be she ever so sad; and walk with him, be she ever so weary; and laugh at his brutal jokes, be she in ever so much pain of body or heart. Caroline's devotion to her husband is a prodigy to read of. What charm had the little man? What was there in those wonderful letters of thirty pages long, which he wrote to her when he was absent, and to his mistresses at Hanover, when he was in London with his wife? Why did Caroline, the most lovely and accomplished princess of Germany, take a little red-faced staring princeling for a husband, and refuse an emperor? Why, to her last hour, did she love him so? She killed herself because she loved him so. She had the gout, and would plunge her feet in cold water in order to walk with him. With the film of death over her eyes, writhing in intolerable pain, she yet had a livid smile and a gentle word for her master. You have read the wonderful history of that death-bed? How she bade him marry again, and the reply the old king blubbered out, "Non, non: j'aurai des maîtresses." There never was such a ghastly farce. I watch the astonishing scene — I stand by that awful bedside, wondering at the ways in which God has ordained the lives, loves, rewards, successes, passions, actions, ends of his creatures — and can't but laugh, in the presence of death, and with the saddest heart. In that often-quoted passage from Lord Hervey, in which the Queen's death-bed is described, the grotesque horror of the details surpasses all satire: the dreadful humor of the scene is more terrible than Swift's blackest pages, or Fielding's fiercest irony. The man who wrote the story had something diabolical about him: the terrible verses which Pope wrote respecting Hervey, in one of his own moods of almost fiendish malignity, I fear are true. I am frightened as I look back into the past, and fancy I behold that ghastly, beautiful face; as I think of the Queen writhing on her death-bed, and crying out, "Pray! — pray!" — of the royal old sinner by her side, who kisses her dead lips with frantic grief, and leaves her to sin no more; — of the bevy of courtly clergymen, and the archbishop, whose prayers she rejects, and who are obliged for propriety's sake to shuffle off the anxious inquiries of the public, and vow that her Majesty quitted this life "in a heavenly frame of mind." What a life! — to what ends devoted! What a vanity of vanities! It is a theme for another pulpit than the lecturer's. For a pulpit? — I think the part which pulpits play in the deaths of kings is the most ghastly of all the ceremonial: the lying eulogies, the blinking of disagreeable truths, the sickening flatteries, the simulated grief, the falsehood and sycophancies — all uttered in the name of Heaven in our State churches: these monstrous threnodies have been sung from time immemorial over kings and queens, good, bad, wicked, licentious. The State parson must bring out his commonplaces; his apparatus of rhetorical black-hangings. Dead king or live king, the clergyman must flatter him — announce his piety whilst living, and when dead, perform the obsequies of "our most religious and gracious king."

I read that Lady Yarmouth (my most religious and gracious King's favorite) sold a bishopric to a clergyman for 5,000*l.* (She betted him 5,000*l.* that he would not be made a bishop, and he lost, and paid her.) Was he the only prelate of his time led up by such hands for consecration? As I peep into George II.'s St. James's, I see crowds of cassocks rustling up the back-stairs of the ladies of the Court; stealthy clergy slipping purses into their laps; that godless old King yawning under his canopy in his Chapel Royal, as the chaplain before him is discoursing. Discoursing about what? — about righteousness and judgment? Whilst the chaplain is preaching, the King is chattering in German almost as loud as the preacher; so loud that the clergyman — it may be one Dr. Young, he who wrote "Night Thoughts," and discoursed on the splendors of the stars, the glories of heaven, and utter vanities of this world — actually burst out crying in his pulpit because the defender of the faith and dispenser of bishoprics would not listen to him! No wonder that the clergy were corrupt and indifferent amidst this indifference and corruption. No wonder that sceptics multiplied and morals degenerated, so far as they depended on the influence of such a king. No wonder that Whitefield cried out in the wilderness, that Wesley quitted the insulted temple to pray on the hill-side. I look with reverence on those men at that time. Which is the sublimer spectacle — the good John Wesley, surrounded by his congregation of miners at the pit's mouth, or the Queen's chaplains mumbling through their morning office in their ante-room, under the picture of the great Venus, with the door opened into the adjoining chamber, where the Queen is dressing, talking scandal to Lord Hervey, or uttering sneers at Lady Suffolk, who is kneeling with the basin at her mistress's side? I say I am scared as I look round at this society — at this king, at these courtiers, at these politicians, at these bishops — at this flaunting vice and levity. Whereabouts in this Court is the honest man? Where is the pure person one may like? The air stifles one with its sickly perfumes. There are some old-world follies and some absurd ceremonials about our Court of the present day, which I laugh at, but as an Englishman, contrasting it with the past, shall I not acknowledge the change of to-day? As the mistress of St. James's passes me now, I salute the sovereign, wise, moderate, exemplary of life; the good mother; the good wife; the accomplished lady; the enlightened friend of art; the tender sympathizer in her people's glories and sorrows.

Of all the Court of George and Caroline, I find no one but Lady Suffolk with whom it seems pleasant and kindly to hold converse. Even the misogynist Croker, who edited her letters, loves her, and has that regard for her with which her sweet graciousness seems to have inspired almost all men and some women who came near her. I have noted many little traits which go to prove the charms of her character (it is not merely because she is charming, but because she is characteristic, that I allude to her). She writes delightfully sober letters. Addressing Mr.

Gay at Tunbridge (he was, you know, a poet, penniless and in disgrace), she says: "The place you are in, has strangely filled your head with physicians and cures; but, take my word for it, many a fine lady has gone there to drink the waters without being sick; and many a man has complained of the loss of his heart, who had it in his own possession. I desire you will keep yours; for I shall not be very fond of a friend without one, and I have a great mind you should be in the number of mine."

When Lord Peterborough was seventy years old, that indomitable youth addressed some flaming love, or rather gallantry, letters to Mrs. Howard — curious relics they are of the romantic manner of wooing sometimes in use in those days. It is not passion; it is not love; it is gallantry: a mixture of earnest and acting; high-flown compliments, profound bows, vows, sighs and ogles, in the manner of the Clelie romances, and Millamont and Doricourt in the comedy. There was a vast elaboration of ceremonies and etiquette, of raptures — a regulated form for kneeling and wooing which has quite passed out of our downright manners. Henrietta Howard accepted the noble old earl's philandering; answered the queer love-letters with due acknowledgment; made a profound courtesy to Peterborough's profound bow; and got John Gay to help her in the composition of her letters in reply to her old knight. He wrote her charming verses, in which there was truth as well as grace. "O wonderful creature!" he writes: —

"O wonderful creature, a woman of reason!
Never grave out of pride, never gay out of season!
When so easy to guess who this angel should be,
Who would think Mrs. Howard ne'er dreamt it was she?"

The great Mr. Pope also celebrated her in lines not less pleasant, and painted a portrait of what must

certainly have been a delightful lady: —

"I know a thing that's most uncommon —
Envy, be silent and attend! —
I know a reasonable woman,
Handsome, yet witty, and a friend:

"Not warped by passion, awed by rumor,
Not grave through pride, or gay through folly:
An equal mixture of good-humor
And exquisite soft melancholy.

"Has she no faults, then (Envy says), sir?
Yes, she has one, I must aver —
When all the world conspires to praise her,
The woman's deaf, and does not hear!"

Even the women concurred in praising and loving her. The Duchess of Queensberry bears testimony to her amiable qualities, and writes to her: "I tell you so and so, because you love children, and to have children love you." The beautiful, jolly Mary Bellenden, represented by contemporaries as "the most perfect creature ever known," writes very pleasantly to her "dear Howard," her "dear Swiss," from the country, whither Mary had retired after her marriage, and when she gave up being a maid of honor. "How do you do, Mrs. Howard?" Mary breaks out. "How do you do, Mrs. Howard? that is all I have to say. This afternoon I am taken with a fit of writing; but as to matter, I have nothing better to entertain you, than news of my farm. I therefore give you the following list of the stock of eatables that I am fatting for my private tooth. It is well known to the whole county of Kent, that I have four fat calves, two fat hogs, fit for killing, twelve promising black pigs, two young chickens, three fine geese, with thirteen eggs under each (several being duck-eggs, else the others do not come to maturity); all this, with rabbits, and pigeons, and carp in plenty, beef and mutton at reasonable rates. Now, Howard, if you have a mind to stick a knife into anything I have named, say so!"

A jolly set must they have been, those maids of honor. Pope introduces us to a whole bevy of them, in a pleasant letter. "I went," he says, "by water to Hampton Court, and met the Prince, with all his ladies, on horseback, coming from hunting. Mrs. Bellenden and Mrs. Lepell took me into protection, contrary to the laws against harboring Papists, and gave me a dinner, with something I liked better, an opportunity of conversation with Mrs. Howard. We all agreed that the life of a maid of honor was of all things the most miserable, and wished that all women who envied it had a specimen of it. To eat Westphalia ham of a morning, ride over hedges and ditches on borrowed hacks, come home in the heat of the day with a fever, and (what is worse a hundred times) with a red mark on the forehead from an uneasy hat — all this may qualify them to make excellent wives for hunters. As soon as they wipe off the heat of the day, they must simper an hour and catch cold in the Princess's apartment; from thence to dinner with what appetite they may; and after that till midnight, work, walk, or think which way they please. No lone house in Wales, with a mountain and rookery, is more contemplative than this Court. Miss Lepell walked with me three or four hours by moonlight, and we met no creature of any quality but the King, who gave audience to the vice-chamberlain all alone under the garden wall."

I fancy it was a merrier England, that of our ancestors, than the island which we inhabit. People high and low amused themselves very much more. I have calculated the manner in which statesmen and persons of condition passed their time — and what with drinking, and dining, and supping, and cards, wonder how they got through their business at all. They played all sorts of games, which, with the exception of cricket and tennis, have quite gone out of our manners now. In the old prints of St. James's Park, you still see the marks along the walk, to note the balls when the Court played at Mall. Fancy Birdcage walk now so laid out, and Lord John and Lord Palmerston knocking balls up and down the avenue! Most of those jolly sports belong to the past, and the good old games of England are only to be found in old novels, in old ballads, or the columns of dingy old newspapers, which say how a main of cocks is to be fought at Winchester between the Winchester men and the Hampton men; or how the Cornwall men and the Devon men are going to hold a great wrestling match at Totnes, and so on.

A hundred and twenty years ago there were not only country towns in England, but people who inhabited them. We were very much more gregarious; we were amused by very simple pleasures. Every town had its fair, every village its wake. The old poets have sung a hundred jolly ditties about great cudgel-playings, famous grinning through horse-collars, great may-pole meetings, and morris-dances. The girls used to run races clad in very light attire; and the kind gentry and good parsons thought no shame in looking on. Dancing bears went about the country with pipe and tabor. Certain well-known tunes were sung all over the land for hundreds of years, and high and low rejoiced in that simple music. Gentlemen who wished to entertain their female friends constantly sent for a band. When Beau Fielding, a mighty fine gentleman, was courting the lady whom he married, he treated her and her companion at his lodgings to a supper from the tavern, and after supper they sent out for a fiddler, three of them. Fancy the three, in a great wainscoted room, in Covent Garden or Soho, lighted by two or three candles in silver sconces, some grapes and a bottle of Florence wine on the table, and the honest fiddler playing old tunes in quaint old minor keys, as the Beau takes out one lady after the other, and solemnly dances with her!

The very great folks, young noblemen, with their governors, and the like, went abroad and made the great tour; the home satirists jeered at the Frenchified and Italian ways which they brought back; but the greater number of people never left the country. The jolly squire often had never been twenty miles from home. Those who did go went to the baths, to Harrogate, or Scarborough, or Bath, or Epsom. Old letters are full of these places of pleasure. Gay writes to us about the fiddlers at Tunbridge; of the ladies having merry little private balls amongst themselves; and the gentlemen entertaining them by turns with tea and music. One of the young beauties whom he met did not care for tea: "We have a young lady here," he says, "that is very particular in her desires. I have known some young ladies, who, if ever they prayed, would ask for some equipage or title, a husband or matadores: but this lady, who is but seventeen, and has 30,000*l.* to her fortune, places all her wishes on a pot of good ale. When her friends, for the sake of her shape and complexion, would dissuade her from it, she answers, with the truest sincerity, that by the loss of shape and complexion she could only lose a husband, whereas ale is her passion."

Every country town had its assembly-room — mouldy old tenements, which we may still see in deserted inn-yards, in decayed provincial cities, out of which the great wen of London has sucked all the life. York, at assize times, and throughout the winter, harbored a large society of northern gentry. Shrewsbury was celebrated for its festivities. At Newmarket, I read of "a vast deal of good company, besides rogues and blacklegs;" at Norwich, of two assemblies, with a prodigious crowd in the hall, the rooms, and the gallery. In Cheshire (it is a maid of honor of Queen Caroline who writes, and who is longing to be back at Hampton Court, and the fun there) I peep into a country house, and see a very merry party: "We meet in the work-room before nine, eat, and break a joke or two till twelve, then we repair to our own chambers and make ourselves ready, for it cannot be called dressing. At noon the great bell fetches us into a parlor, adorned with all sorts of fine arms, poisoned darts, several pairs of old boots and shoes worn by men of might, with the stirrups of King Charles I., taken from him at Edgehill," — and there they have their dinner, after which comes dancing and supper.

As for Bath, all history went and bathed and drank there. George II. and his Queen, Prince Frederick and his court, scarce a character one can mention of the early last century, but was seen in that famous Pump Room where Beau Nash presided, and his picture hung between the busts of Newton and Pope:

"This picture, placed these busts between,
Gives satire all its strength:
Wisdom and Wit are little seen,
But Folly at full length."

I should like to have seen the Folly. It was a splendid, embroidered, beruffled, snuff-boxed, red-heeled, impertinent Folly, and knew how to make itself respected. I should like to have seen that noble old madcap Peterborough in his boots (he actually had the audacity to walk about Bath in boots!), with his blue ribbon and stars, and a cabbage under each arm, and a chicken in his hand, which he had been cheapening for his dinner. Chesterfield came there many a time and gambled for hundreds, and grinned through his gout. Mary Wortley was there, young and beautiful; and Mary Wortley, old, hideous, and snuffy. Miss Chudleigh came there, slipping away from one husband, and on the look-out for another. Walpole passed many a day there; sickly, supercilious, absurdly dandified, and affected; with a brilliant wit, a delightful sensibility; and for his friends, a most tender, generous, and faithful heart. And if you and I had been alive then, and strolling down Milsom Street — hush! we should have taken our hats off, as an awful, long, lean, gaunt figure, swathed in flannels, passed by in its chair, and a livid face looked out from the window — great fierce eyes staring from under a bushy, powdered wig, a terrible frown, a terrible Roman nose — and we whisper to one another, "There he is! There's the great commoner! There is Mr. Pitt!" As we walk away, the abbey bells are set a-ringing; and we meet our testy friend Toby Smollett, on the arm of James Quin the actor, who tells us that the bells ring for Mr. Bullock, an eminent cowkeeper from Tottenham, who has just arrived to drink the waters; and Toby shakes his cane at the door of Colonel Ringworm — the Creole gentleman's lodgings next his own — where the colonel's two negroes are practising on the French horn.

When we try to recall social England, we must fancy it playing at cards for many hours every day. The custom is well nigh gone out among us now, but fifty years ago was general, fifty years before that almost universal, in the country. "Gaming has become so much the fashion," writes Seymour, the author of the "Court Gamester," "that he who in company should be ignorant of the games in vogue, would be reckoned low-bred, and hardly fit for conversation." There were cards everywhere. It was considered ill-bred to read in company. "Books were not fit articles for drawing-rooms," old ladies used to say. People were jealous, as it were, and angry with them. You will find in Hervey that George II. was always furious at the sight of books; and his Queen, who loved reading, had to practise it in secret in her closet. But cards were the resource of all the world. Every night, for hours, kings and queens of England sat down and handled their majesties of spades and diamonds. In European Courts, I believe the practice still remains, not for gambling, but for pastime. Our ancestors generally adopted it. "Books! prithee, don't talk to me about books," said old Sarah Marlborough. "The only books I know are men and cards." "Dear old Sir Roger de Coverley sent all his tenants a string of hogs' puddings and a pack of cards at Christmas," says "The Spectator," wishing to depict a kind landlord. One of the good old lady writers in whose letters I have been dipping cries out, "Sure, cards have kept us women from a great deal of scandal!" Wise old Johnson regretted that he had not learnt to play. "It is very useful in life," he says; "it generates kindness, and consolidates society." David Hume never went to bed without his whist. We have Walpole, in one of his letters, in a transport of gratitude for the cards. "I shall build an altar to Pam," says he, in his pleasant dandified way, "for the escape of my charming Duchess of Grafton." The Duchess had been playing cards at Rome, when she ought to have been at a cardinal's concert, where the floor fell in, and all the monsignors were precipitated into the cellar. Even the Nonconformist clergy looked not unkindly on the practice. "I do not think," says one of them, "that honest Martin Luther committed sin by playing at backgammon for an hour or two after dinner, in order by unbending his mind to promote digestion." As for the High Church parsons, they all played, bishops and all. On Twelfth-day the Court used to play in state. "This being Twelfth-day, his Majesty, the Prince of Wales, and the Knights Companions of the Garter, Thistle, and Bath, appeared in the collars of their respective orders. Their Majesties, the Prince of Wales, and three eldest Princesses, went to the Chapel Royal, preceded by the heralds. The Duke of Manchester carried the sword of State. The King and Prince made offering at the altar of gold, frankincense, and myrrh, according to the annual custom. At night their Majesties played at hazard with the nobility, for the benefit of the groom-porter; and 'twas said the king won 600 guineas; the queen, 360; Princess Amelia, twenty; Princess Caroline, ten; the Duke of Grafton and the Earl of Portmore, several thousands."

Let us glance at the same chronicle, which is of the year 1731, and see how others of our forefathers were engaged.

"Cork, 15th January. — This day, one Tim Croneen was, for the murder and robbery of Mr. St. Leger and his wife, sentenced to be hanged two minutes, then his head to be cut off, and his body divided in four quarters, to be placed in four cross-ways. He was servant to Mr. St. Leger, and committed the murder with the privity of the servant-maid, who was sentenced to be burned; also of the gardener, whom he knocked on the head, to deprive him of his share of the booty."

"January 3. — A postboy was shot by an Irish gentleman on the road near Stone, in Staffordshire, who died in two days, for which the gentleman was imprisoned."

"A poor man was found hanging in a gentleman's stables at Bungay, in Norfolk, by a person who cut him down, and running for assistance, left his penknife behind him. The poor man recovering, cut his throat with the knife; and a river being nigh, jumped into it; but company coming, was dragged out alive, and was like to remain so."

"The Honorable Thomas Finch, brother to the Earl of Nottingham, is appointed ambassador at the Hague, in the room of the Earl of Chesterfield, who is on his return home."

"William Cowper, Esq., and the Rev. Mr. John Cowper, chaplain in ordinary to her Majesty, and rector of Great Berkhamstead, in the county of Hertford, are appointed clerks of the commissioners of bankruptcy."

"Charles Craig, Esq., and —— Macnamara, Esq., between whom an old grudge of three years had subsisted, which had occasioned their being bound over about fifty times for breaking the peace, meeting in company with Mr. Eyres, of Galloway, they discharged their pistols, and all three were killed on the spot, — to the great joy of their peaceful neighbors, say the Irish papers."

"Wheat is 26*s.* to 28*s.*, and barley 20*s.* to 22*s.* a quarter; three per cents., 92; best loaf sugar, 9¼*d.*; Bohea, 12*s.* to 14*s.*; Pekoe, 18*s.*; and Hyson, 35*s.* per pound."

"At Exon was celebrated with great magnificence the birthday of the son of Sir W. Courtney, Bart., at which more than 1,000 persons were present. A bullock was roasted whole; a butt of wine and several tuns of beer and cider were given to the populace. At the same time Sir William delivered to his son, then of age, Powdram Castle, and a great estate."

"Charlesworth and Cox, two solicitors, convicted of forgery, stood on the pillory at the Royal Exchage. The first was severely handled by the populace, but the other was very much favored and protected by six or seven fellows who got on the pillory to protect him from the insults of the mob."

"A boy killed by falling upon iron spikes, from a lamp-post which he climbed to see Mother Needham stand in the pillory."

"Mary Lynn was burnt to ashes at the stake for being concerned in the murder of her mistress."

"Alexander Russell, the foot soldier, who was capitally convicted for a street robbery in January sessions, was reprieved for transportation; but having an estate fallen to him, obtained a free pardon."

"The Lord John Russell married to the Lady Diana Spencer, at Marlborough House. He has a fortune of 30,000*l.* down, and is to have 100,000*l.* at the death of the Duchess

Dowager of Marlborough, his grandmother."

"March 1 being the anniversary of the Queen's birthday, when her Majesty entered the forty-ninth year of her age, there was a splendid appearance of nobility at St. James's. Her Majesty was magnificently dressed, and wore a flowered muslin head-edging, as did also her Royal Highness. The Lord Portmore was said to have the richest dress, though an Italian Count had twenty-four diamonds instead of buttons."

New clothes on the birthday were the fashion for all loyal people. Swift mentions the custom several times. Walpole is constantly speaking of it; laughing at the practice, but having the very finest clothes from Paris, nevertheless. If the King and Queen were unpopular, there were very few new clothes at the drawing-room. In a paper in "The True Patriot," No. 3, written to attack the Pretender, the Scotch, French, and Popery, Fielding supposes the Scotch and the Pretender in possession of London, and himself about to be hanged for loyalty, — when, just as the rope is round his neck, he says: "My little girl entered my bedchamber, and put an end to my dream by pulling open my eyes, and telling me that the tailor had just brought home my clothes for His Majesty's birthday." In his "Temple Beau," the beau is dunned "for a birthday suit of velvet, 40*l*." Be sure that Mr. Harry Fielding was dunned too.

The public days, no doubt, were splendid, but the private court life must have been awfully wearisome. "I will not trouble you," writes Hervey to Lady Sandon, "with any account of our occupations at Hampton Court. No mill-horse ever went in a more constant track, or a more unchanging circle; so, by the assistance of an almanack for the day of the week, and a watch for the hour of the day, you may inform yourself fully, without any other intelligence but your memory, of every transaction within the verge of the Court. Walking, chaises, levées, and audiences fill the morning. At night the King plays at commerce and backgammon, and the Queen at quadrille, where poor Lady Charlotte runs her usual nightly gauntlet, the Queen pulling her hood, and the Princess Royal rapping her knuckles. The Duke of Grafton takes his nightly opiate of lottery, and sleeps as usual between the Princesses Amelia and Caroline. Lord Grantham strolls from one room to another (as Dryden says), like some discontented ghost that oft appears, and is forbid to speak; and stirs himself about as people stir a fire, not with any design, but in hopes to make it burn brisker. At last the King gets up; the pool finishes; and everybody has their dismission. Their Majesties retire to Lady Charlotte and my Lord Lifford; my Lord Grantham, to Lady Frances and Mr. Clark: some to supper, some to bed; and thus the evening and the morning make the day."

The King's fondness for Hanover occasioned all sorts of rough jokes among his English subjects, to whom *sauer-kraut* and sausages have ever been ridiculous objects. When our present Prince Consort came among us, the people bawled out songs in the streets indicative of the absurdity of Germany in general. The sausage-shops produced enormous sausages which we might suppose were the daily food and delight of German princes. I remember the caricatures at the marriage of Prince Leopold with the Princess Charlotte. The bridegroom was drawn in rags. George III.'s wife was called by the people a beggarly German duchess; the British idea being that all princes were beggarly except British princes. King George paid us back. He thought there were no manners out of Germany. Sarah Marlborough once coming to visit the Princess, whilst her Royal Highness was whipping one of the roaring royal children, "Ah!" says George, who was standing by, "you have no good manners in England, because you are not properly brought up when you are young." He insisted that no English cooks could roast, no English coachman could drive: he actually questioned the superiority of our nobility, our horses, and our roast beef!

Whilst he was away from his beloved Hanover, every thing remained there exactly as in the Prince's presence. There were 800 horses in the stables, there was all the apparatus of chamberlains, court-marshals, and equerries; and court assemblies were held every Saturday, where all the nobility of Hanover assembled at what I can't but think a fine and touching ceremony. A large armchair was placed in the assembly-room, and on it the King's portrait. The nobility advanced, and made a bow to the arm-chair, and to the image which Nebuchadnezzar the king had set up; and spoke under their voices before the august picture, just as they would have done had the King Churfürst been present himself.

He was always going back to Hanover. In the year 1729, he went for two whole years, during which Caroline reigned for him in England, and he was not in the least missed by his British subjects. He went again in '35 and '36; and between the years 1740 and 1755 was no less than eight times on the Continent, which amusement he was obliged to give up at the outbreak of the Seven Years' war. Here every day's amusement was the same. "Our life is as uniform as that of a monastery," writes a courtier whom Vehse quotes. "Every morning at eleven, and every evening at six, we drive in the heat to Herrenhausen, through an enormous linden avenue; and twice a day cover our coats and coaches with dust. In the King's society there never is the least change. At table, and at cards, he sees always the same faces, and at the end of the game retires into his chamber. Twice a week there is a French theatre; the other days there is play in the gallery. In this way, were the King always to stop in Hanover, one could make a ten years' calendar of his proceedings; and settle beforehand what his time of business, meals, and pleasure would be."

The old pagan kept his promise to his dying wife. Lady Yarmouth was now in full favor, and treated with profound respect by the Hanover society, though it appears rather neglected in England when she came among us. In 1740, a couple of the King's daughters went to see him at Hanover; Anna, the Princess of Orange (about whom, and whose husband and marriage-day, Walpole and Hervey have left us the most ludicrous descriptions), and Maria of Hesse Cassel, with their respective lords. This made the Hanover court very brilliant. In honor of his high guests, the King gave several *fêtes;* among others, a magnificent masked ball, in the green theatre at Herrenhausen — the garden theatre, with linden and box for screen, and grass for a carpet, where the Platens had danced to George and his father the late sultan. The stage and a great part of the garden were illuminated with colored lamps. Almost the whole court appeared in white dominoes, "like," says the describer of the scene, "like spirits in the Elysian fields. At night, supper was served in the gallery with three great tables, and the King was very merry. After supper dancing was resumed, and I did not get home till five o'clock by full daylight to Hanover. Some days afterwards we had, in the opera-house at Hanover, a great assembly. The King appeared in a Turkish dress; his turban was ornamented with a magnificent agraffe of diamonds; the Lady Yarmouth was dressed as a sultana; nobody was more beautiful than the Princess of Hesse." So, while poor Caroline was resting in her coffin, dapper little George, with his red face and his white eyebrows and goggle-eyes, at sixty years of age, is dancing a pretty dance with Madame Walmoden, and capering about dressed up like a Turk! For twenty years more, that little old Bajazet went on in this Turkish fashion, until the fit came which choked the old man, when he ordered the side of his coffin to be taken out, as well as that of poor Caroline's who had preceded him, so that his sinful old bones and ashes might mingle with those of the faithful creature. O strutting Turkey-cock of Herrenhausen! O naughty little Mahomet! in what Turkish paradise are you now, and where be your painted houris? So Countess Yarmouth appeared as a sultana, and his Majesty in a Turkish dress wore an agraffe of diamonds, and was very merry, was he? Friends! he was your father's King as well as mine — let us drop a respectful tear over his grave.

He said of his wife that he never knew a woman who was worthy to buckle her shoe: he would sit alone weeping before her portrait, and when he had dried his eyes, he would go off to his Walmoden and talk of her. On the 25th day of October, 1760, he being then in the seventy-seventh year of his age, and the thirty-fourth of his reign, his page went to take him his royal chocolate, and behold! the most religious and gracious King was lying dead on the floor. They went and fetched Walmoden; but Walmoden could not wake him. The sacred Majesty was but a lifeless corpse. The King was dead; God save the King! But, of course, poets and clergymen decorously bewailed the late one. Here are some artless verses, in which an English divine deplored the famous departed hero, and over which you may cry or you may laugh, exactly as your humor suits: —

"While at his feet expiring Faction lay,
No contest left but who should best obey,
Saw in his offspring all himself renewed;
The same fair path of glory still pursued;
Saw to young George Augusta's care impart
Whate'er could raise and humanize the heart;
Blend all his grandsire's virtues with his own,
And form their mingled radiance for the throne —
No farther blessing could on earth be given —
The next degree of happiness was — heaven!"

If he had been good, if he had been just, if he had been pure in life, and wise in council, could the poet have said much more? It was a parson who came and went over this grave, with Walmoden sitting on it, and claimed heaven for the poor old man slumbering below. Here was one who had neither dignity, learning, morals, nor wit — who tainted a great society by a bad example; who in youth, manhood, old age, was gross, low, and sensual; and Mr. Porteus, afterwards my Lord Bishop Porteus, says the earth was not good enough for him, and that his only place was heaven! Bravo, Mr. Porteus! The divine who wept these tears over George the Second's memory wore George the Third's lawn. I don't know whether people still admire his poetry or his sermons.

George the Third.

GEORGE THE THIRD.

We have to glance over sixty years in as many minutes. To read the mere catalogue of characters who figured during that long period, would occupy our allotted time, and we should have all text and no sermon. England has to undergo the revolt of the American colonies; to submit to defeat and separation; to shake under the volcano of the French Revolution; to grapple and fight for the life with her gigantic enemy Napoleon; to gasp and rally after that tremendous struggle. The old society, with its courtly splendors, has to pass away; generations of statesmen to rise and disappear; Pitt to follow Chatham to the tomb; the memory of Rodney and Wolfe to be superseded by Nelson's and Wellington's glory; the old poets who unite us to Queen Anne's time to sink into their graves; Johnson to die, and Scott and Byron to arise; Garrick to delight the world with his dazzling dramatic genius, and Kean to leap on the stage and take possession of the astonished theatre. Steam has to be invented; kings to be beheaded, banished, deposed, restored. Napoleon to be but an episode, and George III. is to be alive through all these varied changes, to accompany his people through all these revolutions of thought, government, society; to survive out of the old world into ours.

When I first saw England, she was in mourning for the young Princess Charlotte, the hope of the empire. I came from India as a child, and our ship touched at an island on the way home, where my black servant took me a long walk over rocks and hills until we reached a garden, where we saw a man walking. "That is he," said the black man: "that is Bonaparte! He eats three sheep every day, and all the little children he can lay hands on!" There were people in the British dominions besides that poor Calcutta serving-man, with an equal horror of the Corsican ogre.

With the same childish attendant, I remember peeping through the colonnade at Carleton House, and seeing the abode of the great Prince Regent. I can see yet the Guards pacing before the gates of the place. The place! What place? The palace exists no more than the palace of Nebuchadnezzar. It is but a name now. Where be the sentries who used to salute as the Royal chariots drove in and out? The chariots, with the kings inside, have driven to the realms of Pluto; the tall Guards have marched into darkness, and the echoes of their drums are rolling in Hades. Where the palace once stood, a hundred little children are paddling up and down the steps to St. James's Park. A score of grave gentlemen are taking their tea at the "Athenæum Club;" as many grizzly warriors are garrisoning the "United Service Club" opposite. Pall Mall is the great social Exchange of London now — the mart of news, of politics, of scandal, of rumor — the English forum, so to speak, where men discuss the last despatch from the Crimea, the last speech of Lord Derby, the next move of Lord John. And, now and then, to a few antiquarians whose thoughts are with the past rather than with the present, it is a memorial of old times and old people, and Pall Mall is our Palmyra. Look! About this spot Tom of Ten Thousand was killed by Königsmarck's gang. In that great red house Gainsborough lived, and Culloden Cumberland, George III.'s uncle.

Yonder is Sarah Marlborough's palace, just as it stood when that termagant occupied it. At 25, Walter Scott used to live; at the house, now No. 79,* and occupied by the Society for the Propagation of the Gospel in Foreign Parts, resided Mrs. Eleanor Gwynn, comedian. How often has Queen Caroline's chair issued from under yonder arch! All the men of the Georges have passed up and down the street. It has seen Walpole's chariot and Chatham's sedan; and Fox, Gibbon, Sheridan, on their way to Brookes's; and stately William Pitt stalking on the arm of Dundas; and Hanger and Tom Sheridan reeling out of Raggett's; and Byron limping into Wattier's; and Swift striding out of Bury Street; and Mr. Addison and Dick Steele, both perhaps a little the better for liquor; and the Prince of Wales and the Duke of York clattering over the pavement; and Johnson counting the posts along the streets, after dawdling before Dodsley's window; and Harry Walpole hobbling into his carriage, with a gimcrack just bought at Christie's; and George Selwyn sauntering into White's.

In the published letters to George Selwyn we get a mass of correspondence by no means so brilliant and witty as Walpole's, or so bitter and bright as Hervey's, but as interesting, and even more descriptive of the time, because the letters are the work of many hands. You hear more voices speaking, as it were, and more natural than Horace's dandified treble, and Sporus's malignant whisper. As one reads the Selwyn letters — as one looks at Reynolds's noble pictures illustrative of those magnificent times and voluptuous people — one almost hears the voice of the dead past; the laughter and the chorus; the toast called over the brimming cups; the shout at the racecourse or the gaming-table; the merry joke frankly spoken to the laughing fine lady. How fine those ladies were, those ladies who heard and spoke such coarse jokes; how grand those gentlemen!

* 1856.

I fancy that peculiar product of the past, the fine gentleman, has almost vanished from off the face of the earth, and is disappearing like the beaver or the Red Indian. We can't have fine gentlemen any more, because we can't have the society in which they lived. The people will not obey: the parasites will not be as obsequious as formerly: children do not go down on their knees to beg their parents' blessing: chaplains do not say grace and retire before the pudding: servants do not say "your honor" and "your worship" at every moment: tradesmen do not stand hat in hand as the gentleman passes: authors do not wait for hours in gentlemen's anterooms with a fulsome dedication, for which they hope to get five guineas from his lordship. In the days when there were fine gentlemen, Mr. Secretary Pitt's under-secretaries did not dare to sit down before him; but Mr. Pitt, in his turn, went down on his gouty knees to George II.; and when George III. spoke a few kind words to him, Lord Chatham burst into tears of reverential joy and gratitude; so awful was the idea of the monarch, and so great the distinctions of rank. Fancy Lord John Russell or Lord Palmerston on their knees whilst the Sovereign was reading a despatch, or beginning to cry because Prince Albert said something civil!

At the accession of George III., the patricians were yet at the height of their good fortune. Society recognized their superiority, which they themselves pretty calmly took for granted. They inherited not only titles and estates, and seats in the house of Peers, but seats in the House of Commons. There were a multitude of Government places, and not merely these, but bribes of actual 500*l*. notes, which members of the House took not much shame in receiving. Fox went into Parliament at 20: Pitt when just of age: his father when not much older. It was the good time for Patricians. Small blame to them if they took and enjoyed, and over-enjoyed, the prizes of politics, the pleasures of social life.

In these letters to Selwyn, we are made acquainted with a whole society of these defunct fine gentlemen: and can watch with a curious interest a life which the novel-writers of that time, I think, have scarce touched upon. To Smollett, to Fielding even, a lord was a lord: a gorgeous being with a blue ribbon, a coroneted chair, and an immense star on his bosom, to whom commoners paid reverence. Richardson, a man of humbler birth than either of the above two, owned that he was ignorant regarding the manners of the aristocracy, and besought Mrs. Donnellan, a lady who had lived in the great world, to examine a volume of Sir Charles Grandison, and point out any errors which she might see in this particular. Mrs. Donnellan found so many faults, that Richardson changed color; shut up the book; and muttered that it were best to throw it in the fire. Here, in Selwyn, we have the real original men and women of fashion of the early time of George III. We can follow them to the new club at Almack's: we can travel over Europe with them: we can accompany them not only to the public places, but to their country-houses and private society. Here is a whole company of them; wits and prodigals; some persevering in their bad ways: some repentant, but relapsing; beautiful ladies, parasites, humble chaplains, led captains. Those fair creatures whom we love in Reynolds's portraits, and who still look out on us from his canvases with their sweet calm faces and gracious smiles — those fine gentlemen who did us the honor to govern us; who inherited their boroughs; took their ease in their patient places; and slipped Lord North's bribes so elegantly under their ruffles — we make acquaintance with a hundred of these fine folks, hear their talk and laughter, read of their loves, quarrels, intrigues, debts, duels, divorces; can fancy them alive if we read the book long enough. We can attend at Duke Hamilton's wedding, and behold him marry his bride with the curtain-ring: we can peep into her poor sister's death-bed: we can see Charles Fox cursing over the cards, or March bawling out the odds at Newmarket: we can imagine Burgoyne tripping off from St. James's Street to conquer the Americans, and slinking back into the club somewhat crestfallen after his beating; we can see the young King dressing himself for the drawing-room and asking ten thousand questions regarding all the gentlemen: we can have high or low, the struggle at the Opera to behold the Violetta or the Zamperini — the Macaronies and fine ladies in their chairs trooping to the masquerade or Madame Cornelys's — the crowd at Drury Lane to look at the body of Miss Ray, whom Parson Hackman has just pistolled — or we can peep into Newgate, where poor Mr. Rice the forger is waiting his fate and his supper. "You need not be particular about the sauce for his fowl," says one turnkey to another: "for you know he is to be hanged in the morning." "Yes," replies the second janitor, "but the chaplain sups with him, and he is a terrible fellow for melted butter."

Selwyn has a chaplain and parasite, one Dr. Warner, than whom Plautus, or Ben Jonson, or Hogarth, never painted a better character. In letter after letter he adds fresh strokes to the portrait of himself, and completes a portrait not a little curious to look at now that the man has passed away; all the foul pleasures and gambols in which he revelled, played out; all the rouged faces into which he leered, worms and skulls; all the fine gentlemen whose shoebuckles he kissed, laid in their coffins. This worthy clergyman takes care to tell us that he does not believe in his religion, though, thank heaven, he is not so great a rogue as a lawyer. He goes on Mr. Selwyn's errands, any errands, and is proud, he says, to be that gentleman's proveditor. He waits upon the Duke of Queensberry — old Q. — and exchanges pretty stories with that aristocrat. He comes home "after a hard day's christening," as he says, and writes to his patron before sitting down to whist and partridges for supper. He revels in the thoughts of ox-cheek and burgundy — he is a boisterous, uproarious parasite, licks his master's shoes with explosions of laughter and cunning smack and gusto, and likes the taste of that blacking as much as the best claret in old Q.'s cellar. He has Rabelais and Horace at his greasy fingers' ends. He is inexpressibly mean, curiously jolly; kindly and good-natured in secret — a tender-hearted knave, not a venomous lick-spittle. Jesse says, that at his chapel in Long Acre, "he attained a considerable popularity by the pleasing, manly, and eloquent style of his delivery." Was infidelity endemic, and corruption in the air? Around a young king, himself of the most exemplary life and undoubted piety, lived a court society as dissolute as our country ever knew. George II.'s bad morals bore their fruit in George III.'s early years; as I believe that a knowledge of that good man's example, his moderation, his frugal simplicity, and God-fearing life, tended infinitely to improve the morals of the country and purify the whole nation.

After Warner, the most interesting of Selwyn's correspondents is the Earl of Carlisle, grandfather of the amiable nobleman at present* Viceroy in Ireland. The grandfather, too, was Irish Viceroy, having previously been treasurer of the King's household: and, in 1778, the principal commissioner for treating, consulting, and agreeing upon the means of quieting the divisions subsisting in his Majesty's colonies, plantations, and possessions in North America. You may read his lordship's manifestoes in "The Royal New York Gazette." He returned to England, having by no means quieted the colonies; and speedily afterwards "The Royal New York Gazette" somehow ceased to be published.

This good, clever, kind, highly-bred Lord Carlisle was one of the English fine gentlemen who were well-nigh ruined by the awful debauchery and extravagance which prevailed in the great English society of those days. Its dissoluteness was awful: it had swarmed over Europe after the Peace; it had danced, and raced, and gambled in all the courts. It had made its bow at Versailles; it had run its horses on the plain of Sablons, near Paris, and created the Anglo-mania there: it had exported vast quantities of pictures and marbles from Rome and Florence; it had ruined itself by building great galleries and palaces for the reception of the statues and pictures: it had brought over singing-women and dancing-women from all the operas of Europe, on whom my lords lavished their thousands, whilst they left their honest wives and honest children languishing in the lonely, deserted splendors of the castle and park at home.

Besides the great London society of those days, there was another unacknowledged world, extravagant beyond measure, tearing about in the pursuit of pleasure; dancing, gambling, drinking, singing; meeting the real society in the public places (at Ranelaghs, Vauxhalls, and Ridottos, about which our old novelists talk so constantly), and outvying the real leaders of fashion in luxury, and splendor, and beauty. For instance, when the famous Miss Gunning visited Paris as Lady Coventry, where she expected that her beauty would meet with the applause which had followed her sister through England, it appears she was put to flight by an English lady still more lovely in the

* 1856.

eyes of the Parisians. A certain Mrs. Pitt took a box at the opera opposite the Countess; and was so much handsomer than her ladyship, that the parterre cried out that this was the real English angel, whereupon Lady Coventry quitted Paris in a huff. The poor thing died presently of consumption, accelerated, it was said, by the red and white paint with which she plastered those luckless charms of hers. (We must represent to ourselves all fashionable female Europe, at that time, as plastered with white, and raddled with red.) She left two daughters behind her, whom George Selwyn loved (he was curiously fond of little children), and who are described very drolly and pathetically in these letters, in their little nursery, where passionate little Lady Fanny, if she had not good cards, flung hers into Lady Mary's face; and where they sat conspiring how they should receive a new mother-in-law whom their papa presently brought home. They got on very well with their mother-in-law, who was very kind to them; and they grew up, and they were married, and they were both divorced afterwards — poor little souls! Poor painted mother, poor society, ghastly in its pleasures, its loves, its revelries!

As for my lord commissioner, we can afford to speak about him; because, though he was a wild and weak commissioner at one time, though he hurt his estate, though he gambled and lost ten thousand pounds at a sitting — "five times more," says the unlucky gentleman, "than I ever lost before;" though he swore he never would touch a card again; and yet, strange to say, went back to the table and lost still more: yet he repented of his errors, sobered down, and became a worthy peer and a good country gentleman, and returned to the good wife and the good children whom he had always loved with the best part of his heart. He had married at one and twenty. He found himself, in the midst of a dissolute society, at the head of a great fortune. Forced *into* luxury, and obliged to be a great lord and a great idler, he yielded to some temptations, and paid for them a bitter penalty of manly remorse; from some others he fled wisely, and ended by conquering them nobly. But he always had the good wife and children in his mind, and they saved him. "I am very glad you did not come to me the morning I left London," he writes to G. Selwyn, as he is embarking for America. "I can only say, I never knew till that moment of parting, what grief was." There is no parting now, where they are. The faithful wife, the kind, generous gentleman, have left a noble race behind them: an inheritor of his name and titles, who is beloved as widely as he is known; a man most kind, accomplished, gentle, friendly, and pure; and female descendants occupying high stations and embellishing great names; some renowned for beauty, and all for spotless lives, and pious matronly virtues.

Another of Selwyn's correspondents is the Earl of March, afterwards Duke of Queensberry, whose life lasted into this century; and who certainly as earl or duke, young man or graybeard, was not an ornament to any possible society. The legends about old Q. are awful. In Selwyn, in Wraxall, and contemporary chronicles, the observer of human nature may follow him, drinking, gambling, intriguing to the end of his career; when the wrinkled, palsied, toothless old Don Juan died, as wicked and unrepentant as he had been at the hottest season of youth and passion. There is a house in Piccadilly, where they used to show a certain low window at which old Q. sat to his very last days, ogling through his senile glasses the women as they passed by.

There must have been a great deal of good about this lazy, sleepy George Selwyn, which, no doubt, is set to his present credit. "Your friendship," writes Carlisle to him, "is so different from any thing I have ever met with or seen in the world, that when I recollect the extraordinary proofs of your kindness, it seems to me like a dream." "I have lost my oldest friend and acquaintance, G. Selwyn," writes Walpole to Miss Berry: "I really loved him, not only for his infinite wit, but for a thousand good qualities." I am glad, for my part, that such a lover of cakes and ale should have had a thousand good qualities — that he should have been friendly, generous, warm-hearted, trustworthy. "I rise at six," writes Carlisle to him, from Spa (a great resort of fashionable people in our ancestors' days), "play at cricket till dinner, and dance in the evening, till I can scarcely crawl to bed at eleven. There is a life for you! You get up at nine; play with Raton your dog till twelve, in your dressing-gown; then creep down to 'White's;' are five hours at table; sleep till supper-time; and then make two wretches carry you in a sedan-chair, with three pints of claret in you, three miles for a shilling." Occasionally, instead of sleeping at "White's," George went down and snoozed in the House of Commons by the side of Lord North. He represented Gloucester for many years, and had a borough of his own, Ludgershall, for which, when he was too lazy to contest Gloucester, he sat himself. "I have given directions for the election of Ludgershall to be of Lord Melbourne and myself," he writes to the Premier, whose friend he was, and who was himself as sleepy, as witty, and as good-natured as George.

If, in looking at the lives of princes, courtiers, men of rank and fashion, we must perforce depict them as idle, profligate, and criminal, we must make allowances for the rich men's failings, and recollect that we, too, were very likely indolent and voluptuous, had we no motive for work, a mortal's natural taste for pleasure, and the daily temptation of a large income. What could a great peer, with a great castle and park, and a great fortune, do but be splendid and idle! In these letters of Lord Carlisle's from which I have been quoting, there is many a just complaint made by the kind-hearted young nobleman of the state which he is obliged to keep; the magnificence in which he must live; the idleness to which his position as a peer of England bound him. Better for him had he been a lawyer at his desk, or a clerk in his office; — a thousand times better chance for happiness, education, employment, security from temptation. A few years since the profession of arms was the only one which our nobles could follow. The church, the bar, medicine, literature, the arts, commerce, were below them. It is to the middle class we must look for the safety of England: the working educated men, away from Lord North's bribery in the senate; the good clergy not corrupted into parasites by hopes of preferment; the tradesmen rising into manly opulence; the painters pursuing their gentle calling: the men of letters in their quiet studies; these are the men whom we love and like to read of in the last age. How small the grandees and the men of pleasure look beside them! how contemptible the story of the George III. court-squabbles are beside the recorded talk of dear old Johnson! What is the grandest entertainment at Windsor, compared to a night at the club over its modest cups, with Percy and Langton, and Goldsmith, and poor Bozzy at the table? I declare I think, of all the polite men of that age, Joshua Reynolds was the finest gentleman. And they were good, as well as witty and wise, those dear old friends of the past. Their minds were not debauched by excess, or effeminate with luxury. They toiled their noble day's labor: they rested, and took their kindly pleasure: they cheered their holiday meetings with generous wit and hearty interchange of thought: they were no prudes, but no blush need follow their conversation: they were merry, but no riot came out of their cups. Ah! I would have liked a night at the "Turk's Head," even though bad news had arrived from the colonies, and Dr. Johnson was growling against the rebels; to have sat with him and Goldy; and to have heard Burke, the finest talker in the world; and to have had Garrick flashing in with a story from his theatre!—I like, I say, to think of that society; and not merely how pleasant and how wise, but how *good* they were. I think it was on going home one night from the club that Edmund Burke—his noble soul full of great thoughts, be sure, for they never left him; his heart full of gentleness—was accosted by a poor wandering woman, to whom he spoke words of kindness; and moved by the tears of this Magdalen, perhaps having caused them by the good words he spoke to her, he took her home to the house of his wife and children, and never left her until he had found the means of restoring her to honesty and labor. O you fine gentlemen! you Marches, and Selwyns, and Chesterfields, how small you look by the side of these great men! Good-natured Carlisle plays at cricket all day, and dances in the evening "till he can scarcely crawl," gayly contrasting his superior virtue with George Selwyn's, "carried to bed by two wretches at midnight with three pints of claret in him." Do you remember the verses—the sacred verses—which Johnson wrote on the death of his humble friend, Levett?

"Well tried through many a varying year,
See Levett to the grave descend;
Officious, innocent, sincere,
Of every friendless name the friend.

"In misery's darkest cavern known,
His useful care was ever nigh,
Where hopeless anguish poured the groan,
And lonely want retired to die.

"No summons mocked by chill delay,
No petty gain disdained by pride,
The modest wants of every day
The toil of every day supplied.

"His virtues walked their narrow round,
Nor made a pause, nor left a void;
And sure the Eternal Master found
His single talent well employed."

Whose name looks the brightest now, that of Queensberry the wealthy duke, or Selwyn the wit, or Levett the poor physician?

I hold old Johnson (and shall we not pardon James Boswell some errors for embalming him for us?) to be the great supporter of the British monarchy and church during the last age—better than whole benches of bishops, better than Pitts, Norths, and the great Burke himself. Johnson had the ear of the nation; his immense authority reconciled it to loyalty, and shamed it out of irreligion. When George III. talked with him, and the people heard the great author's good opinion of the sovereign, whole generations rallied to the King. Johnson was revered as a sort of oracle; and the oracle declared for church and king. What a humanity the old man had! He was a kindly partaker of all honest pleasures: a fierce foe to all sin, but a gentle enemy to all sinners. "What, boys, are you for a frolic?" he cries, when Topham Beauclerc comes and wakes him up at midnight: "I'm with you." And away he goes, tumbles on his homely old clothes, and trundles through Covent Garden with the young fellows. When he used to frequent Garrick's theatre, and had "the liberty of the scenes," he says, "All the actresses knew me, and dropped me a courtesy as they passed to the stage." That would make a pretty picture: it is a pretty picture in my mind, of youth, folly, gayety, tenderly surveyed by wisdom's merciful, pure eyes.

George III. and his Queen lived in a very unpretending but elegant-looking house, on the site of the hideous pile under which his granddaughter at present reposes. The King's mother inhabited Carlton House, which contemporary prints represent with a perfect paradise of a garden, with trim lawns, green arcades, and vistas of classic statues. She admired these in company with my Lord Bute, who had a fine classic taste, and sometimes counsel took and sometimes tea in the pleasant green arbors along with that polite nobleman. Bute was hated with a rage of which there have been few examples in English history. He was the butt for everybody's abuse; for Wilkes's devilish mischief; for Churchill's slashing satire; for the hooting of the mob that roasted the boot, his emblem, in a thousand bonfires; that hated him because he was a favorite and a Scotchman, calling him "Mortimer," "Lothario," I know not what names, and accusing his royal mistress of all sorts of crimes — the grave, lean, demure elderly woman, who, I dare say, was quite as good as her neighbors. Chatham lent the aid of his great malice to influence the popular sentiment against her. He assailed, in the House of Lords, "the secret influence, more mighty than the throne itself, which betrayed and clogged every administration." The most furious pamphlets echoed the cry. "Impeach the King's mother," was scribbled over every wall at the Court end of the town, Walpole tells us. What had she done? What had Frederick, Prince of Wales, George's father, done, that he was so loathed by George II. and never mentioned by George III.? Let us not seek for stones to batter that forgotten grave, but acquiesce in the contemporary epitaph over him: —

"Here lies Fred,
Who was alive, and is dead.
Had it been his father,
I had much rather.
Had it been his brother,
Still better than another.
Had it been his sister,
No one would have missed her.
Had it been the whole generation,
Still better for the nation.
But since 'tis only Fred,
Who was alive, and is dead,
There's no more to be said."

The widow with eight children round her, prudently reconciled herself with the King, and won the old man's confidence and good-will. A shrewd, hard, domineering, narrow-minded woman, she educated her children according to her lights, and spoke of the eldest as a dull, good boy: she kept him very close: she held the tightest rein over him: she had curious prejudices and bigotries. His uncle, the burly Cumberland, taking down a sabre once, and drawing it to amuse the child — the boy started back and turned pale. The Prince felt a generous shock: "What must they have told him about me?" he asked.

His mother's bigotry and hatred he inherited with the courageous obstinacy of his own race; but he was a firm believer where his fathers had been free-thinkers, and a true and fond supporter of the Church, of which he was the titular defender. Like other dull men, the King was all his life suspicious of superior people. He did not like Fox; he did not like Reynolds; he did not like Nelson, Chatham, Burke; he was testy at the idea of all innovations, and suspicious of all innovators. He loved mediocrities; Benjamin West was his favorite painter; Beattie was his poet. The King lamented, not without pathos, in his after life, that his education had been neglected. He was a dull lad brought up by narrow-minded people. The cleverest tutors in the world could have done little probably to expand that small intellect, though they might have improved his tastes, and taught his perceptions some generosity.

But he admired as well as he could. There is little doubt that a letter, written by the little Princess Charlotte of Mecklenburg Strelitz, — a letter containing the most feeble commonplaces about the horrors of war, and the most trivial remarks on the blessings of peace, struck the young monarch greatly, and decided him upon selecting the young Princess as the sharer of his throne. I pass over the stories of his juvenile loves — of Hannah Lightfoot, the Quaker, to whom they say he was actually married (though I don't know who has ever seen the register) — of lovely black-haired Sarah Lennox, about whose beauty Walpole has written in raptures, and who used to lie in wait for the young Prince, and make hay at him on the lawn of Holland House. He sighed and he longed, but he rode away from her. Her picture still hangs in Holland House, a magnificent master-piece by Reynolds, a canvas worthy of Titian. She looks from the castle window, holding a bird in her hand, at black-eyed young Charles Fox, her nephew. The royal bird flew away from lovely Sarah. She had to figure as bridesmaid at her little Mecklenburg rival's wedding, and died in our own time a quiet old lady, who had become the mother of the heroic Napiers.

They say the little Princess who had written the fine letter about the horrors of war — a beautiful letter without a single blot, for which she was to be rewarded, like the heroine of the old spelling-book story — was at play one day with some of her young companions in the gardens of Strelitz, and that the young ladies' conversation was, strange to say, about husbands. "Who will take such a poor little princess as me?" Charlotte said to her friend, Ida von Bulow, and at that very moment the postman's horn sounded, and Ida said, "Princess! there is the sweetheart." As she said, so it actually turned out. The postman brought letters from the splendid young King of all England, who said, "Princess! because you have written such a beautiful letter, which does credit to your head and heart, come and be Queen of Great Britain, France, and Ireland, and the true wife of your most obedient servant, George!" So she jumped for joy; and went up stairs and packed all her little trunks; and set off straightway for her kingdom in a beautiful yacht, with a harpsichord on board for her to play upon, and around her a beautiful fleet, all covered with flags and streamers: and the distinguished Madame Auerbach complimented her with an ode, a translation of which may be read in "The Gentleman's Magazine" to the present day: —

"Her gallant navy through the main
  Now cleaves its liquid way.
There to their queen a chosen train
  Of nymphs due reverence pay.

"Europa, when conveyed by Jove
  To Crete's distinguished shore,
Greater attention scarce could prove,
  Or be respected more."

They met, and they were married, and for years they led the happiest, simplest lives sure ever led by married couple. It is said the King winced when he first saw his homely little bride; but, however that may be, he was a true and faithful husband to her, as she was a faithful and loving wife. They had the simplest pleasures — the very mildest and simplest — little country dances, to which a dozen couple were invited, and where the honest King would stand up and dance for three hours at a time to one tune; after which delicious excitement they would go to bed without any supper (the Court people grumbling sadly at that absence of supper), and get up quite early the next morning, and perhaps the next night have another dance; or the Queen would play on the spinet — she played pretty well, Haydn said — or the King would read to her a paper out of "The Spectator," or perhaps one of Ogden's sermons. O Arcadia! what a life it must have been! There used to be Sunday drawing-rooms at Court; but the young King stopped these, as he stopped all that godless gambling whereof we have made mention. Not that George was averse to any innocent pleasures, or pleasures which he thought innocent. He was a patron of the arts, after his fashion; kind and gracious to the artists whom he favored, and respectful to their calling. He wanted once to establish an Order of Minerva for literary and scientific characters; the knights were to take rank after the knights of the Bath, and to sport a straw-colored ribbon and a star of sixteen points. But there was such a row amongst the *literati* as to the persons who should be appointed, that the plan was given up, and Minerva and her star never came down amongst us.

He objected to painting St. Paul's, as Popish practice; accordingly, the most clumsy heathen sculptures decorate that edifice at present. It is fortunate that the paintings, too, were spared, for painting and drawing were wofully unsound at the close of the last century; and it is far better for our eyes to contemplate whitewash (when we turn them away from the clergyman) than to look at Opie's pitchy canvases, or Fuseli's livid monsters.

And yet there is one day in the year — a day when old George loved with all his heart to attend it — when I think St. Paul's presents the noblest sight in the whole world: when five thousand charity children, with cheeks like nosegays, and sweet, fresh voices, sing the hymn which makes every heart thrill with praise and happiness. I have seen a hundred grand sights in the world — coronations, Parisian splendors, Crystal Palace openings, Pope's chapels with their processions of long-tailed cardinals and quavering choirs of fat soprani — but think in all Christendom there is no such sight as Charity Children's day. *Non Angli, sed angeli.* As one looks at that beautiful multitude of innocents: as the first note strikes: indeed one may almost fancy that cherubs are singing.

Of church music the King was always very fond, showing skill in it both as a critic and a performer. Many stories, mirthful and affecting, are told of his behavior at the concerts which he ordered. When he was blind and ill he chose the music for the Ancient Concerts once, and the music and words which he selected were from "Samson Agonistes," and all had reference to his blindness, his captivity, and his affliction. He would beat time with his music-roll as they sang the anthem in the Chapel Royal. If the page below was talkative or inattentive, down would come the music-roll on young scapegrace's powdered head. The theatre was always his delight. His bishops and clergy used to attend it, thinking it no shame to appear where that good man was seen. He is said not to have cared for Shakspeare or tragedy much; farces and pantomimes were his joy; and especially when clown swallowed a carrot or a string of sausages, he would laugh so outrageously that the lovely Princess by his side would have to say, "My gracious monarch, do compose yourself." But he continued to laugh, and at the very smallest farces, as long as his poor wits were left him.

There is something to me exceedingly touching in that simple early life of the King's. As long as his mother lived — a dozen years after his marriage with the little spinet-player — he was a great, shy, awkward boy, under the tutelage of that hard parent. She must have been a clever, domineering, cruel woman. She kept her household lonely and in gloom, mistrusting almost all people who came about her children. Seeing the young Duke of Gloucester silent and unhappy once, she sharply asked him the cause of his silence. "I am thinking," said the poor child. "Thinking, sir! and of what?" "I am thinking if ever I have a son I will not make him so unhappy as you make me." The other sons were all wild, except George. Dutifully every evening George and Charlotte paid their visit to the King's mother at Carlton House. She had a throat-complaint, of which she died; but to the last persisted in driving about the streets to show she was alive. The night before her death the resolute woman talked with her son and daughter-in-law as usual, went to bed, and was found dead there in the morning. "George, be a king!" were the words which she was for ever croaking in the ears of her son: and a king the simple, stubborn, affectionate, bigoted man tried to be.

He did his best; he worked according to his lights; what virtue he knew, he tried to practise; what knowledge he could muster he strove to acquire. He was forever drawing maps, for example, and learned geography with no small care and industry. He knew all about the family histories and genealogies of his gentry, and pretty histories he must have known. He knew the whole *Army List;* and all the facings, and the exact number of the buttons, and all the tags and laces, and the cut of all the cocked hats, pigtails, and gaiters in his army. He knew the *personnel* of the Universities; what doctors were inclined to Socinianism, and who were sound Churchmen; he knew the etiquettes of his own and his grandfather's courts to a nicety, and the smallest particulars regarding the routine of ministers, secretaries, embassies, audiences; the humblest page in the ante-room, or the meanest helper in the stables or kitchen. These parts of the royal business he was capable of learning, and he learned. But, as one thinks of an office, almost divine, performed by any mortal man — of any single being pretending to control the thoughts, to direct the faith, to order the implicit obedience of brother millions, to compel them into war at his offence or quarrel; to command, "In this way you shall trade, in this way you shall think; these neighbors shall be your allies whom you shall help, these others your enemies whom you shall slay at my orders; in this way you shall worship God;" — who can wonder that, when such a man as George took such an office on himself, punishment and humiliation should fall upon people and chief?

Yet there is something grand about his courage. The battle of the King with his aristocracy remains yet to be told by the historian who shall view the reign of George more justly than the trumpery panegyrists who wrote immediately after his decease. It was he, with the people to back him, who made the war with America; it was he and the people who refused justice to the Roman Catholics; and on both questions he beat the patricians. He bribed: he bullied: he darkly dissembled on occasion: he exercised a slippery perseverance, and a vindictive resolution, which one almost admires as one thinks his character over. His courage was never to be beat. It trampled North under foot; it beat the stiff neck of the younger Pitt: even his illness never conquered that indomitable spirit. As soon as his brain was clear, it resumed the scheme, only laid aside when his reason left him: as soon as his hands were out of the strait waistcoat, they took up the pen and the plan which had engaged him up to the moment of his malady. I believe it is by persons believing themselves in the right that nine-tenths of the tyranny of this world has been perpetrated. Arguing on that convenient premiss, the Dey of Algiers would cut off twenty heads of a morning; Father Dominic would burn a score of Jews in the presence of the Most Catholic King, and the Archbishops of Toledo and Salamanca sing Amen. Protestants were roasted, Jesuits hung and quartered at Smithfield, and witches burned at Salem, and all by worthy people, who believed they had the best authority for their actions.

And so, with respect to old George, even Americans, whom he hated and who conquered him, may give him credit for having quite honest reasons for oppressing them. Appended to Lord Brougham's biographical sketch of Lord North are some autograph notes of the King, which let us most curiously into the state of his mind. "The times certainly require," says he, "the concurrence of all who wish to prevent anarchy. I have no wish but the prosperity of my own dominions, therefore I must look upon all who would not heartily assist me as bad men, as well as bad subjects." That is the way he reasoned. "I wish nothing but good, therefore every man who does not agree with me is a traitor and a scoundrel." Remember that he believed himself anointed by a Divine commission; remember that he was a man of slow parts and imperfect education; that the same awful will of Heaven which placed a crown upon his head, which made him tender to his family, pure in his life, courageous and honest, made him dull of comprehension, obstinate of will, and at many times deprived him of reason. He was the father of his people; his rebellious children must be flogged into obedience. He was the defender of the Protestant faith; he would rather lay that stout head upon the block than that Catholics should have a share in the government of England. And you do not suppose that there are not honest bigots enough in all countries to back kings in this kind of statesmanship? Without doubt the American war was popular in England. In 1775 the address in favor of coercing the colonies was carried by 304 to 105 in the Commons, by 104 to 29 in the House of Lords. Popular? — so was the Revocation of the Edict of Nantes popular in France: so was the massacre of St. Bartholomew: so was the Inquisition exceedingly popular in Spain.

Wars and revolutions are, however, the politician's province. The great events of this long reign, the statesmen and orators who illustrated it, I do not pretend to make the subjects of an hour's light talk. Let us return to our humbler duty of court gossip. Yonder sits our little Queen, surrounded by many stout sons and fair daughters whom she bore to her faithful George. The history of the daughters, as little Miss Burney has painted them to us, is delightful. They were handsome — she calls them beautiful; they were most kind, loving, and lady-like; they were gracious to every person, high and low, who served them. They had many little accomplishments of their own. This one drew: that one played the piano: they all worked most prodigiously, and fitted up whole suites of rooms — pretty, smiling Penelopes, — with their busy little needles. As we picture to ourselves the society of eighty years ago, we must imagine hundreds of thousands of groups of women in great high caps, tight bodies, and full skirts, needling away, whilst one of the number, or perhaps a favored gentleman in a pigtail, reads out a novel to the company. Peep into the cottage at Olney, for example, and see there Mrs. Unwin and Lady Hesketh, those high-bred ladies, those sweet, pious women, and William Cowper, that delicate wit, that trembling pietist, that refined gentleman, absolutely reading out Jonathan Wild to the ladies! What a change in our manners, in our amusements, since then!

King George's household was a model of an English gentleman's household. It was early; it was kindly; it was charitable; it was frugal; it was orderly; it must have been stupid to a degree which I shudder now to contemplate. No wonder all the princes ran away from the lap of that dreary domestic virtue. It always rose, rode, dined at stated intervals. Day after day was the same. At the same hour at night the King kissed his daughters' jolly cheeks; the Princesses kissed their mother's hand; and Madame Thielke brought the royal nightcap. At the same hour the equerries and women in waiting had their little dinner, and cackled over their tea. The King had his backgammon or his evening concert; the equerries yawned themselves to death in the anteroom; or the King and his family walked on Windsor slopes, the King holding his darling little Princess Amelia by the hand; and the people crowded round quite

A Little Rebel.

good-naturedly; and the Eton boys thrust their chubby cheeks under the crowd's elbows; and the concert over, the King never failed to take his enormous cocked-hat off, and salute his band, and say, "Thank you, gentlemen."

A quieter household, a more prosaic life than this of Kew or Windsor, cannot be imagined. Rain or shine, the King rode every day for hours; poked his red face into hundreds of cottages round about, and showed that shovel hat and Windsor uniform to farmers, to pig-boys, to old women making apple dumplings; to all sorts of people, gentle and simple, about whom countless stories are told. Nothing can be more undignified than these stories. When Haroun Alraschid visits a subject incog., the latter is sure to be very much the better for the caliph's magnificence. Old George showed no such royal splendor. He used to give a guinea sometimes: sometimes feel in his pockets and find he had no money: often ask a man a hundred questions: about the number of his family, about his oats and beans, about the rent he paid for his house, and ride on. On one occasion he played the part of King Alfred, and turned a piece of meat with a string at a cottager's house. When the old woman came home, she found a paper with an enclosure of money, and a note written by the royal pencil: "Five guineas to buy a jack." It was not splendid, but it was kind and worthy of Farmer George. One day, when the King and Queen were walking together, they met a little boy — they were always fond of children, the good folks — and patted the little white head. "Whose little boy are you?" asks the Windsor uniform. "I am the King's beef-eater's little boy," replied the child. On which the King said, "Then kneel down, and kiss the Queen's hand." But the innocent offspring of the beef-eater declined this treat. "No," said he, "I won't kneel, for if I do, I shall spoil my new breeches." The thrifty King ought to have hugged him and knighted him on the spot. George's admirers wrote pages and pages of such stories about him. One morning, before anybody else was up, the King walked about Gloucester town; pushed over Molly the housemaid with her pail, who was scrubbing the doorsteps; ran up stairs and woke all the equerries in their bedrooms; and then trotted down to the bridge, where, by this time, a dozen of louts were assembled. "What! is this Gloucester New Bridge?" asked our gracious monarch; and the people answered him, "Yes, your Majesty." "Why, then, my boys," said he, "let us have a huzzay!" After giving them which intellectual gratification, he went home to breakfast. Our fathers read these simple tales with fond pleasure; laughed at these very small jokes; liked the old man who poked his nose into every cottage; who lived on plain wholesome roast and boiled; who despised your French kickshaws; who was a true hearty old English gentleman. You may have seen Gilray's famous print of him — in the old wig, in the stout old hideous Windsor uniform — as the King of Brobdingnag, peering at a little Gulliver, whom he holds up in his hand, whilst in the other he has an opera-glass, through which he surveys the pygmy? Our fathers chose to set up George as the type of a great king; and the little Gulliver was the great Napoleon. We prided ourselves on our prejudices; we blustered and bragged with absurd vainglory; we dealt to our enemy a monstrous injustice of contempt and scorn; we fought him with all weapons, mean as well as heroic. There was no lie we would not believe; no charge of crime which our furious prejudices would not credit. I thought at one time of making a collection of the lies which the French had written against us, and we had published against them during the war: it would be a strange memorial of popular falsehood.

Their Majesties were very sociable potentates: and the Court Chronicler tells of numerous visits which they paid to their subjects, gentle and simple: with whom they dined; at whose great country-houses they stopped; or at whose poorer lodgings they affably partook of tea and bread and butter. Some of the great folks spent enormous sums in entertaining their sovereigns. As marks of special favor, the King and Queen sometimes stood as sponsors for the children of the nobility. We find Lady Salisbury was so honored in the year 1786; and in the year 1802, Lady Chesterfield. The "Court News" relates how her ladyship received their Majesties on a state bed "dressed with white satin and a profusion of lace: the counterpane of white satin embroidered with gold, and the bed of crimson satin lined with white." The child was first brought by the nurse to the Marchioness of Bath, who presided as chief nurse. Then the Marchioness handed baby to the Queen. Then the Queen handed the little darling to the Bishop of Norwich, the officiating clergyman; and, the ceremony over, a cup of caudle was presented by the Earl to his Majesty on one knee, on a large gold waiter, placed on a crimson velvet cushion. Misfortunes would occur in these interesting genuflectory ceremonies of royal worship. Bubb Doddington, Lord Melcombe, a very fat, puffy man, in a most gorgeous court-suit, had to kneel, Cumberland says, and was so fat and so tight that he could not get up again. "Kneel, sir, kneel!" cried my lord in waiting to a country mayor who had to read an address, but who went on with his compliment standing. "Kneel, sir, kneel!" cries my lord, in dreadful alarm. "I can't!" says the mayor, turning round; "don't you see I have got a wooden leg?" In the capital "Burney Diary and Letters," the home and court life of good old King George and good old Queen Charlotte are presented at portentous length. The King rose every morning at six: and had two hours to himself. He thought it effeminate to have a carpet in his bedroom. Shortly before eight, the Queen and the royal family were always ready for him, and they proceeded to the King's chapel in the castle. There were no fires in the passages: the chapel was scarcely alight; princesses, governesses, equerries grumbled and caught cold: but cold or hot, it was their duty to go: and, wet or dry, light or dark, the stout old George was always in his place to say amen to the chaplain.

The Queen's character is represented in "Burney" at full length. She was a sensible, most decorous woman; a very grand lady on state occasions, simple enough in ordinary life; well read as times went, and giving shrewd opinions about books; stingy, but not unjust; not generally unkind to her dependants, but invincible in her notions of etiquette, and quite angry if her people suffered ill-health in her service. She gave Miss Burney a shabby pittance, and led the poor young woman a life which well-nigh killed her. She never thought but that she was doing Burney the greatest favor, in taking her from freedom, fame, and competence, and killing her off with languor in that dreary court. It was not dreary to her. Had she been servant instead of mistress, her spirit would never have broken down: she never would have put a pin out of place, or been a moment from her duty. *She* was not weak, and she could not pardon those who were. She was perfectly correct in life, and she hated poor sinners with a rancor such as virtue sometimes has. She must have had awful private trials of her own: not merely with her children, but with her husband, in those long days about which nobody will ever know any thing now; when he was not quite insane; when his incessant tongue was babbling folly, rage, persecution; and she had to smile and be respectful and attentive under this intolerable ennui.

The Queen bore all her duties stoutly, as she expected others to bear them. At a State christening, the lady who held the infant was tired and looked unwell, and the Princess of Wales asked permission for her to sit down. "Let her stand," said the Queen, flicking the snuff off her sleeve. *She* would have stood, the resolute old woman, if she had had to hold the child till his beard was grown. "I am seventy years of age," the Queen said, facing a mob of ruffians who stopped her sedan: "I have been fifty years Queen of England, and I never was insulted before." Fearless, rigid, unforgiving little queen! I don't wonder that her sons revolted from her.

Of all the figures in that large family group which surrounds George and his queen, the prettiest, I think, is the father's darling, the Princess Amelia, pathetic for her beauty, her sweetness, her early death, and for the extreme passionate tenderness with which her father loved her. This was his favorite amongst all the children: of his sons, he loved the Duke of York best. Burney tells a sad story of the poor old man at Weymouth, and how eager he was to have this darling son with him. The King's house was not big enough to hold the Prince; and his father had a portable house erected close to his own, and at huge pains, so that his dear Frederick should be near him. He clung on his arm all the time of his visit: talked to no one else; had talked of no one else for some time before. The Prince, so long expected, staid but a single night. He had business in London the next day, he said. The dulness of the old King's court stupefied York and the other big sons of George III. They scared equerries and ladies, frightened the modest little circle, with their coarse spirits and loud talk. Of little comfort, indeed, were the King's sons to the King.

But the pretty Amelia was his darling; and the little maiden, prattling and smiling in the fond arms of that old father, is a sweet image to look on. There is a family picture in Burney, which a man must be very hard-hearted not to like. She describes an after-dinner walk of the royal family at Windsor: — "It was really a mighty pretty procession," she says. "The little Princess, just turned of three years old, in a robe-coat covered with fine muslin, a dressed close cap, white gloves, and fan, walked on alone and first, highly delighted with the parade, and turning from side to side to see everybody as she passed; for all the terracers stand up against the walls, to make a clear passage for the royal family the moment they come in sight. Then followed the King and Queen, no less delighted with the joy of their little darling. The Princess Royal leaning on Lady Elizabeth Waldegrave, the Princess Augusta holding by the Duchess of Ancaster, the Princess Elizabeth led by Lady Charlotte Bertie, followed. Office here takes place of rank," says Burney, — to explain how it was that Lady E. Waldegrave, as lady of the bed-chamber, walked before a duchess; — "General Bude, and the Duke of Montague, and Major Price as equerry, brought up the rear of the procession. One sees it; the band playing its old music, the sun shining on the happy, loyal club; and lighting the ancient battlements, the rich elms, and purple landscape, and bright greensward; the royal standard drooping from the great tower yonder; as old George passes, followed by his race, preceded by the charming infant, who caresses the crowd with her innocent smiles.

"On sight of Mrs. Delany, the King instantly stopped to speak to her; the Queen, of course, and the little Princess, and all the rest, stood still. They talked a good while with the sweet old lady, during which time the King once or twice addressed himself to me. I caught the Queen's eye, and saw in it a little surprise, but by no means any displeasure, to see me of the party. The little Princess went up to Mrs. Delany, of whom she is very fond, and behaved like a little angel to her. She then, with a look of inquiry and recollection, came behind Mrs. Delany to look at me. 'I am afraid,' said I, in a whisper, and stooping down, 'your Royal Highness does not remember me?' Her answer was an arch little smile, and a nearer approach, with her lips pouted out to kiss me." The Princess wrote verses herself, and there are some pretty plaintive lines attributed to her, which are more touching than better poetry: —

> "Unthinking, idle, wild, and young,
> I laughed, and danced, and talked, and sung:
> And, proud of health, of freedom vain,
> Dreamed not of sorrow, care, or pain;
> Concluding, in those hours of glee,
> That all the world was made for me.
>
> "But when the hour of trial came,
> When sickness shook this trembling frame,
> When folly's gay pursuits were o'er,
> And I could sing and dance no more,
> It then occurred, how sad 'twould be,
> Were this world only made for me."

The poor soul quitted it — and ere yet she was dead the agonized father was in such a state, that the officers round about him were obliged to set watchers over him, and from November, 1810, George III. ceased to reign. All the world knows the story of his malady: all history presents no sadder figure than that of the old man, blind and deprived of reason, wandering through the rooms of his palace, addressing imaginary parliaments, reviewing fancied troops, holding ghostly courts. I have seen his picture as it was taken at this time, hanging in the apartment of his daughter, the Landgravine of Hesse Hombourg — amidst books and Windsor furniture, and a hundred fond reminiscences of her English home. The poor old father is represented in a purple gown, his snowy beard falling over his breast — the star of his famous Order still idly shining on it. He was not only sightless: he became utterly deaf. All light, all reason, all sound of human voices, all the pleasures of this world of God, were taken from him. Some slight lucid moments he had; in one of which, the Queen, desiring to see him, entered the room, and found him singing a hymn, and accompanying himself at the harpsichord. When he had finished, he knelt down and prayed aloud for her, and then for his family, and then for the nation, concluding with a prayer for himself, that it might please God to avert his heavy calamity from him, but if not, to give him resignation to submit. He then burst into tears, and his reason again fled.

What preacher need moralize on this story; what words save the simplest are requisite to tell it? It is too terrible for tears. The thought of such a misery smites me down in submission before the Ruler of kings and men, the Monarch Supreme over empires and republics, the inscrutable Dispenser of life, death, happiness, victory. "O brothers," I said to those who heard me first in America — "O brothers! speaking the same dear mother tongue — O comrades! enemies no more, let us take a mournful hand together as we stand by this royal corpse, and call a truce to battle! Low he lies to whom the proudest used to kneel once, and who was cast lower than the poorest: dead, whom millions prayed for in vain. Driven off his throne; buffeted by rude hands; with his children in revolt; the darling of his old age killed before him untimely; our Lear hangs over her breathless lips and cries, 'Cordelia, Cordelia, stay a little!'

> 'Vex not his ghost — oh! let him pass — he hates him
> That would upon the rack of this tough world
> Stretch him out longer!'

Hush! Strife and Quarrel, over the solemn grave! Sound, trumpets, a mournful march. Fall, dark curtain, upon his pageant, his pride, his grief, his awful tragedy."

George the Fourth.

GEORGE THE FOURTH.

In Twiss's amusing "Life of Eldon," we read how, on the death of the Duke of York, the old Chancellor became possessed of a lock of the defunct Prince's hair; and so careful was he respecting the authenticity of the relic, that Bessie Eldon, his wife, sat in the room with the young man from Hamlet's who distributed the ringlet into separate lockets, which each of the Eldon family afterwards wore. You know how, when George IV. came to Edinburgh, a better man than he went on board the royal yacht to welcome the King to his kingdom of Scotland, seized a goblet from which his Majesty had just drunk, vowed it should remain forever as an heirloom in his family, clapped the precious glass in his pocket, and sat down on it and broke it when he got home. Suppose the good sheriff's prize unbroken now at Abbotsford, should we not smile with something like pity as we beheld it? Suppose one of those lockets of the no-Popery Prince's hair offered for sale at Christie's, *quot libras e duce summo invenies?* how many pounds would you find for the illustrious Duke? Madame Tussaud has got King George's coronation robes; is there any man now alive who would kiss the hem of that trumpery? He sleeps since thirty years: do not any of you who remember him, wonder that you once respected and huzzaed and admired him?

To make a portrait of him at first seemed a matter of small difficulty. There is his coat, his star, his wig, his countenance simpering under it: with a slate and a piece of chalk, I could at this very desk perform a recognizable likeness of him. And yet after reading of him in scores of volumes, hunting him through old magazines and newspapers, having him here at a ball, there at a public dinner, there at races and so forth, you find you have nothing — nothing but a coat and a wig and a mask smiling below it — nothing but a great simulacrum. His sire and grandsires were men. One knows what they were like: what they would do in given circumstances: that on occasions they fought and demeaned themselves like tough good soldiers. They had friends whom they liked according to their natures; enemies whom they hated fiercely; passions, and actions, and individualities of their own. The sailor King who came after George was a man: the Duke of York was a man, big, burly, loud, jolly, cursing, courageous. But this George, what was he? I look through all his life, and recognize but a bow and a grin. I try and take him to pieces, and find silk stockings, padding, stays, a coat with frogs and a fur collar, a star and blue ribbon, a pocket-handkerchief prodigiously scented, one of Truefitt's best nutty-brown whigs reeking with oil, a set of teeth and a huge black stock, under-waistcoats, more under-waistcoats and then nothing. I know of no sentiment that he ever distinctly uttered. Documents are published under his name, but people wrote them — private letters, but people spelt them. He put a great George P. or George R. at the bottom of the page and fancied he had written the paper: some bookseller's clerk, some poor author, some *man* did the work; saw to the spelling, cleaned up the slovenly sentences, and gave the lax maudlin slipslop a sort of consistency. He must have had an individuality: the dancing-master whom he emulated, nay, surpassed — the wig-maker who curled his toupee for him — the tailor who cut his coats, had that. But, about George, one can get at nothing actual. That outside, I am certain, is pad and tailor's work; there may be something behind, but what? We cannot get at the character; no doubt never shall. Will men of the future have nothing better to do than to unswathe and interpret that royal old mummy? I own I once used to think it would be good sport to pursue him, fasten on him, and pull him down. But now I am ashamed to mount and lay good dogs on, to summon a full field, and then to hunt the poor game.

On the 12th August, 1762, the forty-seventh anniversary of the accession of the House of Brunswick to the English throne, all the bells in London pealed in gratulation, and announced that an heir to George III. was born. Five days afterwards the King was pleased to pass letters patent under the great seal, creating H. R. H. the Prince of Great Britain, Electoral Prince of Brunswick Lüneburg, Duke of Cornwall and Rothsay, Earl of Carrick, Baron of Renfrew, Lord of the Isles, and Great Steward of Scotland, Prince of Wales and Earl of Chester.

All the people at his birth thronged to see this lovely child; and behind a gilt china-screen railing in St. James's Palace, in a cradle surmounted by the three princely ostrich feathers, the royal infant was laid to delight the eyes of the lieges. Among the earliest instances of homage paid to him, I read that "a curious Indian bow and arrows were sent to the Prince from his father's faithful subjects in New York." He was fond of playing with these toys; an old statesman, orator, and wit of his grandfather's and great-grandfather's time, never tired of his business, still eager in his old age to be well at court, used to play with the little Prince, and pretend to fall down dead when the Prince shot at him with his toy bow and arrows — and get up and fall down dead over and over again — to the increased delight of the child. So that he was flattered from his cradle upwards; and before his little feet could walk, statesmen and courtiers were busy kissing them.

There is a pretty picture of the royal infant — a beautiful buxom child — asleep in his mother's lap; who turns round and holds a finger to her lip, as if she would bid the courtiers around respect the baby's slumbers. From that day until his decease, sixty-eight years after, I suppose there were more pictures taken of that personage than of any other human being who ever was born and died — in every kind of uniform and every possible court-dress — in long fair hair, with powder, with and without a pig-tail — in every conceivable cocked-hat — in dragoon uniform — in Windsor uniform — in a field-marshal's clothes — in a Scotch kilt and tartans, with dirk and claymore (a stupendous figure) — in a frogged frock-coat with a fur collar and tight breeches and silk stockings — in wigs of every color, fair, brown, and black — in his famous coronation robes finally, with which performance he was so much in love that he distributed copies of the picture to all the courts and British embassies in Europe, and to numberless clubs, town-halls, and private friends. I remember as a young man how almost every dining-room had his portrait.

There is plenty of biographical tattle about the Prince's boyhood. It is told with what astonishing rapidity he learned all languages, ancient and modern; how he rode beautifully, sang charmingly, and played elegantly on the violoncello. That he was beautiful was patent to all eyes. He had a high spirit: and once, when he had had a difference with his father, burst into the royal closet and called out, "Wilkes and liberty forever!" He was so clever, that he confounded his very governors in learning; and one of them, Lord Bruce, having made a false

1780.

1790.

The Regent.

The King.

quantity in quoting Greek, the admirable young Prince instantly corrected him. Lord Bruce could not remain a governor after this humiliation; resigned his office, and, to soothe his feelings, was actually promoted to be an earl! It is the most wonderful reason for promoting a man that ever I heard. Lord Bruce was made an earl for a blunder in prosody; and Nelson was made a baron for the victory of the Nile.

Lovers of long sums have added up the millions and millions which in the course of his brilliant existence this single Prince consumed. Besides his income of 50,000*l.*, 70,000*l.*, 100,000*l.*, 120,000*l.* a year, we read of three applications to Parliament: debts to the amount of 160,000*l.*, of 650,000*l.*; besides mysterious foreign loans, whereof he pocketed the proceeds. What did he do for all this money? Why was he to have it? If he had been a manufacturing town, or a populous rural district, or an army of five thousand men, he would not have cost more. He, one solitary stout man, who did not toil, nor spin, nor fight,—what had any mortal done that he should be pampered so?

In 1784, when he was twenty-one years of age, Carlton Palace was given to him, and furnished by the nation with as much luxury as could be devised. His pockets were filled with money: he said it was not enough; he flung it out of the window: he spent 10,000*l.* a year for the coats on his back. The nation gave him more money, and more, and more. The sum is past counting. He was a prince most lovely to look on, and was christened Prince Florizel on his first appearance in the world. That he was the handsomest prince in the whole world was agreed by men, and alas! by many women.

I suppose he must have been very graceful. There are so many testimonies to the charm of his manner, that we must allow him great elegance and powers of fascination. He, and the King of France's brother, the Count d'Artois, a charming young Prince who danced deliciously on the tight-rope — a poor old tottering exiled King, who asked hospitality of King George's successor, and lived a while in the palace of Mary Stuart — divided in their youth the title of first gentleman of Europe. We in England of course gave the prize to *our* gentleman. Until George's death the propriety of that award was scarce questioned, or the doubters voted rebels and traitors. Only the other day I was reading in the reprint of the delightful "Noctes" of Christopher North. The health of THE KING is drunk in large capitals by the loyal Scotsman. You would fancy him a hero, a sage, a statesman, a pattern for kings and men. It was Walter Scott who had that accident with the broken glass I spoke of anon. He was the king's Scottish champion, rallied all Scotland to him, made loyalty the fashion, and laid about him fiercely with his claymore upon all the Prince's enemies. The Brunswicks had no such defenders as those two Jacobite commoners, old Sam Johnson the Lichfield chapman's son, and Walter Scott, the Edinburgh lawyer's.

Nature and circumstance had done their utmost to prepare the Prince for being spoiled: the dreadful dulness of papa's court, its stupid amusements, its dreary occupations, the maddening humdrum, the stifling sobriety of its routine, would have made a scapegrace of a much less lively prince. All the big princes bolted from that castle of *ennui* where old King George sat, posting up his books and droning over his Handel; and old Queen Charlotte over her snuff and her tambour-frame. Most of the sturdy, gallant sons settled down after sowing their wild oats, and became sober subjects of their father and brother — not ill liked by the nation, which pardons youthful irregularities readily enough, for the sake of pluck, and unaffectedness, and good-humor.

The boy is father of the man. Our Prince signalized his entrance into the world by a feat worthy of his future life. He invented a new shoebuckle. It was an inch long and five inches broad. "It covered almost the whole instep, reaching down to the ground on either side of the foot." A sweet invention! lovely and useful as the Prince on whose foot it sparkled. At his first appearance at a court ball, we read that "his coat was pink silk, with white cuffs; his waistcoat white silk, embroidered with various-colored foil, adorned with a profusion of French paste. And his hat was ornamented with two rows of steel beads, five thousand in number, with a button and loop of the same metal, and cocked in a new military style." What a Florizel! Do these details seem trivial? They are the grave incidents of his life. His biographers say that when he commenced housekeeping in that splendid new palace of his, the Prince of Wales had some windy projects of encouraging literature, science, and the arts; of having assemblies of literary characters; and societies for the encouragement of geography, astronomy, and botany. Astronomy, geography, and botany! Fiddlesticks! French ballet-dancers, French cooks, horse-jockeys, buffoons, procurers, tailors, boxers, fencing-masters, china, jewel, and gimcrack merchants — these were his real companions. At first he made a pretence of having Burke and Fox and Sheridan for his friends. But how could such men be serious before such an empty scapegrace as this lad? Fox might talk dice with him, and Sheridan wine; but what else had these men of genius in common with their tawdry young host of Carlton House? That fribble the leader of such men as Fox and Burke! That man's opinions about the constitution, the India Bill, justice to the Catholics — about any question graver than the button for a waistcoat or the sauce for a partridge — worth any thing! The friendship between the Prince and the Whig chiefs was impossible. They were hypocrites in pretending to respect him, and if he broke the hollow compact between them, who shall blame him? His natural companions were dandies and parasites. He could talk to a tailor or a cook; but, as the equal of great statesmen, to set up a creature, lazy, weak, indolent, besotted, of monstrous vanity, and levity incurable — it is absurd. They thought to use him, and did for a while; but they must have known how timid he was; how entirely heartless and treacherous, and have expected his desertion. His next set of friends were mere table companions, of whom he grew tired too; then we hear of him with a very few select toadies, mere boys from school or the Guards, whose sprightliness tickled the fancy of the worn-out voluptuary. What matters what friends he had? He dropped all his friends; he never could have real friends. An heir to the throne has flatterers, adventurers who hang about him, ambitious men who use him; but friendship is denied him.

And women, I suppose, are as false and selfish in their dealings with such a character as men. Shall we take the Leporello part, flourish a catalogue of the conquests of this royal Don Juan, and tell the names of the favorites to whom, one after the other, George Prince flung his pocket-handkerchief? What purpose would it answer to say how Perdita was pursued, won, deserted, and by whom succeeded? What good in knowing that he did actually marry Mrs. Fitz-Herbert according to the rites of the Roman Catholic Church; that her marriage settlements have been seen in London; that the names of the witnesses to her marriage are known. This sort of vice that we are now come to presents no new or fleeting trait of manners. Debauchees, dissolute, heartless, fickle, cowardly, have been ever since the world began.

This one had more temptations than most, and so much may be said in extenuation for him.

It was an unlucky thing for this doomed one, and tending to lead him yet farther on the road to the deuce, that, besides being lovely, so that women were fascinated by him; and heir-apparent, so that all the world flattered him; he should have a beautiful voice, which led him directly in the way of drink: and thus all the pleasant devils were coaxing on poor Florizel; desire, and idleness, and vanity, and drunkenness, all clashing their merry cymbals and bidding him come on.

We first hear of his warbling sentimental ditties under the walls of Kew Palace by the moonlight banks of Thames, with Lord Viscount Leporello keeping watch lest the music should be disturbed.

Singing after dinner and supper was the universal fashion of the day. You may fancy all England sounding with choruses, some ribald, some harmless, but all occasioning the consumption of a prodigious deal of fermented liquor.

> "The jolly Muse her wings to try no frolic flights need take,
> But round the bowl would dip and fly, like swallows round a lake,"

sang Morris in one of his gallant Anacreontics, to which the Prince many a time joined in chorus, and of which the burden is, —

> "And that I think's a reason fair to drink and fill again."

This delightful boon companion of the Prince's found "a reason fair" to forego filling and drinking, saw the error of his ways, gave up the bowl and chorus, and died retired and religious. The Prince's table no doubt was a very tempting one. The wits came and did their utmost to amuse him. It is wonderful how the spirits rise, the wit brightens, the wine has an aroma, when a great man is at the head of the table. Scott, the loyal cavalier, the king's true liegeman, the very best *raconteur* of his time, poured out with an endless generosity his store of old-world learning, kindness, and humor. Grattan contributed to it his wondrous eloquence, fancy, feeling. Tom Moore perched upon it for a while, and piped his most exquisite little love-tunes on it, flying away in a twitter of indignation afterwards, and attacking the Prince with bill and claw. In such society, no wonder the sitting was long, and the butler tired of drawing corks. Remember what the usages of the time were, and that William Pitt, coming to the House of Commons after having drunk a bottle of port-wine at his own house, would go into Bellamy's with Dundas, and help finish a couple more.

You peruse volumes after volumes about our Prince, and find some half-dozen stock stories — indeed not many more — common to all the histories. He was good-natured; an indolent, voluptuous prince, not unkindly. One story, the most favorable to him of all, perhaps, is that as Prince Regent he was eager to hear all that could be said in behalf of prisoners condemned to death, and anxious, if possible, to remit the capital sentence. He was kind to his servants. There is a story common to all the biographies, of Molly the housemaid, who, when his household was to be broken up, owing to some reforms which he tried absurdly to practise, was discovered crying as she dusted the chairs because she was to leave a master who had a kind word for all his servants. Another tale is that of a groom of the Prince's being discovered in corn and oat peculations, and dismissed by the personage at the head of the stables; the Prince had word of John's disgrace, remonstrated with him very kindly, generously reinstated him, and bade him promise to sin no more — a promise which John kept. Another story is very fondly told of the Prince as a young man hearing of an officer's family in distress, and how he straightway borrowed six or eight hundred pounds, put his long fair hair under his hat, and so disguised carried the money to the starving family. He sent money, too, to Sheridan on his death-bed, and would have sent more had not death ended the career of that man of genius. Besides these, there are a few pretty speeches, kind and graceful, to persons with whom he was brought in contact. But he turned upon twenty friends. He was fond and familiar with them one day, and he passed them on the next without recognition. He used them, liked them, loved them perhaps in his way, and then separated from them. On Monday he kissed and fondled poor Perdita, and on Tuesday he met her and did not know her. On Wednesday he was very affectionate with that wretched Brummell, and on Thursday forgot him; cheated him even out of a snuff-box which he owed the poor dandy; saw him years afterwards in his downfall and poverty, when the bankrupt Beau sent him another snuff-box with some of the snuff he used to love, as a piteous token of remembrance and submission, and the King took the snuff, and ordered his horses and drove on, and had not the grace to notice his old companion, favorite, rival, enemy, superior. In Wraxall there is some gossip about him. When the charming, beautiful, generous Duchess of Devonshire died — the lovely lady whom he used to call his dearest duchess once, and pretend to admire as all English society admired her — he said, "Then we have lost the best bred woman in England." "Then we have lost the kindest heart in England," said noble Charles Fox. On another occasion, when three noblemen were to receive the Garter, says Wraxall, "A great personage observed that never did three men receive the order in so characteristic a manner. The Duke of A. advanced to the sovereign with a phlegmatic, cold, awkward air like a clown; Lord B. came forward fawning and smiling like a courtier; Lord C. presented himself easy, unembarrassed, like a gentleman!" These are the stories one has to recall about the Prince and King — kindness to a housemaid, generosity to a groom, criticism on a bow. There *are* no better stories about him: they are mean and trivial, and they characterize him. The great war of empires and giants goes on. Day by day victories are won and lost by the brave. Torn, smoky flags and battered eagles are wrenched from the heroic enemy and laid at his feet; and he sits there on his throne and smiles, and gives the guerdon of valor to the conqueror. He! Elliston the actor, when the *Coronation* was performed, in which he took the principal part, used to fancy himself the King, burst into tears, and hiccough a blessing on the people. I believe it is certain, about George IV., that he had heard so much of the war, knighted so many people, and worn such a prodigious quantity of marshal's uniforms, cocked-hats, cock's feathers, scarlet and bullion in general, that he actually fancied he had been present in some campaigns, and, under the name of General Brock, led a tremendous charge of the German legion at Waterloo.

He is dead but thirty years, and one asks how a great society could have tolerated him? Would we bear him now? In this quarter of a century, what a silent revolution has been working! how it has separated us from old times and manners! How it has changed men themselves! I can see old gentlemen now among us, of perfect good breeding, of quiet lives, with venerable gray heads, fondling their grandchildren; and look at them, and wonder at what they were once. That gentleman of the grand old school, when he was in the 10th Hussars, and dined at the Prince's table, would fall under it night after night. Night after night, that gentleman sat at Brookes's or Raggett's over the dice. If, in the petulance of play or drink, that gentleman spoke a sharp word to his neighbor, he and the other would infallibly go out and try to shoot each other the next morning. That gentleman would drive his friend Richmond the black boxer down to Moulsey, and hold his coat, and shout and swear, and hurrah with delight, whilst the black man was beating Dutch Sam the Jew. That gentleman would take a manly pleasure in pulling his own coat off, and thrashing a bargeman in a street row. That gentleman has been in a watch-house. That gentleman, so exquisitely polite with ladies in a drawing-room, so loftily courteous, if he talked now as he used among men in his youth, would swear so as to make your hair stand on end. I met lately a very old German gentleman, who had served in our army at the beginning of the century. Since then he has lived on his own estate, but rarely meeting with an Englishman, whose language — the language of fifty years ago that is — he possesses perfectly. When this highly bred old man began to speak English to me almost every other word he uttered was an oath: as they used (they swore dreadfully in Flanders) with the Duke of York before Valenciennes, or at Carlton House over the supper and cards. Read Byron's letters. So accustomed is the young man to oaths that he employs them even in writing to his friends, and swears by the post. Read his account of the doings of young men at Cambridge, of the ribald professors, one of whom "could pour out Greek like a drunken Helot," and whose excesses surpassed even those of the young men. Read Matthews's description of the boyish lordling's housekeeping at Newstead, the skull-cup passed round, the monk's dresses from the masquerade warehouse, in which the young scapegraces used to sit until daylight, chanting appropriate songs round their wine. "We come to breakfast at two or three o'clock," Matthews says. "There are gloves and foils for those who like to amuse themselves, or we fire pistols at a mark in the hall, or we worry the wolf." A jolly life truly! The noble young owner of the mansion writes about such affairs himself in letters to his friend, Mr. John Jackson, pugilist, in London.

All the Prince's time tells a similar strange story of manners and pleasure. In Wraxall we find the Prime Minister himself, the redoubted William Pitt, engaged in high jinks with personages of no less importance than Lord Thurlow the Lord Chancellor, and Mr. Dundas the Treasurer of the Navy. Wraxall relates how these three statesmen, returning after dinner from Addiscombe, found a turnpike open and galloped through it without paying the toll. The turnpike-man, fancying they were highwaymen, fired a blunderbuss after them, but missed them; and the poet sang, —

"How as Pitt wandered darkling o'er the plain,
His reason drowned in Jenkinson's champagne,
A rustic's hand, but righteous fate withstood,
Had shed a premier's for a robber's blood."

Here we have the Treasurer of the Navy, the Lord High Chancellor, and the Prime Minister, all engaged in a most undoubted lark. In Eldon's "Memoirs," about the very same time, I read that the bar loved wine, as well as the woolsack. Not John Scott himself; he was a good boy always; and though he loved port-wine, loved his business and his duty and his fees a great deal better.

He has a Northern Circuit story of those days, about a party at the house of a certain Lawyer Fawcett, who gave a dinner every year to the counsel.

"On one occasion," related Lord Eldon, "I heard Lee say, 'I cannot leave Fawcett's wine. Mind, Davenport, you will go home immediately after dinner, to read the brief in that cause that we have to conduct tomorrow.'

"'Not I,' said Davenport. 'Leave

my dinner and my wine to read a brief! No, no, Lee; that won't do.'

"'Then,' said Lee, 'what is to be done? who else is employed?'

"*Davenport.*—'Oh! young Scott.'

"*Lee.*—'Oh! he must go. Mr. Scott, you must go home immediately, and make yourself acquainted with that cause, before our consultation this evening.'

"This was very hard upon me; but I did go, and there was an attorney from Cumberland, and one from Northumberland, and I do not know how many other persons. Pretty late, in came Jack Lee, as drunk as he could be.

"'I cannot consult to-night; I must go to bed,' he exclaimed, and away he went. Then came Sir Thomas Davenport.

"'We cannot have a consultation to-night, Mr. Wordsworth' (Wordsworth, I think, was the name; it was a Cumberland name), shouted Davenport. 'Don't you see how drunk Mr. Scott is? it is impossible to consult.' Poor me! who had scarce any dinner, and lost all my wine—I was so drunk that I could not consult! Well, a verdict was given against us, and it was all owing to Lawyer Fawcett's dinner. We moved for a new trial; and I must say, for the honor of the bar, that those two gentlemen, Jack Lee and Sir Thomas Davenport, paid all the expenses between them of the first trial. It is the only instance I ever knew; but they did. We moved for a new trial (on the ground, I suppose, of the counsel not being in their senses), and it was granted. When it came on, the following year, the judge rose and said,—

"'Gentlemen, did any of you dine with Lawyer Fawcett yesterday? for, if you did, I will not hear this cause till next year.'

"There was great laughter. We gained the cause that time."

On another occasion, at Lancaster, where poor Bozzy must needs be going the Northern Circuit, "we found him," says Mr. Scott, "lying upon the pavement inebriated. We subscribed a guinea at supper for him, and a half-crown for his clerk"—(no doubt there was a large bar, so that Scott's joke did not cost him much)—"and sent him, when he waked next morning, a brief with instructions to move for what we denominated the writ of *quare adhæsit pavimento?* with observations duly calculated to induce him to think that it required great learning to explain the necessity of granting it, to the judge before whom he was to move." Boswell sent all round the town to attorneys for books that might enable him to distinguish himself—but in vain. He moved, however, for the writ, making the best use he could of the observations in the brief. The judge was perfectly astonished, and the audience amazed. The judge said, "I never heard of such a writ—what can it be that adheres *pavimento?* Are any of you gentlemen at the bar able to explain this?"

The bar laughed. At last one of them said,—

"My lord, Mr. Boswell last night *adhæsit pavimento.* There was no moving him for some time. At last he was carried to bed, and he has been dreaming about himself and the pavement."

The canny old gentleman relishes these jokes. When the Bishop of Lincoln was moving from the deanery of St. Paul's, he says he asked a learned friend of his, by name Will Hay, how he should move some especially fine claret, about which he was anxious.

"Pray, my lord bishop," says Hay, "how much of the wine have you?"

The bishop said six dozen.

"If that is all," Hay answered, "you have but to ask me six times to dinner, and I will carry it all away myself."

There were giants in those days; but this joke about wine is not so fearful as one perpetrated by Orator Thelwall, in the heat of the French

Revolution, ten years later, over a frothing pot of porter. He blew the head off, and said, "This is the way I would serve all kings."

Now we come to yet higher personages, and find their doings recorded in the blushing pages of timid little Miss Burney's "Memoirs." She represents a prince of the blood in quite a royal condition. The loudness, the bigness, boisterousness, creaking boots and rattling oaths of the young princes, appear to have frightened the prim household of Windsor, and set all the teacups twittering on the tray. On the night of a ball and birthday, when one of the pretty, kind princesses was to come out, it was agreed that her brother, Prince William Henry, should dance the opening minuet with her, and he came to visit the household at their dinner.

"At dinner, Mrs. Schwellenberg presided, attired magnificently; Miss Goldsworthy, Mrs. Stanforth, Messrs. Du Luc and Stanhope, dined with us; and while we were still eating fruit, the Duke of Clarence entered.

"He was just risen from the King's table, and waiting for his equipage to go home and prepare for the ball. To give you an idea of the energy of his Royal Highness's language, I ought to set apart an objection to writing, or rather intimating, certain forcible words, and beg leave to show you in genuine colors a royal sailor.

"We all rose, of course, upon his entrance, and the two gentlemen placed themselves behind their chairs, while the footmen left the room. But he ordered us all to sit down, and called the men back to hand about some wine. He was in exceedingly high spirits, and in the utmost good humor. He placed himself at the head of the table, next Mrs. Schwellenberg, and looked remarkably well, gay, and full of sport and mischief; yet clever withal, as well as comical.

"'Well, this is the first day I have ever dined with the King at St. James's on his birthday. Pray, have you all drunk his Majesty's health?'

"'No, your Royal Highness; your Royal Highness might make dem do dat,' said Mrs. Schwellenberg.

"'Oh, by ——, I will! Here, you" (to the footman), "bring champagne; I'll drink the King's health again if I die for it. Yes, I have done it pretty well already; so has the King, I promise you! I believe his Majesty was never taken such good care of before; we have kept his spirits up, I promise you; we have enabled him to go through his fatigues; and I should have done more still, but for the ball and Mary; — I have promised to dance with Mary. I must keep sober for Mary.'"

Indefatigable Miss Burney continues for a dozen pages reporting H. R. H.'s conversation, and indicating, with a humor not unworthy of the clever little author of "Evelina," the increasing state of excitement of the young sailor Prince, who drank more and more champagne, stopped old Mrs. Schwellenberg's remonstrances by giving the old lady a kiss, and telling her to hold her potato-trap, and who did not "keep sober for Mary." Mary had to find another partner that night, for the royal William Henry could not keep his legs.

Will you have a picture of the amusements of another royal prince? It is the Duke of York, the blundering general, the beloved commander-in-chief of the army, the brother with whom George IV. had had many a midnight carouse, and who continued his habits of pleasure almost till death seized his stout body.

In Pückler Muskau's "Letters," that German Prince describes a bout with H. R. H., who in his best time was such a powerful toper that "six bottles of claret after dinner scarce made a perceptible change in his countenance."

"I remember," says Pückler, "that one evening, — indeed, it was past midnight, — he took some of his guests, among whom were the Austrian ambassador, Count Meervelt, Count Beroldingen, and myself, into his beautiful armory. We tried to swing several Turkish sabres, but none of us had a very firm grasp; whence it happened that the Duke and Meervelt both scratched themselves with a sort of straight Indian sword so as to draw blood. Meervelt then wished to try if the sword cut as well as a Damascus, and attempted to cut through one of the wax candles that stood on the table. The experiment answered so ill, that both the candles and candlesticks all fell to the ground and were extinguished. While we were groping in the dark and trying to find the door, the Duke's aide-de-camp stammered out in great agitation, 'By G—, sir, I remember the sword is poisoned!'

"You may conceive the agreeable feelings of the wounded at this intelligence! Happily, on further examination, it appeared that claret, and not poison, was at the bottom of the colonel's exclamation."

And now I have one more story of the bacchanalian sort, in which Clarence and York, and the very highest personage of the realm, the great Prince Regent, all play parts. The feast took place at the Pavilion at Brighton, and was described to me by a gentleman who was present at the scene. In Gilray's caricatures, and amongst Fox's jolly associates, there figures a great nobleman, the Duke of Norfolk, called Jockey of Norfolk in his time, and celebrated for his table exploits. He had quarrelled with the Prince, like the rest of the Whigs; but a sort of reconciliation had taken place; and now, being a very old man, the Prince invited him to dine and sleep at the Pavilion, and the old Duke drove over from his Castle of Arundel with his famous equipage of gray horses, still remembered in Sussex.

The Prince of Wales had concocted with his royal brothers a notable scheme for making the old man drunk. Every person at table was enjoined to drink wine with the Duke — a challenge which the old toper did not refuse. He soon began to see that there was a conspiracy against him; he drank glass for glass; he overthrew many of the brave. At last the First Gentleman of Europe proposed bumpers of brandy. One of the royal brothers filled a great glass for the Duke. He stood up and tossed off the drink. "Now," says he, "I will have my carriage, and go home." The Prince urged upon him his previous promise to sleep under the roof where he had been so generously entertained. "No," he said; he had had enough of such hospitality. A trap had been set for him; he would leave the place at once and never enter its doors more.

The carriage was called, and came; but, in the half-hour's interval, the liquor had proved too potent for the old man; his host's generous purpose was answered, and the Duke's old gray head lay stupefied on the table. Nevertheless, when his post-chaise was announced, he staggered to it as well as he could, and stumbling in, bade the postilions drive to Arundel. They drove him for half an hour round and round the Pavilion lawn; the poor old man fancied he was going home. When he awoke that morning he was in bed at the Prince's hideous house at Brighton. You may see the place now for sixpence: they have fiddlers there every day; and sometimes buffoons and mountebanks hire the Riding House and do their tricks and tumbling there. The trees are still there, and the gravel walks round which the poor old sinner was trotted. I can fancy the flushed faces of the royal princes as they support themselves at the portico pillars, and look on at old Norfolk's disgrace; but I can't fancy how the man who perpetrated it continued to be called a gentleman.

From drinking, the pleased Muse now turns to gambling, of which in his youth our Prince was a great practitioner. He was a famous pigeon for the play-men; they lived upon him. Egalité Orleans, it was believed, punished him severely. A noble lord, whom we shall call the Marquis of Steyne, is said to have mulcted him in immense sums. He frequented the clubs, where play was then almost universal; and as it was known that his debts of honor were sacred, whilst he was gambling Jews waited outside to purchase his notes of hand.* His transactions on the turf were unlucky as well as discreditable: though I believe he, and his jockey, and his horse, Escape, were all innocent in that affair which created so much scandal.

Arthur's, Almack's, Bootle's, and White's were the chief clubs of the young men of fashion. There was play at all, and decayed noblemen and broken-down senators fleeced the unwary there. In Selwyn's "Letters" we find Carlisle, Devonshire, Coventry, Queensberry, all undergoing the probation. Charles Fox, a dreadful gambler, was cheated in very late times — lost 200,000*l.* at play. Gibbon tells of his playing for twenty-two hours at a sitting, and losing 500*l.* an hour. That indomitable punter said that the greatest pleasure in life, after winning, was losing. What hours, what nights, what health did he waste over the devil's books! I was going to say what peace of mind; but he took his losses very philosophically. After an awful night's play, and the enjoyment of the greatest pleasure but *one* in life, he was found on a sofa tranquilly reading an Eclogue of Virgil.

Play survived long after the wild Prince and Fox had given up the dice-box. The dandies continued it. Byron, Brummell — how many names could I mention of men of the world who have suffered by it! In 1837 occurred a famous trial which pretty nigh put an end to gambling in England. A peer of the realm was found cheating at whist, and repeatedly seen to practise the trick called *sauter la coupe*. His friends at the clubs saw him cheat, and went on playing with him. One greenhorn, who had discovered his foul play, asked an old man what he should do. "Do," said the Mammon of Unrighteousness, "*Back him, you fool.*" The best efforts were made to screen him. People wrote him anonymous letters and warned him; but he would cheat, and they were obliged to find him out. Since that day, when my lord's shame was made public, the gaming-table has lost all its splendor. Shabby Jews and blacklegs prowl about racecourses and tavern parlors, and now and then inveigle silly yokels with greasy packs of cards in railroad cars; but play is a deposed goddess, and her worshippers bankrupt and her table in rags.

So is another famous British institution gone to decay — the Ring: the noble practice of British boxing, which in my youth was still almost flourishing.

The Prince, in his early days, was a great patron of this national sport, as his grand-uncle Culloden Cumberland had been before him; but, being present at a fight at Brighton, where one of the combatants was killed, the Prince pensioned the boxer's widow, and declared he never would attend another battle. "But, nevertheless," — I read in the noble language of Pierce Egan (whose smaller work on Pugilism I have the honor to possess), — "he thought it a manly and decided English feature, which ought not to be destroyed. His Majesty had a drawing of the sporting characters in the Fives' Court placed in his boudoir, to remind him of his former attachment and support of true courage; and when any fight of note occurred after he was king, accounts of it were read to him by his desire." That gives one a fine image of a king taking his recreation; — at ease in a royal dressing-gown; too majestic to read himself, ordering the prime minister to read him accounts of battles: how Crib punched Molyneux's eye, or Jack Randall thrashed the Game Chicken.

Where my Prince *did* actually distinguish himself was in driving. He drove once in four hours and a half from Brighton to Carlton House — fifty-six miles. All the young men of that city were fond of that sport. But the fashion of rapid driving deserted England; and, I believe, trotted over to America. Where are the amusements of our youth? I hear of no gambling now but amongst obscure ruffians; of no boxing but amongst the lowest rabble. One solitary four-in-hand still drove round the parks in London last year; but that charioteer must soon disappear. He was very old; he was attired after the fashion of the year 1825. He must drive to the banks of the Styx ere long, — where the ferry-boat waits to carry him over to the defunct revellers who boxed and gambled and drank and drove with King George.

The bravery of the Brunswicks, that all the family must have it, that George possessed it, are points which all English writers have agreed to admit; and yet I cannot see how George IV. should have been endowed with this quality. Swaddling in featherbeds all his life, lazy, obese, perpetually eating and drinking, his education was quite unlike that of his tough old progenitors. His grandsires had confronted hardships and war, and ridden up and fired their pistols undaunted into the face of death. His father had conquered luxury and overcome indolence. Here was one who never resisted temptation; never had a desire but he coddled and pampered it; if ever he had any nerve, frittered it away among the cooks, and tailors, and barbers, and furniture mongers, and opera-dancers. What muscle would not grow flaccid in such a life — a life that was never strung up to any action — an endless Capua without any campaign — all fiddling, and flowers, and feasting, and flattery, and folly? When George III. was pressed by the Catholic question and the India Bill, he said he would retire to Hanover rather than yield upon either point; and he would have done what he said. But, before yielding, he was determined to fight his Ministers and Parliament; and he did, and he beat them. The time came when George IV. was pressed too upon the Catholic claims; the cautious Peel had slipped over to that side; the grim old Wellington had joined it; and Peel tells us, in his "Memoirs," what was the conduct of the King. He at first refused to submit; whereupon Peel and the Duke offered their resignation, which their gracious master accepted. He did these two gentlemen the honor, Peel says, to kiss them both when they went away. (Fancy old Arthur's grim countenance and eagle beak as the monarch kisses it!) When they were gone he sent after them, surrendered, and wrote to them a letter begging them to remain in office, and allowing them to have their way. Then his Majesty had a meeting with Eldon, which is related at curious length in the latter's "Memoirs." He told Eldon what was not true about his interview with the new Catholic converts; utterly misled the old ex-Chancellor; cried, whimpered, fell on his neck, and kissed him too. We know old Eldon's own tears were pumped very freely. Did these two fountains gush together? I can't fancy a behavior more unmanly, imbecile, pitiable. This a defender of the faith! This a chief in the crisis of a great nation! This an inheritor of the courage of the Georges!

Many of my hearers no doubt have journeyed to the pretty old town of Brunswick, in company with that most worthy, prudent, and polite gentleman, the Earl of Malmesbury, and fetched away Princess Caroline for her longing husband, the Prince of Wales. Old Queen Charlotte would have had her eldest son marry a niece of her own, that famous Louisa of Strelitz, afterwards Queen of Prussia, and who shares with Marie Antoinette in the last age the sad pre-eminence of beauty and misfortune. But

George III. had a niece at Brunswick: she was a richer princess than her Serene Highness of Strelitz:—in fine, the Princess Caroline was selected to marry the heir to the English throne. We follow my Lord Malmesbury in quest of her; we are introduced to her illustrious father and royal mother; we witness the balls and fêtes of the old court; we are presented to the Princess herself, with her fair hair, her blue eyes, and her impertinent shoulders—a lively, bouncing, romping Princess, who takes the advice of her courtly English mentor most generously and kindly. We can be present at her very toilette, if we like; regarding which, and for very good reasons, the British courtier implores her to be particular. What a strange court! What a queer privacy of morals and manners do we look into! Shall we regard it as preachers and moralists, and cry Woe, against the open vice and selfishness and corruption; or look at it as we do at the king in the pantomime, with his pantomime wife and pantomime courtiers, whose big heads he knocks together, whom he pokes with his pantomime sceptre, whom he orders to prison under the guard of his pantomime beef-eaters, as he sits down to dine on his pantomime pudding? It is grave, it is sad; it is theme most curious for moral and political speculation; it is monstrous, grotesque, laughable, with its prodigious littlenesses, etiquettes, ceremonials, sham moralities; it is as serious as a sermon, and as absurd and outrageous as Punch's puppet-show.

Malmesbury tells us of the private life of the Duke, Princess Caroline's father, who was to die, like his war-like son, in arms against the French; presents us to his courtiers, his favorite; his Duchess, George III.'s sister, a grim old Princess, who took the British envoy aside, and told him wicked old stories of wicked old dead people and times; who came to England afterwards when her nephew was regent, and lived in a shabby furnished lodging, old, and dingy, and deserted, and grotesque, but somehow royal. And we go with him to the Duke to demand the Princess's hand in form, and we hear the Brunswick guns fire their adieux of salute, as H. R. H. the Princess of Wales departs in the frost and snow; and we visit the domains of the Prince Bishop of Osnaburg—the Duke of York of our early time; and we dodge about from the French revolutionists, whose ragged legions are pouring over Holland and Germany, and gayly trampling down the old world to the tune of *ça ira;* and we take shipping at Slade, and we land at Greenwich, where the Princess's ladies and the Prince's ladies are in waiting to receive her Royal Highness.

What a history follows! Arrived in London, the bridegroom hastened eagerly to receive his bride. When she was first presented to him, Lord Malmesbury says she very properly attempted to kneel. He raised her gracefully enough, embraced her, and turning round to me, said,—

"Harris, I am not well; pray get me a glass of brandy."

I said, "Sir, had you not better have a glass of water?"

Upon which, much out of humor, he said, with an oath, "No; I will go to the Queen."

What could be expected from a wedding which had such a beginning—from such a bridegroom and such a bride? I am not going to carry you through the scandal of that story, or follow the poor Princess through all her vagaries; her balls and her dances, her travels to Jerusalem and Naples, her jigs, and her junketings, and her tears. As I read her trial in history, I vote she is not guilty. I don't say it is an impartial verdict; but as one reads her story the heart bleeds for the kindly, generous, outraged creature. If wrong there be, let it lie at his door who wickedly thrust her from it. Spite of her follies, the great hearty people of England loved, and protected, and pitied her. "God bless you, we will bring your husband back to you," said a mechanic one day, as she told Lady Charlotte Bury with tears streaming down her cheeks. They could not bring that husband back; they could not cleanse that selfish heart. Was hers the only one he had wounded? Steeped in selfishness, impotent for faithful attachment and manly enduring love, — had it not survived remorse, was it not accustomed to desertion?

Malmesbury gives us the beginning of the marriage story; — how the Prince reeled into chapel to be married; how he hiccoughed out his vows of fidelity — you know how he kept them; how he pursued the woman whom he had married; to what a state he brought her; with what blows he struck her; with what malignity he pursued her; what his treatment of his daughter was; and what his own life. *He* the first gentleman of Europe! There is no stronger satire on the proud English society of that day, than that they admired George.

No, thank God, we can tell of better gentlemen; and whilst our eyes turn away, shocked, from this monstrous image of pride, vanity, weakness, they may see in that England over which the last George pretended to reign, some who merit indeed the title of gentlemen, some who make our hearts beat when we hear their names, and whose memory we fondly salute when that of yonder imperial manikin is tumbled into oblivion. I will take men of my own profession of letters. I will take Walter Scott, who loved the King, and who was his sword and buckler, and championed him like that brave Highlander in his own story, who fights round his craven chief. What a good gentleman! What a friendly soul, what a generous hand, what an amiable life was that of the noble Sir Walter! I will take another man of letters, whose life I admire even more, — an English worthy, doing his duty for fifty noble years of labor, day by day storing up learning, day by day working for scant wages, most charitable out of his small means, bravely faithful to the calling which he had chosen, refusing to turn from his path for popular praise or princes' favor; — I mean *Robert Southey*. We have left his old political landmarks miles and miles behind; we protest against his dogmatism; nay, we begin to forget it and his politics: but I hope his life will not be forgotten, for it is sublime in its simplicity, its energy, its honor, its affection. In the combat between Time and Thalaba, I suspect the former destroyer has conquered. Kehama's curse frightens very few readers now; but Southey's private letters are worth piles of epics, and are sure to last among us, as long as kind hearts like to sympathize with goodness and purity, and love and upright life. "If your feelings are like mine," he writes to his wife, "I will not go to Lisbon without you, or I will stay at home, and not part from you. For though not unhappy when away, still without you I am not happy. For your sake, as well as my own and little Edith's, I will not consent to any separation; the growth of a year's love between her and me, if it please God she should live, is a thing too delightful in itself, and too valuable in its consequences, to be given up for any light inconvenience on your part or mine. . . . On these things we will talk at leisure; only, dear, dear Edith, *we must not part!*"

This was a poor literary gentleman. The First Gentleman in Europe had a wife and daughter too. Did he love them so? Was he faithful to them? Did he sacrifice ease for them, or show them the sacred examples of religion and honor? Heaven gave the Great English Prodigal no such good fortune. Peel proposed to make a baronet of Southey; and to this advancement the King agreed. The poet nobly rejected the offered promotion.

"I have," he wrote, "a pension of 200*l.* a year conferred upon me by the good offices of my old friend C. Wynn, and I have the laureateship. The salary of the latter was immediately appropriated, as far as it went, to a life-insurance for 3,000*l.*, which, with an earlier insurance, is the sole provision I have made for my family. All beyond must be derived from my own industry. Writing for a livelihood, a livelihood is all that I have gained; for, having also something better in view, and never, therefore, having courted popularity, nor written for the mere sake of gain, it has not been possible for me to lay by any thing. Last year, for the first time in my life, I was provided with a year's expenditure beforehand. This exposition may show how unbecoming and unwise it would be to accept the rank which, so greatly to my honor, you have solicited for me."

How noble his poverty is, compared to the wealth of his master! His acceptance even of a pension was made the object of his opponents' satire: but think of the merit and modesty of this State pensioner; and that other enormous drawer of public money, who receives 100,000*l.* a year, and comes to Parliament with a request for 650,000*l.* more!

Another true knight of those days was Cuthbert Collingwood; and I think, since heaven made gentlemen, there is no record of a better one than that. Of brighter deeds, I grant you, we may read performed by others; but where of a nobler, kinder, more beautiful life of duty, of a gentler, truer heart? Beyond dazzle of success and blaze of genius, I fancy shining a hundred and a hundred times higher, the sublime purity of Collingwood's gentle glory. His heroism stirs British hearts when we recall it. His love, and goodness, and piety make one thrill with happy emotion. As one reads of him and his great comrade going into the victory with which their names are immortally connected, how the old English word comes up, and that old English feeling of what I should like to call Christian honor! What gentlemen they were, what great hearts they had! "We can, my dear Coll," writes Nelson to him, "have no little jealousies; we have only one great object in view, — that of meeting the enemy, and getting a glorious peace for our country." At Trafalgar, when the "Royal Sovereign" was pressing alone into the midst of the combined fleets, Lord Nelson said to Captain Blackwood: "See how that noble fellow, Collingwood, takes his ship into action! How I envy him!" The very same throb and impulse of heroic generosity was beating in Collingwood's honest bosom. As he led into the fight, he said: "What would Nelson give to be here!"

After the action of the 1st of June, he writes: — "We cruised for a few days, like disappointed people looking for what they could not find, *until the morning of little Sarah's birthday*, between eight and nine o'clock, when the French fleet, of twenty-five sail of the line, was discovered to windward. We chased them, and they bore down within about five miles of us. The night was spent in watching and preparation for the succeeding day; and many a blessing did I send forth to my Sarah, lest I should never bless her more. At dawn, we made our approach on the enemy, then drew up, dressed our ranks, and it was about eight when the admiral made the signal for each ship to engage her opponent, and bring her to close action; and then down we went under a crowd of sail, and in a manner that would have animated the coldest heart, and struck terror into the most intrepid enemy. The ship we were to engage was two ahead of the French admiral, so we had to go through his fire and that of two ships next to him, and received all their broadsides two or three times, before we fired a gun. It was then near ten o'clock. I observed to the admiral, that about that time our wives were going to church, but that I thought the peal we should ring about the Frenchman's ear would outdo their parish bells."

There are no words to tell what the heart feels in reading the simple phrases of such a hero. Here is a victory and courage, but love sublimer and superior. Here is a Christian soldier spending the night before battle in watching and preparing for the succeeding day, thinking of his dearest home, and sending many blessings forth to his Sarah, "lest he should never bless her more." Who would not say Amen to his supplication? It was a benediction to his country — the prayer of that intrepid loving heart.

We have spoken of a good soldier and good men of letters as specimens of English gentlemen of the age just past: may we not also — many of my elder hearers, I am sure, have read, and fondly remember his delightful story — speak of a good divine, and mention Reginald Heber as one of the best of English gentlemen? The charming poet, the happy possessor of all sorts of gifts and accomplishments, birth, wit, fame, high character, competence — he was the beloved parish priest in his own home of Hodnet, "counselling his people in their troubles, advising them in their difficulties, comforting them in distress, kneeling often at their sick beds at the hazard of his own life; exhorting, encouraging where there was need; where there was strife the peacemaker; where there was want the free giver."

When the Indian bishopric was offered to him he refused at first; but after communing with himself (and committing his case to the quarter whither such pious men are wont to carry their doubts), he withdrew his refusal, and prepared himself for his mission and to leave his beloved parish. "Little children, love one another, and forgive one another," were the last sacred words he said to his weeping people. He parted with them, knowing, perhaps, he should see them no more. Like those other good men of whom we have just spoken, love and duty were his life's aim. Happy he, happy they who were so gloriously faithful to both! He writes to his wife those charming lines on his journey: —

" If thou, my love, wert by my side, my babies at my knee,
How gladly would our pinnace glide o'er Gunga's mimic sea!

I miss thee at the dawning gray, when, on our deck reclined,
In careless ease my limbs I lay and woo the cooler wind.

I miss thee when by Gunga's stream my twilight steps I guide;
But most beneath the lamp's pale beam I miss thee by my side.

I spread my books, my pencil try, the lingering noon to cheer;
But miss thy kind approving eye, thy meek attentive ear.

But when of morn and eve the star beholds me on my knee,
I feel, though thou art distant far, thy prayers ascend for me.

Then on! then on! where duty leads my course be onward still, —
O'er broad Hindostan's sultry meads, o'er bleak Almorah's hill.

That course nor Delhi's kingly gates, nor wild Malwah detain,
For sweet the bliss us both awaits by yonder western main.

Thy towers, Bombay, gleam bright, they say, across the dark blue sea:
But ne'er were hearts so blithe and gay as there shall meet in thee!"

Is it not Collingwood and Sarah, and Southey and Edith? His affection is part of his life. What were life without it? Without love, I can fancy no gentleman.

How touching is a remark Heber makes in his "Travels through India," that on inquiring of the natives at a town, which of the governors of India stood highest in the opinion of the people, he found that, though Lord Wellesley and Warren Hastings were honored as the two greatest men who had ever ruled this part of the world, the people spoke with chief affection of Judge Cleaveland, who had died, aged twenty-nine, in 1784. The people have built a monument over him, and still hold a religious feast in his memory. So does his own country still tend with a heart's regard the memory of the gentle Heber.

And Cleaveland died in 1784, and is still loved by the heathen, is he? Why, that year 1784 was remarkable in the life of our friend the First Gentleman of Europe. Do you not know that he was twenty-one in that year, and opened Carlton House with a grand ball to the nobility and gentry, and doubtless wore that lovely pink coat which we have described. I was eager to read about the ball, and looked to the old magazines for information. The entertainment took place on the 10th February. In "The European Magazine" of March, 1784, I came straightway upon it: —

"The alterations at Carlton House being finished, we lay before our readers a description of the state apartments as they appeared on the 10th instant, when H. R. H. gave a grand ball to the principal nobility and gentry. . . . The entrance to the state room fills the mind with an inexpressible idea of greatness and splendor.

"The state chair is of a gold frame, covered with crimson damask; on each corner of the feet is a lion's head, expressive of fortitude and strength; the feet of the chair have serpents twining round them, to denote wisdom. Facing the throne, appears the helmet of Minerva; and over the windows, glory is represented by Saint George with a superb gloria.

"But the saloon may be styled the *chef d'œuvre*, and in every ornament discovers great invention. It is hung with a figured lemon satin. The window-curtains, sofas, and chairs are of the same color. The ceiling is ornamented with emblematical paintings, representing the Graces and Muses, together with Jupiter, Mercury, Apollo, and Paris. Two *ormolu* chandeliers are placed here. It is impossible by expression to do justice to the extraordinary workmanship, as well as design, of the ornaments. They each consist of a palm, branching out in five directions for the reception of lights. A beautiful figure of a rural nymph is represented entwining the stems of the tree with wreaths of flowers. In the centre of the room is a rich chandelier. To see this apartment *dans son plus beau jour*, it should be viewed in the glass over the chimney-piece. The range of apartments from the saloon to the ball-room, when the doors are open, formed one of the grandest spectacles that ever was beheld."

In "The Gentleman's Magazine," for the very same month and year — March, 1784 — is an account of another festival, in which another great gentleman of English extraction is represented as taking a principal share: —

"According to order, H. E. the Commander-in-Chief was admitted to a public audience of Congress; and, being seated, the President, after a pause, informed him that the United States assembled were ready to receive his communications. Whereupon he arose, and spoke as follows: —

"'Mr. President, — The great events on which my resignation depended having at length taken place, I present myself before Congress to surrender into their hands the trust committed to me, and to claim the indulgence of retiring from the service of my country.

"Happy in the confirmation of our independence and sovereignty, I resign the appointment I accepted with diffidence; which, however, was superseded by a confidence in the rectitude of our cause, the support of the supreme power of the nation, and the patronage of Heaven. I close this last act of my official life, by commending the interests of our dearest country to the protection of Almighty God, and those who have the superintendence of them to His holy keeping. Having finished the work assigned me, I retire from the great theatre of action; and, bidding an affectionate farewell to this august body, under whose orders I have so long acted, I here offer my commission and take my leave of the employments of my public life.' To which the President replied: —

"'Sir, having defended the standard of liberty in the New World, having taught a lesson useful to those who inflict and those who feel oppression, you retire with the blessings of your fellow-citizens; though the glory of your virtues will not terminate with your military command, but will descend to remotest ages.'"

Which was the most splendid spectacle ever witnessed; — the opening feast of Prince George in London, or the resignation of Washington? Which is the noble character for after ages to admire; — yon fribble dancing in lace and spangles, or yonder hero who sheathes his sword after a life of spotless honor, a purity unreproached, a courage indomitable, and a consummate victory? Which of these is the true gentleman? What is it to be a gentleman? Is it to have lofty aims, to lead a pure life, to keep your honor virgin; to have the esteem of your fellow-citizens, and the love of your fireside; to bear good fortune meekly; to suffer evil with constancy; and through evil or good to maintain truth always? Show me the happy man whose life exhibits these qualities, and him we will salute as a gentleman, whatever his rank may be; show me the prince who possesses them, and he may be sure of our love and loyalty. The heart of Britain still beats kindly for George III., — not because he was wise and just, but because he was pure in life, honest in intent, and because according to his lights he worshipped Heaven. I think we acknowledge in the inheritrix of his sceptre, a wiser rule, and a life as honorable and pure; and I am sure the future painter of our manners will pay a willing allegiance to that good life, and be loyal to the memory of that unsullied virtue.

THE

ENGLISH HUMORISTS

OF THE EIGHTEENTH CENTURY.

Swift.

THE ENGLISH HUMORISTS

OF THE

EIGHTEENTH CENTURY.

SWIFT.

In treating of the English humorists of the past age, it is of the men and of their lives, rather than of their books, that I ask permission to speak to you; and in doing so, you are aware that I cannot hope to entertain you with a merely humorous or facetious story. Harlequin without his mask is known to present a very sober countenance, and was himself, the story goes, the melancholy patient whom the Doctor advised to go and see Harlequin * — a man full of cares and perplexities like the rest of us, whose Self must always be serious to him, under whatever mask or disguise or uniform he presents it to the public. And as all of you here must needs be grave when you think of your own past and present, you will not look to find, in the histories of those whose lives and feelings I am going to try and describe to you, a story that is otherwise than serious, and often very sad. If Humor only meant laughter, you would scarcely feel more interest about humorous writers than about the private life of poor Harlequin just mentioned, who possesses in common with these the power of making you laugh. But the men regarding whose lives and stories your kind presence here shows that you have curiosity and sympathy, appeal to a great number of our other faculties, besides our mere sense of ridicule. The humorous writer professes to awaken and direct your love, your pity, your kindness — your scorn for untruth, pretension, imposture — your tenderness for the weak, the poor, the oppressed, the unhappy. To the best of his means and ability he comments on all the ordinary actions and passions of life almost. He takes upon himself to be the week-day preacher, so to speak. Accordingly, as he finds, and speaks, and feels the truth best, we regard him, esteem him — sometimes love him. And, as his business is to mark other people's lives and peculiarities, we moralize upon *his* life when he is gone — and yesterday's preacher becomes the text for to-day's sermon.

Of English parents, and of a good English family of clergymen,* Swift

* The anecdote is frequently told of our performer RICH.

* He was from a younger branch of the Swifts of Yorkshire. His grandfather, the Rev. Thomas Swift, vicar of Goodrich, in Herefordshire, suffered for his loyalty in Charles I.'s time. That gentleman married Elizabeth Dryden, a member of the family of the poet. Sir Walter Scott gives, with his characteristic minute-

was born in Dublin in 1667, seven months after the death of his father, who had come to practise there as a lawyer. The boy went to school at Kilkenny, and afterwards to Trinity College, Dublin, where he got a degree with difficulty, and was wild, and witty, and poor. In 1688, by the recommendation of his mother, Swift was received into the family of Sir William Temple, who had known Mrs. Swift in Ireland. He left his patron in 1693, and the next year took orders in Dublin. But he threw up the small Irish preferment which he got and returned to Temple, in whose family he remained until Sir William's death in 1699. His hopes of advancement in England failing, Swift returned to Ireland, and took the living of Laracor. Hither he invited Hester Johnson,* Temple's natural daughter, with whom he had contracted a tender friendship, while they were both dependants of Temple's. And with an occasional visit to England, Swift now passed nine years at home.

In 1709 he came to England, and, with a brief visit to Ireland, during which he took possession of his deanery of St. Patrick, he now passed five years in England, taking the most distinguished part in the political transactions which terminated with the death of Queen Anne. After her death, his party disgraced, and his hopes of ambition over, Swift returned to Dublin, where he remained twelve years. In this time he wrote the famous "Drapier's Letters" and "Gulliver's Travels." He married Hester Johnson, Stella, and buried Esther Vanhomrigh, Vanessa, who had followed him to Ireland from London, where she had contracted a violent passion for him. In 1726 and 1727 Swift was in England, which he quitted for the last time on hearing of his wife's illness. Stella died in January, 1728, and Swift not till 1745, having passed the last five of the seventy-eight years of his life with an impaired intellect and keepers to watch him.*

You know, of course, that Swift has had many biographers; his life has been told by the kindest and most good-natured of men, Scott, who admires but can't bring himself to love him; and by stout old Johnson,†

ness in such points, the exact relationship between these famous men. Swift was "the son of Dryden's second cousin." Swift, too, was the enemy of Dryden's reputation. Witness the "Battle of the Books:"—"The difference was greatest among the horse," says he of the moderns, "where every private trooper pretended to the command, from Tasso and Milton to Dryden and Withers." And in "Poetry, a Rhapsody," he advises the poetaster to—

"Read all the Prefaces of Dryden,
For these our critics much confide in,
Though merely writ, at first for filling,
To raise the volume's price a shilling."

"Cousin Swift, you will never be a poet," was the phrase of Dryden to his kinsman, which remained alive in a memory tenacious of such matters.

* "Miss Hetty," she was called in the family—where her face, and her dress, and Sir William's treatment of her, all made the real fact about her birth plain enough. Sir William left her a thousand pounds.

* Sometimes, during his mental affliction, he continued walking about the house for many consecutive hours; sometimes he remained in a kind of torpor. At times, he would seem to struggle to bring into distinct consciousness, and shape into expression, the intellect that lay smothering under gloomy obstruction in him. A pier-glass falling by accident, nearly fell on him. He said he wished it had! He once repeated slowly several times, "I am what I am." The last thing he wrote was an epigram on the building of a magazine for arms and stores, which was pointed out to him as he went abroad during his mental disease:—

"Behold a proof of Irish sense:
Here Irish wit is seen:
When nothing's left that's worth defence,
They build a magazine!"

† Besides these famous books of Scott's and Johnson's, there is a copious "Life" by Thomas Sheridan (Dr. Johnson's "Sherry"), father of Richard Brinsley, and son of that good-natured, clever Irish Dr. Thomas Sheridan, Swift's intimate, who lost his chaplaincy by so unluckily choosing for a text on the King's birthday, "Sufficient for the day is the evil thereof!" Not to mention less im-

who, forced to admit him into the company of poets, receives the famous Irishman, and takes off his hat to him with a bow of surly recognition, scans him from head to foot, and passes over to the other side of the street. Dr. Wilde of Dublin,* who has written a most interesting volume on the closing years of Swift's life, calls Johnson "the most malignant of his biographers:" it is not easy for an English critic to please Irishmen—perhaps to try and please them. And yet Johnson truly admires Swift: Johnson does not quarrel with Swift's change of politics, or doubt his sincerity of religion: about the famous Stella and Vanessa controversy the Doctor does not bear very hardly on Swift. But he could not give the Dean that honest hand of his; the stout old gentleman puts it into his breast, and moves off from him.†

Would we have liked to live with him? That is a question which, in dealing with these people's works, and thinking of their lives and peculiarities, every reader of biographies must put to himself. Would you have liked to be a friend of the great Dean? I should like to have been Shakspeare's shoeblack—just to have lived in his house, just to have worshipped him—to have run on his errands, and seen that sweet serene face. I should like, as a young man, to have lived on Fielding's staircase in the Temple, and after helping him up to bed perhaps, and opening his door with his latch-key, to have shaken hands with him in the morning, and heard him talk and crack jokes over his breakfast and his mug of small beer. Who would not give something to pass a night at the club with Johnson, and Goldsmith, and James Boswell, Esq., of Auchinleck? The charm of Addison's companionship and conversation has passed to us by fond tradition—but Swift? If you had been his inferior in parts (and that, with a great respect for all persons present, I fear is only very likely), his equal in mere social station, he would have bullied, scorned, and insulted you; if, undeterred by his great reputation, you had met him like a man, he would have quailed before you,* and

portant works, there is also the "Remarks on the Life and Writings of Dr. Jonathan Swift," by that polite and dignified writer, the Earl of Orrery. His lordship is said to have striven for literary renown, chiefly that he might make up for the slight passed on him by his father, who left his library away from him. It is to be feared that the ink he used to wash out that stain only made it look bigger. He had, however, known Swift, and corresponded with people who knew him. His work (which appeared in 1751) provoked a good deal of controversy, calling out, among other *brochures*, the interesting "Observations on Lord Orrery's Remarks," &c., of Dr. Delany.

* Dr. Wilde's book was written on the occasion of the remains of Swift and Stella being brought to the light of day—a thing which happened in 1835, when certain works going on in St. Patrick's Cathedral, Dublin, afforded an opportunity of their being examined. One hears with surprise of these skulls "going the rounds" of houses, and being made the objects of *dilettante* curiosity. The larynx of Swift was actually carried off! Phrenologists had a low opinion of his intellect from the observations they took.

Dr. Wilde traces the symptoms of ill-health in Swift, as detailed in his writings from time to time. He observes, likewise, that the skull gave evidence of "diseased action" of the brain during life—such as would be produced by an increasing tendency to "cerebral congestion."

† "He [Dr. Johnson] seemed to me to have an unaccountable prejudice against Swift; for I once took the liberty to ask him if Swift had personally offended him, and he told me he had not."—BOSWELL'S *Tour to the Hebrides*.

* Few men, to be sure, dared this experiment, but yet their success was encouraging. One gentleman made a point of asking the Dean whether his uncle Godwin had not given him his education. Swift, who hated *that* subject cordially, and, indeed, cared little for his kindred, said, sternly, "Yes; he gave me the education of a dog." "Then, sir," cried the other, striking his fist on the table, "you have not the gratitude of a dog!"

Other occasions there were when a bold face gave the Dean pause, even after his Irish almost-royal position was established. But he brought himself into greater danger on a certain occasion, and the amusing circumstances may be once more repeated here. He had unsparingly

not had the pluck to reply, and gone home, and years after written a foul epigram about you — watched for you in a sewer, and come out to assail you with a coward's blow and a dirty bludgeon. If you had been a lord with a blue ribbon, who flattered his vanity, or could help his ambition, he would have been the most delightful company in the world. He would have been so manly, so sarcastic, so bright, odd, and original, that you might think he had no object in view but the indulgence of his humor, and that he was the most reckless, simple creature in the world. How he would have torn your enemies to pieces for you! and made fun of the Opposition! His servility was so boisterous that it looked like independence; * he would have done your errands, but with the air of patronizing you, and after fighting your battles, masked, in the street or the press, would have kept on his hat before your wife and daughters in the drawing-room, content to take that sort of pay for his tremendous services as a bravo.†

He says as much himself in one of his letters to Bolingbroke: — "All my endeavors to distinguish myself were only for want of a great title and fortune, that I might be used like a lord by those who have an opinion of my parts; whether right or wrong is no great matter. And so the reputation of wit and great learning does the office of a blue ribbon or a coach and six." *

Could there be a greater candor? It is an outlaw, who says, "These are my brains; with these I'll win

lashed the notable Dublin lawyer, Mr. Sergeant Bettesworth —

"So at the bar, the booby Bettesworth,
Though half a crown outpays his sweat's worth,
Who knows in law nor text nor margent,
Calls Singleton his brother-sergeant!"

The Sergeant, it is said, swore to have his life. He presented himself at the deanery. The Dean asked his name. "Sir, I am Sergeant Bett-es-worth."

"*In what regiment, pray?*" asked Swift.

A guard of volunteers formed themselves to defend the Dean at this time.

* "But, my Hamilton, I will never hide the freedom of my sentiments from you. I am much inclined to believe that the temper of my friend Swift might occasion his English friends to wish him happily and properly promoted at a distance. His spirit, for I would give it the proper name, was ever untractable. The motions of his genius were often irregular. He assumed more the air of a patron than of a friend. He affected rather to dictate than to advise." — ORRERY.

† ". . . An anecdote, which, though only told by Mrs. Pilkington, is well attested, bears, that the last time he was in London he went to dine with the Earl of Burlington, who was but newly married. The Earl, it is supposed, being willing to have a little diversion, did not introduce him to his lady nor mention his name. After dinner said the Dean, 'Lady Burlington, I hear you can sing; sing me a song.' The lady looked on this unceremonious manner of asking a favor with distaste, and positively refused. He said, 'She should sing, or he would make her. Why, madam, I suppose you take me for one of your poor English hedge-parsons; sing when I bid you.' As the Earl did nothing but laugh at this freedom, the lady was so vexed that she burst into tears and retired. His first compliment to her when he saw her again was, 'Pray, madam, are you as proud and ill-natured now as when I saw you last?' To which she answered with great good-humor, 'No, Mr. Dean; I'll sing for you if you please.' From which time he conceived a great esteem for her." — SCOTT'S *Life*.

". . . He had not the least tincture of vanity in his conversation. He was, perhaps, as he said himself, too proud to be vain. When he was polite, it was in a manner entirely his own. In his friendships he was constant and undisguised. He was the same in his enmities." — ORRERY.

* "I make no figure but at court, where I affect to turn from the lord to the meanest of my acquaintances." — *Journal to Stella.*

"I am plagued with bad authors, verse and prose, who send me their books and poems, the vilest I ever saw; but I have given their names to my man, never to let them see me." — *Journal to Stella.*

The following curious paragraph illustrates the life of a courtier: —

"Did I ever tell you that the Lord Treasurer hears ill with the left ear, just as I do? . . . I dare not tell him that I am so, *for fear he should think that I counterfeited to make my court!*" — *Journal to Stella.*

titles and compete with fortune. These are my bullets; these I'll turn into gold;" and he hears the sound of coaches and six, takes the road like Macheath, and makes society stand and deliver. They are all on their knees before him. Down go my lord bishop's apron, and his Grace's blue ribbon, and my lady's brocade petticoat in the mud. He eases the one of a living, the other of a patent place, the third of a little snug post about the Court, and gives them over to followers of his own. The great prize has not come yet. The coach with the mitre and crosier in it, which he intends to have for *his* share, has been delayed on the way from St. James's; and he waits and waits until nightfall, when his runners come and tell him that the coach has taken a different road, and escaped him. So he fires his pistol into the air with a curse, and rides away into his own country.*

Swift's seems to me to be as good a name to point a moral or adorn a

* The war of pamphlets was carried on fiercely on one side and the other: and the Whig attacks made the Ministry Swift served very sore. Bolingbroke laid hold of several of the Opposition pamphleteers, and bewails their "factitiousness" in the following letter: —

"Bolingbroke to the Earl of Strafford.

"*Whitehall, July 23d*, 1712.

"It is a melancholy consideration that the laws of our country are too weak to punish effectually those factitious scribblers, who presume to blacken the brightest characters, and to give even scurrilous language to those who are in the first degrees of honor. This, my lord, among others, is a symptom of the decayed condition of our Government, and serves to show how fatally we mistake licentiousness for liberty. All I could do was to take up Hart, the printer, to send him to Newgate, and to bind him over upon bail to be prosecuted; this I have done; and if I can arrive at legal proof against the author, Ridpath, he shall have the same treatment."

Swift was not behind his illustrious friend in this virtuous indignation. In the history of the four last years of the Queen, the Dean speaks in the most edifying manner of the licentiousness of the press and the abusive language of the other party: —

"It must be acknowledged that the bad practices of printers have been such as to deserve the severest animadversion from the public. . . . . The adverse party, full of rage and leisure since their fall, and unanimous in their cause, employ a set of writers by subscription, who are well versed in all the topics of defamation, and have a style and genius levelled to the generality of their readers. . . . . However, the mischiefs of the press were too exorbitant to be cured by such a remedy as a tax upon small papers, and a bill for a much more effectual regulation of it was brought into the House of Commons, but so late in the session that there was no time to pass it, for there always appeared an unwillingness to cramp overmuch the liberty of the press."

But to a clause in the proposed bill, that the names of authors should be set to every printed book, pamphlet or paper, his Reverence objects altogether; for, says he, "besides the objection to this clause from the practice of pious men, who, in publishing excellent writings for the service of religion, have chosen, *out of an humble Christian spirit, to conceal their names*, it is certain that all persons of true genius or knowledge have an invincible modesty and suspicion of themselves upon first sending their thoughts into the world."

This "invincible modesty" was no doubt the sole reason which induced the Dean to keep the secret of the "Drapier's Letters" and a hundred humble Christian works of which he was the author. As for the Opposition, the Doctor was for dealing severely with them: he writes to Stella:

Journal. Letter XIX.

"*London, March 25th*, 1710-11.

" . . . . We have let Guiscard be buried at last, after showing him, pickled in a trough this fortnight for twopence a piece; and the fellow that showed would point to his body and say, 'See, gentlemen, this is the wound that was given him by His Grace the Duke of Ormond;' and, 'This is the wound,' &c.; and then the show was over, and another set of rabble came in. 'Tis hard that our laws would not suffer us to hang his body in chains, because he was not tried; and in the eye of the law every man is innocent till then. . . . ."

Journal. Letter XXVII.

"*London, July 25th*, 1711.

"I was this afternoon with Mr. Secretary at his office, and helped to hinder a man of his pardon, who is condemned for a rape. The Under Secretary was will-

tale of ambition, as any hero's that ever lived and failed. But we must remember that the morality was lax — that other gentlemen besides himself took the road in his day — that public society was in a strange disordered condition, and the State was ravaged by other condottieri. The Boyne was being fought and won, and lost — the bells rung in William's victory, in the very same tone with which they would have pealed for James's. Men were loose upon politics, and had to shift for themselves. They, as well as old beliefs and institutions, had lost their moorings and gone adrift in the storm. As in the South Sea Bubble, almost everybody gambled; as in the railway mania — not many centuries ago — almost every one took his unlucky share: a man of that time, of the vast talents and ambition of Swift, could scarce do otherwise than grasp at his prize, and make his spring at his opportunity. His bitterness, his scorn, his rage, his subsequent misanthropy, are ascribed by some panegyrists to a deliberate conviction of mankind's unworthiness, and a desire to amend them by castigating. His youth was bitter, as that of a great genius bound down by ignoble ties, and powerless in a mean dependence; his age was bitter,* like that of a great genius that had fought the battle and nearly won it, and lost it, and thought of it afterwards writhing in a lonely exile. A man may attribute to the gods, if he likes, what is caused by his own fury, or disappointment, or self-will. What public man — what statesman projecting a *coup* — what king determined on invasion of his neighbor — what satirist meditating an onslaught on society or an individual, can't give a pretext for his move? There was a French general the other day who proposed to march into this country and put it to sack and pillage, in revenge for humanity outraged by our conduct at Copenhagen: there is always some excuse for men of the aggressive turn. They are of their nature warlike, predatory, eager for fight, plunder, dominion.*

As fierce a beak and talon as ever struck — as strong a wing as ever beat, belonged to Swift. I am glad, for one, that fate wrested the prey out of his claws, and cut his wings and chained him. One can gaze, and not without awe and pity, at the lonely eagle chained behind the bars.

That Swift was born at No.7, Hoey's Court, Dublin, on the 30th November, 1667, is a certain fact, of which nobody will deny the sister island the honor and glory; but, it seems to me, he was no more an Irishman than a man born of English parents at Calcutta is a Hindoo.† Goldsmith was

ing to save him; but I told the Secretary he could not pardon him without a favorable report from the Judge; besides, he was a fiddler, and consequently a rogue, and deserved hanging for something else, and so he shall swing."

* It was his constant practice to keep his birthday a day of mourning.

* "These devils of Grub Street rogues, that write the 'Flying Post' and 'Medley' in one paper, will not be quiet. They are always mauling Lord Treasurer, Lord Bolingbroke, and me. We have the dog under prosecution, but Bolingbroke is not active enough; but I hope to swinge him. He is a Scotch rogue, one Ridpath. They get out upon bail, and write on. We take them again, and get fresh bail; so it goes round." — *Journal to Stella.*

† Swift was by no means inclined to forget such considerations; and his English birth makes its mark, strikingly enough, every now and then in his writings. Thus in a letter to Pope (SCOTT'S *Swift*, vol. xix. p. 97), he says: —

"We have had your volume of letters. . . . Some of those who highly value you, and a few who know you personally, are grieved to find you make no distinction between the English gentry of this kingdom, and the savage old Irish (who are only the vulgar, and some gentlemen who live in the Irish parts of the kingdom); but the English colonies, who are three parts in four, are much more civilized than many counties in England, and speak better English, and are much better bred."

And again, in the fourth Drapier's Letter, we have the following: —

"A short paper, printed at Bristol, and reprinted here, reports Mr. Wood to say 'that he wonders at the impudence and insolence of the Irish in refusing his coin.'

an Irishman, and always an Irishman: Steele was an Irishman, and always an Irishman: Swift's heart was English and in England, his habits English, his logic eminently English; his statement is elaborately simple; he shuns tropes and metaphors, and uses his ideas and words with a wise thrift and economy, as he used his money: with which he could be generous and splendid upon great occasions, but which he husbanded when there was no need to spend it. He never indulges in needless extravagance of rhetoric, lavish epithets, profuse imagery. He lays his opinion before you with a grave simplicity and a perfect neatness.* Dreading ridicule too, as a man of his humor — above all an Englishman of his humor — certainly would, he is afraid to use the poetical power which he really possessed; one often fancies in reading him that he dares not be eloquent when he might; that he does not speak above his voice, as it were, and the tone of society.

His initiation into politics, his knowledge of business, his knowledge of polite life, his acquaintance with literature even, which he could not have pursued very sedulously during that reckless career at Dublin, Swift got under the roof of Sir William Temple. He was fond of telling in after life what quantities of books he devoured there, and how King William taught him to cut asparagus in the Dutch fashion. It was at Shene and at Moor Park, with a salary of twenty pounds and a dinner at the upper servants' table, that this great and lonely Swift passed a ten years' apprenticeship — wore a cassock that was only not a livery — bent down a knee as proud as Lucifer's to supplicate my lady's good graces, or run on his honor's errands.* It was here, as he was writing at Temple's table, or following his patron's walk, that he saw and heard the men who had governed the great world — measured himself with them, looking up from his silent corner, gauged their brains, weighed their wits, turned them, and tried them, and marked them. Ah! what platitudes he must have heard! what feeble jokes! what pompous commonplaces! what small men they must have seemed under those enormous periwigs, to the swarthy, un-

When, by the way, it is the true English people of Ireland who refuse it, although we take it for granted that the Irish will do so too whenever they are asked." — SCOTT's *Swift*, vol. iv. p. 143.

He goes further, in a good-humored satirical paper, "On Barbarous Denominations in Ireland," where (after abusing, as he was wont, the Scotch cadence, as well as expression), he advances to the "*Irish brogue*," and speaking of the "censure" which it brings down, says: —

"And what is yet worse, it is too well known that the bad consequence of this opinion affects those among us who are not the least liable to such reproaches farther than the misfortune of being born in Ireland, although of English parents, and whose education has been chiefly in that kingdom." — *Ibid.* vol. vii. p. 149.

But, indeed, if we are to make *any thing* of Race at all, we must call that man an Englishman whose father comes from an old Yorkshire family, and his mother from an old Leicestershire one!

* "The style of his conversation was very much of a piece with that of his writings, concise and clear and strong. Being one day at a Sheriff's feast, who amongst other toasts called out to him, 'Mr. Dean, The Trade of Ireland!' he answered quick: 'Sir, I drink no memories!' . . . .

"Happening to be in company with a petulant young man who prided himself on saying pert things . . . and who cried out — 'You must know, Mr. Dean, that I set up for a wit?' 'Do you so?' says the Dean. 'Take my advice, and sit down again!'

"At another time, being in company, where a lady whisking her long train [long trains were then in fashion] swept down a fine fiddle and broke it; Swift cried out —

"'Mantua væ miseræ nimium vicina Cremonæ!'"

— Dr. DELANY: *Observations upon Lord Orrery's "Remarks, &c. on Swift."* London, 1754.

* "Don't you remember how I used to be in pain when Sir William Temple would look cold and out of humor for three or four days, and I used to suspect a hundred reasons? I have plucked up my spirits since then, faith: he spoiled a fine gentleman." — *Journal to Stella.*

couth, silent Irish secretary. I wonder whether it ever struck Temple, that that Irishman was his master? I suppose that dismal conviction did not present itself under the ambrosial wig, or Temple could never have lived with Swift. Swift sickened, rebelled, left the service — ate humble pie and came back again; and so for ten years went on, gathering learning, swallowing scorn, and submitting with a stealthy rage to his fortune.

Temple's style is the perfection of practised and easy good-breeding. If he does not penetrate very deeply into a subject, he professes a very gentlemanly acquaintance with it; if he makes rather a parade of Latin, it was the custom of his day, as it was the custom for a gentleman to envelop his head in a periwig and his hands in lace ruffles. If he wears buckles and square-toed shoes, he steps in them with a consummate grace, and you never hear their creak, or find them treading upon any lady's train or any rival's heels in the Court crowd. When that grows too hot or too agitated for him, he politely leaves it. He retires to his retreat of Shene or Moor Park; and lets the King's party and the Prince of Orange's party battle it out among themselves. He reveres the Sovereign (and no man perhaps ever testified to his loyalty by so elegant a bow); he admires the Prince of Orange; but there is one person whose ease and comfort he loves more than all the princes in Christendom, and that valuable member of society is himself Gulielmus Temple, Baronettus. One sees him in his retreat; between his study-chair and his tulip-beds,* clipping his apricots and pruning his essays, — the statesman, the ambassador no more; but the philosopher, the Epicurean, the fine gentleman and courtier at St. James's as at Shene; where in place of kings and fair ladies, he pays his court to the Ciceronian majesty; or walks a minuet with the Epic Muse; or dallies by the south wall with the ruddy nymph of gardens.

Temple seems to have received and exacted a prodigious deal of venera-

* ". . . . The Epicureans were more intelligible in their notion, and fortunate in their expression, when they placed a man's happiness in the tranquillity of his mind and indolence of body; for while we are composed of both, I doubt both must have a share in the good or ill we feel. As men of several languages say the same things in very different words, so in several ages, countries, constitutions of laws and religion, the same thing seems to be meant by very different expressions: what is called by the Stoics apathy, or dispassion; by the sceptics, indisturbance; by the Molinists, quietism; by common men, peace of conscience, — seems all to mean but great tranquillity of mind. . . For this reason Epicurus passed his life wholly in his garden; there he studied, there he exercised, there he taught his philosophy; and, indeed, no other sort of abode seems to contribute so much to both the tranquillity of mind and indolence of body, which he made his chief ends. The sweetness of the air, the pleasantness of smell, the verdure of plants, the cleanness and lightness of food, the exercise of working or walking; but, above all, the exemption from cares and solicitude, seem equally to favor and improve both contemplation and health, the enjoyment of sense and imagination, and thereby the quiet and ease both of the body and mind. . . . Where Paradise was, has been much debated, and little agreed; but what sort of a place is meant by it may perhaps easier be conjectured. It seems to have been a Persian word, since Xenophon and other Greek authors mention it as what was much in use and delight among the kings of those eastern countries. Strabo describing Jericho: 'Ibi est palmetum, cui immixtæ sunt etiam aliæ stirpes hortenses, locus ferax palmis abundans, spatio stadiorum centum, totus irriguus: ibi est Regis Balsami paradisus.'" — *Essay on Gardens.*

In the same famous essay Temple speaks of a friend, whose conduct and prudence he characteristically admires:

". . . I thought it very prudent in a gentleman of my friends in Staffordshire, who is a great lover of his garden, to pretend no higher, though his soil be good enough, than to the perfection of plums; and in these (by bestowing south walls upon them) he has very well succeeded, which he could never have done in attempts upon peaches and grapes; and *a good plum is certainly better than an ill peach.*"

tion from his household, and to have been coaxed, and warmed, and cuddled by the people round about him, as delicately as any of the plants which he loved. When he fell ill in 1693, the household was aghast at his indisposition: mild Dorothea his wife, the best companion of the best of men —

"Mild Dorothea, peaceful, wise, and great,
Trembling beheld the doubtful hand of fate."

As for Dorinda, his sister, —

"Those who would grief describe, might come and trace
Its watery footsteps in Dorinda's face.
To see her weep, joy every face forsook,
And grief flung sables on each menial look.
The humble tribe mourned for the quickening soul,
That furnished life and spirit through the whole."

Isn't that line in which grief is described as putting the menials into a mourning livery, a fine image? One of the menials wrote it, who did not like that Temple livery nor those twenty-pound wages. Cannot one fancy the uncouth young servitor, with downcast eyes, books and papers in hand, following at his honor's heels in the garden walk; or taking his honor's orders as he stands by the great chair, where Sir William has the gout, and his feet all blistered with moxa? When Sir William has the gout or scolds it must be hard work at the second table;* the Irish secretary owned as much afterwards: and when he came to dinner, how he must have lashed and growled and torn the household with his gibes and scorn! What would the steward say about the pride of them Irish schollards — and this one had got no great credit even at his Irish college, if the truth were known — and what a contempt his Excellency's own gentleman must have had for Parson Teague from Dublin. (The valets and chaplains were always at war. It is hard to say which Swift thought the more contemptible.) And what must have been the sadness, the sadness and terror, of the housekeeper's little daughter with the curling black ringlets and the sweet smiling face, when the secretary who teaches her to read and write, and whom she loves and reverences above all things — above

* Swift's Thoughts on Hanging.

(*Directions to Servants.*)

"To grow old in the office of a footman is the highest of all indignities: therefore, when you find years coming on without hopes of a place at court, a command in the army, a succession to the stewardship, an employment in the revenue (which two last you cannot obtain without reading and writing), or running away with your master's niece or daughter, I directly advise you to go upon the road, which is the only post of honor left you: there you will meet many of your old comrades, and live a short life and a merry one, and make a figure at your exit, wherein I will give you some instructions.

"The last advice I give you relates to your behavior when you are going to be hanged: which, either for robbing your master, for housebreaking, or going upon the highway, or in a drunken quarrel by killing the first man you meet, may very probably be your lot, and is owing to one of these three qualities: either a love of good-fellowship, a generosity of mind, or too much vivacity of spirits. Your good behavior on this article will concern your whole community: deny the fact with all solemnity of imprecations; a hundred of your brethren, if they can be admitted, will attend about the bar, and be ready upon demand to give you a character before the Court; let nothing prevail on you to confess, but the promise of a pardon for discovering your comrades: but I suppose all this to be in vain; for if you escape now, your fate will be the same another day. Get a speech to be written by the best author in Newgate: some of your kind wenches will provide you with a holland shirt and white cap, crowned with a crimson or black ribbon: take leave cheerfully of all your friends in Newgate: mount the cart with courage; fall on your knees; lift up your eyes; hold a book in your hands, although you cannot read a word; deny the fact at the gallows! kiss and forgive the hangman, and so farewell; you shall be buried in pomp at the charge of the fraternity: the surgeon shall not touch a limb of you; and your fame shall continue until a successor of equal renown succeeds in your place. . ."

mother, above mild Dorothea, above that tremendous Sir William in his square toes and periwig, — when *Mr. Swift* comes down from his master with rage in his heart, and has not a kind word even for little Hester Johnson?

Perhaps, for the Irish Secretary, his Excellency's condescension was even more cruel than his frowns. Sir William *would* perpetually quote Latin and the ancient classics *àpropos* of his gardens and his Dutch statues and *plates-bandes*, and talk about Epicurus and Diogenes Laertius, Julius Cæsar, Semiramis, and the gardens of the Hesperides, Mæcenas, Strabo describing Jericho, and the Assyrian kings. *Apropos* of beans, he would mention Pythagoras's precept to abstain from beans, and that this precept probably meant that wise men should abstain from public affairs. *He* is a placid Epicurean; *he* is a Pythagorean philosopher; *he* is a wise man — that is the deduction. Does not Swift think so? One can imagine the downcast eyes lifted up for a moment, and the flash of scorn which they emit. Swift's eyes were as azure as the heavens; Pope says nobly (as every thing Pope said and thought of his friend was good and noble), "His eyes are as azure as the heavens, and have a charming archness in them." And one person in that household, that pompous, stately, kindly Moor Park, saw heaven nowhere else.

But the Temple amenities and solemnities did not agree with Swift. He was half killed with a surfeit of Shene pippins; and in a garden-seat which he devised for himself at Moor Park, and where he devoured greedily the stock of books within his reach, he caught a vertigo and deafness which punished and tormented him through life. He could not bear the place or the servitude. Even in that poem of courtly condolence, from which we have quoted a few lines of mock melancholy, he breaks out of the funereal procession with a mad shriek, as it were, and rushes away crying his own grief, cursing his own fate, foreboding madness, and forsaken by fortune, and even hope.

I don't know any thing more melancholy than the letter to Temple, in which, after having broke from his bondage, the poor wretch crouches piteously towards his cage again, and deprecates his master's anger. He asks for testimonials for orders. "The particulars required of me are what relate to morals and learning; and the reasons for quitting your honor's family — that is, whether the last was occasioned by any ill action. They are left entirely to your honor's mercy, though in the first I think I cannot reproach myself for any thing further than for *infirmities.* This is all I dare at present beg from your honor, under circumstances of life not worth your regard: what is left me to wish (next to the health and prosperity of your honor and family) is that Heaven would one day allow me the opportunity of leaving my acknowledgments at your feet. I beg my most humble duty and service be presented to my ladies, your honor's lady and sister." — Can prostration fall deeper? could a slave bow lower? *

* "He continued in Sir William Temple's house till the death of that great man." — *Anecdotes of the Family of Swift*, by the DEAN.

"It has since pleased God to take this great and good person to himself." — *Preface to Temple's Works.*

On all *public* occasions, Swift speaks of Sir William in the same tone. But the reader will better understand how acutely he remembered the indignities he suffered in his household, from the subjoined extracts from the *Journal to Stella*: —

"I called at Mr. Secretary the other day, to see what the d—— ailed him on Sunday: I made him a very proper speech; told him I observed he was much out of temper, that I did not expect he would tell me the cause, but would be glad to see he was in better; and one thing I warned him of — never to appear cold to me for I would not be treated like a schoolboy; that I had felt too much of that in my life already" (*meaning Sir William Temple*), &c. &c. — *Journal to Stella.*

"I am thinking what a veneration we

Twenty years afterwards Bishop Kennet, describing the same man, says, "Dr. Swift came into the coffee-house and had a bow from everybody but me. When I came to the antechamber [at Court] to wait before prayers, Dr. Swift was the principal man of talk and business. He was soliciting the Earl of Arran to speak to his brother, the Duke of Ormond, to get a place for a clergyman. He was promising Mr. Thorold to undertake, with my Lord Treasurer, that he should obtain a salary of 200*l.* per annum as member of the English Church at Rotterdam. He stopped F. Gwynne, Esq., going into the Queen with the red bag, and told him aloud, he had something to say to him from my Lord Treasurer. He took out his gold watch, and telling the time of day, complained that it was very late. A gentleman said he was too fast. 'How can I help it,' says the Doctor, 'if the courtiers give me a watch that won't go right?' Then he instructed a young nobleman, that the best poet in England was Mr. Pope (a Papist), who had begun a translation of Homer into English, for which he would have them all subscribe: 'For,' says he, 'he shall not begin to print until I have a thousand guineas for him.'* Lord Treasurer, after leaving the Queen, came through the room, beckoning Dr. Swift to follow him, — both went off just before prayers." There's a little malice in the Bishop's "just before prayers."

This picture of the great Dean seems a true one, and is harsh, though not altogether unpleasant. He was doing good, and to deserving men too, in the midst of these intrigues and triumphs. His journals and a thousand anecdotes of him relate his kind acts and rough manners. His hand was constantly stretched out to relieve an honest man — he was cautious about his money, but ready. — If you were in a strait would you like such a benefactor? I think I would rather have had a potato and a friendly word from Goldsmith than have been beholden to the Dean for a guinea and a dinner.* He insulted

used to have for Sir William Temple because he might have been Secretary of State at fifty; and here is a young fellow hardly thirty in that employment." — *Ibid.*

"The Secretary is as easy with me as Mr. Addison was. I have often thought what a splutter Sir William Temple makes about being Secretary of State." — *Ibid.*

"Lord Treasurer has had an ugly fit of the rheumatism, but is now quite well. I was playing at *one-and-thirty* with him and his family the other night. He gave us all twelvepence apiece to begin with; it put me in mind of Sir William Temple." — *Ibid.*

"I thought I saw Jack Temple [*nephew to Sir William*] and his wife pass by me to-day in their coach; but I took no notice of them. I am glad I have wholly shaken off that family." — *S. to S., Sept.* 1710.

* "Swift must be allowed," says Dr. Johnson, "for a time, to have dictated the political opinions of the English nation."

A conversation on the Dean's pamphlets excited one of the Doctor's liveliest sallies. "One, in particular, praised his 'Conduct of the Allies.' — JOHNSON: 'Sir, his "Conduct of the Allies" is a performance of very little ability. . . Why, sir, Tom Davies might have written the "Conduct of the Allies!"'" — BOSWELL'S *Life of Johnson.*

* "Whenever he fell into the company of any person for the first time, it was his custom to try their tempers and disposition by some abrupt question that bore the appearance of rudeness. If this were well taken, and answered with good humor, he afterwards made amends by his civilities. But if he saw any marks of resentment, from alarmed pride, vanity, or conceit, he dropped all further intercourse with the party. This will be illustrated by an anecdote of that sort related by Mrs. Pilkington. After supper, the Dean having decanted a bottle of wine, poured what remained into a glass, and seeing it was muddy, presented it to Mr. Pilkington to drink it. 'For,' said he, 'I always keep some poor parson to drink the foul wine for me.' Mr. Pilkington, entering into his humor, thanked him, and told him 'he did not know the difference, but was glad to get a glass at any rate.' 'Why, then,' said the Dean, 'you shan't, for I'll drink it myself. Why, —— take you, you are wiser than a paltry curate whom I asked to dine with me a few days ago; for upon my making the same speech to him, he

a man as he served him, made women cry, guests look foolish, bullied unlucky friends, and flung his benefactions into poor men's faces. No; the Dean was no Irishman — no Irishman ever gave but with a kind word and a kind heart.

It is told, as if it were to Swift's credit, that the Dean of St. Patrick's performed his family devotions every morning regularly, but with such secrecy that the guests in his house were never in the least aware of the ceremony. There was no need surely why a church dignitary should assemble his family privily in a crypt, and as if he was afraid of heathen persecution. But I think the world was right, and the bishops who advised Queen Anne, when they counselled her not to appoint the author of the "Tale of a Tub" to a bishopric, gave perfectly good advice. The man who wrote the arguments and illustrations in that wild book, could not but be aware what must be the sequel of the propositions which he laid down. The boon companion of Pope and Bolingbroke, who chose these as the friends of his life, and the recipients of his confidence and affection, must have heard many an argument, and joined in many a conversation over Pope's port, or St. John's burgundy, which would not bear to be repeated at other men's boards.

I know of few things more conclusive as to the sincerity of Swift's religion than his advice to poor John Gay to turn clergyman, and look out for a seat on the Bench. Gay, the author of the "Beggar's Opera" — Gay, the wildest of the wits about town — it was this man that Jonathan Swift advised to take orders — to invest in a cassock and bands — just as he advised him to husband his shillings, and put his thousand pounds out at interest.* The Queen, and the bishops, and the world were right, in mistrusting the religion of that man.

said he did not understand such usage, and so walked off without his dinner. By the same token, I told the gentleman who recommended him to me that the fellow was a blockhead, and I had done with him.'" — SHERIDAN'S *Life of Swift*.

* "FROM THE ARCHBISHOP OF CASHELL.

"*Cashell, May 31st*, 1735.

"DEAR SIR, —

"I HAVE been so unfortunate in all my contests of late, that I am resolved to have no more, especially when I am likely to be overmatched; and as I have some reason to hope what is passed will be forgotten, I confess I did endeavor in my last to put the best color I could think of upon a very bad cause. My friends judge right of my idleness; but, in reality, it has hitherto proceeded from a hurry and confusion, arising from a thousand unlucky unforeseen accidents rather than mere sloth. I have but one troublesome affair now upon my hands, which by the help of the prime sergeant, I hope soon to get rid of; and then you shall see me a true Irish bishop. Sir James Ware has made a very useful collection of the memorable actions of my predecessors. He tells me, they were born in such a town of England or Ireland; were consecrated such a year; and if not translated, were buried in the Cathedral church, either on the north or south side. Whence I conclude that a good bishop has nothing more to do than to eat, drink, grow fat, rich, and die; which laudable example I propose for the remainder of my life to follow; for to tell you the truth, I have for these four or five years past met with so much treachery, baseness, and ingratitude among mankind, that I can hardly think it incumbent on any man to endeavor to do good to so perverse a generation.

"I am truly concerned at the account you give me of your health. Without doubt a southern ramble will prove the best remedy you can take to recover your flesh; and I do not know, except in one stage, where you can choose a road so suited to your circumstances, as from Dublin hither. You have to Kilkenny a turnpike and good inns, at every ten or twelve miles' end. From Kilkenny hither is twenty long miles, bad road, and no inns at all: but I have an expedient for you. At the foot of a very high hill, just midway, there lives in a neat thatched cabin, a parson, who is not poor; his wife is allowed to be the best little woman in the world. Her chickens are the fattest, and her ale the best in all the country. Besides, the parson has a little cellar of his own, of which he keeps the key, where he always has a hogshead of the best wine that can be got, in bottles well corked, upon their side; and he cleans, and pulls out the cork better, I think, than Robin. Here I design to meet you with a coach; if you be tired, you shall stay

I am not here, of course, to speak of any man's religious views, except in so far as they influence his literary character, his life, his humor. The most notorious sinners of all those fellow-mortals whom it is our business to discuss — Harry Fielding and Dick Steele, were especially loud, and I believe really fervent, in their expressions of belief; they belabored freethinkers, and stoned imaginary atheists on all sorts of occasions, going out of their way to bawl their own creed, and persecute their neighbor's, and if they sinned and stumbled, as they constantly did with debt, with drink, with all sorts of bad behavior, they got upon their knees, and cried "Peccavi" with a most sonorous orthodoxy. Yes; poor Harry Fielding and poor Dick Steele were trusty and undoubting Church of England men; they abhorred Popery, Atheism, and wooden shoes, and idolatries in general; and hiccoughed Church and State with fervor.

But Swift? *His* mind had had a different schooling, and possessed a very different logical power. *He* was not bred up in a tipsy guard-room, and did not learn to reason in a Covent Garden tavern. He could conduct an argument from beginning to end. He could see forward with a fatal clearness. In his old age, looking at the "Tale of a Tub," when he said, "Good God, what a genius I had when I wrote that book!" I think he was admiring not the genius, but the consequences to which the genius had brought him — a vast genius, a magnificent genius, a genius wonderfully bright, and dazzling, and strong, — to seize, to know, to see, to flash upon falsehood and scorch it into perdition, to penetrate into the hidden motives, and expose the black thoughts of men, — an awful, an evil spirit.

Ah man! you, educated in Epicurean Temple's library, you whose friends were Pope and St. John — what made you to swear to fatal vows, and bind yourself to a lifelong hypocrisy before the Heaven which you adored with such real wonder, humility, and reverence? For Swift was a reverent, was a pious spirit — for Swift could love and could pray. Through the storms and tempests of his furious mind, the stars of religion and love break out in the blue, shining serenely, though hidden by the driving clouds and the maddened hurricane of his life.

It is my belief that he suffered frightfully from the consciousness of his own scepticism, and that he had bent his pride so far down as to put his apostasy out to hire.* The paper left behind him, called "Thoughts on Religion," is merely a set of excuses for not professing disbelief. He says of his sermons that he preached pamphlets: they have scarce a Christian characteristic; they might be preached from the steps of a synagogue, or the floor of a mosque, or the box of a coffee-house almost. There is little or no cant — he is too great and too proud for that; and, in so far as the badness of his sermons goes, he is honest. But having put that cassock on, it poisoned him; he was strangled in his bands. He goes through life, tearing, like a man possessed with a

all night; if not, after dinner, we will set out about four, and be at Cashell by nine; and by going through fields and by-ways, which the parson will show us, we shall escape all the rocky and stony roads that lie between this place and that, which are certainly very bad. I hope you will be so kind as to let me know a post or two before you set out, the very day you will be at Kilkenny, that I may have all things prepared for you. It may be, if you ask him, Cope will come; he will do nothing for me. Therefore, depending upon your positive promise, I shall add no more arguments to persuade you, and am, with the greatest truth, your most faithful and obedient servant,

"THEO. CASHELL."

* "Mr. Swift lived with him [Sir William Temple] some time, but resolving to settle himself in some way of living, was inclined to take orders. However, although his fortune was very small, he had a scruple against entering into the Church merely for support." — *Anecdotes of the Family of Swift*, by the DEAN.

devil. Like Abudah in the Arabian story, he is always looking out for the Fury, and knows that the night will come and the inevitable hag with it. What a night, my God, it was! what a lonely rage and long agony — what a vulture that tore the heart of that giant!* It is awful to think of the great sufferings of this great man. Through life he always seems alone, somehow. Goethe was so. I can't fancy Shakspeare otherwise. The giants must live apart. The kings can have no company. But this man suffered so; and deserved so to suffer. One hardly reads anywhere of such a pain.

The "sæva indignatio" of which he spoke as lacerating his heart, and which he dares to inscribe on his tombstone — as if the wretch who lay under that stone waiting God's judgment had a right to be angry — breaks out from him in a thousand pages of his writing, and tears and rends him. Against men in office, he having been overthrown; against men in England, he having lost his chance of preferment there, the furious exile never fails to rage and curse. Is it fair to call the famous "Drapier's Letters" patriotism? They are master-pieces of dreadful humor and invective: they are reasoned logically enough too, but the proposition is as monstrous and fabulous as the Lilliputian island. It is not that the grievance is so great, but there is his enemy — the assault is wonderful for its activity and terrible rage. It is Samson, with a bone in his hand, rushing on his enemies and felling them: one admires not the cause so much as the strength, the anger, the fury of the champion. As is the case with madmen, certain subjects provoke him, and awaken his fits of wrath. Marriage is one of these; in a hundred passages in his writings he rages against it; rages against children; an object of constant satire, even more contemptible in his eyes than a lord's chaplain, is a poor curate with a large family. The idea of this luckless paternity never fails to bring down from him gibes and foul language. Could Dick Steele, or Goldsmith, or Fielding, in his most reckless moment of satire, have written any thing like the Dean's famous "modest proposal" for eating children? Not one of these but melts at the thoughts of childhood, fondles and caresses it. Mr. Dean has no such softness, and enters the nursery with the tread and gayety of an ogre.* "I have been assured," says he in the "Modest Proposal," "by a very knowing American of my acquaintance in London, that a young healthy child, well nursed, is, at a year old, a most delicious, nourishing, and wholesome food, whether stewed, roasted, baked, or boiled; and I make no doubt it will equally serve in a *ragoût*." And taking up this pretty joke, as his way is, he argues it with perfect gravity and logic. He turns and twists this subject in a score of different ways: he hashes it; and he serves it up cold; and he garnishes it; and relishes it always. He describes the little animal as "dropped from its dam," advising that the mother should let it suck plentifully in the last month, so as to render it plump and fat for a good table! "A child," says his Reverence, "will make two dishes at an entertainment for friends; and when the family dines alone, the fore or hind quarter will make a reasonable dish," and so on; and, the subject be-

* "Dr. Swift had a natural severity of face, which even his smiles could never soften, or his utmost gayety render placid and serene; but when that sternness of visage was increased by rage, it is scarce possible to imagine looks or features that carried in them more terror and austerity." — ORRERY.

* "*London, April 10th*, 1713.

"Lady Masham's eldest boy is very ill: I doubt he will not live; and she stays at Kensington to nurse him, which vexes us all. She is so excessively fond, it makes me mad. She should never leave the Queen, but leave every thing, to stick to what is so much the interest of the public, as well as her own. . ." — *Journal.*

ing so delightful that he can't leave it, he proceeds to recommend, in place of venison for squires' tables, "the bodies of young lads and maidens not exceeding fourteen or under twelve." Amiable humorist! laughing castigator of morals! There was a process well known and practised in the Dean's gay days: when a lout entered the coffee-house, the wags proceeded to what they called "roasting" him. This is roasting a subject with a vengeance. The Dean had a native genius for it. As the "Almanach des Gourmands" says, *On naît rôtisseur.*

And it was not merely by the sarcastic method that Swift exposed the unreasonableness of loving and having children. In Gulliver, the folly of love and marriage is urged by graver arguments and advice. In the famous Lilliputian kingdom, Swift speaks with approval of the practice of instantly removing children from their parents and educating them by the State; and amongst his favorite horses, a pair of foals are stated to be the very utmost a well-regulated equine couple would permit themselves. In fact, our great satirist was of opinion that conjugal love was unadvisable, and illustrated the theory by his own practice and example — God help him — which made him about the most wretched being in God's world.*

The grave and logical conduct of an absurd proposition, as exemplified in the cannibal proposal just mentioned, is our author's constant method through all his works of humor. Given a country of people six inches or sixty feet high, and by the mere process of the logic, a thousand wonderful absurdities are evolved, at so many stages of the calculation. Turning to the first minister who waited behind him with a white staff near as tall as the mainmast of the "Royal Sovereign," the King of Brobdingnag observes how contemptible a thing human grandeur is, as represented by such a contemptible little creature as Gulliver. "The Emperor of Lilliput's features are strong and masculine" (what a surprising humor there is in this description!) — "The Emperor's features," Gulliver says, "are strong and masculine, with an Austrian lip, an arched nose, his complexion olive, his countenance erect, his body and limbs well proportioned, and his deportment majestic. He is taller *by the breadth of my nail* than any of his court, which alone is enough to strike an awe into beholders."

What a surprising humor there is in these descriptions! How noble the satire is here! How just and honest! How perfect the image! Mr. Macaulay has quoted the charming lines of the poet, where the king of the pygmies is measured by the same standard. We have all read in Milton of the spear that was like "the mast of some tall admiral," but these images are surely likely to come to the comic poet originally. The subject is before him. He is turning it in a thousand ways. He is full of it. The figure suggests itself naturally to him, and comes out of his subject, as in that wonderful passage, when Gulliver's box having been dropped by the eagle into the sea, and Gulliver having been received into the ship's cabin, he calls upon the crew to bring the box into the cabin, and put it on the table, the cabin being only a quarter the size of the box. It is the *veracity* of the blunder which is so admirable. Had a man come from such a country as Brobdingnag he would have blundered so.

But the best stroke of humor, if there be a best in that abounding book, is that where Gulliver, in the unpronounceable country, describes his parting from his master the horse.*

* "My health is somewhat mended, but at best I have an ill head and an aching heart." — *In May*, 1719.

* Perhaps the most melancholy satire in the whole of the dreadful book, is the description of the very old people in the "Voyage to Laputa." At Lugnag, Gulliver hears of some persons who never die, called the Struldbrugs, and expressing a wish to become acquainted with men

"I took," he says, "a second leave of my master, but as I was going to prostrate myself to kiss his hoof, he did me the honor to raise it gently to

who must have so much learning and experience, his colloquist describes the Struldbrugs to him.

"He said: They commonly acted like mortals, till about thirty years old, after which, by degrees, they grew melancholy and dejected, increasing in both till they came to fourscore. This he learned from their own confession: for otherwise there not being above two or three of that species born in an age, they were too few to form a general observation by. When they came to fourscore, which is reckoned the extremity of living in this country, they had not only all the follies and infirmities of other old men, but many more which arose from the prospect of never dying. They were not only opinionative, peevish, covetous, morose, vain, talkative, but incapable of friendship, and dead to all natural affection, which never descended below their grandchildren. Envy and impotent desires are the prevailing passions. But those objects against which their envy seems principally directed, are the vices of the younger sort and the deaths of the old. By reflecting on the former, they find themselves cut off from all possibility of pleasure; and whenever they see a funeral, they lament, and repent that others have gone to a harbor of rest, to which they themselves never can hope to arrive. They have no remembrance of any thing but what they learned and observed in their youth and middle age, and even that is very imperfect. And for the truth or particulars of any fact, it is safer to depend on common tradition than upon their best recollections. The least miserable among them appear to be those who turn to dotage, and entirely lose their memories; these meet with more pity and assistance, because they want many bad qualities which abound in others.

"If a Struldbrug happened to marry one of his own kind, the marriage is dissolved of course, by the courtesy of the kingdom, as soon as the younger of the two comes to be fourscore. For the law thinks it to be a reasonable indulgence that those who are condemned, without any fault of their own, to a perpetual continuance in the world, should not have their misery doubled by the load of a wife.

"As soon as they have completed the term of eighty years, they are looked on as dead in law; their heirs immediately succeed to their estates, only a small pittance is reserved for their support; and the poor ones are maintained at the public charge. After that period they are held incapable of any employment of trust or profit, they cannot purchase lands or take leases, neither are they allowed to be witnesses in any cause, either civil or criminal, not even for the decision of meers and bounds.

"At ninety they lose their teeth and hair; they have at that age no distinction of taste, but eat and drink whatever they can get without relish or appetite. The diseases they were subject to still continue, without increasing or diminishing. In talking, they forget the common appellation of things, and the names of persons, even of those who are their nearest friends and relatives. For the same reason, they can never amuse themselves with reading, because their memory will not serve to carry them from the beginning of a sentence to the end; and by this defect they are deprived of the only entertainment whereof they might otherwise be capable.

"The language of this country being always on the flux, the Struldbrugs of one age do not understand those of another; neither are they able, after two hundred years, to hold any conversation (further than by a few general words) with their neighbors, the mortals; and thus they lie under the disadvantage of living like foreigners in their own country.

"This was the account given me of the Struldbrugs, as near as I can remember. I afterwards saw five or six of different ages, the youngest not above two hundred years old, who were brought to me several times by some of my friends; but although they were told 'that I was a great traveller, and had seen all the world,' they had not the least curiosity to ask me a single question; only desired I would give them slumskudask, or a token of remembrance; which is a modest way of begging, to avoid the law, that strictly forbids it, because they are provided for by the public, although indeed with a very scanty allowance.

"They are despised and hated by all sorts of people; when one of them is born, it is reckoned ominous, and their birth is recorded very particularly; so that you may know their age by consulting the register, which, however, has not been kept above a thousand years past, or at least has been destroyed by time or public disturbances. But the usual way of computing how old they are, is by asking them what kings or great persons they can remember, and then consulting history; for infallibly the last prince in their mind did not begin his reign after they were fourscore years old.

"They were the most mortifying sight I ever beheld, and the women more horrible than the men; besides the usual deformities in extreme old age, they acquired an additional ghastliness, in proportion to

my mouth. I am not ignorant how much I have been censured for mentioning this last particular. Detractors are pleased to think it improbable that so illustrious a person should descend to give so great a mark of distinction to a creature so inferior as I. Neither am I ignorant how apt some travellers are to boast of extraordinary favors they have received. But if these censurers were better acquainted with the noble and courteous disposition of the Houyhnhnms they would soon change their opinion."

The surprise here, the audacity of circumstantial evidence, the astounding gravity of the speaker, who is not ignorant how much he has been censured, the nature of the favor conferred, and the respectful exultation at the receipt of it, are surely complete; it is truth topsy-turvy, entirely logical and absurd.

As for the humor and conduct of this famous fable, I suppose there is no person who reads but must admire; as for the moral, I think it horrible, shameful, unmanly, blasphemous; and giant and great as this Dean is, I say we should hoot him. Some of this audience mayn't have read the last part of Gulliver, and to such I would recall the advice of the venerable Mr. Punch to persons about to marry, and say "Don't." When Gulliver first lands among the Yahoos, the naked howling wretches clamber up trees and assault him, and he describes himself as "almost stifled with the filth which fell about him." The reader of the fourth part of "Gulliver's Travels" is like the hero himself in this instance. It is Yahoo language: a monster gibbering shrieks, and gnashing imprecations against mankind — tearing down all shreds of modesty, past all sense of manliness and shame; filthy in word, filthy in thought, furious, raging, obscene.

their number of years, which is not to be described; and among half a dozen, I soon distinguished which was the eldest, although there was not above a century or two between them."—*Gulliver's Travels.*

And dreadful it is to think that Swift knew the tendency of his creed — the fatal rock towards which his logic desperately drifted. That last part of "Gulliver" is only a consequence of what has gone before; and the worthlessness of all mankind, the pettiness, cruelty, pride, imbecility, the general vanity, the foolish pretension, the mock greatness, the pompous dulness, the mean aims, the base successes — all these were present to him; it was with the din of these curses of the world, blasphemies against heaven, shrieking in his ears, that he began to write his dreadful allegory — of which the meaning is that man is utterly wicked, desperate, and imbecile, and his passions are so monstrous, and his boasted powers so mean, that he is and deserves to be the slave of brutes, and ignorance is better than his vaunted reason. What had this man done? what secret remorse was rankling at his heart? what fever was boiling in him, that he should see all the world blood-shot? We view the world with our own eyes, each of us; and we make from within us the world we see. A weary heart gets no gladness out of sunshine; a selfish man is sceptical about friendship, as a man with no ear doesn't care for music. A frightful self-consciousness it must have been, which looked on mankind so darkly through those keen eyes of Swift.

A remarkable story is told by Scott, of Delany, who interrupted Archbishop King and Swift in a conversation which left the prelate in tears, and from which Swift rushed away with marks of strong terror and agitation in his countenance, upon which the Archbishop said to Delany, "You have just met the most unhappy man on earth; but on the subject of his wretchedness you must never ask a question."

The most unhappy man on earth; — Miserrimus — what a character of him! And at this time all the great wits of England had been at his feet. All Ireland had shouted after him, and worshipped him as a liberator, a saviour, the greatest Irish patriot and citizen. Dean Drapier Bickerstaff Gulliver — the most famous statesmen, and the greatest poets of his day, had applauded him, and done him homage; and at this time, writing over to Bolingbroke from Ireland, he says, "It is time for me to have done with the world, and so I would if I could get into a better before I was called into the best, *and not to die here in a rage, like a poisoned rat in a hole.*"

We have spoken about the men, and Swift's behavior to them; and now it behooves us not to forget that there are certain other persons in the creation who had rather intimate relations with the great Dean.* Two women whom he loved and injured are known by every reader of books so familiarly, that if we had seen them, or if they had been relatives of our own, we scarcely could have known them better. Who hasn't in his mind an image of Stella? Who does not love her? Fair and tender creature: pure and affectionate heart! Boots it to you, now that you have been at rest for a hundred and twenty years, not divided in death from the cold heart which caused yours, whilst it beat, such faithful pangs of love and grief — boots it to you now, that the whole world loves and deplores you? Scarce any man, I believe, ever thought of that grave, that did not cast a flower of pity on it, and write over it a sweet epitaph. Gentle lady, so lovely, so loving, so unhappy! you have had countless champions; millions of manly hearts mourning for you. From generation to generation we take up the fond tradition of your beauty: we watch and follow your tragedy, your bright morning love and purity, your constancy, your grief, your sweet martyrdom. We know your legend by heart. You are one of the saints of English story.

And if Stella's love and innocence are charming to contemplate, I will say that in spite of ill-usage, in spite of drawbacks, in spite of mysterious separation and union, of hope delayed and sickened heart — in the teeth of Vanessa, and that little episodical aberration which plunged Swift into such woful pitfalls and quagmires of amorous perplexity — in spite of the verdicts of most women, I believe, who, as far as my experience and conversation go, generally take Vanessa's part in the controversy — in spite of the tears which Swift caused Stella to shed, and the rocks and the barriers which fate and temper interposed, and which prevented the pure course of that true love from running smoothly — the brightest part of Swift's story, the pure star in that dark and tempestuous life of Swift's, is his love for Hester Johnson. It has been my business, professionally of course, to go through a deal of sentimental reading in my time, and to acquaint myself with love-making, as it has been described in various languages, and at various ages of the

* The name of Varina has been thrown into the shade by those of the famous Stella and Vanessa; but she had a story of her own to tell about the blue eyes of young Jonathan. One may say that the book of Swift's Life opens at places kept by these blighted flowers! Varina must have a paragraph.

She was a Miss Jane Waryng, sister to a college chum of his. In 1696, when Swift was nineteen years old, we find him writing a love-letter to her, beginning, "Impatience is the most inseparable quality of a lover." But absence made a great difference in his feelings; so, four years afterwards, the tone is changed. He writes again, a very curious letter, offering to marry her, and putting the offer in such a way that nobody could possibly accept it.

After dwelling on his poverty, &c., he says, conditionally, "I shall be blessed to have you in my arms, without regarding whether your person be beautiful, or your fortune large. Cleanliness in the first, and competency in the second, is all I ask for!"

The editors do not tell us what became of Varina in life. One would be glad to know that she met with some worthy partner, and lived long enough to see her little boys laughing over Lilliput, without any *arrière pensée* of a sad character about the great Dean!

world; and I know of nothing more manly, more tender, more exquisitely touching, than some of these brief notes, written in what Swift calls "his little language" in his journal to Stella.* He writes to her night and morning often. He never sends away a letter to her but he begins a new one on the same day. He can't bear to let go her kind little hand, as it were. He knows that she is thinking of him, and longing for him far away in Dublin yonder. He takes her letters from under his pillow and talks to them, familiarly, paternally, with fond epithets and pretty caresses — as he would to the sweet and artless creature who loved him. "Stay," he writes one morning — it is the 14th of December, 1710 — "Stay, I will answer some of your letter this morning in bed. Let me see. Come and appear, little letter! Here I am, says he, and what say you to Stella this morning fresh and fasting? And can Stella read this writing without hurting her dear eyes?" he goes on, after more kind prattle and fond whispering. The dear eyes shine clearly upon him then — the good angel of his life is with him and blessing him. Ah, it was a hard fate that wrung from them so many tears, and stabbed pitilessly that pure and tender bosom. A hard fate: but would she have changed it? I have heard a woman say that she would have taken Swift's cruelty to have had his tenderness. He had a sort of worship for her whilst

* A sentimental Champollion might find a good deal of matter for his art, in expounding the symbols of the "Little Language." Usually, Stella is "M. D.," but sometimes her companion Mrs. Dingley, is included in it. Swift is "Presto;" also P. D. F. R. We have "Good-night, M. D.; Night, M. D.; Little, M. D.; Stellakins; Pretty Stella; Dear, roguish, impudent, pretty M. D." Every now and then he breaks into rhyme, as —

"I wish you both a merry new year,
Roast-beef, minced-pies, and good strong beer,
And me a share of your good cheer,
That I was there, as you were here,
And you are a little saucy dear."

he wounded her. He speaks of her after she is gone; of her wit, of her kindness, of her grace, of her beauty, with a simple love and reverence that are indescribably touching; in contemplation of her goodness his hard heart melts into pathos; his cold rhyme kindles and glows into poetry, and he falls down on his knees, so to speak, before the angel whose life he had embittered, confesses his own wretchedness and unworthiness, and adores her with cries of remorse and love: —

"When on my sickly couch I lay,
Impatient both of night and day,
And groaning in unmanly strains,
Called every power to ease my pains,
Then Stella ran to my relief,
With cheerful face and inward grief,
And though by heaven's severe decree
She suffers hourly more than me,
No cruel master could require
From slaves employed for daily hire,
What Stella, by her friendship warmed,
With vigor and delight performed.
Now, with a soft and silent tread,
Unheard she moves about my bed:
My sinking spirits now supplies
With cordials in her hands and eyes.
Best patron of true friends! beware;
You pay too dearly for your care
If, while your tenderness secures
My life, it must endanger yours:
For such a fool was never found
Who pulled a palace to the ground,
Only to have the ruins made
Materials for a house decayed."

One little triumph Stella had in her life — one dear little piece of injustice was performed in her favor, for which I confess, for my part, I can't help thanking fate and the Dean. *That other person* was sacrificed to her — that — that young woman, who lived five doors from Dr. Swift's lodgings in Bury Street, and who flattered him, and made love to him in such an outrageous manner — Vanessa was thrown over.

Swift did not keep Stella's letters to him in reply to those he wrote to her.*

* The following passages are from a paper begun by Swift on the evening of the day of her death, Jan. 28, 1727–8: —

"She was sickly from her childhood, until about the age of fifteen; but then she grew into perfect health, and was looked upon as one of the most beautiful,

He kept Bolingbroke's, and Pope's, and Harley's, and Peterborough's: but Stella, "very carefully," the Lives say, kept Swift's. Of course: that is the way of the world: and so we cannot tell what her style was, or of what sort were the little letters which the Doctor placed there at night, and bade to appear from under his pillow of a morning. But in Letter IV. of that famous collection he describes his lodging in Bury Street, where he has the first-floor, a dining-room and bed-chamber, at eight shillings a week; and in Letter VI. he says "he has visited a lady just come to town," whose name somehow is not mentioned; and in Letter VIII. he enters a query of Stella's — "What do you mean 'that boards near me, that I dine with now and then'? What the deuce! You know whom I have dined with every day since I left you, better than I do." Of course she does. Of course Swift has not the slightest idea of what she means. But in a few letters more it turns out that the Doctor has been to dine "gravely" with a Mrs. Vanhomrigh: then that he has been to "his neighbor:" then that he has been unwell, and means to dine for the whole week with his neighbor! Stella was quite right in her previsions. She saw from the very first hint what was going to happen; and scented Vanessa in the air.* The rival is at the Dean's feet. The pupil and teacher are reading together, and drinking tea together, and going to prayers together, and learning Latin together, and conjugating *amo, amas, amavi* together. The little language is over for poor Stella. By the rule of grammar and the course of conjugation, doesn't *amavi* come after *amo* and *amas?*

The loves of Cadenus and Vanessa†

graceful, and agreeable young women in London — only a little too fat. Her hair was blacker than a raven, and every feature of her face in perfection.

"... Properly speaking" — he goes on, with a calmness which, under the circumstances, is terrible — "she has been dying six months! ...

"Never was any of her sex born with better gifts of the mind, or who more improved them by reading and conversation. ... All of us who had the happiness of her friendship agreed unanimously, that in an afternoon's or evening's conversation she never failed before we parted of delivering the best thing that was said in the company. Some of us have written down several of her sayings, or what the French call *bons mots*, wherein she excelled beyond belief."

The specimens on record, however, in the Dean's paper, called "Bons Mots de Stella," scarcely bear out this last part of the panegyric. But the following prove her wit: —

"A gentleman who had been very silly and pert in her company, at last began to grieve at remembering the loss of a child lately dead. A bishop sitting by comforted him — that he should be easy, because 'the child was gone to heaven.' 'No, my lord,' said she; 'that is it which most grieves him, because he is sure never to see his child there.'

"When she was extremely ill, her physician said, 'Madam, you are near the bottom of the hill, but we will endeavor to get you up again.' She answered, 'Doctor, I fear I shall be out of breath before I get up to the top.'

"A very dirty clergyman of her acquaintance, who affected smartness and repartees, was asked by some of the company how his nails came to be so dirty. He was at a loss; but she solved the difficulty by saying, 'The Doctor's nails grew dirty by scratching himself.'

"A Quaker apothecary sent her a vial, corked; it had a broad brim, and a label of paper about its neck. 'What is that?' — said she — 'my apothecary's son!' The ridiculous resemblance, and the suddenness of the question, set us all a-laughing." — *Swift's Works*, SCOTT's Ed. vol. ix. 295-6.

* "I am so hot and lazy after my morning's walk, that I loitered at Mrs. Vanhomrigh's, where my best gown and periwig was, and *out of mere listlessness dine there, very often*; so I did to-day." — *Journal to Stella.*

Mrs. Vanhomrigh, "Vanessa's" mother, was the widow of a Dutch merchant who held lucrative appointments in King William's time. The family settled in London in 1709, and had a house in Bury Street, St. James's — a street made notable by such residents as Swift and Steele; and, in our own time, Moore and Crabbe.

† "Vanessa was excessively vain. The character given of her by Cadenus is fine painting, but in general fictitious. She was fond of dress; impatient to be admired; very romantic in her turn of mind;

you may peruse in Cadenus's own poem on the subject, and in poor Vanessa's vehement expostulatory verses and letters to him; she adores him, implores him, admires him, thinks him something god-like, and only prays to be admitted to lie at his feet.* As they are bringing him home from church, those divine feet of Dr. Swift's are found pretty often in Vanessa's parlor. He likes to be admired and adored. He finds Miss Vanhomrigh to be a woman of great taste and spirit, and beauty and wit, and a fortune too. He sees her every day; he does not tell Stella about the business: until the impetuous Vanessa becomes too fond of him, until the Doctor is quite frightened by the young woman's ardor, and confounded by her warmth. He wanted to marry neither of them — that I believe was the truth; but if he had not married Stella, Vanessa would have had him in spite of himself. When he went back to Ireland, his Ariadne, not content to remain in her isle, pursued the fugitive Dean. In vain he protested, he vowed, he soothed, and bullied; the news of the Dean's marriage with Stella at last came to her, and it killed her — she died of that passion.*

superior, in her own opinion, to all her sex; full of pertness, gayety, and pride; not without some agreeable accomplishments, but far from being either beautiful or genteel; . . . happy in the thoughts of being reported Swift's concubine, but still aiming and intending to be his wife." — LORD ORRERY.

* "You bid me be easy, and you would see me as often as you could. You had better have said, as often as you can get the better of your inclinations so much; or as often as you remember there was such a one in the world. If you continue to treat me as you do, you will not be made uneasy by me long. It is impossible to describe what I have suffered since I saw you last: I am sure I could have borne the rack much better than those killing, killing words of yours. Sometimes I have resolved to die without seeing you more; but those resolves, to your misfortune, did not last long; for there is something in human nature that prompts one so to find relief in this world I must give way to it, and beg you would see me, and speak kindly to me; for I am sure you'd not condemn any one to suffer what I have done, could you but know it. The reason I write to you is, because I cannot tell it to you, should I see you; for when I begin to complain, then you are angry, and there is something in your looks so awful that it strikes me dumb. Oh! that you may have but so much regard for me left that this complaint may touch your soul with pity. I say as little as ever I can: did you but know what I thought, I am sure it would move you to forgive me; and believe I cannot help telling you this and live." — VANESSA. (M. 1714.)

* "If we consider Swift's behavior, so far only as it relates to women, we shall find that he looked upon them rather as busts than as whole figures." — ORRERY.

"You must have smiled to have found his house a constant seraglio of very virtuous women, who attended him from morning to night." — ORRERY.

A correspondent of Sir Walter Scott's furnished him with the materials on which to found the following interesting passage about Vanessa — after she had retired to cherish her passion in retreat: —

"Marley Abbey, near Celbridge, where Miss Vanhomrigh resided, is built much in the form of a real cloister, especially in its external appearance. An aged man (upwards of ninety, by his own account) showed the grounds to my correspondent. He was the son of Mrs. Vanhomrigh's gardener, and used to work with his father in the garden while a boy. He remembered the unfortunate Vanessa well; and his account of her corresponded with the usual description of her person, especially as to her *embonpoint*. He said she went seldom abroad, and saw little company: her constant amusement was reading, or walking in the garden. . . . She avoided company, and was always melancholy, save when Dean Swift was there, and then she seemed happy. The garden was to an uncommon degree crowded with laurels. The old man said that when Miss Vanhomrigh expected the Dean she always planted with her own hand a laurel or two against his arrival. He showed her favorite seat, still called 'Vanessa's bower.' Three or four trees and some laurels indicate the spot. . . . There were two seats and a rude table within the bower, the opening of which commanded a view of the Liffey. . . . In this sequestered spot, according to the old gardener's account, the Dean and Vanessa used often to sit, with books and writing-materials on the table before them." — SCOTT'S *Swift*, vol. i. pp. 246-7.

". . . But Miss Vanhomrigh, irritated at the situation in which she found herself, determined on bringing to a crisis those expectations of a union with the object of her affections — to the hope of

And when she died, and Stella heard that Swift had written beautifully regarding her, "That doesn't surprise me," said Mrs. Stella, "for we all know the Dean could write beautifully about a broomstick." A woman—a true woman! Would you have had one of them forgive the other?

In a note in his biography, Scott says that his friend Dr. Tuke, of Dublin, has a lock of Stella's hair, enclosed in a paper by Swift, on which are written, in the Dean's hand, the words: "*Only a woman's hair.*" An instance, says Scott, of the Dean's desire to veil his feelings under the mask of cynical indifference.

See the various notions of critics! Do those words indicate indifference or an attempt to hide feeling? Did you ever hear or read four words more pathetic? Only a woman's hair: only love, only fidelity, only purity, innocence, beauty; only the tenderest heart in the world stricken and wounded, and passed away now out of reach of pangs of hope deferred, love insulted, and pitiless desertion:—only that lock of hair left; and memory and remorse, for the guilty, lonely wretch, shuddering over the grave of his victim.

And yet to have had so much love, he must have given some. Treasures of wit and wisdom, and tenderness, too, must that man have had locked up in the caverns of his gloomy heart, and shown fitfully to one or two whom he took in there. But it was not good to visit that place. People did not remain there long, and suffered for having been there.* He shrank away from all affections sooner or later. Stella and Vanessa both died near him, and away from him. He had not heart enough to see them die. He broke from his fastest friend, Sheridan; he slunk away from his fondest admirer, Pope. His laugh jars on one's ear after seven score years. He was always alone—alone and gnashing in the darkness, except when

which she had clung amid every vicissitude of his conduct towards her. The most probable bar was his undefined connection with Mrs. Johnson, which, as it must have been perfectly known to her, had, doubtless, long elicited her secret jealousy, although only a single hint to that purpose is to be found in their correspondence, and that so early as 1713, when she writes to him—then in Ireland—'If you are very happy, it is ill-natured of you not to tell me so, *except 'tis what is inconsistent with mine.*' Her silence and patience under this state of uncertainty for no less than eight years, must have been partly owing to her awe for Swift, and partly, perhaps, to the weak state of her rival's health, which, from year to year, seemed to announce speedy dissolution. At length, however, Vanessa's impatience prevailed, and she ventured on the decisive step of writing to Mrs. Johnson herself, requesting to know the nature of that connection. Stella, in reply, informed her of her marriage with the Dean; and full of the highest resentment against Swift for having given another female such a right in him as Miss Vanhomrigh's inquiries implied, she sent to him her rival's letter of interrogatories, and, without seeing him, or awaiting his reply, retired to the house of Mr. Ford, near Dublin. Every reader knows the consequence. Swift, in one of those paroxysms of fury to which he was liable, both from temper and disease, rode instantly to Marley Abbey. As he entered the apartment, the sternness of his countenance, which was peculiarly formed to express the fiercer passions, struck the unfortunate Vanessa with such terror that she could scarce ask whether he would not sit down. He answered by flinging a letter on the table, and, instantly leaving the house, remounted his horse, and returned to Dublin. When Vanessa opened the packet, she only found her own letter to Stella. It was her death-warrant. She sunk at once under the disappointment of the delayed yet cherished hopes which had so long sickened her heart, and beneath the unrestrained wrath of him for whose sake she had indulged them. How long she survived the last interview is uncertain, but the time does not seem to have exceeded a few weeks."—SCOTT.

* "M. Swift est Rabelais dans son bon sens, et vivant en bonne compagnie. Il n'a pas, à la vérité, la gaîté du premier, mais il a toute la finesse, la raison, le choix, le bon goût qui manquent à notre curé de Meudon. Ses vers sont d'un goût singulier, et presque inimitable; la bonne plaisanterie est son partage en vers et en prose; mais pour le bien entendre il faut faire un petit voyage dans son pays."—VOLTAIRE: *Lettres sur les Anglais.* Let. 22.

Congreve.

Stella's sweet smile came and shone upon him. When that went, silence and utter night closed over him. An immense genius: an awful downfall and ruin. So great a man he seems to me, that thinking of him is like thinking of an empire falling. We have other great names to mention — none I think, however, so great or so gloomy.

CONGREVE AND ADDISON.

A GREAT number of years ago, before the passing of the Reform Bill, there existed at Cambridge a certain debating club, called the "Union;" and I remember that there was a tradition amongst the undergraduates who frequented that renowned school of oratory, that the great leaders of the Opposition and Government had their eyes upon the University Debating Club, and that if a man distinguished himself there he ran some chance of being returned to Parliament as a great nobleman's nominee. So Jones of John's, or Thomson of Trinity, would rise in their might, and draping themselves in their gowns, rally round the monarchy, or hurl defiance at priests and kings, with the majesty of Pitt or the fire of Mirabeau, fancying all the while that the great nobleman's emissary was listening to the debate from the back benches, where he was sitting with the family seat in his pocket. Indeed the legend said that one or two young Cambridge men, orators of the "Union" were actually caught up thence, and carried down to Cornwall or old Sarum, and so into Parliament. And many a young fellow deserted the jogtrot University curriculum, to hang on in the dust behind the fervid wheels of the parliamentary chariot.

Where, I have often wondered, were the sons of Peers and Members of Parliament in Anne's and George's time? Were they all in the army, or hunting in the country, or boxing the watch? How was it that the young gentlemen from the University got such a prodigious number of places? A lad composed a neat copy of verses at Christchurch or Trinity, in which the death of a great personage was bemoaned, the French king assailed, the Dutch or Prince Eugene complimented, or the reverse; and the party in power was presently to provide for the young poet; and a commissionership, or a post in the Stamps, or the secretaryship of an Embassy, or a clerkship in the Treasury, came into the bard's possession. A wonderful fruit-bearing rod was that of Busby's. What have men of letters got in *our* time? Think, not only of Swift, a king fit to rule in any time or empire — but Addison, Steele, Prior, Tickell, Congreve, John Gay, John Dennis, and many others, who got public employment, and pretty little pickings out of the public purse.* The wits

* The following is a *conspectus* of them: —

ADDISON. — Commissioner of Appeals; Under Secretary of State; Secretary to the Lord Lieutenant of Ireland; Keeper of the Records in Ireland; Lord of Trade; and one of the Principal Secretaries of State, successively.

STEELE. — Commissioner of the Stamp Office; Surveyor of the Royal Stables at Hampton Court; and Governor of the Royal Company of Comedians;

of whose names we shall treat in this lecture and two following, all (save one) touched the King's coin, and had, at some period of their lives, a happy quarter-day coming round for them.

They all began at school or college in the regular way, producing panegyrics upon public characters, what were called odes upon public events, battles, sieges, court marriages and deaths, in which the gods of Olympus and the tragic muse were fatigued with invocations, according to the fashion of the time in France and in England. "Aid us, Mars, Bacchus, Apollo," cried Addison, or Congreve, singing of William or Marlborough. "*Accourez, chastes nymphes de Parnasse,*" says Boileau, celebrating the Grand Monarch. "*Des sons que ma lyre enfante* marquez en bien la cadence, *et vous vents, faites silence! je vais parler de Louis!*" Schoolboys' themes and foundation exercises are the only relics left now of this scholastic fashion. The Olympians are left quite undisturbed in their mountain. What man of note, what contributor to the poetry of a country newspaper, would now think of writing a congratulatory ode on the birth of the heir to a dukedom, or the marriage of a nobleman? In the past century the young gentlemen of the Universities all exercised themselves at these queer compositions; and some got fame, and some gained patrons and places for life, and many more took nothing by these efforts of what they were pleased to call their muses.

William Congreve's * Pindaric Odes are still to be found in "Johnson's Poets," that now unfrequented poets'-corner, in which so many forgotten big-wigs have a niche; but though he was also voted to be one of the greatest tragic poets of any day, it was Congreve's wit and humor which first recommended him to courtly fortune. And it is recorded that his first play, the "Old Bachelor," brought our author to the notice of that great patron of English muses, Charles Montague Lord Halifax — who, being desirous to place so eminent a wit in a state of ease and tranquillity, instantly made him one of the Commissioners for licensing hackney-coaches, bestowed on him soon after a place in the Pipe Office, and likewise a post in the Custom House of the value of 600*l*.

A commissionership of hackney-coaches — a post in the Custom House — a place in the Pipe Office, and all for writing a comedy! Doesn't it sound like a fable, that place in the Pipe Office? † "Ah, l'heureux

Commissioner of "Forfeited Estates in Scotland."

PRIOR. — Secretary to the Embassy at the Hague; Gentleman of the Bedchamber to King William; Secretary to the Embassy in France; Under Secretary of State; Ambassador to France.

TICKELL. — Under Secretary of State; Secretary to the Lords Justices of Ireland.

CONGREVE. — Commissioner for licensing Hackney Coaches; Commissioner for Wine Licenses; place in the Pipe Office; post in the Custom House; Secretary of Jamaica.

GAY. — Secretary to the Earl of Clarendon (when Ambassador to Hanover).

JOHN DENNIS. — A place in the Custom House.

"En Angleterre . . . les lettres sont plus en honneur qu'ici." — VOLTAIRE: *Lettres sur les Anglais*. Let. 20.

* He was the son of Colonel William Congreve, and grandson of Richard Congreve, Esq., of Congreve and Stretton in Staffordshire — a very ancient family.

† "PIPE. — *Pipe*, in law, is a roll in the Exchequer, called also the *great roll*.

"*Pipe Office* is an office in which a person called the *Clerk of the Pipe* makes out leases of Crown lands, by warrant from the Lord Treasurer, or Commissioners of the Treasury, or Chancellor of the Exchequer.

"Clerk of the Pipe makes up all accounts of sheriffs, &c." — REES: *Cyclopæd.* Art. PIPE.

"*Pipe Office*. — Spelman thinks so called, because the papers were kept in a large *pipe* or cask.

"'These be at last brought into that office of Her Majesty's Exchequer, which we, by a metaphor, do call the *pipe* . . . because the whole receipt is finally conveyed into it by means of divers small

temps que celui de ces fables!" Men of letters there still be: but I doubt whether any Pipe Offices are left. The public has smoked them long ago.

Words, like men, pass current for a while with the public, and being known everywhere abroad, at length take their places in society; so even the most secluded and refined ladies here present will have heard the phrase from their sons or brothers at school, and will permit me to call William Congreve, Esquire, the most eminent literary "swell" of his age. In my copy of "Johnson's Lives," Congreve's wig is the tallest, and put on with the jauntiest air of all the laurelled worthies. "I am the great Mr. Congreve," he seems to say, looking out from his voluminous curls. People called him the great Mr. Congreve.* From the beginning of his career until the end everybody admired him. Having got his education in Ireland, at the same school and college with Swift, he came to live in the Middle Temple, London, where he luckily bestowed no attention to the law; but splendidly frequented the coffee-houses and theatres, and appeared in the side box, the tavern, the Piazza, and the Mall, brilliant, beautiful, and victorious from the first. Everybody acknowledged the young chieftain. The great Mr. Dryden † declared that he was equal to Shakspeare, and bequeathed to him his own undisputed poetical crown, and writes of him: "Mr. Congreve has done me the favor to review the 'Æneis,' and compare my version with the original. I shall never be ashamed to own that this excellent young man has showed me many faults which I have endeavored to correct."

The "excellent young man" was but three or four and twenty when the great Dryden thus spoke of him: the greatest literary chief in England, the veteran field-marshal of letters, himself the marked man of all Europe, and the centre of a school of wits who daily gathered round his chair and tobacco-pipe at Wills'. Pope dedi-

pipes or quills.'—BACON: *The Office of Alienations*."

[We are indebted to Richardson's *Dictionary* for this fragment of erudition. But a modern man of letters can know little on these points—by experience.]

* "It has been observed that no change of Ministers affected him in the least; nor was he ever removed from any post that was given to him, except to a better. His place in the Custom House, and his office of Secretary in Jamaica, are said to have brought him in upwards of twelve hundred a year."—*Biog. Brit., Art.* CONGREVE.

† Dryden addressed his "twelfth epistle" to "My dear friend, Mr. Congreve," on his comedy called the "Double Dealer," in which he says:—

"Great Jonson did by strength of judgment please;
Yet, doubling Fletcher's force, he wants his ease.
In differing talents both adorned their age:
One for the study, t'other for the stage.
But both to Congreve justly shall submit,
One matched in judgment, both o'ermatched in wit.
In him all beauties of this age we see,"
&c., &c.

The "Double Dealer," however, was not so palpable a hit as the "Old Bachelor," but, at first, met with opposition. The critics first having fallen foul of it, our "Swell" applied the scourge to that presumptuous body, in the "Epistle Dedicatory" to the "Right Honorable Charles Montague."

"I was conscious," said he, "where a true critic might have put me upon my defence. I was prepared for the attack, . . . but I have not heard any thing said sufficient to provoke an answer."

He goes on—

"But there is one thing at which I am more concerned than all the false criticisms that are made upon me; and that is, some of the ladies are offended. I am heartily sorry for it; for I declare, I would rather disoblige all the critics in the world than one of the fair sex. They are concerned that I have represented some women vicious and affected. How can I help it? It is the business of a comic poet to paint the vices and follies of human kind. . . . I should be very glad of an opportunity to make my compliments to those ladies who are offended. But they can no more expect it in a comedy than *to be tickled by a surgeon when he is letting their blood*."

cated his "Iliad" to him; * Swift, Addison, Steele, all acknowledge Congreve's rank, and lavish compliments upon him. Voltaire went to wait upon him as on one of the Representatives of Literature; and the man who scarce praises any other living person — who flung abuse at Pope, and Swift, and Steele, and Addison — the Grub Street Timon, old John Dennis,† was hat in hand to Mr. Congreve; and said that when he retired from the stage, Comedy went with him.

Nor was he less victorious elsewhere. He was admired in the drawing-rooms as well as the coffee-houses; as much beloved in the side-box as on the stage. He loved, and conquered, and jilted the beautiful Bracegirdle, ‡ the heroine of all his plays, the favorite of all the town of her day; and the Duchess of Marlborough, Marlborough's daughter, had such an admiration of him, that when he died she had an ivory figure made to imitate him,* and a large wax doll with gouty feet to be dressed just as the great Congreve's gouty feet were dressed in his great lifetime. He saved some money by his Pipe Office, and his Custom House office, and his Hackney Coach office, and nobly left it, not to Bracegirdle, who wanted it,† but to the Duchess of Marlborough, who didn't. ‡

How can I introduce to you that merry and shameless Comic Muse who won him such a reputation? Nell Gwynn's servant fought the other footman for having called his mistress a bad name: and in like manner, and with pretty like epithets, Jeremy Collier attacked that godless, reckless Jezebel, the English comedy of his time,

* "Instead of endeavoring to raise a vain monument to myself, let me leave behind me a memorial of my friendship with one of the most valuable men as well as finest writers of my age and country — one who has tried, and knows by his own experience, how hard an undertaking it is to do justice to Homer — and one who, I am sure, seriously rejoices with me at the period of my labors. To him, therefore, having brought this long work to a conclusion, I desire to dedicate it, and to have the honor and satisfaction of placing together in this manner the names of Mr. Congreve and of — A. POPE." — *Postscript to Translation of the Iliad of Homer*. Mar. 25, 1720.

† "When asked why he listened to the praises of Dennis, he said he had much rather be flattered than abused. Swift had a particular friendship for our author, and generally took him under his protection in his high authoritative manner." — THOS. DAVIES: *Dramatic Miscellanies*.

‡ "Congreve was very intimate for years with Mrs. Bracegirdle, and lived in the same street, his house very near hers, until his acquaintance with the young Duchess of Marlborough. He then quitted that house. The Duchess showed us a diamond necklace (which Lady Di. used afterwards to wear) that cost seven thousand pounds, and was purchased with the money Congreve left her. How much better would it have been to have given it to poor Mrs. Bracegirdle." — DR. YOUNG. *Spence's Anecdotes*.

* "A glass was put in the hand of the statue, which was supposed to bow to her Grace, and to nod in approbation of what she spoke to it." — THOS. DAVIES: *Dramatic Miscellanies*.

† The sum Congreve left Mrs. Bracegirdle was 200*l*., as is said in the "Dramatic Miscellanies" of Tom Davies; where are some particulars about this charming actress and beautiful woman.

She had a "lively aspect," says Tom, on the authority of Cibber, and "such a glow of health and cheerfulness in her countenance, as inspired everybody with desire." "Scarce an audience saw her that were not half of them her lovers."

Congreve and Rowe courted her in the persons of their lovers. "In Tamerlane, Rowe courted her Selima, in the person of Axalla. . . . Congreve insinuated his addresses in his Valentine to her Angelica, in his 'Love for Love;' in his Osmyn to her Almena, in the 'Mourning Bride;' and, lastly, in his Mirabel, to her Millamant, in the 'Way of the World.' Mirabel, the fine gentleman of the play, is, I believe, not very distant from the real character of Congreve." — *Dramatic Miscellanies*, vol. iii. 1784.

She retired from the stage when Mrs. Oldfield began to be the public favorite. She died in 1748, in the eighty-fifth year of her age.

‡ Johnson calls his legacy the "accumulation of attentive parsimony, which," he continues, "though to her (the Duchess) superfluous and useless, might have given great assistance to the ancient family from which he descended, at that time, by the imprudence of his relation, reduced to difficulties and distress." — *Lives of the Poets*.

and called her what Nell Gwynn's man's fellow-servants called Nell Gwynn's man's mistress. The servants of the theatre, Dryden, Congreve,* and others, defended themselves with the same success, and for the same cause which set Nell's lackey fighting. She was a disreputable, daring, laughing, painted French baggage, that Comic Muse. She came over from the Continent with Charles (who chose many more of his female friends there) at the Restoration — a wild, dishevelled Lais, with eyes bright with wit and wine — a saucy court-favorite that sat at the King's knees, and laughed in his face, and when she showed her bold cheeks at her chariot-window, had some of the noblest and most famous people of the land bowing round her wheel. She was kind and popular enough, that daring Comedy, that audacious poor Nell: she was gay and generous, kind, frank, as such people can afford to be: and the men who lived with her and laughed with her, took her pay and drank her wine, turned out when the Puritans hooted her, to fight and defend her. But the jade was indefensible, and it is pretty certain her servants knew it.

There is life and death going on in every thing: truth and lies always at battle. Pleasure is always warring against self-restraint. Doubt is always crying Psha! and sneering. A man in life, a humorist, in writing about life, sways over to one principle or the other, and laughs with the reverence for right and the love of truth in his heart, or laughs at these from the other side. Didn't I tell you that dancing was a serious business to Harlequin? I have read two or three of Congreve's plays over before speaking of him; and my feelings were rather like those, which I dare say most of us here have had, at Pompeii, looking at Sallust's house and the relics of an orgy: a dried wine-jar or two, a charred supper-table, the breast of a dancing-girl pressed against the ashes, the laughing skull of a jester: a perfect stillness round about, as the cicerone twangs his moral, and the blue sky shines calmly over the ruin. The Congreve Muse is dead, and her song choked in Time's ashes. We gaze at the skeleton, and wonder at the life which once revelled in its mad veins. We take the skull up, and muse over the frolic and daring, the wit, scorn, passion, hope, desire, with which that empty bowl once fermented. We think of the glances that allured, the tears that melted, of the bright eyes that shone in those vacant sockets; and of lips whispering love, and cheeks dimpling with smiles, that once covered yon ghastly yellow framework. They used to call those teeth pearls once. See! there's the cup she drank from, the gold chain she wore on her neck, the vase which held her rouge for her cheeks, her looking-glass, and the harp she used to dance to. Instead of a feast we find a gravestone, and in place of a mistress, a few bones.

Reading in these plays now, is like shutting your ears and looking at

* He replied to Collier, in the pamphlet called "Amendments of Mr. Collier's False and Imperfect Citations," &c. A specimen or two are subjoined: —

"The greater part of these examples which he has produced are only demonstrations of his own impurity: they only savor of his utterance, and were sweet enough till tainted by his breath.

"Where the expression is unblamable in its own pure and genuine signification, he enters into it, himself, like the evil spirit; he possesses the innocent phrase, and makes it bellow forth his own blasphemies.

"If I do not return him civilities in calling him names, it is because I am not very well versed in his nomenclatures. . . . I will only call him Mr. Collier, and that I will call him as often as I think he shall deserve it.

"The corruption of a rotten divine is the generation of a sour critic."

"Congreve," says Dr. Johnson, "a very young man, elated with success, and impatient of censure, assumed an air of confidence and security. . . . The dispute was protracted through two years; but at last Comedy grew more modest, and Collier lived to see the reward of his labors in the reformation of the theatre." — *Life of Congreve.*

people dancing. What does it mean? the measures, the grimaces, the bowing, shuffling and retreating, the cavalier seul advancing upon those ladies — those ladies and men twirling round at the end in a mad galop, after which everybody bows and the quaint rite is celebrated. Without the music we can't understand that comic dance of the last century — its strange gravity and gayety, its decorum or its indecorum. It has a jargon of its own quite unlike life; a sort of moral of its own quite unlike life too. I'm afraid it's a Heathen mystery, symbolizing a Pagan doctrine; protesting — as the Pompeians very likely were, assembled at their theatre and laughing at their games; as Sallust and his friends, and their mistresses, protested, crowned with flowers, with cups in their hands — against the new, hard, ascetic, pleasure-hating doctrine whose gaunt disciples, lately passed over from the Asian shores of the Mediterranean, were for breaking the fair images of Venus, and flinging the altars of Bacchus down.

I fancy poor Congreve's theatre is a temple of Pagan delights, and mysteries not permitted except among heathens. I fear the theatre carries down that ancient tradition and worship, as masons have carried their secret signs and rites from temple to temple. When the libertine hero carries off the beauty in the play, and the dotard is laughed to scorn for having the young wife: in the ballad, when the poet bids his mistress to gather roses while she may, and warns her that old Time is still a-flying: in the ballet, when honest Corydon courts Phillis under the treillage of the pasteboard cottage, and leers at her over the head of grandpapa in red stockings, who is opportunely asleep; and when seduced by the invitations of the rosy youth she comes forward to the footlights, and they perform on each other's tiptoes that *pas* which you all know, and which is only interrupted by old grandpapa awaking from his doze at the pasteboard châlet (whither he returns to take another nap in case the young people get an encore): when Harlequin, splendid in youth, strength, and agility, arrayed in gold and a thousand colors, springs over the heads of countless perils, leaps down the throat of bewildered giants, and, dauntless and splendid, dances danger down: when Mr. Punch, that godless old rebel, breaks every law and laughs at it with odious triumph, outwits his lawyer, bullies the beadle, knocks his wife about the head, and hangs the hangman — don't you see in the comedy, in the song, in the dance, in the ragged little Punch's puppet-show — the Pagan protest? Doesn't it seem as if Life puts in its plea and sings its comment? Look how the lovers walk and hold each other's hands and whisper! Sings the chorus — "There is nothing like love, there is nothing like youth, there is nothing like beauty of your springtime. Look! how old age tries to meddle with merry sport! Beat him with his own crutch, the wrinkled old dotard! There is nothing like youth, there is nothing like beauty, there is nothing like strength. Strength and valor win beauty and youth. Be brave and conquer. Be young and happy. Enjoy, enjoy, enjoy! Would you know the *Segreto per esser felice?* Here it is, in a smiling mistress and a cup of Falernian." As the boy tosses the cup and sings his song — hark! what is that chant coming nearer and nearer? What is that dirge which *will* disturb us? The lights of the festival burn dim — the cheeks turn pale — the voice quavers — and the cup drops on the floor. Who's there? Death and Fate are at the gate, and they *will* come in.

Congreve's comic feast flares with lights, and round the table, emptying their flaming bowls of drink, and exchanging the wildest jests and ribaldry, sit men and women, waited on by rascally valets and attendants as dissolute as their mistresses — perhaps the very worst company in the world.

There doesn't seem to be a pretence of morals. At the head of the table sits Mirabel or Belmour (dressed in the French fashion and waited on by English imitators of Scapin and Frontin). Their calling is to be irresistible, and to conquer everywhere. Like the heroes of the chivalry story, whose long-winded loves and combats they were sending out of fashion, they are always splendid and triumphant — overcome all dangers, vanquish all enemies, and win the beauty at the end. Fathers, husbands, usurers, are the foes these champions contend with. They are merciless in old age, invariably, and an old man plays the part in the dramas which the wicked enchanter or the great blundering giant performs in the chivalry tales, who threatens and grumbles and resists — a huge stupid obstacle always overcome by the knight. It is an old man with a money-box: Sir Belmour his son or nephew spends his money and laughs at him. It is an old man with a young wife whom he locks up: Sir Mirabel robs him of his wife, trips up his gouty old heels and leaves the old hunks. The old fool, what business has he to hoard his money, or to lock up blushing eighteen? Money is for youth, love is for youth, away with the old people. When Millamant is sixty, having of course divorced the first Lady Millamant, and married his friend Doricourt's grand-daughter out of the nursery — it will be his turn; and young Belmour will make a fool of him. All this pretty morality you have in the comedies of William Congreve, Esq. They are full of wit. Such manners as he observes, he observes with great humor; but ah! it's a weary feast, that banquet of wit where no love is. It palls very soon; sad indigestions follow it and lonely blank headaches in the morning.

I can't pretend to quote scenes from the splendid Congreve's plays * — which are undeniably bright, witty, and daring — any more than I could

* The scene of Valentine's pretended madness in "Love for Love" is a splendid specimen of Congreve's daring manner: —

"*Scandal.* — And have you given your master a hint of their plot upon him?

"*Jeremy.* — Yes, Sir; he says he'll favor it, and mistake her for *Angelica.*

"*Scandal.* — It may make us sport.

"*Foresight.* — Mercy on us!

"*Valentine.* — Husht — interrupt me not — I'll whisper predictions to thee, and thou shalt prophesie; — I am truth, and can teach thy tongue a new trick, — I have told thee what's passed — now I'll tell what's to come: — Dost thou know what will happen to-morrow? Answer me not — for I will tell thee. To-morrow knaves will thrive thro' craft, and fools thro' fortune; and honesty will go as it did, frost-nipt in a summer suit. Ask me questions concerning to-morrow.

"*Scandal.* — Ask him, *Mr. Foresight.*

"*Foresight.* — Pray what will be done at Court?

"*Valentine.* — *Scandal* will tell you; — I am truth, I never come there.

"*Foresight.* — In the city?

"*Valentine.* — Oh, prayers will be said in empty churches at the usual hours. Yet you will see such zealous faces behind counters as if religion were to be sold in every shop. Oh, things will go methodically in the city, the clocks will strike twelve at noon, and the horn'd herd buzz in the Exchange at two. Husbands and wives will drive distinct trades, and care and pleasure separately occupy the family. Coffee-houses will be full of smoke and stratagem. And the cropt 'prentice that sweeps his master's shop in the morning, may, ten to one, dirty his sheets before night. But there are two things that you will see very strange; which are, wanton wives with their legs at liberty, and tame cuckolds with chains about their necks. But hold, I must examine you before I go further; you look suspiciously. Are you a husband?

"*Foresight.* — I am married.

"*Valentine.* — Poor creature! Is your wife of Covent-garden *Parish*?

"*Foresight.* — No; St. Martin's-in-the-Fields.

"*Valentine.* — Alas, poor man! his eyes are sunk, and his hands shrivelled; his legs dwindled, and his back bow'd. Pray, pray, for a metamorphosis — change thy shape, and shake off age; get thee *Medea's* kettle and be boiled anew; come forth with lab'ring callous hands, and chine of steel, and *Atlas'* shoulders. Let Taliacotius trim the calves of twenty chairmen, and make thee pedestals to stand erect upon, and look matrimony in the face. Ha, ha, ha! That a man should have a stomach to a wedding-sup-

ask you to hear the dialogue of a witty bargeman and a brilliant fish-woman exchanging compliments at Billingsgate; but some of his verses

per, when the pidgeons ought rather to be laid to his feet! Ha, ha, ha!

"*Foresight.*—His frenzy is very high now, *Mr. Scandal.*

"*Scandal.*—I believe it is a spring-tide.

"*Foresight.* — Very likely — truly; you understand these matters. *Mr. Scandal,* I shall be very glad to confer with you about these things he has uttered. His sayings are very mysterious and hieroglyphical.

"*Valentine.*—Oh, why would *Angelica* be absent from my eyes so long?

"*Jeremy.*—She's here, Sir.

"*Mrs. Foresight.*—Now, Sister!

"*Mrs. Frail.*—O Lord! what must I say?

"*Scandal.*—Humor him, Madam, by all means.

"*Valentine.*—Where is she? Oh! I see her: she comes, like Riches, Health, and Liberty at once, to a despairing, starving, and abandoned wretch. Oh—welcome, welcome!

"*Mrs. Frail.*—How d'ye, Sir? Can I serve you?

"*Valentine.*—Hark'ee—I have a secret to tell you. *Endymion* and the moon shall meet us on *Mount Latmos*, and we'll be married in the dead of night. But say not a word. *Hymen* shall put his torch into a dark lanthorn, that it may be secret; and Juno shall give her peacock poppy-water, that he may fold his ogling tail; and Argus's hundred eyes be shut—ha! Nobody shall know, but *Jeremy.*

"*Mrs. Frail.*—No, no; we'll keep it secret; it shall be done presently.

"*Valentine.*—The sooner the better. *Jeremy*, come hither—closer—that none may overhear us. *Jeremy*, I can tell you news: *Angelica* is turned nun, and I am turning friar, and yet we'll marry one another in spite of the Pope. Get me a cowl and beads, that I may play my part; for she'll meet me two hours hence in black and white, and a long veil to cover the project, and we won't see one another's faces 'till we have done something to be ashamed of, and then we'll blush once for all. . . .

"*Enter* TATTLE.

"*Tattle.*—Do you know me, *Valentine?*

"*Valentine.*—You!—who are you? No, I hope not.

"*Tattle.*—I am *Jack Tattle*, your friend.

"*Valentine.*—My friend! What to do? I am no married man, and thou canst not lye with my wife; I am very poor, and thou canst not borrow money of me. Then, what employment have I for a friend?

"*Tattle.*—Hah! A good open speaker, and not to be trusted with a secret.

"*Angelica.*—Do you know me, *Valentine?*

"*Valentine.*—Oh, very well.

"*Angelica.*—Who am I?

"*Valentine.*—You're a woman, one to whom Heaven gave beauty when it grafted roses on a brier. You are the reflection of Heaven in a pond; and he that leaps at you is sunk. You are all white—a sheet of spotless paper—when you first are born; but you are to be scrawled and blotted by every goose's quill. I know you; for I loved a woman, and loved her so long that I found out a strange thing: I found out what a woman was good for.

"*Tattle.*—Ay! pr'ythee, what's that?

"*Valentine.*—Why, to keep a secret.

"*Tattle.*—O Lord!

"*Valentine.*—Oh, exceeding good to keep a secret; for, though she should tell, yet she is not to be believed.

"*Tattle.*—Hah! Good again, faith.

"*Valentine.*—I would have music. Sing me the song that I like."—CONGREVE: *Love for Love.*

There is a *Mrs. Nickleby*, of the year 1700, in Congreve's Comedy of "The Double Dealer," in whose character the author introduces some wonderful traits of roguish satire. She is practised on by the gallants of the play, and no more knows how to resist them than any of the ladies above quoted could resist Congreve.

"*Lady Plyant.*—Oh! reflect upon the honor of your conduct! Offering to pervert me" [the joke is that the gentleman is pressing the lady for her daughter's hand, not for her own]—"perverting me from the road of virtue, in which I have trod thus long, and never made one trip—not one *faux pas.* Oh, consider it: what would you have to answer for, if you should provoke me to frailty! Alas! humanity is feeble, heaven knows! Very feeble, and unable to support itself.

"*Mellefont.*—Where am I? Is it day? and am I awake? Madam—

"*Lady Plyant.*—O Lord, ask me the question! I'll swear I'll deny it—therefore don't ask me; nay, you shan't ask me, I swear I'll deny it. O Gemini, you have brought all the blood into my face; I warrant I am as red as a turkey-cock. O fie, cousin Mellefont!

"*Mellefont.*—Nay, Madam, hear me; I mean—

"*Lady Plyant.*—Hear you? No, no; I'll deny you first, and hear you afterwards. For one does not know how one's

— they were amongst the most famous lyrics of the time, and pronounced equal to Horace by his contemporaries — may give an idea of his power, of his grace, of his daring manner, his magnificence in compliment, and his polished sarcasm. He writes as if he was so accustomed to conquer, that he has a poor opinion of his victims. Nothing's new except their faces, says he: "every woman is the same." He says this in his first comedy, which he wrote languidly* in illness, when he was an "excellent young man." Richelieu at eighty could have hardly said a more excellent thing.

When he advances to make one of his conquests, it is with a splendid gallantry, in full uniform and with the fiddles playing, like Grammont's French dandies attacking the breach of Lerida.

"Cease, cease to ask her name," he writes of a young lady at the Wells at Tunbridge, whom he salutes with a magnificent compliment —

"Cease, cease to ask her name,
The crowned Muse's noblest theme,
Whose glory by immortal fame
Shall only sounded be.
But if you long to know,
Then look round yonder dazzling row;
Who most does like an angel show,
You may be sure 'tis she."

Here are lines about another beauty, who perhaps was not so well pleased at the poet's manner of celebrating her —

"When Lesbia first I saw, so heavenly fair,
With eyes so bright and with that awful air,
I thought my heart which durst so high aspire
As bold as his who snatched celestial fire.

But soon as e'er the beauteous idiot spoke,
Forth from her coral lips such folly broke:
Like balm the trickling nonsense healed my wound,
And what her eyes enthralled, her tongue unbound."

Amoret is a cleverer woman than the lovely Lesbia, but the poet does not seem to respect one much more than the other; and describes both with exquisite satirical humor —

"Fair Amoret is gone astray:
Pursue and seek her every lover.
I'll tell the signs by which you may
The wandering shepherdess discover.

Coquet and coy at once her air,
Both studied, though both seem neglected;

mind may change upon hearing — hearing is one of the senses, and all the senses are fallible. I won't trust my honor, I assure you; my honor is infallible and uncomatable.

"*Mellefont.* — For heaven's sake, Madam —

"*Lady Plyant.* — Oh, name it no more. Bless me, how can you talk of heaven, and have so much wickedness in your heart? May be, you don't think it a sin. They say some of you gentlemen don't think it a sin; but still, my honor, if it were no sin — But, then, to marry my daughter for the convenience of frequent opportunities — I'll never consent to that: as sure as can be, I'll break the match.

"*Mellefont.* — Death and amazement! Madam, upon my knees —

"*Lady Plyant.* — Nay, nay, rise up! come, you shall see my good-nature. I know love is powerful, and nobody can help his passion. 'Tis not your fault; nor I swear, it is not mine. How can I help it, if I have charms? And how can you help it, if you are made a captive? I swear it is pity it should be a fault; but, my honor. Well, but your honor, too — but the sin! Well, but the necessity. O Lord, here's somebody coming. I dare not stay. Well, you must consider of your crime; and strive as much as can be against it — strive, be sure; but don't be melancholick — don't despair; but never think that I'll grant you any thing. O Lord, no; but be sure you lay all thoughts aside of the marriage, for though I know you don't love Cynthia, only as a blind for your passion to me — yet it will make me jealous. O Lord, what did I say? Jealous! No, I can't be jealous; for I must not love you. Therefore don't hope; but don't despair neither. They're coming; I *must* fly." — *The Double Dealer:* Act 2, sc. v. page 156.

* "There seems to be a strange affectation in authors of appearing to have done every thing by chance. The 'Old Bachelor' was written for amusement in the languor of convalescence. Yet it is apparently composed with great elaborateness of dialogue and incessant ambition of wit." — JOHNSON: *Lives of the Poets.*

Careless she is with artful care,
Affecting to be unaffected.

With skill her eyes dart every glance,
Yet change so soon you'd ne'er suspect them;
For she'd persuade they wound by chance,
Though certain aim and art direct them.

She likes herself, yet others hates
For that which in herself she prizes;
And, while she laughs at them, forgets
She is the thing which she despises."

What could Amoret have done to bring down such shafts of ridicule upon her? Could she have resisted the irresistible Mr. Congreve? Could anybody? Could Sabina, when she woke and heard such a bard singing under her window? "See," he writes —

"See! see, she wakes — Sabina wakes!
And now the sun begins to rise?
Less glorious is the morn that breaks
From his bright beams, than her fair eyes.
With light united, day they give;
But different fates ere night fulfil:
How many by his warmth will live!
How many will her coldness kill!"

Are you melted? Don't you think him a divine man? If not touched by the brilliant Sabina, hear the devout Selinda: —

"Pious Selinda goes to prayers,
If I but ask her favor;
And yet the silly fool's in tears,
If she believes I'll leave her:
Would I were free from this restraint,
Or else had hopes to win her:
Would she could make of me a saint,
Or I of her a sinner!"

What a conquering air there is about these! What an irresistible Mr. Congreve it is! Sinner! of course he will be a sinner, the delightful rascal! Win her! of course he will win her, the victorious rogue! He knows he will: he must — with such a grace, with such a fashion, with such a splendid embroidered suit. You see him with red-heeled shoes deliciously turned out, passing a fair jewelled hand through his dishevelled periwig, and delivering a killing ogle along with his scented billet. And Sabina? What a comparison that is between the nymph and the sun! The sun gives Sabina the *pas*, and does not venture to rise before her ladyship: the morn's *bright beams* are less glorious than her *fair eyes:* but before night everybody will be frozen by her glances: everybody but one lucky rogue who shall be nameless. Louis Quatorze in all his glory is hardly more splendid than our Phœbus Apollo of the Mall and Spring Gardens.*

When Voltaire came to visit the great Congreve, the latter rather affected to despise his literary reputation, and in this perhaps the great Congreve was not far wrong.† A touch of Steele's tenderness is worth all his

* "Among those by whom it ('Wills's') was frequented, Southerne and Congreve were principally distinguished by Dryden's friendship. . . . But Congreve seems to have gained yet farther than Southerne upon Dryden's friendship. He was introduced to him by his first play; the celebrated 'Old Bachelor' being put into the poet's hands to be revised. Dryden, after making a few alterations to fit it for the stage, returned it to the author with the high and just commendation, that it was the best first play he had ever seen." — SCOTT'S *Dryden*, vol. i. p. 370.

† It was in Surrey Street, Strand (where he afterwards died), that Voltaire visited him, in the decline of his life.

The anecdote relating to his saying that he wished "to be visited on no other footing than as a gentleman who led a life of plainness and simplicity," is common to all writers on the subject of Congreve, and appears in the English version of Voltaire's "Letters concerning the English Nation," published in London, 1733, as also in Goldsmith's "Memoir of Voltaire." But it is worthy of remark, that it does not appear in the text of the same Letters in the edition of Voltaire's "Œuvres Complètes" in the "Panthéon Littéraire." Vol. v. of his works. (Paris, 1837.)

"Celui de tous les Anglais qui à porté le plus loin la gloire du théâtre comique est feu M. Congreve. Il n'a fait que peu de pièces, mais toutes sont excellentes dans leur genre. . . . Vous y voyez partout le langage des honnêtes gens avec des actions de fripon; ce qui prouve qu'il connaissait bien son monde, et qu'il vivait dans ce qu'on appelle la bonne compagnie." — VOLTAIRE: *Lettres sur les Anglais.* Let. 19.

finery; a flash of Swift's lightning, a beam of Addison's pure sunshine, and his tawdry playhouse taper is invisible. But the ladies loved him, and he was undoubtedly a pretty fellow.*

* On the death of Queen Mary he published a Pastoral—"The Mourning Muse of Alexis." Alexis and Menalcas sing alternately in the orthodox way. The Queen is called PASTORA.

"I mourn PASTORA dead, let Albion mourn,
And sable clouds her chalky cliffs adorn,"

says Alexis. Among other phenomena, we learn that—

"With their sharp nails themselves the Satyrs wound,
And tug their shaggy beards, and bite with grief the ground"—

(a degree of sensibility not always found in the Satyrs of that period). . . . It continues—

"Lord of these woods and wide extended plains,
Stretched on the ground and close to earth his face,
Scalding with tears the already faded grass.
. . . . .
To dust must all that Heavenly beauty come?
And must Pastora moulder in the tomb?
Ah Death! more fierce and unrelenting far
Than wildest wolves and savage tigers are;
With lambs and sheep their hunger is appeased,
But ravenous Death the shepherdess has seized."

This statement that a wolf eats but a sheep, whilst Death eats a shepherdess—that figure of the "Great Shepherd" lying speechless on his stomach, in a state of despair which neither winds nor floods nor air can exhibit—are to be remembered in poetry surely: and this style was admired in its time by the admirers of the great Congreve!

In the "Tears of Amaryllis for Amyntas" (the young Lord Blandford, the great Duke of Marlborough's only son), Amaryllis represents Sarah Duchess!

The tigers and wolves, nature and motion, rivers and echoes, come into work here again. At the sight of her grief—

"Tigers and wolves their wonted rage forego,
And dumb distress and new compassion show,
Nature herself attentive silence kept,
And motion seemed suspended while she wept!"

And Pope dedicated the "Iliad" to the author of these lines—and Dryden wrote to him in his great hand:—

"Time, place, and action may with pains be wrought,
But Genius must be born, and never can be taught.
This is your portion, this your native store;
Heaven, that but once was prodigal before,
To SHAKSPEARE gave as much she could not give him more.
Maintain your Post: that's all the fame you need,
For 'tis impossible you should proceed;
Already I am worn with cares and age,
And just abandoning the ungrateful stage:
Unprofitably kept at Heaven's expense,
I live a Rent-charge upon Providence:
But you, whom every Muse and Grace adorn,
Whom I foresee to better fortune born,
Be kind to my remains, and oh! defend
Against your Judgment your departed Friend!
Let not the insulting Foe my Fame pursue;
But shade those Laurels which descend to You:
And take for Tribute what these Lines express;
You merit more, nor could my Love do less."

This is a very different manner of welcome to that of our own day. In Shadwell, Higgons, Congreve, and the comic authors of their time, when gentlemen meet they fall into each other's arms, with "Jack, Jack, I must buss thee;" or, "Fore George, Harry, I must kiss thee, lad." And in a similar manner the poets saluted their brethren. Literary gentlemen do not kiss now; I wonder if they love each other better?

Steele calls Congreve "Great Sir" and "Great Author;" says "Well-dressed barbarians knew his awful name," and addresses him as if he were a prince; and speaks of "Pastora" as one of the most famous tragic compositions.

We have seen in Swift a humorous philosopher, whose truth frightens one, and whose laughter makes one melancholy. We have had in Congreve a humorous observer of another school, to whom the world seems to have no moral at all, and whose ghastly doctrine seems to be that we should eat, drink, and be merry when we can, and go to the deuce (if there be a deuce) when the time comes. We come now to a humor that flows from quite a different heart and spirit — a wit that makes us laugh and leaves us good and happy; to one of the kindest benefactors that society has ever had; and I believe you have divined already that I am about to mention Addison's honored name.

From reading over his writings, and the biographies which we have of him, amongst which the famous article in "The Edinburgh Review" * may be cited as a magnificent statue of the great writer and moralist of the last age, raised by the love and the marvellous skill and genius of one of the most illustrious artists of our own; looking at that calm, fair face, and clear countenance — those chiselled features pure and cold, I can't but fancy that this great man — in this respect, like him of whom we spoke in the last lecture — was also one of the lonely ones of the world. Such men have very few equals, and they don't herd with those. It is in the nature of such lords of intellect to be solitary — they are in the world, but not of it; and our minor struggles, brawls, successes, pass under them.

Kind, just, serene, impartial, his fortitude not tried beyond easy endurance, his affections not much used, for his books were his family, and his society was in public; admirably wiser, wittier, calmer, and more instructed than almost every man with whom he met, how could Addison suffer, desire, admire, feel much? I may expect a child to admire me for being taller or writing more cleverly than she; but how can I ask my superior to say that I am a wonder when he knows better than I? In Addison's days you could scarcely show him a literary performance, a sermon, or a poem, or a piece of literary criticism, but he felt he could do better. His justice must have made him indifferent. He didn't praise, because he measured his compeers by a higher standard than common people have.* How was he who was so tall to look up to any but the loftiest genius? He must have stooped to put himself on a level with most men. By that profusion of graciousness and smiles with which Goethe or Scott, for instance, greeted almost every literary beginner, every small literary adventurer who came to his court and went away charmed from the great king's audience, and cuddling to his heart the compliment which his literary majesty had paid him — each of the two good-natured potentates of letters brought their star and ribbon into discredit. Everybody had his majesty's orders. Everybody had his majesty's cheap portrait, on a box surrounded with diamonds worth twopence apiece. A very great and just and wise man ought not to praise indiscriminately, but give his idea of the truth. Addison praises the ingenious Mr. Pinkethman: Addison praises the ingenious Mr. Dog-

* "To Addison himself we are bound by a sentiment as much like affection as any sentiment can be which is inspired by one who has been sleeping a hundred and twenty years in Westminster Abbey. . . . After full inquiry and impartial reflection we have long been convinced that he deserved as much love and esteem as can justly be claimed by any of our infirm and erring race." — MACAULAY.

"Many who praise virtue do no more than praise it. Yet it is reasonable to believe that Addison's profession and practice were at no great variance; since, amidst that storm of faction in which most of his life was passed, though his station made him conspicuous, and his activity made him formidable, the character given him by his friends was never contradicted by his enemies. Of those with whom interest or opinion united him, he had not only the esteem but the kindness; and of others, whom the violence of opposition drove against him, though he might lose the love, he retained the reverence." — JOHNSON.

* "Addison was perfect good company with intimates, and had something more charming in his conversation than I ever knew in any other man; but with any mixture of strangers, and sometimes only with one, he seemed to preserve his dignity much, with a stiff sort of silence." — POPE. *Spence's Anecdotes.*

ADDISON.

gett, the actor, whose benefit is coming off that night: Addison praises Don Saltero: Addison praises Milton with all his heart, bends his knee and frankly pays homage to that imperial genius.* But between those degrees of his men his praise is very scanty. I don't think the great Mr. Addison liked young Mr. Pope, the Papist, much; I don't think he abused him. But when Mr. Addison's men abused Mr. Pope, I don't think Addison took his pipe out of his mouth to contradict them.†

Addison's father was a clergyman of good repute in Wiltshire, and rose in the church.‡ His famous son never lost his clerical training and scholastic gravity, and was called "a parson in a tye-wig" ‖ in London afterwards at a time when tye-wigs were only worn by the laity, and the fathers of theology did not think it decent to appear except in a full bottom. Having been at school at Salisbury, and the Charterhouse, in 1687, when he was fifteen years old, he went to Queen's College, Oxford, where he speedily began to distinguish himself by the making of Latin verses. The beautiful and fanciful poem of "The Pygmies and Cranes," is still read by lovers of that sort of exercise; and verses are extant in honor of King William, by which it appears that it was the loyal youth's custom to toast that sovereign in bumpers of purple Lyæus: many more works are in the Collection, including one on the Peace of Ryswick, in 1697, which was so good that Montague got him a pension of 300*l.* a year, on which Addison set out on his travels.

During his ten years at Oxford, Addison had deeply imbued himself with the Latin poetical literature, and had these poets at his fingers' ends when he travelled in Italy.* His patron went out of office, and his pen-

* "Milton's chief talent, and indeed his distinguishing excellence, lies in the sublimity of his thoughts. There are others of the moderns, who rival him in every other part of poetry; but in the greatness of his sentiments he triumphs over all the poets, both modern and ancient, Homer alone excepted. It is impossible for the imagination of man to disturb itself with greater ideas than those which he has laid together in his first, second, and sixth books."—*Spectator*, No. 279.

"If I were to name a poet that is a perfect master in all these arts of working on the imagination, I think Milton may pass for one."—*Ibid*, No. 417.

These famous papers appeared in each Saturday's "Spectator," from January 19th to May 3d, 1712. Beside his services to Milton, we may place those he did to Sacred Music.

† "Addison was very kind to me at first, but my bitter enemy afterwards."—POPE. *Spence's Anecdotes.*

"'Leave him as soon as you can,' said Addison to me, speaking of Pope; 'he will certainly play you some devilish trick else: he has an appetite to satire.'"—LADY WORTLEY MONTAGU. *Spence's Anecdotes.*

‡ Lancelot Addison, his father, was the son of another Lancelot Addison, a clergyman in Westmoreland. He became Dean of Lichfield and Archdeacon of Coventry.

‖ "The remark of Mandeville, who, when he had passed an evening in his company, declared that he was 'a parson in a tye-wig,' can detract little from his character. He was always reserved to strangers, and was not incited to uncommon freedom by a character like that of Mandeville."—JOHNSON: *Lives of the Poets.*

"Old Jacob Tonson did not like Mr. Addison: he had a quarrel with him, and, after his quitting the secretaryship, used frequently to say of him—'One day or other you'll see that man a bishop—I'm sure he looks that way; and indeed I ever thought him a priest in his heart.'"—POPE. *Spence's Anecdotes.*

"Mr. Addison staid above a year at Blois. He would rise as early as between two and three in the height of summer, and lie abed till between eleven and twelve in the depth of winter. He was untalkative whilst here, and often thoughtful: sometimes so lost in thought, that I have come into his room and staid five minutes there before he has known any thing of it. He had his masters generally at supper with him; kept very little company beside; and had no amour that I know of; and I think I should have known it if he had had any."—ABBÉ PHILIPPEAUX OF BLOIS. *Spence's Anecdotes.*

* His knowledge of the Latin poets, from Lucretius and Catullus down to Claudian and Prudentius, was singularly exact and profound."—MACAULAY.

sion was unpaid: and hearing that this great scholar, now eminent and known to the literati of Europe (the great Boileau,* upon perusal of Mr. Addison's elegant hexameters, was first made aware that England was not altogether a barbarous nation) — hearing that the celebrated Mr. Addison, of Oxford, proposed to travel as governor to a young gentleman on the grand tour, the great Duke of Somerset proposed to Mr. Addison to accompany his son, Lord Hartford.

Mr. Addison was delighted to be of use to his Grace, and his lordship his Grace's son, and expressed himself ready to set forth.

His Grace the Duke of Somerset now announced to one of the most famous scholars of Oxford and Europe that it was his gracious intention to allow my Lord Hartford's tutor one hundred guineas per annum. Mr. Addison wrote back that his services were his Grace's, but he by no means found his account in the recompense for them. The negotiation was broken off. They parted with a profusion of *congées* on one side and the other.

Addison remained abroad for some time, living in the best society of Europe. How could he do otherwise? He must have been one of the finest gentlemen the world ever saw: at all moments of life serene and courteous, cheerful and calm.† He could scarcely ever have had a degrading thought. He might have omitted a virtue or two, or many, but could not have had many faults committed for which he need blush or turn pale. When warmed into confidence, his conversation appears to have been so delightful that the greatest wits sat rapt and charmed to listen to him. No man bore poverty and narrow fortune with a more lofty cheerfulness. His letters to his friends at this period of his life, when he had lost his Government pension, and given up his college chances, are full of courage, and a gay confidence and philosophy: and they are none the worse in my eyes, and I hope not in those of his last and greatest biographer (though Mr. Macaulay is bound to own and lament a certain weakness for wine, which the great and good Joseph Addison notoriously possessed, in common with countless gentlemen of his time), because some of the letters are written when his honest hand was shaking a little in the morning after libations to purple Lyæus over night. He was fond of drinking the healths of his friends: he writes to Wyche,* of Hamburg,

"Mr. Addison to Mr. Wyche.

"Dear Sir,

"My hand at present begins to grow steady enough for a letter, so the properest use I can put it to is to thank ye honest gentleman that set it a shaking. I have had this morning a desperate design in my head to attack you in verse, which I should certainly have done could I have found out a rhyme to rummer. But though you have escaped for ye present, you are not yet out of danger, if I can a little recover my talent at crambo. I am sure, in whatever way I write to you, it will be impossible for me to express ye deep sense I have of ye many favours you have lately shown me. I shall only tell you that Hambourg has been the pleasantest stage I have met with in my travails. If any of my friends wonder at me for living so long in that place, I dare say it will be thought a very good excuse when I tell him Mr. Wyche was there. As your company made our stay at Hambourg agreeable, your wine has given us all ye satisfaction that we have found in our journey through Westphalia. If drinking your health will do you any good, you may expect to be as long-lived as Methuselah, or, to use a more familiar instance, as ye oldest hoc in ye cellar. I hope ye two pair of legs that was left a swelling behind us are by this time come to their shapes again. I can't forbear troubling you with my hearty re-

* "Our country owes it to him, that the famous Monsieur Boileau first conceived an opinion of the English genius for poetry, by perusing the present he made him of the 'Musæ Anglicanæ.'" — Tickell: *Preface to Addison's Works.*

† "It was my fate to be much with the wits; my father was acquainted with all of them. *Addison was the best company in the world.* I never knew anybody that had so much wit as Congreve." — Lady Wortley Montagu. *Spence's Anecdotes.*

gratefully remembering Wyche's "hoc." "I have been drinking your health to-day with Sir Richard Shirley," he writes to Bathurst. "I have lately had the honor to meet my Lord Effingham at Amsterdam, where we have drunk Mr. Wood's health a hundred times in excellent champagne," he writes again. Swift* describes him over his cups, when Joseph yielded to a temptation which Jonathan resisted. Joseph was of a cold nature, and needed perhaps the fire of wine to warm his blood. If he was a parson, he wore a tye-wig, recollect. A better and more Christian man scarcely ever breathed than Joseph Addison. If he had not that little weakness for wine — why, we could scarcely have found a fault with him, and could not have liked him as we do.*

At thirty-three years of age, this most distinguished wit, scholar, and gentleman was without a profession and an income. His book of "Travels" had failed: his "Dialogues on Medals" had had no particular success; his Latin verses, even though reported the best since Virgil, or Statius at any rate, had not brought him a Government place, and Addison was living up two shabby pair of stairs in the Haymarket (in a poverty over which old Samuel Johnson rather chuckles), when in these shabby rooms an emissary from Government and Fortune came and found him.† A poem was wanted about the Duke of Marlborough's victory of Blenheim. Would Mr. Addison write one? Mr. Boyle, afterwards Lord Carleton, took back the reply to the Lord Treasurer Godolphin, that Mr. Addison would. When the poem had reached a certain stage, it was carried to Godolphin; and the last lines which he read were these: —

spects to yᵉ owners of them, and desiring you to believe me always,

"Dear Sir,

"Yours," &c.

"To Mr. Wyche, His Majesty's Resident at Hambourg,

"May, 1703."

— *From the Life of Addison, by* Miss Aikin. Vol. i. p. 146.

* It is pleasing to remember that the relation between Swift and Addison was, on the whole, satisfactory from first to last. The value of Swift's testimony, when nothing personal inflamed his vision or warped his judgment, can be doubted by nobody.

"Sept. 10, 1710. — I sat till ten in the evening with Addison and Steele.

"11. — Mr. Addison and I dined together at his lodgings, and I sat with him part of this evening.

"18. — To-day I dined with Mr. Stratford at Mr. Addison's retirement near Chelsea. . . . I will get what good offices I can from Mr. Addison.

"27. — To-day all our company dined at Will Frankland's, with Steele and Addison, too.

"29. — I dined with Mr. Addison," &c. — *Journal to Stella.*

Addison inscribed a presentation copy of his Travels "To Dr. Jonathan Swift, the most agreeable companion, the truest friend, and the greatest genius of his age." — (Scott. From the information of Mr. Theophilus Swift.)

"Mr. Addison, who goes over first secretary, is a most excellent person; and being my most intimate friend, I shall use all my credit to set him right in his notions of persons and things." — *Letters.*

"I examine my heart, and can find no other reason why I write to you now, besides that great love and esteem I have always had for you. I have nothing to ask you either for my friend or for myself." — Swift to Addison (1717). Scott's *Swift.* Vol. xix. p. 274.

Political differences only dulled for a while their friendly communications. Time renewed them; and Tickell enjoyed Swift's friendship as a legacy from the man with whose memory his is so honorably connected.

* "Addison usually studied all the morning; then met his party at Button's; dined there, and staid five or six hours, and sometimes far into the night. I was of the company for about a year, but found it too much for me: it hurt my health, and so I quitted it." — Pope. *Spence's Anecdotes.*

† "When he returned to England (in 1702), with a meanness of appearance which gave testimony of the difficulties to which he had been reduced, he found his old patrons out of power, and was, therefore for a time, at full leisure for the cultivation of his mind." — Johnson: *Lives of the Poets.*

"But, O my Muse! what numbers wilt thou find
To sing the furious troops in battle joined?
Methinks I hear the drum's tumultuous sound
The victor's shouts and dying groans confound;
The dreadful burst of cannon rend the skies,
And all the thunders of the battle rise.
'Twas then great Marlborough's mighty soul was proved,
That, in the shock of charging hosts unmoved,
Amidst confusion, horror, and despair,
Examined all the dreadful scenes of war:
In peaceful thought the field of death surveyed,
To fainting squadrons lent the timely aid,
Inspired repulsed battalions to engage,
And taught the doubtful battle where to rage.
So when an angel, by divine command,
With rising tempests shakes a guilty land
(Such as of late o'er pale Britannia passed),
Calm and serene he drives the furious blast;
And, pleased the Almighty's orders to perform,
Rides on the whirlwind and directs the storm."

Addison left off at a good moment. That simile was pronounced to be of the greatest ever produced in poetry. That angel, that good angel, flew off with Mr. Addison, and landed him in the place of Commissioner of Appeals — vice Mr. Locke providentially promoted. In the following year Mr. Addison went to Hanover with Lord Halifax, and the year after was made Under Secretary of State. O angel visits! you come "few and far between" to literary gentlemen's lodgings! Your wings seldom quiver at second-floor windows now!

You laugh? You think it is in the power of few writers now-a-days to call up such an angel? Well, perhaps not; but permit us to comfort ourselves by pointing out that there are in the poem of the "Campaign" some as bad lines as heart can desire; and to hint that Mr. Addison did very wisely in not going further with my Lord Godolphin than that angelical simile. Do allow me, just for a little harmless mischief, to read you some of the lines which follow. Here is the interview between the Duke and the King of the Romans after the battle: —

"Austria's young monarch, whose imperial sway
Sceptres and thrones are destined to obey,
Whose boasted ancestry so high extends
That in the Pagan Gods his lineage ends,
Comes from afar, in gratitude to own
The great supporter of his father's throne.
What tides of glory to his bosom ran
Clasped in the embraces of the godlike man!
How were his eyes with pleasing wonder fixed,
To see such fire with so much sweetness mixed!
Such easy greatness, such a graceful port,
So learned and finished for the camp or court!"

How many fourth-form boys at Mr. Addison's school of Charterhouse could write as well as that now? The "Campaign" has blunders, triumphant as it was; and weak points like all campaigns.*

In the year 1718 "Cato" came out. Swift has left a description of the first night of the performance. All the laurels of Europe were scarcely sufficient for the author of this prodigious poem.† Laudations of Whig and Tory chiefs, popular ovations, complimentary garlands from literary

* "Mr. Addison wrote very fluently; but he was sometimes very slow and scrupulous in correcting. He would show his verses to several friends; and would alter almost every thing that any of them hinted at as wrong. He seemed to be too diffident of himself, and too much concerned about his character as a poet, or (as he worded it) too solicitous for that kind of praise which, God knows, is but a very little matter after all!" — POPE. *Spence's Anecdotes.*

† "As to poetical affairs," says Pope, in 1713, "I am content at present to be a bare looker-on. . . . Cato was not so much the wonder of Rome in his days, as he is of Britain in ours; and though all the foolish industry possible has been used to make it thought a party play, yet what the author once said of another may

men, translations in all languages, delight and homage from all — save from John Dennis in a minority of one. Mr. Addison was called the "great Mr. Addison" after this. The Coffee-house Senate saluted him Divus: it was heresy to question that decree.

Meanwhile he was writing political papers and advancing in the political profession. He went Secretary to Ireland. He was appointed Secretary of State in 1717. And letters of his are extant, bearing date some year or two before, and written to young Lord Warwick, in which he addresses him as "my dearest lord," and asks affectionately about his studies, and writes very prettily about nightingales and birds'-nests, which he has found at Fulham for his lordship. Those nightingales were intended to warble in the ear of Lord Warwick's mamma. Addison married her ladyship in 1716; and died at Holland House three years after that splendid but dismal union.*

the most properly in the world be applied to him on this occasion: —

"'Envy itself is dumb — in wonder lost;
And factions strive who shall applaud him most.'

"The numerous and violent claps of the Whig party on the one side of the theatre were echoed back by the Tories on the other; while the author sweated behind the scenes with concern to find their applause proceeding more from the hands than the head. . . . I believe you have heard that, after all the applauses of the opposite faction, my Lord Bolingbroke sent for Booth, who played *Cato*, into the box, and presented him with fifty guineas in acknowledgment (as he expressed it) for defending the cause of liberty so well against a perpetual dictator." — POPE'S *Letter to* SIR W. TRUMBULL.

"Cato" ran for thirty-five nights without interruption. Pope wrote the Prologue, and Garth the Epilogue.

It is worth noticing how many things in "Cato" keep their ground as habitual quotations, *e.g.*: —

". . . big with the fate
Of Cato and of Rome."

"'Tis not in mortals to command success,
But we'll do more, Sempronius, we'll deserve it."

"Blesses his stars, and thinks it luxury."

"I think the Romans call it Stoicism."

"My voice is still for war."

"When vice prevails, and impious men bear sway,
The post of honor is a private station."

Not to mention —

"The woman who deliberates is lost."

And the eternal —

"Plato, thou reasonest well,"

which avenges, perhaps, on the public their neglect of the play!

* "The lady was persuaded to marry him on terms much like those on which a Turkish princess is espoused — to whom the Sultan is reported to pronounce, 'Daughter, I give thee this man for thy slave.' The marriage, if uncontradicted report can be credited, made no addition to his happiness; it neither found them, nor made them, equal. . . . Rowe's ballad of 'The Despairing Shepherd' is said to have been written, either before or after marriage, upon this memorable pair." — DR. JOHNSON.

"I received the news of Mr. Addison's being declared Secretary of State with the less surprise, in that I knew that post was almost offered to him before. At that time he declined it, and I really believe that he would have done well to have declined it now. Such a post as that, and such a wife as the Countess, do not seem to be, in prudence, eligible for a man that is asthmatic, and we may see the day when he will be heartily glad to resign them both." — LADY WORTLEY MONTAGU to POPE: *Works, Lord Wharncliffe's edit.*, vol. ii. p. 111.

The issue of this marriage was a daughter, Charlotte Addison, who inherited, on her mother's death, the estate of Bilton, near Rugby, which her father had purchased. She was of weak intellect, and died, unmarried, at an advanced age.

Rowe appears to have been faithful to Addison during his courtship, for his Collection contains "Stanzas to Lady Warwick, on Mr. Addison's going to Ireland," in which her ladyship is called "Chloe," and Joseph Addison "Lycidas;" besides the ballad mentioned by the Doctor, and which is entitled "Colin's Complaint." But not even the interest attached to the name of Addison could induce the reader to peruse this composition, though one stanza may serve as a specimen: —

"What though I have skill to complain —
Though the Muses my temples have crowned;
What though, when they hear my sweet strain,
The Muses sit weeping around.

But it is not for his reputation as the great author of "Cato" and the "Campaign," or for his merits as Secretary of State, or for his rank and high distinction as my Lady Warwick's husband, or for his eminence as an Examiner of political questions on the Whig side, or a Guardian of British liberties, that we admire Joseph Addison. It is as a Tatler of small talk and a Spectator of mankind, that we cherish and love him, and owe as much pleasure to him as to any human being that ever wrote. He came in that artificial age, and began to speak with his noble, natural voice. He came, the gentle satirist, who hit no unfair blow; the kind judge who castigated only in smiling. While Swift went about, hanging and ruthless — a literary Jeffreys — in Addison's kind court only minor cases were tried: only peccadilloes and small sins against society: only a dangerous libertinism in tuckers and hoops;* or a nuisance in the abuse of beaux' canes and snuff-boxes. It may be a lady is tried for breaking the peace of our sovereign lady Queen Anne, and ogling too dangerously from the side-box: or a Templar for beating the watch, or breaking Priscian's head: or a citizen's wife for caring too much for the puppet-show, and too little for her husband and children: every one of the little sinners brought before him is amusing, and he dismisses each with the pleasantest penalties and the most charming words of admonition.

Addison wrote his papers as gayly as if he was going out for a holiday. When Steele's "Tatler" first began

"Ah, Colin! thy hopes are in vain;
Thy pipe and thy laurel resign;
Thy false one inclines to a swain
Whose music is sweeter than thine."

* One of the most humorous of these is the paper on Hoops, which, "The Spectator" tells us, particularly pleased his friend SIR ROGER:

"MR. SPECTATOR, —

"You have diverted the town almost a whole month at the expense of the country; it is now high time that you should give the country their revenge. Since your withdrawing from this place, the fair sex are run into great extravagances. Their petticoats, which began to heave and swell before you left us, are now blown up into a most enormous concave, and rise every day more and more; in short, sir, since our women knew themselves to be out of the eye of the SPECTATOR, they will be kept within no compass. You praised them a little too soon, for the modesty of their head-dresses; for as the humor of a sick person is often driven out of one limb into another, their superfluity of ornaments, instead of being entirely banished, seems only fallen from their heads upon their lower parts. What they have lost in height they make up in breadth, and, contrary to all rules of architecture, widen the foundations at the same time that they shorten the superstructure.

"The women give out, in defence of these wide bottoms, that they are very airy and very proper for the season; but this I look upon to be only a pretence and a piece of art, for it is well known we have not had a more moderate summer these many years, so that it is certain the heat they complain of cannot be in the weather; besides, I would fain ask these tender-constitutioned ladies, why they should require more cooling than their mothers before them?

"I find several speculative persons are of opinion that our sex has of late years been very saucy, and that the hoop-petticoat is made use of to keep us at a distance. It is most certain that a woman's honor cannot be better intrenched than after this manner, in circle within circle, amidst such a variety of outworks and lines of circumvallation. A female who is thus invested in whalebone is sufficiently secured against the approaches of an ill-bred fellow, who might as well think of Sir George Etheridge's way of making love in a tub as in the midst of so many hoops.

"Among these various conjectures, there are men of superstitious tempers who look upon the hoop-petticoat as a kind of prodigy. Some will have it that it portends the downfall of the *French* king, and observe, that the farthingale appeared in *England* a little before the ruin of the *Spanish* monarchy. Others are of opinion that it foretells battle and bloodshed, and believe it of the same prognostication as the tail of a blazing star. For my part, I am apt to think that it is a sign that multitudes are coming into the world rather than going out of it," &c., &c. — *Spectator*, No. 127.

his prattle Addison, then in Ireland, caught at his friend's notion, poured in paper after paper, and contributed the stores of his mind, the sweet fruits of his reading, the delightful gleanings of his daily observation, with a wonderful profusion, and as it seemed an almost endless fecundity. He was six and thirty years old: full and ripe. He had not worked crop after crop from his brain, manuring hastily, subsoiling indifferently, cutting and sowing and cutting again, like other luckless cultivators of letters. He had not done much as yet; a few Latin poems — graceful prolusions; a polite book of travels; a dissertation on medals, not very deep; four acts of a tragedy, a great classical exercise; and the "Campaign," a large prize poem that won an enormous prize. But with his friend's discovery of "The Tatler," Addison's calling was found, and the most delightful talker in the world began to speak. He does not go very deep: let gentlemen of a profound genius, critics accustomed to the plunge of the bathos, console themselves by thinking that he *couldn't* go very deep. There are no traces of suffering in his writing. He was so good, so honest, so healthy, so cheerfully selfish, if I must use the word. There is no deep sentiment. I doubt, until after his marriage, perhaps, whether he ever lost his night's rest or his day's tranquillity about any woman in his life; * whereas poor Dick Steele had capacity enough to melt, and to languish, and to sigh, and to cry his honest old eyes out, for a dozen. His writings do not show insight into or reverence for the love of women, which I take to be, one the consequence of the other. He walks about the world watching their pretty humors, fashions, follies, flirtations, rivalries; and noting them with the most charming archness. He sees them in public, in the theatre, or the assembly, or the puppet-show; or at the toy-shop higgling for gloves and lace; or at the auction, battling together over a blue porcelain dragon, or a darling monster in Japan; or at church, eying the width of their rival's hoops, or the breadth of their laces, as they sweep down the aisles. Or he looks out of his window at the "Garter" in St. James's Street, at Ardelia's coach, as she blazes to the drawing-room with her coronet and six footmen; and remembering that her father was a Turkey merchant in the city, calculates how many sponges went to purchase her ear-ring, and how many drums of figs to build her coach-box; or he demurely watches behind a tree in Spring Garden as Saccharissa (whom he knows under her mask) trips out of her chair to the alley where Sir Fopling is waiting. He sees only the public life of women. Addison was one of the most resolute club-men of his day. He passed many hours daily in those haunts. Besides drinking — which alas! is past praying for — you must know it, he owned, too, ladies, that he indulged in that odious practice of smoking. Poor fellow! He was a man's man, remember. The only woman he *did* know, he didn't write about. I take it there would not have been much humor in that story.

He likes to go and sit in the smoking-room at the "Grecian," or the "Devil;" to pace 'Change and the Mall * — to mingle in that great club

* "Mr. Addison has not had one epithalamium that I can hear of, and must even be reduced, like a poorer and a better poet, Spenser, to make his own." — POPE's *Letters*.

* "I have observed that a reader seldom peruses a book with pleasure till he knows whether the writer of it be a black or a fair man, of a mild or a choleric disposition, married or a bachelor; with other particulars of a like nature, that conduce very much to the right understanding of an author. To gratify this curiosity, which is so natural to a reader, I design this paper and my next as prefatory discourses to my following writings: and shall give some account in them of the persons that are engaged in this work. As the chief trouble of compiling

of the world — sitting alone in it somehow: having good-will and kindness for every single man and woman in it — having need of some habit and custom binding him to some few; never doing any man a wrong (unless it be a wrong to hint a little doubt about a man's parts, and to damn him with faint praise); and so he looks on the world and plays with the ceaseless humors of all of us — laughs the kindliest laugh — points our neighbor's foible or eccentricity out to us with the most good-natured, smiling confidence; and then, turning over his shoulder, whispers *our* foibles to our neighbor. What would Sir Roger de Coverley be without his follies and his charming little brain-cracks? * If the good knight did not call out to the people sleeping in church, and say "Amen" with such a delightful pomposity: if he did not make a speech in the assize-court *àpropos de bottes*, and merely to show his dignity to Mr. Spectator: † if he did

digesting, and correcting, will fall to my share, I must do myself the justice to open the work with my own history. . . . There runs a story in the family, that when my mother was gone with child of me about three months, she dreamt that she was brought to bed of a judge. Whether this might proceed from a law-suit which was then depending in the family, or my father's being a justice of the peace, I cannot determine; for I am not so vain as to think it presaged any dignity that I should arrive at in my future life, though that was the interpretation which the neighborhood put upon it. The gravity of my behavior at my very first appearance in the world, and all the time that I sucked, seemed to favor my mother's dream; for, as she has often told me, I threw away my rattle before I was two months old, and would not make use of my coral till they had taken away the bells from it.

"As for the rest of my infancy, there being nothing in it remarkable, I shall pass it over in silence. I find that during my nonage I had the reputation of a very sullen youth, but was always the favorite of my schoolmaster, who used to say that *my parts were solid and would wear well.* I had not been long at the university before I distinguished myself by a most profound silence; for during the space of eight years, excepting in the public exercises of the college, I scarce uttered the quantity of an hundred words; and, indeed, I do not remember that I ever spoke three sentences together in my whole life. . . .

"I have passed my latter years in this city, where I am frequently seen in most public places, though there are not more than half a dozen of my select friends that know me. . . . There is no place of general resort wherein I do not often make my appearance; sometimes I am seen thrusting my head into a round of politicians at 'Will's,' and listening with great attention to the narratives that are made in these little circular audiences. Sometimes I smoke a pipe at 'Child's,' and whilst I seem attentive to nothing but 'The Postman,' overhear the conversation of every table in the room. I appear on Tuesday night at 'St. James's Coffee-house;' and sometimes join the little committee of politics in the inner room, as one who comes to hear and improve. My face is likewise very well known at the 'Grecian,' the 'Cocoa-tree,' and in the theatres both of Drury Lane and the Haymarket. I have been taken for a merchant upon the Exchange for above these two years; and sometimes pass for a Jew in the assembly of stock-jobbers at 'Jonathan's.' In short, wherever I see a cluster of people, I mix with them, though I never open my lips but in my own club.

"Thus I live in the world rather as a '*Spectator*' of mankind than as one of the species; by which means I have made myself a speculative statesman, soldier, merchant, and artisan, without ever meddling in any practical part in life. I am very well versed in the theory of a husband or a father, and can discern the errors in the economy, business, and diversions of others, better than those who are engaged in them — as standers-by discover blots which are apt to escape those who are in the game. . . . In short, I have acted, in all the parts of my life, as a looker-on, which is the character I intend to preserve in this paper." — *Spectator*, No. 1.

* "So effectually, indeed, did he retort on vice the mockery which had recently been directed against virtue, that, since his time, the open violation of decency has always been considered, amongst us, the sure mark of a fool." — MACAULAY.

† "The Court was sat before Sir Roger came; but, notwithstanding all the justices had taken their places upon the bench, they made room for the old knight at the head of them; who for his reputation in the country took occasion to whisper in the judge's ear that *he was glad his lordship had met with so much good weather in his circuit.* I was listening

not mistake Madam Doll Tearsheet for a lady of quality in Temple Garden: if he were wiser than he is: if he had not his humor to salt his life, and were but a mere English gentleman and game preserver — of what worth were he to us? We love him for his vanities as much as his virtues. What is ridiculous is delightful in him; we are so fond of him because we laugh at him so. And out of that laughter, and out of that sweet weakness, and out of those harmless eccentricities and follies, and out of that touched brain, and out of that honest manhood and simplicity — we get a result of happiness, goodness, tenderness, pity, piety; such as, if my audience will think their reading and hearing over, doctors and divines but seldom have the fortune to inspire. And why not? Is the glory of Heaven to be sung only by gentlemen in black coats? Must the truth be only expounded in gown and surplice, and out of those two vestments can nobody preach it? Commend me to this preacher without orders — this parson in the tye-wig. When this man looks from the world, whose weaknesses he describes so benevolently, up to the Heaven which shines over us all, I can hardly fancy a human face lighted up with a more serene rapture: a human intellect thrilling with a purer love and adoration than Joseph Addison's. Listen to him: from your childhood you have known the verses: but who can hear their sacred music without love and awe? —

"Soon as the evening shades prevail,
The moon takes up the wondrous tale,
And nightly to the listening earth
Repeats the story of her birth;
And all the stars that round her burn,
And all the planets in their turn,
Confirm the tidings as they roll,
And spread the truth from pole to pole.
What though, in solemn silence, all
Move round this dark terrestrial ball;
What though no real voice nor sound
Among their radiant orbs be found;
In reason's ear they all rejoice,
And utter forth a glorious voice,
Forever singing as they shine,
The hand that made us is divine."

It seems to me those verses shine like the stars. They shine out of a great deep calm. When he turns to Heaven, a Sabbath comes over that man's mind: and his face lights up from it with a glory of thanks and prayer. His sense of religion stirs through his whole being. In the fields, in the town: looking at the birds in the trees: at the children in the streets: in the morning or in the moonlight: over his books in his own room: in a happy party at a country merry-making or a town assembly, good-will and peace to God's creatures, and love and awe of Him who made them, fill his pure heart and shine from his kind face. If Swift's life was the most wretched, I think Addison's was one of the most enviable. A life prosperous and beautiful — a calm death — an immense fame and affection afterwards for his happy and spotless name.*

to the proceedings of the Court with much attention, and infinitely pleased with that great appearance and solemnity which so properly accompanies such a public administration of our laws; when, after about an hour's sitting, I observed, to my great surprise, in the midst of a trial, that my friend Sir Roger was getting up to speak. I was in some pain for him, till I found he had acquitted himself of two or three sentences, with a look of much business and great intrepidity.

"Upon his first rising, the Court was hushed, and a general whisper ran among the country people that Sir Roger *was up*. The speech he made was so little to the purpose, that I shall not trouble my readers with an account of it, and I believe was not so much designed by the knight himself to inform the Court, as to give him a figure in my eyes, and to keep up his credit in the country." — *Spectator*, No. 122.

* "Garth sent to Addison (of whom he had a very high opinion) on his death-bed, to ask him whether the Christian religion was true." — Dr. YOUNG. *Spence's Anecdotes*.

"I have always preferred cheerfulness to mirth. The latter I consider as an act, the former as a habit of the mind. Mirth is short and transient, cheerfulness fixed and permanent. Those are often raised into the greatest transports of mirth who are subject to the greatest depression of

STEELE.

WHAT do we look for in studying the history of a past age? Is it to learn the political transactions and characters of the leading public men? is it to make ourselves acquainted with the life and being of the time? If we set out with the former grave purpose, where is the truth, and who believes that he has it entire? What character of what great man is known to you? You can but make guesses as to character, more or less happy. In common life don't you often judge and misjudge a man's whole conduct, setting out from a wrong impression? The tone of a voice, a word said in joke, or a trifle in behavior — the cut of his hair or the tie of his neckcloth may disfigure him in your eyes, or poison your good opinion; or at the end of years of intimacy it may be your closest friend says something, reveals something which had previously been a secret, which alters all your views about him, and shows that he has been acting on quite a different motive to that which you fancied you knew. And if it is so with those you know, how much more with those you don't know? Say, for example, that I want to understand the character of the Duke of Marlborough. I read Swift's history of the times in which he took a part; the shrewdest of observers and initiated, one would think, into the politics of the age — he hints to me that Marlborough was a coward, and even of doubtful military capacity: he speaks of Walpole as a contemptible boor, and scarcely mentions, except to flout it, the great intrigue of the Queen's latter days, which was to have ended in bringing back the Pretender. Again, I read Marlborough's life by a copious archdeacon, who has the command of immense papers, of sonorous language, of what is called the best information; and I get little or no insight into this secret motive which, I believe, influenced the whole of Marlborough's career, which caused his turnings and windings, his opportune fidelity and treason, stopped his army almost at Paris gate, and landed him finally on the Hanoverian side — the winning side: I get, I say, no truth, or only a portion of it, in the narrative of either writer, and believe that Coxe's portrait, or Swift's portrait, is quite unlike the real Churchill. I take this as a single instance, prepared to be as sceptical about any other, and say to the Muse of History, "O venerable daughter of Mnemosyne, I doubt every single statement you ever made since your ladyship was a Muse! For all your grave airs and high pretensions, you are not a whit more trustworthy than some of your lighter sisters on whom your partisans look down. You bid me listen to a general's oration to his soldiers: Nonsense! He no more made it than Turpin made his dying speech at Newgate. You pronounce a panegyric of a hero: I doubt it, and say you flatter outrageously. You utter the condemnation of a loose character: I doubt it, and think you are prejudiced and take the side of the Dons. You offer me an autobiography: I doubt all autobiographies I ever read; except those, perhaps, of Mr. Robinson Crusoe, Mariner, and writers of his class. *These* have no object in setting themselves right with the public or

melancholy: on the contrary, cheerfulness, though it does not give the mind such an exquisite gladness, prevents us from falling into any depths of sorrow. Mirth is like a flash of lightning that breaks through a gloom of clouds, and glitters for a moment; cheerfulness keeps up a kind of daylight in the mind, and fills it with a steady and perpetual serenity." — ADDISON: *Spectator*, p. 381.

STEELE.

their own consciences; these have no motive for concealment or half-truths; these call for no more confidence than I can cheerfully give, and do not force me to tax my credulity or to fortify it by evidence. I take up a volume of Dr. Smollett, or a volume of 'The Spectator,' and say the fiction carries a greater amount of truth in solution than the volume which purports to be all true. Out of the fictitious book I get the expression of the life of the time; of the manners, of the movement, the dress, the pleasures, the laughter, the ridicules of society — the old times live again, and I travel in the old country of England. Can the heaviest historian do more for me?"

As we read in these delightful volumes of "The Tatler" and "Spectator," the past age returns, the England of our ancestors is revivified. The Maypole rises in the Strand again in London; the churches are thronged with daily worshippers; the beaux are gathering in the coffee-houses; the gentry are going to the drawing-room; the ladies are thronging to the toy-shops; the chairmen are jostling in the streets; the footmen are running with links before the chariots, or fighting round the theatre doors. In the country I see the young Squire riding to Eton with his servants behind him, and Will Wimble, the friend of the family, to see him safe. To make that journey from the Squire's and back, Will is a week on horseback. The coach takes five days between London and Bath. The judges and the bar ride the circuit. If my lady comes to town in her post-chariot, her people carry pistols to fire a salute on Captain Macheath if he should appear, and her couriers ride ahead to prepare apartments for her at the great caravanserais on the road; Boniface receives her under the creaking sign of "The Bell" or "The Ram," and he and his chamberlains bow her up the great stair to the state-apartments, whilst her carriage rumbles into the court-yard, where the "Exeter Fly" is housed that performs the journey in eight days, God willing, having achieved its daily flight of twenty miles, and landed its passengers for supper and sleep. The curate is taking his pipe in the kitchen, where the Captain's man — having hung up his master's half pike — is at his bacon and eggs, bragging of Ramillies and Malplaquet to the town's folk, who have their club in the chimney-corner. The Captain is ogling the chambermaid in the wooden gallery, or bribing her to know who is the pretty young mistress that has come in the coach. The pack-horses are in the great stable, and the drivers and hostlers carousing in the tap. And in Mrs. Landlady's bar, over a glass of strong waters, sits a gentleman of military appearance, who travels with pistols, as all the rest of the world does, and has a rattling gray mare in the stables which will be saddled and away with its owner half an hour before the "Fly" sets out on its last day's flight. And some five miles on the road, as the "Exeter Fly" comes jingling and creaking onwards, it will suddenly be brought to a halt by a gentleman on a gray mare, with a black vizard on his face, who thrusts a long pistol into the coach window, and bids the company to hand out their purses. . . . It must have been no small pleasure even to sit in the great kitchen in those days, and see the tide of humankind pass by. We arrive at places now, but we travel no more. Addison talks jocularly of a difference of manner and costume being quite perceivable at Staines, where there passed a young fellow "with a very tolerable periwig," though, to be sure, his hat was out of fashion, and had a Ramillies cock. I would have liked to travel in those days (being of that class of travellers who are proverbially pretty easy *coram latronibus*) and have seen my friend with the gray mare and the black vizard. Alas! there always came a day in the life of that warrior when it was the fashion to accompany him as he passed — without his black mask, and with a nosegay in his hand, accompanied by halberdiers and attended by the sheriff — in a carriage without springs, and a clergyman jolting beside him, to a spot close by Cumberland Gate and the Marble Arch, where a stone still records that here Tyburn turnpike stood. What a change in a century; in a few years! Within a few yards of that gate the fields began: the fields of his exploits, behind the hedges of which he lurked and robbed. A great and wealthy city has grown over those meadows. Were a man brought to die there now, the windows would be closed and the inhabitants keep their houses in sickening horror. A hundred years back, people crowded to see that last act of a highwayman's life, and make jokes on it. Swift laughed at him, grimly advising him to provide a Holland shirt and white cap crowned with a crimson or black ribbon for his exit, to mount the cart cheerfully — shake hands with the hangman, and so — farewell. Gay wrote the most delightful ballads, and made merry over the same hero. Contrast these with the writings of our present humorists! Compare those morals and ours — those manners and ours!

We can't tell — you would not bear to be told the whole truth regarding those men and manners. You could no more suffer in a British drawing-room, under the reign of Queen Victoria, a fine gentleman or fine lady of Queen Anne's time, or hear what they heard and said, than you would receive an ancient Briton. It is as one reads about savages, that one contemplates the wild ways, the barbarous feasts, the terrific pastimes, of the men of pleasure of that age. We have our fine gentlemen, and our "fast men;" permit me to give you an idea of one particularly fast nobleman of Queen Anne's days, whose biography has been preserved to us by the law reporters.

In 1691, when Steele was a boy at school, my Lord Mohun was tried by his peers for the murder of William Mountford, comedian. In "Howell's State Trials," the reader will find not only an edifying account of this exceedingly fast nobleman, but of the times and manners of those days. My lord's friend, a Captain Hill, smitten with the charms of the beautiful Mrs. Bracegirdle, and anxious to marry her at all hazards, determined to carry her off, and for this purpose hired a hackney-coach with six horses, and a half-dozen of soldiers, to aid him in the storm. The coach with a pair of horses (the four leaders being in waiting elsewhere) took its station opposite my Lord Craven's house in Drury Lane, by which door Mrs. Bracegirdle was to pass on her way from the theatre. As she passed in company of her mamma and a friend, Mr. Page, the Captain seized her by the hand, the soldiers hustled Mr. Page and attacked him sword in hand, and Captain Hill and his noble friend endeavored to force Madam Bracegirdle into the coach. Mr. Page called for help; the population of Drury Lane rose: it was impossible to effect the capture; and bidding the soldiers go about their business, and the coach to drive off, Hill let go of his prey sulkily, and waited for other opportunities of revenge. The man of whom he was most jealous was Will Mountford, the comedian; Will removed, he thought Mrs. Bracegirdle might be his: and accordingly the Captain and his lordship lay that night in wait for Will, and as he was coming out of a house in Norfolk Street, while Mohun engaged him in talk, Hill, in the words of the Attorney-General, made a pass, and ran him clean through the body.

Sixty-one of my lord's peers finding him not guilty of murder, while but fourteen found him guilty, this very fast nobleman was discharged: and made his appearance seven years after in another trial for murder — when he, my Lord Warwick, and three gentlemen of the military profession, were concerned in the fight which ended in the death of Captain Coote.

This jolly company were drinking together at "Lockit's" in Charing Cross, when angry words arose between Captain Coote and Captain French; whom my Lord Mohun and my Lord the Earl of Warwick* and Holland endeavored to pacify. My Lord Warwick was a dear friend of Captain Coote, lent him a hundred pounds to buy his commission in the Guards; once when the captain was arrested for 13*l*. by his tailor, my lord lent him five guineas, often paid his reckoning for him, and showed him other offices of friendship. On this evening the disputants, French and Coote, being separated whilst they were up stairs, unluckily stopped to drink ale again at the bar of "Lockit's." The row began afresh — Coote lunged at French over the bar, and at last all six called for chairs, and went to Leicester Fields, where they fell to. Their lordships engaged on the side of Captain Coote. My Lord of Warwick was severely wounded in the hand, Mr. French also was stabbed, but honest Captain Coote got a couple of wounds — one especially, "a wound in the left side just under the short ribs, and piercing through the diaphragma," which did for Captain Coote. Hence the trials of my Lords Warwick and Mohun: hence the assemblage of peers, the report of the transaction, in which these defunct fast men still live for the observation of the curious. My Lord of Warwick is brought to the bar by the Deputy Governor of the Tower of London, having the axe carried before him by the gentleman jailer, who stood with it at the bar, at the right hand of the prisoner, turning the edge from him; the prisoner, at his approach, making three bows, one to his Grace the Lord High Steward, the other to the peers on each hand; and his Grace and the peers return the salute. And besides these great personages, august in periwigs, and nodding to the right and left, a host of the small come up out of the past and pass before us — the jolly captains brawling in the tavern, and laughing and cursing over their cups — the drawer that serves, the bar-girl that waits, the bailiff on the prowl, the chairmen trudging through the black lampless streets, and smoking their pipes by the railings, whilst swords are clashing in the garden within. "Help there! a gentleman is hurt!" The chairmen put up their pipes, and help the gentleman over the railings, and carry him, ghastly and bleeding, to the Bagnio in Long Acre, where they knock up the surgeon — a pretty tall gentleman: but that wound under the short ribs has done for him. Surgeon, lords, captains, bailiffs, chairmen, and gentleman jailer with your axe, where be you now? The gentleman axeman's head is off his own shoulders; the lords and judges can wag theirs no longer; the bailiff's writs have ceased to run; the honest chairmen's pipes are put out, and with their brawny calves they have walked away into Hades — all as irrecoverably done for as Will Mountford or Captain Coote. The subject of our night's lecture saw all these people — rode in Captain Coote's company of the Guards very proba-

* The husband of the Lady Warwick who married Addison, and the father of the young Earl, who was brought to his stepfather's bed to see "how a Christian could die." He was amongst the wildest of the nobility of that day; and in the curious collection of Chap-Books at the British Museum, I have seen more than one anecdote of the freaks of the gay lord. He was popular in London, as such daring spirits have been in our time. The anecdotists speak very kindly of his practical jokes. Mohun was scarcely out of prison for his second homicide, when he went on Lord Macclesfield's embassy to the Elector of Hanover, when Queen Anne sent the garter to H. E. Highness. The chronicler of the expedition speaks of his lordship as an amiable young man, who had been in bad company, but was quite repentant and reformed. He and Macartney afterwards murdered the Duke of Hamilton between them, in which act Lord Mohun died. This amiable baron's name was Charles, and not Henry, as a recent novelist has christened him.

bly — wrote and sighed for Bracegirdle, went home tipsy in many a chair, after many a bottle, in many a tavern — fled from many a bailiff.

In 1709, when the publication of "The Tatler" began, our great-great-grandfathers must have seized upon that new and delightful paper with much such eagerness as lovers of light literature in a later day exhibited when the Waverley novels appeared, upon which the public rushed, forsaking that feeble entertainment of which the Miss Porters, the Anne of Swanseas, and worthy Mrs. Radcliffe herself, with her dreary castles and exploded old ghosts, had had pretty much the monopoly. I have looked over many of the comic books with which our ancestors amused themselves, from the novels of Swift's coadjutrix, Mrs. Manley, the delectable author of "The New Atlantis," to the facetious productions of Tom Durfey and Tom Brown, and Ned Ward, writer of "The London Spy" and several other volumes of ribaldry. The slang of the taverns and ordinaries, the wit of the Bagnios, form the strongest part of the farrago of which these libels are composed. In the excellent newspaper collection at the British Museum, you may see, besides, the "Craftsmen" and "Postboy" specimens, and queer specimens they are, of the higher literature of Queen Anne's time. Here is an abstract from a notable journal bearing date, Wednesday, October 13th, 1708, and entitled "*The British Apollo; or, curious amusements for the ingenious, by a society of gentlemen.*" "The British Apollo" invited and professed to answer questions upon all subjects of wit, morality, science, and even religion; and two out of its four pages are filled with queries and replies much like some of the oracular penny prints of the present time.

One of the first querists, referring to the passage that a bishop should be the husband of one wife, argues that polygamy is justifiable in the laity. The society of gen'lemen conducting "The British Apollo" are posed by this casuist, and promised to give him an answer. Celinda then wishes to know from "the gentlemen," concerning the souls of the dead, whether they shall have the satisfaction to know those whom they most valued in this transitory life. The gentlemen of "The Apollo" give but cold comfort to poor Celinda. They are inclined to think not: for, say they, since every inhabitant of those regions will be infinitely dearer than here are our nearest relatives — what have we to do with a partial friendship in that happy place? Poor Celinda! it may have been a child or a lover whom she had lost, and was pining after, when the oracle of "British Apollo" gave her this dismal answer. She has solved the question for herself by this time, and knows quite as well as the society of gentlemen.

From theology we come to physics, and Q. asks, "Why does hot water freeze sooner than cold?" *Apollo* replies, "Hot water cannot be said to freeze sooner than cold; but water once heated and cold may be subject to freeze by the evaporation of the spirituous parts of the water, which renders it less able to withstand the power of frosty weather."

The next query is rather a delicate one. "You, Mr. Apollo, who are said to be the God of wisdom, pray give us the reason why kissing is so much in fashion: what benefit one receives by it, and who was the inventor, and you will oblige Corinna." To this queer demand the lips of Phœbus, smiling, answer: "Pretty innocent Corinna! *Apollo* owns that he was a little surprised by your kissing question, particularly at that part of it where you desire to know the benefit you receive by it. Ah! madam, had you a lover, you would not come to *Apollo* for a solution; since there is no dispute but the kisses of mutual lovers give infinite satisfaction. As to its invention, 'tis certain nature was its author, and it began with the first courtship."

After a column more of questions, follow nearly two pages of poems, signed by Philander, Armenia, and the like, and chiefly on the tender passion; and the paper wound up with a letter from Leghorn, an account of the Duke of Marlborough and Prince Eugene before Lille, and proposals for publishing two sheets on the present state of Æthiopia, by Mr. Hill: all of which is printed for the authors by J. Mayo, at the Printing Press against Water Lane in Fleet Street. What a change it must have been — how *Apollo's* oracles must have been struck dumb, when "The Tatler" appeared, and scholars, gentlemen, men of the world, men of genius, began to speak!

Shortly before the Boyne was fought, and young Swift had begun to make acquaintance with English court manners and English servitude, in Sir William Temple's family, another Irish youth was brought to learn his humanities at the old school of Charterhouse, near Smithfield; to which foundation he had been appointed by James, Duke of Ormond, a governor of the House, and a patron of the lad's family. The boy was an orphan, and described, twenty years after, with the sweet pathos and simplicity, some of the earliest recollections of a life which was destined to be checkered by a strange variety of good and evil fortune.

I am afraid no good report could be given by his masters and ushers of that thick-set, square-faced, black-eyed, soft-hearted little Irish boy. He was very idle. He was whipped deservedly a great number of times. Though he had very good parts of his own, he got other boys to do his lessons for him, and only took just as much trouble as should enable him to scuffle through his exercises, and by good fortune escape the flogging-block. One hundred and fifty years after, I have myself inspected, but only as an amateur, that instrument of righteous torture still existing, and in occasional use, in a secluded private apartment of the old Charterhouse School; and have no doubt it is the very counterpart, if not the ancient and interesting machine itself, at which poor Dick Steele submitted himself to the tormentors.

Besides being very kind, lazy, and good-natured, this boy went invariably into debt with the tart-woman; ran out of bounds, and entered into pecuniary, or rather promissory, engagements with the neighboring lollipop-vendors and piemen — exhibited an early fondness and capacity for drinking mum and sack, and borrowed from all his comrades who had money to lend. I have no sort of authority for the statements here made of Steele's early life; but if the child is father of the man, the father of young Steele of Merton, who left Oxford without taking a degree, and entered the Life Guards — the father of Captain Steele of Lucas's Fusiliers, who got his company through the patronage of my Lord Cutts — the father of Mr. Steele the Commissioner of Stamps, the editor of "The Gazette" "The Tatler" and "Spectator," the expelled Member of Parliament, and the author of "The Tender Husband" and "The Conscious Lovers;" if man and boy resembled each other, Dick Steele the schoolboy must have been one of the most generous, good-for-nothing, amiable little creatures that ever conjugated the verb *tupto*, I beat, *tuptomai*, I am whipped, in any school in Great Britain.

Almost every gentleman who does me the honor to hear me will remember that the very greatest character which he has seen in the course of his life, and the person to whom he has looked up with the greatest wonder and reverence, was the head boy at his school. The schoolmaster himself hardly inspires such an awe. The head boy construes as well as the schoolmaster himself. When he begins to speak the hall is hushed, and every little boy listens. He writes off copies of Latin verses as melodiously as Virgil. He is good-natured, and, his own masterpieces achieved, pours out other copies of verses for other boys with an astonishing ease and fluency; the idle ones only trembling lest they should be discovered on giving in their exercises, and whipped because their poems were too good. I have seen great men in my time, but never such a great one as that head boy of my childhood: we all thought he must be Prime Minister, and I was disappointed on meeting him in after-life to find he was no more than six feet high.

Dick Steele, the Charterhouse gownboy, contracted such an admiration in the years of his childhood, and retained it faithfully through his life. Through the school and through the world, whithersoever his strange fortune led this erring, wayward, affectionate creature, Joseph Addison was always his head boy. Addison wrote his exercises. Addison did his best themes. He ran on Addison's messages: fagged for him and blacked his shoes: to be in Joe's company was Dick's greatest pleasure; and he took a sermon or a caning from his monitor with the most boundless reverence, acquiescence, and affection.*

Steele found Addison a stately college Don at Oxford, and himself did not make much figure at this place. He wrote a comedy, which, by the advice of a friend, the humble fellow burned there; and some verses, which I dare say are as sublime as other gentlemen's composition at that age; but being smitten with a sudden love for military glory, he threw up the cap and gown for the saddle and bridle, and rode privately in the Horse Guards, in the Duke of Ormond's troop — the second — and, probably, with the rest of the gentlemen of his troop, "all mounted on black horses with white feathers in their hats, and scarlet coats richly laced," marched by King William, in Hyde Park, in November, 1699, and a great show of the nobility, besides twenty thousand people, and above a thousand coaches. "The Guards had just got their new clothes," "The London Post" said: "they are extraordinary grand, and thought to be the finest body of horse in the world." But Steele could hardly have seen any actual service. He who wrote about himself, his mother, his wife, his loves, his debts, his friends, and the wine he drank, would have told us of his battles if he had seen any. His old patron, Ormond, probably got him his cornetcy in the Guards, from which he was promoted to be a captain in Lucas's Fusiliers, getting his company through the patronage of Lord Cutts, whose secretary he was, and to whom he dedicated his work called "The Christian Hero." As for Dick, whilst writing this ardent devotional work, he was deep in debt, in drink, and in all the follies of the town; it is related that all the officers of Lucas's, and the gentlemen of the Guards, laughed at Dick.* And in

* "Steele had the greatest veneration for Addison, and used to show it, in all companies, in a particular manner. Addison, now and then, used to play a little upon him; but he always took it well." — POPE. *Spence's Anecdotes.*

"Sir Richard Steele was the best-natured creature in the world: even in his worst state of health, he seemed to desire nothing but to please and be pleased." — DR. YOUNG. *Spence's Anecdotes.*

* The gayety of his dramatic tone may be seen in this little scene between two brilliant sisters, from his comedy "The Funeral, or Grief à la Mode." Dick wrote this, he said, from "a necessity of enlivening his character," which, it seemed, the "Christian Hero" had a tendency to make too decorous, grave, and respectable in the eyes of readers of that pious piece.

[*Scene draws and discovers* LADY CHARLOTTE, *reading at a table*, — LADY HARRIET, *playing at a glass, to and fro, and viewing herself.*]

"*L. Ha.* — Nay, good sister, you may as well talk to me [*looking at herself as she speaks*] as sit staring at a book which I know you can't attend. — Good Dr. Lucas may have writ there what he pleases, but there's no putting Francis, Lord Hardy, now Earl of Brumpton, out of

truth a theologian in liquor is not a respectable object, and a hermit, though he may be out at elbows, must not be in debt to the tailor. Steele says of himself that he was always sinning and repenting. He beat his breast and cried most piteously when he *did* repent: but as soon as crying had made him thirsty, he fell to sinning again. In that charming paper in "The Tatler," in which he records his father's death, his mother's griefs, his own most solemn and tender emotions, he says he is interrupted by the arrival of a hamper of wine, "the same as is to be sold at Garraway's, next week;" upon the receipt of which he sends for three friends, and they fall to instantly, "drinking two bottles apiece, with great benefit to themselves, and not separating till two o'clock in the morning."

His life was so. Jack the drawer was always interrupting it, bringing him a bottle from "The Rose," or inviting him over to a bout there with Sir Plume and Mr. Diver; and Dick wiped his eyes, which were whimpering over his papers, took down his laced hat, put on his sword and wig, kissed his wife and children, told them a lie about pressing business, and went off to the "Rose" to the jolly fellows.

While Mr. Addison was abroad, and after he came home in rather a dismal way to wait upon Providence in his shabby lodging in the Haymarket, young Captain Steele was cutting a much smarter figure than that of his classical friend of Charter-

your head, or making him absent from your eyes. Do but look on me, now, and deny it if you can.

"*L. Ch.*—You are the maddest girl [*smiling*].

"*L. Ha.*—Look ye, I knew you could not say it and forbear laughing [*looking over Charlotte*].—Oh! I see his name as plain as you do—F-r-a-n, Fran,—c-i-s, cis, Francis, 'tis in every line of the book.

"*L. Ch.* [*rising*]—It's in vain, I see, to mind any thing in such impertinent company—but granting 'twere as you say, as to my Lord Hardy—'tis more excusable to admire another than one's self.

"*L. Ha.*—No, I think not,—yes, I grant you, than really to be vain of one's person, but I don't admire myself—Pish! I don't believe my eyes to have that softness. [*Looking in the glass.*] They a'n't so piercing: no, 'tis only stuff, the men will be talking.—Some people are such admirers of teeth—Lord, what signifies teeth! [*Showing her teeth.*] A very black-a-moor has as white a set of teeth as I.—No, sister, I don't admire myself, but I've a spirit of contradiction in me: I don't know I'm in love with myself, only to rival the men.

"*L. Ch.*—Ay, but Mr. Campley will gain ground even of that rival of his, your dear self.

"*L. Ha.*—Oh, what have I done to you, that you should name that insolent intruder? A confident, opinionative fop. No, indeed, if I am, as a poetical lover of mine sighed and sung of both sexes,

The public envy and the public care,

I shan't be so easily catched—I thank him—I want but to be sure I should heartily torment him by banishing him, and then consider whether he should depart this life or not.

"*L. Ch.*—Indeed, sister, to be serious with you, this vanity in your humor does not at all become you.

"*L. Ha.*—Vanity! All the matter is, we gay people are more sincere than you wise folks: all your life's an art.—Speak you real.—Look you there.—[*Hauling her to the glass.*] Are you not struck with a secret pleasure when you view that bloom in your look, that harmony in your shape, that promptitude in your mien?

"*L. Ch.*—Well, simpleton, if I am at first so simple as to be a little taken with myself, I know it a fault, and take pains to correct it.

"*L. Ha.*—Pshaw! Pshaw! Talk this musty tale to old Mrs. Fardingale; 'tis tiresome for me to think at that rate.

"*L. Ch.*—They that think it too soon to understand themselves will very soon find it too late.—But tell me honestly, don't you like Campley?

"*L. Ha.*—The fellow is not to be abhorred, if the forward thing did not think of getting me so easily.—Oh, I hate a heart I can't break when I please.—What makes the value of dear china, but that 'tis so brittle?—were it not for that, you might as well have stone mugs in your closet."—*The Funeral*, Oct. 2d.

"We knew the obligations the stage had to his writings [Steele's]; there being scarcely a comedian of merit in our whole company whom his 'Tatlers' had not made better by his recommendation of them."—CIBBER.

house Cloister and Maudlin Walk. Could not some painter give an interview between the gallant captain of Lucas's, with his hat cocked, and his lace, and his face too, a trifle tarnished with drink, and that poet, that philosopher, pale, proud, and poor, his friend and monitor of school-days, of all days? How Dick must have bragged about his chances and his hopes, and the fine company he kept, and the charms of the reigning toasts and popular actresses, and the number of bottles that he and my lord and some other pretty fellows had cracked over night at "The Devil," or "The Garter!" Cannot one fancy Joseph Addison's calm smile and cold gray eyes following Dick for an instant, as he struts down the Mall, to dine with the Guard at St. James's, before he turns, with his sober pace and threadbare suit, to walk back to his lodgings up the two pair of stairs? Steele's name was down for promotion, Dick always said himself, in the glorious, pious, and immortal William's last table-book. Jonathan Swift's name had been written there by the same hand too.

Our worthy friend, the author of "The Christian Hero," continued to make no small figure about town by the use of his wits.* He was appointed Gazetteer: he wrote, in 1703, "The Tender Husband," his second play, in which there is some delightful farcical writing, and of which he fondly owned in after-life, and when Addison was no more, that there were "many applauded strokes" from Addison's beloved hand.† Is it not a pleasant partnership to remember? Can't one fancy Steele full of spirits and youth, leaving his gay company to go to Addison's lodging, where his friend sits in the shabby sitting-room, quite serene, and cheerful, and poor? In 1704, Steele came on the town with another comedy, and behold it was so moral and religious, as poor Dick insisted, — so dull the town thought, — that "The Lying Lover" was damned.

Addison's hour of success now came, and he was able to help our friend the "Christian Hero" in such a way, that, if there had been any chance of keeping that poor tipsy champion upon his legs, his fortune was safe, and his competence assured. Steele procured the place of Commissioner of Stamps: he wrote so richly, so gracefully often, so kindly always, with such a pleasant wit and easy frankness, with such a gush of good spirits and good humor, that his early papers may be compared to Addison's own, and are to be read, by a male reader at least, with quite an equal pleasure.*

* "There is not now in his sight that excellent man, whom Heaven made his friend and superior, to be at a certain place in pain for what he should say or do. I will go on in his further encouragement. The best woman that ever man had cannot now lament and pine at his neglect of himself." — STEELE [of himself]: *The Theatre.* No. 12, Feb. 1719-20.

† "The Funeral" supplies an admirable stroke of humor, — one which Sydney Smith has used as an illustration of the faculty in his Lectures.

The undertaker is talking to his *employés* about their duty.

Sable. — "Ha, you! — A little more upon the dismal [*forming their countenances*]; this fellow has a good mortal look, — place him near the corpse: that wainscot-face must be o' top of the stairs; that fellow's almost in a fright (that looks as if he were full of some strange misery) at the end of the hall. So — But I'll fix you all myself. Let's have no laughing now on any provocation. Look yonder, — that hale, well-looking puppy! You ungrateful scoundrel, did not I pity you, take you out of a great man's service, and show you the pleasure of receiving wages? *Did not I give you ten, then fifteen, and twenty shillings a week to be sorrowful? and the more I give you I think the gladder you are!*"

* "*From my own Apartment. Nov. 16.*

"There are several persons who have many pleasures and entertainments in their possession, which they do not enjoy; it is, therefore, a kind and good office to acquaint them with their own happiness, and turn their attention to such instances of their good fortune as they are apt to overlook. Persons in the married state

After "The Tatler" in 1711, the famous "Spectator" made its appearance, and this was followed, at various intervals, by many periodicals

often want such a monitor; and pine away their days by looking upon the same condition in anguish and murmuring, which carries with it, in the opinion of others, a complication of all the pleasures of life, and a retreat from its inquietudes.

"I am led into this thought by a visit I made to an old friend who was formerly my schoolfellow. He came to town last week, with his family for the winter; and yesterday morning sent me word his wife expected me to dinner. I am, as it were, at home at that house, and every member of it knows me for their well-wisher. I cannot, indeed, express the pleasure it is to be met by the children with so much joy as I am when I go thither. The boys and girls strive who shall come first, when they think it is I that am knocking at the door; and that child which loses the race to me runs back again to tell the father it is Mr. Bickerstaff. This day I was led in by a pretty girl that we all thought must have forgot me; for the family has been out of town these two years. Her knowing me again was a mighty subject with us, and took up our discourse at the first entrance; after which, they began to rally me upon a thousand little stories they heard in the country, about my marriage to one of my neighbors' daughters; upon which, the gentleman, my friend, said, 'Nay; if Mr. Bickerstaff marries a child of any of his old companions, I hope mine shall have the preference: there is Mrs. Mary is now sixteen, and would make him as fine a widow as the best of them. But I know him too well; he is so enamoured with the very memory of those who flourished in our youth, that he will not so much as look upon the modern beauties. I remember, old gentleman, how often you went home in a day to refresh your countenance and dress when Teraminta reigned in your heart. As we came up in the coach, I repeated to my wife some of your verses on her.' With such reflections on little passages which happened long ago, we passed our time during a cheerful and elegant meal. After dinner, his lady left the room, as did also the children. As soon as we were alone, he took me by the hand: 'Well, my good friend,' says he, 'I am heartily glad to see thee; I was afraid you would never have seen all the company that dined with you to-day again. Do not you think the good woman of the house a little altered since you followed her from the playhouse to find out who she was for me?' I perceived a tear fall down his cheek as he spoke, which moved me not a little. But, to turn the discourse, I said, 'She is not, indeed, that creature she was when she returned me the letter I carried from you, and told me, "She hoped, as I was a gentleman, I would be employed no more to trouble her, who had never offended me; but would be so much the gentleman's friend as to dissuade him from a pursuit which he could never succeed in." You may remember I thought her in earnest, and you were forced to employ your cousin Will, who made his sister get acquainted with her for you. You cannot expect her to be forever fifteen.' 'Fifteen!' replied my good friend. 'Ah! you little understand — you, that have lived a bachelor — how great, how exquisite, a pleasure there is in being really beloved! It is impossible that the most beauteous face in nature should raise in me such pleasing ideas as when I look upon that excellent woman. That fading in her countenance is chiefly caused by her watching with me in my fever. This was followed by a fit of sickness, which had liked to have carried me off last winter. I tell you sincerely, I have so many obligations to her that I cannot, with any sort of moderation, think of her present state of health. But, as to what you say of fifteen, she gives me every day pleasure beyond what I ever knew in the possession of her beauty when I was in the vigor of youth. Every moment of her life brings me fresh instances of her complacency to my inclinations, and her prudence in regard to my fortune. Her face is to me much more beautiful than when I first saw it; there is no decay in any feature which I cannot trace from the very instant it was occasioned by some anxious concern for my welfare and interests. Thus, at the same time, methinks, the love I conceived towards her for what she was, is heightened by my gratitude for what she is. The love of a wife is as much above the idle passion commonly called by that name, as the loud laughter of buffoons is inferior to the elegant mirth of gentlemen. Oh! she is an inestimable jewel! In her examination of her household affairs, she shows a certain fearfulness to find a fault, which makes her servants obey her like children; and the meanest we have has an ingenuous shame for an offence not always to be seen in children in other families. I speak freely to you, my old friend; ever since her sickness, things that gave me the quickest joy before turn now to a certain anxiety. As the children play in the next room, I know the poor things by their steps, and am considering what they must do should they lose their mother in their tender years. The pleasure I used to take in telling my boys stories of battles, and

under the same editor, — "The Guardian" — "The Englishman" — "The Lover," whose love was rather insipid — "The Reader," of whom the public saw no more after his second appearance — "The Theatre," under the pseudonyme of Sir John Edgar, which Steele wrote while Governor of the Royal Company of Comedians, to which post, and to that of Surveyor of the Royal Stables at Hampton Court, and to the Commission of the Peace for Middlesex, and to the honor of knighthood, Steele had been preferred soon after the accession of George I.; whose cause honest Dick had nobly fought, through disgrace and danger, against the most formida-

asking my girl questions about the disposal of her baby, and the gossipping of it, is turned into inward reflection and melancholy.'

"He would have gone on in this tender way, when the good lady entered, and, with an inexpressible sweetness in her countenance, told us 'she had been searching her closet for something very good to treat such an old friend as I was.' Her husband's eyes sparkled with pleasure at the cheerfulness of her countenance; and I saw all his fears vanish in an instant. The lady observing something in our looks which showed we had been more serious than ordinary, and seeing her husband receive her with great concern under a forced cheerfulness, immediately guessed at what we had been talking of; and applying herself to me, said, with a smile, 'Mr. Bickerstaff, do not believe a word of what he tells you; I shall still live to have you for my second, as I have often promised you, unless he takes more care of himself than he has done since his coming to town. You must know he tells me, that he finds London is a much more healthy place than the country; for he sees several of his old acquaintances and schoolfellows are here — *young fellows with fair, full-bottomed periwigs.* I could scarce keep him this morning from going out *open-breasted.*' My friend, who is always extremely delighted with her agreeable humor, made her sit down with us. She did it with that easiness which is peculiar to women of sense; and to keep up the good-humor she had brought in with her, turned her raillery upon me. 'Mr. Bickerstaff, you remember you followed me one night from the playhouse; suppose you should carry me thither to-morrow night, and lead me in the front box.' This put us into a long field of discourse about the beauties who were the mothers to the present, and shined in the boxes twenty years ago. I told her, 'I was glad she had transferred so many of her charms, and I did not question but her eldest daughter was within half a year of being a toast.'

"We were pleasing ourselves with this fantastical preferment of the young lady, when, on a sudden, we were alarmed with the noise of a drum, and immediately entered my little godson to give me a point of war. His mother, between laughing and chiding, would have him put out of the room; but I would not part with him so. I found, upon conversation with him, though he was a little noisy in his mirth, that the child had excellent parts, and was a great master of all the learning on the other side of eight years old. I perceived him a very great historian in 'Æsop's Fables:' but he frankly declared to me his mind, 'that he did not delight in that learning, because he did not believe they were true;' for which reason I found he had very much turned his studies, for about a twelvemonth past, into the lives of Don Bellianis of Greece, Guy of Warwick, 'The Seven Champions,' and other historians of that age. I could not but observe the satisfaction the father took in the forwardness of his son, and that these diversions might turn to some profit. I found the boy had made remarks which might be of service to him during the course of his whole life. He would tell you the mismanagement of John Hickerthrift, find fault with the passionate temper in Bevis of Southampton, and loved St. George for being the champion of England; and by this means had his thoughts insensibly moulded into the notions of discretion, virtue, and honor. I was extolling his accomplishments, when his mother told me 'that the little girl who led me in this morning was, in her way, a better scholar than he. Betty,' said she, 'deals chiefly in fairies and sprites; and sometimes in a winter night will terrify the maids with her accounts, until they are afraid to go up to bed.'

"I sat with them until it was very late, sometimes in merry, sometimes in serious discourse, with this particular pleasure, which gives the only true relish to all conversation, a sense that every one of us liked each other. I went home, considering the different conditions of a married life and that of a bachelor; and I must confess it struck me with a secret concern, to reflect, that, whenever I go off, I shall leave no traces behind me. In this pensive mood I return to my family; that is to say, to my maid, my dog, my cat, who only can be the better or worse for what happens to me." — *The Tatler.*

ble enemies, against traitors and bullies, against Bolingbroke and Swift in the last reign. With the arrival of the King, that splendid conspiracy broke up; and a golden opportunity came to Dick Steele, whose hand, alas, was too careless to gripe it.

Steele married twice; and outlived his places, his schemes, his wife, his income, his health, and almost every thing but his kind heart. That ceased to trouble him in 1729, when he died, worn out and almost forgotten by his contemporaries, in Wales, where he had the remnant of a property. Posterity has been kinder to this amiable creature; all women especially are bound to be grateful to Steele, as he was the first of our writers who really seemed to admire and respect them. Congreve the Great, who alludes to the low estimation in which women were held in Elizabeth's time, as a reason why the women of Shakspeare make so small a figure in the poet's dialogues, though he can himself pay splendid compliments to women, yet looks on them as mere instruments of gallantry, and destined, like the most consummate fortifications, to fall after a certain time, before the arts and bravery of the besieger, man. There is a letter of Swift's, entitled "Advice to a very Young Married Lady," which shows the Dean's opinion of the female society of his day, and that if he despised man he utterly scorned women too. No lady of our time could be treated by any man, were he ever so much of a wit or Dean, in such a tone of insolent patronage and vulgar protection. In this performance, Swift hardly takes pains to hide his opinion that a woman is a fool: tells her to read books, as if reading was a novel accomplishment; and informs her that "not one gentleman's daughter in a thousand has been brought to read or understand her own natural tongue." Addison laughs at women equally; but, with the gentleness and politeness of his nature, smiles at them and watches them, as if they were harmless, half-witted, amusing, pretty creatures, only made to be men's playthings. It was Steele who first began to pay a manly homage to their goodness and understanding, as well as to their tenderness and beauty.* In his comedies, the heroes do not rant and rave about the divine beauties of Gloriana or Statira, as the characters were made to do in the chivalry romances and the high-flown dramas just going out of vogue; but Steele admires women's virtue, acknowledges their sense, and adores their purity and beauty, with an ardor and strength which should win the goodwill of all women to their hearty and respectful champion. It is this ardor, this respect, this manliness, which makes his comedies so pleasant and their heroes such fine gentlemen. He paid the finest compliment to a woman that perhaps ever was offered. Of one woman, whom Congreve had also admired and celebrated, Steele says, that "to have loved her was a liberal education." "How often," he says, dedicating a volume to his wife, "how often has your tenderness removed pain from my sick head, how often anguish from my afflicted heart! If there are such beings as guardian angels, they are thus employed. I cannot believe one of them to be more good in inclination, or more charm-

* "As to the pursuits after affection and esteem, the fair sex are happy in this particular, that with them the one is much more nearly related to the other than in men. The love of a woman is inseparable from some esteem of her; and as she is naturally the object of affection, the woman who has your esteem has also some degree of your love. A man that dotes on a woman for her beauty will whisper his friend, 'That creature has a great deal of wit when you are well acquainted with her.' And if you examine the bottom of your esteem for a woman, you will find you have a greater opinion of her beauty than anybody else. As to us men, I design to pass most of my time with the facetious Harry Bickerstaff; but William Bickerstaff, the most prudent man of our family, shall be my executor." — *Tatler*, No. 206.

ing in form, than my wife." His breast seems to warm and his eyes to kindle when he meets with a good and beautiful woman, and it is with his heart as well as with his hat that he salutes her. About children, and all that relates to home, he is not less tender, and more than once speaks in apology of what he calls his softness. He would have been nothing without that delightful weakness. It is that which gives his works their worth, and his style its charm. It, like his life, is full of faults and careless blunders; and redeemed, like that, by his sweet and compassionate nature.

We possess of poor Steele's wild and checkered life some of the most curious memoranda that ever were left of a man's biography.* Most men's letters, from Cicero down to Walpole, or down to the great men

* The Correspondence of Steele passed after his death into the possession of his daughter Elizabeth, by his second wife, Miss Scurlock, of Carmarthenshire. She married the Hon. John, afterwards third Lord Trevor. At her death, part of the letters passed to Mr. Thomas, a grandson of a natural daughter of Steele's; and part to Lady Trevor's next of kin, Mr. Scurlock. They were published by the learned Nichols — from whose later edition of them, in 1809, our specimens are quoted.

Here we have him, in his courtship — which was not a very long one: —

"To Mrs. Scurlock.

"*Aug.* 30, 1707.

"Madam, —

"I beg pardon that my paper is not finer, but I am forced to write from a coffee-house, where I am attending about business. There is a dirty crowd of busy faces all around me, talking of money; while all my ambition, all my wealth, is love! Love which animates my heart, sweetens my humor, enlarges my soul, and affects every action of my life. It is to my lovely charmer I owe, that many noble ideas are continually affixed to my words and actions; it is the natural effect of that generous passion to create in the admirer some similitude of the object admired. Thus, my dear, am I every day to improve from so sweet a companion. Look up, my fair one, to that Heaven which made thee such: and join with me to implore its influence on our tender innocent hours, and beseech the Author of love to bless the rites He has ordained — and mingle with our happiness a just sense of our transient condition, and a resignation to His will, which only can regulate our minds to a steady endeavor to please Him and each other.

"I am forever your faithful servant,

"Rich. Steele."

Some few hours afterwards, apparently, Mistress Scurlock received the next one — obviously written later in the day! —

"*Saturday night* (*Aug.* 30, 1707).

"Dear, Lovely Mrs. Scurlock, —

"I have been in very good company, where your health, under the character of *the woman I loved best*, has been often drunk; so that I may say that I am dead drunk for your sake, which is more than *I die for you.* Rich. Steele."

"To Mrs. Scurlock.

"*Sept.* 1, 1707.

"Madam, —

"It is the hardest thing in the world to be in love, and yet attend business. As for me, all who speak to me find me out, and I must lock myself up, or other people will do it for me.

"A gentleman asked me this morning, 'What news from Lisbon?' and I answered, 'She is exquisitely handsome.' Another desired to know 'when I had last been at Hampton Court?' I replied, 'It will be on Tuesday come se'nnight.' Pr'ythee allow me at least to kiss your hand before that day, that my mind may be in some composure. O Love!

'A thousand torments dwell about thee,
Yet who could live, to live without thee?'

"Methinks I could write a volume to you; but all the language on earth would fail in saying how much, and with what disinterested passion,

"I am ever yours,

"Rich. Steele."

Two days after this, he is found expounding his circumstances and prospects to the young lady's mamma. He dates from "Lord Sunderland's office, Whitehall;" and states his clear income at 1,025*l.* per annum. "I promise myself," says he, "the pleasure of an industrious and virtuous life, in studying to do things agreeable to you."

They were married, according to the most probable conjectures, about the 7th Sept. There are traces of a tiff about the middle of the next month; she being prudish and fidgety, as he was impassioned and reckless. General progress, however, may be seen from the following notes. The "house in Bury Street, St James's," was now taken.

of our own time, if you will, are doctored compositions, and written with an eye suspicious towards posterity. That dedication of Steele's to his wife is an artificial performance, possibly; at least it is written with that degree of artifice which an orator uses in arranging a statement for the House, or a poet employs in preparing a sentiment in verse or for the stage. But there are some 400 letters of Dick Steele's to his wife, which that thrifty woman preserved accurately, and which could have been written but for her and her alone. They contain details of the business, pleasures, quarrels, reconciliations of the pair; they have all the genuineness of conversation; they are as artless as a child's prattle, and as confidential as a curtain-lecture. Some are written from the printing-office, where he is waiting for the proof-sheets of his "Gazette," or his "Tatler;" some are written from the tavern, whence he promises to come to his wife "within a pint of wine," and where he has given a rendezvous to a friend,

"To Mrs. Steele.

"*Oct.* 16, 1707.

"Dearest Being on Earth, —

"Pardon me if you do not see me till eleven o'clock, having met a schoolfellow from India, by whom I am to be informed on things this night which expressly concern your obedient husband,

"Rich. Steele."

"To Mrs. Steele.

"*Eight o'clock, Fountain Tavern, Oct.* 22, 1707.

"My Dear, —

"I beg of you not to be uneasy; for I have done a great deal of business to-day very successfully, and wait an hour or two about my 'Gazette.'"

"*Dec.* 22, 1707.

"My dear, dear Wife, —

"I write to let you know I do not come home to dinner, being obliged to attend some business abroad, of which I shall give you an account (when I see you in the evening), as becomes your dutiful and obedient husband."

"*Devil Tavern, Temple Bar, Jan.* 3, 1707-8.

"Dear Prue, —

"I have partly succeeded in my business to-day, and enclose two guineas as earnest of more. Dear Prue, I cannot come home to dinner. I languish for your welfare, and will never be a moment careless more.

"Your faithful husband," &c.

"*Jan.* 14, 1707-8.

"Dear Wife, —

"Mr. Edgecombe, Ned Ask, and Mr. Lumley have desired me to sit an hour with them at 'The George,' in Pall Mall, for which I desire your patience till twelve o'clock, and that you will go to bed," &c.

"*Gray's Inn, Feb.* 3, 1708.

"Dear Prue, —

"If the man who has my shoemaker's bill calls, let him be answered that I shall call on him as I come home. I stay here in order to get Jonson to discount a bill for me, and shall dine with him for that end. He is expected at home every minute. Your most humble, obedient servant," &c.

"*Tennis-Court Coffee-house, May* 5, 1708.

"Dear Wife, —

"I hope I have done this day what will be pleasing to you; in the mean time shall lie this night at a baker's, one Leg, over against 'The Devil Tavern,' at Charing Cross. I shall be able to confront the fools who wish me uneasy, and shall have the satisfaction to see thee cheerful and at ease.

"If the printer's boy be at home, send him hither; and let Mrs. Todd send by the boy my night-gown, slippers, and clean linen. You shall hear from me early in the morning," &c.

Dozens of similar letters follow, with occasional guineas, little parcels of tea, or walnuts, &c. In 1709 "The Tatler" made its appearance. The following curious note dates April 7, 1710:—

"I enclose to you ['Dear Prue'] a receipt for the saucepan and spoon, and a note of 23*l.* of Lewis's, which will make up the 50*l.* I promised for your ensuing occasion.

"I know no happiness in this life in any degree comparable to the pleasure I have in your person and society. I only beg of you to add to your other charms a fearfulness to see a man that loves you in pain and uneasiness, to make me as happy as it is possible to be in this life. Rising a little in a morning, and being disposed to a cheerfulness . . . would not be amiss."

In another, he is found excusing his coming home, being "invited to supper to Mr. Boyle's:" "Dear Prue," he says on this occasion, "do not send after me, for I shall be ridiculous."

or a money-lender: some are composed in a high state of vinous excitement, when his head is flustered with burgundy, and his heart abounds with amorous warmth for his darling Prue: some are under the influence of the dismal headache and repentance next morning: some, alas, are from the lock-up house, where the lawyers have impounded him, and where he is waiting for bail. You trace many years of the poor fellow's career in these letters. In September, 1707, from which day she began to save the letters, he married the beautiful Mistress Scurlock. You have his passionate protestations to the lady; his respectful proposals to her mamma; his private prayer to Heaven when the union so ardently desired was completed; his fond professions of contrition and promises of amendment, when, immediately after his marriage, there began to be just cause for the one, and need for the other.

Captain Steele took a house for his lady upon their marriage, "the third door from Germain Street, left hand of Berry Street," and the next year he presented his wife with a country house at Hampton. It appears she had a chariot and pair, and sometimes four horses; he himself enjoyed a little horse for his own riding. He paid, or promised to pay, his barber fifty pounds a year, and always went abroad in a laced coat and a large black buckled periwig, that must have cost somebody fifty guineas. He was rather a well-to-do gentleman, Captain Steele, with the proceeds of his estates in Barbadoes (left to him by his first wife), his income as a writer of "The Gazette," and his office of gentleman waiter to his Royal Highness Prince George. His second wife brought him a fortune too. But it is melancholy to relate, that with these houses and chariots and horses and income, the Captain was constantly in want of money, for which his beloved bride was asking as constantly. In the course of a few pages we begin to find the shoemaker calling for money, and some directions from the Captain, who has not thirty pounds to spare. He sends his wife, "the beautifullest object in the world," as he calls her, and evidently in reply to applications of her own, which have gone the way of all waste paper, and lighted Dick's pipes, which were smoked a hundred and forty years ago — he sends his wife now a guinea, then a half-guinea, then a couple of guineas, then half a pound of tea; and again no money and no tea at all, but a promise that his darling Prue shall have some in a day or two: or a request, perhaps, that she will send over his night-gown and shaving-plate to the temporary lodging where the nomadic Captain is lying, hidden from the bailiffs. Oh! that a Christian hero and late Captain in Lucas's should be afraid of a dirty sheriff's officer! That the pink and pride of chivalry should turn pale before a writ! It stands to record in poor Dick's own handwriting — the queer collection is preserved at the British Museum to this present day — that the rent of the nuptial house in Jermyn Street, sacred to unutterable tenderness and Prue, and three doors from Bury Street, was not paid until after the landlord had put in an execution on Captain Steele's furniture. Addison sold the house and furniture at Hampton, and, after deducting the sum in which his incorrigible friend was indebted to him, handed over the residue of the proceeds of the sale to poor Dick, who wasn't in the least angry at Addison's summary proceeding, and I dare say was very glad of any sale or execution, the result of which was to give him a little ready money. Having a small house in Jermyn Street for which he couldn't pay, and a country house at Hampton on which he had borrowed money, nothing must content Captain Dick but the taking, in 1712, a much finer, larger, and grander house, in Bloomsbury Square; where his unhappy landlord got no better satisfaction than his friend in St. James's, and where it is recorded that Dick, giving a grand entertainment, had a half-dozen queer-looking fellows in livery to wait upon his noble guests, and confessed that his servants were bailiffs to a man. "I fared like a distressed prince," the kindly prodigal writes, generously complimenting Addison for his assistance in "The Tatler," — "I fared like a distressed prince, who calls in a powerful neighbor to his aid. I was undone by my auxiliary; when I had once called him in, I could not subsist without dependence on him." Poor, needy Prince of Bloomsbury! think of him in his palace, with his allies from Chancery Lane ominously guarding him.

All sorts of stories are told indicative of his recklessness and his good humor. One narrated by Dr. Hoadly is exceedingly characteristic; it shows the life of the time: and our poor friend very weak, but very kind both in and out of his cups.

"My father," says Dr. John Hoadly, the Bishop's son, "when Bishop of Bangor, was, by invitation, present at one of the Whig meetings, held at 'The Trumpet,' in Shire Lane, when Sir Richard, in his zeal, rather exposed himself, having the double duty of the day upon him, as well to celebrate the immortal memory of King William, it being the 4th November, as to drink his friend Addison up to conversation pitch, whose phlegmatic constitution was hardly warmed for society by that time. Steele was not fit for it. Two remarkable circumstances happened. John Sly, the hatter of facetious memory, was in the house; and John, pretty mellow, took it into his head to come into the company on his knees, with a tankard of ale in his hand to drink off to the *immortal memory*, and to return in the same manner. Steele, sitting next my father, whispered him — *Do laugh. It is humanity to laugh.* Sir Richard, in the evening, being too much in the same condition, was put into a chair, and sent home. Nothing would serve him but being carried to the Bishop of Bangor's, late as it was. However, the chairmen carried him home, and got him up stairs, when his great complaisance would wait on them down stairs, which he did, and then was got quietly to bed." *

There is another amusing story, which, I believe, that renowned collector, Mr. Joseph Miller, or his successors, have incorporated into their work. Sir Richard Steele, at a time when he was much occupied with theatrical affairs, built himself a pretty private theatre, and, before it was opened to his friends and guests, was anxious to try whether the hall was well adapted for hearing. Accordingly he placed himself in the most remote part of the gallery, and begged the carpenter who had built the house to speak up from the stage. The man at first said that he was unaccustomed to public speaking, and did not know what to say to his honor; but the good-natured knight called out to him to say whatever was uppermost; and, after a moment, the carpenter began in a voice perfectly audible: "Sir Richard Steele!" he said, "for three months past me and my men has been a working in this theatre, and we've never seen the color of your honor's money: we will be very much obliged if you'll pay it directly, for until you do we won't drive in another nail." Sir Richard said that his friend's elocution was perfect, but that he didn't like his subject much.

The great charm of Steele's writing is its naturalness. He wrote so quickly and carelessly, that he was forced to make the reader his confidant, and had not the time to deceive him. He had a small share of book-learning, but a vast acquaintance with the world. He had known men and

* Of this famous Bishop, Steele wrote,

"Virtue with so much ease on Bangor sits,
All faults he pardons, though he none commits."

taverns. He had lived with gownsmen, with troopers, with gentlemen ushers of the Court, with men and women of fashion; with authors and wits, with the inmates of the sponging-houses, and with the frequenters of all the club and coffee-houses in the town. He was liked in all company because he liked it; and you like to see his enjoyment as you like to see the glee of a boxful of children at the pantomime. He was not of those lonely ones of the earth whose greatness obliged them to be solitary: on the contrary, he admired, I think, more than any man who ever wrote; and, full of hearty applause and sympathy, wins upon you by calling you to share his delight and good humor. His laugh rings through the whole house. He must have been invaluable at a tragedy, and have cried as much as the most tender young lady in the boxes. He has a relish for beauty and goodness wherever he meets it. He admired Shakspeare affectionately, and more than any man of his time; and, according to his generous expansive nature, called upon all his company to like what he liked himself. He did not damn with faint praise: he was in the world and of it; and his enjoyment of life presents the strangest contrast to Swift's savage indignation and Addison's lonely serenity.* Permit me to read to you a passage from each writer, curiously indicative of his peculiar humor: the subject is the same, and the mood the very gravest. We have said that upon all the actions of man, the most trifling and the most sol-

* Here we have some of his later letters: —

"TO LADY STEELE.

"*Hampton Court, March* 16, 1716–17.

"DEAR PRUE,

"IF you have written any thing to me which I should have received last night, I beg your pardon that I cannot answer till the next post. . . . Your son at the present writing is mighty well employed in tumbling on the floor of the room and sweeping the sand with a feather. He grows a most delightful child, and very full of play and spirit. He is also a very great scholar: he can read his primer; and I have brought down my Virgil. He makes most shrewd remarks about the pictures. We are very intimate friends and playfellows. He begins to be very ragged; and I hope I shall be pardoned if I equip him with new clothes and frocks, or what Mrs. Evans and I shall think for his service."

"TO LADY STEELE.

[Undated.]

"You tell me you want a little flattery from me. I assure you I know no one who deserves so much commendation as yourself, and to whom saying the best things would be so little like flattery. The thing speaks for itself, considering you as a very handsome woman that loves retirement — one who does not want wit, and yet is extremely sincere; and so I could go through all the vices which attend the good qualities of other people, of which you are exempt. But, indeed, though you have every perfection, you have an extravagant fault, which almost frustrates the good in you to me; and that is, that you do not love to dress, to appear, to shine out, even at my request, and to make me proud of you, or rather to indulge the pride I have that you are mine. . . .

"Your most affectionate, obsequious husband, RICHARD STEELE.

"A quarter of Molly's schooling is paid. The children are perfectly well."

"TO LADY STEELE.

"*March* 26, 1717.

"MY DEAREST PRUE,

"I HAVE received yours, wherein you give me the sensible affliction of telling me enow of the continual pain in your head. . . . When I lay in your place, and on your pillow, I assure you I fell into tears last night, to think that my charming little insolent might be then awake and in pain; and took it to be a sin to go to sleep.

"For this tender passion towards you, I must be contented that your *Prueship* will condescend to call yourself my well-wisher." . . .

At the time when the above later letters were written, Lady Steele was in Wales, looking after her estate there. Steele, about this time, was much occupied with a project for conveying fish alive, by which, as he constantly assures his wife, he firmly believed he should make his fortune. It did not succeed, however.

Lady Steele died in December of the succeeding year. She lies buried in Westminster Abbey.

emn, the humorist takes upon himself to comment. All readers of our old masters know the terrible lines of Swift, in which he hints at his philosophy and describes the end of mankind: * —

"Amazed, confused, its fate unknown,
The world stood trembling at Jove's throne;
While each pale singer hung his head,
Jove, nodding, shook the heavens and said:
'Offending race of human kind,
By nature, reason, learning, blind;
You who through frailty stepped aside,
And you who never erred through pride;
You who in different sects were shammed,
And come to see each other damned;
(So some folk told you, but they knew
No more of Jove's designs than you;)
The world's mad business now is o'er,
And I resent your freaks no more;
I to such blockheads set my wit,
I damn such fools — go, go, you're bit!'"

Addison, speaking on the very same theme, but with how different a voice, says, in his famous paper on Westminster Abbey ("Spectator," No. 26): — "For my own part, though I am always serious, I do not know what it is to be melancholy, and can therefore take a view of nature in her deep and solemn scenes with the same pleasure as in her most gay and delightful ones. When I look upon the tombs of the great, every emotion of envy dies within me; when I read the epitaphs of the beautiful, every inordinate desire goes out; when I meet with the grief of parents on a tombstone, my heart melts with compassion; when I see the tomb of the parents themselves, I consider the vanity of grieving for those we must quickly follow." (I have owned that I do not think Addison's heart melted very much, or that he indulged very inordinately in the "vanity of grieving.") "When," he goes on, "when I see kings lying by those who deposed them: when I consider rival wits placed side by side, or the holy men that divided the world with their contests and disputes, — I reflect with sorrow and astonishment on the little competitions, factions, and debates of mankind. And, when I read the several dates on the tombs of some that died yesterday and some 600 years ago, I consider that Great Day when we shall all of us be contemporaries, and make our appearance together."

Our third humorist comes to speak upon the same subject. You will have observed in the previous extracts the characteristic humor of each writer — the subject and the contrast — the fact of Death, and the play of individual thought, by which each comments on it, and now hear the third writer — death, sorrow, and the grave being for the moment also his theme. "The first sense of sorrow I ever knew," Steele says in "The Tatler," "was upon the death of my father, at which time I was not quite five years of age: but was rather amazed at what all the house meant, than possessed of a real understanding why nobody would play with us. I remember I went into the room where his body lay, and my mother sat weeping alone by it. I had my battledore in my hand, and fell a beating the coffin, and calling papa; for, I know not how, I had some idea that he was locked up there. My mother caught me in her arms, and, transported beyond all patience of the silent grief she was before in, she almost smothered me in her embraces, and told me in a flood of tears, 'Papa could not hear me, and would play with me no more; for they were going to put him under ground, whence he would never come to us again.' She was a very beautiful woman, of a noble spirit, and there was a dignity in her grief amidst all the wildness of her transport, which methought struck me with an instinct of sorrow that, before I was sensible what it was to grieve, seized my very soul, and has made pity the weakness of my heart ever since."

Can there be three more character-

* Lord Chesterfield sends these verses to Voltaire in a characteristic letter.

istic moods of minds and men? "Fools, do you know any thing of this mystery?" says Swift, stamping on a grave, and carrying his scorn for mankind actually beyond it. "Miserable, purblind wretches, how dare you to pretend to comprehend the Inscrutable, and how can your dim eyes pierce the unfathomable depths of yonder boundless heaven?" Addison, in a much kinder language and gentler voice, utters much the same sentiment: and speaks of the rivalry of wits, and the contests of holy men, with the same sceptic placidity. "Look what a little vain dust we are," he says, smiling over the tombstones; and catching, as is his wont, quite a divine effulgence as he looks heavenward, he speaks, in words of inspiration almost, of "the Great Day, when we shall all of us be contemporaries, and make our appearance together."

The third, whose theme is Death, too, and who will speak his word of moral as Heaven teaches him, leads you up to his father's coffin, and shows you his beautiful mother weeping, and himself an unconscious little boy wondering at her side. His own natural tears flow as he takes your hand and confidingly asks your sympathy. "See how good and innocent and beautiful women are," he says; "how tender little children! Let us love these and one another, brother — God knows we have need of love and pardon." So it is each man looks with his own eyes, speaks with his own voice, and prays his own prayer.

When Steele asks your sympathy for the actors in that charming scene of Love and Grief and Death, who can refuse it? One yields to it as to the frank advance of a child, or to the appeal of a woman. A man is seldom more manly than when he is what you call unmanned — the source of his emotion is championship, pity, and courage; the instinctive desire to cherish those who are innocent and unhappy, and defend those who are tender and weak. If Steele is not our friend, he is nothing. He is by no means the most brilliant of wits nor the deepest of thinkers: but he is our friend: we love him, as children love their love with an A, because he is amiable. Who likes a man best because he is the cleverest or the wisest of mankind; or a woman because she is the most virtuous, or talks French, or plays the piano better than the rest of her sex? I own to liking Dick Steele the man, and Dick Steele the author, much better than much better men and much better authors.

The misfortune regarding Steele is, that most part of the company here present must take his amiability upon hearsay, and certainly can't make his intimate acquaintance. Not that Steele was worse than his time; on the contrary, a far better, truer, and higher-hearted man than most who lived in it. But things were done in that society, and names were named, which would make you shudder now. What would be the sensation of a polite youth of the present day, if at a ball he saw the young object of his affections taking a box out of her pocket and a pinch of snuff: or if at dinner, by the charmer's side, she deliberately put her knife into her mouth? If she cut her mother's throat with it, mamma would scarcely be more shocked. I allude to these peculiarities of by-gone times as an excuse for my favorite, Steele, who was not worse, and often much more delicate, than his neighbors.

There exists a curious document descriptive of the manners of the last age, which describes most minutely the amusements and occupations of persons of fashions in London at the time of which we are speaking; the time of Swift and Addison and Steele.

When Lord Sparkish, Tom Neverout, and Colonel Alwit, the immortal personages of Swift's polite conversation, came to breakfast with my Lady Smart, at eleven o'clock in the morning, my Lord Smart was absent at the levée. His lordship was at home to dinner at three o'clock to receive his guests; and we may sit down to this meal, like the Barmecide's, and see the fops of the last century before us. Seven of them sat down at dinner, and were joined by a country baronet, who told them they kept court hours. These persons of fashion began their dinner with a sirloin of beef, fish, a shoulder of veal, and a tongue. My Lady Smart carved the sirloin, my Lady Answerall helped the fish, and the gallant Colonel cut the shoulder of veal. All made a considerable inroad on the sirloin and the shoulder of veal with the exception of Sir John, who had no appetite, having already partaken of a beefsteak and two mugs of ale, besides a tankard of March beer as soon as he got out of bed. They drank claret, which the master of the house said should always be drunk after fish; and my Lord Smart particularly recommended some excellent cider to my Lord Sparkish, which occasioned some brilliant remarks from that nobleman. When the host called for wine, he nodded to one or other of his guests, and said, "Tom Neverout, my service to you."

After the first course came almond-pudding, fritters, which the Colonel took with his hands out of the dish, in order to help the brilliant Miss Notable; chickens, black puddings, and soup; and Lady Smart, the elegant mistress of the mansion, finding a skewer in a dish, placed it in her plate with directions that it should be carried down to the cook, and dressed for the cook's own dinner. Wine and small beer were drunk during this second course; and when the Colonel called for beer, he called the butler Friend, and asked whether the beer was good. Various jocular remarks passed from the gentlefolks to the servants; at breakfast several persons had a word and a joke for Mrs. Betty, my lady's maid, who warmed the cream and had charge of the canister (the tea cost thirty shillings a pound in those days). When my Lady Sparkish sent her footman out to my Lady Match to come at six o'clock and play at quadrille, her ladyship warned the man to follow his nose, and if he fell by the way not to stay to get up again. And when the gentlemen asked the hall-porter if his lady was at home, that functionary replied, with manly waggishness, "She was at home just now, but she's not gone out yet."

After the puddings, sweet and black, the fritters and soup, came the third course, of which the chief dish was a hot venison pasty, which was put before Lord Smart, and carved by that nobleman. Besides the pasty, there was a hare, a rabbit, some pigeons, partridges, a goose, and a ham. Beer and wine were freely imbibed during this course, the gentlemen always pledging somebody with every glass which they drank; and by this time the conversation between Tom Neverout and Miss Notable had grown so brisk and lively, that the Derbyshire baronet began to think the young gentlewoman was Tom's sweetheart; on which Miss remarked, that she loved Tom "like pie." After the goose, some of the gentlemen took a dram of brandy, "which was very good for the wholesomes," Sir John said; and now having had a tolerably substantial dinner, honest Lord Smart bade the butler bring up the great tankard full of October to Sir John. The great tankard was passed from hand to hand and mouth to mouth, but when pressed by the noble host upon the gallant Tom Neverout, he said, "No, faith, my lord; I like your wine, and won't put a churl upon a gentleman. Your honor's claret is good enough for me." And so, the dinner over, the host said, "Hang saving, bring us up a ha'porth of cheese."

The cloth was now taken away, and a bottle of burgundy was set down, of which the ladies were invited to partake before they went to their tea. When they withdrew, the gentlemen promised to join them in an hour: fresh bottles were brought; the "dead men," meaning the empty bottles, removed; and "D'you hear, John? bring clean glasses," my Lord Smart said. On which the gallant Colonel Alwit said, "I'll keep my glass; for wine is the best liquor to wash glasses in."

After an hour the gentlemen joined the ladies, and then they all sat and played quadrille until three o'clock in the morning, when the chairs and the flambeaux came, and this noble company went to bed.

Such were manners six or seven score years ago. I draw no inference from this queer picture — let all moralists here present deduce their own. Fancy the moral condition of that society in which a lady of fashion joked with a footman, and carved a sirloin, and provided besides a great shoulder of veal, a goose, hare, rabbit, chickens, partridges, black puddings, and a ham for a dinner for eight Christians. What — what could have been the condition of that polite world in which people openly ate goose after almond-pudding, and took their soup in the middle of dinner? Fancy a Colonel in the Guards putting his hand into a dish of *beignets d'abricot*, and helping his neighbor, a young lady *du monde!* Fancy a noble lord calling out to the servants, before the ladies at his table, "Hang expense, bring us a ha'porth of cheese!" Such were the ladies of Saint James's — such were the frequenters of "White's Chocolate-House," when Swift used to visit it, and Steele described it as the centre of pleasure, gallantry, and entertainment, a hundred and forty years ago!

Dennis, who ran amuck at the literary society of his day, falls foul of poor Steele, and thus depicts him: — "Sir John Edgar, of the county of ———, in Ireland, is of a middle stature, broad shoulders, thick legs, a shape like the picture of somebody over a farmer's chimney — a short chin, a short nose, a short forehead, a broad flat face, and a dusky countenance. Yet with such a face and such a shape, he discovered at sixty that he took himself for a beauty, and appeared to be more mortified at being told that he was ugly, than he was by any reflection made upon his honor or understanding.

"He is a gentleman born, witness himself, of very honorable family; certainly of a very ancient one, for his ancestors flourished in Tipperary long before the English ever set foot in Ireland. He has testimony of this more authentic than the Herald's office, or any human testimony. For God has marked him more abundantly than he did Cain, and stamped his native country on his face, his understanding, his writings, his actions, his passions, and, above all, his vanity. The Hibernian brogue is still upon all these, though long habit and length of days have worn it off his tongue." *

* Steele replied to Dennis in an "Answer to a Whimsical Pamphlet, called the Character of Sir John Edgar." What Steele had to say against the cross-grained old Critic discovers a great deal of humor: —

"Thou never didst let the sun into thy garret, for fear he should bring a bailiff along with him. . . .

"Your years are about sixty-five, an ugly, vinegar face, that if you had any command you would be obeyed out of fear, from your ill-nature pictured there; not from any other motive. Your height is about some five feet five inches. You see I can give your exact measure as well as if I had taken your dimension with a good cudgel, which I promise you to do as soon as ever I have the good fortune to meet you. . . .

"Your doughty paunch stands before you like a firkin of butter, and your duck legs seem to be cast for carrying burdens.

"Thy works are libels upon others, and satires upon thyself; and while they bark at men of sense, call him knave and fool that wrote them. Thou hast a great antipathy to thy own species; and hatest the sight of a fool but in thy glass."

Steele had been kind to Dennis, and once got arrested on account of a pecuniary service which he did him. When John heard of the fact — "S'death!" cries John; "why did not he keep out of the way as I did?"

The "Answer" concludes by mentioning that Cibber had offered Ten Pounds for the discovery of the authorship of

Although this portrait is the work of a man who was neither the friend of Steele nor of any other man alive, yet there is a dreadful resemblance to the original in the savage and exaggerated traits of the caricature, and everybody who knows him must recognize Dick Steele. Dick set about almost all the undertakings of his life with inadequate means, and, as he took and furnished a house with the most generous intentions towards his friends, the most tender gallantry towards his wife, and with this only drawback, that he had not wherewithal to pay the rent when quarter-day came, — so, in his life, he proposed to himself the most magnificent schemes of virtue, forbearance, public and private good, and the advancement of his own and the national religion; but when he had to pay for these articles — so difficult to purchase and so costly to maintain — poor Dick's money was not forthcoming: and when Virtue called with her little bill, Dick made a shuffling excuse that he could not see her that morning, having a headache from being tipsy overnight; or when stern Duty rapped at the door with his account, Dick was absent, and not ready to pay. He was shirking at the tavern; or had some particular business (of somebody's else) at the ordinary: or he was in hiding, or worse than in hiding, in the lock-up house. What a situation for a man! — for a philanthropist — for a lover of right and truth — for a magnificent designer and schemer! Not to dare to look in the face the Religion which he adored and which he had offended: to have to shirk down back lanes and alleys, so as to avoid the friend whom he loved and who had trusted him; to have the house which he had intended for his wife, whom he loved passionately, and for her ladyship's company which he wished to entertain splendidly, in the possession of a bailiff's man; with a crowd of little creditors, — grocers, butchers, and small-coal men — lingering round the door with their bills and jeering at him. Alas! for poor Dick Steele! For nobody else, of course. There is no man or woman in *our* time who makes fine projects and gives them up from idleness or want of means. When Duty calls upon *us*, we no doubt are always at home and ready to pay that grim tax-gatherer. When *we* are stricken with remorse, and promise reform, we keep our promise, and are never angry, or idle, or extravagant any more. There are no chambers in *our* hearts, destined for family friends and affections, and now occupied by some Sin's emissary and bailiff in possession. There are no little sins, shabby peccadilloes, importunate remembrances, or disappointed holders of our promises to reform, hovering at our steps, or knocking at our door! Of course not. We are living in the nineteenth century; and poor Dick Steele stumbled and got up again, and got into jail and out again, and sinned and repented, and loved and suffered, and lived and died, scores of years ago. Peace be with him! Let us think gently of one who was so gentle: let us speak kindly of one whose own breast exuberated with human kindness.

Dennis's pamphlet; on which, says Steele, — "I am only sorry he has offered so much, because the *twentieth part* would have over-valued his whole carcass. But I know the fellow that he keeps to give answers to his creditors will betray him; for he gave me his word to bring officers on the top of the house that should make a hole through the ceiling of his garret, and so bring him to the punishment he deserves. Some people think this expedient out of the way, and that he would make his escape upon hearing the least noise. I say so too; but it takes him up half an hour every night to fortify himself with his old hair trunk, two or three joint-stools, and some other lumber, which he ties together with cords so fast that it takes him up the same time in the morning to release himself."

PRIOR, GAY, AND POPE.

MATTHEW PRIOR was one of those famous and lucky wits of the auspicious reign of Queen Anne, whose name it behooves us not to pass over. Mat was a world-philosopher of no small genius, good nature, and acumen.* He loved, he drank, he sang. He describes himself, in one of his lyrics, "in a little Dutch chaise on a Saturday night; on his left hand his Horace, and a friend on his right," going out of town from the Hague to pass that evening, and the ensuing Sunday, boozing at a Spielhaus with his companions, perhaps bobbing for perch in a Dutch canal, and noting down, in a strain and with a grace not unworthy of his Epicurean master, the charms of his idleness, his retreat, and his Batavian Chloe. A vintner's son in Whitehall, and a distinguished pupil of Busby of the Rod, Prior attracted some notice by writing verses at St. John's College, Cambridge, and, coming up to town, aided Montague * in an attack on the noble old English lion John Dryden; in ridicule of whose work, "The Hind and the Panther," he brought out that remarkable and famous burlesque, "The Town and Country Mouse." Aren't you all acquainted with it? Have you not all got it by heart? What! have you never heard of it?

* Gay calls him — "Dear Prior . . . beloved by every muse." — *Mr. Pope's Welcome from Greece.*

Swift and Prior were very intimate, and he is frequently mentioned in the "Journal to Stella." "Mr. Prior," says Swift, "walks to make himself fat, and I to keep myself down. . . . We often walk round the park together."

In Swift's works there is a curious tract called "Remarks on the Characters of the Court of Queen Anne" [SCOTT's edition, vol. xii.] The "Remarks" are not by the Dean; but at the end of each is an addition in Italics from his hand, and these are always characteristic. Thus, to the Duke of Marlborough, he adds, "*Detestably covetous,*" &c. Prior is thus noticed: —

"MATTHEW PRIOR, Esq., Commissioner of Trade.

"On the Queen's accession to the throne, he was continued in his office; is very well at court with the ministry, and is an entire creature of my Lord Jersey's, whom he supports by his advice; is one of the best poets in England, but very facetious in conversation. A thin, hollow-looked man, turned of forty years old. *This is near the truth.*"

" Yet counting as far as to fifty his years,
His virtues and vices were as other men's are.
High hopes he conceived and he smothered great fears,
In a life party-colored — half pleasure, half care.

" Not to business a drudge, nor to faction a slave,
He strove to make interest and freedom agree;
In public employments industrious and grave,
And alone with his friends, Lord, how merry was he!

" Now in equipage stately, now humble on foot,
Both fortunes he tried, but to neither would trust;
And whirled in the round as the wheel turned about,
He found riches had wings, and knew man was but dust."

— PRIOR's *Poems.* [*For my own monument.*]

* "They joined to produce a parody, entitled 'The town and Country Mouse,' part of which Mr. Bayes is supposed to gratify his old friends, Smart and Johnson, by repeating to them. The piece is therefore founded upon the twice-told jest of the 'Rehearsal.' . . . There is nothing new or original in the idea. . . . In this piece, Prior, though the younger man, seems to have had by far the largest share." — SCOTT's *Dryden*, vol. i. p. 330.

See what fame is made of! The wonderful part of the satire was, that, as a natural consequence of "The Town and Country Mouse," Matthew Prior was made Secretary of Embassy at the Hague! I believe it is dancing, rather than singing, which distinguishes the young English diplomatists of the present day; and have seen them in various parts perform that part of their duty very finely. In Prior's time it appears a different accomplishment led to preferment. Could you write a copy of Alcaics? that was the question. Could you turn out a neat epigram or two? Could you compose "The Town and Country Mouse"? It is manifest that, by the possession of this faculty, the most difficult treaties, the laws of foreign nations, and the interests of our own, are easily understood. Prior rose in the diplomatic service, and said good things that proved his sense and his spirit. When the apartments at Versailles were shown to him, with the victories of Louis XIV. painted on the walls, and Prior was asked whether the palace of the King of England had any such decorations, "The monuments of my master's actions," Mat said, of William whom he cordially revered, "are to be seen everywhere except in his own house." Bravo, Mat! Prior rose to be full ambassador at Paris,* where he somehow was cheated out of his ambassadorial plate; and in an heroic poem, addressed by him to her late lamented Majesty, Queen Anne, Mat makes some magnificent allusions to these dishes and spoons, of which Fate had deprived him. All that he wants, he says, is her Majesty's picture; without that he can't be happy.

"Thee, gracious Anne, thee present I adore:
Thee, Queen of Peace, if Time and Fate have power
Higher to raise the glories of thy reign,
In words sublimer and a nobler strain
May future bards the mighty theme rehearse.
Here, Stator Jove, and Phœbus, king of verse,
The votive tablet I suspend."

With that word the poem stops abruptly. The votive tablet is suspended forever, like Mahomet's coffin. News came that the Queen was dead. Stator Jove, and Phœbus, king of verse, were left there, hovering to this day, over the votive tablet. The picture was never got, any more than the spoons and dishes: the inspiration ceased, the verses were not wanted — the ambassador wasn't wanted. Poor Mat was recalled from his embassy, suffered disgrace along with his patrons, lived under a sort of cloud ever after, and disappeared in Essex. When deprived of all his pensions and emoluments, the hearty and generous Oxford pensioned him. They played for gallant stakes — the bold men of those days — and lived and gave splendidly.

Johnson quotes from Spence a legend, that Prior, after spending an evening with Harley, St. John, Pope, and Swift, would go off and smoke a pipe with a couple of friends of his, a soldier and his wife, in Long Acre. Those who have not read his late Excellency's poems should be warned that they smack not a little of the conversation of his Long Acre friends. Johnson speaks slightingly of his lyrics; but with due deference to the great Samuel, Prior's seem to me amongst the easiest, the richest, the most charmingly humorous of English

* "He was to have been in the same commission with the Duke of Shrewsbury, but that that nobleman," says Johnson, "refused to be associated with one so meanly born. Prior therefore continued to act without a title till the Duke's return next year to England, and then he assumed the style and dignity of ambassador."

He had been thinking of slights of this sort when he wrote his Epitaph: —

"Nobles and heralds, by your leave,
Here lies what once was Matthew Prior,
The son of Adam and of Eve;
Can Bourbon or Nassau claim higher?"

But, in this case, the old prejudice got the better of the old joke.

lyrical poems.* Horace is always in his mind; and his song, and his philosophy, his good sense, his happy, easy turns and melody, his loves and his Epicureanism, bear a great resemblance to that most delightful and accomplished master. In reading his works, one is struck with their modern air, as well as by their happy similarity to the songs of the charming owner of the Sabine farm. In his verses addressed to Halifax, he says, writing of that endless theme to poets, the vanity of human wishes, —

"So when in fevered dreams we sink,
And waking, taste what we desire,
The real draught but feeds the fire,
The dream is better than the drink.

"Our hopes like towering falcons aim
At objects in an airy height:
To stand aloof and view the flight,
Is all the pleasure of the game."

Would not you fancy that a poet of our own days was singing? and in the verses of Chloe weeping and reproaching him for his inconstancy, where he says, —

"The God of us versemen, you know, child, the Sun,
How, after his journey, he sets up his rest.
If at morning o'er earth 'tis his fancy to run,
At night he declines on his Thetis's breast.

"So, when I am wearied with wandering all day,
To thee, my delight, in the evening I come:
No matter what beauties I saw in my way:
They were but my visits, but thou art my home!

"Then finish, dear Chloe, this pastoral war,
And let us like Horace and Lydia agree:
For thou art a girl as much brighter than her,
As he was a poet sublimer than me."

If Prior read Horace, did not Thomas Moore study Prior? Love and pleasure find singers in all days. Roses are always blowing and fading — to-day as in that pretty time when Prior sang of them, and of Chloe lamenting their decay: —

"She sighed, she smiled, and to the flowers
Pointing, the lovely moralist said:
See, friend, in some few leisure hours,
See yonder what a change is made!

"Ah me! the blooming pride of May
And that of Beauty are but one:
At morn both flourisht, bright and gay,
Both fade at evening, pale and gone.

"At dawn poor Stella danced and sung,
The amorous youth around her bowed:
At night her fatal knell was rung;
I saw, and kissed her in her shroud.

"Such as she is who died to-day,
Such I, alas, may be to-morrow:
Go, Damon, bid the Muse display
The justice of thy Chloe's sorrow."

Damon's knell was rung in 1721. May his turf lie lightly on him! *Deus sit propitius huic potatori*, as Walter de Mapes sang.* Perhaps Samuel

* His epigrams have the genuine sparkle.

"THE REMEDY WORSE THAN THE DISEASE.

"I sent for Radcliff; was so ill,
That other doctors gave me over:
He felt my pulse, prescribed a pill,
And I was likely to recover.

"But when the wit began to wheeze,
And wine had warmed the politician,
Cured yesterday of my disease,
I died last night of my physician."

"Yes, every poet is a fool;
By demonstration Ned can show it;
Happy could Ned's inverted rule
Prove every fool to be a poet."

On his death-bed poor Lubin lies,
His spouse is in despair;
With frequent sobs and mutual sighs,
They both express their care.

"'A different cause,' says Parson Sly,
'The same effect may give;
Poor Lubin fears that he shall die,
His wife that he may live.'"

* "PRIOR TO SIR THOMAS HANMER.

Aug. 4, 1709.

"DEAR SIR, —
"FRIENDSHIP may live, I grant you, without being fed and cherished by cor-

Johnson, who spoke slightingly of Prior's verses, enjoyed them more than he was willing to own. The old moralist had studied them as well

respondence; but with that additional benefit I am of opinion it will look more cheerful and thrive better: for in this case, as in love, though a man is sure of his own constancy, yet his happiness depends a good deal upon the sentiments of another, and while you and Chloe are alive, 'tis not enough that I love you both, except I am sure you both love me again; and as one of her scrawls fortifies my mind more against affliction than all Epictetus, with Simplicius's comments into the bargain, so your single letter gave me more real pleasure than all the works of Plato. . . . I must return my answer to your very kind question concerning my health. The Bath waters have done a good deal towards the recovery of it, and the great specific, *Cape caballum*, will, I think, confirm it. Upon this head I must tell you that my mare Betty grows blind, and may one day, by breaking my neck, perfect my cure: if at Rixham fair any pretty nagg that is between thirteen and fourteen hands presented himself, and you would be pleased to purchase him for me, one of your servants might ride him to Euston, and I might receive him there. This, sir, is just as such a thing happens. If you hear, too, of a Welsh widow, with a good jointure, that has her *goings* and is not very skittish, pray, be pleased to cast your eye on her for me too. You see, sir, the great trust I repose in your skill and honor, when I dare put two such commissions in your hand." . . . — *The Hanmer Correspondence*, p. 120.

"FROM MR. PRIOR.

"*Paris*, 1-12 *May*, 1714.

"MY DEAR LORD AND FRIEND, —

"MATTHEW never had so great occasion to write a word to Henry as now: it is noised here that I am soon to return. The question that I wish I could answer to the many that ask, and to our friend Colbert de Torcy (to whom I made your compliments in the manner you commanded) is, what is done for me; and to what I am recalled? It may look like a bagatelle, what is to become of a philosopher like me? but it is not such: what is to become of a person who had the honor to be chosen, and sent hither as intrusted, in the midst of a war, with what the Queen designed should make the peace; returning with the Lord Bolingbroke, one of the greatest men in England, and one of the finest heads in Europe (as they say here, if true or not, *n'importe*); having been left by him in the greatest character (that of Her Majesty's Plenipotentiary), exercising that power conjointly with the Duke of Shrewsbury, and solely after his departure; having here received more distinguished honor than any Minister, except an Ambassador, ever did, and some which were never given to any but who had that character; having had all the success that could be expected; having (God be thanked!) spared no pains, at a time when at home the peace is voted safe and honorable — at a time when the Earl of Oxford is Lord Treasurer and Lord Bolingbroke First Secretary of State? This unfortunate person, I say, neglected, forgot, unnamed to any thing that may speak the Queen satisfied with his services, or his friends concerned as to his fortune.

"Mr. de Torcy put me quite out of countenance, the other day, by a pity that wounded me deeper than ever did the cruelty of the late Lord Godolphin. He said he would write to Robin and Harry about me. God forbid, my lord, that I should need any foreign intercession, or owe the least to any Frenchman living, besides the decency of behavior and the returns of common civility: some say I am to go to Baden, others that I am to be added to the Commissioners for settling the commerce. In all cases I am ready, but in the mean time, *dic aliquid de tribus capellis*. Neither of these two are, I presume, honors or rewards, neither of them (let me say to my dear Lord Bolingbroke, and let him not be angry with me) are what Drift may aspire to, and what Mr. Whitworth, who was his fellow-clerk, has or may possess. I am far from desiring to lessen the great merit of the gentleman I named, for I heartily esteem and love him; but in this trade of ours, my lord, in which you are the general, as in that of the soldiery, there is a certain right acquired by time and long service. You would do any thing for your Queen's service, but you would not be contented to descend, and be degraded to a charge, no way proportioned to that of Secretary of State, any more than Mr. Ross, though he would charge a party with a halbard in his hand, would be content all his life after to be Sergeant. Was my Lord Dartmouth, from Secretary, returned again to be Commissioner of Trade, or from Secretary of War, would Frank Gwyn think himself kindly used to be returned again to be Commissioner? In short, my lord, you have put me above myself, and if I am to return to myself, I shall return to something very discontented and uneasy. I am sure, my lord, you will make the best use you can of this hint for my good. If I am to have any thing, it will certainly be for Her Majesty's service, and the credit of my friends in the Ministry, that it be done

as Mr. Thomas Moore, and defended them, and showed that he remembered them very well too, on an occasion when their morality was called in question by that noted puritan, James Boswell, Esq., of Auchinleck.*

In the great society of the wits, John Gay deserved to be a favorite, and to have a good place.† In his set all were fond of him. His success offended nobody. He missed a fortune once or twice. He was talked of for court favor, and hoped to win it; but the court favor jilted him. Craggs gave him some South Sea Stock; and at one time Gay had very nearly made his fortune. But Fortune shook her swift wings and jilted him too; and so his friends, instead of being angry with him, and jealous of him, were kind and fond of honest Gay. In the portraits of the literary worthies of the early part of the last century, Gay's face is the pleasantest perhaps of all. It appears adorned with neither periwig nor night-cap (the full dress and *negligée* of learning, without which the painters of those days scarcely ever portrayed wits), and he laughs at you over his shoulder with an honest boyish glee — an artless sweet humor. He was so kind, so gentle, so jocular, so delightfully brisk at times, so dismally wobegone at others, such a natural good creature, that the Giants loved him. The great Swift was gentle and sportive with him,* as the enormous Brobdingnag maids of honor were with little Gulliver. He could frisk and fondle round Pope,† and sport

before I am recalled from home, lest the world may think either that I have merited to be disgraced, or that ye dare not stand by me. If nothing is to be done, *fiat voluntas Dei.* I have writ to Lord Treasurer upon this subject, and having implored your kind intercession, I promise you it is the last remonstrance of this kind that I will ever make. Adieu, my lord; all honor, health, and pleasure to you. Yours ever, MATT."

"P.S. — Lady Jersey is just gone from me. We drank your healths together in usquebaugh after our tea: we are the greatest friends alive. Once more, adieu. There is no such thing as the 'Book of Travels' you mentioned; if there be, let friend Tilson send us more particular account of them, for neither I nor Jacob Tonson can find them. Pray send Barton back to me, I hope with some comfortable tidings." — *Bolingbroke's Letters.*

* "I asked whether Prior's poems were to be printed entire; Johnson said they were. I mentioned Lord Hales's censure of Prior in his preface to a collection of sacred poems, by various hands, published by him at Edinburgh a great many years ago, where he mentions 'these impure tales, which will be the eternal opprobrium of their ingenious author.' JOHNSON: 'Sir, Lord Hales has forgot. There is nothing in Prior that will excite to lewdness. If Lord Hales thinks there is, he must be more combustible than other people.' I instanced the tale of 'Paulo Purganti and his wife.' JOHNSON: 'Sir, there is nothing there but that his wife wanted to be kissed, when poor Paulo was out of pocket. No, sir, Prior is a lady's book. No lady is ashamed to have it standing in her library." — BOSWELL'S *Life of Johnson.*

† Gay was of an old Devonshire family, but his pecuniary prospects not being great, was placed in his youth in the house of a silk-mercer in London. He was born in 1688 — Pope's year, and in 1712 the Duchess of Monmouth made him her secretary. Next year he published his "Rural Sports," which he dedicated to Pope, and so made an acquaintance, which became a memorable friendship.

"Gay," says Pope, "was quite a natural man, wholly without art or design, and spoke just what he thought and as he thought it. He dangled for twenty years about a court, and at last was offered to be made usher to the young princess. Secretary Craggs made Gay a present of stock in the South Sea year; and he was once worth 20,000*l.*, but lost it all again. He got about 500*l.* by the first 'Beggar's Opera,' and 1,100*l.* or 1,200*l.* by the second. He was negligent and a bad manager. Latterly, the Duke of Queensberry took his money into his keeping, and let him only have what was necessary out of it, and, as he lived with them, he could not have occasion for much. He died worth upwards of 3,000*l.*" — POPE. *Spence's Anecdotes.*

* "Mr. Gay is, in all regards, as honest and sincere a man as ever I knew." — SWIFT, *To Lady Betty Germaine*, Jan. 1733.

† "Of manners gentle, of affections mild;
In wit a man; simplicity, a child;
With native humor tempering virtuous rage,
Form'd to delight at once and lash the age;

GAY.

and bark, and caper, without offending the most thin-skinned of poets and men; and when he was jilted in that little court affair of which we have spoken, his warm-hearted patrons the Duke and Duchess of Queensberry * (the "Kitty, beautiful and young," of Prior) pleaded his cause with indignation, and quitted the court in a huff, carrying off with them into their retirement their kind, gentle protégé. With these kind lordly folks, a real Duke and Duchess, as delightful as

Above temptation in a low estate,
And uncorrupted e'en among the great:
A safe companion, and an easy friend,
Unblamed through life, lamented in the end.
These are thy honors; not that here thy bust
Is mixed with heroes, or with kings thy dust;
But that the worthy and the good shall say,
Striking their pensive bosoms, '*Here lies Gay.*'"

POPE'S *Epitaph on Gay*.

"A hare who, in a civil way,
Complied with every thing, like Gay."

Fables, "*The Hare and many Friends*."

* "I can give you no account of Gay," says Pope, curiously, "since he was raffled for, and won back by his Duchess." — *Works*, *Roscoe's Ed.*, vol. ix. p. 392.

Here is the letter Pope wrote to him when the death of Queen Anne brought back Lord Clarendon from Hanover, and lost him the secretaryship of that nobleman, of which he had had but a short tenure.

Gay's court prospects were never happy from this time. His dedication of the "Shepherd's Week" to Bolingbroke, Swift used to call the "original sin" which had hurt him with the house of Hanover: —

"*Sept.* 23, 1714.

"DEAR MR. GAY, —

"WELCOME to your native soil! welcome to your friends! thrice welcome to me! whether returned in glory, blest with court interest, the love and familiarity of the great, and filled with agreeable hopes; or melancholy with dejection, contemplative of the changes of fortune, and doubtful for the future; whether returned a triumphant Whig or a desponding Tory, equally all hail! equally beloved and welcome to me! If happy, I am to partake of your elevation; if unhappy, you have still a warm corner in my heart, and a retreat at Benfield in the worst of times at your service. If you are a Tory, or thought so by any man, I know it can proceed from nothing but your gratitude to a few people who endeavored to serve you, and whose politics were never your concern. If you are a Whig, as I rather hope, and as I think your principles and mine (as brother poets) had ever a bias to the side of liberty, I know you will be an honest man and an inoffensive one. Upon the whole, I know you are incapable of being so much of either party as to be good for nothing. Therefore, once more, whatever you are, or in whatever state you are, all hail!

"One or two of your own friends complained they had nothing from you since the Queen's death; I told them no man living loved Mr. Gay better than I, yet I had not once written to him in all his voyage. This I thought a convincing proof, but truly one may be a friend to another without telling him so every month. But they had reasons, too, themselves to allege in your excuse, as men who really value one another will never want such as make their friends and themselves easy. The late universal concern in public affairs threw us all into a hurry of spirits: even I, who am more a philosopher than to expect any thing from any reign, was borne away with the current, and full of the expectation of the successor. During your journeys, I knew not whither to aim a letter after you; that was a sort of shooting flying; add to this the demand Homer had upon me, to write fifty verses a day, besides learned notes, all of which are at a conclusion for this year. Rejoice with me, O my friend! that my labor is over; come and make merry with me in much feasting. We will feed among the lilies (by the lilies I mean the ladies). Are not the Rosalindas of Britain as charming as the Blousalindas of the Hague? or have the two great Pastoral poets of our own nation renounced love at the same time? for Phillips, unnatural Phillips, hath deserted it, yea, and in a rustic manner kicked his Rosalind. Dr. Parnell and I have been inseparable ever since you went. We are now at the Bath, where (if you are not, as I heartily hope, better engaged) your company would be the greatest pleasure to us in the world. Talk not of expenses: Homer shall support his children. I beg a line from you, directed to the Post-house in Bath. Poor Parnell is in an ill state of health.

"Pardon me if I add a word of advice in the poetical way. Write something on the King, or Prince, or Princess. On whatsoever foot you may be with the court, this can do no harm. I shall never

those who harbored Don Quixote, and loved that dear old Sancho, Gay lived, and was lapped in cotton, and had his plate of chicken, and his saucer of cream, and frisked, barked, and wheezed, and grew fat, and so ended.* He became very melancholy and lazy, sadly plethoric, and only occasionally diverting in his latter days. But everybody loved him, and the remembrance of his pretty little tricks; and the raging old Dean of St. Patrick's, chafing in his banishment, was afraid to open the letter which Pope wrote him, announcing the sad news of the death of Gay.†

Swift's letters to him are beautiful; and having no purpose but kindness in writing to him, no party aim to advocate, or slight or anger to wreak, every word the Dean says to his favorite is natural, trustworthy, and kindly. His admiration for Gay's parts and honesty, and his laughter at his weaknesses, were alike just and genuine. He paints his character in wonderful pleasant traits of jocular satire. "I writ lately to Mr. Pope," Swift says, writing to Gay: "I wish you had a little villakin in his neighborhood; but you are yet too volatile, and any lady with a coach and six horses would carry you to Japan." "If your ramble," says Swift, in another letter, "was on horseback, I am glad of it, on account of your health; but I know your arts of packing up a journey between stage-coaches and friends' coaches — for you are as arrant a cockney as any hosier in Cheapside. I have often had it in my head to put it into yours, that you ought to have some great work in scheme, which may take up seven years to finish, besides two or three under-ones that may add another thousand pounds to your stocks, and then I shall be in less pain about you. I know you can find dinners, but you love twelvepenny coaches too well, without considering that the interest of a whole thousand pounds brings you but half a crown a day." And then Swift goes off from Gay to pay some grand compliments to her Grace the Duchess of Queensberry, in whose sunshine Mr. Gay was basking, and in whose radiance the Dean would have liked to warm himself too.

But we have Gay here before us, in these letters — lazy, kindly, uncommonly idle; rather slovenly, I'm afraid; forever eating and saying good things; a little round French abbé of a man, sleek, soft-handed, and soft-hearted.

know where to end, and am confounded in the many things I have to say to you, though they all amount but to this, that I am, entirely, as ever, Yours, &c.

Gay took the advice "in the poetical way," and published "An Epistle to a Lady, occasioned by the arrival of her Royal Highness the Princess of Wales." But though this brought him access to court, and the attendance of the Prince and Princess at his farce of the "What d'ye call it?" it did not bring him a place. On the accession of George II., he was offered the situation of Gentleman Usher to the Princess Louisa (her Highness being then two years old); but "by this offer," says Johnson, "he thought himself insulted."

* "Gay was a great eater. As the French philosopher used to prove his existence by *Cogito, ergo sum*, the greatest proof of Gay's existence is, *Edit, ergo est.*" — CONGREVE, *in a Letter to Pope. Spence's Anecdotes.*

† Swift indorsed the letter — "On my dear friend Mr. Gay's death; received Dec. 15, but not read till the 20th, by an impulse foreboding some misfortune."

"It was by Swift's interest that Gay was made known to Lord Bolingbroke, and obtained his patronage." — SCOTT'S *Swift*, vol. i. p. 156.

Pope wrote on the occasion of Gay's death, to Swift, thus: —

"[*Dec.* 5, 1732.]

". . . One of the dearest and longest ties I have ever had is broken all on a sudden by the unfortunate death of poor Mr. Gay. An inflammatory fever carried him out of this life in three days. . . . He asked of you a few hours before, when in acute torment by the inflammation in his bowels and breast. . . . His sisters, we suppose, will be his heirs, who are two widows. . . . Good God! how often are we to die before we go quite off this stage? In every friend we lose a part of ourselves, and the best part. God keep those we have left! few are worth praying for, and one's self the least of all."

Our object in these lectures is rather to describe the men than their works; or to deal with the latter only in as far as they seem to illustrate the character of their writers. Mr. Gay's "Fables," which were written to benefit that amiable Prince, the Duke of Cumberland, the warrior of Dettingen and Culloden, I have not, I own, been able to peruse since a period of very early youth; and it must be confessed that they did not effect much benefit upon the illustrious young Prince, whose manners they were intended to mollify, and whose natural ferocity our gentle-hearted Satirist perhaps proposed to restrain. But the six pastorals called the "Shepherd's Week," and the burlesque poem of "Trivia," any man fond of lazy literature will find delightful at the present day, and must read from beginning to end with pleasure. They are to poetry what charming little Dresden china figures are to sculpture: graceful, minikin, fantastic; with a certain beauty always accompanying them. The pretty little personages of the pastoral, with gold clocks to their stockings, and fresh satin ribbons to their crooks and waistcoats and bodices, dance their loves to a minuet-tune played on a bird-organ, approach the charmer, or rush from the false one daintily on their red-heeled tip-toes, and die of despair or rapture, with the most pathetic little grins and ogles; or repose, simpering at each other, under an arbor of pea-green crockery; or piping to pretty flocks that have just been washed with the best Naples in a stream of Bergamot. Gay's gay plan seems to me far pleasanter than that of Phillips — his rival and Pope's — a serious and dreary idyllic cockney; not that Gay's "Bumkinets" and "Hobnelias" are a whit more natural than the would-be serious characters of the other posture-master; but the quality of this true humorist was to laugh and make laugh, though always with a secret kindness and tenderness, to perform the drollest little antics and capers, but always with a certain grace, and to sweet music — as you may have seen a Savoyard boy abroad, with a hurdy-gurdy and a monkey, turning over head and heels, or clattering and pirouetting in a pair of wooden shoes, yet always with a look of love and appeal in his bright eyes, and a smile that asks and wins affection and protection. Happy they who have that sweet gift of nature! It was this which made the great folks and court ladies free and friendly with John Gay — which made Pope and Arbuthnot love him — which melted the savage heart of Swift when he thought of him — and drove away, for a moment or two, the dark frenzies which obscured the lonely tyrant's brain, as he heard Gay's voice with its simple melody and artless ringing laughter.

What used to be said about Rubini, *qu'il avait des larmes dans la voix*, may be said of Gay,* and of one other humorist of whom we shall have to speak. In almost every ballad of his, however slight,† in "The Beggar's

* "Gay, like Goldsmith, had a musical talent. 'He could play on the flute,' says Malone, 'and was, therefore, enabled to adapt so happily some of the airs in the "Beggar's Opera."'" — *Notes to Spence.*

† "'Twas when the seas were roaring
With hollow blasts of wind,
A damsel lay deploring,
All on a rock reclined.
Wide o'er the foaming billows
She cast a wistful look;
Her head was crowned with willows
That trembled o'er the brook.

"'Twelve months are gone and over,
And nine long tedious days;
Why didst thou, venturous lover —
Why didst thou trust the seas?
Cease, cease, thou cruel Ocean,
And let my lover rest;
Ah! what's thy troubled motion
To that within my breast?

"'The merchant, robbed of pleasure,
Sees tempests in despair;
But what's the loss of treasure
To losing of my dear?
Should you some coast be laid on,
Where gold and diamonds grow,
You'd find a richer maiden,
But none that loves you so.

Opera"* and in its wearisome continuation (where the verses are to the full as pretty as in the first piece, however), there is a peculiar, hinted, pathetic sweetness and melody. It charms and melts you. It's indefinable, but it exists; and is the property of John Gay's and Oliver Goldsmith's best verse, as fragance is of a violet, or freshness of a rose.

"'How can they say that Nature
Has nothing made in vain;
Why, then, beneath the water
Should hideous rocks remain?
No eyes the rocks discover
That lurk beneath the deep,
To wreck the wandering lover,
And leave the maid to weep?'

"All melancholy lying,
Thus wailed she for her dear;
Repaid each blast with sighing,
Each billow with a tear;
When o'er the white wave stooping,
His floating corpse she spied;
Then like a lily drooping,
She bowed her head, and died."

— *A Ballad from the "What d'ye call it?"*

"What can be prettier than Gay's ballad, or, rather, Swift's, Arbuthnot's, Pope's, and Gay's, in the 'What d'ye call it?' ''Twas when the seas were roaring'? I have been well informed that they all contributed."—*Cowper to Unwin*, 1783.

* "Dr. Swift had been observing once to Mr. Gay, what an odd pretty sort of thing a Newgate pastoral might make. Gay was inclined to try at such a thing for some time, but afterwards thought it would be better to write a comedy on the same plan. This was what gave rise to 'The Beggar's Opera.' He began on it, and when he first mentioned it to Swift, the Doctor did not much like the project. As he carried it on, he showed what he wrote to both of us; and we now and then gave a correction, or a word or two of advice; but it was wholly of his own writing. When it was done, neither of us thought it would succeed. We showed it to Congreve, who, after reading it over, said, 'It would either take greatly, or be damned confoundedly.' We were all, at the first night of it, in great uncertainty of the event, till we were very much encouraged by overhearing the Duke of Argyle, who sat in the next box to us, say, 'It will do—it must do!—I see it in the eyes of them!' This was a good while before the first act was over, and so gave us ease soon; for the Duke [besides his own good taste] has a more particular research than any one now living in discovering the taste of the public. He was quite right in this as usual; the good nature of the audience appeared stronger and stronger every act, and ended in a clamor of applause."—POPE. *Spence's Anecdotes.*

Let me read a piece from one of his letters, which is so famous that most people here are no doubt familiar with it, but so delightful that it is always pleasant to hear:—

"I have just passed part of this summer at an old romantic seat of my Lord Harcourt's which he lent me. It overlooks a common hayfield, where, under the shade of a haycock, sat two lovers—as constant as ever were found in romance—beneath a spreading bush. The name of the one (let it sound as it will) was John Hewet; of the other Sarah Drew. John was a well set man, about five and twenty; Sarah a brave woman of eighteen. John had for several months borne the labor of the day in the same field with Sarah; when she milked, it was his morning and evening charge to bring the cows to her pails. Their love was the talk, but not the scandal, of the whole neighborhood, for all they aimed at was the blameless possession of each other in marriage. It was but this very morning that he had obtained her parents' consent, and it was but till the next week that they were to wait to be happy. Perhaps this very day, in the intervals of their work, they were talking of their wedding-clothes; and John was now matching several kinds of poppies and field-flowers, to make her a present of knots for the day. While they were thus employed (it was on the last of July), a terrible storm of thunder and lightning arose, that drove the laborers to what shelter the trees or hedges afforded. Sarah, frightened and out of breath, sunk on a haycock; and John (who never separated from her) sat by her side, having raked two or three heaps together to secure her. Immediately there was heard so loud a crash, as if heaven had burst asunder. The laborers, all solicitous for each other's safety, called to one another: those that were nearest our lovers, hearing no answer, stepped to the place where they lay: they first saw a little smoke, and after, this faithful pair—John with one arm about his Sarah's neck, and the other held over her face, as if to screen her from the lightning. They were struck dead, and already grown stiff and cold in this tender posture. There was no mark or discoloring on their bodies—only that Sarah's eyebrow was a little singed, and a small spot between her breasts. They were buried the next day in one grave."

And the proof that this description is delightful and beautiful is, that the

Pope.

great Mr. Pope admired it so much that he thought proper to steal it and to send it off to a certain lady and wit, with whom he pretended to be in love in those days — my Lord Duke of Kingston's daughter, and married to Mr. Wortley Montagu, then his Majesty's Ambassador at Constantinople.

We are now come to the greatest name on our list — the highest among the poets, the highest among the English wits and humorists with whom we have to rank him. If the author of "The Dunciad" be not a humorist, if the poet of "The Rape of the Lock" be not a wit, who deserves to be called so? Besides that brilliant genius and immense fame, for both of which we should respect him, men of letters should admire him as being the greatest literary *artist* that England has seen. He polished, he refined, he thought; he took thoughts from other works to adorn and complete his own; borrowing an idea or a cadence from another poet as he would a figure or a simile from a flower, or a river, stream, or any object which struck him in his walk, or contemplation of Nature. He began to imitate at an early age; * and taught himself to write by copying printed books. Then he passed into the hands of the priests, and from his first clerical master, who came to him when he was eight years old, he went to a school at Twyford, and another school at Hyde Park, at which places he unlearned all that he had got from his first instructor. At twelve years old, he went with his father into Windsor Forest, and there learned for a few months under a fourth priest. "And this was all the teaching I ever had," he said, "and God knows it extended a very little way."

When he had done with his priests he took to reading by himself, for which he had a very great eagerness and enthusiasm, especially for poetry. He learned versification from Dryden, he said. In his youthful poem of "Alcander," he imitated every poet, Cowley, Milton, Spenser, Statius, Homer, Virgil. In a few years he had dipped into a great number of the English, French, Italian, Latin, and Greek poets. "This I did," he says, "without any design, except to amuse myself; and got the languages by hunting after the stories in the several poets I read, rather than read the books to get the languages. I followed everywhere as my fancy led me, and was like a boy gathering flowers in the fields and woods, just as they fell in his way. These five or six years I looked upon as the happiest in my life." Is not here a beautiful holiday picture? The

* "Waller, Spenser, and Dryden were Mr. Pope's great favorites, in the order they are named, in his first reading, till he was about twelve years old." — POPE. *Spence's Anecdotes.*

"Mr. Pope's father (who was an honest merchant, and dealt in Hollands, wholesale) was no poet, but he used to set him to make English verses when very young. He was pretty difficult in being pleased; and used often to send him back to new turn them. 'These are not good rhimes;' for that was my husband's word for verses." — POPE'S MOTHER. *Spence.*

"I wrote things, I'm ashamed to say how soon. Part of an Epic Poem when about twelve. The scene of it lay at Rhodes and some of the neighboring islands; and the poem opened under water with a description of the Court of Neptune." — POPE. *Ibid.*

"His perpetual application (after he set to study of himself) reduced him in four years' time to so bad a state of health, that, after trying physicians for a good while in vain, he resolved to give way to his distemper; and sat down calmly in a full expectation of death in a short time. Under this thought, he wrote letters to take a last farewell of some of his more particular friends, and, among the rest, one to the Abbé Southcote. The Abbé was extremely concerned, both for his very ill state of health and the resolution he said he had taken. He thought there might yet be hope, and went immediately to Dr. Radcliffe, with whom he was well acquainted, told him Mr. Pope's case, got full directions from him, and carried them down to Pope in Windsor Forest. The chief thing the Doctor ordered him was to apply less, and to ride every day. The following his advice soon restored him to his health." — POPE. *Spence.*

forest and the fairy story-book — the boy spelling Ariosto or Virgil under the trees, battling with the Cid for the love of Chimène, or dreaming of Armida's garden — peace and sunshine round about — the kindest love and tenderness waiting for him at his quiet home yonder — and Genius throbbing in his young heart, and whispering to him, "You shall be great; you shall be famous; you too shall love and sing; you will sing her so nobly that some kind heart shall forget you are weak and ill formed. Every poet had a love. Fate must give one to you too,"— and day by day he walks the forest, very likely looking out for that charmer. "They were the happiest days of his life," he says, when he was only dreaming of his fame: when he had gained that mistress she was no consoler.

That charmer made her appearance, it would seem, about the year 1705, when Pope was seventeen. Letters of his are extant, addressed to a certain Lady M——, whom the youth courted, and to whom he expressed his ardor in language, to say no worse of it, that is entirely pert, odious, and affected. He imitated love-compositions as he had been imitating love-poems just before — it was a sham mistress he courted, and a sham passion, expressed as became it. These unlucky letters found their way into print years afterwards, and were sold to the congenial Mr. Curll. If any of my hearers, as I hope they may, should take a fancy to look at Pope's correspondence, let them pass over that first part of it; over, perhaps, almost all Pope's letters to women; in which there is a tone of not pleasant gallantry, and, amidst a profusion of compliments and politenesses, a something which makes one distrust the little pert, prurient bard. There is very little indeed to say about his loves, and that little not edifying. He wrote flames and raptures and elaborate verse and prose for Lady Mary Wortley Montagu; but that passion probably came to a climax in an impertinence, and was extinguished by a box on the ear, or some such rebuff, and he began on a sudden to hate her with a fervor much more genuine than that of his love had been. It was a feeble, puny grimace of love, and paltering with passion. After Mr. Pope had sent off one of his fine compositions to Lady Mary, he made a second draft from the rough copy, and favored some other friend with it. He was so charmed with the letter of Gay's that I have just quoted, that he had copied that and amended it, and sent it to Lady Mary as his own. A gentleman who writes letters *à deux fins*, and after having poured out his heart to the beloved, serves up the same dish *rechauffé* to a friend, is not very much in earnest about his loves, however much he may be in his piques and vanities when his impertinence gets its due.

But, save that unlucky part of "The Pope Correspondence," I do not know, in the range of our literature, volumes more delightful.* You live

* "MR. POPE TO THE REV. MR. BROOM, PULHAM, NORFOLK.

"*Aug.* 29*th*, 1730,

"DEAR SIR,—

"I INTENDED to write to you on this melancholy subject, the death of Mr. Fenton, before yours came, but staid to have informed myself and you of the circumstances of it. All I hear is, that he felt a gradual decay, though so early in life, and was declining for five or six months. It was not, as I apprehended, the gout in his stomach, but, I believe, rather a complication first of gross humors, as he was naturally corpulent, not discharging themselves, as he used no sort of exercise. No man better bore the approaches of his dissolution (as I am told), or with less ostentation yielded up his being. The great modesty which you know was natural to him, and the great contempt he had for all sorts of vanity and parade, never appeared more than in his last moments: he had a conscious satisfaction (no doubt) in acting right, in feeling himself honest, true, and unpretending to more than his own. So he died as he lived, with that secret, yet sufficient contentment.

"As to any papers left behind him, I dare say they can be but few; for this reason, he never wrote out of vanity, or

in them in the finest company in the world. A little stately, perhaps; a little *apprêté* and conscious that they are speaking to whole generations

thought much of the applause of men. I know an instance when he did his utmost to conceal his own merit that way; and if we join to this his natural love of ease, I fancy we must expect little of this sort: at least, I have heard of none, except some few further remarks on Waller (which his cautious integrity made him leave an order to be given to Mr. Tonson), and perhaps, though it is many years since I saw it, a translation of the first book of 'Oppian.' He had begun a tragedy of 'Dion,' but made small progress in it.

"As to his other affairs, he died poor, but honest, leaving no debts or legacies, except of a few pounds to Mr. Trumbull and my lady, in token of respect, gratefulness, and mutual esteem.

"I shall with pleasure take upon me to draw this amiable, quiet, deserving, unpretending, Christian, unphilosophical character in his epitaph. There truth may be spoken in a few words; as for flourish and oratory and poetry, I leave them to younger and more lively writers, such as love writing for writing's sake, and would rather show their own fine parts than report the valuable ones of any other man. So the elegy I renounce.

"I condole with you from my heart on the loss of so worthy a man, and a friend to us both. . . .

"Adieu; let us love his memory and profit by his example. Am very sincerely, dear sir,

Your affectionate and real servant."

"To the Earl of Burlington.

"*August*, 1714.

"My Lord,

"If your mare could speak, she would give you an account of what extraordinary company she had on the road, which, since she cannot do, I will.

"It was the enterprising Mr. Lintot, the redoubtable rival of Mr. Tonson, who, mounted on a stone-horse, overtook me in Windsor Forest. He said he heard I designed for Oxford, the seat of the Muses, and would, as my bookseller, by all means accompany me thither.

"I asked him where he got his horse? He answered he got it of his publisher; 'for that rogue, my printer,' said he, 'disappointed me. I hoped to put him in good humor by a treat at the tavern of a brown fricassée of rabbits, which cost ten shillings, with two quarts of wine, besides my conversation. I thought myself cocksure of his horse, which he readily promised me, but said that Mr. Tonson had just such another design of going to Cambridge, expecting there the copy of a new kind of Horace from Dr. ——; and if Mr. Tonson went, he was pre-engaged to attend him, being to have the printing of the said copy. So, in short, I borrowed this stone-horse of my publisher, which he had of Mr. Oldmixon for a debt. He lent me, too, the pretty boy you see after me. He was a smutty dog yesterday, and cost me more than two hours to wash the ink off his face; but the devil is a fair-conditioned devil, and very forward in his catechism. If you have any more bags he shall carry them.'

"I thought Mr. Lintot's civility not to be neglected, so gave the boy a small bag containing three shirts and an Elzevir Virgil, and, mounting in an instant, proceeded on the road, with my man before, my courteous stationer beside, and the aforesaid devil behind.

"Mr. Lintot began in this manner: 'Now, damn them! What if they should put it into the newspaper how you and I went together to Oxford? What would I care? If I should go down into Sussex they would say I was gone to the Speaker; but what of that? If my son were but big enough to go on with the business, by G—d, I would keep as good company as old Jacob.'

"Hereupon, I inquired of his son. 'The lad,' says he, 'has fine parts, but is somewhat sickly, much as you are. I spare for nothing in his education at Westminster. Pray, don't you think Westminster to be the best school in England? Most of the late Ministry came out of it; so did many of this Ministry. I hope the boy will make his fortune.'

"'Don't you design to let him pass a year at Oxford?' 'To what purpose?' said he. 'The Universities do but make pedants, and I intend to breed him a man of business.'

"As Mr. Lintot was talking I observed he sat uneasy on his saddle, for which I expressed some solicitude. 'Nothing,' says he. 'I can bear it well enough; but, since we have the day before us, methinks it would be very pleasant for you to rest a while under the woods.' When we were alighted, 'See, here, what a mighty pretty Horace I have in my pocket? What, if you amused yourself in turning an ode till we mount again? Lord! if you pleased, what a clever miscellany might you make at leisure hours?' 'Perhaps I may,' said I, 'if we ride on: the motion is an aid to my fancy; a round trot very much awakens my spirits; then jog on apace, and I'll think as hard as I can.'

"Silence ensued for a full hour; after which Mr. Lintot lugged the reins, stopped short, and broke out, 'Well, sir, how far have you gone?' I answered, seven miles.

who are listening; but in the tone of their voices — pitched, as no doubt they are, beyond the mere conversation key — in the expression of their

'Z—ds, sir,' said Lintot, 'I thought you had done seven stanzas. Oldsworth, in a ramble round Wimbledon Hill, would translate a whole ode in half this time. I'll say that for Oldsworth [though I lost by his Timothy's], he translates an ode of Horace the quickest of any man in England. I remember Dr. King would write verses in a tavern, three hours after he could not speak: and there is Sir Richard, in that rumbling old chariot of his, between Fleet Ditch and St. Giles's Pound, shall make you half a Job.'

"'Pray, Mr. Lintot,' said I, 'now you talk of translators, what is your method of managing them?' 'Sir,' replied he, 'these are the saddest pack of rogues in the world: in a hungry fit, they'll swear they understand all the languages in the universe. I have known one of them take down a Greek book upon my counter and cry, "Ah, this is Hebrew, and must read it from the latter end." By G—d, I can never be sure in these fellows, for I neither understand Greek, Latin, French, nor Italian myself. But this is my way: I agree with them for ten shillings per sheet, with a proviso that I will have their doings corrected with whom I please; so by one or the other they are led at last to the true sense of an author; my judgment giving the negative to all my translators.' 'Then how are you sure these correctors may not impose upon you?' 'Why, I get any civil gentleman (especially any Scotchman) that comes into my shop, to read the original to me in English; by this I know whether my first translator be deficient, and whether my corrector merits his money or not.

"'I'll tell you what happened to me last month. I bargained with S—— for a new version of "Lucretius," to publish against Tonson's, agreeing to pay the author so many shillings at his producing so many lines. He made a great progress in a very short time, and I gave it to the corrector to compare with the Latin; but he went directly to Creech's translation, and found it the same, word for word, all but the first page. Now, what d'ye think I did? I arrested the translator for a cheat; nay, and I stopped the corrector's pay, too, upon the proof that he had made use of Creech instead of the original.'

"'Pray tell me next how you deal with the critics?' 'Sir,' said he, 'nothing more easy. I can silence the most formidable of them: the rich ones for a sheet apiece of the blotted manuscript, which cost me nothing; they'll go about with it to their acquaintance, and pretend they had it from the author, who submitted it to their correction: this has given some of them such an air, that in time they come to be consulted with and dedicated to as the tip-top critics of the town. As for the poor critics, I'll give you one instance of my management, by which you may guess the rest: A lean man, that looked like a very good scholar, came to me t'other day; he turned over your Homer, shook his head, shrugged up his shoulders, and pished at every line of it. "One would wonder," says he, "at the strange presumption of some men; Homer is no such easy task as every stripling, every versifier" — he was going on when my wife called to dinner. "Sir," said I, "will you please to eat a piece of beef with me?" "Mr. Lintot," said he, "I am very sorry you should be at the expense of this great book: I am really concerned on your account." "Sir, I am much obliged to you: if you can dine upon a piece of beef, together with a slice of pudding"— "Mr. Lintot, I do not say but Mr. Pope, if he would condescend to advise with men of learning" — "Sir, the pudding is upon the table, if you please to go in." My critic complies; he comes to a taste of your poetry, and tells me in the same breath that the book is commendable, and the poetry excellent.

"'Now, sir,' continued Mr. Lintot, 'in return for the frankness I have shown, pray tell me, is it the opinion of your friends at court that my Lord Lansdowne will be brought to the bar or not?' I told him I heard he would not, and I hoped it, my lord being one I had particular obligations to. 'That may be,' replied Mr. Lintot; 'but by G— if he is not, I shall lose the printing of a very good trial.'

"These, my lord, are a few traits with which you discern the genius of Mr. Lintot, which I have chosen for the subject of a letter. I dropped him as soon as I got to Oxford, and paid a visit to my Lord Carleton, at Middleton. . . .

"I am," &c.

"Dr. Swift to Mr. Pope.

"*Sept.* 29, 1725.

"I am now returning to the noble scene of Dublin — into the *grand monde* — for fear of burying my parts; to signalize myself among curates and vicars, and correct all corruptions crept in relating to the weight of bread and butter through those dominions where I govern. I have employed my time (besides ditching) in finishing, correcting, amending, and transcribing my 'Travels' [Gulliver's], in four parts complete, newly augmented, and intended for the press when the world shall deserve them, or rather, when a printer shall be found brave enough to venture his ears. I like the scheme of our thoughts, their various views and natures, there is something generous, and cheering, and ennobling. You are in the society of men who have filled the greatest parts in the world's story —you are with St. John the statesman; Peterborough the conqueror; Swift, the greatest wit of all times; Gay, the kindliest laugher—it is a privilege to sit in that company. Delightful and generous banquet! with a little faith and a little fancy any one of us here may enjoy it, and conjure up those great figures out of the past, and listen to their wit and wisdom. Mind that there is always a certain *cachet* about great men—they may be as mean on many points as you or I, but they carry their great air —they speak of common life more largely and generously than common men do—they regard the world with a manlier countenance, and see its real features more fairly than the timid shufflers who only dare to look up at life through blinkers, or to have

meeting after distresses and dissensions; but the chief end I propose to myself in all my labors is to vex the world rather than divert it; and if I could compass that design without hurting my own person and fortune, I would be the most indefatigable writer you have ever seen, without reading. I am exceedingly pleased that you have done with translations: Lord Treasurer Oxford often lamented that a rascally world should lay you under a necessity of mis-employing your genius for so long a time; but since you will now be so much better employed, when you think of the world, give it one lash the more at my request. I have ever hated all societies, professions, and communities; and all my love is towards individuals —for instance, I hate the tribe of lawyers, but I love Councillor Such-a-one and Judge Such-a-one: it is so with physicians (I will not speak of my own trade), soldiers, English, Scotch, French and the rest. But principally I hate and detest that animal called man—although I heartily love John, Peter, Thomas, and so on.

"... I have got materials towards a treatise proving the falsity of that definition *animal rationale*, and to show it should be only *rationis capax*. ... The matter is so clear that it will admit of no dispute—nay, I will hold a hundred pounds that you and I agree in the point. ...

"Dr. Lewis sent me an account of Dr. Arbuthnot's illness, which is a very sensible affliction to me, who, by living so long out of the world, have lost that hardness of heart contracted by years and general conversation. I am daily losing friends, and neither seeking nor getting others. Oh! if the world had but a dozen Arbuthnots in it, I would burn my 'Travels!'"

"Mr. Pope to Dr. Swift.

"*October* 15, 1725.

"I am wonderfully pleased with the suddenness of your kind answer. It makes me hope you are coming towards us, and that you incline more and more to your old friends. ... Here is one [Lord Bolingbroke] who was once a powerful planet, but has now (after long experience of all that comes of shining) learned to be content with returning to his first point without the thought or ambition of shining at all. Here is another [Edward, Earl of Oxford], who thinks one of the greatest glories of his father was to have distinguished and loved you, and who loves you hereditarily. Here is Arbuthnot, recovered from the jaws of death, and more pleased with the hope of seeing you again than of reviewing a world, every part of which he has long despised but what is made up of a few men like yourself. ...

"Our friend Gay is used as the friends of Tories are by Whigs—and generally by Tories too. Because he had humor, he was supposed to have dealt with Dr. Swift, in like manner as when any one had learning formerly, he was thought to have dealt with the devil. ...

"Lord Bolingbroke had not the least harm by his fall; I wish he had received no more by his other fall. But Lord Bolingbroke is the most improved mind since you saw him, that ever was improved without shifting into a new body, or being *paullo minus ab angelis*. I have often imagined to myself, that if ever all of us meet again, after so many varieties and changes, after so much of the old world and of the old man in each of us has been altered, that scarce a single thought of the one, any more than a single action of the other, remains just the same; I have fancied, I say, that we should meet like the righteous in the millennium, quite at peace, divested of all our former passions, smiling at our past follies, and content to enjoy the kingdom of the just in tranquillity.

. . . .

"I designed to have left the following page for Dr. Arbuthnot to fill, but he is so touched with the period in yours to me, concerning him, that he intends to answer it by a whole letter." ...

an opinion when there is a crowd to back it. He who reads these noble records of a past age salutes and reverences the great spirits who adorn it. You may go home now and talk with St. John; you may take a volume from your library and listen to Swift and Pope.

Might I give counsel to any young hearer, I would say to him, Try to frequent the company of your betters. In books and life that is the most wholesome society; learn to admire rightly; the great pleasure of life is that. Note what the great men admired; they admired great things: narrow spirits admire basely, and worship meanly. I know nothing in any story more gallant and cheering than the love and friendship which this company of famous men bore towards one another. There never has been a society of men more friendly, as there never was one more illustrious. Who dares quarrel with Mr. Pope, great and famous himself, for liking the society of men great and famous? and for liking them for the qualities which made them so? A mere pretty fellow from White's could not have written "The Patriot King," and would very likely have despised little Mr. Pope, the decrepit Papist, whom the great St. John held to be one of the best and greatest of men: a mere nobleman of the court could no more have won Barcelona, than he could have written Peterborough's letters to Pope,* which are as witty as Congreve: a mere Irish Dean could not have written "Gulliver;" and all these men loved Pope, and Pope loved all these men. To name his friends is to name the best men of his time. Addison had a senate; Pope reverenced his equals. He spoke of Swift with respect and admiration always. His admiration for Bolingbroke was so great, that when some one said of his friend, "There is something in that great man which looks as if he was placed here by mistake," "Yes," Pope answered, "and, when the comet appeared to us a month or two ago, I had sometimes an imagination that it might possibly be come to carry him home, as a coach comes to one's door for visitors." So these great spirits spoke of one another. Show me six of the dullest middle-aged gentlemen that ever dawdled round a club table, so faithful and so friendly.

* Of the Earl of Peterborough, Walpole says, — "He was one of those men of careless wit and negligent grace, who scatter a thousand *bon-mots* and idle verses, which we painful compilers gather and hoard, till the authors stare to find themselves authors. Such was this lord, of an advantageous figure and enterprising spirit; as gallant as Amadis, and as brave; but a little more expeditious in his journeys; for he is said to have seen more kings and more postilions than any man in Europe. . . . He was a man, as his friend said, who would neither live nor die like any other mortal."

"FROM THE EARL OF PETERBOROUGH TO POPE.

"You must receive my letter with a just impartiality, and give grains of allowance for a gloomy or rainy day: I sink grievously with the weather-glass, and am quite spiritless when oppressed with the thoughts of a birthday or a return.

"Dutiful affection was bringing me to town; but undutiful laziness, and being much out of order, keep me in the country: however, if alive, I must make my appearance at the birthday. . . .

"You seem to think it vexatious that I shall allow you but one woman at a time either to praise or love. If I dispute with you on this point, I doubt every fairy will give a verdict against me. So, sir, with a Mahometan indulgence, I allow you pluralities, the favorite privileges of our church.

"I find you don't mend upon correction; again I tell you you must not think of women in a reasonable way; you know we always make goddesses of those we adore upon earth; and do not all the good men tell us we must lay aside reason in what relates to the Deity?

". . . I should have been glad of any thing of Swift's. Pray, when you write to him next, tell him I expect him with impatience, in a place as odd and as out of the way as himself. Yours."

Peterborough married Mrs. Anastasia Robinson, the celebrated singer.

We have said before that the chief wits of this time, with the exception of Congreve, were what we should now call men's men. They spent many hours of the four and twenty, a fourth part of each day nearly, in clubs and coffee-houses, where they dined, drank, and smoked. Wit and news went by word of mouth; a journal of 1710 contained the very smallest portion of one or the other. The chiefs spoke, the faithful *habitués* sat round; strangers came to wonder and listen. Old Dryden had his head-quarters at "Will's," in Russell Street, at the corner of Bow Street: at which place Pope saw him when he was twelve years old. The company used to assemble on the first floor — what was called the dining-room floor in those days — and sat at various tables smoking their pipes. It is recorded that the beaux of the day thought it a great honor to be allowed to take a pinch out of Dryden's snuff-box. When Addison began to reign, he with a certain crafty propriety — a policy let us call it — which belonged to his nature, set up his court, and appointed the officers of his royal house. His palace was "Button's," opposite "Will's."* A quiet opposition, a silent assertion of empire, distinguished this great man. Addison's ministers were Budgell, Tickell, Phillips, Carey; his master of the horse, honest Dick Steele, who was what Duroc was to Napoleon, or Hardy to Nelson; the man who performed his master's bidding, and would have cheerfully died in his quarrel. Addison lived with these people for seven or eight hours every day. The male society passed over their punch-bowls and tobacco-pipes about as much time as ladies of that age spent over Spadille and Manille.

For a brief space, upon coming up to town, Pope formed part of King Joseph's court, and was his rather too eager and obsequious humble servant.* Dick Steele, the editor of the "Tatler," Mr. Addison's man, and his own man too — a person of no little figure in the world of letters, patronized the young poet, and set him a task or two. Young Mr. Pope did the tasks very quickly and smartly (he had been at the feet, quite as a boy, of Wycherley's † decrepit repu-

* "Button had been a servant in the Countess of Warwick's family, who, under the patronage of Addison, kept a coffee-house on the south side of Russell Street, about two doors from Covent Garden. Here it was that the wits of that time used to assemble. It is said that when Addison had suffered any vexation from the Countess, he withdrew the company from Button's house.

"From the coffee-house he went again to a tavern, where he often sat late and drank too much wine." — DR. JOHNSON.

Will's coffee-house was on the west side of Bow Street, and "corner of Russell Street." See "Handbook of London."

* "My acquaintance with Mr. Addison commenced in 1712: I liked him then as well as I liked any man, and was very fond of his conversation. It was very soon after that Mr. Addison advised me 'not to be content with the applause of half the nation.' He used to talk much and often to me, of moderation in parties: and used to blame his dear friend Steele for being too much of a party man. He encouraged me in my design of translating the 'Iliad,' which was begun that year, and finished in 1718." — POPE. *Spence's Anecdotes.*

"Addison had Budgell, and I think Phillips, in the house with him. — Gay they would call one of my *élèves*. — They were angry with me for keeping so much with Dr. Swift and some of the late Ministry." — POPE. *Spence's Anecdotes.*

† "TO MR. ALCOURT.

"*Jan.* 21, 1715-16.

"I know of nothing that will be so interesting to you at present as some circumstances of the last act of that eminent comic poet and our friend, Wycherley. He had often told me, and I doubt not he did all his acquaintance, that he would marry as soon as his life was despaired of. Accordingly, a few days before his death, he underwent the ceremony, and joined together those two sacraments which wise men say we should be the last to receive; for, if you observe, matrimony is placed after extreme unction in our catechism, as a kind of hint of the order of time in which they are to be taken. The old man then lay down, satisfied in the consciousness of having, by this one act, obliged a woman who (he was told)

tation, and propped up for a year that doting old wit): he was anxious to be well with the men of letters, to get a footing and a recognition. He thought it an honor to be admitted into their company; to have the confidence of Mr. Addison's friend, Captain Steele. His eminent parts obtained for him the honor of heralding Addison's triumph of "Cato" with his admirable prologue, and heading the victorious procession as it were. Not content with this act of homage and admiration, he wanted to distinguish himself by assaulting Addison's enemies, and attacked John Dennis with a prose lampoon, which highly offended his lofty patron. Mr. Steele was instructed to write to Mr. Dennis, and inform him that Mr. Pope's pamphlet against him was written quite without Mr. Addison's approval.* Indeed, "The Narrative of Dr. Robert Norris on the Phrenzy of J. D." is a vulgar and mean satire, and such a blow as the magnificent Addison could never desire to see any partisan of his strike in any literary quarrel. Pope was closely allied with Swift when he wrote this pamphlet. It is so dirty that it has been printed in Swift's works, too. It bears the foul marks of the master hand. Swift admired and enjoyed with all his heart the prodigious genius of the young Papist lad out of Windsor Forest, who had never seen a university in his life, and came and conquered the Dons and the doctors with his wit. He applauded, and loved him, too, and protected him, and taught him mischief. I wish Addison could have loved him better. The best satire that ever has been penned would never have been written then; and one of the best characters the world ever knew would have been without a flaw. But he who had so few equals could not bear one, and Pope was more than that. When Pope, trying for himself, and soaring on his immortal young wings, found that his, too, was a genius, which no pinion of that age could follow, he rose and left Addison's company, settling on his own eminence, and singing his own song.

It was not possible that Pope should remain a retainer of Mr. Addison; nor likely that after escaping from his vassalage and assuming an independent crown, the sovereign whose allegiance he quitted should view him amicably.† They did not do wrong

had merit, and shown an heroic resentment of the ill-usage of his next heir. Some hundred pounds which he had with the lady discharged his debts; a jointure of 500*l.* a year made her a recompense; and the nephew was left to comfort himself as well as he could with the miserable remains of a mortgaged estate. I saw our friend twice after this was done — less peevish in his sickness than he used to be in his health; neither much afraid of dying, nor (which in him had been more likely) much ashamed of marrying. The evening before he expired, he called his young wife to the bedside, and earnestly entreated her not to deny him one request — the last he should make. Upon her assurances of consenting to it, he told her: 'My dear, it is only this — that you will never marry an old man again.' I cannot help remarking that sickness, which often destroys both wit and wisdom, yet seldom has power to remove that talent which we call humor. Mr. Wycherley showed his even in his last compliment; though I think his request a little hard, for why should he bar her from doubling her jointure on the same easy terms?

"So trivial as these circumstances are, I should not be displeased myself to know such trifles when they concern or characterize any eminent person. The wisest and wittiest of men are seldom wiser or wittier than others in these sober moments; at least, our friend ended much in the same character he had lived in; and Horace's rule for play may as well be applied to him as a playwright: —

"'Servetur ad imum
Qualis ab incepto processerit et sibi constet.'

"I am," &c.

* "Addison, who was no stranger to the world, probably saw the selfishness of Pope's friendship; and resolving that he should have the consequences of his officiousness to himself, informed Dennis by Steele that he was sorry for the insult." — JOHNSON: *Life of Addison.*

† "While I was heated with what I heard, I wrote a letter to Mr. Addison, to let him know 'that I was not unacquainted with this behavior of his; that if I was to speak of him severely in return for it, it

to mislike each other. They but followed the impulse of nature, and the consequence of position. When Bernadotte became heir to a throne, the Prince Royal of Sweden was naturally Napoleon's enemy. "There are many passions and tempers of mankind," says Mr. Addison in "The Spectator," speaking a couple of years before their little differences between him and Mr. Pope took place, "which naturally dispose us to depress and vilify the merit of one rising in the esteem of mankind. All those who made their entrance into the world with the same advantages, and were once looked on as his equals, are apt to think the fame of his merits a reflection on their own deserts. Those who were once his equals envy and defame him, because they now see him the superior; and those who were once his superiors, because they look upon him as their equal." Did Mr. Addison, justly perhaps thinking that, as young Mr. Pope had not had the benefit of a university education, he couldn't know Greek, therefore he couldn't translate Homer, encourage his young friend Mr. Tickell, of Queen's, to translate that poet, and aid him with his own known scholarship and skill? * It was natural that Mr. Addison should doubt of the learning of an amateur Grecian, should have a high opinion of Mr. Tickell, of Queen's, and should help that ingenious young man. It was natural, on the other hand, that Mr. Pope and Mr. Pope's friend should believe that this counter-translation, suddenly advertised and so long written, though Tickell's college friends had never heard of it — though, when Pope first wrote to Addison regarding his scheme, Mr. Addison knew nothing of the similar project of Tickell, of Queen's — it was natural that Mr. Pope and his friends, having interests, passions, and prejudices of their own, should believe that Tickell's translation was but an act of opposition against Pope, and that they should call Mr. Tickell's emulation Mr. Addison's envy — if envy it were.

"And were there one whose fires
True genius kindles and fair fame inspires,
Blest with each talent and each heart to please,
And born to write, converse, and live with ease;
Should such a man, too fond to rule alone,
Bear like the Turk no brother near the throne;
View him with scornful yet with jealous eyes,
And hate, for arts that caused himself to rise;
Damn with faint praise, assent with civil leer,
And without sneering, teach the rest to sneer;
Willing to wound, and yet afraid to strike,
Just hint a fault, and hesitate dislike;
Alike reserved to blame as to commend,
A timorous foe and a suspicious friend;
Dreading even fools, by flatterers besieged,
And so obliging that he ne'er obliged:
Like Cato give his little senate laws,
And sit attentive to his own applause;
While wits and templars every sentence raise,
And wonder with a foolish face of praise;
Who but must laugh if such a man there be,
Who would not weep if Atticus were he?"

"I sent the verses to Mr. Addison," said Pope, "and he used me very civilly ever after that." No wonder he did. It was shame very likely more than fear that silenced him. Johnson recounts an interview between Pope and Addison after their quarrel, in which Pope was angry, and Addison tried to be contemptuous and

should not be in such a dirty way; that I should rather tell him himself fairly of his faults, and allow his good qualities; and that it should be something in the following manner.' I then subjoined the first sketch of what has since been called my satire on Addison. He used me very civilly ever after; and never did me any injustice, that I know of, from that time to his death, which was about three years after." — POPE. *Spence's Anecdotes.*

* "That Tickell should have been guilty of a villany seems to us highly improbable; that Addison should have been guilty of a villany seems to us highly improbable: but that these two men should have conspired together to commit a villany, seems, to us, improbable in a tenfold degree." — MACAULAY.

calm. Such a weapon as Pope's must have pierced any scorn. It flashes forever, and quivers in Addison's memory. His great figure looks out on us from the past — stainless but for that — pale, calm, and beautiful: it bleeds from that black wound. He should be drawn, like St. Sebastian, with that arrow in his side. As he sent to Gay and asked his pardon, as he bade his stepson come and see his death, be sure he had forgiven Pope, when he made ready to show how a Christian could die.

Pope then formed part of the Addisonian court for a short time, and describes himself in his letters as sitting with that coterie until two o'clock in the morning over punch and burgundy amidst the fumes of tobacco. To use an expression of the present day, the "pace" of those *viveurs* of the former age was awful. Peterborough lived into the very jaws of death; Godolphin labored all day and gambled at night; Bolingbroke,* writing to Swift, from Dawley, in his retirement, dating his letter at six o'clock in the morning, and rising, as he says, refreshed, serene, and calm, calls to mind the time of his London life; when about that hour he used to be going to bed, surfeited with pleasure, and jaded with business; his head often full of schemes, and his heart as often full of anxiety. It was too hard, too coarse a life for the sensitive, sickly Pope. He was the only wit of the day, a friend writes to me, who wasn't fat.* Swift was fat; Addison was fat; Steele was fat; Gay and Thomson were preposterously fat — all that fuddling and punch-drinking, that club and coffee-house boozing, shortened the lives and enlarged the waistcoats of the men of that age. Pope withdrew in a great measure from this boisterous London company, and being put into an independence by the gallant exertions of Swift† and his private friends, and by the enthusiastic national admiration which justly rewarded his great achievement of the "Iliad," purchased that famous villa of Twickenham which his song and life celebrated; duteously bringing his old parents to live and die there, entertaining his friends there, and making occasional visits to London in his little chariot, in which Atterbury compared him to "Homer in a nutshell."

"Mr. Dryden was not a genteel man," Pope quaintly said to Spence, speaking of the manner and habits of the famous old patriarch of "Will's." With regard to Pope's own manners, we have the best contemporary authority that they were singularly refined and polished. With his extraordinary sensibility, with his known tastes, with his delicate frame,

* "LORD BOLINGBROKE TO THE THREE YAHOOS OF TWICKENHAM.

"*July* 23, 1726.

"JONATHAN, ALEXANDER, JOHN, MOST EXCELLENT TRIUMVIRS OF PARNASSUS, —

"Though you are probably very indifferent where I am, or what I am doing, yet I resolve to believe the contrary. I persuade myself that you have sent at least fifteen times within this fortnight to Dawley farm, and that you are extremely mortified at my long silence. To relieve you, therefore, from this great anxiety of mind, I can do no less than write a few lines to you; and I please myself beforehand with the vast pleasure which this epistle must needs give you. That I may add to this pleasure, and give further proofs of my beneficent temper, I will likewise inform you, that I shall be in your neighborhood again, by the end of next week: by which time I hope that Jonathan's imagination of business will be succeeded by some imagination more becoming a professor of that divine science, *la bagatelle*. Adieu. Jonathan, Alexander, John, mirth be with you!"

* Prior must be excepted from this observation. "He was lank and lean."

† Swift exerted himself very much in promoting the "Iliad" subscription; and also introduced Pope to Harley and Bolingbroke. — Pope realized by the "Iliad" upwards of 5,000*l.*, which he laid out partly in annuities, and partly in the purchase of his famous villa. Johnson remarks that "it would be hard to find a man so well entitled to notice by his wit, that ever delighted so much in talking of his money."

with his power and dread of ridicule, Pope could have been no other than what we call a highly-bred person.* His closest friends, with the exception of Swift, were among the delights and ornaments of the polished society of their age. Garth,† the accomplished and benevolent, whom Steele has described so charmingly, of whom Codrington said that his character was "all beauty," and whom Pope himself called the best of Christians without knowing it; Arbuthnot,‡ one of the wisest, wittiest, most accomplished, gentlest of mankind; Bolingbroke, the Alcibiades of his age; the generous Oxford; the magnificent, the witty, the famous, and chivalrous Peterborough: these were the fast and faithful friends of Pope, the most brilliant company of friends, let us repeat, that the world has ever seen. The favorite recreation of his leisure hours was the society of painters, whose art he practised. In his correspondence are letters between him and Jervas, whose pupil he loved to be — Richardson, a celebrated art-

* "His (Pope's) voice in common conversation was so naturally musical, that I remember honest Tom Southerne used always to call him 'the little nightingale.'" — ORRERY.

† Garth, whom Dryden calls "generous as his Muse," was a Yorkshireman. He graduated at Cambridge, and was made M.D. in 1691. He soon distinguished himself in his profession, by his poem of "The Dispensary," and in society, and pronounced Dryden's funeral oration. He was a strict Whig, a notable member of the "Kit-Cat," and a friendly, convivial, able man. He was knighted by George I., with the Duke of Marlborough's sword. He died in 1718.

‡ "Arbuthnot was the son of an Episcopal clergyman in Scotland, and belonged to an ancient and distinguished Scotch family. He was educated at Aberdeen; and, coming up to London — according to a Scotch practice often enough alluded to — to make his fortune — first made himself known by 'An Examination of Dr. Woodward's account of the Deluge.' He became physician successively to Prince George of Denmark and to Queen Anne. He is usually allowed to have been the most learned, as well as one of the most witty and humorous members of the Scriblerus Club. The opinion entertained of him by the humorists of the day is abundantly evidenced in their correspondence. When he found himself in his last illness, he wrote thus, from his retreat at Hampstead, to Swift: —

"*Hampstead, Oct.* 4, 1734.

"'MY DEAR AND WORTHY FRIEND, —

"'You have no reason to put me among the rest of your forgetful friends, for I wrote two long letters to you, to which I never received one word of answer. The first was about your health; the last I sent a great while ago, by one De la Mar. I can assure you with great truth that none of your friends or acquaintance has a more warm heart towards you than myself. I am going out of this troublesome world, and you, among the rest of my friends, shall have my last prayers and good wishes.

"'. . . I came out to this place so reduced by a dropsy and an asthma, that I could neither sleep, breathe, eat, nor move. I most earnestly desired and begged of God that he would take me. Contrary to my expectation, upon venturing to ride (which I had forborne for some years), I recovered my strength to a pretty considerable degree, slept, and had my stomach again. . . . What I did, I can assure you was not for life, but ease; for I am at present in the case of a man that was almost in harbor, and then blown back to sea — who has a reasonable hope of going to a good place, and an absolute certainty of leaving a very bad one. Not that I have any particular disgust at the world; for I have as great comfort in my own family and from the kindness of my friends as any man; but the world, in the main, displeases me, and I have too true a presentiment of calamities that are to befall my country. However, if I should have the happiness to see you before I die, you will find that I enjoy the comforts of life with my usual cheerfulness. I cannot imagine why you are frightened from a journey to England: the reasons you assign are not sufficient — the journey I am sure would do you good. In general, I recommend riding, of which I have always had a good opinion, and can now confirm it from my own experience.

"'My family give you their love and service. The great loss I sustained in one of them gave me my first shock, and the trouble I have with the rest to bring them to a right temper to bear the loss of a father who loves them, and whom they love, is really a most sensible affliction to me. I am afraid, my dear friend, we shall never see one another more in this world. I shall, to the last moment, preserve my love and esteem for you, being well assured you will never leave

ist of his time, and who painted for him a portrait of his old mother, and for whose picture he asked and thanked Jervas in one of the most delightful letters that ever was penned,* — and the wonderful Kneller, who bragged more, spelt worse, and painted better than any artist of his day.*

It is affecting to note, through Pope's correspondence, the marked way in which his friends, the greatest, the most famous, and wittiest men of the time — generals and statesmen, philosophers and divines — all have a kind word and a kind thought for the good simple old mother, whom Pope tended so affectionately. Those men would have scarcely valued her, but that they knew how much he loved her, and that they pleased him by thinking of her. If his early letters to women are affected and insincere, whenever he speaks about this one, it is with a childish tenderness and an almost sacred simplicity. In 1713, when young Mr. Pope had, by a series of the most astonishing victories and dazzling achievements, seized the crown of poetry, and the town was in an uproar of admiration, or hostility, for the young chief; when Pope was issuing his famous decrees for the translation of the "Iliad;" when Dennis and the lower critics were hooting and assailing him; when Addison and the gentlemen of his court were sneering with sickening hearts at the prodigious triumphs of the young conqueror; when Pope, in a fever of victory, and genius, and hope, and anger, was struggling through the crowd of shouting friends and furious detractors to his temple of Fame, his old mother writes from the country, "My deare," says she — "My deare, there's Mr. Blount, of Mapel Durom, dead the same day that Mr. Inglefield died.

the paths of virtue and honor; for all that is in this world is not worth the least deviation from the way. It will be great pleasure to me to hear from you sometimes; for none are with more sincerity than I am, my dear friend, your most faithful friend and humble servant.'"

"Arbuthnot," Johnson says, "was a man of great comprehension, skilful in his profession, versed in the sciences, acquainted with ancient literature, and able to animate his mass of knowledge by a bright and active imagination; a scholar with great brilliance of wit; a wit who, in the crowd of life, retained and discovered a noble ardor of religious zeal."

Dugald Stewart has testified to Arbuthnot's ability in a department of which he was particularly qualified to judge: "Let me add, that, in the list of philosophical reformers, the authors of 'Martinus Scriblerus' ought not to be overlooked. Their happy ridicule of the scholastic logic and metaphysics is universally known; but few are aware of the acuteness and sagacity displayed in their allusions to some of the most vulnerable passages in Locke's 'Essay.' In this part of the work it is commonly understood that Arbuthnot had the principal share." — *See Preliminary Dissertation to Encyclopædia Britannica*, note to p. 242, and also note B. B. B., p. 285.

* "TO MR. RICHARDSON.

"*Twickenham, June* 10, 1733.

"As I know you and I mutually desire to see one another, I hope that this day our wishes would have met, and brought you hither. And this for the very reason, which possibly might hinder you coming, that my poor mother is dead. I thank God, her death was as easy as her life was innocent; and as it cost her not a groan, or even a sigh, there is yet upon her countenance such an expression of tranquillity, nay, almost of pleasure, that it is even amiable to behold it. It would afford the finest image of a saint expired that ever painter drew; and it would be the greatest obligation which even that obliging art could ever bestow on a friend, if you could come and sketch it for me. I am sure, if there be no very precedent obstacle, you will leave any common business to do this; and I hope to see you this evening, or to-morrow morning as early, before this winter flower is faded. I will defer her interment till to-morrow night. I know you love me, or I could not have written this — I could not (at this time) have written at all. Adieu! May you die as happy! Yours," &c.

* "Mr. Pope was with Sir Godfrey Kneller one day, when his nephew, a Guinea trader, came in. 'Nephew,' said Sir Godfrey, 'you have the honor of seeing the two greatest men in the world.' — 'I don't know how great you may be,' said the Guinea man, 'but I don't like your looks: I have often bought a man much better than both of you together, all muscles and bones, for ten guineas.'" — DR. WARBURTON. *Spence's Anecdotes.*

Your sister is well; but your brother is sick. My service to Mrs. Blount, and all that ask of me. I hope to hear from you, and that you are well, which is my daily prayer; and this with my blessing." The triumph marches by, and the car of the young conqueror, the hero of a hundred brilliant victories: the fond mother sits in the quiet cottage at home and says, "I send you my daily prayers, and I bless you, my deare."

In our estimate of Pope's character, let us always take into account that constant tenderness and fidelity of affection which pervaded and sanctified his life, and never forget that maternal benediction.* It accompanied him always: his life seems purified by those artless and heartfelt prayers. And he seems to have received and deserved the fond attachment of the other members of his family. It is not a little touching to read in Spence of the enthusiastic admiration with which his half-sister regarded him, and the simple anecdote by which she illustrates her love. "I think no man was ever so little fond of money." Mrs. Rackett says about her brother, "I think my brother when he was young read more books than any man in the world;" and she falls to telling stories of his school-days, and the manner in which his master at Twyford ill-used him. "I don't think my brother knew what fear was," she continues; and the accounts of Pope's friends bear out this character for courage. When he had exasperated the dunces, and threats of violence and personal assault were brought to him, the dauntless little champion never for one instant allowed fear to disturb him, or condescended to take any guard in his daily walks, except occasionally his faithful dog to bear him company. "I had rather die at once," said the gallant little cripple, "than live in fear of those rascals."

As for his death, it was what the noble Arbuthnot asked and enjoyed for himself — a euthanasia — a beautiful end. A perfect benevolence, affection, serenity, hallowed the departure of that high soul. Even in the very hallucinations of his brain, and weaknesses of his delirium, there was something almost sacred. Spence describes him in his last days, looking up and with a rapt gaze as if something had suddenly passed before him. "He said to me, 'What's that?' pointing into the air with a very steady regard, and then looked down and said, with a smile of the greatest softness, ''Twas a vision!' He laughed scarcely ever, but his companions describe his countenance as often illuminated by a peculiar sweet smile.

"When," said Spence,* the kind anecdotist whom Johnson despised — "When I was telling Lord Bolingbroke that Mr. Pope, on every catching and recovery of his mind, was always saying something kindly of his present or absent friends; and that this was so surprising, as it seemed to me as if humanity had outlasted understanding, Lord Bolingbroke said, 'It has so,' and then added, 'I never in my life knew a man who had so tender a heart for his particular friends, or a more general friendship for mankind. I have known him these thirty years, and value myself more for that man's love

* Swift's mention of him as one

"—— whose filial piety excels
Whatever Grecian story tells,"

is well known. And a sneer of Walpole's may be put to a better use than he ever intended it for, *àpropos* of this subject. — He charitably sneers, in one of his letters, at Spence's "fondling an old mother — in imitation of Pope!"

* Joseph Spence was the son of a clergyman, near Winchester. He was a short time at Eton, and afterwards became a Fellow of New College, Oxford, a clergyman, and professor of poetry. He was a friend of Thomson's, whose reputation he aided. He published an "Essay on the Odyssey" in 1726, which introduced him to Pope. Everybody liked him. His "Anecdotes" were placed, while still in MS., at the service of Johnson and also of Malone. They were published by Mr. Singer in 1820.

than'— Here," Spence says, "St. John sunk his head, and lost his voice in tears." The sob which finishes the epitaph is finer than words. It is the cloak thrown over the father's face in the famous Greek picture, which hides the grief and heightens it.

In Johnson's "Life of Pope" you will find described, with rather a malicious minuteness, some of the personal habits and infirmities of the great little Pope. His body was crooked, he was so short that it was necessary to raise his chair in order to place him on a level with other people at table.* He was sewed up in a buckram suit every morning, and required a nurse like a child. His contemporaries reviled these misfortunes with a strange acrimony, and made his poor deformed person the butt for many a bolt of heavy wit. The facetious Mr. Dennis, in speaking of him, says, "If you take the first letter of Mr. Alexander Pope's Christian name, and the first and last letters of his surname, you have A. P. E." Pope catalogues, at the end of the Dunciad, with a rueful precision, other pretty names, besides Ape, which Dennis called him. That great critic pronounced Mr. Pope was a little ass, a fool, a coward, a Papist, and therefore a hater of Scripture, and so forth. It must be remembered that the pillory was a flourishing and popular institution in those days. Authors stood in it in the body sometimes: and dragged their enemies thither morally, hooted them with foul abuse, and assailed them with garbage of the gutter. Poor Pope's figure was an easy one for those clumsy caricaturists to draw. Any stupid hand could draw a hunchback, and write Pope underneath. They did. A libel was published against Pope, with such a frontispiece. This kind of rude jesting was an evidence not only of an ill nature, but a dull one. When a child makes a pun, or a lout breaks out into a laugh, it is some very obvious combination of words, or discrepancy of objects, which provokes the infantine satirist, or tickles the boorish wag; and many of Pope's revilers laughed, not so much because they were wicked, as because they knew no better.

Without the utmost sensibility, Pope could not have been the poet he was; and through his life, however much he protested that he disregarded their abuse, the coarse ridicule of his opponents stung and tore him. One of Cibber's pamphlets coming into Pope's hands, whilst Richardson the painter was with him, Pope turned round and said, "These things are my diversions;" and Richardson, sitting by whilst Pope perused the libel, said he saw his features "writhing with anguish." How little human nature changes! Can't one see that little figure? Can't one fancy one is reading Horace? Can't one fancy one is speaking of to-day?

The tastes and sensibilities of Pope, which led him to cultivate the society of persons of fine manners, or wit, or taste, or beauty, caused him to shrink equally from that shabby and boisterous crew which formed the rank and file of literature in his time: and he was as unjust to these men as they to him. The delicate little creature sickened at habits and company which were quite tolerable to robuster men: and in the famous feud between Pope and the Dunces, and without attributing any peculiar wrong to either, one can quite understand how the two parties should so hate each other. As I fancy, it was a sort of necessity that when Pope's triumph passed, Mr.

* He speaks of Arbuthnot's having helped him through "that long disease, my life." But not only was he so feeble as is implied in his use of the "buckram," but "it now appears," says Mr. Peter Cunningham, "from his unpublished letters, that, like Lord Hervey, he had recourse to ass's-milk for the preservation of his health." It is to his lordship's use of that simple beverage that he alludes when he says:—

"Let Sporus tremble!—A. What, that thing of silk,
Sporus, that mere white-curd of ass's milk?"

Addison and his men should look rather contemptuously down on it from their balcony; so it was natural for Dennis and Tibbald, and Webster and Cibber, and the worn and hungry pressmen in the crowd below, to howl at him and assail him. And Pope was more savage to Grub Street than Grub Street was to Pope. The thong with which he lashed them was dreadful; he fired upon that howling crew such shafts of flame and poison, he slew and wounded so fiercely, that in reading the "Dunciad" and the prose lampoons of Pope, one feels disposed to side against the ruthless little tyrant, at least to pity those wretched folks upon whom he was so unmerciful. It was Pope, and Swift to aid him, who established among us the Grub Street tradition. He revels in base descriptions of poor men's want; he gloats over poor Dennis's garret, and flannel nightcap, and red stockings; he gives instructions how to find Curll's authors, the historian at the tallow-chandler's under the blind arch in Petty France, the two translators in bed together, the poet in the cock-loft in Budge Row, whose landlady keeps the ladder. It was Pope, I fear, who contributed, more than any man who ever lived, to depreciate the literary calling. It was not an unprosperous one before that time, as we have seen; at least there were great prizes in the profession which had made Addison a Minister, and Prior an Ambassador, and Steele a Commissioner, and Swift all but a Bishop. The profession of letters was ruined by that libel of the "Dunciad." If authors were wretched and poor before, if some of them lived in haylofts, of which their landladies kept the ladders, at least nobody came to disturb them in their straw; if three of them had but one coat between them, the two remained invisible in the garret, the third, at any rate, appeared decently at the coffee-house, and paid his twopence like a gentleman. It was Pope that dragged into light all this poverty and meanness, and held up those wretched shifts and rags to public ridicule. It was Pope that has made generations of the reading world (delighted with the mischief, as who would not be that reads it?) believe that author and wretch, author and rags, author and dirt, author and drink, gin, cow-heel, tripe, poverty, duns, bailiffs, squalling children and clamorous landladies, were always associated together. The condition of authorship began to fall from the days of the "Dunciad;" and I believe in my heart that much of that obloquy which has since pursued our calling was occasioned by Pope's libels and wicked wit. Everybody read those. Everybody was familiarized with the idea of the poor devil, the author. The manner is so captivating that young authors practise it, and begin their career with satire. It is so easy to write, and so pleasant to read! to fire a shot that makes a giant wince, perhaps; and fancy one's self his conqueror. It is easy to shoot — but not as Pope did. The shafts of his satire rise sublimely: no poet's verse ever mounted higher than that wonderful flight with which the "Dunciad" concludes: * —

"She comes, she comes! the sable throne behold
Of Night primeval and of Chaos old;
Before her, Fancy's gilded clouds decay,
And all its varying rainbows die away;
Wit shoots in vain its momentary fires,
The meteor drops, and in a flash expires.
As, one by one, at dread Medea's strain
The sickening stars fade off the ethereal plain;
As Argus' eyes, by Hermes' wand oppressed,
Closed, one by one, to everlasting rest; —
Thus, at her fell approach and secret might,
Art after Art goes out, and all is night.
See skulking Faith to her old cavern fled,
Mountains of casuistry heaped o'er her head;

* "He (Johnson) repeated to us, in his forcible melodious manner, the concluding lines of the 'Dunciad.'" — BOSWELL.

Philosophy, that leaned on Heaven before,
Shrinks to her second cause and is no more.
Religion, blushing, veils her sacred fires,
And, unawares, Morality expires.
Nor public flame, nor private, dares to shine,
Nor human spark is left, nor glimpse divine.
Lo! thy dread empire, Chaos, is restored,
Light dies before thy uncreating word;
Thy hand, great Anarch, lets the curtain fall,
And universal darkness buries all."*

In these astonishing lines Pope reaches, I think, to the very greatest height which his sublime art has attained, and shows himself the equal of all poets of all times. It is the brightest ardor, the loftiest assertion of truth, the most generous wisdom, illustrated by the noblest poetic figure, and spoken in words the aptest, grandest, and most harmonious. It is heroic courage speaking: a splendid declaration of righteous wrath and war. It is the gage flung down, and the silver trumpet ringing defiance to falsehood and tyranny, deceit, dulness, superstition. It is Truth, the champion, shining and intrepid, and fronting the great world-tyrant with armies of slaves at his back. It is a wonderful and victorious single combat, in that great battle, which has always been waging since society began.

In speaking of a work of consummate art one does not try to show what it actually is, for that were vain; but what it is like, and what are the sensations produced in the mind of him who views it. And in considering Pope's admirable career, I am forced into similitudes drawn from other courage and greatness, and into comparing him with those who achieved triumphs in actual war. I think of the works of young Pope as I do of the actions of young Bonaparte or young Nelson. In their common life you will find frailties and meannesses, as great as the vices and follies of the meanest men. But in the presence of the great occasion, the great soul flashes out, and conquers transcendent. In thinking of the splendor of Pope's young victories, of his merit, unequalled as his renown, I hail and salute the achieving genius and do homage to the pen of a hero.

HOGARTH, SMOLLETT, AND FIELDING.

I SUPPOSE, as long as novels last and authors aim at interesting their public, there must always be in the story a virtuous and gallant hero, a wicked monster his opposite, and a pretty girl who finds a champion; bravery and virtue conquer beauty; and vice, after seeming to triumph through a certain number of pages, is sure to be discomfited in the last volume, when justice overtakes him and honest folks come by their own. There never was perhaps a greatly popular story but this simple plot was carried through it: mere satiric wit is addressed to a class of readers and thinkers quite different to those simple souls who laugh and weep over the novel. I fancy very few ladies indeed, for instance, could be brought to like "Gulliver" heartily, and (putting the coarseness and difference

* "Mr. Langton informed me that he once related to Johnson (on the authority of Spence), that Pope himself admired these lines so much that when he repeated them his voice faltered. 'And well it might, sir,' said Johnson, 'for they are noble lines.'"—J. BOSWELL, junior.

HOGARTH.

of manners out of the question) to relish the wonderful satire of "Jonathan Wild." In that strange apologue, the author takes for a hero the greatest rascal, coward, traitor, tyrant, hypocrite, that his wit and experience, both large in this matter, could enable him to devise or depict; he accompanies this villain through all the actions of his life, with a grinning deference and a wonderful mock respect: and doesn't leave him, till he is dangling at the gallows, when the satirist makes him a low bow, and wishes the scoundrel good day.

It was not by satire of this sort, or by scorn and contempt, that Hogarth achieved his vast popularity and acquired his reputation.* His art is quite simple,† he speaks popular parables to interest simple hearts, and to inspire them with pleasure or pity or warning and terror. Not one of his tales but is as easy as "Goody Twoshoes;" it is the moral of Tommy was a naughty boy and the master flogged him, and Jacky was a good boy and had plum-cake, which pervades the whole works of the homely and famous English moralist. And if the moral is written in rather too large letters after the fable, we must remember how simple the scholars and schoolmaster both were, and like

* Coleridge speaks of the "beautiful female faces" in Hogarth's pictures, "in whom," he says, "the satirist never extinguished that love of beauty which belonged to him as a poet."—*The Friend.*

† "I was pleased with the reply of a gentleman, who, being asked which book he esteemed most in his library, answered 'Shakspeare:' being asked which he esteemed next best, replied 'Hogarth.' His graphic representations are indeed books: they have the teeming, fruitful, suggestive meaning of *words.* Other pictures we look at—his prints we read. . . .

"The quantity of thought which Hogarth crowds into every picture would almost unvulgarize every subject which he might choose. . . .

"I say not that all the ridiculous subjects of Hogarth have necessarily something in them to make us like them; some are indifferent to us, some in their nature repulsive, and only made interesting by the wonderful skill and truth to nature in the painter; but I contend that there is in most of them that sprinkling of the better nature, which, like holy water, chases away and disperses the contagion of the bad. They have this in them, besides, that they bring us acquainted with the every-day human face,—they give us skill to detect those gradations of sense and virtue (which escape the careless or fastidious observer) in the circumstances of the world about us; and prevent that disgust at common life, that *tædium quotidianarum formarum,* which an unrestricted passion for ideal forms and beauties is in danger of producing. In this, as in many other things, they are analogous to the best novels of Smollett and Fielding."—CHARLES LAMB.

"It has been observed that Hogarth's pictures are exceedingly unlike any other other representations of the same kind of subjects—that they form a class, and have a character, peculiar to themselves. It may be worth while to consider in what this general distinction consists.

"In the first place, they are, in the strictest sense, *historical* pictures; and if what Fielding says be true, that his novel of 'Tom Jones' ought to be regarded as an epic prose-poem, because it contained a regular development of fable, manners, character, and passion, the compositions of Hogarth will, in like manner, be found to have a higher claim to the title of epic pictures than many which have of late arrogated that denomination to themselves. When we say that Hogarth treated his subject historically, we mean that his works represent the manners and humors of mankind in action, and their characters by varied expression. Every thing in his pictures has life and motion in it. Not only does the business of the scene never stand still, but every feature and muscle is put into full play; the exact feeling of the moment is brought out, and carried to its utmost height, and then instantly seized and stamped on the canvas forever. The expression is always taken *en passant,* in a state of progress or change, and, as it were, at the salient point. . . . His figures are not like the back-ground on which they are painted: even the pictures on the wall have a peculiar look of their own. Again, with the rapidity, variety, and scope of history, Hogarth's heads have all the reality and correctness of portraits. He gives the extremes of character and expression, but he gives them with perfect truth and accuracy. This is, in fact, what distinguishes his compositions from all others of the same kind, that they are equally remote from caricature, and from mere still life. . . . His faces go to the very verge of caricature, and yet never (we believe in any single instance) go beyond it."—HAZLITT.

neither the less because they are so artless and honest. "It was a maxim of Dr. Harrison's," Fielding says, in "Amelia," — speaking of the benevolent divine and philosopher who represents the good principle in that novel — "that no man can descend below himself, in doing any act which may contribute to protect an innocent person, *or to bring a rogue to the gallows*." The moralists of that age had no compunction, you see; they had not begun to be sceptical about the theory of punishment, and thought that the hanging of a thief was a spectacle for edification. Masters sent their apprentices, fathers took their children, to see Jack Sheppard or Jonathan Wild hanged, and it was as undoubting subscribers to this moral law, that Fielding wrote and Hogarth painted. Except in one instance, where, in the mad-house scene in "The Rake's Progress," the girl whom he has ruined is represented as still tending and weeping over him in his insanity, a glimpse of pity for his rogues never seems to enter honest Hogarth's mind. There's not the slightest doubt in the breast of the jolly Draco.

The famous set of pictures called "Marriage à la Mode," and which are now exhibited in the National Gallery in London, contains the most important and highly wrought of the Hogarth comedies. The care and method with which the moral grounds of these pictures are laid is as remarkable as the wit and skill of the observing and dexterous artist. He has to describe the negotiations for a marriage pending between the daughter of a rich citizen Alderman and young Lord Viscount Squanderfield, the dissipated son of a gouty old Earl. Pride and pomposity appear in every accessory surrounding the Earl. He sits in gold lace and velvet — as how should such an Earl wear any thing but velvet and gold lace? His coronet is everywhere: on his footstool, on which reposes one gouty toe turned out; on the sconces and looking-glasses; on the dogs; on his lordship's very crutches; on his great chair of state and the great baldaquin behind him; under which he sits pointing majestically to his pedigree, which shows that his race is sprung from the loins of William the Conqueror, and confronting the old Alderman from the City, who has mounted his sword for the occasion, and wears his Alderman's chain, and has brought a bag full of money, mortgage-deeds, and thousand-pound notes, for the arrangement of the transaction pending between them. Whilst the steward (a Methodist — therefore a hypocrite and cheat: for Hogarth scorned a Papist and a Dissenter) is negotiating between the old couple, their children sit together, united but apart. My lord is admiring his countenance in the glass, while his bride is twiddling her marriage-ring on her pocket-handkerchief, and listening with rueful countenance to Counsellor Silvertongue, who has been drawing the settlements. The girl is pretty, but the painter, with a curious watchfulness, has taken care to give her a likeness to her father; as in the young Viscount's face you see a resemblance to the Earl, his noble sire. The sense of the coronet pervades the picture, as it is supposed to do the mind of its wearer. The pictures round the room are sly hints indicating the situation of the parties about to marry. A martyr is led to the fire; Andromeda is offered to sacrifice; Judith is going to slay Holofernes. There is the ancestor of the house (in the picture it is the Earl himself as a young man), with a comet over his head, indicating that the career of the family is to be brilliant and brief. In the second picture, the old lord must be dead, for Madam has now the Countess's coronet over her bed and toilet-glass, and sits listening to that dangerous Counsellor Silvertongue, whose portrait now actually hangs up in her room, whilst the counsellor takes his ease on the sofa by her side, evidently the familiar of the house, and the confidant of the mistress. My lord takes his pleasure elsewhere than at home, whither he returns jaded and tipsy from the "Rose," to find his wife yawning in her drawing-room, her whist-party over, and the daylight streaming in; or he amuses himself with the very worst company abroad, whilst his wife sits at home listening to foreign singers, or wastes her money at auctions, or, worse still, seeks amusement at masquerades. The dismal end is known. My lord draws upon the counsellor, who kills him, and is apprehended whilst endeavoring to escape. My lady goes back perforce to the Alderman in the City, and faints upon reading Counsellor Silvertongue's dying speech at Tyburn, where the counsellor has been executed for sending his lordship out of the world. Moral: — Don't listen to evil silver-tongued counsellors: don't marry a man for his rank, or a woman for her money: don't frequent foolish auctions and masquerade balls unknown to your husband: don't have wicked companions abroad and neglect your wife, otherwise you will be run through the body, and ruin will ensue, and disgrace, and Tyburn. The people are all naughty, and Bogey carries them all off. In "The Rake's Progress," a loose life is ended by a similar sad catastrophe. It is the spendthrift coming into possession of the wealth of the paternal miser; the prodigal surrounded by flatterers, and wasting his substance on the very worst company; the bailiffs, the gambling-house, and Bedlam for an end. In the famous story of "Industry and Idleness," the moral is pointed in a manner similarly clear. Fair-haired Frank Goodchild smiles at his work, whilst naughty Tom Idle snores over his loom. Frank reads the edifying ballads of "Whittington" and "The London 'Prentice," whilst that reprobate Tom Idle prefers "Moll Flanders," and drinks hugely of beer. Frank goes to church of a Sunday, and warbles hymns from the gallery; while Tom lies on a tombstone outside playing at "halfpenny under the hat" with street blackguards, and is deservedly caned by the beadle. Frank is made overseer of the business, whilst Tom is sent to sea. Frank is taken into partnership and marries his master's daughter, sends out broken victuals to the poor, and listens in his nightcap and gown, with the lovely Mrs. Goodchild by his side, to the nuptial music of the City bands and the marrow-bones and cleavers; whilst idle Tom, returned from sea, shudders in a garret lest the officers are coming to take him for picking pockets. The Worshipful Francis Goodchild, Esq., becomes Sheriff of London, and partakes of the most splendid dinners which money can purchase or Aldermen devour; whilst poor Tom is taken up in a night-cellar, with that one-eyed and disreputable accomplice who first taught him to play chuck-farthing on a Sunday. What happens next? Tom is brought up before the justice of his country, in the person of Mr. Alderman Goodchild, who weeps as he recognizes his old brother 'prentice, as Tom's one-eyed friend peaches on him, and the clerk makes out the poor rogue's ticket for Newgate. Then the end comes. Tom goes to Tyburn in a cart with a coffin in it; whilst the Right Honorable Francis Goodchild, Lord Mayor of London, proceeds to his Mansion House in his gilt coach with four footmen and a sword-bearer, whilst the Companies of London march in the august procession, whilst the trainbands of the City fire their pieces and get drunk in his honor; and — O crowning delight and glory of all — whilst his Majesty the King looks out from his royal balcony, with his ribbon on his breast, and his Queen and his star by his side, at the corner house of St. Paul's Churchyard.

How the times have changed! The new Post Office now not disadvantageously occupies that spot where the scaffolding is in the picture, where the tipsy trainband-man is lurching against the post, with his wig over one eye, and the 'prentice-boy is trying to kiss the pretty girl in the gallery. Passed away 'prentice-boy and pretty girl! Passed away tipsy train-band-man with wig and bandolier! On the spot where Tom Idle (for whom I have an unaffected pity) made his exit from this wicked world, and where you see the hangman smoking his pipe as he reclines on the gibbet and views the hills of Harrow or Hampstead beyond, a splendid marble arch, a vast and modern city — clean, airy, painted drab, populous with nursery-maids and children, the abode of wealth and comfort — the elegant, the prosperous, the polite Tyburnia rises, the most respectable district in the habitable globe!

In that last plate of the London Apprentices, in which the apotheosis of the Right Honorable Francis Goodchild is drawn, a ragged fellow is represented in the corner of the simple, kindly piece, offering for sale a broadside, purporting to contain an account of the appearance of the ghost of Tom Idle, executed at Tyburn. Could Tom's ghost have made its appearance in 1847, and not in 1747, what changes would have been remarked by that astonished escaped criminal! Over that road which the hangman used to travel constantly, and the Oxford stage twice a week, go ten thousand carriages every day: over yonder road, by which Dick Turpin fled to Windsor, and Squire Western journeyed into town, when he came to take up his quarters at "The Hercules Pillars" on the outskirts of London, what a rush of civilization and order flows now! What armies of gentlemen with umbrellas march to banks, and chambers, and counting-houses! What regiments of nursery-maids and pretty infantry; what peaceful processions of policemen, what light broughams and what gay carriages, what swarms of busy apprentices and artificers, riding on omnibus-roofs, pass daily and hourly! Tom Idle's times are quite changed: many of the institutions gone into disuse which were admired in his day. There's more pity and kindness and a better chance for poor Tom's successors now than at that simpler period when Fielding hanged him and Hogarth drew him.

To the student of history, these admirable works must be invaluable, as they give us the most complete and truthful picture of the manners, and even the thoughts, of the past century. We look, and see pass before us the England of a hundred years ago — the peer in his drawing-room, the lady of fashion in her apartment, foreign singers surrounding her, and the chamber filled with gewgaws in the mode of that day; the church, with its quaint florid architecture and singing congregation; the parson with his great wig, and the beadle with his cane: all these are represented before us, and we are sure of the truth of the portrait. We see how the Lord Mayor dines in state; how the prodigal drinks and sports at the bagnio; how the poor girl beats hemp in Bridewell; how the thief divides his booty and drinks his punch at the night-cellar, and how he finishes his career at the gibbet. We may depend upon the perfect accuracy of these strange and varied portraits of the bygone generation: we see one of Walpole's Members of Parliament chaired after his election, and the lieges celebrating the event, and drinking confusion to the Pretender: we see the grenadiers and trainbands of the City marching out to meet the enemy; and have before us, with sword and firelock, and white Hanoverian horse embroidered on the cap, the very figures of the men who ran away with Johnny Cope, and who conquered at Culloden. The Yorkshire wagon rolls into the inn yard; the country parson, in his jack-boots, and his bands and short cassock, comes trotting into town, and we fancy it is Parson Adams, with his sermons in his pocket. The Salisbury fly sets forth from the old "Angel" — you see the passengers entering the great heavy vehicle, up the wooden steps, their hats tied down with handkerchiefs over their faces, and under their arms, sword, hanger, and case-bottle; the landlady — apoplectic with the liquors in her own bar — is tugging at the bell; the hunchbacked postilion — he may have ridden the leaders to Humphrey Clinker—is begging a gratuity; the miser is grumbling at the bill; Jack of "The Centurion" lies on the top of the clumsy vehicle, with a soldier by his side — it may be Smollett's Jack Hatchway — it has a likeness to Lismahago. You see the suburban fair and the strolling company of actors; the pretty milk-maid singing under the windows of the enraged French musician: it is such a girl as Steele charmingly described in "The Guardian," a few years before this date, singing, under Mr. Ironside's window in Shire Lane, her pleasant carol of a May morning. You see noblemen and black-legs bawling and betting in the Cockpit: you see Garrick as he was arrayed in "King Richard;" Macheath and Polly in the dresses which they wore when they charmed our ancestors, and when noblemen in blue ribbons sat on the stage and listened to their delightful music. You see the ragged French soldiery, in their white coats and cockades, at Calais Gate: they are of the regiment, very likely, which friend Roderick Random joined before he was rescued by his preserver Monsieur de Strap, with whom he fought on the famous day of Dettingen. You see the judges on the bench; the audience laughing in the pit; the student in the Oxford theatre; the citizen on his country walk; you see Broughton the boxer, Sarah Malcolm the murderess, Simon Lovat the traitor, John Wilkes the demagogue, leering at you with that squint which has become historical, and that face which, ugly as it was, he said he could make as captivating to woman as the countenance of the handsomest beau in town. All these sights and people are with you. After looking in "The Rake's progress" at Hogarth's picture of St. James's Palace Gate, you may people the street, but little altered within these hundred years, with the gilded carriages and thronging chairmen that bore the courtiers your ancestors to Queen Caroline's drawing-room more than a hundred years ago.

What manner of man* was he

* Hogarth (whose family name was Hogart) was the grandson of a Westmoreland yeoman. His father came to London, and was an author and schoolmaster. William was born in 1698 (according to the most probable conjecture) in the parish of St. Martin, Ludgate. He was early apprenticed to an engraver of arms on plate. The following touches are from his "Anecdotes of Himself." (Edition of 1833.)

"As I had naturally a good eye, and a fondness for drawing, shows of all sorts gave me uncommon pleasure when an infant; and mimicry, common to all children, was remarkable in me. An early access to a neighboring painter drew my attention from play; and I was, at every possible opportunity, employed in making drawings. I picked up an acquaintance of the same turn, and soon learned to draw the alphabet with great correctness. My exercises, when at school, were more remarkable for the ornaments which adorned them than for the exercise itself. In the former, I soon found that blockheads with better memories could much surpass me; but for the latter I was particularly distinguished. . . .

"I thought it still more unlikely that by pursuing the common method, and copying *old* drawings, I could ever attain the power of making *new* designs, which was my first and greatest ambition. I therefore endeavored to habituate myself to the exercise of a sort of technical memory; and by repeating in my own mind the parts of which objects were composed, I could by degrees combine and put them down with my pencil. Thus, with all the drawbacks which resulted from the circumstances I have mentioned, I had one material advantage over my competitors, viz., the early habit I thus acquired of retaining in my mind's eye, without coldly copying it on the spot, whatever I intended to imitate.

"The instant I became master of my own time, I determined to qualify myself for engraving on copper. In this I readily got employment; and frontispieces to books, such as prints to 'Hudibras,' in twelves, &c., soon brought me into the

who executed these portraits — so various, so faithful, and so admirable?

In the National Collection of Pictures most of us have seen the best and

way. But the tribe of booksellers remained as my father had left them . . . which put me upon publishing on my own account. But here again I had to encounter a monopoly of printsellers, equally mean and destructive to the ingenious; for the first plate I published, called 'The Taste of the Town,' in which the reigning follies were lashed, had no sooner begun to take a run, than I found copies of it in the print-shops, vending at half price, while the original prints were returned to me again, and I was thus obliged to sell the plate for whatever these pirates pleased to give me, as there was no place of sale but at their shops. Owing to this, and other circumstances, by engraving, until I was near thirty, I could do little more than maintain myself; *but even then, I was a punctual paymaster*.

"I then married, and" —

[But William is going too fast here. He made "a stolen union," on March 23, 1729, with Jane, daughter of Sir James Thornhill, sergeant-painter. For some time Sir James kept his heart and his purse-strings close, but "soon after became both reconciled and generous to the young couple." — *Hogarth's Works*, by NICHOLS and STEEVENS, vol. i. p. 44.]

"— commenced painter of small Conversation Pieces, from twelve to fifteen inches high. This, being a novelty, succeeded for a few years."

[About this time Hogarth had summer lodgings at South Lambeth, and did all kinds of work, "embellishing" the "Spring Gardens" at "Vauxhall," and the like. In 1731, he published a satirical plate against Pope, founded on the well-known imputation against him of his having satirized the Duke of Chandos, under the name of *Timon*, in his poem on "Taste." The plate represented a view of Burlington House, with Pope white-washing it, and bespattering the Duke of Chandos's coach. Pope made no retort, and has never mentioned Hogarth.]

"Before I had done any thing of much consequence in this walk, I entertained some hopes of succeeding in what the puffers in books call *The Great Style of History Painting*; so that without having had a stroke of this *grand* business before, I quitted small portraits and familiar conversations, and with a smile at my own temerity, commenced history-painter, and on a great staircase at St. Bartholomew's Hospital, painted two Scripture stories, the 'Pool of Bethesda' and the 'Good Samaritan,' with features seven feet high. . . . But as religion, the great promoter of this style in other countries, rejected it in England, I was unwilling to sink into a *portrait manufacturer*; and still ambitious of being singular, dropped all expectations of advantage from that source, and returned to the pursuit of my former dealings with the public at large.

"As to portrait-painting, the chief branch of the art by which a painter can procure himself a tolerable livelihood, and the only one by which a lover of money can get a fortune, a man of very moderate talents may have great success in it, as the artifice and address of a mercer is infinitely more useful than the abilities of a painter. By the manner in which the present race of professors in England conduct it, that also becomes still life."

. . . .

"By this inundation of folly and puff" (*he has been speaking of the success of Vanloo, who came over here in* 1737), "I must confess I was much disgusted, and determined to try if by any means I could stem the torrent, and, *by opposing, end it*. I laughed at the pretensions of these quacks in coloring, ridiculed their productions as feeble and contemptible, and asserted that it required neither taste nor talents to excel their most popular performances. This interference excited much enmity, because, as my opponents told me, my studies were in another way. 'You talk,' added they, 'with ineffable contempt of portrait-painting; if it is so easy a task, why do not you convince the world, by painting a portrait yourself?' Provoked at this language, I, one day at the Academy in St. Martin's Lane, put the following question: 'Supposing any man, at this time, were to paint a portrait as well as Vandyke, would it be seen or acknowledged, and could the artist enjoy the benefit or acquire the reputation due to his performance?'

"They asked me in reply, If I could paint one as well? and I frankly answered, I believed I could. . . .

"Of the mighty talents said to be requisite for portrait-painting I had not the most exalted opinion."

Let us now hear him on the question of the Academy: —

"To pester the three great estates of the empire, about twenty or thirty students drawing after a man or a horse, appears, as must be acknowledged, foolish enough: but the real motive is, that a few bustling characters, who have access to people of rank, think they can thus get a superiority over their brethren, be appointed to places, and have salaries, as in France, for telling a lad when a leg or an arm is too long or too short. . . .

"France, ever aping the magnificence of other nations, has in its turn assumed a foppish kind of splendor sufficient to dazzle the eyes of the neighboring states,

most carefully finished series of his comic paintings, and the portrait of his own honest face, of which the bright blue eyes shine out from the canvas, and give you an idea of that keen and brave look with which William Hogarth regarded the world. No man was ever less of a hero; you see him before you, and can fancy what he was — a jovial, honest London citizen, stout and sturdy; a hearty, plain-spoken man,* loving

and draw vast sums of money from this country. . . .

"To return to our Royal Academy: I am told that one of their leading objects will be, sending young men abroad to study the antique statues, for such kind of studies may sometimes improve an exalted genius, but they will not create it; and whatever has been the cause, this same travelling to Italy has, in several instances that I have seen, reduced the student from nature, and led him to paint marble figures, in which he has availed himself of the great works of antiquity, as a coward does when he puts on the armor of an Alexander; for, with similar pretensions and similar vanity, the painter supposes he shall be adored as a second Raphael Urbino."

We must now hear him on his "Sigismunda:" —

"As the most violent and virulent abuse thrown on 'Sigismunda' was from a set of miscreants, with whom I am proud of having been ever at war — I mean the expounders of the mysteries of old pictures — I have been sometimes told they were beneath my notice. This is true of them individually; but as they have access to people of rank, who seem as happy in being cheated as these *merchants* are in cheating them, they have a power of doing much mischief to a modern artist. However mean the vendor of poisons, the mineral is destructive: — to me its operation was troublesome enough. Ill nature spreads so fast that now was the time for every little dog in the profession to bark!"

Next comes a characteristic account of his controversy with Wilkes and Churchill.

"The stagnation rendered it necessary that I should do some *timed thing*, to recover my lost time, and stop a gap in my income. This drew forth my print of 'The Times,' a subject which tended to the restoration of peace and unanimity, and put the opposers of these humane objects in a light which gave great offence to those who were trying to foment disaffection in the minds of the populace. One of the most notorious of them, till now my friend and flatterer, attacked me in 'The North Briton,' in so infamous and malign a style, that he himself, when pushed even by his best friends, was driven to so poor an excuse as to say he was drunk when he wrote it. . . .

"This renowned patriot's portrait drawn like as I could as to features, and marked with some indications of his mind, fully answered my purpose. The ridiculous was apparent to every eye! A Brutus! A saviour of his country with such an aspect — was so arrant a farce, that though it gave rise to much laughter in the lookers-on, galled both him and his adherents to the bone. . . .

"Churchill, Wilkes's toad-echo, put 'The North Briton' into verse, in an Epistle to Hogarth; but as the abuse was precisely the same, except a little poetical heightening, which goes for nothing, it made no impression. . . . However, having an old plate by me, with some parts ready, such as the background and a dog, I began to consider how I could turn so much work laid aside to some account, and so patched up a print of Master Churchill in the character of a Bear. The pleasure and pecuniary advantage which I derived from these two engravings, together with occasionally riding on horseback, restored me to as much health as can be expected at my time of life."

* "It happened in the early part of Hogarth's life, that a nobleman who was uncommonly ugly and deformed came to sit to him for his picture. It was executed with a skill that did honor to the artist's abilities; but the likeness was rigidly observed, without even the necessary attention to compliment or flattery. The peer, disgusted at this counterpart of himself, never once thought of paying for a reflection that would only disgust him with his deformities. Some time was suffered to elapse before the artist applied for his money; but afterwards many applications were made by him (who had then no need of a banker) for payment, without success. The painter, however, at last hit upon an expedient. . . . It was couched in the following card: —

"'Mr. Hogarth's dutiful respects to Lord ——. Finding that he does not mean to have the picture which was drawn for him, is informed again of Mr. Hogarth's necessity for the money. If, therefore, his Lordship does not send for it, in three days it will be disposed of, with the addition of a tail, and some other little appendages, to Mr. Hare, the famous wild-beast man: Mr. Hogarth having given that gentleman a conditional promise of it, for an exhibition-picture, on his Lordship's refusal.'

"This intimation had the desired effect." — *Works*, by NICHOLS and STEEVENS, vol. i. p. 25.

his laugh, his friend, his glass, his roast-beef of Old England, and having a proper *bourgeois* scorn for French frogs, for mounseers, and wooden shoes in general, for foreign fiddlers, foreign singers, and, above all, for foreign painters whom he held in the most amusing contempt.

It must have been great fun to hear him rage against Correggio and the Carracci; to watch him thump the table and snap his fingers, and say "Historical painters be hanged: here's the man that will paint against any of them for a hundred pounds. Correggio's 'Sigismunda!' Look at Bill Hogarth's 'Sigismunda;' look at my altar-piece at St. Mary Redcliffe, Bristol; look at my 'Paul before Felix,' and see whether I'm not as good as the best of them."*

Posterity has not quite confirmed honest Hogarth's opinion about his talents for the sublime. Although Swift could not see the difference between tweedle-dee and tweedle-dum, posterity has not shared the Dean's contempt for Handel; the world has discovered a difference between tweedle-dee and tweedle-dum, and given a hearty applause and admiration to Hogarth, too, but not exactly as a painter of scriptural subjects, or as a rival of Correggio. It does not take away from one's liking for the man, or from the moral of his story, or the humor of it — from one's admiration for the prodigious merit of his performances, to remember that he persisted to the last in believing that the world was in a conspiracy against him with respect to his talents as an historical painter, and that a set of miscreants, as he called them, were employed to run his genius down. They say it was Liston's firm belief, that he was a great and neglected tragic actor; they say that every one of us believes in his heart, or would like to have others believe, that he is something which he is not. One of the most notorious of the "miscreants," Hogarth says, was Wilkes, who assailed him in "The North Briton;" the other was Churchill, who put "The North Briton" attack into heroic verse, and published his "Epistle to Hogarth." Hogarth replied by that caricature of Wilkes, in which the patriot still figures before us, with his Satanic grin and squint, and by a caricature of Churchill, in which he is represented as a bear with a staff, on which, lie the first, lie the second — lie the tenth, are engraved in unmistakable letters. There is very little mistake about honest Hogarth's satire: if he has to paint a man with his throat cut, he draws him with his head almost off; and he tried to do the same for his enemies in this little controversy. "Having an old plate by me," says he, "with some parts ready, such as the background, and a dog, I began to consider how I could turn so much work laid aside to some account, and so patched up a print of Master Churchill, in the character of a bear; the pleasure and pecuniary advantage which I derived from these two engravings, together with occasionally riding on horseback, restored me to as much

* "Garrick himself was not more ductile to flattery. A word in favor of 'Sigismunda' might have commanded a proof-print or forced an original print out of our artist's hands." . . .

"The following authenticated story of our artist (furnished by the late Mr. Belchior, F.R.S., a surgeon of eminence) will also serve to show how much more easy it is to detect ill-placed or hyperbolical adulation respecting others, than when applied to ourselves. Hogarth, being at dinner with the great Cheselden and some other company, was told that Mr. John Freke, surgeon of St. Bartholomew's Hospital, a few evenings before at Dick's Coffee-House, had asserted that Greene was as eminent in composition as Handel. 'That fellow Freke,' replied Hogarth, 'is always shooting his bolt absurdly, one way or another. Handel is a giant in music; Greene only a light Florimel kind of a composer.' 'Ay,' says our artist's informant, 'but at the same time Mr. Freke declared you were as good a portrait-painter as Vandyke.' '*There* he was right,' adds Hogarth, 'and so, by G—, I am, give me my time and let me choose my subject.'" — *Works*, by NICHOLS and STEEVENS, vol. i. pp. 236, 237.

health as I can expect at my time of life."

And so he concludes his queer little book of Anecdotes: "I have gone through the circumstances of a life which till lately passed pretty much to my own satisfaction, and I hope in no respect injurious to any other man. This I may safely assert, that I have done my best to make those about me tolerably happy, and my greatest enemy cannot say I ever did an intentional injury. What may follow, God knows."

A queer account still exists of a holiday jaunt taken by Hogarth and four friends of his, who set out, like the redoubted Mr. Pickwick and his companions, but just a hundred years before those heroes, and made an excursion to Gravesend, Rochester, Sheerness, and adjacent places.* One of the gentlemen noted down the proceedings of the journey, for which Hogarth and a brother artist made drawings. The book is chiefly curious at this moment from showing the citizen life of those days, and the rough jolly style of merriment, not of the five companions merely, but of thousands of jolly fellows of their time. Hogarth and his friends, quitting the "Bedford Arms," Covent Garden, with a song, took water to Billingsgate, exchanging compliments with the bargemen as they went down the river. At Billingsgate, Hogarth made "a caracatura" of a facetious porter, called the Duke of Puddledock, who agreeably entertained the party with the humors of the place. Hence they took a Gravesend boat for themselves; had straw to lie upon, and a tilt over their heads, they say, and went down the river at night, sleeping, and singing jolly choruses.

They arrived at Gravesend at six, when they washed their faces and hands, and had their wigs powdered. Then they sallied forth for Rochester on foot, and drank by the way three pots of ale. At one o'clock they went to dinner with excellent port, and a quantity more beer, and afterwards Hogarth and Scott played at hop-scotch in the town hall. It would appear that they slept, most of them, in one room, and the chronicler of the party describes them all as waking at seven o'clock, and telling each other their dreams. You have rough sketches by Hogarth of the incidents of this holiday excursion. The sturdy little painter is seen sprawling over a plank to a boat at Gravesend; the whole company are represented in one design, in a fisherman's room, where they had all passed the night. One gentleman in a nightcap is shaving himself; another is being shaved by the fisherman; a third, with a handkerchief over his bald pate, is taking his breakfast; and Hogarth is sketching the whole scene.

They describe at night how they returned to their quarters, drank to their friends, as usual, emptied several cans of good flip, all singing merrily.

It is a jolly party of tradesmen engaged at high jinks. These were the manners and pleasures of Hogarth, of his time very likely, of men not very refined, but honest and merry. It is a brave London citizen, with John Bull habits, prejudices, and pleasures.*

* He made this excursion in 1732, his companions being John Thornhill (son of Sir James), Scott the landscape-painter, Tothall, and Forrest.

* "Dr. Johnson made four lines once, on the death of poor Hogarth, which were equally true and pleasing; I know not why Garrick's were preferred to them:—

"'The hand of him here torpid lies,
That drew the essential forms of grace;
Here, closed in death, the attentive eyes,
That saw the manners in the face.'

"Mr. Hogarth, among the variety of kindnesses shown to me when I was too young to have a proper sense of them, was used to be very earnest that I should obtain the acquaintance, and if possible the friendship, of Dr. Johnson; whose conversation was, to the talk of other men, like Titian's painting compared to Hudson's, he said: 'but don't you tell people now that I say so,' continued he;

Of SMOLLETT's associates and manner of life the author of the admirable "Humphrey Clinker" has given us an interesting account, in that most amusing of novels.*

I have no doubt that this picture by Smollett is as faithful a one as any from the pencil of his kindred humorist, Hogarth.

We have before us, and painted by

'for the connoisseurs and I are at war, you know; and because I hate *them*, they think I hate *Titian* — and let them!' . . . Of Dr. Johnson, when my father and he were talking about him one day, 'That man,' says Hogarth, 'is not contented with believing the Bible; but he fairly resolves, I think, to believe nothing *but* the Bible. Johnson,' added he, 'though so wise a fellow, is more like King David than King Solomon, for he says in his haste, *All men are liars*.'" — MRS. PIOZZI.

Hogarth died on the 26th of October, 1764. The day before his death, he was removed from his villa at Chiswick to Leicester Fields, "in a very weak condition, yet remarkably cheerful." He had just received an agreeable letter from Franklin. He lies buried at Chiswick.

* "TO SIR WATKIN PHILLIPS, BART., OF JESUS COLLEGE, OXON.

"DEAR PHILLIPS, — In my last, I mentioned my having spent an evening with a society of authors, who seemed to be jealous and afraid of one another. My uncle was not at all surprised to hear me say I was disappointed in their conversation. 'A man may be very entertaining and instructive upon paper,' said he, 'and exceedingly dull in common discourse. I have observed, that those who shine most in private company are but secondary stars in the constellation of genius. A small stock of ideas is more easily managed, and sooner displayed, than a great quantity crowded together. There is very seldom any thing extraordinary in the appearance and address of a good writer; whereas a dull author generally distinguishes himself by some oddity or extravagance. For this reason I fancy that an assembly of grubs must be very diverting.'

"My curiosity being excited by this hint, I consulted my friend Dick Ivy, who undertook to gratify it the very next day, which was Sunday last. He carried me to dine with S——, whom you and I have long known by his writings. He lives in the skirts of the town; and every Sunday his house is open to all unfortunate brothers of the quill, whom he treats with beef, pudding, and potatoes, port, punch, and Calvert's entire butt beer. He has fixed upon the first day of the week for the exercise of his hospitality, because some of his guests could not enjoy it on any other, for reasons that I need not explain. I was civilly received in a plain, yet decent habitation, which opened backwards into a very pleasant garden, kept in excellent order; and, indeed, I saw none of the outward signs of authorship either in the house or the landlord, who is one of those few writers of the age that stand upon their own foundation, without patronage, and above dependence. If there was nothing characteristic in the entertainer, the company made ample amends for his want of singularity.

"At two in the afternoon, I found myself one of ten messmates seated at table; and I question if the whole kingdom could produce such another assemblage of originals. Among their peculiarities, I do not mention those of dress, which may be purely accidental. What struck me were oddities originally produced by affectation, and afterwards confirmed by habit. One of them wore spectacles at dinner, and another his hat flapped; though (as Ivy told me) the first was noted for having a seaman's eye when a bailiff was in the wind; and the other was never known to labor under any weakness or defect of vision, except about five years ago, when he was complimented with a couple of black eyes by a player, with whom he had quarrelled in his drink. A third wore a laced stocking, and made use of crutches, because, once in his life, he had been laid up with a broken leg, though no man could leap over a stick with more agility. A fourth had contracted such an antipathy to the country, that he insisted upon sitting with his back towards the window that looked into the garden: and when a dish of cauliflower was set upon the table, he snuffed up volatile salts to keep him from fainting; yet this delicate person was the son of a cottager, born under a hedge, and had many years run wild among asses on a common. A fifth affected distraction: when spoke to, he always answered from the purpose. Sometimes he suddenly started up, and rapped out a dreadful oath; sometimes he burst out a-laughing; then he folded his arms, and sighed; and then he hissed like fifty serpents.

"At first, I really thought he was mad; and, as he sat near me, began to be under some apprehensions for my own safety; when our landlord, perceiving me alarmed, assured me aloud that I had nothing to fear. 'The gentleman,' said he, 'is trying to act a part for which he is by no means qualified: if he had all the inclination in the world, it is not in his power to be mad; his spirits are too flat to be

his own hand, Tobias Smollett, the manly, kindly, honest, and irascible; worn and battered, but still brave and full of heart, after a long struggle

kindled into phrensy.' ''Tis no bad p-p-puff, how-owever,' observed a person in a tarnished laced coat: 'aff-ffected m-madness w-ill p-pass for w-wit w-with nine-nineteen out of t-twenty.' 'And affected stuttering for humor,' replied our landlord; 'though, God knows! there is no affinity betwixt them.' It seems this wag, after having made some abortive attempts in plain speaking, had recourse to this defect, by means of which he frequently extorted the laugh of the company, without the least expense of genius; and that imperfection, which he had at first counterfeited, was now become so habitual, that he could not lay it aside.

"A certain winking genius, who wore yellow gloves at dinner, had, on his first introduction, taken such offence at S——, because he looked and talked, and ate and drank, like any other man, that he spoke contemptuously of his understanding ever after, and never would repeat his visit, until he had exhibited the following proof of his caprice. Wat Wyvil, the poet, having made some unsuccessful advances towards an intimacy with S——, at last gave him to understand, by a third person, that he had written a poem in his praise, and a satire against his person: that if he would admit him to his house, the first should be immediately sent to press; but that if he persisted in declining his friendship, he would publish the satire without delay. S—— replied, that he looked upon Wyvil's panegyric as, in effect, a species of infamy, and would resent it accordingly with a good cudgel; but if he published the satire, he might deserve his compassion, and had nothing to fear from his revenge. Wyvil having considered the alternative, resolved to mortify S—— by printing the panegyric, for which he received a sound drubbing. Then he swore the peace against the aggressor, who, in order to avoid a prosecution at law, admitted him to his good graces. It was the singularity in S——'s conduct on this occasion, that reconciled him to the yellow-gloved philosopher, who owned he had some genius; and from that period cultivated his acquaintance.

"Curious to know upon what subjects the several talents of my fellow-guests were employed, I applied to my communicative friend, Dick Ivy, who gave me to understand that most of them were, or had been, understrappers, or journeymen, to more creditable authors, for whom they translated, collated, and compiled, in the business of bookmaking; and that all of them had, at different times, labored in the service of our landlord, though they had now set up for themselves in various departments of literature. Not only their talents, but also their nations and dialects, were so various, that our conversation resembled the confusion of tongues at Babel. We had the Irish brogue, the Scotch accent, and foreign idiom, twanged off by the most discordant vociferation; for as they all spoke together, no man had any chance to be heard, unless he could bawl louder than his fellows. It must be owned, however, there was nothing pedantic in their discourse; they carefully avoided all learned disquisitions, and endeavored to be facetious: nor did their endeavors always miscarry; some droll repartee passed, and much laughter was excited; and if any individual lost his temper so far as to transgress the bounds of decorum, he was effectually checked by the master of the feast, who exerted a sort of paternal authority over this irritable tribe.

"The most learned philosopher of the whole collection, who had been expelled the university for atheism, has made great progress in a refutation of Lord Bolingbroke's metaphysical works, which is said to be equally ingenious and orthodox: but, in the mean time, he has been presented to the grand jury as a public nuisance for having blasphemed in an alehouse on the Lord's-day. The Scotchman gives lectures on the pronunciation of the English language, which he is now publishing by subscription.

"The Irishman is a political writer, and goes by the name of My Lord Potatoe. He wrote a pamphlet in vindication of a Minister, hoping his zeal would be rewarded with some place or pension; but finding himself neglected in that quarter, he whispered about that the pamphlet was written by the Minister himself, and he published an answer to his own production. In this he addressed the author under the title of 'your lordship,' with such solemnity, that the public swallowed the deceit, and bought up the whole impression. The wise politicians of the metropolis declared they were both masterly performances, and chuckled over the flimsy reveries of an ignorant garretteer, as the profound speculations of a veteran statesman, acquainted with all the secrets of the cabinet. The imposture was detected in the sequel, and our Hibernian pamphleteer retains no part of his assumed importance but the bare title of 'my lord,' and the upper part of the table at the potato-ordinary in Shoe Lane.

"Opposite to me sat a Piedmontese, who had obliged the public with a humorous satire, entitled 'The Balance of the English Poets;' a performance which evinced the great modesty and taste of the author, and, in particular, his intimacy with the

against a hard fortune. His brain had been busied with a hundred different schemes; he had been reviewer and historian, critic, medical writer, poet, pamphleteer. He had fought endless literary battles; and braved and wielded for years the cudgels of controversy. It was a hard and savage fight in those days, and a niggard pay. He was oppressed by illness, age, narrow fortune; but his spirit was still resolute, and his courage steady; the battle over, he could do justice to the enemy with whom he had been so fiercely engaged, and give a not unfriendly grasp to the hand that had mauled him. He is like one of those Scotch cadets, of whom history gives us so many examples, and whom, with a national fidelity, the great Scotch novelist has painted so charmingly. Of gentle birth* and

elegancies of the English language. The sage, who labored under the ἀγροφοβία, or, 'horror of green fields,' had just finished a treatise on practical agriculture, though, in fact, he had never seen corn growing in his life, and was so ignorant of grain, that our entertainer, in the face of the whole company, made him own that a plate of hominy was the best rice-pudding he had ever eat.

"The stutterer had almost finished his travels through Europe and part of Asia, without ever budging beyond the liberties of the King's Bench, except in term-time with a tipstaff for his companion: and as for little Tim Cropdale, the most facetious member of the whole society, he had happily wound up the catastrophe of a virgin tragedy, from the exhibition of which he promised himself a large fund of profit and reputation. Tim had made shift to live many years by writing novels, at the rate of five pounds a volume; but that branch of business is now engrossed by female authors, who publish merely for the propagation of virtue, with so much ease, and spirit, and delicacy, and knowledge of the human heart, and all in the serene tranquillity of high life, that the reader is not only enchanted by their genius, but reformed by their morality.

"After dinner, we adjourned into the garden, where I observed Mr. S—— give a short separate audience to every individual in a small remote filbert-walk, from whence most of them dropped off one after another, without further ceremony."

Smollett's house was in Lawrence Lane, Chelsea, and is now destroyed. See *Handbook of London*, p. 115.

"The person of Smollett was eminently handsome, his features prepossessing, and, by the joint testimony of all his surviving friends, his conversation, in the highest degree, instructive and amusing. Of his disposition, those who have read his works (and who has not?) may form a very accurate estimate; for in each of them he has presented, and sometimes under various points of view, the leading features of his own character without disguising the most unfavorable of them. . . . When unseduced by his satirical propensities, he was kind, generous, and humane to others; bold, upright, and independent in his own character; stooped to no patron, sued for no favor, but honestly and honorably maintained himself on his literary labors. . . . He was a doating father, and an affectionate husband; and the warm zeal with which his memory was cherished by his surviving friends showed clearly the reliance which they placed upon his regard." — SIR WALTER SCOTT.

* Smollett of Bonhill, in Dumbartonshire. *Arms*, azure, a bend, or, between a lion rampant, ppr., holding in his paw a banner, argent, and a bugle-horn, also ppr. *Crest*, an oak-tree, ppr. *Motto*, *Viresco*.

Smollett's father, Archibald, was the fourth son of Sir James Smollett of Bonhill, a Scotch Judge and Member of Parliament, and one of the commissioners for framing the Union with England. Archibald married, without the old gentleman's consent, and died early, leaving his children dependent on their grandfather. Tobias, the second son, was born in 1721, in the old house of Dalquharn in the valley of Leven: and all his life loved and admired that valley and Loch Lomond beyond all the valleys and lakes in Europe. He learned the "rudiments" at Dumbarton Grammar School, and studied at Glasgow.

But when he was only eighteen, his grandfather died, and left him without provision (figuring as the old judge in "Roderick Random" in consequence, according to Sir Walter). Tobias, armed with "The Regicide, a Tragedy" — a provision precisely similar to that with which Dr. Johnson had started, just before — came up to London. "The Regicide" came to no good, though at first patronized by Lord Lyttleton ("one of those little fellows who are sometimes called great men," Smollett says); and Smollett embarked as "surgeon's mate" on board a line-of-battle ship, and served in the Carthagena expedition, in 1741. He left the service in the West Indies, and after residing some time in Jamaica, returned to England in 1746.

He was now unsuccessful as a physician, to begin with; published the satires,

narrow means, going out from his northern home to win his fortune in the world, and to fight his way, armed with courage, hunger, and keen wits. His crest is a shattered oak-tree, with green leaves yet springing from it. On his ancient coat-of-arms there is a lion and a horn; this shield of his was battered and dinted in a hundred fights and brawls,* through which the stout Scotchman bore it courageously. You see somehow that he is a gentleman, through all his battling and struggling, his poverty, his hard-fought successes, and his defeats. His novels are recollections of his own adventures; his characters drawn, as I should think, from personages with whom he became acquainted in his own career of life. Strange companions he must have had; queer acquaintances he made in Glasgow College — in the country apothecary's shop; in the gun-room of the man-of-war where he served as surgeon; and in the hard life on shore, where the sturdy adventurer struggled for fortune. He did not invent much, as I fancy, but had the keenest perceptive faculty, and described what he saw with wonderful relish and delightful broad humor. I think Uncle Bowl-

"Advice" and "Reproof," without any luck; and (1747) married the "beautiful and accomplished Miss Lascelles."

In 1748 he brought out his "Roderick Random," which at once made a "hit." The subsequent events of his life may be presented, chronologically, in a bird's-eye view:—

1750. Made a tour to Paris, where he chiefly wrote "Peregrine Pickle."

1751. Published "Peregrine Pickle."

1753. Published "Adventures of Ferdinand Count Fathom."

1755. Published version of "Don Quixote."

1756. Began "The Critical Review."

1738. Published his "History of England."

1763–1766. Travelling in France and Italy; published his "Travels."

1769. Published "Adventures of an Atom."

1770. Set out for Italy; died at Leghorn 21st of October, 1771, in the fifty-first year of his age.

* A good specimen of the old "slashing" style of writing is presented by the paragraph on Admiral Knowles, which subjected Smollett to prosecution and imprisonment. The admiral's defence on the occasion of the failure of the Rochfort expedition came to be examined before the tribunal of "The Critical Review."

"He is," said our author, "an admiral without conduct, an engineer without knowledge, an officer without resolution, and a man without veracity!"

Three months' imprisonment in the King's Bench avenged this stinging paragraph.

But "The Critical" was to Smollett a perpetual fountain of "hot water." Among less important controversies may be mentioned that with Grainger, the translator of "Tibullus." Grainger replied in a pamphlet; and in the next number of "The Review" we find him threatened with "castigation," as an "owl that has broken from his mew!"

In Dr. Moore's biography of him is a pleasant anecdote. After publishing the "Don Quixote," he returned to Scotland to pay a visit to his mother:—

"On Smollett's arrival, he was introduced to his mother with the connivance of Mrs. Telfer (her daughter), as a gentleman from the West Indies, who was intimately acquainted with her son. The better to support his assumed character, he endeavored to preserve a serious countenance, approaching to a frown; but while his mother's eyes were riveted on his countenance, he could not refrain from smiling: she immediately sprung from her chair, and throwing her arms round his neck, exclaimed, 'Ah, my son! my son! I have found you at last!'

"She afterwards told him, that if he had kept his austere looks, and continued to *gloom*, he might have escaped detection some time longer; but 'your old roguish smile,' added she, 'betrayed you at once.'"

"Shortly after the publication of 'The Adventures of an Atom,' disease again attacked Smollett with redoubled violence. Attempts being vainly made to obtain for him the office of Consul in some part of the Mediterranean, he was compelled to seek a warmer climate, without better means of provision than his own precarious finances could afford. The kindness of his distinguished friend and countryman, Dr. Armstrong (then abroad), procured for Dr. and Mrs. Smollett a house at Monte Nero, a village situated on the side of a mountain overlooking the sea, in the neighborhood of Leghorn, a romantic and salutary abode, where he prepared for the press, the last, and like music 'sweetest in the close,' the most pleasing of his compositions, 'The Expedition of Humphrey Clinker.' This delightful work was published in 1771." — Sir Walter Scott.

ing, in "Roderick Random," is as good a character as Squire Western himself: and Mr. Morgan, the Welsh apothecary, is as pleasant as Dr. Caius. What man who has made his inestimable acquaintance — what novel-reader who loves Don Quixote and Major Dalgetty — will refuse his most cordial acknowledgments to the admirable Lieutenant Bismahago. The novel of "Humphrey Clinker" is, I do think, the most laughable story that has ever been written since the goodly art of novel-writing began. Winifred Jenkins and Tabitha Bramble must keep Englishmen on the grin for ages yet to come; and in their letters and the story of their loves there is a perpetual fount of sparkling laughter, as inexhaustible as Bladud's well.

FIELDING, too, has described, though with a greater hand, the characters and scenes which he knew and saw. He had more than ordinary opportunities for becoming acquainted with life. His family and education, first — his fortunes and misfortunes afterwards, brought him into the society of every rank and condition of man. He is himself the hero of his books: he is wild Tom Jones, he is wild Captain Booth; less wild, I am glad to think, than his predecessor: at least heartily conscious of demerit, and anxious to amend.

When Fielding first came upon the town in 1727, the recollection of the great wits was still fresh in the coffee-houses and assemblies, and the judges there declared that young Harry Fielding had more spirits and wit than Congreve or any of his brilliant successors. His figure was tall and stalwart; his face handsome, manly, and noble-looking; to the very last days of his life he retained a grandeur of air, and, although worn down by disease, his aspect and presence imposed respect upon the people round about him.

A dispute took place between Mr. Fielding and the captain of the ship * in which he was making his last voyage, and Fielding relates how the man finally went down on his knees and begged his passenger's pardon. He was living up to the last days of his life, and his spirit never gave in. His vital power must have been immensely strong. Lady Mary Wortley Montagu † prettily characterizes Fielding and this capacity for happiness which he possessed, in a little

* The dispute with the captain arose from the wish of that functionary to intrude on his right to his cabin, for which he had paid thirty pounds. After recounting the circumstances of the apology, he characteristically adds: —

"And here, that I may not be thought the sly trumpeter of my own praises, I do utterly disclaim all praise on the occasion. Neither did the greatness of my mind dictate, nor the force of my Christianity exact, this forgiveness. To speak truth, I forgave him from a motive which would make men much more forgiving, if they were much wiser than they are; because it was convenient for me so to do."

† Lady Mary was his second-cousin — their respective grandfathers being sons of George Fielding, Earl of Desmond, son of William, Earl of Denbigh.

In a letter dated just a week before his death, she says, —

"H. Fielding has given a true picture of himself and his first wife in the characters of *Mr.* and *Mrs. Booth*, some compliments to his own figure excepted; and I am persuaded, several of the incidents he mentions are real matters of fact. I wonder he does not perceive *Tom Jones* and *Mr. Booth* are sorry scoundrels. . . . Fielding has really a fund of true humor, and was to be pitied at his first entrance into the world, having no choice, as he said himself, but to be a hackney writer or a hackney coachman. His genius deserved a better fate; but I cannot help blaming that continued indiscretion, to give it the softest name, that has run through his life, and I am afraid still remains. . . . Since I was born no original appeared excepting Congreve, and Fielding, who would, I believe, have approached nearer to his excellences, if not forced by his necessities to publish without correction, and throw many productions into the world he would have thrown into the fire, if meat could have been got without money, or money without scribbling. . . . I am sorry not to see any more of Peregrine Pickle's performances: I wish you would tell me his name." — *Letters and Works* (Lord WHARNCLIFFE'S, Ed.), vol. iii. pp. 93, 94.

notice of his death, when she compares him to Steele, who was as improvident and as happy as he was, and says that both should have gone on living forever. One can fancy the eagerness and gusto with which a man of Fielding's frame, with his vast health and robust appetite, his ardent spirits, his joyful humor, and his keen and hearty relish for life, must have seized and drunk that cup of pleasure which the town offered to him. Can any of my hearers remember the youthful feats of a college breakfast — the meats devoured and the cups quaffed in that Homeric feast? I can call to mind some of the heroes of those youthful banquets, and fancy young Fielding from Leyden, rushing upon the feast, with his great laugh and immense healthy young appetite, eager and vigorous to enjoy. The young man's wit and manners made him friends everywhere: he lived with the grand Man's society of those days; he was courted by peers and men of wealth and fashion. As he had a paternal allowance from his father, General Fielding, which, to use Henry's own phrase, any man might pay who would; as he liked good wine, good clothes, and good company, which are all expensive articles to purchase, Harry Fielding began to run into debt, and borrow money in that easy manner in which Captain Booth borrows money in the novel: was in nowise particular in accepting a few pieces from the purses of his rich friends, and bore down upon more than one of them, as Walpole tells us only too truly, for a dinner or a guinea. To supply himself with the latter, he began to write theatrical pieces, having already, no doubt, a considerable acquaintance amongst the Oldfields and Bracegirdles behind the scenes. He laughed at these pieces and scorned them. When the audience upon one occasion began to hiss a scene which he was too lazy to correct, and regarding which, when Garrick remonstrated with him, he said that the public was too stupid to find out the badness of his work: when the audience began to hiss, Fielding said, with characteristic coolness — "They have found it out, have they?" He did not prepare his novels in this way, and with a very different care and interest laid the foundations and built up the edifices of his future fame.

Time and shower have very little damaged those. The fashion and ornaments are, perhaps, of the architecture of that age; but the buildings remain strong and lofty, and of admirable proportions — masterpieces of genius and monuments of workmanlike skill.

I cannot offer or hope to make a hero of Harry Fielding. Why hide his faults? Why conceal his weaknesses in a cloud of periphrases? Why not show him, like him as he is, not robed in a marble toga, and draped and polished in an heroic attitude, but with inked ruffles, and claret-stains on his tarnished laced coat, and on his manly face the marks of good-fellowship, of illness, of kindness, of care, and wine. Stained as you see him, and worn by care and dissipation, that man retains some of the most precious and splendid human qualities and endowments. He has an admirable natural love of truth, the keenest instinctive antipathy to hypocrisy, the happiest satirical gift of laughing it to scorn. His wit is wonderfully wise and detective; it flashes upon a rogue, and lightens up a rascal like a policeman's lantern. He is one of the manliest and kindliest of human beings: in the midst of all his imperfections, he respects female innocence and infantine tenderness, as you would suppose such a great-hearted, courageous soul would respect and care for them. He could not be so brave, generous, truth-telling as he is, were he not infinitely merciful, pitiful, and tender. He will give any man his purse — he can't help kindness and profusion. He may have low tastes, but not a mean mind; he admires with all his heart good and virtuous men, stoops to no flattery, bears no rancor, disdains all disloyal arts, does his public duty uprightly, is fondly loved by his family, and dies at his work.*

If that theory be — and I have no doubt it is — the right and safe one, that human nature is always pleased with the spectacle of innocence rescued by fidelity, purity, and courage; I suppose that of the heroes of Fielding's three novels, we should like honest Joseph Andrews the best, and Captain Booth the second, and Tom Jones the third.†

Joseph Andrews, though he wears Lady Booby's cast-off livery, is, I think, to the full as polite as Tom Jones in his fustian-suit, or Captain Booth in regimentals. He has, like those heroes, large calves, broad shoulders, a high courage, and a handsome face. The accounts of Joseph's bravery and good qualities; his voice, too musical to halloo to the dogs; his bravery in riding races for the gentlemen of the county, and his constancy in refusing bribes and temptation, have something affecting in their *naïveté* and freshness, and prepossess one in favor of that handsome young hero. The rustic bloom of Fanny, and the delightful simplicity of Parson Adams, are described with a friendliness which wins the reader of their story; we part from them with more regret than from Booth and Jones.

Fielding, no doubt, began to write this novel in ridicule of "Pamela," for which work one can understand the hearty contempt and antipathy which such an athletic and boisterous genius as Fielding's must have entertained. He couldn't do otherwise than laugh at the puny cockney bookseller, pouring out endless volumes of sentimental twaddle, and hold him up to scorn as a mollcoddle and a milksop. *His* genius had been nursed on sack-posset, and not on dishes of tea. *His* muse had sung the loudest in tavern choruses, had seen the daylight streaming in over thousands of emptied bowls, and reeled home to chambers on the shoulders of the watchman. Richardson's goddess was attended by old maids and dowagers, and fed on muffins and bohea. "Milksop!" roars Harry Fielding, clattering at the timid shop-shutters. "Wretch! Monster! Mohock!" shrieks the sentimental author of "Pamela;" * and all the ladies of his court cackle out an affrighted chorus. Fielding proposes to write a book in ridicule of the author, whom he disliked and utterly scorned and laughed at; but he is himself of so generous, jovial, and kindly a turn that he begins to like the characters which he invents, can't help making them manly and pleasant as well as ridiculous, and before he has done with them all, loves them heartily every one.

Richardson's sickening antipathy for Harry Fielding is quite as natural as the other's laughter and contempt

* He sailed for Lisbon, from Gravesend, on Sunday morning, June 30th, 1754; and began "The Journal of a Voyage" during the passage. He died at Lisbon, in the beginning of October of the same year. He lies buried there, in the English Protestant churchyard, near the Estrella Church, with this inscription over him: —

"HENRICUS FIELDING.
LUGET BRITANNIA GREMIO NON DATUM
FOVERE NATUM."

† Fielding himself is said by Dr. Warton to have preferred "Joseph Andrews" to his other writings.

* "Richardson," says worthy Mrs. Barbauld, in her Memoir of him, prefixed to his Correspondence, "was exceedingly hurt at this ('Joseph Andrews'), the more so as they had been on good terms, and he was very intimate with Fielding's two sisters. He never appears cordially to have forgiven it (perhaps it was not in human nature he should), and he always speaks in his letters with a great deal of asperity of 'Tom Jones,' more indeed than was quite graceful in a rival author. No doubt he himself thought his indignation was solely excited by the loose morality of the work and of its author, but he could tolerate Cibber."

at the sentimentalist. I have not learned that these likings and dislikings have ceased in the present day: and every author must lay his account not only to misrepresentation, but to honest enmity among critics, and to being hated and abused for good as well as for bad reasons. Richardson disliked Fielding's works quite honestly: Walpole quite honestly spoke of them as vulgar and stupid. Their squeamish stomachs sickened at the rough fare and the rough guests assembled at Fielding's jolly revel. Indeed the cloth might have been cleaner: and the dinner and the company were scarce such as suited a dandy. The kind and wise old Johnson would not sit down with him.* But a greater scholar than Johnson could afford to admire that astonishing genius of Harry Fielding: and we all know the lofty panegyric which Gibbon wrote of him, and which remains a towering monument to the great novelist's memory. "Our immortal Fielding," Gibbon writes, "was of the younger branch of the Earls of Denbigh, who drew their origin from the Counts of Hapsburgh. The successors of Charles V. may disdain their brethren of England: but the romance of 'Tom Jones,' that exquisite picture of human manners, will outlive the palace of the Escurial and the Imperial Eagle of Austria."

There can be no gainsaying the sentence of this great judge. To have your name mentioned by Gibbon is like having it written on the dome of St. Peter's. Pilgrims from all the world admire and behold it.

As a picture of manners, the novel of "Tom Jones" is indeed exquisite: as a work of construction quite a wonder: the by-play of wisdom; the power of observation; the multiplied felicitous turns and thoughts; the varied character of the great Comic Epic: keep the reader in a perpetual admiration and curiosity.* But against Mr. Thomas Jones himself we have a right to put in a protest, and quarrel with the esteem the author evidently has for that character. Charles Lamb says finely of Jones, that a single hearty laugh from him "clears the air" — but then it is in a certain state of the atmosphere. It might clear the air when such personages as Blifil or Lady Bellaston poison it. But I fear very much that (except until the very last scene of the story), when Mr. Jones enters Sophia's drawing-room, the pure air there is rather tainted with the young gentleman's tobacco-pipe and punch. I can't say that I think Mr. Jones a virtuous character; I can't say but that I think Fielding's evident liking and admiration for Mr. Jones shows that the great humorist's moral sense was blunted by his life, and that here, in Art and Ethics, there is a great error. If it is right to have a hero whom we may admire, let us at least

* It must always be borne in mind, that besides that the Doctor couldn't be expected to like Fielding's wild life (to say nothing of the fact that they were of opposite sides in politics), Richardson was one of his earliest and kindest friends. Yet Johnson too (as Boswell tells us) read "Amelia" through without stopping.

* "Manners change from generation to generation, and with manners morals appear to change — actually change with some, but appear to change with all but the abandoned. A young man of the present day who should act as Tom Jones is supposed to act at Upton, with Lady Bellaston, &c., would not be a Tom Jones; and a Tom Jones of the present day, without perhaps being in the ground a better man, would have perished rather than submit to be kept by a harridan of fortune. Therefore, this novel is, and indeed pretends to be, no example of conduct. But, notwithstanding all this, I do loathe the cant which can recommend 'Pamela' and 'Clarissa Harlowe' as strictly moral, although they poison the imagination of the young with continued doses of *tinct. lyttæ*, while Tom Jones is prohibited as loose. I do not speak of young women; but a young man whose heart or feelings can be injured, or even his passions excited, by this novel, is already thoroughly corrupt. There is a cheerful, sunshiny, breezy spirit, that prevails everywhere, strongly contrasted with the close, hot, day-dreamy continuity of Richardson." — COLERIDGE: *Literary Remains*, vol. ii. p. 374.

take care that he is admirable: if, as is the plan of some authors (a plan decidedly against their interests, be it said), it is propounded that there exists in life no such being, and therefore that in novels, the picture of life, there should appear no such character; then Mr. Thomas Jones becomes an admissible person, and we examine his defects and good qualities, as we do those of Parson Thwackum or Miss Seagrim. But a hero with a flawed reputation; a hero spunging for a guinea; a hero who can't pay his landlady, and is obliged to let his honor out to hire, is absurd, and his claim to heroic rank untenable. I protest against Mr. Thomas Jones holding such rank at all. I protest even against his being considered a more than ordinary young fellow, ruddy-cheeked, broad-shouldered, and fond of wine and pleasure. He would not rob a church, but that is all; and a pretty long argument may be debated, as to which of these old types, the spendthrift, the hypocrite, Jones and Blifil, Charles and Joseph Surface, — is the worst member of society and the most deserving of censure. The prodigal Captain Booth is a better man than his predecessor Mr. Jones, in so far as he thinks much more humbly of himself than Jones did: goes down on his knees, and owns his weaknesses, and cries out, "Not for my sake, but for the sake of my pure and sweet and beautiful wife Amelia, I pray you, O critical reader, to forgive me." That stern moralist regards him from the bench (the judge's practice out of court is not here the question), and says, "Captain Booth, it is perfectly true that your life has been disreputable, and that on many occasions you have shown yourself to be no better than a scamp — you have been tippling at the tavern, when the kindest and sweetest lady in the world has cooked your little supper of boiled mutton, and awaited you all the night; you have spoiled the little dish of boiled mutton thereby, and caused pangs and pains to Amelia's tender heart.* You have got into debt without the means of paying it. You have gambled the money with which you ought to have paid your rent. You have spent in drink or in worse amusements the sums which your poor wife has raised upon her little home treasures, her own ornaments, and the toys of her children. But, you rascal! you own humbly that you are no better than you should be; you never for one moment pretend that you are any thing but a miserable weak-minded rogue. You do in your heart adore that

* "Nor was she (Lady Mary Wortley Montagu) a stranger to that beloved first wife, whose picture he drew in his 'Amelia,' when, as she said, even the glowing language he knew how to employ, did not do more than justice to the amiable qualities of the original, or to her beauty, although this had suffered a little from the accident related in the novel — a frightful overturn, which destroyed the gristle of her nose. He loved her passionately, and she returned his affection. . . .

"His biographers seem to have been shy of disclosing, that, after the death of this charming woman, he married her maid. And yet the act was not so discreditable to his character as it may sound. The maid had few personal charms, but was an excellent creature, devotedly attached to her mistress, and almost broken-hearted for her loss. In the first agonies of his own grief, which approached to frenzy, he found no relief but from weeping along with her; nor solace, when a degree calmer, but in talking to her of the angel they mutually regretted. This made her his habitual confidential associate, and in process of time he began to think he could not give his children a tenderer mother, or secure for himself a more faithful housekeeper and nurse. At least, this was what he told his friends; and it is certain that her conduct as his wife confirmed it, and fully justified his good opinion." — *Letters and Works of Lady Mary Wortley Montagu.* Edited by Lord WHARNCLIFFE. *Introductory Anecdotes,* vol. i. pp. 80, 81.

Fielding's first wife was Miss Craddock, a young lady from Salisbury, with a fortune of 1,500*l.*, whom he married in 1736. About the same time he succeeded, himself, to an estate of 200*l.* per annum, and on the joint amount he lived for some time as a splendid country gentleman in Derbyshire. Three years brought him to the end of his fortune; when he returned to London, and became a student of law.

angelic woman, your wife, and for her sake, sirrah, you shall have your discharge. Lucky for you and for others like you, that, in spite of your failings and imperfections, pure hearts pity and love you. For your wife's sake you are permitted to go hence without a remand; and I beg you, by the way, to carry to that angelical lady the expression of the cordial respect and admiration of this court." Amelia pleads for her husband, Will Booth: Amelia pleads for her reckless kindly old father, Harry Fielding. To have invented that character is not only a triumph of art, but it is a good action. They say it was in his own home that Fielding knew her and loved her: and from his own wife that he drew the most charming character in English fiction. Fiction! why fiction? why not history? I know Amelia just as well as Lady Mary Wortley Montagu. I believe in Colonel Bath almost as much as in Colonel Gardiner or the Duke of Cumberland. I admire the author of "Amelia," and thank the kind master who introduced me to that sweet and delightful companion and friend. "Amelia" perhaps is not a better story than "Tom Jones," but it has the better ethics; the prodigal repents at least, before forgiveness, — whereas that odious broad-backed Mr. Jones carries off his beauty with scarce an interval of remorse for his manifold errors and short-comings; and is not half punished enough before the great prize of fortune and love falls to his share. I am angry with Jones. Too much of the plum-cake and rewards of life fall to that boisterous, swaggering young scapegrace. Sophia actually surrenders without a proper sense of decorum; the fond, foolish, palpitating little creature! — "Indeed, Mr. Jones," she says, — "it rests with you to appoint the day." I suppose Sophia is drawn from life as well as Amelia; and many a young fellow, no better than Mr. Thomas Jones, has carried by a *coup de main* the heart of many a kind girl who was a great deal too good for him.

What a wonderful art! What an admirable gift of nature was it by which the author of these tales was endowed, and which enabled him to fix our interest, to waken our sympathy, to seize upon our credulity, so that we believe in his people — speculate gravely upon their faults or their excellences, prefer this one or that, deplore Jones's fondness for drink and play, Booth's fondness for play and drink, and the unfortunate position of the wives of both gentlemen — love and admire those ladies with all our hearts, and talk about them as faithfully as if we had breakfasted with them this morning in their actual drawing-rooms, or should meet them this afternoon in the Park! What a genius! what a vigor! what a bright-eyed intelligence and observation! what a wholesome hatred for meanness and knavery! what a vast sympathy! what a cheerfulness! what a manly relish of life! what a love of human kind! what a poet is here! — watching, meditating, brooding, creating! What multitudes of truths has that man left behind him! What generations he has taught to laugh wisely and fairly! What scholars he has formed and accustomed to the exercise of thoughtful humor and the manly play of wit! What a courage he had! What a dauntless and constant cheerfulness of intellect, that burned bright and steady through all the storms of his life, and never deserted its last wreck! It is wonderful to think of the pains and misery which the man suffered; the pressure of want, illness, remorse which he endured; and that the writer was neither malignant nor melancholy, his view of truth never warped, and his generous human kindness never surrendered.*

* In "The Gentleman's Magazine" for 1786, an anecdote is related of Harry Fielding, "in whom," says the correspondent, "good-nature and philanthropy in their extreme degree were known to be the prominent features." It seems that

In the quarrel mentioned before, which happened on Fielding's last voyage to Lisbon, and when the stout captain of the ship fell down on his knees and asked the sick man's pardon — "I did not suffer," Fielding says, in his hearty, manly way, his eyes lighting up as it were with their old fire — "I did not suffer a brave man and an old man to remain a moment in that posture, but immediately forgave him." Indeed, I think,

"some parochial taxes" for his house in Beaufort Buildings had long been demanded by the collector. "At last, Harry went off to Johnson, and obtained by a process of literary mortgage the needful sum. He was returning with it, when he met an old college chum whom he had not seen for many years. He asked the chum to dinner with him at a neighboring tavern; and, learning that he was in difficulties, emptied the contents of his pocket into his. On returning home he was informed that the collector had been twice for the money. 'Friendship has called for the money and had it,' said Fielding; 'let the collector call again.'"

It is elsewhere told of him, that being in company with the Earl of Denbigh, his kinsman, and the conversation turning upon their relationship, the Earl asked him how it was that he spelled his name "Fielding," and not "Feilding," like the head of the house? "I cannot tell, my lord," said he, "except it be that my branch of the family were the first that knew how to spell."

In 1749, he was made Justice of the Peace for Westminster and Middlesex, an office then paid by fees, and very laborious, without being particularly reputable. It may be seen from his own words, in the Introduction to "The Voyage," what kind of work devolved upon him, and in what a state he was, during these last years; and still more clearly, how he comported himself through all.

"Whilst I was preparing for my journey, and when I was almost fatigued to death with several long examinations, relating to five different murders, all committed within the space of a week, by different gangs of street-robbers, I received a message from his Grace the Duke of Newcastle, by Mr. Carrington, the King's messenger, to attend his Grace the next morning in Lincoln's Inn Fields, upon some business of importance: but I excused myself from complying with the message, as, besides being lame, I was very ill with the great fatigues I had lately undergone, added to my distemper.

"His Grace, however, sent Mr. Carrington the very next morning, with another summons; with which, though in the utmost distress, I immediately complied; but the Duke happening, unfortunately for me, to be then particularly engaged, after I had waited some time, sent a gentleman to discourse with me on the best plan which could be invented for these murders and robberies, which were every day committed in the streets; upon which I promised to transmit my opinion in writing to his Grace, who, as the gentleman informed me, intended to lay it before the Privy Council.

"Though this visit cost me a severe cold, I, notwithstanding, set myself down to work, and in about four days sent the Duke as regular a plan as I could form, with all the reasons and arguments I could bring to support it, drawn out on several sheets of paper; and soon received a message from the Duke, by Mr. Carrington, acquainting me that my plan was highly approved of, and that all the terms of it would be complied with.

"The principal and most material of these terms was the immediately depositing 600*l.* in my hands; at which small charge I undertook to demolish the then reigning gangs, and to put the civil policy into such order, that no such gangs should ever be able for the future to form themselves into bodies, or at least to remain any time formidable to the public.

"I had delayed my Bath journey for some time, contrary to the repeated advice of my physical acquaintances and the ardent desire of my warmest friends, though my distemper was now turned to a deep jaundice; in which case the Bath waters are generally reputed to be almost infallible. But I had the most eager desire to demolish this gang of villains and cut-throats." . . .

"After some weeks the money was paid at the Treasury, and within a few days after 200*l.* of it had come into my hands, the whole gang of cut-throats was entirely dispersed. . . .

Further on, he says —

"I will confess that my private affairs at the beginning of the winter had but a gloomy aspect; for I had not plundered the public or the poor of those sums which men, who are always ready to plunder both as much as they can, have been pleased to suspect me of taking; on the contrary, by composing, instead of inflaming, the quarrels of porters and beggars (which I blush when I say hath not been universally practised), and by refusing to take a shilling from a man who most undoubtedly would not have had another left, I had reduced an income of about 500*l.* a year of the dirtiest money upon earth, to little more than 300*l.*, a considerable portion of which remained with my clerk."

Sterne.

with his noble spirit and unconquerable generosity, Fielding reminds one of those brave men of whom one reads in stories of English shipwrecks and disasters —of the officer on the African shore, when disease has destroyed the crew, and he himself is seized by fever, who throws the lead with a death-stricken hand, takes the soundings, carries the ship out of the river or off the dangerous coast, and dies in the manly endeavor — of the wounded captain, when the vessel founders, who never loses his heart, who eyes the danger steadily, and has a cheery word for all, until the inevitable fate overwhelms him, and the gallant ship goes down. Such a brave and gentle heart, such an intrepid and courageous spirit, I love to recognize in the manly, the English Harry Fielding.

STERNE AND GOLDSMITH.

Roger Sterne, Sterne's father, was the second son of a numerous race, descendants of Richard Sterne, Archbishop of York, in the reign of James II.; and children of Simon Sterne and Mary Jaques, his wife, heiress of Elvington, near York.* Roger was a lieutenant in Handyside's regiment, and engaged in Flanders in Queen Anne's wars. He married the daughter of a noted sutler — "N. B., he was in debt to him," his son writes, pursuing the paternal biography — and marched through the world with this companion; she following the regiment and bringing many children to poor Roger Sterne. The captain was an irascible but kind and simple little man, Sterne says, and informs us that his sire was run through the body at Gibraltar, by a brother officer, in a duel which arose out of a dispute about a goose. Roger never entirely recovered from the effects of this rencontre, but died presently at Jamaica, whither he had followed the drum.

Laurence, his second child, was born at Clonmel, in Ireland, in 1713, and travelled, for the first ten years of his life, on his father's march, from barrack to transport, from Ireland to England.*

One relative of his mother's took her and her family under shelter for ten months at Mullingar: another collateral descendant of the Archbishop's housed them for a year at his castle near Carrickfergus. Larry Sterne was put to school at Halifax in England, finally was adopted by his kinsman of Elvington, and parted company with his father, the Captain, who marched on his path of life till he met the fatal goose, which closed his career. The most picturesque and delightful parts of Laurence Sterne's writings, we owe to his recollections of the military life. Trim's montero cap, and Le Fevre's sword, and dear Uncle Toby's roquelaure, are doubtless reminiscences of the boy, who had lived with the followers of William and Marlborough, and had beat

* "He came of a Suffolk family — one of whom settled in Nottinghamshire. The famous "starling" was actually the family crest.

* "It was in this parish (of Animo, in Wicklow), during our stay, that I had that wonderful escape in falling through a mill-race, whilst the mill was going, and of being taken up unhurt; the story is incredible, but known for truth in all that part of Ireland, where hundreds of the common people flocked to see me." — Sterne.

time with his little feet to the fifes of Ramillies in Dublin barrack-yard, or played with the torn flags and halberds of Malplaquet on the parade-ground at Clonmel.

Laurence remained at Halifax school till he was eighteen years old. His wit and cleverness appear to have acquired the respect of his master here; for when the usher whipped Laurence for writing his name on the newly whitewashed school-room ceiling, the pedagogue in chief rebuked the understrapper, and said that the name should never be effaced, for Sterne was a boy of genius, and would come to preferment.

His cousin, the Squire of Elvington, sent Sterne to Jesus College, Cambridge, where he remained five years, and, taking orders, got, through his uncle's interest, the living of Sutton and the prebendary of York. Through his wife's connections, he got the living of Stillington. He married her in 1741; having ardently courted the young lady for some years previously. It was not until the young lady fancied herself dying, that she made Sterne acquainted with the extent of her liking for him. One evening when he was sitting with her, with an almost broken heart to see her so ill (the Rev. Mr. Sterne's heart was a good deal broken in the course of his life), she said — "My dear Laurey, I never can be yours, for I verily believe I have not long to live; but I have left you every shilling of my fortune:" a generosity which overpowered Sterne. She recovered: and so they were married, and grew heartily tired of each other before many years were over. "Nescio quid est materia cum me," Sterne writes to one of his friends (in dog-Latin, and very sad dog-Latin too); "sed sum fatigatus et ægrotus de meâ uxore plus quam unquam:" which means, I am sorry to say, "I don't know what is the matter with me: but I am more tired and sick of my wife than ever." *

This to be sure was five and twenty years after Laurey had been overcome by her generosity and she by Laurey's love. Then he wrote to her of the delights of marriage, saying, "We will be as merry and as innocent as our first parents in Paradise, before the arch fiend entered that indescribable scene. The kindest affections will have room to expand in our retirement: let the human tempest and hurricane rage at a distance, the desolation is beyond the horizon of peace. My L. has seen a polyanthus blow in December? — Some friendly wall has sheltered it from the biting wind. No planetary influence shall reach us but that which presides and cherishes the sweetest flowers. The gloomy family of care and distrust shall be banished from our dwelling, guarded by thy kind and tutelar deity. We will sing our choral songs of gratitude and rejoice to the end of our pilgrimage. Adieu, my L. Return to one who languishes for thy society! — As I take up my pen, my poor pulse quickens, my pale face glows, and tears are trickling down on my paper as I trace the word L."

And it is about this woman, with whom he finds no fault but that she bores him, that our philanthropist writes, "Sum fatigatus et ægrotus" — *Sum mortaliter in amore* with somebody else! That fine flower of love, that polyanthus over which Sterne snivelled so many tears, could not last for a quarter of a century!

Or rather it could not be expected that a gentleman with such a fountain at command should keep it to *arroser* one homely old lady, when a score of younger and prettier people might be refreshed from the same gushing source.* It was in Decem-

* "My wife returns to Toulouse, and proposes to pass the summer at Bignaères. I, on the contrary, go and visit my wife, the church, in Yorkshire. We all live the longer, at least the happier, for having things our own way; this is my conjugal maxim. I own 'tis not the best of maxims, but I maintain 'tis not the worst." — STERNE'S *Letters:* 20th January, 1764.

* In a collection of "Seven Letters by

ber, 1767, that the Rev. Laurence Sterne, the famous Shandean, the charming Yorick, the delight of the fashionable world, the delicious divine, for whose sermons the whole polite world was subscribing,* the occupier of Rabelais's easy-chair, only fresh stuffed and more elegant than when in possession of the cynical old curate of Meudon,* — the more than rival

Sterne and his Friends" (printed for private circulation in 1844) is a letter of M. Tollot, who was in France with Sterne and his family in 1764. Here is a paragraph: —

"Nous arrivâmes le lendemain à Montpellier, où nous trouvâmes notre ami Mr. Sterne, sa femme, sa fille, Mr. Huet, et quelques autres Anglaises. J'eus, je vous l'avoue, beaucoup de plaisir en revoyant le bon et agréable Tristram. . . . Il avait été assez longtemps à Toulouse, où il se serait amusé sans sa femme, qui le poursuivit partout, et qui voulait être de tout. Ces dispositions dans cette bonne dame lui ont fait passer d'assez mauvais momens; il supporte tous ces désagrémens avec une patience d'ange."

About four months after this very characteristic letter, Sterne wrote to the same gentleman to whom Tollot had written; and from his letter we may extract a companion paragraph: —

". . . . All which being premised, I have been for eight weeks smitten with the tenderest passion that ever tender wight underwent. I wish, dear cousin, thou couldst conceive (perhaps thou canst without my wishing it) how deliciously I cantered away with it the first month, two up, two down, always upon my *haunches*, along the streets from my hotel to hers, at first once — then twice, then three times a day, till at length I was within an ace of setting up my hobby-horse in her stable for good and all. I might as well, considering how the enemies of the Lord have blasphemed thereupon. The last three weeks we were every hour upon the doleful ditty of parting; and thou mayst conceive, dear cousin, how it altered my gait and air: for I went and came like any loudened carl, and did nothing but *jouer des sentimens* with her from sun-rising even to the setting of the same; and now she is gone to the south of France; and to finish the comédie, I fell ill, and broke a vessel in my lungs, and half bled to death. Voilà mon histoire!"

Whether husband or wife had most of the "*patience d'ange*" may be uncertain; but there can be no doubt which needed it most!

* "'Tristram Shandy' is still a greater object of admiration, the man as well as the book: one is invited to dinner, when he dines, a fortnight before. As to the volumes yet published, there is much good fun in them and humor sometimes hit and sometimes missed. Have you read his 'Sermons,' with his own comic figure, from a painting by Reynolds, at the head of them? They are in the style I think most proper for the pulpit, and show a strong imagination and a sensible heart; but you see him often tottering on the verge of laughter, and ready to throw his periwig in the face of the audience." — GRAY'S *Letters: June 22d*, 1760.

"It having been observed that there was little hospitality in London — Johnson: 'Nay, sir, any man who has a name, or who has the power of pleasing, will be very generally invited in London. The man, Sterne, I have been told, has had engagements for three months.' Goldsmith: 'And a very dull fellow.' Johnson: 'Why, no, sir.'" — BOSWELL'S *Life of Johnson*.

"Her [Miss Monckton's] vivacity enchanted the sage, and they used to talk together with all imaginable ease. A singular instance happened one evening, when she insisted that some of Sterne's writings were very pathetic. Johnson bluntly denied it. 'I am sure,' said she, 'they have affected me.' 'Why,' said Johnson, smiling, and rolling himself about — 'that is, because, dearest, you're a dunce.' When she some time afterwards mentioned this to him, he said with equal truth and politeness, 'Madam, if I had thought so, I certainly should not have said it.'" — *Ibid.*

* A passage or two from Sterne's "Sermons" may not be without interest here. Is not the following, levelled against the cruelties of the Church of Rome, stamped with the autograph of the author of "The Sentimental Journey"? —

"To be convinced of this, go with me for a moment into the prisons of the Inquisition — behold *religion* with mercy and justice chained down under her feet, — there, sitting ghastly upon a black tribunal, propped up with racks, and instruments of torment. — Hark! — what a piteous groan! — See the melancholy wretch who uttered it, just brought forth to undergo the anguish of a mock-trial, and endure the utmost pain that a studied system of *religious cruelty* has been able to invent. Behold this helpless victim delivered up to his tormentors. *His body so wasted with sorrow and long confinement, you'll see every nerve and muscle as it suffers.* Observe the last movement of that horrid engine. What convulsions it has thrown him into! Consider the nature of the posture in which he now lies stretched. What exquisite torture

of the Dean of St. Patrick's, wrote the above-quoted respectable letter to his friend in London: and it was in April of the same year that he was pouring out his fond heart to Mrs. Elizabeth Draper, wife of "Daniel Draper, Esq., Councillor of Bombay, and, in 1775, chief of the factory of Surat — a gentleman very much respected in that quarter of the globe."

"I got thy letter last night, Eliza," Sterne writes, "on my return from Lord Bathurst's, where I dined" — (the letter has this merit in it, that it contains a pleasant reminiscence of better men than Sterne, and introduces us to a portrait of a kind old gentleman) — "I got thy letter last night, Eliza, on my return from Lord Bathurst's; and where I was heard — as I talked of thee an hour without intermission — with so much pleasure and attention, that the good old Lord toasted your health three different times; and now he is in his 85th year, says he hopes to live long enough to be introduced as a friend to my fair Indian disciple, and to see her eclipse all other Nabobesses as much in wealth as she does already in exterior, and, what is far better" (for Sterne is nothing without his morality), "in interior merit. This nobleman is an old friend of mine. You know he was always the protector of men of wit and genius, and has had those of the last century, Addison, Steele, Pope, Swift, Prior, &c., always at his table. The manner in which his notice began of me was as singular as it was polite. He came up to me one day as I was at the Princess of Wales's court, and said, 'I want to know you, Mr. Sterne; but it is fit you also should know who it is that wishes this pleasure. You have heard of an old Lord Bathurst, of whom your Popes and Swifts have sung and spoken so much? I have lived my life with geniuses of that cast; but have survived them; and, despairing ever to find their equals, it is some years since I have shut up my books and closed my accounts; but you have kindled a desire in me of opening them once more before I die: which I now do: so go home and dine with me.' This nobleman, I say, is a prodigy, for he has all the wit and promptness of a man of thirty; a disposition to be pleased, and a power to please others, beyond whatever I knew: added to which a man of learning, courtesy, and feeling.

"He heard me talk of thee, Eliza,

he endures by it. 'Tis all nature can bear. Good GOD! see how it keeps his weary soul hanging upon his trembling lips, willing to take its leave, but not suffered to depart. Behold the unhappy wretch led back to his cell, — dragged out of it again to meet the flames — and the insults in his last agonies, which this principle — this principle, that there can be religion without morality — has prepared for him." — *Sermon 27th.*

The next extract is preached on a text to be found in Judges xix. vv. 1, 2, 3, concerning a "certain Levite:" —

"Such a one the Levite wanted to share his solitude and fill up that uncomfortable blank in the heart in such a situation: for, notwithstanding all we meet with in books, in many of which, no doubt, there are a good many handsome things said upon the sweets of retirement, &c. . . . yet still 'it *is not good for man to be alone:*' nor can all which the cold-hearted pedant stuns our ears with upon the subject, ever give one answer of satisfaction to the mind; in the midst of the loudest vauntings of philosophy, nature will have her yearnings for society and friendship; — a good heart wants some object to be kind to — and the best parts of our blood, and the purest of our spirits, suffer most under the destitution.

"Let the torpid monk seek Heaven comfortless and alone. God speed him! For my own part, I fear I should never so find the way: *let me be wise and religious, but let me be* MAN; wherever thy Providence places me, or whatever be the road I take to Thee, give me some companion in my journey, be it only to remark to, 'How our shadows lengthen as our sun goes down;' — to whom I may say, 'How fresh is the face of Nature! how sweet the flowers of the field! how delicious are these fruits!'" — *Sermon 18th.*

The first of these passages gives us another drawing of the famous "Captive." The second shows that the same reflection was suggested to the Rev. Laurence by a text in Judges as by the *fille-de-Chambre.*

Sterne's Sermons were published as those of "Mr. Yorick."

with uncommon satisfaction — for there was only a third person, *and of sensibility*, with us: and a most sentimental afternoon till nine o'clock have we passed!* But thou, Eliza, wert the star that conducted and enlivened the discourse! And when I talked not of thee, still didst thou fill my mind, and warm every thought I uttered, for I am not ashamed to acknowledge I greatly miss thee. Best of all good girls! — the sufferings I have sustained all night in consequence of thine, Eliza, are beyond the power of words. . . . And so thou hast fixed thy Bramin's portrait over thy writing-desk, and will consult it in all doubts and difficulties? — Grateful and good girl! Yorick smiles contentedly over all thou dost: his picture does not do justice to his own complacency. I am glad your shipmates are friendly beings" (Eliza was at Deal, going back to the Councillor at Bombay, and indeed it was high time she should be off). "You could least dispense with what is contrary to your own nature, which is soft and gentle, Eliza; it would civilize savages — though pity were it thou shouldst be tainted with the office. Write to me, my child, thy delicious letters. Let them speak the easy carelessness of a heart that opens itself anyhow, everyhow. Such, Eliza, I write to thee!" (The artless rogue, of course he did!) "And so I should ever love thee, most artlessly, most affectionately, if Providence permitted thy residence in the same section of the globe: for I am all that honor and affection can make me 'THY BRAMIN.'"

The Bramin continues addressing Mrs. Draper until the departure of the "Earl of Chatham" Indiaman from Deal, on the 2d of April, 1767. He is amiably anxious about the fresh paint for Eliza's cabin; he is uncommonly solicitous about her companions on board: "I fear the best of your shipmates are only genteel by comparison with the contrasted crew with which thou beholdest them. So was — you know who — from the same fallacy which was put upon your judgment when — but I will not mortify you!"

"You know who" was, of course, Daniel Draper, Esq., of Bombay — a gentleman very much respected in that quarter of the globe, and about whose probable health our worthy Bramin writes with delightful candor: —

"I honor you, Eliza, for keeping secret some things which, if explained, had been a panegyric on yourself. There is a dignity in venerable affliction which will not allow it to appeal to the world for pity or redress. Well have you supported that character, my amiable, my philosophic friend! And, indeed, I begin to think you have as many virtues as my Uncle Toby's widow. Talking of widows — pray, Eliza, if ever you are such, do not think of giving yourself to some wealthy Nabob, because I design to marry you myself. My wife cannot live long, and I know not the woman I should like so well for her substitute as yourself. 'Tis true I am ninety-five in constitution, and you but twenty-five; but what I want in youth, I will make up in wit and good-

* "I am glad that you are in love: 'twill cure you at least of the spleen, which has a bad effect on both man and woman. I myself must ever have some Dulcinea in my head; it harmonizes the soul; and in these cases I first endeavor to make the lady believe so, or rather, I begin first to make myself believe that I am in love; but I carry on my affairs quite in the French way, sentimentally: '*L'amour*,' say they, '*n'est rien sans sentiment*.' Now, notwithstanding they make such a pother about the *word*, they have no precise idea annexed to it. And so much for that same subject called love." — STERNE'S *Letters*: May 23, 1765.

"P.S. — My 'Sentimental Journey' will please Mrs. J—— and my Lydia" [his daughter, afterwards Mrs. Medalle] — "I can answer for those two. It is a subject which works well, and suits the frame of mind I have been in for some time past. I told you my design in it was to teach us to love the world and our fellow creatures better than we do — so it runs most upon those gentler passions and affections which aid so much to it." — *Letters* [1767].

humor. Not Swift so loved his Stella, Scarron his Maintenon, or Waller his Saccharissa. Tell me, in answer to this, that you approve and honor the proposal."

Approve and honor the proposal! The coward was writing gay letters to his friends this while, with sneering allusions to this poor foolish *Bramine*. Her ship was not out of the Downs, and the charming Sterne was at the "Mount Coffee-house," with a sheet of gilt-edged paper before him, offering that precious treasure, his heart, to Lady P——, asking whether it gave her pleasure to see him unhappy? whether it added to her triumph that her eyes and lips had turned a man into a fool? — quoting the Lord's Prayer, with a horrible baseness of blasphemy, as a proof that he had desired not to be led into temptation, and swearing himself the most tender and sincere fool in the world. It was from his home at Coxwould that he wrote the Latin letter, which, I suppose, he was ashamed to put into English. I find in my copy of the Letters, that there is a note of I can't call it admiration, at Letter 112, which seems to announce that there was a No. 3 to whom the wretched, worn-out old scamp was paying his addresses; * and the year after, having come back to his lodgings in Bond Street, with his "Sentimental Journey" to launch upon the town, eager as ever for praise and pleasure — as vain, as wicked, as witty, as false as he had ever been — death at length seized the feeble wretch, and, on the 18th of March, 1768, that "bale of cadaverous goods," as he calls his body, was consigned to Pluto.* In his last letter there is one sign of grace — the real affection with which he entreats a friend to be a guardian to his daughter Lydia. All his letters to her are artless, kind, affectionate, and

* "To Mrs. H——.

"*Coxwould*, Nov. 15, 1767.

"Now be a good dear woman, my H——, and execute those commissions well, and when I see you I will give you a kiss — there's for you! But I have something else for you which I am fabricating at a great rate, and that is my 'Sentimental Journey,' which shall make you cry as much as it has affected me, or I will give up the business of sentimental writing. . . . I am yours, &c. &c.,

"T. Shandy."

"To the Earl of ——.

"*Coxwould*, Nov. 28, 1767.

"My Lord, — 'Tis with the greatest pleasure I take my pen to thank your lordship for your letter of inquiry about Yorick: he was worn out, both his spirits and body, with the 'Sentimental Journey.' 'Tis true, then, an author must feel himself, or his reader will not; but I have torn my whole frame into pieces by my feelings: I believe the brain stands as much in need of recruiting as the body. Therefore I shall set out for town the twentieth of next month, after having recruited myself a week at York. I might indeed solace myself with my wife (who is come from France); but, in fact, I have long been a sentimental being, whatever your lordship may think to the contrary."

* "In February, 1768, Laurence Sterne, his frame exhausted by long debilitating illness, expired at his lodgings in Bond Street, London. There was something in the manner of his death singularly resembling the particulars detailed by *Mrs. Quickly* as attending that of *Falstaff*, the compeer of *Yorick* for infinite jest, however unlike in other particulars. As he lay on his bed totally exhausted, he complained that his feet were cold, and requested the female attendant to chafe them. She did so, and it seemed to relieve him. He complained that the cold came up higher; and whilst the assistant was in the act of chafing his ankles and legs, he expired without a groan. It was also remarkable that his death took place much in the manner which he himself had wished; and that the last offices were rendered him, not in his own house, or by the hand of kindred affection, but in an inn, and by strangers.

"We are well acquainted with Sterne's features and personal appearance, to which he himself frequently alludes. He was tall and thin, with a hectic and consumptive appearance." — Sir Walter Scott.

"It is known that Sterne died in hired lodgings, and I have been told that his attendants robbed him even of his gold sleeve-buttons while he was expiring." — Dr. Ferriar.

"He died at No. 41 (now a cheesemonger's) on the west side of Old Bond Street." — *Handbook of London.*

not sentimental; as a hundred pages in his writings are beautiful, and full, not of surprising humor merely, but of genuine love and kindness. A perilous trade, indeed, is that of a man who has to bring his tears and laughter, his recollections, his personal griefs and joys, his private thoughts and feelings, to market, to write them on paper, and sell them for money. Does he exaggerate his grief, so as to get his reader's pity for a false sensibility? feign indignation, so as to establish a character for virtue? elaborate repartees, so that he may pass for a wit? steal from other authors, and put down the theft to the credit side of his own reputation for ingenuity and learning? feign originality? affect benevolence or misanthropy? appeal to the gallery gods with claptraps and vulgar baits to catch applause?

How much of the paint and emphasis is necessary for the fair business of the stage, and how much of the rant and rouge is put on for the vanity of the actor. His audience trusts him: can he trust himself? How much was deliberate calculation and imposture — how much was false sensibility — and how much true feeling? Where did the lie begin, and did he know where? and where did the truth end in the art and scheme of this man of genius, this actor, this quack? Some time since, I was in the company of a French actor, who began after dinner, and at his own request, to sing French songs of the sort called *des chansons grivoises*, and which he performed admirably, and to the dissatisfaction of most persons present. Having finished these, he commenced a sentimental ballad — it was so charmingly sung, that it touched all persons present, and especially the singer himself, whose voice trembled, whose eyes filled with emotion, and who was snivelling and weeping quite genuine tears by the time his own ditty was over. I suppose Sterne had this artistical sensibility; he used to blubber perpetually in his study, and finding his tears infectious, and that they brought him a great popularity, he exercised the lucrative gift of weeping: he utilized it, and cried on every occasion. I own that I don't value or respect much the cheap dribble of those fountains. He fatigues me with his perpetual disquiet and his uneasy appeals to my risible or sentimental faculties. He is always looking in my face, watching his effect, uncertain whether I think him an impostor or not; posture-making, coaxing, and imploring me. "See what sensibility I have — own now that I'm very clever — do cry now, you can't resist this." The humor of Swift and Rabelais, whom he pretended to succeed, poured from them as naturally as song does from a bird; they lose no manly dignity with it, but laugh their hearty great laugh out of their broad chests, as Nature bade them. But this man — who can make you laugh, who can make you cry too — never lets his reader alone, or will permit his audience repose: when you are quiet, he fancies he must rouse you, and turns over head and heels, or sidles up and whispers a nasty story. The man is a great jester, not a great humorist. He goes to work systematically and of cold blood; paints his face, puts on his ruff and motley clothes, and lays down his carpet, and tumbles on it.

For instance, take "The Sentimental Journey," and see in the writer the deliberate propensity to make points and seek applause. He gets to "Dessein's Hotel," he wants a carriage to travel to Paris, he goes to the inn-yard, and begins what the actors call "business" at once. There is that little carriage (the *désobligeante*). "Four months had elapsed since it had finished its career of Europe in the corner of Monsieur Dessein's courtyard, and having sallied out thence but a vamped-up business at first, though it had been twice taken to pieces on Mount Sennis, it had not profited much by its adventures, but by none so little as the standing so many months unpitied in the corner of Monsieur Dessein's coach-yard. Much, indeed, was not to be said for it — but something might — and when a few words will rescue misery out of her distress, I hate the man who can be a churl of them."

Le tour est fait! Paillasse has tumbled! Paillasse has jumped over the *désobligeante*, cleared it, hood and all, and bows to the noble company. Does anybody believe that this is a real Sentiment? that this luxury of generosity, this gallant rescue of Misery — out of an old cab, is genuine feeling? It is as genuine as the virtuous oratory of Joseph Surface when he begins, "The man who," &c., &c., and wishes to pass off for a saint with his credulous, good-humored dupes.

Our friend purchases the carriage: after turning that notorious old monk to good account, and effecting (like a soft and good-natured Paillasse as he was, and very free with his money when he had it) an exchange of snuff-boxes with the old Franciscan, jogs out of Calais; sets down in immense figures on the credit side of his account the sous he gives away to the Montreuil beggars; and, at Nampont, gets out of the chaise, and whimpers over that famous dead donkey, for which any sentimentalist may cry who will. It is agreeably and skilfully done — that dead jackass: like M. de Soubise's cook on the campaign, Sterne dresses it, and serves it up quite tender and with a very piquant sauce. But tears, and fine feelings, and a white pocket-handkerchief, and a funeral sermon, and horses and feathers, and a procession of mutes, and a hearse with a dead donkey inside! Psha, mountebank! I'll not give thee one penny more for that trick, donkey and all!

This donkey had appeared once before with signal effect. In 1765, three years before the publication of "The Sentimental Journey," the seventh and eighth volumes of "Tristram Shandy" were given to the world, and the famous Lyons donkey makes his entry in those volumes (pp. 315, 316): —

"'Twas by a poor ass, with a couple of large panniers at his back, who had just turned in to collect eleemosynary turnip-tops and cabbage-leaves, and stood dubious, with his two forefeet at the inside of the threshold, and with his two hinder feet towards the street, as not knowing very well whether he was to go in or no.

"Now 'tis an animal (be in what hurry I may) I cannot bear to strike: there is a patient endurance of suffering wrote so unaffectedly in his looks and carriage which pleads so mightily for him, that it always disarms me, and to that degree that I do not like to speak unkindly to him: on the contrary, meet him where I will, whether in town or country, in cart or under panniers, whether in liberty or bondage, I have ever something civil to say to him on my part; and, as one word begets another (if he has as little to do as I), I generally fall into conversation with him; and surely never is my imagination so busy as in framing responses from the etchings of his countenance; and where those carry me not deep enough, in flying from my own heart into his, and seeing what is natural for an ass to think — as well as a man, upon the occasion. In truth, it is the only creature of all the classes of beings below me with whom I can do this. . . . With an ass I can commune forever.

"'Come, Honesty,' said I, seeing it was impracticable to pass betwixt him and the gate, 'art thou for coming in or going out?'"

"The ass twisted his head round to look up the street.

"'Well!' replied I, 'we'll wait a minute for thy driver.'

"He turned his head thoughtful about, and looked wistfully the opposite way.

"'I understand thee perfectly,' answered I: 'if thou takest a wrong step in this affair, he will cudgel thee to death. Well! a minute is but a minute; and if it saves a fellow-creature a drubbing, it shall not be set down as ill spent.'

"He was eating the stem of an artichoke as this discourse went on, and, in the little peevish contentions between hunger and unsavoriness, had dropped it out of his mouth half a dozen times, and had picked it up again. 'God help thee, Jack!' said I, 'thou hast a bitter breakfast on't — and many a bitter day's labor, and many a bitter blow, I fear, for its wages! 'Tis all, all bitterness to thee — whatever life is to others! And now thy mouth, if one knew the truth of it, is as bitter, I dare say, as soot' (for he had cast aside the stem), 'and thou hast not a friend perhaps in all this world that will give thee a macaroon.' In saying this, I pulled out a paper of 'em, which I had just bought, and gave him one; — and, at this moment that I am telling it, my heart smites me that there was more of pleasantry in the conceit of seeing *how* an ass would eat a macaroon, than of benevolence in giving him one, which presided in the act.

"When the ass had eaten his macaroon, I pressed him to come in. The poor beast was heavy loaded — his legs seemed to tremble under him — he hung rather backwards, and, as I pulled at his halter, it broke in my hand. He looked up pensive in my face: 'Don't thrash me with it; but if you will you may.' 'If I do,' said I, 'I'll be d——.'"

A critic who refuses to see in this charming description wit, humor, pathos, a kind nature speaking, and a real sentiment, must be hard indeed to move and to please. A page or two farther we come to a description not less beautiful — a landscape and figures, deliciously painted by one who had the keenest enjoyment and the most tremulous sensibility: —

"'Twas in the road between Nismes and Lunel, where is the best Muscatto wine in all France: the sun was set, they had done their work: the nymphs had tied up their hair afresh, and the swains were preparing for a carousal. My mule made a dead point. ''Tis the pipe and tambourine,' said I — 'I never will argue a point with one of your family as long as I live;' so leaping off his back, and kicking off one boot into this ditch and t'other into that, 'I'll take a dance,' said I, 'so stay you here.'

"A sun-burnt daughter of labor rose up from the group to meet me as I advanced towards them; her hair, which was of a dark chestnut approaching to a black, was tied up in a knot, all but a single tress.

"'We want a cavalier,' said she, holding out both her hands, as if to offer them. 'And a cavalier you shall have,' said I, taking hold of both of them. 'We could not have done without you,' said she, letting go one hand, with self-taught politeness, and leading me up with the other.

"A lame youth, whom Apollo had recompensed with a pipe, and to which he had added a tambourine of his own accord, ran sweetly over the prelude, as he sat upon the bank. 'Tie me up this tress instantly,' said Nannette, putting a piece of string into my hand. It taught me to forget I was a stranger. The whole knot fell down — we had been seven years acquainted. The youth struck the note upon the tambourine, his pipe followed, and off we bounded.

"The sister of the youth — who had stolen her voice from heaven — sang alternately with her brother. 'Twas a Gascoigne roundelay: '*Viva la joia, fidon la tristessa.*' The nymphs joined in unison, and their swains an octave below them.

"*Viva la joia* was in Nannette's lips, *viva la joia* in her eyes. A transient spark of amity shot across the space betwixt us. She looked amiable. Why could I not live and end my days thus? 'Just Disposer of our joys and sorrows!' cried I, 'why could not a man sit down in the lap of content here, and dance, and sing, and say his prayers, and go to heaven with this nut-brown maid?' Capriciously did she bend her head on one side, and dance up insidious. 'Then 'tis time to dance off,' quoth I."

And with this pretty dance and chorus, the volume artfully concludes. Even here one can't give the whole description. There is not a page in Sterne's writing but has something that were better away, a latent corruption — a hint, as of an impure presence.*

Some of that dreary *double entendre* may be attributed to freer times and manners than ours, but not all. The foul Satyr's eyes leer out of the leaves constantly: the last words the famous author wrote were bad and wicked — the last lines the poor stricken wretch penned were for pity and pardon. I think of these past writers and of one who lives amongst us now, and am grateful for the innocent laughter and the sweet and unsullied page which the author of "David Copperfield" gives to my children.

" Jeté sur cette boule,
Laid, chétif et souffrant;
Etouffé dans la foule,
Faute d'être assez grand:

" Une plainte touchante
De ma bouche sortit.
Le bon Dieu me dit: Chante,
Chante, pauvre petit!

" Chanter, ou je m'abuse,
Est ma tâche ici bas.
Tous ceux qu'ainsi j'amuse,
Ne m'aimeront-ils pas?"

In those charming lines of Béranger, one may fancy described the career, the sufferings, the genius, the gentle nature, of GOLDSMITH, and the esteem in which we hold him. Who, of the millions whom he has amused, doesn't love him? To be the most beloved of English writers, what a title that is for a man!* A

* "With regard to Sterne, and the charge of licentiousness which presses so seriously upon his character as a writer, I would remark that there is a sort of knowingness, the wit of which depends, 1st, on the modesty it gives pain to: or, 2dly, on the innocence and innocent ignorance over which it triumphs; or, 3dly, on a certain oscillation in the individual's own mind between the remaining good and the encroaching evil of his nature — a sort of dallying with the devil — a fluxionary art of combining courage and cowardice, as when a man snuffs a candle with his fingers for the first time, or better still, perhaps, like that trembling daring with which a child touches a hot tea-urn, because it has been forbidden; so that the mind has its own white and black angel; the same or similar amusement as may be supposed to take placebetween an old debauchee and a prude — the feeling resentment, on the one hand, from a prudential anxiety to preserve appearances and have a character; and on the other, an inward sympathy with the enemy. We have only to suppose society innocent, and then nine-tenths of this sort of wit would be like a stone that falls in snow, making no sound, because exciting no resistance; the remainder rests on its being an offence against the good manners of human nature itself.

"This source, unworthy as it is, may doubtless be combined with wit, drollery, fancy, and even humor; and we have only to regret the misalliance; but that the latter are quite distinct from the former, may be made evident by abstracting in our imagination the morality of the characters of Mr. Shandy, my Uncle Toby, and Trim, which are all antagonists to this spurious sort of wit, from the rest of 'Tristram Shandy,' and by supposing, instead of them, the presence of two or three callous debauchees. The result will be pure disgust. Sterne cannot be too severely censured for thus using the best dispositions of our nature as the panders and condiments for the basest." — COLERIDGE: *Literary Remains*, vol. i. pp. 141, 142.

* "He was a friend to virtue, and in his most playful pages never forgets what is due to it. A gentleness, delicacy, and purity of feeling, distinguishes whatever he wrote, and bears a correspondence to the generosity of a disposition which knew no bounds but his last guinea. . . .

"The admirable ease and grace of the narrative, as well as the pleasing truth with which the principal characters are designed, make 'The Vicar of Wakefield' one of the most delicious morsels of fictitious composition on which the human mind was ever employed.

". . . We read 'The Vicar of Wakefield' in youth and in age — we return to it again and again, and bless the memory of an author who contrives so well to reconcile us to human nature." — Sir WALTER SCOTT.

wild youth, wayward, but full of tenderness and affection, quits the country village where his boyhood has been passed in happy musing, in idle shelter, in fond longing to see the great world out of doors, and achieve name and fortune; and after years of dire struggle, and neglect and poverty, his heart turning back as fondly to his native place as it had longed eagerly for change when sheltered there, he writes a book and a poem, full of the recollections and feelings of home; he paints the friends and scenes of his youth, and peoples Auburn and Wakefield with remembrances of Lissoy. Wander he must, but he carries away a home-relic with him, and dies with it on his breast. His nature is truant; in repose it longs for change: as on the journey it looks back for friends and quiet. He passes to-day in building an air-castle for to-morrow, or in writing yesterday's elegy; and he would fly away this hour, but that a cage and necessity keep him. What is the charm of his verse, of his style, and humor? His sweet regrets, his delicate compassion, his soft smile, his tremulous sympathy, the weakness which he owns? Your love for him is half pity. You come hot and tired from the day's battle, and this sweet minstrel sings to you. Who could harm the kind vagrant harper? Whom did he ever hurt? He carries no weapon, save the harp on which he plays to you; and with which he delights great and humble, young and old, the captains in the tents, or the soldiers round the fire, or the women and children in the villages, at whose porches he stops and sings his simple songs of love and beauty. With that sweet story of "The Vicar of Wakefield"* he has found entry into every castle and every hamlet in Europe. Not one of

* "Now Herder came," says Goethe in his Autobiography, relating his first acquaintance with Goldsmith's masterpiece, "and together with his great knowledge brought many other aids, and the later publications besides. Among these he announced to us 'The Vicar of Wakefield' as an excellent work, with the German translation of which he would make us acquainted by reading it aloud to us himself. . . .

"A Protestant country clergyman is perhaps the most beautiful subject for a modern idyl; he appears like Melchisedek, as priest and king in one person. To the most innocent situation which can be imagined on earth, to that of a husbandman, he is, for the most part, united by similarity of occupation as well as by equality in family relationships; he is a father, a master of a family, an agriculturist, and thus perfectly a member of the community. On this pure, beautiful, earthly foundation rests his higher calling; to him is it given to guide men through life, to take care of their spiritual education, to bless them at all the leading epochs of their existence, to instruct, to strengthen, to console them, and, if consolation is not sufficient for the present, to call up and guarantee the hope of a happier future. Imagine such a man with pure human sentiments, strong enough not to deviate from them under any circumstances, and by this already elevated above the multitude of whom one cannot expect purity and firmness: give him the learning necessary for his office, as well as a cheerful, equable activity, which is even passionate, as it neglects no moment to do good — and you will have him well endowed. But at the same time add the necessary limitation, so that he must not only pause in a small circle, but may also, perchance, pass over to a smaller; grant him good-nature, placability, resolution, and every thing else praiseworthy that springs from a decided character, and over all this a cheerful spirit of compliance, and a smiling toleration of his own failings and those of others, — then you will have put together pretty well the image of our excellent Wakefield.

"The delineation of this character on his course of life through joys and sorrows, the ever-increasing interest of the story, by the combination of the entirely natural with the strange and the singular, make this novel one of the best which has ever been written; besides this, it has the great advantage that it is quite moral, nay, in a pure sense, Christian — represents the reward of a good-will and perseverance in the right, strengthens an unconditional confidence in God, and attests the final triumph of good over evil; and all this without a trace of cant or pedantry. The author was preserved from both of these by an elocution of mind that shows itself throughout in the form of irony, by which this little work must appear to us as wise as it is amiable. The author, Dr. Goldsmith, has, without ques-

us, however busy or hard, but once or twice in our lives has passed an evening with him, and undergone the charm of his delightful music.

Goldsmith's father was no doubt the good Dr. Primrose, whom we all of us know.* Swift was yet alive, when the little Oliver was born at Pallas, or Pallasmore, in the county of Longford, in Ireland. In 1730, two years after the child's birth, Charles Goldsmith removed his family to Lissoy, in the county Westmeath, that sweet "Auburn" which every person who hears me has seen in fancy. Here the kind parson † brought up his eight children; and loving all the world, as his son says, fancied all the world loved him. He had a crowd of poor dependants besides those hungry children. He kept an open table; round which sat flatterers and poor friends, who laughed at the honest rector's many jokes, and ate the produce of his seventy acres of farm. Those who have seen an Irish house

tion, a great insight into the moral world, into its strength and its infirmities; but at the same time he can thankfully acknowledge that he is an Englishman, and reckon highly the advantages which his country and his nation afford him. The family, with the delineation of which he occupies himself, stands upon one of the last steps of citizen comfort, and yet comes in contact with the highest; its narrow circle, which becomes still more contracted, touches upon the great world through the natural and civil course of things; this little skiff floats on the agitated waves of English life, and in weal or woe it has to expect injury or help from the vast fleet which sails around it.

"I may suppose that my readers know this work, and have it in memory; whoever hears it named for the first time here, as well as he who is induced to read it again, will thank me." — GOETHE: *Truth and Poetry; from my own Life.* (English Translation, vol. i. pp. 378, 379.)

"He seems from infancy to have been compounded of two natures, one bright, the other blundering; or to have had fairy gifts laid in his cradle by the 'good people' who haunted his birthplace, the old goblin mansion on the banks of the Inny.

"He carries with him the wayward elfin spirit, if we may so term it, throughout his career. His fairy gifts are of no avail at school, academy, or college; they unfit him for close study and practical science, and render him heedless of every thing that does not address itself to his poetical imagination and genial and festive feelings; they dispose him to break away from restraint, to stroll about hedges, green lanes, and haunted streams, to revel with jovial companions, or to rove the country like a gypsy in quest of odd adventures. . . .

"Though his circumstances often compelled him to associate with the poor, they never could betray him into companionship with the depraved. His relish for humor, and for the study of character, as we have before observed, brought him often into convivial company of a vulgar kind; but he discriminated between their vulgarity and their amusing qualities, or rather wrought from the whole store familiar features of life which form the staple of his most popular writings." — WASHINGTON IRVING.

* "The family of Goldsmith, Goldsmyth, or, as it was occasionally written, Gouldsmith, is of considerable standing in Ireland, and seems always to have held a respectable station in society. Its origin is English, supposed to be derived from that which was long settled at Crayford in Kent." — PRIOR'S *Life of Goldsmith.*

Oliver's father, great-grandfather, and great-great-grandfather were clergymen; and two of them married clergymen's daughters.

† "At church, with meek and unaffected grace,
His looks adorned the venerable place;
Truth from his lips prevailed with double sway,
And fools who came to scoff remained to pray.
The service past, around the pious man,
With steady zeal each honest rustic ran;
E'en children followed with endearing wile,
And plucked his gown to share the good man's smile.
His ready smile a parent's warmth expressed,
Their welfare pleased him, and their cares distressed;
To them his heart, his love, his griefs were given,
But all his serious thoughts had rest in Heaven.
As some tall cliff that lifts his awful form,
Swells from the vale, and midway leaves the storm,
Though round its breast the rolling clouds are spread,
Eternal sunshine settles on its head." — *The Deserted Village.*

in the present day can fancy that one of Lissoy. The old beggar still has his allotted corner by the kitchen turf; the maimed old soldier still gets his potatoes and butter-milk; the poor cottier still asks his honor's charity, and prays God bless his reverence for the sixpence: the ragged pensioner still takes his place by right and sufferance. There's still a crowd in the kitchen and a crowd round the parlor-table, profusion, confusion, kindness, poverty. If an Irishman comes to London to make his fortune, he has a half-dozen of Irish dependants who take a percentage of his earnings. The good Charles Goldsmith* left but little provision for his hungry race when death summoned him: and one of his daughters being engaged to a Squire of rather superior dignity, Charles Goldsmith impoverished the rest of his family to provide the girl with a dowry.

The small-pox, which scourged all Europe at that time, and ravaged the roses off the cheeks of half the world, fell foul of poor little Oliver's face, when the child was eight years old, and left him scarred and disfigured for his life. An old woman in his father's village taught him his letters, and pronounced him a dunce: Paddy Byrne, the hedge-schoolmaster, took him in hand; and from Paddy Byrne, he was transmitted to a clergyman at Elphin. When a child was sent to school in those days, the classic phrase was that he was placed under Mr. So-and-so's *ferule*. Poor little ancestors! It is hard to think how ruthlessly you were birched; and how much of needless whipping and tears our small forefathers had to undergo! A relative — kind uncle Contarine, took the main charge of little Noll; who went through his school-days righteously doing as little work as he could: robbing orchards, playing at ball, and making his pocket-money fly about whenever fortune sent it to him. Everybody knows the story of that famous "Mistake of a Night," when the young schoolboy, provided with a guinea and a nag, rode up to the "best house" in Ardagh, called for the landlord's company over a bottle of wine at supper, and for a hot cake for breakfast in the morning; and found, when he asked for the bill, that the best house was Squire Featherstone's, and not the inn for which he mistook it. Who does not know every story about Goldsmith? That is a delightful and fantastic picture of the child dancing and capering about in the kitchen at home, when the old fiddler gibed at him for his ugliness, and called him Æsop; and little Noll made his repartee of "Heralds proclaim aloud this saying — See Æsop dancing and his monkey playing." One can fancy a queer pitiful look of humor and appeal upon that little scarred face, the funny little dancing figure, the funny little brogue. In his life, and his writings, which are the honest expression of it, he is constantly bewailing that homely face and person: anon, he surveys them in the glass ruefully; and presently assumes the most comical dignity.

* "In May this year (1768), he lost his brother, the Rev. Henry Goldsmith, for whom he had been unable to obtain preferment in the church. . . .

" . . . To the curacy of Kilkenny West, the moderate stipend of which, forty pounds a year, is sufficiently celebrated by his brother's lines. It has been stated that Mr. Goldsmith added a school, which, after having been held at more than one place in the vicinity, was finally fixed at Lissoy. Here his talents and industry gave it celebrity, and under his care the sons of many of the neighboring gentry received their education. A fever breaking out among the boys about 1765, they dispersed for a time, but re-assembling at Athlone, he continued his scholastic labors there until the time of his death, which happened, like that of his brother, about the forty-fifth year of his age. He was a man of an excellent heart and an amiable disposition." — PRIOR'S *Goldsmith*.

"Where'er I roam, whatever realms to see,
My heart, untravelled, fondly turns to thee:
Still to my brother turns with ceaseless pain,
And drags at each remove a lengthening chain." — *The Traveller*.

He likes to deck out his little person in splendor and fine colors. He presented himself to be examined for ordination in a pair of scarlet breeches, and said honestly that he did not like to go into the church, because he was fond of colored clothes. When he tried to practice as a doctor, he got by hook or by crook, a black velvet suit, and looked as big and grand as he could, and kept his hat over a patch on the old coat: in better days he bloomed out in plum-color, in blue silk, and in new velvet. For some of those splendors the heirs and assignees of Mr. Filby, the tailor, have never been paid to this day: perhaps the kind tailor and his creditor have met and settled the little account in Hades.*

They showed until lately a window at Trinity College, Dublin, on which the name of O. Goldsmith was engraved with a diamond. Whose diamond was it? Not the young sizar's, who made but a poor figure in that place of learning. He was idle, penniless, and fond of pleasure: † he learned his way early to the pawnbroker's shop. He wrote ballads, they say, for the street-singers, who paid him a crown for a poem: and his pleasure was to steal out at night and hear his verses sung. He was chastised by his tutor for giving a dance in his rooms, and took the box on the ear so much to heart, that he packed up his all, pawned his books and little property, and disappeared from college and family. He said he intended to go to America, but when his money was spent, the young prodigal came home ruefully, and the good folks there killed their calf — it was but a lean one — and welcomed him back.

After college, he hung about his mother's house, and lived for some years the life of a buckeen — passed a month with this relation and that, a year with one patron, a great deal of time at the public-house.* Tired of this life, it was resolved that he should go to London and study at the Temple; but he got no farther on the road to London and the woolsack than Dublin, where he gambled away the fifty pounds given to him for his outfit, and whence he returned to the indefatigable forgiveness of home. Then he determined to be a doctor, and uncle Contarine helped him to a couple of years at Edinburgh. Then from Edinburgh he felt that he ought to hear the famous professors of Leyden and Paris, and wrote most amusing pompous letters to his uncle about the great Farheim, Du Petit, and Duhamel du Monceau, whose lectures he proposed to follow. If uncle Contarine believed those letters — if Oliver's mother believed that story which the youth related of his going to Cork, with the purpose of embarking for America, of his having paid his passage money, and having sent his kit on board; of the anonymous captain sailing away with Oliver's valuable luggage, in a nameless ship, never to return; if uncle Contarine and the mother at Ballymahon believed his stories, they must have been a very simple pair; as it was a very simple rogue indeed who cheated them. When the lad, after failing in his clerical examination, after failing in his plan for studying the law, took

* "When Goldsmith died, half the unpaid bill he owed to Mr. William Filby (amounting in all to 79*l.*) was for clothes supplied to this nephew Hodson." — FORSTER'S *Goldsmith*, p. 520.

As this nephew Hodson ended his days (see the same page) "a prosperous Irish gentleman," it is not unreasonable to wish that he had cleared off Mr. Filby's bill.

† "Poor fellow! He hardly knew an ass from a mule, nor a turkey from a goose, but when he saw it on the table." — CUMBERLAND'S *Memoirs*.

* "These youthful follies, like the fermentation of liquors, often disturb the mind only in order to its future refinement: a life spent in phlegmatic apathy resembles those liquors which never ferment, and are consequently always muddy." — GOLDSMITH: *Memoir of Voltaire*.

"He [Johnson] said 'Goldsmith was a plant that flowered late. There appeared nothing remarkable about him when he was young.'" — BOSWELL.

leave of these projects and of his parents, and set out for Edinburgh, he saw mother, and uncle, and lazy Ballymahon, and green native turf, and sparkling river for the last time. He was never to look on old Ireland more, and only in fancy, revisit her.

"But me not destined such delights to share,
My prime of life in wandering spent and care,
Impelled, with step unceasing, to pursue
Some fleeting good that mocks me with the view;
That like the circle bounding earth and skies
Allures from far, yet, as I follow, flies:
My fortune leads to traverse realms unknown,
And find no spot of all the world my own."

I spoke in a former lecture of that high courage which enabled Fielding, in spite of disease, remorse, and poverty, always to retain a cheerful spirit and to keep his manly benevolence and love of truth, intact, as if these treasures had been confided to him for the public benefit, and he was accountable to posterity for their honorable employ; and a constancy equally happy and admirable I think was shown by Goldsmith, whose sweet and friendly nature bloomed kindly always in the midst of a life's storm, and rain, and bitter weather.* The poor fellow was never so friendless but he could befriend some one; never so pinched and wretched but he could give of his crust, and speak his word of compassion. If he had but his flute left, he could give that, and make the children happy in the dreary London court. He could give the coals in that queer coal-scuttle we read of to his poor neighbor: he could give away his blankets in college to the poor widow, and warm himself as he best might in the feathers: he could pawn his coat to save his landlord from jail: when he was a school-usher he spent his earnings in treats for the boys, and the good-natured schoolmaster's wife said justly that she ought to keep Mr. Goldsmith's money as well as the young gentlemen's. When he met his pupils in later life nothing would satisfy the Doctor but he must treat them still. "Have you seen the print of me after Sir Joshua Reynolds?" he asked of one of his old pupils. "Not seen it? not bought it? Sure, Jack, if your picture had been published, I'd not have been without it half an hour." His purse and his heart were everybody's, and his friends' as much as his own. When he was at the height of his reputation, and the Earl of Northumberland, going as Lord Lieutenant to Ireland, asked if he could be of any service to Dr. Goldsmith, Goldsmith recommended his brother, and not himself, to the great man. "My patrons," he gallantly said, "are the booksellers, and I want no others."* Hard

* "An 'inspired idiot,' Goldsmith, hangs strangely about him [Johnson]. . . . Yet, on the whole, there is no evil in the 'gooseberry-fool,' but rather much good; of a finer, if of a weaker sort than Johnson's; and all the more genuine that he himself could never become *conscious* of it, — though unhappily never cease *attempting* to become so: the author of the genuine 'Vicar of Wakefield,' nill he will he, must needs fly towards such a mass of genuine manhood." — CARLYLE'S *Essays* (2d ed.), vol. iv. p. 91.

* "At present, the few poets of England no longer depend on the great for subsistence; they have now no other patrons but the public, and the public, collectively considered, is a good and a generous master. It is indeed too frequently mistaken as to the merits of every candidate for favor; but to make amends, it is never mistaken long. A performance indeed may be forced for a time into reputation, but, destitute of real merit, it soon sinks; time, the touchstone of what is truly valuable, will soon discover the fraud, and an author should never arrogate to himself any share of success till his works have been read at least ten years with satisfaction.

'A man of letters at present, whose works are valuable, is perfectly sensible of their value. Every polite member of the community, by buying what he writes, contributes to reward him. The ridicule, therefore, of living in a garret might have been wit in the last age, but continues

patrons they were, and hard work he did; but he did not complain much: if in his early writings some bitter words escaped him, some allusions to neglect and poverty, he withdrew these expressions when his works were republished, and better days seemed to open for him; and he did not care to complain that printer or publisher had overlooked his merit, or left him poor. The Court face was turned from honest Oliver, the Court patronized Beattie; the fashion did not shine on him — fashion adored Sterne.† Fashion pronounced Kelly to be the great writer of comedy of his day. A little, not ill-humor, but plaintiveness — a little betrayal of wounded pride which he showed, render him not the less amiable. The author of "The Vicar of Wakefield" had a right to protest when Newbery kept back the MS. for two years; had a right to be a little peevish with Sterne; a little angry when Colman's actors declined their parts in his delightful comedy, when the manager refused to have a scene painted for it, and pronounced its damnation before hearing. He had not the great public with him; but he had the noble Johnson, and the admirable Reynolds, and the great Gibbon, and the great Burke, and the great Fox — friends and admirers illustrious indeed, as famous as those, who, fifty years before, sat round Pope's table.

Nobody knows, and I dare say Goldsmith's buoyant temper kept no account of, all the pains which he endured during the early period of his literary career. Should any man of letters in our day have to bear up against such, heaven grant he may come out of the period of misfortune with such a pure kind heart as that which Goldsmith obstinately bore in his breast. The insults to which he had to submit are shocking to read of — slander, contumely, vulgar satire, brutal malignity perverting his commonest motives and actions; he had his share of these, and one's anger is roused at reading of them, as it is at seeing a woman insulted or a child assaulted, at the notion that a creature so very gentle and weak, and full of love, should have had to suffer so. And he had worse than insult to undergo — to own to fault and deprecate the anger of ruffians. There is a letter of his extant to one Griffiths, a bookseller, in which poor Goldsmith is forced to confess that certain books sent by Griffiths are in the hands of a friend from whom Goldsmith had been forced to borrow money. "He was wild, sir," Johnson said, speaking of Goldsmith to Boswell, with his great, wise benevolence and noble mercifulness of heart — "Dr. Goldsmith was wild,

such no longer, because no longer true. A writer of real merit now may easily be rich, if his heart be set only on fortune: and for those who have no merit, it is but fit that such should remain in merited obscurity." — GOLDSMITH: *Citizen of the World*, Let. 84.

† Goldsmith attacked Sterne obviously enough, censuring his indecency, and slighting his wit, and ridiculing his manner, in the 53d letter in "The Citizen of the World."

"As in common conversation," says he, "the best way to make the audience laugh is by first laughing yourself; so in writing, the properest manner is to show an attempt at humor, which will pass upon most for humor in reality. To effect this, readers must be treated with the most perfect familiarity; in one page the author is to make them a low bow, and in the next to pull them by the nose; he must talk in riddles, and then send them to bed in order to dream for the solution," &c.

Sterne's humorous *mot* on the subject of the gravest part of the charges, then, as now, made against him, may perhaps be quoted here, from the excellent, the respectable, Sir Walter Scott: —

"Soon after 'Tristram' had appeared, Sterne asked a Yorkshire lady of fortune and condition, whether she had read his book. 'I have not, Mr. Sterne,' was the answer; 'and to be plain with you, I am informed it is not proper for female perusal.' 'My dear good lady,' replied the author, 'do not be gulled by such stories; the book is like your young heir there' (pointing to a child of three years old, who was rolling on the carpet in his white tunic); 'he shows at times a good deal that is usually concealed, but it is all in perfect innocence.'"

sir; but he is so no more." Ah! if we pity the good and weak man who suffers undeservedly, let us deal very gently with him from whom misery extorts not only tears, but shame; let us think humbly and charitably of the human nature that suffers so sadly and falls so low. Whose turn may it be to-morrow? What weak heart, confident before trial, may not succumb under temptation invincible? Cover the good man who has been vanquished — cover his face, and pass on.

For the last half-dozen years of his life, Goldsmith was far removed from the pressure of any ignoble necessity; and in the receipt, indeed, of a pretty large income from the booksellers his patrons. Had he lived but a few years more, his public fame would have been as great as his private reputation, and he might have enjoyed alive a part of that esteem which his country has ever since paid to the vivid and versatile genius who has touched on almost every subject of literature, and touched nothing that he did not adorn. Except in rare instances, a man is known in our profession, and esteemed as a skilful workman, years before the lucky hit which trebles his usual gains, and stamps him a popular author. In the strength of his age, and the dawn of his reputation, having for backers and friends the most illustrious literary men of his time,* fame and prosperity might have been in store for Goldsmith, had fate so willed it; and, at forty-six, had not sudden disease carried him off. I say prosperity rather than competence, for it is probable that no sum could have put order into his affairs or sufficed for his irreclaimable habits of dissipation. It must be remembered that he owed 2,000*l.*, when he died. "Was ever poet," Johnson asked, "so trusted before?" As has been the case with many another good fellow of his nation, his life was tracked and his substance wasted by crowds of hungry beggars and lazy dependants. If they came at a lucky time (and be sure they knew his affairs better than he did himself, and watched his pay-day), he gave them of his money; if they begged on empty-purse days he gave them his promissory bills: or he treated them to a tavern where he had credit; or he obliged them with an order upon honest Mr. Filby for coats, for which he paid as long as he could earn, and until the shears of Filby were to cut for him no more. Staggering under a load of debt and labor, tracked by bailiffs and reproachful creditors, running from a hundred poor dependants, whose appealing looks were perhaps the hardest of all pains for him to bear, devising fevered plans for the morrow, new histories, new comedies, all sorts of new literary schemes, flying from all these into seclusion, and out of seclusion into pleasure — at last, at five and forty, death seized him and closed his career.* I have been many a time in the chambers in the Temple

* "Goldsmith told us that he was now busy in writing a Natural History; and that he might have full leisure for it he had taken lodgings at a farmer's house, near to the six-mile stone in the Edgware Road, and had carried down his books in two returned postchaises. He said he believed the farmer's family thought him an odd character, similar to that in which 'The Spectator' appeared to his landlady and her children; he was 'The Gentleman.' Mr. Mickle, the translator of 'The Lusiad,' and I went to visit him at this place a few days afterwards. He was not at home; but, having a curiosity to see his apartment, we went in, and found curious scraps of descriptions of animals scrawled upon the wall with a blacklead pencil." — BOSWELL.

* "When Goldsmith was dying, Dr. Turton said to him, 'Your pulse is in greater disorder than it should be, from the degree of fever which you have; is your mind at ease?' Goldsmith answered it was not." — DR. JOHNSON (*in Boswell*).

"Chambers, you find, is gone far, and poor Goldsmith is gone much farther. He died of a fever, exasperated, as I believe, by the fear of distress. He had raised money and squandered it, by every artifice of acquisition and folly of expense. But let not his failings be remembered; he was a very great man." — DR. JOHNSON to *Boswell, July 5th*, 1774.

which were his, and passed up the staircase, which Johnson, and Burke, and Reynolds trod to see their friend, their poet, their kind Goldsmith — the stair on which the poor women sat weeping bitterly when they heard that the greatest and most generous of all men was dead within the black oak door.* Ah, it was a different lot from that for which the poor fellow sighed, when he wrote with heart yearning for home those most charming of all fond verses in which he fancies he revisits Auburn: —

"Here, as I take my solitary rounds,
Amidst thy tangled walks and ruined grounds,
And, many a year elapsed, return to view
Where once the cottage stood, the hawthorn grew,
Remembrance wakes, with all her busy train,
Swells at my heart, and turns the past to pain.

In all my wanderings round this world of care,
In all my griefs — and God has given my share —
I still had hopes my latest hours to crown,
Amidst these humble bowers to lay me down;
To husband out life's taper at the close,
And keep the flame from wasting by repose;
I still had hopes — for pride attends us still —
Amidst the swains to show my book-learned skill,
Around my fire an evening group to draw,
And tell of all I felt and all I saw;
And, as a hare, whom hounds and horns pursue,
Pants to the place from whence at first she flew —
I still had hopes — my long vexations past,
Here to return, and die at home at last.

O blest retirement, friend to life's decline!
Retreats from care that never must be mine —
How blest is he who crowns, in shades like these,
A youth of labor with an age of ease;
Who quits a world where strong temptations try,
And, since 'tis hard to combat, learns to fly!
For him no wretches born to work and weep
Explore the mine or tempt the dangerous deep;
No surly porter stands in guilty state
To spurn imploring famine from his gate;
But on he moves to meet his latter end,
Angels around befriending virtue's friend;
Sinks to the grave with unperceived decay,
Whilst resignation gently slopes the way:
And all his prospects brightening at the last,
His heaven commences ere the world be past."

In these verses, I need not say with what melody, with what touching truth, with what exquisite beauty of comparison — as indeed in hundreds more pages of the writings of this honest soul — the whole character of the man is told — his humble confession of faults and weakness; his pleasant little vanity, and desire that his village should admire him; his simple scheme of good in which everybody was to be happy — no beggar was to be refused his dinner — nobody in fact was to work much, and he to be the harmless chief of the Utopia, and the monarch of the Irish Yvetot. He would have told again, and without fear of their failing, those famous

* "When Burke was told [of Goldsmith's death] he burst into tears. Reynolds was in his painting-room when the messenger went to him; but at once he laid his pencil aside, which in times of great family distress he had not been known to do, left his painting room, and did not re-enter it that day. . . .

"The staircase of Brick Court is said to have been filled with mourners, the reverse of domestic; women without a home, without domesticity of any kind, with no friend but him they had come to weep for; outcasts of that great, solitary, wicked city, to whom he had never forgotten to be kind and charitable. And he had domestic mourners, too. His coffin was re-opened at the request of Miss Horneck and her sister (such was the regard he was known to have for them!) that a lock might be cut from his hair. It was in Mrs. Gwyn's possession when she died, after nearly seventy years." — FORSTER'S *Goldsmith*.

jokes * which had hung fire in London; he would have talked of his great friends of the Club — of my Lord Clare and my Lord Bishop, my Lord Nugent—sure he knew them intimately, and was hand and glove with some of the best men in town — and he would have spoken of Johnson and of Burke, and of Sir Joshua who had painted him — and he would have told wonderful sly stories of Ranelagh and the Pantheon, and the masquerades at Madame Cornelis'; and he would have toasted, with a sigh, the Jessamy Bride — the lovely Mary Horneck.

The figure of that charming young lady forms one of the prettiest recollections of Goldsmith's life. She and her beautiful sister, who married Bunbury, the graceful and humorous amateur artist of those days when Gilray had but just begun to try his powers, were among the kindest and dearest of Goldsmith's many friends, cheered and pitied him, travelled abroad with him, made him welcome at their home, and gave him many a pleasant holiday. He bought his finest clothes to figure at their country-house at Barton — he wrote them droll verses. They loved him, laughed at him, played him tricks, and made him happy. He asked for a loan from Garrick, and Garrick kindly supplied him, to enable him to go to Barton: but there were to be no more holidays, and only one brief struggle more for

* "Goldsmith's incessant desire of being conspicuous in company was the occasion of his sometimes appearing to such disadvantage as one should hardly have supposed possible in a man of his genius. When his literary reputation had risen deservedly high, and his society was much courted, he became very jealous of the extraordinary attention which was everywhere paid to Johnson. One evening, in a circle of wits, he found fault with me for talking of Johnson as entitled to the honor of unquestionable superiority. 'Sir,' said he, 'you are for making a monarchy of what should be a republic.'

"He was still more mortified, when, talking in a company with fluent vivacity, and, as he flattered himself, to the admiration of all present, a German who sat next him, and perceived Johnson rolling himself as if about to speak, suddenly stopped him, saying, 'Stay, stay — Toctor Shonson is going to zay zomething.' This was no doubt very provoking, especially to one so irritable as Goldsmith, who frequently mentioned it with strong expressions of indignation.

"It may also be observed that Goldsmith was sometimes content to be treated with an easy familiarity, but upon occasions would be consequential and important. An instance of this occurred in a small particular. Johnson had a way of contracting the names of his friends, as Beauclerk, Beau; Boswell, Bozzy. . . . I remember one day, when Tom Davies was telling that Dr. Johnson said — 'We are all in labor for a name to *Goldy's* play,' Goldsmith seemed displeased that such a liberty should be taken with his name, and said, 'I have often desired him not to call me *Goldy.*'"

This is one of several of Boswell's depreciatory mentions of Goldsmith — which may well irritate biographers and admirers — and also those who take that more kindly and more profound view of Boswell's own character, which was opened up by Mr. Carlyle's famous article on his book. No wonder that Mr. Irving calls Boswell an "incarnation of toadyism." And the worst of it is, that Johnson himself has suffered from this habit of the Laird of Auchinleck's. People are apt to forget under what Boswellian stimulus the great Doctor uttered many hasty things: — things no more indicative of the nature of the depths of his character than the phosphoric gleaming of the sea, when struck at night, is indicative of radical corruption of nature! In truth, it is clear enough on the whole that both Johnson and Goldsmith *appreciated* each other, and that they mutually knew it. They were — as it were, tripped up and flung against each other, occasionally, by the blundering and silly gambolling of people in company.

Something must be allowed for Boswell's "rivalry for Johnson's good graces" with Oliver (as Sir Walter Scott has remarked), for Oliver was intimate with the Doctor before his biographer was, — and, as we all remember, marched off with him to "take tea with Mrs. Williams," before Boswell had advanced to that honorable degree of intimacy. But, in truth, Boswell — though he perhaps showed more talent in his delineation of the Doctor than is generally ascribed to him — had not faculty to take a fair view of *two* great men at a time. Besides, as Mr. Forster justly remarks, "he was impatient of Goldsmith from the first hour of their acquaintance." — *Life and Adventures*, p. 292.

poor Goldsmith. A lock of his hair was taken from the coffin and given to the Jessamy Bride. She lived quite into our time. Hazlitt saw her an old lady, but beautiful still, in Northcote's painting-room, who told the eager critic how proud she always was that Goldsmith had admired her. The younger Colman has left a touching reminiscence of him. Vol. i. 63, 64.

"I was only five years old," he says, "when Goldsmith took me on his knee one evening whilst he was drinking coffee with my father, and began to play with me, which amiable act I returned, with the ingratitude of a peevish brat, by giving him a very smart slap on the face: it must have been a tingler, for it left the marks of my spiteful paw on his cheek. This infantile outrage was followed by summary justice, and I was locked up by my indignant father in an adjoining room to undergo solitary imprisonment in the dark. Here I began to howl and scream most abominably, which was no bad step towards my liberation, since those who were not inclined to pity me might be likely to set me free for the purpose of abating a nuisance.

"At length a generous friend appeared to extricate me from jeopardy, and that generous friend was no other than the man I had so wantonly molested by assault and battery — it was the tender-hearted Doctor himself, with a lighted candle in his hand, and a smile upon his countenance, which was still partially red from the effects of my petulance. I sulked and sobbed as he fondled and soothed, till I began to brighten. Goldsmith seized the propitious moment of returning good-humor, when he put down the candle and began to conjure. He placed three hats, which happened to be in the room, and a shilling under each. The shillings he told me were England, France, and Spain. 'Hey presto cockalorum!' cried the Doctor, and lo, on uncovering the shillings, which had been dispersed each beneath a separate hat, they were all found congregated under one. I was no politician at five years old, and therefore might not have wondered at the sudden revolution which brought England, France, and Spain all under one crown; but, as also I was no conjurer, it amazed me beyond measure. . . . From that time, whenever the Doctor came to visit my father, 'I plucked his gown to share the good man's smile;' a game at romps constantly ensued, and we were always cordial friends and merry playfellows. Our unequal companionship varied somewhat as to sports as I grew older; but it did not last long: my senior playmate died in his forty-fifth year, when I had attained my eleventh. . . . In all the numerous accounts of his virtues and foibles, his genius and absurdities, his knowledge of nature and ignorance of the world, his 'compassion for another's woe' was always predominant; and my trivial story of his humoring a froward child weighs but as a feather in the recorded scale of his benevolence."

Think of him reckless, thriftless, vain if you like — but merciful, gentle, generous, full of love and pity. He passes out of our life, and goes to render his account beyond it. Think of the poor pensioners weeping at his grave; think of the noble spirits that admired and deplored him; think of the righteous pen that wrote his epitaph — and of the wonderful and unanimous response of affection with which the world has paid back the love he gave it. His humor delighting us still: his song fresh and beautiful as when first he charmed with it: his words in all our mouths: his very weaknesses beloved and familiar — his benevolent spirit seems still to smile upon us: to do gentle kindnesses: to succor with sweet charity: to soothe, caress, and forgive: to plead with the fortunate for the unhappy and the poor.

His name is the last in the list of those men of humor who have formed the themes of the discourses which you have heard so kindly.

Long before I had ever hoped for such an audience, or dreamed of the possibility of the good fortune which has brought me so many friends, I was at issue with some of my literary brethren upon a point — which they held from tradition I think rather than experience — that our profession was neglected in this country; and that men of letters were ill received and held in slight esteem. It would hardly be grateful of me now to alter my old opinion that we do meet with good-will and kindness, with generous helping hands in the time of our necessity, with cordial and friendly recognition. What claim had any one of these of whom I have been speaking, but genius? What return of gratitude, fame, affection, did it not bring to all?

What punishment befell those who were unfortunate among them, but that which follows reckless habits and careless lives? For these faults a wit must suffer like the dullest prodigal that ever ran in debt. He must pay the tailor if he wears the coat; his children must go in rags if he spends his money at the tavern; he can't come to London and be made Lord Chancellor if he stops on the road and gambles away his last shilling at Dublin. And he must pay the social penalty of these follies too, and expect that the world will shun the man of bad habits, that women will avoid the man of loose life, that prudent folks will close their doors as a precaution, and before a demand should be made on their pockets by the needy prodigal. With what difficulty had any one of these men to contend, save that eternal and mechanical one of want of means and lack of capital, and of which thousands of young lawyers, young doctors, young soldiers and sailors, of inventors, manufacturers, shopkeepers, have to complain? Hearts as brave and resolute as ever beat in the breast of any wit or poet, sicken and break daily in the vain endeavor and unavailing struggle against life's difficulty. Don't we see daily ruined inventors, gray-haired midshipmen, balked heroes, blighted curates, barristers pining a hungry life out in chambers, the attorneys never mounting to their garrets, whilst scores of them are rapping at the door of the successful quack below? If these suffer, who is the author, that he should be exempt? Let us bear our ills with the same constancy with which others endure them, accept our manly part in life, hold our own, and ask no more. I can conceive of no kings or laws causing or curing Goldsmith's improvidence, or Fielding's fatal love of pleasure, or Dick Steele's mania for running races with the constable. You never can outrun that sure-footed officer — not by any swiftness or by dodges devised by any genius, however great; and he carries off the Tatler to the spunging-house, or taps the Citizen of the World on the shoulder as he would any other mortal.

Does society look down on a man because he is an author? I suppose if people want a buffoon they tolerate him only in so far as he is amusing; it can hardly be expected that they should respect him as an equal. Is there to be a guard of honor provided for the author of the last new novel or poem? how long is he to reign, and keep other potentates out of possession? He retires, grumbles, and prints a lamentation that literature is despised. If Captain A. is left out of Lady B.'s parties he does not state that the army is despised: if Lord C. no longer asks Counsellor D. to dinner, Counsellor D. does not announce that the bar is insulted. He is not fair to society if he enters it with this suspicion hankering about him; if he is doubtful about his reception, how hold up his head honestly, and look frankly in the face that world about which he is full of suspicion? Is he place-hunting, and thinking in his mind that he ought to be made an Ambassador, like Prior, or a Secretary of State, like Addison? his pretence of equality falls to the ground at once: he is scheming for a patron, not shaking the hand of a friend, when he meets the world. Treat such a man as he deserves; laugh at his buffoonery, and give him a dinner and a *bon jour;* laugh at his self-sufficiency and absurd assumptions of superiority, and his equally ludicrous airs of martyrdom: laugh at his flattery and his scheming, and buy it, if it's worth the having. Let the wag have his dinner and the hireling his pay, if you want him, and make a profound bow to the *grand homme incompris,* and the boisterous martyr, and show him the door. The great world, the great aggregate experience, has its good sense, as it has its good humor. It detects a pretender, as it trusts a loyal heart. It is kind in the main: how should it be otherwise than kind, when it is so wise and clear-headed? To any literary man who says, "It despises my profession," I say, with all my might — no, no, no. It may pass over your individual case — how many a brave fellow has failed in the race, and perished unknown in the struggle! — but it treats you as you merit in the main. If you serve it, it is not unthankful; if you please, it is pleased; if you cringe to it, it detects you, and scorns you if you are mean; it returns your cheerfulness with its good humor; it deals not ungenerously with your weaknesses; it recognizes most kindly your merits; it gives you a fair place and fair play. To any one of those men of whom we have spoken was it in the main ungrateful? A king might refuse Goldsmith a pension, as a publisher might keep his masterpiece and the delight of all the world in his desk for two years; but it was mistake, and not ill-will. Noble and illustrious names of Swift, and Pope, and Addison! dear and honored memories of Goldsmith and Fielding! kind friends, teachers, benefactors! who shall say that our country, which continues to bring you such an unceasing tribute of applause, admiration, love, sympathy, does not do honor to the literary calling in the honor which it bestows upon *you!*

CHARITY AND HUMOR.

A LECTURE.

CHARITY AND HUMOR.

SEVERAL charitable ladies of this city, to some of whom I am under great personal obligation, having thought that a Lecture of mine would advance a benevolent end which they had in view, I have preferred, in place of delivering a Discourse, which many of my hearers no doubt know already, upon a subject merely literary or biographical, to put together a few thoughts which may serve as a supplement to the former Lectures,* if you like, and which have this at least in common with the kind purpose which assembles you here, that they rise out of the same occasion, and treat of charity.

Besides contributing to our stock of happiness, to our harmless laughter and amusement, to our scorn for falsehood and pretension, to our righteous hatred of hypocrisy, to our education in the perception of truth, our love of honesty, our knowledge of life, and shrewd guidance through the world, have not our humorous writers, our gay and kind week-day preachers, done much in support of that holy cause which has assembled you in this place; and which you are all abetting, the cause of love and charity, the cause of the poor, the weak, and the unhappy; the sweet mission of love and tenderness, and peace and good-will towards men? That same theme which is urged upon you by the eloquence and example of good men to whom you are delighted listeners on Sabbath-days, is taught in his way and according to his power by the humorous writer, the commentator on every-day life and manners.

And as you are here assembled for a charitable purpose, giving your contributions at the door to benefit deserving people who need them without, I like to hope and think that the men of our calling have done something in aid of the cause of charity, and have helped, with kind words and kind thoughts at least, to confer happiness and to do good. If the humorous writers claim to be week-day preachers, have they conferred any benefit by their sermons? Are people happier, better, better disposed to their neighbors, more inclined to do works of kindness, to love, forbear, forgive, pity, after reading in Addison, in Steele, in Fielding, in Goldsmith, in Hood, in Dickens? I hope and believe so, and fancy that in writing they are also acting charitably, contributing with the means which Heaven supplies them, to forward the end which brings you, too, together.

A love of the human species is a very vague and indefinite kind of virtue, sitting very easily on a man, not confining his actions at all, shining in print, or exploding in

* This Lecture was delivered as supplementary to the course on the English Humorists.

paragraphs, after which efforts of benevolence, the philanthropist is sometimes said to go home, and be no better than his neighbors. Tartuffe and Joseph Surface, Stiggins and Chadband, who are always preaching fine sentiments, and are no more virtuous than hundreds of those whom they denounce and whom they cheat, are fair objects of mistrust and satire; but their hypocrisy, the homage, according to the old saying, which vice pays to virtue, has this of good in it, that its fruits are good: a man may preach good morals, though he may be himself but a lax practitioner; a Pharisee may put pieces of gold into the charity-plate out of mere hypocrisy and ostentation, but the bad man's gold feeds the widow and the fatherless as well as the good man's. The butcher and baker must needs look, not to motives, but to money, in return for their wares.

I am not going to hint that we of the Literary calling resemble Monsieur Tartuffe or Monsieur Stiggins, though there may be such men in our body, as there are in all.

A literary man of the humoristic turn is pretty sure to be of a philanthropic nature, to have a great sensibility, to be easily moved to pain or pleasure, keenly to appreciate the varieties of temper of people round about him, and sympathize in their laughter, love, amusement, tears. Such a man is philanthropic, man-loving by nature, as another is irascible, or red-haired, or six feet high. And so I would arrogate no particular merit to literary men for the possession of this faculty of doing good which some of them enjoy. It costs a gentleman no sacrifice to be benevolent on paper; and the luxury of indulging in the most beautiful and brilliant sentiments never makes any man a penny the poorer. A literary man is no better than another, as far as my experience goes; and a man writing a book, no better nor no worse than one who keeps accounts in a ledger, or follows any other occupation. Let us, however, give him credit for the good, at least, which he is the means of doing, as we give credit to a man with a million for the hundred which he puts into the plate at a charity-sermon. He never misses them. He has made them in a moment by a lucky speculation, and parts with them, knowing that he has an almost endless balance at his bank, whence he can call for more. But in esteeming the benefaction, we are grateful to the benefactor, too, somewhat; and so of men of genius, richly endowed, and lavish in parting with their mind's wealth, we may view them at least kindly and favorably, and be thankful for the bounty of which Providence has made them the dispensers.

I have said myself somewhere, I do not know with what correctness (for definitions never are complete), that humor is wit and love; I am sure, at any rate, that the best humor is that which contains most humanity, that which is flavored throughout with tenderness and kindness. This love does not demand constant utterance or actual expression, as a good father, in conversation with his children or wife, is not perpetually embracing them, or making protestations of his love; as a lover in the society of his mistress is not, at least as far as I am led to believe, forever squeezing her hand or sighing in her ear, "My soul's darling, I adore you!" He shows his love by his conduct, by his fidelity, by his watchful desire to make the beloved person happy; it lightens from his eye when she appears, though he may not speak it; it fills his heart when she is present or absent; influences all his words and actions; suffuses his whole being; it sets the father cheerily to work through the long day, supports him through the tedious labor of the weary absence or journey, and sends him happy home again, yearning towards the wife and children. This kind of love is not a spasm, but a life. It fondles and caresses at due seasons, no doubt; but the fond heart is always beating fondly and truly, though the wife is not sitting hand in hand with him, or the children hugging at his knee. And so with a loving humor: I think it is a genial writer's habit of being; it is the kind, gentle spirit's way of looking out on the world — that sweet friendliness which fills his heart and his style. You recognize it, even though there may not be a single point of wit, or a single pathetic touch in the page; though you may not be called upon to salute his genius by a laugh or a tear. That collision of ideas which provokes the one or the other must be occasional. They must be like papa's embraces, which I spoke of anon, who only delivers them now and again, and cannot be expected to go on kissing the children all night. And so the writer's jokes and sentiment, his ebullitions of feeling, his outbreaks of high spirits, must not be too frequent. One tires of a page of which every sentence sparkles with points, of a sentimentalist who is always pumping the tears from his eyes or your own. One suspects the genuineness of the tear, the naturalness of the humor; these ought to be true and manly in a man, as every thing else in his life should be manly and true; and he loses his dignity by laughing or weeping out of place, or too often.

When the Reverend Laurence Sterne begins to sentimentalize over the carriage in Monsieur Dessein's court-yard, and pretends to squeeze a tear out of a rickety old shandrydan; when, presently, he encounters the dead donkey on his road to Paris, and snivels over that asinine corpse, I say: "Away you drivelling quack: do not palm off these grimaces of grief upon simple folks who know no better, and cry, misled by your hypocrisy." Tears are sacred. The tributes of kind hearts to misfortune, the mites which gentle souls drop into the collections made for God's poor and unhappy, are not to be tricked out of them by a whimpering hypocrite, handing round a begging-box for your compassion, and asking your pity for a lie. When that same man tells me of Lefévre's illness and Uncle Toby's charity; of the noble at Rennes coming home and reclaiming his sword, I thank him for the generous emotion, which, springing genuinely from his own heart, has caused mine to admire benevolence, and sympathize with honor; and to feel love, and kindness, and pity.

If I do not love Swift, as, thank God, I do not, however immensely I may admire him, it is because I revolt from the man who placards himself as a professional hater of his own kind; because he chisels his savage indignation on his tomb-stone, as if to perpetuate his protest against being born of our race — the suffering, the weak, the erring, the wicked, if you will, but still the friendly, the loving children of God our Father: it is because, as I read through Swift's dark volumes, I never find the aspect of nature seems to delight him; the smiles of children to please him; the sight of wedded love to soothe him. I do not remember in any line of his writing a passing allusion to a natural scene of beauty. When he speaks about the families of his comrades and brother clergymen, it is to assail them with gibes and scorn, and to laugh at them brutally for being fathers, and for being poor. He does mention in the Journal to Stella, a sick child, to be sure — a child of Lady Masham, that was ill of the small-pox — but then it is to confound the brat for being ill, and the mother for attending to it, when she should have been busy about a court intrigue, in which the Dean was deeply engaged. And he alludes to a suitor of Stella's, and a match she might have made, and would have made, very likely, with an honorable and faithful and attached man, Tisdall, who loved her, and of whom Swift speaks, in a letter to this lady, in language so foul that you would not bear to hear it. In treating of the good the humorists have done, of the love and kindness they have taught and left behind them, it is not of this one I dare speak. Heaven help the lonely misanthrope! be kind to that multitude of sins, with so little charity to cover them!

Of Mr. Congreve's contributions to the English stock of benevolence, I do not speak; for, of any moral legacy to posterity, I doubt whether that brilliant man ever thought at all. He had some money, as I have told; every shilling of which he left to his friend the Duchess of Marlborough, a lady of great fortune and the highest fashion. He gave the gold of his brains to persons of fortune and fashion too. There is no more feeling in his comedies than in as many books of Euclid. He no more pretends to teach love for the poor, and good-will for the unfortunate, than a dancing-master does; he teaches pirouettes and flic-flacs; and how to bow to a lady, and to walk a minuet. In his private life, Congreve was immensely liked — more so than any man of his age, almost; and to have been so liked, must have been kind and good-natured. His good-nature bore him through extreme bodily ills and pain, with uncommon cheerfulness and courage. Being so gay, so bright, so popular, such a grand seigneur, be sure he was kind to those about him, generous to his dependants, serviceable to his friends. Society does not like a man so long as it liked Congreve, unless he is likable; it finds out a quack very soon; it scorns a poltroon or a curmudgeon; we may be certain that this man was brave, good-tempered, and liberal; so, very likely, is Monsieur Pirouette, of whom we spoke; he cuts his capers, he grins, bows, and dances to his fiddle. In private he may have a hundred virtues; in public, he teaches dancing. His business is cotillons, not ethics.

As much may be said of those charming and lazy Epicureans, Gay and Prior, sweet lyric singers, comrades of Anacreon, and disciples of love and the bottle. "Is there any moral shut within the bosom of a rose?" sings our great Tennyson. Does a nightingale preach from a bough, or the lark from his cloud? Not knowingly; yet we may be grateful, and love larks and roses, and the flower-crowned minstrels, too, who laugh and who sing.

Of Addison's contributions to the charity of the world, I have spoken before, in trying to depict that noble figure; and say now, as then, that we should thank him as one of the greatest benefactors of that vast and immeasurably spreading family which speaks our common tongue. Wherever it is spoken, there is no man that does not feel, and understand, and use the noble English word "gentleman." And there is no man that teaches us to be gentlemen better than Joseph Addison. Gentle in our bearing through life; gentle and courteous to our neighbor; gentle in dealing with his follies and weaknesses; gentle in treating his opposition; deferential to the old; kindly to the poor, and those below us in degree; for people above us and below us we must find, in whatever hemisphere we dwell, whether kings or presidents govern us; and in no republic or monarchy that I know of, is a citizen exempt from the tax of befriending poverty and weakness, of respecting age, and of honoring his father and mother. It has just been whispered to me — I have not been three months in the country, and, of course, cannot venture to express an opinion of my own — that, in regard to paying this latter tax of respect and honor to age, some very few of the Republican youths are occasionally a little remiss. I have heard of young Sons of Freedom publishing their Declaration of Independence before they could well spell it; and cutting the connection between father and mother before they had learned to shave. My own time of life having been stated by various enlightened organs of public opinion, at almost any figure from forty-five to sixty, I cheerfully own that I belong to the Fogy interest, and ask leave to rank in, and plead for, that respectable class. Now a gentleman can but be a gentleman, in Broadway or the backwoods, in Pall-Mall or California; and where and whenever he lives, thousands of miles away in the wilderness, or hundreds of years hence, I am sure that reading the writings of this true gentleman, this true Christian, this noble Joseph Addison, must do him good. He may take Sir Roger de Coverley to the Diggings with him, and learn to be gentle and good-humored, and urbane, and friendly in the midst of that struggle in which his life is engaged. I take leave to say that the most brilliant youth of this city may read over this delightful memorial of a bygone age, of fashions long passed away; of manners long since changed and modified; of noble gentlemen, and a great, and a brilliant and polished society; and find in it much to charm and polish, to refine and instruct him. A courteousness, which can be out of place at no time, and under no flag. A politeness and simplicity, a truthful manhood, a gentle respect and deference, which may be kept as the unbought grace of life, and cheap defence of mankind, long after its old artificial distinctions, after periwigs, and small-swords, and ruffles, and red-heeled shoes, and titles, and stars and garters, have passed away. I will tell you when I have been put in mind of two of the finest gentlemen books bring us any mention of. I mean *our* books (not books of history, but books of humor). I will tell you when I have been put in mind of the courteous gallantry of the noble knight, Sir Roger de Coverley of Coverley Manor, of the noble Hidalgo Don Quixote of La Mancha: here in your own omnibus-carriages and railway-cars, when I have seen a woman step in, handsome or not, well-dressed or not, and a workman in hob-nail shoes, or a dandy in the height of the fashion, rise up and give her his place. I think Mr. Spectator, with his short face, if he had seen such a deed of courtesy, would have smiled a sweet smile to the doer of that gentleman-like action, and have made him a low bow from under his great periwig, and have gone home and written a pretty paper about him.

I am sure Dick Steele would have hailed him, were he dandy or mechanic, and asked him to a tavern to share a bottle, or perhaps half a dozen. Mind, I do not set down the five last flasks to Dick's score for virtue, and look upon them as works of the most questionable supererogation.

Steele, as a literary benefactor to the world's charity, must rank very high, indeed, not merely from his givings, which were abundant, but because his endowments are prodigiously increased in value since he bequeathed them, as the revenues of the lands, bequeathed to our Foundling-Hospital at London, by honest Captain Coram, its founder, are immensely enhanced by the houses since built upon them. Steele was the founder of sentimental writing in English, and how the land has been since occupied, and what hundreds of us have laid out gardens and built up tenements on Steele's ground! Before his time, readers or hearers were never called upon to cry except at a tragedy, and compassion was not expected to express itself otherwise than in blank verse, or for personages much lower in rank than a dethroned monarch, or a widowed or a jilted empress. He stepped off the high-heeled cothurnus, and came down into common life; he held out his great hearty arms, and embraced us all; he had a bow for all women; a kiss for all children; a shake of the hand for all men, high or low; he showed us Heaven's sun shining every day on quiet homes; not gilded palace-roofs only, or court processions, or heroic warriors fighting for princesses and pitched battles.

He took away comedy from behind the fine lady's alcove, or the screen where the libertine was watching her. He ended all that wretched business of wives jeering at their husbands, of rakes laughing wives, and husbands too, to scorn. That miserable rouged, tawdry, sparkling, hollow-hearted comedy of the Restoration fled before him, and, like the wicked spirit in the Fairy-books, shrank, as Steele let the daylight in, and shrieked, and shuddered, and vanished. The stage of humorists has been common-life ever since Steele's and Addison's time; the joys and griefs, the aversions and sympathies, the laughter and tears of nature.

And here, coming off the stage, and throwing aside the motley habit, or satiric disguise, in which he had before entertained you, mingling with the world, and wearing the same coat as his neighbor, the humorist's service became straightway immensely more available; his means of doing good infinitely multiplied; his success, and the esteem in which he was held, proportionately increased. It requires an effort, of which all minds are not capable, to understand Don Quixote; children and common people still read Gulliver for the story merely. Many more persons are sickened by Jonathan Wild than can comprehend the satire of it. Each of the great men who wrote those books was speaking from behind the satiric mask I anon mentioned. Its distortions appall many simple spectators: its settled sneer or laugh is unintelligible to thousands, who have not the wit to interpret the meaning of the visored satirist preaching from within. Many a man was at fault about Jonathan Wild's greatness, who could feel and relish Allworthy's goodness in Tom Jones, and Doctor Harrison's in Amelia, and dear Parson Adams, and Joseph Andrews. We love to read; we may grow ever so old, but we love to read of them still — of love and beauty, of frankness, and bravery, and generosity. We hate hypocrites and cowards; we long to defend oppressed innocence, and to soothe and succor gentle women and children. We are glad when vice is foiled and rascals punished; we lend a foot to kick Blifil down stairs; and as we attend the brave bridegroom to his wedding on the happy marriage day, we ask the groomsman's privilege to salute the blushing cheek of Sophia. A lax morality in many a vital point I own in Fielding, but a great hearty sympathy and benevolence; a great kindness for the poor; a great gentleness and pity for the unfortunate; a great love for the pure and good: these are among the contributions to the charity of the world with which this erring but noble creature endowed it.

As for Goldsmith, if the youngest and most unlettered person here has not been happy with the family at Wakefield; has not rejoiced when Olivia returned, and been thankful for her forgiveness and restoration; has not laughed with delighted good humor over Moses's gross of green spectacles; has not loved with all his heart the good Vicar, and that kind spirit which created these charming figures, and devised the beneficent fiction which speaks to us so tenderly — what call is there for me to speak? In this place, and on this occasion, remembering these men, I claim from you your sympathy for the good they have done, and for the sweet charity which they have bestowed on the world.

When humor joins with rhythm and music, and appears in song, its influence is irresistible; its charities are countless, it stirs the feelings to love, peace, friendship, as scarce any moral agent can. The songs of Béranger are hymns of love and tenderness; I have seen great whiskered Frenchmen warbling the "Bonne Vielle," the "Soldats au pas, au pas;" with tears rolling down their mustaches. At a Burns's Festival, I have seen Scotchmen singing

Burns, while the drops twinkled on their furrowed cheeks: while each rough hand was flung out to grasp its neighbor's; while early scenes and sacred recollections, and dear and delightful memories of the past, came rushing back at the sound of the familiar words and music, and the softened heart was full of love and friendship and home. Humor! if tears are the alms of gentle spirits, and may be counted, as sure they may, among the sweetest of life's charities. Of that kindly sensibility, and sweet sudden emotion, which exhibits itself at the eyes, I know no such provocative as humor. It is an irresistible sympathizer; it surprises you into compassion; you are laughing and disarmed, and suddenly forced into tears. I heard a humorous balladist not long since, a minstrel with wool on his head, and an ultra-Ethiopian complexion, who performed a negro ballad, that I confess moistened these spectacles in the most unexpected manner. They have gazed at dozens of tragedy-queens, dying on the stage, and expiring in appropriate blank verse, and I never wanted to wipe them. They have looked up, with deep respect be it said, at many scores of clergymen in pulpits, and without being dimmed; and behold a vagabond with a corked face and a banjo sings a little song, strikes a wild note which sets the whole heart thrilling with happy pity. Humor! humor is the mistress of tears; she knows the way to the *fons lachrymarum*, strikes in dry and rugged places with her enchanting wand, and bids the fountain gush and sparkle. She has refreshed myriads more from her natural springs, than ever tragedy has watered from her pompous old urn.

Popular humor, and especially modern popular humor, and the writers, its exponents, are always kind and chivalrous, taking the side of the weak against the strong. In our plays, and books, and entertainments for the lower classes in England, I scarce remember a story or theatrical piece in which a wicked aristocrat is not bepommelled by a dashing young champion of the people. There was a book which had an immense popularity in England, and I believe has been greatly read here, in which the Mysteries of the Court of London were said to be unveiled by a gentleman, who I suspect knows about as much about the court of London as he does of that of Pekin. Years ago I treated myself to sixpennyworth of this performance at a railway station, and found poor dear George the Fourth, our late most religious and gracious king, occupied in the most flagitious designs against the tradesmen's families in his metropolitan city. A couple of years after, I took sixpennyworth more of the same delectable history: George the Fourth was still at work, still ruining the peace of tradesmen's families; he had been at it for two whole years, and a bookseller at the Brighton station told me that this book was by many, many times the most popular of all periodical tales then published, because, says he, "it lashes the aristocracy!" Not long since, I went to two penny-theatres in London; immense eager crowds of people thronged the buildings, and the vast masses thrilled and vibrated with the emotion produced by the piece represented on the stage, and burst into applause or laughter, such as many a polite actor would sigh for in vain. In both these pieces there was a wicked Lord kicked out of the window — there is always a wicked Lord kicked out of the window. First piece: — "Domestic drama — Thrilling interest! — Weaver's family in distress! — Fanny gives away her bread to little Jacky, and starves! — Enter wicked Lord: tempts Fanny with offer of Diamond Necklace, Champagne Suppers, and Coach to ride in! — Enter sturdy Blacksmith. — Scuffle between Blacksmith and Aristocratic minion: exit wicked Lord out of the window." Fanny, of course, becomes Mrs. Blacksmith.

The second piece was a nautical

drama, also of thrilling interest, consisting chiefly of hornpipes, and acts of most tremendous oppression on the part of certain Earls and Magistrates towards the people. Two wicked Lords were in this piece the atrocious scoundrels: one Aristocrat, a deep-dyed villain, in short duck trowsers and Berlin cotton gloves; while the other minion of wealth enjoyed an eye-glass with a blue ribbon, and whisked about the stage with a penny cane. Having made away with Fanny Forester's lover, Tom Bowling, by means of a press-gang, they meet her all alone on a common, and subject her to the most opprobrious language and behavior: "Release me, villains!" says Fanny, pulling a brace of pistols out of her pockets, and crossing them over her breast so as to cover wicked Lord to the right, wicked Lord to the left; and they might have remained in that position ever so much longer (for the aristocratic rascals had pistols too), had not Tom Bowling returned from sea at the very nick of time, armed with a great marlinespike, with which — whack! whack! down goes wicked Lord, No. 1 — wicked Lord, No. 2. Fanny rushes into Tom's arms with an hysterical shriek, and I dare say they marry and are very happy ever after. — Popular fun is always kind: it is the champion of the humble against the great. In all popular parables, it is Little Jack that conquers, and the Giant that topples down. I think our popular authors are rather hard upon the great folks. Well, well! their Lordships have all the money, and can afford to be laughed at.

In our days, in England, the importance of the humorous preacher has prodigiously increased; his audiences are enormous; every week or month his happy congregations flock to him; they never tire of such sermons. I believe my friend Mr. Punch is as popular to-day as he has been any day since his birth; I believe that Mr. Dickens's readers are even more numerous than they have ever been since his unrivalled pen commenced to delight the world with its humor. We have among us other literary parties; we have Punch, as I have said, preaching from his booth; we have a Jerrold party very numerous, and faithful to that acute thinker and distinguished wit; and we have also — it must be said, and it is still to be hoped — a Vanity-Fair party, the author of which work has lately been described by "The London Times" newspaper as a writer of considerable parts, but a dreary misanthrope, who sees no good anywhere, who sees the sky above him green I think, instead of blue, and only miserable sinners round about him. So we are; so is every writer and every reader I ever heard of; so was every being who ever trod this earth, save One. I cannot help telling the truth as I view it, and describing what I see. To describe it otherwise than it seems to me would be falsehood in that calling in which it has pleased Heaven to place me; treason to that conscience which says that men are weak; that truth must be told; that fault must be owned; that pardon must be prayed for; and that love reigns supreme over all.

I look back at the good which of late years the kind English Humorists have done; and if you are pleased to rank the present speaker among that class, I own to an honest pride at thinking what benefits society has derived from men of our calling. That "Song of the Shirt," which Punch first published, and the noble, the suffering, the melancholy, the tender Hood sang, may surely rank as a great act of charity to the world, and call from it its thanks and regard for its teacher and benefactor. That astonishing poem, which you all of you know, of the "Bridge of Sighs,"*

* THE BRIDGE OF SIGHS.

"Drowned! Drowned!" — HAMLET.

One more Unfortunate,
Weary of breath,
Rashly importunate,
Gone to her death.

who can read it without tenderness, without reverence to Heaven, charity to man, and thanks to the beneficent genius which sang for us so nobly?

I never saw the writer but once; but shall always be glad to think that some words of mine, printed in a periodical of that day, and in praise of these amazing verses (which, strange to say, appeared almost unnoticed at first in the magazine in which Mr. Hood published them) — I am proud, I say, to think that some words of appreciation of mine reached him on his death-bed, and pleased

Take her up tenderly,
Lift her with care;
Fashioned so slenderly,
Young, and so fair!

Look at her garments
Clinging like cerements;
Whilst the wave constantly
Drips from her clothing;
Take her up instantly,
Loving, not loathing.

Touch her not scornfully;
Think of her mournfully,
Gently, and humanly;
Not of the stains of her:
All that remains of her
Now, is pure womanly.

Make no deep scrutiny
Into her mutiny
Rash and undutiful;
Past all dishonor,
Death has left on her
Only the beautiful.

Still, for all slips of hers,
One of Eve's family —
Wipe those poor lips of hers
Oozing so clammily.

Loop up her tresses
Escaped from the comb, —
Her fair auburn tresses, —
Whilst wonderment guesses
Where was her home?

Who was her Father?
Who was her Mother?
Had she a sister?
Had she a brother?
Or was there a dearer one
Still, and a nearer one
Yet, than all other?

Alas for the rarity
Of Christian charity
Under the sun!
Oh! it was pitiful!
Near a whole city full,
Home she had none.

Sisterly, brotherly,
Fatherly, motherly
Feelings had changed:
Love by harsh evidence
Thrown from its eminence;
Even God's providence
Seeming estranged.

Where the lamps quiver
So far in the river,
With many a light
From window and casement,
From garret to basement,
She stood with amazement,
Houseless by night.

The bleak wind of March
Made her tremble and shiver,
But not the dark arch,
Or the black flowing river.

Mad from life's history,
Glad to death's mystery,
Swift to be hurled
Anywhere, anywhere
Out of the world!

In she plunged boldly,
No matter how coldly
The rough river ran,
Over the brink of it,
Picture it — think of it,
Dissolute man!
Lave in it, drink of it,
Then, if you can!

Take her up tenderly,
Lift her with care;
Fashioned so slenderly,
Young, and so fair!

Ere her limbs frigidly
Stiffen too rigidly,
Decently — kindly —
Smoothe and compose them;
And her eyes, close them,
Staring so blindly!

Dreadfully staring
Through muddy impurity,
As when with the daring
Last look of despairing
Fixed on futurity.

Perishing gloomily,
Spurred by contumely,
Cold inhumanity,
Burning insanity
Into her rest.
Cross her hands humbly
As if praying dumbly,
Over her breast!

Owning her weakness,
Her evil behavior,
And leaving with meekness
Her sins to her Saviour!"

and soothed him in that hour of manful resignation and pain.

As for the charities of Mr. Dickens, multiplied kindnesses which he has conferred upon us all; upon our children; upon people educated and uneducated; upon the myriads here and at home, who speak our common tongue; have not you, have not I, all of us, reason to be thankful to this kind friend, who soothed and charmed so many hours, brought pleasure and sweet laughter to so many homes; made such multitudes of children happy; endowed us with such a sweet store of gracious thoughts, fair fancies, soft sympathies, hearty enjoyments? There are creations of Mr. Dickens's which seem to me to rank as personal benefits; figures so delightful, that one feels happier and better for knowing them, as one does for being brought into the society of very good men and women. The atmosphere in which these people live is wholesome to breathe in; you feel that to be allowed to speak to them is a personal kindness; you come away better for your contact with them; your hands seem cleaner from having the privilege of shaking theirs. Was there ever a better charity sermon preached in the world than Dickens's Christmas Carol? I believe it occasioned immense hospitality throughout England; was the means of lighting up hundreds of kind fires at Christmas time; caused a wonderful outpouring of Christmas good feeling; of Christmas punch-brewing; an awful slaughter of Christmas turkeys, and roasting and basting of Christmas beef. As for this man's love of children, that amiable organ at the back of his honest head must be perfectly monstrous. All children ought to love him. I know two that do, and read his books ten times for once that they peruse the dismal preachments of their father. I know one who, when she is happy, reads Nicholas Nickleby; when she is unhappy, reads Nicholas Nickleby; when she is tired, reads Nicholas Nickleby; when she is in bed, reads Nicholas Nickleby; when she has nothing to do, reads Nicholas Nickleby; and when she has finished the book, reads Nicholas Nickleby over again. This candid young critic, at ten years of age, said, "I like Mr. Dickens's books much better than your books, papa;" and frequently expressed her desire that the latter author should write a book like one of Mr. Dickens's books. Who can? Every man must say his own thoughts in his own voice, in his own way; *

* The following is from "The Curate's Walk," in Punch, for 1847.

"It was the third out of the four bell-buttons at the door at which the Curate pulled; and the summons was answered after a brief interval.

"I must premise that the house before which we stopped was No. 14, Sedan Buildings, leading out of Great Guelph Street—Dettingen Street, Culloden Street, Minden Square and Upper and Lower Caroline Row form part of the same quarter—a very queer and solemn quarter to walk in, I think, and one which always suggests Fielding's novels to me. I can fancy Captain Booth strutting before the very door at which we were standing, in tarnished lace, with his hat cocked over his eye, and his hand on his hanger; or Lady Bellaston's chair and bearers coming swinging down Great Guelph Street, which we have just quitted to enter Sedan Buildings.

"Sedan Buildings is a little flagged square, ending abruptly with the huge walls of Bluck's Brewery. The houses, by many degrees smaller than the large decayed tenements in Great Guelph Street, are still not uncomfortable, although shabby. There are brass plates on the doors, two on some of them; or simple names, as 'Lunt,' 'Padgemore,' &c. (as if no other statement about Lunt and Padgemore were necessary at all), under the bells. There are pictures of mangles before two of the houses, and a gilt arm with a hammer sticking out from one. I never saw a Goldbeater. What sort of a being is he, that he always sticks out his ensign in dark, mouldy, lonely, dreary, but somewhat respectable places? What powerful Mulciberian fellows they must be, those Goldbeaters, whacking and thumping with huge mallets at the precious metals all day. I wonder what is Goldbeater's skin? and if they get impregnated with the metal? and are their great arms under their clean shirts on Sundays, all gilt and shining? It is a quiet, kind, respectable place somehow,

lucky is he who has such a charming gift of nature as this, which brings all the children in the world trooping to him, and being fond of him.

in spite of its shabbiness. Two pewter pints and a jolly little half-pint are hanging on the railings in perfect confidence, basking in what little sun comes into the Court. A group of small children are making an ornament of oyster-shells in one corner. Who has that half-pint? Is it for one of those small ones, or for some delicate female recommended to take beer? The windows in the Court, upon some of which the sun glistens, are not cracked, and pretty clean; it is only the black and dreary look behind which gives them a poverty-stricken appearance. No curtains or blinds. A bird-cage and a very few pots of flowers here and there. This — with the exception of a milkman talking to a whitey-brown woman, made up of bits of flannel and strips of faded chintz and calico seemingly, and holding a long bundle which cried — this was all I saw in Sedan Buildings while we were waiting until the door should open.

"At last the door was opened, and by a porteress so small, that I wonder how she could ever have reached up to the latch. She bobbed a courtesy and smiled at the Curate, whose face gleamed with benevolence too, in reply to that salutation.

"'Mother not at home?' says Frank Whitestock, patting the child on the head.

"'Mother's out charing, sir,' replied the girl; 'but please to walk up, sir.' And she led the way up one or two pairs of stairs to that apartment in the house which is called the second-floor front; in which was the abode of the charwoman.

"There were two young persons in the room, of the respective ages of eight and five, I should think. She of five years of age was hemming a duster, being perched on a chair at the table in the middle of the room. The elder, of eight, politely wiped a chair with a cloth for the accommodation of the good-natured Curate, and came and stood between his knees, immediately alongside of his umbrella, which also reposed there, and which she by no means equalled in height.

"'These children attend my school at Saint Timothy's,' Mr. Whitestock said; 'and Betsy keeps the house while her mother is from home.'

"Any thing cleaner or neater than this house it was impossible to conceive. There was a big bed, which must have been the resting-place of the whole of this little family. There were three or four religious prints on the walls, besides two framed and glazed, of Prince Coburg and the Princess Charlotte. There were brass candlesticks, and a lamb on the chimney-piece, and a cupboard in the corner, decorated with near half a dozen of plates, yellow bowls, and crockery. And on the table there were two or three bits of dry bread, and a jug with water, with which these three young people (it being then near three o'clock) were about to make their meal called tea.

"That little Betsy, who looks so small, is nearly ten years old; and has been a mother ever since the age of about five. I mean to say, that her own mother having to go out upon her charing operations, Betsy assumes command of the room during her parent's absence: has nursed her sisters from babyhood up to the present time: keeps order over them, and the house as clean as you see it: and goes out occasionally and transacts the family purchases of bread, moist sugar, and mother's tea. They dine upon bread, tea and breakfast upon bread when they have it, or go to bed without a morsel. Their holiday is Sunday, which they spend at Church and Sunday-school. The younger children scarcely ever go out save on that day, but sit sometimes in the sun, which comes in pretty pleasantly; sometimes blue in the cold, for they very seldom see a fire except to heat irons by, when mother has a job of linen to get up. Father was a journeyman book-binder, who died four years ago, and is buried among thousands and thousands of the nameless dead who lie crowding the black churchyard of St. Timothy's parish.

"The Curate evidently took especial pride in Victoria, the youngest of these three children of the charwoman, and caused Betsy to fetch a book which lay at the window, and bade her read. It was a Missionary Register which the Curate opened hap-hazard, and this baby began to read out in an exceedingly clear and resolute voice about —

"'The island of Raritongo is the least frequented of all the Caribbean Archipelago. Wankyfungo is four leagues south-east by east, and the peak of the crater of Shuagnahua is distinctly visible. "The Irascible" entered Raritongo Bay on the evening of Thursday 29th, and the next day the Rev. Mr. Flethers, Mrs. Flethers, and their nine children, and Shangpooky, the native converted at Cacabawgo, landed and took up their residence at the house of Ratatua, the principal chief, who entertained us with a yam, a pig,' &c., &c., &c.

"Raritongo, Wankifungo, Archipelago. I protest this little woman read off each of these long words with an ease which perfectly astonished me. Many a lieutenant in Her Majesty's Heavies would be puzzled with words of half the length. Whitestock, by way of reward for her

I remember when that famous Nicholas Nickleby came out, seeing a letter from a pedagogue in the north of England, which, dismal as it was, was immensely comical. "Mr. Dickens's ill-advised publication," wrote the poor schoolmaster, "has passed like a whirlwind over the schools of the North." He was a proprietor of a cheap school; Dotheboys-Hall was a cheap school. There were many such establishments in the northern counties. Parents were ashamed, that never were ashamed before, until the kind satirist laughed at them; relatives were frightened; scores of little scholars were taken away; poor school-masters had to shut their shops up; every pedagogue was voted a Squeers, and many suffered, no doubt unjustly; but afterwards school-boys' backs were not so much caned; school-boys' meat was less tough and more plentiful; and school-boys' milk was not so sky-blue. What a kind light of benevolence it is that plays round Crummles and the Phenomenon, and all those poor theatre people in that charming book! What a humor? and what a good-humor! I coincide with the youthful critic, whose opinion has just been mentioned, and own to a family admiration for Nicholas Nickleby.

One might go on, though the task would be endless and needless, chronicling the names of kind folks with whom this kind genius has made us familiar. Who does not love the Marchioness, and Mr. Richard Swiv-

scholarship, gave her another pat on the head; having received which present with a courtesy, she went and put back the book into the window, and, clambering back into the chair, resumed the hemming of the blue duster.

"I suppose it was the smallness of these people, as well as their singular, neat, and tidy behavior, which interested me so. Here were three creatures not so high as the table, with all the labors, duties, and cares of life upon their little shoulders, working and doing their duty like the biggest of my readers; regular, laborious, cheerful — content with small pittances, practising a hundred virtues of thrift and order.

"Elizabeth, at ten years of age, might walk out of this house, and take the command of a small establishment. She can wash, get up linen, cook, make purchases, and buy bargains. If I were ten years old and three feet in height, I would marry her, and we would go and live in a cupboard, and share the little half-pint pot of porter for dinner. 'Melia, eight years of age, though inferior in accomplishments to her sister, is her equal in size, and can wash, scrub, hem, go errands, put her hand to the dinner, and make herself generally useful. In a word, she is fit to be a little housemaid, to make every thing but the beds, which she cannot as yet reach up to. As for Victoria's qualifications, they have been mentioned before. I wonder whether the Princess Alice can read off 'Raritongo,' &c., as glibly as this surprising little animal.

"I asked the Curate's permission to make these young ladies a present, and accordingly produced the sum of sixpence to be divided amongst the three. 'What will you do with it?' I said, laying down the coin.

"They answered all three at once, and in a little chorus, 'We'll give it to mother.' This verdict caused the disbursement of another sixpence, and it was explained to them that the sum was for their own private pleasures, and each was called upon to declare what she would purchase.

"Elizabeth says, 'I would like two penn'orth of meat, if you please, sir.'

"'Melia: 'Ha'porth of treacle, three farthings' worth of milk, and the same of fresh bread.'

"Victoria, speaking very quick, and gasping in an agitated manner. 'Ha'pny — aha — orange, and ha'pny — aha — apple, and ha'pny — aha — treacle, and, and aha' — here her imagination failed her. She did not know what to do with the rest of the money.

"At this 'Melia actually interposed, 'Suppose she and Victoria subscribed a farthing a piece out of their money, so that Betsy might have a quarter of a pound of meat?' She added that her sister wanted it, and that it would do her good. Upon my word, she made the proposals and the calculations in an instant, and all of her own accord. And before we left them, Betsy had put on the queerest little black shawl and bonnet, and had a mug and basket ready to receive the purchases in question.

"Sedan Court has a particularly friendly look to me since that day. Peace be with you, O thrifty, kindly, simple, loving little maidens! May their voyage in life prosper! Think of that great journey before them, and the little cock-boat manned by babies venturing over the stormy sea." — Spec.

eller! Who does not sympathize, not only with Oliver Twist, but his admirable young friend the Artful Dodger? Who has not the inestimable advantage of possessing a Mrs. Nickleby in his own family? Who does not bless Sairey Gamp, and wonder at Mrs. Harris? Who does not venerate the chief of that illustrious family who, being stricken by misfortune, wisely and greatly turned his attention to "coals," the accomplished, the Epicurean, the dirty, the delightful Micawber?

I may quarrel with Mr. Dickens's art a thousand and a thousand times, I delight and wonder at his genius; I recognize in it — I speak with awe and reverence — a commission from that Divine Beneficence, whose blessed task we know it will one day be to wipe every tear from every eye. Thankfully I take my share of the feast of love and kindness, which this gentle, and generous, and charitable soul has contributed to the happiness of the world. I take and enjoy my share, and say a Benediction for the meal.

ROUNDABOUT PAPERS.

A Lazy Idle Boy.

ROUNDABOUT PAPERS.

ON A LAZY IDLE BOY.

I HAD occasion to pass a week in the autumn in the little old town of Coire or Chur, in the Grisons, where lies buried that very ancient British king, saint, and martyr, Lucius,* who founded the Church of St. Peter, on Cornhill. Few people note the church now-a-days, and fewer ever heard of the saint. In the cathedral at Chur, his statue appears surrounded by other sainted persons of his family. With tight red breeches, a Roman habit, a curly brown beard, and a neat little gilt crown and sceptre, he stands, a very comely and cheerful image: and, from what I may call his peculiar position with regard to Cornhill, I beheld this figure of St. Lucius with more interest than I should have bestowed upon personages who, hierarchically, are, I dare say, his superiors.

The pretty little city stands, so to speak, at the end of the world — of the world of to-day, the world of rapid motion, and rushing railways, and the commerce and intercourse of men. From the northern gate, the iron road stretches away to Zürich, to Basle, to Paris, to home. From the old southern barriers, before which a little river rushes, and around which stretch the crumbling battlements of the ancient town, the road bears the slow diligence or lagging vetturino by the shallow Rhine, through the awful gorges of the Via Mala, and presently over the Splügen to the shores of Como.

I have seldom seen a place more quaint, pretty, calm, and pastoral, than this remote little Chur. What need have the inhabitants for walls and ramparts, except to build summer-houses, to trail vines, and hang clothes to dry on them? No enemies approach the great mouldering gates: only at morn and even the cows come lowing past them, the village maidens chatter merrily round the fountains, and babble like the ever-voluble stream that flows under the old walls. The schoolboys, with book and satchel, in smart uniforms, march up to the gymnasium, and return thence at their stated time. There is one coffee-house in the town, and I see one old gentleman goes to it. There are shops with no customers seemingly, and the lazy tradesmen look out of their little

* Stow quotes the inscription, still extant, "from the table fast chained in St. Peter's Church, Cornhill;" and says, "he was after some chronicle buried at London, and after some chronicle buried at Glowcester" — but, oh! these incorrect chroniclers! when Alban Butler, in "The Lives of the Saints," v. xii., and Murray's "Handbook," and the Sacristan at Chur, all say Lucius was killed there, and I saw his tomb with my own eyes!

windows at the single stranger sauntering by. There is a stall with baskets of queer little black grapes and apples, and a pretty brisk trade with half a dozen urchins standing round. But, beyond this, there is scarce any talk or movement in the street. There's nobody at the book-shop. "If you will have the goodness to come again in an hour," says the banker, with his mouthful of dinner at one o'clock, "you can have the money." There is nobody at the hotel, save the good landlady, the kind waiters, the brisk young cook who ministers to you. Nobody is in the Protestant church — (oh! strange sight, the two confessions are here at peace!) — nobody in the Catholic church: until the sacristan, from his snug abode in the cathedral close, espies the traveller eying the monsters and pillars before the old shark-toothed arch of his cathedral, and comes out (with a view to remuneration possibly) and opens the gate, and shows you the venerable church, and the queer old relics in the sacristy, and the ancient vestments (a black velvet cope, amongst other robes, as fresh as yesterday, and presented by that notorious "pervert," Henry of Navarre and France), and the statue of St. Lucius who built St. Peter's Church, on Cornhill.

What a quiet, kind, quaint, pleasant, pretty old town! Has it been asleep these hundreds and hundreds of years, and is the brisk young Prince of the Sidereal Realms in his screaming car drawn by his snorting steel elephant coming to waken it? Time was when there must have been life and bustle and commerce here. Those vast, venerable walls were not made to keep out cows, but men-at-arms, led by fierce captains, who prowled about the gates, and robbed the traders as they passed in and out with their bales, their goods, their pack-horses, and their wains. Is the place so dead that even the clergy of the different denominations can't quarrel? Why, seven or eight, or a dozen, or fifteen hundred years ago (they haven't the register at St. Peter's up to that remote period. I dare say it was burnt in the fire of London) — a dozen hundred years ago, when there was some life in the town, St. Lucius was stoned here on account of theological differences, after founding our church in Cornhill.

There was a sweet pretty river walk we used to take in the evening and mark the mountains round glooming with a deeper purple; the shades creeping up the golden walls; the river brawling, the cattle calling, the maids and chatterboxes round the fountains babbling and bawling; and several times in the course of our sober walks we overtook a lazy slouching boy, or hobble-de-hoy, with a rusty coat, and trousers not too long, and big feet trailing lazily one after the other, and large lazy hands dawdling from out the tight sleeves, and in the lazy hands a little book, which my lad held up to his face, and which I dare say so charmed and ravished him, that he was blind to the beautiful sights around him; unmindful, I would venture to lay any wager, of the lessons he had to learn for to-morrow; forgetful of mother waiting supper, and father preparing a scolding; — absorbed utterly and entirely in his book.

What was it that so fascinated the young student, as he stood by the river shore? Not the *Pons Asinorum*. What book so delighted him, and blinded him to all the rest of the world, so that he did not care to see the apple-woman with her fruit, or (more tempting still to sons of Eve) the pretty girls with their apple cheeks, who laughed and prattled round the fountain! What was the book? Do you suppose it was Livy, or the Greek grammar? No; it was a NOVEL that you were reading, you lazy, not very clean, good-for-nothing, sensible boy! It was D'Artagnan locking up General Monk in a box, or almost succeeding in keeping Charles the First's head on. It was the prisoner of the Chateau d'If cutting himself out of the sack fifty feet under water (I mention the novels I like best myself — novels without love or talking, or any of that sort of nonsense, but containing plenty of fighting, escaping, robbery, and rescuing) — cutting himself out of the sack, and swimming to the island of Monte Cristo. O Dumas! O thou brave, kind, gallant old Alexandre! I hereby offer thee homage, and give thee thanks for many pleasant hours. I have read thee (being sick in bed) for thirteen hours of a happy day, and had the ladies of the house fighting for the volumes. Be assured that lazy boy was reading Dumas (or I will go so far as to let the reader here pronounce the eulogium, or insert the name of his favorite author); and as for the anger, or it may be, the reverberations of his schoolmaster, or the remonstrances of his father, or the tender pleadings of his mother that he should not let the supper grow cold — I don't believe the scapegrace cared one fig. No! Figs are sweet, but fictions are sweeter.

Have you ever seen a score of white-bearded, white-robed warriors, or grave seniors of the city, seated at the gate of Jaffa or Beyrout, and listening to the story-teller reciting his marvels out of "Antar" or "The Arabian Nights"? I was once present when a young gentleman at table put a tart away from him, and said to his neighbor, the Younger Son (with rather a fatuous air), "I never eat sweets."

"Not eat sweets! and do you know why?" says T.

"Because I am past that kind of thing," says the young gentleman.

"Because you are a glutton and a sot!" cries the Elder (and Juvenis winces a little). "All people who have natural, healthy appetites, love sweets; all children, all women, all Eastern people, whose tastes are not corrupted by gluttony and strong drink." And a plateful of raspberries and cream disappeared before the philosopher.

You take the allegory? Novels are sweets. All people with healthy literary appetites love them — almost all women; — a vast number of clever, hard-headed men. Why, one of the most learned physicians of England said to me only yesterday, "I have just read 'So-and-So' for the second time" (naming one of Jones's exquisite fictions). Judges, bishops, chancellors, mathematicians, are notorious novel-readers; as well as young boys and sweet girls, and their kind, tender mothers. Who has not read about Eldon, and how he cried over novels every night when he was not at whist?

As for that lazy naughty boy at Chur, I doubt whether *he* will like novels when he is thirty years of age. He is taking too great a glut of them now. He is eating jelly until he will be sick. He will know most plots by the time he is twenty, so that *he* will never be surprised when the Stranger turns out to be the rightful earl, — when the old waterman, throwing off his beggarly gabardine, shows his stars and the collars of his various orders, and clasping Antonia to his bosom, proves himself to be the prince, her long-lost father. He will recognize the novelist's same characters, though they appear in red-heeled pumps and *ailes-de-pigeon*, or the garb of the nineteenth century. He will get weary of sweets, as boys of private schools grow (or used to grow, for I have done growing some little time myself, and the practice may have ended too) — as private school-boys used to grow tired of the pudding before their mutton at dinner.

And pray what is the moral of this apologue? The moral I take to be this: the appetite for novels extending to the end of the world; far away in the frozen deep, the sailors reading them to one another during the endless night; — far away under the Syrian stars, the solemn sheiks and elders hearkening to the poet as he recites his tales; far away in the Indian camps, where the soldiers listen to ——'s tales, or ——'s, after the hot day's march; far away in the little Chur yonder, where the lazy boy pores over the fond volume, and drinks it in with all his eyes; — the demand being what we know it is, the merchant must supply it, as he will supply saddles and pale ale for Bombay or Calcutta.

But as surely as the cadet drinks too much pale ale, it will disagree with him; and so surely, dear youth, will too much novels cloy on thee. I wonder, do novel-writers themselves read many novels? If you go into Gunter's, you don't see those charming young ladies (to whom I present my most respectful compliments) eating tarts and ices, but at the proper even-tide they have good plain wholesome tea and bread and butter. Can anybody tell me does the author of "The Tale of Two Cities" read novels? does the author of "The Tower of London" devour romances? does the dashing "Harry Lorrequer" delight in "Plain or Ringlets" or "Sponge's Sporting Tour"? Does the veteran, from whose flowing pen we had the books which delighted our young days, "Darnley," and "Richelieu," and "Delorme,"* relish the works of Alexandre the Great, and thrill over "The Three Musqueteers"? Does the accomplished author of "The Caxtons" read the other tales in "Blackwood"? (For example, that ghost-story printed last August, and which for my part, though I read it in the public reading room at "The Pavilion Hotel" at Folkestone, I protest frightened me so that I scarce dared look over my shoulder.) Does "Uncle Tom" admire "Adam Bede;" and does the author of "The Vicar of Wrexhill" laugh over "The Warden" and "The Three Clerks"? Dear youth of ingenuous countenance and ingenuous pudor! I make no doubt that the eminent parties above named all partake of novels in moderation — eat jellies — but mainly nourish themselves upon wholesome roast and boiled.

Here, dear youth aforesaid! our "Cornhill Magazine" owners strive to provide thee with facts as well as fiction; and though it does not become them to brag of their Ordinary, at least they invite thee to a table where thou shalt sit in good company. That story of "The Fox"* was written by one of the gallant seamen who sought for poor Franklin under the awful Arctic Night; that account of China † is told by the man of all the empire most likely to know of what he speaks: those pages regarding Volunteers ‡ come from an honored hand that has borne the sword in a hundred famous fields, and pointed the British guns in the greatest siege in the world.

Shall we point out others? We are fellow-travellers, and shall make acquaintance as the voyage proceeds. In the Atlantic steamers, on the first day out (and on high and holy days subsequently), the jellies set down on table are richly ornamented; *medioque in fonte leporum* rise the American and British flags nobly emblazoned in tin. As the passengers remark this pleasing phenomenon, the Captain no doubt improves the occasion by expressing a hope, to his right and left, that the flag of Mr. Bull and his younger Brother may always float side by side in friendly emulation. Novels having been previously compared to jellies — here are two (one perhaps not entirely saccharine, and flavored with an *amari aliquid* very

* By the way, what a strange fate is that which befell the veteran novelist! He was appointed her Majesty's Consul-General in Venice, the only city in Europe where the famous "Two Cavaliers" cannot by any possibility be seen riding together.

* "The Search for Sir John Franklin. (From the Private Journal of an Officer of 'The Fox.')"

† "The Chinese and the Outer Barbarians." By Sir John Bowring.

‡ "Our Volunteers." By Sir John Burgoyne.

distasteful to some palates) — two novels * under two flags, the one that ancient ensign which has hung before the well-known booth of "Vanity Fair;" the other that fresh and handsome standard which has lately been hoisted on "Barchester Towers." Pray, sir, or madam, to which dish will you be helped?

So have I seen my friends Captain Lang and Captain Comstock press their guests to partake of the fare on that memorable "First day out," when there is no man, I think, who sits down but asks a blessing on his voyage, and the good ship dips over the bar, and bounds away into the blue water.

* "Lovel the Widower" and "Framley Parsonage."

ON TWO CHILDREN IN BLACK.

Montaigne and "Howel's Letters" are my bedside books. If I wake at night, I have one or other of them to prattle me to sleep again. They talk about themselves forever, and don't weary me. I like to hear them tell their old stories over and over again. I read them in the dozy hours, and only half remember them. I am informed that both of them tell coarse stories. I don't heed them. It was the custom of their time, as it is of Highlanders and Hottentots, to dispense with a part of dress which we all wear in cities. But people can't afford to be shocked either at Cape Town or at Inverness every time they meet an individual who wears his national airy raiment. I never knew "The Arabian Nights" was an improper book until I happened once to read it in a "family edition." Well, *qui s'excuse*. . . . Who, pray, has accused me as yet? Here am I smothering dear good old Mrs. Grundy's objections, before she has opened her mouth. I love, I say, and scarce ever tire of hearing, the artless prattle of those two dear old friends, the Perigourdin gentleman and the priggish little Clerk of King Charles's Council. Their egotism in nowise disgusts me. I hope I shall always like to hear men, in reason, talk about themselves. What subject does a man know better? If I stamp on a friend's corn, his outcry is genuine — he confounds my clumsiness in the accents of truth. He is speaking about himself, and expressing his emotion of grief or pain in a manner perfectly authentic and veracious. I have a story of my own, of a wrong done to me by somebody, as far back as the year 1838: whenever I think of it, and have had a couple glasses of wine, I *cannot* help telling it. The toe is stamped upon: the pain is just as keen as ever: I cry out, and perhaps utter imprecatory language. I told the story only last Wednesday at dinner: —

"Mr. Roundabout," says a lady sitting by me, "how comes it that in your books there is a certain class (it may be of men, or it may be of women, but that is not the question in point) — how comes it, dear sir, there is a certain class of persons whom you always attack in your writings, and savagely rush at, goad, poke, toss up in the air, kick, and trample on?"

I couldn't help myself. I knew I ought not to do it. I told her the whole story, between the entrées and roast. The wound began to bleed again. The horrid pang was there, as keen and as fresh as ever. If I live half as long as Tithonus,* that crack across my heart can never be cured. There are wrongs and griefs that *can't* be mended. It is all very well of you, my dear Mrs. G., to say that this spirit is unchristian, and that we ought to forgive and forget, and so forth. How can I forget at will? How forgive? I can forgive the occasional waiter who broke my

* "Tithonus," by Tennyson, had appeared in the preceding (the 2d) number of "The Cornhill Magazine."

beautiful old decanter at that very dinner. I am not going to do him any injury. But all the powers on earth can't make that claret-jug whole.

So, you see, I told the lady the inevitable story. I was egotistical. I was selfish, no doubt; but I was natural, and was telling the truth. You say you are angry with a man for talking about himself. It is because you yourself are selfish, that that other person's Self does not interest you. Be interested by other people and with their affairs. Let them prattle and talk to you, as I do my dear old egotists just mentioned. When you have had enough of them, and sudden hazes come over your eyes, lay down the volume; pop out the candle, and *dormez bien*. I should like to write a nightcap book — a book that you can muse over, that you can smile over, that you can yawn over — a book of which you can say, "Well, this man is so and so and so and so; but he has a friendly heart (although some wiseacres have painted him as black as Bogey), and you may trust what he says." I should like to touch you sometimes with a reminiscence that shall waken your sympathy, and make you say, *Io anchè* have so thought, felt, smiled, suffered. Now, how is this to be done except by egotism? *Linea recta brevissima*. That right line "I" is the very shortest, simplest, straightforwardest means of communication between us, and stands for what it is worth, and no more. Sometimes authors say, "The present writer has often remarked;" or "The undersigned has observed;" or "Mr. Roundabout presents his compliments to the gentle reader, and begs to state," &c.: but "I" is better and straighter than all these grimaces of modesty: and although these are Roundabout Papers, and may wander who knows whither, I shall ask leave to maintain the upright and simple perpendicular. When this bundle of egotisms is bound up together, as they may be one day, if no accident prevents this tongue from wagging, or this ink from running, they will bore you very likely; so it would to read through "Howel's Letters" from beginning to end, or to eat up the whole of a ham: but a slice on occasion may have a relish: a dip into the volume at random and so on for a page or two: and now and then a smile; and presently a gape; and the book drops out of your hand; and so, *bon soir*, and pleasant dreams to you. I have frequently seen men at clubs asleep over their humble servant's works, and am always pleased. Even at a lecture I don't mind, if they don't snore. Only the other day when my friend A. said, "You've left off that Roundabout business, I see; very glad you have," I joined in the general roar of laughter at the table. I don't care a fig whether Archilochus likes the papers or no. You don't like partridge, Archilochus, or porridge, or what not? Try some other dish. I am not going to force mine down your throat, or quarrel with you if you refuse it. Once in America a clever and candid woman said to me, at the close of a dinner, during which I had been sitting beside her, "Mr. Roundabout, I was told I should not like you; and I don't." "Well, ma'am," says I, in a tone of the most unfeigned simplicity, "I don't care." And we became good friends immediately, and esteemed each other ever after.

So, my dear Archilochus, if you come upon this paper, and say, "Fudge!" and pass on to another, I for one shall not be in the least mortified. If you say, "What does he mean by calling this paper *On Two Children in Black*, when there's nothing about people in black at all, unless the ladies he met (and evidently bored) at dinner, were black women? What is all this egotistical pother? A plague on his I's!" My dear fellow, if you read "Montaigne's Essays," you must own that he might call almost any one by the name of any other, and that an essay on the

Moon or an essay on Green Cheese would be as appropriate a title as one of his on Coaches, on the Art of Discoursing, or Experience, or what you will. Besides, if I *have* a subject (and I have) I claim to approach it in a roundabout manner.

You remember Balzac's tale of the *Peau de Chagrin,* and how every time the possessor used it for the accomplishment of some wish the fairy *Peau* shrank a little and the owner's life correspondingly shortened? I have such a desire to be well with my public that I am actually giving up my favorite story. I am killing my goose, I know I am. I can't tell my story of the children in black after this; after printing it, and sending it through the country. When they are gone to the printer's these little things become public property. I take their hands. I bless them. I say, "Good-by, my little dears." I am quite sorry to part with them: but the fact is, I have told all my friends about them already, and don't dare to take them about with me any more.

Now every word is true of this little anecdote, and I submit that there lies in it a most curious and exciting little mystery. I am like a man who gives you the last bottle of his '25 claret. It is the pride of his cellar; he knows it, and he has a right to praise it. He takes up the bottle, fashioned so slenderly — takes it up tenderly, cants it with care, places it before his friends, declares how good it is, with honest pride, and wishes he had a hundred dozen bottles more of the same wine in his cellar. *Si quid novisti,* &c., I shall be very glad to hear from you. I protest and vow I am giving you the best I have.

Well, who those little boys in black were, I shall never probably know to my dying day. They were very pretty little men, with pale faces, and large, melancholy eyes; and they had beautiful little hands, and little boots, and the finest little shirts, and black paletots lined with the richest silk; and they had picture-books in several languages, English, and French, and German, I remember. Two more aristocratic-looking little men I never set eyes on. They were travelling with a very handsome, pale lady in mourning, and a maid-servant dressed in black, too; and on the lady's face there was the deepest grief. The little boys clambered and played about the carriage, and she sat watching. It was a railway-carriage from Frankfort to Heidelberg.

I saw at once that she was the mother of those children, and going to part from them. Perhaps I have tried parting with my own, and not found the business very pleasant. Perhaps I recollect driving down (with a certain trunk and carpet-bag on the box) with my own mother to the end of the avenue, where we waited — only a few minutes — until the whirring wheels of that "Defiance" coach were heard rolling towards us as certain as death. Twang goes the horn; up goes the trunk; down come the steps. Bah! I see the autumn evening: I hear the wheels now: I smart the cruel smart again: and, boy or man, have never been able to bear the sight of people parting from their children.

I thought these little men might be going to school for the first time in their lives; and mamma might be taking them to the doctor, and would leave them with many fond charges, and little wistful secrets of love, bidding the elder to protect his younger brother, and the younger to be gentle, and to remember to pray to God always for his mother, who would pray for her boy too. Our party made friends with these young ones during the little journey; but the poor lady was too sad to talk except to the boys now and again, and sat in her corner, pale, and silently looking at them.

The next day, we saw the lady and her maid driving in the direction of the railway-station, *without the boys.* The parting had taken place, then.

That night they would sleep among strangers. The little beds at home were vacant, and poor mother might go and look at them. Well, tears flow, and friends part, and mothers pray every night all over the world. I dare say we went to see Heidelberg Castle, and admired the vast shattered walls, and quaint gables; and the Neckar running its bright course through that charming scene of peace and beauty; and ate our dinner, and drank our wine with relish. The poor mother would eat but little *Abendessen* that night; and, as for the children — that first night at school — hard bed, hard words, strange boys bullying, and laughing, and jarring you with their hateful merriment — as for the first night at a strange school, we most of us remember what *that* is. And the first is not the *worst*, my boys, there's the rub. But each man has his share of troubles, and, I suppose, you must have yours.

From Heidelberg we went to Baden-Baden: and, I dare say, saw Madame de Schlangenbad and Madame de la Cruchecassee, and Count Punter, and honest Captain Blackball. And whom should we see in the evening, but our two little boys, walking on each side of a fierce, yellow-faced, bearded man! We wanted to renew our acquaintance with them, and they were coming forward quite pleased to greet us. But the father pulled back one of the little men by his paletot, gave a grim scowl, and walked away. I can see the children now looking rather frightened away from us and up into the father's face, or the cruel uncle's — which was he? I think he was the father. So this was the end of them. Not school, as I at first had imagined. The mother was gone, who had given them the heaps of pretty books, and the pretty studs in the shirts, and the pretty silken clothes, and the tender — tender cares; and they were handed to this scowling practitioner of Trente et Quarante. Ah! this is worse than school. Poor little men! poor mother sitting by the vacant little beds! We saw the children once or twice after, always in Scowler's company; but we did not dare to give each other any marks of recognition.

From Baden we went to Basle, and thence to Lucerne, and so over the St. Gothard into Italy. From Milan we went to Venice; and now comes the singular part of my story. In Venice there is a little court of which I forget the name: but in it is an apothecary's shop, whither I went to buy some remedy for the bites of certain animals which abound in Venice. Crawling animals, skipping animals, and humming, flying animals; all three will have at you at once; and one night nearly drove me into a strait-waistcoat. Well, as I was coming out of the apothecary's with the bottle of spirits of hartshorn in my hand (it really does do the bites a great deal of good), whom should I light upon but one of my little Heidelberg-Baden boys!

I have said how handsomely they were dressed as long as they were with their mother. When I saw the boy at Venice, who perfectly recognized me, his only garb was a wretched yellow cotton gown. His little feet, on which I had admired the little shiny boots, were *without shoe or stocking*. He looked at me, ran to an old hag of a woman, who seized his hand; and with her he disappeared down one of the thronged lanes of the city.

From Venice we went to Trieste (the Vienna railway at that time was only opened as far as Laybach, and the magnificent Semmering Pass was not quite completed). At a station between Laybach and Graetz, one of my companions alighted for refreshment, and came back to the carriage, saying: —

"There's that horrible man from Baden, with the two little boys."

Of course, we had talked about the appearance of the little boy at Venice, and his strange altered garb.

My companion said they were pale, wretched-looking, and *dressed quite shabbily*.

I got out at several stations, and looked at all the carriages. I could not see my little men. From that day to this I have never set eyes on them. That is all my story. Who were they? What could they be? How can you explain that mystery of the mother giving them up; of the remarkable splendor and elegance of their appearance while under her care; of their bare-footed squalor in Venice, a month afterwards; of their shabby habiliments at Laybach? Had the father gambled away his money, and sold their clothes? How came they to have passed out of the hands of a refined lady (as she evidently was, with whom I first saw them) into the charge of quite a common woman like her with whom I saw one of the boys at Venice? Here is but one chapter of the story. Can any man write the next, or that preceding the strange one on which I happened to light? Who knows? the mystery may have some quite simple solution. I saw two children, attired like little princes, taken from their mother and consigned to other care; and a fortnight afterwards, one of them bare-footed and like a beggar. Who will read this riddle of The Two Children in Black?

ON RIBBONS.

The uncle of the present Sir Louis N. Bonaparte, K. G., &c., inaugurated his reign as Emperor over the neighboring nation by establishing an Order, to which all citizens of his country, military, naval, and civil — all men most distinguished in science, letters, arts, and commerce — were admitted. The emblem of the Order was but a piece of ribbon, more or less long or broad, with a toy at the end of it. The Bourbons had toys and ribbons of their own, blue, black, and all-colored; and on their return to dominion such good old Tories would naturally have preferred to restore their good old Orders of Saint Louis, Saint Esprit, and Saint Michel; but France had taken the ribbon of the Legion of Honor so to her heart that no Bourbon sovereign dared to pluck it thence.

In England, until very late days, we have been accustomed rather to pooh-pooh national Orders, to vote ribbons and crosses tinsel gewgaws, foolish foreign ornaments, and so forth. It is known how the Great Duke (the breast of whose own coat was plastered with some half-hundred decorations) was averse to the wearing of ribbons, medals, clasps, and the like, by his army. We have all of us read how uncommonly distinguished Lord Castlereagh looked at Vienna, where he was the only gentleman present without any decoration whatever. And the Great Duke's theory was, that clasps and ribbons, stars and garters, were good and proper ornaments for himself, for the chief officers of his distinguished army, and for gentlemen of high birth, who might naturally claim to wear a band of garter blue across their waistcoats; but that for common people your plain coat, without stars and ribbons, was the most sensible wear.

And no doubt you and I are as happy, as free, as comfortable; we can walk and dine as well; we can keep the winter's cold out as well, without a star on our coats, as without a feather in our hats. How often we have laughed at the absurd mania of the Americans for dubbing their senators, members of Congress, and States' representatives, Honorable! We have a right to call *our* Privy Councillors Right Honorable, our Lords' sons Honorable, and so forth: but for a nation as numerous, well educated, strong, rich, civilized, free as our own, to dare to give its distinguished citizens titles of honor — monstrous assumption of low-bred arrogance and *parvenu* vanity! Our titles are respectable, but theirs absurd. Mr. Jones, of London, a Chancellor's son, and a tailor's grandson, is justly Honorable, and entitled to be Lord Jones at his noble father's decease: but Mr. Brown, the senator from New York, is a silly upstart for tacking Honorable to his name, and our sturdy British good sense laughs at him. Who has not laughed (I have myself) at Honorable Nahum Dodge, Honorable Zeno Scudder, Honorable Hiram Boake, and the rest? A score of such queer names and titles I have smiled at in America. And, *mutato nomine*? I meet a born idiot, who is a peer and born legislator. This drivelling noodle and his descendants through life are your natural superiors and mine — your and my children's superiors. I read of an alderman kneeling and knighted at court: I see a gold-stick waddling backwards before Majesty in a procession, and if we laugh, don't you suppose the Americans laugh too?

Yes, stars, garters, orders, knighthoods, and the like, are folly. Yes, Bobus, citizen and soap-boiler, is a good man, and no one laughs at him or good Mrs. Bobus, as they have their dinner at one o'clock. But who will not jeer at Sir Thomas on a melting day, and Lady Bobus, at Margate, eating shrimps in a donkey-chaise? Yes, knighthood is absurd: and chivalry an idiotic superstition: and Sir Walter Manny was a zany: and Nelson, with his flaming stars and cordons, splendent upon a day of battle, was a madman: and Murat, with his crosses and orders, at the head of his squadrons charging victorious, was only a crazy mountebank, who had been a tavern-waiter, and was puffed up with absurd vanity about his dress and legs. And the men of the French line at Fontenoy, who told Messieurs de la Garde to fire first, were smirking French dancing-masters; and the Black Prince, waiting upon his royal prisoner, was acting an inane masquerade: and Chivalry is nought; and Honor is humbug; and Gentlemanhood is an extinct folly; and Ambition is madness; and desire of distinction is criminal vanity; and glory is bosh; and fair fame is idleness; and nothing is true but two and two; and the color of all the world is drab; and all men are equal; and one man is as tall as another; and one man is as good as another — and a great dale betther, as the Irish philosopher said.

Is this so? Titles and badges of honor are vanity; and in the American Revolution you have his Excellency General Washington sending back, and with proper spirit sending back, a letter in which he is not addressed as Excellency and General. Titles are abolished; and the American Republic swarms with men claiming and bearing them. You have the French soldier cheered and happy in his dying agony, and kissing with frantic joy the chief's hand who lays the little cross on the bleeding bosom. At home you have the Dukes and Earls jobbing and intriguing for the Garter; the Military Knights grumbling at the Civil Knights of the Bath; the little ribbon eager for the collar; the soldiers and seamen from India and the Crimea marching in procession before the Queen, and receiving from her hands the cross bearing her royal name. And, remember, there are not only the cross wearers, but all the fathers and friends; all the women who have prayed for their absent heroes; Harry's wife, and Tom's mother, and Jack's daughter, and Frank's sweetheart, each of whom wears in her heart of hearts afterwards the badge which son, father, lover, has won by his merit; each of whom is made happy and proud, and is bound to the country by that little bit of ribbon.

I have heard, in a lecture about George the Third, that, at his accession, the King had a mind to establish an order for literary men. It was to have been called the Order of Minerva — I suppose with an Owl for a badge. The knights were to have worn a star of sixteen points, and a yellow ribbon; and good old Samuel Johnson was talked of as President, or Grand Cross, or Grand Owl, of the society. Now about such an order as this there certainly may be doubts. Consider the claimants, the difficulty of settling their claims, the rows and squabbles amongst the candidates, and the subsequent decision of posterity! Dr. Beattie would have ranked as first poet, and twenty years after the sublime Mr. Hayley would, no doubt, have claimed the Grand Cross. Mr. Gibbon would not have been eligible, on account of his dangerous freethinking opinions; and her sex, as well as her republican sentiments, might have interfered with the knighthood of the immortal Mrs. Catherine Macaulay. How Goldsmith would have paraded the ribbon at Madame Cornelys's, or the Academy dinner! How Peter Pindar would have railed at it! Fifty years later, the noble Scott would have worn the Grand Cross and deserved it; but Gifford would have had it; and Byron, and Shelley, and Hazlitt, and Hunt would have been without it; and had Keats been proposed as officer, how the Tory prints would have yelled with rage and scorn! Had the star of Minerva lasted to our present time — but I pause, not because the idea is dazzling, but too awful. Fancy the claimants, and the row about their precedence? Which philosopher shall have the grand cordon? — which the collar? — which the little scrap no bigger than a butter-cup? Of the historians — A, say, — and C, and F, and G, and S, and T, — which shall be Companion and which Grand Owl? Of the poets, who wears, or claims, the largest and brightest star? Of the novelists, there is A, and B, and CD; and E (star of first magnitude, newly discovered), and F (a magazine of wit), and fair G, and H, and I, and brave old J, and charming K, and L, and M, and N, and O (fair twinklers), and I am puzzled between three P's — Peacock, Miss Pardoe, and Paul Pry — and Queechy, and R, and S, and T, *mère et fils*, and very likely U, O gentle reader, for who has not written his novel now-a-days? — who has not a claim to the star and straw-colored ribbon? — and who shall have the biggest and largest? Fancy the struggle! Fancy the squabble! Fancy the distribution of prizes!

Who shall decide on them? Shall it be the sovereign? shall it be the Minister for the time being? and has Lord Palmerston made a deep study of novels? In this matter the late Ministry,* to be sure, was better qualified; but even then, grumblers who had not got their canary cordons, would have hinted at professional jealousies entering the Cabinet; and, the ribbons being awarded, Jack would have scowled at his because Dick had a broader one; Ned been indignant because Bob's was as large: Tom would have thrust his into the drawer, and scorn to wear it at all. No — no: the so-called literary world was well rid of Minerva and her yellow ribbon. The great poets would have been indifferent, the little poets jealous, the funny men furious, the philosophers satirical, the historians supercilious, and, finally, the jobs without end. Say, ingenuity and cleverness are to be rewarded by State tokens and prizes — and take for granted the Order of Minerva is established — who shall have it? A great philosopher? no doubt we cordially salute him G. C. M. A great historian? G. C. M. of course. A great engineer? G. C. M. A great poet? received with acclamation G. C. M. A great painter? oh! certainly, G. C. M. If a great painter, why not a great novelist? Well, pass, great novelist, G. C. M. But if a poetic, a pictorial, a story-telling or music-composing artist, why not a singing artist? Why not a basso-profondo? Why not a primo tenore? And if a singer, why should not a ballet-dancer

* That of Lord Derby, in 1859, which included Mr. Disraeli and Sir Edward Bulwer Lytton.

come bounding on the stage with his cordon, and cut capers to the music of a row of decorated fiddlers? A chemist puts in his claim for having invented a new color; an apothecary for a new pill; the cook for a new sauce; the tailor for a new cut of trousers. We have brought the star of Minerva down from the breast to the pantaloons. Stars and garters! can we go any farther; or shall we give the shoemaker the yellow ribbon of the order for his shoe-tie?

When I began this present Roundabout excursion, I think I had not quite made up my mind whether we would have an Order of all the Talents or not: perhaps I rather had a hankering for a rich ribbon and gorgeous star, in which my family might like to see me at parties in my best waistcoat. But then the door opens, and there come in, and by the same right too, Sir Alexis Soyer! Sir Alessandro Tamburini! Sir Agostino Velluti! Sir Antonio Paganini (violinist)! Sir Sandy McGuffog (piper to the most noble the Marquis of Farintosh)! Sir Alcide Flicflac (premier danseur of H. M. Theatre)! Sir Harley Quin and Sir Joseph Grimaldi (from Covent Garden)! They have all the yellow ribbon. They are all honorable, and clever, and distinguished artists. Let us elbow through the rooms, make a bow to the lady of the house, give a nod to Sir George Thrum, who is leading the orchestra, and go and get some champagne and seltzer-water from Sir Richard Gunter, who is presiding at the buffet. A national decoration might be well and good: a token awarded by the country to all its *bene-merentibus:* but most gentlemen with Minerva stars would, I think, be inclined to wear very wide breast-collars to their coats. Suppose yourself, brother penman, decorated with this ribbon, and looking in the glass, would you not laugh? Would not wife and daughters laugh at that canary-colored emblem?

But suppose a man, old or young, of figure ever so stout, thin, stumpy, homely, indulging in looking-glass reflections with that hideous ribbon and cross called V. C. on his coat, would he not be proud? and his family, would not they be prouder? For your noblemen there is the famous old blue garter and star, and welcome. If I were a marquis — if I had thirty — forty thousand a year (settle the sum, my dear Alnaschar, according to your liking), I should consider myself entitled to my seat in Parliament and to my garter. The garter belongs to the Ornamental Classes. Have you seen the new magnificent *Pavo Spicifer* at the Zoological Gardens, and do you grudge him his jewelled coronet and the azure splendor of his waistcoat? I like my Lord Mayor to have a gilt coach; my magnificent monarch to be surrounded by magnificent nobles: I huzzah respectfully when they pass in procession. It is good for Mr. Briefless (50 Pump Court, fourth floor) that there should be a Lord Chancellor with a gold robe and fifteen thousand a year. It is good for a poor curate that there should be splendid bishops at Fulham and Lambeth: their Lordships were poor curates once, and have won, so to speak, their ribbon. Is a man who puts into a lottery to be sulky because he does not win the twenty thousand pounds prize? Am I to fall into a rage, and bully my family when I come home, after going to see Chatsworth or Windsor, because we have only two little drawing rooms? Welcome to your garter, my Lord, and shame upon him *qui mal y pense!*

So I arrive in my roundabout way near the point towards which I have been trotting ever since we set out.

In a voyage to America, some nine years since, on the seventh or eighth day out from Liverpool, Captain L—— came to dinner at eight bells as usual, talked a little to the persons right and left of him, and helped the soup with his accustomed politeness. Then he went on deck, and was back in a minute, and operated on the fish, looking rather grave the while.

Then he went on deck again; and this time was absent, it may be, three or five minutes, during which the fish disappeared, and the *entrées* arrived, and the roast beef. Say ten minutes passed — I can't tell after nine years.

Then L—— came down with a pleased and happy countenance this time, and began carving the sirloin: "We have seen the light," he said. "Madam, may I help you to a little gravy, or a little horse-radish?" or what not?

I forget the name of the light; nor does it matter. It was a point off Newfoundland for which he was on the look-out, and so well did "The Canada" know where she was, that, between soup and beef, the captain had sighted the headland by which his course was lying.

And so through storm and darkness, through fog and midnight, the ship had pursued her steady way over the pathless ocean and roaring seas, so surely that the officers who sailed her knew her place within a minute or two, and guided us with a wonderful providence safe on our way. Since the noble Cunard Company has run its ships, but one accident, and that through the error of a pilot, has happened on the line.

By this little incident (hourly of course repeated, and trivial to all sea-going people) I own I was immensely moved, and never can think of it but with a heart full of thanks and awe. We trust our lives to these seamen, and how nobly they fulfil their trust! They are, under heaven, as a providence for us. Whilst we sleep, their untiring watchfulness keeps guard over us. All night through that bell sounds at its season, and tells how our sentinels defend us. It rang when "The Amazon" was on fire, and chimed its heroic signal of duty, and courage, and honor. Think of the dangers these seamen undergo for us: the hourly peril and watch; the familiar storm; the dreadful iceberg; the long winter nights when the decks are as glass, and the sailor has to climb through icicles to bend the stiff sail on the yard! Think of their courage and their kindnesses in cold, in tempest, in hunger, in wreck! "The women and children to the boats," says the captain of "The Birkenhead," and, with the troops formed on the deck, and the crew obedient to the word of glorious command, the immortal ship goes down. Read the story of "The Sarah Sands:" —

"SARAH SANDS.

"The screw steam-ship 'Sarah Sands,' 1,330 registered tons, was chartered by the East India Company in the autumn of 1858, for the conveyance of troops to India. She was commanded by John Squire Castle. She took out a part of the 54th Regiment, upwards of 350 persons, besides the wives and children of some of the men, and the families of some of the officers. All went well till the 11th November, when the ship had reached lat. 14 S., long. 56 E., upwards of 400 miles from the Mauritius.

"Between three and four p.m. on that day a very strong smell of fire was perceived arising from the after-deck, and upon going below into the hold, Captain Castle found it to be on fire, and immense volumes of smoke arising from it. Endeavors were made to reach the seat of the fire, but in vain; the smoke and heat were too much for the men. There was, however, no confusion. Every order was obeyed with the same coolness and courage with which it was given. The engine was immediately stopped. All sail was taken in, and the ship brought to the wind, so as to drive the smoke and fire, which was in the after-part of the ship, astern. Others were, at the same time, getting fire-hoses fitted and passed to the scene of the fire. The fire, however, continued to increase, and attention was directed to the ammunition contained in the powder-magazines, which were situated one on each side the ship immediately above the fire. The starboard magazine was soon cleared. But by this time the whole of the after-part of the ship was so much enveloped in smoke that it was scarcely possible to stand, and great fears were entertained on account of the port magazine. Volunteers were called for, and came immediately, and, under the guidance of Lieutenant Hughes, attempted to clear the port magazine, which they succeeded in doing, with the exception, as was supposed, of one or two barrels. It was most dangerous work. The men became overpowered with the smoke and heat, and fell; and several, while thus engaged, were dragged up by ropes, senseless.

"The flames soon burst up through the deck, and running rapidly along the various cabins, set the greater part on fire.

"In the mean time Captain Castle took steps for lowering the boats. There was a heavy gale at the time, but they were launched without the least accident. The soldiers were mustered on deck; — there was no rush to the boats; — and the men obeyed the word of command as if on parade. The men were informed that Captain Castle did not despair of saving the ship, but that they must be prepared to leave her if necessary. The women and children were lowered into the port life-boat, under the charge of Mr. Very, third officer, who had orders to keep clear of the ship until recalled.

"Captain Castle then commenced constructing rafts of spare spars. In a short time, three were put together, which would have been capable of saving a great number of those on board. Two were launched overboard, and safely moored alongside, and then a third was left across the deck forward, ready to be launched.

"In the mean time the fire had made great progress. The whole of the cabins were one body of fire, and at about 8.30 p.m. flames burst through the upper deck, and shortly after the mizzen rigging caught fire. Fears were entertained of the ship paying off, in which case the flames would have been swept forwards by the wind; but fortunately the after-braces were burnt through, and the main-yard swung round, which kept the ship's head to wind. About nine p.m., a fearful explosion took place in the port magazine, arising, no doubt, from the one or two barrels of powder which it had been impossible to remove. By this time the ship was one body of flame, from the stern to the main rigging, and thinking it scarcely possible to save her, Captain Castle called Major Brett (then in command of the troops, for the Colonel was in one of the boats) forward, and, telling him that he feared the ship was lost, requested him to endeavor to keep order amongst the troops till the last, but, at the same time, to use every exertion to check the fire. Providentially, the iron bulkhead in the after-part of the ship withstood the action of the flames, and here all efforts were concentrated to keep it cool.

"'No person,' says the captain, 'can describe the manner in which the men worked to keep the fire back; one party were below, keeping the bulkhead cool, and when several were dragged up senseless, fresh volunteers took their places, who were, however, soon in the same state. At about ten p.m., the maintopsail-yard took fire. Mr. Welch, one quartermaster, and four or five soldiers, went aloft with wet blankets, and succeeded in extinguishing it, but not until the yard and mast were nearly burnt through. The work of fighting the fire below continued for hours, and about midnight it appeared that some impression was made; and after that, the men drove it back, inch by inch, until daylight, when they had completely got it under. The ship was now in a frightful plight. The after-part was literally burnt out — merely the shell remaining — the port quarter blown out by the explosion: fifteen feet of water in the hold.'

"The gale still prevailed, and the ship was rolling and pitching in a heavy sea, and taking in large quantities of water abaft: the tanks, too, were rolling from side to side in the hold.

"As soon as the smoke was partially cleared away, Captain Castle got spare sails and blankets aft to stop the leak, passing two hawsers round the stern, and setting them up. The troops were employed baling and pumping. This continued during the whole morning.

"In the course of the day the ladies joined the ship. The boats were ordered alongside, but they found the sea too heavy to remain there. The gig had been abandoned during the night, and the crew, under Mr. Wood, fourth officer, had got into another of the boats. The troops were employed the remainder of the day baling and pumping, and the crew securing the stern. All hands were employed during the following night baling and pumping, the boats being moored alongside, where they received some damage. At daylight, on the 13th, the crew were employed hoisting the boats, the troops were working manfully baling and pumping. Latitude at noon, 13 deg. 12 min. south. At five p.m., the foresail and foretopsail were set, the rafts were cut away, and the ship bore for the Mauritius. On Thursday, the 19th, she sighted the Island of Rodrigues, and arrived at Mauritius on Monday the 23d."

The Nile and Trafalgar are not more glorious to our country, are not greater victories, than these won by our merchant seamen. And if you look in the Captains' reports of any maritime register, you will see similar acts recorded every day I have such a volume, for last year, now lying before me. In the second number, as I open it at hazard, Captain Roberts, master of the ship "Empire," from Shields to London, reports how on the 14th ult. (the 14th December, 1859), he, "being off Whitby, discovered the ship to be on fire between the main hold and boilers: got the hose from the engine laid on, and succeeded in subduing the fire; but only apparently; for at seven the next morning, 'The Dudgeon' bear-S. S. E. seven miles' distance, the fire again broke out, causing the ship to be enveloped in flames on both sides of midships: got the hose again into play and all hands to work with buckets to combat with the fire. Did not succeed in stopping it till four P.M., to effect which, were obliged to cut away the deck and top sides, and throw overboard part of the cargo. The vessel was very much damaged and leaky: determined to make for the Humber. Ship was run on shore, on the mud, near Grimsby harbor, with five feet of water in her hold. The donkey-engine broke down. The water increased so fast as to put out the furnace fires, and render the ship almost unmanageable. On the tide flowing, a tug towed the ship off the mud, and got her into Grimsby to repair."

On the 2d of November, Captain Strickland, of "The Purchase" brigantine, from Liverpool to Yarmouth, U. S., "encountered heavy gales from W.N.W. to W.S.W., in lat. 43° N., long. 34° W., in which we lost jib, foretopmast, staysail, topsail, and carried away the foretopmast stays, bobstays, and bowsprit, head-sails, cut-water, and stern, also started the wood ends, which caused the vessel to leak. Put her before the wind and sea, and hove about twenty-five tons of cargo overboard to lighten the ship forward. Slung myself in a bowline, and by means of thrusting 2½-inch rope in the opening, contrived to stop a great portion of the leak.

"*December* 16*th.* — The crew continuing night and day at the pumps, could not keep the ship free; deemed it prudent for the benefit of those concerned to bear up for the nearest port. On arriving in lat. 48° 45′ N., long. 23° W., observed a vessel with a signal of distress flying. Made towards her, when she proved to be the barque 'Carleton,' water-logged. The captain and crew asked to be taken off. Hove to, and received them on board, consisting of thirteen men: and their ship was abandoned. We then proceeded on our course, the crew of the abandoned vessel assisting all they could to keep my ship afloat. We arrived at Cork harbour on the 27th ult."

Captain Coulson, master of the brig "Othello," reports that his brig foundered off Portland, December 27; — encountering a strong gale, and shipping two heavy seas in succession, which hove the ship on her beam-ends. "Observing no chance of saving the ship, took to the long-boat, and, within ten minutes of leaving her, saw the brig founder. We were picked up the same morning by the French ship 'Commerce de Paris,' Captain Tombarel."

Here, in a single column of a newspaper, what strange, touching pictures do we find of seamen's dangers, vicissitudes, gallantry, generosity! The ship on fire — the captain in the gale slinging himself in a bowline to stop the leak — the Frenchman in the hour of danger coming to his British comrade's rescue — the brigantine, almost a wreck, working up to the barque with the signal of distress flying, and taking off her crew of thirteen men. "We then proceeded on our course, *the crew of the abandoned vessel assisting all they could to keep my ship afloat.*" What noble, simple words! What courage, devotedness, brotherly love! Do they not cause the heart to beat, and the eyes to fill?

This is what seamen do daily, and for one another. One lights occasionally upon different stories. It happened, not very long since, that the passengers by one of the great ocean steamers were wrecked, and, after undergoing the most severe hardships, were left, destitute and helpless, at a miserable coaling port. Amongst them were old men, ladies, and children. When the next steamer arrived, the passengers by that steamer took alarm at the haggard and miserable appearance of their unfortunate predecessors, and actually *remonstrated with their own captain, urging him not to take the poor creatures on board.* There was every excuse, of course. The last-arrived steamer was already dangerously full; the cabins were crowded; there were sick and delicate people on board — sick and delicate people who had paid a large price to the company for room, food, comfort, already not too sufficient. If fourteen of us are in an omnibus, will we see three or four women outside, and say, "Come in, because this is the last 'bus, and it rains"? Of course not: but think of that remonstrance, and of that Samaritan master of "The Purchase" brigantine!

In the winter of '53, I went from Marseilles to Civita Vecchia, in one of the magnificent P. and O. ships, "The Valetta," the master of which subsequently did distinguished service in the Crimea. This was his first Mediterranean voyage, and he sailed his ship by the charts alone, going into each port as surely as any pilot. I remember walking the deck at night with this most skilful, gallant, well-bred, and well-educated gentleman, and the glow of eager enthusiasm with which he assented, when I asked him whether he did not think a RIBBON or ORDER would be welcome or useful in his service.

Why is there not an ORDER OF BRITANNIA for British seamen? In the Merchant and the Royal Navy alike, occur almost daily instances and occasions for the display of science, skill, bravery, fortitude in trying circumstances, resource in danger. In the first number of "The Cornhill Magazine," a friend contributed a most touching story of the M'Clintock expedition, in the dangers and dreadful glories of which he shared; and the writer was a merchant captain. How many more are there (and, for the honor of England, may there be many like him!) — gallant, accomplished, high-spirited, enterprising masters of their noble profession! Can our fountain of Honor not be brought to such men? It plays upon captains and colonels in seemly profusion. It pours forth not illiberal rewards upon doctors and judges. It sprinkles mayors and aldermen. It bedews a painter now and again. It has spirted a baronetcy upon two, and bestowed a coronet upon one noble man of letters. Diplomatists take their Bath in it as of right; and it flings out a profusion of glittering stars upon the nobility of the three kingdoms. Cannot Britannia find a ribbon for her sailors? The Navy, royal or mercantile, is a *Service.* The command of a ship, or the conduct of her, implies danger, honor, science, skill, subordination, good faith. It may be a victory, such as that of "The Sarah Sands;" it may be discovery, such as that of "The Fox;" it may be heroic disaster, such as that of "The Birkenhead;" and in such events merchant seamen, as well as royal seamen, take their share.

Why is there not, then, an Order of Britannia? One day a young officer of "The Euryalus" * may win it: and, having just read the memoirs of LORD DUNDONALD, I know who ought to have the first Grand Cross.

ON SOME LATE GREAT VICTORIES.

ON the 18th day of April last I went to see a friend in a neighboring Crescent, and on the steps of the next house beheld a group something

* Prince Alfred was serving on board the frigate "Euryalus" when this was written.

like that here depicted. A news-boy had stopped in his walk, and was reading aloud the journal which it was his duty to deliver; a pretty orange-girl, with a heap of blazing fruit, rendered more brilliant by one of those great blue papers in which oranges are now artfully wrapped, leant over the railing and listened; and opposite the *nympham discentem* there was a capering and acute-eared young satirist of a crossing-sweeper, who had left his neighboring professional avocation and chance of profit in order to listen to the tale of the little news-boy.

That intelligent reader, with his hand following the line as he read it out to his audience, was saying:— "And — now — Tom — coming up smiling — after his fall — dee — delivered a rattling clinker upon the Benicia Boy's — potato-trap — but was met by a — punisher on the nose — which," &c., &c.; or words to that effect. Betty at 52 let me in, while the boy was reading his lecture; and, having been some twenty minutes or so in the house and paid my visit, I took leave.

The little lecturer was still at work on the 51 doorstep, and his audience had scarcely changed their position. Having read every word of the battle myself in the morning, I did not stay to listen further; but if the gentleman who expected his paper at the usual hour that day experienced delay and a little disappointment I shall not be surprised.

I am not going to expatiate on the battle. I have read in the correspondent's letter of a Northern newspaper, that in the midst of the company assembled, the reader's humble servant was present, and in a very polite society, too, of "poets, clergymen, men of letters, and members of both Houses of Parliament." If so, I must have walked to the station in my sleep, paid three guineas in a profound fit of mental abstraction, and returned to bed unconscious, for I certainly woke there about the time when history relates that the fight was over. I do not know whose colors I wore — the Benician's, or those of the Irish champion; nor remember where the fight took place, which, indeed, no somnambulist is bound to recollect. Ought Mr. Sayers to be honored for being brave, or punished for being naughty? By the shade of Brutus the elder, I don't know.

In George II.'s time, there was a turbulent navy lieutenant (Handsome Smith he was called — his picture is at Greenwich now, in brown velvet, and gold and scarlet; his coat handsome, his waistcoat exceedingly handsome; but his face by no means the beauty) — there was, I say, a turbulent young lieutenant who was broke on a complaint of the French ambassador, for obliging a French ship of war to lower her topsails to his ship at Spithead. But, by the King's orders, Tom was next day made Captain Smith. Well, if I were absolute king, I would send Tom Sayers to the mill for a month, and make him Sir Thomas on coming out of Clerkenwell. You are a naughty boy, Tom! but then, you know, we ought to love our brethren, though ever so naughty. We are moralists, and reprimand you; and you are hereby reprimanded accordingly. But in case England should ever have need of a few score thousand champions, who laugh at danger; who cope with giants; who, stricken to the ground, jump up and gayly rally, and fall, and rise again, and strike, and die rather than yield — in case the country should need such men, and you should know them, be pleased to send lists of the misguided persons to the principal police stations, where means may some day be found to utilize their wretched powers, and give their deplorable energies a right direction. Suppose, Tom, that you and your friends are pitted against an immense invader — suppose you are bent on holding the ground, and dying there, if need be — suppose it is life, freedom, honor, home, you are fighting for, and there is a death-dealing sword or rifle in your hand, with which you are going to resist some tremendous enemy who challenges your championship on your native shore? Then, Sir Thomas, resist him to the death, and it is all right: kill him, and heaven bless you. Drive him into the sea, and there destroy, smash, and drown him; and let us sing *Laudamus.* In these national cases, you see, we override the indisputable first laws of morals. Loving your neighbor is very well, but suppose your neighbor comes over from Calais and Boulogne to rob you of your laws, your liberties, your newspapers, your parliament (all of which *some* dear neighbors of ours have given up in the most self-denying manner): suppose any neighbor were to cross the water and propose this kind of thing to us? Should we not be justified in humbly trying to pitch him into the water? If it were the King of Belgium himself we must do so. I mean that fighting, of course, is wrong; but that there are occasions when, &c. — I suppose I mean that that one-handed fight of Sayers is one of the most spirit-stirring little stories ever told: and, with every love and respect for Morality — my spirit says to her, "Do, for goodness' sake, my dear madam, keep your true, and pure, and womanly, and gentle remarks for another day. Have the great kindness to stand a *leetle* aside and just let us see one or two more rounds between the men. That little man with the one hand powerless on his breast facing yonder giant for hours, and felling him, too, every now and then! It is the little 'Java' and the 'Constitution' over again."

I think it is a most fortunate event for the brave Heenan, who has acted and written since the battle with a true warrior's courtesy, and with a great deal of good logic too, that the battle was a drawn one. The advantage was all on Mr. Sayers' side. Say a young lad of sixteen insults me in the street, and I try and thrash him, and do it. Well, I have thrashed a young lad. You great, big tyrant, couldn't you hit one of your own size? But say the lad thrashes me? In either case I walk away discomfited: but in the latter, I am positively put to shame. Now, when the ropes were cut from that death-grip, and Sir Thomas released, the gentleman of Benicia was confessedly blind of one eye, and speedily afterwards was blind of both. Could Mr. Sayers have held out for three minutes, for five minutes, for ten minutes more? He says he could. So we say *we* could have held out, and did, and had beaten off the enemy at Waterloo, even if the Prussians hadn't come up. The opinions differ pretty much according to the nature of the opinants. I say the Duke and Tom could have held out, that they meant to hold out, that they did hold out, and that there has been fistifying enough. That crowd which came in and stopped the fight ought to be considered like one of those divine clouds which the gods send in Homer:

> "Apollo shrouds
> The godlike Trojan in a veil of clouds."

It is the best way of getting the godlike Trojan out of the scrape, don't you see? The *nodus* is cut; Tom is out of chancery; the Benicia Boy not a bit the worse, nay, better than if he had beaten the little man. He has not the humiliation of conquest. He is greater, and will be loved more hereafter by the gentle sex. Suppose he had overcome the god-like Trojan? Suppose he had tied Tom's corpse to his cab-wheels, and driven to Farnham, smoking the pipe of triumph? Faugh! the great hulking conqueror! Why did you not hold your hand from yonder hero? Everybody, I say, was relieved by that opportune appearance of the British gods, protectors of native valor, who interfered, and "withdrew" their champion.

Now, suppose six feet two conqueror, and five feet eight beaten; would Sayers have been a whit the less gallant and meritorious? If Sancho had been allowed *really* to reign in Barataria, I make no doubt that, with his good sense and kindness of heart, he would have devised some means of rewarding the brave vanquished, as well as the brave victors in the Baratarian army, and that a champion who had fought a good fight would have been a knight of King Don Sancho's orders, whatever the upshot of the combat had been. Suppose Wellington overwhelmed on the plateau of Mont St. John; suppose Washington attacked and beaten at Valley Forge — and either supposition is quite easy — and what becomes of the heroes? They would have been as brave, honest, heroic, wise; but their glory, where would it have been? Should we have had their portraits hanging in our chambers? have been familiar with their histories? have pondered over their letters, common lives, and daily sayings? There is not only merit, but luck which goes to making a hero out of a gentleman. Mind, please you, I am not saying that the hero is after all not so very heroic; and have not the least desire to grudge him his merit because of his good fortune.

Have you any idea whither this Roundabout Essay on some late great victories is tending? Do you suppose that by those words I mean Trenton, Brandywine, Salamanca, Vittoria, and so forth? By a great victory I can't mean that affair at Farnham, for it was a drawn fight. Where, then, are the victories, pray, and when are we coming to them?

My good sir, you will perceive that in this Nicæan discourse, I have only as yet advanced as far as this — that a hero, whether he wins or loses, is a hero; and that if a fellow will but be honest and courageous, and do his best, we are for paying all honor to him. Furthermore, it has been asserted that Fortune has a good deal to do with the making of heroes; and thus hinted for the consolation of those who don't happen to be engaged in any stupendous victories, that, had opportunity so served, they might have been heroes too. If you are not, friend, it is not your fault, whilst I don't wish to detract from any gentleman's reputation who is. There. My worst enemy can't take objection to that. The point might have been put more briefly perhaps; but, if you please, we will not argue that question.

Well, then. The victories which I wish especially to commemorate in this paper, are the six great, complete, prodigious, and undeniable victories, achieved by the corps which the editor of "The Cornhill Magazine" has the honor to command. When I seem to speak disparagingly but now of generals, it was that chief I had in my I (if you will permit me the expression). I wished him not to be elated by too much prosperity; I warned him against assuming heroic imperatorial airs, and cocking his laurels too jauntily over his ear. I was his conscience, and stood on the splash-board of his triumph-car, whispering, "*Hominem memento te.*" As we rolled along the way, and passed the weathercocks on the temples, I saluted the symbol of the goddess Fortune with a reverent awe. "We have done our little endeavor," I said, bowing my head, "and mortals can do no more. But we might have fought bravely, and *not* won. We might have cast the coin, calling, 'Head,' and lo! Tail might have come uppermost." O thou Ruler of Victories! — thou Awarder of Fame! — thou Giver of Crowns (and shillings) — if thou hast smiled upon us, shall we not be thankful? There is a Saturnine philosopher, standing at the door of his book-shop, who, I fancy, has a pooh-pooh expression as the triumph passes. (I can't see quite clearly for the laurels, which have fallen down over my nose.) One hand is reining in the two white elephants that draw the car; I raise the other hand up to — to the laurels, and pass on, waving him a graceful recognition. Up the Hill of Ludgate — around the Pauline Square — by the side of Chepe — until it reaches our own Hill of Corn — the procession passes. The Imperator is bowing to the people; the captains of the legions are riding round the car, their gallant minds struck by the thought, "Have we not fought as well as yonder fellow, swaggering in the chariot, and are we not as good as he?" Granted, with all my heart, my dear lads. When your consulship arrives, may you be as fortunate. When these hands, now growing old, shall lay down sword and truncheon, may you mount the car, and ride to the temple of Jupiter. Be yours the laurels then. *Neque me myrtus dedecet*, looking cosily down from the arbor where I sit under the arched vine.

I fancy the Imperator standing on the steps of the temple (erected by Titus) on the Mons Frumentarius, and addressing the citizens: "Quirites!" he says, "in our campaign of six months, we have been engaged six times, and in each action have taken near upon a *hundred thousand prisoners*. Go to! What are other magazines compared to our magazine? (Sound, trumpeter!) What banner is there like that of Cornhill? You, philosopher yonder!" (He shirks under his mantle.) "Do you know what it is to have a hundred and ten thousand readers? A hundred thousand readers? a hundred thousand *buyers!*" (Cries of "No!" — "Pooh!" "Yes, upon my honor!" "Oh, come!" and murmurs of applause and derision) — "I say more than a hundred thousand purchasers — and I believe *as much as a million* readers!" (Immense sensation.) "To these have we said an unkind word? We have enemics; have we hit them an unkind blow? Have we sought to pursue party aims, to forward private jobs, to advance selfish schemes? The only persons to whom wittingly we have given pain are some who have volunteered for our corps — and of these volunteers we have had *thousands*." (Murmurs and grumbles.) "What commander, citizens, could place all these men — could make officers of all these men?" (cries of "No — no!" and laughter) — "could say, 'I accept this recruit, though he is too short for our standard, because he is poor, and has a mother at home who wants bread?' could enroll this other, who is too weak to bear arms, because he says, 'Look, sir, I shall be stronger anon.' The leader of such an army as ours must select his men, not because they are good and virtuous, but because they are strong and capable. To these our ranks are ever open, and in addition to the warriors who surround me" — (the generals look proudly conscious) — "I tell you, citizens, that I am in treaty with other and most tremendous champions, who will march by the side of our veterans to the achievement of fresh victories. Now, blow trumpets! Bang, ye gongs! and drummers, drub the thundering skins! Generals and chiefs, we go to sacrifice to the gods."

Crowned with flowers, the captains enter the temple, the other Magazines walking modestly behind them. The people huzza; and, in some instances, kneel and kiss the fringes of the robes of the warriors. The Philosopher puts up his shutters, and retires into his shop, deeply moved. In ancient times, Pliny (*apud* Smith) relates it was the custom of the Imperator "to paint his whole body a bright red;" and, also, on ascending the Hill, to have some of the hostile chiefs led aside "to the adjoining prison, and put to death." We propose to dispense with both these ceremonies.

THORNS IN THE CUSHION.

In the Essay with which this volume commences, "The Cornhill Magazine" was likened to a ship sailing forth on her voyage, and the captain uttered a very sincere prayer for her prosperity. The dangers of storm and rock, the vast outlay upon ship and cargo, and the certain risk of the venture, gave the chief officer a feeling of no small anxiety; for who could say from what quarter danger might arise, and how his owner's property might be imperilled? After a six months' voyage, we with very thankful hearts could acknowledge our good fortune: and, taking up the apologue in the Roundabout manner, we composed a triumphal procession in honor of the Magazine, and imagined the Imperator thereof riding in a sublime car to return thanks in the Temple of Victory. Cornhill is accustomed to grandeur and greatness, and has witnessed, every ninth of November, for I don't know how many centuries, a prodigious annual pageant, chariot, progress and flourish of trumpetry; and being so very near the Mansion House, I am sure the reader will understand how the idea of pageant and procession came naturally to my mind. The imagination easily supplied a gold coach, eight cream-colored horses of your true Pegasus breed, huzzaing multitudes, running footmen, and clanking knights in armor, a chaplain and a sword-bearer with a muff on his head, scowling out of the coach-window, and a Lord Mayor all crimson, fur, gold-chain, and white ribbons, solemnly occupying the place of state. A playful fancy could have carried the matter farther, could have depicted the feast in the Egyptian Hall, the Ministers, Chief Justices, and right reverend prelates taking their seats round about his lordship, the turtle and other delicious viands, and Mr. Toole behind the central throne, bawling out to the assembled guests and dignitaries: "My Lord So-and-so, my Lord What-d'ye-call-'im, my Lord Etcætera, the Lord Mayor pledges you all in a loving-cup." Then the noble proceedings come to an end; Lord Simper proposes the ladies; the company rises from table, and adjourns to coffee and muffins. The carriages of the nobility and guests roll back to the West. The Egyptian Hall, so bright just now, appears in a twilight glimmer, in which waiters are seen ransacking the dessert, and rescuing the spoons. His lordship and the Lady Mayoress go into their private apartments. The robes are doffed, the collar and white ribbons are removed. The Mayor becomes a man, and is pretty surely in a fluster about the speeches which he has just uttered; remembering too well now, wretched creature, the principal points which he *didn't* make when he rose to speak. He goes to bed to headache, to care, to repentance, and, I dare say, to a dose of something which his body-physician has prescribed for him. And there are ever so many men in the city who fancy that man happy!

Now, suppose that all through that 9th of November his lordship has had a racking rheumatism, or a toothache, let us say, during all dinner-time — through which he has been obliged to grin and mumble his poor old speeches. Is he enviable? Would you like to change with his lordship? Suppose that bumper which his golden footman brings him, instead i'fackins of ypocras or canary, contains some abomination of senna? Away! Remove the golden goblet, insidious cup-bearer! You now begin to perceive the gloomy moral which I am about to draw.

Last month we sang the song of glorification, and rode in the chariot of triumph. It was all very well. It was right to huzza, and be thankful, and cry, Bravo, our side! and besides, you know, there was the enjoyment of thinking how pleased Brown, and Jones, and Robinson (our dear friends) would be at this announcement of success. But now that the performance is over, my good sir, just step into my private room, and see that it is not all pleasure — this winning of successes. Cast your eye over those newspapers, over those letters. See what the critics say of your harmless jokes, neat little trim sentences, and pet waggeries! Why, you are no better than an idiot; you are drivelling; your powers have left you; this always overrated writer is rapidly sinking to, &c.

This is not pleasant; but neither is this the point. It may be the critic is right and the author wrong. It may be that the archbishop's sermon is not so fine as some of those discourses twenty years ago which used to delight the faithful in Granada. Or it may be (pleasing thought!) that the critic is a dullard, and does not understand what he is writing about. Everybody who has been to an exhibition has heard visitors discoursing about the pictures before their faces. One says, "This is very well!" another says, "This is stuff and rubbish;" another cries, "Bravo! this is a masterpiece:" and each has a right to his opinion. For example, one of the pictures I admired most at the Royal Academy is by a gentleman on whom I never, to my knowledge, set eyes. This picture is No. 346, "Moses," by Mr. S. Solomon. I thought it had a great intention, I thought it finely drawn and composed. It nobly represented, to my mind, the dark children of the Egyptian bondage, and suggested the touching story. My newspaper says, "Two ludicrously ugly women looking at a dingy baby, do not form a pleasing object;" and so good-by, Mr. Solomon. Are not most of our babies served so in life? and doesn't Mr. Robinson consider Mr. Brown's cherub an ugly, squalling little brat? So cheer up, Mr. S. S. It may be the critic who discoursed on your baby is a bad judge of babies. When Pharaoh's kind daughter found the child, and cherished and loved it, and took it home, and found a nurse for it, too, I dare say there were grim, brickdust-colored chamberlains, or some of the tough, old, meagre, yellow princesses at court, who never had children themselves, who cried out, "Faugh! the horrid little squalling wretch!" and knew he would never come to good; and said, "Didn't I tell you so?" when he assaulted the Egyptian.

Never mind, then, Mr. S. Solomon, I say, because a critic pooh-poohs your work of art — your Moses — your child — your foundling. Why, did not a wiseacre in "Blackwood's Magazine" lately fall foul of "Tom Jones?" O hypercritic! So, to be sure, did good old Mr. Richardson, who could write novels himself — but you, and I, and Mr. Gibbon, my dear sir, agree in giving our respect and wonder and admiration, to the brave old master.

In these last words I am supposing the respected reader to be endowed with a sense of humor, which he may or may not possess; indeed, don't we know many an honest man who can no more comprehend a joke than he can turn a tune? But I take for granted, my dear sir, that you are brimming over with fun — you mayn't make jokes, but you could if you would — you know you could: and in your quiet way you enjoy them extremely. Now, many people neither make them, nor understand them when made, nor like them when understood, and are suspicious, testy, and angry with jokers. Have you ever watched an elderly male or female — an elderly "party," so to speak, who begins to find out that some young wag of the company is "chaffing" him? Have you ever tried the sarcastic or Socratic method with a child? Little simple he or she, in the innocence of the simple heart, plays some silly freak, or makes some absurd remark, which you turn to ridicule. The little creature dimly perceives that you are making fun of him, writhes, blushes, grows uneasy, bursts into tears, — upon my word it is not fair to try the weapon of ridicule upon that innocent young victim. The awful objurgatory practice he is accustomed to. Point out his fault, and lay bare the dire consequences thereof: expose it roundly, and give him a proper, solemn, moral whipping — but do not attempt to *castigare ridendo.* Do not laugh at him writhing, and cause all the other boys in the school to laugh. Remember your own young days at school, my friend — the tingling cheeks, burning ears, bursting heart, and passion of desperate tears, with which you looked up, after having performed some blunder, whilst the doctor held you to public scorn before the class, and cracked his great clumsy jokes upon you — helpless, and a prisoner! Better the block itself, and the lictors, with their fasces of birch-twigs, than the maddening torture of those jokes!

Now, with respect to jokes — and the present company of course excepted — many people, perhaps most people, are as infants. They have little sense of humor. They don't like jokes. Raillery in writing annoys and offends them. The coarseness apart, I think I have met very, very few women who liked the banter of Swift and Fielding. Their simple, tender natures revolt at laughter. Is the satyr always a wicked brute at heart, and are they rightly shocked at his grin, his leer, his horns, hoofs, and ears? *Fi donc, le vilain monstre* with his shrieks, and his capering crooked legs! Let him go and get a pair of well-wadded black silk stockings, and pull them over those horrid shanks; put a large gown and bands over beard and hide; and pour a dozen of lavender-water into his lawn handkerchief, and cry, and never make a joke again. It shall all be highly-distilled poesy, and perfumed sentiment, and gushing eloquence; and the foot *shan't* peep out, and plague take it. Cover it up with the surplice. Out with your cambric, dear ladies, and let us all whimper together.

Now, then, hand on heart, we declare that it is not the fire of adverse critics which afflicts or frightens the editorial bosom. They may be right; they may be rogues who have a personal spite; they may be dullards who kick and bray as their nature is to do, and prefer thistles to pine-apples; they may be conscientious, acute, deeply learned, delightful judges, who see your joke in a moment, and the profound wisdom lying underneath. Wise or dull, laudatory or otherwise, we put their opinions aside. If they applaud, we are pleased: if they shake their quick pens, and fly off with a hiss, we resign their favors and put on all the fortitude we can muster. I would rather have the lowest man's good word than his bad one, to be sure; but as for coaxing a compliment, or wheedling him into good-humor, or stopping his angry mouth with a good dinner, or accepting his contributions for a certain Magazine, for fear of his barking or snapping elsewhere — *allons donc!* These shall not be our acts. Bow-wow, Cerberus! Here shall be no sop for thee, unless — unless Cerberus is an uncommonly good dog, when we shall bear no malice because he flew at us from our neighbor's gate.

What, then, is the main grief you spoke of as annoying you — the toothache in the Lord Mayor's jaw, the thorn in the cushion of the editorial chair? It is there. Ah! it stings me now as I write. It comes with almost every morning's post. At night I come home, and take my letters up to bed (not daring to open them), and in the morning I find one, two, three thorns on my pillow. Three I extracted yesterday; two I found this morning. They don't sting quite so sharply as they did; but a skin is a skin, and they bite, after all, most wickedly. It is all very fine to advertise on the Magazine, "Contributions are only to be sent to Messrs. Smith, Elder, and Co., and not to the Editor's private residence." My dear sir, how little you know man or woman kind, if you fancy they will take that sort of warning! How am I to know (though, to be sure, I begin to know now), as I take the letters off the tray, which of those envelopes contains a real *bonâ fide* letter, and which a thorn? One of the best invitations this year I mistook for a thorn-letter, and kept it without opening. This is what I call a thorn-letter :—

"Camberwell, June 4.

"SIR,—May I hope, may I entreat, that you will favor me by perusing the enclosed lines, and that they may be found worthy of insertion in "The Cornhill Magazine." We have known better days, sir. I have a sick and widowed mother to maintain, and little brothers and sisters who look to me. I do my utmost as a governess to support them. I toil at night when they are at rest, and my own hand and brain are alike tired. If I could add but *a little* to our means by my pen, many of my poor invalid's wants might be supplied, and I could procure for her comforts to which she is now a stranger. Heaven knows it is not for want of *will* or for want of *energy* on my part, that she is now in ill-health, and our little household almost without bread. Do—do cast a kind glance over my poem, and if you can help us, the widow, the orphans, will bless you! I remain, sir, in anxious expectancy,

"Your faithful servant,

"S. S. S."

And enclosed is a little poem or two, and an envelope with its penny stamp—heaven help us!—and the writer's name and address.

Now you see what I mean by a thorn. Here is the case put with true female logic. "I am poor; I am good; I am ill; I work hard; I have a sick mother and hungry brothers and sisters dependent on me. You can help us if you will." And then I look at the paper, with the thousandth part of a faint hope that it may be suitable, and I find it won't do: and I knew it wouldn't do: and why is this poor lady to appeal to my pity and bring her poor little ones kneeling to my bedside, and calling for bread which I can give them if I choose? No day passes but that argument *ad misericordiam* is used. Day and night that sad voice is crying out for help. Thrice it appealed to me yesterday. Twice this morning it cried to me: and I have no doubt when I go to get my hat, I shall find it with its piteous face and its pale family about it, waiting for me in the hall. One of the immense advantages which women have over our sex is, that they actually like to read these letters. Like letters? O mercy on us! Before I was an editor I did not like the postman much:—but now!

A very common way with these petitioners is to begin with a fine flummery about the merits and eminent genius of the person whom they are addressing. But this artifice, I state publicly, is of no avail. When I see *that* kind of herb, I know the snake within it, and fling it away before it has time to sting. Away, reptile, to the waste-paper basket, and thence to the flames!

But of these disappointed people, some take their disappointment and meekly bear it. Some hate and hold you their enemy because you could not be their friend. Some, furious and envious, say, "Who is this man who refuses what I offer, and how dares he, the conceited coxcomb, to deny my merit?"

Sometimes my letters contain not mere thorns, but bludgeons. Here are two choice slips from that noble Irish oak, which has more than once supplied alpeens for this meek and unoffending skull:—

"Theatre Royal, Donnybrook.

"SIR,—I have just finished reading the first portion of your Tale, *Lovel the Widower*, and am much surprised at the unwarrantable strictures you pass therein on the *corps de ballet*.

"I have been for more than ten years connected with the theatrical profession, and I beg to assure you that the majority of the *corps de ballet* are virtuous, well-conducted girls, and, consequently, that snug cottages are not taken for them in the Regent's Park.

"I also have to inform you that theatrical managers are in the habit of speaking good English, possibly better English than authors.

"You either know nothing of the subject in question, or you assert a wilful falsehood.

"I am happy to say that the characters of the *corps de ballet*, as also those of actors and actresses, are superior to the snarlings of dyspeptic libellers, or the spiteful attacks and *brutum fulmen* of ephemeral authors.

"I am, sir, your obedient servant,

A. B. C.

"The Editor of 'The Cornhill Magazine.'"

"Theatre Royal, Donnybrook.

"SIR,—I have just read, in 'The Cornhill Magazine,' for January, the first portion of a Tale written by you, and entitled *Lovel the Widower*.

"In the production in question you employ all your malicious spite (and you have great capabilities that way) in trying to degrade the character of the *corps de ballet*. When you imply that the majority of ballet-girls have villas taken for them in the Regent's Park, *I say you tell a deliberate falsehood.*

"Having been brought up to the stage from infancy, and, though now an actress, having been seven years principal dancer at the opera, I am competent to speak on the subject. I am only surprised that so vile a libeller as yourself should be allowed to preside at the Dramatic Fund dinner on the 22d instant. I think it would be much better if you were to reform your own life, instead of telling lies of those who are immeasurably your superiors.

"Yours in supreme disgust,
"A. D."

The signatures of the respected writers are altered, and for the site of their Theatre Royal an adjacent place is named, which (as I may have been falsely informed) used to be famous for quarrels, thumps, and broken heads. But, I say, is this an easy chair to sit on, when you are liable to have a pair of such shillelaghs flung at it? And, prithee, what was all the quarrel about? In the little history of "Lovel the Widower" I described, and brought to condign punishment, a certain wretch of a ballet-dancer, who lived splendidly for a while on ill-gotten gains, had an accident, and lost her beauty, and died poor, deserted, ugly, and every way odious. In the same page, other little ballet-dancers are described, wearing homely clothing, doing their duty, and carrying their humble savings to the family at home. But nothing will content my dear correspondents but to have me declare that the majority of ballet-dancers have villas in the Regent's Park, and to convict me of "deliberate falsehood." Suppose, for instance, I had chosen to introduce a red-haired washerwoman into a story? I might get an expostulatory letter saying, "Sir, in stating that the majority of washerwomen are red-haired, you are a liar! and you had best not speak of ladies who are immeasurably your superiors." Or suppose I had ventured to describe an illiterate haberdasher? One of the craft might write to me, "Sir, in describing haberdashers as illiterate, you utter a wilful falsehood. Haberdashers use much better English than authors." It is a mistake, to be sure. I have never said what my correspondents say I say. There is the text under their noses, but what if they choose to read it their own way? "Hurroo, lads! Here's for a fight. There's a bald head peeping out of the hut. There's a bald head! It must be Tim Malone's." And whack! come down both the bludgeons at once.

Ah me! we wound where we never intended to strike; we create anger where we never meant harm; and these thoughts are the thorns in our Cushion. Out of mere malignity, I suppose, there is no man who would like to make enemies. But here, in this editorial business, you can't do otherwise: and a queer, sad, strange, bitter thought it is, that must cross the mind of many a public man: "Do what I will, be innocent or spiteful, be generous or cruel, there are A and B, and C and D, who will hate me to the end of the chapter—to the chapter's end—to the Finis of the page—when hate, and envy, and fortune, and disappointment shall be over."

ON SCREENS IN DINING-ROOMS.

A GRANDSON of the late Rev. Dr. Primrose (of Wakefield, vicar) wrote me a little note from his country living this morning, and the kind fellow had the precaution to write "No thorn" upon the envelope, so that, ere I broke the seal, my mind might be relieved of any anxiety lest the letter should contain one of those lurking stabs which are so painful to the present gentle writer. Your epigraph, my dear P., shows your kind and artless nature; but don't you see it is of no use? People who are bent upon assassinating you in the manner mentioned will write "No thorn" upon their envelopes too; and you open the case, and presently out flies a poisoned stiletto, which springs into a man's bosom, and makes the wretch howl with anguish. When the bailiffs are after a man, they adopt all sorts of disguises, pop out on him from all conceivable corners, and tap his miserable shoulder. His wife is taken ill; his sweetheart, who remarked his brilliant, too brilliant appearance at the Hyde Park review, will meet him at Cremorne, or where you will. The old friend who has owed him that money these five years will meet him at so-and-so and pay. By one bait or other the victim is hooked, netted, landed, and down goes the basket-lid. It is not your wife, your sweetheart, your friend, who is going to pay you. It is Mr. Nab the bailiff. *You* know —— you are caught. You are off in a cab to Chancery Lane.

You know, I say? *Why* should you know? I make no manner of doubt you never were taken by a bailiff in your life. I never was. I have been in two or three debtors' prisons, but not on my own account. Goodness be praised! I mean you can't escape your lot; and Nab only stands here metaphorically as the watchful, certain, and untiring officer of Mr. Sheriff Fate. Why, my dear Primrose, this morning along with your letter, comes another, bearing the well known superscription of another old friend, which I open without the least suspicion, and what do I find? A few lines from my friend Johnson, it is true, but they are written on a page covered with feminine handwriting. "Dear Mr. Johnson," says the writer, "I have just been perusing with delight a most charming tale by the Archbishop of Cambray. It is called 'Telemachus;' and I think it would be admirably suited to 'The Cornhill Magazine.' As you know the Editor, will you have the great kindness, dear Mr. Johnson, to communicate with him *personally* (as that is much better than writing in a roundabout way to the Publishers, and waiting goodness knows how long for an answer), and state my readiness to translate this excellent and instructive story. I do not wish to breathe *a word* against 'Lovel Parsonage,' 'Framley the Widower,' or any of the novels which have appeared in 'The Cornhill Magazine,' but I *am sure* 'Telemachus' is as good as new to English readers, and in point of interest and morality *far*," &c., &c., &c.

There it is. I am stabbed through Johnson. He has lent himself to this attack on me. He is weak about women. Other strong men are. He submits to the common lot, poor fellow. In my reply I do not use a word of unkindness. I write him back gently that I fear "Telemachus" won't suit us. He can send the letter on to his fair correspondent. But however soft the answer, I question whether the wrath will be turned away. Will there not be a coolness between him and the lady? and is it not possible that henceforth her fine eyes will look with darkling glances upon the pretty orange cover of our magazine?

Certain writers, they say, have a bad opinion of women. Now am I very whimsical in supposing that this disappointed candidate will be hurt at her rejection, and angry or cast down according to her nature? "Angry, indeed!" says Juno, gathering up her purple robes and royal raiment. "Sorry, indeed!" cries Minerva, lacing on her corselet again, and scowling under her helmet. (I imagine the well known Apple case has just been argued and decided.) "Hurt, forsooth! Do you suppose *we* care for the opinion of that hobnailed lout of a Paris? Do you suppose that I, the Goddess of Wisdom, can't make allowances for mortal ignorance, and am so base as to bear malice against a poor creature who knows no better? You little know the goddess nature when you dare to insinuate that our divine minds are actuated by motives so base. A love of justice influences *us*. We are above mean revenge. We are too magnanimous to be angry at the award of such a judge in favor of such a creature." And rustling out their skirts, the ladies walk away together. This is all very well. You are bound to believe them. They are actuated by no hostility: not they. They bear no malice—of course not. But when the Trojan war occurs presently, which side will they take? Many brave souls will be sent to Hades. Hector will perish. Poor old Priam's bald numskull will be cracked, and Troy town will burn, because Paris prefers golden-haired Venus to ox-eyed Juno and gray-eyed Minerva.

The last Essay of this Roundabout Series, describing the griefs and miseries of the editorial chair, was written, as the kind reader will acknowledge, in a mild and gentle, not in a warlike or satirical spirit. I showed how cudgels were applied; but surely the meek object of persecution hit no blows in return. The beating did not hurt much, and the person assaulted could afford to keep his good-humor; indeed, I admired that brave though illogical little actress, of the T. R. D-bl-n, for her fiery vindication of her profession's honor. I assure her I had no intention to tell l—s — well, let us say, monosyllables — about my superiors: and I wish her nothing but well, and when Macmahon (or shall it be Mulligan?) *Roi d'Irlande* ascends his throne, I hope she may be appointed professor of English to the princesses of the royal house. *Nuper* — in former days — I too have militated; sometimes, as I now think, unjustly; but always I vow, without personal rancor. Which of us has not idle words to recall, flippant jokes to regret? Have you never committed an imprudence? Have you never had a dispute, and found out that you were wrong? So much the worse for you. Woe be to the man *qui croit toujours avoir raison.* His anger is not a brief madness, but a permanent mania. His rage is not a fever-fit, but a black poison inflaming him, distorting his judgment, disturbing his rest, imbittering his cup, gnawing at his pleasures, causing him more cruel suffering than ever he can inflict on his enemy. *O la belle morale!* As I write it, I think about one or two little affairs of my own. There is old Dr. Squaretoso (he certainly was very rude to me, and that's the fact); there is Madame Pomposa (and certainly her ladyship's behavior was about as cool as cool could be). Never mind, old Squaretoso: never mind, Madame Pomposa! Here is a hand. Let us be friends, as we once were, and have no more of this rancor.

I had hardly sent that last Roundabout Paper to the printer (which, I submit, was written in a placable and not unchristian frame of mind), when Saturday came, and with it, of course, my "Saturday Review." I remember at New York coming down to breakfast at the hotel one morning, after a criticism had appeared in "The New York Herald," in which an Irish waiter had given me a dressing for a certain lecture on Swift. Ah! my dear little enemy of the T. R. D., what were the cudgels in *your* little *billet-doux* compared to those noble New York shillelaghs? All through the Union, the literary sons of Erin have marched *alpeen*-stock in hand, and in every city of the States they call each other and everybody else the finest names. Having come to breakfast, then, in the public room, I sit down, and see — that the nine people opposite have all got "New York Heralds" in their hands. One dear little lady, whom I knew, and who sat opposite, gave a pretty blush, and popped her paper under the tablecloth. I told her I had had my whipping already in my own private room, and begged her to continue her reading. I may have undergone agonies, you see, but every man who has been bred at an English public school comes away from a private interview with Dr. Birch with a calm, even a smiling face. And this is not impossible, when you are prepared. You screw your courage up — you go through the business. You come back and take your seat on the form, showing not the least symptom of uneasiness or of previous unpleasantries. But to be caught suddenly up, and whipped in the bosom of your family — to sit down to breakfast, and cast your innocent eye on a paper, and find, before you are aware, that "The Saturday Monitor" or "Black Monday Instructor" has hoisted you and is laying on — that is indeed a trial. Or perhaps the family has looked at the dreadful paper beforehand, and weakly tries to hide it. "Where is 'The Instructor,' or 'The Monitor'?" say you. "Where is that paper?" says mamma to one of the young ladies. Lucy hasn't it. Fanny hasn't seen it. Emily thinks that the governess has it. At last, out it is brought, that awful paper! Papa is amazingly tickled with the article on Thomson; thinks that show-up of Johnson is very lively; and now — heaven be good to us! — he has come to the critique on himself — "Of all the rubbish which we have had from Mr. Tomkins, we do protest and vow that this last cartload is" &c. Ah, poor Tomkins! — but most of all, ah! poor Mrs. Tomkins, and poor Emily, and Fanny, and Lucy, who have to sit by and see *paterfamilias* put to the torture!

Now, on this eventful Saturday, I did not cry, because it was not so much the Editor as the Publisher of "The Cornhill Magazine" who was brought out for a dressing; and it is wonderful how gallantly one bears the misfortunes of one's friends. That a writer should be taken to task about his books, is fair, and he must abide the praise or the censure. But that a publisher should be criticised for his dinners, and for the conversation which did *not* take place there, — is this tolerable press practice, legitimate joking, or honorable warfare? I have not the honor to know my next door neighbor, but I make no doubt that he receives his friends at dinner; I see his wife and children pass constantly; I even know the carriages of some of the people who call upon him, and could tell their names. Now, suppose his servants were to tell mine what the doings are next door, who comes to dinner, what is eaten and said, and I were to publish an account of these transactions in a newspaper, I could assuredly get money for the report; but ought I to write it, and what would you think of me for doing so?

And suppose, Mr. Saturday Reviewer — you *censor morum*, you who pique yourself (and justly and honorably in the main) upon your character of gentleman, as well of writer, — suppose, not that you yourself invent and indite absurd twaddle about gentlemen's private meetings and transactions, but pick this wretched garbage out of a New York street, and hold it up for your readers' amusement—don't you think, my friend, that you might have been better employed? Here, is my "Saturday Review," and in an American paper subsequently sent to me, I light, astonished, on an account of the dinners of my friend and publisher, which are described as "tremendously heavy," of the conversation (which does not take place), and of the guests assembled at the table. I am informed that the proprietor of "The Cornhill" and the host on these occasions, is "a very good man, but totally unread;" and that on my asking him whether Dr. Johnson was dining behind the screen, he said, "God bless my soul, my dear sir, there's no person by the name of Johnson here, nor any one behind the screen," and that a roar of laughter cut him short. I am informed by the same New York correspondent that I have touched up a contributor's article; that I once said to a literary gentleman, who was proudly pointing to an anonymous article as his writing, "Ah! I thought I recognized *your hoof* in it." I am told by the same authority that "The Cornhill Magazine" "shows symptoms of being on the wane," and having sold nearly a hundred thousand copies, he (the correspondent) "should think forty thousand was now about the mark." Then the graceful writer passes on to the dinners, at which it appears the Editor of the Magazine "is the great gun, and comes out with all the geniality in his power."

Now suppose this charming intelligence is untrue? Suppose the publisher (to recall the words of my friend the Dublin actor of last month) is a gentleman to the full as well informed as those whom he invites to his table? Suppose he never made the remark, beginning — "God bless my soul, my dear sir," &c., nor any thing resembling it? Suppose nobody roared with laughing? Suppose the Editor of "The Cornhill Magazine" never "touched up" one single line of the contribution which bears "marks of his hand"? Suppose he never said to any literary gentleman, "I recognized *your hoof*" in any periodical whatever? Suppose the 40,000 subscribers, which the writer to New York "considered to be about the mark," should be between 90,000 and 100,000 (and as he will have figures, there they are)? Suppose this back-door gossip should be utterly blundering and untrue, would any one wonder? Ah! if we had only enjoyed the happiness to number this writer among the contributors to our Magazine, what a cheerfulness and easy confidence his presence would impart to our meetings! He would find that "poor Mr. Smith" had heard that recondite anecdote of Dr. Johnson behind the screen; and as for "the great gun of those banquets," with what geniality should not I "come out" if I had an amiable companion close by me, dotting down my conversation for "The New York Times"!

Attack our books, Mr. Correspondent, and welcome. They are fair subjects for just censure or praise. But woe be to you, if you allow private rancors or animosities to influence you in the discharge of your public duty. In the little court where you are paid to sit as judge, as critic, you owe it to your employers, to your conscience, to the honor of your calling, to deliver just sentences; and you shall have to answer to heaven for your dealings, as surely as my Lord Chief Justice on the Bench. The dignity of letters, the honor of the literary calling, the slights put by haughty and unthinking people upon literary men, — don't we hear outcries upon these subjects raised daily? As dear Sam Johnson sits behind the screen, too proud to show his threadbare coat and patches among the more prosperous brethren of his trade, there is no want of dignity in *him*, in that homely image of labor ill rewarded, genius as yet unrecognized, independence sturdy and uncomplaining. But Mr. Nameless, behind the publisher's screen uninvited, peering at the company and the meal, catching up scraps of the jokes, and noting down the guests' behavior and conversation, — what a figure his is! *Allons*, Mr. Nameless! Put up your notebook; walk out of the hall; and leave gentlemen alone who would be private, and wish you no harm.

TUNBRIDGE TOYS.

I WONDER whether those little silver pencil-cases with a movable almanac at the butt-end are still favorite implements with boys, and whether peddlers still hawk them about the country? Are there peddlers and hawkers still, or are rustics and children grown too sharp to deal with them? Those pencil-cases, as far as my memory serves me, were not of much use. The screw upon which the movable almanac turned was constantly getting loose. The I of the table would work from its moorings, under Tuesday or Wednesday, as the case might be, and you would find, on examination, that Th. or W. was the 23½ of the month (which was absurd on the face of the thing), and in a word your cherished pencil-case an utterly unreliable time-keeper. Nor was this a matter of wonder. Consider the position of a pencil-case in a boy's pocket. You had hard-bake in it; marbles, kept in your purse when the money was all gone; your mother's purse, knitted so fondly and supplied with a little bit of gold, long since — prodigal little son! — scattered amongst the swine — I mean amongst brandy-balls, open tarts, three-cornered puffs, and similar abominations. You had a top and string; a knife; a piece of cobbler's wax; two or three bullets; a *Little Warbler;* and I, for my part, remember, for a considerable period, a brass-barrelled pocket-pistol (which would fire beautifully, for with it I shot off a button from Butt Major's jacket); — with all these things, and ever so many more, clinking and rattling in your pockets, and your hands, of course, keeping them in perpetual movement, how could you expect your movable almanac not to be twisted out of its place now and again — your pencil-case to be bent — your licorice water not to leak out of your bottle over the cobbler's wax, your bull's-eyes not to ram up the lock and barrel of your pistol, and so forth?

In the month of June, thirty-seven years ago, I bought one of those pencil-cases from a boy whom I shall call Hawker, and who was in my form. Is he dead? Is he a millionnaire? Is he a bankrupt now? He was an immense screw at school, and I believe to this day that the value of the thing for which I owed and eventually paid three-and-sixpence, was in reality not one-and-nine.

I certainly enjoyed the case at first a good deal, and amused myself with twiddling round the movable calendar. But this pleasure wore off. The jewel, as I said, was not paid for, and Hawker, a large and violent boy, was exceedingly unpleasant as a creditor. His constant remark was, "When are you going to pay me that three-and-sixpence? What sneaks your relations must be? They come to see you. You go out to them on Saturdays and Sundays, and they never give you any thing! Don't tell *me*, you little humbug!" and so forth. The truth is that my relations were respectable; but my parents were making a tour in Scotland; and my friends in London, whom I used to go and see, were most kind to me, certainly, but somehow never tipped me. That term, of May to August, 1823, passed in agonies then, in consequence of my debt to Hawker. What was the pleasure of a calendar pencil-case in comparison with the doubt and torture of mind occasioned by the sense of the debt, and the constant reproach in that fellow's scowling eyes and gloomy, coarse reminders? How was I to pay off such a debt out of sixpence a week? ludicrous! Why did not some one come to see me, and tip me? Ah! my dear sir, if you have any little friends at school, go and see them, and do the natural thing by them. You won't miss the sovereign. You don't know what a blessing it will be to them. Don't fancy they are too old — try 'em. And they will remember you, and bless you in future days; and their gratitude shall accompany your dreary after-life; and they shall meet you kindly when thanks for kindness are scant. O mercy! shall I ever forget that sovereign you gave me, Captain Bob? or the agonies of being in debt to Hawker? In that very term, a relation of mine was going to India. I actually was fetched from school in order to take leave of him. I am afraid I told Hawker of this circumstance. I own I speculated upon my friend's giving me a pound. A pound? Pooh! A relation going to India, and deeply affected at parting from his darling kinsman, might give five pounds to the dear fellow! . . . There was Hawker when I came back — of course there he was. As he looked in my scared face, his turned livid with rage. He muttered curses, terrible from the lips of so young a boy. My relation, about to cross the ocean to fill a lucrative appointment, asked me with much interest about my progress at school, heard me construe a passage of Eutropius, the pleasing Latin work on which I was then engaged; gave me a God bless you, and sent me back to school; upon my word of honor, without so much as a half-crown! It is all very well, my dear sir, to say that boys contract habits of expecting tips from their parents' friends, that they become avaricious, and so forth. Avaricious! fudge! Boys contract habits of tart and toffee eating, which they do not carry into after-life. On the contrary, I wish I *did* like 'em. What raptures of pleasure one could have now for five shillings, if one could but pick it off the pastrycook's tray! No. If you have any little friends at school, out with your half-crowns, my friend, and impart to those little ones the little fleeting joys of their age.

Well, then. At the beginning of August, 1823, Bartlemy-tide holidays came, and I was to go to my parents, who were at Tunbridge Wells. My place in the coach was taken by my tutor's servants — "Bolt-in-Tun," Fleet Street, seven o'clock in the morning, was the word. My Tutor, the Rev. Edward P——, to whom I hereby present my best compliments, had a parting interview with me: gave me my little account for my governor: the remaining part of the coach-hire; five shillings for my own expenses; and some five and twenty shillings on an old account which had been overpaid, and was to be restored to my family.

Away I ran and paid Hawker his three-and-six. Ouf! what a weight it was off my mind! (He was a Norfolk boy, and used to go home from Mrs. Nelson's "Bell Inn," Aldgate — but that is not to the point.) The next morning, of course, we were an hour before the time. I and another boy shared a hackney-coach; two-and-six; porter for putting luggage on coach, threepence. I had no more money of my own left. Rasherwell, my companion, went into the "Bolt-in-Tun" coffee-room, and had a good breakfast. I couldn't; because, though I had five and twenty shillings of my parents' money, I had none of my own, you see.

I certainly intended to go without breakfast, and still remember how strongly I had that resolution in my mind. But there was that hour to wait. A beautiful August morning — I am very hungry. There is Rasherwell "tucking" away in the coffee-room. I pace the street, as sadly almost as if I had been coming to school, not going thence. I turn into a court by mere chance — I vow it was by mere chance — and there I see a coffee-shop with a placard in the window, *Coffee, Twopence. Round of buttered toast, Twopence.* And here am I, hungry, penniless, with five and twenty shillings of my parents' money in my pocket.

What would you have done? You see I had had my money, and spent it in that pencil-case affair. The five and twenty shillings were a trust — by me to be handed over.

But then would my parents wish their only child to be actually without breakfast? Having this money, and being so hungry, so *very* hungry, mightn't I take ever so little? Mightn't I at home eat as much as I chose.

Well, I went into the coffee-shop and spent fourpence. I remember the taste of the coffee and toast to this day — a peculiar, muddy, not-sweet-enough, most fragrant coffee — a rich, rancid, yet not-buttered-enough, delicious toast. The waiter had nothing. At any rate, fourpence I know was the sum I spent. And the hunger appeased, I got on the coach a guilty being.

At the last stage, — what is its name? I have forgotten in seven and thirty years, — there is an inn with a little green and trees before it; and by the trees there is an open carriage. It is our carriage. Yes, there are Prince and Blucher, the horses; and my parents in the carriage. Oh! how I had been counting the days until this one came! Oh! how happy had I been to see them yesterday! But there was that fourpence. All the journey down the toast had choked me, and the coffee poisoned me.

I was in such a state of remorse about the fourpence, that I forgot the maternal joy and caresses, the tender paternal voice. I pull out the twenty-four shillings and eightpence with a trembling hand.

"Here's your money," I gasp out, "which Mr. P—— owes you, all but fourpence. I owed three-and-sixpence to Hawker out of my money for a pencil-case, and I had none left, and I took fourpence of yours, and had some coffee at a shop."

I suppose I must have been choking whilst uttering this confession.

"My dear boy," says the governor, "why didn't you go and breakfast at the hotel?"

"He must be starved," says my mother.

I had confessed; I had been a prodigal; I had been taken back to my parents' arms again. It was not a very great crime as yet, or a very long career of prodigality; but don't we know that a boy who takes a pin which is not his own will take a thousand pounds when occasion serves, bring his parents' gray heads with sorrow to the grave, and carry his own to the gallows? Witness the career of Dick Idle, upon whom our friend Mr. Sala has been discoursing. Dick only began by playing pitch-and toss on a tombstone: playing fair, for what we know: and even for that sin he was promptly caned by the beadle. The bamboo was ineffectual to cane that reprobate's bad courses out of him. From pitch-and-toss he proceeded to man-slaughter if necessary: to highway robbery; to Tyburn and the rope there. Ah! heaven be thanked, my parents' heads are still above the grass, and mine still out of the noose.

As I look up from my desk, I see Tunbridge Wells Common and the rocks, the strange familiar place which I remember forty years ago. Boys saunter over the green with stumps and cricket-bats. Other boys gallop by on the riding-master's hacks. I protest it is *Cramp, Riding Master*, as it used to be in the reign of George IV., and that Centaur Cramp must be at least a hundred years old. Yonder comes a footman with a bundle of novels from the library. Are they as good as *our* novels? Oh! how delightful they were! Shades of Valancour, awful ghost of Manfroni, how I shudder at your appearance! Sweet image of Thaddeus of Warsaw, how often has this almost infantile hand tried to depict you in a Polish cap and richly embroidered tights! And as for Corinthian Tom in light blue pantaloons and Hessians, and Jerry Hawthorn from the country, can all the fashion, can all the splendor of real life which these eyes have subsequently beheld, can all the wit I have heard or read in later times, compare with your fashion, with your brilliancy, with your delightful grace, and sparkling vivacious rattle?

Who knows? They *may* have kept those very books at the library still — at the well-remembered library on the Pantiles, where they sell that delightful, useful Tunbridge ware. I will go and see. I went my way to the Pantiles, the queer little old-world Pantiles, where, a hundred years since, so much good company came to take its pleasure. Is it possible that in the past century, gentlefolks of the first rank (as I read lately in a lecture on George II. in "The Cornhill Magazine") assembled here and entertained each other with gaming, dancing, fiddling, and tea? There are fiddlers, harpers, and trumpeters performing at this moment in a weak old balcony, but where is the fine company? Where are the earls, duchesses, bishops, and magnificent embroidered gamesters? A half-dozen of children and their nurses are listening to the musicians: an old lady or two in a poke bonnet passes, and for the rest, I see but an uninteresting population of native tradesmen. As for the library, its window is full of pictures of burly theologians and their works, sermons, apologues, and so forth. Can I go in and ask the young ladies at the counter for "Manfroni, or the One-Handed Monk," and "Life in London, or the Adventures of Corinthian Tom, Jeremiah Hawthorn, Esq., and their friend Bob Logic"? — absurd. I turn away abashed from the casement — from the Pantiles — no longer Pantiles but Parade. I stroll over the Common, and survey the beautiful purple hills around, twinkling with a thousand bright villas, which have sprung up over this charming ground since first I saw it. What an admirable scene of peace and plenty! What a delicious air breathes over the heath, blows the cloud shadows across it, and murmurs through the full-clad trees! Can the world show a land fairer, richer, more cheerful? I see a portion of it when I look up from the window at which I write. But fair scene, green woods, bright terraces gleaming in sunshine, and purple clouds swollen with summer rain — nay, the very pages over which my head bends — disappear from before my eyes. They are looking backwards, back into forty years off, into a dark room, into a little house hard by on the Common here, in the Bartlemy-tide holidays. The parents have gone to town for two days: the house is all his own, his own and a grim old maid-servant's, and a little boy is seated at night in the lonely drawing-room, poring over "Manfroni, or the One-Handed Monk," so frightened that he scarcely dares to turn round.

DE JUVENTUTE.

Our last paper of this veracious and roundabout series related to a period which can only be historical to a great number of readers of this Magazine. Four I saw at the station to-day with orange-covered books in their hands, who can but have known George IV. by books, and statues, and pictures. Elderly gentlemen were in their prime, old men in their middle age, when he reigned over us. His image remains on coins; on a picture or two hanging here and there in a Club or old-fashioned dining-room; on horseback, as at Trafalgar Square, for example, where I defy any monarch to look more uncomfortable. He turns up in sundry memoirs and histories which have been published of late days; in Mr. Massey's "History;" in "The Buckingham and Grenville Correspondence;" and gentlemen who have accused a certain writer of disloyalty are referred to those volumes to see whether the picture drawn of George is overcharged. Charon has paddled him off; he has mingled with the crowded republic of the dead. His effigy smiles from a canvas or two. Breechless he bestrides his steed in Trafalgar Square. I believe he still wears his robes at Madame Tussaud's (Madame herself having quitted Baker Street and life, and found him she modelled t'other side the Stygian stream). On the head of a five-shilling piece we still occasionally come upon him, with St. George, the dragon-slayer, on the other side of the coin. Ah me! did this George slay many dragons? Was he a brave, heroic champion, and rescuer of virgins? Well! well! have you and I overcome all the dragons that assail *us*?

come alive and victorious out of all the caverns which we have entered in life, and succored, at risk of life and limb, all poor distressed persons in whose naked limbs the dragon Poverty is about to fasten his fangs, whom the dragon Crime is poisoning with his horrible breath, and about to crunch up and devour? O my royal liege! O my gracious prince and warrior! *You* a champion to fight that monster? Your feeble spear ever pierce that slimy paunch or plated back? See how the flames come gurgling out of his red-hot brazen throat! What a roar! Nearer and nearer he trails, with eyes flaming like the lamps of a railroad engine. How he squeals, rushing out through the darkness of his tunnel! Now he is near. Now he is *here*. And now — what? — lance, shield, knight, feathers, horse and all? O horror, horror! Next day, round the monster's cave, there lie a few bones more. You, who wish to keep yours in your skins, be thankful that you are not called upon to go out and fight dragons. Be grateful that they don't sally out and swallow you. Keep a wise distance from their caves, lest you pay too dearly for approaching them. Remember that years passed, and whole districts were ravaged, before the warrior came who was able to cope with the devouring monster. When that knight *does* make his appearance, with all my heart let us go out and welcome him with our best songs, huzzas, and laurel wreaths, and eagerly recognize his valor and victory. But he comes only seldom. Countless knights were slain before St. George won the battle. In the battle of life are we all going to try for the honors of championship? If we can do our duty, if we can keep our place pretty honorably through the combat, let us say, *Laus Deo!* at the end of it, as the firing ceases, and the night falls over the field.

The old were middle-aged, the elderly were in their prime, then, thirty years since, when yon royal George was still fighting the dragon. As for you, my pretty lass, with your saucy hat and golden tresses tumbled in your net, and you, my spruce young gentleman in your mandarin's cap (the young folks at the country-place where I am staying are so attired), your parents were unknown to each other, and wore short frocks and short jackets, at the date of this five-shilling piece. Only to-day I met a dog-cart crammed with children — children with mustaches and mandarin caps — children with saucy hats and hair-nets — children in short frocks and knickerbockers (surely the prettiest boy's dress that has appeared these hundred years) — children from twenty years of age to six; and father, with mother by his side, driving in front — and on father's countenance I saw that very laugh which I remember perfectly in the time when this crown-piece was coined — in *his* time, in King George's time, when we were school-boys seated on the same form. The smile was just as broad, as bright, as jolly, as I remember it in the past — unforgotten, though not seen or thought of, for how many decades of years, and quite and instantly familiar, though so long out of sight.

Any contemporary of that coin who takes it up and reads the inscription round the laurelled head, "Georgius IV. Britanniarum Rex. Fid. Def. 1823," if he will but look steadily enough at the round, and utter the proper incantation, I dare say may conjure back his life there. Look well, my elderly friend, and tell me what you see? First, I see a Sultan, with hair, beautiful hair, and a crown of laurels round his head, and his name is Georgius Rex. Fid. Def., and so on. Now the Sultan has disappeared; and what is that I see? A boy, — a boy in a jacket. He is at a desk; he has great books before him, Latin and Greek books and dictionaries. Yes, but behind the great books, which he pretends to read, is a little one, with pictures, which he is really reading. It is — yes, I can read now — it is "The Heart of Mid Lothian," by the author of "Waverley" — or, no, it is "Life in London, or the Adventures of Corinthian Tom, Jeremiah Hawthorn, and their friend Bob Logic," by Pierce Egan; and it has pictures,— oh! such funny pictures! As he reads, there comes behind the boy, a man, a dervish, in a black gown, like a woman, and a black square cap, and he has a book in each hand, and he seizes the boy who is reading the picture-book, and lays his head upon one of his books, and smacks it with the other. The boy makes faces, and so that picture disappears.

Now the boy has grown bigger. *He* has got on a black gown and cap, something like the dervish. He is at a table, with ever so many bottles on it, and fruit, and tobacco; and other young dervishes come in. They seem as if they were singing. To them enters an old moollah, he takes down their names, and orders them all to go to bed. What is this? a carriage, with four beautiful horses all galloping — a man in red is blowing a trumpet. Many young men are on the carriage — one of them is driving the horses. Surely they won't drive into that? — ah! they have all disappeared. And now I see one of the young men alone. He is walking in a street — a dark street — presently a light comes to a window. There is the shadow of a lady who passes. He stands there till the light goes out. Now he is in a room scribbling on a piece of paper, and kissing a miniature every now and then. They seem to be lines each pretty much of a length. I can read *heart, smart, dart; Mary, fairy; Cupid, stupid; true, you;* and never mind what more. Bah! it is bosh. Now see, he has got a gown on again, and a wig of white hair on his head, and he is sitting with other dervishes in a great room full of them, and on a throne in the middle is an old Sultan in scarlet, sitting before a desk, and he wears a wig too — and the young man gets up and speaks to him. And now what is here? He is in a room with ever so many children, and the miniature hanging up. Can it be a likeness of that woman who is sitting before that copper urn, with a silver vase in her hand, from which she is pouring hot liquor into cups? Was *she* ever a fairy? She is as fat as a hippopotamus now. He is sitting on a divan by the fire. He has a paper on his knees. Read the name of the paper. It is "The Superfine Review." It inclines to think that Mr. Dickens is not a true gentleman, that Mr. Thackeray is not a true gentleman, and that when the one is pert and the other is arch, we, the gentlemen of "The Superfine Review," think, and think rightly, that we have some cause to be indignant. The great cause why modern humor and modern sentimentalism repel us, is that they are unwarrantably familiar. Now, Mr. Sterne, "The Superfine Reviewer" thinks, "was a true sentimentalist, because he was *above all things* a true gentleman." The flattering inference is obvious: let us be thankful for having an elegant moralist watching over us, and learn, if not too old, to imitate his high-bred politeness and catch his unobtrusive grace. If we are unwarrantably familiar, we know who is not. If we repel by pertness, we know who never does. If our language offends, we know whose is always modest. O pity! The vision has disappeared off the silver, the images of youth and the past are vanishing away! We who have lived before railways were made, belong to another world. In how many hours could the Prince of Wales drive from Brighton to London, with a light carriage built expressly, and relays of horses longing to gallop the next stage? Do you remember Sir Somebody, the coachman of the Age, who took our half-crown so affably? It was only yesterday; but what a gulf between now and then! *Then* was the old world. Stage-coaches, more or less swift riding-horses, pack-horses, highwaymen, knights in armor, Norman invaders, Roman legions, Druids, Ancient Britons painted blue, and so forth — all these belong to the old period. I will concede a halt in the midst of it, and allow that gunpowder and printing tended to modernize the world. But your railroad starts the new era, and we of a certain age belong to the new time and the old one. We are of the time of chivalry as well as the Black Prince or Sir Walter Manny. We are of the age of steam. We have stepped out of the old world on to "Brunel's" vast deck, and across the waters *ingens patet tellus*. Towards what new continent are we wending? to what new laws, new manners, new politics, vast new expanses of liberties unknown as yet, or only surmised? I used to know a man who had invented a flying-machine. "Sir," he would say, "give me but five hundred pounds, and I will make it. It is so simple of construction that I tremble daily lest some other person should light upon and patent my discovery." Perhaps faith was wanting; perhaps the five hundred pounds. He is dead, and somebody else must make the flying-machine. But that will only be a step forward on the journey already begun since we quitted the old world. There it lies on the other side of yonder embankments. You young folks have never seen it; and Waterloo is to you no more than Agincourt, and George IV. than Sardanapalus. We elderly people have lived in that pre-railroad world, which has passed into limbo and vanished from under us. I tell you it was firm under our feet once, and not long ago. They have raised those railroad embankments up, and shut off the old world that was behind them. Climb up that bank on which the irons are laid, and look to the other side — it is gone. There *is* no other side. Try and catch yesterday. Where is it? Here is a "Times" newspaper, dated Monday 26th, and this is Tuesday 27th. Suppose you deny there was such a day as yesterday?

We who lived before railways, and survive out of the ancient world, are like Father Noah and his family out of the Ark. The children will gather round and say to us patriarchs, "Tell us, grandpapa, about the old world." And we shall mumble our old stories; and we shall drop off one by one; and there will be fewer and fewer of us, and these very old and feeble. There will be but ten pre-railroadites left: then three — then two — then one — then 0! If the hippopotamus had the least sensibility (of which I cannot trace any signs either in his hide or his face), I think he would go down to the bottom of his tank, and never come up again. Does he not see that he belongs to bygone ages, and that his great hulking barrel of a body is out of place in these times? What has he in common with the brisk young life surrounding him? In the watches of the night, when the keepers are asleep, when the birds are on one leg, when even the little armadillo is quiet, and the monkeys have ceased their chatter, — he, I mean the hippopotamus, and the elephant, and the long-necked giraffe, perhaps may lay their heads together and have a colloquy about the great silent antediluvian world which they remember, where mighty monsters floundered through the ooze, crocodiles basked on the banks, and dragons darted out of the caves and waters before men were made to slay them. We who lived before railways are antediluvians — we must pass away. We are growing scarcer every day; and old — old — very old relicts of the times when George was still fighting the Dragon.

Not long since, a company of horseriders paid a visit to our watering-place. We went to see them, and I bethought me that young Walter Juvenis, who was in the place, might like also to witness the performance. A pantomime is not always amusing to persons who have attained a certain age; but a boy at a pantomime is always amused and amusing, and to see his pleasure is good for most hypochondriacs.

We sent to Walter's mother, requesting that he might join us, and the kind lady replied that the boy had already been at the morning performance of the equestrians, but was most eager to go in the evening likewise. And go he did; and laughed at all Mr. Merryman's remarks, though he remembered them with remarkable accuracy, and insisted upon waiting to the very end of the fun, and was only induced to retire just before its conclusion by representations that the ladies of the party would be incommoded if they were to wait and undergo the rush and trample of the crowd round about. When this fact was pointed out to him, he yielded at once, though with a heavy heart, his eyes looking longingly towards the ring as we retreated out of the booth. We were scarcely clear of the place, when we heard "God save the Queen," played by the equestrian band, the signal that all was over. Our companion entertained us with scraps of the dialogue on our way home — precious crumbs of wit which he had brought away from that feast. He laughed over them again as we walked under the stars. He has them now, and takes them out of the pocket of his memory, and crunches a bit, and relishes it with a sentimental tenderness, too, for he is, no doubt, back at school by this time; the holidays are over; and Doctor Birch's young friends have re-assembled.

Queer jokes, which caused a thousand simple mouths to grin! As the jaded Merryman uttered them to the old gentleman with the whip, some of the old folks in the audience, I dare say, indulged in reflections of their own. There was one joke — I utterly forget it — but it began with Merryman saying what he had for dinner. He had mutton for dinner, at one o'clock, after which "he had to *come to business.*" And then came the point. Walter Juvenis, Esq., Rev. Doctor Birch's, Market Rodborough, if you read this, will you please send me a line, and let me know what was the joke Mr. Merryman made about having his dinner? *You* remember well enough. But do I want to know? Suppose a boy takes a favorite, long-cherished lump of cake out of his pocket, and offers you a bite? *Merci!* The fact is, I *don't* care much about knowing that joke of Mr. Merryman's.

But whilst he was talking about his dinner, and his mutton, and his landlord, and his business, I felt a great interest about Mr. M., in private life — about his wife, lodgings, earnings, and general history, and I dare say was forming a picture of those in my mind: — wife cooking the mutton; children waiting for it; Merryman in his plain clothes, and so forth; during which contemplation the joke was uttered and laughed at, and Mr. M., resuming his professional duties, was tumbling over head and heels. Do not suppose I am going *sicut est mos*, to indulge in moralities about buffoons, paint, motley, and mountebanking. Nay, Prime Ministers rehearse their jokes; Opposition leaders prepare and polish them; Tabernacle preachers must arrange them in their minds before they utter them. All I mean is, that I would like to know any one of these performers thoroughly, and out of his uniform; that preacher, and why in his travels this and that point struck him; wherein lies his power of pathos, humor, eloquence; — that Minister of State, and what moves him, and how his private heart is working; — I would only say that, at a certain time of life, certain things cease to interest: but about *some* things when we cease to care, what will be the use of life, sight, hearing? Poems are written, and we cease to admire. Lady Jones invites us, and we yawn; she ceases to invite us, and we are resigned. The last time I saw a ballet at the opera — oh! it is many years ago — I fell asleep in the stalls, wagging my head in insane dreams, and I hope affording amusement to the company, while the feet of five hundred nymphs were cutting flicflacs on the stage at a few paces' distance. Ah, I remember a different state of things! *Credite posteri.* To see those nymphs — gracious powers, how beautiful they were! That leering, painted, shrivelled, thin-armed, thick-ankled old thing, cutting dreary capers, coming thumping down on her board out of time — *that* an opera-dancer? Pooh! My dear Walter, the great difference between *my* time and yours, who will enter life some two or three years hence, is that, now, the dancing women and singing women are ludicrously old, out of time, and out of tune; the paint is so visible, and the dinge and wrinkles of their wretched old cotton stockings, that I am surprised how anybody can like to look at them. And as for laughing at *me* for falling asleep, I can't understand a man of sense doing otherwise. In *my* time, *à la bonne heure*. In the reign of George IV., I give you my honor, all the dancers at the opera were as beautiful as Houris. Even in William IV.'s time, when I think of Duvernay prancing in as the Bayadère, — I say it was a vision of loveliness such as mortal eyes can't see now-a-days. How well I remember the tune to which she used to appear! Kaled used to say to the Sultan, "My lord, a troop of those dancing and singing gurls called Bayadères approaches," and, to the clash of cymbals, and the thumping of my heart, in she used to dance! There has never been any thing like it — never. There never will be — I laugh to scorn old people who tell me about your Noblet, your Montessu, your Vestris, your Parisot — pshaw, the senile twaddlers! And the impudence of the young men, with their music and their dancers of to-day: I tell you the women are dreary old creatures. I tell you one air in an opera is just like another, and they send all rational creatures to sleep. Ah, Ronzi de Begnis, thou lovely one! Ah, Caradori, thou smiling angel! Ah, Malibran! Nay, I will come to modern times, and acknowledge that Lablache was a very good singer thirty years ago (though Porto was the boy for me): and then we had Ambrogetti, and Curioni, and Donzelli, a rising young singer.

But what is most certain and lamentable is the decay of stage beauty since the days of George IV. Think of Sontag! I remember her in *Otello* and the *Donna del Lago* in '28. I remember being behind the scenes at the opera (where numbers of us young fellows of fashion used to go), and seeing Sontag let her hair fall down over her shoulders previous to her murder by Donzelli. Young fellows have never seen beauty like *that*, heard such a voice, seen such hair, such eyes. Don't tell *me!* A man who has been about town since the reign of George IV., ought he not to know better than you young lads who have seen nothing? The deterioration of women is lamentable; and the conceit of the young fellows more lamentable still, that they won't see this fact, but persist in thinking their time as good as ours.

Bless me! when I was a lad, the stage was covered with angels, who sang, acted, and danced. When I remember the Adelphi, and the actresses there: when I think of Miss Chester, and Miss Love, and Mrs. Serle at Sadler's Wells, and her forty glorious pupils — of the Opera and Noblet, and the exquisite young Taglioni, and Pauline Leroux, and a host more! One much-admired being of those days I confess I never cared for, and that was the chief *male* dancer — a very important personage then, with a bare neck, bare arms, a tunic, and a hat and feathers, who used to divide the applause with the ladies, and who has now sunk down a trap-door for ever. And this frank admission ought to show that I am not your mere twaddling *laudator temporis acti* — your old fogy who can see no good except in his own time.

They say that claret is better now-a-days, and cookery much improved since the days of *my* monarch — of George IV. *Pastry Cookery* is certainly not so good. I have often eaten half a crown's worth (including, I trust, ginger beer) at our school pastrycook's, and that is a proof that the pastry must have been very good, for could I do as much now? I passed by the pastrycook's shop lately, having occasion to visit my old school. It looked a very dingy old baker's; misfortunes may have come over him — those penny tarts certainly did *not* look so nice as I remember them: but he may have grown careless as he has grown old (I should judge him to be now about ninety-six years of age), and his hand may have lost its cunning.

Not that we were not great epicures. I remember how we constantly grumbled at the quantity of the food in our master's house — which on my conscience I believe was excellent and plentiful — and how we tried once or twice to eat him out of house and home. At the pastrycook's we may have over-eaten ourselves (I have admitted half a crown's worth for my own part, but I don't like to mention the *real* figure for fear of perverting the present generation of boys by my monstrous confession) — we may have eaten too much, I say. We did; but what then? The school apothecary was sent for: a couple of small globules, at night, a trifling preparation of senna in the morning, and we had not to go to school, so that the draught was an actual pleasure.

For our amusements, besides the games in vogue, which were pretty much in old times as they are now (except cricket, *par exemple* — and I wish the present youth joy of their bowling, and suppose Armstrong and Whitworth will bowl at them with light field-pieces next), there were novels — ah! I trouble you to find such novels in the present day! O "Scottish Chiefs," didn't we weep over you! O "Mysteries of Udolpho," didn't I and Briggs Minor draw pictures out of you, as I have said? Efforts, feeble indeed, but still giving pleasure to us and our friends. "I say, old boy, draw us Vivaldi tortured in the Inquisition," or "Draw us Don Quixote and the windmills, you know," amateurs would say, to boys who had a love of drawing. "Peregrine Pickle" we liked, our fathers admiring it, and telling us (the sly old boys) it was capital fun; but I think I was rather bewildered by it, though "Roderick Random" was and remains delightful. I don't remember having Sterne in the school library, no doubt because the works of that divine were not considered decent for young people. Ah! not against thy genius, O father of Uncle Toby and Trim, would I say a word in disrespect. But I am thankful to live in times when men no longer have the temptation to write so as to call blushes on women's cheeks, and would shame to whisper wicked allusions to honest boys. Then, above all, we had Walter Scott, the kindly, the generous, the pure — the companion of what countless delightful hours; the purveyor of how much happiness; the friend whom we recall as the constant benefactor of our youth! How well I remember the type and the brownish paper of the old duodecimo "Tales of My Landlord"! I have never dared to read "The Pirate," and "The Bride of Lammermoor," or "Kenilworth," from that day to this, because the finale is unhappy, and people die, and are murdered at the end. But "Ivanhoe," and "Quentin Durward!" Oh! for a half-holiday, and a quiet corner, and one of those books again! Those books, and perhaps those eyes with which we read them; and, it may be, the brains behind the eyes! It may be the tart was good; but how fresh the appetite was! If the gods would give me the desire of my heart, I should be able to write a story which boys would relish for the next few dozen of centuries. The boy critic loves the story: grown-up, he loves the author who wrote the story. Hence the kindly tie is established between writer and reader, and lasts pretty nearly for life. I meet people now who don't care for Walter Scott, or "The Arabian Nights;" I am sorry for them, unless they in their time have found *their* romancer — their charming Scheherazade. By the way, Walter, when you are writing, tell me who is the favorite novelist in the fourth form now? Have you got any thing so good and kindly as dear Miss Edgeworth's *Frank?* It used to belong to a fellow's sisters generally; but though he pretended to despise it, and said, "Oh, stuff for girls!" he read it; and I think there were one or two passages which would try my eyes now, were I to meet with the little book.

As for Thomas and Jeremiah (it is only my witty way of calling Tom and Jerry), I went to the British Museum the other day on purpose to get it; but somehow, if you will press the question so closely, on re-perusal, Tom and Jerry is not so brilliant as I had supposed it to be. The pictures are just as fine as ever; and I shook hands with broad-backed Jerry Hawthorn and Corinthian Tom with delight, after many years' absence. But the style of the writing, I own, was not pleasing to me; I even thought it a little vulgar — well! well! other writers have been considered vulgar — and as a description of the sports and amusements of London in the ancient times, more curious than amusing.

But the pictures! — oh! the pictures are noble still! First, there is Jerry arriving from the country, in a green coat and leather gaiters, and being measured for a fashionable suit at Corinthian House, by Corinthian Tom's tailor. Then away for the career of pleasure and fashion. The park! delicious excitement! The theatre! the saloon!! the green-room!!! Rapturous bliss — the opera itself! and then perhaps to Temple Bar, to *knock down a Charley* there! There are Jerry and Tom, with their tights and little cocked hats, coming from the opera — very much as gentlemen in waiting on royalty are habited now. There they are at Almack's itself, amidst a crowd of high-bred personages, with the Duke of Clarence himself looking at them dancing. Now, strange change, they are in Tom Cribb's parlor, where they don't seem to be a whit less at home than in fashion's gilded halls: and now they are at Newgate, seeing the irons knocked off the malefactors' legs previous to execution. What hardened ferocity in the countenance of the desperado in yellow breeches! What compunction in the face of the gentleman in black (who, I suppose, has been forging), and who clasps his hands, and listens to the chaplain! Now we haste away to merrier scenes: to Tattersall's (ah, gracious powers! what a funny fellow that actor was who performed Dicky Green in that scene at the play!); and now we are at a private party, at which Corinthian Tom is waltzing (and very gracefully, too, as you must confess) with Corinthian Kate, whilst Bob Logic, the Oxonian, is playing on the piano!

"After," the text says, "*the Oxonian* had played several pieces of lively music, he requested as a favor that Kate and his friend Tom would perform a waltz. Kate without any hesitation immediately stood up. Tom offered his hand to his fascinating partner, and the dance took place. The plate conveys a correct representation of the 'gay scene' at that precise moment. The anxiety of *the Oxonian* to witness the attitudes of the elegant pair had nearly put a stop to their movements. On turning round from the pianoforte and presenting his comical *mug*, Kate could scarcely suppress a laugh."

And no wonder; just look at it now, and compare Master Logic's countenance and attitude with the splendid elegance of Tom! Now every London man is weary and *blasé*. There is an enjoyment of life in these young bucks of 1823 which contrasts strangely with our feelings of 1860. Here, for instance, is a specimen of their talk and walk. "'If,' says LOGIC — 'if *enjoyment* is your *motto*, you may make the most of an evening at Vauxhall, more than at any other place in the metropolis. It is all free and easy. Stay as long as you like, and depart when you think proper.' — 'Your description is so flattering,' replied JERRY, 'that I do not care how soon the time arrives for us to start.' LOGIC proposed a '*bit of a stroll*' in order to get rid of an hour or two, which was immediately accepted by Tom and Jerry. A *turn* or two in Bond Street, a *stroll* through Piccadilly, a *look in* at TATTERSALL'S, a *ramble* through Pall Mall, and a *strut* on the Corinthian path, fully occupied the time of our heroes until the hour for dinner arrived, when a few glasses of TOM'S rich wines soon put them on the *qui vive*. VAUXHALL was then the object in view, and the TRIO started, bent upon enjoying the pleasures which this place so amply affords."

How nobly those inverted commas, those Italics, those capitals, bring out the writer's wit and relieve the eye! They are as good as jokes, though you mayn't quite perceive the point. Mark the varieties of lounge in which the young men indulge — now *a stroll*, then *a look in*, then *a ramble*, and presently *a strut*. When George, Prince of Wales, was twenty, I have read in an old Magazine, "The Prince's Lounge" was a peculiar manner of walking which the young bucks imitated. At Windsor George III. had *a cat's path* — a sly early walk which the good old king took in the gray morning before his household was astir. What was the Corinthian path here recorded? Does any antiquary know? And what were the rich wines which our friends took, and which enabled them to enjoy Vauxhall? Vauxhall is gone, but the wines which could occasion such a delightful perversion of the intellect as to enable it to enjoy ample pleasures there, what were they?

So the game of life proceeds, until Jerry Hawthorn, the rustic, is fairly knocked up by all this excitement and is forced to go home, and the last picture represents him getting into the coach at the "White Horse Cellar," he being one of six inside; whilst his friends shake him by the hand; whilst the sailor mounts on the roof; whilst the Jews hang round with oranges, knives, and sealing-wax; whilst the guard is closing the door. Where are they now, those sealing-wax venders? where are the guards? where are the jolly teams? where are the coaches? and where the youth that climbed inside and out of them; that heard the merry horn which sounds no more; that saw the sun rise over Stonehenge; that rubbed away the bitter tears at night after parting as the coach sped on the journey to school and London; that looked out with beating heart as the milestones flew by, for the welcome corner where began home and holidays?

It is night now: and here is home. Gathered under the quiet roof, elders and children lie alike at rest. In the midst of a great peace and calm, the stars look out from the heavens. The silence is peopled with the past; sorrowful remorses for sins and shortcomings — memories of passionate joys and griefs rise out of their graves, both now alike calm and sad. Eyes, as I shut mine, look at me, that have long ceased to shine. The town and the fair landscape sleep under the starlight, wreathed in the autumn mists. Twinkling among the houses, a light keeps watch, here and there, in what may be a sick chamber or two. The clock tolls sweetly in the silent air. Here is night and rest. An awful sense of thanks makes the heart swell, and the head bow, as I pass to my room through the sleeping house, and feel as though a hushed blessing were upon it.

ON A JOKE I ONCE HEARD FROM THE LATE THOMAS HOOD.

THE good-natured reader who has perused some of these rambling papers has long since seen (if to see has been worth his trouble) that the writer belongs to the old-fashioned classes of this world, loves to remember very much more than to prophesy, and though he can't help being carried onward and downward, perhaps, on the hill of life, the swift milestones marking their forties, fifties — how many tens or lustres shall we say? — he sits under Time, the white-wigged charioteer, with his back to the horses, and his face to the past, looking at the receding landscape and the hills fading into the gray distance. Ah me! those gray, distant hills were green once, and *here*, and covered with smiling people! As we came *up* the hill there was difficulty, and here and there a hard pull to be sure, but strength and spirits, and all sorts of cheery incident and companionship on the road; there were the tough struggles (by heaven's merciful will) overcome, the pauses, the faintings, the weakness, the lost way, perhaps, the bitter weather, the dreadful partings, the lonely night, the passionate grief—towards these I turn my thoughts as I sit and think in my hobby-coach under Time, the silver-wigged charioteer. The young folks in the same carriage meanwhile are looking forwards. Nothing escapes their keen eyes — not a flower at the side of a cottage garden, nor a bunch of rosy-faced children at the gate: the landscape is all bright, the air brisk and jolly, the town yonder looks beautiful, and do you think they have learned to be difficult about the dishes at the inn?

Now, suppose Paterfamilias on his journey with his wife and children in the sociable, and he passes an ordinary brick house on the road with an ordinary little garden in the front, we will say, and quite an ordinary knocker to the door, and as many sashed windows as you please, quite common and square, and tiles, windows, chimney-pots, quite like others; or suppose, in driving over such and such a common, he sees an ordinary tree, and an ordinary donkey browsing under it, if you like — wife and daughter look at these objects without the slightest particle of curiosity or interest. What is a brass knocker to them but a lion's head, or what not? and a thorn-tree with a pool beside it, but a pool in which a thorn and a jackass are reflected?

But you remember how once upon a time your heart used to beat, as you beat on that brass knocker, and whose eyes looked from the window above. You remember how by that thorn-tree and pool, where the geese were performing a prodigious evening concert, there might be seen, at a certain hour, somebody in a certain cloak and bonnet, who happened to be coming from a village yonder, and whose image has flickered in that pool. In that pool, near the thorn? Yes, in that goose-pool, never mind how long ago, when there were reflected the images of the geese — and two geese more. Here, at least, an oldster may have the advantage of his young fellow-travellers, and so Putney Heath or the New Road may be invested with a halo of brightness invisible to them, because it only beams out of his own soul.

I have been reading "The Memorials of Hood" by his children,* and wonder whether the book will have the same interest for others and for younger people, as for persons of my own age and calling. Books of travel to any country become interesting to us who have been there. Men

* *Memorials of Thomas Hood.* Moxon, 1860. 2 vols.

Sir J-sh- R-yn-lds in a Domino, Dr. G-ldsm-th in an Old English Dress.

revisit the old school, though hateful to them, with ever so much kindliness and sentimental affection. There was the tree under which the bully licked you: here the ground where you had to fag out on holidays, and so forth. In a word, my dear sir, *You* are the most interesting subject to yourself, of any that can occupy your worship's thoughts. I have no doubt a Crimean soldier, reading a history of that siege, and how Jones and the gallant 99th were ordered to charge or what not, thinks, "Ah, yes, we of the 100th were placed so and so, I perfectly remember." So with this memorial of poor Hood, it may have, no doubt, a greater interest for me than for others, for I was fighting, so to speak, in a different part of the field, and engaged, a young subaltern, in the Battle of Life, in which Hood fell, young still, and covered with glory. "The Bridge of Sighs" was his Corunna, his Heights of Abraham — sickly, weak, wounded, he fell in the full blaze and fame of that great victory.

What manner of man was the genius who penned that famous song? What like was Wolfe, who climbed and conquered on those famous Heights of Abraham? We all want to know details regarding men who have achieved famous feats, whether of war, or wit, or eloquence, or endurance, or knowledge. His one or two happy and heroic actions take a man's name and memory out of the crowd of names and memories. Henceforth he stands eminent. We scan him: we want to know all about him; we walk round and examine him, are curious, perhaps, and think are we not as strong and tall and capable as yonder champion; were we not bred as well, and could we not endure the winter's cold as well as he? Or we look up with all our eyes of admiration; will find no fault in our hero: declare his beauty and proportions perfect; his critics envious detractors, and so forth. Yesterday, before he performed his feat, he was nobody. Who cared about his birthplace, his parentage, or the color of his hair? To-day, by some single achievement, or by a series of great actions to which his genius accustoms us, he is famous, and antiquarians are busy finding out under what schoolmaster's ferule he was educated, where his grandmother was vaccinated, and so forth. If half a dozen washing-bills of Goldsmith's were to be found to-morrow, would they not inspire a general interest, and be printed in a hundred papers? I lighted upon Oliver, not very long since, in an old Town and Country Magazine, at the Pantheon masquerade "in an old English habit." Straightway my imagination ran out to meet him, to look at him, to follow him about. I forgot the names of scores of fine gentlemen of the past age, who were mentioned besides. We want to see this man who has amused and charmed us; who has been our friend, and given us hours of pleasant companionship and kindly thought. I protest when I came, in the midst of those names of people of fashion, and beaux, and demireps, upon those names "*Sir J. R-yn-lds, in a domino; Mr. Cr-d-ck and Dr. G-ldsm-th, in two old English dresses,*" I had, so to speak, my heart in my mouth. What, *you* here, my dear Sir Joshua? Ah, what an honor and privilege it is to see you! This is Mr. Goldsmith? And very much, sir, the ruff and the slashed doublet become you! O Doctor! what a pleasure I had and have in reading the *Animated Nature*. How *did* you learn the secret of writing the decasyllable line, and whence that sweet wailing note of tenderness that accompanies your song? Was Beau Tibbs a real man, and will you do me the honor of allowing me to sit at your table at supper? Don't you think you know how he would have talked? Would you not have liked to hear him prattle over the champagne?

Now, Hood is passed away — passed off the earth as much as Goldsmith or Horace. The times in which he lived, and in which very many of us lived and were young, are changing or changed. I saw Hood once as a young man at a dinner which seems almost as ghostly now as that masquerade at the Pantheon (1772), of which we were speaking anon. It was at a dinner of the Literary Fund, in that vast apartment which is hung round with the portraits of very large Royal Freemasons, now unsubstantial ghosts. There at the end of the room was Hood. Some publishers, I think, were our companions. I quite remember his pale face; he was thin and deaf, and very silent; he scarcely opened his lips during the dinner, and he made one pun. Some gentleman missed his snuff-box, and Hood said, — (the Freemasons' Tavern was kept, you must remember, by Mr. CUFF in those days, not by its present proprietors). Well, the box being lost, and asked for, and CUFF (remember that name) being the name of the landlord, Hood opened his silent jaws and said . . . Shall I tell you what he said? It was not a very good pun which the great punster then made. Choose your favorite pun out of "Whims and Oddities," and fancy that was the joke which he contributed to the hilarity of our little table.

Where those points are drawn on the page, you must know, a pause occurred, during which I was engaged with "Hood's Own," having been referred to the book by this life of the author which I have just been reading. I am not going to dissert on Hood's humor; I am not a fair judge. Have I not said elsewhere that there are one or two wonderfully old gentlemen still alive who used to give me tips when I was a boy? I can't be a fair critic about them. I always think of that sovereign, that rapture of raspberry-tarts, which made my young days happy. Those old sovereign-contributors may tell stories ever so old, and I shall laugh; they may commit murder, and I shall believe it was justifiable homicide. There is my friend Baggs, who goes about abusing me, and of course our dear mutual friends tell me. Abuse away, *mon bon!* You were so kind to me when I wanted kindness, that you may take the change out of that gold now, and say I am a cannibal and negro if you will. Ha, Baggs! Dost thou wince as thou readest this line? Does guilty conscience throbbing at thy breast tell thee of whom the fable is narrated? Puff out thy wrath, and, when it has ceased to blow, my Baggs shall be to me as the Baggs of old — the generous, the gentle, the friendly.

No, on second thoughts, I am determined I will not repeat that joke which I heard Hood make. He says he wrote these jokes with such ease that he sent manuscripts to the publishers faster than they could acknowledge the receipt thereof. I won't say that they were all good jokes, or that to read a great book full of them is a work at present altogether jocular. Writing to a friend respecting some memoir of him which had been published, Hood says, "You will judge how well the author knows me, when he says my mind is rather serious than comic." At the time when he wrote these words, he evidently undervalued his own serious power, and thought that in punning and broad grinning lay his chief strength. Is not there something touching in that simplicity and humility of faith? "To make laugh is my calling," says he; "I must jump, I must grin, I must tumble, I must turn language head over heels, and leap through grammar;" and he goes to his work humbly and courageously, and what he has to do that does he with all his might, through sickness, through sorrow, through exile, poverty, fever, depression — there he is, always ready to his work, and with a jewel of genius in his pocket! Why, when he laid down his puns and pranks, put the motley off and spoke out of his heart, all England and America listened with tears and wonder! Other men have delusions of conceit, and fancy themselves greater than they are, and that the world slights them. Have we not heard how Liston always thought he ought to play Hamlet? Here is a man with a power to touch the heart almost unequalled, and he passes days and years in writing, "Young Ben he was a nice young man!" and so forth. To say truth, I have been reading in a book of "Hood's Own" until I am perfectly angry. "You great man, you good man, you true genius and poet," I cry out, as I turn page after page. "Do, do, make no more of these jokes, but be yourself and take your station."

When Hood was on his deathbed, Sir Robert Peel, who only knew of his illness, not of his imminent danger, wrote to him a noble and touching letter, announcing that a pension was conferred on him: —

> "I am more than repaid," writes Peel, "by the personal satisfaction which I have had in doing that for which you return me warm and characteristic acknowledgments.
>
> "You perhaps think that you are known to one with such multifarious occupations as myself, merely by general reputation as an author; but I assure you that there can be little, which you have written and acknowledged, which I have not read; and that there are few who can appreciate and admire more than myself the good sense and good feeling which have taught you to infuse so much fun and merriment into writings correcting folly and exposing absurdities, and yet never trespassing beyond those limits within which wit and facetiousness are not very often confined. You may write on with the consciousness of independence, as free and unfettered as if no communication had ever passed between us. I am not conferring a private obligation upon, but am fulfilling the intentions of the legislature, which has placed at the disposal of the Crown a certain sum (miserable, indeed, in amount) to be applied to the recognition of public claims on the bounty of the Crown. If you will review the names of those whose claims have been admitted on account of their literary or scientific eminence, you will find an ample confirmation of the truth of my statement.
>
> "One return, indeed, I shall ask of you, — that you will give me the opportunity of making your personal acquaintance."

And Hood, writing to a friend, enclosing a copy of Peel's letter, says, "Sir R. Peel came from Burleigh on Tuesday night, and went down to Brighton on Saturday. If he had written by post, I should not have had it till to-day. So he sent his servant with the enclosed on *Saturday night;* another mark of considerate attention." He is frightfully unwell, he continues: his wife says he looks *quite green;* but ill as he is, poor fellow, "his well is not dry. He has pumped out a sheet of Christmas fun, is drawing some cuts, and shall write a sheet more of his novel."

Oh, sad, marvellous picture of courage, of honesty, of patient endurance, of duty struggling against pain! How noble Peel's figure is standing by that sick-bed! how generous his words, how dignified and sincere his compassion! And the poor dying man, with a heart full of natural gratitude towards his noble benefactor, must turn to him and say — "If it be well to be remembered by a Minister, it is better still not to be forgotten by him in a 'hurly Burleigh!'" Can you laugh? Is not the joke horribly pathetic from the poor dying lips? As dying Robin Hood must fire a last shot with his bow — as one reads of Catholics on their death-beds putting on a Capuchin dress to go out of the world — here is poor Hood at his last hour putting on his ghastly motley, and uttering one joke more.

He dies, however, in dearest love and peace with his children, wife, friends; to the former especially his whole life had been devoted, and every day showed his fidelity, simplicity, and affection. In going through the record of his most pure, modest, honorable life, and living along with him, you come to trust him thoroughly, and feel that here is a most loyal, affectionate, and upright soul, with whom you have been brought into communion. Can we say as much of the lives of all men of letters? Here is one at least without guile, without pretension, without scheming, of a pure life, to his family and little modest circle of friends tenderly devoted.

And what a hard work, and what a slender reward! In the little domestic details with which the book abounds, what a simple life is shown to us! The most simple little pleasures and amusements delight and occupy him. You have revels on shrimps; the good wife making the pie; details about the maid, and criticisms on her conduct; wonderful tricks played with the plum-pudding — all the pleasures centring round the little humble home. One of the first men of his time, he is appointed editor of a Magazine at a salary of 300*l.* per annum, signs himself exultingly "Ed. N. M. M.," and the family rejoice over the income as over a fortune. He goes to a Greenwich dinner — what a feast and a rejoicing afterwards! —

"Well, we drank 'the Boz' with a delectable clatter, which drew from him a good warm-hearted speech. . . . He looked very well, and had a younger brother along with him. . . . Then we had songs. Barham chanted a Robin Hood ballad, and Cruikshank sang a burlesque ballad of Lord H——; and somebody, unknown to me, gave a capital imitation of a French showman. Then we toasted Mrs. Boz, and the Chairman, and Vice, and the Traditional Priest sang the 'Deep, deep sea,' in his deep, deep voice; and then we drank to Proctor, who wrote the said song; also Sir J. Wilson's good health, and Cruikshank's, and Ainsworth's: and a Manchester friend of the latter sang a Manchester ditty, so full of trading stuff, that it really seemed to have been not composed, but manufactured. Jerdan, as Jerdanish as usual on such occasions — you know how paradoxically he is *quite at home* in *dining out.* As to myself, I had to make my *second maiden speech*, for Mr. Monckton Milnes proposed my health in terms my modesty might allow me to repeat to *you*, but my memory won't. However, I ascribed the toast to my notoriously bad health, and assured them that their wishes had already improved it — that I felt a brisker circulation — a more genial warmth about the heart, and explained that a certain trembling of my hand was not from palsy, or my old ague, but an inclination in my hand to shake itself with every one present. Whereupon I had to go through the friendly ceremony with as many of the company as were within reach, besides a few more who came express from the other end of the table. *Very* gratifying, wasn't it? Though I cannot go quite so far as Jane, who wants me to have that hand chopped off, bottled, and preserved in spirits. She was sitting up for me, very anxiously, as usual when I go out, because I am so domestic and steady, and was down at the door before I could ring at the gate, to which Boz kindly sent me in his own carriage. Poor girl! what *would* she do if she had a wild husband instead of a tame one?"

And the poor anxious wife is sitting up, and fondles the hand which has been shaken by so many illustrious men! The little feast dates back only eighteen years, and yet somehow it seems as distant as a dinner at Mr. Thrale's, or a meeting at Will's.

Poor little gleam of sunshine! very little good cheer enlivens that sad simple life. We have the triumph of the Magazine: then a new Magazine projected and produced: then illness and the last scene, and the kind Peel by the dying man's bedside speaking noble words of respect and sympathy, and soothing the last throbs of the tender honest heart.

I like, I say, Hood's life even better than his books, and I wish with all my heart, *Monsieur et cher confrère*, the same could be said for both of us, when the inkstream of our life hath ceased to run. Yes: if I drop first, dear Baggs, I trust you may find reason to modify some of the unfavorable views of my character, which you are so freely imparting to our mutual friends. What ought to be the literary man's point of honor now-a-days? Suppose, friendly reader, you are one of the craft, what legacy would you like to leave to your children? First of all (and by heaven's gracious help) you would pray and strive to give them such an endowment of love as should last certainly for all their lives, and perhaps be transmitted to their children. You would (by the same aid and blessing) keep your honor pure, and transmit a name unstained to those who have a right to bear it. You would — though this faculty of giving is one of the easiest of the literary man's qualities — you would out of your earnings, small or great, be able to help a poor brother in need, to dress his wounds, and, if it were but twopence, to give him succor. Is the money which the noble Macaulay gave to the poor lost to his family? God forbid. To the loving hearts of his kindred is it not rather the most precious part of their inheritance? It was invested in love and righteous doing, and it bears interest in heaven. You will, if letters be your vocation, find saving harder than giving and spending. To save be your endeavor, too, against the night's coming, when no man may work; when the arm is weary with the long day's labor; when the brain perhaps grows dark; when the old, who can labor no more, want warmth and rest, and the young ones call for supper.

I copied the little galley-slave who is made to figure in the initial letter of this paper, from a quaint old silver spoon which we purchased in a curiosity-shop at the Hague. It is one of the gift spoons so common in Holland, and which have multiplied so astonishingly of late years at our dealers in old silverware. Along the stem of the spoon are written the words: "Anno 1609, *Bin ick aldus ghekledt gheghaen*" — "In the year 1609 I went thus clad." The good Dutchman was released from his Algerine captivity (I imagine his figure looks like that of a slave amongst the Moors), and in his thank-offering to some godchild at home, he thus piously records his escape.

Was not poor Cervantes also a captive amongst the Moors? Did not Fielding, and Goldsmith, and Smollett, too, die at the chain as well as poor Hood? Think of Fielding going on board his wretched ship in the Thames, with scarce a hand to bid him farewell; of brave Tobias Smollett, and his life, how hard, and how poorly rewarded; of Goldsmith, and the physician whispering, "Have you something on your mind?" and the wild dying eyes answering, "Yes." Notice how Boswell speaks of Goldsmith, and the splendid contempt with which he regards him. Read Hawkins on Fielding, and the scorn with which Dandy Walpole and Bishop Hurd speak of him. Galley-slaves doomed to tug the oar and wear the chain, whilst my lords and dandies take their pleasure, and hear fine music, and disport with fine ladies in the cabin!

But stay. Was there any cause for this scorn? Had some of these great men weaknesses which gave inferiors advantage over them? Men of letters cannot lay their hands on their hearts, and say, "No, the fault was fortune's, and the indifferent world's, not Goldsmith's nor Fielding's." There was no reason why Oliver should always be thriftless; why Fielding and Steele should sponge upon their friends; why Sterne should make love to his neighbors' wives. Swift, for a long time, was as poor as any wag that ever laughed: but he owed no penny to his neighbors: Addison, when he wore his most threadbare coat, could hold his head up, and maintain his dignity: and, I dare vouch, neither of those gentlemen, when they were ever so poor, asked any man alive to pity their condition, and have a regard to the weaknesses incidental to the literary profession. Galley-slave, forsooth! If you are sent to prison for some error for which the law awards that sort of laborious seclusion, so much the more shame for you. If you are chained to the oar a prisoner of war, like Cervantes, you have the pain, but not the shame, and the friendly compassion of mankind to reward you. Galley-slaves, indeed! What man has not his oar to pull? There is that wonderful old stroke-oar in the Queen's galley. How many years has he pulled? Day and night, in rough water or smooth, with what invincible vigor and surprising gayety, he plies his arms. There is in the same *Galère Capitaine*, that well-known, trim figure, the bow-oar; how he tugs, and with what a will! How both of them have been abused in their time! Take the Lawyer's galley, and that dauntless octogenarian in command; when has *he* ever complained or repined about his slavery? There is the Priest's galley — black and lawn sails — do any mariners out of Thames work harder? When lawyer, and statesman, and divine, and writer are snug in bed, there is a ring at the poor Doctor's bell. Forth he must go, in rheumatism or snow; a galley-slave bearing his galley-pots to quench the flames of fever, to succor mothers and young children in their hour of peril, and, as gently and soothingly as may be, to carry the hopeless patient over to the silent shore. And have we not just read of the actions of the Queen's galleys and their brave crews in the Chinese waters? — men not more worthy of human renown and honor to-day in their victory, than last year in their glorious hour of disaster. So with stout hearts may we ply the oar, messmates all, till the voyage is over, and the Harbor of Rest is found!

ROUND ABOUT THE CHRISTMAS TREE.

THE kindly Christmas tree, from which I trust every gentle reader has pulled a bonbon or two, is yet all aflame whilst I am writing, and sparkles with the sweet fruits of its season. You young ladies, may you have plucked pretty giftlings from it; and out of the cracker sugar-plum which you have split with the captain or the sweet young curate may you have read one of those delicious conundrums which the confectioners introduce into the sweetmeats, and which apply to the cunning passion of love. Those riddles are to be read at *your* age, when I dare say they are amusing. As for Dolly, Merry, and Bell, who are standing at the tree, they don't care about the love-riddle part, but understand the sweet-almond portion very well. They are four, five, six years old. Patience, little people! A dozen merry Christmases more, and you will be reading those wonderful love-conundrums, too. As for us elderly folks, we watch the babies at their sport, and the young people pulling at the branches: and instead of finding bonbons or sweeties in the packets which *we* pluck off the boughs, we find enclosed Mr. Carnifex's review of the quarter's meat; Mr. Sartor's compliments, and little statement for self and the young gentlemen; and Madame de Sainte-Crinoline's respects to the young ladies, who encloses her account, and will send on Saturday, please; or we stretch our hand out to the educational branch of the Christmas tree, and there find a lively and amusing article from the Rev. Henry Holyshade, containing our dear Tommy's exceedingly moderate account for the last term's school expenses.

The tree yet sparkles, I say. I am writing on the day before Twelfth Day, if you must know; but already ever so many of the fruits have been pulled, and the Christmas lights have gone out. Bobby Miseltow, who has been staying with us for a week (and who has been sleeping mysteriously in the bath-room), comes to say he is going away to spend the rest of the holidays with his grandmother — and I brush away the manly tear of regret as I part with the dear child. "Well, Bob, good-by, since you *will* go. Compliments to grandmamma. Thank her for the turkey. Here's" —— (*A slight pecuniary transaction takes place at this juncture, and Bob nods and winks, and puts his hand in his waistcoat pocket.*) "You have had a pleasant week?"

BOB. — "Haven't I!" (*And exit, anxious to know the amount of the coin which has just changed hands.*)

He is gone, and as the dear boy vanishes through the door (behind which I see him perfectly), I too cast up a little account of our past Christmas week. When Bob's holidays are over, and the printer has sent me back this manuscript, I know Christmas will be an old story. All the fruit will be off the Christmas tree then; the crackers will have cracked off; the almonds will have been crunched; and the sweet-bitter riddles will have been read; the lights will have perished off the dark green boughs; the toys growing on them will have been distributed, fought for, cherished, neglected, broken. Ferdinand and Fidelia will each keep out of it (be still, my gushing heart!) the remembrance of a riddle read together, of a double-almond munched together, and the moiety of an exploded cracker. . . . The maids, I say, will have taken down all that holly stuff and nonsense about the clocks, lamps, and looking-glasses, the dear boys will be back at school, fondly thinking of the pantomime-fairies whom they have seen; whose gaudy gossamer wings are battered by this time; and whose pink cotton (or silk is it?) lower extremities are all dingy and dusty. Yet but a few days, Bob, and flakes of paint will have cracked off the fairy flower-bowers, and the revolving temples of adamantine lustre will be as shabby as the city of Pekin. When you read this, will Clown still be going on lolling his tongue out of his mouth, and saying, "How are you to-morrow?" To-morrow, indeed! He must be almost ashamed of himself (if that cheek is still capable of the blush of shame) for asking the absurd question. To-morrow, indeed! To-morrow the diffugient snows will give place to Spring; the snowdrops will lift their heads; Ladyday may be expected, and the pecuniary duties peculiar to that feast; in place of bonbons, trees will have an eruption of light green knobs; the whitebait season will bloom . . . as if one need go on describing these vernal phenomena, when Christmas is still here, though ending, and the subject of my discourse!

We have all admired the illustrated papers, and noted how boisterously jolly they become at Christmas time. What wassail-bowls, robin-redbreasts, waits, snow landscapes, bursts of Christmas song! And then to think that these festivities are prepared months before — that these Christmas pieces are prophetic! How kind of artists and poets to devise the festivities beforehand, and serve them pat at the proper time! We ought to be grateful to them, as to the cook who gets up at midnight and sets the pudding a-boiling, which is to feast us at six o'clock. I often think with gratitude of the famous Mr. Nelson Lee — the author of I don't know how many hundred glorious pantomimes — walking by the summer wave at Margate, or Brighton perhaps, revolving in his mind the idea of some new gorgeous spectacle of faëry, which the winter shall see complete. He is like cook at midnight (*si parva licet*). He watches and thinks. He pounds the sparkling sugar of benevolence, the plums of fancy, the sweetmeats of fun, the figs of — well, the figs of fairy fiction, let us say, and pops the whole in the seething caldron of imagination, and at due season serves up THE PANTOMIME.

Very few men in the course of nature can expect to see *all* the pantomimes in one season, but I hope to the end of my life I shall never forego reading about them in that delicious sheet of "The Times" which appears on the morning after Boxing-day. Perhaps reading is even better than seeing. The best way, I think, is to say you are ill, lie in bed, and have the paper for two hours, reading all the way down from Drury Lane to the Britannia at Hoxton. Bob and I went to two pantomimes. One was at the Theatre of Fancy, and the other at the Fairy Opera, and I don't know which we liked the best.

At the Fancy, we saw "Harlequin Hamlet, or Daddy's Ghost and Nunky's Pison," which is all very well — but, gentlemen, if you don't respect Shakspeare, to whom will you be civil? The palace and ramparts of

Elsinore by moon and snow light is one of Loutherbourg's finest efforts. The banqueting hall of the palace is illuminated: the peaks and gables glitter with the snow: the sentinels march blowing their fingers with the cold — the freezing of the nose of one of them is very neatly and dexterously arranged: the snow-storm rises: the winds howl awfully along the battlements: the waves come curling, leaping, foaming to shore. Hamlet's umbrella is whirled away in the storm. He and his two friends stamp on each other's toes to keep them warm. The storm-spirits rise in the air, and are whirled howling round the palace and the rocks. My eyes! what tiles and chimney-pots fly hurtling through the air! As the storm reaches its height (here the wind instruments come in with prodigious effect, and I compliment Mr. Brumby and the violoncellos) — as the snow-storm rises (queek, queek, queek, go the fiddles, and then thrumpty thrump comes a pizzicato movement in Bob Major, which sends a shiver into your very boot-soles), the thunder-clouds deepen (bong, bong, bong, from the violoncellos). The forked lightning quivers through the clouds in a ziz-zag scream of violins — and look, look, look! as the frothing, roaring waves come rushing up the battlements, and over the reeling parapet, each hissing wave becomes a ghost, sends the gun-carriages rolling over the platform, and plunges howling into the water again.

Hamlet's mother comes on to the battlements to look for her son. The storm whips her umbrella out of her hands, and she retires screaming in pattens.

The cabs on the stand in the great market-place at Elsinore are seen to drive off, and several people are drowned. The gas-lamps along the street are wrenched from their foundations, and shoot through the troubled air. Whist, rush, hish! how the rain roars and pours! The darkness becomes awful, always deepened by the power of the music — and see — in the midst of a rush, and whirl, and scream of spirits of air and wave — what is that ghastly figure moving hither? It becomes bigger, bigger, as it advances down the platform — more ghastly, more horrible, enormous! It is as tall as the whole stage. It seems to be advancing on the stalls and pit, and the whole house screams with terror, as the GHOST OF THE LATE HAMLET comes in, and begins to speak. Several people faint, and the light-fingered gentry pick pockets furiously in the darkness.

In the pitchy darkness, this awful figure throwing his eyes about, the gas in the boxes shuddering out of sight, and the wind-instruments bugling the most horrible wails, the boldest spectator must have felt frightened. But hark! what is that silver shimmer of the fiddles? Is it — can it be — the gray dawn peeping in the stormy east? The ghost's eyes look blankly towards it, and roll a ghastly agony. Quicker, quicker ply the violins of Phœbus Apollo. Redder, redder grow the orient clouds. Cockadoodledoo! crows that great cock which has just come out on the roof of the palace. And now the round sun himself pops up from behind the waves of night. Where is the ghost? He is gone! Purple shadows of morn "slant o'er the snowy sward," the city wakes up in life and sunshine, and we confess we are very much relieved at the disappearance of the ghost. We don't like those dark scenes in pantomimes.

After the usual business, that Ophelia should be turned into Columbine was to be expected; but I confess I was a little shocked when Hamlet's mother became Pantaloon, and was instantly knocked down by Clown Claudius. Grimaldi is getting a little old now, but for real humor there are few clowns like him. Mr. Shuter, as the gravedigger, was chaste and comic, as he always is, and the scene-painters surpassed themselves.

"Harlequin Conqueror and the Field of Hastings," at the other house, is very pleasant too. The irascible William is acted with great vigor by Snoxall, and the battle of Hastings is a good piece of burlesque. Some trifling liberties are taken with history, but what liberties will not the merry genius of pantomime permit himself? At the battle of Hastings, William is on the point of being defeated by the Sussex volunteers, very elegantly led by the always pretty Miss Waddy (as Haco Sharpshooter), when a shot from the Normans kills Harold. The fairy Edith hereupon comes forward, and finds his body, which straightway leaps up a live harlequin, whilst the Conqueror makes an excellent clown, and the Archbishop of Bayeux a diverting pantaloon, &c., &c., &c., &c.

Perhaps these are not the pantomimes we really saw; but one description will do as well as another. The plots, you see, are a little intricate and difficult to understand in pantomimes; and I may have mixed up one with another. That I was at the theatre on Boxing-night is certain — but the pit was so full that I could only see fairy legs glittering in the distance, as I stood at the door. And if I was badly off, I think there was a young gentleman behind me worse off still. I own that he has good reason (though others have not) to speak ill of me behind my back, and hereby beg his pardon.

Likewise to the gentleman who picked up a party in Piccadilly, who had slipped and fallen in the snow, and was there on his back, uttering energetic expressions; that party begs to offer thanks, and compliments of the season.

Bob's behavior on New Year's day, I can assure Dr. Holyshade, was highly creditable to the boy. He had expressed a determination to partake of every dish which was put on the table; but after soup, fish, roast-beef, and roast-goose, he retired from active business until the pudding and mince-pies made their appearance, of which he partook liberally, but not too freely. And he greatly advanced in my good opinion by praising the punch, which was of my own manufacture, and which some gentlemen present (Mr. O'M—g—n, amongst others) pronounced to be too weak. Too weak! A bottle of rum, a bottle of Madeira, half a bottle of brandy, and two bottles and half of water — *can* this mixture be said to be too weak for any mortal? Our young friend amused the company during the evening, by exhibiting a two-shilling magic-lantern, which he had purchased, and likewise by singing "Sally, come up!" a quaint but rather monotonous melody, which I am told is sung by the poor negro on the banks of the broad Mississippi.

What other enjoyments did we proffer for the child's amusement during the Christmas week? A great philosopher was giving a lecture to young folks at the British Institution. But when this diversion was proposed to our young friend Bob, he said, "Lecture? No, thank you. Not as I knows on," and made sarcastic signals on his nose. Perhaps he is of Dr. Johnson's opinion about lectures: "Lectures, sir! what man would go to hear that imperfectly at a lecture, which he can read at leisure in a book?" *I* never went, of my own choice, to a lecture; that I can vow. As for sermons, they are different; I delight in them, and they cannot, of course, be too long.

Well, we partook of yet other Christmas delights besides pantomime, pudding, and pie. One glorious, one delightful, one most unlucky and pleasant day, we drove in a brougham, with a famous horse, which carried us more quickly and briskly than any of your vulgar railways, over Battersea Bridge, on which the horse's hoofs rung as if it had been iron; through suburban villages, plum-caked with snow; under a leaden sky, in which the sun hung like a red-hot warming-pan; by pond after pond, where not only men and boys, but scores after scores of women and girls, were sliding, and roaring, and clapping their lean old sides with laughter, as they tumbled down, and their hobnailed shoes flew up in the air; the air frosty with a lilac haze, through which villas, and commons, and churches, and plantations glimmered. We drive up the hill, Bob and I; we make the last two miles in eleven minutes; we pass that poor, armless man who sits there in the cold, following you with his eyes. I don't give any thing, and Bob looks disappointed. We are set down neatly at the gate, and a horse-holder opens the brougham door. I don't give any thing; again disappointment on Bob's part. I pay a shilling apiece, and we enter into the glorious building, which is decorated for Christmas, and straightway forgetfulness on Bob's part of every thing but that magnificent scene. The enormous edifice is all decorated for Bob and Christmas. The stalls, the columns, the fountains, courts, statues, splendors, are all crowned for Christmas. The delicious negro is singing his Alabama choruses for Christmas and Bob. He has scarcely done, when, Tootarootatoo! Mr. Punch is performing his surprising actions, and hanging the beadle. The stalls are decorated. The refreshment-tables are piled with good things; at many fountains "MULLED CLARET" is written up in appetizing capitals. "Mulled Claret — oh, jolly! How cold it is!" says Bob; I pass on. "It's only three o'clock," says Bob. "No, only three," I say, meekly. "We dine at seven," sighs Bob, "and it's so-o-o coo-old." I still would take no hints. No claret, no refreshment, no sandwiches, no sausage-rolls for Bob. At last I am obliged to tell him all. Just before we left home, a little Christmas bill popped in at the door and emptied my purse at the threshold. I forgot all about the transaction, and had to borrow half a crown from John Coachman to pay for our entrance into the palace of delight. *Now* you see, Bob, why I could not treat you on that second of January when we drove to the palace together; when the girls and boys were sliding on the ponds at Dulwich; when the darkling river was full of floating ice, and the sun was like a warming-pan in the leaden sky.

One more Christmas sight we had, of course; and that sight I think I like as well as Bob himself at Christmas, and at all seasons. We went to a certain garden of delight, where, whatever your cares are, I think you can manage to forget some of them, and muse, and be not unhappy; to a garden beginning with a Z, which is as lively as Noah's ark; where the fox has brought his brush, and the cock has brought his comb, and the elephant has brought his trunk, and the kangaroo has brought his bag, and the condor his old white wig and black satin hood. On this day it was so cold that the white bears winked their pink eyes, as they plapped up and down by their pool, and seemed to say, "Aha, this weather reminds us of dear home!" "Cold! bah! I have got such a warm coat," says brother Bruin, "I don't mind;" and he laughs on his pole, and clucks down a bun. The squealing hyenas gnashed their teeth and laughed at us quite refreshingly at their window; and, cold as it was, Tiger, Tiger, burning bright, glared at us red-hot through his bars, and snorted blasts of hell. The woolly camel leered at us quite kindly as he paced round his ring on his silent pads. We went to our favorite places. Our dear wambat came up, and had himself scratched very affably. Our fellow-creatures in the monkey-room held out their little black hands, and piteously asked us for Christmas alms. Those darling alligators on their rock winked at us in the most friendly way. The solemn eagles sat alone, and scowled at us from their peaks; whilst little Tom Ratel tumbled over head and heels for us in his usual diverting manner. If I have cares in my mind, I come to the Zoo, and fancy they don't pass the gate. I recognize my friends, my enemies, in countless cages. I entertained the eagle, the vulture, the old billy-goat, and the black-pated, crimson-necked, blear-eyed, baggy, hook-beaked old marabou stork yesterday at dinner; and when Bob's aunt came to tea in the evening, and asked him what he had seen, he stepped up to her gravely, and said —

> "First I saw the white bear, then I saw the black,
> Then I saw the camel with a hump upon his back.
>
> *Chorus of Children.* } Then I saw the camel with a HUMP upon his back!
>
> Then I saw the gray wolf, with mutton in his maw;
> Then I saw the wambat waddle in the straw;
> Then I saw the elephant with his waving trunk,
> Then I saw the monkeys — mercy, how unpleasantly they — smelt!"

There. No one can beat that piece of wit, can he, Bob? And so it is all over; but we had a jolly time, whilst you were with us, hadn't we? Present my respects to the doctor; and I hope, my boy, we may spend another merry Christmas next year.

ON A CHALK-MARK ON THE DOOR.

On the doorpost of the house of a friend of mine, a few inches above the lock, is a little chalk-mark, which some sportive boy in passing has probably scratched on the pillar. The door-steps, the lock, handle, and so forth, are kept decently enough; but this chalk-mark, I suppose some three inches out of the housemaid's beat, has already been on the door for more than a fortnight, and I wonder whether it will be there whilst this paper is being written, whilst it is at the printer's, and, in fine, until the month passes over? I wonder whether the servants in that house will read these remarks about the chalk-mark? That "The Cornhill Magazine" is taken in in that house I know. In fact I have seen it there. In fact I have read it there. In fact I have written it there. In a word, the house to which I allude is mine — the "editor's private residence," to which, in spite of prayers, entreaties, commands, and threats, authors, and ladies especially, *will* send their communications, although they won't understand that they injure their own interests by so doing; for how is a man who has his own work to do, his own exquisite inventions to form and perfect — Maria to rescue from the unprincipled Earl — the atrocious General to confound in his own machinations — the angelic Dean to promote to a bishopric, and so forth — how is a man to do all this, under a hundred interruptions, and keep his nerves and temper in that just and equable state in which they ought to be when he comes to assume the critical office? As you will send here, ladies, I must tell you you have a much worse chance than if you forward your valuable articles to Cornhill. Here your papers arrive, at dinner-time, we will say. Do you suppose that is a pleasant period, and that we are to criticise you between the *ovum* and *malum*, between the soup and the dessert? I have touched, I think, on this subject before. I say again, if you want real justice shown you, don't send your papers to the private residence. At home, for instance, yesterday, having given strict orders that I was to receive nobody, "except on business," do you suppose a smiling young Scottish gentleman, who forced himself into my study, and there announced himself as agent of a Cattle-food Company, was received with pleasure? There, as I sat in my arm-chair, suppose he had proposed to draw a couple of my teeth, would I have been pleased? I could have throttled that agent. I dare say the whole of that day's work will be found tinged with a ferocious misanthropy, occasioned by my clever young friend's intrusion. Cattle-food, indeed! As if beans, oats, warm mashes, and a ball, are to be pushed down a man's throat just as he is meditating on the great social problem, or (for I think it was my epic I was going to touch up) just as he was about to soar to the height of the empyrean!

Having got my cattle-agent out of the door, I resume my consideration of that little mark on the doorpost, which is scored up as the text of the present little sermon; and which I hope will relate, not to chalk, nor to any of its special uses or abuses (such as milk, neck-powder, and the like), but to servants. Surely ours might remove that unseemly little mark. Suppose it were on my coat, might I not request its removal? I remember, when I was at school, a little careless boy, upon whose forehead an ink-mark remained, and was perfectly recognizable for three weeks after its first appearance. May I take any notice of this chalk-stain on the forehead of my house? Whose business is it to wash that forehead? and ought I to fetch a brush and a little hot water, and wash it off myself?

Yes. But that spot removed, why not come down at six, and wash the doorsteps? I dare say the early rising and exercise would do me a great deal of good. The housemaid, in that case, might lie in bed a little later, and have her tea and the morning paper brought to her in bed: then, of course, Thomas would expect to be helped about the boots and knives; cook about the saucepans, dishes, and what not; the lady's-maid would want somebody to take the curl-papers out of her hair, and get her bath ready. You should have a set of servants for the servants, and these under-servants should have slaves to wait on them. The king commands the first lord in waiting to desire the second lord to intimate to the gentleman usher to request the page of the antechamber to entreat the groom of the stairs to implore John to ask the captain of the buttons to desire the maid of the still-room to beg the housekeeper to give out a few more lumps of sugar, as his Majesty has none for his coffee, which probably is getting cold during the negotiation. In our little Brentfords we are all kings, more or less. There are orders, gradations, hierarchies, everywhere. In your house and mine there are mysteries unknown to us. I am not going into the horrid old question of "followers." I don't mean cousins from the country, love-stricken policemen, or gentlemen in mufti from Knightsbridge Barracks; but people who have an occult right on the premises; the uncovenanted servants of the house; gray women who are seen at evening with baskets flitting about area-railings; dingy shawls which drop you furtive courtesies in your neighborhood; demure little Jacks, who start up from behind boxes in the pantry. Those outsiders wear Thomas's crest and livery, and call him "Sir;" those silent women address the female servants as "Mum," and courtesy before them, squaring their arms over their wretched lean aprons. Then, again, those *servi servorum* have dependants in the vast, silent, poverty-stricken world outside your comfortable kitchen fire, in the world of darkness, and hunger, and miserable cold, and dank, flagged cellars, and huddled straw, and rags, in which pale children are swarming. It may be your beer (which runs with great volubility) has a pipe or two which communicates with those dark caverns where hopeless anguish pours the groan, and would scarce see light but for a scrap or two of candle which has been whipped away from your worship's kitchen. Not many years ago — I don't know whether before or since that white mark was drawn on the door — a lady occupied the confidential place of housemaid in this "private residence," who brought a good character, who seemed to have a cheerful temper, whom I used to hear clattering and bumping overhead or on the stairs long before daylight —

there, I say, was poor Camilla, scouring the plain, trundling and brushing, and clattering with her pans and brooms, and humming at her work. Well, she had established a smuggling communication of beer over the area frontier. This neat-handed Phyllis used to pack up the nicest baskets of my provender, and convey them to somebody outside —I believe, on my conscience, to some poor friend in distress. Camilla was consigned to her doom. She was sent back to her friends in the country; and when she was gone we heard of many of her faults. She expressed herself, when displeased, in language that I shall not repeat. As for the beer and meat, there was no mistake about them. But *après*? Can I have the heart to be very angry with that poor jade for helping another poorer jade out of my larder? on your honor and conscience, when you were boy, and the apples looked temptingly over Farmer Quarringdon's hedge, did you never? — When there was a grand dinner at home, and you were sliding, with Master Bacon, up and down the stairs, and the dishes came out, did you ever do such a thing as just to? — Well, in many and many a respect servants are like children. They are under domination. They are subject to reproof, to ill temper, to petty exactions and stupid tyrannies not seldom. They scheme, conspire, fawn, and are hypocrites. "Little boys should not loll on chairs." "Little girls should be seen, and not heard;" and so forth. Have we not almost all learnt these expressions of old foozles: and uttered them ourselves when in the square-toed state? The Eton master, who was breaking a lance with our Paterfamilias of late, turned on Paterfamilias, saying, He knows not the nature and exquisite candor of well-bred English boys. Exquisite fiddlestick's end, Mr. Master! Do you mean for to go for to tell us that the relations between young gentlemen and their schoolmasters are entirely frank and cordial; that the lad is familiar with the man who can have him flogged; never shirks his exercises; never gets other boys to do his verses; never does other boys' verses; never breaks bounds; never tells fibs —I mean the fibs permitted by scholastic honor? Did I know of a boy who pretended to such a character, I would forbid my scapegraces to keep company with him. Did I know a schoolmaster who pretended to believe in the existence of many hundred such boys in one school at one time, I would set that man down as a baby in knowledge of the world. "Who was making that noise?" "I don't know, sir." And he knows it was the boy next him in school. "Who was climbing over that wall?" "I don't know, sir." And it is in the speaker's own trousers, very likely, the glass bottle-tops have left their cruel scars. And so with servants. "Who ate up the three pigeons which went down in the pigeon-pie at breakfast this morning?" "O dear me! sir, it was John, who went away last month!" —or, "I think it was Miss Mary's canary-bird, which got out of the cage, and is so fond of pigeons, it never can have enough of them." Yes, it *was* the canary-bird; and Eliza saw it; and Eliza is ready to vow she did. These statements are not true; but please don't call them lies. This not lying; this is voting with your party. You *must* back your own side. The servants'-hall stands by the servants'-hall against the dining-room. The schoolboys don't tell tales of each other. They agree not to choose to know who has made the noise, who has broken the window, who has eaten up the pigeons, who has picked all the plovers'-eggs out of the aspic, how it is that liqueur brandy of Gledstane's is in such porous glass bottles — and so forth. Suppose Brutus had a footman, who came and told him that the butler drank the Curaçoa, which of these servants would you dismiss? —

the butler, perhaps, but the footman certainly.

No. If your plate and glass are beautifully bright, your bell quickly answered, and Thomas ready, neat, and good-humored, you are not to expect absolute truth from him. The very obsequiousness and perfection of his service prevents truth. He may be ever so unwell in mind or body, and he must go through his service — hand the shining plate, replenish the spotless glass, lay the glittering fork — never laugh when you yourself or your guests joke — be profoundly attentive, and yet look utterly impassive — exchange a few hurried curses at the door with that unseen slavey who ministers without, and with you be perfectly calm and polite. If you are ill, he will come twenty times in an hour to your bell; or leave the girl of his heart — his mother, who is going to America — his dearest friend, who has come to say farewell — his lunch, and his glass of beer just freshly poured out — any or all of these, if the door-bell rings, or the master calls out "THOMAS" from the hall. Do you suppose you can expect absolute candor from a man whom you may order to powder his hair? As between the Rev. Henry Holyshade and his pupil, the idea of entire unreserve is utter bosh; so the truth as between you and Jeames or Thomas, or Mary the housemaid, or Betty the cook, is relative, and not to be demanded on one side or the other. Why, respectful civility is itself a lie, which poor Jeames often has to utter or perform to many a swaggering vulgarian, who should black Jeames's boots, did Jeames wear them, and not shoes. There is your little Tom, just ten, ordering the great, large, quiet, orderly young man about — shrieking calls for hot water — bullying Jeames because the boots are not varnished enough, or ordering him to go to the stables, and ask Jenkins why the deuce Tomkins hasn't brought his pony round — or what you will. There is mamma rapping the knuckles of Pincot the lady's-maid, and little Miss scolding Martha, who waits up five-pair of stairs in the nursery. Little Miss, Tommy, papa, mamma, you all expect from Martha, from Pincot, from Jenkins, from Jeames, obsequious civility and willing service. My dear, good people, you can't have truth too. Suppose you ask for your newspaper, and Jeames says, "I'm reading it, and jest beg not to be disturbed;" or suppose you ask for a can of water, and he remarks, "You great, big, 'ulking fellar, ain't you big enough to bring it hup yoursulf?" what would your feelings be? Now, if you made similar proposals or requests to Mr. Jones next door, this is the kind of answer Jones would give you. You get truth habitually from equals only; so my good Mr. Holyshade, don't talk to me about the habitual candor of the young Etonian of high birth, or I have my own opinion of *your* candor or discernment when you do. No. Tom Bowling is the soul of honor and has been true to Black-eyed Syousan since the last time they parted at Wapping Old Stairs; but do you suppose Tom is perfectly frank, familiar, and above-board in his conversation with Admiral Nelson, K.C.B.? There are secrets, prevarications, fibs, if you will, between Tom and the Admiral — between your crew and *their* captain. I know I hire a worthy, clean, agreeable, and conscientious male or female hypocrite, at so many guineas a year, to do so and so for me. Were he other than hypocrite I would send him about his business. Don't let my displeasure be too fierce with him for a fib or two on his own account.

Some dozen years ago, my family being absent in a distant part of the country, and my business detaining me in London, I remained in my own house with three servants on board wages. I used only to breakfast at home; and future ages will be interested to know that this meal used to consist, at that period, of tea, a penny roll, a pat of butter, and, perhaps, an egg. My weekly bill used invariably to be about fifty shillings; so that, as I never dined in the house, you see, my breakfast, consisting of the delicacies before mentioned, cost about seven shillings and threepence per diem. I must, therefore, have consumed daily —

	s.	*d.*
A quarter of a pound of tea (say)...	1	3
A penny roll (say)..................	1	0
One pound of butter (say)..........	1	3
One pound of lump sugar...........	1	0
A new-laid egg	2	9

Which is the only possible way I have for making out the sum.

Well, I fell ill while under this regimen, and had an illness which, but for a certain doctor, who was brought to me by a certain kind friend I had in those days, would, I think, have prevented the possibility of my telling this interesting anecdote now a dozen years after. Don't be frightened, my dear madam; it is not a horrid, sentimental account of a malady you are coming to — only a question of grocery. This illness, I say, lasted some seventeen days, during which the servants were admirably attentive and kind; and poor John, especially, was up at all hours, watching night after night — amiable, cheerful, untiring, respectful, the very best of Johns and nurses.

Twice or thrice in the seventeen days I may have had a glass of *eau sucrée* — say a dozen glasses of *eau sucrée* — certainly not more. Well, this admirable, watchful, cheerful, tender, affectionate John brought me in a little bill for seventeen pounds of sugar consumed during the illness — "Often 'ad sugar and water; always was a callin' for it," says John, wagging his head quite gravely. You are dead, years and years ago, poor John — so patient, so friendly, so kind, so cheerful to the invalid in the fever. But confess now, wherever you are, that seventeen pounds of sugar to make six glasses of *eau sucrée* was a *little* too strong, wasn't it, John? Ah, how frankly, how trustily, how bravely he lied, poor John! One evening, being at Brighton, in the convalescence, I remember John's step was unsteady, his voice thick, his laugh queer — and having some quinine to give me, John brought the glass to me — not to my mouth, but struck me with it pretty smartly in the eye, which was not the way in which Dr. Elliotson had intended his prescription should be taken. Turning that eye upon him, I ventured to hint that my attendant had been drinking. Drinking! I never was more humiliated at the thought of my own injustice than at John's reply. "Drinking! Sulp me! I have had ony one pint of beer with my dinner at one o'clock!" — and he retreats, holding on by a chair. These are fibs, you see, appertaining to the situation. John is drunk. "*Sulp* him, he has only had an 'alf-pint of beer with his dinner six hours ago;" and none of his fellow-servants, will say otherwise. Polly is smuggled on board ship. Who tells the lieutenant when he comes his rounds? Boys are playing cards in the bedroom. The outlying fag announces master coming — out go candles — cards popped into bed — boys sound asleep. Who had that light in the dormitory? Law bless you! the poor dear innocents are every one snoring. Every one snoring, and every snore is a lie told through the nose! Suppose one of your boys or mine is engaged in that awful crime, are we going to break our hearts about it? Come, come. We pull a long face, waggle a grave head, and chuckle within our waistcoats.

Between me and those fellow-creatures of mine who are sitting in the room below, how strange and wonderful is the partition! We meet at every hour of the daylight, and are indebted to each other for a hundred offices of duty and comfort of life; and we live together for years, and don't know each other. John's voice to me is quite different from John's voice when it addresses his mates below. If I met Hannah in the street with a bonnet on, I doubt whether I should know her. And all these good people with whom I may live for years and years have cares, interests, dear friends and relatives, mayhap schemes, passions, longing hopes, tragedies of their own, from which a carpet and a few planks and beams utterly separate me. When we were at the seaside, and poor Ellen used to look so pale and run after the postman's bell, and seize a letter in a great scrawling hand, and read it, and cry in a corner, how should we know that the poor little thing's heart was breaking? She fetched the water, and she smoothed the ribbons, and she laid out the dresses, and brought the early cup of tea in the morning, just as if she had had no cares to keep her awake. Henry (who lived out of the house) was the servant of a friend of mine who lived in chambers. There was a dinner one day, and Henry waited all through the dinner. The champagne was properly iced, the dinner was excellently served; every guest was attended to; the dinner disappeared; the dessert was set; the claret was in perfect order, carefully decanted, and more ready. And then Henry said, "If you please, sir, may I go home?" He had received word that his house was on fire; and, having seen through his dinner, he wished to go and look after his children, and little sticks of furniture. Why, such a man's livery is a uniform of honor. The crest on his button is a badge of bravery.

Do you see — I imagine I do myself — in these little instances a tinge of humor? Ellen's heart is breaking for handsome Jeames of Buckley Square, whose great legs are kneeling, and who has given a lock of his precious powdered head, to some other than Ellen. Henry is preparing the sauce for his master's wild-ducks while the engines are squirting over his own little nest and brood. Lift these figures up but a story from the basement to the ground-floor, and the fun is gone. We may be *en pleine tragédie.* Ellen may breathe her last sigh in blank verse, calling down blessings upon James the profligate who deserts her. Henry is a hero, and epaulets are on his shoulders. *Atqui sciebat*, &c., whatever tortures are in store for him, he will be at his post of duty.

You concede, however, that there is a touch of humor in the two tragedies here mentioned. Why? Is it that the idea of persons at service is somehow ludicrous? Perhaps it is made more so in this country by the splendid appearance of the liveried domestics of great people. When you think that we dress in black ourselves, and put our fellow-creatures in green, pink, or canary-colored breeches; that we order them to plaster their hair with flour, having brushed that nonsense out of our own heads fifty years ago; that some of the most genteel and stately among us cause the men who drive their carriages to put on little Albino wigs, and sit behind great nosegays — I say I suppose it is this heaping of gold lace, gaudy colors, blooming plushes, on honest John Trot, which makes the man absurd in our eyes, who need be nothing but a simple reputable citizen and in-door laborer. Suppose, my dear sir, that you yourself were suddenly desired to put on a full dress, or even undress, domestic uniform with our friend Jones's crest repeated in varied combinations of button on your front and back? Suppose, madam, your son were told, that he could not get out except in lower garments of carnation or amber-colored plush — would you let him? ... But as you justly say, this is not the question, and besides it is a question fraught with danger, sir; and radicalism, sir; and subversion of the very foundations of the social fabric, sir. ... Well, John, we won't enter on your great domestic question. Don't let us disport with Jeames's dangerous strength, and the edge-tools about his knife-board: but with Betty and Susan who wield the playful mop, and set on the simmering kettle. Surely you have heard Mrs. Toddles talking to Mrs. Doddles about their mutual maids. Miss Susan must have a silk gown, and Miss Betty must wear flowers under her bonnet when she goes to church if you please, and did you ever hear such impudence? The servant in many small establishments is a constant and endless theme of talk. What small wage, sleep, meal, what endless scouring, scolding, tramping on messages, fall to that poor Susan's lot; what indignation at the little kindly passing word with the grocer's young man, the pot-boy, the chubby butcher! Where such things will end, my dear Mrs. Toddles, I don't know. What wages they will want next, my dear Mrs. Doddles, &c.

Here, dear ladies, is an advertisement which I cut out of "The Times" a few days since, expressly for you: —

"A LADY is desirous of obtaining a SITUATION for a very respectable young woman as HEAD KITCHEN-MAID under a man-cook. She has lived four years under a very good cook and housekeeper. Can make ice, and is an excellent baker. She will only take a place in a very good family, where she can have the opportunity of improving herself, and, if possible, staying for two years. Apply by letter to," &c., &c.

There, Mrs. Toddles, what do you think of that, and did you ever? Well, no, Mrs. Doddles. Upon my word now, Mrs. T., I don't think I ever did. A respectable young woman — as head kitchen-maid — under a man-cook, will only take a place in a very good family, where she can improve, and stay two years. Just note up the conditions, Mrs. Toddles, mum, if you please, mum, and *then* let us see: —

1. This young woman is to be HEAD kitchen-maid, that is to say, there is to be a chorus of kitchen-maids, of which Y. W. is to be chief.
2. She will only be situated under a man-cook. (A) Ought he to be a French cook; and (B), if so, would the lady desire him to be a Protestant?
3. She will only take a place in a *very good family*. How old ought the family to be, and what do you call good? that is the question. How long after the Conquest will do? Would a banker's family do, or is a baronet's good enough? Best say what rank in the peerage would be sufficiently high. But the lady does not say whether she would like a High Church or a Low Church family. Ought there to be unmarried sons, and may they follow a profession? and please say how many daughters; and would the lady like them to be musical? And how many company dinners a week? Not too many, for fear of fatiguing the upper kitchen-maid; but sufficient, so as to keep the upper kitchen-maid's hand in. [N. B. — I think I can see a rather bewildered expression on the countenances of Mesdames Doddles and Toddles as I am prattling on in this easy bantering way.]
4. The head kitchen-maid wishes to stay for two years, and improve herself under the man-cook, and having of course sucked the brains (as the phrase is) from under the chef's nightcap, then the head kitchen-maid wishes to go.

And upon my word, Mrs. Toddles, mum, I will go and fetch the cab for her. The cab? Why not her ladyship's own carriage and pair, and the head coachman to drive away the head kitchen-maid? You see she stipulates for every thing — the time to come; the time to stay; the family she will be with; and as soon as she has improved herself enough, of course the upper kitchen-maid will step into the carriage and drive off.

Well, upon my word and conscience if things are coming to *this* pass, Mrs. Toddles and Mrs. Doddles, mum, I think I will go up stairs and get a basin and a sponge, and then down stairs and get some hot water; and then I will go and scrub that chalk-mark off my own door with my own hands.

It is wiped off, I declare! After ever so many weeks! Who has done it? It was just a little round-about mark, you know, and it was there for days and weeks, before I ever thought it would be the text of a Roundabout Paper.

ON BEING FOUND OUT.

At the close (let us say) of Queen Anne's reign, when I was a boy at a private and preparatory school for young gentlemen, I remember the wiseacre of a master ordering us all, one night, to march into a little garden at the back of the house, and thence to proceed one by one into a tool or hen house (I was but a tender little thing just put into short clothes, and can't exactly say whether the house was for tools or hens), and in that house to put our hands into a sack which stood on a bench, a candle burning beside it. I put my hand into the sack. My hand came out quite black. I went and joined the other boys in the school-room; and all their hands were black too.

By reason of my tender age (and there are some critics, who, I hope, will be satisfied by my acknowledging that I am a hundred and fifty-six next birthday) I could not understand what was the meaning of this night excursion — this candle, this tool-house, this bag of soot. I think we little boys were taken out of our sleep to be brought to the ordeal. We came, then, and showed our little hands to the master; washed them or not — most probably, I should say, not — and so went bewildered back to bed.

Something had been stolen in the school that day; and Mr. Wiseacre having read in a book of an ingenious method of finding out a thief by making him put his hand into a sack (which, if guilty, the rogue would shirk from doing), all we boys were subjected to the trial. Goodness knows what the lost object was, or who stole it. We all had black hands to show to the master. And the thief, whoever he was, was not Found Out that time.

I wonder if the rascal is alive — an elderly scoundrel he must be by this time; and a hoary old hypocrite to whom an old schoolfellow presents his kindest regards — parenthetically remarking what a dreadful place that private school was; cold, chilblains, bad dinners, not enough victuals, and caning awful! — Are you alive still, I say, you nameless villain, who escaped discovery on that day of crime? I hope you have escaped often since, old sinner. Ah, what a lucky thing it is, for you and me, my man, that we are *not* found out in all our peccadilloes; and that our backs can slip away from the master and the cane!

Just consider what life would be, if every rogue was found out, and flogged *coram populo!* What a butchery, what an indecency, what an endless swishing of the rod! Don't cry out about my misanthropy. My good friend Mealymouth, I will trouble you to tell me, do you go to church? When there, do you say, or do you not, that you are a miserable sinner? and saying so, do you believe or disbelieve it? If you are a M. S., don't you deserve correction, and aren't you grateful if you are to be let off? I say again, what a blessed thing it is that we are not all found out!

Just picture to yourself everybody who does wrong being found out, and punished accordingly. Fancy all the boys in all the school being whipped; and then the assistants, and then the head master (Dr. Badford let us call him). Fancy the provost-marshal being tied up, having previously superintended the correction of the whole army. After the young gentlemen have had their turn for the faulty exercises, fancy Dr. Lincolnsinn being taken up for certain faults in *his* Essay and Review. After the clergyman has cried his peccavi, suppose we hoist up a bishop, and give him a couple of dozen! (I see my Lord Bishop of Double-Gloucester sitting in a very uneasy posture on his right reverend bench.) After we have cast off the bishop, what are we to say to the Minister who appointed him? My Lord Cinqwarden, it is painful to have to use personal correction to a boy of your age; but really . . . *Siste tandem carnifex!* The butchery is too horrible. The hand drops powerless, appalled at the quantity of birch which it must cut and brandish. I am glad we are not all found out, I say again; and protest, my dear brethren, against our having our deserts.

To fancy all men found out and punished is bad enough; but imagine all women found out in the distinguished social circle in which you and I have the honor to move. Is it not a mercy that a many of these fair criminals remain unpunished and undiscovered? There is Mrs. Longbow, who is forever practising, and who shoots poisoned arrows, too; when you meet her you don't call her liar, and charge her with the wickedness she has done, and is doing. There is Mrs. Painter, who passes for a most respectable woman, and a model in society. There is no use in saying what you really know regarding her and her goings on. There is Diana Hunter—what a little haughty prude it is; and yet *we* know stories about her which are not altogether edifying. I say it is best, for the sake of the good, that the bad should not all be found out. You don't want your children to know the history of that lady in the next box, who is so handsome, and whom they admire so. Ah me! what would life be if we were all found out, and punished for all our faults? Jack Ketch would be in permanence; and then who would hang Jack Ketch?

They talk of murderers being pretty certainly found out. Psha! I have heard an authority awfully competent vow and declare that scores and hundreds of murders are committed, and nobody is the wiser. That terrible man mentioned one or two ways of committing murder, which he maintained were quite common, and were scarcely ever found out. A man, for instance, comes home to his wife, and . . . but I pause—I know that this Magazine has a very large circulation. Hundreds and hundreds of thousands—why not say a million of people at once?—well, say a million, read it. And amongst these countless readers, I might be teaching some monster how to make away with his wife without being found out, some fiend of a woman how to destroy her dear husband. I will *not* then tell this easy and simple way of murder, as communicated to me by a most respectable party in the confidence of private intercourse. Suppose some gentle reader were to try this most simple and easy receipt—it seems to me almost infallible—and come to grief in consequence, and be found out and hanged? Should I ever pardon myself for having been the means of doing injury to a single one of our esteemed subscribers? The prescription whereof I speak—that is to say, whereof I *don't* speak—shall be buried in this bosom. No, I am a humane man. I am not one of your Bluebeards to go and say to my wife, "My dear! I am going away for a few days to Brighton. Here are all the keys of the house. You may open every door and closet, except the one at the end of the oak-room opposite the fire-place, with the little bronze Shakspeare on the mantelpiece (or what not)." I don't say this to a woman—unless, to be sure, I want to get rid of her—because, after such a caution, I know she'll peep into the closet. I say nothing about the closet at all. I keep the key in my pocket, and a being whom I love, but who, as I know, has many weaknesses, out of harm's way. You toss up your head, dear angel, drub on the ground with your lovely little feet, on the table with your sweet rosy fingers, and cry, "Oh, sneerer! You don't know the depth of woman's feeling, the lofty scorn of all deceit, the entire absence of mean curiosity in the sex, or never, never would you libel us so!" Ah, Delia! dear, dear Delia! It is because I fancy I *do* know something about you (not all, mind — no, no; no man knows that) — Ah, my bride, my ringdove, my rose, my poppet — choose, in fact, whatever name you like — bulbul of my grove, fountain of my desert, sunshine of my darkling life, and joy of my dungeoned existence, it is because I *do* know a little about you that I conclude to say nothing of that private closet, and keep my key in my pocket. You take away that closet-key then, and the house-key. You lock Delia in. You keep her out of harm's way and gadding, and so she never *can* be found out.

And yet by little strange accidents and coincidents how we are being found out every day! You remember that old story of the Abbé Kakatoes, who told the company at supper one night how the first confession he ever received was — from a murderer let us say. Presently enters to supper the Marquis de Croquemitaine. "Palsambleu, abbé!" says the brilliant marquis, taking a pinch of snuff, "are you here? Gentlemen and ladies! I was the abbé's first penitent, and I made him a confession which I promise you astonished him."

To be sure how queerly things are found out! Here is an instance. Only the other day I was writing in these Roundabout Papers about a certain man, whom I facetiously called Baggs, and who had abused me to my friends, who of course told me. Shortly after that paper was published another friend — Sacks let us call him — scowls fiercely at me as I am sitting in perfect good-humor at the club, and passes on without speaking. A cut. A quarrel. Sacks thinks it is about him that I was writing: whereas, upon my honor and conscience, I never had him once in my mind, and was pointing my moral from quite another man. But don't you see, by this wrath of the guilty-conscienced Sacks, that he had been abusing me too? He has owned himself guilty, never having been accused. He has winced when nobody thought of hitting him. I did but put the cap out, and madly butting and chafing, behold my friend rushes to put his head into it! Never mind, Sacks, you are found out; but I bear you no malice, my man.

And yet to be found out, I know from my own experience, must be painful and odious, and cruelly mortifying to the inward vanity. Suppose I am a poltroon, let us say. With fierce mustache, loud talk, plentiful oaths, and an immense stick, I keep up, nevertheless, a character for courage. I swear fearfully at cabmen and women; brandish my bludgeon, and perhaps knock down a little man or two with it; brag of the images which I break at the shooting-gallery, and pass amongst my friends for a whiskery fire-eater, afraid of neither man nor dragon. Ah me! Suppose some brisk little chap steps up and gives me a caning in St. James's Street, with all the heads of my friends looking out of all the club windows. My reputation is gone. I frighten no man more. My nose is pulled by whipper-snappers, who jump up on a chair to reach it. I am found out. And in the days of my triumphs, when people were yet afraid of me, and were taken in by my swagger, I always knew that I was a lily-liver, and expected that I should be found out some day.

That certainty of being found out must haunt and depress many a bold braggadocio spirit. Let us say it is a clergyman, who can pump copious floods of tears out of his own eyes and those of his audience. He thinks to himself, "I am but a poor swindling, chattering rogue. My bills are unpaid. I have jilted several women whom I have promised to marry. I don't know whether I believe what I preach, and I know I have stolen the very sermon over which I have been snivelling. Have they found me out?" says he, as his head drops down on the cushion.

Then your writer, poet, historian, novelist, or what not? "The Beacon" says that "Jones's work is one of the first order." "The Lamp" declares that "Jones's tragedy surpasses every work since the days of Him of Avon." The "Comet" asserts that "J.'s 'Life of Goody Twoshoes' is a *κτῆμα ἐς ἀεὶ*, a noble and enduring monument to the fame of that admirable Englishwoman," and so forth. But then Jones knows that he has lent the critic of "The Beacon" five pounds; that his publisher has a half-share in "The Lamp;" and that "The Comet" comes repeatedly to dine with him. It is all very well. Jones is immortal until he is found out; and then down comes the extinguisher, and the immortal is dead and buried. The idea (*dies iræ!*) of discovery must haunt many a man, and make him uneasy, as the trumpets are puffing in his triumph. Brown, who has a higher place than he deserves, cowers before Smith, who has found him out. What is a chorus of critics shouting "Bravo"?—a public clapping hands and flinging garlands? Brown knows that Smith has found him out. Puff, trumpets! Wave, banners! Huzza, boys, for the immortal Brown! "This is all very well," B. thinks (bowing the while, smiling, laying his hand to his heart); "but there stands Smith at the window: *he* has measured me; and some day the others will find me out too." It is a very curious sensation to sit by a man who has found you out, and who, as you know, has found you out, or, *vice versâ*, to sit with a man whom *you* have found out. His talent? Bah! His virtue? We know a little story or two about his virtue, and he knows we know it. We are thinking over friend Robinson's antecedents, as we grin, bow, and talk; and we are both humbugs together. Robinson a good fellow, is he? You know how he behaved to Hicks? A good-natured man, is he? Pray do you remember that little story of Mrs. Robinson's black eye? How men have to work, to talk, to smile, to go to bed, and try and sleep, with this dread of being found out on their consciences! Bardolph, who has robbed a church, and Nym, who has taken a purse, go to their usual haunts, and smoke their pipes with their companions. Mr. Detective Bullseye appears, and says, "Oh, Bardolph! I want you about that there pyx business!" Mr. Bardolph knocks the ashes out of his pipe, puts out his hands to the little steel cuffs, and walks away quite meekly. He is found out. He must go. "Good-by, Doll Tearsheet! Good-by, Mrs. Quickly, ma'am!" The other gentlemen and ladies *de la société* look on and exchange mute adieux with the departing friends. And an assured time will come when the other gentlemen and ladies will be found out too.

What a wonderful and beautiful provision of nature it has been, that, for the most part, our womankind are not endowed with the faculty of finding us out! *They* don't doubt, and probe, and weigh, and take your measure. Lay down this paper, my benevolent friend and reader, go into your drawing-room now, and utter a joke ever so old, and I wager sixpence the ladies there will all begin to laugh. Go to Brown's house, and tell Mrs. Brown and the young ladies what you think of him, and see what a welcome you will get! In like manner, let him come to your house, and tell *your* good lady his candid opinion of you, and fancy how she will receive him! Would you have your wife and children know you exactly for what you are, and esteem you precisely at your worth? If so, my friend, you will live in a dreary house, and you will have but a chilly fireside. Do you suppose the people round it don't see your homely face as under a glamour, and, as it were, with a halo of love round it? You don't fancy you *are*, as you seem to them? No such thing, my man. Put away that monstrous conceit, and be thankful that *they* have not found you out.

ON A HUNDRED YEARS HENCE.

Where have I just read of a game played at a country house? The party assembles round a table with pens, ink, and paper. Some one narrates a tale containing more or less incidents and personages. Each person of the company then writes down, to the best of his memory and ability, the anecdote just narrated, and finally the papers are to be read out. I do not say I should like to play often at this game, which might possibly be a tedious and lengthy pastime, not by any means so amusing as smoking a cigar in the conservatory; or even listening to the young ladies playing their piano-pieces; or to Hobbs and Nobbs lingering round the bottle and talking over the morning's run with the hounds; but surely it is a moral and ingenious sport. They say the variety of narratives is often very odd and amusing. The original story becomes so changed and distorted that at the end of all the statements you are puzzled to know where the truth is at all. As time is of small importance to the cheerful persons engaged in this sport, perhaps a good way of playing it would be to spread it over a couple of years. Let the people who played the game in '60 all meet and play it once more in '61, and each write his story over again. Then bring out your original and compare notes. Not only will the stories differ from each other, but the writers will probably differ from themselves. In the course of the year the incidents will grow or will dwindle strangely. The least authentic of the statements will be so lively or so malicious, or so neatly put, that it will appear most like the truth. I like these tales and sportive exercises. I had begun a little print collection once. I had Addison in his nightgown in bed at Holland House, requesting young Lord Warwick to remark how a Christian should die. I had Cambronne clutching his cocked-hat, and uttering the immortal *la Garde meurt et ne se rend pas.* I had "The Vengeur" going down, and all the crew hurrahing like madmen. I had Alfred toasting the muffin; Curtius (Haydon) jumping into the gulf; with extracts from Napoleon's bulletins, and a fine authentic portrait of Baron Munchausen.

What man who has been before the public at all has not heard similar wonderful anecdotes regarding himself and his own history? In these humble essaykins I have taken leave to egotize. I cry out about the shoes which pinch me, and, as I fancy, more naturally and pathetically than if my neighbor's corns were trodden under foot. I prattle about the dish which I love, the wine which I like, the talk I heard yesterday — about Brown's absurd airs — Jones's ridiculous elation when he thinks he has caught me in a blunder (a part of the fun, you see, is that Jones will read this, and will perfectly well know that I mean him, and that we shall meet and grin at each other with entire politeness). This is not the highest kind of speculation, I confess, but it is a gossip which amuses some folks. A brisk and honest small-beer will refresh those who do not care for the frothy outpourings of heavier taps. A two of clubs may be a good, handy little card sometimes, and able to tackle a king of diamonds, if it is a little trump. Some philosophers get their wisdom with deep thought and out of ponderous libraries; I pick up my small crumbs of cogitation at a dinner-table; or from Mrs. Mary and Miss Louisa, as they are prattling over their five-o'clock tea.

Well, yesterday at dinner Jucundus was good enough to tell me a story about myself which he had heard from a lady of his acquaintance, to whom I send my best compliments. The tale is this. At nine o'clock on the evening of the 31st of November last, just before sunset, I was seen leaving No. 96, Abbey Road, St. John's Wood, leading two little children by the hand, one of them in a nankeen pelisse, and the other having a mole on the third finger of his left hand (she thinks it was the third finger, but is quite sure it was the left hand). Thence I walked with them to Charles Boroughbridge's, pork and sausage man, No. 29, Upper Theresa Road. Here, whilst I left the little girl innocently eating a polony in the front shop, I and Boroughbridge retired with the boy into the back parlor, where Mrs. Boroughbridge was playing cribbage. She put up the cards and boxes, took out a chopper and a napkin, and we cut the little boy's little throat (which he bore with great pluck and resolution), and made him into sausage-meat by the aid of Purkis's excellent sausage-machine. The little girl at first could not understand her brother's absence, but, under the pretence of taking her to see Mr. Fechter in *Hamlet*, I led her down to the New River at Sadler's Wells, where a body of a child in a nankeen pelisse was subsequently found, and has never been recognized to the present day. And this Mrs. Lynx can aver, because she saw the whole transaction with her own eyes, as she told Mr. Jucundus.

I have altered the little details of the anecdote somewhat. But this story is, I vow and declare, as true as Mrs. Lynx's. Gracious goodness! how do lies begin? What are the averages of lying? Is the same amount of lies told about every man, and do we pretty much all tell the same amount of lies? Is the average greater in Ireland than in Scotland, or *vice versâ* — among women than among men? Is this a lie I am telling now? If I am talking about you, the odds are, perhaps, that it is. I look back at some which have been told about me, and speculate on them with thanks and wonder. Dear friends have told them of me, have told them to me of myself. Have they not to and of you, dear friend? A friend of mine was dining at a large dinner of clergymen, and a story, as true as the sausage story above given, was told regarding me, by one of those reverend divines, in whose frocks sit some anile chatterboxes, as any man who knows this world knows. They take the privilege of their gown. They cabal, and tattle, and hiss, and cackle comminations under their breath. I say the old women of the other sex are not more talkative or more mischievous than some of these. "Such a man ought not to be spoken to," says Gobemouche, narrating the story — and such a story! "And I am surprised he is admitted into society at all." Yes, dear Gobemouche, but the story wasn't true; and I had no more done the wicked deed in question than I had run away with the Queen of Sheba.

I have always longed to know what that story was (or what collection of histories), which a lady had in her mind to whom a servant of mine applied for a place, when I was breaking up my establishment once, and going abroad. Brown went with a very good character from us, which, indeed, she fully deserved after several years' faithful service. But when Mrs. Jones read the name of the person out of whose employment Brown came, "That is quite sufficient," says Mrs. Jones. "You may go. I will never take a servant out of *that* house." Ah, Mrs. Jones, how I should like to know what that crime was, or what that series of villanies, which made you determine never to take a servant out of my house. Do you believe in the story of the little boy and the sausages? Have you swallowed that little minced infant? Have you devoured that young Polonius? Upon my word you have maw enough. We somehow greedily gobble down all stories in which the characters of our friends are chopped up, and believe wrong of them without inquiry. In a late serial work written by this hand, I remember making some pathetic remarks about our propensity to believe ill of our neighbors — and I remember the remarks, not because they were valuable, or novel, or ingenious, but because, within three days after they had appeared in print, the moralist who wrote them, walking home with a friend, heard a story about another friend, which story he straightway believed, and which story was scarcely more true than that sausage fable which is here set down. *O mea culpa, mea maxima culpa!* But though the preacher trips, shall not the doctrine be good? Yea, brethren! Here be the rods. Look you, here are the scourges. Choose me a nice long, swishing, buddy one, light and well-poised in the handle, thick and bushy at the tail. Pick me out a whip-cord thong with some dainty knots in it — and now — we all deserve it — whish, whish, whish. Let us cut into each other all round.

A favorite liar and servant of mine was a man I once had to drive a brougham. He never came to my house, except for orders, and once when he helped to wait at dinner so clumsily that it was agreed we would dispense with his further efforts. The (job) brougham horse used to look dreadfully lean and tired, and the livery-stable keeper complained that we worked him too hard. Now, it turned out that there was a neighboring butcher's lady who liked to ride in a brougham; and Tomkins lent her ours, drove her cheerfully to Richmond and Putney, and, I suppose, took out a payment in mutton-chops. We gave this good Tomkins wine and medicine for his family when sick — we supplied him with little comforts and extras which need not now be remembered — and the grateful creature rewarded us by informing some of our tradesmen whom he honored with his custom, "Mr. Roundabout? Lor' bless you! I carry him up to bed drunk every night in the week." He, Tomkins, being a man of seven stone weight and five feet high; whereas his employer was — but here modesty interferes, and I decline to enter into the avoirdupois question.

Now, what was Tomkins's motive for the utterance and dissemination of these lies? They could further no conceivable end or interest of his own. Had they been true stories, Tomkins's master would still, and reasonably, have been more angry than at the fables. It was but suicidal slander on the part of Tomkins — must come to a discovery — must end in a punishment. The poor wretch had got his place under, as it turned out, a fictitious character. He might have stayed in it, for of course Tomkins had a wife and poor innocent children. He might have had bread, beer, bed, character, coats, coals. He might have nestled in our little island, comfortably sheltered from the storms of life; but we were compelled to cast him out, and send him driving, lonely, perishing, tossing, starving, to sea — to drown. To drown? There be other modes of death whereby rogues die. Good-by, Tomkins. And so the night-cap is put on, and the bolt is drawn for poor T.

Suppose we were to invite volunteers amongst our respected readers to send in little statements of the lies which they know have been told about themselves; what a heap of correspondence, what an exaggeration of malignities, what a crackling bonfire of incendiary falsehoods, might we not gather together! And a lie once set going, having the breath of life breathed into it by the father of lying, and ordered to run its diabolical little course, lives with a prodigious vitality. You say, "*Magna est veritas et prævalebit.*" Psha! Great lies are as great as great truths, and prevail constantly, and day after day. Take an instance or two out of my own little budget. I sit near a gentleman at dinner, and the conversation turns upon a certain anonymous literary performance which at the time is amusing the town. "Oh," says the gentleman, "everybody knows who wrote that paper: it is Momus's." I was a young author at the time, perhaps proud of my bantling: "I beg your pardon," I say, "it was written by your humble servant." "Indeed!" was all that the man replied, and he shrugged his shoulders, turned his back, and talked to his other neighbor. I never heard sarcastic incredulity more finely conveyed than by that "indeed." "Impudent liar," the gentleman's face said, as clear as face could speak. Where was Magna Veritas, and how did she prevail then? She lifted up her voice, she made her appeal, and she was kicked out of court. In New York I read a newspaper criticism one day (by an exile from our shores who has taken up his abode in the Western Republic), commenting upon a letter of mine which had appeared in a contemporary volume, and wherein it was stated that the writer was a lad in such and such a year, and, in point of fact, I was, at the period spoken of, nineteen years of age. "Falsehood, Mr. Roundabout," says the noble critic: "you were then not a lad; you were then six and twenty years of age." You see he knew better than papa and mamma and parish register. It was easier for him to think and say I lied, on a twopenny matter connected with my own affairs, than to imagine he was mistaken. Years ago, in a time when we were very mad wags, Arcturus and myself met a gentleman from China who knew the language. We began to speak Chinese against him. We said we were born in China. We were two to one. We spoke the mandarin dialect with perfect fluency. We had the company with us; as in the old, old days, the squeak of the real pig was voted not to be so natural as the squeak of the sham pig. O Arcturus, the sham pig squeaks in our streets now to the applause of multitudes, and the real porker grunts unheeded in his sty!

I once talked for some little time with an amiable lady: it was for the first time; and I saw an expression of surprise on her kind face, which said as plainly as face could say, "Sir, do you know that up to this moment I have had a certain opinion of you, and that I begin to think I have been mistaken or misled?" I not only know that she had heard evil reports of me, but I know who told her—one of those acute fellows, my dear brethren, of whom we spoke in a previous sermon, who has found me out—found out actions which I never did, found out thoughts and sayings which I never spoke, and judged me accordingly. Ah, my lad! have I found *you* out? *O risum teneatis.* Perhaps the person I am accusing is no more guilty than I.

How comes it that the evil which men say spreads so widely and lasts so long, whilst our good, kind words don't seem somehow to take root and bear blossom? Is it that in the stony hearts of mankind these pretty flowers can't find a place to grow? Certain it is that scandal is good brisk talk, whereas praise of one's neighbor is by no means lively hearing. An acquaintance grilled, scored, devilled, and served with mustard and cayenne pepper, excites the appetite; whereas a slice of cold friend with currant jelly is but a sickly, unrelishing meat.

Now, such being the case, my dear worthy Mrs. Candor, in whom I know there are a hundred good and generous qualities: it being perfectly clear that the good things which we say of our neighbors don't fructify, but somehow perish in the ground where they are dropped, whilst the evil words are wafted by all the winds of scandal, take root in all soils, and flourish amazingly — seeing, I say, that this conversation does not give us a fair chance, suppose we give up censoriousness altogether, and decline uttering our opinions about Brown, Jones, and Robinson (and Mesdames B., J., and R.) at all. We may be mistaken about every one of them, as, please goodness, those anecdote-mongers against whom I have uttered my meek protest have been mistaken about me. We need not go to the extent of saying that Mrs. Manning was an amiable creature, much misunderstood; and Jack Thurtell a gallant, unfortunate fellow, not near so black as he was painted; but we will try and avoid personalities altogether in talk, won't we? We will range the fields of science, dear madam, and communicate to each other the pleasing results of our studies. We will, if you please, examine the infinitesimal wonders of nature through the microscope. We will cultivate entomology. We will sit with our arms round each other's waists on the *pons asinorum*, and see the stream of mathematics flow beneath. We will take refuge in cards, and play at "beggar my neighbor," not abuse my neighbor. We will go to the Zoological Gardens and talk freely about the gorilla and his kindred, but not talk about people who can talk in their turn. Suppose we praise the High Church? we offend the Low Church. The Broad Church? High and Low are both offended. What do you think of Lord Derby as a politician? and what is your opinion of Lord Palmerston? If you please, will you play me those lovely variations of "In my cottage near a wood?" It is a charming air (you know it in French, I suppose? *Ah! te dirai-je maman!*) and was a favorite with poor Marie Antoinette. I say "poor" because I have a right to speak with pity of a sovereign who was renowned for so much beauty and so much misfortune. But as for giving any opinion on her conduct, saying that she was good or bad, or indifferent, goodness forbid! We have agreed we will not be censorious. Let us have a game at cards — at *écarté*, if you please. You deal. I ask for cards. I lead the deuce of clubs. . . .

What? there is no deuce! Deuce take it! What? People *will* go on talking about their neighbors, and won't have their mouths stopped by cards, or ever so much microscopes and aquariums? Ah, my poor dear Mrs. Candor, I agree with you. By the way, did you ever see any thing like Lady Godiva Trotter's dress last night? People *will* go on chattering, although we hold our tongues; and, after all, my good soul, what will their scandal matter a hundred years hence?

SMALL-BEER CHRONICLE.

Not long since, at a certain banquet, I had the good fortune to sit by Doctor Polymathesis, who knows every thing, and who, about the time when the claret made its appearance, mentioned that old dictum of the grumbling Oxford Don, that "All Claret *would be port if it could!*" Imbibing a bumper of one or the other not ungratefully, I thought to myself, "Here surely, Mr. Roundabout, is a good text for one of your reverence's sermons." Let us apply to the human race, dear brethren, what is here said of the vintages of Portugal and Gascony, and we shall have no difficulty in perceiving how many clarets aspire to be ports in their way; how most men and women of our acquaintance, how we ourselves, are Aquitanians giving ourselves Lusitanian airs; how we wish to have credit for being stronger, braver, more beautiful, more worthy, than we really are.

Nay, the beginning of this hypocrisy — a desire to excel, a desire to be hearty, fruity, generous, strength-imparting — is a virtuous and noble ambition; and it is most difficult for a man in his own case, or his neighbor's, to say at what point this ambition transgresses the boundary of virtue, and becomes vanity, pretence, and self-seeking. You are a poor man, let us say, showing a bold face to adverse fortune, and wearing a confident aspect. Your purse is very narrow, but you owe no man a penny; your means are scanty, but your wife's gown is decent; your old coat well brushed; your children at a good school; you grumble to no one; ask favors of no one; truckle to no neighbors on account of their superior rank, or (a worse, and a meaner, and a more common crime still) envy none for their better fortune. To all outward appearances you are as well to do as your neighbors, who have thrice your income. There may be in this case some little mixture of pretension in your life and behavior. You certainly *do* put on a smiling face whilst fortune is pinching you. Your wife and girls, so smart and neat at evening parties, are cutting, patching, and cobbling all day to make both ends of life's haberdashery meet. You give a friend a bottle of wine on occasion, but are content yourself with a glass of whiskey and water. You avoid a cab, saying that of all things you like to walk home after dinner (which you know, my good friend, is a fib). I grant you that in this scheme of life there does enter ever so little hypocrisy; that this claret is loaded, as it were; but your desire to *portify* yourself is amiable, is pardonable, is perhaps honorable: and were there no other hypocrisies than yours in the world, we should be a set of worthy fellows; and sermonizers, moralizers, satirizers, would have to hold their tongues, and go to some other trade to get a living.

But you know you *will* step over that boundary line of virtue and modesty, into the district where humbug and vanity begin, and there the moralizer catches you, and makes an example of you. For instance, in a certain novel in another place, my friend Mr. Talbot Twysden is mentioned — a man whom you and I know to be a wretched ordinaire, but who persists in treating himself as if he was the finest '20 port. In our Britain there are hundreds of men like him; forever striving to swell beyond their natural size, to strain beyond their natural strength, to step beyond their natural stride. Search, search within your own waistcoats, dear brethren — *you* know in your hearts, which of your ordinaire qualities you would pass off, and fain consider as first-rate port. And why not you yourself, Mr. Preacher? says the congregation. Dearly beloved, neither in nor out of this pulpit do I profess to be bigger, or cleverer, or wiser, or better than any of you. A short while since, a certain Reviewer announced that I gave myself great pretensions as a philosopher. I a philosopher! I advance pretensions! My dear Saturday friend, And you? Don't you teach every thing to everybody? and punish the naughty boys if they don't learn as you bid them? You teach politics to Lord John and Mr. Gladstone. You teach poets how to write; painters, how to paint; gentlemen, manners; and opera-dancers, how to pirouette. I was not a little amused of late by an instance of the modesty of our Saturday friend, who, more Athenian than the Athenians, and àpropos of a Greek book by a Greek author, sat down and gravely showed the Greek gentleman how to write his own language.

No, I do not, as far as I know, try to be port at all; but offer in these presents, a sound genuine ordinaire, at 18*s.* per doz. let us say, grown on my own hill-side, and offered *de bon cœur* to those who will sit down under my *tonnelle*, and have a half-hour's drink and gossip. It is none of your hot porto, my friend. I know there is much better and stronger liquor elsewhere. Some pronounce it sour: some say it is thin; some that it has woefully lost its flavor. This may or may not be true. There are good and bad years; years that surprise everybody; years of which the produce is small and bad, or rich and plentiful. But if my tap is not genuine it is naught, and no man should give himself the trouble to drink it. I do not even say that I would be port if I could; knowing that port (by which I would imply much stronger, deeper, richer, and more durable liquor than my vineyard can furnish) is not relished by all palates or suitable to all heads. We will assume, then, dear brother, that you and I are tolerably modest people; and, ourselves being thus out of the question, proceed to show how pretentious our neighbors are, and how very many of them would be port if they could.

Have you never seen a small man from college placed amongst great folk, and giving himself the airs of a man of fashion? He goes back to his common room with fond reminiscences of Ermine Castle or Strawberry Hall. He writes to the dear countess, to say that dear Lord Lollypop is getting on very well at St. Boniface, and that the accident which he met with in a scuffle with an inebriated bargeman only showed his spirit and honor, and will not permanently disfigure his lordship's nose. He gets his clothes from dear Lollypop's London tailor, and wears a mauve or magenta tie when he rides out to see the hounds. A love of fashionable people is a weakness, I do not say of all, but of some tutors. Witness that Eton tutor t'other day, who intimated that in Cornhill we could not understand the perfect purity, delicacy, and refinement of those genteel families who sent their sons to Eton. O usher, *mon ami!* Old Sam Johnson, who, too, had been an usher in his early life, kept a little of that weakness always. Suppose Goldsmith had knocked him up at three in the morning and proposed a boat to Greenwich, as Topham Beauclerc and his friends did, would he have said, "What, my boy, are you for a frolic? I'm with you!" and gone and put on his clothes? Rather he would have pitched poor Goldsmith down stairs. He would have liked to be port if he could. Of course *we* wouldn't. Our opinion of the Portugal grape is known. It grows very high, and is very sour, and we don't go for that kind of grape at all.

"I was walking with Mr. Fox"— and sure this anecdote comes very pat after the grapes—"I was walking with Mr. Fox in the Louvre," says Benjamin West (*apud* some paper I have just been reading), "and I remarked how many people turned round to look at *me*. This shows the respect of the French for the fine arts." This is a curious instance of a very small claret indeed, which imagined itself to be port of the strongest body. There are not many instances of a faith so deep, so simple so satisfactory, as this. I have met many who would like to be port; but with few of the Gascon sort, who absolutely believed they *were* port. George III. believed in West's port, and thought Reynolds's overrated stuff. When I saw West's pictures at Philadelphia, I looked at them with astonishment and awe. Hide, blushing glory, hide your head under your old night-cap. O immortality! is this the end of you? Did any of you, my dear brethren, ever try and read "Blackmore's Poems," or "The Epics of Baour-Lormian," or "The Henriade," or — what shall we say? — Pollok's "Course of Time"? They were thought to be more lasting than brass by some people, and where are they now? And *our* masterpieces of literature — *our* ports — that, if not immortal, at any rate are to last their fifty, their hundred years — oh, sirs, don't you think a very small cellar will hold them?

Those poor people in brass, on pedestals, hectoring about Trafalgar Square and that neighborhood, don't you think many of them — apart even from the ridiculous execution — cut rather a ridiculous figure, and that we are too eager to set up our ordinaire heroism and talent for port? A Duke of Wellington or two I will grant, though even of these idols a moderate supply will be sufficient. Some years ago, a famous and witty French critic was in London, with whom I walked the streets. I am ashamed to say that I informed him (being in hopes that he was about to write some papers regarding the manners and customs of this country) that all the statues he saw represented the Duke of Wellington. That on the arch opposite Apsley House? the Duke in a cloak, and cocked-hat, on horseback. That behind Apsley House in an airy fig-leaf costume? the Duke again. That in Cockspur Street? the Duke with a pigtail — and so on. I showed him an army of Dukes. There are many bronze heroes who after a few years look already as foolish, awkward, and out of place as a man, say at Shoolbred's or Swan and Edgar's. For example, those three Grenadiers in Pall Mall, who have been up only a few months, don't you pity those unhappy household troops, who have to stand frowning and looking fierce there; and think they would like to step down and go to barracks? That they fought very bravely there is no doubt; but so did the Russians fight very bravely; and the French fight very bravely; and so did Colonel Jones and the 99th, and Colonel Brown and the 100th; and I say again that ordinaire should not give itself port airs, and that an honest ordinaire would blush to be found swaggering so. I am sure if you could consult the Duke of York, who is impaled on his column between the two clubs, and ask his late Royal Highness whether he thought he ought to remain there, he would say no. A brave, worthy man, not a braggart or boaster, to be put upon that heroic perch must be painful to him. Lord George Bentinck, I suppose, being in the midst of the family park in Cavendish Square, may conceive that he has a right to remain in his place. But look at William of Cumberland, with his hat cocked over his eye, prancing behind Lord George on his Roman-nosed charger; he, depend on it, would be for getting off his horse if he had the permission. He did not hesitate about trifles, as we know; but he was a very truth-telling and honorable soldier: and as for heroic rank and statuesque dignity, I would wager a dozen of '20 port against a bottle of pure and sound Bordeaux, at 18s. per dozen (bottles included), that he never would think of claiming any such absurd distinction. They have got a statue of Thomas Moore at Dublin, I hear. Is he on horseback? Some men should have, say, a fifty years' lease of glory. After a while some gentlemen now in brass should go to the melting furnace, and reappear in some other gentleman's shape. Lately I saw that Melville column rising over Edinburgh; come, good men and true, don't you feel a little awkward and uneasy when you walk under it? Who was this to stand in heroic places? and is yon the man whom Scotchmen most delight to honor? I must own deferentially that there is a tendency in North Britain to over-esteem its heroes. Scotch ale is very good and strong, but it is not stronger than all the other beer in the world, as some Scottish patriots would insist. When there has been a war, and stout old Sandy Sansculotte returns home from India or Crimea, what a bagpiping, shouting, hurraying, and self-glorification takes place round about him! You would fancy, to hear Mc Orator after dinner, that the Scotch had fought all the battles, killed all the Russians, Indian rebels, or what not. In Cupar-Fife, there's a little inn called "The Battle of Waterloo," and what do you think the sign is? "The Battle of Waterloo" is one broad Scotchman laying about him with a broadsword. Yes, yes, my dear Mac, you are wise, you are good, you are clever, you are handsome, you are brave, you are rich, &c.; but so is Jones over the border. Scotch salmon is good, but there are other good fish in the sea. I once heard a Scotchman lecture on poetry in London. Of course the pieces he selected were chiefly by Scottish authors, and Walter Scott was his favorite poet. I whispered to my neighbor, who was a Scotchman (by the way, the audience were almost all Scotch, and the room was All-Mac's — I beg your pardon, but I could't help it, I really couldn't help it) — "The professor has said the best poet was a Scotchman: I wager that he will say the worst poet was a Scotchman, too." And sure enough that worst poet, when he made his appearance, was a Northern Briton.

And as we are talking of bragging, and I am on my travels, can I forget one mighty republic — one — two mighty republics, where people are notoriously fond of passing off their claret for port? I am very glad, for the sake of a kind friend, that there is a great and influential party in the United, and, I trust, in the Confederate States,* who believe that Catawba wine is better than the best Champagne. Opposite that famous old White House at Washington, whereof I shall ever have a grateful memory, they have set up an equestrian statue of General Jackson, by a self-taught American artist of no inconsiderable genius and skill. At an evening party a member of Congress seized me in a corner of the room, and asked me if I did not think this was *the finest equestrian statue in the world?* How was I to deal with this plain question, put to me in a corner? I was bound to reply, and accordingly said that I did *not* think it was the finest statue in the world. "Well, sir," says the member of Congress, "but you must remember that Mr. M—— had never seen a statue when he made this!" I suggested that to see other statues might do Mr. M—— no harm. Nor was any man more willing to own his defects, or more modest regarding his merits, than the sculptor himself, whom I met subsequently. But oh! what a charming article there was in a Washington paper next day about the impertinence of criticism and offensive tone of arrogance which Englishmen adopted towards men and works of genius in America! "Who was this man, who," &c., &c.? The Washington writer was angry because I would not accept this American claret as the finest port-wine in the world. Ah, me! It is about blood and not wine that the quarrel now is, and who shall foretell its end?

How much claret that would be port if it could is handed about in every society! In the House of Commons what small-beer orators try to pass for strong? Stay: have I a spite against any one? It is a fact that the wife of the member for Bungay has left off asking me and Mrs. Roundabout to her evening parties. Now is the time to have a slap at him. I will say that he was always overrated, and that now he is lamentably falling off even from what he has been. I will back the Member for Stoke Poges against him; and show that the dashing young Member for Islington is a far sounder man than either. Have I any little literary animosities? Of course not. Men of letters never have. Otherwise, how I could serve out a competitor here, make a face over his works, and show that his would-be port is very meagre ordinaire indeed! Nonsense, man! Why so squeamish? Do they spare *you!* Now you have the whip in your hand, won't you lay on? You used to be a pretty whip enough as a young man, and liked it too. Is there no enemy who would be the better for

* Written in July, 1861.

a little thonging? No. I have militated in former times, not without glory; but I grow peaceable as I grow old. And if I have a literary enemy, why, he will probably write a book ere long, and then it will be *his* turn, and my favorite review will be down upon him.

My brethren, these sermons are professedly short; for I have that opinion of my dear congregation, which leads me to think that were I to preach at great length they would yawn, stamp, make noises, and perhaps go straightway out of church; and yet with this text I protest I could go on for hours. What multitudes of men, what multitudes of women, my dears, pass off their ordinaire for port, their small beer for strong! In literature, in politics, in the army, the navy, the church, at the bar, in the world, what an immense quantity of cheap liquor is made to do service for better sorts! Ask Sergeant Roland his opinion of Oliver Q.C. "Ordinaire, my good fellow, ordinaire, with a port-wine label." Ask Oliver his opinion of Roland. "Never was a man so overrated by the world and by himself." Ask Tweedledumski his opinion of Tweedledeestein's performance, "A quack, my tear sir! an ignoramus, I geef you my vort? He gombose an opera! He is not fit to make dance a bear!" Ask Paddington and Buckmister, those two "swells" of fashion, what they think of each other? They are notorious ordinaire. You and I remember when they passed for very small wine, and now how high and mighty they have become! What do you say to Tomkins's sermons? Ordinaire, trying to go down as orthodox port, and very meagre ordinaire too! To Hopkins's historical works? — to Pumkins's poetry? Ordinaire, ordinaire again — thin, feeble, overrated; and so down the whole list. And when we have done discussing our men friends, have we not all the women? Do these not advance absurd pretensions? Do these never give themselves airs? With feeble brains, don't they often set up to be *esprits forts?* Don't they pretend to be women of fashion, and cut their betters? Don't they try and pass off their ordinary-looking girls as beauties of the first order? Every man in his circle knows women who give themselves airs, and to whom we can apply the port-wine simile.

Come, my friends. Here is enough of ordinaire and port for to-day. My bottle has run out. Will anybody have any more? Let us go up stairs, and get a cup of tea from the ladies.

OGRES.

I DARESAY the reader has remarked that the upright and independent vowel, which stands in the vowel-list between E and O, has formed the subject of the main part of these essays. How does that vowel feel this morning?—fresh, good-humored, and lively? The Roundabout lines, which fall from this pen, are correspondingly brisk and cheerful. Has any thing, on the contrary, disagreed with the vowel? Has its rest been disturbed, or was yesterday's dinner too good, or yesterday's wine not good enough? Under such circumstances, a darkling, misanthropic tinge, no doubt, is cast upon the paper. The jokes, if attempted, are elaborate and dreary. The bitter temper breaks out. That sneering manner is adopted, which you know, and which exhibits itself so especially when the writer is speaking about women. A moody carelessness comes over him. He sees no good in any body or thing: and treats gentlemen, ladies, history, and things in general, with a like gloomy flippancy. Agreed. When the vowel in question is in that mood, if you like airy gayety and tender gushing benevolence —if you want to be satisfied with yourself and the rest of your fellow-beings; I recommend you, my dear creature, to go to some other shop in Cornhill, or turn to some other article. There are moods in the mind of the vowel of which we are speaking, when it is ill conditioned and captious. Who always keeps good health, and good humor? Do not philosophers grumble? Are not sages sometimes out of temper? and do not angel-women go off in tantrums? To-day my mood is dark. I scowl as I dip my pen in the inkstand.

Here is the day come round — for every thing here is done with the utmost regularity; — intellectual labor, sixteen hours; meals, thirty-two minutes; exercise, a hundred and forty-eight minutes; conversation with the family, chiefly literary, and about the housekeeping, one hour and four minutes; sleep, three hours and fifteen minutes (at the end of the month, when the Magazine is complete, I own I take eight minutes more); and the rest for the toilette and the world. Well, I say, "The Roundabout Paper Day" being come, and the subject long since settled in my mind, an excellent subject — a most telling, lively and popular subject — I go to breakfast determined to finish that meal in nine and three-fourths minutes, as usual, and then retire to my desk and work, when — oh, provoking! — here in the paper is the very subject treated, on which I was going to write! Yesterday another paper which I saw treated it — and of course, as I need not tell you, spoiled it. Last Saturday, another paper had an article on the subject; perhaps you may guess what it was — but I won't tell you. Only this is true, my favorite subject, which was about to make the best paper we have had for a long time: my bird, my game that I was going to shoot and serve up with such a delicate sauce, has been found by other sportsmen; and pop, pop, pop, a half-dozen of guns have banged at it, mangled it, and brought it down.

"And can't you take some other text?" say you. All this is mighty well. But if you have set your heart on a certain dish for dinner, be it cold boiled veal, or what you will, and they bring you turtle and venison, don't you feel disappointed? During your walk you have been making up your mind that that cold meat, with moderation and a pickle, will be a very sufficient dinner: you have accustomed your thoughts to it; and here, in place of it, is a turkey, surrounded by coarse sausages, or a reeking pigeon-pie or a fulsome roast pig. I have known many a good and kind man made furiously angry by such a *contretemps*. I have known him lose his temper, call his wife and servants names, and a whole household made miserable. If, then, as is notoriously the case, it is too dangerous to balk a man about his dinner, how much more about his article? I came to my meal with an ogre-like appetite and gusto. Fee, faw, fum! Wife, where is that tender little Princekin? Have you trussed him, and did you stuff him nicely, and have you taken care to baste him and do him, not too brown, as I told you? Quick! I am hungry! I begin to whet my knife, to roll my eyes about, and roar, and clap my huge chest like a gorilla; and then my poor Ogrina has to tell me that the little princes have all run away whilst she was in the kitchen, making the paste to bake them in! I pause in the description. I won't condescend to report the bad language, which you know must ensue, when an ogre, whose mind is ill regulated, and whose habits of self-indulgence are notorious, finds himself disappointed of his greedy hopes. What treatment of his wife, what abuse and brutal behavior to his children, who, though ogrillons, are children! My dears, you may fancy, and need not ask my delicate pen to describe, the language and behavior of a vulgar, coarse, greedy, large man with an immense mouth and teeth, which are too frequently employed in the gobbling and crunching of raw man's meat.

And in this circuitous way you see

I have reached my present subject, which is, Ogres. You fancy they are dead or only fictitious characters — mythical representatives of strength, cruelty, stupidity, and lust for blood? Though they had seven-leagued boots, you remember all sorts of little whipping-snapping Tom Thumbs used to elude and outrun them. They were so stupid that they gave into the most shallow ambuscades and artifices: witness that well-known ogre, who, because Jack cut open the hasty-pudding, instantly ripped open his own stupid waistcoat and interior. They were cruel, brutal, disgusting, with their sharpened teeth, immense knives, and roaring voices! but they always ended by being overcome by little Tom Thumbkins, or some other smart little champion.

Yes; they were conquered in the end there is no doubt. They plunged headlong (and uttering the most frightful bad language) into some pit where Jack came with his smart *couteau de chasse*, and whipped their brutal heads off. They would be going to devour maidens,

> "But ever when it seemed
> Their need was at the sorest,
> A knight, in armor bright,
> Came riding through the forest."

And down, after a combat, would go the brutal persecutor, with a lance through his midriff. Yes, I say, this is very true and well. But you remember that round the ogre's cave the ground was covered, for hundreds and hundreds of yards, *with the bones of the victims* whom he had lured into the castle. Many knights and maids came to him and perished under his knife and teeth. Were dragons the same as ogres? monsters dwelling in caverns, whence they rushed, attired in plate armor, wielding pikes and torches, and destroying stray passengers who passed by their lair? Monsters, brutes, rapacious tyrants, ruffians, as they were, doubtless they ended by being overcome. But, before they were destroyed, they did a deal of mischief. The bones round their caves were countless. They had sent many brave souls to Hades, before their own fled, howling out of their rascal carcasses, to the same place of gloom.

There is no greater mistake than to suppose that fairies, champions, distressed damsels, and by consequence ogres, have ceased to exist. It may not be *ogreable* to them (pardon the horrible pleasantry, but as I am writing in the solitude of my chamber, I am grinding my teeth — yelling, roaring, and cursing — brandishing my scissors and paper-cutter, and as it were, have become an ogre). I say there is no greater mistake than to suppose that ogres have ceased to exist. We all *know* ogres. Their caverns are round us, and about us. There are the castles of several ogres within a mile of the spot where I write. I think some of them suspect I am an ogre myself. I am not: but I know they are. I visit them. I don't mean to say that they take a cold roast prince out of the cupboard, and have a cannibal feast before *me*. But I see the bones lying about the roads to their houses, and in the areas and gardens. Politeness, of course, prevents me from making any remarks; but I know them well enough. One of the ways to know 'em is to watch the scared looks of the ogres' wives and children. They lead an awful life. They are present at dreadful cruelties. In their excesses those ogres will stab about, and kill not only strangers who happen to call in and ask a night's lodging, but they will outrage, murder, and chop up their own kin. We all know ogres, I say, and have been in their dens often. It is not necessary that ogres who ask you to dine should offer their guests the *peculiar dish* which they like. They cannot always get a Tom Thumb family. They eat mutton and beef too; and I dare say even go out to tea, and invite you to drink it. But I tell you there are numbers of them going about in the world. And now you have my word for it, and this little hint, it is quite curious what an interest society may be made to have for you, by your determining to find out the ogres you meet there.

What does the man mean? says Mrs. Downright, to whom a joke is a very grave thing. I mean, madam, that in the company assembled in your genteel drawing-room, who bow here and there, and smirk in white neckcloths, you receive men who elbow through life successfully enough, but who are ogres in private: men wicked, false, rapacious, flattering; cruel hectors at home, smiling courtiers abroad; causing wives, children, servants, parents, to tremble before them, and smiling and bowing as they bid strangers welcome into their castles. I say, there are men who have crunched the bones of victim after victim; in whose closets lie skeletons picked frightfully clean. When these ogres come out into the world, you don't suppose they show their knives, and their great teeth? A neat simple white neckcloth, a merry, rather obsequious manner, a cadaverous look, perhaps, now and again, and a rather dreadful grin; but I know ogres very considerably respected: and when you hint to such and such a man, "My dear sir, Mr. Sharpus, whom you appear to like, is, I assure you, a most dreadful cannibal;" the gentleman cries, "Oh, psha, nonsense! Dare say not so black as he is painted. Dare say not worse than his neighbors." We condone every thing in this country — private treason, falsehood, flattery, cruelty at home, roguery, and double dealing. What! Do you mean to say in your acquaintance you don't know ogres guilty of countless crimes of fraud and force, and that knowing them you don't shake hands with them; dine with them at your table; and meet them at their own? Depend upon it, in the time when there were real live ogres in real caverns or castles, gobbling up real knights and virgins, when they went into the world — the neighboring market-town, let us say, or earl's castle — though their nature and reputation were pretty well known, their notorious foibles were never alluded to. You would say, "What, Blunderbore, my boy! How do you do? How well and fresh you look! What's the receipt you have for keeping so young and rosy?" And your wife would softly ask after Mrs. Blunderbore and the dear children. Or it would be, "My dear Humguffin! try that pork. It is home-bred, home-fed, and, I promise you, tender. Tell me if you think it as good as yours? John, a glass of Burgundy to Colonel Humguffin!" You don't suppose there would be any unpleasant allusions to disagreeable home-reports regarding Humguffin's manner of furnishing his larder? I say we all of us know ogres. We shake hands and dine with ogres. And if inconvenient moralists tell us we are cowards for our pains, we turn round with a *tu quoque*, or say that we don't meddle with other folk's affairs; that people are much less black than they are painted, and so on. What! Won't half the county go to Ogreham Castle? Won't some of the clergy say grace at dinner? Won't the mothers bring their daughters to dance with the young Rawheads? And if Lady Ogreham happens to die — I won't say to go the way of all flesh, that is too revolting — I say if Ogreham is a widower, do you aver, on your conscience and honor, that mothers will not be found to offer their young girls to supply the lamented lady's place? How stale this misanthropy is! Something must have disagreed with this cynic. Yes, my good woman. I dare say you would like to call another subject. Yes, my fine fellow; ogre at home; supple as a dancing-master abroad, and shaking in thy pumps, and wearing a horrible grin of sham gayety to conceal thy terror, lest I should point thee out: — thou art prosperous and honored, art thou? I say thou hast been a tyrant and a robber. Thou hast plundered the poor. Thou hast bullied the weak. Thou hast laid violent hands on the goods of the innocent and confiding. Thou hast made a prey of the meek and gentle who asked for thy protection. Thou hast been hard to thy kinsfolk, and cruel to thy family. Go, monster! Ah, when shall little Jack come and drill daylight through thy wicked cannibal carcass? I see the ogre pass on, bowing right and left to the company; and he gives a dreadful sidelong glance of suspicion as he is talking to my lord bishop in the corner there.

Ogres in our days need not be giants at all. In former times, and in children's books, where it is necessary to paint your moral in such large letters that there can be no mistake about it, ogres are made with that enormous mouth and *ratelier* which you know of, and with which they can swallow down a baby, almost without using that great knife which they always carry. They are too cunning now-a-days. They go about in society, slim, small, quietly dressed, and showing no especially great appetite. In my own young days there used to be play ogres — men who would devour a young fellow in one sitting, and leave him without a bit of flesh on his bones. They were quiet, gentlemanlike-looking people. They got the young fellow into their cave. Champagne pâté-de-foie-gras, and numberless good things, were handed about; and then, having eaten, the young man was devoured in his turn. I believe these card and dice ogres have died away almost as entirely as the hasty-pudding giants whom Tom Thumb overcame. Now, there are ogres in City courts who lure you into their dens. About our Cornish mines I am told there are many most plausible ogres, who tempt you into their caverns, and pick your bones there. In a certain newspaper there used to be lately a whole column of advertisements from ogres who would put on the most plausible, nay, piteous appearance, in order to inveigle their victims. You would read, "A tradesman, established for seventy years in the City, and known, and much respected by Messrs. N. M. Rothschild and Baring Brothers, has pressing need for three pounds until next Saturday. He can give security for half a million, and forty thousand pounds will be given for the use of the loan," and so on; or, "An influential body of capitalists are about to establish a company, of which the business will be enormous and the profits proportionately prodigious. They will require A SECRETARY, of good address and appearance, at a salary of two thousand per annum. He need not be able to write, but address and manners are absolutely necessary. As a mark of confidence in the company, he will have to deposit," &c.; or, "A young widow (of pleasing manners and appearance) who has a pressing necessity for four pounds ten for three weeks, offers her Erard's grand piano valued at three hundred guineas; a diamond cross of eight hundred pounds; and board and lodging in her elegant villa near Banbury Cross, with the best references and society, in return for the loan." I suspect these people are ogres. There are ogres and ogres. Polyphemus was a great, tall, one-eyed, notorious ogre, fetching his victims out of a hole, and gobbling them one after another. There could be no mistake about him. But so were the Sirens ogres — pretty blue-eyed things, peeping at you coaxingly from out of the water, and singing their melodious wheedles. And the bones round their caves were more numerous than the ribs, skulls, and thigh-bones round the cavern of hulking Polypheme.

To the castle-gates of some of these monsters up rides the dapper champion of the pen; puffs boldly upon the horn which hangs by the chain; enters the hall resolutely, and challenges the big tyrant sulking within.

We defy him to combat, the enormous roaring ruffian! We give him a meeting on the green plain before his castle. Green? No wonder it should be green: it is manured with human bones. After a few graceful wheels and curvets, we take our ground. We stoop over our saddle. 'Tis but to kiss the locket of our lady-love's hair. And now the visor is up: the lance is in rest (Gillott's iron is the point for me). A touch of the spur in the gallant sides of Pegasus, and we gallop at the great brute.

"Cut off his ugly head, Flibbertygibbet, my squire!" And who are these who pour out of the castle? the imprisoned maidens, the maltreated widows, the poor old hoary grandfathers, who have been locked up in the dungeons these scores and scores of years, writhing under the tyranny of that ruffian! Ah ye knights of the pen! May honor be your shield, and truth tip your lances! Be gentle to all gentle people. Be modest to women. Be tender to children. And as for the Ogre Humbug, out sword, and have at him.

ON TWO ROUNDABOUT PAPERS WHICH I INTENDED TO WRITE.*

We have all heard of a place paved with good intentions:—a place which I take to be a very dismal, useless and unsatisfactory terminus for many pleasant thoughts, kindly fancies, gentle wishes, merry little quips and pranks, harmless jokes which die as it were the moment of their birth. Poor little children of the brain! He was a dreary theologian who huddled you under such a melancholy cenotaph, and laid you in the vaults under the flagstones of Hades! I trust that some of the best actions we have all of us committed in our lives have been committed in fancy. It is not all wickedness we are thinking, *que diable!* Some of our thoughts are bad enough, I grant you. Many a one you and I have had here below. Ah, mercy, what a monster! what crooked horns! what leering eyes! what a flaming mouth! what cloven feet, and what a hideous writhing tail! Oh, let us fall down on our knees, repeat our most potent exorcisms, and overcome the brute. Spread your black pinions, fly—fly to the dusky realms of Eblis, and bury thyself under the paving-stones of his hall, dark genie! But *all* thoughts are not so. No—no. There are the pure: there are the kind: there are the gentle. There are sweet unspoken thanks before a fair scene of nature: at a sun-setting below a glorious sea; or a moon and a host of stars shining over it; at a bunch of children playing in the street, or a group of flowers by the hedge-side, or a bird singing there. At a hundred moments or occurrences of the day good thoughts pass through the mind, let us trust, which never are spoken; prayers are made which never are said; and Te Deum is sung without church, clerk, choristers, parson, or organ. Why, there's my enemy: who got the place I wanted; who maligned me to the woman I wanted to be well with; who supplanted me in the good graces of my patron. I don't say any thing about the matter: but, my poor old enemy, in my secret mind I have movements of as tender charity towards you, you old scoundrel, as ever I had when we were boys together at school. You ruffian! do you fancy I forget that we were fond of each other? We are still. We share our toffy; go halves at the tuck-shop; do each other's exercises; prompt each other with the word in construing or repetition; and tell the most frightful fibs to prevent each other from being found out. We meet each other in public. Ware a fight! Get them into different parts

* The following paper was written in 1861, after the extraordinary affray between Major Murray and the money-lender in a house in Northumberland Street, Strand, and subsequent to the appearance of M. Du Chaillu's book on Gorillas.

of the room! Our friends hustle round us. Capulet and Montague are not more at odds than the houses of Roundabout and Wrightabout, let us say. It is, "My dear Mrs. Buffer, do kindly put yourself in the chair between those two men!" Or, "My dear Wrightabout, will you take that charming Lady Blancmange down to supper? She adores your poems; and gave five shillings for your autograph at the fancy fair." In like manner the peace-makers gather round Roundabout on his part; he is carried to a distant corner, and coaxed out of the way of the enemy with whom he is at feud.

When we meet in the Square at Verona, out flash rapiers, and we fall to. But in his private mind Tybalt owns that Mercutio has a rare wit, and Mercutio is sure that his adversary is a gallant gentleman. Look at the amphitheatre yonder. You do not suppose those gladiators who fought and perished, as hundreds of spectators in that grim Circus held thumbs down, and cried, "Kill, kill!" — you do not suppose the combatants of necessity hated each other? No more than the celebrated trained bands of literary sword-and-buckler men hate the adversaries whom they meet in the arena. They engage at the given signal; feint and parry; slash, poke, rip each other open, dismember limbs, and hew off noses: but in the way of business, and, I trust, with mutual private esteem. For instance, I salute the warriors of the Superfine Company with the honors due among warriors. Here's at you, Spartacus, my lad. A hit, I acknowledge. A palpable hit! Ha! how do you like that poke in the eye in return? When the trumpets sing truce, or the spectators are tired, we bow to the noble company: withdraw; and get a cool glass of wine in our *rendezvous des braves gladiateurs.*

By the way, I saw that amphitheatre of Verona under the strange light of a lurid eclipse some years ago: and I have been there in spirit for these twenty lines past, under a vast gusty awning, now with twenty thousand fellow-citizens looking on from the benches, now in the circus itself, a grim gladiator with sword and net, or a meek martyr — was I? — brought out to be gobbled up by the lions? or a huge, shaggy, tawny lion myself, on whom the dogs were going to be set? What a day of excitement I have had to be sure! But I must get away from Verona, or who knows how much farther the Roundabout Pegasus may carry me?

We were saying, my Muse, before we dropped and perched on earth for a couple of sentences, that our unsaid words were in some limbo or other, as real as those we have uttered; that the thoughts which have passed through our brains are as actual as any to which our tongues and pens have given currency. For instance, besides what is here hinted at, I have thought ever so much more about Verona: about an early Christian church I saw there; about a great dish of rice we had at the inn; about the bugs there; about ever so many more details of that day's journey from Milan to Venice; about lake Garda, which lay on the way from Milan, and so forth. I say what fine things we have thought of, haven't we, all of us? Ah, what a fine tragedy that was I thought of, and never wrote! On the day of the dinner of the Oystermongers' Company, what a noble speech I thought of in the cab, and broke down — I don't mean the cab, but the speech. Ah, if you could but read some of the unwritten Roundabout Papers—how you would be amused! Aha! my friend, I catch you saying, "Well, then, I wish *this* was unwritten with all my heart." Very good. I owe you one. I do confess a hit, a palpable hit.

One day in the past month, as I was reclining on the bench of thought, with that ocean "The Times" newspaper spread before me, the ocean cast up on the shore at my feet two famous subjects for Roundabout Papers, and

I picked up those waifs, and treasured them away until I could polish them and bring them to market. That scheme is not to be carried out. I can't write about those subjects. And though I cannot write about them, I may surely tell what are the subjects I am going not to write about.

The first was that Northumberland Street encounter, which all the papers have narrated. Have any novelists of our days a scene and catastrophe more strange and terrible than this which occurs at noonday within a few yards of the greatest thoroughfare in Europe? At the theatres they have a new name for their melodramatic pieces, and call them "Sensation Dramas." What a sensation Drama this is! What have people been flocking to see at the Adelphi Theatre for the last hundred and fifty nights? A woman pitched overboard out of a boat, and a certain Miles taking a tremendous "header," and bringing her to shore? Bagatelle! What is this compared to the real life-drama, of which a mid-day representation takes place just opposite the Adelphi in Northumberland Street? The brave Dumas, the intrepid Ainsworth, the terrible Eugene Sue, the cold-shudder-inspiring "Woman in White," the astounding author of the "Mysteries of the Court of London," never invented any thing more tremendous than this. It might have happened to you and me. We want to borrow a little money. We are directed to an agent. We propose a pecuniary transaction at a short date. He goes into the next room, as we fancy, to get the bank-notes, and returns with "two very pretty, delicate little ivory-handled pistols," and blows a portion of our heads off. After this, what is the use of being squeamish about the probabilities and possibilities in the writing of fiction? Years ago I remember making merry over a play of Dumas, called *Kean*, in which the "Coal-Hole Tavern" was represented on the Thames, with a fleet of pirate-ships moored alongside. Pirate-ships? Why not? What a cavern of terror was this in Northumberland Street, with its splendid furniture covered with dust, its empty bottles, in the midst of which sits a grim "agent," amusing himself by firing pistols, aiming at the unconscious mantelpiece, or at the heads of his customers!

After this, what is not possible? It is possible Hungerford Market is mined, and will explode some day. Mind how you go in for a penny ice unawares. "Pray, step this way," says a quiet person at the door. You enter — into a back room: — a quiet room; rather a dark room. "Pray, take your place in a chair." And she goes to fetch the penny ice. *Malheureux!* The chair sinks down with you — sinks, and sinks, and sinks — a large wet flannel suddenly envelops your face and throttles you. Need we say any more? After Northumberland Street, what is improbable? Surely there is no difficulty in crediting Bluebeard. I withdraw my last month's opinions about ogres. Ogres? Why not? I protest I have seldom contemplated any thing more terribly ludicrous than this "agent" in the dingy splendor of his den, surrounded by dusty ormolu and piles of empty bottles, firing pistols for his diversion at the mantelpiece until his clients come in! Is pistol-practice so common in Northumberland Street, that it passes without notice in the lodging-houses there?

We spake anon of good thoughts. About bad thoughts? Is there some Northumberland Street chamber in your heart and mine, friend: close to the every-day street of life: visited by daily friends: visited by people on business; in which affairs are transacted; jokes are uttered; wine is drunk; through which people come and go; wives and children pass; and in which murder sits unseen until the terrible moment when he rises up and kills? A farmer, say, has a gun over the mantelpiece in his room where he sits at his daily meals and rest: caressing his children, joking with his friends, smoking his pipe in his calm. One night the gun is taken down: the farmer goes out: and it is a murderer who comes back and puts the piece up and drinks by that fire-side. Was he a murderer yesterday when he was tossing the baby on his knee, and when his hands were playing with his little girl's yellow hair? Yesterday there was no blood on them at all: they were shaken by honest men: have done many a kind act in their time very likely. He leans his head on one of them, the wife comes in with her anxious looks of welcome, the children are prattling as they did yesterday round the father's knee at the fire, and Cain is sitting by the embers, and Abel lies dead on the moor. Think of the gulf between now and yesterday. Oh, yesterday! Oh, the days when those two loved each other and said their prayers side by side! He goes to sleep, perhaps, and dreams that his brother is alive. Be true, O dream! Let him live in dreams, and wake no more. Be undone, O crime, O crime! But the sun rises: and the officers of conscience come: and yonder lies the body on the moor. I happened to pass, and looked at the Northumberland Street house the other day. A few loiterers were gazing up at the dingy windows. A plain ordinary face of a house enough — and in a chamber in it one man suddenly rose up, pistol in hand, to slaughter another. Have you ever killed any one in your thoughts? Has your heart compassed any man's death? In your mind, have you ever taken a brand from the altar, and slain your brother? How many plain ordinary faces of men do we look at, unknowing of murder behind those eyes? Lucky for you and me, brother, that we have good thoughts unspoken. But the bad ones? I tell you that the sight of those blank windows in Northumberland Street — through which, as it were, my mind could picture the awful tragedy glimmering behind — set me thinking, "Mr. Street-Preacher, here is a text for one of your pavement sermons. But it is too glum and serious. You eschew dark thoughts: and desire to be cheerful and merry in the main." And, such being the case, you see we must have no Roundabout Essay on this subject.

Well, I had another arrow in my quiver. (So, you know, had William Tell a bolt for his son, the apple of his eye; and a shaft for Gessler, in case William came to any trouble with the first poor little target.) And this, I must tell you, was to have been a rare Roundabout performance — one of the very best that has ever appeared in this series. It was to have contained all the deep pathos of Addison; the logical precision of Rabelais; the childlike playfulness of Swift; the manly stoicism of Sterne; the metaphysical depth of Goldsmith; the blushing modesty of Fielding; the epigrammatic terseness of Walter Scott; the uproarious humor of Sam Richardson; and the gay simplicity of Sam Johnson; — it was to have combined all these qualities, with some excellences of modern writers whom I could name: — but circumstances have occurred which have rendered this Roundabout Essay also impossible.

I have not the least objection to tell you what was to have been the subject of that other admirable Roundabout Paper. Gracious powers! the Dean of St. Patrick's never had a better theme. The paper was to have been on the Gorillas, to be sure. I was going to imagine myself to be a young surgeon apprentice from Charleston, in South Carolina, who ran away to Cuba on account of unhappy family circumstances, with which nobody has the least concern; who sailed thence to Africa in a large, roomy schooner with an extraordinary vacant space between decks. I was subject to dreadful ill treatment from the first mate of the ship, who, when I found she was a slaver, altogether declined to put me on shore. I was chased — we were chased — by three British frigates and a seventy-four, which we engaged and captured; but were obliged to scuttle, and sink, as we could sell them in no African port: and I never shall forget the look of manly resignation, combined with considerable disgust, of the British Admiral as he walked the plank, after cutting off his pigtail, which he handed to me, and which I still have in charge for his family at Boston, Lincolnshire, England.

We made the port of Bpoopoo, at the confluence of the Bungo and Sgglolo rivers (which you may see in Swammerdahl's map) on the 31st April last year. Our passage had been so extraordinarily rapid, owing to the continued drunkenness of the captain and chief officers, by which I was obliged to work the ship and take her in command that we reached Bpoopoo six weeks before we were expected, and five before the coffres from the interior and from the great slave dépôt at Zbabblo were expected. Their delay caused us not a little discomfort, because, though we had taken the four English ships, we knew that Sir Byam Martin's iron-cased squadron, with "The Warrior," "The Impregnable," "The Sanconiathon," and "The Berosus," were cruising in the neighborhood, and might prove too much for us.

It not only became necessary to quit Bpoopoo before the arrival of the British fleet or the rainy season, but to get our people on board as soon as might be. While the chief mate, with a detachment of seamen, hurried forward to the Pgogo lake, where we expected a considerable part of our cargo, the second mate, with six men, four chiefs, King Fbumbo, an Obi man, and myself, went N.W. by W., towards King Mtoby's-town, where we knew many hundreds of our between-deck passengers were to be got together. We went down the Pdodo river, shooting snipes, ostriches, and rhinoceros in plenty, and I think a few elephants, until, by the advice of a guide, who, I now believe, was treacherous, we were induced to leave the Pdodo, and march N.E., by N.N. Here Lieutenant Larkins, who had persisted in drinking rum from morning to night, and thrashing me in his sober moments during the whole journey, died, and I have too good reason to know was eaten with much relish by the natives. At Mgoo, where there are barracoons and a dépôt for our cargo we had no news of our expected freight; accordingly, as time pressed exceedingly, parties were despatched in advance towards the great Washaboo lake, by which the caravans usually come towards the coast. Here we found no caravan, but only four negroes down with the ague, whom I treated, I am bound to say, unsuccessfully, whilst we waited for our friends. We used to take watch and watch in front of the place, both to guard ourselves from attack, and get early news of the approaching caravan.

At last, on the 23d September, as I was in advance with Charles Rogers, second mate, and two natives with bows and arrows, we were crossing a great plain skirted by a forest, when we saw emerging from a ravine what I took to be three negroes — a very tall one, one of a moderate size, and one quite little.

Our native guide shrieked out some words in their language, of which Charles Rogers knew something. I thought it was the advance of the negroes whom we expected. "No!" said Rogers (who swore dreadfully in conversation), "it is the Gorillas!" And he fired both barrels of his gun, bringing down the little one first, and the female afterwards.

The male, who was untouched, gave a howl that you might have heard a league off; advanced towards us as if he would attack us, and then turned and ran away with inconceivable celerity towards the wood.

We went up towards the fallen brutes. The little one by the female appeared to be about two years old.

It lay bleating and moaning on the ground, stretching out its little hands, with movements and looks so strangely resembling human, that my heart sickened with pity. The female, who had been shot through both legs, could not move. She howled most hideously when I approached the little one.

"We must be off," said Rogers, "or the whole Gorilla race may be down upon us." "The little one is only shot in the leg," I said. "I'll bind the limb up, and we will carry the beast with us on board."

The poor little wretch held up its leg to show it was wounded, and looked to me with appealing eyes. It lay quite still whilst I looked for and found the bullet, and, tearing off a piece of my shirt, bandaged up the wound. I was so occupied in this business, that I hardly heard Rogers cry, "Run! run!" and when I looked up —

When I looked up, with a roar the most horrible I ever heard — a roar? ten thousand roars — a whirling army of dark beings rushed by me. Rogers, who had bullied me so frightfully during the voyage, and who had encouraged my fatal passion for play, so that I own I owed him 1,500 dollars, was overtaken, felled, brained, and torn into ten thousand pieces; and I dare say the same fate would have fallen on me, but that the little Gorilla, whose wound I had dressed, flung its arms round my neck (their arms, you know, are much longer than ours). And when an immense gray Gorilla, with hardly any teeth, brandishing the trunk of a gollybosh-tree about sixteen feet long, came up to me roaring, the little one squeaked out something plaintive, which, of course, I could not understand; on which suddenly the monster flung down his tree, squatted down on his huge hams by the side of the little patient, and began to bellow and weep.

And now, do you see whom I had rescued? I had rescued the young Prince of the Gorillas, who was out walking with his nurse and footman. The footman had run off to alarm his master, and certainly I never saw a footman run quicker. The whole army of Gorillas rushed forward to rescue their prince, and punish his enemies. If the King Gorilla's emotion was great, fancy what the queen's must have been when *she* came up! She arrived, on a litter, neatly enough made with wattled branches, on which she lay, with her youngest child, a prince of three weeks old.

My little *protégé*, with the wounded leg, still persisted in hugging me with its arms (I think I mentioned that they are longer than those of men in general), and as the poor little brute was immensely heavy, and the Gorillas go at a prodigious pace, a litter was made for us likewise; and my thirst much refreshed by a footman (the same domestic who had given the alarm) running hand over hand up a cocoanut-tree, tearing the rinds off, breaking the shell on his head, and handing me the fresh milk in its cup. My little patient partook of a little, stretching out its dear little unwounded foot, with which, or with its hand, a Gorilla can help itself indiscriminately. Relays of large Gorillas relieved each other at the litters at intervals of twenty minutes, as I calculated by my watch, one of Jones and Bates's, of Boston, Mass., though I have been unable to this day to ascertain how these animals calculate time with such surprising accuracy. We slept for that night under —

And now, you see, we arrive at really the most interesting part of my travels in the country which I intended to visit, viz. the manners and habits of the Gorillas *chez eux*. I give the heads of this narrative only, the full account being suppressed for a reason which shall presently be given. The heads, then, of the chapters, are briefly as follows: —

The author's arrival in the Gorilla country. Its geographical position. Lodgings assigned to him up a gum-tree. Constant attachment of the little prince.

His royal highness's gratitude. Anecdotes of his wit, playfulness, and extraordinary precocity. Am offered a portion of poor Larkins for my supper, but decline with horror. Footman brings me a young crocodile: fishy but very palatable. Old crocodiles too tough: ditto rhinoceros. Visit the queen mother — an enormous old Gorilla, quite white. Prescribe for her majesty. Meeting of Gorillas at what appears a parliament amongst them: presided over by old Gorilla in cocoa-nut-fibre wig. Their sports. Their customs. A privileged class amongst them. Extraordinary likeness of Gorillas to people at home, both at Charleston, S.C., my native place; and London, England, which I have visited. Flat-nosed Gorillas and blue-nosed Gorillas; their hatred, and wars between them. In a part of the country (its geographical position described) I see several negroes under Gorilla domination. Well treated by their masters. Frog-eating Gorillas across the Salt Lake. Bull-headed Gorillas — their mutual hostility. Green Island Gorillas. More quarrelsome than the Bull-heads, and howl much louder. I am called to attend one of the princesses. Evident partiality of H.R.H. for me. Jealousy and rage of large red-headed Gorilla. How shall I escape?

Ay, how indeed? Do you wish to know? Is your curiosity excited? Well, I *do* know how I escaped. I could tell the most extraordinary adventures that happened to me. I could show you resemblances to people at home, that would make them blue with rage and you crack your sides with laughter. . . . And what is the reason I cannot write this paper, having all the facts before me? The reason is, that walking down St. James Street yesterday, I met a friend who says to me, "Roundabout, my boy, have you seen your picture? Here it is!" And he pulls out a portrait, executed in photography, of your humble servant, as an immense and most unpleasant-featured baboon, with long hairy hands, and called by the waggish artist "A Literary Gorilla." O horror! And now you see why I can't play off this joke myself, and moralize on the fable, as it has been narrated already *de me.*

A MISSISSIPPI BUBBLE.

This group * of dusky children of the captivity is copied out of a little sketch-book which I carried in many a roundabout journey, and will point a moral as well as any other sketch in the volume. Yonder drawing was made in a country where there was such hospitality, friendship, kindness shown to the humble designer, that his eyes do not care to look out for faults, or his pen to note them. How they sang! how they laughed and grinned! how they scraped, bowed, and complimented you and each other, those negroes of the cities of the Southern parts of the then United States! My business kept me in the towns; I was but in one negro-plantation village, and there were only women and little children, the men being out a-field. But there was plenty of cheerfulness in the huts, under the great trees — I speak of what I saw — and amidst the dusky bondsmen of the cities. I witnessed a curious gayety; heard amongst the black folk endless singing, shouting, and laughter; and saw on holidays black gentlemen and ladies arrayed in such splendor and comfort as free-born workmen in our towns seldom exhibit. What a grin and bow that dark gentleman performed, who was the porter at the colonel's, when he said, "You write your name, mas'r, else I will forgot." I am not going into the slavery question, I am not an advocate for "the institution," as I know, madam, by that angry toss of your head, you are about to declare me to be. For domestic purposes, my dear lady, it seemed to me about

* Alluding to the woodcut which accompanied this paper when it first appeared.

the dearest institution that can be devised. In a house in a Southern city you will find fifteen negroes doing the work which John, the cook, the housemaid, and the help, do perfectly in your own comfortable London house. And these fifteen negroes are the pick of a family of some eighty or ninety. Twenty are too sick, or too old for work, let us say: twenty too clumsy: twenty are too young, and have to be nursed and watched by ten more.* And master has to maintain the immense crew to do the work of half a dozen willing hands. No, no; let Mitchell, the exile from poor dear enslaved Ireland, wish for a gang of "fat niggers;" I would as soon you should make me a present of a score of Bengal elephants, when I need but a single stout horse to pull my brougham.

How hospitable they were, those Southern men! In the North itself the welcome was not kinder, as I, who have eaten Northern and Southern salt, can testify. As for New Orleans, in spring-time, — just when the orchards were flushing over with peach-blossoms, and the sweet herbs came to flavor the juleps — it seemed to me the city of the world where you can eat and drink the most and suffer the least. At Bordeaux itself, claret is not better to drink than at New Orleans. It was all good — believe an expert Robert — from the half-dollar Médoc of the public hotel table, to the private gentleman's choicest wine. Claret is, somehow, good in that gifted place at dinner, at supper, and at breakfast in the morning. It is good: it is superabundant — and there is nothing to pay. Find me speaking ill of such a country! When I do, *pone me pigris campis:* smother me in a desert, or let Mississippi or Garonne drown me! At that comfortable tavern on Pontchartrain we had a *bouillabaisse* than which a better was never eaten at Marseilles: and not the least headache in the morning, I give you my word; on the contrary, you only wake with a sweet refreshing thirst for claret and water. They say there is fever there in the autumn: but not in the spring-time, when the peach-blossoms blush over the orchards, and the sweet herbs come to flavor the juleps.

I was bound from New Orleans to Saint Louis; and our walk was constantly on the Levee, whence we could see a hundred of those huge white Mississippi steamers at their moorings in the river: "Look," said my friend Lochlomond to me, as we stood one day on the quay — "look at that post! Look at that coffee-house behind it! Sir, last year a steamer blew up in the river yonder, just where you see those men pulling off in the boat. By that post where you are standing a mule was cut in two by a fragment of the burst machinery, and a bit of the chimney-stove in that first-floor window of the coffee-house killed a negro who was cleaning knives in the top-room!" I looked at the post, at the coffee-house window, at the steamer in which I was going to embark, at my friend, with a pleasing interest not divested of melancholy. Yesterday, it was the mule, thinks I, who was cut in two: it may be *cras mihi.* Why, in the same little sketch-book, there is a drawing of an Alabama river steamer which blew up on the very next voyage after that in which your humble servant was on board! Had I but waited another week, I might have. . . . These incidents give a queer zest to the voyage down the life-stream in America. When our huge, tall, white, paste-board castle of a steamer began to work up stream, every limb in her creaked and groaned, and quivered, so that you might fancy she would burst right off. Would she hold together, or would she split into ten million of shivers? O my home and children! Would

* This was an account given by a gentleman at Richmond of his establishment. Six European servants would have kept his house and stables well. "His farm," he said, "barely sufficed to maintain the negroes residing on it."

your humble servant's body be cut in two across yonder chain on the Levee, or be precipitated into yonder first-floor, so as to damage the chest of a black man cleaning boots at the window? The black man is safe for me, thank goodness. But you see the little accident *might* have happened. It has happened; and if to a mule, why not to a more docile animal? On our journey up the Mississippi, I give you my honor we were on fire three times, and burned our cook-room down. The deck at night was a great firework — the chimney spouted myriads of stars, which fell blackening on our garments, sparkling on to the deck, or gleaming into the mighty stream through which we labored — the mighty yellow stream with all its snags.

How I kept up my courage through these dangers shall now be narrated. The excellent landlord of the "Saint Charles Hotel," when I was going away, begged me to accept two bottles of the very finest Cognac, with his compliments; and I found them in my state-room with my luggage. Lochlomond came to see me off, and as he squeezed my hand at parting, "Roundabout," says he, "the wine mayn't be very good on board, so I have brought a dozen-case of the Médoc which you liked;" and we grasped together the hands of friendship and farewell. Whose boat is this pulling up to the ship? It is our friend Glenlivat, who gave us the dinner on Lake Pontchartrain. "Roundabout," says he, "we have tried to do what we could for you, my boy; and it has been done *de bon cœur*" (I detect a kind tremulousness in the good fellow's voice as he speaks). "I say — hem! — the a — the wine isn't too good on board, so I've brought you a dozen of Médoc for your voyage, you know. And God bless you; and when I come to London in May I shall come and see you. Hallo! here's Johnson come to see you off, too!"

As I am a miserable sinner, when Johnson grasped my hand, he said, "Mr. Roundabout, you can't be sure of the wine on board these steamers, so I thought I would bring you a little case of that light claret which you liked at my house." *Et de trois!* No wonder I could face the Mississippi with so much courage supplied to me! Where are you, honest friends, who gave me of your kindness and your cheer? May I be considerably boiled, blown up, and snagged, if I speak hard words of you. May claret turn sour ere I do!

Mounting the stream, it chanced that we had very few passengers. How far is the famous city of Memphis from New Orleans? I do not mean the Egyptian Memphis, but the American Memphis, from which to the American Cairo we slowly toiled up the river — to the American Cairo at the confluence of the Ohio and Mississippi rivers. And at Cairo we parted company from the boat, and from some famous and gifted fellow-passengers who joined us at Memphis, and whose pictures we had seen in many cities of the South. I do not give the names of these remarkable people, unless, by some wondrous chance, in inventing a name I should light upon that real one which some of them bore; but if you please I will say that our fellow-passengers whom we took in at Memphis were no less personages than the Vermont Giant and the famous Bearded Lady of Kentucky and her son. Their pictures I had seen in many cities through which I travelled with my own little performance. I think the Vermont Giant was a trifle taller in his pictures than he was in life (being represented in the former, as, at least, some two stories high): but the lady's prodigious beard received no more than justice at the hands of the painter; that portion of it which I saw being really most black, rich, and curly — I say the portion of beard, for this modest or prudent woman kept I don't know how much of the beard covered up with a red handkerchief, from which I suppose it only emerged when she went to bed, or when she exhibited it professionally.

The Giant, I must think, was an overrated giant. I have known gentlemen, not in the profession, better made, and I should say taller, than the Vermont gentleman. A strange feeling I used to have at meals; when, on looking round our little society, I saw the Giant, the Bearded Lady of Kentucky, the little Bearded Boy of three years old, the Captain (this I *think;* but at this distance of time I would not like to make the statement on affidavit), and the three other passengers, all with their knives in their mouths making play at the dinner — a strange feeling I say it was, and as though I was in a castle of ogres. But, after all, why so squeamish? A few scores of years back, the finest gentlemen and ladies of Europe did the like. Belinda ate with her knife; and Saccharissa had only that weapon, or a two-pronged fork, or a spoon, for her pease. Have you ever looked at Gilray's print of the Prince of Wales, a languid voluptuary, retiring after his meal, and noted the toothpick which he uses? . . . You are right, madam; I own that the subject is revolting and terrible. I will not pursue it. Only — allow that a gentleman, in a shaky steamboat, on a dangerous river, in a far-off country, which caught fire three times during the voyage — (of course I mean the steamboat, not the country), — seeing a giant, a voracious supercargo, a bearded lady, and a little boy not three years of age, with a chin already quite black and curly, all plying their victuals down their throats with their knives — allow, madam, that in such a company a man had a right to feel a little nervous. I don't know whether you have ever remarked the Indian jugglers swallowing their knives, or seen, as I have, a whole table of people performing the same trick, but if you look at their eyes when they do it, I assure you there is a roll in them which is dreadful.

Apart from this usage, which they practise in common with many thousand most estimable citizens, the Vermont gentleman, and the Kentucky whiskered lady — or did I say the reverse? — whichever you like, my dear sir — were quite quiet, modest, unassuming people. She sat working with her needle, if I remember right. He, I suppose, slept in the great cabin, which was seventy feet long at the least, nor, I am bound to say, did I hear in the night any snores or roars, such as you would fancy ought to accompany the sleep of ogres. Nay, this giant had quite a small appetite, (unless, to be sure, he went forward and ate a sheep or two in private with his horrid knife — oh, the dreadful thought! — but *in public,* I say, he had quite a delicate appetite), and was also a tea-totaller. I don't remember to have heard the lady's voice, though I might, not unnaturally, have been curious to hear it. Was her voice a deep, rich, magnificent bass; or was it soft, fluty, and mild? I shall never know now. Even if she comes to this country, I shall never go and see her. I *have* seen her, and for nothing.

You would have fancied that, as after all we were only some half-dozen on board, she might have dispensed with her red handkerchief, and talked, and eaten her dinner in comfort: but in covering her chin there was a kind of modesty. That beard was her profession: that beard brought the public to see her: out of her business she wished to put that beard aside as it were: as a barrister would wish to put off his wig. I know some who carry theirs into private life, and who mistake you and me for jury-boxes when they address us: but these are not your modest barristers, not your true gentlemen.

Well, I own I respected the lady for the modesty with which, her public business over, she retired into private life. She respected her life, and her beard. That beard having done its day's work, she puts it away in a handkerchief; and becomes, as far as in her lies, a private ordinary person. All public men and women of good sense, I should think, have this modesty. When, for instance, in my small way, poor Mrs. Brown comes simpering up to me, with her album in one hand, a pen in the other, and says, "Ho, ho, dear Mr. Roundabout, write us one of your amusing," &c., &c., my beard drops behind my handkerchief instantly. Why am I to wag my chin and grin for Mrs. Brown's good pleasure? My dear madam, I have been making faces all day. It is my profession. I do my comic business with the greatest pains, seriousnesss, and trouble: and with it make, I hope, a not dishonest livelihood. If you ask Mons. Blondin to tea, you don't have a rope stretched from your garret window to the opposite side of the square, and request Monsieur to take his tea out on the centre of the rope? I lay my hand on this waistcoat, and declare that not once in the course of our voyage together did I allow the Kentucky Giant to suppose I was speculating on his stature, or the Bearded Lady to surmise that I wished to peep under the handkerchief which muffled the lower part of her face.

"And the more fool you," says some cynic. (Faugh, those cynics, I hate 'em!) Don't you know, sir, that a man of genius is pleased to have his genius recognized; that a beauty likes to be admired; that an actor likes to be applauded; that stout old Wellington himself was pleased, and smiled when the people cheered him as he passed? Suppose you had paid some respectful elegant compliment to that lady? Suppose you had asked that giant, if, for once, he would take any thing at the liquor-bar? you might have learned a great deal of curious knowledge regarding giants and bearded ladies, about whom you evidently now know very little. There was that little boy of three years old, with a fine beard already, and his little legs and arms, as seen out of his little frock, covered with a dark down. What a queer little capering satyr! He was quite good-natured, childish, rather solemn. He had a little Norval dress, I remember: the drollest little Norval.

I have said the B. L. had another child. Now this was a little girl of some six years old, as fair and as smooth of skin, dear madam, as your own darling cherubs. She wandered about the great cabin quite melancholy. No one seemed to care for her. All the family affections were centred on Master Esau yonder. His little beard was beginning to be a little fortune already, whereas Miss Rosalba was of no good to the family. No one would pay a cent to see *her* little fair face. No wonder the poor little maid was melancholy. As I looked at her, I seemed to walk more and more in a fairy tale, and more and more in a cavern of ogres. Was this a little fondling whom they had picked up in some forest, where lie the picked bones of the queen, her tender mother, and the tough old defunct monarch, her father? No. Doubtless they were quite good-natured people, these. I don't believe they were unkind to the little girl without the mustaches. It may have been only my fancy that she repined because she had a cheek no more bearded than a rose's.

Would you wish your own daughter, madam, to have a smooth cheek, a modest air, and a gentle feminine behavior, or to be — I won't say a whiskered prodigy, like this Bearded Lady of Kentucky — but a masculine wonder, a virago, a female personage of more than female strength, courage, wisdom? Some authors, who shall be nameless, are, I know, accused of depicting the most feeble, brainless, namby-pamby heroines, forever whimpering tears and prattling commonplaces. *You* would have the heroine of your novel so beautiful that she should charm the captain (or hero, whoever he may be) with her appearance; surprise and confound the bishop with her learning; outride the squire and get the brush, and, when he fell from his horse, whip out a lancet and bleed him; rescue from fever and death the poor cottager's family whom the doctor had given up; make 21 at the butts with the rifle, when the poor captain only scored 18; give him twenty in fifty at billiards and beat him; and draw tears from the professional Italian people by her exquisite performance (of voice and violoncello) in the evening; — I say, if a novelist would be popular with ladies — the great novel-readers of the world — this is the sort of heroine who would carry him through half a dozen editions. Suppose I had asked that Bearded Lady to sing? Confess, now, miss, you would not have been displeased if I had told you that she had a voice like Lablache, only ever so much lower.

My dear, you would like to be a heroine? You would like to travel in triumphal caravans; to see your effigy placarded on city walls; to have your levées attended by admiring crowds, all crying out, "Was there ever such a wonder of a woman?" You would like admiration? Consider the tax you pay for it. You would be alone were you eminent. Were you so distinguished from your neighbors — I will not say by a beard and whiskers, that were odious — but by a great and remarkable intellectual superiority — would you, do you think, be any the happier? Consider envy. Consider solitude. Consider the jealousy and torture of mind which this Kentucky lady must feel, suppose she should hear that there is, let us say, a Missouri prodigy, with a beard larger than hers? Consider how she is separated from her kind by the possession of that wonder of a beard? When that beard grows gray, how lonely she will be, the poor old thing! If it falls off, the public admiration falls off too; and how she will miss it — the compliments of the trumpeters, the admiration of the crowd, the gilded progress of the car. I see an old woman alone in a decrepit old caravan, with cobwebs on the knocker, with a blistered ensign flapping idly over the door. Would you like to be that deserted person? Ah, Chloe! To be good, to be simple, to be modest, to be loved, be thy lot. Be thankful thou art not taller, nor stronger, nor richer, nor wiser, than the rest of the world!

ON LETTS'S DIARY.

Mine is one of your No. 12 diaries, three shillings cloth boards; silk limp, gilt edges, three-and-six; French morocco, tuck ditto, four-and-six. It has two pages, ruled with faint lines for memoranda, for every week, and a ruled account at the end, for the twelve months from January to December, where you may set down your incomings and your expenses. I hope yours, my respected reader, are large; that there are many fine round sums of figures on each side of the page: liberal on the expenditure side, greater still on the receipt. I hope, sir, you will be "a better man," as they say, in '62 than in this moribund '61, whose career of life is just coming to its terminus. A better man in purse? in body? in soul's health? Amen, good sir, in all. Who is there so good in mind, body, or estate, but bettering won't still be good for him? O unknown Fate, presiding over next year, if you will give me better health, a better appetite, a better digestion, a better income, a better temper in '62 than you have bestowed in '61, I think your servant will be the better for the changes. For instance, I should be the better for a new coat. This one, I acknowledge, is very old. The family says so. My good friend, who amongst us would not be the better if he would give up some old habits? Yes, yes. You agree with me. You take the allegory? Alas!

at our time of life we don't like to give up those old habits, do we? It is ill to change. There is the good old loose, easy, slovenly bedgown, laziness, for example. What man of sense likes to fling it off and put on a tight *guindé* prim dress-coat that pinches him? There is the cosey wraprascal, self-indulgence — how easy it is! How warm! How it always seems to fit! You can walk out in it; you can go down to dinner in it. You can say of such what Tully says of his books: *Pernoctat nobiscum, peregrinatur, rusticatur.* It is a little slatternly — it is a good deal stained — it isn't becoming — it smells of cigar-smoke; but, *allons donc!* let the world call me idle and sloven. I love my ease better than my neighbor's opinion. I live to please myself; not you, Mr. Dandy, with your supercilious airs. I am a philosopher. Perhaps I live in my tub, and don't make any other use of it — We won't pursue further this unsavory metaphor; but, with regard to some of your old habits, let us say, —

1. The habit of being censorious, and speaking ill of your neighbors.

2. The habit of getting into a passion with your man-servant, your maid-servant, your daughter, wife, &c.

3. The habit of indulging too much at table.

4. The habit of smoking in the dining-room after dinner.

5. The habit of spending insane sums of money in *bric-à-brac*, tall copies, binding, Elzevirs, &c.; '20 Port, outrageously fine horses, ostentatious entertainments, and what not? or,

6. The habit of screwing meanly, when rich, and chuckling over the saving of half a crown, whilst you are poisoning your friends and family with bad wine.

7. The habit of going to sleep immediately after dinner, instead of cheerfully entertaining Mrs. Jones and the family: or,

8. Ladies! The habit of running up bills with the milliners, and swindling paterfamilias on the house bills.

9. The habit of keeping him waiting for breakfast.

10. The habit of sneering at Mrs. Brown and the Miss Browns, because they are not quite *du monde,* or quite so genteel as Lady Smith.

11. The habit of keeping your wretched father up at balls till five o'clock in the morning, when he has to be at his office at eleven.

12. The habit of fighting with each other, dear Louisa, Jane, Arabella, Amelia.

13. The habit of *always* ordering John Coachman three-quarters of an hour before you want him.

Such habits, I say, sir or madam, if you have had to note in your diary of '61, I have not the slightest doubt you will enter in your pocket-book of '62. There are habits Nos. 4 and 7, for example. I am morally sure that some of us will not give up those bad customs, though the women cry out and grumble, and scold ever so justly. There are habits Nos. 9 and 13. I feel perfectly certain, my dear young ladies, that you will continue to keep John Coachman waiting; that you will continue to give the most satisfactory reasons for keeping him waiting: and as for (9), you will show that you once (on the 1st of April last, let us say) came to breakfast first, and that you are *always* first in consequence.

Yes; in our '62 diaries, I fear we may all of us make some of the '61 entries. There is my friend Freehand, for instance. (Aha! Master Freehand, how you will laugh to find yourself here!) F. is in the habit of spending a little, ever so little, more than his income. He shows you how Mrs. Freehand works, and works (and, indeed, Jack Freehand, if you say she is an angel, you don't say too much of her); how they toil, and how they mend, and patch, and pinch; and how they *can't* live on their means. And I very much fear — nay, I will bet him half a bottle of Gladstone 14*s*. per dozen claret — that the account which is a little on the wrong side this year will be a little on the wrong side in the next ensuing year of grace.

A diary. Dies. Hodie. How queer to read are some of the entries in the journal! Here are the records of dinners eaten, and gone the way of flesh. The lights burn blue somehow, and we sit before the ghosts of victuals. Hark at the dead jokes resurging! Memory greets them with the ghost of a smile. Here are the lists of the individuals who have dined at your own humble table. The agonies endured before and during those entertainments are renewed, and smart again. What a failure that special grand dinner was! How those dreadful occasional waiters did break the old china! What a dismal hash poor Mary, the cook, made of the French dish which she *would* try out of *Francatelli!* How angry Mrs. Pope was at not going down to dinner before Mrs. Bishop! How Trimalchio sneered at your absurd attempt to give a feast; and Harpagon cried out at your extravagance and ostentation! How Lady Almack bullied the other ladies in the drawing-room (when no gentlemen were present): never asked you back to dinner again: left her card by her footman: and took not the slightest notice of your wife and daughters at Lady Hustleby's assembly! On the other hand, how easy, cosey, merry, comfortable, those little dinners were; got up at one or two days' notice; when everybody was contented; the soup as clear as amber; the wine as good as Trimalchio's own; and the people kept their carriages waiting, and would not go away till midnight!

Along with the catalogue of bygone pleasures, balls, banquets, and the like, which the pages record, comes a list of much more important occurrences, and remembrances of graver import. On two days of Dives's diary are printed notices that "Dividends are due at the Bank." Let us hope, dear sir, that this announcement considerably interests you; in which case, probably, you have no need of the almanac-maker's printed reminder. If you look over poor Jack Reckless's note-book, amongst his memoranda of racing odds given and taken, perhaps you may read:—"Nabbam's bill, due 29th September, 142*l.* 15*s.* 6*d.*" Let us trust, as the day has passed, that the little transaction here noted has been satisfactorily terminated. If you are paterfamilias, and a worthy kind gentleman, no doubt you have marked down on your register, 17th December (say), "Boys come home." Ah, how carefully that blest day is marked in *their* little calendars! In my time it used to be, Wednesday, 13th November, "5 *weeks from the holidays;*" Wednesday, 20th NOVEMBER, "4 *weeks from the holidays;*" until sluggish time sped on, and we came to WEDNESDAY 18TH DECEMBER. O rapture! Do you remember pea-shooters? I think we only had them on going home for holidays from private schools,—at public schools, men are too dignified. And then came that glorious announcement, Wednesday, 27th, "Papa took us to the Pantomime;" or if not papa, perhaps you condescended to go to the pit, under charge of the footman.

That was near the end of the year—and mamma gave you a new pocket-book, perhaps, with a little coin, God bless her, in the pocket. And that pocket-book was for next year, you know; and, in that pocket-book you had to write down that sad day, Wednesday, January 24th, eighteen hundred and never mind what,—when Dr. Birch's young friends were expected to re-assemble.

Ah me! Every person who turns this page over has his own little diary, in paper or ruled in his memory tablets, and in which are set down the transactions of the now dying year. Boys and men, we have our calendar, mothers and maidens. For example, in your calendar pocket-book, my good Eliza, what a sad, sad day that is — how fondly and bitterly remembered — when your boy went off to his regiment, to India, to danger, to battle perhaps! What a day was that last day at home, when the tall brother sat yet amongst the family, the little ones round about him wondering at saddle-boxes, uniforms, sword-cases, gun-cases, and other wonderous apparatus of war and travel which poured in and filled the hall; the new dressing-case for the beard not yet grown; the great sword-case at which little brother Tom looks so admiringly! What a dinner that was, that last dinner, when little and grown children assembled together, and all tried to be cheerful! What a night was that last night, when the young ones were at roost for the last time together under the same roof, and the mother lay alone in her chamber counting the fatal hours as they tolled one after another, amidst her tears, her watching, her fond prayers! What a night that was, and yet how quickly the melancholy dawn came! Only too soon the sun rose over the houses. And now in a moment more the city seemed to wake. The house began to stir. The family gathers together for the last meal. For the last time in the midst of them the widow kneels amongst her kneeling children, and falters a prayer in which she commits her dearest, her eldest born, to the care of the Father of all. O night, what tears you hide — what prayers you hear! And so the nights pass and the days succeed, until that one comes when tears and parting shall be no more.

In your diary, as in mine, there are days marked with sadness, not for this year only, but for all. On a certain day — and the sun, perhaps, shining ever so brightly — the house-mother comes down to her family with a sad face, which scares the children round about in the midst of their laughter and prattle. They may have forgotten — but she has not — a day which came, twenty years ago it may be, and which she remembers only too well: the long night-watch; the dreadful dawning and the rain beating at the pane; the infant speechless, but moaning in its little crib; and then the awful calm, the awful smile on the sweet cherub face, when the cries have ceased, and the little suffering breast heaves no more. Then the children, as they see their mother's face, remember this was the day on which their little brother died. It was before they were born; but she remembers it. And as they pray together, it seems almost as if the spirit of the little lost one was hovering round the group. So they pass away: friends, kindred, the dearest-loved, grown people, aged, infants. As we go on the down-hill journey, the mile-stones are grave-stones, and in each more and more names are written; unless haply you live beyond man's common age, when friends have dropped off, and tottering, and feeble, and unpitied, you reach the terminus alone.

In this past year's diary is there any precious day noted on which you have made a new friend? This is a piece of good fortune bestowed but grudgingly on the old. After a certain age a new friend is a wonder, like Sarah's child. Aged persons are seldom capable of bearing friendships. Do you remember how warmly you loved Jack and Tom when you were at school; what a passionate regard you had for Ned when you were at college, and the immense letters you wrote to each other? How often do you write, now that postage costs nothing? There is the age of blossoms and sweet budding green: the age of generous summer; the autumn when the leaves drop; and then winter, shivering and bare. Quick, children, and sit at my feet: for they are cold, very cold: and it seems as if neither wine nor worsted will warm 'em.

In this past year's diary is there any dismal day noted in which you have lost a friend? In mine there is.

I do not mean by death. Those who are gone, you have. Those who departed loving you, love you still; and you love them always. They are not really gone, those dear hearts and true; they are only gone into the next room: and you will presently get up and follow them, and yonder door will close upon *you*, and you will be no more seen. As I am in this cheerful mood, I will tell you a fine and touching story of a doctor which I heard lately. About two years since there was, in our or some other city, a famous doctor, into whose consulting-room crowds came daily, so that they might be healed. Now this doctor had a suspicion that there was something vitally wrong with himself, and he went to consult another famous physician at Dublin, or it may be at Edinburgh. And he of Edinburgh punched his comrade's sides; and listened at his heart and lungs; and felt his pulse, I suppose; and looked at his tongue; and when he had done, Doctor London said to Doctor Edinburgh, "Doctor, how long have I to live?" And Doctor Edinburgh said to Doctor London, "Doctor, you may last a year."

Then Doctor London came home, knowing that what Doctor Edinburgh said was true. And he made up his accounts, with man and heaven, I trust. And he visited his patients as usual. And he went about healing, and cheering, and soothing, and doctoring; and thousands of sick people were benefited by him. And he said not a word to his family at home; but lived amongst them cheerful and tender, and calm, and loving; though he knew the night was at hand when he should see them and work no more.

And it was winter time, and they came and told him that some man at a distance — very sick, but very rich — wanted him; and, though Doctor London knew that he was himself at death's door, he went to the sick man; for he knew the large fee would be good for his children after him. And he died; and his family never knew until he was gone, that he had been long aware of the inevitable doom.

This is a cheerful carol for Christmas, is it not? You see, in regard to these Roundabout discourses, I never know whether they are to be merry or dismal. My hobby has the bit in his mouth; goes his own way; and sometimes trots through a park, and sometimes paces by a cemetery. Two days since came the printer's little emissary, with a note saying, "We are waiting for the Roundabout Paper!" A Roundabout Paper about what or whom? How stale it has become, that printed jollity about Christmas! Carols, and wassail-bowls, and holly, and mistletoe, and yule-logs *de commande* — what heaps of these have we not had for years past! Well, year after year the season comes. Come frost, come thaw, come snow, come rain, year after year my neighbor the parson has to make his sermon. They are getting together the bonbons, iced cakes, Christmas trees at Fortnum and Mason's now. The genii of the theatres are composing the Christmas pantomime, which our young folks will see and note anon in their little diaries.

And now, brethren, may I conclude this discourse with an extract out of that great diary, the newspaper? I read it but yesterday, and it has mingled with all my thoughts since then. Here are the two paragraphs, which appeared following each other: —

"Mr. R., the Advocate-General of Calcutta, has been appointed to the post of Legislative Member of the Council of the Governor-General."

"Sir R. S., Agent to the Governor-General for Central India, died on the 29th of October, of bronchitis."

These two men, whose different fates are recorded in two paragraphs and half a dozen lines of the same newspaper, were sisters' sons. In one of the stories by the present writer, a man is described tottering "up the steps of the ghaut," having just parted with his child, whom he is despatching to England from India. I wrote this, remembering in long, long distant days, such a ghaut, or river-stair, at Calcutta; and a day when, down those steps, to a boat which was in waiting, came two children, whose mothers remained on the shore. One of those ladies was never to see her boy more; and he, too, is just dead in India, "of bronchitis, on the 29th October." We were first-cousins; had been little playmates and friends from the time of our birth; and the first house in London to which I was taken was that of our aunt, the mother of his Honor the Member of Council. His Honor was even then a gentleman of the long robe, being, in truth, a baby in arms. We Indian children were consigned to a school of which our deluded parents had heard a favorable report, but which was governed by a horrible little tyrant, who made our young lives so miserable that I remember kneeling by my little bed of a night, and saying, "Pray God, I may dream of my mother!" Thence we went to a public school: and my cousin to Addiscombe and to India.

"For thirty-two years," the paper says, "Sir Richmond Shakespear faithfully and devotedly served the Government of India, and during that period but once visited England, for a few months and on public duty. In his military capacity he saw much service, was present in eight general engagements, and was badly wounded in the last. In 1840, when a young lieutenant, he had the rare good fortune to be the means of rescuing from almost hopeless slavery in Khiva 416 subjects of the Emperor of Russia; and, but two years later, greatly contributed to the happy recovery of our own prisoners from a similar fate in Cabul. Throughout his career this officer was ever ready and zealous for the public service, and freely risked life and liberty in the discharge of his duties. Lord Canning, to mark his high sense of Sir Richmond Shakespear's public services, had lately offered him the Chief Commissionership of Mysore, which he had accepted, and was about to undertake, when death terminated his career."

When he came to London the cousins and playfellows of early Indian days met once again, and shook hands. "Can I do any thing for you?" I remember the kind fellow asking. He was always asking that question: of all kinsmen; of all widows and orphans; of all the poor; of young men who might need his purse or his service. I saw a young officer yesterday to whom the first words Sir Richmond Shakespear wrote on his arrival in India were, "Can I do any thing for you?" His purse was at the command of all. His kind hand was always open. It was a gracious fate which sent him to rescue widows and captives. Where could they have had a champion more chivalrous, a protector more loving and tender?

I write down his name in my little book, among those of others dearly loved, who, too, have been summoned hence. And so we meet and part: we struggle and succeed; or we fail and drop unknown on the way. As we leave the fond mother's knee, the rough trials of childhood and boyhood begin; and then manhood is upon us, and the battle of life with its chances, perils, wounds, defeats, distinctions. And Fort William guns are saluting in one man's honor,* while the troops are firing the last volleys over the other's grave — over the grave of the brave, the gentle, the faithful Christian soldier.

NOTES OF A WEEK'S HOLIDAY.

Most of us tell old stories in our families. The wife and children laugh

* W. R. obiit March 22, 1862.

Little Dutchmen.

for the hundredth time at the joke. The old servants (though old servants are fewer every day) nod and smile a recognition at the well-known anecdote. "Don't tell that story of Grouse in the gun-room," says Diggory to Mr. Hardcastle in the play, "or I must laugh." As we twaddle, and grow old and forgetful, we may tell an old story; or, out of mere benevolence, and a wish to amuse a friend when conversation is flagging, disinter a Joe Miller now and then; but the practice is not quite honest, and entails a certain necessity of hypocrisy on story hearers and tellers. It is a sad thing to think that a man with what you call a fund of anecdote is a humbug, more or less amiable and pleasant. What right have I to tell my "Grouse in the gun-room" over and over in the presence of my wife, mother, mother-in-law, sons, daughters, old footman or parlormaid, confidential clerk, curate, or what not? I smirk and go through the history, giving my admirable imitations of the characters introduced: I mimic Jones's grin, Hobbs's squint, Brown's stammer, Grady's brogue, Sandy's Scotch accent, to the best of my power: and the family part of my audience laughs good-humoredly. Perhaps the stranger, for whose amusement the performance is given, is amused by it, and laughs too. But this practice continued is not moral. This self-indulgence on your part, my dear Paterfamilias, is weak, vain — not to say culpable. I can imagine many a worthy man, who begins unguardedly to read this page, and comes to the present sentence, lying back in his chair, thinking of that story which he has told innocently for fifty years, and rather piteously owning to himself, "Well, well, it *is* wrong; I have no right to call on my poor wife to laugh, my daughters to affect to be amused, by that old, old jest of mine. And they would have gone on laughing, and they would have pretended to be amused, to their dying day, if this man had not flung his damper over our hilarity." . . . I lay down the pen, and think, "Are there any old stories which I still tell myself in the bosom of my family? Have I any 'Grouse in my gun-room'?" If there are such, it is because my memory fails, not because I want applause, and wantonly repeat myself. You see, men with the so-called fund of anecdote will not repeat the same story to the same individual; but they do think that, on a new party, the repetition of a joke ever so old may be honorably tried. I meet men walking the London street, bearing the best reputation, men of anecdotal powers: — I know such, who very likely will read this. and say, "Hang the fellow, he means *me!*" And so I do. No — no man ought to tell an anecdote more than thrice, let us say, unless he is sure he is speaking only to give pleasure to his hearers — unless he feels that it is not a mere desire for praise which makes him open his jaws.

And is it not with writers as with *raconteurs?* Ought they not to have their ingenuous modesty? May authors tell old stories, and how many times over? When I come to look at a place which I have visited any time these twenty or thirty years, I recall not the place merely, but the sensations I had at first seeing it, and which are quite different to my feelings to-day. That first day at Calais; the voices of the women crying out at night, as the vessel came alongside the pier: the supper at Quillacq and the flavor of the cutlets and wine; the red-calico canopy under which I slept: the tiled floor, and the fresh smell of the sheets; the wonderful postilion in his jack-boots and pigtail; — all return with perfect clearness to my mind, and I am seeing them and not the objects which are actually under my eyes. Here is Calais. Yonder is that commissioner I have known this score of years. Here are the women screaming and bustling over the baggage; the people at the passport-barrier who take your papers. My good people, I hardly see you. You no more interest me than a dozen orange-women in Covent Garden, or a shop book-keeper in Oxford Street. But you make me think of a time when you were indeed wonderful to behold — when the little French soldiers wore white cockades in their shakos — when the diligence was forty hours going to Paris; and the great-booted postilion, as surveyed by youthful eyes from the coupé, with his *jurons*, his ends of rope for the harness, and his clubbed pigtail, was a wonderful being, and productive of endless amusement. You young folks don't remember the apple-girls who used to follow the diligence up the hill beyond Boulogne, and the delights of the jolly road? In making continental journeys with young folks, an oldster may be very quiet, and, to outward appearance, melancholy; but really he has gone back to the days of his youth, and he is seventeen or eighteen years of age (as the case may be), and is amusing himself with all his might. He is noting the horses as they come squealing out of the post-house yard at midnight; he is enjoying the delicious meals at Beauvais and Amiens, and quaffing *ad libitum* the rich table-d'hôte wine; he is hail-fellow with the conductor, and alive to all the incidents of the road. A man can be alive in 1860 and 1830 at the same time, don't you see? Bodily, I may be in 1860, inert, silent, torpid; but in the spirit I am walking about in 1828, let us say; — in a blue dress-coat and brass buttons, a sweet figured silk waistcoat (which I button round a slim waist with perfect ease), looking at beautiful beings with gigot sleeves and tea-tray hats under the golden chestnuts of the Tuileries, or round the Place Vendôme, where the *drapeau blanc* is floating from the statueless column. Shall we go and dine at "Bombarda's," near the "Hôtel Breteuil," or at the "Café Virginie?" — Away! "Bombarda's" and the "Hôtel Breteuil" have been pulled down ever so long. They knocked down the poor old Virginia Coffee-house last year. My spirit goes and dines there. My body, perhaps, is seated with ever so many people in a railway-carriage, and no wonder my companions find me dull and silent. Have you read Mr. Dale Owen's "Footfalls on the Boundary of Another World"? — (My dear sir, it will make your hair stand quite refreshingly on end). In that work you will read that when gentlemen's or ladies' spirits travel off a few score or thousand miles to visit a friend, their bodies lie quiet and in a torpid state in their beds or in their arm-chairs at home. So in this way, I am absent. My soul whisks away thirty years back into the past. I am looking out anxiously for a beard. I am getting past the age of loving Byron's poems, and pretend that I like Wordsworth and Shelley much better. Nothing I eat or drink (in reason) disagrees with me; and I know whom I think to be the most lovely creature in the world. Ah, dear maid (of that remote but well-remembered period), are you a wife or widow now? — are you dead? — are you thin and withered and old? — or are you grown much stouter, with a false front? and so forth.

O Eliza, Eliza! — Stay, *was* she Eliza? Well, I protest I have forgotten what your Christian name was. You know I only met you for two days, but your sweet face is before me now, and the roses blooming on it are as fresh as in that time of May. Ah, dear Miss X——, my timid youth and ingenuous modesty would never have allowed me, even in my private thoughts, to address you otherwise than by your paternal name, but *that* (though I conceal it) I remember perfectly well, and that your dear and respected father was a brewer.

Carillon. — I was awakened this morning with the chime which Antwerp cathedral clock plays at half-hours. The tune has been haunting me ever since, as tunes will. You dress, eat, drink, walk, and talk to yourself to their tune: their inaudible jingle accompanies you all day: you read the sentences of the paper to their rhythm. I tried uncouthly to imitate the tune to the ladies of the family at breakfast, and they say it is "the shadow dance of *Dinorah.*" It may be so. I dimly remember that my body was once present during the performance of that opera, whilst my eyes were closed, and my intellectual faculties dormant at the back of the box; howbeit, I have learned that shadow dance from hearing it pealing up ever so high in the air, at night, morn, noon.

How pleasant to lie awake and listen to the cheery peal! whilst the old city is asleep at midnight, or waking up rosy at sunrise, or basking in noon, or swept by the scudding rain which drives in gusts over the broad places, and the great shining river; or sparkling in snow which dresses up a hundred thousand masts, peaks, and towers; or wrapped round with thunder-cloud canopies, before which the white gables shine whiter; day and night the kind little carillon plays its fantastic melodies overhead. The bells go on ringing. *Quot vivos vocant, mortuos plangunt, fulgura frangunt;* so on to the past and future tenses, and for how many nights, days, and years! Whilst the French were pitching their *fulgura* into Chassé's citadel, the bells went on ringing quite cheerfully. Whilst the scaffolds were up and guarded by Alva's soldiery, and regiments of penitents, blue, black, and gray, poured out of churches and convents, droning their dirges, and marching to the place of the Hôtel de Ville, where heretics and rebels were to meet their doom, the bells up yonder were chanting at their appointed half-hours and quarters, and rang the *mauvais quart d'heure* for many a poor soul. This bell can see as far away as the towers and dykes of Rotterdam. That one can call a greeting to St. Ursula's at Brussels, and toss a recognition to that one at the town-hall of Oudenarde, and remember how after a great struggle there a hundred and fifty years ago the whole plain was covered with the flying French cavalry — Burgundy, and Berri, and the Chevalier of St. George flying like the rest. "What is your clamor about Oudenarde?" says another bell (Bob Major *this* one must be). "Be still, thou querulous old clapper! *I* can see over to Hougoumont and St. John. And about forty-five years since, I rang all through one Sunday in June, when there was such a battle going on in the corn-fields there, as none of you others ever heard tolled of. Yes, from morning service until after vespers, the French and English were all at it, ding-dong." And then calls of business intervening, the bells have to give up their private jangle, resume their professional duty, and sing their hourly chorus out of *Dinorah.*

What a prodigious distance those bells can be heard! I was awakened this morning to their tune, I say. I have been hearing it constantly ever since. And this house whence I write, Murray says, is two hundred and ten miles from Antwerp. And it is a week off; and there is the bell still jangling its shadow dance out of *Dinorah.* An audible shadow you understand, and an invisible sound, but quite distinct; and a plague take the tune!

Under the Bells. — Who has not seen the church under the bells? Those lofty aisles, those twilight chapels, that cumbersome pulpit with its huge carvings, that wide gray pavement flecked with various light from the jewelled windows, those famous pictures between the voluminous columns over the altars, which twinkle with their ornaments, their votive little silver hearts, legs, limbs, their little guttering tapers, cups of sham roses, and what not? I saw two regiments of little scholars creeping in and forming square, each in its appointed place, under the vast roof; and teachers presently coming to them. A stream of light from the jewelled windows beams slanting down upon each little squad of children, and the tall background of the church retires into a grayer gloom. Pattering little feet of laggards arriving echo through the great nave. They trot in and join their regiments, gathered under the slanting sunbeams. What are they learning? Is it truth? Those two gray ladies with their books in their hands in the midst of these little people have no doubt of the truth of every word they have printed under their eyes. Look, through the windows jewelled all over with saints, the light comes streaming down from the sky, and heaven's own illuminations paint the book! A sweet, touching picture indeed it is, that of the little children assembled in this immense temple, which has endured for ages, and grave teachers bending over them. Yes, the picture is very pretty of the children and the teachers, and their book — but the text? Is it the truth, the only truth, nothing but the truth? If I thought so, I would go and sit down on the form *cum parvulis*, and learn the precious lesson with all my heart.

Beadle. — But I submit, an obstacle to conversions is the intrusion and impertinence of that Swiss fellow with the baldric — the officer who answers to the beadle of the British Islands, and is pacing about the church with an eye on the congregation. Now the boast of Catholics is that their churches are open to all; but in certain places and churches there are exceptions. At Rome I have been into St. Peter's at all hours: the doors are always open, the lamps are always burning, the faithful are forever kneeling at one shrine or the other. But at Antwerp not so. In the afternoon you can go to the church, and be civilly treated; but you must pay a franc at the side gate. In the forenoon the doors are open, to be sure, and there is no one to levy an entrance-fee. I was standing ever so still, looking through the great gates of the choir at the twinkling lights, and listening to the distant chants of the priests performing the service, when a sweet chorus from the organ-loft broke out behind me overhead, and I turned round. My friend the drum-major ecclesiastic was down upon me in a moment. "Do not turn your back to the altar during divine service," says he, in very intelligible English. I take the rebuke, and turn a soft right-about face, and listen a while as the service continues. See it I cannot, nor the altar and its ministrants. We are separated from these by a great screen and closed gates of iron, through which the lamps glitter and the chant comes by gusts only. Seeing a score of children trotting down a side aisle, I think I may follow them. I am tired of looking at that hideous old pulpit with its grotesque monsters and decorations. I slip off to the side aisle; but my friend the drum-major is instantly after me — almost I thought he was going to lay hands on me. "You mustn't go there," says he; "you mustn't disturb the service." I was moving as quietly as might be, and ten paces off there were twenty children kicking and clattering at their ease. I point them out to the Swiss. "They come to pray," says he. "*You* don't come to pray, you" — "When I come to pay," says I, "I am welcome;" and with this withering sarcasm, I walk out of church in a huff. I don't envy the feelings of that beadle after receiving point blank such a stroke of wit.

Leo Belgicus. — Perhaps you will say after this I am a prejudiced critic. I see the pictures in the cathedral fuming under the rudeness of that beadle, or at the lawful hours and prices, pestered by a swarm of shabby touters, who come behind me chattering in bad English, and who would have me see the sights through their mean, greedy eyes. Better see Rubens anywhere than in a church. At the Academy, for example, where you may study him at your leisure. But at church? — I would as soon ask Alexandre Dumas for a sermon. Either would paint you a martyrdom very fiercely and picturesquely — writhing muscles flaming coals, scowling captains and executioners, swarming groups, and light, shade, color, most dexterously brilliant or dark; but in Rubens I am admiring the performer rather than the piece. With what astonishing rapidity he travels over his canvas! how tellingly the cool lights and warm shadows are made to contrast and relieve each other! how that blazing, blowsy penitent in yellow satin and glittering hair carries down the stream of light across the picture! This is the way to work, my boys, and earn a hundred florins a day. See! I am as sure of my line as a skater of making his figure of eight! and down with a sweep goes a brawny arm or a flowing curl of drapery. The figures arrange themselves as if by magic. The paint-pots are exhausted in furnishing brown shadows. The pupils look wondering on, as the master careers over the canvas. Isabel or Helena, wife No. 1 or No. 2, are sitting by, buxom, exuberant, ready to be painted; and the children are boxing in the corner, waiting till they are wanted to figure as cherubs in the picture. Grave burghers and gentlefolks come in on a visit. There are oysters and Rhenish always ready on yonder table. Was there ever such a painter? He has been an ambassador, an actual Excellency, and what better man could be chosen? He speaks all the languages. He earns a hundred florins a day. Prodigious! Thirty-six thousand five hundred florins a year. Enormous! He rides out to his castle with a score of gentlemen after him, like the Governor. That is his own portrait as St. George. You know he is an English knight? Those are his two wives as the two Maries. He chooses the handsomest wives. He rides the handsomest horses. He paints the handsomest pictures. He gets the handsomest prices for them. That slim young Van Dyck, who was his pupil, has genius too, and is painting all the noble ladies in England, and turning the heads of some of them. And Jordaens — what a droll dog and clever fellow! Have you seen his fat Silenus? The master himself could not paint better. And his altar-piece at St. Bavon's? He can paint you any thing that Jordaens can — a drunken jollification of boors and doxies, or a martyr howling with half his skin off. What a knowledge of anatomy! But there is nothing like the master — nothing. He can paint you his thirty-six thousand five hundred florins' worth a year. Have you heard of what he has done for the French Court? Prodigious! I can't look at Rubens' pictures without fancying I see that handsome figure swaggering before the canvas. And Hans Hemmelinck at Bruges? Have you never seen that dear old hospital of St. John, on passing the gate of which you enter into the fifteenth century? I see the wounded soldier still lingering in the house, and tended by the kind gray sisters. His little panel on its easel is placed at the light. He covers his board with the most wondrous, beautiful little figures, in robes as bright as rubies and amethysts. I think he must have a magic glass, in which he catches the reflection of little cherubs with many-colored wings, very little and bright. Angels, in long crisp robes of white, surrounded with halos of gold, come and flutter across the mirror, and he draws them. He hears mass every day. He fasts through Lent. No monk is more austere and holy than Hans. Which do you love best to behold, the lamb or the lion? the eagle rushing through the storm, and pouncing mayhap on carrion; or the linnet warbling on the spray?

By much the most delightful of the *Christopher* set of Rubens to my mind (and *ego* is introduced on these occasions, so that the opinion may pass only for my own, at the reader's humble service to be received or declined) is the "Presentation in the Temple:" splendid in color, in sentiment sweet and tender, finely conveying the story. To be sure, all the others tell their tale unmistakably — witness that coarse "Salutation," that magnificent "Adoration of the Kings" (at the Museum), by the same strong downright hands; that wonderful "Communion of St. Francis," which, I think, gives the key to the artist's *faire* better than any of his performances. I have passed hours before that picture in my time, trying and sometimes fancying I could understand by what masses and contrasts the artist arrived at his effect. In many others of the pictures parts of his method are painfully obvious, and you see how grief and agony are produced by blue lips, and eyes rolling blood-shot with dabs of vermilion. There is something simple in the practice. Contort the eyebrow sufficiently, and place the eyeball near it, — by a few lines you have anger or fierceness depicted. Give me a mouth with no special expression, and pop a dab of carmine at each extremity — and there are the lips smiling. This is art if you will, but a very naïve kind of art: and now you know the trick, don't you see how easy it is?

Tu Quoque. — Now you know the trick, suppose you take a canvas and see whether *you* can do it? There are brushes, palettes, and gallipots full of paint and varnish. Have you tried, my dear sir — you, who set up to be a connoisseur? Have you tried? I have — and many a day. And the end of the day's labor? O dismal conclusion! Is this puerile niggling, this feeble scrawl, this impotent rubbish, all you can produce — you, who but now found Rubens commonplace and vulgar, and were pointing out the tricks of his mystery? Pardon, O great chief, magnificent master and poet! You can *do*. We critics, who sneer and are wise, can but pry, and measure, and doubt, and carp. Look at the lion. Did you ever see such a gross, shaggy, mangy, roaring brute? Look at him eating lumps of raw meat — positively bleeding, and raw and tough — till, faugh! it turns one's stomach to see him — O the coarse wretch! Yes, but he is a lion. Rubens has lifted his great hand, and the mark he has made has endured for two centuries, and we still continue wondering at him, and admiring him. What a strength in that arm! What splendor of will hidden behind that tawny beard, and those honest eyes! Sharpen your pen, my good critic. Shoot a feather into him; hit him, and make him wince. Yes, you may hit him fair, and make him bleed, too; but, for all that, he is a lion — a mighty, conquering, generous, rampagious Leo Belgicus — monarch of his wood. And he is not dead yet, and I will not kick at him.

Sir Antony. — In that "Pietà" of Van Dyck, in the Museum, have you ever looked at the yellow-robed angel, with the black scarf thrown over her wings and robe? What a charming figure of grief and beauty! What a pretty compassion it inspires! It soothes and pleases me like a sweet rhythmic chant. See how delicately the yellow robe contrasts with the blue sky behind, and the scarf binds the two! If Rubens lacked grace, Van Dyck abounded in it. What a consummate elegance! What a perfect cavalier! No wonder the fine ladies in England admired Sir Antony. Look at —

Here the clock strikes three, and the three gendarmes who keep the Musée cry out, "*Allons! Sortons! Il est trois heures! Allez! Sortez!*" and they skip out of the gallery as happy as boys running from school. And we must go too, for though many stay behind — many Britons with Murray's handbooks in their handsome hands — they have paid a franc for entrance-fee, you see; and we knew nothing about the franc for entrance until those gendarmes with sheathed sabres had driven us out of this Paradise.

But it was good to go and drive on the great quays, and see the ships unlading, and by the citadel, and wonder howabouts and whereabouts it was so strong. We expect a citadel to look like Gibraltar or Ehrenbreitstein at least. But in this one there is nothing to see but a flat plain and some ditches, and some trees, and mounds of uninteresting green. And then I remember how there was a boy at school, a little dumpy fellow of no personal appearance whatever, who couldn't be overcome except by a much bigger champion, and the immensest quantity of thrashing. A perfect citadel of a boy, with a General Chassé sitting in that bomb-proof casemate, his heart, letting blow after blow come thumping about his head, and never thinking of giving in.

And we go home, and we dine in the company of Britons, at the comfortable Hôtel du Parc, and we have bought a novel apiece for a shilling, and every half-hour the sweet carillon plays the waltz from *Dinorah* in the air. And we have been happy; and it seems about a month since we left London yesterday; and nobody knows where we are, and we defy care and the postman.

Spoorweg. — Vast green flats, speckled by spotted cows, and bound by a gray frontier of windmills; shining canals stretching through the green; odors like those exhaled from the Thames in the dog-days, and a fine pervading smell of cheese; little trim houses, with tall roofs, and great windows of many panes; gazebos, or summer-houses, hanging over pea-green canals; kind-looking, dumpling-faced farmers' women, with laced caps and golden frontlets and ear-rings; about the houses and towns which we pass a great air of comfort and neatness; a queer feeling of wonder that you can't understand what your fellow-passengers are saying, the tone of whose voices, and a certain comfortable dowdiness of dress, are so like our own; — whilst we are remarking on these sights, sounds, smells, the little railway journey from Rotterdam to the Hague comes to an end. I speak to the railway porters and hackney coachmen in English, and they reply in their own language, and it seems somehow as if we understood each other perfectly. The carriage drives to the handsome, comfortable, cheerful hotel. We sit down a score at the table; and there is one foreigner and his wife, — I mean every other man and woman at dinner are English. As we are close to the sea, and in the midst of endless canals, we have no fish. We are reminded of dear England by the noble prices which we pay for wines. I confess I lost my temper yesterday at Rotterdam, where I had to pay a florin for a bottle of ale (the water not being drinkable, and country or Bavarian beer not being genteel enough for the hotel); — I confess, I say, that my fine temper was ruffled, when the bottle of pale ale turned out to be a pint bottle; and I meekly told the waiter that I had bought beer at Jerusalem at a less price. But then Rotterdam is eighteen hours from London, and the steamer with the passengers and beer comes up to the hotel windows; whilst to Jerusalem they have to carry the ale on camels' backs from Beyrout or Jaffa, and through hordes of marauding Arabs, who evidently don't care for pale ale, though I am told it is not forbidden in the Koran. Mine would have been very good, but I choked with rage whilst drinking it. A florin for a bottle, and that bottle having the words "imperial pint," in bold relief, on the surface! It was too much. I intended not to say any thing about it; but I *must* speak. A florin a bottle, and that bottle a pint! Oh, for shame! for shame! I can't cork down my indignation; I froth up with fury; I am pale with wrath, and bitter with scorn.

As we drove through the old city at night, how it swarmed and hummed with life! What a special clatter, crowd, and outcry there was in the Jewish quarter, where myriads of young ones were trotting about the fishy street! Why don't they have lamps? We passed by canals seeming so full that a pailful of water more would overflow the place. The *laquais-de-place* calls out the names of the buildings: the town-hall, the cathedral, the arsenal, the synagogue, the statue of Erasmus. Get along! *We* know the statue of Erasmus well enough. We pass over drawbridges by canals where thousands of barges are at roost. At roost—at rest! Shall *we* have rest in those bedrooms, those ancient lofty bedrooms, in that inn where we have to pay a florin for a pint of pa—psha at the "New Bath Hotel" on the Boompjes? If this dreary edifice is the "New Bath," what must the Old Bath be like? As I feared to go to bed, I sat in the coffee-room as long as I might; but three young men were imparting their private adventures to each other with such freedom and liveliness that I felt I ought not to listen to their artless prattle. As I put the light out, and felt the bedclothes and darkness overwhelm me, it was with an awful sense of terror—that sort of sensation which I should think going down in a diving-bell would give. Suppose the apparatus goes wrong, and they don't understand your signal to mount? Suppose your matches miss fire when you wake; when you *want* them, when you will have to rise in half an hour, and do battle with the horrid enemy who crawls on you in the darkness? I protest I never was more surprised than when I woke and beheld the light of dawn. Indian birds and strange trees were visible on the ancient gilt hangings of the lofty chamber, and through the windows the Boompjes and the ships along the quay. We have all read of deserters being brought out, and made to kneel, with their eyes bandaged, and hearing the word to "Fire" given! I declare I underwent all the terrors of execution that night, and wonder how I ever escaped unwounded.

But if ever I go to the "Bath Hotel," Rotterdam, again, I am a Dutchman. A guilder for a bottle of pale ale, and that bottle a pint! Ah! for shame—for shame!

Mine Ease in Mine Inn.—Do you object to talk about inns? It always seems to me to be very good talk. Walter Scott is full of inns. In "Don Quixote" and "Gil Blas" there is plenty of inn-talk. Sterne, Fielding, and Smollett constantly speak about them; and, in their travels, the last two tot up the bill, and describe the dinner quite honestly; whilst Mr. Sterne becomes sentimental over a cab, and weeps generous tears over a donkey.

How I admire and wonder at the information in Murray's Handbooks—wonder how it is got, and admire the travellers who get it. For instance, you read: Amiens (please select your towns), 60,000 inhabitants. Hotels, &c.—"Lion d'Or," good and clean. "Le Lion d'Argent," so so. "Le Lion Noir," bad, dirty, and dear. Now say, there are three travellers—three inn-inspectors, who are sent forth by Mr. Murray on a great commission, and who stop at every inn in the world. The eldest goes to the "Lion d'Or"—capital house, good table-d'hôte, excellent wine, moderate charges. The second commissioner tries the "Silver Lion"—tolerable house, bed, dinner, bill, and so forth. But fancy commissioner No. 3—the poor fag, doubtless, and boots of the party. He has to go to the "Lion Noir." He knows he is to have a bad dinner—he eats it uncomplainingly. He is to have bad wine. He swallows it, grinding his wretched teeth, and aware that he will be unwell in consequence. He knows he is to have a dirty bed, and what he is to expect there. He pops out the candle. He sinks into those dingy sheets. He delivers over his body to the nightly tormentors, he pays an exorbitant bill, and he writes down "Lion Noir, bad, dirty, dear." Next day the commission sets out for Arras, we will say, and they begin again: "Le Cochon d'Or," "Le Cochon d'Argent," "Le Cochon Noir"—and that is poor Boots's inn, of course. What a life that poor man must lead! What horrors of dinners he has to go through! What a hide he must have! And yet not impervious; for unless he is bitten, how is he to be able to warn others? No; on second thoughts, you will perceive that he ought to have a very delicate skin. The monsters ought to troop to him eagerly, and bite him instantaneously and freely, so that he may be able to warn all future handbook buyers of their danger. I fancy this man devoting himself to danger, to dirt, to bad dinners, to sour wine, to damp beds, to midnight agonies, to extortionate bills. I admire him, I thank him. Think of this champion, who devotes his body for us—this dauntless gladiator going to do battle alone in the darkness, with no other armor than a light helmet of cotton, and a *lorica* of calico. I pity and honor him. Go, Sparticus! Go, devoted man—to bleed, to groan, to suffer—and smile in silence as the wild beasts assail thee!

How did I come into this talk? I protest it was the word inn set me off—and here is one, the "Hôtel de Belle Vue," at the Hague, as comfortable, as handsome, as cheerful, as any I ever took mine ease in. And the Bavarian beer, my dear friend, how good and brisk and light it is! Take another glass—it refreshes and does not stupefy—and then we will sally out, and see the town and the park and the pictures.

The prettiest little brick city, the pleasantest little park to ride in, the neatest comfortable people walking about, the canals not unsweet, and busy and picturesque with old-world life. Rows upon rows of houses, built with the neatest little bricks, with windows fresh painted, and tall doors polished and carved to a nicety. What a pleasant spacious garden our inn has, all sparkling with autumn flowers, and bedizened with statues! At the end is a row of trees, and a summer-house, over the canal, where you might go and smoke a pipe with Mynheer Van Dunch, and quite cheerfully catch the ague. Yesterday, as we passed, they were making hay, and stacking it in a barge which was lying by the meadow, handy. Round about Kensington Palace there are houses, roofs, chimneys, and bricks like these. I feel that a Dutchman is a man and a brother. It is very funny to read the newspaper, one can understand it somehow. Sure it is the neatest, gayest little city—scores and hundreds of mansions looking like Cheyne Walk, or the ladies' schools about Chiswick and Hackney.

Le Gros Lot.—To a few lucky men the chance befalls of reaching fame at once, and (if it is of any profit *morituro*) retaining the admiration of the world. Did poor Oliver, when he was at Leyden yonder, ever think that he should paint a little picture which should secure him the applause and pity of all Europe for a century after? He and Sterne drew the twenty thousand prize of fame. The latter had splendid instalments during his lifetime. The ladies pressed round him; the wits admired him, the fashion hailed the successor of Rabelais. Goldsmith's little gem was hardly so valued until later days. Their works still form the wonder and delight of the lovers of English art; and the pictures of the Vicar and Uncle Toby are among the masterpieces of our English school. Here in the Hague Gallery is Paul

Potter's pale, eager face, and yonder is the magnificent work by which the young fellow achieved his fame. How did you, so young, come to paint so well? What hidden power lay in that weakly lad that enabled him to achieve such a wonderful victory? Could little Mozart, when he was five years old, tell you how he came to play those wonderful sonatas? Potter was gone out of the world before he was thirty, but left this prodigy (and I know not how many more specimens of his genius and skill) behind him. The details of this admirable picture are as curious as the effect is admirable and complete. The weather being unsettled, and clouds and sunshine in the gusty sky, we saw in our little tour numberless Paul Potters — the meadows streaked with sunshine and spotted with the cattle, the city twinkling in the distance, the thunder-clouds glooming overhead. Napoleon carried off the picture (*vide* Murray) amongst the spoils of his bow and spear to decorate his triumph of the Louvre. If I were a conquering prince, I would have this picture certainly, and the Raphael "Madonna" from Dresden, and the Titian "Assumption" from Venice, and that matchless Rembrandt of the "Dissection." The prostrate nations would howl with rage as my gendarmes took off the pictures, nicely packed, and addressed to "Mr. the Director of my Imperial Palace of the Louvre, at Paris. This side uppermost." The Austrians, Prussians, Saxons, Italians, &c., should be free to come and visit my capital, and bleat with tears before the pictures torn from their native cities. Their ambassadors would meekly remonstrate, and with faded grins make allusions to the feeling of despair occasioned by the absence of the beloved works of art. Bah! I would offer them a pinch of snuff out of my box as I walked along my gallery, with their Excellencies cringing after me. Zenobia was a fine woman and a queen, but she had to walk in Aurelian's triumph. The *procédé* was *peu délicat? En usez vous, mon cher monsieur!* (The marquis says the "Macaba" is delicious.) What a splendor of color there is in that cloud! What a richness, what a freedom of handling, and what a marvellous precision! I trod upon your Excellency's corn? — a thousand pardons. His Excellency grins and declares that he rather likes to have his corns trodden on. Were you ever very angry with Soult — about that Murillo which we have bought? The veteran loved that picture because it saved the life of a fellow-creature — the fellow-creature who hid it, and whom the Duke intended to hang unless the picture was forthcoming.

We gave several thousand pounds for it — how many thousand? About its merit is a question of taste which we will not here argue. If you choose to place Murillo in the first class of painters, founding his claim upon these Virgin altar-pieces, I am your humble servant. Tom Moore painted altar-pieces as well as Milton, and warbled Sacred Songs and Loves of the Angels after his fashion. I wonder did Watteau ever try historical subjects? And as for Greuze, you know that his heads will fetch 1,000*l.*, 1,500*l.*, 2,000*l.*, — as much as a Sêvres "cabaret" of Rose du Barri. If cost price is to be your criterion of worth, what shall we say to that little receipt for 10*l.* for the copyright of "Paradise Lost," which used to hang in old Mr. Rogers's room? When living painters, as frequently happens in our days, see their pictures sold at auctions for four or five times the sums which they originally received, are they enraged or elated? A hundred years ago the state of the picture-market was different: that dreary old Italian stock was much higher than at present; Rembrandt himself, a close man, was known to be in difficulties. If ghosts are fond of money still, what a wrath his must be at the present value of his works!

The Hague Rembrandt is the greatest and grandest of all his pieces to my mind. Some of the heads are as sweetly and lightly painted as Gainsborough; the faces not ugly, but delicate and high-bred; the exquisite gray tones are charming to mark and study; the heads not plastered, but painted with a free, liquid brush: the result, one of the great victories won by this consummate chief, and left for the wonder and delight of succeeding ages.

The humblest volunteer in the ranks of art, who has served a campaign or two ever so ingloriously, has at least this good fortune of understanding, or fancying he is able to understand, how the battle has been fought, and how the engaged general won it. This is the Rhinelander's most brilliant achievement — victory along the whole line. "The Night-watch" at Amsterdam is magnificent in parts, but on the side to the spectator's right, smoky and dim. "The Five Masters of the Drapers" is wonderful for depth, strength, brightness, massive power. What words are these to express a picture! to describe a description! I once saw a moon riding in the sky serenely, attended by her sparkling maids of honor, and a little lady said, with an air of great satisfaction, "*I must sketch it.*" Ah, my dear lady, if with an H. B., a Bristol board, and a bit of india-rubber, you can sketch the starry firmament on high, and the moon in her glory, I make you my compliment! I can't sketch "The Five Drapers" with any ink or pen at present at command — but can look with all my eyes, and be thankful to have seen such a masterpiece.

They say he was a moody, ill-conditioned man, the old tenant of the mill. What does he think of the "Vander Helst" which hangs opposite his "Night-watch," and which is one of the great pictures of the world? It is not painted by so great a man as Rembrandt; but there it is — to see it is an event of your life. Having beheld it you have lived in the year 1648, and celebrated the treaty of Munster. You have shaken the hands of the Dutch Guardsmen, eaten from their platters, drunk their Rhenish, heard their jokes, as they wagged their jolly beards. The Amsterdam Catalogue discourses thus about it: — a model catalogue: it gives you the prices paid, the signatures of the painters, a succinct description of the work.

"This masterpiece represents a banquet of the civic guard, which took place on the 18th June, 1648, in the great hall of the St. Joris Doele, on the Singel at Amsterdam, to celebrate the conclusion of the Peace at Munster. The thirty-five figures composing the picture are all portraits.

"'The Captain WITSE' is placed at the head of the table, and attracts our attention first. He is dressed in black velvet, his breast covered with a cuirass, on his head a broad-brimmed black hat with white plumes. He is comfortably seated on a chair of black oak, with a velvet cushion, and holds in his left hand, supported on his knee, a magnificent drinking-horn, surrounded by a St. George destroying the dragon, and ornamented with olive-leaves. The captain's features express cordiality and good-humor; he is grasping the hand of 'Lieutenant VAN WAVERN' seated near him, in a habit of dark gray, with lace and buttons of gold, lace-collar and wristbands, his feet crossed, with boots of yellow leather, with large tops, and gold spurs, on his head a black hat and dark-brown plumes. Behind him, at the centre of the picture, is the standard-bearer, 'JACOB BANNING,' in an easy martial attitude, hat in hand, his right hand on his chair, his right leg on his left knee. He holds the flag of blue silk, in which the Virgin is embroidered (such a silk! such a flag! such a piece of painting!) emblematic of the town of Amsterdam. The banner covers his shoulder, and he looks towards the spectator frankly and complacently.

"The man behind him is probably one of the sergeants. His head is bare. He wears a cuirass, and yellow gloves, gray stockings, and boots with large tops, and kneecaps of cloth. He has a napkin on his knees, and in his hand a piece of ham, a slice of bread, and a knife. The old man behind is probably 'WILLIAM THE DRUMMER.' He has his hat in his right hand, and in his left a gold-footed wineglass, filled with white wine. He wears a red scarf, and a black satin doublet, with little slashes of yellow silk. Behind the drummer, two matchlock-men are seated at the end of the table. One in a large black habit, a napkin on his knee, a *hausse-col* of iron, and a linen scarf and collar. He is eating with his knife. The other holds a long glass of white wine. Four musketeers, with different shaped hats, are behind these, one holding a glass, the three others with their guns on their shoulders. Other guests are placed between the personage who is giving the toast and the standard-bearer. One with his hat off, and his hand uplifted, is talking to another. The second is carving a fowl. A third holds a silver plate; and another, in the background, a silver flagon, from which he fills a cup. The corner behind the captain is filled by two seated personages, one of whom is peeling an orange. Two others are standing, armed with halberts, of whom one holds a plumed hat. Behind him are other three individuals, one of them holding a pewter pot, on which the name 'Poock,' the landlord of the 'Hotel Doele,' is engraved. At the back, a maid-servant is coming in with a pasty, crowned with a turkey. Most of the guests are listening to the captain. From an open window in the distance, the façades of two houses are seen, surmounted by stone figures of sheep."

There, now you know all about it: now you can go home and paint just such another. If you do, do pray remember to paint the hands of the figures as they are here depicted; they are as wonderful portraits as the faces. None of your slim Van Dyck elegances, which have done duty at the cuffs of so many doublets; but each man with a hand for himself, as with a face for himself. I blushed for the coarseness of one of the chiefs in this great company, that fellow behind "WILLIAM THE DRUMMER," splendidly attired, sitting full in the face of the public; and holding a pork-bone in his hand. Suppose "The Saturday Review" critic were to come suddenly on this picture? Ah! what a shock it would give that noble nature! Why is that knuckle of pork not painted out? at any rate, why is not a little fringe of lace painted round it? or a cut pink paper? or couldn't a smelling-bottle be painted in instead, with a crest and a gold top, or a cambric pocket-handkerchief, in lieu of the horrid pig, with a pink coronet in the corner? or suppose you covered the man's hand (which is very coarse and strong), and gave him the decency of a kid glove? But a piece of pork in a naked hand? O nerves and eau de Cologne, hide it, hide it!

In spite of this lamentable coarseness, my noble sergeant, give me thy hand as nature made it! A great, and famous, and noble handiwork I have seen here. Not the greatest picture in the world — not a work of the highest genius — but a performance so great, various, and admirable, so shrewd of humor, so wise of observation, so honest and complete of expression, that to have seen it has been a delight, and to remember it will be a pleasure for days to come. Well done, Bartholomeus Vander Helst! Brave, meritorious, victorious, happy Bartholomew, to whom it has been given to produce a masterpiece!

May I take off my hat and pay a respectful compliment to Jan Steen, Esq.? He is a glorious composer

His humor is as frank as Fielding's. Look at his own figure sitting in the window-sill yonder, and roaring with laughter! What a twinkle in the eyes! what a mouth it is for a song, or a joke, or a noggin! I think the composition in some of Jan's pictures amounts to the sublime, and look at them with the same delight and admiration which I have felt before works of the very highest style. This gallery is admirable — and the city in which the gallery is, is perhaps even more wonderful and curious to behold than the gallery.

The first landing at Calais (or, I suppose, on any foreign shore) — the first sight of an Eastern city — the first view of Venice — and this of Amsterdam, are among the delightful shocks which I have had as a traveller. Amsterdam is as good as Venice, with a superadded humor and grotesqueness, which gives the sight-seer the most singular zest and pleasure. A run through Pekin I could hardly fancy to be more odd, strange, and yet familiar. This rush, and crowd, and prodigious vitality; this immense swarm of life; these busy waters, crowding barges, swinging drawbridges, piled ancient gables, spacious markets teeming with people; that ever-wonderful Jews' quarter; that dear old world of painting and the past, yet alive, and throbbing, and palpable — actual, and yet passing before you swiftly and strangely as a dream! Of the many journeys of this Roundabout life, that drive through Amsterdam is to be specially and gratefully remembered. You have never seen the palace of Amsterdam, my dear sir? Why, there's a marble hall in that palace that will frighten you as much as any hall in "Vathek," or a nightmare. At one end of that old, cold, glassy, glittering, ghostly, marble hall there stands a throne, on which a white marble king ought to sit with his white legs gleaming down into the white marble below, and his white eyes looking at a great white marble Atlas, who bears on his icy shoulders a blue globe as big as the full moon. If he were not a genie, and enchanted, and with a strength altogether hyperatlantean, he would drop the moon with a shriek on to the white marble floor, and it would splitter into perdition. And the palace would rock, and heave, and tumble; and the waters would rise, rise, rise; and the gables sink, sink, sink; and the barges would rise up to the chimneys; and the water-souchee fishes would flap over the Boompjes, where the pigeons and storks used to perch; and the Amster, and the Rotter, and the Saar, and the Op, and all the dams of Holland, would burst, and the Zuyder Zee roll over the dykes; and you would wake out of your dream, and find yourself sitting in your arm-chair.

Was it a dream? it seems like one. Have we been to Holland? have we heard the chimes at midnight at Antwerp? Were we really away for a week, or have I been sitting up in the room dozing, before this stale old desk? Here's the desk; yes. But, if it has been a dream, how could I have learned to hum that tune out of *Dinorah?* Ah, is it that tune, or myself that I am humming? If it was a dream, how comes this yellow NOTICE DES TABLEAUX DU MUSÉE D'AMSTERDAM AVEC FACSIMILE DES MONOGRAMMES before me, and this signature of the gallant

Bartholomeus Vander Helst fecit A° 1648.

Yes, indeed, it was a delightful little holiday; it lasted a whole week. With the exception of that little pint of *amari aliquid* at Rotterdam, we were all very happy. We might have gone on being happy for whoever knows how many days more? a week more, ten days more: who knows how long that dear teetotum happiness can be made to spin without toppling over?

But one of the party had desired letters to be sent *poste restante*, Amsterdam. The post-office is hard by that awful palace where the Atlas is, and which we really saw.

There was only one letter, you see. Only one chance of finding us. There it was. "The post has only this moment come in," says the smirking commissioner. And he hands over the paper, thinking he has done something clever.

Before the letter had been opened, I could read COME BACK, as clearly as if it had been painted on the wall. It was all over. The spell was broken. The sprightly lightly holiday fairy that had frisked and gambolled so kindly beside us for eight days of sunshine — or rain which was as cheerful as sunshine — gave a parting piteous look, and whisked away and vanished. And yonder scuds the postman, and here is the old desk.

NIL NISI BONUM.

ALMOST the last words which Sir Walter spoke to Lockhart, his biographer, were, "Be a good man, my dear!" and with the last flicker of breath on his dying lips he sighed a farewell to his family, and passed away blessing them.

Two men, famous, admired, beloved, have just left us, the Goldsmith and the Gibbon of our time.* Ere a few weeks are over, many a critic's pen will be at work, reviewing their lives, and passing judgment on their works. This is no review or history or criticism: only a word in testimony of respect and regard from a man of letters, who owes to his own professional labor the honor of becoming acquainted with these two eminent literary men. One was the first ambassador whom the New World of Letters sent to the Old. He was born almost with the Republic; the *pater patriæ* had laid his hand on the child's head. He bore Washington's name: he came amongst us bringing the kindest sympathy, the most artless, smiling goodwill. His new country (which some people here might be disposed to regard rather superciliously) could send us, as he showed in his own person, a gentleman, who, though himself born in no very high sphere, was most finished, polished, easy, witty, quiet, and, socially, the equal of the most refined Europeans. If Irving's welcome in England was a kind one, was it not also gratefully remembered? If he ate our salt, did he not pay us with a thankful heart? Who can calculate the amount of friendliness and good feeling for our country which this writer's generous and untiring regard for us disseminated in his own? His books are read by millions* of his countrymen whom he has taught to love England, and why to love her. It would have been easy to speak otherwise than he did: to inflame national rancors, which, at the time when he first became known as a public writer, war had just renewed: to cry down the old civilization at the expense of the new: to point out our faults, arrogance, short-comings, and give the republic to infer how much she was the parent state's superior. There are writers enough in the United States, honest and otherwise, who preach that kind of doctrine. But the good Irving, the peaceful, the

* Washington Irving died, Nov. 28, 1859; Lord Macaulay died, Dec. 28, 1859.

* See his *Life* in the most remarkable "Dictionary of Authors," published lately at Philadelphia, by Mr. Alibone.

friendly, had no place for bitterness in his heart, and no scheme but kindness. Received in England with extraordinary tenderness and friendship (Scott, Southey, Byron, a hundred others have borne witness to their liking for him), he was a messenger of goodwill and peace between his country and ours. "See, friends!" he seems to say, "these English are not so wicked, rapacious, callous, proud, as you have been taught to believe them. I went amongst them a humble man; won my way by my pen; and, when known, found every hand held out to me with kindliness and welcome. Scott is a great man, you acknowledge. Did not Scott's King of England give a gold medal to him, and another to me, your countryman, and a stranger?"

Tradition in the United States still fondly retains the history of the feasts and rejoicings which awaited Irving on his return to his native country from Europe. He had a national welcome; he stammered in his speeches, hid himself in confusion, and the people loved him all the better. He had worthily represented America in Europe. In that young community a man who brings home with him abundant European testimonials is still treated with respect (I have found American writers, of wide-world reputation, strangely solicitous about the opinions of quite obscure British critics, and elated or depressed by their judgments); and Irving went home medalled by the King, diplomatized by the University, crowned and honored and admired. He had not in any way intrigued for his honors, he had fairly won them; and in Irving's instance, as in others, the old country was glad and eager to pay them.

In America, the love and regard for Irving was a national sentiment. Party wars are perpetually raging there, and are carried on by the press with a rancor and fierceness against individuals which exceed British, almost Irish, virulence. It seemed to me, during a year's travel in the country, as if no one ever aimed a blow at Irving. All men held their hand from that harmless, friendly peacemaker. I had the good fortune to see him at New York, Philadelphia, Baltimore, and Washington,* and remarked how in every place he was honored and welcome. Every large city has its "Irving House." The country takes pride in the fame of its men of letters. The gate of his own charming little domain on the beautiful Hudson River was forever swinging before visitors who came to him. He shut out no one.† I had seen many pictures of this house, and read descriptions of it, in both of which it was treated with a not unusual American exaggeration. It was but a pretty little cabin of a place; the gentleman of the press who took notes of the place, whilst his kind old host was sleeping, might have visited the whole house in a couple of minutes.

And how came it that this house was so small, when Mr. Irving's books were sold by hundreds of thousands, nay, millions, when his profits were known to be large, and the habits of life of the good old bachelor were notoriously modest and simple? He had loved once in his life. The lady he loved died; and he, whom all the world loved, never sought to replace

* At Washington, Mr. Irving came to a lecture given by the writer, which Mr. Filmore and General Pierce, the President and President Elect, were also kind enough to attend together. "Two Kings of Brentford smelling at one rose," says Irving, looking up with his good-humored smile.

† Mr. Irving described to me, with that humor and good humor which he always kept, how, amongst other visitors, a member of the British press, who had carried his distinguished pen to America (where he employed it in vilifying his own country), came to Sunnyside, introduced himself to Irving, partook of his wine and luncheon, and in two days described Mr. Irving, his house, his nieces, his meal, and his manner of dozing afterwards, in a New York paper. On another occasion, Irving said, laughing, "Two persons came to me, and one held me in conversation whilst the other miscreant took my portrait!"

her. I can't say how much the thought of that fidelity has touched me. Does not the very cheerfulness of his after-life add to the pathos of that untold story? To grieve always was not in his nature; or, when he had his sorrow, to bring all the world in to condole with him and bemoan it. Deep and quiet he lays the love of his heart, and buries it; and grass and flowers grow over the scarred ground in due time.

Irving had such a small house and such narrow rooms, because there was a great number of people to occupy them. He could only afford to keep one old horse (which, lazy and aged as it was, managed once or twice to run away with that careless old horseman). He could only afford to give plain sherry to that amiable British paragraph-monger from New York, who saw the patriarch asleep over his modest, blameless cup, and fetched the public into his private chamber to look at him. Irving could only live very modestly, because the wifeless, childless man had a number of children to whom he was as a father. He had as many as nine nieces, I am told — I saw two of these ladies at his house — with all of whom the dear old man had shared the produce of his labor and genius.

"*Be a good man, my dear.*" One can't but think of these last words of the veteran Chief of Letters, who had tasted and tested the value of worldly success, admiration, prosperity. Was Irving not good, and, of his works, was not his life the best part? In his family, gentle, generous, good-humored, affectionate, self-denying: in society, a delightful example of complete gentlemanhood; quite unspoiled by prosperity; never obsequious to the great (or, worse still, to the base and mean, as some public men are forced to be in his and other countries); eager to acknowledge every contemporary's merit; always kind and affable to the young members of his calling; in his professional bargains and mercantile dealings delicately honest and grateful; one of the most charming masters of our lighter language; the constant friend to us and our nation; to men of letters doubly dear, not for his wit and genius merely, but as an examplar of goodness, probity, and pure life: — I don't know what sort of testimonial will be raised to him in his own country, where generous and enthusiastic acknowledgment of American merit is never wanting: but Irving was in our service as well as theirs: and as they have placed a stone at Greenwich yonder in memory of that gallant young Bellot, who shared the perils and fate of some of our Arctic seamen, I would like to hear of some memorial raised by English writers and friends of letters in affectionate remembrance of the dear and good Washington Irving.

As for the other writer, whose departure many friends, some few most dearly-loved relatives, and multitudes of admiring readers deplore, our republic has already decreed his statue, and he must have known that he had earned this posthumous honor. He is not a poet and man of letters merely, but citizen, statesman, a great British worthy. Almost from the first moment when he appears, amongst boys, amongst college students, amongst men, he is marked, and takes rank as a great Englishman. All sorts of successes are easy to him: as a lad he goes down into the arena with others, and wins all the prizes to which he has a mind. A place in the senate is straightway offered to the young man. He takes his seat there; he speaks, when so minded, without party anger or intrigue, but not without party faith and a sort of heroic enthusiasm for his cause. Still he is poet and philosopher even more than orator. That he may have leisure and means to pursue his darling studies, he absents himself for a while, and accepts a richly-remunerative post in the East. As learned a man may live in a cottage or a college common-room; but it always seemed to me that ample means and recognized rank were Macaulay's as of right. Years ago there was a wretched outcry raised because Mr. Macaulay dated a letter from Windsor Castle, where he was staying. Immortal gods! Was this man not a fit guest for any palace in the world? or a fit companion for any man or woman in it? I dare say, after Austerlitz, the old K. K. court officials and footmen sneered at Napoleon for dating from Schönbrunn. But that miserable "Windsor Castle" outcry is an echo out of fast-retreating old-world remembrances. The place of such a natural chief was amongst the first of the land; and that country is best, according to our British notion at least, where the man of eminence has the best chance of investing his genius and intellect.

If a company of giants were got together, very likely one or two of the mere six-feet-six people might be angry at the incontestable superiority of the very tallest of the party: and so I have heard some London wits, rather peevish at Macaulay's superiority, complain that he occupied too much of the talk, and so forth. Now that wonderful tongue is to speak no more, will not many a man grieve that he no longer has the chance to listen? To remember the talk is to wonder: to think not only of the treasures he had in his memory, but of the trifles he had stored there, and could produce with equal readiness. Almost on the last day I had the fortune to see him, a conversation happened suddenly to spring up about senior wranglers, and what they had done in after life. To the almost terror of the persons present, Macaulay began with the senior wrangler of 1801-2-3-4, and so on, giving the name of each, and relating his subsequent career and rise. Every man who has known him has his story regarding that astonishing memory. It may be that he was not ill pleased that you should recognize it; but to those prodigious intellectual feats, which were so easy to him, who would grudge his tribute of homage? His talk was, in a word, admirable, and we admired it.

Of the notices which have appeared regarding Lord Macaulay, up to the day when the present lines are written (the 9th of January), the reader should not deny himself the pleasure of looking especially at two. It is a good sign of the times when such articles as these (I mean the articles in "The Times" and "Saturday Review") appear in our public prints about our public men. They educate us, as it were, to admire rightly. An uninstructed person in a museum or at a concert may pass by without recognizing a picture or a passage of music, which the connoisseur by his side may show him is a masterpiece of harmony, or a wonder of artistic skill. After reading these papers you like and respect more the person you have admired so much already. And so with regard to Macaulay's style there may be faults of course — what critic can't point them out? But for the nonce we are not talking about faults: we want to say *nil nisi bonum*. Well — take at hazard any three pages of the "Essays" or "History;"— and, glimmering below the stream of the narrative, as it were, you, an average reader, see one, two, three, a half-score of allusions to other historic facts, characters, literature, poetry, with which you are acquainted. Why is this epithet used? Whence is that simile drawn? How does he manage, in two or three words, to paint an individual, or to indicate a landscape? Your neighbor, who has *his* reading, and his little stock of literature stowed away in his mind, shall detect more points, allusions, happy touches, indicating not only the prodigious memory and vast learning of this master, but the wonderful industry, the honest, humble previous toil of this great scholar. He reads twenty books to write a sentence; he travels a hundred miles to make a line of description.

Many Londoners — not all — have seen the British Museum Library. I speak *à cœur ouvert*, and pray the kindly reader to bear with me. I have seen all sorts of domes of Peters and Pauls, Sophia, Pantheon, — what not? — and have been struck by none of them so much as by that catholic dome in Bloomsbury, under which our million volumes are housed. What peace, what love, what truth, what beauty, what happiness, for all, what generous kindness for you and me, are here spread out! It seems to me one cannot sit down in that place without a heart full of grateful reverence. I own to have said my grace at the table, and to have thanked heaven for this my English birthright, freely to partake of these bountiful books, and to speak the truth I find there. Under the dome which held Macaulay's brain, and from which his solemn eyes looked out on the world but a fortnight since, what a vast, brilliant, and wonderful store of learning was ranged! what strange lore would he not fetch for you at your bidding! A volume of law, or history, a book of poetry familiar or forgotten (except by himself, who forgot nothing), a novel ever so old, and he had it at hand. I spoke to him once about "Clarissa." "Not read 'Clarissa!'" he cried out. "If you have once thoroughly entered on 'Clarissa' and are infected by it, you can't leave it. When I was in India I passed one hot season at the hills, and there were the Governor-General, and the Secretary of Government, and the Commander-in-Chief, and their wives. I had 'Clarissa' with me: and, as soon as they began to read, the whole station was in a passion of excitement about Miss Harlowe and her misfortunes, and her scoundrelly Lovelace! The Governor's wife seized the book, and the Secretary waited for it, and the Chief Justice could not read it for tears!" He acted the whole scene: he paced up and down the "Athenæum" library: I dare say he could have spoken pages of the book — of that book, and of what countless piles of others!

In this little paper let us keep to the text of *nil nisi bonum*. One paper I have read regarding Lord Macaulay says "he had no heart." Why, a man's books may not always speak the truth, but they speak his mind in spite of himself: and it seems to me this man's heart is beating through every page he penned. He is always in a storm of revolt and indignation against wrong, craft, tyranny. How he cheers heroic resistance! how he backs and applauds freedom struggling for its own! how he hates scoundrels, ever so victorious and successful! how he recognizes genius, though selfish villains possess it! The critic who says Macaulay had no heart, might say that Johnson had none: and two men more generous, and more loving, and more hating, and more partial, and more noble, do not live in our history. Those who knew Lord Macaulay knew how admirably tender and generous,* and affectionate he was. It was not his business to bring his family before the theatre footlights, and call for bouquets from the gallery as he wept over them.

If any young man of letters reads this little sermon — and to him, indeed, it is addressed — I would say to him, "Bear Scott's words in your mind, and '*be good, my dear.*'" Here are two literary men gone to their account, and, *laus Deo*, as far as we know, it is fair, and open, and clean. Here is no need of apologies for shortcomings, or explanations of vices which would have been virtues but for unavoidable, &c. Here are two examples of men most differently gifted: each pursuing his calling; each speaking his truth as God bade him; each honest in his life; just and irreproachable in his dealings; dear to his friends; honored by his

* Since the above was written, I have been informed that it has been found, on examining Lord Macaulay's papers, that he was in the habit of giving away *more than a fourth part* of his annual income.

country; beloved at his fireside. It has been the fortunate lot of both to give incalculable happiness and delight to the world, which thanks them in return with an immense kindliness, respect, affection. It may not be our chance, brother scribe, to be endowed with such merit, or rewarded with such fame. But the rewards of these men are rewards paid to *our service*. We may not win the bâton or epaulettes; but God give us strength to guard the honor of the flag!

ON HALF A LOAF.

A LETTER TO MESSRS. BROADWAY, BATTERY, AND CO., OF NEW YORK, BANKERS.

Is it all over? May we lock up the case of instruments? Have we signed our wills; settled up our affairs; pretended to talk and rattle quite cheerfully to the women at dinner, so that they should not be alarmed; sneaked away under some pretext, and looked at the children sleeping in their beds with their little unconscious thumbs in their mouths, and a flush on the soft-pillowed cheek; made every arrangement with Colonel MacTurk, who acts as our second, and knows the other principal a great deal too well to think he will ever give in; invented a monstrous figment about going to shoot pheasants with Mac in the morning, so as to soothe the anxious fears of the dear mistress of the house; early as the hour appointed for the — the little affair — was, have we been awake hours and hours sooner; risen before daylight, with a faint hope, perhaps, that MacTurk might have come to some arrangement with the other side; at seven o'clock (confound his punctuality!) heard his cab-wheel at the door, and let him in looking perfectly trim, fresh, jolly, and well shaved; driven off with him in the cold morning, after a very unsatisfactory breakfast of coffee and stale bread and butter (which choke, somehow, in the swallowing); driven off to Wormwood Scrubs in the cold, muddy, misty, moonshiny morning; stepped out of the cab, where Mac has bid the man to halt on a retired spot in the common; in one minute more, seen another cab arrive, from which descend two gentlemen, one of whom has a case like MacTurk's under his arm; — looked round and round the solitude, and seen not one single sign of a policeman — no, no more than in a row in London; — deprecated the horrible necessity which drives civilized men to the use of powder and bullet; — taken ground as firmly as may be, and looked on whilst Mac is neatly loading his weapons; and when all ready, and one looked for the decisive One, Two, Three — have we even heard Captain O'Toole (the second of the other principal) walk up, and say, "Colonel MacTurk, I am desired by my principal to declare at this eleventh — this twelfth hour, that he is willing to own that he sees HE HAS BEEN WRONG in the dispute which has arisen between him and your friend; that he apologizes for offensive expressions which he has used in the heat of the quarrel; and regrets the course he has taken?" If something like this has happened to you, however great your courage, you have been glad not to fight; — however accurate your aim, you have been pleased not to fire.

On the sixth day of January in this year sixty-two, what hundreds of thousands — I may say, what millions of Englishmen, were in the position of the personage here sketched — Christian men, I hope, shocked at the dreadful necessity of battle; aware of the horrors which the conflict must produce, and yet feeling that the moment was come, and that there was no arbitrament left but that of steel and cannon! My reader, perhaps, has been in America. If he has, he knows what good people are to be found there; how polished, how generous, how gentle, how courteous. But it is not the voices of these you hear in the roar of hate, defiance, folly, falsehood, which comes to us across the Atlantic. You can't hear gentle voices; very many who could speak are afraid. Men must go forward, or be crushed by the maddened crowd behind them. I suppose after the perpetration of that act of — what shall we call it? — of sudden war, which Wilkes did, and Everett approved, most of us believed that battle was inevitable. Who has not read the American papers for six weeks past? Did you ever think the United States Government would give up those Commissioners? I never did, for my part. It seems to me the United States Government have done the most courageous act of the war. Before that act was done, what an excitement prevailed in London! In every Club there was a parliament sitting in permanence: in every domestic gathering this subject was sure to form a main part of the talk. Of course I have seen many people who have travelled in America, and heard them on this matter — friends of the South, friends of the North, friends of peace, and American stockholders in plenty. "They will never give up the men, sir," that was the opinion on all sides; and, if they would not, we knew what was to happen.

For weeks past this nightmare of war has been riding us. The City was already gloomy enough. When a great domestic grief and misfortune visits the chief person of the State, the heart of the people, too, is sad and awe-stricken. It might be this sorrow and trial were but presages of greater trials and sorrow to come. What if the sorrow of war is to be added to the other calamity? Such forebodings have formed the theme of many a man's talk, and darkened many a fireside. Then came the rapid orders for ships to arm and troops to depart. How many of us have had to say farewell to friends whom duty called away with their regiments; on whom we strove to look cheerfully, as we shook their hands, it might be for the last time; and whom our thoughts depicted, treading the snows of the immense Canadian frontier, where their intrepid little band might have to face the assaults of other enemies than winter and rough weather! I went to a play one night, and protest I hardly know what was the entertainment which passed before my eyes. In the next stall was an American gentleman, who knew me. "Good heavens, sir," I thought, "is it decreed that you and I are to be authorized to murder each other next week; that my people shall be bombarding your cities, destroying your navies, making a hideous desolation of your coast; that our peaceful frontiers shall be subject to fire, rapine, and murder?" "They will never give up the men," said the Englishman. "They will never give up the men," said the American. And the Christmas piece which the actors were playing proceeded like a piece in a dream. To make the grand comic performance doubly comic, my neighbor presently informed me how one of the best friends I had in America — the most hospitable, kindly, amiable of men, from whom I had twice received the warmest welcome and the most delightful hospitality — was a prisoner in Fort Warren, on charges by which his life perhaps might be risked. I think that was the most dismal Christmas fun which these eyes ever looked on.

Carry out that notion a little further, and depict ten thousand, a hundred thousand homes in England saddened by the thought of the coming calamity, and oppressed by the pervading gloom. My next-door neighbor perhaps has parted with her son. Now the ship in which he is, with a thousand brave comrades, is ploughing through the stormy midnight ocean. Presently (under the flag we know of) the thin red line in which her boy forms a speck, is winding its way through the vast Canadian snows. Another neighbor's boy is not gone, but is expecting orders to sail; and some one else, besides the circle at home maybe, is in prayer and terror, thinking of the summons which calls the young sailor away. By firesides modest and splendid, all over the three kingdoms, that sorrow is keeping watch, and myriads of hearts beating with that thought, "Will they give up the men?"

I don't know how, on the first day after the capture of the Southern Commissioners was announced, a rumor got abroad in London that the taking of the men was an act according to law, of which our nation could take no notice. It was said that the law authorities had so declared, and a very noble testimony to the *loyalty* of Englishmen, I think, was shown by the instant submission of high-spirited gentlemen, most keenly feeling that the nation had been subject to a coarse outrage, who were silent when told that the law was with the aggressor. The relief which presently came, when, after a pause of a day, we found that law was on our side, was indescribable. The nation *might* then take notice of this insult to its honor. Never were people more eager than ours when they found they had a right to reparation.

I have talked during the last week with many English holders of American securities, who, of course, have been aware of the threat held over them. "England," says "The New York Herald," "cannot afford to go to war with us, for six hundred millions' worth of American stock is owned by British subjects, which, in event of hostilities, would be confiscated; and we now call upon the Companies not to take it off their hands on any terms. *Let its forfeiture be held over England as a weapon in terrorem.* British subjects have two or three hundred millions of dollars invested in shipping and other property in the United States. All this property, together with the stocks, would be seized, amounting to nine hundred millions of dollars. Will England incur this tremendous loss for a mere abstraction?"

Whether "a mere abstraction" here means the abstraction of the two Southern Commissioners from under our flag, or the abstract idea of injured honor, which seems ridiculous to "The Herald," it is needless to ask. I have spoken with many men who have money invested in the States; but I declare I have not met one English gentleman whom the publication of this threat has influenced for a moment. Our people have nine hundred millions of dollars invested in the United States, have they? And "The Herald" "calls upon the Companies" not to take any of this debt off our hands. Let us, on our side, entreat the English press to give this announcement every publicity. Let us do every thing in our power to make this "call upon the Americans" well known in England. I hope English newspaper editors will print it, and print it again and again. It is not we who say this of American citizens, but American citizens who say this of themselves. "Bull is odious. We can't bear Bull. He is haughty, arrogant, a braggart, and a blusterer; and we can't bear brag and bluster in our modest and decorous country. We hate Bull, and if he quarrels with us on a point in which we are in the wrong, we have goods of his in our custody, and we will rob him!" Suppose your London banker saying to you, "Sir, I have always thought your manners disgusting, and your arrogance insupportable. You dare to complain of my conduct because I have wrongfully imprisoned Jones. My answer to your vulgar interference is, that I confiscate your balance!"

What would be an English merchant's character after a few such transactions? It is not improbable that the moralists of "The Herald" would call him a rascal. Why have the United States been paying seven, eight, ten per cent for money for years past, when the same commodity can be got elsewhere at half that rate of interest? Why, because, though among the richest proprietors in the world, creditors were not sure of them. So the States have had to pay eighty millions yearly for the use of money which would cost other borrowers but thirty. Add up this item of extra interest alone for a dozen years, and see what a prodigious penalty the States have been paying for repudiation here and there, for sharp practice, for doubtful credit. Suppose the peace is kept between us, the remembrance of this last threat alone will cost the States millions and millions more. If they must have money, we must have a greater interest to insure our jeopardized capital. Do American Companies want to borrow money — as want to borrow they will? Mr. Brown, show the gentlemen that extract from "The New York Herald," which declares that the United States will confiscate private property in the event of a war. As the country newspapers say, "Please, country papers, copy this paragraph." And, gentlemen in America, when the honor of *your* nation is called in question, please to remember that it is the American press which glories in announcing that you are prepared to be rogues.

And when this war has drained uncounted hundreds of millions more out of the United States exchequer, will they be richer or more inclined to pay debts, or less willing to evade them, or more popular with their creditors, or more likely to get money from men whom they deliberately announce that they will cheat? I have not followed "The Herald" on the "stone-ship" question — that great naval victory appears to me not less horrible and wicked than suicidal. Block the harbors forever; destroy the inlets of the commerce of the world; perish cities, — so that we may wreak an injury on them. It is the talk of madmen, but not the less wicked. The act injures the whole Republic: but it is perpetrated. It is to deal harm to ages hence; but it is done. The Indians of old used to burn women and their unborn children. This stone-ship business is Indian warfare. And it is performed by men who tell us every week that they are at the head of civilization, and that the Old World is decrepit, and cruel, and barbarous, as compared to theirs.

The same politicians who throttle commerce at its neck, and threaten to confiscate trust-money, say that when the war is over, and the South is subdued, then the turn of the old country will come, and a direful retribution shall be taken for our conduct. This has been the cry all through the war. "We should have conquered the South," says an American paper which I read this very day, "but for England." Was there ever such puling heard from men who have an army of a million, and who turn and revile a people who have stood as aloof from their contest as we have from the war of Troy? Or is it an outcry made with malice prepense? And is the song of "The New York Times" a variation of "The Herald" tune? "The conduct of the British in folding their arms and taking no part in the fight, has been so base that it has caused the prolongation of the war, and occasioned a prodigious expense on our part. Therefore, as we have British property in our hands, we, &c., &c." The lamb troubled the water dreadfully, and the wolf, in a righteous indignation, "confiscated" him. Of course we have heard that at an undisturbed time Great Britain would never have dared to press its claims for redress. Did the United States wait until we were at peace with France before they went to war with us last? Did Mr. Seward yield the claim which he confesses to be just, until he himself was menaced with war? How long were the Southern gentlemen kept in prison? What caused them to be set free? and did the Cabinet of Washington see its error before or after the demand for redress? * The captor was feasted at Boston, and the captives in prison hard by. If the wrong-doer was to be punished, it was Captain Wilkes who ought to have gone into limbo. At any rate, as "the Cabinet of Washington could not give its approbation to the commander of 'The San Jacinto,'" why were the men not sooner set free? To sit at the Tremont House, and hear the captain after dinner give his opinion on international law, would have been better sport for the prisoners than the grim *salle-à-manger* at Fort Warren.

I read in the commercial news brought by "The Teutonia," and published in London on the present 13th January, that the pork market was generally quiet on the 29th December last; that lard, though with more activity, was heavy and decidedly lower; and at Philadelphia, whiskey is steady and stocks firm. Stocks are firm: that is a comfort for the English holders, and the confiscating process recommended by "The Herald" is at least deferred. But presently comes an announcement which is not quite so cheering:—"The Saginaw Central Railway Company (let us call it) has postponed its January dividend on account of the disturbed condition of public affairs."

A la bonne heure. The bond and share holders of the Saginaw must look for loss and depression in times of war. This is one of war's dreadful taxes and necessities; and all sorts of innocent people must suffer by the misfortune. The corn was high at Waterloo when a hundred and fifty thousand men came and trampled it down on a Sabbath morning. There was no help for that calamity, and the Belgian farmers lost their crops for the year. Perhaps I am a farmer myself—an innocent *colonus;* and instead of being able to get to church with my family, have to see squadrons of French dragoons thundering upon my barley, and squares of English infantry forming and trampling all over my oats. (By the way, in writing of "Panics," an ingenious writer in "The Atlantic Magazine" says that the British panics at Waterloo were frequent and notorious). Well I am a Belgian peasant, and I see the British running away and the French cutting the fugitives down. What have I done that these men should be kicking down my peaceful harvest for me, on which I counted to pay my rent, to feed my horses, my household, my children? It is hard. But it is the fortune of war. But suppose the battle over; the Frenchman says, "You scoundrel! why did you not take a part with me? and why did you stand like a double-faced traitor looking on? I should have won the battle but for you. And I hereby confiscate the farm you stand on, and you and your family may go to the workhouse."

The New York press holds this argument over English people *in terrorem.* "We Americans may be ever so wrong in the matter in dispute, but if you push us to war, we will confiscate your English property." Very good. It is peace now. Confidence of course

* "At the beginning of December the British fleet on the West Indian station mounted 850 guns, and comprised five liners, ten first-class frigates, and seventeen powerful corvettes. . . . In little more than a month the fleet available for operations on the American shore had been more than doubled. The re-enforcements prepared at the various dockyards included two line-of-battle ships, twenty-nine magnificent frigates—such as 'The Shannon,' 'The Sutlej,' 'The Euryalus,' 'The Orlando,' 'The Galatea;' eight corvettes, armed like the frigates in part, with 100 and 40 pounder Armstrong guns; and the two tremendous iron-cased ships, 'The Warrior' and 'The Black Prince;' and their smaller sisters 'The Resistance,' and 'The Defence.' There was work to be done which might have delayed the commission of a few of these ships for some weeks longer; but if the United States had chosen war instead of peace, the blockade of their coasts would have been supported by a steam fleet of more than sixty splendid ships, armed with 1,800 guns, many of them of the heaviest and most effective kind."—*Saturday Review:* Jan. 11.

is restored between us. Our eighteen hundred peace commissioners have no occasion to open their mouths; and the little question of confiscation is postponed. Messrs. Battery, Broadway, and Co., of New York, have the kindness to sell my Saginaws for what they will fetch. I shall lose half my loaf very likely; but for the sake of a quiet life, let us give up a certain quantity of farinaceous food; and half a loaf, you know, is better than no bread at all.

THE NOTCH ON THE AXE. A STORY À LA MODE.

PART I.

"EVERY one remembers in the Fourth Book of the immortal poem of your Blind Bard (to whose sightless orbs no doubt Glorious Shapes were apparent, and Visions Celestial) how Adam discourses to Eve of the Bright Visitors who hovered round their Eden—

'Millions of spiritual creatures walk the earth,
Unseen, both when we wake and when we sleep.'

"'How often,' says Father Adam, 'from the steep of echoing hill or thicket, have we heard celestial voices to the midnight air, sole, or responsive to each other's notes, singing!' After the Act of Disobedience, when the erring pair from Eden took their solitary way, and went forth to toil and trouble on common earth—though the Glorious Ones no longer were visible, you cannot say they were gone. It was not that the Bright Ones were absent, but that the dim eyes of rebel man no longer could see them. In your chamber hangs a picture of one whom you never knew, but whom you have long held in tenderest regard, and who was painted for you by a friend of mine, the Knight of Plympton. She communes with you. She smiles on you. When your spirits are low, her bright eyes shine on you and cheer you. Her innocent sweet smile is a caress to you. She never fails to soothe you with her speechless prattle. You love her. She is alive with you. As you extinguish your candle and turn to sleep, though your eyes see her not, is she not there still smiling? As you lie in the night awake, and thinking of your duties, and the morrow's inevitable toil oppressing the busy, weary, wakeful brain as with a remorse, the crackling fire flashes up for a moment in the grate, and she is there, your little Beauteous Maiden, smiling with her sweet eyes! When moon is down, when fire is out, when curtains are drawn, when lids are closed, is she not there, the little Beautiful One, though invisible, present and smiling still? Friend, the Unseen Ones are round about us. Does it not seem as if the time were drawing near when it shall be given to men to behold them?"

The print of which my friend spoke, and which, indeed, hangs in my room, though he has never been there, is that charming little winter piece of Sir Joshua, representing the little Lady Caroline Montague, afterwards Duchess of Buccleuch. She is represented as standing in the midst of a winter landscape, wrapped in muff and cloak; and she looks out of her picture with a smile so exquisite that a Herod could not see her without being charmed.

"I beg your pardon, Mr. PINTO," I said to the person with whom I was conversing. (I wonder, by the way, that I was not surprised at his knowing how fond I am of this print.) "You spoke of the Knight of Plympton. Sir Joshua died, 1792: and you say he was your dear friend?"

As I spoke I chanced to look at Mr. Pinto; and then it suddenly struck me: Gracious powers! Perhaps you *are* a hundred years old, now I think of it. You look more than a hundred. Yes, you may be a thousand years old for what I know. Your teeth are false. One eye is evidently false. Can I say that the other is not? If a man's age may be calculated by the rings round his eyes, this man may be as old as Methusaleh. He has no beard. He wears a large curly glossy brown wig, and his eyebrows are painted a deep olive-green. It was odd to hear this man, this walking mummy, talking sentiment, in these queer old chambers in Shepherd's Inn.

Pinto passed a yellow bandanna handkerchief over his awful white teeth, and kept his glass eye steadily fixed on me. "Sir Joshua's friend?" said he (you perceive, eluding my direct question). "Is not every one that knows his pictures Reynolds's friend? Suppose I tell you that I have been in his painting room scores of times, and that his sister Thé has made me tea, and his sister Toffy has made coffee for me? You will only say I am an old ombog." (Mr. Pinto, I remarked, spoke all languages with an accent equally foreign.) "Suppose I tell you that I knew Mr. Sam Johnson, and did not like him? that I was at that very ball at Madame Cornelis's, which you have mentioned in one of your little — what do you call them? — bah! my memory begins to fail me — in one of your little Whirligig Papers? Suppose I tell you that Sir Joshua has been here, in this very room?"

"Have you, then, had these apartments for — more — than — seventy years?" I asked.

"They look as if they had not been swept for that time — don't they? Hey? I did not say that I had them for seventy years, but that Sir Joshua has visited me here."

"When?" I asked, eying the man sternly, for I began to think he was an impostor.

He answered me with a glance still more stern: "Sir Joshua Reynolds was here this very morning, with Angelica Kaufmann and Mr. Oliver Goldschmidt. He is still very much attached to Angelica, who still does not care for him. Because he is dead (and I was in the fourth mourning coach at his funeral) is that any reason why he should not come back to earth again? My good sir, you are laughing at me. He has sat many a time on that very chair which you are occupying. There are several spirits in the room now, whom you cannot see. Excuse me." Here he turned round as if he was addressing somebody, and began rapidly speaking a language unknown to me.

"It is Arabic," he said; "a bad patois I own. I learned it in Barbary, when I was a prisoner amongst the Moors. In anno 1609, bin ick aldus ghekledt gheghaen. Ha! you doubt me: look at me well. At least I am like" —

Perhaps some of my readers remember a paper of which the figure of a man carrying a barrel formed the initial letter, and which I copied from an old spoon now in my possession. As I looked at Mr. Pinto I do declare he looked so like the figure on that old piece of plate that I started and felt very uneasy. "Ha!" said he, laughing through his false teeth (I declare they were false — I could see utterly toothless gums working up and down behind the pink coral), "you see I wore a beard den; I am shafed now; perhaps you tink I am *a spoon*. Ha, ha!" And as he laughed he gave a cough which I thought would have coughed his teeth out, his glass eye out, his wig off, his very head off; but he stopped this convulsion by stumping across the room and seizing a little bottle of bright pink medicine, which, being opened, spread a singular acrid aromatic odor through the apartment; and I thought I saw — but of this I cannot take an affirmation — a light green and violet flame flickering round the neck of the phial as he opened it. By the way, from the peculiar stumping noise which he made in crossing the bare-boarded apartment, I knew at once that my strange entertainer had a wooden leg. Over the dust which lay quite thick on the boards, you could see the mark of one foot very neat and pretty, and then a round O, which was naturally the impression made by the wooden stump. I own I had a queer thrill as I saw the mark, and felt a comfort that it was not *cloven*.

In this desolate apartment in which Mr. Pinto had invited me to see him, there were three chairs, one bottomless, a little table on which you might put a breakfast-tray, and not a single other article of furniture. In the next room, the door of which was open, I could see a magnificent gilt dressing-case, with some splendid diamond and ruby shirt-studs lying by it, and a chest of drawers, and a cupboard apparently full of clothes.

Remembering him in Baden Baden in great magnificence, I wondered at his present denuded state. "You have a house elsewhere, Mr. Pinto?" I said.

"Many," says he. "I have apartments in many cities. I lock dem up, and do not carry mosh logish."

I then remembered that his apartment at Baden, where I first met him, was bare, and had no bed in it.

"There is, then, a sleeping-room beyond?"

"This is the sleeping-room." (He pronounces it *dis*. Can this, by the way, give any clew to the nationality of this singular man?)

"If you sleep on these two old chairs you have a rickety couch; if on the floor, a dusty one."

"Suppose I sleep up dere?" said this strange man, and he actually pointed up to the ceiling. I thought him mad, or what he himself called "an ombog." "I know. You do not believe me; for why should I deceive you? I came but to propose a matter of business to you. I told you I could give you the clew to the mystery of the Two Children in Black, whom you met at Baden, and you came to see me. If I told you, you would not believe me. What for try and convinz you? Ha hey?" And he shook his hand once, twice, thrice, at me, and glared at me out of his eye in a peculiar way.

Of what happened now I protest I cannot give an accurate account. It seemed to me that there shot a flame from his eye into my brain, whilst behind his *glass* eye there was a green illumination as if a candle had been lit in it. It seemed to me that from his long fingers two quivering flames issued, sputtering, as it were, which penetrated me, and forced me back into one of the chairs — the broken one — out of which I had much difficulty in scrambling, when the strange glamor was ended. It seemed to me that, when I was so fixed, so transfixed in the broken chair, the man floated up to the ceiling, crossed his legs, folded his arms as if he was lying on a sofa, and grinned down at me. When I came to myself, he was down from the ceiling, and, taking me out of the broken cane-bottomed chair, kindly enough — "Bah!" said he, "it is the smell of my medicine. It often gives the vertigo. I thought you would have had a little fit. Come into the open air." And we went down the steps, and into Shepherd's Inn, where the setting sun was just shining on the statue of Shepherd; the laundresses where trapesing about; the porters were leaning against the railings; and the clerks were playing at marbles, to my inexpressible consolation.

"You said you were going to dine at the 'Gray's-inn Coffee-house,'" he said. I was. I often dine there. There is excellent wine at the "Gray's-inn Coffee-house;" but I declare I NEVER SAID SO. I was not astonished at his remark; no more astonished than if I was in a dream. Perhaps I *was* in a dream. Is life a dream? Are dreams facts? Is sleeping being really awake? I don't know. I tell you I am puzzled. I have read "The Woman in White," "The Strange Story" — not to mention that story "Stranger than Fiction" in "The Cornhill Magazine" —

that story for which THREE credible witnesses are ready to vouch. I have had messages from the dead; and not only from the dead, but from people who never existed at all. I own I am in a state of much bewilderment; but, if you please, will proceed with my simple, my artless story.

Well, then. We passed from Shepherd's Inn into Holborn, and looked for a while at Woodgate's bric-à-brac shop, which I never can pass without delaying at the windows — indeed, if I were going to be hung, I would beg the cart to stop, and let me have one look more at that delightful *omnium gatherum*. And passing Woodgate's, we come to Gale's little shop, "No. 47," which is also a favorite haunt of mine.

Mr. Gale happened to be at his door, and as we exchanged salutations, "Mr. Pinto," I said, "will you like to see a real curiosity in this curiosity shop? Step into Mr. Gale's little back room."

In that little back parlor there are Chinese gongs; there are old Saxe and Sêvres plates; there is Fürstenberg, Carl Theodor, Worcester, Amstel, Nankin and other jimcrockery. And in the corner what do you think there is? There is an actual GUILLOTINE. If you doubt me, go and see — Gale, High Holborn, No. 47. It is a slim instrument, much slighter than those which they make now; — some nine feet high, narrow, a pretty piece of upholstery enough. There is the hook over which the rope used to play which unloosened the dreadful axe above; and look! dropped into the orifice where the head used to go — there is THE AXE itself, all rusty, with A GREAT NOTCH IN THE BLADE.

As Pinto looked at it — Mr. Gale was not in the room, I recollect; happening to have been just called out by a customer who offered him three pound fourteen and sixpence for a blue Shepherd in *pâte tendre*, — Mr. Pinto gave a little start, and seemed *crispé* for a moment. Then he looked steadily towards one of those great porcelain stools which you see in gardens — and — it seemed to me — I tell you I won't take my affidavit — I may have been maddened by the six glasses I took of that pink elixir — I may have been sleep-walking: perhaps am as I write now — I may have been under the influence of that astounding MEDIUM into whose hands I had fallen — but I vow I heard Pinto say, with rather a ghastly grin at the porcelain stool,

"Nay, nefer shague your gory locks at me,
Dou canst not say I did it."

(He pronounced it, by the way, I *dit* it, by which I *know* that Pinto was a German.)

I heard Pinto say those very words, and sitting on the porcelain stool, I saw, dimly at first, then with an awful distinctness — a ghost — an *eidolon* — a form — A HEADLESS MAN seated, with his head in his lap, which wore an expression of piteous surprise.

At this minute, Mr. Gale entered from the front shop to show a customer some delf plates; and he did not see — but *we did* — the figure rise up from the porcelain stool, shake its head, which it held in its hand, and which kept its eyes fixed sadly on us, and disappear behind the guillotine.

"Come to the 'Gray's-inn Coffee-house,'" Pinto said, "and I will tell you how *the notch came to the axe*." And we walked down Holborn at about thirty-seven minutes past six o'clock.

If there is any thing in the above statement which astonishes the reader, I promise him that in the next chapter of this little story he will be astonished still more.

PART II.

"You will excuse me," I said to my companion, "for remarking, that when you addressed the individual sitting on the porcelain stool, with his head in his lap, your ordinarily benevolent features" — (this I confess was a bouncer, for between ourselves a more sinister and ill-looking rascal than Mons. P. I have seldom set eyes on)—"your ordinarily handsome face wore an expression that was by no means pleasing. You grinned at the individual just as you did at me when you went up to the cei—, pardon me as I *thought* you did, when I fell down in a fit in your chambers;" and I qualified my words in a great flutter and tremble; I did not care to offend the man — I did not *dare* to offend the man. I thought once or twice of jumping into a cab, and flying; of taking refuge in Day and Martin's Blacking Warehouse; of speaking to a policeman, but not one would come. I was this man's slave. I followed him like his dog. I *could* not get away from him. So, you see, I went on meanly conversing with him, and affecting a simpering confidence. I remember when I was a little boy at school, going up fawning and smiling in this way to some great hulking bully of a sixth-form boy. So I said in a word, "Your ordinarily handsome face wore a disagreeable expression," &c.

"It is ordinarily *very* handsome," said he, with such a leer at a couple of passers-by that one of them cried, "Oh, crikey, here's a precious guy!" and a child in its nurse's arms, screamed itself into convulsions. "*Oh, oui, che suis très-choli garçon, bien peau, cerdainement,*" continued Mr. Pinto; "but you were right. That — that person was not very well pleased when he saw me. There was no love lost between us, as you say; and the world never knew a more worthless miscreant. I hate him, *voyez-vouz?* I hated him alife; I hate him dead. I hate him man; I hate him ghost: and he know it, and tremble before me. If I see him twenty tausend years hence — and why not? — I shall hate him still. You remarked how he was dressed?"

"In black satin breeches and striped stockings; a white piqué waistcoat, a gray coat, with large metal buttons, and his hair in powder. He must have worn a pigtail — only" —

"Only it was *cut off!* Ha, ha, ha!" Mr. Pinto cried, yelling a laugh, which I observed made the policemen stare very much. "Yes. It was cut off by the same blow which took off the scoundrel's head — ho, ho, ho!" And he made a circle with his hook-nailed finger round his own yellow neck, and grinned with a horrible triumph. "I promise you that fellow was surprised when he found his head in the pannier. Ha! ha! Do you ever cease to hate those whom you hate?" — fire flashed terrifically from his glass eye, as he spoke — "or to love dose whom you once loved. Oh, never, never!" And here his natural eye was bedewed with tears. "But here we are at the 'Gray's-inn Coffee-house.' James, what is the joint?"

That very respectful and efficient waiter brought in the bill of fare, and I, for my part, chose boiled leg of pork and pease-pudding, which my acquaintance said would do as well as any thing else; though I remarked he only trifled with the pease-pudding, and left all the pork on the plate. In fact, he scarcely ate any thing. But he drank a prodigious quantity of wine; and I must say that my friend Mr. Hart's port-wine is so good that I myself took — well, I should think, I took three glasses. Yes, three, certainly. *He* — I mean Mr. P.,— the old rogue, was insatiable: for we had to call for a second bottle in no time. When that was gone, my companion wanted another. A little red mounted up to his yellow cheeks as he drank the wine, and he winked at it in a strange manner. "I remember," said he, musing, "when port-wine was scarcely drunk in this country — though the Queen liked it, and so did Harley; but Bolingbroke didn't — he drank Florence and Champagne. Dr. Swift put water to his wine.

'Jonathan,' I once said to him — but bah! *autres temps, autres mœurs.* Another magnum, James."

This was all very well. "My good sir," I said, "it may suit *you* to order bottles of '20 port, at a guinea a bottle; but that kind of price does not suit me. I only happen to have thirty-four and sixpence in my pocket, of which I want a shilling for the waiter, and eighteenpence for my cab. You rich foreigners and *swells* may spend what you like" (I had him there: for my friend's dress was as shabby as an old-clothes-man's); "but a man with a family, Mr. What-d'you-call'im, cannot afford to spend seven or eight hundred a year on his dinner alone."

"Bah!" he said. "Nunkey pays for all, as you say. I will what you call stant the dinner, if you are *so poor!*" and again he gave that disagreeable grin, and placed an odious crooked-nailed and by no means clean finger to his nose. But I was not so afraid of him now, for we were in a public place; and the three glasses of port-wine had, you see, given me courage.

"What a pretty snuff-box!" he remarked as I handed him mine, which I am still old-fashioned enough to carry. It is a pretty old gold box enough, but valuable to me especially as a relic of an old, old relative, whom I can just remember as a child, when she was very kind to me. "Yes; a pretty box. I can remember when many ladies —most ladies, carried a box — nay, two boxes — *tabatière* and *bonbonnière.* What lady carries snuff-box now, hey? Suppose your astonishment if a lady in an assembly were to offer you a *prise?* I can remember a lady with such a box as this, with a *tour,* as we used to call it then; with *paniers,* with a tortoise-shell cane, with the prettiest little high-heeled velvet shoes in the world! — ah! that was a time, that was a time! Ah, Eliza, Eliza, I have thee now in my mind's eye! At Bungay on the Waveney, did I not walk with thee, Eliza? Aha, did I not love thee? Did I not walk with thee then? Do I not see thee still?"

This was passing strange. My ancestress — but there is no need to publish her revered name — did indeed live at Bungay Saint Mary's, where she lies buried. She used to walk with a tortoise-shell cane. She used to wear little black velvet shoes, with the prettiest high heels in the world.

"Did you — did you — know, then, my great gr-ndm-ther?" I said.

He pulled up his coat-sleeve — "Is that her name?" he said.

"Eliza ——"

There, I declare, was the very name of the kind old creature written in red on his arm.

"*You* knew her old," he said, divining my thoughts (with his strange knack); "*I* knew her young and lovely. I danced with her at the Bury ball. Did I not, dear, dear Miss ——?"

As I live, he here mentioned dear gr-nny's *maiden* name. Her maiden name was ——. Her honored married name was ——.

"She married your great gr-nd-f-th-r the year Poseidon won the Newmarket Plate," Mr. Pinto dryly remarked.

Merciful powers! I remember, over the old shagreen knife and spoon case on the sideboard in my gr-nny's parlor, a print by Stubbs of that very horse. My grandsire, in a red coat, and his fair hair flowing over his shoulders, was over the mantelpiece, and Poseidon won the Newmarket Cup in the year 1783!

"Yes; you are right. I danced a minuet with her at Bury that very night, before I lost my poor leg. And I quarrelled with your grandf—, ha!"

As he said "Ha!" there came three quiet little taps on the table — it is the middle table in the "Gray's-inn Coffee-house," under the bust of the late Duke of W-ll-ngt-n.

"I fired in the air," he continued;

"did I not?" (Tap, tap, tap.) "Your grandfather hit me in the leg. He married three months afterwards. 'Captain Brown,' I said, 'who could see Miss Sm-th without loving her?' She is there! She is there!" (Tap, tap, tap.) "Yes, my first love"—

But here there came tap, tap, which everybody knows means "No."

"I forgot," he said with a faint blush stealing over his wan features, "she was not my first love. In Germ — in my own country — there *was* a young woman"—

Tap, tap, tap. There was here quite a lively little treble knock; and when the old man said, "But I loved thee better than all the world, Eliza," the affirmative signal was briskly repeated.

And this I declare UPON MY HONOR. There was, I have said, a bottle of port-wine before us — I should say a decanter. That decanter was LIFTED UP, and out of it into our respective glasses two bumpers of wine were poured. I appeal to Mr. Hart, the landlord — I appeal to James, the respectful and intelligent waiter, if this statement is not true? And when we had finished that magnum, and I said — for I did not now in the least doubt of her presence — "Dear gr-nny, may we have another magnum?" — the table *distinctly* rapped "No."

"Now, my good sir," Mr. Pinto said, who really began to be affected by the wine, "you understand the interest I have taken in you. I loved Eliza ——" (of course I don't mention family names). "I knew you had that box which belonged to her — I will give you what you like for that box. Name your price at once, and I pay you on the spot."

"Why, when we came out, you said you had not sixpence in your pocket."

"Bah! give you any thing you like — fifty — a hundred — a tausend pound."

"Come, come," said I, "the gold of the box may be worth nine guineas, and the *façon* we will put at six more."

"One tausend guineas!" he screeched. "One tausend and fifty pound, dere!" and he sank back in his chair — no, by the way, on his bench, for he was sitting with his back to one of the partitions of the boxes, as I dare say James remembers.

"*Don't* go on in this way," I continued, rather weakly, for I did not know whether I was in a dream. "If you offer me a thousand guineas for this box I *must* take it. Mustn't I, dear gr-nny?"

The table most distinctly said, "Yes;" and putting out his claws to seize the box, Mr. Pinto plunged his hooked nose into it and eagerly inhaled some of my 47 with a dash of Hardman.

"But stay, you old harpy!" I exclaimed, being now in a sort of rage, and quite familiar with him. "Where is the money. Where is the check?"

"James, a piece of note-paper and a receipt stamp!"

"This is all mighty well, sir," I said, "but I don't know you; I never saw you before. I will trouble you to hand me that box back again, or give me a check with some known signature."

"Whose? Ha, HA, HA!"

The room happened to be very dark. Indeed, all the waiters were gone to supper, and there were only two gentlemen snoring in their respective boxes. I saw a hand come quivering down from the ceiling — a very pretty hand, on which was a ring with a coronet, with a lion rampant gules for a crest. *I saw that hand take a dip of ink and write across the paper.* Mr. Pinto, then, taking a gray receipt-stamp out of his blue leather pocket-book, fastened it on to the paper by the usual process; and the hand then wrote across the receipt stamp, went across the table and shook hands with Pinto, and then, as if waving him an adieu, vanished in the direction of the ceiling.

There was the paper before me, wet with the ink. There was the pen which THE HAND had used. Does anybody doubt me? *I have that pen now.* A cedar-stick of a not uncommon sort, and holding one of Gillott's pens. It is in my inkstand now, I tell you. Anybody may see it. The handwriting on the check, for such the document was, was the writing of a female. It ran thus: — "London, midnight, March 31, 1862. Pay the bearer one thousand and fifty pounds. Rachel Sidonia. To Messrs. Sidonia, Pozzosanto and Co., London."

"Noblest and best of women!" said Pinto, kissing the sheet of paper with much reverence. "My good Mr. Roundabout, I suppose you do not question *that* signature?"

Indeed, the house of Sidonia, Pozzosanto, and Co., is known to be one of the richest in Europe, and as for the Countess Rachel, she was known to be the chief manager of that enormously wealthy establishment. There was only one little difficulty, *the Countess Rachel died last October.*

I pointed out this circumstance, and tossed over the paper to Pinto with a sneer.

"*C'est a brendre ou à laisser,*" he said with some heat. "You literary men are all imprudent; but I did not tink you such a fool *wie* dis. Your box is not worth twenty pound, and I offer you a tausend because I know you want money to pay dat rascal Tom's college bills." (This strange man actually knew that my scapegrace Tom has been a source of great expense and annoyance to me.) "You see money costs me nothing, and you refuse to take it! Once, twice; will you take this check in exchange for your trumpery snuff-box?"

What could I do? My poor granny's legacy was valuable and dear to me, but after all a thousand guineas are not to be had every day. "Be it a bargain," said I. "Shall we have a glass of wine on it?" says Pinto; and to this proposal I also unwillingly acceded, reminding him, by the way, that he had not yet told me the story of the headless man.

"Your poor gr-ndm-ther was right just now, when she said she was not my first love. 'Twas one of those *banale* expressions" (here Mr. P. blushed once more) "which we use to women. We tell each she is our first passion. They reply with a similar illusory formula. No man is any woman's first love; no woman any man's. We are in love in our nurse's arms, and women coquette with their eyes before their tongue can form a word. How could your lovely relative love me? I was far, far too old for her. I am older than I look. I am so old that you would not believe my age were I to tell you. I have loved many and many a woman before your relative. It has not always been fortunate for them to love me. Ah, Sophronia! Round the dreadful circus where you fell, and whence I was dragged corpse-like by the heels, there sat multitudes more savage than the lions which mangled your sweet form! Ah, tenez! when we marched to the terrible stake together at Valladolid — the Protestant and the J— But away with memory! Boy! it was happy for thy grandam that she loved me not.

"During that strange period," he went on "when the teeming Time was great with the revolution that was speedily to be born, I was on a mission in Paris with my excellent, my maligned friend, Cagliostro. Mesmer was one of our band. I seemed to occupy but an obscure rank in it: though, as you know, in secret societies the humble man may be a chief and director — the ostensible leader but a puppet moved by unseen hands. Never mind who was chief, or who was second. Never mind my age. It boots not to tell it; why shall I expose myself to your scornful incredulity — or reply to your questions in words that are familiar to you, but which yet you cannot understand? Words are symbols of things which you know, or of things which you don't know. If you don't know them, to speak is idle." (Here I confess Mr. P. spoke for exactly thirty-eight minutes, about physics, metaphysics, language, the origin and destiny of man, during which time I was rather bored, and, to relieve my *ennui*, drank a half glass or so of wine.) "LOVE, friend, is the fountain of youth! It may not happen to me once — once in an age: but when I love, then I am young, I loved when I was in Paris. Bathilde, Bathilde, I loved thee — ah, how fondly! Wine, I say, more wine! Love is ever young. I was a boy at the little feet of Bathilde de Béchamel — the fair, the fond, the fickle, ah, the false!" the strange old man's agony was here really terrific, and he showed himself much more agitated than he had been when speaking about my gr-ndm-th-r.

"I thought Blanche might love me. I could speak to her in the language of all countries, and tell her the lore of all ages. I could trace the nursery legends which she loved up to their Sanscrit source, and whisper to her the darkling mysteries of Egyptian Magi. I could chant for her the wild chorus that rang in the dishevelled Eleusinian revel: I could tell her, and I would, the watchword never known but to one woman, the Saban Queen, which Hiram breathed in the abysmal ear of Solomon — You don't attend. Psha! you have drunk too much wine!" Perhaps I may as well own that I was *not* attending, for he had been carrying on for about fifty-seven minutes; and I don't like a man to have *all* the talk to himself.

"Blanche de Béchamel was wild, then, about this secret of Masonry. In early, early days I loved, I married a girl fair as Blanche, who, too, was tormented by curiosity, who, too, would peep into my closet — into the only secret I guarded from her. A dreadful fate befell poor Fatima. An *accident* shortened her life. Poor thing! she had a foolish sister who urged her on. I always told her to beware of Ann. She died. They said her brothers killed me. A gross falsehood. *Am* I dead? If I were, could I pledge you in this wine?"

"Was your name," I asked, quite bewildered, "was your name, pray, then, ever Blueb — ?"

"Hush! the waiter will overhear you. Methought we were speaking of Blanche de Béchamel. I loved her, young man. My pearls, and diamonds, and treasure, my wit, my wisdom, my passion, I flung them all into the child's lap. I was a fool! Was strong Samson not as weak as I? Was Solomon the Wise much better when Balkis wheedled him? I said to the king — But enough of that, I spake of Blanche de Béchamel.

"Curiosity was the poor child's foible. I could see, as I talked to her, that her thoughts were elsewhere (as yours, my friend, have been absent once or twice to-night). To know the secret of Masonry was the wretched child's mad desire. With a thousand wiles, smiles, caresses, she strove to coax it from me — from *me* — ha! ha!

"I had an apprentice — the son of a dear friend, who died by my side at Rossbach, when Soubise, with whose army I happened to be, suffered a dreadful defeat for neglecting my advice. The young Chevalier Goby de Mouchy was glad enough to serve as my clerk, and help in some chemical experiments in which I was engaged with my friend Dr. Mesmer. Bathilde saw this young man. Since women were, has it not been their business to smile and deceive, to fondle and lure? Away! From the very first it has been so!" And as my companion spoke, he looked as wicked as the serpent that coiled round the tree, and hissed a poisoned counsel to the first woman.

"One evening I went, as was my

wont, to see Blanche. She was radiant: she was wild with spirits: a saucy triumph blazed in her blue eyes. She talked, she rattled in her childish way. She uttered, in the course of her rhapsody, a hint, an intimation, so terrible that the truth flashed across me in a moment. Did I ask her? She would lie to me. But I know how to make falsehood impossible. And I *ordered her to go to sleep*."

At this moment the clock (after its previous convulsions) sounded TWELVE. And as the new Editor* of "The Cornhill Magazine"— and *he*, I promise you, won't stand any nonsense — will only allow seven pages, I am obliged to leave off at THE VERY MOST INTERESTING POINT OF THE STORY.

PART III.

"ARE you of our fraternity? I see you are not. The secret which Mademoiselle de Béchamel confided to me in her mad triumph and wild hoyden spirits — she was but a child, poor thing, poor thing, scarce fifteen: — but I love them young — a folly not unusual with the old!" (Here Mr. Pinto thrust his knuckles into his hollow eyes; and, I am sorry to say, so little regardful was he of personal cleanliness, that his tears made streaks of white over his gnarled dark hands.) "Ah, at fifteen, poor child, thy fate was terrible! Go to! It is not good to love me, friend. They prosper not who do. I divine you. You need not say what you are thinking" —

In truth, I was thinking, if girls fall in love with this sallow, hook-nosed, glass-eyed, wooden-legged, dirty, hideous old man, with the sham teeth, they have a queer taste. *That* is what I was thinking.

"Jack Wilkes said the handsomest man in London had but half an hour's start of him. And without vanity, I am scarcely uglier than Jack Wilkes. We were members of the same club at Medenham Abbey, Jack and I, and had many a merry night together. Well, sir, I — Mary of Scotland knew me but as a little hunch-backed music-master; and yet, and yet, I think *she* was not indifferent to her David Riz — and *she* came to misfortune. They all do — they all do!"

"Sir, you are wandering from your point!" I said, with some severity. For, really, for this old humbug to hint that he had been the baboon who frightened the club at Medenham, that he had been in the Inquisition at Valladolid — that under the name of D. Riz, as he called it, he had known the lovely Queen of Scots — was a *little* too much. "Sir," then I said, "you were speaking about a Miss de Béchamel. I really have not time to hear all your biography."

"Faith, the good wine gets into my head." (I should think so, the old toper! Four bottles all but two glasses.) "To return to poor Blanche. As I sat laughing, joking with her, she let slip a word, a little word, which filled me with dismay. Some one had told her a part of the Secret — the secret which has been divulged scarce thrice in three thousand years — the Secret of the Freemasons. Do you know what happens to those uninitiate who learn that secret? to those wretched men, the initiate who reveal it?"

As Pinto spoke to me, he looked through and through me with his horrible piercing glance, so that I sat quite uneasily on my bench. He continued: "Did I question her awake? I knew she would lie to me. Poor child! I loved her no less because I did not believe a word she said. I loved her blue eye, her golden hair, her delicious voice, that was true in song, though when she spoke, false as Eblis! You are aware that I possess in rather a remarkable degree what we have agreed to call the mesmeric power. I set the unhappy girl to sleep. *Then* she was obliged to

* Mr. Thackeray retired from the Editorship of "The Cornhill Magazine" in March, 1862.

tell me all. It was as I had surmised. Goby de Mouchy, my wretched, besotted, miserable secretary, in his visits to the château of the old Marquis de Béchamel, who was one of our society, had seen Blanche. I suppose it was because she had been warned that he was worthless and poor, artful, and a coward, she loved him. She wormed out of the besotted wretch the secrets of our Order. 'Did he tell you the NUMBER ONE?' I asked.

"She said, 'Yes.'

"'Did he,' I further inquired, 'tell you the'—

"'Oh, don't ask me, don't ask me!' she said, writhing on the sofa, where she lay in the presence of the Marquis de Béchamel, her most unhappy father. Poor Béchamel, poor Béchamel! How pale he looked as I spoke! 'Did he tell you,' I repeated with a dreadful calm, 'the NUMBER TWO?' She said, 'Yes.'

"The poor old marquis rose up, and clasping his hands, fell on his knees before Count Cagl—— Bah! I went by a different name then. Vat's in a name? Dat vich ve call a Rosicrucian by any other name vil smell as sveet. 'Monsieur,' he said, 'I am old—I am rich. I have five hundred thousand livres of rentes in Picardy. I have half as much in Artois. I have two hundred and eighty thousand on the Grand Livre. I am promised by my Sovereign a dukedom and his orders with a reversion to my heir. I am a grandee of Spain of the First Class, and Duke of Volovento. Take my titles, my ready money, my life, my honor, every thing I have in the world, but don't ask the THIRD QUESTION.'

"'Godefroid de Bouillon, Comte de Béchamel, Grandee of Spain and Prince of Volovento, in our Assembly what was the oath you swore?'" The old man writhed as he remembered its terrific purport.

"Though my heart was racked with agony, and I would have died, ay, cheerfully" (died, indeed, as if *that* were a penalty!) "to spare yonder lovely child a pang, I said to her calmly, 'Blanche de Béchamel, did Goby de Mouchy tell you secret NUMBER THREE?'

"She whispered a *oui* that was quite faint, faint and small. But her poor father fell in convulsions at her feet.

"She died suddenly that night. Did I not tell you those I love come to no good? When General Bonaparte crossed the Saint Bernard, he saw in the convent an old monk with a white beard, wandering about the corridors, cheerful and rather stout, but mad—mad as a March hare. 'General,' I said to him, 'did you ever see that face before?' He had not. He had not mingled much with the higher classes of our society before the Revolution. *I* knew the poor old man well enough; he was the last of a noble race, and I loved his child."

"And did she die by?"—

"Man! did I say so? Do I whisper the secrets of the Vehmgericht? I say she died that night; and he—he, the heartless, the villain, the betrayer,—you saw him seated in yonder curiosity shop, by yonder guillotine, with his scoundrelly head in his lap.

"You saw how slight that instrument was? It was one of the first which Guillotin made, and which he showed to private friends in a *hangar* in the Rue Picpus, where he lived. The invention created some little conversation amongst scientific men at the time, though I remember a machine in Edinburgh of a very similar construction, two hundred—well, many, many years ago—and at a breakfast which Guillotin gave, he showed us the instrument, and much talk arose amongst us as to whether people suffered under it.

"And now I must tell you what befell the traitor who had caused all this suffering. Did he know that the poor child's death was a SENTENCE? He felt a cowardly satisfaction that with her was gone the secret of his treason. Then he began to doubt. I had MEANS to penetrate all his thoughts, as well as to know his acts. Then he became a slave to a horrible fear. He fled in abject terror to a convent. They still existed in Paris; and behind the walls of Jacobins the wretch thought himself secure. Poor fool! I had but to set one of my somnambulists to sleep. Her spirit went forth and spied the shuddering wretch in his cell. She described the street, the gate, the convent, the very dress which he wore, and which you saw to-day.

"And now *this* is what happened. In his chamber in the Rue St. Honoré, at Paris, sat a man *alone* — a man who has been maligned, a man who has been called a knave and charlatan, a man who has been persecuted even to the death, it is said, in Roman Inquisitions, forsooth, and elsewhere. Ha! ha! A man who has a mighty will.

"And looking towards the Jacobins convent (of which, from his chamber, he could see the spires and trees), this man WILLED. And it was not yet dawn. And he willed; and one who was lying in his cell in the convent of Jacobins, awake and shuddering with terror for a crime which he had committed, fell asleep.

"But though he was asleep, his eyes were open.

"And after tossing and writhing, and clinging to the pallet, and saying, 'No, I will not go,' he rose up and donned his clothes — a gray coat, a vest of white piqué, black satin small-clothes, ribbed silk stockings, and a white stock with a steel buckle; and he arranged his hair, and he tied his cue, all the while being in that strange somnolence which walks, which moves, which FLIES sometimes, which sees, which is indifferent to pain, which OBEYS. And he put on his hat, and he went forth from his cell; and though the dawn was not yet, he trod the corridors as seeing them. And he passed into the cloister, and then into the garden where lie the ancient dead. And he came to the wicket, which Brother Jerome was opening just at the dawning. And the crowd was already waiting with their cans and bowls to receive the alms of the good brethren.

"And he passed through the crowd and went on his way, and the few people then abroad who marked him, said, 'Tiens! How very odd he looks! He looks like a man walking in his sleep!' This was said by various persons: —

"By milk-women, with their cans and carts, coming into the town.

"By roysterers who had been drinking at the taverns of the Barrier, for it was Mid-Lent.

"By the sergeants of the watch, who eyed him sternly as he passed near their halberds.

"But he passed on unmoved by the halberds,

"Unmoved by the cries of the roysterers,

"By the market-women coming with their milk and eggs.

"He walked through the Rue St. Honoré, I say: —

"By the Rue Rambuteau,

"By the Rue St. Antoine,

"By the King's Château of the Bastile,

"By the Faubourg St. Antoine.

"And he came to No. 29 in the Rue Picpus — a house which then stood between a court and garden —

"That is, there was a building of one story, with a great coach-door.

"Then there was a court, around which were stables, coach-houses, offices.

"Then there was a house — a two storied house, with a *perron* in front.

"Behind the house was a garden — a garden of two hundred and fifty French feet in length.

"And as one hundred feet of France equal one hundred and six feet of England, this garden, my friends, equalled exactly two hundred and sixty-five feet of British measure.

"In the centre of the garden was a fountain and a statue — or, to speak more correctly, two statues. One was recumbent,—a man. Over him, sabre in hand, stood a woman.

"The man was Olofernes. The woman was Judith. From the head, from the trunk, the water gushed. It was the taste of the doctor;—was it not a droll of taste?

"At the end of the garden was the doctor's cabinet of study. My faith, a singular cabinet, and singular pictures!—

"Decapitation of Charles Premier at Vitehall.

"Decapitation of Montrose at Edimbourg.

"Decapitation of Cinq Mars. When I tell you that he was a man of taste, charming!

"Through this garden, by these statues, up these stairs, went the pale figure of him who, the porter said, knew the way of the house. He did. Turning neither right nor left, he seemed to walk *through* the statues, the obstacles, the flower-beds, the stairs, the door, the tables, the chairs.

"In the corner of the room was THAT INSTRUMENT which Guillotin had just invented and perfected. One day he was to lay his own head under his own axe. Peace be to his name! With him I deal not!

"In a frame of mahogany, neatly worked, was a board with a half-circle in it, over which another board fitted. Above was a heavy axe, which fell—you know how. It was held up by a rope, and when this rope was untied, or cut, the steel fell.

"To the story which I now have to relate you may give credence, or not, as you will. The sleeping man went up to that instrument.

"He laid his head in it, asleep."

"Asleep!"

"He then took a little penknife out of the pocket of his white dimity waistcoat.

"He cut the rope asleep.

"The axe descended on the head of the traitor and villain. The notch in it was made by the steel buckle of his stock, which was cut through.

"A strange legend has got abroad that after the deed was done, the figure rose, took the head from the basket, walked forth through the garden, and by the screaming porters at the gate, and went and laid itself down at the Morgue. But for this I will not vouch. Only of this be sure. 'There are more things in heaven and earth, Horatio, than are dreamed of in your philosophy.' More and more the light peeps through the chinks. Soon, amidst music ravishing, the curtain will rise, and the glorious scene be displayed. Adieu! Remember me. Ha! 'tis dawn," Pinto said. And he was gone.

I am ashamed to say that my first movement was to clutch the check which he had left with me, and which I was determined to present the very moment the bank opened. I know the importance of these things, and that men *change their mind* sometimes. I sprang through the streets to the great banking house of Manasseh in Duke Street. It seemed to me as if I actually flew as I walked. As the clock struck ten I was at the counter and laid down my check.

The gentleman who received it, who was one of the Hebrew persuasion, as were the other two hundred clerks of the establishment, having looked at the draft with terror in his countenance, then looked at me, then called to himself two of his fellow-clerks, and queer it was to see all their aquiline beaks over the paper.

"Come, come?" said I, "don't keep me here all day. Hand me over the money, short, if you please!" for I was, you see, a little alarmed, and so determined to assume some extra bluster.

"Will you have the kindness to step into the parlor to the partners?" the clerk said, and I followed him.

"What, *again?*" shrieked a bald-headed, red-whiskered gentleman, whom I knew to be Mr. Manasseh. "Mr. Salathiel, this is too bad! Leave me with this gentleman, S." And the clerk disappeared.

"Sir," he said, "I know how you came by this; the Count de Pinto gave it you. It is too bad! I honor my parents; I honor *their* parents; I honor their bills! But this one of grandma's is too bad — it is upon my word, now. She've been dead these five and thirty years. And this last four months she has left her burial-place and took to drawing on our 'ouse! It's too bad, grandma; it is too bad!" and he appealed to me, and tears actually trickled down his nose.

"Is it the Countess Sidonia's check or not?" I asked haughtily.

"But, I tell you, she's dead! It's a shame! — it's a shame! — it is, grandmamma!" and he cried, and wiped his great nose in his yellow pocket-handkerchief. "Look year — will you take pounds instead of guineas? She's dead, I tell you! It's no go! Take the pounds — one tausend pound! — ten nice, neat, crisp hundred-pound notes, and go away vid you, do!"

"I will have my bond, sir, or nothing," I said; and I put on an attitude of resolution which I confess surprised even myself.

"Wery vell," he shrieked, with many oaths, "then you shall have noting — ha, ha, ha! — noting but a policeman! Mr. Abednego, call a policeman! Take that, you humbug and impostor!" and here with an abundance of frightful language, which I dare not repeat, the wealthy banker abused and defied me.

Au bout du compte, what was I to do, if a banker did not choose to honor a check drawn by his dead grandmother? I began to wish I had my snuff-box back. I began to think I was a fool for changing that little old-fashioned gold for this slip of strange paper.

Meanwhile the banker had passed from his fit of anger to a paroxysm of despair. He seemed to be addressing some person invisible, but in the room: "Look here, ma'am, you've really been coming it too strong. A hundred thousand in six months, and now a thousand more! The 'ouse can't stand it; it *won't* stand it, I say! What? Oh! mercy, mercy!"

As he uttered these words, A HAND fluttered over the table in the air! It was a female hand: that which I had seen the night before. That female hand took a pen from the green baize table, dipped it in a silver inkstand, and wrote on a quarter of a sheet of foolscap on the blotting-book, "How about the diamond robbery? If you do not pay, I will tell him where they are."

What diamonds? what robbery? what was this mystery? That will never be ascertained, for the wretched man's demeanor instantly changed. "Certainly, sir; — oh, certainly," he said, forcing a grin. "How will you have the money, sir? All right, Mr. Abednego. This way out."

"I hope I shall often see you again," I said; on which I own poor Manasseh gave a dreadful grin, and shot back into his parlor.

I ran home, clutching the ten delicious, crisp hundred pounds, and the dear little fifty which made up the account. I flew through the streets again. I got to my chambers. I bolted the outer doors. I sank back in my great chair, and slept. . . .

My first thing on waking was to feel for my money. Perdition! Where was I? Ha! — on the table before me was my grandmother's snuff-box, and by its side one of those awful — those admirable — sensation novels, which I had been reading, and which are full of delicious wonder.

But that the guillotine is still to be seen at Mr. Gale's, No. 47, High Holborn, I give you MY HONOR. I suppose I was dreaming about it. I don't know. What is dreaming? What is life? Why shouldn't I sleep on the ceiling? — and am I sitting on it now, or on the floor? I am puzzled. But enough. If the fashion for sensation novels goes on, I tell you I will write one in fifty volumes. For the present, DIXI. But between ourselves, this Pinto, who fought at the Colosseum, who was nearly being roasted by the Inquisition, and sang duets at Holyrood, I am rather sorry to lose him after three little bits of Roundabout Papers. *Et vous?*

DE FINIBUS.

WHEN Swift was in love with Stella, and despatching her a letter from London thrice a month by the Irish packet, you may remember how he would begin letter No. XXIII., we will say, on the very day when XXII. had been sent away, stealing out of the coffee-house or the assembly so as to be able to prattle with his dear; "never letting go her kind hand, as it were," as some commentator or other has said in speaking of the Dean and his amour. When Mr. Johnson, walking to Dodsley's, and touching the posts in Pall Mall as he walked, forgot to pat the head of one of them, he went back and imposed his hands on it, — impelled I know not by what superstition. I have this I hope not dangerous mania too. As soon as a piece of work is out of hand, and before going to sleep, I like to begin another: it may be to write only half a dozen lines: but that is something towards Number the Next. The printer's boy has not yet reached Green Arbor Court with the copy. Those people who were alive half an hour since, Pendennis, Clive Newcome, and (what do you call him? what was the name of the last hero? I remember now!) Philip Firmin, have hardly drunk their glass of wine, and the mammas have only this minute got the children's cloaks on, and have been bowed out of my premises — and here I come back to the study again: *tamen usque recurro.* How lonely it looks now all these people are gone! My dear good friends, some folks are utterly tired of you, and say, "What a poverty of friends the man has? He is always asking us to meet those Pendennises, Newcomes, and so forth. Why does he not introduce us to some new characters? Why is he not thrilling like Twostars, learned and profound like Threestars, exquisitely humorous and human like Fourstars? Why, finally, is he not somebody else?" My good people, it is not only impossible to please you all, but it is absurd to try. The dish which one man devours, another dislikes. Is the dinner of to-day not to your taste? Let us hope to-morrow's entertainment will be more agreeable. . . . I resume my original subject. What an odd, pleasant, humorous, melancholy feeling it is to sit in the study, alone and quiet, now all these people are gone who have been boarding and lodging with me for twenty months! They have interrupted my rest: they have plagued me at all sorts of minutes: they have thrust themselves upon me when I was ill, or wished to be idle, and I have growled out a "Be hanged to you, can't you leave me alone now?" Once or twice they have prevented my going out to dinner. Many and many a time they have prevented my coming home, because I knew they were there waiting in the study, and a plague take them! and I have left home and family, and gone to dine at the Club, and told nobody where I went. They have bored me, those people. They have plagued me at all sorts of uncomfortable hours. They have made such a disturbance in my mind and house, that sometimes I have hardly known what was going on in my family, and scarcely have heard what my neighbor said to me. They are gone at last; and you would expect me to be at ease? Far from it. I should almost be glad if Woolcomb would walk in and talk to me; or Twysden reappear, take his place in that chair opposite me, and begin one of his tremendous stories.

Madmen, you know, see visions, hold conversations with, even draw the likeness of, people invisible to you and me. Is this making of people out of fancy madness? and are novel-writers at all entitled to strait-waistcoats? I often forget people's names in life; and in my own stories contritely own that I make dreadful blunders regarding them; but I declare, my dear sir, with respect to the personages introduced into your humble servant's fables, I know the people utterly — I know the sound of their voices. A gentleman came in to see me the other day, who was so like the picture of Philip Firmin in Mr. Walker's charming drawings in "The Cornhill Magazine," that he was quite a curiosity to me. The same eyes, beard, shoulders, just as you have seen them from month to month. Well, he is not like the Philip Firmin in my mind. Asleep, asleep in the grave, lies the bold, the generous, the reckless, the tender-hearted creature whom I have made to pass through those adventures which have just been brought to an end. It is years since I heard the laughter ringing, or saw the bright blue eyes. When I knew him, both were young. I become young as I think of him. And this morning he was alive again in this room, ready to laugh, to fight, to weep. As I write, do you know, it is the gray of evening; the house is quiet; everybody is out: the room is getting a little dark, and I look rather wistfully up from the paper with perhaps ever so little fancy that HE MAY COME IN —— No? No movement. No gray shade, growing more palpable, out of which at last look the well-known eyes. No, the printer came and took him away with the last page of the proofs. And with the printer's boy did the whole cortège of ghosts flit away, invisible? Ha! stay! what is this? Angels and ministers of grace! The door opens, and a dark form — enters, bearing a black — a black suit of clothes. It is John. He says it is time to dress for dinner.

. . . .

Every man who has had his German tutor, and has been coached through the famous "Faust" of Goethe (thou wert my instructor, good old Weissenborn, and these eyes beheld the great master himself in dear little Weimar town!) has read those charming verses which are prefixed to the drama, in which the poet reverts to the time when his work was first composed, and recalls the friends now departed, who once listened to his song. The dear shadows rise up around him, he says; he lives in the past again. It is to-day which appears vague and visionary. We humbler writers cannot create Fausts, or raise up monumental works that shall endure for all ages: but our books are diaries, in which our own feelings must of necessity be set down. As we look to the page written last month, or ten years ago, we remember the day and its events; the child ill, mayhap, in the adjoining room, and the doubts and fears which racked the brain as it still pursued its work; the dear old friend who read the commencement of the tale, and whose gentle hand shall be laid in ours no more. I own for my part that, in reading pages which this hand penned formerly, I often lose sight of the text under my eyes. It is not the words I see; but that past day; that bygone page of life's history; that tragedy, comedy it may be, which our little home company was enacting; that merrymaking which we shared; that funeral which we followed; that bitter, bitter grief which we buried.

And, such being the state of my mind, I pray gentle readers to deal kindly with their humble servant's manifold short-comings, blunders, and slips of memory. As sure as I read a page of my own composition, I find a fault or two, half a dozen. Jones is called Brown. Brown, who is dead, is brought to life. Aghast, and months after the number was printed, I saw that I had called Philip Firmin, Clive Newcome. Now Clive Newcome is the hero of another story by the reader's most obedient writer. The two men are as different, in my mind's eye, as — as Lord Palmerston and Mr. Disraeli let us say. But there is that blunder at page 990, line 76, volume 84 of "The Cornhill Magazine," and it is past mending; and I wish in my life I had made no worse blunders or errors than that which is hereby acknowledged.

Another Finis written. Another mile-stone passed on this journey from birth to the next world! Sure it is a subject for solemn cogitation. Shall we continue this story-telling business, and be voluble to the end of our age? Will it not be presently time, O prattler, to hold your tongue, and let younger people speak? I have a friend, a painter, who, like other persons who shall be nameless, is growing old. He has never painted with such laborious finish as his works now show. This master is still the most humble and diligent of scholars. Of Art, his mistress, he is always an eager, reverent pupil. In his calling, in yours, in mine, industry and humility will help and comfort us. A word with you. In a pretty large experience I have not found the men who write books superior in wit or learning to those who don't write at all. In regard of mere information, non-writers must often be superior to writers. You don't expect a lawyer in full practice to be conversant with all kinds of literature; he is too busy with his law; and so a writer is commonly too busy with his own books to be able to bestow attention on the works of other people. After a day's work (in which I have been depicting, let us say, the agonies of Louisa on parting with the Captain, or the atrocious behavior of the wicked Marquis to Lady Emily), I march to the Club, proposing to improve my mind and keep myself "posted up," as the Americans phrase it, with the literature of the day. And what happens? Given, a walk after luncheon, a pleasing book, and a most comfortable arm-chair by the fire, and you know the rest. A doze ensues. Pleasing book drops suddenly, is picked up once with an air of some confusion, is laid presently softly in lap: head falls on comfortable arm-chair cushion: eyes close: soft nasal music is heard. Am I telling Club secrets? Of afternoons, after lunch, I say, scores of sensible fogies have a doze. Perhaps I have fallen asleep over that very book to which "Finis" has just been written. "And if the writer sleeps, what happens to the readers?" says Jones, coming down upon me with his lightning wit. What? You *did* sleep over it? And a very good thing too. These eyes have more than once seen a friend dozing over pages which this hand has written. There is a vignette somewhere in one of my books of a friend so caught napping with "Pendennis," or the "Newcomes," in his lap; and if a writer can give you a sweet, soothing, harmless sleep, has he not done you a kindness? So is the author who excites and interests you worthy of your thanks and benedictions. I am troubled with fever and ague, that seizes me at odd intervals and prostrates me for a day. There is cold fit, for which, I am thankful to say, hot brandy and water is prescribed, and this induces hot fit, and so on. In one or two of these fits I have read novels with the most fearful contentment of mind. Once, on the Mississippi, it was my dearly beloved "Jacob Faithful:" once at Frankfort O. M., the delightful "Vingt Ans Après" of Monsieur Dumas: once at Tunbridge Wells, the thrilling "Woman in White:" and these books gave me amusement from morning till sunset. I remember those ague fits with a great deal of pleasure and gratitude. Think of a whole day in bed, and a good novel for a companion! No cares: no remorse about idleness: no visitors: and the Woman in White or the Chevalier d'Artagnan to tell me stories from dawn till night! "Please, ma'am, my master's compliments, and can h.. have the third volume?" (This message was sent to an astonished friend and neighbor who lent me volume by volume, the *W. in W.*) How do you like your novels? I like mine strong, "hot with," and no mistake: no love-making: no observations about society: little dialogue, except where the characters are bullying each other: plenty of fighting: and a villain in the cupboard, who is to suffer tortures just before Finis. I don't like your melancholy Finis. I never read the history of a consumptive heroine twice. If I might give a short hint to an impartial writer (as "The Examiner" used to say in old days), it would be to act *not* à la mode le pays de Pole (I think that was the phraseology), but *always* to give quarter. In the story of Philip, just come to an end, I have the permission of the author to state that he was going to drown the two villains of the piece — a certain Doctor F—— and a certain Mr. T. H—— on board "The President," or some other tragic ship — but you see I relented. I pictured to myself Firmin's ghastly face amid the crowd of shuddering people on that reeling deck in the lonely ocean, and thought, "Thou ghastly lying wretch, thou shall not be drowned: thou shalt have a fever only; a knowledge of thy danger; and a chance — ever so small a chance — of repentance." I wonder whether he *did* repent when he found himself in the yellow-fever in Virginia? The probability is, he fancied that his son had injured him very much, and forgave him on his deathbed. Do you imagine there is a great deal of genuine right-down remorse in the world? Don't people rather find excuses which make their minds easy; endeavor to prove to themselves that they have been lamentably belied and misunderstood; and try and forgive the persecutors who *will* present that bill when it is due; and not bear malice against the cruel ruffian who takes them to the police-office for stealing the spoons? Years ago I had a quarrel with a certain well-known person (I believed a statement regarding him which his friends imparted to me, and which turned out to be quite incorrect). To his dying day that quarrel was never quite made up. I said to his brother, "Why is your brother's soul still dark against me? It is I who ought to be angry and unforgiving: for I was in the wrong." In the region which they now inhabit (for Finis has been set to the volumes of the lives of both here below), if they take any cognizance of our squabbles, and tittle-tattles, and gossips on earth here, I hope they admit that my little error was not of a nature unpardonable. If you have never committed a worse, my good sir, surely the score against you will not be heavy. Ha, *dilectissimi fratres!* It is in regard of sins *not* found out that we may say or sing (in an undertone, in a most penitent and lugubrious minor-key), *Miserere nobis miseris peccatoribus.*

Among the sins of commission which novel-writers not seldom perpetrate, is the sin of grandiloquence, or tall-talking, against which for my part, I will offer up a special *libera me.* This is the sin of schoolmasters, governesses, critics, sermoners, and instructors of young or old people. Nay (for I am making a clean breast, and liberating my soul), perhaps of all the novel-spinners now extant, the present speaker is the most addicted to preaching. Does he not stop perpetually in his story and begin to preach to you? When he ought to be engaged with business, is he not forever taking the Muse by the sleeve, and plaguing her with some of his cynical sermons? I cry *peccavi* loudly and heartily. I tell you I would like to be able to write a story which should show no egotism whatever — in which there should be no reflections, no cynicism, no vulgarity (and so forth), but an incident in every other page, a villain, a battle, a mystery, in every chapter. I should like to be able to feed a reader so spicily as to leave him hungering and thirsting for more at the end of every monthly meal.

Alexandre Dumas describes himself, when inventing the plan of a work, as lying silent on his back for two whole days on the deck of a yacht in a Mediterranean port. At the end of the two days he arose and called for dinner. In those two days he had built his plot. He had moulded a mighty clay, to be cast presently in perennial brass. The chapters, the characters, the incidents, the combinations, were all arranged in the artist's brain ere he set a pen to paper. My Pegasus won't fly, so as to let me survey the field below me. He has no wings, he is blind of one eye certainly, he is restive, stubborn, slow; crops a hedge when he ought to be galloping, or gallops when he ought to be quiet. He never will show off when I want him. Sometimes he goes at a pace which surprises me. Sometimes, when I most wish him to make the running, the brute turns restive, and I am obliged to let him take his own time. I wonder do other novel-writers experience this fatalism? They *must* go a certain way, in spite of themselves. I have been surprised at the observations made by some of my characters. It seems as if an occult Power was moving the pen. The personage does or says something, and I ask, how the dickens did he come to think of that? Every man has remarked in dreams the vast dramatic power which is sometimes evinced; I won't say the surprising power, for nothing does surprise you in dreams. But those strange characters you meet make instant observations of which you never can have thought previously. In like manner, the imagination foretells things. We spake anon of the inflated style of some writers. What also if there is an *afflated* style, — when a writer is like a Pythoness on her oracle tripod, and mighty words, words which he cannot help, come blowing, and bellowing, and whistling, and moaning through the speaking pipes of his bodily organ? I have told you it was a very queer shock to me the other day when, with a letter of introduction in his hand, the artist's (not my) Philip Firmin walked into this room, and sat down in the chair opposite. In the novel of "Pendennis," written ten years ago, there is an account of a certain Costigan, whom I had invented (as I suppose authors invent their personages out of scraps, heel-taps, odds and ends of characters). I was smoking in a tavern parlor one night — and this Costigan came into the room alive — the very man: — the most remarkable resemblance of the printed sketches of the man, of the rude drawings in which I had depicted him. He had the same little coat, the same battered hat, cocked on one eye, the same twinkle in that eye. "Sir," said I, knowing him to be an old friend whom I had met in unknown regions, "sir," I said, "may I offer you a glass of brandy and water?" "*Bedad, ye may,*" says he, "*and I'll sing ye a song tu.*" Of course he spoke with an Irish brogue. Of course he had been in the army. In ten minutes he pulled out an Army Agent's account, whereon his name was written. A few months after we read of him in a police court. How had I come to know him, to divine him? Nothing shall convince me that I have not seen that man in the world of spirits. In the world of spirits and water I know I did: but that is a mere quibble of words. I was not surprised when he spoke in an Irish brogue. I had had cognizance of him before somehow. Who has not felt that little shock which arises when a person, a place, some words in a book (there is always a collocation) present themselves to you, and you know that you have before met the same person, words, scene, and so forth?

They used to call the good Sir Walter the "Wizard of the North." What if some writer should appear who can write so *enchantingly* that he shall be able to call into actual life the people whom he invents? What if Mignon, and Margaret, and Goetz von Berlichingen are alive now (though I don't say they are visible), and Dugald Dalgetty and Ivanhoe were to step in at that open window by the little garden yonder? Suppose Uncas and our noble old Leather Stocking were to glide silent in? Suppose Athos, Porthos, and Aramis should enter with a noiseless swagger, curling their mustaches? And dearest Amelia Booth, on Uncle Toby's arm; and Tittlebat Titmouse, with his hair dyed green; and all the Crummles company of comedians, with the Gil Blas troop; and Sir Roger De Coverley; and the greatest of all crazy gentlemen, the Knight of La Mancha, with his blessed squire? I say to you, I look rather wistfully towards the window, musing upon these people. Were any of them to enter, I think I should not be very much frightened. Dear old friends what pleasant hours I have had with them! We do not see each other very often, but when we do, we are ever happy to meet. I had a capital half hour with Jacob Faithful last night; when the last sheet was corrected, when "Finis" had been written, and the printer's boy, with the copy, was safe in Green Arbor Court.

So you are gone, little printer's boy with the last scratches and corrections on the proof, and a fine flourish by way of Finis at the story's end. The last corrections? I say those last corrections seem never to be finished. A plague upon the weeds! Every day, when I walk in my own little literary garden-plot, I spy some, and should like to have a spud, and root them out. Those idle words, neighbor, are past remedy. That turning back to the old pages produces any thing but elation of mind. Would you not pay a pretty fine to be able to cancel some of them? Oh, the sad old pages, the dull old pages! Oh, the cares, the *ennui*, the squabbles, the repetitions, the old conversations over and over again! But now and again a kind thought is recalled, and now and again a dear memory. Yet a few chapters more, and then the last: after which, behold Finis itself come to an end, and the Infinite begun.

ON A PEAL OF BELLS.

As some bells in a church hard by are making a great holiday clanging in the summer afternoon, I am reminded, somehow, of a July day, a garden, and a great clanging of bells years and years ago, on the very day when George IV. was crowned. I remember a little boy lying in that garden reading his first novel. It was called "The Scottish Chiefs." The little boy (who is now ancient and not little) read this book in the summer-house of his great grandmamma. She was eighty years of age then. A most lovely and picturesque old lady, with a long tortoise-shell cane, with a little puff, or *tour*, of snow-white (or was it powdered?) hair under her cap, with the prettiest little black-velvet slippers and high heels you ever saw. She had a grandson, a lieutenant in the navy; son of her son, a captain in the navy; grandson of her husband, a captain in the navy. She lived for scores and scores of years in a dear little old Hampshire town inhabited by the wives, widows, daughters of navy captains, admirals, lieutenants. Dear me! Don't I remember Mrs. Duval, widow of Admiral Duval; and the Miss Dennets, at the Great House at the other end of the town, Admiral Dennet's daughters; and the Miss Barrys, the late Captain Barry's daughters; and the good old Miss Maskews, Admiral Maskews's daughter; and that dear little Miss Norval, and the kind Miss Bookers, one of whom married Captain, now Admiral, Sir Henry Excellent, K.C.B? Far,

far away into the past I look and see the little town with its friendly glimmer. That town was so like a novel of Miss Austen's that I wonder was she born and bred there? No, we should have known, and the good old ladies would have pronounced her to be a little idle thing, occupied with her silly books, and neglecting her housekeeping. There were other towns in England, no doubt, where dwelt the widows and wives of other navy captains; where they tattled, loved each other, and quarrelled; talked about Betty the maid, and her fine ribbons indeed! took their dish of tea at six, played at quadrille every night till ten, when there was a little bit of supper, after which Betty came with the lanthorn; and next day came, and next, and next, and so forth, until a day arrived when the lanthorn was out, when Betty came no more: all that little company sank to rest under the daisies, whither some folks will presently follow them. How did they live to be so old, those good people? *Moi qui vous parle*, I perfectly recollect old Mr. Gilbert, who had been to sea with Captain Cook; and Captain Cook, as you justly observe, dear Miss, quoting out of your "Mangnall's Questions," was murdered by the natives of Owhyhee, anno 1779. Ah! don't you remember his picture, standing on the seashore, in tights and gaiters, with a musket in his hand, pointing to his people not to fire from the boats, whilst a great tattooed savage is going to stab him in the back? Don't you remember those houris dancing before him and the other officers at the great Otaheite ball? Don't you know that Cook was at the siege of Quebec, with the glorious Wolfe, who fought under the Duke of Cumberland, whose royal father was a distinguished officer at Ramillies, before he commanded in chief at Dettingen? Huzza! Give it them, my lads! My horse is down? Then I know I shall not run away. Do the French run? then I die content. Stop. Wo! *Quo me rapis?* My Pegasus is galloping off, goodness knows where, like his Majesty's charger at Dettingen.

How do these rich historical and personal reminiscences come out of the subject at present in hand? What *is* that subject, by the way? My dear friend, if you look at the last essaykin (though you may leave it alone, and I shall not be in the least surprised or offended), if you look at the last paper, where the writer imagines Athos and Porthos, Dalgetty and Ivanhoe, Amelia and Sir Charles Grandison, Don Quixote and Sir Roger, walking in at the garden-window, you will at once perceive that NOVELS and their heroes and heroines are our present subject of discourse, into which we will presently plunge. Are you one of us, dear sir, and do you love novel-reading? To be reminded of your first novel will surely be a pleasure to you. Hush! I never read quite to the end of my first, "The Scottish Chiefs." I couldn't. I peeped in an alarmed furtive manner at some of the closing pages. Miss Porter, like a kind dear tender-hearted creature, would not have Wallace's head chopped off at the end of Vol. V. She made him die in prison,* and if I remember right (protesting I have not read the book for forty two or three years), Robert Bruce made a speech to his soldiers, in which he said, "And Bannockburn shall equal Cambuskenneth." † But I repeat, I could not

* I find, on reference to the novel, that Sir William died on the scaffold, not in prison. His last words were, "'My prayer is heard. Life's cord is cut by heaven. Helen! Helen! May heaven preserve my country, and'—— He stopped. He fell. And with that mighty shock the scaffold shook to its foundation."

† The remark of Bruce (which I protest I had not read for forty-two years), I find to be as follows:—"When this was uttered by the English heralds, Bruce turned to Ruthven, with an heroic smile, 'Let him come, my brave barons! and he shall find that Bannockburn shall page with Cambuskenneth!'" In the same amiable author's famous novel of "Thad

read the end of the fifth volume of that dear delightful book for crying. Good heavens! It was as sad, as sad as going back to school.

The glorious Scott cycle of romances came to me some four or five years afterwards; and I think boys of our year were specially fortunate in coming upon those delightful books at that special time when we could best enjoy them. Oh, that sunshiny bench on half-holidays, with Claverhouse or Ivanhoe for a companion! I have remarked of very late days some little men in a great state of delectation over the romances of Captain Mayne Reid, and Gustave Aimard's Prairie and Indian Stories, and during occasional holiday visits, lurking off to bed with the volume under their arms. But are those Indians and warriors so terrible as *our* Indians and warriors were? (I say, are they? Young gentlemen, mind, I do not say they are not.) But as an oldster I can be heartily thankful for the novels of the 1–10 Geo. IV., let us say, and so downward to a period not unremote. Let us see; there is, first, our dear Scott. Whom do I love in the works of that dear old master? Amo —

The Baron of Bradwardine, and Fergus. (Captain Waverley is certainly very mild.)

Amo Ivanhoe; LOCKSLEY; the Templar.

Amo Quentin Durward, and specially Quentin's uncle, who brought the Boar to bay. I forget the gentleman's name.

I have never cared for the Master of Ravenswood, or fetched his hat out of the water since he dropped it there when I last met him (circa 1825).

Amo SALADIN and the Scotch knight in "The Talisman." The Sultan best.

Amo CLAVERHOUSE.

Amo MAJOR DALGETTY. Delightful Major! To think of him is to desire to jump up, run to the book, and get the volume down from the shelf. About all those heroes of Scott, what a manly bloom there is, and honorable modesty! They are not at all heroic. They seem to blush somehow in their position of hero, and as it were to say, "Since it must be done, here goes!" They are handsome, modest, upright, simple, courageous, not too clever. If I were a mother (which is absurd), I should like to be mother-in-law to several young men of the Walter-Scott-hero sort.

Much as I like those most unassuming, manly, unpretending gentlemen, I have to own that I think the heroes of another writer, viz, —

LEATHER-STOCKING,
UNCAS,
HARDHEART,
TOM COFFIN,

are quite the equals of Scott's men; perhaps Leather-stocking is better than any one in "Scott's lot." *La Longue Carabine* is one of the great prize-men of fiction. He ranks with your Uncle Toby, Sir Roger de Coverley, Falstaff — heroic figures, all — American or British, and the artist has deserved well of his country who devised them.

At school, in my time, there was a public day, when the boys' relatives, an examining bigwig or two from the universities, old schoolfellows, and so forth, came to the place. The boys were all paraded; prizes were administered; each lad being in a new suit of clothes — and magnificent dandies, I promise you, some of us were. Oh, the chubby cheeks, clean collars, glossy new raiment, beaming faces, glorious in youth — *fit tueri cœlum* — bright with truth, and mirth, and

deus of Warsaw," there is more crying than in any novel I ever remember to have read. See, for example, the last page. . . . "Incapable of speaking, Thaddeus led his wife back to her carriage. . . . His tears gushed out in spite of himself, and mingling with hers, poured those thanks, those assurances, of animated approbation through her heart, which made it even ache with excess of happiness." . . . And a sentence or two further. "Kosciusko did bless him, and embalmed the benediction with a shower of tears."

honor! To see a hundred boys marshalled in a chapel or old hall; to hear their sweet fresh voices when they chant, and look in their brave calm faces; I say, does not the sight and sound of them smite you, somehow, with a pang of exquisite kindness? . . . Well. As about boys, so about Novelists. I fancy the boys of Parnassus School all paraded. I am a lower boy myself in that academy. I like our fellows to look well, upright, gentlemanlike. There is Master Fielding — he with the black eye. What a magnificent build of a boy! There is Master Scott, one of the heads of the school. Did you ever see the fellow more hearty and manly? Yonder lean, shambling, cadaverous lad, who is always borrowing money, telling lies, leering after the housemaids, is Master Laurence Sterne — a bishop's grandson, and himself intended for the Church; for shame, you little reprobate! But what a genius the fellow has! Let him have a sound flogging, and as soon as the young scamp is out of the whipping-room give him a gold medal. Such would be my practice if I were Doctor Birch, and master of the school.

Let us drop this school metaphor, this birch, and all pertaining thereto. Our subject, I beg leave to remind the reader's humble servant, is novel heroes and heroines. How do you like your heroes, ladies? Gentlemen, what novel heroines do you prefer? When I set this essay going, I sent the above question to two of the most inveterate novel-readers of my acquaintance. The gentleman refers me to Miss Austen; the lady says Athos, Guy Livingston, and (pardon my rosy blushes) Colonel Esmond, and owns that in youth she was very much in love with Valancourt.

"Valancourt? and who was he?" cry the young people. Valancourt, my dears, was the hero of one of the most famous romances which ever was published in this country. The beauty and elegance of Valancourt made your young grandmammas' gentle hearts to beat with respectful sympathy. He and his glory have passed away. Ah, woe is me that the glory of novels should ever decay; that dust should gather round them on the shelves; that the annual checks from Messieurs the publishers should dwindle, dwindle! Inquire at Mudie's, or the London Library, who asks for "The Mysteries of Udolpho" now? Have not even "The Mysteries of Paris" ceased to frighten? Alas! our novels are but for a season; and I know characters whom a painful modesty forbids me to mention, who shall go to limbo along with "Valancourt," and "Doricourt," and "Thaddeus of Warsaw."

A dear old sentimental friend, with whom I discoursed on the subject of novels yesterday, said that her favorite hero was Lord Orville, in "Evelina," that novel which Doctor Johnson loved so. I took down the book from a dusty old crypt at a club, where Mrs. Barbauld's novelists repose; and this is the kind of thing, ladies and gentlemen, in which your ancestors found pleasure: —

"And here, whilst I was looking for the books, I was followed by Lord Orville. He shut the door after he came in, and, approaching me with a look of anxiety, said, 'Is this true, Miss Anville — are you going?'

"'I believe so, my lord,' said I, still looking for the books.

"'So suddenly, so unexpectedly: must I lose you?'

"'No great loss, my lord,' said I, endeavoring to speak cheerfully.

"'Is it possible,' said he gravely, 'Miss Anville can doubt my sincerity?'

"'I can't imagine,' cried I, 'what Mrs. Selwyn has done with those books.'

"'Would to heaven,' continued he, 'I might flatter myself you would allow me to prove it!'

"'I must run up stairs,' cried I, greatly confused, 'and ask what she has done with them.'

"'You are going, then,' cried he, taking my hand, 'and you give me not the smallest hope of any return! Will you not, my too lovely friend, will you not teach me, with fortitude like your own, to support your absence?'

"'My lord,' cried I, endeavoring to disengage my hand, 'pray let me go!'

"'I will,' cried he, to my inexpressible confusion, dropping on one knee, 'if you wish me to leave you.'

"'Oh, my lord,' exclaimed I, 'rise, I beseech you; rise. Surely your lordship is not so cruel as to mock me.'

"'Mock you!' repeated he earnestly, 'no, I revere you. I esteem and admire you above all human beings! You are the friend to whom my soul is attached, as to its better half. You are the most amiable, the most perfect of women; and you are dearer to me than language has the power of telling.'

"I attempt not to describe my sensations at that moment; I scarce breathed; I doubted if I existed; the blood forsook my cheeks, and my feet refused to sustain me. Lord Orville hastily rising supported me to a chair upon which I sank almost lifeless.

"I cannot write the scene that followed, though every word is engraven on my heart; but his protestations, his expressions, were too flattering for repetition; nor would he, in spite of my repeated efforts to leave him, suffer me to escape; in short, my dear sir, I was not pooof against his solicitations, and he drew from me the most sacred secret of my heart!"*

Other people may not much like this extract, madam, from your favorite novel, but when you come to read it, *you* will like it. I suspect that when you read that book which you so love, you read it *à deux*. Did you not yourself pass a winter at Bath, when you were the belle of the assembly? Was there not a Lord Orville in your case too? As you think of him eleven lustres pass away. You look at him with the bright eyes of those days, and your hero stands before you, the brave, the accomplished, the simple, the true gentleman; and he makes the most elegant of bows to one of the most beautiful young women the world ever saw; and he leads you out to the cotillon, to the dear unforgotten music. Hark to the horns of Elfland, blowing, blowing! *Bonne Vieille*, you remember their melody, and your heart-strings thrill with it still.

Of your heroic heroes, I think our friend Monseigneur Athos, Count de la Fère, is my favorite. I have read about him from sunrise to sunset with the utmost contentment of mind. He has passed through how many volumes? Forty? Fifty? I wish for my part there were a hundred more,

* Contrast this old perfumed, powdered D'Arblay conversation with the present modern talk. If the two young people wished to hide their emotions now-a-days, and express themselves in modest language, the story would run:—

"Whilst I was looking for the books, Lord Orville came in. He looked uncommonly down in the mouth, as he said, 'Is this true, Miss Anville; are you going to cut?'

"'To absquatulate, Lord Orville,' said I, still pretending that I was looking for the books.

"'You're very quick about it,' said he.

"'Guess it's no great loss,' I remarked, as cheerfully as I could.

"'You don't think I'm chaffing?' said Orville, with much emotion.

"'What has Mrs. Selwyn done with the books?' I went on.

"'What, going?' said he, 'and going for good? I wish I was such a good-plucked one as you, Miss Anville,'" &c.

The conversation, you perceive, might be easily written down to this key; and if the hero and heroine were modern, they would not be suffered to go through their dialogue on stilts, but would converse in the natural graceful way at present customary. By the way, what a strange custom that is in modern lady novelists to make the men bully the women! In the time of Miss Porter and Madame D'Arblay, we have respect, profound bows and courtesies, graceful courtesy, from men to women. In the time of Miss Brontë, absolute rudeness. Is it true, mesdames, that you like rudeness, and are pleased at being ill-used by men? I could point to more than one lady novelist who so represents you.

and would never tire of him rescuing prisoners, punishing ruffians, and running scoundrels through the midriff with his most graceful rapier. Ah, Athos, Porthos, and Aramis, you are a magnificent trio. I think I like d'Artagnan in his own memoirs best. I bought him years and years ago, price fivepence, in a little parchment-covered Colonge-printed volume, at a stall in Gray's Inn Lane. Dumas glorifies him and makes a Marshal of him; if I remember rightly, the original d'Artagnan was a needy adventurer, who died in exile very early in Louis XIV.'s reign. Did you ever read the "Chevalier d'Harmenthal"? Did you ever read the "Tulipe Noire," as modest as a story by Miss Edgeworth? I think of the prodigal banquets to which this Lucullus of a man has invited me, with thanks and wonder. To what a series of splendid entertainments he has treated me! Where does he find the money for these prodigious feasts? They say that all the works bearing Dumas's name are not written by him. Well? Does not the chief cook have *aides* under him? Did not Rubens's pupils paint on his canvases? Had not Lawrence assistants for his backgrounds? For myself, being also *du métier*, I confess I would often like to have a competent, respectable, and rapid clerk for the business part of my novels; and on his arrival, at eleven o'clock, would say, "Mr. Jones, if you please, the archbishop must die this morning in about five pages. Turn to article 'Dropsy' (or what you will) in Encyclopædia. Take care there are no medical blunders in his death. Group his daughters, physicians, and chaplains round him. In Wales's 'London,' letter B, third shelf, you will find an account of Lambeth, and some prints of the place. Color in with local coloring. The daughter will come down, and speak to her lover in his wherry at Lambeth Stairs," &c., &c. Jones (an intelligent young man) examines the medical, historical, topographical books necessary; his chief points out to him in Jeremy Taylor (fol., London, M.DCLV.) a few remarks such as might befit a dear old archbishop departing this life. When I come back to dress for dinner, the archbishop is dead on my table in five pages; medicine, topography, theology, all right, and Jones has gone home to his family some hours. Sir Christopher is the architect of St. Paul's. He has not laid the stones or carried up the mortar. There is a great deal of carpenter's and joiner's work in novels which surely a smart professional hand might supply. A smart professional hand? I give you my word, there seem to me parts of novels — let us say the love-making, the "business," the villain in the cupboard, and so forth, which I should like to order John Footman to take in hand, as I desire him to bring the coals and polish the boots. Ask *me* indeed to pop a robber under a bed, to hide a will which shall be forthcoming in due season, or at my time of life to write a namby-pamby love conversation between Emily and Lord Arthur! I feel ashamed of myself, and especially when my business obliges me to do the love-passages, I blush so, though quite alone in my study, that you would fancy I was going off in an apoplexy. Are authors affected by their own works? I don't know about other gentlemen, but if I make a joke myself I cry; if I write a pathetic scene I am laughing wildly all the time — at least Tomkins thinks so. You know I am such a cynic!

The editor of "The Cornhill Magazine" (no soft and yielding character like his predecessor, but a man of stern resolution) will only allow these harmless papers to run to a certain length. But for this veto I should gladly have prattled over half a sheet more, and have discoursed on many heroes and heroines of novels whom fond memory brings back to me. Of these books I have been a diligent student from those early days, which are recorded at the commencement of this little essay. Oh, delightful novels, well remembered! Oh, novels, sweet and delicious as the raspberry open-tarts of budding boyhood! Do I forget one night after prayers (when we under-boys were sent to bed) lingering at my cupboard to read one little half-page more of my dear Walter Scott — and down came the monitor's dictionary upon my head! Rebecca, daughter of Isaac of York, I have loved thee faithfully for forty years! Thou wert twenty years old (say), and I but twelve, when I knew thee. At sixty odd, love, most of the ladies of thy Orient race have lost the bloom of youth, and bulged beyond the line of beauty; but to me thou art ever young and fair, and I will do battle with any felon Templar who assails thy fair name.

ON A PEAR-TREE.

A GRACIOUS reader no doubt has remarked that these humble sermons have for subjects some little event which happens at the preacher's own gate, or which falls under his peculiar cognizance. Once, you may remember, we discoursed about a chalk-mark on the door. This morning Betsy, the housemaid, comes with a frightened look, and says, "Law, mum! there's three bricks taken out of the garden wall, and the branches broke, and all the pears taken off the pear-tree!" Poor peaceful suburban pear-tree! Jail-birds have hopped about thy branches, and robbed them of their smoky fruit. But those bricks removed; that ladder evidently prepared, by which unknown marauders may enter and depart from my little Englishman's castle; is not this a subject of thrilling interest, and may it not *be continued in a future number?* — that is the terrible question. Suppose, having escaladed the outer wall, the miscreants take a fancy to storm the castle? Well — well! we are armed; we are numerous; we are men of tremendous courage, who will defend our spoons with our lives; and there are barracks close by (thank goodness!) whence, at the noise of our shouts and firing, at least a thousand bayonets will bristle to our rescue.

What sound is yonder? A church bell. I might go myself, but how listen to the sermon? I am thinking of those thieves who have made a ladder of my wall, and a prey of my pear-tree. They may be walking to church at this moment, neatly shaved, in clean linen, with every outward appearance of virtue. If I went, I know I should be watching the congregation, and thinking, "Is that one of the fellows who came over my wall?" If, after the reading of the eighth Commandment, a man sang out with particular energy, "Incline our hearts to keep this law," I should think, "Aha, Master Basso, did you have pears for breakfast this morning?" Crime is walking round me, that is clear. Who is the perpetrator? . . . What a changed aspect the world has, since these last few lines were written! I have been walking round about my premises, and in consultation with a gentleman in a single-breasted blue coat, with pewter buttons, and a tape ornament on the collar. He has looked at the holes in the wall, and the amputated tree. We have formed our plan of defence —*perhaps of attack*. Perhaps some day you may read in the papers, "DARING ATTEMPT AT BURGLARY — HEROIC VICTORY OVER THE VILLAINS," &c., &c. Rascals as yet unknown! perhaps you, too, may read these words, and may be induced to pause in your fatal intention. Take the advice of a sincere friend, and keep off. To find a man writhing in my man-trap, another mayhap impaled in my ditch, to pick off another from my tree (scoundrel! as though he were a pear), will give me no pleasure; but such things may happen. Be warned in time, villains!

Or, if you *must* pursue your calling as cracksmen, have the goodness to try some other shutters. Enough! subside into your darkness, children of night! Thieves! we seek not to have *you* hanged — you are but as pegs whereon to hang others.

I may have said before, that if I were going to be hanged myself, I think I should take an accurate note of my sensations, request to stop at some public-house on the road to Tyburn, and be provided with a private room and writing-materials, and give an account of my state of mind. Then, gèe up, carter! I beg your reverence to continue your apposite, though not novel, remarks on my situation; and so we drive up to Tyburn turnpike, where an expectant crowd, the obliging sheriffs, and the dexterous and rapid Mr. Ketch are already in waiting.

A number of laboring people are sauntering about our streets and taking their rest on this holiday — fellows who have no more stolen my pears than they have robbed the crown jewels out of the Tower — and I say I cannot help thinking in my own mind, "Are you the rascal who got over my wall last night?" Is the suspicion haunting my mind written on my countenance? I trust not. What if one man after another were to come up to me and say, "How dare you, sir, suspect me in your mind of stealing your fruit? Go be hanged, you and your jargonels!" You rascal thief! it is not merely three halfp'orth of sooty fruit you rob me of; it is my peace of mind — my artless innocence and trust in my fellow-creatures, my childlike belief that every thing they say is true. How can I hold out the hand of friendship in this condition, when my first impression is, "My good sir, I strongly suspect that you were up my pear-tree last night?" It is a dreadful state of mind. The core is black; the death-stricken fruit drops on the bough, and a great worm is within — fattening, and feasting, and wriggling! Who stole the pears, I say? Is it you, brother? Is it you, madam? Come, are you ready to answer — *respondere parati et cantare pares?* (O shame! shame!)

Will the villains ever be discovered and punished who stole my fruit? Some unlucky rascals who rob orchards are caught up the tree at once. Some rob through life with impunity. If I, for my part, were to try and get up the smallest tree, on the darkest night, in the most remote orchard, I wager any money I should be found out — be caught by the leg in a man-trap, or have Towler fastening on me. I always am found out; have been; shall be. It's my luck. Other men will carry off bushels of fruit, and get away undetected, unsuspected; whereas I know woe and punishment would fall upon me were I to lay my hand on the smallest pippin. So be it. A man who has this precious self-knowledge will surely keep his hands from picking and stealing, and his feet upon the paths of virtue.

I will assume, my benevolent friends and present reader, that you yourself are virtuous, not from a fear of punishment, but from a sheer love of good. but as you and I walk through life, consider what hundreds of thousands of rascals we must have met, who have not been found out at all. In high places and low, in Clubs and on 'Change, at church or the balls and routs of the nobility and gentry, how dreadful it is for benevolent beings like you and me to have to think these undiscovered though not unsuspected scoundrels are swarming! What is the difference between you and a galley-slave? Is yonder poor wretch at the hulks not a man and a brother too? Have you ever forged, my dear sir? Have you ever cheated your neighbor? Have you ever ridden to Hounslow Heath, and robbed the mail? Have you ever entered a first-class railway-carriage, where an old gentleman sat alone in a sweet sleep, daintily murdered him, taken his pocket-book, and got out at the next station? You know that this circumstance occurred in France a few months since. If we have travelled in France this autumn, we may have met the ingenious gentleman who perpetrated this daring and successful *coup*. We may have found him a well-informed and agreeable man. I have been acquainted with two or three gentlemen who have been discovered after — after the performance of illegal actions. What? That agreeable rattling fellow we met was the celebrated Mr. John Sheppard? Was that amiable quiet gentleman in spectacles the well-known Mr. Fauntleroy? In Hazlitt's admirable paper, "Going to a Fight," he describes a dashing sporting fellow who was in the coach, and who was no less a man than the eminent destroyer of Mr. William Weare. Don't tell me that you would not like to have met (out of business) Captain Sheppard, the Reverend Doctor Dodd, or others rendered famous by their actions and misfortunes, by their lives and their deaths. They are the subjects of ballads, the heroes of romance. A friend of mine had the house in May Fair, out of which poor Doctor Dodd was taken handcuffed. There was the paved hall over which he stepped. That little room at the side was, no doubt, the study where he composed his elegant sermons. Two years since I had the good fortune to partake of some admirable dinners in Tyburnia — magnificent dinners indeed; but rendered doubly interesting from the fact that the house was that occupied by the late Mr. Sadleir. One night the late Mr. Sadleir took tea in that dining-room, and, to the surprise of his butler, went out, having put into his pocket his own cream-jug. The next morning, you know, he was found dead on Hampstead Heath, with the cream-jug lying by him, into which he had poured the poison by which he died. The idea of the ghost of the late gentleman flitting about the room gave a strange interest to the banquet. Can you fancy him taking his tea alone in the dining-room? He empties that cream-jug and puts it in his pocket; and then he opens yonder door, through which he is never to pass again. Now he crosses the hall: and hark! the hall-door shuts upon him, and his steps die away. They are gone into the night. They traverse the sleeping city. They lead him into the fields, where the gray morning is beginning to glimmer. He pours something from a bottle into a little silver jug. It touches his lips, the lying lips. Do they quiver a prayer ere that awful draught is swallowed? When the sun rises they are dumb.

I neither knew this unhappy man, nor his countryman — Laërtes let us call him — who is at present in exile, having been compelled to fly from remorseless creditors. Laërtes fled to America, where he earned his bread by his pen. I own to having a kindly feeling towards this scapegrace, because, though an exile, he did not abuse the country whence he fled. I have heard that he went away taking no spoil with him, penniless almost; and on his voyage he made acquaintance with a certain Jew; and when he fell sick, at New York, this Jew befriended him, and gave him help and money out of his own store, which was but small. Now, after they had been a while in the strange city, it happened that the poor Jew spent all his little money, and he too fell ill, and was in great penury. And now it was Laërtes who befriended that Ebrew Jew. He feed doctors; he fed and tended the sick and hungry. Go to, Laërtes! I know thee not. It may be thou art justly *exul patriæ*. But the Jew shall intercede for thee, thou not, let us trust, hopeless Christian sinner.

Another exile to the same shore I knew: who did not? Julius Cæsar hardly owed more money than Cucedicus: and, gracious powers! Cucedicus, how did you manage to spend and owe so much? All day he was at work for his clients; at night he was occupied in the Public Council. He neither had wife nor children. The rewards which he received for his orations were enough to maintain twenty rhetoricians. Night after night I have seen him eating his frugal meal, consisting but of a fish, a small portion of mutton, and a small measure of Iberian or Trinacrian wine, largely diluted with the sparkling waters of Rhenish Gaul. And this was all he had; and this man earned and paid away talents upon talents; and fled, owing who knows how many more! Does a man earn fifteen thousand pounds a year, toiling by day, talking by night, having horrible unrest in his bed, ghastly terrors at waking, seeing an officer lurking at every corner, a sword of justice forever hanging over his head — and have for his sole diversion a newspaper, a lonely mutton-chop, and a little sherry and seltzer-water? In the German stories we read how men sell themselves to — a certain Personage, and that Personage cheats them. He gives them wealth; yes, but the gold-pieces turn into worthless leaves. He sets them before splendid banquets; yes, but what an awful grin that black footman has who lifts up the dish-cover; and don't you smell a peculiar sulphurous odor in the dish? Faugh! take it away; I can't eat. He promises them splendors and triumphs. The conqueror's car rolls glittering through the city, the multitudes shout and huzza. Drive on, coachman. Yes, but who is that hanging on behind the carriage? Is this the reward of eloquence, talents, industry? Is this the end of a life's labor? Don't you remember how, when the dragon was infesting the neighborhood of Babylon, the citizens used to walk dismally out of evenings, and look at the valleys round about strewed with the bones of the victims whom the monster had devoured? O insatiate brute, and most disgusting, brazen, and scaly reptile! Let us be thankful, children, that it has not gobbled us up too. Quick. Let us turn away, and pray that we may be kept out of the reach of his horrible maw, jaw, claw!

When I first came up to London, as innocent as Monsieur Gil Blas, I also fell in with some pretty acquaintances, found my way into several caverns, and delivered my purse to more than one gallant gentleman of the road. One I remember especially — one who never eased me personally of a single maravedi — one than whom I never met a bandit more gallant, courteous, and amiable. Rob me? Rolando feasted me; treated me to his dinner and his wine; kept a generous table for his friends, and I know was most liberal to many of them. How well I remember one of his speculations! It was a great plan for smuggling tobacco. Revenue officers were to be bought off; silent ships were to ply on the Thames; cunning depôts were to be established, and hundreds of thousands of pounds to be made by the *coup*. How his eyes kindled as he propounded the scheme to me! How easy and certain it seemed! It might have succeeded: I can't say: but the bold and merry, the hearty and kindly Rolando came to grief — a little matter of imitated signatures occasioned a Bank persecution of Rolando the Brave. He walked about armed, and vowed he would never be taken alive: but taken he was; tried, condemned, sentenced to perpetual banishment; and I heard that for some time he was universally popular in the colony which had the honor to possess him. What a song he could sing! 'Twas when the cup was sparkling before us, and heaven gave a portion of its blue, boys, blue, that I remember the song of Roland at "The Old Piazza Coffee-house." And now where is "The Old Piazza Coffee-house?" Where is Thebes? where is Troy? where is the Colossus of Rhodes? Ah, Rolando, Rolando! thou wert a gallant captain, a cheery, a handsome, a merry. At *me* thou never presentedst pistol. Thou badest the bumper of Burgundy fill, fill for me, giving those who preferred it Champagne. *Cœlum non animum*, &c. Do you think he has reformed now that he has crossed the sea, and changed the air? I have my own opinion. Howbeit, Rolando, thou wert a most kind and hospitable bandit. And I love not to think of thee with a chain at thy shin.

Do you know how all these memories of unfortunate men have come upon me? When they came to frighten me this morning by speaking of my robbed pears, my perforated garden wall, I was reading an article in "The Saturday Review" about Rupilius. I have sat near that young man at a public dinner, and beheld him in a gilded uniform. But yesterday he lived in splendor, had long hair, a flowing beard, a jewel at his neck, and a smart surtout. So attired, he stood but yesterday in court; and to-day he sits over a bowl of prison cocoa, with a shaved head, and in a felon's jerkin.

That beard and head shaved, that gaudy deputy-lieutenant's coat exchanged for felon uniform, and your daily bottle of champagne for prison cocoa, my poor Rupilius, what a comfort it must be to have the business brought to an end! Champagne was the honorable gentleman's drink in the House of Commons dining-room, as I am informed. What uncommonly dry champagne that must have been! When we saw him outwardly happy, how miserable he must have been! when we thought him prosperous, how dismally poor! When the great Mr. Harker, at the public dinners, called out — "Gentlemen, charge your glasses, and please silence for the Honorable Member for Lambeth!" how that Honorable Member must have writhed inwardly! One day, when there was a talk of a gentleman's honor being questioned, Rupilius said, "If any man doubted mine, I would knock him down." But that speech was in the way of business. The Spartan boy, who stole the fox, smiled while the beast was gnawing him under his cloak: I promise you Rupilius had some sharp fangs gnashing under his. We have sat at the same feast, I say: we have paid our contribution to the same charity. Ah! when I ask this day for my daily bread, I pray not to be led into temptation, and to be delivered from evil.

DESSEIN'S.

I ARRIVED by the night-mail packet from Dover. The passage had been rough, and the usual consequences had ensued. I was disinclined to travel farther that night on my road to Paris, and knew the Calais hotel of old as one of the cleanest, one of the dearest, one of the most comfortable hotels on the continent of Europe. There is no town more French than Calais. That charming old "Hôtel Dessein," with its court, its gardens, its lordly kitchen, its princely waiter — a gentleman of the old school, who has welcomed the finest company in Europe — have long been known to me. I have read complaints in "The Times," more than once, I think, that the Dessein bills are dear. A bottle of soda-water certainly costs — well, never mind how much. I remember as a boy, at the "Ship" at Dover (imperante Carolo Decimo), when, my place to London being paid, I had but 12*s*. left after a certain little Paris excursion (about which my benighted parents never knew any thing), ordering for dinner a whiting, a beefsteak, and a glass of negus, and the bill was, dinner 7*s*., glass of negus 2*s*., waiter 6*d*., and only half a crown left, as I was a sinner, for the guard and coachman on the way to London! And I *was* a sinner. I had gone without leave. What a long, dreary, guilty forty hours' journey it was from Paris to Calais, I remember! How did I come to think of this escapade, which occurred in the Easter vacation of the year 1830? I always think of it when I am crossing to Calais. Guilt, sir, guilt remains stamped on the memory, and I feel easier in my mind now that it is liberated of this old peccadillo. I met my college tutor only yesterday. We were travelling, and stopped at the same hotel. He had the very next room to mine. After he had gone into his apartment, having shaken me quite kindly by the hand, I felt inclined to knock at his door and say, "Doctor Bentley, I beg your pardon, but do you remember, when I was going down at the Easter vacation in 1830, you asked me where I was going to spend my vacation? And I said, With my friend Slingsby, in Huntingdonshire. Well, sir, I grieve to have to confess that I told you a fib. I had got 20*l.* and was going for a lark to Paris, where my friend Edwards was staying." There, it is out. The Doctor will read it, for I did not wake him up after all to make my confession, but protest he shall have a copy of this Roundabout sent to him when he returns to his lodge.

They gave me a bed-room there; a very neat room on the first floor, looking into the pretty garden. The hotel must look pretty much as it did a hundred years ago when *he* visited it. I wonder whether he paid his bill? Yes: his journey was just begun. He had borrowed or got the money somehow. Such a man would spend it liberally enough when he had it, give generously — nay, drop a tear over the fate of the poor fellow whom he relieved. I don't believe a word he says, but I never accused him of stinginess about money. That is a fault of much more virtuous people than he. Mr. Laurence is ready enough with his purse when there are anybody's guineas in it. Still when I went to bed in the room, in *his* room; when I think how I admire, dislike, and have abused him, a certain dim feeling of apprehension filled my mind at the midnight hour. What if I should see his lean figure in the black-satin breeches, his sinister smile, his long thin finger pointing to me in the moonlight (for I am in bed, and have popped my candle out), and he should say, "You mistrust me, you hate me, do you? And you, don't you know how Jack, Tom, and Harry, your brother authors, hate *you?*" I grin and laugh in the moonlight, in the midnight, in the silence. "O you ghost in black-satin breeches and a wig! I like to be hated by some men," I say. "I know men whose lives are a scheme, whose laughter is a conspiracy, whose smile means something else, whose hatred is a cloak, and I had rather these men should hate me than not."

"My good sir," says he, with a ghastly grin on his lean face, "you have your wish."

"*Après?*" I say. "Please let me go to sleep. I shan't sleep any the worse because" —

"Because there are insects in the bed, and they sting you?" (This is only by way of illustration, my good sir; the animals don't bite me now. All the house at present seems to me excellently clean.) "'Tis absurd to affect this indifference. If you are thin-skinned, and the reptiles bite, they keep you from sleep."

"There are some men who cry out at a flea-bite as loud as if they were torn by a vulture," I growl.

"Men of the *genus irritabile,* my worthy good gentleman! — and you are one."

"Yes, sir, I am of the profession, as you say; and I dare say make a great shouting and crying at a small hurt."

"You are ashamed of that quality by which you earn your subsistence, and such reputation as you have? Your sensibility is your livelihood, my worthy friend. You feel a pang of pleasure or pain? It is noted in your memory, and some day or other makes its appearance in your manuscript. Why, in your last Roundabout rubbish you mention reading your first novel on the day when

King George IV. was crowned. I remember him in his cradle at St. James's, a lovely little babe; a gilt Chinese railing was before him, and I dropped the tear of sensibility as I gazed on the sleeping cherub."

"A tear — a fiddlestick, Mr. STERNE," I growled out, for of course I knew my friend in the wig and satin breeches to be no other than the notorious, nay, celebrated Mr. Laurence Sterne.

"Does not the sight of a beautiful infant charm and melt you, *mon ami?* If not, I pity you. Yes, he was beautiful. I was in London the year he was born. I used to breakfast at the 'Mount Coffee-house.' I did not become the fashion until two years later, when my 'Tristram' made his appearance, who has held his own for a hundred years. By the way, *mon bon monsieur*, how many authors of your present time will last till the next century? Do you think Brown will?"

I laughed with scorn as I lay in my bed (and so did the ghost give a ghastly snigger).

"Brown!" I roared. "One of the most over-rated men that ever put pen to paper!"

"What do you think of Jones?"

I grew indignant with this old cynic. "As a reasonable ghost, come out of the other world, you don't mean," I said, "to ask me a serious opinion of Mr. Jones? His books may be very good reading for maid-servants and school-boys, but you don't ask *me* to read them? As a scholar yourself you must know that" —

"Well, then, Robinson?"

"Robinson, I am told, has merit. I dare say; I never have been able to read his books, and can't, therefore, form any opinion about Mr. Robinson. At least you will allow that I am not speaking in a prejudiced manner about *him.*"

"Ah! I see you men of letters have your cabals and jealousies, as we had in my time. There was an Irish fellow by the name of Gouldsmith, who used to abuse me; but he went into no genteel company — and faith! it mattered little, his praise or abuse. I never was more surprised than when I heard that Mr. Irving, an American gentleman of parts and elegance, had wrote the fellow's life. To make a hero of that man, my dear sir, 'twas ridiculous! You followed in the fashion, I hear, and chose to lay a wreath before this queer little idol. Preposterous! A pretty writer, who has turned some neat couplets. Bah! I have no patience with Master Posterity, that has chosen to take up this fellow, and make a hero of him! And there was another gentleman of my time, Mr. Thiefcatcher Fielding, forsooth! a fellow with the strength, and the tastes, and the manners of a porter! What madness has possessed you all to bow before that Calvert Butt of a man? — a creature without elegance or sensibility! The dog had spirits, certainly. I remember my Lord Bathurst praising them: but as for reading his books — *ma foi,* I would as lief go and dive for tripe in a cellar. The man's vulgarity stifles me. He wafts me whiffs of gin. Tobacco and onions are in his great coarse laugh, which chokes me, *pardi;* and I don't think much better of the other fellow — the Scots' gallipot purveyor — Peregrine Clinker, Humphrey Random — how did the fellow call his rubbish? Neither of these men had the *bel air*, the *bon ton*, the *je ne sçais quoi*. Pah! If I meet them in my walks by our Stygian river, I give them a wide berth, as that hybrid apothecary fellow would say. An ounce of civet, good apothecary; horrible, horrible! The mere thought of the coarseness of those men gives me the *chair de poule*. Mr. Fielding, especially, has no more sensibility than a butcher in Fleet Market. He takes his heroes out of ale-house kitchens, or worse places still. And this is the person whom Posterity has chosen to honor along with me — *me!* Faith, Monsieur Posterity, you have put me in pretty company, and I see you are no wiser than we were in our time. Mr. Fielding, forsooth! Mr. Tripe and Onions! Mr. Cow-heel and Gin! Thank you for nothing, Monsieur Posterity!"

"And so," thought I, "even among these Stygians this envy and quarrelsomeness (if you will permit me the word) survive? What a pitiful meanness! To be sure, I can understand this feeling to a certain extent; a sense of justice will prompt it. In my own case, I often feel myself forced to protest against the absurd praises lavished on contemporaries. Yesterday, for instance, Lady Jones was good enough to praise one of my works. *Très bien.* But in the very next minute she began, with quite as great enthusiasm, to praise Miss Hobson's last romance. My good creature, what is that woman's praise worth who absolutely admires the writings of Miss Hobson? I offer a friend a bottle of '44 claret, fit for a pontifical supper. 'This is capital wine,' says he; 'and now we have finished the bottle, will you give me a bottle of that ordinaire we drank the other day?' Very well, my good man. You are a good judge — of ordinaire, I dare say. Nothing so provokes my anger, and rouses my sense of justice, as to hear other men undeservedly praised. In a word, if you wish to remain friends with me, don't praise anybody. You tell me that the Venus de' Medici is beautiful, or Jacob Omnium is tall. *Que diable!* Can't I judge for myself? Haven't I eyes and a foot-rule? I don't think the Venus *is* so handsome, since you press me. She is pretty, but she has no expression. And as for Mr. Omnium, I can see much taller men in a fair for twopence."

"And so," I said, turning round to Mr. Sterne, you are actually jealous of Mr. Fielding? O you men of letters, you men of letters! Is not the world (your world, I mean) big enough for all of you?"

I often travel in my sleep. I often of a night find myself walking in my night-gown about the gray streets. It is awkward at first, but somehow nobody makes any remark. I glide along over the ground with my naked feet. The mud does not wet them. The passers-by do not tread on them. I am wafted over the ground. down the stairs, through the doors. This sort of travelling, dear friends, I am sure you have all of you indulged.

Well, on the night in question (and if you wish to know the precise date, it was the 31st of September last), after having some little conversation with Mr. Sterne in our bed-room, I must have got up, though I protest I don't know how, and come down stairs with him into the coffee-room of the "Hôtel Dessein," where the moon was shining, and a cold supper was laid out. I forget what we had —"vol-au-vent d'œufs de Phénix— agneau aux pistaches à la Barmécide,"—what matters what we had?

"As regards supper this is certain, the less you have of it the better."

That is what one of the guests remarked, — a shabby old man, in a wig, and such a dirty, ragged, disreputable dressing-gown that I should have been quite surprised at him, only one never *is* surprised in dr— under certain circumstances.

"I can't eat 'em now," said the greasy man (with his false teeth, I wonder he could eat any thing). "I remember Alvanley eating three suppers once at Carlton House — one night *de petite comité.*"

"*Petit comité,* sir," said Mr. Sterne,

"Dammy, sir, let me tell my own story my own way. I say, one night at Carlton House, playing at blind hookey with York, Wales, Tom Raikes, Prince Boothby, and Dutch Sam the boxer, Alvanley ate three suppers, and won three and twenty hundred pounds in ponies. Never saw a fellow with such an appetite, except Wales in his *good* time. But he destroyed the finest digestion a man ever had with maraschino, by Jove — always at it."

"Try mine," said Mr. Sterne.

"What a doosid queer box!" says Mr. Brummell.

"I had it from a Capuchin friar in this town. The box is but a horn one; but to the nose of sensibility Araby's perfume is not more delicate."

"I call it doosid stale old rappee," says Mr. Brummell — (as for me I declare I could not smell any thing at all in either of the boxes). "Old boy in smock-frock, take a pinch?"

The old boy in the smock-frock, as Mr. Brummell called him, was a very old man, with long white beard, wearing, not a smock-frock, but a shirt; and he had actually nothing else save a rope round his neck, which hung behind his chin in the queerest way.

"Fair sir," he said, turning to Mr. Brummell, "when the Prince of Wales and his father laid siege to our town" —

"What nonsense are you talking, old cock?" says Mr. Brummell; "Wales was never here. His late Majesty George IV. passed through on his way to Hanover. My good man, you don't seem to know what's up at all. What is he talkin' about the siege of Calais? I lived here fifteen years! Ought to know. What's his old name?"

"I am Master Eustace of Saint Peter's," said the old gentleman in the shirt. "When my Lord King Edward laid siege to this city" —

"Laid siege to Jericho!" cries Mr. Brummell. "The old man is cracked — cracked, sir!"

"— Laid siege to this city," continued the old man, "I and five more promised Messire Gautier de Mauny that we would give ourselves up as ransom for the place. And we came before our Lord King Edward, attired as you see, and the fair queen begged our lives out of her gramercy."

"Queen, nonsense! you mean the Princess of Wales — pretty woman, *petit nez retroussé*, grew monstrous stout?" suggested Mr. Brummell, whose reading was evidently not extensive. "Sir Sidney Smith was a fine fellow, great talker, hook nose, so has Lord Cochrane, so has Lord Wellington. She was very sweet on Sir Sidney."

"Your acquaintance with the history of Calais does not seem to be considerable," said Mr. Sterne to Mr. Brummell, with a shrug.

"Don't it, bishop? — for I conclude you are a bishop by your wig. I know Calais as well as any man. I lived here for years before I took that confounded consulate at Caen. Lived in this hotel, then at Leleux's. People used to stop here. Good fellows used to ask for poor George Brummell; Hertford did, so did the Duchess of Devonshire. Not know Calais indeed! That is a good joke. Had many a good dinner here: sorry I ever left it."

"My Lord King Edward," chirped the queer old gentleman in the shirt, "colonized the place with his English, after we had yielded it up to him. I have heard tell they kept it for nigh three hundred years, till my Lord de Guise took it from a fair Queen, Mary of blessed memory, a holy woman. Eh, but Sire Gautier of Mauny was a good knight, a valiant captain, gentle and courteous withal! Do you remember his ransoming the?" —

"What is the old fellow twaddlin' about?" cries Brummell. "He is talking about some knight? — I never spoke to a knight, and very seldom to a baronet. Firkins, my butterman, was a knight — a knight and alderman. Wales knighted him once on going into the City."

"I am not surprised that the gentleman should not understand Messire Eustace of St. Peter's," said the ghostly individual addressed as Mr. Sterne. "Your reading doubtless has not been very extensive?"

"Dammy, sir, speak for yourself!" cries Mr. Brummell, testily. "I never professed to be a reading man, but I was as good as my neighbors. Wales wasn't a reading man; York wasn't a reading man; Clarence wasn't a reading man; Sussex was, but he wasn't a man in society. I remember reading your 'Sentimental Journey,' old boy: read it to the Duchess at Beauvoir, I recollect, and she cried over it. Doosid clever amusing book, and does you great credit. Birron wrote doosid clever books, too; so did Monk Lewis. George Spencer was an elegant poet, and my dear Duchess of Devonshire, if she had not been a grande dame, would have beat 'em all, by George. Wales couldn't write: he could sing, but he couldn't spell."

"Ah, you know the great world? so did I in my time, Mr. Brummell. I have had the visiting tickets of half the nobility at my lodgings in Bond Street. But they left me there no more cared for than last year's calendar," sighed Mr. Sterne. "I wonder who is the mode in London now? One of our late arrivals, my Lord Macaulay, has prodigious merit and learning, and, faith, his histories are more amusing than any novels, my own included."

"Don't know, I'm sure; not in my line. Pick this bone of chicken," says Mr. Brummell, trifling with a skeleton bird before him.

"I remember in this city of Calais worse fare than yon bird," said old Mr. Eustace of St. Peter's. "Marry, sirs, when my Lord King Edward laid siege to us, lucky was he who could get a slice of horse for his breakfast, and a rat was sold at the price of a hare."

"Hare is coarse food, never tasted rat," remarked the Beau. "Table-d'hôte poor fare enough for a man like me, who has been accustomed to the best of cookery. But rat — stifle me! I couldn't swallow that: never could bear hardship at all."

"We had to bear enough when my Lord of England pressed us. 'Twas pitiful to see the faces of our women as the siege went on, and hear the little ones asking for dinner."

"Always a bore, children. At dessert, they are bad enough, but at dinner they're the deuce and all," remarked Mr. Brummell.

Messire Eustace of St. Peter's did not seem to pay much attention to the Beau's remarks, but continued his own train of thought as old men will do.

"I hear," said he, "that there has actually been no war between us of France and you men of England for well nigh fifty year. Ours has ever been a nation of warriors. And besides her regular found men-at-arms, 'tis said the English of the present time have more than a hundred thousand of archers with weapons that will carry for half a mile. And a multitude have come amongst us of late from a great Western country, never so much as heard of in my time — valiant men and great drawers of the long-bow, and they say they have ships in armor that no shot can penetrate. Is it so? Wonderful; wonderful! The best armor, gossips, is a stout heart."

"And if ever manly heart beat under shirt-frill, thine is that heart, Sir Eustace!" cried Mr. Sterne enthusiastically.

"We, of France, were never accused of lack of courage, sir, in so far as I know," said Messire Eustace. "We have shown as much in a thousand wars with you English by sea and land; and sometimes we conquered, and sometimes, as is the fortune of war, we were discomfited. And notably in a great sea-fight which befell off Ushant on the first of June — Our Admiral, Messire Villaret de Joyeuse, on board his galleon named 'The Vengeur,' being sore pressed by an English bombard, rather than yield the crew of his ship to mercy, determined to go down with all on board of her: and to the cry of Vive la Répub — or, I would say, of Notre Dame à la Rescousse, he and his crew all sank to an immortal grave" —

"Sir," said I, looking with amazement at the old gentleman, "surely, surely, there is some mistake in your statement. Permit me to observe that the action of the first of June took place five hundred years after your time, and" —

"Perhaps I am confusing my dates," said the old gentleman, with a faint blush. "You say I am mixing up the transactions of my time on earth with the story of my successors? It may be so. We take no count of a few centuries more or less in our dwelling by the darkling Stygian river. Of late, there came amongst us a good knight, Messire de Cambronne, who fought against you English in the country of Flanders, being captain of the guard of my Lord the King of France, in a famous battle where you English would have been utterly routed but for the succor of the Prussian heathen. This Messire de Cambronne, when bidden to yield by you of England, answered this, 'The guard dies, but never surrenders;' and fought a long time afterwards, as became a good knight. In our wars with you of England it may have pleased the Fates to give you the greater success, but on our side, also, there has been no lack of brave deeds performed by brave men."

"King Edward may have been the victor, sir, as being the strongest, but you are the hero of the siege of Calais!" cried Mr. Sterne. "Your story is sacred, and your name has been blessed for five hundred years. Wherever men speak of patriotism and sacrifice, Eustace of Saint Pierre shall be beloved and remembered. I prostrate myself before the bare feet which stood before King Edward. What collar of chivalry is to be compared to that glorious order which you wear? Think, sir, how out of the myriad millions of our race, you, and some few more, stand forth as exemplars of duty and honor. *Fortunati nimium!*"

"Sir," said the old gentleman, "I did but my duty at a painful moment; and 'tis matter of wonder to me that men talk still, and glorify such a trifling matter. By our Lady's grace, in the fair kingdom of France, there are scores of thousands of men, gentle and simple, who would do as I did. Does not every sentinel at his post, does not every archer in the front of battle, brave it, and die where his captain bids him? Who am I that I should be chosen out of all France to be an example of fortitude? I braved no tortures, though these I trust I would have endured with a good heart. I was subject to threats only. Who was the Roman knight of whom the Latin clerk Horatius tells?"

"A Latin clerk? Faith, I forget my Latin," says Mr. Brummell. "Ask the parson here."

"Messire Regulus, I remember, was his name. Taken prisoner by the Saracens, he gave his knightly word, and was permitted to go seek a ransom among his own people. Being unable to raise the sum that was a fitting ransom for such a knight, he returned to Afric, and cheerfully submitted to the tortures which the Paynims inflicted. And 'tis said he took leave of his friends as gayly as though he were going to a village kermes, or riding to his garden house in the suburb of the city."

"Great, good, glorious man!" cried Mr. Sterne, very much moved. "Let me embrace that gallant hand, and bedew it with my tears! As long as honor lasts thy name shall be remembered. See this dew-drop twinkling on my cheek! 'Tis the sparkling tribute that Sensibility pays to Valor. Though in my life and practice I may turn from Virtue, believe me, I never have ceased to honor her! Ah, Virtue! Ah, Sensibility! Oh" —

Here Mr. Sterne was interrupted by a monk of the Order of St. Francis, who stepped into the room, and begged us all to take a pinch of his famous old rappee. I suppose the snuff was very pungent, for, with a great start, I woke up; and now perceived that I must have been dreaming altogether. "Dessein's" of nowadays is not the "Dessein's" which Mr. Sterne, and Mr. Brummell, and I recollect in the good old times. The town of Calais has bought the old hotel, and "Dessein" has gone over to "Quillacq's." And I was there yesterday. And I remember old diligences, and old postilions in pigtails and jack-boots, who were once as alive as I am, and whose cracking whips I have heard in the midnight many and many a time. Now, where are they? Behold! they have been ferried over Styx, and have passed away into limbo.

I wonder what time does my boat go? Ah! Here comes the waiter bringing me my little bill.

ON SOME CARP AT SANS SOUCI.

We have lately made the acquaintance of an old lady of ninety, who has passed the last twenty-five years of her old life in a great metropolitan establishment, the workhouse, namely, of the parish of Saint Lazarus. Stay — twenty three or four years ago, she came out once, and thought to earn a little money by hop-picking; but being overworked, and having to lie out at night, she got a palsy which has incapacitated her from all further labor, and has caused her poor old limbs to shake ever since.

An illustration of that dismal proverb which tells us how poverty makes us acquainted with strange bed-fellows, this poor old shaking body has to lay herself down every night in her work-house bed by the side of some other old woman with whom she may or may not agree. She herself can't be a very pleasant bed-fellow, poor thing! with her shaking old limbs and cold feet. She lies awake a deal of the night, to be sure, not thinking of happy old times, for hers never were happy; but sleepless with aches, and agues, and rheumatism of old age. "The gentleman gave me brandy and water," she said, her old voice shaking with rapture at the thought. I never had a great love for Queen Charlotte, but I like her better now from what this old lady told me. The Queen, who loved snuff herself, has left a legacy of snuff to certain poor-houses; and, in her watchful nights, this old woman takes a pinch of Queen Charlotte's snuff, "and it do comfort me, sir, that it do!" *Pulveris exigui munus.* Here is a forlorn aged creature, shaking with palsy, with no soul among the great struggling multitude of mankind to care for her, not quite trampled out of life, but past and forgotten in the rush, made a little happy, and soothed in her hours of unrest by this penny legacy. Let me think as I write. (The next month's sermon, thank goodness! is safe to press.) This discourse will appear at the season when I have read that wassail-bowls make their appearance; at the season of pantomime, turkey, and sausages, plum-puddings, jollifications for schoolboys; Christmas bills, and reminiscences more or less sad and sweet for elders. If we oldsters are not merry, we shall be having a semblance of merriment. We shall see the young folks laughing round the holly-bush. We shall pass the bottle round cosily as we sit by the fire. That old thing will have a sort of festival too. Beef, beer, and pudding will be served to her for that day also. Christmas falls on a Thursday. Friday is the workhouse day for coming out. Mary, remember that old Goody Twoshoes has her invitation for Friday, 26th December! Ninety is she, poor old soul? Ah! what a bonny face to catch under a mistletoe! "Yes, ninety, sir," she says, "and my mother was a hundred, and my grandmother was a hundred and two."

Herself ninety, her mother a hundred, her grandmother a hundred and two? What a queer calculation!

Ninety! Very good, granny: you were born, then, in 1772.

Your mother, we will say, was twenty-seven when you were born, and was born therefore in 1745.

Your grandmother was thirty when her daughter was born, and was born therefore in 1715.

We will begin with the present granny first. My good old creature, you can't of course remember, but that little gentleman for whom your mother was laundress in the Temple was the ingenious Mr. Goldsmith, author of a "History of England," "The Vicar of Wakefield," and many diverting pieces. You were brought almost an infant to his chambers, in Brick Court, and he gave you some sugar-candy, for the doctor was always good to children. That gentleman who well-nigh smothered you by sitting down on you as you lay in a chair asleep was the learned Mr. S. Johnson, whose history of "Rasselas" you have never read, my poor soul; and whose tragedy of "Irene" I don't believe any man in these kingdoms ever perused. That tipsy Scotch gentleman who used to come to the chambers sometimes, and at whom everybody laughed, wrote a more amusing book than any of the scholars, your Mr. Burke and your Mr. Johnson, and your Doctor Goldsmith. Your father often took him home in a chair to his lodgings; and has done as much for Parson Sterne in Bond Street, the famous wit. Of course, my good creature, you remember the Gordon Riots, and crying No Popery before Mr. Langdale's house, the Popish distiller's and that bonny fire of my Lord Mansfield's books in Bloomsbury Square? Bless us, what a heap of illuminations you have seen! For the glorious victory over the Americans at Breed's Hill; for the peace in 1814, and the beautiful Chinese bridge in St. James's Park; for the coronation of his Majesty, whom you recollect as Prince of Wales, Goody, don't you? Yes; and you went in a procession of laundresses to pay your respects to his good lady, the injured Queen of England, at Brandenburg House; and you remember your mother told you how she was taken to see the Scotch lords executed at the Tower. And as for your grandmother, she was born five years after the battle of Malplaquet, she was; where her poor father was killed, fighting like a bold Briton for the Queen. With the help of a "Wade's Chronology," I can make out ever so queer a history for you, my poor old body, and a pedigree as authentic as many in the peerage-books.

Peerage-books and pedigrees? What does she know about them? Battles and victories, treasons, kings, and beheadings, literary gentlemen, and the like, what have they ever been to her? Granny, did you ever hear of General Wolfe? Your mother may have seen him embark, and your father may have carried a musket under him. Your grandmother may have cried huzza for Marlborough; but what is the Prince Duke to you, and did you ever so much as hear tell of his name? How many hundred or thousand of years had that toad lived who was in the coal at the defunct Exhibition? — and yet he was not a bit better informed than toads seven or eight hundred years younger.

"Don't talk to me your nonsense about Exhibitions, and Prince Dukes, and toads in coals, or coals in toads, or what is it?" says granny. "I know there was a good Queen Charlotte, for she left me snuff; and it comforts me of a night when I lie awake."

To me there is something very touching in the notion of that little pinch of comfort doled out to granny, and gratefully inhaled by her in the darkness. Don't you remember what traditions there used to be of chests of plate, bulses of diamonds, laces of inestimable value, sent out of the country privately by the old Queen to enrich certain relations in M-ckl-nb-rg

Str-l-tz? Not all the treasure went. *Non omnis moritur.* A poor old palsied thing at midnight is made happy sometimes as she lifts her shaking old hand to her nose. Gliding noiselessly among the beds where lie the poor creatures huddled in their cheerless dormitory, I fancy an old ghost with a snuff-box that does not creak. "There, Goody, take of my rappee. You will not sneeze, and I shall not say 'God bless you.' But you will think kindly of old Queen Charlotte, won't you? Ah! I had a many troubles, a many troubles. I was a prisoner almost so much as you are. I had to eat boiled mutton every day: *entre nous,* I abominated it. But I never complained. I swallowed it. I made the best of a hard life. We have all our burdens to bear. But hark! I hear the cock-crow, and snuff the morning air." And with this the royal ghost vanishes up the chimney — if there be a chimney in that dismal harem, where poor old Twoshoes and her companions pass their nights — their dreary nights, their restless nights, their cold long nights, shared in what glum companionship, illumined by what a feeble taper!

"Did I understand you, my good Twoshoes, to say that your mother was seven and twenty years old when you were born, and that she married your esteemed father when she herself was twenty-five? 1745, then, was the date of your dear mother's birth. I dare say her father was absent in the Low Countries, with his Royal Highness the Duke of Cumberland, under whom he had the honor of carrying a halberd at the famous engagement of Fontenoy — or if not there, he may have been at Preston Pans, under General Sir John Cope, when the wild Highlanders broke through all the laws of discipline, and the English lines; and, being on the spot, did he see the famous ghost which didn't appear to Colonel Gardiner of the Dragoons? My good creature, is it possible you don't remember that Doctor Swift, Sir Robert Walpole (my Lord Orford, as you justly say), old Sarah Marlborough, and little Mr. Pope, of Twitnam, died in the year of your birth? What a wretched memory you have! What? haven't they a library, and the commonest books of reference at the old convent of Saint Lazarus, where you dwell?"

"Convent of Saint Lazarus, Prince William, Dr. Swift, Atossa, and Mr. Pope, of Twitnam! What is the gentleman talking about?" says old Goody, with a "Ho! ho!" and a laugh like an old parrot — you know they live to be as old as Methuselah, parrots do, and a parrot of a hundred is comparrotively young (ho! ho! ho!). Yes, and likewise carps live to an immense old age. Some which Frederick the Great fed at Sans Souci are there now, with great humps of blue mould on their old backs; and they could tell all sorts of queer stories, if they chose to speak — but they are very silent, carps are — of their nature *peu communicatives.* Oh! what has been thy long life, old Goody, but a dole of bread and water and a perch on a cage; a dreary swim round and round a Lethe of a pond? What are Rossbach or Jena to those mouldy ones, and do they know it is a grandchild of England who brings bread to feed them?

No! Those Sans Souci carps may live to be a thousand years old, and have nothing to tell but that one day is like another; and the history of friend Goody Twoshoes has not much more variety than theirs. Hard labor, hard fare, hard bed, numbing cold all night, and gnawing hunger most days. That is her lot. Is it lawful in my prayers to say, "Thank heaven, I am not as one of these"? If I were eighty, would I like to feel the hunger always gnawing, gnawing? to have to get up and make a bow when Mr. Bumble the beadle entered the common room? to have to listen to Miss Prim, who came to give me her ideas of the next world? If I were eighty, I own I should not like to have to sleep with another gentleman of my own age, gouty, a bad sleeper, kicking in his old dreams, and snoring; to march down my vale of years at word of command, accommodating my tottering old steps to those of the other prisoners in my dingy, hopeless old gang; to hold out a trembling hand for a sickly pittance of gruel, and say, "Thank you, ma'm," to Miss Prim, when she has done reading her sermon. John! when Goody Twoshoes comes next Friday, I desire she may not be disturbed by theological controversies. You have a very fair voice, and I heard you and the maids singing a hymn very sweetly the other night, and was thankful that our humble household should be in such harmony. Poor old Twoshoes is so old and toothless and quaky, that she can't sing a bit; but don't be giving yourself airs over her, because she can't sing and you can. Make her comfortable at our kitchen hearth. Set that old kettle to sing by our hob. Warm her old stomach with nut-brown ale and a toast laid in the fire. Be kind to the poor old school-girl of ninety, who has had leave to come out for a day of Christmas holiday. Shall there be many more Christmases for thee? Think of the ninety she has seen already; the fourscore and ten cold, cheerless, nipping New Years!

If you were in her place, would you like to have a remembrance of better early days, when you were young, and happy, and loving, perhaps; or would you prefer to have no past on which your mind could rest? About the year 1788, Goody, were your cheeks rosy, and your eyes bright, and did some young fellow in powder and a pigtail look in them? We may grow old, but to us some stories never are old. On a sudden they rise up, not dead, but living — not forgotten, but freshly remembered. The eyes gleam on us as they used to do. The dear voice thrills in our hearts. The rapture of the meeting, the terrible, terrible parting, again and again the tragedy is acted over. Yesterday, in the street, I saw a pair of eyes so like two which used to brighten at my coming once, that the whole past came back as I walked lonely, in the rush of the Strand, and I was young again in the midst of joys and sorrows, alike sweet and sad, alike sacred and fondly remembered.

If I tell a tale out of school, will any harm come to my old school-girl? Once, a lady gave her a half-sovereign, which was a source of great pain and anxiety to Goody Twoshoes. She sewed it away in her old stays somewhere, thinking here at least was a safe investment — (vestis — a vest — an investment, — pardon me, thou poor old thing, but I cannot help the pleasantry). And what do you think? Another pensionnaire of the establishment cut the coin out of Goody's stays — *an old woman who went upon two crutches!* Faugh, the old witch! What? Violence amongst these toothless, tottering, trembling, feeble ones? Robbery amongst the penniless? Dogs coming and snatching Lazarus's crumbs out of his lap? Ah, how indignant Goody was as she told the story! To that pond at Potsdam where the carps live for hundreds of hundreds of years, with hunches of blue mould on their back, I dare say the little Prince and Princess of Preussen-Britannien come sometimes with crumbs and cakes to feed the mouldy ones. Those eyes may have goggled from beneath the weeds at Napoleon's jack-boots: they have seen Frederick's lean shanks reflected in their pool; and perhaps Monsieur de Voltaire has fed them — and now, for a crumb of biscuit they will fight, push, hustle, rob, squabble, gobble, relapsing into their tranquillity when the ignoble struggle is over. Sans souci, indeed! It is mighty well writing "Sans souci" over the gate; but where is the gate through which care has not slipped? She perches on the shoulders of the sentry in the sentry-box: she whispers the porter sleeping in his arm-chair: she glides up the staircase, and lies down between the king and queen in their bed-royal; this very night I dare say she will perch upon poor old Goody Twoshoes's meagre bolster, and whisper, "Will the gentleman and those ladies ask me again? No, no; they will forget poor old Twoshoes." Goody! For shame of yourself! Do not be cynical. Do not mistrust your fellow-creatures. What? Has the Christmas morning dawned upon thee ninety times? For fourscore and ten years has it been thy lot to totter on this earth, hungry and obscure? Peace and goodwill to thee, let us say at this Christmas season. Come, drink, eat, rest a while at our hearth, thou poor old pilgrim! And of the bread which God's bounty gives us, I pray, brother reader, we may not forget to set aside a part for those noble and silent poor, from whose innocent hands war has torn the means of labor. Enough! As I hope for beef at Christmas, I vow a note shall be sent to Saint Lazarus Union House, in which Mr. Roundabout requests the honor of Mrs. Twoshoes's company on Friday, 26th December.

AUTOUR DE MON CHAPEAU.

Never have I seen a more noble tragic face. In the centre of the forehead there was a great furrow of care, towards which the brows rose piteously. What a deep solemn grief in the eyes! They looked blankly at the object before them, but through it, as it were, and into the grief beyond. In moments of pain, have you not looked at some indifferent object so? It mingles dumbly with your grief, and remains afterwards connected with it in your mind. It may be some indifferent thing — a book which you were reading at the time when you received her farewell letter (how well you remember the paragraph afterwards — the shape of the words, and their position on the page); the words you were writing when your mother came in, and said it was all over — she was MARRIED — Emily married — to that insignificant little rival at whom you have laughed a hundred times in her company. Well, well; my friend and reader, whoe'er you be — old man or young, wife or maiden — you have had your grief-pang. Boy, you have lain awake the first night at school, and thought of home. Worse still, man, you have parted from the dear ones with bursting heart; and, lonely boy, recall the bolstering an unfeeling comrade gave you; and lonely man, just torn from your children — their little tokens of affection yet in your pocket — pacing the deck at evening in the midst of the roaring ocean, you can remember how you were told that supper was ready, and how you went down to the cabin and had brandy and water and biscuit. You remember the taste of them. Yes; forever. You took them whilst you and your Grief were sitting together, and your Grief clutched you round the soul. Serpent, how you have writhed round me, and bitten me! Remorse, Remembrance, &c., come in the night season, and I feel you gnawing, gnawing! . . . I tell you that man's face was like Laocoon's (which, by the way, I always think over-rated. The real head is at Brussels, at the Duke Daremberg's, not at Rome).

That man! What man? That man of whom I said that his magnificent countenance exhibited the noblest tragic woe. He was not of European blood. He was handsome, but not of European beauty. His face white — not of a Northern whiteness; his eyes protruding somewhat, and rolling in their grief. Those eyes had seen the Orient sun, and his beak was the eagle's. His lips were full. The beard, curling round them, was unkempt and tawny. The locks were of a deep, deep coppery red. The hands, swart and powerful, accustomed to the rough grasp of the wares in which he dealt, seemed unused to the flimsy artifices of the bath. He came from the Wilderness, and its sands were on his robe, his cheek, his tattered sandal, and the hardy foot it covered.

And his grief — whence came his sorrow? I will tell you. He bore it in his hand. He had evidently just concluded the compact by which it became his. His business was that of a purchaser of domestic raiment. At early dawn — nay, at what hour when the city is alive — do we not all hear the nasal cry of "Clo?" In Paris, *Habits Galons, Marchand d'habits*, is the twanging signal with which the wandering merchant makes his presence known. It was in Paris I saw this man. Where else have I not seen him? In the Roman Ghetto — at the Gate of David, in his fathers' once imperial city. The man I mean was an itinerant vender and purchaser of wardrobes — what you call an . . . Enough! You know his name.

On his left shoulder hung his bag; and he held in that hand a white hat, which I am sure he had just purchased, and which was the cause of the grief which smote his noble features. Of course I cannot particularize the sum, but he had given too much for that hat. He felt he might have got the thing for less money. It was not the amount, I am sure; it was the principle involved. He had given fourpence (let us say) for that which threepence would have purchased. He had been done: and a manly shame was upon him, that he, whose energy, acuteness, experience, point of honor, should have made him the victor in any mercantile duel in which he should engage, had been overcome by a porter's wife, who very likely sold him the old hat, or by a student who was tired of it. I can understand his grief. Do I seem to be speaking of it in a disrespectful or flippant way? Then you mistake me. He had been outwitted. He had desired, coaxed, schemed, haggled, got what he wanted, and now found he had paid too much for his bargain. You don't suppose I would ask you to laugh at that man's grief? It is you, clumsy cynic, who are disposed to sneer, whilst it may be tears of genuine sympathy are trickling down this nose of mine. What do you mean by laughing? If you saw a wounded soldier on the field of battle, would you laugh? If you saw a ewe robbed of her lamb, would you laugh, you brute? It is you who are the cynic, and have no feeling: and you sneer because that grief is unintelligible to you which touches my finer sensibility. The OLD-CLOTHES'-MAN had been defeated in one of the daily battles of his most interesting, checkered, adventurous life.

Have you ever figured to yourself what such a life must be? The pursuit and conquest of twopence must be the most eager and fascinating of occupations. We might all engage in that business if we would. Do not whist-players, for example, toil and think, and lose their temper over sixpenny points? They bring study, natural genius, long forethought, memory, and careful historical experience to bear upon their favorite labor. Don't tell me that it is the sixpenny points, and five shillings the rub, which keeps them for hours over their painted pasteboard. It is the desire to conquer. Hours pass by. Night glooms. Dawn, it may be, rises unheeded; and they sit calling for fresh cards at the "Portland," or the "Union," while waning candles splutter in the sockets, and languid waiters snooze in the ante-room. Sol rises. Jones has lost four pounds: Brown has won two; Robinson lurks away to his family house and (mayhap, indignant) Mrs. R. Hours of evening, night, morning, have passed away whilst they have been waging this sixpenny battle. What is the loss of four pounds to Jones, the gain of two to Brown? B. is, perhaps, so rich that two pounds more or less are as nought to him; J. is so hopelessly involved that to win four pounds cannot benefit his creditors, or alter his condition; but they play for that stake: they put forward their best energies: they ruff, finesse (what are the technical words, and how do I know?) It is but a sixpenny game if you like; but they want to win it. So as regards my friend yonder with the hat. He stakes his money: he wishes to win the game, not the hat merely. I am not prepared to say that he is not inspired by a noble ambition. Cæsar wished to be first in a village. If first of a hundred yokels, why not first of two? And my friend the old-clothes'-man wishes to win his game, as well as to turn his little sixpence.

Suppose in the game of life — and it is but a twopenny game after all — you are equally eager of winning. Shall you be ashamed of your ambition, or glory in it? There are games, too, which are becoming to particular periods of life. I remember in the days of our youth, when my friend Arthur Bowler was an eminent cricketer. Slim, swift, strong, well-built, he presented a goodly appearance on the ground in his flannel uniform. *Militâsti non sine gloria*, Bowler, my boy! Hush! We tell no tales. Mum is the word. Yonder comes Charley his son. Now Charley his son has taken the field, and is famous among the eleven of his school. Bowler senior, with his capacious waistcoat, &c., waddling after a ball, would present an absurd object, whereas it does the eyes good to see Bowler junior scouring the plain — a young exemplar of joyful health, vigor, activity. The old boy wisely contents himself with amusements more becoming his age and waist; takes his sober ride; visits his farm soberly — busies himself about his pigs, his ploughing, his peaches, or what not? Very small *routinier* amusements interest him; and (thank goodness!) nature provides very kindly for kindly-disposed fogies. We relish those things which we scorned in our lusty youth. I see the young folks of an evening kindling and glowing over their delicious novels. I look up and watch the eager eye flashing down the page, being, for my part, perfectly contented with my twaddling old volume of "Howel's Letters," or "The Gentleman's Magazine." I am actually arrived at such a calm frame of mind that I like batter-pudding. I never should have believed it possible; but it is so. Yet a little while, and I may relish water-gruel. It will be the age of *mon lait de poule et mon bonnet de nuit*. And then — the cotton extinguisher is pulled over the old noddle, and the little flame of life is popped out.

Don't you know elderly people who make learned notes in Army Lists, Peerages, and the like? This is the batter-pudding, water-gruel of old age. The worn-out old digestion does not care for stronger food. Formerly it could swallow twelve hours' tough reading, and digest an encyclopædia.

If I had children to educate, I would, at ten or twelve years of age, have a professor, or professoress, of whist for them, and cause them to be well grounded in that great and useful game. You cannot learn it well when you are old, any more than you can dancing or billiards. In our house at home we youngsters did not play whist because we were dear obedient children, and the elders said playing at cards was "a waste of time." A waste of time, my good people! *Allons!* What do elderly home-keeping people do of a night after dinner? Darby gets his newspaper; my dear Joan her "Missionary Magazine" or her volume of Cumming's Sermons — and don't you know what ensues? Over the arm of Darby's arm-chair the paper flutters to the ground unheeded, and he performs the trumpet obligato *que vous savez* on his old nose. My dear old Joan's head nods over her sermon (awakening though the doctrine may be). Ding, ding, ding: can that be ten o'clock? It is time to send the servants to bed, my dear — and to bed master and mistress go too. But they have not wasted their time playing at cards. Oh, no! I belong to a Club where there is whist of a night; and not a little amusing is it to hear Brown speak of Thompson's play, and *vice versâ*. But there is one man — Greatorex let us call him — who is the acknowledged captain and primus of all the whist-players. We all secretly admire him. I, for my part, watch him in private life, hearken to what he says, note what he orders for dinner, and have that feeling of awe for him that I used to have as a boy for the cock of the school. Not play at whist? "*Quelle triste vieillesse vous vous préparez!*" were the words of the great and good Bishop of Autun. I can't. It is too late now. Too late! too late! Ah! humiliating confession! That joy might have been clutched, but the life-stream has swept us by it — the swift life-stream rushing to the nearing sea. Too late! too late! Twenty-stone my boy! When you read in the papers "Valse à deux temps," and all the fashionable dances taught to adults by "Miss Lightfoots," don't you feel that you would like to go in and learn? Ah, it is too late! You have passed the *choreas*, Master Twenty-stone, and the young people are dancing without you.

I don't believe much of what my Lord Byron the poet says; but when he wrote, "So, for a good old gentlemanly vice, I think I shall put up with avarice," I think his lordship meant what he wrote, and if he practised what he preached, shall not quarrel with him. As an occupation in declining years, I declare I think saving is useful, amusing, and not unbecoming. It must be a perpetual amusement. It is a game that can be played by day, by night, at home and abroad, and at which you must win in the long-run. I am tired and want a cab. The fare to my house, say, is two shillings. The cabman will naturally want half a crown. I pull out my book. I show him the distance is exactly three miles and fifteen hundred and ninety yards. I offer him my card — my winning card. As he retires with the two shillings, blaspheming inwardly, every curse is a compliment to my skill. I have played him and beat him; and a sixpence is my spoil and just reward. This is a game, by the way, which women play far more cleverly than we do. But what an interest it imparts to life! During the whole drive home I know I shall have my game at the journey's end; am sure of my hand, and shall beat my adversary. Or I can play in another way. I won't have a cab at all, I will wait for the omnibus: I will be one of the damp fourteen in that steaming vehicle. I will wait about in the rain for an hour, and 'bus after 'bus shall pass, but I will not be beat. I *will* have a place, and get it at length, with my boots wet through, and an umbrella dripping between my legs. I have a rheumatism, a cold, a sore throat, a sulky evening, — a doctor's bill tomorrow perhaps? Yes, but I have won my game, and am gainer of a shilling on this rubber.

If you play this game all through life it is wonderful what daily interest it has, and amusing occupation. For instance, my wife goes to sleep after dinner over her volume of sermons. As soon as the dear soul is sound asleep, I advance softly and puff out her candle. Her pure dreams will be all the happier without that light; and, say she sleeps an hour, there is a penny gained.

As for clothes, *parbleu!* there is not much money to be saved in clothes, for the fact is, as a man advances in life — as he becomes an *Ancient Briton* (mark the pleasantry) — he goes without clothes. When my tailor proposes something in the way of a change of raiment, I laugh in his face. My blue coat and brass buttons will last these ten years. It is seedy? What then? I don't want to charm anybody in particular. You say that my clothes are shabby? What do I care? When I wished to look well in somebody's eyes, the matter may have been different. But now, when I receive my bill of 10*l.* (let us say) at the year's end, and contrast it with old tailors' reckonings, I feel that I have played the game with master tailor, and beat him; and my old clothes are a token of the victory.

I do not like to give servants board-wages, though they are cheaper than household bills; but I know they save out of board-wages, and so beat me. This shows that it is not the money but the game which interests me. So about wine. I have it good and dear. I will trouble you to tell me where to get it good and cheap. You may as well give me the address of a shop where I can buy meat for fourpence a pound, or sovereigns for fifteen shillings apiece. At the game of auctions, docks, shy wine-merchants, depend on it there is *no* winning; and I would as soon think of buying jewelry at an auction in Fleet Street as of purchasing wine from one of your dreadful needy wine-agents such as infest every man's door. Grudge myself good wine? As soon grudge my horse corn. *Merci!* that would be a very losing game indeed, and your humble servant has no relish for such.

But in the very pursuit of saving there must be a hundred harmless delights and pleasures which we who are careless necessarily forego. What do you know about the natural history of your household? Upon your honor and conscience, do you know the price of a pound of butter? Can you say what sugar costs, and how much your family consumes and ought to consume? How much lard do you use in your house? As I think on these subjects I own I hang down the head of shame. I suppose for a moment that you, who are reading this, are a middle-aged gentleman, and paterfamilias. Can you answer the above questions? You know, sir, you cannot. Now turn round, lay down the book, and suddenly ask Mrs. Jones and your daughters if *they* can answer. They cannot. They look at one another. They pretend they can answer. They can tell you the plot and principal characters of the last novel. Some of them know something about history, geology, and so forth. But of the natural history of home — *Nichts,* and for shame on you all! *Honnis soyez!* For shame on you? for shame on us!

In the early morning I hear a sort of call or *jodel* under my window, and know 'tis the matutinal milkman leaving his can at my gate. O household gods! have I lived all these years, and don't know the price or the quantity of the milk which is delivered in that can? Why don't I know? As I live, if I live till to-morrow morning, as soon as I hear the call of Lactantius, I will dash out upon him. How many cows? How much milk, on an average, all the year round? What rent? What cost of food and dairy servants? What loss of animals, and average cost of purchase? If I interested myself properly about my pint (or hogshead, whatever it be) of milk, all this knowledge would ensue; all this additional interest in life. What is this talk of my friend, Mr. Lewes, about objects at the seaside, and so forth?* Objects at the seaside? Objects at the area-bell: objects before my nose: objects which the butcher brings me in his tray: which the cook dresses and puts down before me, and over which I say grace! My daily life is surrounded with objects which ought to interest me. The pudding I eat (or refuse, that is neither here nor there; and, between ourselves, what I have said about batter-pudding may be taken *cum grano* — we are not come to *that* yet, except for the sake of argument or illustration) — the pudding, I say, on my plate, the eggs that made it, the fire that cooked it, the tablecloth on which it is laid, and so forth — are each and all of these objects a knowledge of which I may acquire — a knowledge of the cost

* "Seaside Studies." By G. H. Lewes.

and production of which I might advantageously learn? To the man who *does* know these things, I say the interest of life is prodigiously increased. The milkman becomes a study to him; the baker a being he curiously and tenderly examines. Go, Lewes, and clap a hideous sea-anemone into a glass: I will put a cabman under mine, and make a vivisection of a butcher. O Lares, Penates, and gentle household gods, teach me to sympathize with all that comes within my doors! Give me an interest in the butcher's book. Let me look forward to the ensuing number of the grocer's account with eagerness. It seems ungrateful to my kitchen-chimney not to know the cost of sweeping it; and I trust that many a man who reads this, and muses on it, will feel, like the writer, ashamed of himself, and hang down his head humbly.

Now, if to this household game you could add a little money interest, the amusement would be increased far beyond the mere money value, as a game at cards for sixpence is better than a rubber for nothing. If you can interest yourself about sixpence, all life is invested with a new excitement. From sunrise to sleeping you can always be playing that game — with butcher, baker, coal-merchant, cabman, omnibus-man — nay, diamond-merchant and stock-broker. You can bargain for a guinea over the price of a diamond necklace, or for a sixteenth per cent in a transaction at the Stock Exchange. We all know men who have this faculty who are not ungenerous with their money. They give it on great occasions. They are more able to help than you and I who spend ours, and say to poor Prodigal who comes to us out at elbow, "My dear fellow, I should have been delighted, but I have already anticipated my quarter, and am going to ask Screwby if he can do any thing for me."

In this delightful, wholesome, ever-novel twopenny game, there is a danger of excess, as there is in every other pastime or occupation of life. If you grow too eager for your twopence, the acquisition or the loss of it may affect your peace of mind, and peace of mind is better than any amount of twopences. My friend, the old-clothes'-man, whose agonies over the hat have led to this rambling disquisition, has, I very much fear, by a too eager pursuit of small profits, disturbed the equanimity of a mind that ought to be easy and happy. "Had I stood out," he thinks, "I might have had the hat for threepence," and he doubts whether, having given fourpence for it, he will ever get back his money. My good Shadrach, if you go through life passionately deploring the irrevocable, and allow yesterday's transactions to imbitter the cheerfulness of to-day and to-morrow — as lief walk down to the Seine, souse in, hats, body, clothes-bag, and all, and put an end to your sorrow and sordid cares. Before and since Mr. Franklin wrote his pretty apologue of the Whistle have we not all made bargains of which we repented, and coveted and acquired objects for which we have paid too dearly? Who has not purchased his hat in some market or other? There is General M'Clellan's cocked-hat for example: I dare say he was eager enough to wear it, and he has learned that it is by no means cheerful wear. There were the military beavers of Messeigneurs of Orleans:* they wore them gallantly in the face of battle; but I suspect they were glad enough to pitch them into the James River and come home in mufti. Ah, *mes amis! à chacun son schakot!* I was looking at a bishop the other day, and thinking, "My right reverend lord, that broad-brim and rosette must bind your great broad forehead very tightly, and give you many a headache. A good easy

* Two cadets of the House of Orleans who served as Volunteers under General M'Clellan in his campaign against Richmond.

wide-awake were better for you, and I would like to see that honest face with a cutty-pipe in the middle of it." There is my Lord Mayor. My once dear lord, my kind friend, when your two years' reign was over, did not you jump for joy and fling your chapeau-bras out of window: and hasn't *that* hat cost you a pretty bit of money? There, in a splendid travelling chariot, in the sweetest bonnet, all trimmed with orange-blossoms and Chantilly lace, sits my Lady Rosa, with old Lord Snowden by her side. Ah, Rosa! what a price have you paid for that hat which you wear; and is your ladyship's coronet not purchased too dear? Enough of hats. Sir, or Madam, I take off mine, and salute you with profound respect.

ON ALEXANDRINES.*

A LETTER TO SOME COUNTRY COUSINS.

Dear Cousins, — Be pleased to receive herewith a packet of Mayall's photographs, and copies of "Illustrated News," "Illustrated Times," "London Review," "Queen," and "Observer," each containing an account of the notable festivities of the past week. If, besides these remembrances of home, you have a mind to read a letter from an old friend, behold here it is. When I was at school, having left my parents in India, a good-natured captain or colonel would come sometimes and see us Indian boys, and talk to us about papa and mamma, and give us coins of the realm, and write to our parents, and say, "I drove over yesterday, and saw Tommy at Dr. Birch's. I took him to 'The George,' and gave him a dinner. His appetite is fine. He states that he is reading 'Cornelius Nepos,' with which he is much interested. His masters report," &c. And though Dr. Birch wrote by the same mail a longer, fuller, and official statement, I have no doubt the distant parents preferred the friend's letter, with its artless, possibly ungrammatical, account of their little darling.

I have seen the young heir of Britain. These eyes have beheld him and his bride, on Saturday in Pall Mall, and on Tuesday in the nave of St. George's Chapel at Windsor, when the young Princess Alexandra of Denmark passed by with her blooming procession of bridesmaids; and half an hour later, when the Princess of Wales came forth from the chapel, her husband by her side robed in the purple mantle of the famous Order which his forefather established here five hundred years ago. We were to see her yet once again, when her open carriage passed out of the Castle gate to the station of the near railway which was to convey her to Southampton.

Since womankind existed, has any woman ever had such a greeting? At ten hours' distance, there is a city far more magnificent than ours. With every respect for Kensington turnpike, I own that the Arc de l'Étoile at Paris is a much finer entrance to an imperial capital. In our black, orderless, zigzag streets, we can show nothing to compare with the magnificent array of the Rue de Rivoli, that enormous regiment of stone stretching for five miles and presenting arms before the Tuileries. Think of the late Fleet Prison and Waithman's Obelisk, and of the Place de la Concorde and the Luxor Stone! "The finest site in Europe," as Trafalgar Square has been called by some obstinate British optimist, is disfigured by trophies, fountains, columns, and statues so puerile, disorderly, and hideous, that a lover of the arts must hang the head of shame as he passes to see our dear old queen city arraying herself so absurdly; but when all is said and done, we can show one or two

* This paper, it is almost needless to say, was written just after the marriage of the Prince and Princess of Wales in March, 1863.

of the greatest sights in the world. I doubt if any Roman festival was as vast or striking as the Derby day, or if any Imperial triumph could show such a prodigious muster of faithful people as our young Princess saw on Saturday, when the nation turned out to greet her. The calculators are squabbling about the numbers of hundreds of thousands, of millions, who came forth to see her and bid her welcome. Imagine beacons flaming, rockets blazing, yards manned, ships and forts saluting with their thunder, every steamer and vessel, every town and village from Ramsgate to Gravesend, swarming with happy gratulation; young girls with flowers, scattering roses before her; staid citizens and aldermen pushing and squeezing and panting to make the speech, and bow the knee, and bid her welcome! Who is this who is honored with such a prodigious triumph, and received with a welcome so astonishing? A year ago we had never heard of her. I think about her pedigree and family not a few of us are in the dark still, and I own, for my part, to be much puzzled by the allusions of newspaper genealogists and bards and skalds to Vikings, Berserkers, and so forth. But it would be interesting to know how many hundreds of thousands of photographs of the fair bright face have by this time made it beloved and familiar in British homes. Think of all the quiet country nooks from Land's End to Caithness, where kind eyes have glanced at it! The farmer brings it home from market; the curate from his visit to the Cathedral town; the rustic folk peer at it in the little village shop-window; the squire's children gaze on it round the drawing-room table: every eye that beholds it looks tenderly on its bright beauty and sweet artless grace, and young and old pray God bless her. We have an elderly friend (a certain Goody Twoshoes) who inhabits, with many other old ladies, the Union House of the parish of St. Lazarus in Soho. One of your cousins from this house went to see her, and found Goody and her companion crones all in a flutter of excitement about the marriage. The whitewashed walls of their bleak dormitory were ornamented with prints out of the illustrated journals, and hung with festoons and true-lovers' knots of tape and colored paper; and the old bodies had had a good dinner, and the old tongues were chirping and clacking away, all eager, interested, sympathizing; and one very elderly and rheumatic Goody, who is obliged to keep her bed (and has, I trust, an exaggerated idea of the cares attending on royalty), said, "Pore thing, pore thing! I pity her." Yes, even in that dim place there was a little brightness and a quavering huzza, a contribution of a mite subscribed by those dozen poor old widows to the treasure of loyalty with which the nation endows the Prince's bride.

Three hundred years ago, when our dread Sovereign Lady Elizabeth came to take possession of her realm and capital city, Holingshed, if you please (whose pleasing history of course you carry about with you), relates in his fourth volume folio, that—"At hir entring the citie, she was of the people received maruellous intierlie, as appeared by the assemblies, praiers, welcommings, cries, and all other signes which argued a woonderfull earnest loue:" and at various halting-places on the royal progress children habited like angels appeared out of allegoric edifices and spoke verses to her—

"Welcome, O Queen, as much as heart can think,
Welcome again, as much as tongue can tell,
Welcome to joyous tongues and hearts that will not shrink.
God thee preserve, we pray, and wish thee ever well!"

Our new Princess, you may be sure, has also had her Alexandrines, and many minstrels have gone before her, singing her praises. Mr. Tupper, who begins in very great force and strength, and who proposes to give her no less than eight hundred thousand welcomes in the first twenty lines of his ode, is not satisfied with this most liberal amount of acclamation, but proposes at the end of his poem a still more magnificent subscription. Thus we begin, "A hundred thousand welcomes, a hundred thousand welcomes." In my copy the figures are in the well-known Arabic numerals, but let us have the numbers literally accurate:—

"A hundred thousand welcomes!
A hundred thousand welcomes!
And a hundred thousand more!
O happy heart of England,
Shout aloud and sing, land,
As no land sang before;
And let the pæans soar
And ring from shore to shore,
A hundred thousand welcomes,
And a hundred thousand more;
And let the cannons roar
The joy-stunned city o'er.
And let the steeples chime it
A hundred thousand welcomes
And a hundred thousand more;
And let the people rhyme it
From neighbor's door to door,
From every man's heart's core,
A hundred thousand welcomes
And a hundred thousand more."

This contribution, in twenty not long lines, of 900,000 (say nine hundred thousand) welcomes, is handsome indeed; and shows that when our bard is inclined to be liberal, he does not look to the cost. But what is a sum of 900,000 to his further proposal?—

"O let all these declare it,
Let miles of shouting swear it,
In all the years of yore,
Unparalleled before!
And thou, most welcome Wanderer
Across the Northern Water,
Our England's ALEXANDRA,
Our dear adopted daughter—
Lay to thine heart, conned o'er and o'er,
In future years remembered well,
The magic fervor of this spell
That shakes the land from shore to shore,
And makes all hearts and eyes brim o'er;
Our hundred thousand welcomes,
Our fifty million welcomes,
And a hundred million more!"

Here we have, besides the most liberal previous subscription, a further call on the public for no less than one hundred and fifty million one hundred thousand welcomes for her Royal Highness. How much is this per head for all of us in the three kingdoms? Not above five welcomes apiece, and I am sure many of us have given more than five hurrahs to the fair young Princess.

Each man sings according to his voice, and gives in proportion to his means. The guns at Sheerness, "from their adamantine lips" (which had spoken in quarrelsome old times a very different language), roared a hundred thundering welcomes to the fair Dane. The maidens of England strewed roses before her feet at Gravesend when she landed. Mr. Tupper, with the million and odd welcomes, may be compared to the thundering fleet; Mr. Chorley's song, to the flowerets scattered on her Royal Highness's happy and carpeted path:—

"Blessings on that fair face!
Safe on the shore
Of her home-dwelling place,
Stranger no more.
Love, from her household shrine,
Keep sorrow far!
May for her hawthorn twine,
June bring sweet eglantine,
Autumn, the golden vine,
Dear Northern Star!"

Hawthorn for May, eglantine for June, and in autumn a little tass of the golden vine for our Northern Star. I am sure no one will grudge the Princess these simple enjoyments, and of the produce of the last-named pleasing plant, I wonder how many bumpers were drunk to her health on the happy day of her bridal? As for the Laureate's verses, I would respectfully liken his Highness to a giant showing a beacon torch on "a windy headland." His flaring torch is a pine-tree, to be sure, which nobody can wield but himself. He waves it: and four times in the midnight he shouts mightily, "Alexandra!" and the Pontic pine is whirled into the ocean, and Enceladus goes home.

Whose muse, whose cornemuse,

sounds with such plaintive sweetness from Arthur's Seat, while Edinburgh and Musselburgh lie rapt in delight, and the mermaids come flapping up to Leith shore to hear the exquisite music? Sweeter piper Edina knows not than Aytoun, the Bard of the Cavaliers, who has given in his frank adhesion to the reigning dynasty. When a most beautiful, celebrated, and unfortunate princess whose memory the Professor loves — when Mary, wife of Francis the Second, King of France, and by her own right proclaimed Queen of Scotland and England (poor soul!) entered Paris with her young bridegroom, good Peter Ronsard wrote of her —

"Toi qui as veu l'excellence de celle
Qui rend le ciel de l'Escosse envieux,
Dy hardiment, contentez vous mes yeux,
Vous ne verrez jamais chose plus belle."*

"*Vous ne verrez jamais chose plus belle.*" Here is an Alexandrine written three hundred years ago, as simple as *bon jour*. Professor Aytoun is more ornate. After elegantly complimenting the spring, and a description of her Royal Highness's well-known ancestors the "Berserkers," he bursts forth —

"The Rose of Denmark comes, the Royal Bride!
O loveliest Rose! our paragon and pride —
Choice of the Prince whom England holds so dear —
What homage shall we pay
To one who has no peer?
What can the bard or wildered minstrel say
More than the peasant who on bended knee
Breathes from his heart an earnest prayer for thee?
Words are not fair, if that they would express
Is fairer still; so lovers in dismay
Stand all abashed before that loveliness
They worship most, but find no words to pray.
Too sweet for incense! (*bravo!*) Take our loves instead —
Most freely, truly, and devoutly given;
Our prayer for blessings on that gentle head,
For earthly happiness and rest in Heaven!
May never sorrow dim those dove-like eyes,
But peace as pure as reigned in Paradise,
Calm and untainted on creation's eve,
Attend thee still! May holy angels," &c.

This is all very well, my dear country cousins. But will you say "Amen" to this prayer? I won't. Assuredly our fair Princess will shed many tears out of the "dove-like eyes," or the heart will be little worth. Is she to know no parting, no care, no anxious longing, no tender watches by the sick, to deplore no friends and kindred, and feel no grief? Heaven forbid! When a bard or wildered minstrel writes so, best accept his own confession, that he is losing his head. On the day of her entrance into London who looked more bright and happy than the Princess? On the day of the marriage, the fair face wore its marks of care already, and looked out quite grave, and frightened almost, under the wreaths and lace and orange-flowers. Would you have had her feel no tremor? A maiden on the bridegroom's threshold, a Princess led up to the steps of a throne? I think her pallor and doubt became her as well as her smiles. That, I can tell you, was *our* vote who sat in X compartment, let us say, in the nave of St. George's Chapel at Windsor, and saw a part of one of the brightest ceremonies ever performed there.

My dear cousin Mary, you have an account of the dresses; and I promise you there were princesses besides the bride whom it did the eyes good to behold. Around the bride sailed a bevy of young creatures so fair, white, and graceful, that I thought of those fairy-tale beauties who are sometimes princesses, and sometimes white swans. The Royal Princesses and the Royal Knights of the Garter swept by in prodigious robes and trains of purple velvet, thirty shil-

* Quoted in Mignet's "Life of Mary."

lings a yard, my dear, not of course including the lining, which, I have no doubt, was of the richest satin, or that costly "miniver" which we used to read about in poor Jerrold's writings. The young princes were habited in kilts; and by the side of the Princess Royal trotted such a little wee solemn Highlander! He is the young heir and chief of the famous clan of Brandenburg. His eyrie is amongst the Eagles, and I pray no harm may befall the dear little chieftain.

The heralds in their tabards were marvellous to behold, and a nod from Rouge Croix gave me the keenest gratification. I tried to catch Garter's eye, but either I couldn't or he wouldn't. In his robes, he is like one of the Three Kings in old missal illuminations. Goldstick in waiting is even more splendid. With his gold rod and robes and trappings of many colors, he looks like a royal enchanter, and as if he had raised up all this scene of glamor by a wave of his glittering wand. The silver trumpeters wear such quaint caps, as those I have humbly tried to depict on the playful heads of children. Behind the trumpeters came a drum-bearer, on whose back a gold-laced drummer drubbed his march.

When the silver clarions had blown, and under a clear chorus of white-robed children chanting round the organ, the noble procession passed into the chapel, and was hidden from our sight for a while, there was silence, or from the inner chapel ever so faint a hum. Then hymns arose, and in the lull we knew that prayers were being said, and the sacred rite performed which joined Albert Edward to Alexandra his wife. I am sure hearty prayers were offered outside the gate as well as within for that princely young pair, and for their Mother and Queen. The peace, the freedom, the happiness, the order which her rule guarantees, are part of my birthright as an Englishman, and I bless God for my share. Where else shall I find such liberty of action, thought, speech, or laws which protect me so well? Her part of her compact with her people, what sovereign ever better performed? If ours sits apart from the festivities of the day, it is because she suffers from a grief so recent that the loyal heart cannot master it as yet, and remains *treu und fest* to a beloved memory. A part of the music which celebrates the day's service was composed by the husband who is gone to the place where the just and pure of life meet the reward promised by the Father of all of us to good and faithful servants who have well done here below. As this one gives in his account, surely we may remember how the Prince was the friend of all peaceful arts and learning; how he was true and fast always to duty, home, honor; how, through a life of complicated trials, he was sagacious, righteous, active, and self-denying. And as we trace in the young faces of his many children the father's features and likeness, what Englishman will not pray that they may have inherited also some of the great qualities which won for the Prince Consort the love and respect of our country?

The papers tell us how, on the night of the marriage of the Prince of Wales, all over England and Scotland illuminations were made, the poor and children were feasted, and in village and city thousands of kindly schemes were devised to mark the national happiness and sympathy. "The bonfire on Coptpoint at Folkestone was seen in France," "The Telegraph" says, "more clearly than even the French marine lights could be seen at Folkestone." Long may the fire continue to burn! There are European coasts (and inland places) where the liberty light has been extinguished, or is so low that you can't see to read by it — there are great Atlantic shores where it flickers and smokes very gloomily. Let us be thankful to the honest guardians of ours, and for the kind sky under which it burns bright and steady.

ON A MEDAL OF GEORGE THE FOURTH.

BEFORE me lies a coin bearing the image and superscription of King George IV., and of the nominal value of two-and-sixpence. But an official friend at a neighboring turnpike says the piece is hopelessly bad; and a chemist tested it, returning a like unfavorable opinion. A cabman, who had brought me from a Club, left it with the Club porter, appealing to the gent who gave it a pore cabby, at ever so much o'clock of a rainy night, which he hoped he would give him another. I have taken that cabman at his word. He has been provided with a sound coin. The bad piece is on the table before me, and shall have a hole drilled through it, as soon as this essay is written, by a loyal subject who does not desire to deface the Sovereign's image, but to protest against the rascal who has taken his name in vain. *Fid. Def.* indeed! Is this what you call defending the faith? You dare to forge your Sovereign's name, and pass your scoundrel pewter as his silver? I wonder who you are, wretch and most consummate trickster? This forgery is so complete that even now I am deceived by it — I can't see the difference between the base and sterling metal. Perhaps this piece is a little lighter; — I don't know. A little softer: — is it? I have not bitten it, not being a connoisseur in the tasting of pewter or silver. I take the word of three honest men, though it goes against me: and though I have given two-and-sixpence worth of honest consideration for the counter, I shall not attempt to implicate anybody else in my misfortune, or transfer my ill-luck to a deluded neighbor.

I say the imitation is so curiously successful, the stamping, milling of the edges, lettering, and so forth, are so neat, that even now, when my eyes are open, I cannot see the cheat. How did those experts, the cabman, and pikeman, and tradesman, come to find it out? How do they happen to be more familiar with pewter and silver than I am? You see, I put out of the question another point which I might argue without fear of defeat, namely, the cabman's statement that I gave him this bad piece of money. Suppose every cabman who took me a shilling fare were to drive away and return presently with a bad coin and an assertion that I had given it to him! This would be absurd and mischievous; an encouragement of vice amongst men who already are subject to temptations. Being *homo*, I think if I were a cabman myself, I might sometimes stretch a furlong or two in my calculation of distance. But don't come *twice*, my man, and tell me I have given you a bad half-crown. No, no! I have paid once like a gentleman, and once is enough. For instance, during the Exhibition time I was stopped by an old country-woman in black, with a huge umbrella, who, bursting into tears, said to me, "Master, be this the way to Harlow, in Essex?" "This the way to Harlow? This is the way to Exeter, my good lady, and you will arrive there if you walk about 170 miles in your present direction," I answered courteously, replying to the old creature. Then she fell a-sobbing as though her old heart would break. She had a daughter a-dying at Harlow. She had walked already "vifty-dree mile that day." Tears stopped the rest of her discourse, so artless, genuine, and abundant that—I own the truth — I gave her, in I believe genuine silver, a piece of the exact size of that coin which forms the subject of this essay. Well. About a month since, near to the very spot where I had met my old woman, I was accosted by a person in black, a person in a large draggled cap, a person with a huge umbrella, who was beginning, "I say, Master, can you tell me if this be the way to Har" — but here she stopped. Her eyes goggled wildly. She started from me, as Macbeth turned from Macduff. She would not engage with me. It was my old friend of Harlow, in Essex. I dare say she has informed many other people of her daughter's illness, and her anxiety to be put upon the right way to Harlow. Not long since, a very gentleman-like man, Major Delamere let us call him (I like the title of Major very much), requested to see me, named a dead gentleman who he said had been our mutual friend, and on the strength of this mutual acquaintance, begged me to cash his check for five pounds!

It is these things, my dear sir, which serve to make a man cynical. I do conscientiously believe that had I cashed the Major's check there would have been a difficulty about payment on the part of the respected bankers on whom he drew. On your honor and conscience, do you think that old widow who was walking from Tunbridge Wells to Harlow had a daughter ill, and was an honest woman at all? The daughter couldn't always, you see, be being ill, and her mother on her way to her dear child through Hyde Park. In the same way some habitual sneerers may be inclined to hint that the cabman's story was an invention — or at any rate, choose to ride off (so to speak) on the doubt. No. My opinion, I own, is unfavorable as regards the widow from Tunbridge Wells, and Major Delamere; but believing the cabman was honest, I am glad to think he was not injured by the reader's most humble servant.

What a queer, exciting life this rogue's march must be; this attempt of the bad half-crowns to get into circulation! Had my distinguished friend the Major knocked at many doors that morning, before operating on mine? The sport must be something akin to the pleasure of tiger or elephant hunting. What ingenuity the sportsman must have in tracing his prey — what daring and caution in coming upon him! What coolness in facing the angry animal (for, after all, a man on whom you draw a check *à bout portant* will be angry). What a delicious thrill of triumph, if you can bring him down! If I have money at the banker's, and draw for a portion of it over the counter, that is mere prose — any dolt can do that. But, having no balance, say I drive up in a cab, present a check at Coutts's, and, receiving the amount, drive off? What a glorious morning's sport that has been! How superior in excitement to the common transactions of every-day life! . . . I must tell a story; it is against myself, I know, but it *will* out, and perhaps my mind will be the easier.

More than twenty years ago, in an island remarkable for its verdure, I met four or five times one of the most agreeable companions with whom I have passed a night. I heard that evil times had come upon this gentleman; and, overtaking him in a road near my own house one evening, I asked him to come home to dinner. In two days, he was at my door again. At breakfast-time was this second appearance. He was in a cab (of course he was in a cab, they always are, these unfortunate, these courageous men). To deny myself was absurd. My friend could see me over the parlor blinds, surrounded by my family, and cheerfully partaking of the morning meal. Might he have a word with me? and can you imagine its purport? By the most provoking delay, his uncle the admiral not being able to come to town till Friday— would I cash him a check? I need not say it would be paid on Saturday without fail. I tell you that man went away with money in his pocket, and I regret to add that his gallant relative has not *come to town yet!*

Laying down the pen, and sinking back in my chair, here, perhaps, I fall into a five minutes' reverie, and think of one, two, three, half a dozen cases in which I have been content to accept that sham promissory coin in return for sterling money advanced. Not a reader, whatever his age, but could tell a like story. I vow and believe there are men of fifty, who will dine well to-day, who have not paid their school debts yet, and who have not taken up their long-protested promises to pay. Tom, Dick, Harry, my boys, I owe you no grudge, and rather relish that wince with which you will read these meek lines and say, "He means me." Poor Jack in Hades! Do you remember a certain pecuniary transaction, and a little sum of money you borrowed "until the meeting of Parliament?" Parliament met often in your lifetime: Parliament has met since: but I think I should scarce be more surprised if your ghost glided into the room now, and laid down the amount of our little account, than I should have been if you had paid me in your lifetime with the actual acceptances of the Bank of England. You asked to borrow, but you never intended to pay. I would as soon have believed that a promissory note of Sir John Falstaff (accepted by Messrs. Bardolph and Nym, and payable in Aldgate) would be as sure to find payment, as that note of the departed — nay, lamented — Jack Thriftless.

He who borrows, meaning to pay, is quite a different person from the individual here described. Many — most, I hope — took Jack's promise for what it was worth — and quite well knew that when he said, "Lend me," he meant "Give me" twenty pounds. "Give me change for this half-crown," said Jack; "I know it's a pewter piece;" and you gave him the change in honest silver, and pocketed the counterfeit gravely.

What a queer consciousness that must be which accompanies such a man in his sleeping, in his waking, in his walk through life, by his fireside with his children round him! "For what we are going to receive," &c. — he says grace before his dinner. "My dears! Shall I help you to some mutton? I robbed the butcher of the meat. I don't intend to pay him. Johnson my boy, a glass of champagne? Very good, isn't it? Not too sweet. Forty-six. I get it from So-and-so, whom I intend to cheat." As eagles go forth and bring home to their eaglets the lamb or the pavid kid, I say there are men who live and victual their nests by plunder. We all know highway robbers in white neckcloths, domestic bandits, marauders, passers of bad coin. What was yonder check which Major Delamere proposed I should cash but a piece of bad money? What was Jack Thriftless's promise to pay? Having got his booty, I fancy Jack or the Major returning home, and wife and children gathering round about him. Poor wife and children! They respect papa very likely. They don't know he is false coin. Maybe the wife has a dreadful inkling of the truth, and, sickening, tries to hide it from the daughters and sons. Maybe she is an accomplice: herself a brazen forgery. If Turpin and Jack Sheppard were married, very likely Mesdames Sheppard and Turpin did not know, at first, what their husband's real profession was, and fancied, when the men left home in the morning, they only went away to follow some regular and honorable business. Then a suspicion of the truth may have come: then a dreadful revelation; and presently we have the guilty pair robbing together, or passing forged money each on his own account. You know Doctor Dodd? I wonder whether his wife knows that he is a forger and scoundrel? Has she had any of the plunder, think you, and were the darling children's new dresses bought with it? The doctor's sermon last Sunday was certainly charming, and we all cried. Ah, my poor Dodd! Whilst he is preaching most beautifully, pocket-handkerchief in hand, he is peering over the pulpit cushions, looking out piteously for Messrs. Peachum and Lockit from the police-office. By Doctor Dodd you understand I would typify the rogue of respectable exterior, not committed to jail yet, but not undiscovered. We all know one or two such. This very sermon perhaps will be read by some, or more likely — for, depend upon it, your solemn hypocritic scoundrels don't care much for light literature — more likely, I say, this discourse will be read by some of their wives, who think, "Ah, mercy! does that horrible cynical wretch know how my poor husband blacked my eye, or abstracted mamma's silver teapot, or forced me to write So-and-so's name on that piece of stamped paper, or what not?" My good creature, I am not angry with *you*. If your husband has broken your nose, you will vow that he had authority over your person, and a right to demolish any part of it: if he has conveyed away your mamma's teapot, you will say that she gave it to him at your marriage, and it was very ugly, and what not? if he takes your aunt's watch, and you love him, you will carry it erelong to the pawnbroker's, and perjure yourself — oh, how you will perjure yourself — in the witness-box! I know this is a degrading view of woman's noble nature, her exalted mission, and so forth, and so forth. I know you will say this is bad morality. Is it? Do you, or do you not, expect your womankind to stick by you for better or for worse? Say I have committed a forgery, and the officers come in search of me, is my wife, Mrs. Dodd, to show them into the dining-room and say, "Pray step in, gentlemen! My husband has just come home from church. That bill with my Lord Chesterfield's acceptance, I am bound to own, was never written by his lordship, and the signature is in the doctor's handwriting?" I say, would any man of sense or honor, or fine feeling, praise his wife for telling the truth under such circumstances? Suppose she made a fine grimace, and said, "Most painful as my position is, most deeply as I feel for my William, yet truth must prevail, and I deeply lament to state that the beloved partner of my life *did* commit the flagitious act with which he is charged, and is at this present moment located in the two-pair back, up the chimney, whither it is my duty to lead you." Why, even Dodd himself, who was one of the greatest humbugs who ever lived, would not have had the face to say that he approved of his wife telling the truth in such a case. Would you have had Flora Macdonald beckon the officers, saying, "This way, gentlemen! You will find the young chevalier asleep in that cavern." Or don't you prefer her to be *splendide mendax*, and ready at all risks to save him? If ever I lead a rebellion, and my women betray me, may I be hanged but I will not forgive them: and if ever I steal a teapot, and *my* women don't stand up for me, pass the article under their shawls, whisk down the street with it, outbluster the policeman, and utter any amount of fibs before Mr. Beak, those beings are not what I take them to be, and — for a fortune — I won't give them so much as a bad half-crown.

Is conscious guilt a source of unmixed pain to the bosom which harbors it? Has not your criminal, on the contrary, an excitement, an enjoyment within quite unknown to you and me who never did any thing wrong in our lives? The housebreaker must snatch a fearful joy as he walks unchallenged by the policeman with his sack full of spoons and tankards. Do not cracksmen, when assembled together, entertain themselves with stories of glorious old burglaries which they or bygone heroes have committed? But that my age is mature and my habits formed, I should really just like to try a little criminality. Fancy passing a forged bill to your banker; calling on a friend and sweeping his sideboard of plate, his hall of umbrellas and coats; and then going home to dress for dinner, say — and to meet a bishop, a judge, and a police magistrate or so, and talk more morally than any man at table! How I should chuckle (as my host's spoons clinked softly in my pocket) whilst I was uttering some noble speech about virtue, duty, charity! I wonder do we meet garotters in society? In an average tea-party, now, how many returned convicts are there? Does John Footman, when he asks permission to go and spend the evening with some friends, pass his time in thuggee; waylay and strangle an old gentleman, or two; let himself into your house, with the house-key of course, and appear as usual with the shaving-water when you ring your bell in the morning? The very possibility of such a suspicion invests John with a new and romantic interest in my mind. Behind the grave politeness of his countenance I try and read the lurking treason. Full of this pleasing subject, I have been talking thief-stories with a neighbor. The neighbor tells me how some friends of hers used to keep a jewel-box under a bed in their room; and, going into the room, they thought they heard a noise under the bed. They had the courage to look. The cook was under the bed — under the bed with the jewel-box. Of course she said she had come for purposes connected with her business; but this was absurd. A cook under a bed is not there for professional purposes. A relation of mine had a box containing diamonds under her bed, which diamonds she told me were to be mine. Mine! One day, at dinner-time, between the entrées and the roast, a cab drove away from my relative's house containing the box wherein lay the diamonds. John laid the dessert, brought the coffee, waited all the evening — and oh, how frightened he was when he came to learn that his mistress's box had been conveyed out of her own room, and it contained diamonds — "Law bless us, did it now?" I wonder whether John's subsequent career has been prosperous? Perhaps the gentlemen from Bow Street were all in the wrong when they agreed in suspecting John as the author of the robbery. His noble nature was hurt at the suspicion. You conceive he would not like to remain in a family where they were mean enough to suspect him of stealing a jewel-box out of a bed-room — and the injured man and my relatives soon parted. But, inclining (with my usual cynicism) to think that he did steal the valuables, think of his life for the month or two whilst he still remains in the service! He shows the officers over the house, agrees with them that the *coup* must have been made by persons familiar with it; gives them every assistance; pities his master and mistress with a manly compassion; points out what a cruel misfortune it is to himself as an honest man, with his living to get and his family to provide for, that this suspicion should fall on him. Finally, he takes leave of his place, with a deep though natural melancholy that ever he had accepted it. What's a thousand pounds to gentlefolks! A loss certainly, but they will live as well without the diamonds as with them. But to John his Hhhonour was worth more than diamonds, his Hhonour was. Whohever is to give him back his character? Who is to prevent hany one from saying, "Ho yes. This is the footman which was in the family where the diamonds was stole?" &c.

I wonder has John prospered in life subsequently? If he is innocent, he does not interest me in the least. The interest of the case lies in John's behavior, supposing him to be guilty. Imagine the smiling face, the daily service, the orderly performance of duty, whilst within John is suffering pangs lest discovery should overtake him. Every bell of the door which he is obliged to open may bring a police-officer. The accomplices may peach. What an exciting life John's must have been for a while! And now, years and years after, when pursuit has long ceased, and detection is impossible, does he ever revert to the little transaction? Is it possible those diamonds cost a thousand pounds? What a rogue the fence must have been who only gave him so and so! And I pleasingly picture to myself an old ex-footman and an ancient receiver of stolen goods meeting and talking over this matter, which dates from times so early that her present Majesty's fair image could only just have begun to be coined or forged.

I choose to take John at the time when his little peccadillo is suspected, perhaps, but when there is no specific charge of robbery against him. He is not yet convicted: he is not even on his trial; how then can we venture to say he is guilty? Now think what scores of men and women walk the world in a like predicament; and what false coin passes current! Pinchbeck strives to pass off his history as sound coin. He knows it is only base metal, washed over with a thin varnish of learning. Poluphloisbos puts his sermons in circulation: sounding brass, lacquered over with white metal, and marked with the stamp and image of piety. What say you to Drawcansir's reputation as a military commander? to Tibbs's pretensions to be a fine gentleman? to Sapphira's claims as a poetess, or Rodoessa's as a beauty? His bravery, his piety, high birth, genius, beauty — each of these deceivers would palm his falsehood on us, and have us accept his forgeries as sterling coin. And we talk here, please to observe, of weaknesses rather than crimes. Some of us have more serious things to hide than a yellow cheek behind a raddle of rouge, or a white poll under a wig of jetty curls. You know, neighbor, there are not only false teeth in this world, but false tongues: and some make up a bust and an appearance of strength with padding, cotton, and what not? while another kind of artist tries to take you in by wearing under his waistcoat, and perpetually thumping, an immense sham heart. Dear sir, may yours and mine be found, at the right time, of the proper size and in the right place.

And what has this to do with half-crowns, good or bad? Ah, friend! may our coin, battered and clipped and defaced though it be, be proved to be Sterling Silver on the day of the Great Assay!

"STRANGE TO SAY, ON CLUB PAPER."

Before the Duke of York's column, and between "The Athenæum" and "United Service" Clubs, I have seen more than once, on the esplanade, a preacher holding forth to a little congregation of *badauds* and street-boys, whom he entertains with a discourse on the crimes of a rapacious aristocracy, or warns of the imminent peril of their own souls. Sometimes this orator is made to "move on" by brutal policemen. Sometimes, on a Sunday, he points to a white head or two visible in the windows of the Clubs to the right and left of him, and volunteers a statement that those quiet and elderly Sabbath-breakers will very soon be called from this world to another, where their lot will by no means be so comfortable as that which the reprobates enjoy here, in their arm-chairs by their snug fires.

At the end of last month, had I been a Pall Mall preacher, I would have liked to send a whip round to all the Clubs in St. James's, and convoke the few members remaining in London to hear a discourse *sub Dio* on a text from "The Observer" newspaper. I would have taken post under the statue of Fame, say, where she stands distributing wreaths to the three Crimean Guardsmen. (The crossing-sweeper does not obstruct the path, and I suppose is away at his villa on Sundays.) And, when the congregation was pretty quiet, I would have begun: —

In "The Observer" of the 27th September, 1863, in the fifth page and the fourth column, it is thus written: —

"The codicil appended to the will of the late Lord Clyde, executed at Chatham, and bearing the signature of Clyde, F. M., is written, strange to say, on a sheet of paper *bearing 'The Athenæum Club' mark.*"

What the codicil is, my dear brethren, it is not our business to inquire. It conveys a benefaction to a faithful and attached friend of the good Field-Marshal. The gift may be a lakh of rupees, or it may be a house and its contents — furniture, plate, and wine-cellar. My friends, I know the wine-merchant, and, for the sake of the legatee, hope heartily that the stock is large.

Am I wrong, dear brethren, in supposing that you expect a preacher to say a seasonable word on death here? If you don't, I fear you are but little familiar with the habits of preachers, and are but lax hearers of sermons. We might contrast the vault where the warrior's remains lie shrouded and coffined, with that in which his worldly provision of wine is stowed away. Spain and Portugal and France — all the lands which supplied his store — as hardy and obedient subaltern, as resolute captain, as colonel daring but prudent — he has visited the fields of all. In India and China he marches always unconquered; or at the head of his dauntless Highland brigade he treads the Crimean snow; or he rides from conquest to conquest in India once more; succoring his countrymen in the hour of their utmost need; smiting down the scared mutiny, and trampling out the embers of rebellion; at the head of an heroic army, a consummate chief. And now his glorious old sword is sheathed, and his honors are won; and he has bought him a house, and stored it with modest cheer for his friends (the good old man put water in his own wine, and a glass or two sufficed him) — behold the end comes, and his legatee inherits these modest possessions by virtue of a codicil to his lordship's will, written, "*strange to say, upon a sheet of paper, bearing 'The Athenæum Club' mark.*"

It is to this part of the text, my brethren, that I propose to address myself particularly, and if the remarks I make are offensive to any of you, you know the doors of our meeting-house are open, and you can walk out when you will. Around us are magnificent halls and palaces frequented by such a multitude of men as not even the Roman Forum assembled together. Yonder are the Martium and the Palladium. Next to the Palladium is the elegant Viatorium, which Barry gracefully stole from Rome. By its side is the massive Reformatorium: and the — the Ultratorium rears its granite columns beyond. Extending down the street palace after palace rises magnificent, and under their lofty roofs warriors and lawyers, merchants and nobles, scholars and seamen, the wealthy, the poor, the busy, the idle assemble. Into the halls built down this little street and its neighborhood, the principal men of all London come to hear or impart the news; and the affairs of the state or of private individuals, the quarrels of empires or of authors, the movements of the court, or the splendid vagaries of fashion, the intrigues of statesmen or of persons of another sex yet more wily, the last news of battles in the great occidental continents, nay the latest betting for the horse-races, or the advent of a dancer at the theatre — all that men do is discussed in these Pall Mall agoræ, where we of London daily assemble.

Now among so many talkers, consider how many false reports must fly about: in such multitudes imagine how many disappointed men there must be; how many chatterboxes; how many feeble and credulous (whereof I mark some specimens in my congregation); how many mean, rancorous, prone to believe ill of their betters, eager to find fault; and then, my brethren, fancy how the words of my text must have been read and received in Pall Mall! (I perceive several of the congregation looking most uncomfortable. One old boy with a dyed mustache turns purple in the face, and struts back to the Martium: another, with a shrug of the shoulder and a murmur of "Rubbish," slinks away in the direction of the Togatorium, and the preacher continues.) The will of Field-Marshal Lord Clyde — signed *at Chatham*, mind, where his lordship died — is written, *strange to say*, on a sheet of paper bearing "The Athenæum Club" mark!

The inference is obvious. A man cannot get Athenæum paper except at "The Athenæum." Such paper is not sold at Chatham, where the last codicil to his lordship's will is dated. And so the painful belief is forced upon us, that a Peer, a Field-Marshal, wealthy, respected, illustrious, could pocket paper at his Club, and carry it away with him to the country. One fancies the hall-porter conscious of the old lord's iniquity, and holding down his head as the Marshal passes the door. What is that roll which his lordship carries? Is it his Marshal's bâton gloriously won? No; it is a roll of foolscap conveyed from the Club. What has he on his breast, under his great-coat? Is it his Star of India? No; it is a bundle of envelopes, bearing the head of Minerva, some sealing-wax, and a half-score of pens.

Let us imagine how in the hall of one or other of these Clubs this strange anecdote will be discussed.

"Notorious screw," says Sneer. "The poor old fellow's avarice has long been known."

"Suppose he wishes to imitate the Duke of Marlborough," says Simper.

"Habit of looting contracted in India, you know; ain't so easy to get over, you know," says Snigger.

"When officers dined with him in India," remarks Solemn, "it was notorious that the spoons were all of a different pattern."

"Perhaps it isn't true. Suppose he wrote his paper at the Club?" interposes Jones.

"It is dated at Chatham, my good man," says Brown. "A man if he is in London says he is in London. A man if he is in Rochester says he is in Rochester. This man happens to forget that he is using the Club paper: and he happens to be found out: many men *don't* happen to be found out. I've seen literary fellows at Clubs writing their rubbishing articles; I have no doubt they take away reams of paper. They crib thoughts: why shouldn't they crib stationery? One of your literary vagabonds who is capable of stabbing a reputation, who is capable of telling any monstrous falsehood to support his party, is surely capable of stealing a ream of paper."

"Well, well, we have all our weaknesses," sighs Robinson. "Seen that article, Thompson, in 'The Observer' about Lord Clyde and the Club paper? You'll find it up stairs. In the third column of the fifth page towards the bottom of the page. I suppose he was so poor he couldn't afford to buy a quire of paper. Hadn't fourpence in the world. Oh, no!"

"And they want to get up a testimonial to this man's memory — a statue or something!" cries Jawkins. "A man who wallows in wealth and takes paper away from his Club! I don't say he is not brave. Brutal courage most men have. I don't say he was not a good officer: a man with such experience *must* have been a good officer, unless he was born fool. But to think of this man loaded with honors — though of a low origin — so lost to self-respect as actually to take away 'The Athenæum' paper! These parvenus, sir, betray their origin — betray their origin. I said to my wife this very morning, 'Mrs. Jawkins,' I said, 'there is talk of a testimonial to this man. I will not give one shilling. I have no idea of raising statues to fellows who take away Club paper. No, by George, I have not. Why, they will be raising statues to men who take Club spoons next! Not one penny of *my* money shall they have!'"

And now, if you please, we will tell the real story which has furnished this scandal to a newspaper, this tattle to Club gossips and loungers. The Field-Marshal, wishing to make a further provision for a friend, informed his lawyer what he desired to do. The lawyer, a member of "The Athenæum Club," there wrote the draft of such a codicil as he would advise, and sent the paper by the post to Lord Clyde at Chatham. Lord Clyde, finding the paper perfectly satisfactory, signed it and sent it back: and hence we have the story of "the codicil bearing the signature of Clyde, F. M., and written, strange to say, upon paper bearing 'The Athenæum Club' mark."

Here I have been imagining a dialogue between a half-dozen gossips such as congregate round a Club fireplace of an afternoon. I wonder how many people besides—whether any chance reader of this very page has read and believed this story about the good old lord. Have the country papers copied the anecdote, and our "own correspondents" made their remarks on it? If, my good sir, or madam, you have read it and credited it, don't you own to a little feeling of shame and sorrow, now that the trumpery little mystery is cleared? To "the new inhabitants of light," passed away and out of reach of our censure, misrepresentation, scandal, dulness, malice, a silly falsehood matters nothing. Censure and praise are alike to him —

> "The music warbling to the deafened ear,
> The incense wasted on the funeral bier,"

the pompous eulogy pronounced over the gravestone, or the lie that slander spits on it. Faithfully though this brave old chief did his duty, honest and upright though his life was, glorious his renown—you see he could write at Chatham on London paper; you see men can be found to point out how "strange" his behavior was.

And about ourselves? My good people, do you by chance know any man or woman who has formed unjust conclusions regarding his neighbor? Have you ever found yourself willing, nay, eager to believe evil of some man whom you hate? Whom you hate because he is successful, and you are not: because he is rich, and you are poor: because he dines with great men who don't invite you: because he wears a silk gown, and yours is still stuff: because he has been called in to perform the operation though you lived close by: because his pictures have been bought, and yours returned home unsold: because he fills his church, and you are preaching to empty pews? If your rival prospers, have you ever felt a twinge of anger? If his wife's carriage passes you and Mrs. Tomkins, who are in a cab, don't you feel that those people are giving themselves absurd airs of importance? If he lives with great people, are you not sure he is a sneak? And if you ever felt envy towards another, and if your heart has ever been black towards your brother, if you have been peevish at his success, pleased to hear his merit depreciated, and eager to believe all that is said in his disfavor — my good sir, as you yourself contritely own that you are unjust, jealous, uncharitable, so you may be sure, some men are uncharitable, jealous, and unjust regarding *you*.

The proofs and manuscript of this little sermon have just come from the printer's, and as I look at the writing, I perceive, not without a smile, that one or two of the pages bear, "strange to say," the mark of a Club of which I have the honor to be a member. Those lines quoted in a foregoing page are from some noble verses written by one of Mr. Addison's men, Mr. Tickell, on the death of Cadogan, who was amongst the most prominent "of Marlborough's captains and

Eugenio's friends." If you are acquainted with the history of those times, you have read how Cadogan had his feuds and hatreds too, as Tickell's patron had his, as Cadogan's great chief had his. "The Duke of Marlborough's character has been so variously drawn" (writes a famous contemporary of the duke's), "that it is hard to pronounce on either side without the suspicion of flattery or detraction. I shall say nothing of his military accomplishments, which the opposite reports of his friends and enemies among the soldiers have rendered problematical. Those maligners who deny him personal valor seem not to consider that this accusation is charged at a venture, since the person of a general is too seldom exposed, and that fear which is said sometimes to have disconcerted him before action might probably be more for his army than himself." If Swift could hint a doubt of Marlborough's courage, what wonder that a nameless scribe of our day should question the honor of Clyde?

THE LAST SKETCH.

Not many days since I went to visit a house where in former years I had received many a friendly welcome. We went into the owner's — an artist's — studio. Prints, pictures, and sketches hung on the walls as I had last seen and remembered them. The implements of the painter's art were there. The light which had shone upon so many, many hours of patient and cheerful toil, poured through the northern window upon print and bust, lay figure and sketch, and upon the easel before which the good, the gentle, the beloved Leslie labored. In this room the busy brain had devised, and the skilful hand executed, I know not how many of the noble works which have delighted the world with their beauty and charming humor. Here the poet called up into pictorial presence, and informed with life, grace, beauty, infinite friendly mirth and wondrous naturalness of expression, the people of whom his dear books told him the stories, — his Shakspeare, his Cervantes, his Molière, his Le Sage. There was his last work on the easel — a beautiful, fresh, smiling shape of Titania, such as his sweet guileless fancy imagined "The Midsummer Night's" queen to be. Gracious, and pure, and bright, the sweet smiling image glimmers on the canvas. Fairy elves, no doubt, were to have been grouped around their mistress in laughing clusters. Honest Bottom's grotesque head and form are indicated as reposing by the side of the consummate beauty. The darkling forest would have grown around them, with the stars glittering from the midsummer sky: the flowers at the queen's feet, and the boughs and foliage about her, would have been peopled with gambolling sprites and fays. They were dwelling in the artist's mind no doubt, and would have been developed by that patient, faithful, admirable genius; but the busy brain stopped working, the skilful hand fell lifeless, the loving, honest heart ceased to beat. What was she to have been — that fair Titania — when perfected by the patient skill of the poet, who in imagination saw the sweet innocent figure, and with tender courtesy and caresses, as it were, posed and shaped and traced the fair form? Is there record kept anywhere of fancies conceived, beautiful, unborn? Some day will they assume form in some yet undeveloped light? If our bad unspoken thoughts are registered against us, and are written in the awful account, will not the good thoughts unspoken, the love and tenderness, the pity, beauty, charity, which pass through the breast, and cause the heart to throb with silent good, find a remembrance too? A few weeks more, and this lovely offspring of the poet's conception would have been complete — to charm the world with its beautiful mirth. May there not be some sphere unknown to us where it may have an existence? They say our words, once out of our lips, go travelling in *omne ævum*, reverberating for ever and ever. If our words, why not our thoughts? If the Has Been, why not the Might Have Been?

Some day our spirits may be permitted to walk in galleries of fancies more wondrous and beautiful than any achieved works which at present we see, and our minds to behold and delight in masterpieces which poets' and artists' minds have fathered and conceived only.

With a feeling much akin to that with which I looked upon the friend's — the admirable artist's — unfinished work, I can fancy many readers turning to the last pages which were traced by Charlotte Brontë's hand. Of the multitude that have read her books, who has not known and deplored the tragedy of her family, her own most sad and untimely fate? Which of her readers has not become her friend? Who that has known her books has not admired the artist's noble English, the burning love of truth, the bravery, the simplicity, the indignation at wrong, the eager sympathy, the pious love and reverence, the passionate honor, so to speak, of the woman? What a story is that of that family of poets in their solitude yonder on the gloomy northern moors! At nine o'clock at night, Mrs. Gaskell tells, after evening prayers, when their guardian and relative had gone to bed, the three poetesses — the three maidens, Charlotte, and Emily, and Anne — Charlotte being the "motherly friend and guardian to the other two" — "began, like restless wild animals, to pace up and down their parlor, 'making out' their wonderful stories, talking over plans and projects, and thoughts of what was to be their future life."

One evening, at the close of 1854, as Charlotte Nicholls sat with her husband by the fire, listening to the howling of the wind about the house, she suddenly said to her husband, "If you had not been with me, I must have been writing now." She then ran up stairs, and brought down, and read aloud, the beginning of a new tale. When she had finished, her husband remarked, "The critics will accuse you of repetition." She replied, "Oh! I shall alter that. I always begin two or three times before I can please myself." But it was not to be. The trembling little hand was to write no more. The heart newly awakened to love and happiness, and throbbing with maternal hope, was soon to cease to beat; that intrepid outspeaker and champion of truth, that eager, impetuous redresser of wrong, was to be called out of the world's fight and struggle, to lay down the shining arms, and to be removed to a sphere where even a noble indignation *cor ulterius nequit lacerare*, and where truth complete, and right triumphant, no longer need to wage war.

I can only say of this lady, *vidi tantum*. I saw her first just as I rose out of an illness from which I had never thought to recover. I remember the trembling little frame, the little hand, the great honest eyes. An impetuous honesty seemed to me to characterize the woman. Twice I recollect she took me to task for what she held to be errors in doctrine. Once about Fielding we had a disputation. She spoke her mind out. She jumped too rapidly to conclusions. (I have smiled at one or two passages in the "Biography," in which my own disposition or behavior forms the subject of talk.) She formed conclusions that might be wrong, and built up whole theories of character upon them. New to the London world, she entered it with an independent, indomitable spirit of her own; and judged of contemporaries, and especially spied out arrogance or affectation, with extraordinary keenness of vision. She was angry with her favorites if their conduct or conversation fell below her ideal. Often she seemed to me to be judging the London folk prematurely; but perhaps the city is rather angry at being judged. I fancied an austere little Joan of Arc marching in upon us, and rebuking our easy lives, our easy morals. She gave me the impression of being a very pure, and lofty, and high-minded person. A great and holy reverence of right and truth seemed to be with her always. Such, in our brief interview, she appeared to me. As one thinks of that life so noble, so lonely — of that passion for truth — of those nights and nights of eager study, swarming fancies, invention, depression, elation, prayer; as one reads the necessarily incomplete, though most touching and admirable history of the heart that throbbed in this one little frame — of this one amongst the myriads of souls that have lived and died on this great earth — this great earth? — this little speck in the infinite universe of God, — with what wonder do we think of to-day, with what awe await to-morrow, when that which is now but darkly seen shall be clear! As I read this little fragmentary sketch, I think of the rest. Is it? And where is it? Will not the leaf be turned some day, and the story be told? Shall the deviser of the tale somewhere perfect the history of little EMMA's griefs and troubles? Shall TITANIA come forth complete with her sportive court, with the flowers at her feet, the forest around her, and all the stars of summer glittering overhead?

How well I remember the delight, and wonder, and pleasure with which I read "Jane Eyre," sent to me by an author whose name and sex were then alike unknown to me; the strange fascinations of the book; and how with my own work pressing upon me, I could not, having taken the volumes up, lay them down until they were read through! Hundreds of those who, like myself, recognized and admired that master-work of a great genius, will look with a mournful interest and regard and curiosity upon the last fragmentary sketch from the noble hand which wrote "Jane Eyre."

THE

SECOND FUNERAL OF NAPOLEON.

By MICHAEL ANGELO TITMARSH.

THE

SECOND FUNERAL OF NAPOLEON.

I.

ON THE DISINTERMENT OF NAPOLEON AT ST. HELENA.

MY DEAR ——, — It is no easy task in this world to distinguish between what is great in it, and what is mean; and many and many is the puzzle that I have had in reading History (or the works of fiction which go by that name), to know whether I should laud up to the skies, and endeavor, to the best of my small capabilities, to imitate the remarkable character about whom I was reading, or whether I should fling aside the book and the hero of it, as things altogether base, unworthy, laughable, and get a novel, or a game of billiards, or a pipe of tobacco, or the report of the last debate in the House, or any other employment which would leave the mind in a state of easy vacuity, rather than pester it with a vain set of dates relating to actions which are in themselves not worth a fig, or with a parcel of names of people whom it can do one no earthly good to remember.

It is more than probable, my love, that you are acquainted with what is called Grecian and Roman history, chiefly from perusing, in very early youth, the little sheepskin-bound volumes of the ingenious Dr. Goldsmith, and have been indebted for your knowledge of our English annals to a subsequent study of the more voluminous works of Hume and Smollett. The first and the last-named authors, dear Miss Smith, have written each an admirable history, — that of the Rev. Dr. Primrose, Vicar of Wakefield, and that of Mr. Robert Bramble, of Bramble Hall, — in both of which works you will find true and instructive pictures of human life, and which you may always think over with advantage. But let me caution you against putting any considerable trust in the other works of these authors, which were placed in your hands at school and afterwards, and in which you were taught to believe. Modern historians, for the most part, know very little, and, secondly, only tell a little of what they know.

As for those Greeks and Romans whom you have read of in "sheepskin," were you to know really what those monsters were, you would blush all over as red as a hollyhock, and put down the history-book in a fury. Many of our English worthies are no better. You are not in a situation to know the real characters of any one of them. They appear before you in their public capacities, but the individuals you know not. Suppose, for instance, your mamma had purchased her tea in the Borough from a grocer living there by the name of Greenacre: suppose you had been asked out to dinner, and the gentleman of the house had said, "Ho! François! a glass of champagne for Miss Smith;" Courvoisier would have served you just as any other footman would; you would never have known that there was any thing extraordinary in these individuals, but would have thought of them only in their respective public characters of Grocer and Footman. This, Madam, is History, in which a man always appears dealing with the world in his apron, or his laced livery, but which has not the power or the leisure, or, perhaps, is too high and mighty, to condescend to follow and study him in his privacy. Ah, my dear, when big and little men come to be measured rightly, and great and small actions to be weighed properly, and people to be stripped of their royal robes, beggars' rags, generals' uniforms, seedy out-at-elbowed coats, and the like—or the contrary say, when souls come to be stripped of their wicked, deceiving bodies, and turned out stark naked as they were before they were born—what a strange startling sight shall we see, and what a pretty figure shall some of us cut! Fancy how we shall see Pride, with his Stultz clothes and padding pulled off, and dwindled down to a forked radish! Fancy some Angelic Virtue, whose white raiment is suddenly whisked over his head, showing us cloven feet and a tail! Fancy Humility, eased of its sad load of cares, and want, and scorn, walking up to the very highest place of all, and blushing as he takes it! Fancy—but we must not fancy such a scene at all, which would be an outrage on public decency. Should we be any better than our neighbors? No, certainly. And as we can't be virtuous, let us be decent. Fig-leaves are a very decent, becoming wear, and have been now in fashion for four thousand years. And so, my dear, History is written on fig-leaves. Would you have any thing further? O fie!

Yes, four thousand years ago, that famous tree was planted. At their very first lie, our first parents made for it, and there it is still the great Humbug Plant, stretching its wide arms, and sheltering beneath its leaves, as broad and green as ever, all the generations of men. Thus, my dear, coquettes of your fascinating sex cover their persons with figgery, fantastically arranged, and call their masquerading, modesty. Cowards fig themselves out fiercely as "salvage men," and make us believe that they are warriors. Fools look very solemnly out from the dusk of the leaves, and we fancy in the gloom that they are sages. And many a man sets a great wreath about his pate, and struts abroad a hero, whose claims we would all of us laugh at, could we but remove the ornament and see his numskull bare.

And such—(excuse my sermonizing)—such is the constitution of mankind, that men have, as it were, entered into a compact among themselves to pursue the fig-leaf system *à l'outrance*, and to cry down all who oppose it. Humbug they will have. Humbugs themselves, they will respect humbugs. Their daily victuals of life must be seasoned with humbug. Certain things are there in the world that they will not allow to be called by their right names, and will insist upon our admiring, whether we will or no. Woe be to the man who would enter too far into the recesses of that magnificent temple where our Goddess is enshrined, peep through the vast embroidered curtains indiscreetly, penetrate the secret of secrets, and expose the Gammon of Gammons! And as you must not peer too curiously within, so neither must you remain scornfully without. Humbug-worshippers, let us come into our great temple regularly and decently: take our seats, and settle our clothes decently; open our books, and go through the service with decent gravity; listen, and be decently affected by the expositions of the decent priest of the place; and if by chance some straggling vagabond, loitering in the sunshine out of doors, dares to laugh or to sing, and disturb the sanctified dulness of the faithful; — quick! a couple of big beadles rush out and belabor the wretch, and his yells make our devotions more comfortable.

Some magnificent religious ceremonies of this nature are at present taking place in France; and thinking that you might perhaps while away some long winter evening with an account of them, I have compiled the following pages for your use. Newspapers have been filled, for some days past, with details regarding the Saint Helena expedition, many pamphlets have been published, men go about crying little books and broadsheets filled with real or sham particulars; and from these scarce and valuable documents the following pages are chiefly compiled.

We must begin at the beginning; premising, in the first place, that Monsieur Guizot, when French Ambassador at London, waited upon Lord Palmerston with a request that the body of the Emperor Napoleon should be given up to the French nation, in order that it might find a final resting-place in French earth. To this demand the English Government gave a ready assent; nor was there any particular explosion of sentiment upon either side, only some pretty cordial expressions of mutual good-will. Orders were sent out to St. Helena that the corpse should be disinterred in due time, when the French expedition had arrived in search of it, and that every respect and attention should be paid to those who came to carry back to their country the body of the famous dead warrior and sovereign.

This matter being arranged in very few words (as in England, upon most points, is the laudable fashion), the French Chambers began to debate about the place in which they should bury the body when they got it; and numberless pamphlets and newspapers out of doors joined in the talk. Some people there were who had fought and conquered and been beaten with the great Napoleon, and loved him and his memory. Many more were there who, because of his great genius and valor, felt excessively proud in their own particular persons, and clamored for the return of their hero. And if there were some few individuals in this great hot-headed, gallant, boasting, sublime, absurd French nation, who had taken a cool view of the dead Emperor's character; if, perhaps, such men as Louis Philippe, and Monsieur A. Thiers, Minister and Deputy, and Monsieur François. Guizot, Deputy and Excellency, had, from interest or conviction, opinions at all differing from those of the majority; why, they knew what was what, and kept their opinions to themselves, coming with a tolerably good grace and flinging a few handfuls of incense upon the altar of the popular idol.

In the succeeding debates, then, various opinions were given with regard to the place to be selected for the Emperor's sepulture. "Some demanded," says an eloquent anonymous Captain in the Navy who has written an "Itinerary from Toulon to St. Helena," "that the coffin should be deposited under the bronze taken from the enemy by the French army — under the Column of the Place Vendôme. The idea was a fine one. This is the most glorious monument that was ever raised in a conqueror's honor. This column has been melted out of foreign cannon. These same cannons have furrowed the bosoms of our braves with noble cicatrices; and this metal — conquered by the soldier first, by the artist afterwards — has allowed to be imprinted on its front its own defeat and our glory. Napoleon might sleep in peace under this audacious trophy. But, would his ashes find a shelter sufficiently vast beneath this pedestal? And his puissant statue dominating Paris, beams with sufficient grandeur on this place: whereas the wheels of carriages and the feet of passengers would profane the funereal sanctity of the spot in trampling on the soil so near his head."

You must not take this description, dearest Amelia, "at the foot of the letter," as the French phrase it, but you will here have a masterly exposition of the arguments for and against the burial of the Emperor under the Column of the Place Vendôme. The idea was a fine one, granted; but, like all other ideas, it was open to objections. You must not fancy that the cannon, or rather the cannon-balls, were in the habit of furrowing the bosoms of French braves, or any other braves, with cicatrices: on the contrary, it is a known fact that cannon-balls make wounds, and not cicatrices (which, my dear, are wounds partially healed); nay, that a man generally dies after receiving one such projectile on his chest, much more after having his bosom furrowed by a score of them. No, my love; no bosom, however heroic, can stand such applications, and the author only means that the French soldiers faced the cannon and took them. Nor, my love, must you suppose that the column was melted: it was the cannon was melted, not the column; but such phrases are often used by orators when they wish to give a particular force and emphasis to their opinions.

Well, again, although Napoleon might have slept in peace under "this audacious trophy," how could he do so, and carriages go rattling by all night, and people with great iron heels to their boots pass clattering over the stones? Nor indeed could it be expected that a man whose reputation stretches from the Pyramids to the Kremlin, should find a column, of which the base is only five and twenty feet square, a shelter vast enough for his bones. In a word, then, although the proposal to bury Napoleon under the column was ingenious, it was found not to suit; whereupon somebody else proposed the Madelaine.

"It was proposed," says the before-quoted author with his usual felicity, "to consecrate the Madelaine to his exiled manes" — that is, to his bones when they were not in exile any longer. "He ought to have, it was said, a temple entire. His glory fills the world. His bones could not contain themselves in the coffin of a man — in the tomb of a king!" In this case what was Mary Magdalen to do? "This proposition, I am happy to say, was rejected, and a new one — that of the President of the Council — adopted. Napoleon and his braves ought not to quit each other. Under the immense gilded dome of the Invalides he would find a sanctuary worthy of himself. A dome imitates the vault of heaven, and that vault alone" (meaning of course the other vault) "should dominate above his head. His old mutilated Guard shall watch around him: the last veteran, as he has shed his blood in his combats, shall breathe his last sigh near his tomb, and all these tombs shall sleep under the tattered standards that have been won from all the nations of Europe."

The original words are "sous les lambeaux criblés des drapeaux cueillis chez toutes les nations;" in English, "under the riddled rags of the flags that have been culled or plucked" (like roses or buttercups) "in all the nations." Sweet, innocent flowers of victory! there they are, my dear, sure enough, and a pretty considerable *hortus siccus* may any man examine who chooses to walk to the Invalides. The burial-place being thus agreed on, the expedition was prepared, and on the 7th July the "Belle Poule" frigate, in company with "La Favorite" corvette, quitted Toulon harbor. A couple of steamers, "The Trident" and "The Ocean," escorted the ships as far as Gibraltar, and there left them to pursue their voyage.

The two ships quitted the harbor in the sight of a vast concourse of people, and in the midst of a great roaring of cannons. Previous to the departure of the "Belle Poule," the Bishop of Fréjus went on board, and gave to the cenotaph, in which the Emperor's remains were to be deposited, his episcopal benediction. Napoleon's old friends and followers, the two Bertrands, Gourgaud, Emanuel Las Cases, "companions in exile, or sons of the companions in exile of the prisoner of the *infame* Hudson," says a French writer, were passengers on board the frigate. Marchand, Denis, Pierret, Novaret, his old and faithful servants, were likewise in the vessel. It was commanded by his Royal Highness Francis Ferdinand Philip Louis Marie d'Orleans, Prince de Joinville, a young prince two and twenty years of age, who was already distinguished in the service of his country and king.

On the 8th of October, after a voyage of six and sixty days, the "Belle Poule" arrived in James Town harbor; and on its arrival, as on its departure from France, a great firing of guns took place. First, the "Oreste" French brig-of-war began roaring out a salutation to the frigate; then "The Dolphin" English schooner gave her one and twenty guns; then the frigate returned the compliment of "The Dolphin" schooner; then she blazed out with one and twenty guns more, as a mark of particular politeness to the shore — which kindness the forts acknowledged by similar detonations.

These little compliments concluded on both sides, Lieutenant Middlemore, son and aide-de-camp of the Governor of St. Helena, came on board the French frigate, and brought his father's best respects to his Royal Highness. The Governor was at home ill, and forced to keep his room; but he had made his house at James Town ready for Captain Joinville and his suite, and begged that they would make use of it during their stay.

On the 9th, H. R. H. the Prince of Joinville put on his full uniform and landed, in company with Generals Bertrand and Gourgaud, Baron Las Cases, M. Marchand, M. Coquereau, the chaplain of the expedition, and M. de Rohan Chabot, who acted as chief mourner. All the garrison were under arms to receive the illustrious Prince and the other members of the expedition — who forthwith repaired to Plantation House, and had a conference with the Governor regarding their mission.

On the 10th, 11th, 12th, these conferences continued: the crews of the French ships were permitted to come on shore and see the tomb of Napoleon. Bertrand, Gourgaud, Las Cases, wandered about the island and revisited the spots to which they had been partial in the lifetime of the Emperor.

The 15th October was fixed on for the day of the exhumation: that day five and twenty years, the Emperor Napoleon first set his foot upon the island.

On the day previous, all things had been made ready; the grand coffins and ornaments brought from France, and the articles necessary for the operation were carried to the valley of the Tomb.

The operations commenced at midnight. The well-known friends of Napoleon before named, and some other attendants of his, the chaplain and his acolytes, the doctor of the "Belle Poule," the captains of the French ships, and Captain Alexander of the Engineers, the English Commissioner, attended the disinterment. His Royal Highness Prince de Joinville could not be present because the workmen were under English command.

The men worked for nine hours incessantly, when at length the earth was entirely removed from the vault, all the horizontal strata of masonry demolished, and the large slab which covered the place where the stone sarcophagus lay, removed by a crane. This outer coffin of stone was perfect, and could scarcely be said to be damp.

"As soon as the Abbé Coquereau had recited the prayers, the coffin was removed with the greatest care, and carried by the engineer-soldiers, bare-headed, into a tent that had been prepared for the purpose. After the religious ceremonies, the inner coffins were opened. The outermost coffin was slightly injured: then came one of lead, which was in good condition, and enclosed two others — one of tin and one of wood. The last coffin was lined inside with white satin, which, having become detached by the effect of time, had fallen upon the body, and enveloped it like a winding-sheet, and had become slightly attached to it.

"It is difficult to describe with what anxiety and emotion those who were present waited for the moment which was to expose to them all that death had left of Napoleon. Notwithstanding the singular state of preservation of the tomb and coffins, we could scarcely hope to find any thing but some misshapen remains of the least perishable part of the costume to evidence the identity of the body. But when Doctor Guillard raised the sheet of satin, an indescribable feeling of surprise and affection was expressed by the spectators, many of whom burst into tears. The Emperor was himself before their eyes! The features of the face, though changed, were perfectly recognized; the hands extremely beautiful; his well-known costume had suffered but little, and the colors were easily distinguished. The attitude itself was full of ease, and but for the fragments of the satin lining which covered, as with a fine gauze, several parts of the uniform, we might have believed we still saw Napoleon before us lying on his bed of state. General Bertrand and M. Marchand, who were both present at the interment, quickly pointed out the different articles which each had deposited in the coffin and remained in the precise position in which they had previously described them to be.

"The two inner coffins were carefully closed again; the old leaden coffin was strongly blocked up with wedges of wood, and both were once more soldered up with the most minute precautions, under the direction of Doctor Guillard. These different operations being terminated, the ebony sarcophagus was closed as well as its oak case. On delivering the key of the ebony sarcophagus to Count de Chabot, the King's Commissioner, Captain Alexander declared to him, in the name of the Governor, that this coffin, containing the mortal remains of the Emperor Napoleon, was considered as at the disposal of the French Government from that day, and from the moment at which it should arrive at the place of embarkation, towards which it was about to be sent under the orders of General Middlemore. The King's Commissioner replied that he was charged by his Government, and in its name, to accept the coffin from the hands of the British authorities, and that he and the other persons composing the French mission were ready to follow it to James Town, where the Prince de Joinville, superior commandant of the expedition, would be ready to receive it and conduct it on board his frigate. A car drawn by four horses, decked with funereal emblems, had been prepared before the arrival of the expedition, to receive the coffin, as well as a pall, and all the other suitable trappings of mourning. When the sarcophagus was placed on the car, the whole was covered with a magnificent imperial mantle brought from Paris, the four corners of which were borne by Generals Bertrand and Gourgaud, Baron Las Cases and M. Marchand. At half-past three o'clock the funeral car began to move, preceded by a chorister bearing the cross, and by the Abbé Coquereau. M. de Chabot acted as chief mourner. All the authorities of the island, all the principal inhabitants, and the whole of the garrison, followed in procession from the tomb to the quay. But with the exception of the artillerymen necessary to lead the horses, and occasionally support the car when descending some steep parts of the way, the places nearest the coffin were reserved for the French mission. General Middlemore, although in a weak state of health, persisted in following the whole way on foot, together with General Churchill, chief of the staff in India, who had arrived only two days before from Bombay. The immense weight of the coffins, and the unevenness of the road, rendered the utmost carefulness necessary throughout the whole distance. Colonel Trelawney commanded in person the small detachment of artillerymen who conducted the car, and, thanks to his great care, not the slightest accident took place. From the moment of departure to the arrival at the quay, the cannons of the forts and the 'Belle Poule' fired minute-guns. After an hour's march, the rain ceased for the first time since the commencement of the operations; and on arriving in sight of the town, we found a brilliant sky and beautiful weather. From the morning, the three French vessels of war had assumed the usual signs of deep mourning: their yards crossed and their flags lowered. Two French merchantmen, 'Bonne Amie' and 'Indien,' which had been in the roads for two days, had put themselves under the Prince's orders, and followed during the ceremony all the manœuvres of the 'Belle Poule.' The forts of the town, and the houses of the consuls, had also their flags half-mast high.

"On arriving at the entrance of the town, the troops of the garrison and the militia formed in two lines as far as the extremity of the quay. According to the order for mourning prescribed for the English army, the men had their arms reversed, and the officers had crape on their arms, with their swords reversed. All the inhabitants had been kept away from the line of march, but they lined the terraces commanding the town, and the streets were occupied only by the troops, the 91st Regiment being on the right, and the militia on the left. The cortége advanced slowly between two ranks of soldiers to the sound of a funeral march, while the cannons of the forts were fired, as well as those of the 'Belle Poule,' and the 'Dolphin;' the echoes being repeated a thousand times by the rocks above James Town. After two hours' march, the cortége stopped at the end of the quay, where the Prince de Joinville had stationed himself at the head of the officers of the three French ships of war. The greatest official honors had been rendered by the English authorities to the memory of the Emperor — the most striking testimonials of respect had marked the adieu given by St. Helena to his coffin; and from this moment the mortal remains of the Emperor were about to belong to France. When the funeral-car stopped, the Prince de Joinville advanced alone, and in presence of all around, who stood with their heads uncovered, received, in a solemn manner, the imperial coffin from the hands of General Middlemore. His Royal Highness then thanked the Governor, in the name of France, for all the testimonials of sympathy and respect with which the authorities and inhabitants of St. Helena had surrounded the memorable ceremonial. A cutter had been expressly prepared to receive the coffin. During the embarkation, which the Prince directed himself, the bands played funeral-airs, and all the boats were stationed round with their oars shipped. The moment the sarcophagus touched the cutter, a magnificent royal flag, which the ladies of James Town had embroidered for the occasion, was unfurled, and the 'Belle Poule' immediately squared her masts and unfurled her colors. All the manœuvres of the frigate were immediately followed by the other vessels. Our mourning had ceased with the exile of Napoleon, and the French naval division dressed itself out in all its festal ornaments to receive the imperial coffin under the French flag. The sarcophagus was covered in the cutter with the imperial mantle. The Prince de Joinville placed himself at the rudder, Commandant Guyet at the head of the boat; Generals Bertrand and Gourgaud, Baron Las Cases, M. Marchand, and the Abbé Coquereau occupied the same places as during the march. Count Chabot and Commandant Hernoux were astern, a little in advance of the Prince. As soon as the cutter had pushed off from the quay, the batteries ashore fired a salute of twenty-one guns, and our ships returned the salute with all their artillery. Two other salutes were fired during the passage from the quay to the frigate; the cutter advancing very slowly, and surrounded by the other boats. At half-past six o'clock, it reached the 'Belle Poule,' all the men being on the yards with their hats in their hands. The Prince had arranged on the deck a chapel, decked with flags and trophies of arms, the altar being placed at the foot of the mizzenmast. The coffin, carried by our sailors, passed between two ranks of officers with drawn swords, and was placed on the quarter-deck. The absolution was pronounced by the Abbé Coquereau the same evening. Next day, at ten o'clock, a solemn mass was celebrated on the deck, in presence of the officers and part of the crews of the ships. His Royal Highness stood at the foot of the coffin. The cannon of the 'Favorite' and 'Oreste' fired minute-guns during this ceremony, which terminated by a solemn absolution; and the Prince de Joinville, the gentlemen of the mission, the officers, and the *premiers maîtres* of the ship, sprinkled holy water on the coffin. At eleven, all the ceremonies of the church were accomplished, all the honors done to a sovereign had been paid to the mortal remains of Napoleon. The coffin was carefully lowered between decks, and placed in the *chapelle ardente* which had been prepared at Toulon for its reception. At this moment, the vessels fired a last salute with all their artillery, and the frigate took in her flags, keeping up only her flag at the stern and the royal standard at the maintopgallant-mast. On Sunday, the 18th, at eight in the morning, the 'Belle Poule' quitted St. Helena with her precious deposit on board.

"During the whole time that the mission remained at James Town, the best understanding never ceased to exist between the population of the island and the French. The Prince de Joinville and his companions met in all quarters and at all times with the greatest good-will and the warmest testimonials of sympathy. The authorities and the inhabitants must have felt, no doubt, great regret at seeing taken away from their island the coffin that had rendered it so celebrated; but they repressed their feelings with a courtesy that does honor to the frankness of their character."

II.

ON THE VOYAGE FROM ST. HELENA TO PARIS.

On the 18th October the French frigate quitted the island with its precious burden on board.

His Royal Highness the Captain acknowledged cordially the kindness and attention which he and his crew had received from the English authorities and the inhabitants of the Island of St. Helena; nay, promised a pension to an old soldier who had been for many years the guardian of the imperial tomb, and went so far as to take into consideration the petition of a certain lodging-house keeper, who prayed for a compensation for the loss which the removal of the Emperor's body would occasion to her. And although it was not to be expected that the great French nation should forego its natural desire of recovering the remains of a hero so dear to it foi the sake of the individual interest of the landlady in question, it must have been satisfactory to her to find that the peculiarity of her position was so delicately appreciated by the august Prince who commanded the expedition, and carried away with him *animæ dimidium suæ* — the half of the genteel independence which she derived from the situation of her hotel. In a word, politeness and friendship could not be carried further. The Prince's realm and the landlady's were bound together by the closest ties of amity. M. Thiers was Minister of France, the great patron of the English alliance. At London M. Guizot was the worthy representative of the French good-will towards the British people; and the remark frequently made by our orators at public dinners, that "France and England, while united, might defy the world," was considered as likely to hold good for many years to come, — the union that is. As for defying the world, that was neither here nor there; nor did English politicians ever dream of doing any such thing, except perhaps at the tenth glass of port at "Freemason's Tavern."

Little, however, did Mrs. Corbett, the Saint Helena landlady, little did his Royal Highness Prince Ferdinand Philip Marie de Joinville, know what was going on in Europe all this time (when I say in Europe, I mean in Turkey, Syria, and Egypt); how clouds, in fact, were gathering upon what you call the political horizon; and how tempests were rising that were to blow to pieces our Anglo-Gallic temple of friendship. Oh, but it is sad to think that a single wicked old Turk should be the means of setting our two Christian nations by the ears!

Yes, my love, this disreputable old man had been for some time past the object of the disinterested attention of the great sovereigns of Europe. The Emperor Nicolas (a moral character, though following the Greek superstition, and adored for his mildness and benevolence of disposition), the Emperor Ferdinand, the King of Prussia, and our own gracious Queen, had taken such just offence at his conduct and disobedience towards a young and interesting sovereign, whose authority he had disregarded, whose fleet he had kidnapped, whose fair provinces he had pounced upon, that they determined to come to the aid of Abdul Medjid the First, Emperor of the Turks, and bring his rebellious vassal to reason. In this project, the French nation was invited to join; but they refused the invitation, saying, that it was necessary for the maintenance of the balance of power in Europe that his Highness Mehemet Ali should keep possession of what by hook or by crook he had gotten, and that they would have no hand in injuring him. But why continue this argument, which you have read in the newspapers for many months past? You, my dear, must know as well as I, that the balance of power in Europe could not possibly be maintained in any such way; and though, to be sure, for the last fifteen years, the progress of the old robber has not made much difference to us in the neighborhood of Russell Square, and the battle of Nezib did not in the least affect our taxes, our homes, our institutions, or the price of butcher's meat, yet there is no knowing what *might* have happened had Mehemet Ali been allowed to remain quietly as he was: and the balance of power in Europe might have been — the deuce knows where.

Here, then, in a nutshell, you have the whole matter in dispute. While Mrs. Corbett and the Prince de Joinville were innocently interchanging compliments at Saint Helena, — bang! bang! Commodore Napier was pouring broadsides into Tyre and Sidon; our gallant navy was storming breeches and routing armies; Colonel Hodges had seized upon the green standard of Ibraham Pacha; and the powder-magazine of St. John of Acre was blown up sky-high, with eighteen hundred Egyptian soldiers in company with it. The French said that *l'or Anglais* had achieved all these successes, and no doubt believed that the poor fellows at Acre were bribed to a man.

It must have been particularly unpleasant to a high-minded nation like the French — at the very moment when the Egyptian affair and the balance of Europe had been settled in this abrupt way — to find out all of a sudden that the Pacha of Egypt was their dearest friend and ally. They had suffered in the person of their friend; and though, seeing that the dispute was ended, and the territory out of his hand, they could not hope to get it back for him, or to aid him in any substantial way, yet Monsieur Thiers determined, just as a mark of politeness to the Pasha, to fight all Europe for maltreating him, — all Europe, England included. He was bent on war, and an immense majority of the nation went with him. He called for a million of soldiers, and would have had them too, had not the King been against the project and delayed the completion of it at least for a time.

Of these great European disputes Captain Joinville received a notification while he was at sea on board his frigate: as we find by the official account which has been published of his mission.

"Some days after quitting Saint Helena," says that document, "the expedition fell in with a ship coming from Europe, and was thus made acquainted with the warlike rumors then afloat, by which a collision with the English marine was rendered possible. The Prince de Joinville immediately assembled the officers of the 'Belle Poule,' to deliberate on an event so unexpected and important.

"The council of war having expressed its opinion that it was necessary at all events to prepare for an energetic defence, preparations were made to place in battery all the guns that the frigate could bring to bear against the enemy. The provisional cabins that had been fitted up in the battery were demolished, the partitions removed, and, with all the elegant furniture of the cabins, flung into the sea. The Prince de Joinville was the first 'to execute himself,' and the frigate soon found itself armed with six or eight more guns.

"That part of the ship where these cabins had previously been, went by the name of Lacedæmon; every thing luxurious being banished to make way for what was useful.

"Indeed, all persons who were on board agree in saying that Monseigneur the Prince de Joinville most worthily acquitted himself of the great and honorable mission which had been confided to him. All affirm not only that the commandant of the expedition did every thing at St. Helena which as a Frenchman he was bound to do in order that the remains of the Emperor should receive all the honors due to them, but moreover that he accomplished his mission with all the measured solemnity, all the pious and severe dignity, that the son of the Emperor himself would have shown upon a like occasion. The commandant had also comprehended that the remains of the Emperor must never fall into the hands of the stranger, and being himself decided rather to sink his ship than to give up his precious deposit, he had inspired every one about him with the same energetic resolution that he had himself taken '*against an extreme eventuality*.'"

Monseigneur, my dear, is really one of the finest young fellows it is possible to see. A tall, broad-chested, slim-waisted, brown-faced, dark-eyed young prince, with a great beard (and other martial qualities no doubt) beyond his years. As he strode into the Chapel of the Invalides on Tuesday at the head of his men, he made no small impression, I can tell you, upon the ladies assembled to witness the ceremony. Nor are the crew of the "Belle Poule" less agreeable to look at than their commander. A more clean, smart, active, well-limbed set of lads never "did dance" upon the deck of the famed "Belle Poule" in the days of her memorable combat with the "Saucy Arethusa." "These five hundred sailors," says a French newspaper, speaking of them in the proper French way, "sword in hand, in the severe costume of board-ship (*la sevère tenue du bord*), seemed proud of the mission that they had just accomplished. Their blue jackets, their red cravats, the turned-down collars of blue shirts edged with white, *above all* their resolute appearance and martial air, gave a favorable specimen of the present state of our marine — a marine of which so much might be expected and from which so little has been required." — *Le Commerce:* 16th December.

There they were, sure enough; a cutlass upon one hip, a pistol on the other — a gallant set of young men indeed. I doubt, to be sure, whether the *sevère tenue du bord* requires that the seaman should be always furnished with these ferocious weapons, which in sundry maritime manœuvres, such as going to sleep in your hammock for instance, or twinkling a binnacle, or luffing a marlinspike, or keelhauling a maintopgallant (all naval operations, my dear, which any seafaring novelist will explain to you) — I doubt, I say, whether these weapons are *always* worn by sailors, and have heard that they are commonly, and very sensibly too, locked up until they are wanted. Take another example: suppose artillerymen were incessantly compelled to walk about with a pyramid of twenty-four-pound shot in one pocket, a lighted fuse and a few barrels of gunpowder in the other — these objects would, as you may imagine, greatly inconvenience the artilleryman in his peaceful state.

The newspaper writer is therefore most likely mistaken in saying that the seamen were in the *sevère tenue du bord*, or by "*bord*" meaning "*abordage*," — which operation they were not, in a harmless church hung round with velvet and wax-candles, and filled with ladies, surely called upon to perform. Nor, indeed, can it be reasonably supposed that the picked men of the crack frigate of the French navy are a "good specimen" of the rest of the French marine, any more than a cuirassed colossus at the gate of the Horse Guards can be considered a fair sample of the British soldier of the line. The sword and pistol, however, had no doubt their effect — the former was in its sheath, the latter not loaded, and I hear that the French ladies are quite in raptures with these charming *loups-de-mer*.

Let the warlike accoutrements then pass. It was necessary, perhaps, to strike the Parisians with awe, and therefore the crew were armed in this fierce fashion; but why should the Captain begin to swagger as well as his men? and why did the Prince de Joinville lug out sword and pistol so early? or why, if he thought fit to make preparations, should the official journals brag of them afterwards as proofs of his extraordinary courage?

Here is the case. The English Government makes him a present of the bones of Napoleon: English workmen work for nine hours without ceasing, and dig the coffin out of the ground: the English Commissioner hands over the key of the box to the French representative, Monsieur Chabot: English horses carry the funeral-car down to the sea-shore, accompanied by the English Governor, who has actually left his bed to walk in the procession and to do the French nation honor.

After receiving and acknowledging these politenesses, the French captain takes his charge on board, and the first thing we afterwards hear of him is the determination "*qu'il a su faire passer*" into all his crew, to sink rather than yield up the body of the Emperor *aux mains de l'étranger* — into the hand of the foreigner. My dear Monseigneur, is not this *par trop fort?* Suppose "the foreigner" had wanted the coffin, could he not have kept it? Why show this uncalled-for valor, this extraordinary alacrity at sinking? Sink or blow yourself up as much as you please, but your Royal Highness must see that the genteel thing would have been to wait until you were asked to do so, before you offended good-natured, honest people, who—heaven help them!—have never shown themselves at all murderously inclined towards you. A man knocks up his cabins forsooth, throws his tables and chairs overboard, runs guns into the portholes, and calls *le quartier du bord où existaient ces chambres, Lacedæmon.* Lacedæmon! There is a province, O Prince, in your royal father's dominions, a fruitful parent of heroes in its time which would have given a much better nickname to your *quartier du bord:* you should have called it Gascony.

> "Sooner than strike we'll all ex-pi-er
> On board of the Bell-e Pou-le."

Such fanfaronnading is very well on the part of Tom Dibdin, but a person of your Royal Highness's "pious and severe dignity" should have been above it. If you entertained an idea that war was imminent, would it not have been far better to have made your preparations in quiet, and when you found the war-rumor blown over, to have said nothing about what you intended to do? Fie upon such cheap Lacedæmonianism! There is no poltroon in the world but can brag about what he *would* have done: however, to do your Royal Highnesses's nation justice, they brag and fight too.

This narrative, my dear Miss Smith, as you will have remarked, is not a simple tale merely, but is accompanied by many moral and pithy remarks which form its chief value, in the writer's eyes at least, and the above account of the sham Lacedæmon on board the "Belle Poule" has a double-barrelled morality, as I conceive. Besides justly reprehending the French propensity towards braggadocio, it proves very strongly a point on which I am the only statesman in Europe who has strongly insisted. In "The Paris Sketch Book" it was stated that *the French hate us.* They hate us, my dear, profoundly and desperately, and there never was such a hollow humbug in the world as the French alliance. Men get a character for patriotism in France merely by hating England. Directly they go into strong opposition (where, you know, people are always more patriotic than on the ministerial side), they appeal to the people, and have their hold on the people by hating England in common with them. Why? It is a long story, and the hatred may be accounted for by many reasons, both political and social. Any time these eight hundred years this ill-will has been going on, and has been transmitted on the French side from father to son. On the French side, not on ours: we have had no, or few, defeats to complain of, no invasions to make us angry; but you see that to discuss such a period of time would demand a considerable number of pages, and for the present we will avoid the examination of the question.

But they hate us, that is the long and short of it; and you see how this hatred has exploded just now, not upon a serious cause of difference, but upon an argument: for what is the Pacha of Egypt to us or them but a mere abstract opinion? For the same reason the Little-endians in Liliput abhorred the Big-endians; and I beg you to remark how his Royal Highness Prince Ferdinand Mary, upon hearing that this argument was in the course of debate between us, straightway flung his furniture overboard and expressed a preference for sinking his ship rather than yielding it to the *étranger*. Nothing came of this wish of his, to be sure; but the intention is everything. Unlucky circumstances denied him the power, but he had the will.

Well, beyond this disappointment, the Prince de Joinville had nothing to complain of during the voyage, which terminated happily by the arrival of the "Belle Poule" at Cherbourg, on the 30th of November, at five o'clock in the morning. A telegraph made the glad news known at Paris, where the Minister of the Interior, Tanneguy-Duchâtel (you will read the name, Madam, in the old Anglo-French wars), had already made "immense preparations" for receiving the body of Napoleon.

The entry was fixed for the 15th of December.

On the 8th of December, at Cherbourg, the body was transferred from the "Belle Poule" frigate to the "Normandie" steamer; on which occasion the mayor of Cherbourg deposited in the name of his town, a gold laurel branch upon the coffin — which was saluted by the forts and dikes of the place with ONE THOUSAND GUNS! There was a treat for the inhabitants.

There was on board the steamer a splendid receptacle for the coffin: "a temple with twelve pillars and a dome to cover it from the wet and moisture, surrounded with velvet hangings and silver fringes. At the head was a gold cross, at the foot a gold lamp: other lamps were kept constantly burning within, and vases of burning incense were hung around. An altar, hung with velvet and silver, was at the mizzen-mast of the vessel, *and four silver eagles at each corner of the altar*." It was a compliment at once to Napoleon and — excuse me for saying so, but so the facts are — to Napoleon and to God Almighty.

Three steamers, the "Normandie," the "Véloce," and the "Courrier," formed the expedition from Cherbourg to Havre, at which place they arrived on the evening of the 9th of December, and where the "Véloce" was replaced by the Seine steamer, having in tow one of the state-coasters, which was to fire the salute at the moment when the body was transferred into one of the vessels belonging to the Seine.

The expedition passed Havre the same night, and came to anchor at Val de la Haye on the Seine, three leagues below Rouen.

Here the next morning (10th), it was met by the flotilla of steamboats of the Upper Seine, consisting of the three "Dorades," the three "Etoiles," the "Elbeuvien," the "Parisien," the "Parisienne," and the "Zampa." The Prince de Joinville, and the persons of the expedition, embarked immediately in the flotilla, which arrived the same day at Rouen.

At Rouen, salutes were fired, the National Guard on both sides of the river paid military honors to the body, and over the middle of the suspension-bridge a magnificent cenotaph was erected, decorated with flags, fasces, violet hangings, and the imperial arms. Before the cenotaph the expedition stopped, and the absolution was given by the archbishop and the clergy. After a couple of hours' stay, the expedition proceeded to Pont de l'Arche. On the 11th it reached Vernon, on the 12th Mantes, on the 13th Maisons-sur-Seine.

"Everywhere," says the official account from which the above particulars are borrowed, "the authorities, the National Guard, and the people, flocked to the passage of the flotilla, desirous to render the honors due to his glory, which is the glory of France. In seeing its hero return, the nation seemed to have found its Palladium again,— the sainted relics of victory."

At length, on the 14th, the coffin was transferred from the "Dorade" steamer on board the imperial vessel arrived from Paris. In the evening, the imperial vessel arrived at Courbevoie, which was the last stage of the journey.

Here it was that M. Guizot went to examine the vessel, and was very nearly flung into the Seine, as report goes, by the patriots assembled there. It is now lying on the river, near the Invalides, amidst the drifting ice, whither the people of Paris are flocking out to see it.

The vessel is of a very elegant antique form, and I can give you on the Thames no better idea of it than by requesting you to fancy an immense wherry, of which the stern has been cut straight off, and on which a temple on steps has been elevated. At the figure-head is an immense gold eagle, and at the stern is a little terrace, filled with evergreens and a profusion of banners. Upon pedestals along the sides of the vessel are tripods in which incense was burned, and underneath them are garlands of flowers called here "immortals." Four eagles surmount the temple, and a great scroll or garland, held in their beaks, surrounds it. It is hung with velvet and gold; four gold caryatides support the entry of it; and in the midst, upon a large platform hung with velvet, and bearing the imperial arms, stood the coffin. A steamboat, carrying two hundred musicians playing funereal marches and military symphonies, preceded this magnificent vessel to Courbevoie, where a funereal temple was erected, and "a statue of Notre Dame de Grâce, before which the seamen of the 'Belle Poule' inclined themselves, in order to thank her for having granted them a noble and glorious voyage."

Early on the morning of the 15th December, amidst clouds of incense, and thunder of cannon, and innumerable shouts of people, the coffin was transferred from the barge, and carried by the seamen of the "Belle Poule" to the Imperial Car.

And now, having conducted our hero almost to the gates of Paris, I must tell you what preparations were made in the capital to receive him.

Ten days before the arrival of the body, as you walked across the Deputies' Bridge, or over the Esplanade of the Invalides, you saw on the bridge eight, on the esplanade thirty-two, mysterious boxes erected, wherein a couple of score of sculptors were at work night and day.

In the middle of the Invalid Avenue, there used to stand, on a kind of shabby fountain or pump, a bust of Lafayette, crowned with some dirty wreaths of "immortals," and looking down at the little streamlet which occasionally dribbled below him. The spot of ground was now clear, and Lafayette and the pump had been consigned to some cellar, to make way for the mighty procession that was to pass over the place of their habitation.

Strange coincidence! If I had been Mr. Victor Hugo, my dear, or a poet of any note, I would, in a few hours, have made an impromptu concerning that Lafayette-crowned pump, and compared its lot now to the fortune of its patron some fifty years back. From him then issued, as from his fountain now, a feeble dribble of pure words; then, as now, some faint circle of disciples were willing to admire him. Certainly in the midst of the war and storm without, this pure fount of eloquence went dribbling, dribbling on, till of a sudden the revolutionary workmen knocked down statue and fountain, and the gorgeous imperial cavalcade trampled over the spot where they stood.

As for the Champs Elysées, there was no end to the preparations: the first day you saw a couple of hundred scaffoldings erected at intervals between the handsome gilded gas-lamps that at present ornament that avenue; next day, all these scaffoldings were filled with brick and mortar. Presently, over the bricks and mortar rose pediments of statues, legs of urns, legs of goddesses, legs and bodies of goddesses, legs, bodies, and busts of goddesses. Finally, on the 13th December, goddesses complete. On the 14th, they were painted marble-color; and the basements of wood and canvas on which they stood were made to resemble the same costly material. The funereal urns were ready to receive the frankincense and precious odors which were to burn in them. A vast number of white columns stretched down the avenue, each bearing a bronze buckler on which was written, in gold letters, one of the victories of the Emperor, and each decorated with enormous imperial flags. On these columns golden eagles were placed; and the newspapers did not fail to remark the ingenious position in which the royal birds had been set: for while those on the right-hand side of the way had their heads turned *towards* the procession, as if to watch its coming, those on the left were looking exactly the other way, as if to regard its progress. Do not fancy I am joking: this point was gravely and emphatically urged in many newspapers; and I do believe no mortal Frenchman ever thought it any thing but sublime.

Do not interrupt me, sweet Miss Smith. I feel that you are angry. I can see from here the pouting of your lips, and know what you are going to say. You are going to say, "I will read no more of this Mr. Titmarsh; there is no subject, however solemn, but he treats it with flippant irreverence, and no character, however great, at whom he does not sneer."

Ah, my dear! you are young now and enthusiastic; and your Titmarsh is old, very old, sad, and gray-headed. I have seen a poor mother buy a halfpenny wreath at the gate of Montmartre burying-ground, and go with it to her little child's grave, and hang it there over the little humble stone; and if ever you saw me scorn the mean offering of the poor shabby creature, I will give you leave to be as angry as you will. They say that on the passage of Napoleon's coffin down the Seine, old soldiers and country people walked miles from their villages just to catch a sight of the boat which carried his body, and to kneel down on the shore and pray for him. God forbid that we should quarrel with such prayers and sorrow, or question their sincerity. Something great and good must have been in this man, something loving and kindly, that has kept his name so cherished in the popular memory, and gained him such lasting reverence and affection.

But, Madam, one may respect the dead without feeling awe-stricken at the plumes of the hearse; and I see no reason why one should sympathize with the train of mutes and undertakers, however deep may be their mourning. Look, I pray you, at the manner in which the French nation has performed Napoleon's funeral. Time out of mind, nations have raised, in memory of their heroes, august mausoleums, grand pyramids, splendid statues of gold or marble, sacrificing whatever they had that was most costly and rare, or that was most beautiful in art, as tokens of their respect and love for the dead person. What a fine example of this sort of sacrifice is that (recorded in a book of which Simplicity is the great characteristic) of the poor woman who brought her pot of precious ointment — her all, and laid it at the feet of the Object which, upon earth, she most loved and respected. "Economists and calculators" there were even in those days who quarrelled with the manner in which the poor woman lavished so much "capital;" but you will remember how nobly and generously the sacrifice was appreciated, and how the economists were put to shame.

With regard to the funeral ceremony that has just been performed here, it is said that a famous public personage and statesman, Monsieur Thiers indeed, spoke with the bitterest indignation of the general style of the preparations, and of their mean and tawdry character. He would have had a pomp as magnificent, he said, as that of Rome at the triumph of Aurelian: he would have decorated the bridges and avenues through which the procession was to pass, with the costliest marbles and the finest works of art, and have had them to remain there forever as monuments of the great funeral.

The economists and calculators might here interpose with a great deal of reason; for, indeed, there was no reason why a nation should impoverish itself to do honor to the memory of an individual for whom, after all, it can feel but a qualified enthusiasm: but it surely might have employed the large sum voted for the purpose more wisely and generously, and recorded its respect for Napoleon by some worthy and lasting memorial, rather than have erected yonder thousand vain heaps of tinsel, paint, and plaster, that are already cracking and crumbling in the frost, at three days old.

Scarcely one of the statues, indeed, deserves to last a month: some are odious distortions and caricatures, which never should have been allowed to stand for a moment. On the very day of the fête, the wind was shaking the canvas pedestals, and the flimsy wood-work had begun to gape and give way. At a little distance, to be sure, you could not see the cracks; and pedestals and statutes *looked* like marble. At some distance you could not tell but that the wreaths and eagles were gold embroidery, and not gilt paper — the great tricolor flags damask, and not striped calico. One would think that these sham splendors betokened sham respect, if one had not known that the name of Napoleon is held in real reverence, and observed somewhat of the character of the nation. Real feelings they have, but they distort them by exaggeration; real courage, which they render ludicrous by intolerable braggadocio; and I think the above official account of the Prince de Joinville's proceedings, of the manner in which the Emperor's remains have been treated in their voyage to the capital, and of the preparations made to receive him in it, will give my dear Miss Smith some means of understanding the social and moral condition of this worthy people of France.

III.

ON THE FUNERAL CEREMONY.

SHALL I tell you, my dear, that when François woke me at a very early hour on this eventful morning, while the keen stars were still glittering overheard, a half-moon, as sharp as a razor, beaming in the frosty sky, and a wicked north wind blowing, that blew the blood out of one's fingers and froze your leg as you put it out of bed; — shall I tell you, my dear, that when François called me, and said, "V'là vot' café, Monsieur Titemasse, buvez-le, tiens, il est tout chaud," I felt myself, after imbibing the hot breakfast, so comfortable under three blankets and a mackintosh, that for at least a quarter of an hour no man in Europe could say whether Titmarsh would or would not be present at the burial of the Emperor Napoleon.

Besides, my dear, the cold, there was another reason for doubting. Did the French nation, or did they not, intend to offer up some of us English over the imperial grave? And were the games to be concluded by a massacre? It was said in the newspapers that Lord Granville had despatched circulars to all the English resident in Paris, begging them to keep their homes. The French journals announced this news, and warned us charitably of the fate intended for us. Had Lord Granville written? Certainly not to me. Or had he written to all *except me?* And was I *the victim* — the doomed one? — to be seized directly I showed my face in the Champs Elysées, and torn in pieces by French Patriotism to the frantic chorus of the "Marseillaise"? Depend on it, Madam, that high and low in this city on Tuesday were not altogether at their ease, and that the bravest felt no small tremor! And be sure of this, that, as his Majesty Louis Philippe took his night-cap off his royal head that morning, he prayed heartily that he might, at night, put it on in safety.

Well, as my companion and I came out of doors, being bound for the Church of the Invalides, for which a Deputy had kindly furnished us with tickets, we saw the very prettiest sight of the whole day, and I can't refrain from mentioning it to my dear, tender-hearted Miss Smith.

In the same house where I live (but about five stories nearer the ground), lodges an English family, consisting of — 1. A great-grandmother, a hale, handsome old lady of seventy, the very best dressed and neatest old lady in Paris. 2. A grandfather and grandmother, tolerably young to bear that title. 3. A daughter. And 4. Two little great-grand, or grand-children, that may be of the age of three and one, and belong to a son and daughter who are in India. The grandfather, who is as proud of his wife as he was thirty years ago when he married, and pays her compliments still twice or thrice in a day, and when he leads her into a room looks round at the persons assembled, and says in his heart, "Here, gentlemen, here is my wife — show me such another woman in England," — this gentleman had hired a room on the Champs Elysées, for he would not have his wife catch cold by exposing her to the balconies in the open air.

When I came to the street, I found the family assembled in the following order of march: —

— No. 1, the great-grandmother walking daintily along, supported by No. 3, her grand-daughter.

— A nurse carrying No. 4 junior, who was sound asleep: and a huge basket containing saucepans, bottles of milk, parcels of infants' food, certain dimity napkins, a child's coral, and a little horse belonging to No. 4 senior.

— A servant bearing a basket of condiments.

— No. 2, grandfather, spick and span, clean shaved, hat brushed, white buckskin gloves, bamboo cane, brown great-coat, walking as upright and solemn as may be, having his lady on his arm.

— No. 4, senior, with mottled legs and a tartan costume, who was frisking about between his grandpapa's legs, who heartily wished him at home.

"My dear," his face seemed to say to his lady, "I think you might have left the little things in the nursery, for we shall have to squeeze through a terrible crowd in the Champs Elysées."

The lady was going out for a day's pleasure, and her face was full of care: she had to look first after her old mother, who was walking ahead, then after No. 4 junior with the nurse — he might fall into all sorts of danger, wake up, cry, catch cold; nurse might slip down, or heaven knows what. Then she had to look her husband in the face, who had gone to such expense, and been so kind for her sake, and make that gentleman believe she was thoroughly happy; and, finally, she had to keep an eye upon No. 4 senior, who, as she was perfectly certain, was about in two minutes to be lost forever, or trampled to pieces in the crowd.

These events took place in a quiet little street leading into the Champs Elysées, the entry of which we had almost reached by this time. The four detachments above described, which had been straggling a little in their passage down the street, closed up at the end of it, and stood for a moment huddled together. No. 3, Miss X——, began speaking to her companion the great-grandmother.

"Hush, my dear," said that old lady, looking round alarmed at her daughter. "*Speak French.*" And she straightway began nervously to make a speech which she supposed to be in the language, but which was as much like French as Iroquois. The whole secret was out: you could read it in the grandmother's face, who was do ing all she could to keep from crying, and looked as frightened as she dared to look. The two elder ladies had settled between them that there was going to be a general English slaughter that day, and had brought the children with them, so that they might all be murdered in company.

God bless you, O women, moist-eyed and tender-hearted! In those gentle silly tears of yours there is something touches one, be they never so foolish. I don't think there were many such natural drops shed that day as those which just made their appearance in the grandmother's eyes, and then went back again as if they had been ashamed of themselves, while the good lady and her little troop walked across the road. Think how happy she will be when night comes, and there has been no murder of English, and the brood is all nestled under her wings sound asleep, and she is lying awake thanking God that the day and its pleasures and pains are over. Whilst we were considering these things, the grandfather had suddenly elevated No. 4 senior upon his left shoulder, and I saw the tartan hat of that young gentleman, and the bamboo-cane which had been transferred to him, high over the heads of the crowd on the opposite side through which the party moved.

After this little procession had passed away — you may laugh at it, but upon my word and conscience, Miss Smith, I saw nothing in the course of the day which affected me more — after this little procession had passed away, the other came, accompanied by gun-banging, flag-waving, incense-burning, trumpets pealing, drums rolling, and at the close, received by the voice of six hundred choristers, sweetly modulated to the tones of fifteen score of fiddlers. Then you saw horse and foot, jackboots and bearskin, cuirass and bayonet, national guard and line, marshals and generals all over gold, smart aides-de-camp galloping about like mad, and high in the midst of all, riding on his golden buckler, Solomon in all his glory, forsooth — Imperial Cæsar, with his crown over his head, laurels and standards waving about his gorgeous chariot, and a million of people looking on in wonder and awe.

His Majesty the Emperor and King reclined on his shield, with his head a little elevated. His Majesty's skull is voluminous, his forehead broad and large. We remarked that his Imperial Majesty's brow was of a yellowish color, which appearance was also visible about the orbits of the eyes. He kept his eyelids constantly closed, by which we had the opportunity of observing that the upper lids were garnished with eyelashes. Years and climate have effected upon the face of this great monarch only a trifling alteration; we may say, indeed, that Time has touched his Imperial and Royal Majesty with the lightest feather in his wing. In the nose of the Conqueror of Austerlitz we remarked very little alteration: it is of the beautiful shape which we remember it possessed five and twenty years since, ere unfortunate circumstances induced him to leave us for a while. The nostril and the tube of the nose appear to have undergone some slight alteration, but in examining a beloved object the eye of affection is perhaps too critical. *Vive l'Empereur!* the soldier of Marengo is among us again. His lips are thinner, perhaps, than they were before! how white his teeth are! you can just see three of them pressing his under-lip; and pray remark the fulness of his cheeks and the round contour of his chin. Oh, those beautiful white hands! many a time have they patted the cheek of poor Josephine, and played with the black ringlets of her hair. She is dead now, and cold, poor creature; and so are Hortense and bold Eugene, "than whom the world never saw a curtier knight," as was said of King Arthur's Sir Lancelot. What a day would it have been for those three could they but have lived until now, and seen their hero returning! Where's Ney? His wife sits looking out from M. Flahaut's window yonder, but the bravest of the brave is not with her. Murat too is absent: honest Joachim loves the Emperor at heart, and repents that he was not at Waterloo: who knows but that at the sight of the handsome swordsman those stubborn English "canaille" would have given way? A king, Sire, is, you know, the greatest of slaves — State affairs of consequence — his Majesty the King of Naples is detained no doubt. When we last saw the King, however, and his Highness the Prince of Elchingen, they looked to have as good health as ever they had in their lives, and we heard each of them calmly calling out "*Fire!*" as they have done in numberless battles before.

Is it possible? can the Emperor forget? We don't like to break it to him, but has he forgotten all about the farm at Pizzo, and the garden of the Observatory? Yes, truly: there he lies on his golden shield, never stirring, never so much as lifting his eyelids, or opening his lips any wider.

O vanitas vanitatum! Here is our Sovereign in all his glory, and they fired a thousand guns at Cherbourg and never woke him!

However, we are advancing matters by several hours, and you must give just as much credence as you please to the subjoined remarks concerning the Procession, seeing that your humble servant could not possibly be present at it, being bound for the church elsewhere.

Programmes, however, have been published of the affair, and your vivid fancy will not fail to give life to them, and the whole magnificent train will pass before you.

Fancy, then, that the guns are fired at Neuilly: the body landed at daybreak from the funereal barge and transferred to the car; and fancy the car, a huge Juggernaut of a machine, rolling on four wheels of an antique shape, which supported a basement adorned with golden eagles, banners, laurels, and velvet hangings. Above the hangings stand twelve golden statues with raised arms supporting a huge shield, on which the coffin lay. On the coffin was the imperial crown, covered with violet velvet crape, and the whole vast machine was drawn by horses in superb housings, led by valets in the imperial livery.

Fancy at the head of the procession first of all —

The Gendarmerie of the Seine, with their trumpets and Colonel.

The Municipal Guard (horse), with their trumpets, standard, and Colonel.

Two squadrons of the 7th Lancers, with Colonel, standard, and music.

The Commandant of Paris and his Staff.

A battalion of Infantry of the Line, with their flag, sappers, drums, music, and Colonel.

The Municipal Guard (foot), with flag, drums, and Colonel.

The Sapper-pumpers, with ditto.

Then picture to yourself more squadrons of Lancers and Cuirassiers. The General of the Division and his Staff; all officers of all arms employed at Paris, and unattached; the Military School of Saint Cyr, the Polytechnic School, the School of the Etat-Major; and the Professors, and Staff of each. Go on imagining more battalions of Infantry, of Artillery, companies of Engineers, squadrons of Cuirassiers, ditto of the Cavalry, of the National Guard, and the first and second legions of ditto.

Fancy a carriage, containing the Chaplain of the St. Helena expedition, the only clerical gentleman that formed a part of the procession.

Fancy you hear the funereal music, and then figure in your mind's eye —

THE EMPEROR'S CHARGER, that is, Napoleon's own saddle and bridle (when First Consul) upon a white horse. The saddle (which has been kept ever since in the Garde Meuble of the Crown) is of amaranth velvet, embroidered in gold: the holsters and housings are of the same rich material. On them you remark the attributes of War, Commerce, Science, and Art. The bits and stirrups are silver-gilt chased. Over the stirrups, two eagles were placed at the time of the empire. The horse was covered with a violet crape embroidered with golden bees.

After this, came more Soldiers, General Officers, Sub-Officers, Marshals, and what was said to be the prettiest sight almost of the whole, the banners of the eighty-six Departments of France. These are due to the invention of M. Thiers, and were to have been accompanied by federates from each Department. But the Government very wisely mistrusted this and some other projects of Monsieur Thiers; and as for a federation, my dear, *it has been tried.* Next comes—

His Royal Highness the Prince de Joinville.

The 500 sailors of the "Belle Poule" marching in double file on each side of

THE CAR.

[Hush! the enormous crowd thrills as it passes, and only some few voices cry *Vive l'Empereur!* Shining golden in the frosty sun — with hundreds of thousands of eyes upon it, from houses and housetops, from balconies, black, purple, and tricolor, from tops of leafless trees, from behind long lines of glittering bayonets under schakos and bear-skin caps, from behind the Line and the National Guard again, pushing, struggling, heaving, panting, eager, the heads of an enormous multitude stretching out to meet and follow it, amidst long avenues of columns and statues gleaming white, of standards rainbow-colored, of golden eagles, of pale funereal urns, of discharging odors amidst huge volumes of pitch-black smoke,

THE GREAT IMPERIAL CHARIOT

ROLLS MAJESTICALLY ON.

The cords of the pall are held by two Marshals, and Admiral and General Bertrand; who are followed by—

The Prefects of the Seine and Police, &c.

The Mayors of Paris, &c.

The Members of the Old Guard, &c.

A Squadron of Light Dragoons, &c.

Lieutenant-General Schneider, &c.

More cavalry, more infantry, more artillery, more everybody; and as the procession passes, the Line and the National Guard forming line on each side of the road fall in and follow it, until it arrives at the Church of the Invalides, where the last honors are to be paid to it.]

Among the company assembled under the dome of that edifice, the casual observer would not perhaps have remarked a gentleman of the name of Michael Angelo Titmarsh, who nevertheless was there. But as, my dear Miss Smith, the descriptions in this letter, from the words in page 418, line 36 — *the party moved* — up to the words *paid to it,* on this page, have purely emanated from your obedient servant's fancy, and not from his personal observation (for no being on earth, except a newspaper reporter, can be in two places at once), permit me now to communicate to you what little circumstances fell under my own particular view on the day of the 15th of December.

As we came out, the air and the buildings round about were tinged with purple, and the clear sharp half-moon before-mentioned was still in the sky, where it seemed to be lingering as if it would catch a peep of the commencement of the famous procession. The Arc de Triomphe was shining in a keen frosty sunshine, and looking as clean and rosy as if it had just made its toilet. The canvas or pasteboard image of Napoleon, of which only the gilded legs had been erected the night previous, was now visible, body, head, crown, sceptre, and all, and made an imposing show. Long gilt banners were flaunting about, with the imperial cipher and eagle, and the names of the battles and victories glittering in gold. The long avenues of the Champs Elysées had been covered with sand for the convenience of the great procession that was to tramp across it that day. Hundreds of people were marching to and fro, laughing, chattering, singing, gesticulating as happy Frenchmen do. There is no pleasanter sight than a French crowd on the alert for a festival, and nothing more catching than their good-humor. As for the notion which has been put forward by some of the opposition newspapers that the populace were on this occasion unusually solemn or sentimental, it would be paying a bad compliment to the natural gayety of the nation, to say that it was, on the morning at least of the 15th of December, affected in any such absurd way. Itinerant merchants were shouting out lustily their commodities of cigars and brandy, and the weather was so bitter cold, that they could not fail to find plenty of customers. Carpenters and workmen were still making a huge banging and clattering among the sheds which were built for the accommodation of the visitors. Some of these sheds were hung with black, such as one sees before churches in funerals; some were robed in violet, in compliment to the Emperor whose mourning they put on. Most of them had fine tricolor hangings with appropriate inscriptions to the glory of the French arms.

All along the Champs Elysées were urns of plaster-of-Paris destined to contain funereal incense and flames; columns decorated with huge flags of blue, red, and white embroidered with shining crowns, eagles, and N's in gilt paper, and statues of plaster representing Nymphs, Triumphs, Victories, or other female personages, painted in oil so as to represent marble. Real marble could have had no better effect, and the appearance of the whole was lively and picturesque in the extreme. On each pillar was a buckler of the color of bronze, bearing the name and date of a battle in gilt letters: you had to walk through a mile-long avenue of these glorious reminiscences, telling of spots where, in the great imperial days, throats had been victoriously cut.

As we passed down the avenue, several troops of soldiers met us: the *garde-municipale à cheval*, in brass helmets and shining jack-boots, noble-looking men, large, on large horses, the pick of the old army, as I have heard, and armed for the special occupation of peace-keeping: not the most glorious, but the best part of the soldier's duty, as I fancy. Then came a regiment of Carabineers, one of Infantry — little, alert, brown-faced, good-humored men, their band at their head playing sounding marches. These were followed by a regiment or detachment of the Municipals on foot — two or three inches taller than the men of the Line, and conspicuous for their neatness and discipline. By and by came a squadron or so of dragoons of the National Guards: they are covered with straps, buckles, aiguillettes, and cartouche-boxes, and made under their tricolor cock's plumes a show sufficiently war-like. The point which chiefly struck me on beholding these military men of the National Guard and the Line, was the admirable manner in which they bore a cold that seemed to me as sharp as the weather in the Russian retreat, through which cold the troops were trotting without trembling and in the utmost cheerfulness and good-humor. An aide-de-camp galloped past in white pantaloons. By heavens! it made me shudder to look at him.

With this profound reflection, we turned away to the right, towards the hanging-bridge (where we met a detachment of young men of the École de l'État Major, fine-looking lads, but sadly disfigured by the wearing of stays or belts, that make the waists of the French dandies of a most absurd tenuity), and speedily passed into the avenue of statues leading up to the Invalides. All these were statues of warriors from Ney to Charlemagne, modelled in clay for the nonce, and placed here to meet the corpse of the greatest warrior of all. Passing these, we had to walk to a little door at the back of the Invalides, where was a crowd of persons plunged in the deepest mourning, and pushing for places in the chapel within.

The chapel is spacious, and of no great architectural pretensions, but was on this occasion gorgeously decorated in honor of the great person to whose body it was about to give shelter.

We had arrived at nine: the ceremony was not to begin, they said, till two: we had five hours before us to see all that from our places could be seen.

We saw that the roof, up to the first lines of architecture, was hung with violet; beyond this with black. We saw N's, eagles, bees, laurel-wreaths, and other such imperial emblems, adorning every nook and corner of the edifice. Between the arches, on each side of the aisle, were painted trophies, on which were written the names of some of Napoleon's Generals and of their principal deeds of arms — and not their deeds of arms alone, *pardi*, but their coats of arms too. O stars and garters! but this is too much. What was Ney's paternal coat, prithee, or honest Junot's quarterings, or the venerable escutcheon of King Joachim's father, the innkeeper?

You and I, dear Miss Smith, know the exact value of heraldic bearings. We know that though the greatest pleasure of all is to *act* like a gentleman, it is a pleasure, nay a merit, to *be* one — to come of an old stock, to have an honorable pedigree, to be able to say that centuries back our fathers had gentle blood, and to us transmitted the same. There *is* a good in gentility: the man who questions it is envious, or a coarse dullard not able to perceive the difference between high breeding and low. One has in the same way heard a man brag that he did not know the difference between wines, not he — give him a good glass of port, and he would pitch all your claret to the deuce. My love, men often brag about their own dulness in this way.

In the matter of gentlemen, democrats cry, "Psha! Give us one of Nature's gentlemen, and hang your aristocrats." And so indeed Nature does make *some* gentlemen — a few here and there. But Art makes most. Good birth, that is, good handsome well-formed fathers and mothers, nice cleanly nursery-maids, good meals, good physicians, good education, few cares, pleasant, easy habits of life, and luxuries not too great or enervating, but only refining — a course of these going on for a few generations are the best gentlemen-makers in the world, and beat Nature hollow.

If, respected Madam, you say, that there is something *better* than gentility in this wicked world, and that honesty and personal worth are more valuable than all the politeness and high-breeding that ever wore red-heeled pumps, knights' spurs, or Hoby's boots, Titmarsh for one is never going to say you nay. If you even go so far as to say that the very existence of this super-genteel society among us, from the slavish respect that we pay to it, from the dastardly manner in which we attempt to imitate its airs and ape its vices, goes far to destroy honesty of intercourse, to make us meanly ashamed of our natural affections, and honest, harmless usages, and so does a great deal more harm than it is possible it can do good by its example — perhaps, Madam, you speak with some sort of reason. Potato myself, I can't help seeing that the tulip yonder has the best place in the garden, and the most sunshine, and the most water, and the best tending — and not liking him over well. But I can't help acknowledging that Nature has given him a much finer dress than ever I can hope to have, and of this, at least, must give him the benefit.

Or say, we are so many cocks and hens, my dear (*sans arrière pensée*), with our crops pretty full, our plumes pretty sleek, decent picking here and there in the straw-yard, and tolerable snug roosting in the barn: yonder on the terrace, in the sun, walks Peacock, stretching his proud neck, squealing every now and then in the most pert fashionable voice, and flaunting his great supercilious dandified tail. Don't let us be too angry, my dear, with the useless, haughty, insolent creature, because he despises us. *Something* is there about Peacock that we don't possess. Strain your neck ever so, you can't make it as long or as blue as his — cock your tail as much as you please, and it will never be half so fine to look at. But the most absurd, disgusting, contemptible sight in the world would you and I be, leaving the barn-door for my lady's flower-garden, forsaking our natural sturdy walk for the peacock's genteel rickety stride, and adopting the squeak of his voice in the place of our gallant lusty cock-a-doodle-dooing.

Do you take the allegory? I love to speak in such, and the above types have been presented to my mind while sitting opposite a gimcrack coat-of-arms and coronet that are painted in the Invalides Church, and assigned to one of the Emperor's Generals.

Ventrebleu! Madam, what need have *they* of coats-of-arms and coronets, and wretched imitations of old exploded aristocratic gewgaws that they had flung out of the country — with the heads of the owners in them sometimes, for indeed they were not particular — a score of years before? What business, forsooth, had they to be meddling with gentility, and aping its ways, who had courage, merit, daring, genius sometimes, and a pride of their own to support, if proud they were inclined to be? A clever young man (who was not of high family himself, but had been bred up genteelly at Eton and the university) — young Mr. George Canning, at the commencement of the French Revolution, sneered at "Roland the Just, with ribbons in his shoes," and the dandies, who then wore buckles, voted the sarcasm monstrous killing. It was a joke, my dear, worthy of a lackey, or of a silly smart parvenu, not knowing the society into which his luck had cast him (God help him! in later years, they taught him what they were!), and fancying in his silly intoxication that simplicity was ludicrous and fashion respectable. See, now, fifty years are gone, and where are shoebuckles? Extinct, defunct, kicked into the irrevocable past off the toes of all Europe!

How fatal to the parvenu, throughout history, has been this respect for shoebuckles. Where, for instance, would the Empire of Napoleon have been, if Ney and Lannes had never sported such a thing as a coat-of-arms, and had only written their simple names on their shields, after the fashion of Desaix's scutcheon yonder? — the bold Republican who led the crowning charge at Marengo, and sent the best blood of the Holy Roman Empire to the right-about, before the wretched, misbegotten, imperial heraldry was born, that was to prove so disastrous to the father of it. It has always been so. They won't amalgamate. A country must be governed by the one principle or the other. But give, in a republic, an aristocracy ever so little chance, and it works and plots and sneaks and bullies and sneers itself into place, and you find democracy out of doors. Is it good that the aristocracy should so triumph? — that is a question that you may settle according to your own notions and tastes; and permit me to say, I do not care twopence how you settle it. Large books have been written upon the subject in a variety of languages, and coming to a variety of conclusions. Great statesmen are there in our country, from Lord Londonderry down to Mr. Vincent, each in his degree maintaining his different opinion. But here, in the matter of Napoleon, is a simple fact: he founded a great, glorious, strong, potent republic, able to cope with the best aristocracies in the world, and perhaps to beat them all; he converts his republic into a monarchy, and surrounds his monarchy with what he calls aristocratic institutions; and you know what becomes of him. The people estranged, the aristocracy faithless (when did they ever pardon one who was not of themselves?) — the imperial fabric tumbles to the ground. If it teaches nothing else, my dear, it teaches one a great point of policy, — namely, to stick by one's party.

While these thoughts (and sundry others relative to the horrible cold of the place, the intense dulness of delay, the stupidity of leaving a warm bed and a breakfast in order to witness a procession that is much better performed at a theatre) — while these thoughts were passing in the mind, the church began to fill apace, and you saw that the hour of the ceremony was drawing near.

Imprimis, came men with lighted staves, and set fire to at least ten thousand wax-candles that were hanging in brilliant chandeliers, in various parts of the chapel. Curtains were dropped over the upper windows as these illuminations were effected, and the church was left only to the funereal light of the spermaceti. To the right was the dome, round the cavity of which sparkling lamps were set, that designed the shape of it brilliantly against the darkness. In the midst, and where the altar used to stand, rose the catafalque. And why not? Who is God here but Napoleon? and in him the sceptics have already ceased to believe; but the people does still somewhat. He and Louis XIV. divide the worship of the place between them.

As for the catafalque, the best that I can say for it is that it is really a noble and imposing-looking edifice, with tall pillars supporting a grand dome, with innumerable escutcheons, standards, and allusions military and funereal. A great eagle of course tops the whole: tripods burning spirits of wine stand round this kind of dead man's throne, and as we saw it (by peering over the heads of our neighbors in the front rank), it looked, in the midst of the black concave, and under the effect of half a thousand flashing cross-lights, properly grand and tall. The effect of the whole chapel, however (to speak the jargon of the painting-room), was spoiled by being *cut up:* there were too many objects for the eye to rest upon: the ten thousand wax-candles, for instance, in their numberless twinkling chandeliers, the raw *tranchant* colors of the new banners, wreaths, bees, N's, and other emblems dotting the place all over, and incessantly puzzling, or rather *bothering* the beholder.

High overhead, in a sort of mist, with the glare of their original colors worn down by dust and time, hung long rows of dim ghostly-looking standards, captured in old days from the enemy. They were, I thought, the best and most solemn part of the show.

To suppose that the people were bound to be solemn during the ceremony is to exact from them something quite needless and unnatural. The very fact of a squeeze dissipates all solemnity. One great crowd is always, as I imagine, pretty much like another. In the course of the last few years I have seen three: that attending the coronation of our present sovereign, that which went to see Courvoisier hanged, and this which witnessed the Napoleon ceremony. The people so assembled for hours together are jocular rather than solemn, seeking to pass away the weary time with the best amusements that will offer. There was, to be sure, in all the scenes above alluded to, just one moment — one particular moment — when the universal people feels a shock and is for that second serious.

But, except for that second of time, I declare I saw no seriousness here beyond that of ennui. The church began to fill with personages of all ranks and conditions. First, opposite our seats came a company of fat grenadiers of the National Guard, who presently, at the word of command, put their muskets down against benches and wainscots, until the arrival of the procession. For seven hours these men formed the object of the most anxious solicitude of all the ladies and gentlemen seated on our benches: they began to stamp their feet, for the cold was atrocious, and we were frozen where we sat. Some of them fell to blowing their fingers; one executed a kind of dance, such as one sees often here in cold weather — the individual jumps repeatedly upon one leg, and kicks out the other violently, meanwhile his hands are flapping across his chest. Some fellows opened their cartouche-boxes, and from them drew eatables of various kinds. You can't think how anxious we were to know the qualities of the same. "Tiens, ce gros qui mange une cuisse de volaille!" — "Il a du jambon, celui-là." "I should like some, too," growls an Englishman, "for I hadn't a morsel of breakfast," and so on. This is the way, my dear, that we see Napoleon buried.

Did you ever see a chicken escape from clown in a pantomime, and hop over into the pit, or amongst the fiddlers? and have you not seen the shrieks of enthusiastic laughter that the wondrous incident occasions? We had our chicken, of course: there never was a public crowd without one. A poor, unhappy woman in a greasy plaid cloak, with a battered rose-colored, plush bonnet, was seen taking her place among the stalls allotted to the grandees. "Voyez donc l'Anglaise," said everybody, and it was too true. You could swear the wretch was an Englishwoman: a bonnet was never made or worn so in any other country. Half an hour's delightful amusement did this lady give us all. She was whisked from seat to seat by the *huissiers*, and at every change of place woke a peal of laughter. I was glad, however, at the end of the day to see the old pink bonnet over a very comfortable seat, which somebody had not claimed and she had kept.

Are not these remarkable incidents? The next wonder we saw was the arrival of a set of tottering old Invalids, who took their places under us with drawn sabres. Then came a superb drum-major, a handsome, smiling, good-humored giant of a man, his breeches astonishingly embroidered with silver lace. Him a dozen little drummer-boys followed — "the little darlings!" all the ladies cried out in a breath: they were indeed pretty little fellows, and came and stood close under us: the huge drum-major smiled over his little red-capped flock, and for many hours in the most perfect contentment twiddled his mustaches and played with the tassels of his cane.

Now the company began to arrive thicker and thicker. A whole covey of *Conseillers-d'État* came in, in blue coats, embroidered with blue silk, then came a crowd of lawyers in toques and caps, among whom were sundry venerable Judges in scarlet, purple velvet, and ermine — a kind of Bajazet costume. Look there! there is the Turkish Ambassador in his red cap, turning his solemn brown face about, and looking preternaturally wise. The Deputies walk in in a body. Guizot is not there: he passed by just now in full ministerial costume. Presently little Thiers saunters back: what a clear, broad, sharp-eyed face the fellow has, with his gray hair cut down so demure! A servant passes, pushing through the crowd a shabby wheel-chair. It has just brought old Moncey the Governor of the Invalids, the honest old man who defended Paris so stoutly in 1814. He has been very ill, and is worn down almost by infirmities: but in his illness he was perpetually asking, "Doctor, shall I live till the 15th? Give me till then, and I die contented." One can't help believing that the old man's wish is honest, however one may doubt the piety of another illustrious Marshal, who once carried a candle before Charles X. in a procession, and has been this morning to Neuilly to kneel and pray at the foot of Napoleon's coffin. He might have said his prayers at home, to be sure; but don't let us ask too much: that kind of reserve is not a Frenchman's characteristic.

Bang — bang! At about half-past two a dull sound of cannonading was heard without the church, and signals took place between the Commandant of the Invalids, of the National Guards, and the big drum-major. Looking to these troops (the fat Nationals were shuffling into line again), the two Commandants uttered, as nearly as I could catch them, the following words: —

"Harrum Hump!"

At once all the National bayonets were on the present, and the sabres of the old Invalids up. The big drum-major looked round at the children, who began very slowly and solemnly on their drums, Rub-dub-dub — rub-dub-dub — (count two between each) — rub-dub-dub, and a great procession of priests came down from the altar.

First, there was a tall handsome cross-bearer, bearing a long gold cross, of which the front was turned towards his grace the Archbishop. Then came a double row of about sixteen incense-boys, dressed in white surplices: the first boy, about six years old, the last with whiskers, and of the height of a man. Then followed a regiment of priests in black tippets and white gowns: they had black hoods, like the moon when she is at her third quarter, wherewith those who were bald (many were, and fat too) covered themselves. All the reverend men held their heads meekly down, and affected to be reading in their breviaries.

After the Priests came some Bishops of the neighboring districts, in purple, with crosses sparkling on their episcopal bosoms.

Then came, after more priests, a set of men whom I have never seen before — a kind of ghostly heralds, young and handsome men, some of them in stiff tabards of black and silver, their eyes to the ground, their hands placed at right angles with their chests.

Then came two gentlemen bearing remarkable tall candlesticks, with candles of corresponding size. One was burning brightly, but the wind (that chartered libertine) had blown out the other, which nevertheless kept its place in the procession — I wondered to myself whether the reverend gentleman who carried the extinguished candle felt disgusted, humiliated, mortified — perfectly conscious that the eyes of many thousands of people were bent upon that bit of refractory wax. We all of us looked at it with intense interest.

Another cross-bearer, behind whom came a gentleman carrying an instrument like a bed-room candlestick.

His Grandeur Monseigneur Affre, Archbishop of Paris: he was in black and white, his eyes were cast to the earth, his hands were together at right angles from his chest: on his hands were black gloves, and on the black gloves sparkled the sacred episcopal — what do I say? — archiepiscopal ring. On his head was the mitre. It is unlike the godly coronet that figures upon the coach-panels of our own Right Reverend Bench. The Archbishop's mitre may be about a yard high: formed within probably of consecrated pasteboard, it is without covered by a sort of watered silk of white and silver. On the two peaks at the top of the mitre are two very little spangled tassels, that frisk and twinkle about in a very agreeable manner.

Monseigneur stood opposite to us for some time, when I had the opportunity to note the above remarkable phenomena. He stood opposite me for some time, keeping his eyes steadily on the ground, his hands before him, a small clerical train following after. Why didn't they move? There was the National Guard keeping on presenting arms, the little drummers going on rub-dub-dub — rub-dub-dub — in the same steady, slow way, and the Procession never moved an inch. There was evidently, to use an elegant phrase, a hitch somewhere.

[*Enter a fat priest, who bustles up to the drum-major.*]

Fat priest — "Taisez-vous."

Little drummer — Rub-dub-dub — rub-dub-dub, — rub-dub-dub, &c.

Drum major — "Qu'est-ce donc?"

Fat priest — 'Taisez-vous, vous dis-je; ce n'est pas le corps. Il n'arrivera pas — pour une heure."

The little drums were instantly hushed, the procession turned to the right about, and walked back to the altar again, the blown-out candle that had been on the near side of us before was now on the off side, the National Guards set down their muskets and began at their sandwiches again. We had to wait an hour and a half at least before the great procession arrived. The guns without went on booming all the while at intervals, and as we heard each, the audience gave a kind of "*ahahah!*" such as you hear when the rockets go up at Vauxhall.

At last the real Procession came.

Then the drums began to beat as formerly, the Nationals to get under arms, the clergymen were sent for and went, and presently — yes, there was the tall cross-bearer at the head of the procession, and they came *back!*

They chanted something in a weak, snuffling, lugubrious manner, to the melancholy bray of a serpent.

Crash! however, Mr. Habeneck and the fiddlers in the organ-loft pealed out a wild shrill march, which stopped the reverend gentlemen, and in the midst of this music —

And of a great trampling of feet and clattering,

And of a great crowd of Generals and Officers in fine clothes,

With the Prince de Joinville marching quickly at the head of the procession,

And while everybody's heart was thumping as hard as possible,

NAPOLEON'S COFFIN PASSED.

It was done in an instant. A box covered with a great red cross — a dingy-looking crown lying on the top of it — Seamen on one side and Invalids on the other — they had passed in an instant and were up the aisle.

A faint snuffling sound, as before, was heard from the officiating priests, but we knew of nothing more. It is said that old Louis Philippe was standing at the catafalque, whither the Prince de Joinville advanced and said, "Sire, I bring you the body of the Emperor Napoleon."

Louis Philippe answered, "I receive it in the name of France." Bertrand put on the body the most glorious victorious sword that ever has been forged since the apt descendants of the first murderer learned how to hammer steel; and the coffin was placed in the temple prepared for it.

The six hundred singers and the fiddlers now commenced the playing and singing of a piece of music; and a part of the crew of the "Belle Poule" skipped into the places that had been kept for them under us, and listened to the music, chewing tobacco. While the actors and fiddlers were going on, most of the spirits-of-wine lamps on altars went out.

When we arrived in the open air, we passed through the court of the Invalides, where thousands of people had been assembled, but where the benches were now quite bare. Then we came on to the terrace before the place; the old soldiers were firing off the great guns, which made a dreadful stunning noise, and frightened some of us, who did not care to pass before the cannon and be knocked down even by the wadding. The guns were fired in honor of the King, who was going home by a back door. All the forty thousand people who covered the great stands before the Hôtel had gone away too. The Imperial Barge had been dragged up the river, and was lying lonely along the Quay, examined by some few shivering people on the shore.

It was five o'clock when we reached home: the stars were shining keenly out of the frosty sky, and François told me that dinner was just ready.

In this manner, my dear Miss Smith, the great Napoleon was buried.

Farewell.

LITTLE TRAVELS AND ROADSIDE SKETCHES.

By TITMARSH.

LITTLE TRAVELS AND ROAD-SIDE SKETCHES.

I. — FROM RICHMOND IN SURREY TO BRUSSELS IN BELGIUM.

I QUITTED "The Rose Cottage Hotel" at Richmond, one of the comfortablest, quietest, cheapest, neatest little inns in England, and a thousand times preferable, in my opinion, to "The Star and Garter," whither, if you go alone, a sneering waiter, with his hair curled, frightens you off the premises; and where, if you are bold enough to brave the sneering waiter, you have to pay ten shillings for a bottle of claret; and whence, if you look out of the window, you gaze on a view which is so rich that it seems to knock you down with its splendor — a view that has its hair curled like the swaggering waiter: I say, I quitted "The Rose Cottage Hotel" with deep regret, believing that I should see nothing so pleasant as its gardens, and its veal cutlets, and its dear little bowling-green, elsewhere. But the time comes when people must go out of town, and so I got on the top of the omnibus, and the carpet-bag was put inside.

If I were a great prince, and rode outside of coaches (as I should if I were a great prince), I would, whether I smoked or not, have a case of the best Havannas in my pocket — not for my own smoking, but to give them to the snobs on the coach, who smoke the vilest cheroots. They poison the air with the odor of their filthy weeds. A man at all easy in his circumstances would spare himself much annoyance by taking the above simple precaution.

A gentleman sitting behind me tapped me on the back, and asked for a light. He was a footman, or rather valet. He had no livery, but the three friends who accompanied him were tall men in pepper-and-salt undress jackets, with a duke's coronet on their buttons.

After tapping me on the back, and when he had finished his cheroot, the gentleman produced another wind instrument, which he called a "kinopium," a sort of trumpet, on which he showed a great inclination to play. He began puffing out of the "kinopium" a most abominable air, which he said was "The Duke's March." It was played by particular request of one of the pepper-and-salt gentry.

The noise was so abominable that even the coachman objected (although my friend's brother footmen were ravished with it), and said that it was not allowed to play toons on *his* 'bus. "Very well," said the valet, "*we're only of the Duke of B——'s establishment*, THAT'S ALL." The coachman could not resist that appeal to his fashionable feelings. The valet was allowed to play his infernal kinopium, and the poor fellow (the coachman), who had lived in some private families, was quite anxious to conciliate the footmen "of the Duke of B.'s establishment, that's all," and told several stories of his having been groom in Captain Hoskins's family, *nephew of Governor Hoskins;* which stories the footmen received with great contempt.

The footmen were like the rest of the fashionable world in this respect. I felt for my part that I respected them. They were in daily communication with a duke! They were not the rose, but they had lived beside it. There is an odor in the English aristocracy which intoxicates plebeians. I am sure that any commoner in England, though he would die rather than confess it, would have a respect for those great big hulking Duke's footmen.

The day before, her Grace the Duchess had passed us alone in a chariot-and-four, with two outriders. What better mark of innate superiority could man want? Here was a slim lady who required four — six horses to herself, and four servants (kinopium was, no doubt, one of the number) to guard her.

We were sixteen inside and out, and had consequently an eighth of a horse apiece.

A duchess = 6, a commoner = $\frac{1}{8}$; that is to say,

1 duchess = 48 commoners.

If I were a duchess of the present day, I would say to the duke my noble husband, "My dearest grace, I think, when I travel alone in my chariot from Hammersmith to London, I will not care for the outriders. In these days, when there is so much poverty and so much disaffection in the country, we should not *éclabousser* the *canaille* with the sight of our preposterous prosperity."

But this is very likely only plebeian envy, and I dare say if I were a lovely duchess of the realm, I would ride in a coach-and-six, with a coronet on the top of my bonnet and a robe of velvet and ermine even in the dog-days.

Alas! these are the dog-days. Many dogs are abroad — snarling dogs, biting dogs, envious dogs, mad dogs; beware of exciting the fury of such with your flaming red velvet and dazzling ermine. It makes ragged Lazarus doubly hungry to see Dives feasting in cloth-of-gold; and so if I were a beauteous duchess . . . Silence, vain man! Can the Queen herself make you a duchess? Be content, then, nor gibe at thy betters of "the Duke of B——'s establishment — that's all."

On board "The Antwerpen," off everywhere.

We have bidden adieu to Billingsgate, we have passed the Thames Tunnel; it is one o'clock, and of course people are thinking of being hungry. What a merry place a steamer is on a calm sunny summer forenoon, and what an appetite every one seems to have! We are, I assure you, no less than 170 noblemen and gentlemen together, pacing up and down under the awning, or lolling on the sofas in the cabin, and hardly have we passed Greenwich when the feeding begins. The company was at the brandy and soda-water in an instant (there is a sort of legend that the beverage is a preservative against sea-sickness), and I admired the penetration of gentlemen who partook of the drink. In the first place, the steward *will* put so much brandy into the tumbler that it is fit to choke you; and, secondly, the soda-water, being kept as near as possible to the boiler of the engine, is of a fine wholesome heat when presented to the hot and thirsty traveller. Thus he is prevented from catching any sudden cold which might be dangerous to him.

The forepart of the vessel is crowded to the full as much as the genteeler quarter. There are four carriages, each with piles of imperials and aristocratic gimcracks of travel, under the wheels of which those personages have to clamber who have a mind to look at the bowsprit, and perhaps to smoke a cigar at ease. The carriages overcome, you find yourself confronted by a huge penful of Durham oxen, lying on hay, and surrounded by a barricade of oars. Fifteen of these horned monsters maintain an incessant mooing and bellowing. Beyond the cows come a heap of cotton-bags, beyond the cotton-bags more carriages, more pyramids of travelling trunks, and valets and couriers bustling and swearing round about them. And already, and in various corners and niches, lying on coils of rope, black tar-cloths, ragged cloaks, or hay, you see a score of those dubious fore-cabin passengers, who are never shaved, who always look unhappy, and appear getting ready to be sick.

At one, dinner begins in the after-cabin — boiled salmon, boiled beef, boiled mutton, boiled cabbage, boiled potatoes, and parboiled wine for any gentlemen who like it, and two roast-ducks between seventy. After this, knobs of cheese are handed round on a plate, and there is a talk of a tart somewhere at some end of the table. All this I saw peeping through a sort of meat-safe which ventilates the top of the cabin, and very happy and hot did the people seem below.

"How the deuce *can* people dine at such an hour?" say several genteel fellows who are watching the manœuvres. "I can't touch a morsel before seven."

But somehow at half-past three o'clock we had dropped a long way down the river. The air was delightfully fresh, the sky of a faultless cobalt, the river shining and flashing like quicksilver, and at this period steward runs against me bearing two great smoking dishes covered by two great glistening hemispheres of tin. "Fellow," says I, "what's that?"

He lifted up the cover: it was ducks and green pease, by jingo!

"What! haven't they done *yet* the greedy creatures?" I asked. "Have the people been feeding for three hours?"

"Law, bless you, sir, it's the second dinner. Make haste, or you won't get a place." At which words a genteel party, with whom I had been conversing, instantly tumbled down the hatchway, and I find myself one of the second relay of seventy who are attacking the boiled salmon, boiled beef, boiled cabbage, &c. As for the ducks, I certainly had some pease, very fine yellow stiff pease, that ought to have been split before they were boiled; but, with regard to the ducks, I saw the animals gobbled up before my eyes by an old widow lady and her party just as I was shrieking to the steward to bring a knife and fork to carve them. The fellow! (I mean the widow lady's whiskered companion) — I saw him eat pease with the very knife with which he had dissected the duck!

After dinner (as I need not tell the keen observer of human nature who peruses this) the human mind, if the body be in a decent state, expands into gayety and benevolence, and the intellect longs to measure itself in friendly converse with the divers intelligences around it. We ascend upon deck, and after eying each other for a brief space and with a friendly modest hesitation, we begin anon to converse about the weather and other profound and delightful themes of English discourse. We confide to each other our respective opinions of the ladies round about us. Look at that charming creature in a pink bonnet and a dress of the pattern of a Kilmarnock snuff-box: a stalwart Irish gentleman in a green coat and bushy red whiskers is whispering something very agreeable into her ear, as is the wont of gentlemen of his nation; for her dark eyes kindle, her red lips open and give an opportunity to a dozen beautiful pearly teeth to display themselves, and glance brightly in the sun; while round the teeth and the lips a number of lovely dimples make their appearance, and her whole countenance assumes a look of perfect health and happiness. See her companion in shot silk and a dove-colored parasol; in what a graceful Watteau-like attitude she reclines. The tall courier who has been bouncing about the deck in attendance upon these ladies (it is his first day of service, and he is eager to make a favorable impression on them and the lady's maids too) has just brought them from the carriage a small paper of sweet cakes (nothing is prettier than to see a pretty woman eating sweet biscuits) and a bottle that evidently contains Malmsey madeira. How daintily they sip it; how happy they seem; how that lucky rogue of an Irishman prattles away! Yonder is a noble group indeed: an English gentleman and his family. Children, mother, grandmother, grown-up daughters, father, and domestics, twenty-two in all. They have a table to themselves on the deck, and the consumption of eatables among them is really endless. The nurses have been bustling to and fro, and bringing, first, slices of cake; then dinner; then tea with huge family jugs of milk; and the little people have been playing hide-and-seek round the deck, coquetting with the other children, and making friends of every soul on board. I love to see the kind eyes of women fondly watching them as they gambol about; a female face, be it ever so plain, when occupied in regarding children, becomes celestial almost, and a man can hardly fail to be good and happy while he is looking on at such sights. "Ah, sir!" says a great big man, whom you would not accuse of sentiment, "I have a couple of those little things at home;" and he stops and heaves a great big sigh and swallows down a half tumbler of cold something and water. We know what the honest fellow means well enough. He is saying to himself, "God bless my girls and their mother!" but, being a Briton, is too manly to speak out in a more intelligible way. Perhaps it is as well for him to be quiet, and not chatter and gesticulate like those Frenchmen a few yards from him, who are chirping over a bottle of champagne.

There is, as you may fancy, a number of such groups on the deck, and a pleasant occupation it is for a lonely man to watch them and build theories upon them, and examine those two personages seated cheek by jowl. One is an English youth, travelling for the first time, who has been hard at his Guide-book, during the whole journey. He has a "Manuel du Voyageur" in his pocket: a very pretty, amusing little oblong work it is too, and might be very useful, if the foreign people in three languages, among whom you travel, would but give the answers set down in the book, or understand the questions you put to them out of it. The other honest gentleman in the fur cap, what can his occupation be? We know him at once for what he is. "Sir," says he, in a fine German accent, "I am a brofessor of languages, and will gif you lessons in Danish, Swedish, English, Bortuguese, Spanish, and Bersian." Thus occupied in meditations, the rapid hours and the rapid steamer pass quickly on, The sun is sinking, and, as he drops, the ingenious luminary sets the Thames on fire: several worthy gentlemen, watch in hand, are eagerly examining the phenomena attending his disappearance, — rich clouds of purple and gold, that form the curtains of his bed, —little barks that pass black across his disc, his disc every instant dropping nearer and nearer into the water. "There he goes!" says one sagacious observer. "No, he doesn't," cries another. Now he is gone, and the steward is already threading the deck, asking the passengers, right and left, if they will take a little supper. What a grand object is a sunset, and what a wonder is an appetite at sea! Lo! the horned moon shines pale over Margate, and the red beacon is gleaming from distant Ramsgate pier.

. . . .

A great rush is speedily made for the mattresses that lie in the boat at the ship's side; and as the night is delightfully calm, many fair ladies and worthy men determine to couch on deck for the night. The proceedings of the former, especially if they be young and pretty, the philosopher watches with indescribable emotion and interest. What a number of pretty coquetries do the ladies perform, and into what pretty attitudes do they take care to fall! All the little children have been gathered up by the nursery-maids, and are taken down to roost below. Balmy sleep seals the eyes of many tired wayfarers, as you see in the case of the Russian nobleman asleep among the portmanteaus; and Titmarsh, who has been walking the deck for some time with a great mattress on his shoulders, knowing full well that were he to relinquish it for an instant, some other person would seize on it, now stretches his bed upon the deck, wraps his cloak about his knees, draws his white cotton nightcap tight over his head and ears; and, as the smoke of his cigar rises calmly upwards to the deep sky and the cheerful twinkling stars, he feels himself exquisitely happy, and thinks of thee, my Juliana!

. . . .

Why people, because they are in a steam-boat, should get up so deucedly early I cannot understand. Gentlemen have been walking over my legs ever since three o'clock this morning, and, no doubt, have been indulging in personalities (which I hate) regarding my appearance and manner of sleeping, lying, snoring. Let the wags laugh on; but a far pleasanter occupation is to sleep until breakfast-time, or near it.

The tea, and ham and eggs, which, with a beef-steak or two, and three or four rounds of toast, form the component parts of the above-named elegant meal, are taken in the River Scheldt. Little neat, plump-looking churches and villages are rising here and there among tufts of trees and pastures that are wonderfully green. To the right, as "The Guide Book" says, is Walcheren: and on the left Cadsand, memorable for the English expedition of 1809, when Lord Chatham, Sir Walter Manny, and Henry Earl of Derby, at the head of the English gained a great victory over the Flemish mercenaries in the pay of Philippe of Valois. The cloth-yard shafts of the English archers did great execution. Flushing was taken, and Lord Chatham returned to England, where he distinguished himself greatly in the debates on the American war, which he called the brightest jewel of the British crown. You see, my love, that, though an artist by profession, my education has by no means been neglected; and what, indeed, would be the pleasure of travel, unless these charming historical recollections were brought to bear upon it?

Antwerp.

As many hundreds of thousands of English visit this city (I have met at least a hundred of them in this half-hour walking the streets, "Guide-book" in hand), and as the ubiquitous Murray has already depicted the place, there is no need to enter into a long description of it, its neatness, its beauty, and its stiff antique splendor. The tall pale houses have many of them crimped gables, that look like Queen Elizabeth ruffs. There are as many people in the streets as in London at three o'clock in the morning; the market-women wear bonnets of a flower-pot shape, and have shining brazen milk-pots, which are delightful to the eyes of a painter. Along the quays of the lazy Scheldt are innumerable good-natured groups of beer-drinkers (small-beer is the most good-natured drink in the world); along the barriers outside of the town, and by the glistening canals, are more beer-shops, and more beer-drinkers. The city is defended by the queerest fat military. The chief traffic is between the hotels and the railroad. The hotels give wonderful good dinners, and especially at "The Grand Laboreur" may be mentioned a peculiar tart, which is the best of all tarts that ever a man ate since he was ten years old. A moonlight walk is delightful. At ten o'clock the whole city is quiet; and so little changed does it seem to be, that you may walk back three hundred years into time, and fancy yourself a majestical Spaniard, or an oppressed and patriotic Dutchman at your leisure. You enter the inn, and the old Quentin Durward courtyard, on which the old towers look down. There is a sound of singing — singing at midnight. Is it Don Sombrero, who is singing an Andalusian seguidilla under the window of the Flemish burgomaster's daughter? Ah, no! it is a fat Englishman in a zephyr coat: he is drinking cold gin and water in the moonlight, and warbling softly —

"Nix my dolly, pals, fake away,
N-ix my dolly, pals, fake a—a—way." *

I wish the good people would knock off the top part of Antwerp Cathedral spire. Nothing can be more gracious and elegant than the lines of the first two compartments; but near the top there bulges out a little round, ugly, vulgar Dutch monstrosity (for which the architects have, no doubt, a name) which offends the eye cruelly. Take the Apollo, and set upon him a bob-wig and a little cocked-hat; imagine "God Save the King" ending with a jig; fancy a polonaise, or procession of slim, stately elegant court beauties, headed by a buffoon dancing a hornpipe. Marshal Gérard should have discharged a bomb-shell at that abomination, and have given the noble steeple a chance to be finished in the grand style of the early fifteenth century, in which it was begun.

* In 1844.

This style of criticism is base and mean, and quite contrary to the orders of the immortal Goethe, who was only for allowing the eye to recognize the beauties of a great work, but would have its defects passed over. It is an unhappy, luckless organization which will be perpetually fault-finding, and in the midst of a grand concert of music will persist only in hearing that unfortunate fiddle out of tune.

Within — except where the rococo architects have introduced their ornaments (here is the fiddle out of tune again) — the cathedral is noble. A rich, tender sunshine is streaming in through the windows, and gilding the stately edifice with the purest light. The admirable stained-glass windows are not too brilliant in their colors. The organ is playing a rich, solemn music; some two hundred of people are listening to the service; and there is scarce one of the women kneeling on her chair, enveloped in her full, majestic black drapery, that is not a fine study for a painter. These large black mantles of heavy silk brought over the heads of the women, and covering their persons, fall into such fine folds of drapery, that they cannot help being picturesque and noble. See, kneeling by the side of two of those fine devout-looking figures, is a lady in a little twiddling Parisian hat and feather, in a little lace mantelet, in a tight gown and a bustle. She is almost as monstrous as yonder figure of the Virgin, in a hoop, and with a huge crown and a ball and a sceptre; and a bambino dressed in a little hoop, and in a little crown, round which are clustered flowers and pots of orange-trees, and before which many of the faithful are at prayer. Gentle clouds of incense come wafting through the vast edifice; and in the lulls of the music you hear the faint chant of the priest and the silver tinkle of the bell.

Six Englishmen, with the commissionaires, and the "Murray's Guide-books" in their hands, are looking at the "Descent from the Cross." Of this picture "The Guide-book" gives you orders how to judge. If it is the end of religious painting to express the religious sentiment, a hundred of inferior pictures must rank before Rubens. Who was ever piously affected by any picture of the master? He can depict a livid thief writhing upon the cross, sometimes a blonde Magdalen weeping below it; but it is a Magdalen a very short time indeed after her repentance: her yellow brocades and flaring satins are still those which she wore when she was of the world; her body has not yet lost the marks of the feasting and voluptousness in which she used to indulge, according to the legend. Not one of the Rubens pictures, among all the scores that decorate chapels and churches here, has the least tendency to purify, to touch the affections, or to awaken the feelings of religious respect and wonder. The "Descent from the Cross" is vast, gloomy, and awful; but the awe inspired by it is, as I take it, altogether material. He might have painted a picture of any criminal broken on the wheel, and the sensation inspired by it would have been precisely similar. Nor in a religious picture do you want the *savoir-faire* of the master to be always protruding itself; it detracts from the feeling of reverence, just as the thumping of cushion and the spouting of tawdry oratory does from a sermon: meek religion disappears, shouldered out of the desk by the pompous, stalwart, big-chested, fresh-colored, bushy-whiskered pulpiteer. Rubens's piety has always struck us as of this sort. If he takes a pious subject, it is to show you in what a fine way he, Peter Paul Rubens, can treat it. He never seems to doubt but that he is doing it a great honor. His "Descent from the Cross," and its accompanying wings and cover, are a set of puns upon the word Christopher, of which the taste is more odious than that of the hooped-petticoated Virgin yonder, with her artificial flowers and her rings and brooches. The people who made an offering of that hooped petticoat did their best, at any rate; they knew no better. There is humility in that simple, quaint present; trustfulness and kind intention. Looking about at other altars, you see (much to the horror of pious Protestants) all sorts of queer little emblems hanging up under little pyramids of penny candles that are sputtering and flaring there. Here you have a silver arm, or a little gold toe, or a wax leg, or a gilt eye, signifying or commemorating cures that have been performed by the supposed intercession of the saint over whose chapel they hang. Well, although they are abominable superstitions, yet these queer little offerings seem to me to be a great deal more pious than Rubens's big pictures; just as is the widow with her poor little mite compared to the swelling Pharisee who flings his purse of gold into the plate.

A couple of days of Rubens and his church-pictures makes one thoroughly and entirely sick of him. His very genius and splendor pall upon one, even taking the pictures as worldly pictures. One grows weary of being perpetually feasted with this rich, coarse, steaming food. Considering them as church pictures, I don't want to go to church to hear, however splendid, an organ play "The British Grenadiers."

The Antwerpians have set up a clumsy bronze statue of their divinity in a square of the town; and those who have not enough of Rubens in the churches may study him, and indeed to much greater advantage, in a good, well-lighted museum. Here, there is one picture, a dying saint taking the communion, a large piece ten or eleven feet high, and painted in an incredibly short space of time, which is extremely curious indeed for the painter's study. The picture is scarcely more than an immense magnificent sketch; but it tells the secret of the artist's manner, which, in the midst of its dash and splendor, is curiously methodical. Where the shadows are warm the lights are cold, and *vice versâ;* and the picture has been so rapidly painted, that the tints lie raw by the side of one another, the artist not having taken the trouble to blend them.

There are two exquisite Vandykes (whatever Sir Joshua may say of them), and in which the very management of the gray tones which the President abuses forms the principal excellence and charm. Why, after all, are we not to have our opinion? Sir Joshua is not the Pope. The color of one of those Vandykes is as fine as *fine* Paul Veronese, and the sentiment beautifully tender and graceful.

I saw, too, an exhibition of the modern Belgian artists (1843), the remembrance of whose pictures after a month's absence has almost entirely vanished. Wappers's hand, as I thought, seemed to have grown old and feeble, Verboeckhoven's cattle-pieces are almost as good as Paul Potter's, and Keyser has dwindled down into namby-pamby prettiness, pitiful to see in the gallant young painter who astonished the Louvre artists ten years ago by a hand almost as dashing and ready as that of Rubens himself. There were besides, many caricatures of the new German school, which are in themselves caricatures of the masters before Raphael.

An instance of honesty may be mentioned here with applause. The writer lost a pocket-book containing a passport and a couple of modest ten-pound notes. The person who found the portfolio ingeniously put it into the box of the post-office, and it was faithfully restored to the owner; but somehow the two ten-pound notes were absent. It was, however, a great comfort to get the passport, and the pocket-book, which must be worth about ninepence.

Brussels.

It was night when we arrived by the railroad from Antwerp at Brussels; the route is very pretty and interesting, and the flat countries through which the road passes in the highest state of peaceful, smiling cultivation. The fields by the roadside are enclosed by hedges as in England, the harvest was in part down, and an English country gentleman who was of our party pronounced the crops to be as fine as any he had ever seen. Of this matter a cockney cannot judge accurately, but any man can see with what extraordinary neatness and care all these little plots of ground are tilled, and admire the richness and brilliancy of the vegetation. Outside of the moat of Antwerp, and at every village by which we passed, it was pleasant to see the happy congregations of well-clad people that basked in the evening sunshine, and soberly smoked their pipes and drank their Flemish beer. Men who love this drink must, as I fancy, have something essentially peaceful in their composition, and must be more easily satisfied than folks on our side of the water. The excitement of Flemish beer is, indeed, not great. I have tried both the white beer and the brown; they are both of the kind which schoolboys denominate "swipes," very sour and thin to the taste, but served, to be sure, in quaint Flemish jugs that do not seem to have changed their form since the days of Rubens, and must please the lovers of antiquarian knickknacks. Numbers of comfortable-looking women and children sat beside the head of the family upon the tavern-benches, and it was amusing to see one little fellow of eight years old smoking, with much gravity, his father's cigar. How the worship of the sacred plant of tobacco has spread through all Europe! I am sure that the persons who cry out against the use of it are guilty of superstition and unreason, and that it would be a proper and easy task for scientific persons to write an encomium upon the weed. In solitude it is the pleasantest companion possible, and in company never *de trop.* To a student it suggests all sorts of agreeable thoughts, it refreshes the brain when weary, and every sedentary cigar-smoker will tell you how much good he has had from it, and how he has been able to return to his labor, after a quarter of an hour's mild interval of the delightful leaf of Havanna. Drinking has gone from among us since smoking came in. It is a wicked error to say that smokers are drunkards; drink they do, but of gentle diluents mostly, for fierce stimulants of wine or strong liquors are abhorrent to the real lover of the Indian weed. Ah! my Juliana, join not in the vulgar cry that is raised against us. Cigars and cool drinks beget quiet conversations, good-humor, meditation; not hot blood such as mounts into the head of drinkers of apoplectic port or dangerous claret. Are we not more moral and reasonable than our forefathers? Indeed I think so somewhat; and many improvements of social life and converse must date with the introduction of the pipe.

We were a dozen tobacco-consumers in the wagon of the train that brought us from Antwerp; nor did the women of the party (sensible women!) make a single objection to the fumigation. But enough of this; only let me add, in conclusion, that an excellent Israelitish gentleman, Mr. Hartog of Antwerp, supplies cigars for a penny apiece, such as are not to be procured in London for four times the sum.

Through smiling corn-fields, then, and by little woods from which rose here and there the quaint peaked towers of some old-fashioned *châteaux*, our train went smoking along at thirty miles an hour. We caught a glimpse of Mechlin steeple, at first dark against the sunset, and afterwards bright as we came to the other side of it, and admired long glistening canals or moats that surrounded the queer old town, and were lighted up in that wonderful way which the sun only understands, and not even Mr. Turner, with all his vermilion and gamboge, can put down on canvas. The verdure was everywhere astonishing, and we fancied we saw many golden Cuyps as we passed by these quiet pastures.

Steam-engines and their accompaniments, blazing forges, gaunt manufactories, with numberless windows and long black chimneys, of course take away from the romance of the place; but, as we whirled into Brussels, even these engines had a fine appearance. Three or four of the snorting, galloping monsters had just finished their journey, and there was a quantity of flaming ashes lying under the brazen bellies of each that looked properly lurid and demoniacal. The men at the station came out with flaming torches — awful-looking fellows indeed! Presently the different baggage was handed out, and in the very worst vehicle I ever entered, and at the very slowest pace, we were borne to the "Hôtel de Suède," from which house of entertainment this letter is written.

We strolled into the town, but though the night was excessively fine, and it was not yet eleven o'clock, the streets of the little capital were deserted, and the handsome blazing *cafés* round about the theatres contained no inmates. Ah, what a pretty sight is the Parisian Boulevard on a night like this! how many pleasant hours has one passed in watching the lights, and the hum, and the stir, and the laughter of those happy, idle people! There was none of this gayety here; nor was there a person to be found, except a skulking commissioner or two (whose real name in French is that of a fish that is eaten with fennel-sauce), and who offered to conduct us to certain curiosities in the town. What must we English not have done that in every town in Europe we are to be fixed upon by scoundrels of this sort; and what a pretty reflection it is on our country that such rascals find the means of living on us!

Early the next morning we walked through a number of streets in the place, and saw certain sights. The Park is very pretty, and all the buildings round about it have an air of neatness — almost of stateliness. The houses are tall, the streets spacious, and the roads extremely clean. In the Park is a little theatre, a *café* somewhat ruinous, a little palace for the king of this little kingdom, some smart public buildings (with S. P. Q. B. emblazoned on them, at which pompous inscription one cannot help laughing), and other rows of houses somewhat resembling a little Rue de Rivoli. Whether from my own natural greatness and magnanimity, or from that handsome share of national conceit that every Englishman possesses, my impressions of this city are certainly any thing but respectful. It has an absurd kind of Liliput look with it. There are soldiers, just as in Paris, better dressed, and doing a vast deal of drumming and bustle; and yet, somehow, far from being frightened at them, I feel inclined to laugh in their faces. There are little Ministers, who work at their little bureaux; and to read the journals, how fierce they are! A great thundering "Times" could hardly talk more big. One reads about the rascally Ministers, the miserable Opposition, the designs of tyrants, the eyes of Europe, &c., just as one would in real journals. The "Moniteur" of Ghent belabors the "Independent" of Brussels; the "Independent" falls foul of the "Lynx"; and really it is difficult not to suppose, sometimes, that these worthy people are in earnest. And yet how happy were they *sua si bona nôrint!* Think what a comfort it would be to belong to a little state like this; not to abuse their privilege, but philosophically to use it. If I were a Belgian, I would not care one single fig about politics. I would not read thundering leading-articles. I would not have an opinion. What's the use of an opinion here? Happy fellows! do not the French, the English, and the Prussians, spare them the trouble of thinking, and make all their opinions for them? Think of living in a country free, easy, respectable, wealthy, and with the nuisance of talking politics removed from out of it. All this might the Belgians have, and a part do they enjoy, but not the best part; no, these people will be brawling and by the ears, and parties run as high here as at Stoke Pogis or little Pedlington.

These sentiments were elicited by the reading of a paper at the *café* in the Park, where we sat under the trees for a while and sipped our cool lemonade. Numbers of statues decorate the place, the very worst I ever saw. These Cupids must have been erected in the time of the Dutch dynasty, as I judge from the immense posterior developments. Indeed the arts of the country are very low. The statues here, and the lions before the Prince of Orange's palace, would disgrace almost the figure-head of a ship.

Of course we paid our visit to this little lion of Brussels (the Prince's palace, I mean). The architecture of the building is admirably simple and firm; and you remark about it, and all other works here, a high finish in doors, wood-works, paintings, &c., that one does not see in France, where the buildings are often rather sketched than completed, and the artist seems to neglect the limbs, as it were, and extremities of his figures.

The finish of this little place is exquisite. We went through some dozen of state-rooms, paddling along over the slippery floors of inlaid woods in great slippers, without which we must have come to the ground. How did his Royal Highness the Prince of Orange manage when he lived here, and her Imperial Highness the Princess, and their excellencies the chamberlains and the footmen? They must have been on their tails many times a day, that's certain, and must have cut queer figures.

The ball-room is beautiful — all marble, and yet with a comfortable, cheerful look; the other apartments are not less agreeable, and the people looked with intense satisfaction at some great lapis-lazuli tables, which the guide informed us were worth four millions, more or less; adding with a very knowing look, that they were *un peu plus cher que l'or*. This speech has a tremendous effect on visitors, and when we met some of our steamboat companions in the Park or elsewhere — in so small a place as this one falls in with them a dozen times a day — "Have you seen the tables?" was the general question. Prodigious tables are they, indeed! Fancy a table, my dear — a table four feet wide — a table with legs. Ye heavens! the mind can hardly picture to itself any thing so beautiful and so tremendous!

There are some good pictures in the palace, too, but not so extraordinarily good as the guide-books and the guide would have us to think. The latter, like most men of his class, is an ignoramus, who showed us an Andrea del Sarto (copy or original), and called it a Correggio, and made other blunders of a like nature. As is the case in England, you are hurried through the rooms without being allowed time to look at the pictures, and, consequently, to pronounce a satisfactory judgment on them.

In the Museum more time was granted me, and I spent some hours with pleasure there. It is an absurd little gallery, absurdly imitating the Louvre, with just such compartments and pillars as you see in the noble Paris gallery; only here the pillars and capitals are stucco and white in place of marble and gold, and plaster-of-Paris busts of great Belgians are placed between the pillars. An artist of the country has made a picture containing them, and you will be ashamed of your ignorance when you hear many of their names. Old Tilly of Magdeburg figures in one corner; Rubens, the endless Rubens, stands in the midst. What a noble countenance it is, and what a manly, swaggering consciousness of power!

The picture to see here is a portrait, by the great Peter Paul, of one of the governesses of the Netherlands. It is just the finest portrait that ever was seen. Only a half-length, but such a majesty, such a force, such a splendor, such a simplicity about it! The woman is in a stiff black dress, with a ruff and a few pearls; a yellow curtain is behind her — the simplest arrangement that can be conceived; but this great man knew how to rise to his occasion; and no better proof can be shown of what a fine gentleman he was than this his homage to the vice-Queen. A common bungler would have painted her in her best clothes, with crown and sceptre, just as our Queen has been painted by — but comparisons are odious. Here stands this majestic woman in her every-day working-dress of black satin, *looking your hat off*, as it were. Another portrait of the same personage hangs elsewhere in the gallery, and it is curious to observe the difference between the two, and see how a man of genius paints a portrait, and how a common limner executes it.

Many more pictures are there here by Rubens, or rather from Rubens's manufactory, — odious and vulgar most of them are; fat Magdalens, coarse Saints, vulgar Virgins, with the scene-painter's tricks far too evident upon the canvas. By the side of one of the most astonishing color-pieces in the world, the "Worshipping of the Magi," is a famous picture of Paul Veronese that cannot be too much admired. As Rubens sought in the first picture to dazzle and astonish by gorgeous variety, Paul in his seems to wish to get his effect by simplicity, and has produced the most noble harmony that can be conceived. Many more works are there that merit notice,— a singularly clever, brilliant, and odious Jordaens, for example; some curious costume-pieces; one or two works by the Belgian Raphael, who was a very

Belgian Raphael indeed; and a long gallery of pictures of the very oldest school, that, doubtless, afford much pleasure to the amateurs of ancient art. I confess that I am inclined to believe in very little that existed before the time of Raphael. There is, for instance, the Prince of Orange's picture by Perugino, very pretty indeed, up to a certain point, but all the heads are repeated, all the drawing is bad and affected; and this very badness and affectation is what the so-called Catholic school is always anxious to imitate. Nothing can be more juvenile or paltry than the works of the native Belgians here exhibited. Tin crowns are suspended over many of them, showing that the pictures are prize compositions: and pretty things, indeed, they are! Have you ever read an Oxford prize-poem? Well, these pictures are worse even than the Oxford poems — an awful assertion to make.

In the matter of eating, dear sir, which is the next subject of the fine arts, a subject that, after many hours' walking, attracts a gentleman very much, let me attempt to recall the transactions of this very day at the *table-d'hôte*. 1, green pea-soup; 2, boiled salmon; 3, mussels; 4, crimped skate; 5, roast-meat; 6, patties; 7, melon; 8, carp, stewed with mushrooms and onions; 9, roast-turkey; 10, cauliflower and butter; 11, fillets of venison *piqués*, with assafœtida sauce; 12, stewed calf's-ear; 13, roast-veal; 14, roast-lamb; 15, stewed cherries; 16, rice-pudding; 17, Gruyère cheese, and about twenty-four cakes of different kinds. Except 5, 13, and 14, I give you my word I ate of all written down here, with three rolls of bread and a score of potatoes. What is the meaning of it? How is the stomach of man brought to desire and to receive all this quantity? Do not gastronomists complain of heaviness in London after eating a couple of mutton-chops? Do not respectable gentlemen fall asleep in their arm-chairs? Are they fit for mental labor? Far from it. But look at the difference here: after dinner here one is as light as a gossamer. One walks with pleasure, reads with pleasure, writes with pleasure — nay, there is the supper-bell going at ten o'clock, and plenty of eaters, too. Let lord mayors and aldermen look to it, this fact of the extraordinary increase of appetite in Belgium, and, instead of steaming to Blackwall, come a little further to Antwerp.

Of ancient architectures in the place, there is a fine old Port de Halle, which has a tall, gloomy, bastille look; a most magnificent town-hall, that has been sketched a thousand of times, and opposite it, a building that I think would be the very model for a Conservative club-house in London. Oh! how charming it would be to be a great painter, and give the character of the building, and the numberless groups round about it. The booths lighted up by the sun, the market-women in their gowns of brilliant hue, each group having a character and telling its little story, the troops of men lolling in all sorts of admirable attitudes of ease round the great lamp. Half a dozen light blue dragoons are lounging about, and peeping over the artist as the drawing is made, and the sky is more bright and blue than one sees it in a hundred years in London.

The priests of the country are a remarkably well-fed and respectable race, without that scowling, hang-dog look which one has remarked among reverend gentlemen in the neighboring country of France. Their reverences wear buckles to their shoes, light-blue neckcloths, and huge three-cornered hats in good condition. To-day, strolling by the cathedral, I heard the tinkling of a bell in the street, and beheld certain persons, male and female, suddenly plump down on their knees before a little procession that was passing. Two men in black held a tawdry red canopy, a priest walked beneath it holding the sacrament covered with a cloth, and before him marched a couple of little altar-boys in short white surplices, such as you see in Rubens, and holding lacquered lamps. A small train of street-boys followed the procession, cap in hand, and the clergyman finally entered a hospital for old women, near the church, the canopy and the lamp-bearers remaining without.

It was a touching scene, and as I staid to watch it, I could not but think of the poor old soul who was dying within, listening to the last words of prayer, led by the hand of the priest to the brink of the black, fathomless grave. How bright the sun was shining without all the time and how happy and careless every thing around us looked!

The Duke d'Arenberg has a picture-gallery worthy of his princely house. It does not contain great pieces, but tit-bits of pictures, such as suit an aristocratic epicure. For such persons a great huge canvas is too much, it is like sitting down alone to a roasted ox; and they do wisely, I think, to patronize small, high-flavored, delicate *morceaux*, such as the Duke has here.

Among them may be mentioned, with special praise, a magnificent small Rembrandt, a Paul Potter of exceeding minuteness and beauty, an Ostade, which reminds one of Wilkie's early performances, and a Dusart quite as good as Ostade. There is a Berghem, much more unaffected than that artist's works generally are; and, what is more, precious in the eyes of many ladies as an object of art, there is, in one of the grand saloons, some needlework done by the Duke's own grandmother, which is looked at with awe by those admitted to see the palace.

The chief curiosity, if not the chief ornament, of a very elegant library, filled with vases and bronzes, is a marble head, supposed to be the original head of the Laocoon. It is, unquestionably, a finer head than that which at present figures upon the shoulders of the famous statue. The expression of woe is more manly and intense; in the group as we know it, the head of the principal figure has always seemed to me to be a grimace of grief, as are the two accompanying young gentlemen with their pretty attitudes, and their little silly, open-mouthed despondency. It has always had upon me the effect of a trick, that statue, and not of a piece of true art. It would look well in the vista of a garden; it is not august enough for a temple, with all its jerks, and twirls, and polite convulsions. But who knows what susceptibilities such a confession may offend? Let us say no more about the Laocoon, nor its head, nor its tail. The Duke was offered its weight in gold, they say, for this head, and refused. It would be a shame to speak ill of such a treasure, but I have my opinion of the man who made the offer.

In the matter of sculpture almost all the Brussels churches are decorated with the most laborious wooden pulpits, which may be worth their weight in gold, too, for what I know, including his reverence preaching inside. At St. Gudule the preacher mounts into no less a place than the garden of Eden, being supported by Adam and Eve, by Sin and Death, and numberless other animals; he walks up to his desk by a rustic railing of flowers, fruits, and vegetables, with wooden peacocks, paroquets, monkeys biting apples, and many more of the birds and beasts of the field. In another church the clergyman speaks from out a hermitage; in a third from a carved palm-tree, which supports a set of oak clouds that form the canopy of the pulpit, and are, indeed, not much heavier in appearance than so many huge sponges. A priest, however tall or stout, must be lost in the midst of all these queer gimcracks; in order to be consistent, they ought to dress him up, too, in some odd fantastical suit. I can fancy the Curé of Meudon preaching out of such a place, or the

Rev. Sidney Smith, or that famous clergyman of the time of the League, who brought all Paris to laugh and listen to him.

But let us not be too supercilious and ready to sneer. It is only bad taste. It may have been very true devotion which erected these strange edifices.

II. — GHENT. — BRUGES.

GHENT. (1840.)

The Béguine College or Village is one of the most extraordinary sights that all Europe can show. On the confines of the town of Ghent you come upon an old-fashioned brick gate, that seems as if it were one of the city barriers; but, on passing it, one of the prettiest sights possible meets the eye: At the porter's lodge you see an old lady, in black, and a white hood, occupied over her book; before you is a red church with a tall roof and fantastical Dutch pinnacles, and all around it rows upon rows of small houses, the queerest, neatest, nicest that ever were seen (a doll's house is hardly smaller or prettier). Right and left, on each side of little alleys, these little mansions rise; they have a courtlet before them, in which some green plants or holly-hocks are growing; and to each house is a gate, that has mostly a picture or queer-carved ornament upon or about it, and bears the name, not of the Béguine who inhabits it, but of the saint to whom she may have devoted it — the house of St. Stephen, the house of St. Donatus, the English or Angel Convent and so on. Old ladies in black are pacing in the quiet alleys here and there, and drop the stranger a courtesy as he passes them and takes off his hat. Never were such patterns of neatness seen as these old ladies and their houses. I peeped into one or two of the chambers, of which the windows were open to the pleasant evening sun, and saw beds scrupulously plain, a quaint old chair or two, and little pictures of favorite saints decorating the spotless white walls. The old ladies kept up a quick, cheerful clatter, as they paused to gossip at the gates of their little domiciles; and with a great deal of artifice, and lurking behind walls, and looking at the church as if I intended to design that, I managed to get a sketch of a couple of them.

But what white paper can render the whiteness of their linen; what black ink can do justice to the lustre of their gowns and shoes? Both of the ladies had a neat ankle and a tight stocking; and I fancy that heaven is quite as well served in this costume as in the dress of a scowling, stockingless friar, whom I had seen passing just before. The look and dress of the man made me shudder. His great red feet were bound up in a shoe open at the toes, a kind of compromise for a sandal. I had just seen him and his brethren at the Dominican Church, where a mass of music was sung, and orange-trees, flags, and banners decked the aisle of the church.

One begins to grow sick of these churches, and the hideous exhibitions of bodily agonies that are depicted on the sides of all the chapels. Into one wherein we went this morning was what they called a Calvary: a horrible, ghastly image of a Christ in a tomb, the figure of the natural size, and of the livid color of death; gaping red wounds on the body and round the brows: the whole piece enough to turn one sick, and fit only to brutalize the beholder of it. The Virgin is commonly represented with a dozen swords stuck in her heart; bleeding throats of headless John Baptists are perpetually thrust before your eyes. At the Cathedral gate was a papier-mâché church-ornament shop — most of the carvings and reliefs of the same dismal character. One, for instance, represented a heart with a great gash in it, and a double row of large blood-drops dribbling from it; nails and a knife were thrust into the heart; round the whole was a crown of thorns. Such things are dreadful to think of. The same gloomy spirit which made a religion of them, and worked upon the people by the grossest of all means, terror, distracted the natural feelings of man to maintain its power — shut gentle women into lonely, pitiless convents — frightened poor peasants with tales of torment — taught that the end and labor of life was silence, wretchedness, and the scourge — murdered those by fagot and prison who thought otherwise. How has the blind and furious bigotry of man perverted that which God gave us as our greatest boon, and bid us hate where God bade us love! Thank heaven that monk has gone out of sight! It is pleasant to look at the smiling, cheerful old Béguine, and think no more of yonder livid face.

One of the many convents in this little religious city seems to be the specimen-house, which is shown to strangers, for all the guides conduct you thither, and I saw in a book kept for the purpose the names of innumerable Smiths and Joneses registered.

A very kind, sweet-voiced, smiling nun (I wonder, do they always choose the most agreeable and best-humored sister of the house to show it to strangers?) came tripping down the steps and across the flags of the little garden-court, and welcomed us with much courtesy into the neat little old-fashioned, red-bricked, gable-ended, shining-windowed Convent of the Angels. First she showed us a whitewashed parlor, decorated with a grim picture or two and some crucifixes and other religious emblems, where, upon stiff old chairs, the sisters sit and work. Three or four of them were still there, pattering over their laces and bobbins; but the chief part of the sisterhood were engaged in an apartment hard by, from which issued a certain odor which I must say resembled onions: it was in fact the kitchen of the establishment.

Every Béguine cooks her own little dinner in her own little pipkin; and there was half a score of them, sure enough, busy over their pots and crockery, cooking a repast which, when ready, was carried off to a neighboring room, the refectory, where, at a ledge-table which is drawn out from under her own particular cupboard, each nun sits down and eats her meal in silence. More religious emblems ornamented the carved cupboard-doors, and within, every thing was as neat as neat could be: shining pewter-ewers and glasses, snug baskets of eggs and pats of butter, and little bowls with about a farthing's-worth of green tea in them — for some great day of fête, doubtless. The old ladies sat round as we examined these things, each eating soberly at her ledge and never looking round. There was a bell ringing in the chapel hard by. "Hark!" said our guide, "that is one of the sisters dying. Will you come up and see the cells?"

The cells, it need not be said, are the snuggest little nests in the world, with serge-curtained beds and snowy linen, and saints and martyrs pinned against the wall. "We may sit up till twelve o'clock, if we like," said the nun; "but we have no fire and candle, and so what's the use of sitting up? When we have said our prayers, we are glad enough to go to sleep."

I forget, although the good soul told us, how many times in the day, in public and in private, these devotions are made, but fancy that the morning service in the chapel takes place at too early an hour for most easy travellers. We did not fail to attend in the evening, when likewise is a general muster of the seven hundred, minus the absent and sick, and the sight is not a little curious and striking to a stranger.

The chapel is a very big whitewashed place of worship, supported by half a dozen columns on either side, over each of which stands the statue of an Apostle, with his emblem of martyrdom. Nobody was as yet at the distant altar, which was too far off to see very distinctly; but I could perceive two statues over it, one of which (St. Laurence, no doubt) was leaning upon a huge gilt gridiron that the sun lighted up in a blaze — a painful but not a romantic instrument of death. A couple of old ladies in white hoods were tugging and swaying about at two bell-ropes that came down into the middle of the church, and at least five hundred others in white veils were seated all round about us in mute contemplation until the service began, looking very solemn, and white, and ghastly, like an army of tombstones by moonlight.

The service commenced as the clock finished striking seven: the organ pealed out, a very cracked and old one, and presently some weak old voice from the choir overhead quavered out a canticle; which done, a thin old voice of a priest at the altar far off (and which had now become quite gloomy in the sunset) chanted feebly another part of the service; then the nuns warbled once more overhead; and it was curious to hear, in the intervals of the most lugubrious chants, how the organ went off with some extremely cheerful military or profane air. At one time was a march, at another a quick tune; which ceasing, the old nuns began again, and so sung until the service was ended.

In the midst of it one of the white-veiled sisters approached us with a very mysterious air, and put down her white veil close to our ears, and whispered. Were we doing any thing wrong, I wondered? Were they come to that part of the service where heretics and infidels ought to quit the church? What have you to ask, O sacred, white-veiled maid?

All she said was, "Deux centièmes pour les suisses," which sum was paid; and presently the old ladies, rising from their chairs one by one, came in face of the altar, where they knelt down and said a short prayer; then, rising, unpinned their veils, and folded them up all exactly in the same folds and fashion, and laid them square like napkins on their heads, and tucked up their long black outer dresses, and trudged off to their convents.

The novices wear black veils, under one of which I saw a young, sad, handsome face; it was the only thing in the establishment that was the least romantic or gloomy: and, for the sake of any reader of a sentimental turn, let us hope that the poor soul has been crossed in love, and that over some soul-stirring tragedy that black curtain has fallen.

Ghent has, I believe, been called a vulgar Venice. It contains dirty canals and old houses that must satisfy the most eager antiquary, though the buildings are not quite in so good preservation as others that may be seen in the Netherlands. The commercial bustle of the place seems considerable, and it contains more beer-shops than any city I ever saw.

These beer-shops seem the only amusement of the inhabitants, until at least, the theatre shall be built, of which the elevation is now complete, a very handsome and extensive pile. There are beer-shops in the cellars of the houses, which are frequented, it is to be presumed, by the lower sort; there are beer-shops at the barriers, where the citizens and their families repair; and beer-shops in the town, glaring with gas, with long gauze blinds, however, to hide what I hear is a rather questionable reputation.

Our inn, "The Hotel of the Post," a spacious and comfortable residence, is on a little place planted round with trees, and that seems to be the Palais Royal of the town. Three clubs, which look from without to be very comfortable, ornament this square with their gas-lamps. Here stands, too, the theatre that is to be; there is a café, and on evenings a military band plays the very worst music I ever remember to have heard. I went out to-night to take a quiet walk upon this place, and the horrid brazen discord of these trumpeters set me half mad.

I went to the café for refuge, passing on my way a subterraneous beer-shop, where men and women were drinking to the sweet music of a cracked barrel-organ. They take in a couple of French papers at this café, and the same number of Belgian journals. You may imagine how well the latter are informed, when you hear that the battle of Boulogne, fought by the immortal Louis Napoleon, was not known here until some gentlemen out of Norfolk brought the news from London, and until it had travelled to Paris, and from Paris to Brussels. For a whole hour I could not get a newspaper at the café. The horrible brass band in the mean time had quitted the place, and now, to amuse the Ghent citizens, a couple of little boys came to the café, and set up a small concert: one played ill on the guitar, but sang, very sweetly, plaintive French ballads; the other was the comic singer; he carried about with him a queer, long, damp-looking mouldy white hat, with no brim. "Ecoutez," said the waiter to me, "il va faire l'Anglais; c'est très drôle!" The little rogue mounted his immense brimless hat, and, thrusting his thumbs into the armholes of his waistcoat, began to *faire l'Anglais*, with a song in which swearing was the principal joke. We all laughed at this, and indeed the little rascal seemed to have a good deal of humor.

How they hate us, these foreigners, in Belgium as much as in France! What lies they tell of us; how gladly they would see us humiliated! Honest folks at home over their port-wine say, "Ay, ay, and very good reason they have too. National vanity, sir, wounded — we have beaten them so often." My dear sir, there is not a greater error in the world than this. They hate you because you are stupid, hard to please, and intolerably insolent and air-giving. I walked with an Englishman yesterday, who asked the way to a street of which he pronounced the name very badly to a little Flemish boy: the Flemish boy did not answer; and there was my Englishman quite in a rage, shrieking in the child's ear as if he must answer. He seemed to think that it was the duty of "the snob," as he called him, to obey the gentleman. This is why we are hated — for pride. In our free country a tradesman, a lackey, or a waiter will submit to almost any given insult from a gentleman: in these benighted lands one man is as good as another; and pray God it may soon be so with us! Of all European people, which is the nation that has the most haughtiness, the strongest prejudices, the greatest reserve, the greatest dulness? I say an Englishman of the genteel classes. An honest groom jokes and hobs-and-nobs, and makes his way with the kitchen-maids, for there is good social nature in the man; his master dare not unbend. Look at him, how he scowls at you on your entering an inn-room; think how you scowl yourself to meet his scowl. To-day, as we were walking and staring about the place, a worthy old gentleman in a carriage, seeing a pair of strangers, took off his hat and bowed very gravely with his old powdered head out of the window: I am sorry to say that our first impulse was to burst out laughing — it seemed so supremely ridiculous that a stranger should notice and welcome another.

As for the notion that foreigners hate us because we have beaten them so often, my dear sir, this is the greatest error in the world: well-educated Frenchmen *do not believe that we have beaten them*. A man was once ready to call me out in Paris because I said that we had beaten the French in Spain; and here before me is a French paper, with a London correspondent discoursing about Louis Bonaparte and his jackass expedition to Boulogne. "He was received at Eglintoun, it is true," says the correspondent, "but what do you think was the reason? Because the English nobility were anxious *to revenge upon his person* (with some *coups de lance*) *the checks which the 'grand homme' his uncle had inflicted on us in Spain.*"

This opinion is so general among the French, that they would laugh at you with scornful incredulity if you ventured to assert any other. Foy's history of the Spanish War does not, unluckily, go far enough. I have read a French history which hardly mentions the war in Spain, and calls the battle of Salamanca a French victory. You know how the other day, and in the teeth of all evidence, the French swore to their victory of Toulouse: and so it is with the rest; and you may set it down as pretty certain, 1st, That only a few people know the real state of things in France, as to the matter in dispute between us; 2d, That those who do, keep the truth to themselves, and so it is as if it had never been.

These Belgians have caught up, and quite naturally, the French tone. We are *perfide Albion* with them still. Here is the Ghent paper, which declares that it is beyond a doubt that Louis Napoleon was sent by the English and Lord Palmerston; and though it states in another part of the journal (from English authority) that the Prince had never seen Lord Palmerston, yet the lie will remain uppermost — the people and the editor will believe it to the end of time. . . . See to what a digression yonder little fellow in the tall hat has given rise! Let us make his picture, and have done with him.

I could not understand, in my walks about this place, which is certainly picturesque enough, and contains extraordinary charms in the shape of old gables, quaint spires, and broad shining canals — I could not at first comprehend why, for all this, the town was especially disagreeable to me, and have only just hit on the reason why. Sweetest Juliana, you will never guess it: it is simply this, that I have not seen a single decent-looking woman in the whole place; they look all ugly, with coarse mouths, vulgar figures, mean mercantile faces; and so the traveller walking among them finds the pleasure of his walk excessively damped, and the impressions made upon him disagreeable.

In the Academy there are no pictures of merit; but sometimes a second-rate picture is as pleasing as the best, and one may pass an hour here very pleasantly. There is a room appropriated to Belgian artists, of which I never saw the like: they are, like all the rest of the things in this country, miserable imitations of the French school — great nude Venuses, and Junos *à la* David, with the drawing left out.

BRUGES.

The change from vulgar Ghent, with its ugly women and coarse bustle, to this quiet, old, half-deserted, cleanly Bruges, was very pleasant. I have seen old men at Versailles, with shabby coats and pigtails, sunning themselves on the benches in the walls; they had seen better days, to be sure, but they were gentlemen still: and so we found, this morning, old dowager Bruges basking in the pleasant August sun, and looking if not prosperous, at least cheerful and well-bred. It is the quaintest and prettiest of all the quaint and pretty towns I have seen. A painter might spend months here, and wander from church to church, and admire old towers and pinnacles, tall gables, bright canals, and pretty little patches of green garden and moss-grown wall, that reflect in the clear quiet water. Before the inn-window is a garden, from which in the early morning issues a most wonderful odor of stocks and wall-flowers; next comes a road with trees of admirable green; numbers of little children are playing in this road (the place is so clean that they may roll in it all day without soiling their pinafores), and on the other side of the trees are little old-fashioned, dumpy, whitewashed, red-tiled houses. A poorer landscape to draw never was known, nor a pleasanter to see — the children especially, who are inordinately fat and rosy. Let it be remembered, too, that here we are out of the country of ugly women: the expression of the face is almost uniformly gentle and pleasing, and the figures of the women, wrapped in long black, monk-like cloaks and hoods, very picturesque. No wonder there are so many children: "The Guide-book" (omniscient Mr. Murray!) says there are fifteen thousand paupers in the town, and we know how such multiply. How the deuce do their children look so fat and rosy? By eating dirt-pies, I suppose. I saw a couple making a very nice savory one, and another employed in gravely sticking strips of stick betwixt the pebbles at the house-door, and so making for herself a stately garden. The men and women don't seem to have much more to do. There are a couple of tall chimneys at either suburb of the town, where no doubt manufactories are at work, but within the walls everybody seems decently idle.

We have been, of course, abroad to visit the lions. The tower in the Grand Place is very fine, and the bricks of which it is built do not yield a whit in color to the best stone. The great building round this tower is very like the pictures of the Ducal Palace at Venice; and there is a long market area, with columns down the middle, from which hung shreds of rather lean-looking meat, that would do wonders under the hands of Cattermole or Haghe. In the tower there is a chime of bells that keep ringing perpetually. They not only play tunes of themselves, and every quarter of an hour, but an individual performs selections from popular operas on them at certain periods of the morning, afternoon, and evening. I have heard to-day "Suoni la Tromba," "Son Vergin Vezzosa," from "The Puritani," and other airs, and very badly they were played too; for such a great monster as a tower-bell cannot be expected to imitate Madame Grisi or even Signor Lablache. Other churches indulge in the same amusement, so that one may come here and live in melody all day or night, like the young woman in Moore's "Lalla Rookh."

In the matter of art, the chief attractions of Bruges are the pictures of Hemling, that are to be seen in the churches, the hospital, and the picture-gallery of the place. There are no more pictures of Rubens to be seen, and, indeed, in the course of a fortnight, one has had quite enough of the great man and his magnificent, swaggering canvases. What a difference is here with simple Hemling and the extraordinary creations of his pencil! The hospital is particularly rich in them; and the legend there is that the painter, who had served Charles the Bold in his war against the Swiss, and his last battle and defeat, wandered back wounded and penniless to Bruges, and here found cure and shelter.

This hospital is a noble and curious sight. The great hall is almost as it was in the twelfth century; it is spanned by Saxon arches, and lighted by a multiplicity of Gothic windows of all sizes; it is very lofty, clean, and perfectly well ventilated; a screen runs across the middle of the room, to divide the male from the female patients, and we were taken to examine each ward, where the poor people seemed happier than possibly they would have been in health and starvation without it. Great yellow blankets were on the iron beds, the linen was scrupulously clean, glittering pewter-jugs and goblets stood by the side of each patient, and they were provided with godly books (to judge from the binding), in which several were reading at leisure. Honest old comfortable nuns, in queer dresses of blue, black, white, and flannel, were bustling through the room, attending to the wants of the sick. I saw about a dozen of these kind women's faces; one was young — all were healthy and cheerful. One came with bare blue arms and a great pile of linen from an out-house — such a grange as Cedric the Saxon might have given to a guest for the night. A couple were in a laboratory, a tall, bright, clean room, 500 years old at least. "We saw you were not very religious," said one of the old ladies, with a red, wrinkled, good-humored face, "by your behavior yesterday in chapel." And yet we did not laugh and talk as we used at college, but were profoundly affected by the scene that we saw there. It was a fête-day: a mass of Mozart was sung in the evening — not well sung, and yet so exquisitely tender and melodious, that it brought tears into our eyes. There were not above twenty people in the church: all, save three or four, were women in long black cloaks. I took them for nuns at first. They were, however, the common people of the town, very poor indeed, doubtless, for the priest's box that was brought round was not added to by most of them, and their contributions were but two-cent pieces, — five of these go to a penny; but we know the value of such, and can tell the exact worth of a poor woman's mite! The box-bearer did not seem at first willing to accept our donation — we were strangers and heretics; however, I held out my hand, and he came perforce as it were. Indeed it had only a franc in it: but *que voulez-vous?* I had been drinking a bottle of Rhine wine that day, and how was I to afford more? The Rhine wine is dear in this country, and costs four francs a bottle.

Well, the service proceeded. Twenty poor women, two Englishmen, four ragged beggars, cowering on the steps; and there was the priest at the altar, in a great robe of gold and damask, two little boys in white surplices serving him, holding his robe as he rose and bowed, and the money-gatherer swinging his censer, and filling the little chapel with smoke. The music pealed with wonderful sweetness; you could see the prim white heads of the nuns in their gallery. The evening light streamed down upon old statues of saints and carved brown stalls, and lighted up the head of the golden-haired Magdalen in a picture of the entombment of Christ. Over the gallery, and, as it were, a kind protectress to the poor below, stood the statue of the Virgin.

III. — WATERLOO.

It is, my dear, the happy privilege of your sex in England, to quit the dinner-table after the wine-bottles have once or twice gone round it, and you are thereby saved (though, to be sure, I can't tell what the ladies do up stairs) — you are saved two or three hours' excessive dulness, which the men are obliged to go through.

I ask any gentleman who reads this — the letters to my Juliana being written with an eye to publication — to remember especially how many times, how many hundred times, how many thousand times, in his hearing, the battle of Waterloo has been discussed after dinner, and to call to mind how cruelly he has been bored by the discussion. "Ah, it was lucky for us that the Prussians came up!" says one little gentleman, looking particularly wise and ominous. "Hang the Prussians!" (or, perhaps, something stronger, "the Prussians!") says a stout old major on half-pay. "We beat the French without them, sir, as beaten them we always have! We were thundering down the hill of Belle Alliance, sir, at the backs of them, and the French were crying 'Sauve qui peut' long before the Prussians ever touched them!" And so the battle opens, and for many mortal hours, amid rounds of claret, rages over and over again.

I thought to myself, considering the above things, what a fine thing it will be in after-days to say that I have been to Brussels, and never seen the field of Waterloo; indeed, that I am such a philosopher as not to care a fig about the battle — nay, to regret, rather, that when Napoleon came back, the British Government had not spared their men and left him alone.

But this pitch of philosophy was unattainable. This morning, after having seen the Park, the fashionable boulevard, the pictures, the cafés — having sipped, I say, the sweets of every flower that grows in this paradise of Brussels, quite weary of the place, we mounted on a Namur diligence, and jingled off at four miles an hour for Waterloo.

The road is very neat and agreeable: the Forest of Soignies here and there interposes pleasantly, to give your vehicle a shade: the country, as usual, is vastly fertile and well cultivated. A farmer and the conducteur were my companions in the imperial, and, could I have understood their conversation, my dear, you should have had certainly a report of it. The jargon which they talked was, indeed, most queer and puzzling — French, I believe, strangely hashed up and pronounced, for here and there one could catch a few words of it. Now and anon, however, they condescended to speak in the purest French they could muster; and, indeed, nothing is more curious than to hear the French of the country. You can't understand why all the people insist upon speaking it so badly. I asked the conductor if he had been at the battle; he burst out laughing like a philosopher, as he was, and said, "Pas si bête." I asked the farmer whether his contributions were lighter now than in King William's time, and lighter than those in the time of the Emperor? He vowed that in war-time he had not more to pay than in time of peace (and this strange fact is vouched for by every person of every nation), and being asked wherefore the King of Holland had been ousted from his throne, replied at once, "Parceque c'étoit un voleur:" for which accusation I believe there is some show of reason, his Majesty having laid hands on much Belgian property before the lamented outbreak which cost him his crown. A vast deal of laughing and roaring passed between these two worldly people and the postilion whom they called "baron," and I thought, no doubt that this talk was one of the many jokes that my companions were in the habit of making. But not so: the postilion was an actual baron, the bearer of an ancient name, the descendant of gallant gentlemen. Good heavens! what would Mrs. Trollope say to see his lordship here? His father the old baron had dissipated the family fortune, and here was this young nobleman, at about five-and-forty, compelled to bestride a clattering Flemish stallion, and bump over dusty pavements at the rate of five miles an hour. But see the beauty of high blood: with what a calm grace the man of family accommodates himself to fortune! Far from being cast down, his lordship met his fate like a man: he swore and laughed the whole of the journey, and as we changed horses, condescended to partake of half a pint of Louvain beer, to which the farmer treated him — indeed the worthy rustic treated me to a glass too.

Much delight and instruction have I had in the course of the journey from my guide, philosopher, and friend, the author of "Murray's Handbook." He has gathered together, indeed, a store of information, and must, to make his single volume, have gutted many hundreds of guide-books. How the Continental ciceroni must hate him, whoever he is! Every English party I saw had this infallible red book in their hands, and gained a vast deal of historical and general information from it. Thus I heard, in confidence, many remarkable anecdotes of Charles V., the Duke of Alva, Count Egmon, all of which I had before perceived, with much satisfaction, not only in "The Handbook," but even in other works.

The Laureate is among the English poets evidently the great favorite of our guide: the choice does honor to his head and heart. A man must have a very strong bent for poetry, indeed, who carries Southey's works in his portmanteau, and quotes them in proper time and occasion. Of course at Waterloo a spirit like our guide's cannot fail to be deeply moved, and to turn to his favorite poet for sympathy. Hark how the laureated bard sings about the tombstones at Waterloo:—

"That temple to our hearts was hallowed now,
For many a wounded Briton there was laid,
With such for help as time might then allow,
From the fresh carnage of the field conveyed.
And they whom human succor could not save,
Here, in its precincts, found a hasty grave.
And here, on marble tablets, set on high,
In English lines by foreign workmen traced,
The names familiar to an English eye,
Their brethren here the fit memorial placed;
Whose unadorned inscriptions briefly tell
Their gallant comrades' rank, and where they fell.
The stateliest monument of human pride,
Enriched with all magnificence of art,
To honor chieftains who in victory died,
Would wake no stronger feelings in the heart
Than these plain tablets by the soldier's hand
Raised to his comrades in a foreign land."

There are lines for you! wonderful for justice, rich in thought and novel ideas. The passage concerning their gallant comrades' rank should be specially remarked. There indeed they lie, sure enough: the Honorable Colonel This of the Guards, Captain That of the Hussars, Major So-and-So of the Dragoons, brave men and good, who did their duty by their country on that day, and died in the performance of it.

Amen. But I confess fairly, that in looking at these tablets, I felt very much disappointed at not seeing the names of the *men* as well as the officers. Are they to be counted for nought? A few more inches of marble to each monument would have given space for all the names of the men; and the men of that day were the winners of the battle. We have a right to be as grateful individually to any given private as to any given officer; their duties were very much the same. Why should the country reserve its gratitude for the genteel occupiers of the army-list, and forget the gallant fellows whose humble names were written in the regimental books? In reading of the Wellington wars, and the conduct of the men engaged in them, I don't know whether to respect them or to wonder at them most. They have death, wounds, and poverty in contemplation; in possession, poverty, hard labor, hard fare, and small thanks. If they do wrong, they are handed over to the inevitable provost-marshal; if they are heroes, heroes they may be, but they remain privates still, handling the old brown-bess, starving on the old twopence a day. They grow gray in battle and victory, and after thirty years of bloody service, a young gentleman of fifteen, fresh from a preparatory school, who can scarcely read, and came but yesterday with a pinafore in to papa's dessert — such a young gentleman, I say, arrives in a spick-and-span red coat, and calmly takes the command over our veteran, who obeys him as if God and nature had ordained that so throughout time it should be.

That privates should obey, and that they should be smartly punished if they disobey, this one can understand very well. But to say obey for ever and ever — to say that private John Styles is, by some physical disproportion, hopelessly inferior to Cornet Snooks — to say that Snooks shall have honors, epaulets, and a marble tablet if he dies, and that Styles shall fight his fight, and have his twopence a day, and when shot down shall be shovelled into a hole with other Styleses, and so forgotten; and to think that we had in the course of the last war some 400,000 of these Styleses, and some 10,000, say, of the Snooks sort — Styles being by nature exactly as honest, clever, and brave as Snooks — and to think that the 400,000 should bear this, is the wonder!

Suppose Snooks makes a speech. "Look at these Frenchmen, British soldiers," says he, "and remember who they are. Two and twenty years since they hurled their King from his throne and murdered him" (groans). "They flung out of their country their ancient and famous nobility — they published the audacious doctrine of equality — they made a cadet of artillery, a beggarly lawyer's son, into an Emperor, and took ignoramuses from the ranks — drummers and privates, by Jove! — of whom they made kings, generals, and marshals! Is this to be borne?" (Cries of "No! no!") "Upon them, boys! down with these godless revolutionists, and rally round the British lion!"

So saying, Ensign Snooks (whose flag, which he can't carry, is held by a huge grisly color-sergeant) draws a little sword, and pipes out a feeble huzza. The men of his company, roaring curses at the Frenchmen, prepare to receive and repel a thundering charge of French cuirassiers. The men fight, and Snooks is knighted because the men fought so well.

But live or die, win or lose, what do *they* get? English glory is too genteel to meddle with those humble fellows. She does not condescend to ask the names of the poor devils whom she kills in her service. Why was not every private man's name written upon the stones in Waterloo Church as well as every officer's? Five hundred pounds to the stone-cutters would have served to carve the whole catalogue, and paid the poor compliment of recognition to men who died in doing their duty. If the officers deserved a stone, the men did. But come, let us away and drop a tear over the Marquis of Anglesea's leg!

As for Waterloo, has it not been talked of enough after dinner? Here are some oats that were plucked before Hougoumont, where grow not only oats, but flourishing crops of grape-shot, bayonets, and legion-of-honor crosses, in amazing profusion.

Well, though I made a vow not to talk about Waterloo either here or after dinner, there is one little secret admission that one must make after seeing it. Let an Englishman go and see that field, and he *never forgets it.* The sight is an event in his life; and, though it has been seen by millions of peaceable *gents* — grocers from Bond Street, meek attorneys from Chancery Lane, and timid tailors from Piccadilly — I will wager that there is not one of them but feels a glow as he looks at the place, and remembers that he, too, is an Englishman.

It is a wrong, egotistical, savage, unchristian feeling, and that's the truth of it. A man of peace has no right to be dazzled by that red-coated glory, and to intoxicate his vanity with those remembrances of carnage and triumph. The same sentence which tells us that on earth there ought to be peace and goodwill amongst men, tells us to whom GLORY belongs.

THE FITZ-BOODLE PAPERS.

THE FITZ-BOODLE PAPERS.*

FITZ-BOODLE'S CONFESSIONS.

PREFACE.

GEORGE FITZ-BOODLE, ESQUIRE, TO OLIVER YORKE, ESQUIRE.

Omnium Club, May 20, 1842.

DEAR SIR, — I have always been considered the third-best whist-player in Europe, and (though never betting more than five pounds) have for many years past added considerably to my yearly income by my skill in the game, until the commencement of the present season, when a French gentleman, Monsieur Lalouette, was admitted to the club where I usually play. His skill and reputation were so great, that no men of the club were inclined to play against us two of a side; and the consequence has been, that we have been in a manner pitted against one another. By a strange turn of luck (for I cannot admit the idea of his superiority), Fortune, since the Frenchman's arrival, has been almost constantly against me, and I have lost two and thirty nights in the course of a couple score of nights' play.

Everybody knows that I am a poor man; and so much has Lalouette's luck drained my finances, that only last week I was obliged to give him that famous gray cob on which you have seen me riding in the Park (I can't afford a thorough-bred, and hate a cocktail), — I was, I say, forced to give him up my cob in exchange for four ponies which I owed him. Thus, as I never walk, being a heavy man whom nobody cares to mount, my time hangs heavily on my hands; and as I hate home, or that apology for it — a bachelor's lodgings — and as I have nothing earthly to do now until I can afford to purchase another horse, I spend my time in sauntering from one club to another, passing many rather listless hours in them before the men come in.

You will say, Why not take to backgammon, or écarté, or amuse yourself with a book? Sir (putting out of the question the fact that I do not play upon credit), I make a point never to play before candles are lighted; and as for books, I must candidly confess to you I am not a reading man. 'Twas but the other day that some one recommended me to read your Magazine after dinner, saying it contained an exceedingly witty article upon — I forget what. I give you my honor, sir, that I took up the work at six, meaning to amuse myself till seven, when Lord Trumpington's dinner was to come off, and egad! in two minutes I fell asleep, and never woke till midnight. Nobody ever thought of looking for me in the library, where nobody ever

* "The Fitz-Boodle Papers" first appeared in "Fraser's Magazine" for the year 1842.

goes; and so ravenously hungry was I, that I was obliged to walk off to Crockford's for supper.

What is it that makes you literary persons so stupid? I have met various individuals in society who I was told were writers of books, and that sort of thing, and, expecting rather to be amused by their conversation, have invariably found them dull to a degree, and as for information, without a particle of it. Sir, I actually asked one of these fellows, "What was the nick to seven?" and he stared in my face, and said he didn't know. He was hugely over-dressed in satin, rings, chains, and so forth; and at the beginning of dinner was disposed to be rather talkative and pert; but my little sally silenced *him*, I promise you, and got up a good laugh at his expense too. "Leave George alone," said little Lord Cinqbars, "I warrant he'll be a match for any of you literary fellows." Cinqbars is no great wiseacre; but, indeed, it requires no great wiseacre to know *that*.

What is the simple deduction to be drawn from this truth? Why, this — that a man to be amusing and well-informed, has no need of books at all, and had much better go to the world and to men for his knowledge. There was Ulysses, now, the Greek fellow engaged in the Trojan war, as I dare say you know; well, he was the cleverest man possible, and how? From having seen men and cities, their manners noted and their realms surveyed, to be sure. So have I. I have been in every capital, and can order a dinner in every language in Europe.

My notion, then, is this. I have a great deal of spare time on my hands, and as I am told you pay a handsome sum to persons writing for you, I will furnish you occasionally with some of my views upon men and things; occasional histories of my acquaintance, which I think may amuse you; personal narratives of my own; essays, and what not. I am told that I do not spell correctly. This, of course, I don't know; but you will remember that Richelieu and Marlborough could not spell, and, egad! I am an honest man, and desire to be no better than they. I know that it is the matter, and not the manner, which is of importance. Have the goodness, then, to let one of your understrappers correct the spelling and the grammar of my papers; and you can give him a few shillings in my name for his trouble.

Begging you to accept the assurance of my high consideration, I am, sir,

Your obedient servant,
GEORGE SAVAGE FITZ-BOODLE.

P.S. — By the way, I have said in my letter that I found *all* literary persons vulgar and dull. Permit me to contradict this with regard to yourself. I met you once at Blackwall, I think it was, and really did not remark any thing offensive in your accent or appearance.

BEFORE commencing the series of moral disquisitions, &c., which I intend, the reader may as well know who I am, and what my past course of life has been. To say that I am a Fitz-Boodle is to say at once that I am a gentleman. Our family has held the estate of Boodle ever since the reign of Henry II.; and it is out of no ill will to my elder brother, or unnatural desire for his death, but only because the estate is a very good one, that I wish heartily it was mine: I would say as much of Chatsworth or Eton Hall.

I am not, in the first place, what is called a ladies' man, having contracted an irrepressible habit of smoking after dinner, which has obliged me to give up a great deal of the dear creatures' society; nor can I go much to country-houses for the same reason. Say what they will, ladies do not like you to smoke in their bed-rooms; their silly little noses scent out the odor upon the chintz, weeks after you have left them. Sir John has been caught coming to bed particularly merry and redolent of cigar-smoke; young George, from Eton, was absolutely found in the little green-house puffing an Havanna; and when discovered, they both lay the blame upon Fitz-Boodle. "It was Mr. Fitz-Boodle, mamma," says George, "who offered me the cigar, and I did not like to refuse him." "That rascal Fitz seduced us, my dear," says Sir John, "and kept us laughing until past midnight." Her ladyship instantly sets me down as a person to be avoided. "George," whispers she to her boy, "promise me, on your honor, when you go to town, not to know that man." And when she enters the breakfast-room for prayers, the first greeting is a peculiar expression of countenance, and inhaling of breath, by which my lady indicates the presence of some exceedingly disagreeable odor in the room. She makes you the faintest of courtesies, and regards you, if not with a "flashing eye," as in the novels, at least with a "distended nostril." During the whole of the service, her heart is filled with the blackest gall towards you; and she is thinking about the best means of getting you out of the house.

What is this smoking that it should be considered a crime? I believe in my heart that women are jealous of it, as of a rival. They speak of it as of some secret, awful vice that seizes upon a man, and makes him a pariah from genteel society. I would lay a guinea that many a lady who has just been kind enough to read the above lines lays down the book, after this confession of mine that I am a smoker, and says, "Oh, the vulgar wretch!" and passes on to something else.

The fact is, that the cigar *is* a rival to the ladies, and their conqueror too. In the chief pipe-smoking nations they are kept in subjection. While the chief, Little White Belt, smokes, the women are silent in his wigwam; while Mahomet Ben Jawbrahim causes volumes of odorous incense of Latakia to play round his beard, the women of the harem do not disturb his meditations, but only add to the delight of them by tinkling on a dulcimer and dancing before him. When Professor Strumpff of Göttingen takes down No. 13 from the wall, with a picture of Beatrice Cenci upon it, and which holds a pound of canaster, the Frau Professorin knows that for two hours Hermann is engaged, and takes up her stockings and knits in quiet. The constitution of French society has been quite changed within the last twelve years: an ancient and respectable dynasty has been overthrown; an aristocracy which Napoleon could never master has disappeared: and from what cause? I do not hesitate to say,—*from the habit of smoking.* Ask any man whether, five years before the revolution of July, if you wanted a cigar at Paris, they did not bring you a roll of tobacco with a straw in it? Now, the whole city smokes; society is changed; and be sure of this, ladies, a similar combat is going on in this country at present between cigar-smoking and you. Do you suppose you will conquer? Look over the wide world, and see that your adversary has overcome it. Germany has been puffing for threescore years; France smokes to a man. Do you think you can keep the enemy out of England? Psha! look at his progress. Ask the club-houses, Have they smoking-rooms, or not? Are they not obliged to yield to the general want of the age, in spite of the resistance of the old women on the committees? I, for my part, do not despair to see a bishop lolling out of "The Athenæum" with a cheroot in his mouth, or, at any rate, a pipe stuck in his shovel-hat.

But as in all great causes and in promulgating new and illustrious theories, their first propounders and exponents are generally the victims of their enthusiasm, of course the first preachers of smoking have been martyrs, too; and George Fitz-Boodle is one. The first gas-man was ruined; the inventor of steam-engine printing became a pauper. I began to smoke in days when the task was one of some danger, and paid the penalty of my crime. I was flogged most fiercely for my first cigar; for, being asked to dine one Sunday evening with a half-pay colonel of dragoons (the gallant, simple, humorous Shortcut — heaven bless him! — I have had many a guinea from him who had so few), he insisted upon my smoking in his room at "The Salopian," and the consequence was, that I became so violently ill as to be reported intoxicated upon my return to Slaughter-House School, where I was a boarder, and I was whipped the next morning for my peccadillo. At Christ Church, one of our tutors was the celebrated lamented Otto Rose, who would have been a bishop under the present Government, had not an immoderate indulgence in water-gruel cut short his elegant and useful career. He was a good man, a pretty scholar and poet (the episode upon the discovery of eau-de-Cologne, in his prize-poem on "The Rhine," was considered a masterpiece of art, though I am not much of a judge myself upon such matters), and he was as remarkable for his fondness for a tuft as for his nervous antipathy to tobacco. As ill-luck would have it, my rooms (in Tom Quad) were exactly under his; and I was grown by this time to be a confirmed smoker. I was a baronet's son (we are of James the First's creation), and I do believe our tutor could have pardoned any crime in the world but this. He had seen me in a tandem, and at that moment was seized with a violent fit of sneezing — (sternutatory paroxysm he called it) — at the conclusion of which I was a mile down the Woodstock Road. He had seen me in pink, as we used to call it, swaggering in the open sunshine across a grass-plat in the court; but spied out opportunely a servitor, one Todhunter by name, who was going to morning chapel with his shoestring untied, and forthwith sprung towards that unfortunate person, to set him an imposition. Every thing, in fact, but tobacco he could forgive. Why did cursed fortune bring him into the rooms over mine? The odor of the cigars made his gentle spirit quite furious; and one luckless morning, when I was standing before my "oak," and chanced to puff a great *bouffée* of Varinas into his face, he forgot his respect for my family altogether (I was the second son, and my brother a sickly creature *then*, — he is now sixteen stone in weight, and has a half-score of children); gave me a severe lecture, to which I replied rather hotly, as was my wont. And then came demand for an apology; refusal on my part; appeal to the dean; convocation; and rustication of George Savage Fitz-Boodle.

My father had taken a second wife (of the noble house of Flintskinner), and Lady Fitz-Boodle detested smoking, as a woman of her high principles should. She had an entire mastery over the worthy old gentleman, and thought I was a sort of demon of wickedness. The old man went to his grave with some similar notion, — heaven help him! and left me but the wretched twelve thousand pounds secured to me on my poor mother's property.

In the army, my luck was much the same. I joined the ——th Lancers, Lieut.-Col. Lord Martingale, in the year 1817. I only did duty with the regiment for three months. We were quartered at Cork, where I found the Irish doodheen and tobacco the pleasantest smoking possible; and was found by his lordship, one day upon stable duty, smoking the shortest, dearest little dumpy clay-pipe in the world.

"Cornet Fitz-Boodle," said my lord, in a towering passion, "from what blackguard did you get that pipe?"

I omit the oaths which garnished invariably his lordship's conversation.

"I got it, my lord," said I, "from

one Terence Mullins, a jingle-driver, with a packet of his peculiar tobacco. You sometimes smoke Turkish, I believe; do try this. Isn't it good?" And in the simplest way in the world I puffed a volume into his face. "I see you like it," said I, so coolly, that the men — and I do believe the horses — burst out laughing.

He started back — choking almost, and recovered himself only to vent such a storm of oaths and curses that I was compelled to request Captain Rawdon (the captain on duty) to take note of his lordship's words; and unluckily could not help adding a question which settled my business. "You were good enough," I said, "to ask me, my lord, from what blackguard I got my pipe; might I ask from what blackguard you learned your language?"

This was quite enough. Had I said, "From what *gentleman* did your lordship learn your language?" the point would have been quite as good, and my Lord Martingale would have suffered in my place: as it was, I was so strongly recommended to sell out by his Royal Highness the Commander-in-Chief, that, being of a good-natured disposition, never knowing how to refuse a friend, I at once threw up my hopes of military distinction and retired into civil life.

My lord was kind enough to meet me afterwards in a field in the Glanmire Road, where he put a ball into my leg. This I returned to him some years later with about twenty-three others — black ones — when he came to be balloted for at a club of which I have the honor to be a member.

Thus by the indulgence of a simple and harmless propensity, — of a propensity which can inflict an injury upon no person or thing except the coat and the person of him who indulges in it, — of a custom honored and observed in almost all the nations of the world, — of a custom which, far from leading a man into any wickedness or dissipation to which youth is subject, on the contrary, begets only benevolent silence and thoughtful good-humored observation — I found at the age of twenty all my prospects in life destroyed. I cared not for woman in those days: the calm smoker has a sweet companion in his pipe. I did not drink immoderately of wine; for though a friend to trifling potations, to excessively strong drinks tobacco is abhorrent. I never thought of gambling, for the lover of the pipe has no need of such excitement; but I was considered a monster of dissipation in my family, and bade fair to come to ruin.

"Look at George," my mother-in-law said to the genteel and correct young Flintskinners. "He entered the world with every prospect in life, and see in what an abyss of degradation his fatal habits have plunged him! At school he was flogged and disgraced, he was disgraced and rusticated at the university, he was disgraced and expelled from the army! He might have had the living of Boodle" (her ladyship gave it to one of her nephews), "but he would not take his degree; his papa would have purchased him a troop — nay, a lieutenant-colonelcy some day, but for his fatal excesses. And now as long as my dear husband will listen to the voice of a wife who adores him — never, never shall he spend a shilling upon so worthless a young man. He has a small income from his mother (I cannot but think that the first Lady Fitz-Boodle was a weak and misguided person); let him live upon his mean pittance as he can, and I heartily pray we may not hear of him in jail!"

My brother, after he came to the estate, married the ninth daughter of our neighbor, Sir John Spreadeagle; and Boodle Hall has seen a new little Fitz-Boodle with every succeeding spring. The dowager retired to Scotland with a large jointure and a wondrous heap of savings. Lady Fitz is a good creature, but she thinks me something diabolical, trembles when she sees me, and gathers all her children about her, rushes into the nursery whenever I pay that little seminary a visit, and actually slapped poor little Frank's ears one day when I was teaching him to ride upon the back of a Newfoundland dog.

"George," said my brother to me the last time I paid him a visit at the old hall, "don't be angry, my dear fellow, but Maria is in a — hum — in a delicate situation, expecting her — hum" — (the eleventh) — "and do you know you frighten her? It was but yesterday you met her in the rookery — you were smoking that enormous German pipe — and when she came in she had an hysterical seizure, and Drench says that in her situation it's dangerous. And I say, George, if you go to town you'll find a couple of hundred at your banker's." And with this the poor fellow shook me by the hand, and called for a fresh bottle of claret.

Afterwards he told me, with many hesitations, that my room at Boodle Hall had been made into a second nursery. I see my sister-in-law in London twice or thrice in the season, and the little people, who have almost forgotten to call me uncle George.

It's hard, too, for I am a lonely man after all, and my heart yearns to them. The other day I smuggled a couple of them into my chambers, and had a little feast of cream and strawberries to welcome them. But it had like to have cost the nursery-maid (a Swiss girl that Fitz-Boodle hired somewhere in his travels) her place. My step-mamma, who happened to be in town, came flying down in her chariot, pounced upon the poor thing and the children in the midst of the entertainment; and when I asked her with rather a bad grace to be sure, to take a chair and a share of the feast —

"Mr. Fitz-Boodle," said she, "I am not accustomed to sit down in a place that smells of tobacco like an ale-house — an ale-house inhabited by a *serpent*, sir! A *serpent!* — do you understand me? — who carries his poison into his brother's own house, and purshues his eenfamous designs before his brother's own children. Put on Miss Maria's bonnet this instant. Mamsell, ontondy-voo? *Metty le bonny à mamsell.* And I shall take care, Mamsell, that you return to Switzerland to-morrow. I've no doubt you are a relation of Courvoisier — *oui! oui! Courvoisier, vous comprenny* — and you shall certainly be sent back to your friends."

With this speech, and with the children and their maid sobbing before her, my lady retired; but for once my sister-in-law was on my side, not liking the meddlement of the elder lady.

I know, then, that from indulging in that simple habit of smoking, I have gained among the ladies a dreadful reputation. I see that they look coolly upon me, and darkly at their husbands when they arrive at home in my company. Men, I observe, in consequence, ask me to dine much oftener at the club, or "The Star and Garter" at Richmond, or at "Lovegrove's," than in their own houses; and with this sort of arrangement I am fain to acquiesce; for, as I said before, I am of an easy temper, and can at any rate take my cigar-case out after dinner at Blackwall, when my lady or the duchess is not by. I know, of course, the best *men* in town; and as for ladies' society, not having it (for I will have none of your pseudo-ladies, such as sometimes honor bachelors' parties, — actresses, couturieres, opera-dancers, and so forth) — as for ladies' society, I say, I cry pish! 'tis not worth the trouble of the complimenting, and the bother of pumps and black silk stockings.

Let any man remember what ladies' society was when he had an opportunity of seeing them among themselves, as What-d'ye-call'im does in the Thesmophoria — I beg pardon, I was on the verge of a classical allusion, which I abominate) — I mean at that period of his life when the intellect is pretty acute, though the body is small — namely, when a young gentleman is about eleven years of age, dining at his father's table during the holidays, and is requested by his papa to quit the dinner-table when the ladies retire from it.

Corbleu! I recollect their whole talk as well as if it had been whispered but yesterday; and can see, after a long dinner, the yellow summer sun throwing long shadows over the lawn before the dining-room windows, and my poor mother and her company of ladies sailing away to the music-room in old Boodle Hall. The Countess Dawdley was the great lady in our county, a portly lady who used to love crimson satin in those days, and birds-of-paradise. She was flaxen-haired, and the Regent once said she resembled one of King Charles's beauties.

When Sir John Todcaster used to begin his famous story of the exciseman (I shall not tell it here, for very good reasons), my poor mother used to turn to Lady Dawdley, and give that mystic signal at which all females rise from their chairs. Tufthunt, the curate, would spring from his seat, and be sure to be the first to open the poor for the retreating ladies; and my brother Tom and I, though remaining stoutly in our places, were speedily ejected from them by the governor's invariable remark, "Tom and George, if you have had *quite* enough of wine, you had better go and join your mamma." Yonder she marches, heaven bless her! through the old oak hall (how long the shadows of the antlers are on the wainscot, and the armor of Rollo Fitz-Boodle looks in the sunset as if it were emblazoned with rubies) — yonder she marches, stately and tall, in her invariable pearl-colored tabinet, followed by Lady Dawdley, blazing like a flamingo; next comes Lady Emily Tufthunt (she was Lady Emily Flintskinner), who will not for all the world take precedence of rich, vulgar, kind, good-humored Mrs. *Colonel* Grogwater, as she would be called, with a yellow little husband from Madras, who first taught me to drink sangaree. He was a new arrival in our county, but paid nobly to the hounds, and occupied hospitably a house which was always famous for its hospitality — Sievely Hall (poor Bob Cullender ran through seven thousand a year before he was thirty years old). Once when I was a lad, Colonel Grogwater gave me two gold mohurs out of his desk for whist-markers, and I'm sorry to say I ran up from Eton and sold them both for seventy-three shillings at a shop in Cornhill. But to return to the ladies, who are all this while kept waiting in the hall, and to their usual conversation after dinner.

Can any man forget how miserably flat it was? Five matrons sit on sofas, and talk in a subdued voice: —

First Lady (*mysteriously*). — "My dear Lady Dawdley, do tell me about poor Susan Tuckett."

Second Lady. — "All three children are perfectly well, and I assure you as fine babies as I ever saw in my life. I made her give them Daffy's Elixir the first day; and it was the greatest mercy that I had some of Frederick's baby-clothes by me; for you know I had provided Susan with sets for one only, and really" —

Third Lady. — "Of course one couldn't; and for my part I think your ladyship is a great deal too kind to these people. A little gardener's boy dressed in Lord Dawdley's frocks indeed! I recollect that one at his christening had the sweetest lace in the world!"

Fourth Lady. — "What do you think of this, ma'am — Lady Emily, I mean? I have just had it from Howell and James: — guipure, they call it. Isn't it an odd name for lace? And they charge me, upon my conscience, four guineas a yard!"

Third Lady. — "My mother, when she came to Flintskinner, had lace upon her robe that cost sixty guineas a yard, ma'am! 'Twas sent from

Malines direct by our relation, the Count d'Araignay."

Fourth Lady (*aside*). — "I thought she would not let the evening pass without talking of her Malines lace and her Count d'Araignay. Odious people! they don't spare their backs, but they pinch their" —

Here Tom upsets a coffee-cup over his white jean trousers, and another young gentleman bursts into a laugh, saying, "By Jove, that's a good 'un!"

"George, my dear," says mamma, "had not you and your young friend better go into the garden? But mind, no fruit, or Dr. Glauber must be called in again immediately!" And we all go, and in ten minutes I and my brother are fighting in the stables.

If, instead of listening to the matrons and their discourse, we had taken the opportunity of attending to the conversation of the Misses, we should have heard matter not a whit more interesting.

First Miss. — "They were all three in blue crape; you never saw any thing so odious. And I know for a certainty that they wore those dresses at Muddlebury, at the archery-ball, and I dare say they had them in town."

Second Miss. — "Don't you think Jemima decidedly crooked? And those fair complexions, they freckle so, that really Miss Blanche ought to be called Miss Brown."

Third Miss. — "He, he he!"

Fourth Miss. — "Don't you think Blanche is a pretty name?"

First Miss. — "La! do you think so, dear? Why, it's my second name!"

Second Miss. — "Then I'm sure Captain Travers thinks it a *beautiful* name!"

Third Miss. — "He, he, he!"

Fourth Miss. — "What was he telling you at dinner that seemed to interest you so?"

First Miss. — "O law, nothing! — that is yes! Charles — that is, — Captain, Travers, is a sweet poet, and was reciting to me some lines that he had composed upon a faded violet: —

"'The odor from the flower is gone,
That like thy' —

like thy something, I forget what it was; but his lines are sweet, and so original too! I wish that horrid Sir John Todcaster had not begun his story of the exciseman, for Lady Fitz-Boodle always quits the table when he begins."

Third Miss. — "Do you like those tufts that gentlemen wear sometimes on their chins?"

Second Miss. — "Nonsense, Mary!"

Third Miss. — "Well, I only asked Jane. Frank thinks, you know, that he shall very soon have one, and puts bear's-grease on his chin every night."

Second Miss. — "Mary, nonsense!"

Third Miss. — "Well, only ask him. You know he came to our dressing-room last night and took the pomatum away; and he says that when boys go to Oxford, they always" —

First Miss. — "O heavens! have you heard the news about the Lancers? Charles — that is, Captain Travers, told it me!"

Second Miss. — "Law! they won't go away before the ball, I hope!"

First Miss. — "No, but on the 15th they are to shave their mustaches! He says that Lord Tufto is in a perfect fury about it!"

Second Miss. — "And poor George Beardmore, too!" &c.

Here Tom upsets the coffee over his trousers, and the conversations end. I can recollect a dozen such, and ask any man of sense whether such talk amuses him?

Try again to speak to a young lady while you are dancing — what we call in this country — a quadrille. What nonsense do you invariably give and receive in return! No, I am a woman-scorner, and don't care to own it. I hate young ladies! Have I not been in love with several, and has any one of them ever treated me decently? I hate married women! Do they not hate me? and, simply because I smoke, try to draw their husbands away from my society? I hate dowagers! Have I not cause? Does not every dowager in London point to George Fitz-Boodle as to a dissolute wretch whom young and old should avoid?

And yet do not imagine that I have not loved. I have, and madly, many, many times! I am but eight and thirty,* not past the age of passion, and may very likely end by running off with an heiress — or a cook-maid (for who knows what strange freaks Love may choose to play in his own particular person? and I hold a man to be a mean creature who calculates about checking any such sacred impulse as lawful love) — I say, though despising the sex in general for their conduct to me, I know of particular persons belonging to it who are worthy of all respect and esteem, and as such I beg leave to point out the particular young lady who is perusing these lines. Do not, dear madam, then imagine that if I knew you I should be disposed to sneer at you. Ah, no! Fitz-Boodle's bosom has tenderer sentiments than from his way of life you would fancy, and stern by rule is only too soft by practice. Shall I whisper to you the story of one or two of my attachments? All terminating fatally (not in death, but in disappointment, which, as it occurred, I used to imagine a thousand times more bitter than death, but from which one recovers somehow more readily than from the other-named complaint) — all, I say, terminating wretchedly to myself, as if some fatality pursued my desire to become a domestic character.

My first love — no, let us pass *that* over. Sweet one! thy name shall profane no hireling page. Sweet, sweet memory! Ah, ladies, those delicate hearts of yours have, too, felt the throb. And between the last *ob* in the word throb and the words now written, I have passed a delicious period of perhaps an hour, perhaps a minute, I know not how long, thinking of that holy first love and of her who inspired it. How clearly every single incident of the passion is remembered by me! and yet, 'twas long, long since. I was but a child then — a child at school — and, if the truth must be told, L—ra R–ggl–s (I would not write her whole name to be made one of the Marquess of Hertford's executors) was a woman full thirteen years older than myself; at the period of which I write she must have been at least five and twenty. She and her mother used to sell tarts, hard-bake, lollipops, and other such simple comestibles, on Wednesdays and Saturdays (half-holidays), at a private school where I received the first rudiments of a classical education. I used to go and sit before her tray for hours, but I do not think the poor girl ever supposed any motive led me so constantly to her little stall beyond a vulgar longing for her tarts and her ginger-beer. Yes, even at that early period, my actions were misrepresented, and the fatality which has oppressed my whole life began to show itself, — the purest passion was misinterpreted by her and my schoolfellows, and they thought I was actuated by simple gluttony. They nicknamed me Alicompayne.

Well, be it so. Laugh at early passion ye who will; a high-born boy madly in love with a lowly ginger-beer girl! She married afterwards, took the name of Latter, and now keeps with her old husband a turnpike, through which I often ride; but I can recollect her bright and rosy of a sunny summer afternoon, her red cheeks shaded by a battered straw bonnet, her tarts and ginger-beer upon a neat white cloth before her, mending blue worsted stockings until the young gentlemen should interrupt her by coming to buy.

Many persons will call this description low; I do not envy them their gentility, and have always observed through life (as, to be sure, every

* He is five and forty, if he is a day old. — O. Y.

other *gentleman* has observed as well as myself) that it is your *parvenu* who stickles most for what he calls the genteel, and has the most squeamish abhorrence for what is frank and natural. Let us pass at once, however, as all the world must be pleased, to a recital of an affair which occurred in the very best circles of society, as they are called, viz. my next unfortunate attachment.

It did not occur for several years after that simple and platonic passion just described: for, though they may talk of youth as the season of romance, it has always appeared to me that there are no beings in the world so entirely unromantic and selfish as certain young English gentlemen from the age of fifteen to twenty. The oldest Lovelace about town is scarcely more hard-hearted and scornful than they; they ape all sorts of selfishness and *rouerie:* they aim at excelling at cricket, at billiards, at rowing, and drinking, and set more store by a red coat and a neat pair of top-boots than by any other glory. A young fellow staggers into college-chapel of a morning, and communicates to all his friends that he was "*so cut* last night," with the greatest possible pride. He makes a joke of having sisters and a kind mother at home who loves him; and if he speaks of his father, it is with a knowing sneer to say that he has a tailor's and a horse-dealer's bill that will surprise "the old governor." He would be ashamed of being in love. I, in common with my kind, had these affectations, and my perpetual custom of smoking added not a little to my reputation as an accomplished *roué.* What came of this custom in the army and at college, the reader has already heard. Alas! in life it went no better with me, and many pretty chances I had went off in that accursed smoke.

After quitting the army in the abrupt manner stated, I passed some short time at home, and was tolerated by my mother-in-law, because I had formed an attachment to a young lady of good connections and with a considerable fortune, which was really very nearly becoming mine. Mary M'Alister was the only daughter of Colonel M'Alister, late of the Blues, and Lady Susan his wife. Her ladyship was no more; and, indeed, of no family compared to ours (which has refused a peerage any time these two hundred years); but being an earl's daughter and a Scotchwoman, Lady Emily Fitz-Boodle did not fail to consider her highly. Lady Susan was daughter of the late Admiral Earl of Marlingspike and Baron Plumduff. The Colonel, Miss M'Alister's father, had a good estate, of which his daughter was the heiress, and as I fished her out of the water upon a pleasure-party, and swam with her to shore, we became naturally intimate, and Colonel M'Alister forgot, on account of the service rendered to him, the dreadful reputation for profligacy which I enjoyed in the county.

Well, to cut a long story short, which is told here merely for the moral at the end of it, I should have been Fitz-Boodle M'Alister at this minute most probably, and master of four thousand a year, but for the fatal cigar-box. I bear Mary no malice in saying that she was a high-spirited little girl, loving, before all things, her own way; nay, perhaps I do not, from long habit and indulgence in tobacco-smoking, appreciate the delicacy of female organizations, which were oftentimes most painfully affected by it. She was a keen-sighted little person, and soon found that the world had belied poor George Fitz-Boodle; who, instead of being the cunning monster people supposed him to be, was a simple, reckless, good-humored, honest fellow, marvellously addicted to smoking, idleness, and telling the truth. She called me Orson, and I was happy enough on the 14th February, in the year 18 — (it's of no consequence), to send her such a pretty little copy of verses about Orson and Valentine, in which the rude habits of the savage man were shown to be overcome by the polished graces of his kind and brilliant conqueror, that she was fairly overcome, and said to me, "George Fitz-Boodle, if you give up smoking for a year I will marry you."

I swore I would, of course, and went home and flung four pounds of Hudson's cigars, two meerschaum pipes that had cost me ten guineas at the establishment of Mr. Gattie at Oxford, a tobacco-bag that Lady Fitz-Boodle had given me *before* her marriage with my father (it was the only present that I ever had from her or any member of the Flintskinner family), and some choice packets of Varinas and Syrian, into the lake in Boodle Park. The weapon amongst them all which I most regretted was — will it be believed? — the little black doodheen which had been the cause of the quarrel between Lord Martingale and me. However, it went along with the others. I would not allow my groom to have so much as a cigar, lest I should be tempted hereafter; and the consequence was that a few days after many fat carps and tenches in the lake (I must confess 'twas no bigger than a pond) nibbled at the tobacco, and came floating on their backs on the top of the water quite intoxicated. My conversion made some noise in the county, being emphasized as it were by this fact of the fish. I can't tell you with what pangs I kept my resolution; but keep it I did for some time.

With so much beauty and wealth, Mary M'Alister had of course many suitors, and among them was the young Lord Dawdley, whose mamma has previously been described in her gown of red satin. As I used to thrash Dawdley at school, I thrashed him in after-life in love; he put up with his disappointment pretty well, and came after a while and shook hands with me, telling me of the bets that there were in the county, where the whole story was known, for and against me. For the fact is, as I must own, that Mary M'Alister, the queerest, frankest of women, made no secret of the agreement or the cause of it.

"I did not care a penny for Orson," she said, "but he would go on writing me such dear pretty verses that at last I couldn't help saying yes. But if he breaks his promise to me, I declare, upon my honor, I'll break mine, and nobody's heart will be broken either."

This was the perfect fact, as I must confess, and I declare that it was only because she amused me and delighted me, and provoked me, and made me laugh very much, and because, no doubt, she was very rich, that I had any attachment for her.

"For heaven's sake, George," my father said to me, as I quitted home to follow my beloved to London, "remember that you are a younger brother and have a lovely girl and four thousand a year within a year's reach of you. Smoke as much as you like, my boy, after marriage," added the old gentleman, knowingly (as if *he*, honest soul, after his second marriage, dared drink an extra pint of wine without my lady's permission!) "but eschew the tobacco-shops till then."

I went to London resolving to act upon the paternal advice, and oh! how I longed for the day when I should be married, vowing in my secret soul that I would light a cigar as I walked out of St. George's Hanover Square.

Well, I came to London, and so carefully avoided smoking that I would not even go into Hudson's shop to pay his bill, and as smoking was not the fashion then among young men as (thank heaven!) it is now, I had not many temptations from my friends' examples in my clubs or elsewhere; only little Dawdley began to smoke, as if to spite me. He had never done so before, but confessed — the rascal! — that he enjoyed a cigar now, if it were but to mortify me. But I took to other and more dangerous excitements, and upon the nights when not in attendance upon Mary M'Alister, might be found in very dangerous proximity to a polished mahogany table, round which claret-bottles circulated a great deal too often, or worse still, to a table covered with green cloth and ornamented with a couple of wax-candles and a couple of packs of cards, and four gentlemen playing the enticing game of whist. Likewise, I came to carry a snuff-box, and to consume in secret huge quantities of rappee.

For ladies' society I was even then disinclined, hating and despising small-talk, and dancing, and hot routs, and vulgar scrambles for suppers. I never could understand the pleasure of acting the part of lackey to a dowager, and standing behind her chair, or bustling through the crowd for her carriage. I always found an opera too long by two acts, and have repeatedly fallen asleep in the presence of Mary M'Alister herself, sitting at the back of the box shaded by the huge beret of her old aunt Lady Betty Plumduff; and many a time has Dawdley, with Miss M'Alister on his arm, wakened me up at the close of the entertainment in time to offer my hand to Lady Betty, and lead the ladies to their carriage. If I attended her occasionally to any ball or party of pleasure, I went, it must be confessed, with clumsy, ill-disguised ill-humor. Good heavens! have I often and often thought in the midst of a song, or the very thick of a ball-room, can people prefer this to a book and a sofa, and a dear, dear cigar-box, from thy stores, O charming Mariana Woodville! Deprived of my favorite plant, I grew sick in mind and body, moody, sarcastic, and discontented.

Such a state of things could not long continue, nor could Miss M'Alister continue to have much attachment for such a sullen, ill-conditioned creature as I then was. She used to make me wild with her wit and her sarcasm, nor have I ever possessed the readiness to parry or reply to those fine points of woman's wit, and she treated me the more mercilessly as she saw that I could not resist her.

Well, the polite reader must remember a great fête that was given at B—— House, some years back, in honor of his Highness the Hereditary Prince of Kalbsbraten-Pumpernickel, who was then in London on a visit to his illustrious relatives. It was a fancy ball, and the poems of Scott being at that time all the fashion, Mary was to appear in the character of the "Lady of the Lake," old M'Alister making a very tall and severe-looking harper; Dawdley, a most insignificant Fitz-james; and your humble servant a stalwart manly Roderick Dhu. We were to meet at B—— House at twelve o'clock, and as I had no fancy to drive through the town in my cab dressed in a kilt and philibeg, I agreed to take a seat in Dawdley's carriage, and to dress at his house in May Fair. At eleven I left a very pleasant bachelors' party, growling to quit them and the honest, jovial claret-bottle, in order to scrape and cut capers like a harlequin from the theatre. When I arrived at Dawdley's, I mounted to a dressing-room, and began to array myself in my cursed costume.

The art of costuming was by no means so well understood in those days as it has been since, and mine was out of all correctness. I was made to sport an enormous plume of black ostrich-feathers, such as never was worn by any Highland chief, and had a huge tiger-skin sporran to dangle like an apron before innumerable yards of plaid petticoat. The tartan cloak was outrageously hot and voluminous; it was the dog-days, and all these things I was condemned to wear in the midst of a crowd of a thousand people!

Dawdley sent up word, as I was dressing, that his dress had not arrived, and he took my cab and drove off in a rage to his tailor.

There was no hurry, I thought, to make a fool of myself; so having put on a pair of plaid trews, and very neat pumps, with shoe-buckles, my courage failed me as to the rest of the dress, and taking down one of his dressing-gowns, I went down stairs to the study, to wait untill he should arrive.

The windows of the pretty room were open, and a snug sofa, with innumerable cushions, drawn towards one of them. A great tranquil moon was staring into the chamber, in which stood, amidst books and all sorts of bachelor's lumber, a silver tray with a couple of tall Venice glasses, and a bottle of Maraschino bound with straw. I can see now the twinkle of the liquor in the moonshine, as I poured it into the glass; and I swallowed two or three little cups of it, for my spirits were downcast. Close to the tray of Maraschino stood — must I say it? — a box, a mere box of cedar, bound rudely together with pink paper, branded with the name of "Hudson" on the side, and bearing on the cover the arms of Spain. I thought I would just take up the box and look in it.

Ah heaven!" there they were — a hundred and fifty of them, in calm, comfortable rows: lovingly side by side they lay, with the great moon shining down upon them — thin at the tip, full in the waist, elegantly round and full, a little spot here and there shining upon them — beauty-spots upon the cheek of Sylvia. The house was quite quiet. Dawdley always smoked in his room; — I had not smoked for four months and eleven days.

. . . .

When Lord Dawdley came into the study, he did not make any remarks; and oh, how easy my heart felt! He was dressed in his green and boots, after Westall's picture, correctly.

"It's time to be off, George," said he; "they told me you were dressed long ago. Come up, my man, and get ready."

I rushed up into the dressing-room and madly dashed my head and arms into a pool of eau-de-Cologne. I drank, I believe, a tumblerful of it. I called for my clothes, and, strange to say, they were gone. My servant brought them, however, saying that he had put them away — making some stupid excuse. I put them on, not heeding them much, for I was half tipsy with the exitement of the ci — of the smo — of what had taken place in Dawdley's study, and with the Maraschino and the eau-de-Cologne I had drunk.

"What a fine odor of lavender-water!" said Dawdley, as we rode in the carriage.

I put my head out of the window and shrieked out a laugh; but made no other reply.

"What's the joke, George?" said Dawdley. "Did I say any thing witty?"

"No," cried I, yelling still more wildly; "nothing more witty than usual."

"Don't be severe, George," said he, with a mortified air; and we drove on to B—— House.

. . . .

There must have been something strange and wild in my appearance, and those awful black plumes, as I passed through the crowd; for I observed people looking and making a strange nasal noise (it is called sniffing, and I have no other more delicate term for it), and making way as I pushed on. But I moved forward very fiercely, for the wine, the Maraschino, the eau-de-Cologne, and the — the excitement had rendered me almost wild; and at length I arrived at the place where my lovely Lady of the Lake and her Harper stood. How beautiful she looked, — all eyes were upon her as she stood blushing. When she saw me, however, her countenance assumed an appearance of alarm. "Good heavens, George!" she said, stretching her hand to me, "what makes you look so wild and pale?" I advanced, and was going to take her hand, when she dropped it with a scream.

"Ah — ah — ah!" she said. "Mr. Fitz-Boodle, you've been smoking!"

There was an immense laugh from four hundred people round about us, and the scoundrelly Dawdley joined in the yell. I rushed furiously out, and, as I passed, hurtled over the fat Hereditary Prince of Kalbsbraten-Pumpernickel.

"Es riecht hier ungeheuer stark von Tabak!" I heard his Highness say, as I madly flung myself through the aides-de-camp.

The next day Mary M'Alister, in a note full of the most odious good sense and sarcasm, reminded me of our agreement; said that she was quite convinced that we were not by any means fitted for one another, and begged me to consider myself henceforth quite free. The little wretch had the impertinence to send me a dozen boxes of cigars, which, she said, would console me for my lost love; as she was perfectly certain that I was not mercenary, and that I loved tobacco better than any woman in the world.

I believe she was right, though I have never to this day been able to pardon the scoundrelly stratagem by which Dawdley robbed me of a wife and won one himself. As I was lying on his sofa, looking at the moon and lost in a thousand happy contemplations, Lord Dawdley, returning from the tailor's, saw me smoking at my leisure. On entering his dressing-room, a horrible, treacherous thought struck him. "I must not betray my friend," said he; "but in love all is fair, and he shall betray himself." There were my tartans, my cursed feathers, my tiger-skin sporran, upon the sofa.

He called up my groom; he made the rascal put on all my clothes, and, giving him a guinea and four cigars, bade him lock himself into the little pantry and smoke them *without taking the clothes off*. John did so, and was very ill in consequence, and so when I came to B—— House, my clothes were redolent of tobacco, and I lost lovely Mary M'Alister.

I am godfather to one of Lady Dawdley's boys, and hers is the only house where I am allowed to smoke unmolested; but I have never been able to admire Dawdley, a sly, *sournois*, spiritless, lily-livered fellow, that took his name off all his clubs the year he married.

MISS LÖWE.

"I AM sick of this squeamish English world," said I, in bitter scorn, as I sat in my lonely lodgings smoking Mary M'Alister's cigars; "a curse upon their affectations of propriety and silly obedience to the dictates of whimpering woman! I will away to some other country where thought is free, and honest men have their way. I will have no more of your rose-water passion, or cringing drawing-room tenderness. Pshaw! is George Fitz-Boodle to be bound up in the scented ringlets of a woman, or made to fetch and carry her reticule? No, I will go where women shall obey and not command me. I will be a sheik, and my wife shall cook my couscous, and dance before me, and light my narghilé. I will be a painted savage spearing the fish, and striking the deer, and my wife shall sing my great actions to me as I smoke my calumet in my lodge. Away! land of dowagers and milk-sops, Fitz-Boodle disowns you; he will wander to some other clime, where man is respected, and woman takes her proper rank in the creation, as the pretty smiling slave she should be."

I received at this time, in an abrupt enclosure from my father, 120*l.*, being a quarter's income, and a polite intimation from Lady Fitz-Boodle, that as I had disappointed every one of my parents' expectations (*she* my parent! faugh!), I must never look to the slightest pecuniary aid from them.

Such a sum would not enable me to travel across the Atlantic or to the shores of the Red Sea, as was my first intention ; I determined, therefore, to visit a country where, if woman was still too foolishly worshipped, at least smoking was tolerated, and took my departure at the Tower Stairs for Rotterdam and the Rhine.

There were no incidents of the voyage worth recounting, nor am I so absurd as to attempt to give the reader an account of Holland or any other country. This memoir is purely personal; and relates rather to what I suffered than to what I saw. Not a word then about Cologne and the eleven thousand British virgins whom a storm drove into that port, and who were condemned, as I am pleased to think, to a most merited death. Ah, Mary M'Alister! in my rage and fury I wished that there had been eleven thousand and one spinsters so destroyed. Ah! Minna Löwe, Jewess as thou wert, thou merited no better a fate than that which overtook those Christian damsels.

Minna Löwe was the daughter of Moses Löwe, banker at Bonn. I passed through the town last year, fifteen years after the event I am about to relate, and heard that Moses was imprisoned for forgery and fraudulent bankruptcy. He merited the punishment which the merciful Prussian law inflicted on him.

Minna was the most beautiful creature that my eyes ever lighted on. Sneer not, ye Christian maidens; but the fact was so. I saw her for the first time seated at a window covered with golden vine-leaves, with grapes just turning to purple, and tendrils twisting in the most fantastical arabesques. The leaves cast a pretty checkered shadow over her sweet face, and the simple, thin, white muslin gown in which she was dressed. She had bare white arms, and a blue ribbon confined her little waist. She was knitting, as all German women do, whether of the Jewish sort or otherwise: and in the shadow of the room sat her sister Emma, a powerful woman with a powerful voice. Emma was at the piano, singing, "Herz mein herz warum so trau-au-rig," — singing much out of tune.

I had come to change one of Coutts's circulars at Löwe's bank, and was looking for the door of the caisse.

"*Links, mein herr!*" said Minna Löwe, making the gentlest inclination with her pretty little head; and blushing ever so little, and raising up tenderly a pair of heavy blue eyes, and then dropping them again, overcome by the sight of the stranger. And no wonder, I was a sight worth contemplating then, — I had golden hair which fell gracefully over my shoulders, and a slim waist (where are you now, slim waist and golden hair?), and a pair of brown mustachios that curled gracefully under a firm Roman nose, and a tuft to my chin that could not but vanquish *any* woman. "Links, mein herr," said lovely Minna Löwe.

That little word *links* dropped upon my wounded soul like balm. There is nothing in *links;* it is not a pretty word. Minna Löwe simply told me to turn to the left, when I was debating between that side and its opposite, in order to find the cash-room door. Any other person might have said *links* (or *rechts* for that matter), and would not have made the slightest impression upon me ; but Minna's full red lips, as they let slip the monosyllable, wore a smile so tender, and uttered it with such inconceivable sweetness, that I was overcome at once. "Sweet bell!" I could have said, "tinkle that dulcet note forever, —

links, clinks, linx! I love the chime. It soothes and blesses me." All this I could have said, and much more, had I had my senses about me, and had I been a proficient in the German language; but I could not speak, both from ignorance and emotion. I blushed, stuttered, took off my cap, made an immensely foolish bow, and began forthwith fumbling at the door-handle.

The reason why I have introduced the name of this siren is to show that if tobacco in a former unlucky instance proved my enemy, in the present case it was my firmest friend. I, the descendant of the Norman Fitz-Boodle, the relative of kings and emperors, might, but for tobacco, have married the daughter of Moses Löwe, the Jew forger and convict of Bonn. I would have done it; for I hold the man a slave who calculates in love, and who thinks about prudence when his heart is in question. Men marry their cook-maids, and the world looks down upon them. *Ne sit ancillæ amor pudori!* I exclaim with a notorious poet, if you heartily and entirely love your cook-maid, you are a fool and a coward not to wed her. What more can you want than to have your heart filled up? Can a duchess do more? You talk of the difference of rank and the decencies of society. Away, sir! love is divine, and knows not your paltry, worldly calculations. It is not love you worship, O heartless, silly calculator! it is the interest of thirty thousand pounds in the three per cents, and the blessing of a genteel mother-in-law in Harley Street, and the ineffable joy of snug dinners, and a butler behind your chair. Fool! love is eternal, butlers and mothers-in-law are perishable; you have but the enjoyment of your three per cents for forty years; and *then*, what do they avail you? But if you believe that she whom you choose, and to whom your heart clings, is to be your soul's companion, not now merely, but for *ever and ever;* then what a paltry item of money or time has deterred you from your happiness, what a miserable penny-wise economist you have been!

And here, if, as a man of the world, I might be allowed to give advice to fathers and mothers of families, it would be this; young men fall in love with people of a lower rank, and they are not strong enough to resist the dread of disinheritance, or of the world's scorn, or of the cursed tyrant gentility, and dare not marry the woman they love above all. But if prudence is strong, passion is strong too, and principle is not, and women (heaven keep them!) are weak. We all know what happens then. Prudent papas and mammas say, "George will sow his wild oats soon, he will be tired of that odious woman one day, and we'll get a good marriage for him; meanwhile it is best to hush the matter up, and pretend to know nothing about it." But suppose George does the only honest thing in his power, and marries the woman he loves above all; *then* what a cry you have from parents and guardians, what shrieks from aunts and sisters, what excommunications and disinheriting! "What a weak fool George is!" say his male friends in the clubs; and no hand of sympathy is held out to poor *Mrs.* George, who is never forgiven, but shunned like a plague, and sneered at by a relentless pharisaical world until death sets her free. As long as she is *unmarried* avoid her if you will; but as soon as she is married, go! be kind to her, and comfort her, and pardon and forget, if you can! And lest some charitable people should declare that I am setting up here an apology for vice, let me here, and by way of precaution, flatly contradict them, and declare that I only would offer a *plea for marriage.*

But where has Minna Löwe been left during this page of disquisition? Blushing under the vine-leaves positively, whilst I was thanking my stars that she never became Mrs. George

Fitz-Boodle. And yet who knows what thou mightst have become, Minna, had such a lot fallen to thee? She was too pretty and innocent-looking to have been by nature that artful, intriguing huzzy that education made her, and that my experience found her. The case was simply this, not a romantic one by any means.

. . . .

[At this very juncture, perhaps, it will be as well to pause, and leave the world to wait for a month until it learns the result of the loves of Minna Löwe and George Fitz-Boodle. I have other tales still more interesting in store; and, though I have never written a line until now, I doubt not before long to have excited such a vast sympathy in my favor, that I shall become as popular as the oldest (I mean the handsomest and most popular) literary character of this or any other age or country. Artists and print publishers, desirous of taking my portrait, may as well, therefore, begin sending in their proposals to Mr. Nickisson; nor shall I so much look to a high remuneration for sitting (egad! it is a frightful operation), as to a clever and skilful painter, who must likewise be a decently bred and companionable person.

Nor is it merely upon matters relating to myself (for egotism I hate, and the reader will remark that there is scarcely a single "I" in the foregoing pages) that I propose to speak. Next month, for instance (besides the continuation of my own and other people's memoirs), I shall acquaint the public with a discovery which is intensely interesting to all fathers of families: I have in my eye *three new professions* which a gentleman may follow with credit and profit, which are to this day unknown, and which in the present difficult times, cannot fail to be eagerly seized upon.

Before submitting them to public competition, I will treat privately with parents and guardians, or with young men of good education and address; such only will suit. G. S. F. B.]

It has twice been my lot to leave Minna Löwe under the vine-leaves; on one occasion to break off into a dissertation about marriage, which, to my surprise, nobody has pronounced to be immoral; and, secondly, Minna was obliged to give place to that great essay on professions which appeared in July, and which enables me, as "The Kelso Warder" observes, "to take my place among the proudest and wisest of England's literary men." This praise is, to be sure, rather qualified; and I beg leave to say once more that I am *not* a literary character in the least, but simply a younger brother of a good house wanting money.

Well, twice has Minna Löwe been left. I was very nearly being off from her in the above sentence, but luckily paused in time; for if any thing were to occur in this paragraph, calling me away from her yet a third time, I should think it a solemn warning to discontinue her history, which is, I confess, neither very romantic in its details, nor very creditable to myself.

Let us take her where we left her in the June number of this Magazine,* gazing through a sunny cluster of vine-leaves upon a young and handsome stranger of noble face and exquisite proportions, who was trying to find the door of her father's bank. That entrance being through her amiable directions discovered, I entered and found Messrs. Moses and Solomon Löwe in the counting-house. Herr Solomon being the son of Moses, and head-clerk or partner in the business. That I was cheated in my little matter of exchange stands to reason. A Jew banker (or such as I have had the honor to know) cannot forego the privilege of cheating; no, if it be but for a shilling. What do I say, — a shilling? — a penny! He

* Fraser's.

will cheat you in the first place, in the exchanging your note; he will then cheat you in giving gold for your silver; and though very likely he will invite you to a splendid repast afterwards that shall have cost him a score of thalers to procure, he will have had the satisfaction of robbing you of your *groschen*, as no doubt he would rob his own father or son.

Herr Moses Löwe must have been a very sharp Israelite indeed, to rob Herr Solomon, or *vice versâ*. The poor fellows are both in prison for a matter of forgery, as I heard last year when passing through Bonn; and I confess it was not without a little palpitation of the heart (it is a sausage-merchant's now) that I went and took one look at the house where I had first beheld the bright eyes of Minna Löwe.

For let them say as they will, that woman whom a man has once loved *cannot* be the same to him as another. Whenever one of my passions comes into a room, my cheeks flush, — my knees tremble, — I look at her with pleased tenderness and (for the objects of my adoration do not once in forty times know their good fortune) with melancholy secret wonder. There they are, the same women, and yet not the same; it is the same nose and eyes, if you will, but not the same looks; the same voice, but not the same sweet words as of old. The figure moves, and looks, and talks to you; you know how dear and how different its speech and actions once were; 'tis the hall with all the lights put out and the garlands dead (as I have said in one of my poems). Did you ever have a pocket-book that once contained five thousand pounds? Did you ever look at that pocket-book with the money lying in it? Do you remember how you respected and admired that pocket-book, investing it with a secret awe, imagining it had a superiority to other pocket-books? I have such a pocket-book; I keep it now, and often look at it rather tenderly. It cannot be as other portfolios to me. I remember that it once held five thousand pounds.

Thus it is with love. I have empty pocket-books scattered all over Europe of this kind; and I always go and look at them just for a moment, and the spirit flies back to days gone by, kind eyes look at me as of yore, and echoes of old gentle voices fall tenderly upon the ear. Away! to the true heart the past *never* is past; and some day when Death has cleared our dull faculties, and past and future shall be rolled into one, we shall . . .

Well, you were quite right, my good sir, to interrupt me, I can't help it, I am too apt to grow sentimental, and always on the most absurd pretexts. I never know when the fit will come on me, or *àpropos* of what. I never was so jolly in my whole life as one day coming home from a funeral; and once went to a masked ball at Paris, the gayety of which made me so profoundly miserable, that, egad! I wept like Xerxes (wasn't that the fellow's name?), and was sick — sick at heart. This premised, permit me, my friend, to indulge in sentiment *àpropos* of Minna Löwe; for, *corbleu!* for three weeks, at least, I adored the wench; and could give any person curious that way a complete psychological history of the passion's rise, progress, and decay; — decay indeed, why do I say decay? A man does not "decay" when he tumbles down a well, he drowns there; so is love choked sometimes by abrupt conclusions, falls down wells, and, oh the dismal truth at the bottom of them!

"If, my lord," said Herr Moses, counting out the gold fredericks to me, you intend to shtay in our town, I hope my daughtersh and I vill have shometimesh de pleashure of your high vell-born shoshiety?"

The town is a most delightful one, Mr. Löwe," answered I. "I am myself an Oxford man, and exceedingly interested about — ahem — about the Byzantine historians, of which I see the university is producing an edition; and I shall make, I think, a considerable stay." Heaven bless us! 'twas Miss Minna's eyes that had done the business. But for them I should have slept at Coblentz that very night; where, by the way, the Hôtel de la Poste is one of the very best inns in Europe.

A friend had accompanied me to Bonn, — a jolly dragoon, who was quite versed in the German language, having spent some time in the Austrian service before he joined us; or in the "Awthtwian thervith," as he would call it, with a double-distilled gentility of accent, very difficult to be acquired out of Regent Street. We had quarrelled already thrice on the passage from England — viz., at Rotterdam, at Cologne, and once here; so that when he said he intended to go to Mayence, I at once proclaimed that I intended to stay where I was; and with Miss Minna Löwe's image in my heart, went out and selected lodgings for myself as near as possible to her father's house. Wilder said I might go to — any place I liked; he remained in his quarters at the hotel, as I found a couple of days afterwards, when I saw the fellow smoking at the gateway in the company of a score of Prussian officers, with whom he had made acquaintance.

I for my part have never been famous for that habit of extemporaneous friendship-making, which some lucky fellows possess. Like most of my countrymen, when I enter a room I always take care to look about with an air as if I heartily despised every one, and wanted to know what the d—l they did there! Among foreigners I feel this especially; for the truth is, right or wrong, I can't help despising the rogues, and feeling manifestly my own superiority. In consequence of this amiable quality, then (in this particular instance of my life), I gave up the *table-d'hôte* dinner at the Star as something low and ungentlemanlike, made a point of staring and not answering when people spoke to me, and thus I have no doubt impressed all the world with a sense of my dignity. Instead of dining at the public place, then, I took my repasts alone; though, as Wilder said with some justice, though with a good deal too much *laisser-aller* of tongue, "You gweat fool, if it'th only becauth you want to be thilent, why don't you thtill dine with uth? You'll get a wegular good dinner inthtead of a bad one; and ath for *thpeaking* to you, deped on it every man in the room will thee you hanged futht!"

"Pray allow me to dine in my own way, Wilder," says I, in the most dignified way.

"Dine and be d—d!" said the lieutenant, and so I lived solitary and had my own way.

I proposed to take some German lessons; and for this purpose asked the banker, Mr. Löwe, to introduce me to a master. He procured one, a gentleman of his own persuasion; and further, had the kindness to say that his clerk, Mr. Hirsch, should come and sit with me every morning, and perfect me in the tongue; so that, with the master I had and the society I kept, I might look to acquire a very decent German pronunciation.

This Hirsch was a little Albino of a creature with pinkish eyes, white hair, flame-colored whiskers, and ear-rings. His eyes jutted out enormously from his countenance, as did his two large swollen red lips, which had the true Israelitish coarseness. He was always, after a short time, in and out of my apartments. He brought a dozen messages and run as many errands for me in the course of the day. My way of addressing him was, "Hirsch, you scoundrel, get my boots!" "Hirsch, my Levite, brush my coat for me!" "Run, you stag of Israel, and put this letter in the post!" and with many similar compliments. The little rascal was, to do him justice, as willing as possible, never minded by what name I called him, and above all, — came from

Minna. He was not the rose; no, indeed, nor any thing like it; but, as the poet says, "he had lived beside it;" and was there in all Sharon such a rose as Minna Löwe?

If I did not write with a moral purpose, and because my unfortunate example may act wholesomely upon other young men of fashion, and induce them to learn wisdom, I should not say a single syllable about Minna Löwe, nor all the blunders I committed, nor the humiliation I suffered. There is about a young Englishman of twenty a degree of easy self-confidence, hardly possessed even by a Frenchman. The latter swaggers and bullies about his superiority, taking all opportunities to shriek it into your ears, and to proclaim the infinite merits of himself and his nation; but, upon my word, the bragging of the Frenchman is not so conceited or intolerable as that calm, silent, contemptuous conceit, of us young Britons, who think our superiority so well established that it is really not worth arguing upon, and who take upon us to despise thoroughly the whole world through which we pass. We are hated on the Continent, they say, and no wonder. If any other nation were to attempt to domineer over us as we do over Europe, we would hate them as heartily and furiously as many a Frenchman and Italian does us.

Now, when I went abroad I fancied myself one of the finest fellows under the sun. I patronized a banker's dinners as if I did him honor in eating them; I took my place before grave professors and celebrated men, and talked vapid nonsense to them in infamous French, laughing heartily in return at their own manner of pronouncing that language. I set down as a point beyond question that their customs were inferior to our own, and would not in the least scruple, in a calm way, to let my opinion be known. What an agreeable young fellow I must have been!

With these opinions, and my pleasant way of expressing them, I would sit for hours by the side of lovely Minna Löwe, ridiculing, with much of that elegant satire for which the English are remarkable, every one of the customs of the country,—the dinners, with the absurd un-English pudding in the very midst of them; the dresses of the men, with their braided coats and great seal-rings. As for little Hirsch, he formed the constant subject of my raillery with Mademoiselle Minna; and I gave it as my fixed opinion, that he was only fit to sell sealing-wax, and oranges to the coaches in Piccadilly.

"O fous afez tant d'esprit, fous autres jeunes Anglais," would she say; and I said, "Oui, nous avons beaucoup d'esprit, beaucoup plus que les Allemands," with the utmost simplicity; and then would half close my eyes, and give her a look that I thought must kill her.

Shall I tell the result of our conversation? In conversation 1, Minna asked me if I did not think the tea remarkably good, with which she and her sister treated me. She said it came overland from China, that her papa's correspondent at Petersburg forwarded it to them, and that no such tea was to be had in Germany. On this I seriously believed the tea to be excellent; and next morning at breakfast little Hirsch walked smirking into my room, with a parcel of six pounds of congo, for which I had the honor of paying eighteen Prussian thalers, being two pounds fourteen shillings of our money.

The next time I called, Herr Moses insisted on regaling me with a glass of Cyprus wine. His brother Löwe of Constantinople was the only person in the world who possessed this precious liquor. Four days afterwards Löwe came to know how I liked the Cyprus wine which I had ordered and would I like another dozen? On saying that I had not ordered any, that I did not like sweet wine, he answered "*Pardon!*" it had been in my cellar three days, and he would send some excellent Médoc at a moderate price, and would take no refusal. A basket of Médoc came that very night in my absence, with a bill directed to the "High Well-born Count von Fitz-Boodle." This excessive desire of the Löwe family to serve me made me relax my importunities somewhat. "Ah!" says Minna, with a sigh, the next time I saw her, "have we offended you, Herr George? You don't come to see us any more now!"

"I'll come to-morrow," says I; and she gave me a look and a smile which, oh!—"I am a fool, I know I am!" as the honorable member for Montrose said t'other day. And was not Samson ditto? was not Hercules another? Next day she was seated at the vine-leaves as I entered the court. She smiled, and then retreated. She had been on the lookout for me, I knew she had. She held out her little hand to me as I came into the room. Oh, how soft it was and how round! and with a little apricot-colored glove that—that I have to this day! I had been arranging a little compliment as I came along, something quite new and killing. I had only the heart to say, "*Es ist sehr warm.*"

"Oh, Herr George!" says she; "*Lieber* Herr George, what a progress have you made in German! You speak it like a native!"

But somehow I preferred to continue the conversation in French; and it was made up, as I am bound to say, of remarks equally brilliant and appropriate with that one above given. When old Löwe came in, I was winding a skein of silk, seated in an enticing attitude, gazing with all my soul at Delilah, who held down her beautiful eyes.

That day they did not sell me any bargains at all; and the next found me, you may be very sure, in the same parlor again, where, in his *schlafrock*, the old Israelite was smoking his pipe.

"Get away, papa," said Minna, "English lords can't bear smoke. I'm sure Herr George dislikes it."

"Indeed, I smoke occasionally myself," answered your humble servant.

"Get his lordship a pipe, Minna, my soul's darling!" exclaimed the banker.

"Oh, yes! the beautiful long Turkish one," cried Minna, springing up, and presently returned, bearing a long cherry-stick covered with a scarlet and gold cloth, at one end an enamelled amber mouth-piece, a gilded pipe at the other. In she came dancing, wand in hand, and looking like a fairy!

"Stop!" she said: "I must light it for Herr George." (By Jupiter! there was a way that girl had of pronouncing my name, "George," which I never heard equalled before or since.) And accordingly, bidding her sister get fire, she put herself in the prettiest attitude ever seen: with one little foot put forward, and her head thrown back, and a little hand holding the pipe-stick between finger and thumb, and a pair of red lips kissing the amber mouth-piece with the sweetest smile ever mortal saw. Her sister, giggling, lighted the tobacco, and presently you saw issuing from between those beautiful, smiling, red lips of Minna's a little curling, graceful, white smoke, which rose soaring up to the ceiling. I swear, I felt quite faint with the fragrance of it.

When the pipe was lighted, she brought it to me with quite as pretty an attitude and a glance that—Psha! I gave old Moses Löwe fourteen pounds sterling for that pipe that very evening; and as for the mouth-piece, I would not part with it away from me, but I wrapped it up in a glove that I took from the table, and put both into my breast-pocket; and next morning, when Charley Wilder burst suddenly into my room, he found me sitting up in bed in a green silk night-cap, a little apricot-colored glove lying on the counterpane before me, your humble servant employed in mumbling the mouth-piece as if it were a bit of barley-sugar.

He stopped, stared, burst into a shriek of laughter, and made a rush at the glove on the counterpane; but, in a fury, I sent a large single-volumed Tom Moore (I am not a poetical man, but I must confess I was reading some passages in "Lalla Rookh" that I found applicable to my situation) — I sent, I say, a Tom Moore at his head, which, luckily, missed him; and to which he responded by seizing a bolster and thumping me outrageously. It was lucky that he was a good-natured fellow, and had only resorted to that harmless weapon, for I was in such a fury that I certainly would have murdered him at the least insult.

I did not murder him then; but if he peached a single word upon the subject, I swore I would, and Wilder knew I was a man of my word. He was not unaware of my *tendre* for Minna Löwe, and was for passing some of his delicate light-dragoon jokes upon it and her; but these, too, I sternly cut short.

"Why, cuth me, if I don't think you want to mawwy her!" blurted out Wilder.

"Well, sir," said I, "and suppose I do?"

"What! mawwy the daughter of that thwindling old clotheman? I tell you what, Fitth-Boodle, they alwayth thaid you were mad in the weg'ment, and, run me thwough, if I don't think you are."

"The man," says I, "sir, who would address Mademoiselle Löwe in any but an honorable way is a scoundrel; and the man who says a word against her character is a liar!"

After a little further parley (which Wilder would not have continued but that he wanted to borrow money of me), that gentleman retired, declaring that "I wath ath thulky ath a bear with a thaw head," and left me to my apricot-colored glove and my amber mouth-piece.

Wilder's assertion that I was going to act up to opinions which I had always professed, and to marry Minna Löwe, certainly astounded me, and gave me occasion for thought. Marry the daughter of a Jew banker! I, George Fitz-Boodle! That would never do; not unless she had a million to her fortune, at least, and it was not probable that a humble dealer at Bonn could give her so much. But, marry her or not, I could not refrain from the sweet pleasure of falling in love with her, and shut my eyes to the morrow that I might properly enjoy the day. Shortly after Wilder's departure, little Hirsch paid his almost daily visit to me. I determined — and wondered that I had never thought of the scheme before — sagely to sound him regarding Minna's fortune, and to make use of him as my letter and message carrier.

"Ah, Hirsch! my lion of Judah!" says I, "you have brought me the pipe-stick, have you?"

"Yes, my lord, and seven pounds of the tobacco you said you liked. 'Tis real Syrian, and a great bargain you get it, I promise."

"Egad!" replied I, affecting an air of much careless ingenuousness. "Do you know, Hirsch, my boy, that the youngest of the Miss Löwes — Miss Anna, I think you call her" —

"Minna," said Hirsch, with a grin.

"Well, Minna — Minna Hirsch, is a devilish fine girl; upon my soul now, she is."

"Do you really think so?" says Hirsch.

"'Pon my honor, I do. And yesterday, when she was lighting the pipe-stick, she looked so confoundedly handsome that I — I quite fell in love with her; really I did."

"Ho! Vell, you do our people great honor, I'm sure," answered Hirsch.

"Father a warm man?"

"Varm! How do you mean varm?"

"Why, *rich*. We call a rich man

warm in England; only you don't understand the language. How much will he give his daughter?"

"Oh! very little. Not a veek of your income, my lord," said Hirsch.

"Pooh, pooh! You always talk of me as if I'm rich; but I tell you I am poor — exceedingly poor."

"Go away vid you!" said Hirsch, increduously. "*You* poor! I vish I had a year of your income; that I do" (and I have no doubt he did, or of the revenue of any one else). "I'd be a rich man, and have de best house in Bonn."

"Are you so very poor yourself, Hirsch, that you talk in this way?" asked I.

To which the young Israelite replied, that he had not one dollar to rub against another; that Mr. Löwe was a close man; and finally (upon my pressing the point, like a cunning dog as I was!), that he would do any thing to earn a little money.

"Hirsch," said I, like a wicked young reprobate and Don Juan, "will you carry a letter to Miss Minna Löwe?"

Now there was no earthly reason why I should have made a twopenny-postman of Mr. Hirsch. I might with just as much ease have given Minna the letter myself. I saw her daily and for hours, and it would be hard if I could not find her for a minute alone, or at least slip a note into her glove or pocket-handkerchief, if secret the note must be. But, I don't care to own it, I was as ignorant of any love-making which requires mystery as any bishop on the bench, and pitched upon Hirsch, as it were, because in comedies and romances that I had read, the hero has always a go-between — a valet, or humble follower — who performs the intrigue of the piece. So I asked Hirsch the above question, "Would he carry a letter to Miss Minna Löwe?"

"Give it me," said he, with a grin.

But the deuce of it was, it wasn't written. Rosina, in the opera, has hers ready in her pocket, and says "*Eccolo qua*" when Figaro makes the same request, so I told Hirsch that I would get it ready. And a very hard task I found it too, in sitting down to compose the document. It shall be in verse, thought I, for Minna understands some English; but there is no rhyme to Minna, as everybody knows, except a cockney, who might make "thinner, dinner, winner," &c., answer to it. And as for Löwe, it is just as bad. Then it became, as I thought, my painful duty to send her a note in French; and in French finally it was composed, and I blush now when I think of the nonsense and bad grammar it contained — the conceit above all. The easy vulgar assurance of victory with which I, a raw lad from the stupidest country in Europe, assailed one of the most beautiful women in the world!

Hirsch took the letter, and to bribe the fellow to silence, I agreed to purchase a great hideous amethyst brooch, which he had offered me a dozen times for sale, and which I had always refused till now. He said it had been graciously received, but as all the family were present in the evening when I called, of course no allusion could be made to the note; but I thought Minna looked particularly kind, as I sat and lost a couple of fredericks at *écarté* to a very stout Israelite lady, Madame Löwe, junior, the wife of Monsieur Solomon Löwe. I think it was on this night, or the next, that I was induced to purchase a bale of remarkably fine lawn for shirts, for old Löwe had every thing to sell, as is not uncommon with men of his profession and persuasion; and had I expressed a fancy for a coffin or a hod of mortar, I have no doubt Hirsch would have had it at my door next morning.

I went on sending letters to Minna, copying them out of a useful little work called "Le Petit Sécrétaire Français," and easily adapting them to circumstances, by altering a phrase here and there. Day and night I used to dangle about the house. It was provoking, to be sure, that Minna was never alone now: her sister or Madame Solomon were always with her, and as they naturally spoke German, of which language I knew but few words, my evenings were passed in sighing, ogling, and saying nothing. I must have been a very charming companion. One evening was pretty much like another. Four or five times in the week, old Löwe would drop in and sell me a bargain. Berlin-iron chains and trinkets for my family at home, Naples soap, a case of *eau de Cologne;* a beautiful dressing-gown, lined with fur for the winter; a rifle, one of the famous Frankfort make; a complete collection of the German classics; and finally, to my awful disgust, a set of the Byzantine historians.

I must tell you that, although my banking friend had furnished me with half a stone of Syrian tobacco from his brother at Constantinople, and though the most beautiful lips in the world had first taught me to smoke it, I discovered, after a few pipes of the weed, that it was not so much to my taste as that grown in the West Indies; and as his Havanna cigars were also not to my liking, I was compelled, not without some scruples of conscience at my infidelity, to procure my smoking supplies elsewhere.

And now I come to the fatal part of my story. Wilder, who was likewise an amateur of the weed, once came to my lodgings in the company of a tobacconist whom he patronized, and who brought several boxes and samples for inspection. Herr Rohr, which was the gentleman's name, sat down with us, his wares were very good, and — must I own it? — I thought it would be a very clever and prudent thing on my part to exchange some of my rare Syrian against his canaster and Havannas. I vaunted the quality of goods to him, and going into the inner room, returned with a packet of the real Syrian. Herr Rohr looked at the parcel rather contemptuously, I thought.

"I have plenty of these goods in my shop," said he.

"Why, you don't thay tho," says Wilder, with a grin; "ith the weal wegular Thywian. My friend Fitth-Boodle got it from hith bankerth, and no mithtake!"

"Was it from Mr. Löwe?" says Rohr, with another provoking sneer.

"Exactly. His brother Israel sent it from Constantinople."

"Bah!" says Rohr. "I sold this very tobacco, seven pounds of it, at fourteen groschen a pound, to Miss Minna Löwe and little Mr. Hirsch, who came express to my shop for it. Here's my seal," says Mr. Rohr. And sure enough he produced, from a very fat and dirty forefinger, a seal, which bore the engraving on the packet.

"You sold that to Miss Minna Löwe?" groaned poor George Fitz-Boodle.

"Yes, and she bated me down half a gros in the price. Heaven help you, sir! she *always* makes the bargains for her father. There's something so pretty about her that we can't resist her."

"And do you thell *wineth,* too, — Thypwuth and Médoc, hay?" continued the brute Wilder, enjoying the joke.

"No," answered Mr. Rohr, with another confounded sneer. "He makes those himself; but I *have* some very fine Médoc and Greek wine, if his high well-born lordship would like a few dozen. Shall I send a pannier?"

"*Leave the room,* sir!" here shouted I, in a voice of uncontrollable ferocity, and looked so wildly that little Rohr rushed away in a fright, and Wilder burst into one of his demoniacal laughs again.

"Don't you thee, my good fwiend," continued he, "how wegularly thethe people have been doing you? I tell you their chawacterth are known all over the town. There'th not a thtudent in the place but can give you a hithtory of the family. Löwe ith an infarnal old uthuwer, and hith daughterth wegular mantwapth. At the Thtar, where I dine with the officerth of the garrithon, you and Minna are a thtandard joke. Captain Heerpauk wath caught himself for near six weekth; young Von Twommel wath wemoved by hith fwiends: old Colonel Blitz wath at one time tho nearly gone in love with the elder, that he would have had a divorce from hith lady. Among the thtudentth the mania hath been jutht the thame. Whenever one wath worth plucking, Löwe uthed to have him to hith houthe and wob him, until at latht the wathcal'th chawacter became tho well known, that the thtudentth in a body have detherted him, and you will find that not one of them will dance with hith daughterth, handsome ath they are. Go down to Godesberg to-night and thee."

"I *am* going," answered I; "the young ladies asked me to drive down in their carriage;" and I flung myself back on the sofa and puffed away volumes of smoke, and tossed and tumbled the live-long day, with a horrible conviction that something of what Wilder had told me might be true, and with a vow to sacrifice, at least, one of the officers who had been laughing at me.

There they were, the scoundrels! in their cursed tight frock-coats and hay-colored mustachios, twirling round in the waltzes with the citizens' daughters, when, according to promise, I arrived with the Israelitish ladies at the garden at Godesberg, where dancing is carried on twice or thrice in a week. There were the students, with their long pipes, and little caps, and long hair, tippling at the tables under the leaves, or dancing that absurd waltz which has always been the object of my contempt. The fact is, I am not a dancing man.

Students and officers, I thought, every eye was looking at me, as I entered the garden with Miss Minna Löwe on my arm. Wilder tells me that I looked blue with rage, and as if I should cut the throat of any man I met.

We had driven down in old Löwe's landau, the old gentleman himself acting as coachman, with Mr. Hirsch in his best clothes by his side. In the carriage came Madam Solomon, in yellow satin; Miss Löwe in light green (it is astonishing how persons of a light complexion will wear this detestable color); Miss Minna was in white muslin, with a pair of black knit gloves on her beautiful arms, a pink ribbon round her delicate waist, and a pink scarf on her shoulders, for in those days — and the fashion exists still somewhat on the Rhine — it was the custom of ladies to dress themselves in what we call an evening costume for dinner time; and so was the lovely Minna attired. As I sat by her on the back seat, I did not say one single word, I confess, but looked unutterable things, and forgot in her beauty all the suspicions of the morning. I hadn't asked her to waltz, — for, the fact is, I didn't know how to waltz (though I learned afterwards, as you shall hear), and so only begged her hand for a quadrille.

We entered thus Mr. Blintzner's garden as I have described, the men staring at us, the lovely Minna on my arm. I ordered refreshments for the party; and we sat at a table near the boarded place where the people were dancing. No one came up to ask Minna to waltz, and I confess I was not sorry for it,— for I own to that dog-in-the-manger jealousy which is common to love,— no one came but poor little Hirsch, who had been absent to get sandwiches for the ladies, and came up making his bow just as I was asking Minna whether she would give no response to my letters. She looked surprised, — looked at Hirsch, who looked at me, and laying his hand (rather familiarly) upon my arm, put the other paw to his great, red, blubber lips, as if enjoining silence; and, before a word, carries off Minna, and began twisting her round in waltz.

The little brute had assumed his best clothes for the occasion. He had a white hat and a pair of white gloves; a green satin stock, with profuse studs of jewels in his shirt; a yellow waistcoat, with one of pink Cashmere underneath; very short nankeen trousers, and striped silk stockings; and a swallow-tailed, short-waisted, light-brown coat, with brass buttons; the tails whirled in the wind as he and his partner spun round to a very quick waltz,— not without agility, I confess, on the little scoundrel's part,— and oh, with what incomparable grace on Minna's! The other waltzers cleared away, doubtless to look at her performance; but though such a reptile was below my jealousy, I felt that I should have preferred to the same music to kick the little beast round the circle rather than see his hand encircling such a waist as that.

They only made one or two turns, however, and came back. Minna was blushing very red, and very much agitated.

"Will you take one turn, Fräulein Lisa?" said the active Hirsch; and after a little to-do on the part of the elder sister, she got up, and advanced to the dancing place.

What was my surprise when the people again cleared off, and left the pair to perform alone! Hirsch and his partner enjoyed their waltz however, and returned, looking as ill-humored as possible. The band struck up presently a quadrille tune. I would not receive any of Minna's excuses. She did not wish to dance; she was faint, — she had no *vis-à-vis* "Hirsch," said I, with much courtesy, "take out Madam Solomon, and come and dance." We advanced, — big Mrs. Solomons and Hirsch, Minna and I, — Miss Lisa remaining with her papa over the Rhine wine and sandwiches.

There were at least twenty couple, who were mustering to make a quadrille when we advanced. Minna blushed scarlet, and I felt her trembling on my arm; no doubt 'twas from joy at dancing with the fashionable young Englander. Hirsch, with a low bow and a scrape, led Madam Solomon opposite us, and put himself in the fifth position. It *was* rather disgusting, certainly, for George Savage Fitz-Boodle to be dancing *vis-à-vis* such an animal as that!

Mr. Hirsch clapped his hands with a knowing air, to begin. I looked up from Minna (what I had been whispering to her must not be concealed, — in fact, I had said so previously, *es ist sehr warm;* but I said it with an accent that must have gone to her heart), — when I say I looked up from her lovely face, I found that every one of the other couples had retired, and that we four were left to dance the quadrille by ourselves!

Yes, by Heavens! it was so! Minna, from being scarlet, turned ghastly pale, and would have fallen back, had I not encircled her with my arm. "I'm ill," said she; "let me go back to my father." "You *must dance,*" said I, and held up my clinched fist at Hirsch, who I thought would have moved off too; on which the little fellow was compelled to stop. And so we four went through the quadrille.

The first figure seemed to me to last a hundred thousand years. I don't know how Minna did not fall down and faint; but gathering courage all of a sudden, and throwing a quick, fierce look round about her, as if in defiance, and a look which made my little angel for a moment look like a little demon, she went through the dance with as much gracefulness as a duchess. As for me, — at first the whole air seemed to be peopled with grinning faces, and I moved about almost choked with rage and passion. Then gradually the film of fury wore off, and I became wonderfully calm, — nay, had the leisure to look at Monsieur

Hirsch, who performed all the steps with wonderful accuracy; and at every one of the faces round about it, officers, students, and citizens. None of the gentlemen, probably, liked my face, — for theirs wore, as I looked at them, a very grave and demure expression. But as Minna was dancing, I heard a voice behind her cry, sneeringly, "Brava!" I turned quickly round, and caught the speaker. He turned very red, and so betrayed himself. Our eyes met, — it was a settled thing. There was no need of any further arrangement, and it was then, as I have said, that the film cleared off; and I have to thank Capt. Heerpauk for getting through the quadrille without an apoplexy.

"Did you hear that — that voice, Herr George?" said Miss Minna, looking beseechingly in my face, and trembling on my arm, as I led her back to her father. Poor soul! I saw it all at once. She loved me, — I knew she did, and trembled lest I should run into any danger. I stuttered, stammered, vowed I did not hear it; at the same time swearing inwardly an oath of the largest dimensions, that I would cut the throat whence that "Brava!" issued. I left my lady for a moment, and finding Wilder out, pointed the man to him.

"Oh, Heerpauk," says he. "What do you want with him?"

"Charley," says I, with much heroism and ferocity, "*I want to shoot him;* just tell him so." And when, on demurring, I swore I would go and pull the captain's nose on the ground, Wilder agreed to settle the business for me; and I returned to our party.

It was quite clear that we could not stay longer in the gardens. Löwe's carriage was not to come for an hour yet; for the banker would not expend money in stabling his horses at the inn, and had accordingly sent them back to Bonn. What should we do? There is a ruined castle at Godesberg, which looks down upon the fair green plain of the Rhine, where Mr. Blintzner's house stands (and let the reader be thankful that I don't give a description of scenery here): there is, I say, a castle at Godesberg. "*Explorons le shatto,*" says I; which elegant French Hirsch translated; and this suggestion was adopted by the five Israelites, to the fairest of whom I offered my arm. The lovely Minna took it, and away we went; Wilder, who was standing at the gate, giving me a nod, to say all was right. I saw him presently strolling up the hill after me, with a Prussian officer, with whom he was talking. Old Löwe was with his daughter, and as the old banker was infirm, the pair walked but slowly. Monsieur Hirsch had given his arm to Madam Solomon. She was a fat woman; the consequence was, that Minna and I were soon considerably ahead of the rest of the party, and were ascending the hill alone. I said several things to her, such as only lovers say. *Com il fay bo issy,*" says I, in the most insinuating way. No answer. *Es ist etwas kalt,*" even I continued, admirably varying my phrase. She did not speak: she was agitated by the events of the evening, and no wonder.

That fair round arm resting on mine, — that lovely creature walking by my side in the calm moonlight, — the silver Rhine flashing before us, with Drachenfels and the Seven Mountains rising clear in the distance, — the music of the dance coming up to us from the plain below, — the path winding every now and then into the darkest foliage, and at the next moment giving us rich views of the moonlit river and plain below. Could any man but feel the influence of a scene so exquisitely lovely?

"Minna," says I, as she wouldn't speak, — "Minna, I love you; you have known it long, long ago, I know you have. Nay, do not withdraw your hand; your heart has spoken for me.

Be mine, then!" and taking her hand, I kissed it rapturously, and should have proceeded to her cheek, no doubt, when — she gave me a swinging box on the ear, started back, and incontinently fell a screaming as loudly as any woman ever did.

"Minna, Minna!" I heard the voice of that cursed Hirsch shouting. "Minna, *meine gattin!*" and he rushed up the hill; and Minna flung herself in his arms, crying, "Lorenzo, my husband, save me!"

The Löwe family, Wilder, and his friend, came skurrying up the hill at the same time; and we formed what in the theatres they call a tableau.

"You coward!" says Minna, her eyes flashing fire, "who could see a woman insulted, and never defend her?"

"You coward!" roared Hirsch; "coward as well as profligate! You communicated to me your lawless love for this angel, — to me, her affianced husband; and you had the audacity to send her letters, not one of which, so help me Heaven, has been received. Yes, you will laugh at Jews, — will you, you brutal Englishman? You will insult our people, — will you, you stupid islander? Psha! I spit upon you!" and here Monsieur Hirsch snapped his fingers in my face, holding Minna at the same time round the waist, who thus became the little monster's buckler.

. . . .

They presently walked away, and left me in a pleasant condition. I was actually going to fight a duel on the morrow for the sake of this fury, and it appeared she had flung me off for cowardice. I had allowed myself to be swindled by her father, and insulted by her filthy little bridegroom, and for what? All the consolation I got from Wilder was, — "I told you tho, my boy, but you wouldn't lithn, you gweat thoopid, blundewing ignowamuth; and now I shall have to thee you shot and buwied to-morrow; and I dare thay you won't even remember me in your will. Captain Schläger," continued he, presenting me to his companion, "Mr. Fitz-Boodle; the captain acts for Heerpauk in the morning, and we were just talking matters over, when Webecca yonder quied out, and we found her in the armth of Bwian de Bois Guilbert here."

Captain Schläger was a little, social, good-humored man, with a mustachio of a straw and silver mixed, and a brilliant purple sabre-cut across a rose-colored nose. He had the iron cross at his button-hole, and looked, as he was, a fierce little fighter. But he was too kind-hearted to allow of two boys needlessly cutting each other's throats; and much to the disappointment of Wilder, doubtless, who had been my second in the Martingale affair, and enjoyed no better sport, he said, in English, laughing, "Vell, make your mint easy, my goot young man, I tink you af got into enough sgrabes about dis tam Shewess; and dat you and Heerpauk haf no need to blow each other's brains off."

"Ath for Fitth apologithing," burst out Wilder, "that'th out of the quethtion. He gave the challenge, you know; and how the *dooth* ith he to apologithe now?"

"He gave the challenge, and you took it, and you are de greatest fool of de two. I say the two young men shall not fight;" and then the honest captain entered into a history of the worthy family of Israel, which would have saved me at least fifty pounds had I known it sooner. It did not differ in substance from what Rohr and Wilder had both told me in the morning. The venerable Löwe was a great thief and extortioner; the daughters were employed as decoy-ducks, in the first place, for the university and the garrison, and afterwards for young strangers, such as my wise self, who visited the place. There was some very sad story about the elder Miss Löwe and a tutor from St. John's College, Cambridge, who came to Bonn on a reading tour; but I am not at liberty to set down here the particulars. And with regard to Minna, there was a still more dismal history. A fine, handsome young student, the pride of the university, had first ruined himself through the offices of the father, and then shot himself for love of the daughter; from which time the whole town had put the family into Coventry; nor had they appeared for two years in public until upon the present occasion with me. As for Monsieur Hirsch, he did not care. He was of a rich Frankfort family of the peoples, serving his apprenticeship with Löwe, a cousin, and the destined husband of the younger daughter. He traded as much as he could on his own account, and would run upon any errand and buy or sell any thing for a consideration. And so, instead of fighting Captain Heerpauk, I agreed willingly enough to go back to the hotel at Godesberg, and shake hands with that officer. The reconciliation, or, rather, the acquaintance between us, was effected over a bottle of wine, at Mr. Blintzner's hotel; and we rode comfortably back in a drosky together to Bonn, where the friendship was still more closely cemented by a supper. At the close of the repast, Heerpauk make a speech on England, fatherland, and German truth and love, and kindly saluted me with a kiss, which is at any lady's service who peruses this little narrative.

As for Mr. Hirsch, it must be confessed, to my shame, that the next morning a gentleman having the air of an old clothesman off duty presented me with an envelope, containing six letters of my composition addressed to Miss Minna Löwe (among them was a little poem in English, which has since called tears from the eyes of more than one lovely girl); and, furthermore, a letter from himself, in which he, Baron Hirsch, of Hirschenwald (the scoundrel, like my friend Wilder, purchased his title in "The Awthtwian Thervith") — in which he, I say, Baron Hirsch, of Hirschenwald, challenges me for insulting Miss Minna Löwe, or demanded an apology.

This, I said, Mr. Hirsch might have whenever he chose to come and fetch it, pointing to a horsewhip which lay in a corner; but that he must come early, as I proposed to quit Bonn the next morning. The baron's friend, hearing this, asked whether I would like some remarkably fine cigars for my excursion, which he could give me at a great bargain? He was then shown to the door by my body-servant; nor did Hirsch von Hirschenwald come for the apology.

Twice every year, however, I get a letter from him, dated Frankfort, and proposing to make me a present of a splendid palace in Austria or Bohemia, or 200,000 florins, should I prefer money. I saw his lady at Frankfort only last year, in a front box at the theatre, loaded with diamonds, and at least sixteen stone in weight.

Ah! Minna, Minna! thou mayest grow to be as ugly as sin, and as fat as Daniel Lambert, but I have the amber mouth-piece still, and swear that the prettiest lips in Jewry have kissed it!

The MS. here concludes with a rude design of a young lady smoking a pipe.

DOROTHEA.

The reason why my memoirs have not been continued with that regularity, which, I believe, is considered requisite by professional persons, in order to insure the success of their work, is a very simple one, — I have been otherwise engaged; and as I do not care one straw whether the public do or do not like my speculations (heartily pitying, and at the same time despising those poor devils who write under different circumstances) — as I say, I was in Scotland shooting grouse for some time past, coming home deucedly tired of evenings, which I devoted to a cigar and a glass of toddy, it was quite impossible to satisfy the curiosity of the public. I bagged 1114 brace of grouse in sixty days, besides dancing in kilt before her M—y at Bl—r Ath—l. By the way, when Mr. F—x M—le gives away cairngorums, he may as well say *whose property* they are. I lent the man the very stone out of a snuff-mull with which Charles Edward complimented my great-great-aunt, Flora MacWhirter.

The worthy publisher sent me down his Magazine to Dunkeld (a good deal of it will be found in wadding over the moors, and perhaps in the birds which I sent him), and, at the same time, he despatched some critiques, both epistolary and newspaperacious, upon the former chapter of my Memoirs. The most indignant of the manuscript critiques came from a member of the Hebrew persuasion. And what do you think is the opinion of this Lion of Judah? Simply that George Savage Fitz-Boodle is a false name, assumed by some coward, whose intention it is to insult the Jewish religion! He says that my history of the Löwe family is a dastardly attack upon the people! How is it so? If I say that an individual Christian is a rogue, do I impugn the professors of the whole Christian religion? Can my Hebrew critic say that a Hebrew banker never cheated in matters of exchange, or that a Hebrew was never guilty of a roguery? If so, what was the gold-dust robbery, and why is Ikey Solomons at Botany Bay? No; the Lion of Judah may be a good lion, but he is a deucedly bad arguer, — nay, he is a bad lion, he roars before he is hurt. Be calm, thou red-maned desert-roarer, the arrows of Fitz-Boodle have no poison at their tip, and are shot only in play.

I never wished to attack the Jewish nation, far from it, I have three bills now out; nor is he right in saying that I have made a dastardly statement, which I have given under a false name; just the contrary, my name is, as everybody knows, my real name, — it is the *statement* which is false, and I confess there is not one word of truth in it — I never knew, to my knowledge, any Hirsch or Löwe in my life; I never was with Minna Löwe; the adventures never did occur at Bonn. Is my friend now satisfied? Let him remember, in the first place, that the tale is related of individuals, and not of his people at large; and in the second place, that the statement is not true. If *that* won't satisfy him, what will? Rabbi, let us part in peace! Neither thee nor thy like would George Fitz-Boodle ever willingly harm — neither thee nor any bearded nor unbearded man. If there be no worse rogues in Jewry, the people is more lucky than the rest of the world, and the fact is good to be known.

And now for the second objections. These are mainly of one kind — most of the journalists, from whose works pleasing extracts have been made, concurring in stating, that the last paper, which the Hebrew thought so dangerous, was, what is worse still, exceedingly stupid.

This disgusting unanimity of sentiment at first annoyed me a good deal, for I was pained to think that success so soon bred envy, and that the members of the British press could not bear to see an amateur enter the lists with them, and carry off laurels for which they had been striving long years in vain. Is there no honesty left in the world, I thought? And the thought gave me extreme pain, for, though (as in the Hebrew case above mentioned) I love occasionally to disport with the follies and expose the vices of individuals, to attribute envy to a whole class is extremely disagreeable to one whose feelings are more than ordinarily benevolent and pure.

An idea here struck me. I said to myself, "Fitz-Boodle! perhaps the paper *is* stupid, and the critics are right." I read the paper: I found that it *was* abominably stupid, and, as I fell asleep over it, an immense repose and calm came over my mind, and I woke reconciled with human nature.

Let authors consider this above fact well, and draw their profit from it. I have met with many men, who, like myself, fancy themselves the victims of a conspiracy — martyrs; but, in the long-run, the world and the critics of nowadays are generally right; they praise too much perhaps, they puff a small reputation into a huge one, but they do not neglect much that is good; and, if literary gentlemen would but bear this truth in mind, what a deal of pain and trouble might they spare themselves! There would be no despair, ill-humor, no quarrelling with your fellow-creatures, nor jaundiced moody looks upon nature and the world. Instead of crying the world is wicked — all men are bad, is it not wiser, my brethren, to say, "I am an ass"? let me be content to know that, nor anathematize universal mankind for not believing in me. It is a well-known fact, that no natural man can see the length of his own ears; it is only the glass — the reflection that shows them to him. Let the critics be our glass, I am content to believe that they are pretty honest, that they are not actuated by personal motives of hatred in falling foul of me and others; and this being premised, I resume the narration of my adventures. If *this* chapter don't please them, they *must*, indeed, be very hard to amuse.

Beyond sparring and cricket, I do not recollect I learned any thing useful at Slaughter-House School, where I was educated (according to an old family tradition, which sends particular generations of gentlemen to particular schools in the kingdom; and such is the force of habit, that though I hate the place, I shall send my own son thither, too, should I marry any day). I say I learned little that was useful at Slaughter House, and nothing that was ornamental. I would as soon have thought of learning to dance, as of learning to climb chimneys. Up to the age of seventeen, as I have shown, I had a great contempt for the female race, and when age brought with it warmer and juster sentiments, where was I? — I could no more dance nor prattle to a young girl than a young bear could. I have seen the ugliest little low-bred wretches carrying off young and lovely creatures, twirling with them in waltzes, whispering between their glossy curls in quadrilles, simpering with perfect equanimity, and cutting *pas* in that abominable "cavalier seul," until my soul grew sick with fury. In a word, I determined to learn to dance.

But such things are hard to be acquired late in life, when the bones and the habits of a man are formed. Look at a man in a hunting-field who has not been taught to ride as a boy. All the pluck and courage in the world will not make the man of him that I am, or as any man who has had the advantages of early education in the field.

In the same way with dancing. Though I went to work with immense energy, both in Brewer Street, Golden Square (with an advertising fellow), and afterwards with old Coulon at Paris, I never was able to be *easy* in dancing; and though little Coulon instructed me in a smile, it was a cursed forced one, that looked like the grin of a person in extreme agony. I once caught sight of it in a glass, and have hardly ever smiled since.

Most young men about London have gone through that strange secret ordeal of the dancing-school. I am given to understand that young snobs from attorneys' offices, banks, shops, and the like, make not the least mystery of their proceedings in the saltatory line, but trip gayly, with pumps in hand, to some dancing-place about Soho, waltz and quadrille it with Miss Greengrocer or Miss Butcher, and fancy they have had rather a pleasant evening. There is one house in Dover Street, where, behind a dirty curtain, such figures may be seen hopping every night, to a perpetual fiddling; and I have stood sometimes wondering in the street, with about six blackguard boys wondering too, at the strange contortions of the figures jumping up and down to the mysterious squeaking of the kit. Have they no shame *ces gens?* are such degrading initiations to be held in public? No, the snob may, but the man of refined mind never can submit to show himself in public laboring at the apprenticeship of this most absurd art. It is owing, perhaps, to this modesty, and the fact that I had no sisters at home, that I have never thoroughly been able to dance; for though I always arrive at the end of a quadrille (and thank heaven for it too!) and though, I believe, I make no mistake in particular, yet I solemnly confess I have never been able thoroughly to comprehend the mysteries of it, or what I have been about from the beginning to the end of the dance. I always look at the lady opposite, and do as she does: if *she* did not know how to dance, *par hasard*, it would be all up. But if they can't do any thing else, women can dance; let us give them that praise at least.

In London, then, for a considerable time, I used to get up at eight o'clock in the morning, and pass an hour alone with Mr. Wilkinson, of the Theatres Royal, in Golden Square;— an hour alone. It was "one, two, three; one, two, three — now jump — right foot more out, Mr. Smith; and if you *could* try and look a little more cheerful; your partner, sir, would like you hall the better." Wilkinson called me Smith, for the fact is, I did not tell him my real name, nor (thank heaven!) does he know it to this day.

I never breathed a word of my doings to any soul among my friends: once a pack of them met me in the strange neighborhood, when, I am ashamed to say, I muttered something about a "little French milliner," and walked off, looking as knowing as I could.

In Paris, two Cambridge-men and myself, who happened to be staying at a boarding-house together, agreed to go to Coulon, a little creature of four feet high with a pigtail. His room was hung round with glasses. He made us take off our coats, and dance each before a mirror. Once he was standing before us playing on his kit — the sight of the little master and the pupil was so supremely ridiculous, that I burst into a yell of laughter, which so offended the old man that he walked away abruptly, and begged me not to repeat my visits. Nor did I. I was just getting into waltzing then, but determined to drop waltzing, and content myself with quadrilling for the rest of my days.

This was all very well in France and England; but in Germany what was I to do? What did Hercules do when Omphale captivated him?

What did Rinaldo do when Armida fixed upon him her twinkling eyes? Nay, to cut all historical instances short, by going at once to the earliest, what did Adam do when Eve tempted him? He yielded and became her slave; and so I do heartily trust every honest man will yield until the end of the world — he has no heart who will not. When I was in Germany, I say, I began to learn to *waltz*. The reader from this will no doubt expect that some new love-adventures befell me — nor will his gentle heart be disappointed. Two deep and tremendous incidents occurred which shall be notified on the present occasion.

The reader, perhaps, remembers the brief appearance of his Highness the Duke of Kalbsbraten-Pumpernickel at B—— House, in the first part of my Memoirs, at that unlucky period of my life when the Duke was led to remark the odor about my clothes, which lost me the hand of Mary M'Alister. I somehow found myself in his Highness's territories, of which anybody may read a description in the "Almanach de Goth." His Highness's father, as is well known, married Emilia Kunegunda Thomasina Charleria Emanela Louisa Georgina, Princess of Saxe-Pumpernickel and a cousin of his Highness the Duke. Thus the two principalities were united under one happy sovereign in the person of Philibert Sigismund Emanuel Maria, the reigning Duke, who has received from his country (on account of the celebrated pump which he erected in the market place of Kalbsbraten) the well-merited appellation of the Magnificent. The allegory which the statues round about the pump represent is of a very mysterious and complicated sort. Minerva is observed leading up Ceres to a river-god, who has his arms round the neck of Pomona; while Mars (in a full-bottomed wig) is driven away by Peace, under whose mantle two lovely children, representing the Duke's two provinces, repose. The celebrated Speck is, as need scarcely be said, the author of this piece; and of other magnificent edifices in the Residenz, such as the guard-room, the skittle-hall (*Grossherzoglich Kalbsbratenpumpernickelisch Schkittelspielsaal*), &c., and the superb sentry-boxes before the Grand-Ducal Palace. He is Knight Grand Cross of the Ancient Kartoffel Order, as, indeed, is almost every one else in his Highness's dominions.

The town of Kalbsbraten contains a population of two thousand inhabitants, and a palace which would accommodate about six times that number. The principality sends three and a half men to the German Confederation, who are commanded by a General (Excellency), two Major-Generals, and sixty-four officers of lower grades; all noble, all knights of the Order, and almost all chamberlains to his Highness the Grand Duke. An excellent band of eighty performers is the admiration of the surrounding country, and leads the Grand-Ducal troops to battle in time of war. Only three of the contingent of soldiers returned from the Battle of Waterloo, where they won much honor; the remainder was cut to pieces on that glorious day.

There is a chamber of representatives (which, however, nothing can induce to sit), home and foreign ministers, residents from neighboring courts, law presidents, town councils, &c., all the adjuncts of a big or little government. The court has its chamberlains and marshals, the Grand Duchess her noble ladies in waiting, and blushing maids of honor. Thou wert one, Dorothea! Dost remember the poor young Engländer? We parted in anger; but I think — I think thou hast not forgotten him.

The way in which I have Dorothea von Speck present to my mind is this: not as I first saw her in the garden — for her hair was in bandeaux then, and a large Leghorn hat with a deep ribbon covered half her fair face, — not in a morning-dress, which, by the way, was none of the newest nor the best made — but as I saw her afterwards at a ball at the pleasant splendid little court, where she moved the most beautiful of the beauties of Kalbsbraten. The grand saloon of the palace is lighted — the Grand Duke and his officers, the Duchess and her ladies, have passed through. I, in my uniform of the ——th, and a number of young fellows (who are evidently admiring my legs and envying my *distingué* appearance), are waiting round the entrance-door, where a huge Heyduke is standing, and announcing the titles of the guests as they arrive.

"Herr Oberhof und Bauinspektor von Speck!" shouts the Heyduke; and the little Inspector comes in. His lady is on his arm — huge, in towering plumes, and her favorite costume of light blue. Fair women always dress in light blue or light green; and Frau von Speck is very fair and stout.

But who comes behind her? Lieber Himmel! It is Dorothea! Did earth, among all the flowers which have sprung from its bosom, produce ever one more beautiful? She was none of your heavenly beauties, I tell you. She had nothing ethereal about her. No, sir; she was of the earth, earthy, and must have weighed ten stone four or five, if she weighed an ounce. She had none of your Chinese feet nor waspy, unhealthy waists, which those may admire who will. No; Dora's foot was a good stout one; you could see her ankle (if her robe was short enough) without the aid of a microscope; and that envious little, sour, skinny Amalia von Mangelwürzel used to hold up her four fingers and say (the two girls were most intimate friends, of course), "Dear Dorothea's vaist is so much dicker as dis." And so I have no doubt it was.

But what then? Goethe sings in one of his divine epigrams: —

"Epicures vaunting their taste, entitle me vulgar and savage,
Give them their Brussel-sprouts, but I am contented with cabbage."

I hate your little women — that is, when I am in love with a tall one; and who would not have loved Dorothea?

Fancy her, then, if you please, about five feet four inches high — fancy her in the family color of light blue, a little scarf covering the most brilliant shoulders in the world; and a pair of gloves clinging close round an arm that may, perhaps, be somewhat too large now, but that Juno might have envied then. After the fashion of young ladies on the continent, she wears no jewels or gimcracks: her only ornament is a wreath of vine-leaves in her hair, with little clusters of artificial grapes. Down on her shoulders falls the brown hair, in rich, liberal clusters; all that health, and good-humor, and beauty can do for her face, kind nature has done for hers. Her eyes are frank, sparkling, and kind. As for her cheeks, what paint-box or dictionary contains pigments or words to describe their red? They say she opens her mouth and smiles always to show the dimples in her cheeks. Psha! she smiles because she is happy, and kind, and good-humored, and not because her teeth are little pearls.

All the young fellows crowd up to ask her to dance, and, taking from her waist a little mother-of-pearl remembrancer, she notes them down. Old Schnabel for the polonaise; Klingenspohr, first waltz; Haarbart, second waltz; Count Hornpieper (the Danish envoy), third; and so on. I have said why *I* could not ask her to waltz, and I turned away with a pang, and played écarté with Colonel Trumpenpack all night.

In thus introducing this lovely creature in her ball-costume, I have been somewhat premature, and had best go back to the beginning of the history of my acquaintance with her.

Dorothea, then, was the daughter of the celebrated Speck before mentioned. It is one of the oldest names in Germany, where her father's and mother's houses, those of Speck and

Eyer, are loved wherever they are known. Unlike his warlike progenitor, Lorenzo von Speck, Dorothea's father, had early shown himself a passionate admirer of art; had quitted home to study architecture in Italy, and had become celebrated throughout Europe and been appointed Oberhofarchitect and Kunst und Bau-inspektor of the united principalities. They are but four miles wide, and his genius has, consequently, but little room to play. What art can do, however, he does. The palace is frequently whitewashed under his eyes; the theatre painted occasionally; the noble public buildings erected, of which I have already made mention.

I had come to Kalbsbraten, scarce knowing whither I went; and having, in about ten minutes, seen the curiosities of the place (I did not care to see the King's palace, for chairs and tables have no great charm for me), I had ordered horses, and wanted to get on, I cared not whither, when fate threw Dorothea in my way. I was yawning back to the hotel, through the palace-garden, a *valet-de-place* at my side, when I saw a young lady seated under a tree reading a novel, her mamma on the same bench (a fat woman in light blue) knitting a stocking, and two officers, choked in their stays, with various orders on their spinach-colored coats, standing by in first attitudes: the one was caressing the fat-lady-in-blue's little dog; the other was twirling his own mustache, which was already as nearly as possible curled into his own eye.

I don't know how it is, but I hate to see men evidently intimate with nice-looking women, and on good terms with themselves. There's something annoying in their cursed complacency—their evident sunshiny happiness. I've no woman to make sunshine for *me;* and yet my heart tells me that not one, but several such suns, would do good to my system.

"Who are those pert-looking officers," says I, peevishly, to the guide, "who are talking to those vulgar-looking women?"

"The big one, with the epaulets, is Major von Schnabel; the little one, with the pale face, is Stiefel von Klingenspohr."

"And the big blue woman?"

"The Grand-Ducal Pumpernickelian-court-architectress and Upper-Palace-and-building-inspectress Von Speck, born V. Eyer," replied the guide. "Your well-born honor has seen the pump in the market-place; that is the work of the great Von Speck."

"And yonder young person?"

"Mr. Court-architect's daughter; the Fräulein Dorothea."

. . . .

Dorothea looked up from her novel here, and turned her face towards the stranger who was passing, and then, blushing, turned it down again. Schnabel looked at me with a scowl, Klingenspohr with a simper, the dog with a yelp, the fat lady in blue just gave one glance, and seemed, I thought, rather well pleased. "Silence, Lischen!" said she to the dog. "Go on, darling Dorothea," she added, to her daughter, who continued her novel.

Her voice was a little tremulous, but very low and rich. For some reason or other, on getting back to the inn, I countermanded the horses, and said I would stay for the night.

I not only staid that night, but many, many afterwards; and as for the manner in which I became acquainted with the Speck family, why it was a good joke against me at the time, and I did not like then to have it known; but now it may as well come out at once. Speck, as everybody knows, lives in the market-place, opposite his grand work of art, the town pump, or fountain. I bought a large sheet of paper, and having a knack at drawing, sat down with the greatest gravity, before the pump, and sketched it for several hours. I knew it would bring out old Speck to see. At first he contented himself by flattening his nose against the window-glasses of his study, and looking what the Engländer was about. Then he put on his gray cap with the huge green shade, and sauntered to the door: then he walked round me, and formed one of a band of street-idlers who were looking on: then at last he could restrain himself no more, but, pulling off his cap, with a low bow, began to discourse upon arts, and architecture in particular.

"It is curious," says he, "that you have taken the same view of which a print has been engraved."

"That *is* extraordinary," says I (though it wasn't, for I had traced my drawing at a window off the very print in question). I added that I was, like all the world, immensely struck with the beauty of the edifice; heard of it at Rome, where it was considered to be superior to any of the celebrated fountains of that capital of the fine arts; finally, that unless, perhaps, the celebrated fountain of Aldgate in London might compare with it, Kalbsbraten building, *except* in that case, was incomparable.

This speech I addressed in French, of which the worthy Hofarchitect understood somewhat, and, continuing to reply in German, our conversation grew pretty close. It is singular that I can talk to a man and pay him compliments with the utmost gravity, whereas, to a woman, I at once lose all self-possession, and have never said a pretty thing in my life.

My operations on old Speck were so conducted, that in a quarter of an hour I had elicited from him an invitation to go over the town with him, and see its architectural beauties. So we walked through the huge half-furnished chambers of the palace, we panted up the copper pinnacle of the church-tower, we went to see the Museum and Gymnasium, and coming back into the market-place again, what could the Hofarchitect do but offer me a glass of wine and a seat in his house? He introduced me to his Gattinn, his Leocadia (the fat woman in blue), "as a young world-observer, and worthy art-friend, a young scion of British Adel, who had come to refresh himself at the Urquellen of his race, and see his brethren of the great family of Hermann."

I saw instantly that the old fellow was of a romantic turn, from this rodomontade to his lady: nor was she a whit less so; nor was Dorothea less sentimental than her mamma. She knew every thing regarding the literature of Albion, as she was pleased to call it; and asked me news of all the famous writers there. I told her that Miss Edgeworth was one of the loveliest young beauties at our court; I described to her Lady Morgan, herself as beautiful as the wild Irish girl she drew; I promised to give her a signature of Mrs. Hemans (which I wrote for her that very evening); and described a fox-hunt, at which I had seen Thomas Moore and Samuel Rogers, Esquires; and a boxing-match, in which the athletic author of "Pelham" was pitched against the hardy mountain bard, Wordsworth. You see my education was not neglected, for though I have never read the works of the above-named ladies and gentlemen, yet I knew their names well enough.

Time passed away. I, perhaps, was never so brilliant in conversation as when excited by the Asmanshauser and the brilliant eyes of Dorothea that day. She and her parents had dined at their usual heathen hour; but I was, I don't care to own it, so smitten, that for the first time in my life I did not even miss the meal, and talked on until six o'clock, when tea was served. Madame Speck said they always drank it; and so placing a teaspoonful of bohea in a caldron of water, she placidly handed out this decoction, which we took with cakes and tartines. I leave you to imagine how disgusted Klingenspohr and Schnabel looked when they stepped in as usual that evening to make their party of whist with the Speck family!

Down they were obliged to sit; and the lovely Dorothea, for that night, declined to play altogether, and — sat on the sofa by me.

What we talked about, who shall tell? I would not, for my part, break the secret of one of those delicious conversations, of which I and every man in his time have held so many. You begin, very probably, about the weather — 'tis a common subject, but what sentiments the genius of Love can fling into it! I have often, for my part, said to the girl of my heart for the time being, "It's a fine day," or, "It's a rainy morning!" in a way that has brought tears to her eyes. Something beats in your heart, and twangle! a corresponding string thrills and echoes in hers. You offer her any thing — her knitting-needles, a slice of bread and butter — what causes the grateful blush with which she accepts the one or the other? Why, she sees your heart handed over to her upon the needles, and the bread and butter is to her a sandwich with love inside it. If you say to your grandmother, "Ma'am, it is a fine day," or what not, she would find in the words no other meaning than their outward and visible one; but say so to the girl you love, and she understands a thousand mystic meanings in them. Thus, in a word, though Dorothea and I did not, probably, on the first night of our meeting, talk of any thing more than the weather, or trumps, or some subjects which to such listeners as Schnabel and Klingenspohr and others might appear quite ordinary, yet to *us* they had a different signification, of which Love alone held the key.

Without further ado then, after the occurrences of that evening, I determined on staying at Kalbsbraten, and presenting my card the next day to the Hof-Marshal, requesting to have the honor of being presented to his Highness the Prince, at one of whose court-balls my Dorothea appeared as I have described her.

It was summer when I first arrived at Kalbsbraten. The little court was removed to Siegmundslust, his Highness's country-seat: no balls were taking place, and, in consequence, I held my own with Dorothea pretty well. I treated her admirer, Lieutenant Klingenspohr, with perfect scorn, had a manifest advantage over Major Schnabel, and used somehow to meet the fair one every day, walking in company with her mamma in the palace garden, or sitting under the acacias, with Belotte in her mother's lap, and the favorite romance beside her. Dear, dear Dorothea! what a number of novels she must have read in her time! She confesses to me that she had been in love with Uncas, with Saint Preux, with Ivanhoe, and with hosts of German heroes of romance; and when I asked her if she, whose heart was so tender towards imaginary youths, had never had a preference for any one of her living adorers, she only looked, and blushed, and sighed, and said nothing.

You see I had got on as well as man could do, until the confounded court season and the balls began, and then — why, then came my usual luck.

Waltzing is a part of a German girl's life. With the best will in the world — which, I doubt not, she entertains for me, for I never put the matter of marriage directly to her — Dorothea could not go to balls and not waltz. It was madness to me to see her whirling round the room with officers, *attachés*, prim little chamberlains with gold keys and embroidered coats, her hair floating in the wind, her hand reposing upon the abominable little dancer's epaulet, her good-humored face lighted up with still greater satisfaction. I saw that I must learn to waltz too, and took my measures accordingly.

The leader of the ballet at the Kalbsbraten theatre in my time was Springbock, from Vienna. He had been a regular Zephyr once, 'twas said, in his younger days; and though he is now fifteen stone weight, I can, *hélas!* recommend him conscientiously as a master; and I determined to take some lessons from him in the art which I had neglected so foolishly in early life.

It may be said, without vanity that I was an apt pupil, and in the course of half a dozen lessons I had arrived at very considerable agility in the waltzing line, and could twirl round the room with him at such a pace as made the old gentleman pant again, and hardly left him breath enough to puff out a compliment to his pupil. I may say, that in a single week I became an expert waltzer; but as I wished, when I came out publicly in that character, to be quite sure of myself, and as I had hitherto practised not with a lady, but with a very fat old man, it was agreed that he should bring a lady of his acquaintance to perfect me, and accordingly, at my eighth lesson, Madame Springbock herself came to the dancing-room, and the old Zephyr performed on the violin.

If any man ventures the least sneer with regard to this lady, or dares to insinuate any thing disrespectful to her or myself, I say at once that he is an impudent calumniator. Madame Springbock is old enough to be my grandmother, and as ugly a woman as I ever saw; but, though old, she was *passionnée pour la danse,* and not having (on account, doubtless, of her age and unprepossessing appearance) many opportunities of indulging in her favorite pastime, made up for lost time by immense activity whenever she could get a partner. In vain, at the end of the hour, would Springbock exclaim, "Amalia, my soul's blessing, the time is up!" "Play on, dear Alphonso!" would the old lady exclaim, whisking me round: and though I had not the least pleasure in such a homely partner, yet for the sake of perfecting myself, I waltzed and waltzed with her, until we were both half dead with fatigue.

At the end of three weeks I could waltz as well as any man in Germany.

At the end of four weeks there was a grand ball at court in honor of H. H. the Prince of Dummerland, and his Princess, and *then* I determined I would come out in public. I dressed myself with unusual care and splendor. My hair was curled and my mustache dyed to a nicety; and of the four hundred gentlemen present, if the girls of Kalbsbraten *did* select one who wore an English hussar uniform, why should I disguise the fact? In spite of my silence, the news had somehow got abroad, as news will in such small towns, — Herr von Fitz-Boodle was coming out in a waltz that evening. His highness the Duke even made an allusion to the circumstance. When on this eventful night, I went, as usual, and made him my bow in the presentation, "Vous, Monsieur," said he — "vous qui êtes si jeune, devez aimer la danse." I blushed as red as my trousers, and, bowing, went away.

I stepped up to Dorothea. Heavens! how beautiful she looked! and how archly she smiled, as, with a thumping heart, I asked her hand for a *waltz!* She took out her little mother-of-pearl dancing-book, she wrote down my name with her pencil: we were engaged for the fourth waltz, and till then I left her to other partners.

Who says that his first waltz is not a nervous moment? I vow I was more excited than by any duel I ever fought. I would not dance any contre-danse or galop. I repeatedly went to the buffet and got glasses of punch (dear simple Germany! 'tis with rum-punch and egg-flip thy children strengthen themselves for the dance!) I went into the ball-room and looked — the couples bounded before me, the music clashed and rung in my ears — all was fiery, feverish, indistinct. The gleaming white columns, the polished oaken floors in which the innumerable tapers were reflected — all together swam before my eyes, and I was in a pitch of madness almost when the fourth waltz at length came. "*Will you dance with your sword on?*" said the sweetest voice in the world. I blushed and stammered and trembled, as I laid down that weapon and my cap, and hark! the music began!

Oh, how my hand trembled as I placed it round the waist of Dorothea! With my left hand I took her right — did she squeeze it? I think she did — to this day I think she did. Away we went! we tripped over the polished oak floor like two young fairies. "Courage, monsieur," said she, with her sweet smile. Then it was "Très bien, monsieur." Then I heard the voices humming and buzzing about. "Il danse bien l'Anglais." "Ma foi, oui," says another. On we went, twirling and twisting, and turning and whirling; couple after couple dropped panting off. Little Klingenspohr himself was obliged to give in. All eyes were upon us — we were going round *alone*. Dorothea was almost exhausted, when

. . . .

I have been sitting for two hours since I marked the points, thinking — thinking. I have committed crimes in my life — who hasn't? But talk of remorse, what remorse is there like *that* which rushes up in a flood to my brain sometimes when I am alone, and causes me to blush when I'm abed in the dark?

I fell, sir, on that infernal slippery floor. Down we came like shot; we rolled over and over in the midst of the ball-room, the music going ten miles an hour, 800 pairs of eyes fixed upon us, a cursed shriek of laughter bursting out from all sides. Heavens! how clear I heard it, as we went on rolling and rolling! "My child! my Dorothea!" shrieked out Madame Speck, rushing forward, and as soon as she had breath to do so, Dorothea of course screamed too; then she fainted, then she was disentangled from out my spurs, and borne off by a bevy of tittering women. "Clumsy brute!" said Madame Speck, turning her fat back upon me. I remained upon my *séant*, wild, ghastly, looking about. It was all up with me — I knew it was. I wished I could have died there, and I wish so still.

Klingenspohr married her, that is the long and short; but before that event I placed a sabre-cut across the young scoundrel's nose, which destroyed *his* beauty forever.

O Dorothea! you can't forgive me — you oughtn't to forgive me; but I love you madly still.

My next flame was Ottilia: but let us keep her for another number; my feelings overpower me at present.

OTTILIA.

CHAPTER I.

THE ALBUM. — THE MEDITERRANEAN HEATH.

TRAVELLING some little time back in a wild part of Connemara, where I had been for fishing and seal-shooting, I had the good luck to get admission to the château of a hospitable Irish gentleman, and to procure some news of my once dear Ottilia.

Yes, of no other than Ottilia v. Schlippenschlopp, the Muse of Kalbsbraten-Pumpernickel, the friendly little town far away in Sachsenland — where old Speck built the town pump, where Klingenspohr was slashed across the nose, — where Dorothea rolled over and over in that horrible waltz with Fitz-Boo—— Psha! — away with the recollection: but wasn't it strange to get news of

Ottilia in the wildest corner of Ireland, where I never should have thought to hear her gentle name? Walking on that very Urrisbeg Mountain under whose shadow I heard Ottilia's name, Mackay, the learned author of "The Flora Patlandica," discovered the Mediterranean heath, — such a flower as I have often plucked on the sides of Vesuvius, and as Proserpine, no doubt, amused herself in gathering as she strayed in the fields of Enna. Here it is — the self-same flower, peering out at the Atlantic from Roundstone Bay; here, too, in this wild lonely place, nestles the fragrant memory of my Ottilia!

In a word, after a day on Ballylynch Lake (where, with a brown fly and a single hair, I killed fourteen salmon, the smallest twenty-nine pounds weight, the largest somewhere about five stone ten), my young friend Blake Bodkin Lynch Browne (a fine lad who has made his continental tour) and I adjourned, after dinner, to the young gentleman's private room, for the purpose of smoking a certain cigar; which is never more pleasant than after a hard day's sport, or a day spent in-doors, or after a good dinner, or a bad one, or at night when you are tired, or in the morning when you are fresh, or of a cold winter's day, or of a scorching summer's afternoon, or at any other moment you choose to fix upon.

What should I see in Blake's room but a rack of pipes, such as are to be found in almost all the bachelors' rooms in Germany, and amongst them was a porcelain pipe-head bearing the image of the Kalbsbraten pump! There it was: the old spout, the old familiar allegory of Mars, Bacchus, Apollo virorum, and the rest, that I had so often looked at from Hofarchitect Speck's window, as I sat there by the side of Dorothea. The old gentleman had given me one of these very pipes; for he had hundreds of them painted, wherewith he used to gratify almost every stranger who came into his native town.

Any old place with which I have once been familiar (as, perhaps, I have before stated in these "Confessions" — but never mind that) is in some sort dear to me; and were I Lord Shootingcastle or Colonel Popland, I think after a residence of six months there I should love the Fleet Prison. As I saw the old familiar pipe, I took it down, and crammed it with Cavendish tobacco, and lay down on a sofa, and puffed away for an hour well-nigh, thinking of old, old times.

"You're very entertaining to-night, Fitz," says young Blake, who had made several tumblers of Punch for me, which I had gulped down without saying a word. "Don't ye think ye'd be more easy in bed than snorting and sighing there on my sofa, and groaning fit to make me go hang myself?"

"I am thinking, Blake," says I, "about Pumpernickel, where old Speck gave you this pipe."

"'Deed he did," replies the young man; "and did ye know the old Bar'n?"

"I did," said I. "My friend, I have been by the banks of the Bendemeer. Tell me, are the nightingales still singing there, and do the roses still bloom?"

"The *hwhat*?" cries Blake. "What the divvle, Fitz, are you growling about? Bendemeer Lake's in Westmoreland, as I preshume; and as for roses and nightingales, I give ye my word it's Greek ye're talking to me." And Greek it very possibly was, for my young friend, though as good across country as any man in his county, has not the fine feeling and tender perception of beauty which may be found elsewhere, dear madam.

"Tell me about Speck, Blake, and Kalbsbraten, and Dorothea, and Klingenspohr her husband."

"He with the cut across the nose, is it?" cries Blake. "I know him well, and his old wife."

"His old what, sir!" cries Fitz-

Boodle, jumping up from his seat. "Klingensphor's wife old! — Is he married again? — Is Dorothea, then, d-d-dead?"

"Dead! — no more dead than you are, only I take her to be five and thirty. And when a woman has had nine children, you know, she looks none the younger; and I can tell ye, that when she trod on my corruns at a ball at the Grand Juke's, I felt something heavier than a feather on my foot."

"Madame de Klingensphor, then," replied I, hesitating somewhat, "has grown rather — rather st-st-out?" I could hardly get out the *out*, and trembled I don't know why as I asked the question.

"Stout, begad! — she weighs fourteen stone, saddle and bridle. That's right, down goes my pipe; flop! crash falls the tumbler into the fender! Break away, my boy, and remember, whoever breaks a glass here pays a dozen."

The fact was, that the announcement of Dorothea's changed condition caused no small disturbance within me, and I expressed it in the abrupt manner mentioned by young Blake.

Roused thus from my reverie, I questioned the young fellow about his residence at Kalbsbraten, which has been always since the war a favorite place for our young gentry, and heard with some satisfaction that Potzdorff was married to the Behrenstein, Haarbart had left the dragoons, the Crown Prince had broken with the — but mum! of what interest are all these details to the reader, who has never been at friendly little Kalbsbraten?

Presently Lynch reaches me down one of the three books that formed his library ("The Racing Calendar" and a book of fishing-flies making up the remainder of the set). "And there's my album," says he. "You'll find plenty of hands in it that you'll recognize, as you are an old Pumpernickelaner." And so I did, in truth: it was a little book after the fashion of German albums, in which good simple little ledger every friend or acquaintance of the owner inscribes a poem or stanza from some favorite poet or philosopher with the transcriber's own name, as thus: —

"To the true house-friend, and beloved Irelandish youth.

"'*Sera nunquam est ad bonos mores via.*'

"WACKERBART,

"Professor at the Grand-Ducal Kalbsbraten-Pumpernickelisch Gymnasium."

Another writes, —

"'*Wander on roses and forget me not.*'

"AMALIA V. NACHTMUTZE,
GEB. V. SCHLAFROCK,"

with a flourish, and the picture, mayhap, of a rose. Let the reader imagine some hundreds of these interesting inscriptions, and he will have an idea of the book.

Turning over the leaves, I came presently on *Dorothea's* hand. There it was, the little neat, pretty handwriting, the dear old up-and-down-strokes that I had not looked at for many a long year, — the Mediterranean heath, which grew on the sunniest banks of Fitz-Boodle's existence, and here found, dear, dear little sprig! in rude Galwagian boglands.

"Look at the other side of the page" says Lynch, rather sarcastically (for I don't care to confess that I kissed the name of "Dorothea v. Klingenspohr, born v. Speck" written under an extremely feeble passage of verse). "Look at the other side of the paper!"

I did, and what do you think I saw?

I saw the writing of five of the little Klingenspohrs, who have all sprung up since my time.

. . . .

"Ha! ha! haw!" screamed the impertinent young Irishman, and the story was all over Connemara and Joyce's Country in a day after.

CHAPTER II.

OTTILIA IN PARTICULAR.

Some kind critic who peruses these writings will, doubtless, have the goodness to point out that the simile of the Mediterranean heath is applied to two personages in this chapter — to Ottilia and Dorothea, and say, Psha! the fellow is but a poor unimaginative creature not to be able to find a simile apiece at least for the girls; how much better would *we* have done the business!

Well, it is a very pretty simile. The girls were rivals, were beautiful, I loved them both, — which should have the sprig of heath? Mr. Cruikshank (who has taken to serious painting) is getting ready for the exhibition a fine piece, representing Fitz-Boodle on the Urrisbeg Mountain, county Galway, Ireland, with a sprig of heath in his hand, hesitating, like Paris, on which of the beauties he should bestow it. In the background is a certain animal between two bundles of hay; but that I take to represent the critic, puzzled to which of my young beauties to assign the choice.

If Dorothea had been as rich as Miss Coutts, and had come to me the next day after the accident at the ball, and said, "George, will you marry me?" it must not be supposed I would have done any such thing. *That* dream had vanished forever: rage and pride took the place of love; and the only chance I had of recovering from my dreadful discomfiture was by bearing it bravely, and trying, if possible, to awaken a little compassion in my favor. I limped home (arranging my scheme with great presence of mind as I actually sat spinning there on the ground) — I limped home, sent for Pflastersticken, the court-surgeon, and addressed him to the following effect: "Pflastersticken," says I, "there has been an accident at court of which you will hear. You will send in leeches, pills, and the deuce knows what, and you will say that I have dislocated my leg: for some days you will state that I am in considerable danger. You are a good fellow and a man of courage I know, for which very reason you can appreciate those qualities in another; so mind, if you breathe a word of my secret, either you or I must lose a life."

Away went the surgeon, and the next day all Kalbsbraten knew that I was on the point of death: I had been delirious all night, had had eighty leeches, besides I don't know how much medicine; but Kalbsbrateners knew to a scruple. Whenever anybody was ill, this little kind society knew what medicines were prescribed. Everybody in the town knew what everybody had for dinner. If Madame Rumpel had her satin dyed ever so quietly, the whole society was on the *qui vive;* if Countess Pultuski sent to Berlin for a new set of teeth, not a person in Kalbsbraten but what was ready to compliment her as she put them on; if Potzdorff paid his tailor's bill, or Muffinstein bought a piece of black wax for his mustaches, it was the talk of the little city. And so, of course, was my accident. In their sorrow for my misfortune, Dorothea's was quite forgotten, and those eighty leeches saved me. I became interesting; I had cards left at my door; and I kept my room for a fortnight, during which time I read every one of M. Kotzebue's plays.

At the end of that period I was convalescent, though still a little lame. I called at old Speck's house and apologized for my clumsiness, with the most admirable coolness; I appeared at court, and stated calmly that I did not intend to dance any more; and when Klingenspohr grinned, I told that young gentleman such a piece of my mind as led to his wearing a large sticking-plaster patch on his nose: which was split as neatly down the middle as you would split an orange at dessert. In a word, what man could do to repair my defeat, I did.

There is but one thing now of which I am ashamed — of those killing epigrams which I wrote (*mon Dieu!* must I own it? — but even the fury of my anger proves the extent of my love!) against the Speck family. They were handed about in confidence at court, and made a frightful sensation: —

"*Is it possible?*

"There happened at Schloss P-mp-r-n-ckel,
A strange mishap our sides to tickle,
And set the people in a roar; —
A strange caprice of fortune fickle:
I never thought at Pumpernickel
To see a SPECK *upon the floor!*"

"*La Perfide Albion; or, a Caution to Waltzers.*

"'Come to the dance,' the Briton said,
And forward D-r-th-a led,
Fair, fresh, and three and twenty!
Ah, girls, beware of Britons red!
What wonder that it *turned her head?*
SAT VERBUM SAPIENTI."

"*Reasons for not Marrying.*

"'The lovely Miss S.
Will surely say "yes,"
You've only to ask and try;'
'That subject we'll quit,'
Says Georgy the wit,
'*I've a much better* SPEC *in my eye!*'"

This last epigram especially was voted so killing that it flew like wildfire; and I know for a fact that our Chargé-d'Affaires at Kalbsbraten sent a courier express with it to the Foreign Office in England, whence, through our amiable Foreign Secretary, Lord P-lm-rston, it made its way into every fashionable circle: nay, I have reason to believe caused a smile on the cheek of R-y-lty itself. Now that Time has taken away the sting of these epigrams, there can be no harm in giving them; and 'twas well enough then to endeavor to hide under the lash of wit the bitter pangs of humiliation: but my heart bleeds now to think that I should have ever brought a tear on the gentle cheek of Dorothea.

Not content with this — with humiliating her by satire, and with wounding her accepted lover across the nose — I determined to carry my revenge still further, and to fall in love with somebody else. This person was Ottilia v. Schlippenschlopp.

Otho Sigismund Freyherr von Schlippenschlopp, Knight Grand Cross of the Ducal Order of the Two-Necked Swan of Pumpernickel, of the Porc-et-Siflet of Kalbsbraten, Commander of the George and Blue-Boar of Dummerland, Excellency, and High Chancellor of the United Duchies, lived in the second floor of a house in the Schwapsgasse; where, with his private income and his revenues as Chancellor, amounting together to some 300*l.* per annum, he maintained such a state as very few other officers of the Grand-Ducal Crown could exhibit. The Baron is married to Maria Antoinetta, a Countess of the house of Kartoffelstadt, branches of which have taken root all over Germany. He has no sons, and but one daughter, the Fräulein OTTILIA.

The Chancellor is a worthy old gentleman, too fat and wheezy to preside at the Privy Council, fond of his pipe, his ease, and his rubber. His lady is a very tall and pale Roman-nosed Countess, who looks as gentle as Mrs. Robert Roy, where, in the novel, she is for putting Baillie Nicol Jarvie into the lake, and who keeps the honest Chancellor in the greatest order. The Fräulein Ottilia had not arrived at Kalbsbraten when the little affair between me and Dorothea was going on; or rather had only just come in for the conclusion of it, being presented for the first time that year at the ball where I — where I met with my accident.

At the time when the Countess was young, it was not the fashion in her country to educate the young ladies so highly as since they have been educated; and provided they could waltz, sew, and make puddings, they were thought to be decently bred; being seldom called upon for algebra or Sanscrit in the discharge of the honest duties of their lives. But Fräulein Ottilia was of the modern school in this respect, and came back from her *pension* at Strasburg speaking all the languages, dabbling in all the sciences: an historian, a poet, — a blue of the ultramarinest sort, in a word. What a difference there was, for instance, between poor, simple Dorothea's love of novel-reading and the profound encyclopædic learning of Ottilia!

Before the latter arrived from Strasburg (where she had been under the care of her aunt the canoness, Countess Ottilia of Kartoffelstadt, to whom I here beg to offer my humblest respects), Dorothea had passed for a *bel esprit* in the little court circle, and her little simple stock of accomplishments had amused us all very well. She used to sing "Herz, mein Herz" and "T'en souviens-tu," in a decent manner (*once*, before heaven, I thought her singing better than Grisi's), and then she had a little album in which she drew flowers, and used to embroider slippers wonderfully, and was very merry at a game of loto or forfeits, and had a hundred small *agrémens de société* which rendered her an acceptable member of it.

But when Ottilia arrived, poor Dolly's reputation was crushed in a month. The former wrote poems both in French and German; she painted landscapes and portraits in real oil; and she twanged off a rattling piece of Listz or Kalkbrenner in such a brilliant way, that Dora scarcely dared to touch the instrument after her, or venture, after Ottilia had trilled and gurgled through "Una voce," or "Di piacer" (Rossina was in fashion then), to lift up her little modest pipe in a ballad. What was the use of the poor thing going to sit in the park, where so many of the young officers used ever to gather round her? Whirr! Ottilia went by galloping on a chestnut mare with a groom after her, and presently all the young fellows who could buy or hire horseflesh were prancing in her train.

When they met, Ottilia would bounce towards her soul's darling, and put her hands round her waist, and call her by a thousand affectionate names, and then talk of her as only ladies or authors can talk of one another. How tenderly she would hint at Dora's little imperfections of education! — how cleverly she would insinuate that the poor girl had no wit! and, thank God, no more she had. The fact is, that do what I will I see I'm in love with her still, and would be if she had fifty children; but my passion blinded me *then*, and every arrow that fiery Ottilia discharged I marked with savage joy. Dolly, thank heaven, didn't mind the wit much; she was too simple for that. But still the recurrence of it would leave in her heart a vague, indefinite feeling of pain, and somehow she began to understand that her empire was passing away, and that her dear friend hated her like poison; and so she married Klingenspohr. I have written myself almost into a reconciliation with the silly fellow; for the truth is, he has been a good, honest husband to her, and she has children, and makes puddings, and is happy.

Ottilia was pale and delicate. She wore her glistening black hair in bands, and dressed in vapory white muslin. She sang her own words to her harp, and they commonly insinuated that she was alone in the world, — that she suffered some inexpressible and mysterious heart-pangs, the lot of all finer geniuses, — that though she lived and moved in the world, she was not of it, — that she was of a consumptive tendency and might look for a premature interment. She even had fixed on the spot where she should lie: the violets grew there, she said, the river went moaning by; the gray willow whispered sadly over her head, and her heart pined to be at rest. "Mother," she would say, turning to her parent, "promise me — promise me to lay me in that spot when the parting hour has come!"

At which Madame de Schlippenschlopp would shriek, and grasp her in her arms; and at which, I confess, I would myself blubber like a child. She had six darling friends at school, and every courier from Kalbsbraten carried off whole reams of her letter-paper.

In Kalbsbraten, as in every other German town, there are a vast number of literary characters, of whom our young friend quickly became the chief. They set up a literary journal, which appeared once a week, upon light-blue or primrose paper, and which, in compliment to the lovely Ottilia's maternal name, was called "The Kartoffelnkranz." Here are a couple of her ballads extracted from "The Kranz," and by far the most cheerful specimen of her style. For in her songs she never would willingly let off the heroines without a suicide or a consumption. She never would hear of such a thing as a happy marriage, and had an appetite for grief quite amazing in so young a person. As for her dying and desiring to be buried under the willow-tree, of which the first ballad is the subject, though I believed the story then, I have at present some doubts about it. For, since the publication of my Memoirs, I have been thrown much into the society of literary persons (who admire my style hugely), and egad! though some of them are dismal enough in their works, I find them in their persons the least sentimental class that ever a gentleman fell in with.

"THE WILLOW-TREE.

"Know ye the willow-tree
Whose gray leaves quiver,
Whispering gloomily
To yon pale river?
Lady, at even-tide
Wander not near it:
They say its branches hide
A sad, lost spirit!

"Once to the willow-tree
A maid came fearful,
Paled seemed her cheek to be,
Her blue eye tearful;
Soon as she saw the tree,
Her step moved fleeter.
No one was there — ah me!
No one to meet her!

"Quick beat her heart to hear
The far bell's chime
Toll from the chapel-tower
The trysting time:
But the red sun went down
In golden flame,
And though she looked round,
Yet no one came!

"Presently came the night,
Sadly to greet her, —
Moon in her silver light,
Stars in their glitter.
Then sank the moon away
Under the billow,
Still wept the maid alone —
There by the willow!

"Through the long darkness,
By the stream rolling,
Hour after hour went on
Tolling and tolling.
Long was the darkness,
Lonely and stilly;
Shrill came the night-wind,
Piercing and chilly.

"Shrill blew the morning breeze,
Biting and cold,
Bleak peers the gray dawn
Over the wold.
Bleak over moor and stream
Looks the gray dawn,
Gray, with dishevelled hair,
Still stands the willow there —
THE MAID IS GONE!

"*Domine, Domine!*
Sing we a litany, —
Sing for poor maiden-hearts broken and weary;
Domine, Domine!
Sing we a litany,
Wail we and weep we a wild Miserere!"

One of the chief beauties of this ballad (for the translation of which I received some well merited compliments) is the delicate way in which the suicide of the poor young woman under the willow-tree is hinted at; for that she threw herself into the water, and became one among the lilies of the stream, is as clear as a pikestaff. Her suicide is committed some time in the darkness, when the slow hours move on tolling and tolling, and is hinted at darkly as befits the time and the deed.

But that unromantic brute, Van Cutsem, the Dutch Chargé-d'Affaires, sent to "The Kartoffelnkranz" of the week after a conclusion of the ballad, which shows what a poor creature he must be. His pretext for writing it was, he said, because he could not bear such melancholy endings to poems and young women, and therefore he submitted the following lines: —

I.

"Long by the willow-trees
Vainly they sought her,
Wild rang the mother's screams
O'er the gray water:
'Where is my lovely one?
Where is my daughter?

II.

"'Rouse thee, Sir Constable —
Rouse thee and look;
Fisherman, bring your net,
Boatman, your hook.
Beat in the lily-beds,
Dive in the brook!'

III.

"Vainly the constable
Shouted and called her;
Vainly the fisherman
Beat the green alder;
Vainly he flung the net,
Never it hauled her!

IV.

"Mother, beside the fire
Sat, her night-cap in;
Father, in easy-chair,
Gloomily napping;
When at the window-sill
Came a light tapping!

V.

"And a pale countenance
Looked through the casement.
Loud beat the mother's heart,
Sick with a amazement;
And at the vision, which
Came to surprise her,
Shrieked in an agony —
'Lor'! it's Elizar!'

VI.

"Yes, 'twas Elizabeth —
Yes, 'twas their girl;
Pale was her cheek, and her
Hair out of curl.
'Mother!' the loving one,
Blushing, exclaimed,
'Let not your innocent
Lizzy be blamed.

VII.

"'Yesterday, going to aunt
Jones's to tea,
Mother, dear mother, I
Forgot the door-key!
And as the night was cold,
And the way steep,
Mrs. Jones kept me to
Breakfast and sleep.'

VIII.

"Whether her Pa and Ma
Fully believed her,
That we shall never know:
Stern they received her;
And for the work of that
Cruel, though short, night,
Sent her to bed without
Tea for a fortnight.

IX.

"MORAL.

"*Hey diddle diddlety,*
Cat and the Fiddlety,
Maidens of England, take caution by she!
Let love and suicide
Never tempt you aside,
And always remember to take the door-key!"

Some people laughed at this parody, and even preferred it to the original; but for myself I have no patience with the individual who can turn the finest sentiments of our nature into ridicule, and make every thing sacred a subject of scorn. The next ballad is less gloomy than that of the willow-tree, and in it the lovely writer expresses her longing for what has charmed us all, and, as it were, squeezes the whole spirit of the fairy tale into a few stanzas: —

"FAIRY DAYS.

"Beside the old hall-fire — upon my nurse's knee,
Of happy fairy days — what tales were told to me!
I thought the world was once — all peopled with princesses,
And my heart would beat to hear — their loves and their distresses:
And many a quiet night, — in slumber sweet and deep,
The pretty fairy people — would visit me in sleep.

"I saw them in my dreams — come flying east and west,
With wondrous fairy gifts — the new-born babe they blessed;

One has brought a jewel — and one a crown of gold,
And one has brought a curse — but she is wrinkled and old.
The gentle queen turns pale — to hear those words of sin,
But the king he only laughs — and bids the dance begin.

"The babe has grown to be — the fairest of the land
And rides the forest green — a hawk upon her hand.
An ambling palfrey white — a golden robe and crown;
I've seen her in my dreams — riding up and down;
And heard the ogre laugh — as she fell into his snare,
At the little tender creature — who wept and tore her hair!

"But ever when it seemed — her need was at the sorest
A prince in shining mail — comes prancing through the forest.
A waving ostrich-plume — a buckler burnished bright;
I've seen him in my dreams — good sooth! a gallant knight.
His lips are coral red — beneath a dark mustache;
See how he waves his hand — and how his blue eyes flash!

"'Come forth, thou Paynim knight!' — he shouts in accents clear.
The giant and the maid — both tremble his voice to hear.
Saint Mary guard him well! — he draws his falchion keen,
The giant and the knight — are fighting on the green.
I see them in my dreams — his blade gives stroke on stroke,
The giant pants and reels — and tumbles like an oak!

"With what a blushing grace — he falls upon his knee
And takes the lady's hand — and whispers, 'You are free!'
Ah! happy childish tales — of knight and faërie!
I waken from my dreams — but there's ne'er a knight for me;
I waken from my dreams — and wish that I could be
A child by the old hall-fire — upon my nurse's knee."

Indeed, Ottilia looked like a fairy herself: pale, small, slim, and airy. You could not see her face, as it were, for her eyes, which were so wild, and so tender, and shone so that they would have dazzled an eagle, much more a poor goose of a Fitz-Boodle. In the theatre, when she sat on the opposite side of the house, those big eyes used to pursue me as I sat pretending to listen to the "Zauber-flöte," or to "Don Carlos," or "Egmont," and at the tender passages, especially, they would have such a winning, weeping, imploring look with them as flesh and blood could not bear.

Shall I tell how I became a poet for the dear girl's sake? 'Tis surely unnecessary after the reader has perused the above versions of her poems. Shall I tell what wild follies I committed in prose as well as in verse? how I used to watch under her window of icy evenings, and with chilblainy fingers sing serenades to her on the guitar? Shall I tell how, in a sledging-party, I had the happiness to drive her, and of the delightful privilege which is, on these occasions, accorded to the driver?

Any reader who has spent a winter in Germany perhaps knows it. A large party of a score or more of sledges is formed. Away they go to some pleasure-house that has been previously fixed upon, where a ball and collation are prepared, and where each man, as his partner descends, has the delicious privilege of saluting her. O heavens and earth! I may grow to be a thousand years old, but I can never forget the rapture of that salute.

"The keen air has given me an appetite," said the dear angel, as we entered the supper-room; and to say the truth, fairy as she was, she made a remarkably good meal — consuming a couple of basins of white soup, several kinds of German sausages, some Westphalia ham, some white puddings, an anchovy-salad made with cornichons and onions, sweets innumerable, and a considerable quantity of old Steinwein and rum-punch afterwards. Then she got up and danced as brisk as a fairy; in which operation I of course did not follow her, but had the honor, at the close of the evening's amusement, once more to have her by my side in the sledge, as we swept in the moonlight over the snow.

Kalbsbraten is a very hospitable place as far as tea-parties are concerned, but I never was in one where dinners were so scarce. At the palace they occurred twice or thrice in a month; but on these occasions spinsters were not invited, and I seldom had the opportunity of seeing my Ottilia except at evening-parties.

Nor are these, if the truth must be told, very much to my taste. Dancing I have forsworn, whist is too severe a study for me, and I do not like to play écarté with old ladies, who are sure to cheat you in the course of an evening's play.

But to have an occasional glance at Ottilia was enough; and many and many a napoleon did I lose to her mamma, Madame de Schlippenschlopp, for the blest privilege of looking at her daughter. Many is the tea-party I went to, shivering into cold clothes after dinner (which is my abomination) in order to have one little look at the lady of my soul.

At these parties there were generally refreshments of a nature more substantial than mere tea — punch, both milk and rum, hot wine, *consommé*, and a peculiar and exceedingly disagreeable sandwich made of a mixture of cold white puddings and garlic, of which I have forgotten the name, and always detested the savor.

Gradually a conviction came upon me that Ottilia *ate a great deal.*

I do not dislike to see a woman eat comfortably. I even think that an agreeable woman ought to be *friande*, and should love certain little dishes and knicknacks. I know that though at dinner they commonly take nothing, they have had roast-mutton with the children at two, and laugh at their pretensions to starvation.

No! a woman who eats a grain of rice, like Amina, in "The Arabian Nights," is absurd and unnatural; but there is a *modus in rebus:* there is no reason why she should be a ghoul, a monster, an ogress, a horrid gormandizeress — faugh!

It was, then, with a rage amounting almost to agony, that I found Ottilia ate too much at every meal. She was always eating, and always eating too much. If I went there in the morning, there was the horrid familiar odor of those oniony sandwiches; if in the afternoon, dinner had been just removed, and I was choked by reeking reminiscences of roast meat. Tea we have spoken of. She gobbled up more cakes than any six people present; then came the supper and the sandwiches again, and the egg-flip and the horrible rum-punch.

She was as thin as ever — paler if possible than ever: — but, by heavens! *her nose began to grow red!*

Mon Dieu! how I used to watch and watch it! Some days it was purple, some days had more of the vermilion — I could take an affidavit that after a heavy night's supper it was more swollen, more red than before.

I recollect one night when we were playing a round game (I had been looking at her nose very eagerly and sadly for some time), she of herself brought up the conversation about eating, and confessed that she had five meals a day.

"*That accounts for it!*" says I, flinging down the cards, and springing up and rushing like a madman out of the room. I rushed away into the night, and wrestled with my passion. "What! Marry," said I, "a woman who eats meat twenty-one times in a week, besides breakfast and tea? Marry a sarcophagus, a cannibal, a butcher's shop? — Away!" I strove and strove. I drank, I groaned, I wrestled and fought with my love — but it overcame me: one look of those eyes brought me to her feet again. I yielded myself up like a slave; I fawned and whined for her;

I thought her nose was not so *very* red.

Things came to this pitch that I sounded his Highness's Minister to know whether he would give me service in the Duchy; I thought of purchasing an estate there. I was given to understand that I should get a chamberlain's key and some post of honor did I choose to remain, and I even wrote home to my brother Tom in England, hinting a change in my condition.

At this juncture, the town of Hamburg sent his Highness the Grand Duke (*àpropos* of a commercial union which was pending between the two States) a singular present: no less than a certain number of barrels of oysters, which are considered extreme luxuries in Germany, especially in the inland parts of the country, where they are almost unknown.

In honor of the oysters and the new commercial treaty (which arrived in *fourgons* despatched for the purpose), his Highness announced a grand supper and ball, and invited all the quality of all the principalities round about. It was a splendid affair: the grand saloon brilliant with hundreds of uniforms and brilliant toilets — not the least beautiful among them, I need not say, was Ottilia.

At midnight the supper-rooms were thrown open, and we formed into little parties of six, each having a table, nobly served with plate, a lackey in attendance, and a gratifying ice-pail or two of champagne to *égayer* the supper. It was no small cost to serve

22*

five hundred people on silver, and the repast was certainly a princely and magnificent one.

I had, of course, arranged with Mademoiselle Schlippenschlopp. Captains Frumpel and Fridelberger of the Duke's Guard, Mesdames de Butterbrod and Bopp, formed our little party.

The first course, of course, consisted of *the oysters*. Ottilia's eyes gleamed with double brilliancy as the lackey opened them. There were nine apiece for us — how well I recollect the number!

I never was much of an oyster-eater, nor can I relish them *in naturalibus* as some do, but require a quantity of sauces, lemons, cayenne peppers, bread and butter, and so forth, to render them palatable.

By the time I had made my preparations, Ottilia, the Captains, and the two ladies, had well-nigh finished theirs. Indeed Ottilia had gobbled up all hers, and there were only my nine left in the dish.

I took one — IT WAS BAD. The scent of it was enough, — they were all bad. Ottilia had eaten nine bad oysters.

I put down the horrid shell. Her eyes glistened more and more; she could not take them off the tray.

"Dear Herr George," she said, "*will you give me your oysters?*"

. . . .

She had them all down — before — I could say — Jack — Robinson!

. . . .

I left Kalbsbraten that night, and have never been there since.

FITZ-BOODLE'S PROFESSIONS.

BEING APPEALS TO THE UNEMPLOYED YOUNGER SONS OF THE NOBILITY.

FIRST PROFESSION.

THE fair and honest proposition in which I offered to communicate privately with parents and guardians, relative to two new and lucrative professions which I had discovered, has, I find from the publisher, elicited not one single inquiry from those personages, who I can't but think are very little careful of their children's welfare to allow such a chance to be thrown away. It is not for myself I speak, as my conscience proudly tells me; for though I actually gave up Ascot in order to be in the way should any father of a family be inclined to treat with me regarding my discoveries, yet I am grieved, not on my own account, but on theirs, and for the wretched penny-wise policy that has held them back.

That they must feel an interest in my announcement is unquestionable. Look at the way in which the public prints of all parties have noticed my appearance in the character of a literary man! Putting aside my personal narrative, look at the offer I made to the nation, — a choice of no less than two new professions! Suppose I had invented as many new kinds of butcher's-meat; does any one pretend that the world, tired as it is of the perpetual recurrence of beef, mutton, veal, cold beef, cold veal, cold mutton, hashed ditto, would not have jumped eagerly at the delightful intelligence that their old, stale, stupid meals were about to be varied at last?

Of course people would have come forward. I should have had deputations from Mr. Gibletts and the fashionable butchers of this world; petitions would have poured in from Whitechapel salesmen; the speculators panting to know the discovery; the cautious with stock in hand eager to bribe me to silence, and prevent the certain depreciation of the goods which they already possessed. I should have dealt with them, not greedily or rapaciously, but on honest principles of fair barter. "Gentlemen," I should have said, or rather, "Gents" — which affectionate diminutive is, I am given to understand, at present much in use among commercial persons — "Gents, my researches, my genius, or my good fortune, have brought me to the valuable discovery about which you are come to treat. Will you purchase it outright, or will you give the discoverer an honest share of the profits resulting from your speculation? My position in the world puts *me* out of the power of executing the vast plan I have formed, but 'twill be a certain fortune to him who engages in it; and why should not I, too, participate in that fortune?"

Such would have been my manner of dealing with the world, too, with regard to my discovery of the new professions. Does not the world want new professions? Are there not thousands of well-educated men panting, struggling, pushing, starving, in the old ones? Grim tenants of chambers looking out for attorneys who never come? — wretched physicians practising the stale joke of being called out of church until people no longer think fit even to laugh or to pity? Are there not hoary-headed midshipmen, antique ensigns growing mouldy upon fifty years' half-pay? Nay, are there not men who would pay any thing to be employed rather than remain idle? But such is the glut of professionals, the horrible cut-throat competition among them, that there is no chance for one in a thousand, be he ever so willing, or brave, or clever: in the great ocean of life he makes a few strokes, and puffs, and sputters, and sinks, and the innumerable waves overwhelm him, and he is heard of no more.

Walking to my banker's t'other day — and I pledge my sacred honor this story is true — I met a young fellow whom I had known *attaché* to an embassy abroad, a young man of tolerable parts, unwearied patience, with some fortune too, and, moreover, allied to a noble Whig family, whose interest had procured him his appointment to the legation at Krähwinkel, where I knew him. He remained for ten years a diplomatic character; he was the working-man of the legation: he sent over the most diffuse translations of the German papers for the use of the Foreign Secretary: he signed passports with most astonishing ardor; he exiled himself for ten long years in a wretched German town, dancing attendance at court-balls, and paying no end of money for uniforms. And for what? At the end of the ten years — during which period of labor he never received a single shilling from the Government which employed him (rascally spendthrift of a Government, *va!*), — he was offered the paid *attaché-ship* to the court of H. M. the King of the Mosquito Islands, and refused that appointment a week before the Whig Ministry retired. Then he knew that there was no further chance for him, and incontinently quitted the diplomatic service forever, and I have no doubt will sell his uniform a bargain. The Government had *him* a bargain certainly; nor is he by any means the first person who has been sold at that price.

Well, my worthy friend met me in the street and informed me of these facts with a smiling countenance, — which I thought a master-piece of diplomacy. Fortune had been belaboring and kicking him for ten whole years, and here he was grinning in my face; could Monsieur de Talleyrand have acted better? "I have given up diplomacy," said Protocol, quite simply and good-humoredly, "for between you and me, my good fellow, it's a very slow profession; sure perhaps, but slow. But though I gained no actual pecuniary remuneration in the service, I have learned all the languages in Europe, which will be invaluable to me in my new profession — the mercantile one — in which directly I looked out for a post I found one."

"What! and a good pay?" said I.

"Why, no; that's absurd, you know. No young men, strangers to business, are paid much to speak of. Besides, I don't look to a paltry clerk's pay. Some day, when thoroughly acquainted with the business (I shall learn it in about seven years), I shall go into a good house with my capital, and become junior partner."

"And meanwhile?"

"Meanwhile I conduct the foreign correspondence of the eminent house of Jam, Ram, and Johnson: and very heavy it is, I can tell you. From nine till six every day, except foreign post days, and then from nine till eleven. Dirty dark court to sit in: snobs to talk to, — great change, as you may fancy."

"And you do all this for nothing?"

"I do it to learn the business." And so saying Protocol gave me a knowing nod, and went his way.

Good heavens! I thought, and is this a true story? Are there hundreds of young men in a similar situation at the present day, giving away the best years of their youth for the sake of a mere windy hope of something in old age, and dying before they come to the goal? In seven years, he hopes to have a business, and then to have the pleasure of risking his money? He will be admitted into some great house as a particular favor, and three months after the house will fail. Has it not happened to a thousand of our acquaintance? I thought I would run after him and tell him about the new professions that I have invented.

"Oh! ay! those you wrote about in 'Fraser's Magazine.' Egad! George, Necessity makes strange fellows of us all. Who would ever have thought of you *spelling*, much more writing?"

"Never mind that. Will you, if I tell you of a new profession, that, with a little cleverness and instruction from me, you may bring to a most successful end — will you, I say, make me a fair return?"

"My dear creature," replied young Protocol, "what nonsense you talk! I saw that very humbug in the magazine. You say you have made a great discovery — very good; you puff your discovery — very right; you ask money for it — nothing can be more reasonable; and then you say that you intend to make your discovery public in the next number of the Magazine. Do you think I will be such a fool as to give you money for a thing which I can have next month for nothing? Good-by, George, my boy; the *next* discovery you make, I'll tell you how to get a better price for it." And with this the fellow walked off, looking supremely knowing and clever.

This tale of the person I have called Protocol is not told without a purpose, you may be sure. In the first place, it shows what are the reasons that nobody has made application to me concerning the new professions, namely, because I have passed my word to make them known in this Magazine, which persons may have for the purchasing, stealing, borrowing, or hiring, and, therefore, they will never think of applying personally to me. And, secondly, his story proves also my assertion, viz., that all professions are most cruelly crowded at present, and that men will make the most absurd outlay and sacrifices for the smallest chance of success at some future period. Well, then, I will be a benefactor to my race, if I cannot be to one single member of it, whom I love better than most men. What I have discovered I will make known; there shall be no shilly-shallying work here, no circumlocution, no bottle-conjuring business. But, oh! I wish for all our sakes that I had had an opportunity to impart the secret to one or two persons only; for, after all, but one or two can live in the manner I would suggest. And when the discovery is made known, I am sure ten thousand will try. The rascals! I can see their brass plates gleaming over scores of doors. Competition will ruin my professions, as it has all others.

It must be premised that the two professions are intended for gentlemen, and gentlemen only — men of birth and education. No others could support the parts which they will be called upon to play.

And, likewise, it must be honestly confessed, that these professions have, to a certain degree, been exercised before. Do not cry out at this and say it is no discovery! I say it *is* a discovery. It is a discovery if I show you — a gentleman — a profession which you may exercise without derogation, or loss of standing, with certain profit, nay, possibly with honor, and of which, until the reading of this present page, you never thought but as of a calling beneath your rank and quite below your reach. Sir, I do not mean to say that I create a profession. I cannot create gold; but if, when discovered, I find the means of putting it in your pocket, do I or do I not deserve credit?

I see you sneer contemptuously when I mention to you the word AUCTIONEER. "Is this all," you say, "that this fellow brags and prates about? An auctioneer, forsooth! he might as well have 'invented' chimney-sweeping."

No such thing. A little boy of seven, be he ever so low of birth, can do this as well as you. Do you suppose that little stolen Master Montague made a better sweeper than the lowest bred chummy that yearly commemorates his release? No, sir. And he might have been ever so much a genius or a gentleman, and not have been able to make his trade respectable.

But all such trades as can be rendered decent the aristocracy has adopted one by one. At first they followed the profession of arms, flouting all others as unworthy, and thinking it ungentlemanlike to know how to read or write. They did not go into the church in very early days, till the money to be got from the church was strong enough to tempt them. It is but of later years that they have condescended to go to the bar, and since the same time only that we see some of them following trades. I know an English lord's son who is, or was, a wine-merchant (he may have been a bankrupt for what I know). As for bankers, several partners in banking-houses have four balls to their coronets, and I have no doubt that another sort of banking, viz., that practised by gentlemen who lend small sums of money upon deposited securities, will be one day followed by the noble order, so that they may have four balls on their coronets and carriages, and three in front of their shops.

Yes, the nobles come peoplewards as the people, on the other hand, rise and mingle with the nobles. With the *plebs*, of course, Fitz-Boodle, in whose veins flows the blood of a thousand kings, can have nothing to do; but, watching the progress of the world, 'tis impossible to deny that the good old days of our race are passed away. We want money still, as much as ever we did; but we cannot go down from our castles with horse and sword and waylay fat merchants — no, no, confounded new policemen and the assize-courts prevent that. Younger brothers cannot be pages to noble houses, as of old they were, serving gentle dames without disgrace, handing my lord's rose-water to wash, or holding his stirrup as he mounted for the chase. A page, forsooth! A pretty figure would George Fitz-Boodle or any other man of fashion cut, in a jacket covered with sugar-loafed buttons, and handing in penny-post notes on a silver tray. The *plebs* have robbed us of *that* trade among others: nor, I confess, do I much grudge them their *trouvaille*. Neither can we collect together a few scores of free lances, like honest Hugh Calverly, in the Black Prince's time, or brave Harry Butler of Wallenstein's dragoons, and serve this or that prince, Peter the Cruel or Henry of Trastamare, Gustavus or the Emperor, at our leisure; or, in default of service, fight and rob on our own gallant account, as the good gentlemen of old did. Alas! no. In South America or Texas, perhaps, a man might have a chance that way; but in the ancient world no man can fight except in the king's service (and a mighty bad service that is too), and the lowest European sovereign, were it Baldomero Espartero himself, would think nothing of seizing the best-born condottiere that ever drew sword, and shooting him down like the vulgarest deserter.

What, then, is to be done? We must discover fresh fields of enterprise — of peaceable and commercial enterprise in a peaceful and commercial age. I say, then, that the auctioneer's pulpit has never yet been ascended by a scion of the aristocracy, and am prepared to prove that they might scale it, and do so with dignity and profit.

For the auctioneer's pulpit is just the peculiar place where a man of social refinement, of elegant wit, of polite perceptions, can bring his wit, his eloquence, his taste, and his experience of life, most delightfully into play. It is not like the bar, where the better and higher qualities of a man of fashion find no room for exercise. In defending John Jorrocks in an action of trespass, for cutting down a stick in Sam Snooks's field, what powers of mind do you require? — powers of mind, that is, which Mr. Sergeant Snorter, a butcher's son with a great loud voice, a sizar at Cambridge, a wrangler, and so forth, does not possess as well as yourself? Snorter has never been in decent society in his life. He thinks the bar-mess the most fashionable assemblage in Europe, and the jokes of "grand day" the *ne plus ultra* of wit. Snorter lives near Russell Square, eats beef and Yorkshire-pudding, is a judge of port-wine, is in all social respects your inferior. Well, it is ten to one but in the case of Snooks *v.* Jorrocks, before mentioned, he will be a better advocate than you; he knows the law of the case entirely, and better probably than you. He can speak long, loud, to the point, grammatically — more grammatically than you, no doubt, will condescend to do. In the case of Snooks *v.* Jorrocks he is all that can be desired. And so about dry disputes, respecting real property, he knows the law; and, beyond this, has no more need to be a gentleman than my body-servant has — who, by the way, from constant intercourse with the best society, *is* almost a gentleman. But this is apart from the question.

Now, in the matter of auctioneering, this, I apprehend, is not the case, and I assert that a high-bred gentleman, with good powers of mind and speech, must, in such a profession, make a fortune. I do not mean in all auctioneering matters. I do not mean that such a person should be called upon to sell the good-will of a public-house, or discourse about the value of the beer-barrels, or bars with pewter fittings, or the beauty of a trade doing a stroke of so many hogsheads a week. I do not ask a gentleman to go down and sell pigs, ploughs, and cart-horses, at Stoke Pogis; or to enlarge at the Auction-Rooms, Wapping, upon the beauty of "The Lively Sally" schooner. These articles of commerce or use can be better appreciated by persons in a different rank of life to his.

But there are a thousand cases in which a gentleman only can do justice to the sale of objects which the necessity or convenience of the genteel world may require to change hands. All articles properly called of taste should be put under his charge. Pictures, — he is a travelled man, has seen and judged the best galleries of Europe, and can speak of them as a common person cannot. For, mark you, you must have the confidence of your society, you must be able to be familiar with them, to plant a happy *mot* in a graceful manner, to appeal to my lord or the duchess in such a modest, easy, pleasant way as that her grace should not be hurt by your allusion to her — nay, amused (like the rest of the company) by the manner in which it was done.

What is more disgusting than the familiarity of a snob? What more loathsome than the swaggering quackery of some present holders of the hammer? There was a late sale, for instance, which made some noise in the world (I mean the late Lord Gimcrack's, at Dilberry Hill). Ah! what an opportunity was lost there! I declare solemnly that I believe, but for the absurd quackery and braggadocio of the advertisements, much more money would have been bid; people were kept away by the vulgar trumpeting of the auctioneer, and could not help thinking the things were worthless that were so outrageously lauded.

They say that sort of Bartholomew-fair advocacy (in which people are invited to an entertainment by the medium of a hoarse yelling beef-eater, twenty-four drums, and a jack-pudding turning head over heels) is absolutely necessary to excite the public attention. What an error! I say that the refined individual so accosted is more likely to close his ears, and, shuddering, run away from the booth. Poor Horace Waddlepoodle! to think that thy gentle accumulation of bricabrac should have passed away in such a manner! by means of a man who brings down a butterfly with a blunderbuss, and talks of a pin's head through a speaking-trumpet! Why, the auctioneer's very voice was enough to crack the Sèvres porcelain, and blow the lace into annihilation. Let it be remembered that I speak of the gentleman in his public character merely, meaning to insinuate nothing more than I would by stating that Lord Brougham speaks with a northern accent, or that the voice of Mr. Sheil is sometimes unpleasantly shrill.

Now the character I have formed to myself of a great auctioneer is this. I fancy him a man of first-rate and irreproachable birth and fashion. I fancy his person so agreeable that it must be a pleasure for ladies to behold and tailors to dress it. As a private man he must move in the very best society, which will flock round his pulpit when he mounts it in his public calling. It will be a privilege for vulgar people to attend the hall where he lectures; and they will consider it an honor to be allowed to pay their money for articles the value of which is stamped by his high recommendation. Nor can such a person be a mere fribble; nor can any loose hanger-on of fashion imagine he may assume the character. The gentleman auctioneer must be an artist above all, adoring his profession; and adoring it, what must he not know? He must have a good knowledge of the history and language of all nations; not the knowledge of the mere critical scholar, but of the lively and elegant man of the world. He will not commit the gross blunders of pronunciation that untravelled Englishmen perpetrate; he will not degrade his subject by coarse eulogy, or sicken his audience with vulgar banter. He will know where to apply praise and wit properly; he will have the tact only acquired in good society, and know where a joke is in place, and how far a compliment may go. He will not outrageously and indiscriminately laud all objects committed to his charge, for he knows the value of praise; that diamonds, could we have them by the bushel, would be used as coals; that, above all, he has a character of sincerity to support; that he is not merely the advocate of the person who employs him, but that the public is his client too, who honors him and confides in him. Ask him to sell a copy of Raffaelle for an original; a trumpery modern Brussels counterfeit for real old Mechlin; some common French forged crockery for the old delightful, delicate Dresden china; and he will quit you with scorn, or order his servant to show you the door of his study.

Study, by the way, — no, "study" is a vulgar word; every word is vulgar which a man uses to give the world an exaggerated notion of himself or his condition. When the wretched bagman, brought up to give evidence before Judge Coltman, was asked what his trade was, and replied that "he represented the house of Dobson and Hobson," he showed himself to be a vulgar, mean-souled wretch, and was most properly reprimanded by his lordship. To be a bagman is to be humble but not of necessity vulgar. Pomposity is vulgar, to ape a higher rank than your own is vulgar, for an ensign of militia to call himself captain is vulgar, or for a bagman to style himself the "representative" of Dobson and Hobson. The honest auctioneer, then, will not call his room his study; but his "private room," or his office, or whatever may be the phrase commonly used among auctioneers.

He will not for the same reason call himself (as once in a momentary feeling of pride and enthusiasm for the profession I thought he should) — he will not call himself an "advocate," but an auctioneer. There is no need to attempt to awe people by big titles; let each man bear his own name without shame. And a very gentlemanlike and agreeable, though exceptional position (for it is clear that there cannot be more than two of the class), may the auctioneer occupy.

He must not sacrifice his honesty, then, either for his own sake or his clients', in any way, nor tell fibs about himself or them. He is by no means called upon to draw the long bow in their behalf; all that his office obliges him to do — and let us hope his disposition will lead him to do it also — is to take a favorable, kindly, philanthropic view of the world; to say what can fairly be said by a good-natured and ingenious man in praise of any article for which he is desirous to awaken public sympathy. And how readily and pleasantly may this be done! I will take upon myself, for instance, to write an eulogium upon So-and-So's last novel, which shall be every word of it true; and which work, though to some discontented spirits it might appear dull, may be shown to be really amusing and instructive, — nay, *is* amusing and instructive, — to those who have the art of discovering where those precious qualities lie.

An auctioneer should have the organ of truth large; of imagination and comparison, considerable; of wit, great; of benevolence, excessively large.

And how happy might such a man be, and cause others to be! He should go through the world laughing, merry, observant, kind-hearted. He should love every thing in the world, because his profession regards every thing. With books of lighter literature (for I do not recommend the genteel auctioneer to meddle with heavy antiquarian and philological works) he should be elegantly conversant, being able to give a neat history of the author, a pretty sparkling kind criticism of the work, and an appropriate eulogium upon the binding, which would make those people read who never read before; or buy, at least, which is his first consideration. Of pictures, we have already spoken. Of china, of jewelry, of gold-headed canes, valuable arms, picturesque antiquities, with what eloquent *entrainement* might he not speak! He feels every one of these things in his heart. He has all the tastes of the fashionable world. Dr. Meyrick cannot be more enthusiastic about an old suit of armor than he; Sir Harris Nicholas not more eloquent regarding the gallant times in which it was worn, and the brave histories connected with it. He takes up a pearl necklace with as much delight as any beauty who was sighing to wear it round her own snowy throat, and hugs a china monster with as much joy as the oldest duchess could do. Nor must he affect these things; he must feel them. He is a glass in which all the tastes of fashion are reflected. He must be every one of the characters to whom he addresses himself — a genteel Goethe or Shakspeare, a fashionable world-spirit.

How can a man be all this and not be a gentleman; and not have had an education in the midst of the best company — an insight into the most delicate feelings, and wants, and usages? The pulpit oratory of such a man would be invaluable; people would flock to listen to him from far and near. He might out of a single teacup cause streams of world-philosophy to flow, which would be drunk in by grateful thousands; and draw out of an old pincushion points of wit, morals, and experience, that would make a nation wise.

Look round, examine THE ANNALS OF AUCTIONS, as Mr. Robins remarks, and (with every respect for him and his brethren) say, is there in the profession SUCH A MAN? Do we want such a man? Is such a man likely or not likely to make an immense fortune? Can we get such a man, except out of the very best society, and among the most favored there?

Everybody answers "No!" I knew you would answer no. And now, gentlemen, who have laughed at my pretension to discover a profession, say, have I not? I have laid my finger upon the spot where the social deficit exists. I have shown that we labor under a want; and when the world wants, do we not know that a man will step forth to fill the vacant space that Fate has left for him? Pass we now to the —

SECOND PROFESSION.

This profession, too, is a great, lofty, and exceptional one, and discovered by me considering these things, and deeply musing upon the necessities of society. Nor let honorable gentlemen imagine that I am enabled to offer them in this profession, more than any other, a promise of what is called future glory, deathless fame, and so forth. All that I say is, that I can put young men in the way of making a comfortable livelihood, and leaving behind them, not a name, but, what is better, a decent maintenance to their children. Fitz-Boodle is as good a name as any in England. General Fitz-Boodle, who, in Marlborough's time and in conjunction with the famous Van Slaap, beat the French in the famous action of Vischzouchee, near Mardyk, in Holland, on the 14th of February, 1709, is promised an immortality upon his tomb in Westminster Abbey; but he died of apoplexy, deucedly in debt, two years afterwards: and what after that is the use of a name?

No, no; the age of chivalry is past. Take the twenty-four first men who come into the club, and ask who they are, and how they made their money? There's Woolsey-Sackville: his father was Lord Chancellor, and sat on the woolsack, whence he took his title; his grandfather dealt in coal-sacks, and not in wool-sacks,—small coal-sacks, dribbling out little supplies of black diamonds to the poor. Yonder comes Frank Leveson, in a huge broad-brimmed hat, his shirt-cuffs turned up to his elbows. Leveson is as gentlemanly a fellow as the world contains, and if he has a fault, is perhaps too finikin. Well, you fancy him related to the Sutherland family: nor, indeed, does honest Frank deny it; but *entre nous*, my good sir, his father was an attorney, and his grandfather a bailiff in Chancery Lane, bearing a name still older than that of Leveson, namely, Levy. So it is that this confounded equality grows and grows, and has laid the good old nobility by the heels. Look at that venerable Sir Charles Kitely, of Kitely Park: he is interested about the Ashantees, and is just come from Exeter Hall. Kitely discounted bills in the City in the year 1787, and gained his baronetcy by a loan to the French princes. All these points of history are perfectly well known; and do you fancy the world cares? Psha! Profession is no disgrace to a man: be what you like, provided you succeed. If Mr. Fauntleroy could come to life with a million of money, you and I would dine with him: you know we would; for why should we be better than our neighbors?

Put, then, out of your head, the idea that this profession is unworthy of you: take any that may bring you profit, and thank him that puts you in the way of being rich.

The profession I would urge (upon a person duly qualified to undertake it) has, I confess, at the first glance, something ridiculous about it; and will not appear to young ladies so romantic as the calling of a gallant soldier, blazing with glory, gold lace, and vermilion coats; or a dear delightful clergyman, with a sweet blue eye, and a pocket-handkerchief scented charmingly with lavender-water. The profession I allude to *will*, I own, be to young women disagreeable, to sober men trivial, to great stupid moralists unworthy.

But mark my words for it, that in the religious world (I have once or twice, by mistake no doubt, had the honor of dining in "serious" houses, and can vouch for the fact that the dinners there are of excellent quality)

— in the serious world, in the great mercantile world, among the legal community (notorious feeders), in every house in town (except some half-dozen which can afford to do without such aid), the man I propose might speedily render himself indispensable.

Does the reader now begin to take? Have I hinted enough for him that he may see with eagle glance the immense beauty of the profession I am about to unfold to him? We have all seen Gunter and Chevet; Fregoso, on the Puerta del Sol (a relation of the ex-Minister Calomarde), is a good purveyor enough for the benighted olla-eaters of Madrid; nor have I any fault to find with Guimard, a Frenchman, who has lately set up in the Toledo, at Naples, where he furnishes people with decent food. It has given me pleasure, too, in walking about London — in the Strand, in Oxford Street, and elsewhere, to see fournisseurs and comestible-merchants newly set up. Messrs. Morell have excellent articles in their warehouses; Fortnum and Mason are known to most of my readers.

But what is not known, what is wanted, what is languished for in England is *a dinner-master,*— a gentleman who is not a provider of meat or wine, like the parties before named, who can have no earthly interest in the price of truffled turkeys or dry champagne beyond that legitimate interest which he may feel for his client, and which leads him to see that the latter is not cheated by his tradesmen. For the dinner-giver is almost naturally an ignorant man. How in mercy's name can Mr. Sergeant Snorter, who is all day at Westminster, or in chambers, know possibly the mysteries, the delicacy, of dinner-giving? How can Alderman Pogson know any thing beyond the fact that venison is good with currant-jelly, and that he likes lots of green fat with his turtle? Snorter knows law, Pogson is acquainted with the state of the tallow market; but what should he know of eating, like you and me, who have given up our time to it? (I say *me* only familiarly, for I have only reached so far in the science as to know that I know nothing.) But men there are, gifted individuals, who have spent years of deep thought — not merely intervals of labor, but hours of study every day — over the gormandizing science — who like alchemists, have let their fortunes go, guinea by guinea, into the all-devouring pot,— who, ruined as they sometimes are, never get a guinea by chance but they will have a plate of pease in May with it, or a little feast of ortolans, or a piece of Glo'ster salmon, or one more flask from their favorite claret-bin.

It is not the ruined gastronomist that I would advise a person to select as his *table-master;* for the opportunities of peculation would be too great in a position of such confidence — such complete abandonment of one man to another. A ruined man would be making bargains with the tradesmen. They would offer to cash bills for him, or send him opportune presents of wine, which he could convert into money, or bribe him in one way or another. Let this be done, and the profession of table-master is ruined. Snorter and Pogson may almost as well order their own dinners, as be at the mercy of a "gastronomic agent" whose faith is not beyond all question.

A vulgar mind, in reply to these remarks regarding the gastronomic ignorance of Snorter and Pogson, might say, "True, these gentlemen know nothing of household economy, being occupied with other more important business elsewhere. But what are their wives about? Lady Pogson in Harley Street has nothing earthly to do but to mind her poodle, and her mantua-maker's and housekeeper's bills. Mrs. Snorter in Bedford Place, when she has taken her drive in the Park with the young ladies, may surely have time to attend to her husband's guests and preside over the preparations of his kitchen, as she does worthily at his hospitable mahogany."

To this I answer, that a man who expects a woman to understand the philosophy of dinner-giving, shows the strongest evidence of a low mind. He is unjust towards that lovely and delicate creature, woman, to suppose that she heartily understands and cares for what she eats and drinks. No: taken as a rule, women have no real appetites. They are children in the gormandizing way; loving sugar, sops, tarts, trifles, apricot-creams, and such gewgaws. They would take a sip of Malmsey, and would drink currant-wine just as happily, if that accursed liquor were presented to them by the butler. Did you ever know a woman who could lay her fair hand upon her gentle heart and say on her conscience that she preferred dry sillery to sparkling champagne? Such a phenomenon does not exist. They are not made for eating and drinking; or, if they make a pretence to it, become downright odious. Nor can they, I am sure, witness the preparations of a really great repast without a certain jealousy. They grudge spending money (ask guards, coachmen, inn-waiters, whether this be not the case). They will give their all, heaven bless them! to serve a son, a grandson, or a dear relative, but they have not the heart to pay for small things magnificently. They are jealous of good dinners, and no wonder. I have shown in a former discourse how they are jealous of smoking, and other personal enjoyments of the male. I say, then, that Lady Pogson or Mrs. Snorter can never conduct their husbands' table properly. Fancy either of them consenting to allow a calf to be stewed down into gravy for one dish, or a dozen hares to be sacrificed to a single *purée* of game, or the best Madeira to be used for a sauce, or half a dozen of champagne to boil a ham in. They will be for bringing a bottle of Marsala in place of the old particular, or for having the ham cooked in water. But of these matters — of kitchen philosophy — I have no practical or theoretic knowledge; and must beg pardon if, only understanding the goodness of a dish when cooked, I may have unconsciously made some blunder regarding the preparation.

Let it, then, be set down as an axiom, without further trouble of demonstration, that a woman is a bad dinner-caterer; either too great and simple for it, or too mean — I don't know which it is; and gentlemen, according as they admire or contemn the sex, may settle that matter their own way. In brief, the mental constitution of lovely woman is such that she cannot give a great dinner. It must be done by a man. It can't be done by an ordinary man, because he does not understand it. Vain fool! and he sends off to the pastry-cook in Great Russell Street or Baker Street, he lays on a couple of extra waiters (green-grocers in the neighborhood), he makes a great bother with his butler in the cellar, and fancies he has done the business.

Bon Dieu! Who has not been at those dinners? — those monstrous exhibitions of the pastrycook's art? Who does not know those made dishes with the universal sauce to each? — fricandeaux, sweet-breads, damp dumpy cutlets, &c., seasoned with the compound of grease, onions, bad port-wine, cayenne pepper, curry-powder (Warren's Blacking, for what I know, but the taste is always the same) — there they lie in the old corner dishes, the poor wiry Moselle and sparkling Burgundy in the ice-coolers, and the old story of white and brown soup, turbot, little smelts, boiled turkey, saddle-of-mutton, and so forth. "Try a little of that fricandeau," says Mrs. Snorter, with a kind smile. "You'll find it, I think, very nice." Be sure it has come in a green tray from Great Russell Street. "Mr. Fitz-Boodle, you have been in Germany," cries Snorter, knowingly; "taste the hock, and tell me what you think of *that*."

How should he know better, poor benighted creature; or she, dear good soul that she is? If they would have a leg of mutton and an apple pudding, and a glass of sherry and port (or simple brandy and water called by its own name) after dinner, all would be very well; but they must shine, they must dine as their neighbors. There is no difference in the style of dinners in London; people with five hundred a year treat you exactly as those of five thousand. They *will* have their Moselle or hock, their fatal side-dishes brought in the green trays from the pastrycook's.

Well, there is no harm done; not as regards the dinner-givers at least, though the dinner-eaters may have to suffer somewhat; it only shows that the former are hospitably inclined, and wish to do the very best in their power, — good honest fellows! If they do wrong, how can they help it? they know no better.

And now, is it not as clear as the sun at noon-day, that A WANT exists in London for a superintendent of the table — a gastronomic agent — a dinner-master, as I have called him before? A man of such a profession would be a metropolitan benefit; hundreds of thousands of people of the respectable sort, people in white waistcoats, would thank him daily. Calculate how many dinners are given in the City of London, and calculate the numbers of benedictions that "the Agency" might win.

And as no doubt the observant man of the world has remarked that the freeborn Englishman of the respectable class is, of all others, the most slavish and truckling to a lord; that there is no fly-blown peer but he is pleased to have him at his table, proud beyond measure to call him by his surname (without the lordly prefix); and that those lords whom he does not know, he yet (the freeborn Englishman) takes care to have their pedigrees and ages by heart from his world-bible, the "Peerage:" as this is an indisputable fact, and as it is in this particular class of Britons that our agent must look to find clients, I need not say it is necessary that the agent should be as high-born as possible, and that he should be able to tack, if possible, an honorable or some other handle to his respectable name. He must have it on his professional card —

The Honorable George Gormand Gobbleton, *Apician Chambers, Pall Mall.*

Or,

Sir Augustus Carver Cramley Cramley, *Amphitryonic Council Office, Swallow St.*

or, in some such neat way, Gothic letters on a large handsome crockery-ware card, with possibly a gilt coat-of-arms and supporters, or the blood-red hand of baronetcy duly displayed. Depend on it plenty of guineas will fall in it, and that Gobbleton's supporters will support him comfortably enough.

For this profession is not like that of the auctioneer, which I take to be a far more noble one, because more varied and more truthful; but in the Agency case, a little humbug at least is necessary. A man cannot be a successful agent by the mere force of his simple merit or genius in eating and drinking. He must of necessity impose upon the vulgar to a certain degree. He must be of that rank which will lead them naturally to respect him, otherwise they might be led to jeer at his profession; but let a noble exercise, it, and bless your soul, all the "Court Guide" is dumb!

He will then give out in a manly and somewhat pompous address what has before been mentioned, namely, that he has seen the fatal way in which the hospitality of England has been perverted hitherto, *accaparé*'d by a few cooks with green trays. (He must use a good deal of French in his language, for that is considered very gentleman-like by vulgar people.) He will take a set of chambers in Carlton Gardens, which will be richly though severely furnished, and the door of which will be opened by a French valet (he *must* be a Frenchman, remember), who will say, on letting Mr. Snorter or Sir Benjamin Pogson in, that "*Milor* is at home." Pogson will then be shown into a library furnished with massive bookcases, containing all the works on cookery and wines (the titles of them) in all the known languages in the world. Any books, of course, will do, as you will have them handsomely bound, and keep them under plate-glass. On a side-table will be little sample-bottles of wine, a few truffles on a white porcelain saucer, a prodigious strawberry or two, perhaps, at the time when such fruit costs much money. On the library will be busts marked Ude, Carème, Béchamel, in marble (never mind what heads, of course); and, perhaps, on the clock should be a figure of the Prince of Condé's cook killing himself because the fish had not arrived in time: there may be a wreath of *immortelles* on the figure to give it a more decidedly Frenchified air. The walls will be of a dark rich paper, hung round with neat gilt frames, containing plans of *menus* of various great dinners, those of Cambacères, Napoleon, Louis XIV., Louis XVIII., Heliogabalus, if you like, each signed by the respective cook.

After the stranger has looked about him at these things, which he does not understand in the least, especially the truffles, which look like dirty potatoes, you will make your appearance, dressed in a dark dress, with one handsome enormous gold chain, and one large diamond ring; a gold snuff-box, of course, which you will thrust into the visitor's paw before saying a word. You will be yourself a portly grave man, with your hair a little bald and gray. In fact, in this, as in all other professions, you had best try to look as like Canning as you can.

When Pogson has done sneezing with the snuff, you will say to him, "Take a *fauteuil*. I have the honor of addressing Sir Benjamin Pogson, I believe?" And then you will explain to him your system.

This, of course, must vary with every person you address. But let us lay down a few of the heads of a plan which may be useful, or may be modified infinitely, or may be cast aside altogether, just as circumstances dictate. After all *I* am not going to turn gastronomic agent, and speak only for the benefit perhaps of the very person who is reading this: —

"SYNOPSIS OF THE GASTRONOMIC AGENCY OF THE HONORABLE GEORGE GOBBLETON.

"THE Gastronomic Agent having traversed Europe, and dined with the best society of the world, has been led naturally, as a patriot, to turn his thoughts homeward, and cannot but deplore the lamentable ignorance regarding gastronomy displayed in a country for which Nature has done almost every thing.

"But it is ever singularly thus. Inherent ignorance belongs to man; and The Agent, in his Continental travels, has always remarked, that the countries most fertile in themselves were invariably worse tilled than those more barren. The Italians and the Spaniards leave their fields to Nature, as we leave our vegetables, fish, and meat. And, heavens! what richness do we fling away, — what dormant qualities in our dishes do we disregard, — what glorious gastronomic crops (if The Agent may be permitted the expression) — what glorious gastronomic crops do we sacrifice, allowing our goodly meats and fishes to lie fallow! 'Chance,' it is said by an ingenious historian, who, having been long a secretary in the East India House, must certainly have had access to the best information upon Eastern matters — 'Chance' it is said by Mr. Charles Lamb, 'which burnt down a Chinaman's house, with a litter of sucking-pigs that were unable to escape from the interior, discovered to the world the excellence of roast-pig.' Gunpowder, we know, was invented by a similar fortuity." [The reader will observe that my style in the supposed character of a Gastronomic Agent is purposely pompous and loud.] "So, 'tis said, was printing, — so glass. — We should have drunk our wine poisoned with the villanous odor of the borachio, had not some Eastern merchants, lighting their fires in the Desert, marked the strange composition which now glitters on our sideboards, and holds the costly produce of our vines.

"We have spoken of the natural riches of a country. Let the reader think but for one moment of the gastronomic wealth of our country of England, and he will be lost in thankful amazement as he watches the astonishing riches poured out upon us from Nature's bounteous cornucopia! Look at our fisheries! — the trout and salmon tossing in our brawling streams; the white and full-breasted turbot struggling in the mariner's net; the purple lobster lured by hopes of greed into his basket-prison, which he quits only for the red ordeal of the pot. Look at whitebait, great heavens! look at whitebait, and a thousand frisking, glittering, silvery things besides, which the nymphs of our native streams bear kindly to the deities of our kitchens — our kitchens such as they are.

"And though it may be said that other countries produce the freckle-backed salmon and the dark broad-shouldered turbot; though trout frequent many a stream besides those of England, and lobsters sprawl on other sands than ours; yet, let it be remembered, that our native country possesses these altogether, while other lands only know them separately; that, above all, whitebait is peculiarly our country's — our city's own! Blessings and eternal praises be on it, and, of course, on brown bread and butter! And the Briton should further remember, with honest pride and thankfulness, the situation of his capital, of London: the lordly turtle floats from the sea into the stream, and from the stream to the city; the rapid fleets of all the world *se donnent rendezvous* in the docks of our silvery Thames; the produce of our coasts and provincial cities, east and west, is borne to us on the swift lines of lightning railroads. In a word — and no man but one who, like The Agent, has travelled Europe over, can appreciate the gift — there is no city on earth's surface so well supplied with fish as London!

"With respect to our meats, all praise is supererogatory. Ask the wretched hunter of *chevreuil*, the poor devourer of *rehbraten*, what they think of the noble English haunch, that after bounding in the Park of Knole or Windsor, exposes its magnificent flank upon some broad silver platter at our tables? It is enough to say of foreign venison, that *they are obliged to lard it*. Away! ours is the palm of roast; whether of the crisp mutton that crops the thymy herbage of our downs, or the noble ox who revels on lush Althorpian oil-cakes. What game is like to ours? Mans excels us in poultry, 'tis true; but 'tis only in merry England that the partridge has a flavor, that the turkey can almost *se passer de truffes*, that the jolly juicy goose can be eaten as he deserves.

"Our vegetables, moreover, surpass all comment; Art (by the means of glass) has wrung fruit out of the bosom of Nature, such as she grants to no other clime. And if we have no vineyards on our hills, we have gold to purchase their best produce. Nature, and enterprise that masters

Nature, have done every thing for our land.

"But with all these prodigious riches in our power, is it not painful to reflect how absurdly we employ them? Can we say that we are in the habit of dining well? Alas, no! and The Agent, roaming o'er foreign lands, and seeing how, with small means and great ingenuity and perseverance, great ends were effected, comes back sadly to his own country, whose wealth he sees absurdly wasted, whose energies are misdirected, and whose vast capabilities are allowed to lie idle." . . . [Here should follow what I have only hinted at previously, a vivid and terrible picture of the degradation of our table.] . . . "Oh, for a master spirit, to give an impetus to the land, to see its great power directed in the right way, and its wealth not squandered or hidden, but nobly put out to interest and spent!

"The Agent dares not hope to win that proud station — to be the destroyer of a barbarous system wallowing in abusive prodigality — to become a dietetic reformer — the Luther of the table.

"But convinced of the wrongs which exist, he will do his humble endeavor to set them right, and to those who know that they are ignorant (and this is a vast step to knowledge) he offers his counsels, his active co-operation, his frank and kindly sympathy. The Agent's qualifications are these: —

"1. He is of one of the best families in England; and has in himself, or through his ancestors, been accustomed to good living for centuries. In the reign of Henry V., his maternal great-great-grandfather, Roger de Gobylton" [*the name may be varied, of course, or the king's reign, or the dish invented*], "was the first who discovered the method of roasting a peacock whole with his tail-feathers displayed; and the dish was served to the two kings at Rouen. Sir Walter Cramley, in Elizabeth's reign, produced before her Majesty, when at Killingworth Castle, mackerel with the famous *gooseberry sauce*, &c.

"2. He has, through life, devoted himself to no other study than that of the table, and has visited to that end the courts of all the monarchs of Europe; taking the receipts of the cooks, with whom he lives on terms of intimate friendship, often at enormous expense to himself.

"3. He has the same acquaintance with all the vintages of the Continent; having passed the autumn of 1811 (the comet year) on the great Weinberg of Johannisberg; being employed similarly at Bordeaux, in 1834: at Oporto, in 1820; and at Xeres de la Frontera, with his excellent friends, Duff, Gordon, and Co., the year after. He travelled to India and back in company with fourteen pipes of Madeira (on board of 'The Samuel Snob' East Indiaman, Captain Scuttler), and spent the vintage season in the island, with unlimited powers of observation granted to him by the great houses there.

"4. He has attended Mr. Groves of Charing Cross, and Mr. Giblett of Bond Street, in a course of purchases of fish and meat; and is able at a glance to recognize the age of mutton, the primeness of beef, the firmness and freshness of fish of all kinds.

"5. He has visited the parks, the grouse-manors, and the principal gardens of England, in a similar professional point of view."

The Agent then, through his subordinates, engages to provide gentlemen who are about to give dinner-parties —

"1. With cooks to dress the dinners; a list of which gentlemen he has by him, and will recommend none who are not worthy of the strictest confidence.

"2. With a *menu* for the table, according to the price which the Amphitryon chooses to incur.

"3. He will, through correspondences with the various fournisseurs of the metropolis, provide them with viands, fruit, wine, &c., sending to Paris, if need be, where he has a regular correspondence with Messrs. Chevet.

"4. He has a list of dexterous table-waiters (all answering to the name of John for fear of mistakes, the butler's name to be settled according to pleasure), and would strongly recommend that the servants of the house should be locked in the back-kitchen or servants' hall during the time the dinner takes place.

"5. He will receive and examine all the accounts of the fournisseurs, — of course pledging his honor as a gentleman not to receive one shilling of paltry gratification from the tradesmen he employs, but to see that the bills are more moderate, and their goods of better quality, than they would provide to any person of less experience than himself.

"6. His fee for superintending a dinner will be five guineas : and The Agent entreats his clients to trust *entirely* to him and his subordinates for the arrangement of the repast, — *not to think* of inserting dishes of their own invention, or producing wine from their own cellars, as he engages to have it brought in the best order, and fit for immediate drinking. Should the Amphitryon, however, desire some particular dish or wine, he must consult The Agent in the first case by writing, in the second, by sending a sample to The Agent's chambers. For it is manifest that the whole complexion of a dinner may be altered by the insertion of a single dish ; and, therefore, parties will do well to mention their wishes on the first interview with The Agent. He cannot be called upon to recompose his bill of fare, except at great risk to the *ensemble* of the dinner and enormous inconvenience to himself.

"7. The Agent will be at home for consultation from ten o'clock until two — earlier, if gentlemen who are engaged at early hours in the City desire to have an interview : and be it remembered, that a *personal interview* is always the best: for it is greatly necessary to know not only the number but the character of the guests whom the Amphitryon proposes to entertain, — whether they are fond of any particular wine or dish, what is their state of health, rank, style, profession, &c.

"8. At two o'clock, he will commence his rounds ; for as the metropolis is wide, it is clear that he must be early in the field in some districts. From 2 to 3 he will be in Russell Square and the neighborhood ; 3 to 3¾, Harley Street, Portland Place, Cavendish Square, and the environs ; 3¾ to 4¼, Portman Square, Gloucester Place, Baker Street, &c. ; 4¼ to 5, the new district about Hyde Park Terrace ; 5 to 5¾, St. John's Wood and the Regent's Park. He will be in Grosvenor Square by 6, and in Belgrave Square, Pimlico, and its vicinity, by 7. Parties there are requested not to dine until 8 o'clock ; and The Agent, once for all, peremptorily announces that he will NOT go to the palace, where it is utterly impossible to serve a good dinner."

"TO TRADESMEN.

"Every Monday evening during the season the Gastronomic Agent proposes to give a series of trial-dinners, to which the principal gourmands of the metropolis, and a few of The Agent's most respectable clients, will be invited. Covers will be laid for *ten* at nine o'clock precisely. And as The Agent does not propose to exact a single shilling of profit from their bills, and as his recommendation will be of infinite value to them, the tradesmen he employs will furnish the weekly dinner gratis. Cooks will attend (who have acknowledged characters) upon the same terms. To save trouble, a book will be kept where butchers, poulterers, fishmongers, &c., may inscribe their names in order, taking it by turns to supply the trial-table. Wine-merchants will naturally compete every week promiscuously, sending what they consider their best samples, and leaving with the hall-porter tickets of the prices. Confectionery to be done out of the house. Fruiterers, market-men, as butchers and poulterers. The Agent's *maître d'hôtel* will give a receipt to each individual for the articles he produces; and let all remember that The Agent is a *very keen judge*, and woe betide those who serve him or his clients ill!

"GEORGE GORMAND GOBBLETON.

"*Carlton Gardens, June* 10, 1842."

Here I have sketched out the heads of such an address as I conceive a gastronomic agent might put forth; and appeal pretty confidently to the British public regarding its merits and my own discovery. If this be not a profession — a new one — a feasible one — a lucrative one, — I don't know what is. Say that a man attends but fifteen dinners daily, that is seventy-five guineas, or five hundred and fifty pounds weekly, or fourteen thousand three hundred pounds for a season of six months; and how many of our younger sons have such a capital even? Let, then, some unemployed gentleman with the requisite qualifications come forward. It will not be necessary that he should have done all that is stated in the prospectus; but, at any rate, let him *say* he has: there can't be much harm in an innocent fib of that sort; for the gastronomic agent must be a sort of dinner-pope, whose opinions cannot be supposed to err.

And as he really will be an excellent judge of eating and drinking, and will bring his whole mind to bear upon the question, and will speedily acquire an experience which no person out of the profession can possibly have; and as, moreover, he will be an honorable man, not practising upon his client in any way, or demanding sixpence beyond his just fee, the world will gain vastly by the coming forward of such a person,— gain in good dinners, and absolutely save money: for what is five guineas for a dinner of sixteen? The sum may be *gaspillé* by a cook-wench, or by one of those abominable, before-named pastrycooks, with their green trays.

If any man take up the business, he will invite me, of course, to the Monday dinners. Or does ingratitude go so far as that a man should forget the author of his good fortune? I believe it does. Turn we away from the sickening theme!

And now, having concluded my professions, how shall I express my obligations to the discriminating press of this country for the unanimous applause which hailed my first appearance? It is the more wonderful, as I pledge my sacred word, I never wrote a document before much longer than a laundress's bill, or the acceptance of an invitation to dinner. But enough of this egotism: thanks for praise conferred sound like vanity; gratitude is hard to speak of, and at present it swells the full heart of

GEORGE SAVAGE FITZ-BOODLE.

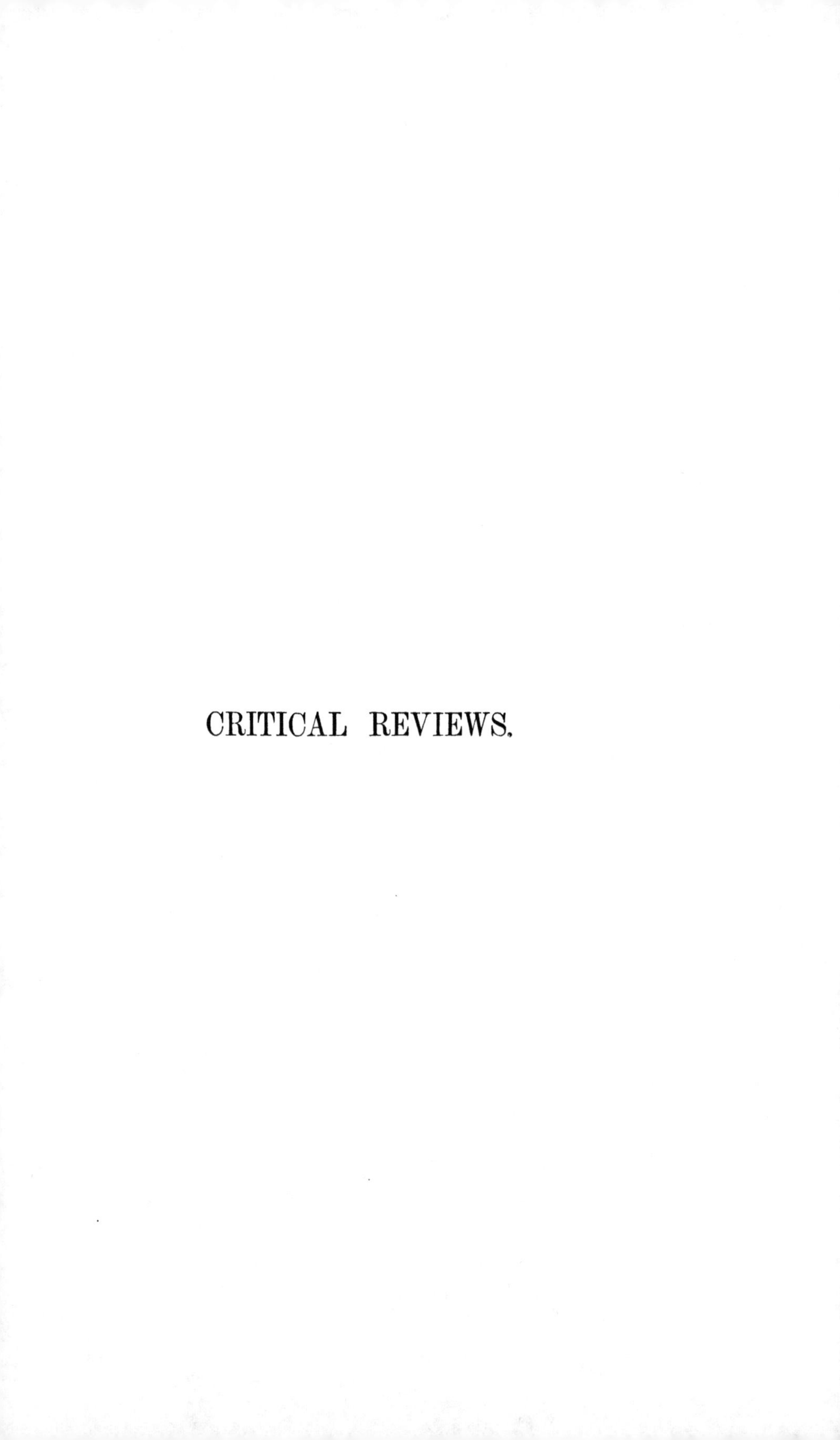

CRITICAL REVIEWS.

CRITICAL REVIEWS.

GEORGE CRUIKSHANK.*

ACCUSATIONS of ingratitude, and just accusations, no doubt, are made against every inhabitant of this wicked world, and the fact is, that a man who is ceaselessly engaged in its trouble and turmoil, borne hither and thither upon the fierce waves of the crowd, bustling, shifting, struggling to keep himself somewhat above water — fighting for reputation, or more likely for bread, and ceaselessly occupied to-day with plans for appeasing the eternal appetite of inevitable hunger to-morrow — a man in such straits has hardly time to think of any thing but himself, and, as in a sinking ship, must make his own rush for the boats, and fight, struggle, and trample for safety. In the midst of such a combat as this, the "ingenious arts, which prevent the ferocity of the manners, and act upon them as an emollient" (as the philosophic bard remarks in the Latin Grammar) are likely to be jostled to death, and then forgotten. The world will allow no such compromises between it and that which does not belong to it — no two gods must we serve; but (as one has seen in some old portraits) the horrible glazed eyes of Necessity are always fixed upon you; fly away as you will, black Care sits behind you, and with his ceaseless gloomy croaking drowns the voice of all more cheerful companions. Happy he whose fortune has placed him where there is calm and plenty, and who has the wisdom not to give up his quiet in quest of visionary gain.

Here is, no doubt, the reason why a man, after the period of his boyhood, or first youth, makes so few friends. Want and ambition (new acquaintances which are introduced to him along with his beard) thrust away all other society from him. Some old friends remain, it is true, but these are become as a habit — a part of your selfishness; and, for new ones, they are selfish as you are. Neither member of the new partnership has the capital of affection and kindly feeling, or can even afford the time that is requisite for the establishment of the new firm. Damp and chill the shades of the prison-house begin to close round us, and that "vision splendid" which has accompanied our steps in our journey daily farther from the east, fades away and dies into the light of common day.

And what a common day! what a foggy, dull, shivering apology for light is this kind of muddy twilight through which we are about to tramp and flounder for the rest of our existence, wandering farther and farther from the beauty and freshness and from the kindly gushing springs of clear gladness that made all around us green in our youth! One wanders and gropes in a slough of

* Reprinted from "The Westminster Review" for June, 1840. (No. 66.)

stock-jobbing, one sinks or rises in a storm of politics, and in either case it is as good to fall as to rise—to mount a bubble on the crest of the wave, as to sink a stone to the bottom.

The reader who has seen the name affixed to the head of this article scarcely expected to be entertained with a declamation upon ingratitude, youth, and the vanity of human pursuits, which may seem at first sight to have little to do with the subject in hand. But (although we reserve the privilege of discoursing upon whatever subject shall suit us, and by no means admit the public has any right to ask in our sentences for any meaning, or any connection whatever) it happens that, in this particular instance, there is an undoubted connection. In Susan's case, as recorded by Wordsworth, what connection had the corner of Wood Street with a mountain ascending, a vision of trees, and a nest by the Dove? Why should the song of a thrush cause bright volumes of vapor to glide through Lothbury, and a river to flow on through the vale of Cheapside? As she stood at that corner of Wood Street, a mop and a pail in her hand most likely, she heard the bird singing, and straightway began pining and yearning for the days of her youth, forgetting the proper business of the pail and mop. Even so we are moved by the sight of some of Mr. Cruikshank's works — the "Busen fühlt sich jugendlich erschüttert," the "schwankende Gestalten" of youth flit before one again, — Cruikshank's thrush begins to pipe and carol, as in the days of boyhood; hence misty moralities, reflections, and sad and pleasant remembrances arise. He is the friend of the young especially. Have we not read all the story-books that his wonderful pencil has illustrated? Did we not forego tarts, in order to buy his "Breaking-up," or his "Fashionable Monstrosities" of the year eighteen hundred and something? Have we not before us, at this very moment, a print, —one of the admirable "Illustrations of Phrenology"—which entire work was purchased by a joint-stock company of boys, each drawing lots afterwards for the separate prints, and taking his choice in rotation? The writer of this, too, had the honor of drawing the first lot, and seized immediately upon "Philoprogenitiveness"—a marvellous print (our copy is not at all improved by being colored, which operation we performed on it ourselves)—a marvellous print, indeed, —full of ingenuity and fine, jovial humor. A father, possessor of an enormous nose and family, is surrounded by the latter, who are, some of them, embracing the former. The composition writhes and twists about like the Kermes of Rubens. No less than seven little men and women in nightcaps, in frocks, in bibs, in breeches, are clambering about the head, knees, and arms of the man with the nose; their noses, too, are preternaturally developed — the twins in the cradle have noses of the most considerable kind. The second daughter, who is watching them; the youngest but two, who sits squalling in a certain wicker chair; the eldest son, who is yawning; the eldest daughter, who is preparing, with the gravy of two mutton-chops, a savory dish of Yorkshire pudding for eighteen persons; the youths who are examining her operations (one a literary gentleman, in a remarkably neat nightcap and pinafore, who has just had his finger in the pudding); the genius who is at work on the slate, and the two honest lads who are hugging the good-humored washerwoman, their mother, — all, all, save this worthy woman, have noses of the largest size. Not handsome certainly are they, and yet everybody must be charmed with the picture. It is full of grotesque beauty. The artist has at the back of his own skull, we are certain, a huge bump of philoprogenitiveness. He loves children in his heart;

every one of those he has drawn is perfectly happy, and jovial, and affectionate, and innocent as possible. He makes them with large noses, but he loves them, and you always find something kind in the midst of his humor, and the ugliness redeemed by a sly touch of beauty. The smiling mother reconciles one with all the hideous family: they have all something of the mother in them — something kind, and generous, and tender.

Knight's, in Sweeting's Alley; Fairburn's, in a court off Ludgate Hill; Hone's, in Fleet Street — bright, enchanted palaces, which George Cruikshank used to people with grinning, fantastical imps, and merry, harmless sprites, — where are they? Fairburn's shop knows him no more; not only has Knight disappeared from Sweeting's Alley, but, as we are given to understand, Sweeting's Alley has disappeared from the face of the globe. Slop, the atrocious Castlereagh, the sainted Caroline (in a tight pelisse, with feathers in her head), the "Dandy of sixty," who used to glance at us from Hone's friendly windows — where are they? Mr. Cruikshank may have drawn a thousand better things since the days when these were; but they are to us a thousand times more pleasing than any thing else he has done. How we used to believe in them! to stray miles out of the way on holidays, in order to ponder for an hour before that delightful window in Sweeting's Alley! in walks through Fleet Street, to vanish abruptly down Fairburn's passage, and there make one at his "charming gratis" exhibition. There used to be a crowd round the window in those days, of grinning, good-natured mechanics, who spelt the songs, and spoke them out for the benefit of the company, and who received the points of humor with a general sympathizing roar. Where are these people now? You never hear any laughing at HB.; his pictures are a great deal too genteel for that — polite points of wit, which strike one as exceedingly clever and pretty, and cause one to smile in a quiet, gentleman-like kind of way.

There must be no smiling with Cruikshank. A man who does not laugh outright is a dullard, and has no heart; even the old dandy of sixty must have laughed at his own wondrous grotesque image, as they say Louis Philippe did, who saw all the caricatures that were made of himself. And there are some of Cruikshank's designs which have the blessed faculty of creating laughter as often as you see them. As Diggory says in the play, who is bidden by his master not to laugh while waiting at table — "Don't tell the story of Grouse in the Gunroom, master, or I can't help laughing." Repeat that history ever so often, and at the proper moment, honest Diggory is sure to explode. Every man, no doubt, who loves Cruikshank has his "Grouse in the Gunroom." There is a fellow in the "Points of Humor" who is offering to eat up a certain little general, that has made us happy any time these sixteen years: his huge mouth is a perpetual well of laughter — buckets full of fun can be drawn from it. We have formed no such friendships as that boyish one of the man with the mouth. But though, in our eyes, Mr. Cruikshank reached his apogee some eighteen years since, it must not be imagined that such is really the case. Eighteen sets of children have since then learned to love and admire him, and may many more of their successors be brought up in the same delightful faith. It is not the artist who fails, but the men who grow cold — the men, from whom the illusions (why illusions? realities) of youth disappear one by one; who have no leisure to be happy, no blessed holidays, but only fresh cares at Midsummer and Christmas, being the inevitable seasons which bring us bills instead of pleasures. Tom, who comes bounding home from school, has the doctor's account in his trunk, and his father goes to sleep at the pantomime to which he takes him. *Pater infelix*, you too have laughed at clown, and the magic wand of spangled harlequin; what delightful enchantment did it wave around you, in the golden days "when George the Third was king!" But our clown lies in his grave; and our harlequin, Ellar, prince of how many enchanted islands, was he not at Bow Street the other day,* in his dirty, tattered, faded motley — seized as a law-breaker, for acting at a penny theatre, after having well-nigh starved in the streets, where nobody would listen to his old guitar? No one gave a shilling to bless him: not one of us who owe him so much.

We know not if Mr. Cruikshank will be very well pleased at finding his name in such company as that of Clown and Harlequin; but he, like them, is certainly the children's friend. His drawings abound in feeling for these little ones, and hideous as in the course of his duty he is from time to time compelled to design them, he never sketches one without a certain pity for it, and imparting to the figure a certain grotesque grace. In happy school-boys he revels; plum-pudding and holidays his needle has engraved over and over again; there is a design in one of the comic almanacs of some young gentlemen who are employed in administering to a schoolfellow the correction of the pump, which is as graceful and elegant as a drawing of Stothard. Dull books about children George Cruikshank makes bright with illustrations — there is one published by the ingenious and opulent Mr. Tegg. It is entitled "Mirth and Morality," the mirth being, for the most part, on the side of the designer — the morality, unexceptionable certainly, the author's capital. Here are then, to these moralities, a smiling train of mirths supplied by George Cruikshank. See yonder little fellows butterfly-hunting across a common! Such a light, brisk, airy, gentleman-like drawing was never made upon such a theme. Who, cries the author —

> "Who has not chased the butterfly,
> And crushed its slender legs and wings,
> And heaved a moralizing sigh:
> Alas! how frail are human things!"

A very unexceptionable morality truly; but it would have puzzled another than George Cruikshank to make mirth out of it as he has done. Away, surely not on the wings of these verses, Cruikshank's imagination begins to soar; and he makes us three darling little men on a green common, backed by old farm-houses, somewhere about May. A great mixture of blue and clouds in the air, a strong fresh breeze stirring, Tom's jacket flapping in the same, in order to bring down the insect queen or king of spring that is fluttering above him, — he renders all this with a few strokes on a little block of wood not two inches square, upon which one may gaze for hours, so merry and life-like a scene does it present. What a charming creative power is this, what a privilege — to be a god, and create little worlds upon paper, and whole generations of smiling, jovial men, women, and children half inch high, whose portraits are carried abroad, and have the faculty of making us monsters of six feet curious and happy in our turn. Now, who would imagine that an artist could make any thing of such a subject as this? The writer begins by stating, —

> "I love to go back to the days of my youth,
> And to reckon my joys to the letter,
> And to count o'er the friends that I have in the world,
> *Ay, and those who are gone to a better.*"

This brings him to the consideration of his uncle. "Of all the men I have ever known," says he, "my uncle united the greatest degree of cheerfulness with the sobriety of

* This was written in 1840.

manhood. Though a man when I was a boy, he was yet one of the most agreeable companions I ever possessed. . . . He embarked for America, and nearly twenty years passed by before he came back again; . . . but oh, how altered! — he was in every sense of the word an old man, his body and mind were enfeebled, and second childishness had come upon him. How often have I bent over him, vainly endeavoring to recall to his memory the scenes we had shared together: and how frequently, with an aching heart, have I gazed on his vacant and lustreless eye, while he has amused himself in clapping his hands, and singing with a quavering voice a verse of a psalm." Alas! such are the consequences of long residences in America, and of old age even in uncles! Well, the point of this morality is, that the uncle one day in the morning of life vowed that he would catch his two nephews and tie them together, ay, and actually did so, for all the efforts the rogues made to run away from him; but he was so fatigued that he declared he never would make the attempt again, whereupon the nephew remarks, — "Often since then, when engaged in enterprises beyond my strength, have I called to mind the determination of my uncle."

Does it not seem impossible to make a picture out of this? And yet George Cruikshank has produced a charming design, in which the uncles and nephews are so prettily portrayed that one is reconciled to their existence, with all their moralities. Many more of the mirths in this little book are excellent, especially a great figure of a parson entering church on horseback, — an enormous parson truly, calm, unconscious, unwieldy. As Zeuxis had a bevy of virgins in order to make his famous picture — his express virgin — a clerical host must have passed under Cruikshank's eyes before he sketched this little, enormous parson of parsons.

Being on the subject of children's books, how shall we enough praise the delightful German nursery-tales, and Cruikshank's illustrations of them? We coupled his name with pantomime a while since, and sure never pantomimes were more charming than these. Of all the artists that ever drew, from Michael Angelo upwards and downwards, Cruikshank was the man to illustrate these tales, and give them just the proper admixture of the grotesque, the wonderful, and the graceful. May all Mother Bunch's collection be similarly indebted to him; may "Jack the Giant Killer," may "Tom Thumb," may "Puss in Boots," be one day revivified by his pencil! Is not Whittington sitting yet on Highgate Hill, and poor Cinderella (in that sweetest of all fairy stories) still pining in her lonely chimney nook? A man who has a true affection for these delightful companions of his youth is bound to be grateful to them if he can, and we pray Mr. Cruikshank to remember them.

It is folly to say that this or that kind of humor is too good for the public, that only a chosen few can relish it. The best humor that we know of has been as eagerly received by the public as by the most delicate connoisseur. There is hardly a man in England who can read, but will laugh at Falstaff and the humor of Joseph Andrews; and honest Mr. Pickwick's story can be felt and loved by any person above the age of six. Some may have a keener enjoyment of it than others, but all the world can be merry over it, and is always ready to welcome it. The best criterion of good humor is success, and what a share of this has Mr. Cruikshank had! how many millions of mortals has he made happy! We have heard very profound persons talk philosophically of the marvellous and mysterious manner in which he has suited himself to the time — *fait vibrer la fibre populaire* (as Napoleon boasted of himself), supplied a peculiar want felt at a peculiar period, the simple secret of which is, as we take it, that he, living amongst the public, has with them a general wide-hearted sympathy, that he laughs at what they laugh at, that he has a kindly spirit of enjoyment, with not a morsel of mysticism in his composition; that he pities and loves the poor, and jokes at the follies of the great, and that he addresses all in a perfectly sincere and manly way. To be greatly successful as a professional humorist, as in any other calling, a man must be quite honest, and show that his heart is in his work. A bad preacher will get admiration and a hearing with this point in his favor, where a man of three times his acquirements will only find indifference and coldness. Is any man more remarkable than our artist for telling the truth after his own manner? Hogarth's honesty of purpose was as conspicuous in an earlier time, and we fancy that Gilray would have been far more successful and more powerful but for that unhappy bribe, which turned the whole course of his humor into an unnatural channel. Cruikshank would not for any bribe say what he did not think, or lend his aid to sneer down any thing meritorious, or to praise any thing or person that deserved censure. When he levelled his wit against the Regent, and did his very prettiest for the Princess, he most certainly believed, along with the great body of the people whom he represents, that the Princess was the most spotless, pure-mannered darling of a princess that ever married a heartless debauchee of a Prince Royal. Did not millions believe with him, and noble and learned lords take their oaths to her Royal Highness's innocence? Cruikshank would not stand by and see a women ill-used, and so struck in for her rescue, he and the people belaboring with all their might the party who were making the attack, and determining, from pure sympathy and indignation, that the woman must be innocent because her husband treated her so foully.

To be sure we have never heard so much from Mr. Cruikshank's own lips; but any man who will examine these odd drawings, which first made him famous, will see what an honest, hearty hatred the champion of woman has for all who abuse her, and will admire the energy with which he flings his wood-blocks at all who side against her. Canning, Castlereagh, Bexley, Sidmouth, he is at them, one and all; and as for the Prince, up to what a whipping-post of ridicule did he tie that unfortunate old man! And do not let squeamish Tories cry out about disloyalty; if the crown does wrong, the crown must be corrected by the nation, out of respect, of course, for the crown. In those days, and by those people who so bitterly attacked the son, no word was ever breathed against the father, simply because he was a good husband, and a sober, thrifty, pious, orderly man.

This attack upon the Prince Regent we believe to have been Mr. Cruikshank's only effort as a party politician. Some early manifestoes against Napoleon we find, it is true, done in the regular John Bull style, with the Gilray model for the little upstart Corsican: but as soon as the Emperor had yielded to stern fortune, our artist's heart relented (as Béranger's did on the other side of the water), and many of our readers will doubtless recollect a fine drawing of "Louis XVIII. trying on Napoleon's boots," which did not certainly fit the gouty son of Saint Louis. Such satirical hits as these, however, must not be considered as political, or as any thing more than the expression of the artist's national British idea of Frenchmen.

It must be confessed that for that great nation Mr. Cruikshank entertains a considerable contempt. Let the reader examine the "Life in Paris," or the five hundred designs in which Frenchmen are introduced, and he will find them almost invariably thin, with ludicrous spindle-shanks, pigtails, outstretched hands, shrugging shoulders, and queer hair and mustachios. He has the British idea of a Frenchman; and if he does not believe that the inhabitants of France are for the most part dancing-masters and barbers, yet takes care to depict such in preference, and would not speak too well of them. It is curious how these traditions endure. In France, at the present moment, the Englishman on the stage is the caricatured Englishman at the time of the war, with a shock red head, a long white coat, and invariable gaiters. Those who wish to study this subject should peruse Monsieur Paul de Kock's histories of "Lord Boulingrog" and "Lady Crockmilove." On the other hand, the old *émigré* has taken his station amongst us, and we doubt if a good British gallery would understand that such and such a character *was* a Frenchman unless he appeared in the ancient traditional costume.

A curious book, called "Life in Paris," published in 1822, contains a number of the artist's plates in the aquatint style; and though we believe he had never been in that capital, the designs have a great deal of life in them, and pass muster very well. A villanous race of shoulder-shrugging mortals are his Frenchmen indeed. And the heroes of the tale, a certain Mr. Dick Wildfire, Squire Jenkins, and Captain O'Shuffleton, are made to show the true British superiority on every occasion when Britons and French are brought together. This book was one among the many that the designer's genius has caused to be popular; the plates are not carefully executed, but, being colored, have a pleasant, lively look. The same style was adopted in the once famous book called "Tom and Jerry, or Life in London," which must have a word of notice here, for, although by no means Mr. Cruikshank's best work, his reputation was extraordinarily raised by it. Tom and Jerry were as popular twenty years since as Mr. Pickwick and Sam Weller now are; and often have we wished, while reading the biographies of the latter celebrated personages, that they had been described as well by Mr. Cruikshank's pencil as by Mr. Dickens's pen.

As for Tom and Jerry, to show the mutability of human affairs and the evanescent nature of reputation, we have been to the British Museum, and no less than five circulating libraries, in quest of the book, and "Life in London," alas, is not to be found at any one of them. We can only, therefore, speak of the work from recollection, but have still a very clear remembrance of the leather-gaiters of Jerry Hawthorn, the green spectacles of Logic, and the hooked nose of Corinthian Tom. They were the school-boy's delight; and in the days when the work appeared we firmly believed the three heroes above named to be types of the most elegant, fashionable young fellows the town afforded, and thought their occupations and amusements were those of all high-bred English gentlemen. Tom knocking down the watchman at Temple Bar; Tom and Jerry dancing at Almack's; or flirting in the saloon at the theatre; at the night-houses, after the play; at Tom Cribb's, examining the silver cup then in the possession of that champion; at the chambers of Bob Logic, who, seated at a cabinet piano, plays a waltz to which Corinthian Tom and Kate are dancing; ambling gallantly in Rotten Row; or examining the poor fellow at Newgate who was having his chains knocked off before hanging: all these scenes remain indelibly engraved upon the mind, and so far we are independent of all the circulating libraries in London.

As to the literary contents of the book, they have passed sheer away. It was, most likely, not particularly refined; nay, the chances are that it was absolutely vulgar. But it must have had some merit of its own, that is clear; it must have given striking descriptions of life in some part or other of London, for all London read it, and went to see it in its dramatic shape. The artist, it is said, wished to close the career of the three heroes by bringing them all to ruin, but the writer, or publishers, would not allow any such melancholy subjects to dash the merriment of the public, and we believe Tom, Jerry, and Logic, were married off at the end of the tale, as if they had been the most moral personages in the world. There is some goodness in this pity, which authors and the public are disposed to show towards certain agreeable, disreputable characters of romance. Who would mar the prospects of honest Roderick Random, or Charles Surface, or Tom Jones? only a very stern moralist indeed. And in regard of Jerry Hawthorn and that hero without a surname, Corinthian Tom, Mr. Cruikshank, we make little doubt, was glad in his heart that he was not allowed to have his own way.

Soon after "The Tom and Jerry" and "The Life in Paris," Mr. Cruikshank produced a much more elaborate set of prints, in a work which was called "Points of Humor." These "Points" were selected from various comic works, and did not, we believe, extend beyond a couple of numbers, containing about a score of copperplates. The collector of humorous designs cannot fail to have them in his portfolio, for they contain some of the very best efforts of Mr. Cruikshank's genius, and though not quite so highly labored as some of his later productions, are none the worse, in our opinion, for their comparative want of finish. All the effects are perfectly given, and the expression is as good as it could be in the most delicate engraving upon steel. The artist's style, too, was then completely formed; and, for our parts, we should say that we preferred his manner of 1825 to any other which he has adopted since. The first picture, which is called "The Point of Honor," illustrates the old story of the officer, who, being accused of cowardice for refusing to fight a duel, came among his brother officers, and flung a lighted grenade down upon the floor, before which his comrades fled ignominiously. This design is capital, and the outward rush of heroes, walking, trampling, twisting, scuffling at the door, is in the best style of the grotesque. You see but the back of most of these gentlemen; into which, nevertheless, the artist has managed to throw an expression of ludicrous agony that one could scarcely have expected to find in such a part of the human figure. The next plate is not less good. It represents a couple, who, having been found one night tipsy, and lying in the same gutter, were, by a charitable though misguided gentleman, supposed to be man and wife, and put comfortably to bed together. The morning came; fancy the surprise of this interesting pair when they awoke and discovered their situation. Fancy the manner, too, in which Cruikshank has depicted them, to which words cannot do justice. It is needless to state that this fortuitous and temporary union was followed by one more lasting and sentimental, and that these two worthy persons were married, and lived happily ever after.

We should like to go through every one of these prints. There is the jolly miller, who, returning home at night, calls upon his wife to get him a supper, and falls to upon rashers of bacon and ale. How he gormandizes, that jolly miller! rasher after rasher, how they pass away frizzling and smoking from the gridiron down that immense grinning gulf of a mouth. Poor wife! how she pines and frets, at that untimely hour of midnight to be obliged to fry, fry, fry perpetually, and minister to the monster's appetite. And yonder in the clock: what agonized face is that we see? By heavens, it is the squire of the parish. What business has he there? Let us not ask. Suffice it to say, that he has, in the hurry of the moment, left up stairs his br——; his—psha! a part of his dress, in short, with a number of bank-notes in the pockets. Look in the next page, and you will see the ferocious, bacon-devouring ruffian of a miller is actually causing this garment to be carried through the village and cried by the town-crier. And we blush to be obliged to say that the demoralized miller never offered to return the bank-notes, although he was so mighty scrupulous in endeavoring to find an owner for the corduroy portfolio in which he had found them.

Passing from this painful subject, we come, we regret to state, to a series of prints representing personages not a whit more moral. Burns's famous "Jolly Beggars" have all had their portraits drawn by Cruikshank. There is the lovely "hempen widow," quite as interesting and romantic as the famous Mrs. Sheppard, who has at the lamented demise of her husband adopted the very same consolation.

"My curse upon them every one,
They've hanged my braw John Highlandman;

. . . .

And now a widow I must mourn
Departed joys that ne'er return;
No comfort but a hearty can
When I think on John Highlandman."

Sweet "raucle carlin," she has none of the sentimentality of the English highwayman's lady; but being wooed by a tinker and

"A pygmy scraper wi' his fiddle
Wha us'd to trystes and fairs to driddle,"

prefers the practical to the merely musical man. The tinker sings with a noble candor, worthy of a fellow of his strength of body and station in life—

"My bonnie lass, I work in brass,
A tinker is my station;
I've travell'd round all Christian ground
In this my occupation.
I've ta'en the gold, I've been enroll'd
In many a noble squadron;
But vain they search'd when off I march'd
To go an' clout the caudron."

It was his ruling passion. What was military glory to him, forsooth? He had the greatest contempt for it, and loved freedom and his copper kettle a thousand times better—a kind of hardware Diogenes. Of fiddling he has no better opinion. The picture represents the "sturdy caird" taking "poor gut-scraper" by the beard,—drawing his "roosty rapier," and swearing to "speet him like a pliver" unless he would relinquish the bonnie lassie forever—

"Wi' ghastly ee, poor tweedle-dee
Upon his hunkers bended,
An' pray'd for grace wi' ruefu' face,
An' so the quarrel ended."

Hark how the tinker apostrophizes the violinist, stating to the widow at the same time the advantages which she might expect from an alliance with himself:—

"Despise that shrimp, that wither'd imp,
Wi' a' his noise and caperin';
And take a share with those that bear
The budget and the apron!

"And by that stowp, my faith an' houpe,
An' by that dear Kilbaigie!
If e'er ye want, or meet wi' scant,
May I ne'er weet my craigie."

Cruikshank's caird is a noble creature; his face and figure show him to be fully capable of doing and saying all that is above written of him.

In the second part, the old tale of "The Three Hunchbacked Fiddlers" is illustrated with equal felicity. The famous classical dinners and duel in "Peregrine Pickle" are also excellent in their way; and the connoisseur of prints and etchings may see in the latter plate, and in another in this volume, how great the artist's mechanical skill is as an etcher. The distant view of the city in the duel, and of a market-place in "The Quack Doctor," are delightful specimens of the artist's skill in depicting buildings and backgrounds. They are touched with a grace, truth, and dexterity of workmanship that leave nothing to desire. We have before mentioned the man with the mouth, which appears in this number emblematical of gout and indigestion, in which the artist has shown all the fancy of Callot. Little demons, with long saws for noses, are making dreadful incisions into the toes of the unhappy sufferer; some are bringing pans of hot coals to keep the wounded member warm; a huge, solemn nightmare sits on the invalid's chest, staring solemnly into his eyes; a monster, with a pair of drumsticks, is banging a devil's tattoo on his forehead; and a pair of imps are nailing great tenpenny nails into his hands to make his happiness complete.

The late Mr. Clark's excellent work, "Three Courses and a Dessert," was published at a time when the rage for comic stories was not so great as it since has been, and Messrs. Clark and Cruikshank only sold their hundreds where Messrs. Dickens and Phiz dispose of their thousands. But if our recommendation can in any way influence the reader, we would enjoin him to have a copy of "The Three Courses," that contains some of the best designs of our artist, and some of the most amusing tales in our language. The invention of the pictures, for which Mr. Clark takes credit to himself, says a great deal for his wit and fancy. Can we, for instance, praise too highly the man who invented that wonderful oyster?

Examine him well; his beard, his pearl, his little round stomach, and his sweet smile. Only oysters know how to smile in this way; cool, gentle, waggish, and yet inexpressibly innocent and winning. Dando himself must have allowed such an artless native to go free, and consigned him to the glassy, cool, translucent wave again.

In writing upon such subjects as these with which we have been furnished, it can hardly be expected that we should follow any fixed plan and order — we must therefore take such advantage as we may, and seize upon our subject when and wherever we can lay hold of him.

For Jews, sailors, Irishmen, Hessian boots, little boys, beadles, policemen, tall life-guardsmen, charity children, pumps, dustmen, very short pantaloons, dandies in spectacles, and ladies with aquiline noses, remarkably taper waists, and wonderfully long ringlets, Mr. Cruikshank has a special predilection. The tribe of Israelites he has studied with amazing gusto; witness the Jew in Mr. Ainsworth's "Jack Sheppard," and the immortal Fagin of "Oliver Twist." Whereabouts lies the comic *vis* in these persons and things? Why should a beadle be comic, and his opposite a charity boy? Why should a tall life-guardsman have something in him essentially absurd? Why are short breeches more ridiculous than long? What is there particularly jocose about a pump, and wherefore does a long nose always provoke the beholder to laughter? These points may be metaphysically elucidated by those who list. It is probable that Mr. Cruikshank could not give an accurate definition of that which is ridiculous in these objects, but his instinct has told him that fun lurks in them, and cold must be the heart that can pass by the pantaloons of his charity boys, the Hessian boots of his dandies, and the fan-tail hats of his dustmen, without respectful wonder.

He has made a complete little gallery of dustmen. There is, in the first place, the professional dustman, who, having in the enthusiastic exercise of his delightful trade, laid hands upon property not strictly his own, is pursued, we presume, by the right owner, from whom he flies as fast as his crooked shanks will carry him.

What a curious picture it is — the horrid rickety houses in some dingy suburb of London, the grinning cobbler, the smothered butcher, the very trees which are covered with dust — it is fine to look at the different expressions of the two interesting fugitives. The fiery charioteer who belabors the poor donkey has still a glance for his brother on foot, on whom punishment is about to descend.

And not a little curious is it to think of the creative power of the man who has arranged this little tale of low life. How logically it is conducted! how cleverly each one of the accessories is made to contribute to the effect of the whole! What a deal of thought and humor has the artist expended on this little block of wood! A large picture might have been painted out of the very same materials, which Mr. Cruikshank, out of his wondrous fund of merriment and observation, can afford to throw away upon a drawing not two inches long. From the practical dustmen we pass to those purely poetical. There are three of them who rise on clouds of their own raising, the very genii of the sack and shovel.

Is there no one to write a sonnet to these? and yet a whole poem was written about Peter Bell the Waggoner, a character by no means so poetic.

And lastly, we have the dustman in love: the honest fellow, having seen a young beauty stepping out of a gin-shop on a Sunday morning, is pressing eagerly his suit.

Gin has furnished many subjects to Mr. Cruikshank, who labors in his own sound and hearty way to teach his countrymen the dangers of that drink. In "The Sketch-Book" is a plate upon the subject, remarkable for fancy and beauty of design; it is called the "Gin Juggernaut," and represents a hideous moving palace, with a reeking still at the roof, and vast gin barrels for wheels, under which unhappy millions are crushed to death. An immense black cloud of desolation covers over the country through which the gin monster has passed, dimly looming through the darkness whereof you see an agreeable prospect of gibbets with men dangling, burnt houses, &c. The vast cloud comes sweeping on in the wake of this horrible body-crusher; and you see, by way of contrast, a distant, smiling, sunshiny tract of old English country, where gin as yet is not known. The allegory is as good, as earnest, and as fanciful, as one of John Bunyan's, and we have often fancied there was a similarity between the men.

The reader will examine the work called "My Sketch-Book" with not a little amusement, and may gather from it, as we fancy, a good deal of information regarding the character of the individual man, George Cruikshank: what points strike his eye as a painter; what move his anger or admiration as a moralist; what classes he seems most especially disposed to observe, and what to ridicule. There are quacks of all kinds, to whom he has a mortal hatred; quack dandies, who assume under his pencil, perhaps in his eye, the most grotesque appearance possible — their hats grow larger, their legs infinitely more crooked and lean; the tassels of their canes swell out to a most preposterous size; the tails of their coats dwindle away, and finish where coat-tails generally begin. Let us lay a wager that Cruikshank, a man of the people, if ever there was one, heartily hates and despises these supercilious, swaggering young gentlemen; and his contempt is not a whit the less laudable because there may be *tant soit peu* of prejudice in it. It is right and wholesome to scorn dandies, as Nelson said it was to hate Frenchmen; in which sentiment (as we have before said) George Cruikshank undoubtedly shares. In "The Sunday in London,"* Monsieur the Chef is instruct-

* The following lines — ever fresh — by the author of "Headlong Hall," published years ago in "The Globe and Traveller," are an excellent comment on several of the cuts from "The Sunday in London:"—

I.

"The poor man's sins are glaring;
In the face of ghostly warning
He is caught in the fact
Of an overt act,
Buying greens on Sunday morning.

II.

"The rich man's sins are hidden
In the pomp of wealth and station,

ing a kitchen-maid how to compound some rascally French kickshaw or the other — a pretty scoundrel truly! with what an air he wears that nightcap of his, and shrugs his lank shoulders, and chatters, and ogles, and grins! they are all the same, these mounseers; there are two other fellows — *morbleu!* one is putting his dirty fingers into the saucepan; there are frogs cooking in it, no doubt; and just over some other dish of abomination, another dirty rascal is taking snuff! Never mind, the sauce won't be hurt by a few ingredients more or less. Three such fellows as these are not worth one Englishman, that's clear. There is one in the very midst of them, the great burly fellow with the beef: he could beat all three in five minutes. We cannot be certain that such was the process going on in Mr. Cruikshank's mind when he made the design; but some feelings of the sort were no doubt entertained by him.

Against dandy footmen he is particularly severe. He hates idlers, pretenders, boasters, and punishes these fellows as best he may. Who does not recollect the famous picture, "What *is* Taxes, Thomas?" What is taxes indeed; well may that vast, over-fed, lounging flunky ask the question of his associate Thomas: and yet not well, for all that Thomas says in reply is, "*I don't know.*" "O beati *plushicolæ*," what a charming state of ignorance is yours! In "The Sketch-Book" many footmen make their appearance: one is a huge fat Hercules of a Portman Square porter, who calmly surveys another poor fellow, a porter likewise, but out of livery, who comes staggering forward with a box that Hercules might lift with his little finger. Will Hercules do so? not he. The giant can carry nothing heavier than a cocked-hat note on a silver tray, and his labors are to walk from his sentry-box to the door, and from the door back to his sentry-box, and to read the Sunday paper, and to poke the hall fire twice or thrice, and to make five meals a day. Such a fellow does Cruikshank hate and scorn worse even than a Frenchman.

The man's master, too, comes in for no small share of our artist's wrath. There is a company of them at church, who humbly designate themselves "miserable sinners!" Miserable sinners indeed! Oh, what floods of turtle-soup, what tons of turbot and lobster-sauce must have been sacrificed to make those sinners properly miserable. My lady with the ermine tippet and draggling feather, can we not see that she lives in Portland Place, and is the wife of an East India Director? She has been to the Opera over-night (indeed her husband, on her right, with his fat hand dangling over the pew-door, is at this minute thinking of Mademoiselle Léocadie, whom he saw behind the scenes) — she has been at the Opera overnight, which with a trifle of supper afterwards — a white and brown soup,

---

And escape the sight
Of the children of light,
Who are wise in their generation.

III.

"The rich man has a kitchen,
And cooks to dress his dinner;
The poor who would roast,
To the baker's must post,
And thus becomes a sinner.

IV.

"The rich man's painted windows
Hide the concerts of the quality;
The poor can but share
A cracked fiddle in the air,
Which offends all sound morality.

V.

"The rich man has a cellar,
And a ready butler by him;
The poor must steer
For his pint of beer [him.
Where the saint can't choose but spy

VI.

"The rich man is invisible
In the crowd of his gay society;
But the poor man's delight
Is a sore in the sight
And a stench in the nose of piety."

a lobster-salad, some woodcocks, and a little champagne — sent her to bed quite comfortable. At half-past eight her maid brings her chocolate in bed, at ten she has fresh eggs and muffins, with, perhaps, a half-hundred of prawns for breakfast, and so can get over the day and the sermon till lunch-time pretty well. What an odor of musk and bergamot exhales from the pew! — how it is wadded and stuffed, and spangled over with brass nails! what hassocks are there for those who are not too fat to kneel! what a flustering and flapping of gilt prayer-books; and what a pious whirring of Bible leaves one hears all over the church, as the doctor blandly gives out the text! To be miserable at this rate you must, at the very least, have four thousand a year: and many persons are there so enamored of grief and sin, that they would willingly take the risk of the misery to have a life-interest in the consols that accompany it, quite careless about consequences, and sceptical as to the notion that a day is at hand when you must fulfil *your share of the bargain*.

Our artist loves to joke at a soldier; in whose livery there appears to him to be something almost as ridiculous as in the uniform of the gentleman of the shoulder-knot. Tall life-guardsmen and fierce grenadiers figure in many of his designs, and almost always in a ridiculous way. Here again we have the honest popular English feeling which jeers at pomp or pretension of all kinds, and is especially jealous of all display of military authority. "Raw Recruit," "ditto dressed," ditto "served up," as we see them in "The Sketch-Book," are so many satires upon the army: Hodge with his ribbons flaunting in his hat, or with red coat and musket, drilled stiff and pompous, or at last, minus leg and arm, tottering about on crutches, does not fill our English artist with the enthusiasm that follows the soldier in every other part of Europe. Jeanjean, the conscript in France, is laughed at to be sure, but then it is because he is a bad soldier: when he comes to have a huge pair of mustachios and the *croix-d'honneur* to *briller* on his *poitrine cicatrisée*, Jeanjean becomes a member of a class that is more respected than any other in the French nation. The veteran soldier inspires our people with no such awe — we hold that democratic weapon the fist in much more honor than the sabre and bayonet, and laugh at a man tricked out in scarlet and pipe-clay.

That regiment of heroes is "marching to divine service," to the tune of "The British Grenadiers." There they march in state, and a pretty contempt our artist shows for all their gimcracks and trumpery. He has drawn a perfectly English scene — the little blackguard boys are playing pranks round about the men, and shouting, "Heads up, soldier," "Eyes right, lobster," as little British urchins will do. Did one ever hear the like sentiments expressed in France? Shade of Napoleon, we insult you by asking the question. In England, however, see how different the case is; and designedly or undesignedly, the artist has opened to us a piece of his mind. In the crowd the only person who admires the soldiers is the poor idiot, whose pocket a rogue is picking. There is another picture, in which the sentiment is much the same, only, as in the former drawing we see Englishmen laughing at the troops of the line, here are Irishmen giggling at the militia.

We have said that our artist has a great love for the drolleries of the Green Island. Would any one doubt what was the country of the merry fellows depicted in his group of Paddies?

"Place me amid O'Rourkes, O'Tooles,
 The ragged royal race of Tara;
Or place me where Dick Martin rules
 The pathless wilds of Connemara."

We know not if Mr. Cruikshank has ever had any such good luck as to see the Irish in Ireland itself, but he certainly has obtained a knowledge of their looks, as if the country had been all his life familiar to him. Could Mr. O'Connell himself desire any thing more national than the scene of a drunken row, or could Father Mathew have a better text to preach upon? There is not a broken nose in the room that is not thoroughly Irish.

We have then a couple of compositions treated in a graver manner, as characteristic, too, as the other. We call attention to the comical look of poor Teague, who has been pursued and beaten by the witch's stick, in order to point out also the singular neatness of the workmanship, and the pretty, fanciful little glimpse of landscape that the artist has introduced in the background. Mr. Cruikshank has a fine eye for such homely landscapes, and renders them with great delicacy and taste. Old villages, farm-yards, groups of stacks, queer chimneys, churches, gable-ended cottages, Elizabethan mansion-houses, and other old English scenes, he depicts with evident enthusiasm.

Famous books in their day were Cruikshank's "John Gilpin" and "Epping Hunt;" for though our artist does not draw horses very scientifically, — to use a phrase of the atelier, — he *feels* them very keenly; and his queer animals, after one is used to them, answer quite as well as better. Neither is he very happy in trees, and such rustical produce; or rather, we should say, he is very original, his trees being decidedly of his own make and composition, not imitated from any master.

But what then? Can a man be supposed to imitate every thing? We know what the noblest study of mankind is, and to this Mr. Cruikshank has confined himself. That postilion with the people in the broken-down chaise roaring after him is as deaf as the post by which he passes. Suppose all the accessories were away, could not one swear that the man was stone-deaf, beyond the reach of trumpet? What is the peculiar character in a deaf man's physiognomy? — can any person define it satisfactorily in words? — not in pages; and Mr. Cruikshank has expressed it on a piece of paper not so big as the tenth part of your thumb-nail. The horses of John Gilpin are much more of the equestrian order; and as here the artist has only his favorite suburban buildings to draw, not a word is to be said against his design. The inn and old buildings are charmingly designed, and nothing can be more prettily or playfully touched.

"At Edmonton his loving wife
From the balcony spied
Her tender husband, wond'ring much
To see how he did ride.

"'Stop, stop, John Gilpin! Here's the house!'
They all at once did cry;
'The dinner waits, and we are tired' —
Said Gilpin — 'So am I!'

"Six gentlemen upon the road
Thus seeing Gilpin fly,
With post-boy scamp'ring in the rear,
They raised the hue and cry: —

"'Stop thief! stop thief! — a highwayman!'
Not one of them was mute;
And all and each that passed that way
Did join in the pursuit.

"And now the turnpike gates again
Flew open in short space;
The toll-men thinking, as before,
That Gilpin rode a race."

The rush and shouting and clatter are excellently depicted by the artist; and we, who have been scoffing at his manner of designing animals, must here make a special exception in favor of the hens and chickens; each has a different action, and is curiously natural.

Happy are children of all ages who have such a ballad and such pictures as this in store for them! It is a comfort to think that woodcuts never wear out, and that the book still may be had for a shilling, for those who can command that sum of money.

In "The Epping Hunt," which we owe to the facetious pen of Mr. Hood, our artist has not been so successful.

There is here too much horsemanship and not enough incident for him; but the portrait of Roundings the huntsman is an excellent sketch, and a couple of the designs contain great humor. The first represents the Cockney hero, who, "like a bird, was singing out while sitting on a tree."

And in the second the natural order is reversed. The stag, having taken heart, is hunting the huntsman, and the Cheapside Nimrod is most ignominiously running away.

The Easter Hunt, we are told, is no more; and as "The Quarterly Review" recommends the British public to purchase Mr. Catlin's pictures, as they form the only record of an interesting race now rapidly passing away, in like manner we should exhort all our friends to purchase Mr. Cruikshank's designs of *another* interesting race, that is run already and for the last time.

Besides these, we must mention, in the line of our duty, the notable tragedies of "Tom Thumb" and "Bombastes Furioso," both of which have appeared with many illustrations by Mr. Cruikshank. The "brave army" of Bombastes exhibits a terrific display of brutal force, which must shock the sensibilities of an English radical. And we can well understand the caution of the general who bids this *soldatesque effrénée* to begone, and not to kick up a row.

Such a troop of lawless ruffians let loose upon a populous city would play sad havoc in it; and we fancy the massacres of Birmingham renewed, or at least of Badajoz, which, though not quite so dreadful, if we may believe his Grace the Duke of Wellington, as the former scenes of slaughter, were nevertheless severe enough; but we must not venture upon any ill-timed pleasantries in presence of the disturbed King Arthur and the awful ghost of Gaffer Thumb.

We are thus carried at once into the supernatural, and here we find Cruikshank reigning supreme. He has invented in his time a little comic pandemonium, peopled with the most droll, good-natured fiends possible. We have before us Chamisso's "Peter Schlemihl," with Cruikshank's designs translated into German, and gaining nothing by the change. The "Kinder und Hans-Maerchen" of Grimm are likewise ornamented with a frontispiece, copied from that one which appeared to the amusing version of the English work. The books on Phrenology and Time have been imitated by the same nation; and even in France, whither reputation travels slower than to any country except China, we have seen copies of the works of George Cruikshank.

He in return has complimented the French by illustrating a couple of Lives of Napoleon, and the "Life in Paris" before mentioned. He has also made designs for Victor Hugo's "Hans of Iceland." Strange, wild etchings were those, on a strange, mad subject; not so good in our notion as the designs for the German books, the peculiar humor of which latter seemed to suit the artist exactly. There is a mixture of the awful and the ridiculous in these, which perpetually excites and keeps awake the reader's attention; the German writer and the English artist seem to have an entire faith in their subject. The reader, no doubt, remembers the awful passage in "Peter Schlemihl," where the little gentleman purchases the shadow of that hero — "Have the kindness, noble sir, to examine and try this bag." "He put his hand into his pocket, and drew thence a tolerably large bag of Cordovan leather, to which a couple of thongs were fixed. I took it from him, and immediately counted out ten gold pieces, and ten more, and ten more, and still other ten, whereupon I held out my hand to him. Done, said I, it is a bargain; you shall have my shadow for your bag. The bargain was concluded; he knelt down before me, and I saw him with a wonderful neatness take my shadow from head to foot, lightly lift it up from the grass, roll and fold it up neatly, and at last pocket it. He then rose up, bowed to me once more, and walked away again, disappearing behind the rose-bushes. I don't know, but I thought I heard him laughing a little. I, however, kept fast hold of the bag. Every thing around me was bright in the sun, and as yet I gave no thought to what I had done."

This marvellous event, narrated by Peter with such a faithful, circumstantial detail, is painted by Cruikshank in the most wonderful poetic way, with that happy mixture of the real and supernatural that makes the narrative so curious, and like truth. The sun is shining with the utmost brilliancy in a great quiet park or garden; there is a palace in the background, and a statue basking in the sun quite lonely and melancholy; there is a sun-dial, on which is a deep shadow, and in the front stands Peter Schlemihl, bag in hand: the old gentleman is down on his knees to him, and has just lifted off the ground the *shadow of one leg;* he is going to fold it back neatly, as one does the tails of a coat, and will stow it, without any creases or crumples, along with the other black garments that lie in that immense pocket of his. Cruikshank has designed all this as if he had a very serious belief in the story; he laughs, to be sure, but one fancies that he is a little frightened in his heart, in spite of all his fun and joking.

The German tales we have mentioned before. "The Prince riding on the Fox," "Hans in Luck," "The Fiddler and his Goose," "Heads off," are all drawings, which, albeit not before us now, nor seen for ten years, remain indelibly fixed on the memory. "*Heisst du etwa Rumpelstilzchen?*" There sits the Queen on her throne, surrounded by grinning beef-eaters, and little Rumpelstiltskin stamps his foot through the floor in the excess of his tremendous despair. In one of these German tales, if we remember rightly, there is an account of a little orphan who is carried away by a pitying fairy for a term of seven years, and passing that period of sweet apprenticeship among the imps and sprites of fairy-land. Has our artist been among the same company, and brought back their portraits in his sketch-book? He is the only designer fairy-land has had. Callot's imps, for all their strangeness, are only of the earth earthy. Fuseli's fairies belong to the infernal regions; they are monstrous, lurid, and hideously melancholy. Mr. Cruikshank alone has had a true insight into the character of the "little people." They are something like men and women, and yet not flesh and blood; they are laughing and mischievous, but why we know not. Mr. Cruikshank, however, has had some dream or the other, or else a natural mysterious instinct (as the Seherinn of Prevorst had for beholding ghosts), or else some preternatural fairy revelation, which has made him acquainted with the looks and ways of the fantastical subjects of Oberon and Titania.

We have, unfortunately, no fairy portraits; but, on the other hand, can descend lower than fairy-land, and have seen some fine specimens of devils. One has already been raised, and the reader has seen him tempting a fat Dutch burgomaster, in an ancient gloomy market-place, such as George Cruikshank can draw as well as Mr. Prout, Mr. Nash, or any man living. There is our friend once more; our friend the burgomaster, in a highly excited state, and running as hard as his great legs will carry him, with our mutual enemy at his tail.

What are the bets; will that long-legged bond-holder of a devil come up with the honest Dutchman? It serves him right: why did he put his name to stamped paper? And yet we should not wonder if some lucky chance should turn up in the burgomaster's favor, and his infernal creditor lose his labor; for one so proverbially cunning as yonder tall individual with the saucer eyes, it must be confessed that he has been very often outwitted.

There is, for instance, the case of "The Gentleman in Black," which has been illustrated by our artist. A young French gentleman, by name M. Desonge, who, having expended his patrimony in a variety of taverns and gaming-houses, was one day pondering upon the exhausted state of his finances, and utterly at a loss to think how he should provide means for future support, exclaimed very naturally, "What the devil shall I do?" He had no sooner spoken than a GENTLEMAN IN BLACK made his appearance, whose authentic portrait Mr. Cruikshank has had the honor to paint. This gentleman produced a black-edged book out of a black bag, some black-edged papers tied up with black crape, and sitting down familiarly opposite M. Desonge, began conversing with him on the state of his affairs.

It is needless to state what was the result of the interview. M. Desonge was induced by the gentleman to sign his name to one of the black-edged papers, and found himself at the close of the conversation to be possessed of an unlimited command of capital. This arrangement completed, the Gentleman in Black posted (in an extraordinarily rapid manner) from Paris to London, there found a young English merchant in exactly the same situation in which M. Desonge had been, and concluded a bargain with the Briton of exactly the same nature.

The book goes on to relate how these young men spent the money so miraculously handed over to them, and how both, when the period drew near that was to witness the performance of *their* part of the bargain, grew melancholy, wretched, nay, so absolutely dishonorable as to seek for every means of breaking through their agreement. The Englishman living in a country where the lawyers are more astute than any other lawyers in the world, took the advice of a Mr. Bagsby, of Lyon's Inn; whose name, as we cannot find it in the "Law List," we presume to be fictitious. Who could it be that was a match for the devil? Lord —— very likely; we shall not give his name, but let every reader of this Review fill up the blank according to his own fancy, and on comparing it with the copy purchased by his neighbors, he will find that fifteen out of twenty have written down the same honored name.

Well, the Gentleman in Black was anxious for the fulfilment of his bond. The parties met at Mr. Bagsby's chambers to consult, the Black Gentleman foolishly thinking that he could act as his own counsel, and fearing no attorney alive. But mark the superiority of British law, and see how the black pettifogger was defeated.

Mr. Bagsby simply stated that he would take the case into Chancery, and his antagonist, utterly humiliated and defeated, refused to move a step farther in that matter.

And now the French gentleman, M. Desonge, hearing of his friend's escape, became anxious to be free from his own rash engagements. He employed the same counsel who had been successful in the former instance, but the Gentleman in Black was a great deal wiser by this time, and whether M. Desonge escaped, or whether he is now in that extensive place which is paved with good intentions, we shall not say. Those who are anxious to know had better purchase the book wherein all these interesting matters are duly set down. There is one more diabolical picture in our budget, engraved by Mr. Thompson, the same dexterous artist who has rendered the former *diableries* so well.

We may mention Mr. Thompson's name as among the first of the engravers to whom Cruikshank's designs have been intrusted; and next to him (if we may be allowed to make such arbitrary distinctions) we may place Mr. Williams; and the reader is not possibly aware of the immense difficulties to be overcome in the rendering of these little sketches, which, traced by the designer in a few hours, require weeks' labor from the engraver. Mr. Cruikshank has not been educated in the regular schools of drawing (very luckily for him, as we think), and consequently has had to make a manner for himself, which is quite unlike that of any other draftsman. There is nothing in the least mechanical about it; to produce his particular effects he uses his own particular lines, which are queer, free, fantastical, and must be followed in all their infinite twists and vagaries by the careful tool of the engraver. Those three lovely heads, for instance, imagined out of the rinds of lemons, are worth examining, not so much for the jovial humor and wonderful variety of feature exhibited in these darling countenances as for the engraver's part of the work. See the infinite delicate cross-lines and hatchings which he is obliged to render; let him go, not a hair's breadth, but the hundredth part of a hair's breadth, beyond the given line, and the *feeling* of it is ruined. He receives these little dots and specks, and fantastical quirks of the pencil, and cuts away with a little knife round each, not too much nor too little. Antonio's pound of flesh did not puzzle the Jew so much; and so well does the engraver succeed at last, that we never remember to have met with a single artist who did not vow that the wood-cutter had utterly ruined his design.

Of Messrs. Thompson and Williams we have spoken as the first engravers in point of rank; however, the regulations of professional precedence are certainly very difficult, and the rest of their brethren we shall not endeavor to class. Why should the artists who executed the cuts of the admirable "Three Courses" yield the *pas* to any one?

There, for instance, is an engraving by Mr. Landells, nearly as good in our opinion as the very best woodcut that ever was made after Cruikshank, and curiously happy in rendering the artist's peculiar manner: this cut does not come from the facetious publications which we have consulted; but is a contribution by Mr. Cruikshank to an elaborate and splendid botanical work upon the Orchidaceæ of Mexico, by Mr. Bateman. Mr. Bateman despatched some extremely choice roots of this valuable plant to a friend in England, who, on the arrival of the case, consigned it to his gardener to unpack. A great deal of anxiety with regard to the contents was manifested by all concerned, but, on the lid of the box being removed, there issued from it three or four fine specimens of the enormous Blatta beetle that had been preying upon the plants during the voyage; against these the gardeners, the grooms, the porters, and the porters' children issued forth in arms, and this scene the artist has immortalized.

We have spoken of the admirable way in which Mr. Cruikshank has depicted Irish character and Cockney character; English country character is quite as faithfully delineated in the person of the stout porteress and her children, and of the "Chawbacon" with the shovel, on whose face is written "Zummerzetsheer." Chawbacon appears in another plate, or else Chawbacon's brother. He has come up to Lunnan, and is looking about him at raaces.

How distinct are these rustics from those whom we have just been examining! They hang about the purlieus of the metropolis: Brook Green, Epsom, Greenwich, Ascot, Goodwood, are their haunts. They visit London professionally once a year, and that is at the time of Bartholomew fair. How one may speculate upon the different degrees of rascality, as exhibited in each face of the thimblerigging trio, and form little histories for these worthies, charming Newgate romances, such as have been of late the fashion! Is any man so blind that he cannot see the exact face that is writhing under the thimblerigged hero's hat? Like Timanthes of old our artist expresses great passions without the aid of the human countenance. There is another specimen — a street row of inebriated bottles. Is there any need of having a face after this? "Come on!" says Claret-bottle, a dashing, genteel fellow, with his hat on one ear — "Come on! has any man a mind to tap me?" Claret-bottle, is a little screwed (as one may see by his legs), but full of gayety and courage; not so that stout, apoplectic Bottle-of-rum, who has staggered against the wall, and has his hand upon his liver: the fellow hurts himself with smoking, that is clear, and is as sick as sick can be. See, Port is making away from the storm, and Double X is as flat as ditch-water. Against these, awful in their white robes, the sober watchmen come.

Our artist, then, can cover up faces, and yet show them quite clearly, as in the thimblerig group; or he can do without faces altogether; or he can, at a pinch, provide a countenance for a gentleman out of any given object — a beautiful Irish physiognomy being moulded upon a keg of whiskey; and a jolly English countenance frothing out of a pot of ale (the spirit of brave Toby Philpot come back to re-animate his clay); while in a fungus may be recognized the physiognomy of a mushroom peer. Finally, if he is at a loss, he can make a living head, body, and legs out of steel or tortoise-shell, as in the case of the vivacious pair of spectacles that are jockeying the nose of Caddy Cuddle.

Of late years, Mr. Cruikshank has busied himself very much with steel engraving, and the consequences of that lucky invention have been, that his plates are now sold by thousands, where they could only be produced by hundreds before. He has made many a bookseller's and author's fortune (we trust that in so doing he may not have neglected his own). Twelve admirable plates, furnished yearly to that facetious little publication, "The Comic Almanac," have gained for it a sale, as we hear, of nearly twenty thousand copies. The idea of the work was novel: there was, in the first number especially, a great deal of comic power, and Cruikshank's designs were so admirable that "The Almanac" at once became a vast favorite with the public, and has so remained ever since.

Besides the twelve plates, this almanac contains a prophetic woodcut, accompanying an awful Blarneyhum Astrologicum that appears in this and other almanacs. There is one that hints in pretty clear terms that with the Reform of Municipal Corporations the ruin of the great Lord Mayor of London is at hand. His Lordship is meekly going to dine at an eightpenny ordinary, — his giants in pawn, his men in armor dwindled to "one poor knight," his carriage to be sold, his stalwart aldermen vanished, his sheriffs, alas! and alas! in jail! Another design shows that Rigdum, if a true, is also a moral and instructive prophet. John Bull is asleep, or rather in a vision; the cunning demon, Speculation, blowing a thousand bright bubbles about him. Meanwhile the rooks are busy at his fob, a knave has cut a cruel hole in his pocket, a rattlesnake has coiled safe round his feet, and will in a trice swallow Bull, chair, money and all; the rats are at his corn-bags (as if, poor devil, he had corn to spare); his faithful dog is bolting his leg of mutton — nay, a thief has gotten hold of his very candle, and there, by way of moral, is his ale-pot, which looks and winks in his face, and seems to say, O Bull, all this is froth, and a cruel satirical picture of a certain rustic who had a goose that laid certain golden eggs, which goose the rustic slew in expectation of finding all the eggs at once. This is goose and sage too, to borrow the pun of "learned Dr. Gill;" but we shrewdly suspect that Mr. Cruikshank is becoming a little conservative in his notions.

We love these pictures so that it is hard to part us, and we still fondly endeavor to hold on, but this wild word, farewell, must be spoken by the best friends at last, and so good-by, brave woodcuts: we feel quite a sadness in coming to the last of our collection.

In the earlier numbers of "The Comic Almanac" all the manners and customs of Londoners that would afford food for fun were noted down; and if during the last two years the mysterious personage who, under the title of "Rigdum Funnidos," compiles this ephemeris, has been compelled to resort to romantic tales, we must suppose that he did so because the great metropolis was exhausted; and it was necessary to discover new worlds in the cloud-land of fancy. The character of Mr. Stubbs, who made his appearance in "The Almanac" for 1839, had, we think, great merit, although his adventures were somewhat of too tragical a description to provoke pure laughter.

We should be glad to devote a few pages to "The Illustrations of Time," "The Scraps and Sketches" and "The Illustrations of Phrenology," which are among the most famous of our artist's publications; but it is very difficult to find new terms of praise, as find them one must, when reviewing Mr. Cruikshank's publications, and more difficult still (as the reader of this notice will no doubt have perceived for himself long since) to translate his design into words, and go to the printer's box for a description of all that fun and humor which the artist can produce by a few skilful turns of his needle. A famous article upon "The Illustrations of Time" appeared some dozen years since in "Blackwood's Magazine," of which the conductors have always been great admirers of our artist, as became men of honor and genius. To these grand qualities do not let it be supposed that we are laying claim, but, thank heaven, Cruikshank's humor is so good and benevolent, that any man must love it, and on this score we may speak as well as another.

Then there are "The Greenwich Hospital" designs, which must not be passed over. "Greenwich Hospital" is a hearty, good-natured book, in the Tom Dibdin school, treating of the virtue of British tars, in approved nautical language. They maul Frenchmen and Spaniards, they go out in brigs and take frigates, they relieve women in distress, and are yard-arm and yard-arming, athwart-hawsing, marlinspiking, binnacling, and helm's-a-leeing, as honest seamen invariably do, in novels, on the stage, and doubtless on board ship. This we cannot take upon us to say, but the artist, like a true Englishman, as he is, loves dearly these brave guardians of Old England, and chronicles their rare or fanciful exploits with the greatest good-will. Let any one look at the noble head of Nelson in "The Family Library," and they will, we are sure, think with us that the designer must have felt and loved what he drew. There are to this abridgment of Southey's admirable book many more cuts after Cruikshank; and about a dozen pieces by the same hand will be found in a work equally popular, Lockhart's excellent "Life of Napoleon." Among these the retreat from Moscow is very fine; the Mamlouks most vigorous, furious, and barbarous, as they should be. At the end of these three volumes Mr. Cruikshank's contributions to "The Family Library" seem suddenly to have ceased.

We are not at all disposed to undervalue the works and genius of Mr. Dickens, and we are sure that he would admit as readily as any man the wonderful assistance that he has derived from the artist who has given us the portraits of his ideal personages, and made them familiar to all the world. Once seen, these figures remain impressed on the memory, which otherwise would have had no hold upon them, and the heroes and heroines of Boz become personal acquaintances with each of us. Oh that Hogarth could have illustrated Fielding in the same way! and fixed down on paper those grand figures of Parson Adams, and Squire Allworthy, and the great Jonathan Wild.

With regard to the modern romance of "Jack Sheppard," in which the latter personage makes a second appearance, it seems to us that Mr. Cruikshank really created the tale, and that Mr. Ainsworth, as it were, only put words to it. Let any reader of the novel think over it for a while, now that it is some months since he has perused and laid it down — let him think, and tell us what he remembers of the tale. George Cruikshank's pictures — always George Cruikshank's pictures. The storm in the Thames, for instance: all the author's labored description of that event has passed clean away — we have only before the mind's eye the fine plates of Cruikshank: the poor wretch cowering under the bridge arch, as the waves come rushing in, and the boats are whirling away in the drift of the great swollen black waters. And let any man look at that second plate of the murder on the Thames, and he must acknowledge how much more brilliant the artist's description is than the writer's, and what a real genius for the terrible as well as for the ridiculous the former has; how awful is the gloom of the old bridge, a few lights glimmering from the houses here and there, but not so as to be reflected on the water at all, which is too turbid and raging: a great heavy rack of clouds goes sweeping over the bridge, and men with flaring torches, the murderers, are borne away with the stream.

The author requires many pages to describe the fury of the storm, which Mr. Cruikshank has represented in one. First, he has to prepare you with the something inexpressibly melancholy in sailing on a dark night upon the Thames: "the ripple of the water," "the darkling current," "the indistinctively seen craft," "the solemn shadows" and other phenomena visible on rivers at night are detailed (with not unskilful rhetoric) in order to bring the reader into a proper frame of mind for the deeper gloom and horror which is to ensue. Then follow pages of description. "As Rowland sprang to the helm, and gave the signal for pursuit, a war like a volley of ordnance was heard aloft, and the wind again burst its bondage. A moment before, the surface of the stream was as black as ink. It was now whitening, hissing, and seething, like an enormous caldron. The blast once more swept over the agitated river, whirled off the sheets of foam, scattered them far and wide in rain-drops, and left the raging torrent blacker than before. Destruction everywhere marked the course of the gale. Steeples toppled and towers reeled beneath its fury. All was darkness, horror, confusion, ruin. Men fled from their tottering habitations and returned to them, scared by greater danger. The end of the world seemed at hand. . . . The hurricane had now reached its climax. The blast shrieked, as if exulting in its wrathful mission. Stunning and continuous, the din seemed almost to take away the power of hearing. He who had faced the gale *would have been instantly stifled,*" &c., &c. See with what a tremendous war of words (and good loud words too; Mr. Ainsworth's description is a good and spirited one) the author is obliged to pour in upon the reader before he can effect his purpose upon the latter, and inspire him with a proper terror. The painter does it at a glance, and old Wood's dilemma in the midst of that tremendous storm, with the little infant at his bosom, is remembered afterwards, not from the words, but from the visible image of them that the artist has left us.

It would not, perhaps, be out of place to glance through the whole of "The Jack Sheppard" plates, which are among the most finished and the most successful of Mr. Cruikshank's performances, and say a word or two concerning them. Let us begin with finding fault with No. 1, "Mr. Wood offers to adopt little Jack Sheppard." A poor print, on a poor subject; the figure of the woman not as carefully designed as it might be, and the expression of the eyes (not an uncommon fault with our artist) much caricatured. The print is cut up, to use the artist's phrase, by the number of accessories which the engraver has thought proper, after the author's elaborate description, elaborately to reproduce. The plate of "Wild discovering Darrell in the loft" is admirable—ghastly, terrible, and the treatment of it extraordinarily skilful, minute, and bold. The intricacies of the tile-work, and the mysterious twinkling of light among the beams, are excellently felt and rendered; and one sees here, as in the two next plates of the storm and murder, what a fine eye the artist has, what a skilful hand, and what a sympathy for the wild and dreadful. As a mere imitation of nature, the clouds and the bridge in the murder picture may be examined by painters who make far higher pretensions than Mr. Cruikshank. In point of workmanship, they are equally good, the manner quite unaffected, the effect produced without any violent contrast, the whole scene evidently well and philosophically arranged in the artist's brain, before he began to put it upon copper.

The famous drawing of "Jack carving the name on the beam," which has been transferred to half the play-bills in town, is over-loaded with accessories, as the first plate; but they are much better arranged than in the last-named engraving, and do not injure the effect of the principal figure. Remark, too, the conscientiousness of the artist, and that shrewd pervading idea of *form* which is one of his principal characteristics. Jack is surrounded by all sorts of implements of his profession; he stands on a regular carpenter's table: away in the shadow under it lie shavings and a couple of carpenter's hampers. The glue-pot, the mallet, the chisel-handle, the planes, the saws, the hone with its cover, and the other paraphernalia are all represented with extraordinary accuracy and forethought. The man's mind has retained the exact *drawing* of all these minute objects (unconsciously perhaps to himself), but we can see with what keen eyes he must go through the world, and what a fund of facts (as such a knowledge of the shape of objects is in his profession) this keen student of nature has stored away in his brain. In the next plate, where Jack is escaping from his mistress, the figure of that lady, one of the deepest of the *βαθύκολποι*, strikes us as disagreeable and unrefined; that of Winifred is, on the contrary, very pretty and graceful; and Jack's puzzled, slinking look must not be forgotten. All the accessories are good, and the apartment has a snug, cosey air; which is not remarkable, except that it shows how faithfully the designer has performed his work, and how curiously he has entered into all the particulars of the subject.

Master Thames Darrell, the handsome young man of the book, is, in Mr. Cruikshank's portraits of him, no favorite of ours. The lad seems to wish to make up for the natural insignificance of his face by frowning on all occasions most portentously. This figure, borrowed from the compositor's desk, will give a notion of what we mean. Wild's face is too violent for the great man of history (if we may call Fielding history), but this is in consonance with the ranting, frowning, braggadocio character that Mr. Ainsworth has given him.

"The Interior of Willesden Church" is excellent as a composition, and a piece of artistical workmanship; the groups are well arranged; and the figure of Mrs. Sheppard looking round alarmed, as her son is robbing the dandy Kneebone, is charming, simple, and unaffected. Not so "Mrs. Sheppard ill in bed," whose face is screwed up to an expression vastly too tragic. The little glimpse of the church seen through the open door of the room is very beautiful and poetical: it is in such small hints that an artist especially excels; they are the morals which he loves to append to his stories, and are always appropriate and welcome. The boozing ken is not to our liking; Mrs. Sheppard is there with her horrified eyebrows again. Why this exaggeration — is it necessary for the public? We think not, or if they require such excitement, let our artist, like a true painter as he is, teach them better things.*

"The Escape from Willesden Cage" is excellent; "The Burglary in Wood's house" has not less merit; "Mrs. Sheppard in Bedlam," a ghastly picture indeed, is finely conceived, but not, as we fancy, so carefully executed; it would be better for a little more careful drawing in the female figure.

"Jack sitting for his picture" is a very pleasing group, and savors of the manner of Hogarth, who is introduced in the company. "The Murder of Trenchard" must be noticed too as remarkable for the effect and terrible vigor which the artist has given to the scene. "The Willesden Churchyard" has great merit too, but the gems of the book are the little vignettes illustrating the escape from Newgate. Here, too, much anatomical care of drawing is not required; the figures are so small that the outline and attitude need only to be indicated, and the designer has produced a series of figures quite remarkable for reality and poetry too. There are no less than ten of Jack's feats so described by Mr. Cruikshank. (Let us say a word here in praise of the excellent manner in which the author has carried us through the adventure.) Here is Jack clattering up the chimney, now peering into the lonely red room, now opening "the door between the red room and the chapel." What a wild, fierce, scared look he has, the young ruffian, as cautiously he steps in, holding light his bar of iron. You can see by his face how his heart is beating. If any one were there! but no! And this is a very fine characteristic of the prints, the extreme *loneliness* of them all. Not a soul is there to disturb him — woe to him who should — and Jack drives in the chapel gate, and shatters down the passage door, and there you have him on the leads. Up he goes! it is but a spring of a few feet from the blanket, and he is gone — *abiit, evasit, erupit!* Mr. Wild must catch him again if he can.

We must not forget to mention "Oliver Twist," and Mr. Cruikshank's famous designs to that work.* The sausage scene at Fagin's, Nancy seizing the boy; that capital piece of humor, Mr. Bumble's courtship, which is even better in Cruikshank's version than in Boz's exquisite ac-

* A gentleman (whose wit is so celebrated that one should be very cautious in repeating his stories) gave the writer a good illustration of the philosophy of exaggeration. Mr. —— was once behind the scenes at the Opera when the scene-shifters were preparing for the ballet. Flora was to sleep under a bush, whereon were growing a number of roses, and amidst which was fluttering a gay covey of butterflies. In size, the roses exceeded the most expansive sun-flowers, and the butterflies were as large as cocked hats; — the scene-shifter explained to Mr. ——, who asked the reason why every thing was so magnified, that the galleries could never see the objects unless they were enormously exaggerated. How many of our writers and designers work for the galleries?

* Or his new work, "The Tower of London," which promises even to surpass Mr. Cruikshank's former productions.

count of the interview; Sykes's farewell to the dog; and the Jew,—the dreadful Jew — that Cruikshank drew! What a fine touching picture of melancholy desolation is that of Sykes and the dog! The poor cur is not too well drawn, the landscape is stiff and formal; but in this case the faults, if faults they be, of execution rather add to than diminish the effect of the picture: it has a strange, wild, dreary, broken-hearted look; we fancy we see the landscape as it must have appeared to Sykes, when ghastly and with bloodshot eyes he looked at it. As for the Jew in the dungeon, let us say nothing of it — what can we say to describe it? What a fine homely poet is the man who can produce this little world of mirth or woe for us! Does he elaborate his effects by slow process of thought, or do they come to him by instinct? Does the painter ever arrange in his brain an image so complete, that he afterwards can copy it exactly on the canvas, or does the hand work in spite of him?

A great deal of this random work of course every artist has done in his time; many men produce effects of which they never dreamed, and strike off excellences, haphazard, which gain for them reputation; but a fine quality in Mr. Cruikshank, the quality of his success, as we have said before, is the extraordinary earnestness and good faith with which he executes all he attempts — the ludicrous, the polite, the low, the terrible. In the second of these he often, in our fancy, fails, his figures lacking elegance and descending to caricature; but there is something fine in this too: it is good that he *should* fail, that he should have these honest *naïve* notions regarding the *beau monde*, the characteristics of which a namby-pamby tea-party painter could hit off far better than he. He is a great deal too downright and manly to appreciate the flimsy delicacies of small society — you cannot expect a lion to roar you like any sucking dove, or frisk about a drawing-room like a lady's little spaniel.

If then, in the course of his life and business, he has been occasionally obliged to imitate the ways of such small animals, he has done so, let us say it at once, clumsily, and like as a lion should. Many artists, we hear, hold his works rather cheap; they prate about bad drawing, want of scientific knowledge; — they would have something vastly more neat, regular, anatomical.

Not one of the whole band most likely but can paint an Academy figure better than himself; nay, or a portrait of an alderman's lady and family of children. But look down the list of the painters and tell us who are they? How many among these men are *poets* (makers), possessing the faculty to create, the greatest among the gifts with which Providence has endowed the mind of man? Say how many there are, count up what they have done, and see what in the course of some nine and twenty years has been done by this indefatigable man.

What amazing energetic fecundity do we find in him! As a boy he began to fight for bread, has been hungry (twice a day we trust) ever since, and has been obliged to sell his wit for his bread week by week. And his wit, sterling gold as it is, will find no such purchasers as the fashionable painter's thin pinchbeck, who can live comfortably for six weeks, when paid for and painting a portrait, and fancies his mind prodigiously occupied all the while. There was an artist in Paris, an artist hairdresser, who used to be fatigued and take restoratives after inventing a new coiffure. By no such gentle operation of head-dressing has Cruikshank lived: time was (we are told so in print) when for a picture with thirty heads in it he was paid three guineas — a poor week's pittance truly, and a dire week's labor. We make no doubt that the same labor would at present bring him twenty times the sum; but whether it be ill paid or well, what labor has Mr. Cruikshank's been! Week by week, for thirty years, to produce something new; some smiling offspring of painful labor, quite independent and distinct from its ten thousand jovial brethren; in what hours of sorrow and ill-health to be told by the world, "Make us laugh or you starve — Give us fresh fun; we have eaten up the old, and are hungry." And all this has he been obliged to do — to wring laughter day by day, sometimes, perhaps, out of want, often certainly from ill-health or depression — to keep the fire of his brain perpetually alight: for the greedy public will give it no leisure to cool. This he has done, and done well. He has told a thousand truths in as many strange and fascinating ways; he has given a thousand new and pleasant thoughts to millions of people; he has never used his wit dishonestly; he has never, in all the exuberance of his frolicsome humor, caused a single painful or guilty blush: how little do we think of the extraordinary power of this man, and how ungrateful we are to him!

Here, as we are come round to the charge of ingratitude, the starting-post from which we set out, perhaps we had better conclude. The reader will perhaps wonder at the high-flown tone in which we speak of the services and merits of an individual, whom he considers a humble scraper on steel, that is wonderfully popular already. But none of us remember all the benefits we owe him; they have come one by one, one driving out the memory of the other; it is only when we come to examine them all together, as the writer has done, who has a pile of books on the table before him — a heap of personal kindnesses from George Cruikshank (not presents, if you please, for we bought, borrowed, or stole every one of them) — that we feel what we owe him. Look at one of Mr. Cruikshank's works, and we pronounce him an excellent humorist. Look at all: his reputation is increased by a kind of geometrical progression; as a whole diamond is a hundred times more valuable than the hundred splinters into which it might be broken would be. A fine rough English diamond is this about which we have been writing.

JOHN LEECH'S PICTURES OF LIFE AND CHARACTER.*

WE, who can recall the consulship of Plancus, and quite respectable, old-fogyfied times, remember, amongst other amusements which we had as children, the pictures at which we were permitted to look. There was Boydell's Shakspeare, black and ghastly gallery of murky Opies, glum Northcotes, straddling Fuselis! there were Lear, Oberon, Hamlet, with starting muscles, rolling eyeballs, and long pointing quivering fingers; there was little Prince Arthur (Northcote) crying, in white satin, and bidding good Hubert not put out his eyes; there was Hubert crying; there was little Rutland being run through the poor little body by bloody Clifford; there was Cardinal Beaufort (Reynolds) gnashing his teeth, and grinning and howling demoniacally on his deathbed (a picture

* Reprinted from "The Quarterly Review," No. 191, Dec. 1854, by permission of Mr. John Murray.

frightful to the present day); there was Lady Hamilton (Romney) waving a torch, and dancing before a black background, — a melancholy museum indeed. Smirke's delightful "Seven Ages" only fitfully relieved its general gloom. We did not like to inspect it unless the elders were present, and plenty of lights and company were in the room.

Cheerful relatives used to treat us to Miss Linwood's. Let the children of the present generation thank their stars *that* tragedy is put out of their way. Miss Linwood's was worsted-work. Your grandmother or grand-aunts took you there, and said the pictures were admirable. You saw "The Woodman" in worsted, with his axe and dog, trampling through the snow; the snow bitter cold to look at, the woodman's pipe wonderful; a gloomy piece, that made you shudder. There were large dingy pictures of woollen martyrs, and scowling warriors with limbs strongly knitted; there was especially, at the end of a black passage, a den of lions, that would frighten any boy not born in Africa, or Exeter 'Change, and accustomed to them.

Another exhibition used to be West's Gallery, where the pleasing figures of Lazarus in his grave-clothes, and Death on the pale horse, used to impress us children. The tombs of Westminster Abbey, the vaults at St. Paul's, the men in armor at the Tower, frowning ferociously out of their helmets, and wielding their dreadful swords; that superhuman Queen Elizabeth at the end of the room, a livid sovereign with glass eyes, a ruff, and a dirty satin petticoat, riding a horse covered with steel: who does not remember these sights in London in the consulship of Plancus? and the wax-work in Fleet Street, not like that of Madame Tussaud's, whose chamber of death is gay and brilliant; but a nice old gloomy wax-work, full of murderers; and as a chief attraction, the Dead Baby and the Princess Charlotte lying in state?

Our story-books had no pictures in them for the most part. Frank (dear old Frank!) had none; nor "The Parent's assistant;" nor "The Evenings at Home;" nor our copy of the "Ami des Enfans:" there were a few just at the end of the Spelling-Book, beside the allegory at the beginning, of Education leading up Youth to the temple of Industry, where Dr. Dilworth and Professor Walkinghame stood with crowns of laurel. There were, we say, just a few pictures, at the end of the Spelling-Book, little oval gray woodcuts of Bewick's, mostly of the Wolf and the Lamb, the Dog and the Shadow, and Brown, Jones, and Robinson with long ringlets and little tights; but for pictures, so to speak, what had we? The rough old wood-blocks in the old harlequin-backed fairy-books had served hundreds of years; before *our* Plancus, in the time of Priscus Plancus — in Queen Anne's time, who knows? We were flogged at school; we were fifty boys in our boarding-house, and had to wash in a leaden trough, under a cistern, with lumps of fat yellow soap floating about in the ice and water. Are *our* sons ever flogged? Have they not dressing-rooms, hair-oil, hip-baths, and Baden towels? And what picture-books the young villains have? What have these children done that they should be so much happier than we were?

We had "The Arabian Nights" and Walter Scott, to be sure. Smirke's illustrations to the former are very fine. We did not know how good they were then; but we doubt whether we did not prefer the little old "Miniature Library Nights" with frontispieces by Uwins; for *these* books the pictures don't count. Every boy of imagination does his own pictures to Scott and "The Arabian Nights" best.

Of funny pictures there were none especially intended for us children. There was Rowlandson's "Doctor Syntax:" Doctor Syntax, in a fuzz-wig, on a horse with legs like sausages, riding races, making love, frolicking with rosy exuberant damsels. Those pictures were very funny, and that aqua-tinting and the gay-colored plates very pleasant to witness; but if we could not read the poem in those days, could we digest it in this? Nevertheless, apart from the text which we could not master, we remember Doctor Syntax pleasantly, like those cheerful painted hieroglyphics in the Nineveh Court at Sydenham. What matter for the arrow-head, illegible, stuff? give us the placid grinning kings, twanging their jolly bows over their rident horses, wounding those good-humored enemies, who tumble gayly off the towers, or drown, smiling, in the dimpling waters, amidst the anerithmon gelasma of the fish.

After Doctor Syntax, the apparition of Corinthian Tom, Jerry Hawthorn, and the facetious Bob Logic, must be recorded — a wondrous history indeed theirs was! When the future student of our manners comes to look over the pictures and the writing of these queer volumes, what will he think of our society, customs, and language in the consulship of Plancus? "Corinthian," it appears, was the phrase applied to men of fashion and *ton* in Plancus's time: they were the brilliant predecessors of the "swell" of the present period — brilliant, but somewhat barbarous, it must be confessed. The Corinthians were in the habit of drinking a great deal too much in Tom Cribb's parlor: they used to go and see "life" in the gin-shops; of nights, walking home (as well as they could), they used to knock down "Charleys," poor harmless old watchmen with lanterns, guardians of the streets of Rome, Planco Consule. They perpetrated a vast deal of boxing; they put on the "mufflers" in Jackson's rooms; they "sported their prads" in the Ring in the Park; they attended cock-fights, and were enlightened patrons of dogs and destroyers of rats. Besides these sports, the *délassemens* of gentlemen mixing with the people, our patricians, of course, occasionally enjoyed the society of their own class. What a wonderful picture that used to be of Corinthian Tom dancing with Corinthian Kate at Almack's! What a prodigious dress Kate wore! With what graceful *abandon* the pair flung their arms about as they swept through the mazy quadrille, with all the noblemen standing round in their stars and uniforms! You may still, doubtless, see the pictures at the British Museum, or find the volumes in the corner of some old country-house library. You are led to suppose that the English aristocracy of 1820 *did* dance and caper in that way, and box and drink at Tom Cribb's, and knock down watchmen; and the children of to-day, turning to their elders, may say, "Grandmamma, did you wear such a dress as that when you danced at Almack's? There was very little of it, grandmamma. Did grandpapa kill many watchmen when he was a young man, and frequent thieves' gin-shops, cock-fights, and the ring, before you married him? Did he use to talk the extraordinary slang and jargon which is printed in this book? He is very much changed. He seems a gentlemanly old boy enough now."

In the above-named consulate, when *we* had grandfathers alive, there would be in the old gentleman's library in the country two or three old mottled portfolios, or great swollen scrap-books of blue paper, full of the comic prints of grandpapa's time, ere Plancus ever had the fasces borne before him. These prints were signed Gilray, Bunbury, Rowlandson, Woodward, and some actually George Cruikshank — for George is a veteran now, and he took the etching needle in hand as a child. He caricatured "Boney," borrowing not a little from Gilray in his first puerile efforts. He drew Louis XVIII. trying on Boney's boots. Before the century was actually in its teens we believe that George Cruikshank was amusing the public.

In those great colored prints in our grandfathers' portfolios in the library, and in some other apartments of the house, where the caricatures used to be pasted in those days, we found things quite beyond our comprehension. Boney was represented as a fierce dwarf, with goggle eyes, a huge laced hat and tricolored plume, a crooked sabre, reeking with blood: a little demon revelling in lust, murder, massacre. John Bull was shown kicking him a good deal: indeed he was prodigiously kicked all through that series of pictures; by Sidney Smith and our brave allies the gallant Turks; by the excellent and patriotic Spaniards; by the amiable and indignant Russians, — all nations had boots at the service of poor Master Boney. How Pitt used to defy him! How good old George, King of Brobdingnag, laughed at Gulliver-Boney, sailing about in his tank to make sport for their Majesties! This little fiend, this beggar's brat, cowardly, murderous, and atheistic as he was (we remember, in those old portfolios, pictures representing Boney and his family in rags, gnawing raw bones in a Corsican hut; Boney murdering the sick at Jaffa; Boney with a hookah and a large turban, having adopted the Turkish religion, &c.) — this Corsican monster, nevertheless, had some devoted friends in England, according to the Gilray chronicle, — a set of villains who loved atheism, tyranny, plunder, and wickedness in general, like their French friend. In the pictures, these men were all represented as dwarfs, like their ally. The miscreants got into power at one time, and, if we remember right, were called the Broad-backed Administration. One with shaggy eyebrows and a bristly beard, the hirsute ringleader of the rascals, was, it appears, called Charles James Fox; another miscreant, with a blotched countenance, was a certain Sheridan; other imps were hight Erskine, Norfolk (Jockey of), Moira, Henry Petty. As in our childish innocence we used to look at these demons, now sprawling and tipsy in their cups; now scaling heaven, from which the angelic Pitt hurled them down; now cursing the light (their atrocious ringleader Fox was represented with hairy cloven feet, and a tail and horns); now kissing Boney's boot, but inevitably discomfited by Pitt and the other good angels: we hated these vicious wretches, as good children should; we were on the side of Virtue and Pitt and Grandpapa. But if our sisters wanted to look at the portfolios, the good old grandfather used to hesitate. There were some prints among them very odd indeed; some that girls could not understand; some that boys, indeed, had best not see. We swiftly turn over those prohibited pages. How many of them there were in the wild, coarse, reckless, ribald, generous book of old English humor!

How savage the satire was — how fierce the assault — what garbage hurled at opponents — what foul blows were hit — what language of Billingsgate flung! Fancy a party in a country-house now looking over Woodward's facetiæ or some of the Gilray comicalities, or the slatternly Saturnalia of Rowlandson! Whilst we live we must laugh, and have folks to make us laugh. We cannot afford to lose Satyr with his pipe and dances and gambols. But we have washed, combed, clothed, and taught the rogue good manners: or rather, let us say, he has learned them himself; for he is of nature soft and kindly, and he has put aside his mad pranks and tipsy habits; and, frolicsome always, has become gentle and harmless, smitten into shame by the pure presence of our women and the sweet, confiding smiles of our children. Among the veterans, the old pictorial satirists, we have mentioned the famous name of one humorous designer who is still alive and at work. Did we not see, by his own hand, his own portrait of his own famous face, and whiskers, in "The Illustrated London

News" the other day? There was a print in that paper of an assemblage of Teetotallers in "Sadler's Wells Theatre," and we straightway recognized the old Roman hand — the old Roman's of the time of Plancus — George Cruikshank's. There were the old bonnets and droll faces and shoes, and short trousers, and figures of 1820 sure enough. And there was George (who has taken to the water-doctrine, as all the world knows) handing some teetotallesses over a plank to the table where the pledge was being administered. How often has George drawn that picture of Cruikshank! Where haven't we seen it? How fine it was, facing the effigy of Mr. Ainsworth in "Ainsworth's Magazine" when George illustrated that periodical! How grand and severe he stands in that design in G. C.'s "Omnibus," where he represents himself tonged like St. Dunstan, and tweaking a wretch of a publisher by the nose! The collectors of George's etchings — oh, the charming etchings! — oh, the dear old "German Popular Tales!" — the capital "Points of Humor" — the delightful "Phrenology" and "Scrap-books," of the good time, *our* time — Plancus's in fact! — the collectors of the Georgian etchings, we say, have at least a hundred pictures of the artist. Why, we remember him in his favorite Hessian boots in "Tom and Jerry" itself; and in woodcuts as far back as the Queen's trial. He has rather deserted satire and comedy of late years, having turned his attention to the serious, and warlike, and sublime. Having confessed our age and prejudices, we prefer the comic and fanciful to the historic, romantic, and at present didactic George. May respect, and length of days, and comfortable repose attend the brave, honest, kindly, pure-minded artist, humorist, moralist! It was he first who brought English pictorial humor and children acquainted. Our young people and their fathers and mothers owe him many a pleasant hour and harmless laugh. Is there no way in which the country could acknowledge the long services and brave career of such a friend and benefactor?

Since George's time humor has been converted. Comus and his wicked satyrs and leering fauns have disappeared, and fled into the lowest haunts; and Comus's lady (if she had a taste for humor, which may be doubted) might take up our funny picture-books without the slightest precautionary squeamishness. What can be purer than the charming fancies of Richard Doyle? In all Mr. Punch's huge galleries can't we walk as safely as through Miss Pinkerton's school-rooms? And as we look at Mr. Punch's pictures, at the "Illustrated News" pictures, at all the pictures in the book-shop windows at this Christmas season, as oldsters, we feel a certain pang of envy against the youngsters — they are too well off. Why hadn't *we* picture-books? Why were we flogged so? A plague on the lictors and their rods in the time of Plancus!

And now, after this rambling preface, we are arrived at the subject in hand — Mr. John Leech and his "Pictures of Life and Character," in the collection of Mr. Punch. This book is better than plum-cake at Christmas. It is an enduring plum-cake, which you may eat, and which you may slice, and deliver to your friends; and to which, having cut it, you may come again and welcome, from year's end to year's end. In the frontispiece you see Mr. Punch examining the pictures in his gallery — a portly, well-dressed, middle-aged, respectable gentleman, in a white neckcloth, and a polite evening costume — smiling in a very bland and agreeable manner upon one of his pleasant drawings, taken out of one of his handsome portfolios. Mr. Punch has very good reason to smile at the work, and be satisfied with the artist. Mr. Leech, his chief contributor, and some kindred humorists, with pencil and pen have served Mr.

Punch admirably. Time was, if we remember Mr. P.'s history rightly, that he did not wear silk stockings nor well made clothes (the litle dorsal irregularity in his figure is almost an ornament now, so excellent a tailor has he). He was of humble beginnings. It is said he kept a ragged little booth, which he put up at corners of streets; associated with beadles, policemen, his own ugly wife (whom he treated most scandalously), and persons in a low station of life; earning a precarious livelihood by the cracking of wild jokes, the singing of ribald songs, and half-pence extorted from passers-by. He is the Satyric genius we spoke of anon: he cracks his jokes still, for satire must live; but he is combed, washed, neatly clothed, and perfectly presentable. He goes into the very best company; he keeps a stud at Melton; he has a moor in Scotland; he rides in the Park; has his stall at the Opera; is constantly dining out at clubs and in private society; and goes every night in the season to balls and parties, where you see the most beautiful women possible. He is welcomed amongst his new friends the great; though, like the good old English gentleman of the song, he does not forget the small. He pats the heads of street boys and girls; relishes the jokes of Jack the costermonger and Bob the dustman; good-naturedly spies out Molly the cook flirting with policeman X, or Mary the nursemaid as she listens to the fascinating guardsman. He used rather to laugh at guardsmen, "plungers," and other military men; and was until latter days very contemptuous in his behavior towards Frenchmen. He has a natural antipathy to pomp and swagger, and fierce demeanor. But now that the guardsmen are gone to war, and the dandies of "The Rag"—dandies no more—are battling like heroes at Balaklava and Inkermann * by the side of their heroic allies, Mr. Punch's laughter is changed to hearty respect and enthusiasm. It is not against courage and honor he wars: but this great moralist—must it be owned?—has some popular British prejudices, and these led him in peace time to laugh at soldiers and Frenchmen. If those hulking footmen who accompanied the carriages to the opening of Parliament the other day, would form a plush brigade, wear only gunpowder in their hair, and strike with their great canes on the enemy, Mr. Punch would leave off laughing at Jeames, who meanwhile remains among us, to all outward appearance regardless of satire, and calmly consuming his five meals per diem. Against lawyers, beadles, bishops and clergy, and authorities, Mr. Punch is still rather bitter. At the time of the Papal aggression he was prodigiously angry; and one of the chief misfortunes which happened to him at that period was that, through the violent opinions which he expressed regarding the Roman Catholic hierarchy, he lost the invaluable services, the graceful pencil, the harmless wit, the charming fancy, of Mr. Doyle. Another member of Mr. Punch's cabinet, the biographer of Jeames, the author of "The Snob Papers," resigned his functions on account of Mr. Punch's assaults upon the present Emperor of the French nation, whose anger Jeames thought it was unpatriotic to arouse. Mr. Punch parted with these contributors; he filled their places with others as good. The boys at the railroad stations cried "Punch" just as cheerily, and sold just as many numbers, after these events as before.

There is no blinking the fact that in Mr. Punch's cabinet, John Leech is the right-hand man. Fancy a number of "Punch" without Leech's pictures! What would you give for it? The learned gentlemen who write the work must feel that, without him, it were as well left alone. Look at the rivals whom the popularity of "Punch" has brought into the

* This was written in 1854.

field; the direct imitators of Mr. Leech's manner — the artists with a manner of their own — how inferior their pencils are to his in humor, in depicting the public manners, in arresting, amusing the nation! The truth, the strength, the free vigor, the kind humor, the John Bull pluck and spirit of that hand are approached by no competitor. With what dexterity he draws a horse, a woman, a child! He feels them all, so to speak, like a man. What plump young beauties those are with which Mr. Punch's chief contributor supplies the old gentleman's pictorial harem! What famous thews and sinews Mr. Punch's horses have, and how Briggs, on the back of them, scampers across country! You see youth, strength, enjoyment, manliness, in those drawings, and in none more so, to our thinking, than in the hundred pictures of children which this artist loves to design. Like a brave, hearty, good-natured Briton, he becomes quite soft and tender with the little creatures, pats gently their little golden heads, and watches with unfailing pleasure their ways, their sports, their jokes, laughter, caresses. *Enfans terribles* come home from Eton; young Miss practising her first flirtation; poor little ragged Polly making dirt-pies in the gutter, or staggering under the weight of Jacky, her nurse-child, who is as big as herself — all these little ones, patrician and plebeian, meet with kindness from this kind heart, and are watched with curious nicety by this amiable observer.

We remember, in one of those ancient Gilray portfolios, a print which used to cause a sort of terror in us youthful spectators, and in which the Prince of Wales (his Royal Highness was a Foxite then) was represented as sitting alone in a magnificent hall after a voluptuous meal, and using a great steel fork in the guise of a toothpick. Fancy the first young gentleman living employing such a weapon in such a way! The most elegant Prince of Europe engaged with a two-pronged iron fork — the heir of Britannia with a *bident!* The man of genius who drew that picture saw little of the society which he satirized and amused. Gilray watched public characters as they walked by the shop in St. James's Street, or passed through the lobby of the House of Commons. His studio was a garret, or little better; his place of amusement a tavern-parlor, where his club held its nightly sittings over their pipes and sanded floor. You could not have society represented by men to whom it was not familiar. When Gavarni came to England a few years since — one of the wittiest of men, one of the most brilliant and dexterous of draughtsmen — he published a book of "Les Anglais," and his *Anglais* were all Frenchmen. The eye, so keen and so long practised to observe Parisian life, could not perceive English character. A social painter must be of the world which he depicts, and native to the manners which he portrays.

Now, any one who looks over Mr. Leech's portfolio must see that the social pictures which he gives us are authentic. What comfortable little drawing-rooms and dining-rooms, what snug libraries, we enter; what fine young-gentlemanly wags they are, those beautiful little dandies who wake up gouty old grandpapa to ring the bell; who decline aunt's pudding and custards, saying that they will reserve themselves for an anchovy toast with the claret; who talk together in ball-room doors, where Fred whispers Charley — pointing to a dear little partner seven year old — "My dear Charley she has very much gone off; you should have seen that girl last season!" Look well at every thing appertaining to the economy of the famous Mr. Briggs: how snug, quiet, appropriate all the appointments are! What a comfortable, neat, clean, middle-class house Briggs's is (in the Bayswater suburb of London, we should guess from the sketches of the surrounding scenery)! What a good stable he has, with a loose box for those celebrated hunters which he rides! How pleasant, clean, and warm his breakfast-table looks! What a trim little maid brings in the top-boots which horrify Mrs. B.! What a snug dressing-room he has, complete in all its appointments, and in which he appears trying on the delightful hunting-cap which Mrs. Briggs flings into the fire! How cosey all the Briggs party seem in their dining-room: Briggs reading a Treatise on Dog-breaking by a lamp; Mamma and Grannie with their respective needle-works; the children clustering round a great book of prints — a great book of prints such as this before us, which, at this season, must make thousands of children happy by as many firesides! The inner life of all these people is represented: Leech draws them as naturally as Teniers depicts Dutch boors, or Morland pigs and stables. It is your house and mine: we are looking at everybody's family circle. Our boys coming from school give themselves such airs, the young scapegraces! our girls, going to parties, are so tricked out by fond mammas — a social history of London in the middle of the nineteenth century. As such, future students — lucky they to have a book so pleasant — will regard these pages: even the mutations of fashion they may follow here if they be so inclined. Mr. Leech has as fine an eye for tailory and millinery as for horse-flesh. How they change those cloaks and bonnets! How we have to pay milliners' bills from year to year! Where are those prodigious châtelaines of 1850 which no lady could be without? Where those charming waistcoats, those "stunning" waistcoats, which our young girls used to wear a few brief seasons back, and which cause 'Gus, in the sweet little sketch of "La Mode," to ask Ellen for her tailor's address. 'Gus is a young warrior by this time, very likely facing the enemy at Inkermann; and pretty Ellen, and that love of a sister of hers, are married and happy, let us hope, superintending one of those delightful nursery scenes which our artist depicts with such tender humor. Fortunate artist, indeed! You see he must have been bred at a good public school; that he has ridden many a good horse in his day; paid, no doubt, out of his own purse for the originals of some of those lovely caps and bonnets; and watched paternally the ways, smiles, frolics, and slumbers of his favorite little people.

As you look at the drawings, secrets come out of them, — private jokes, as it were, imparted to you by the author for your special delectation. How remarkably, for instance, has Mr. Leech observed the hair-dressers of the present age! Look at "Mr. Tongs," whom that hideous old bald woman, who ties on her bonnet at the glass, informs that "she has used the whole bottle of Balm of California, but her hair comes off yet." You can see the bear's-grease not only on Tongs's head, but on his hands, which he is clapping clammily together. Remark him who is telling his client "there is cholera in the hair:" and that lucky rogue whom the young lady bids to cut off "a long thick piece" — for somebody, doubtless. All these men are different and delightfully natural and absurd. Why should hair-dressing be an absurd profession?

The amateur will remark what an excellent part hands play in Mr. Leech's pieces: his admirable actors use them with perfect naturalness. Look at Betty, putting the urn down; at cook, laying her hands on the kitchen table, whilst her policeman grumbles at the cold meat. They are cook's and housemaid's hands without mistake, and not without a certain beauty too. The bald old lady, who is tying her bonnet at Tongs's, has hands which you see are trembling. Watch the fingers of the two old harridans who are talking scandal: for what long years past they have pointed out holes in their neighbors' dresses, and mud on their flounces; "Here's a go! I've lost my diamond ring." As the dustman utters this pathetic cry, and looks at his hand, you burst out laughing. These are among the little points of humor. One could indicate hundreds of such as one turns over the pleasant pages.

There is a little snob or gent, whom we all of us know, who wears little tufts on his little chin, outrageous pins and pantaloons, smokes cigars on tobacconists' counters, sucks his cane in the streets, struts about with Mrs. Snob and the baby (Mrs. S. an immense woman, whom Snob nevertheless bullies), who is a favorite abomination of Leech, and pursued by that savage humorist into a thousand of his haunts. There he is, choosing waistcoats at the tailor's — such waistcoats! Yonder he is giving a shilling to the sweeper, who calls him "Capting;" now he is offering a paletot to a huge giant who is going out in the rain. They don't know their own pictures, very likely; if they did, they would have a meeting, and thirty or forty of them would be deputed to thrash Mr. Leech. One feels a pity for the poor little bucks. In a minute or two, when we close this discourse and walk the streets, we shall see a dozen such.

Ere we shut the desk up, just one word to point out to the unwary specially to note the backgrounds of landscapes in Leech's drawings — homely drawings of moor and wood, and seashore and London street — the scenes of his little dramas. They are as excellently true to nature as the actors themselves; our respect for the genius and humor which invented both increases as we look and look again at the designs. May we have more of them; more pleasant Christmas volumes, over which we and our children can laugh together. Can we have too much of truth and fun and beauty and kindness?

THE WOLVES AND THE LAMB.

DRAMATIS PERSONÆ.

Mr. HORACE MILLIKEN, *a Widower, a wealthy City Merchant.*
GEORGE MILLIKEN, *a Child, his Son.*
Captain TOUCHIT, *his Friend.*
CLARENCE KICKLEBURY, *brother to Milliken's late Wife.*
JOHN HOWELL, *M.'s Butler and confidential Servant.*
CHARLES PAGE, *Foot-boy.*
BULKELEY, *Lady Kicklebury's Servant.*
Mr. BONNINGTON.
Coachman, Cabman; a Bluecoat Boy, another Boy (Mrs. Prior's Sons).

LADY KICKLEBURY, *Mother-in-law to Milliken.*
Mrs. BONNINGTON, *Milliken's Mother (married again).*
Mrs. PRIOR.
Miss PRIOR, *her Daughter, Governess to Milliken's Children.*
ARABELLA MILLIKEN, *a Child.*
MARY BARLOW, *School-room Maid.*
A grown-up Girl and Child of Mrs. Prior's, Lady's K.'s Maid, Cook.

THE WOLVES AND THE LAMB.

ACT I.

SCENE. — MILLIKEN'S *villa at Richmond; two drawing-rooms opening into one another. The late* Mrs. MILLIKEN'S *portrait over the mantelpiece; book-cases, writing-tables, piano, newspapers, a handsomely furnished saloon. The back-room opens, with very large windows, on the lawn and pleasure-ground; gate, and wall — over which the heads of a cab and a carriage are seen, as persons arrive. Fruit, and a ladder on the walls. A door to the dining-room, another to the sleeping-apartments, &c.*

JOHN. — Everybody out; governor in the city; governess (heigh-ho!) walking in the Park with the children; ladyship gone out in the carriage. Let's sit down and have a look at the papers. Buttons! fetch "The Morning Post" out of Lady Kicklebury's room. Where's "The Daily News," sir?

PAGE. — Think it's in Milliken's room.

JOHN. — Milliken! you scoundrel! What do you mean by Milliken? Speak of your employer as your governor, if you like, but not as simple Milliken. Confound your impudence! you'll be calling me Howell next.

PAGE. — Well! I didn't know. *You* call him Milliken.

JOHN. — Because I know him, because I'm intimate with him, because there's not a secret he has but I may have it for the asking; because the letters addressed to Horace Milliken, Esq., might as well be addressed John Howell, Esq., for I read 'em, I put 'em away and docket 'em, and remember 'em. I know his affairs better than he does: his income to a shilling, pay his tradesmen, wear his coats if I like. *I* may call Mr. Milliken what I please; but not *you*, you little scamp of a clod-hopping ploughboy. Know your station and do your business, or you don't wear *them* buttons long, I promise you. [*Exit* Page.]

Let me go on with the paper [*reads*]. How brilliant this writing is! "Times," "Chronicle," "Daily News," they're all good, blest if they ain't. How much better the nine leaders in them three daily papers is, than nine speeches in the House of Commons! Take a very best speech in the 'Ouse now, and compare it with an article in "The Times!" I say, the newspaper has the best of it for philosophy, for wit, novelty, good sense, too. And the party that writes the leading article is nobody, and the chap that speaks in the House of Commons is a hero. Lord, Lord, how the world is 'umbugged! Pop'lar representation! what *is* pop'lar representation? Dammy, it's a farce. Hallo! this article is stole! I remember a passage in Montesquieu uncommonly like it. [*Goes and gets the book. As he is standing upon sofa to get it, and sitting down to read it,* Miss PRIOR *and the* Children *have come in at the garden.* Children *pass across stage.* Miss PRIOR *enters by open window, bringing flowers into the room.*]

JOHN. — It *is* like it. [*He slaps the book, and seeing* Miss PRIOR *who enters, then jumps up from sofa, saying very respectfully,*]

JOHN. — I beg your pardon, Miss.

MISS P. [*sarcastically*]. — Do I disturb you, Howell?

JOHN. — Disturb! I have no right to say — a servant has no right to be disturbed, but I hope I may be pardoned for venturing to look at a volume in the libery, Miss, just in reference to a newspaper harticle — that's all, Miss.

MISS P. — You are very fortunate in finding any thing to interest you in the paper, I'm sure.

JOHN. — Perhaps, Miss, you are not accustomed to political discussion, and ignorant of — ah — I beg your pardon: a servant, I know, has no right to speak. [*Exit into dining-room, making a low bow.*]

MISS PRIOR. — The coolness of some people is really quite extraordinary! the airs they give themselves, the way in which they answer one, the books they read! Montesquieu: "Esprit des Lois!" [*takes book up, which J. has left on sofa.*] I believe the man has actually taken this from the shelf. I am sure Mr. Milliken, or her ladyship, never would. The other day "Helvetius" was found in Mr. Howell's pantry, forsooth! It is wonderful how he picked up French whilst we were abroad. "Esprit des Lois!" what is it? it must be dreadfully stupid. And as for reading "Helvetius" (who, I suppose, was a Roman general), I really can't understand how — Dear, dear! what airs these persons give themselves! What will come next? A footman — I beg Mr. Howell's pardon — a butler and confidential valet lolls on the drawing-room sofa, and reads Montesquieu! Impudence! And add to this, he follows me for the last two or three months with eyes that are quite horrid. What can the creature mean? But I forgot — I am only a governess. A governess is not a lady — a governess is but a servant — a governess is to work and walk all day with the children, dine in the school-room, and come to the drawing-room to play the man of the house to sleep. A governess is a domestic, only her place is not the servants' hall, and she is paid not quite so well as the butler who serves her her glass of wine. Odious! George! Arabella! there are those little wretches quarrelling again! [*Exit.* Children *are heard calling out, and seen quarrelling in garden.*]

JOHN [*re-entering*]. — See where she moves! grace is in all her steps. 'Eaven in her high — no—a-heaven in her heye, in every gesture dignity and love — ah, I wish I could say it! I wish you may procure it, poor fool! She passes by me — she tr-r-amples on me. Here's the chair she sets in [*kisses it*]. Here's the piano she plays on. Pretty keys, them fingers outhivories you! When she plays on it, I stand and listen at the drawing-room door, and my heart thr-obs in time! Fool, fool, fool! why did you look on her, John Howell! why did you beat for her, busy heart! You were tranquil till you knew her! I thought I could have been a-happy with Mary till then. That girl's affection soothed me. Her conversation didn't amuse me much, her ideers ain't exactly elevated, but they are just and proper. Her attentions pleased me. She ever kep' the best cup of tea for me. She crisped my buttered toast, or mixed my quiet tumbler for me, as I sat of hevenings and read my newspaper in the kitching. She respected the sanctaty of my pantry. When I was a-studying there, she never interrupted me. She darned my stockings for me, she starched and folded my chokers, and she sowed on the habsent buttons of which time and chance had bereft my linning. She has a good heart, Mary has. I know she'd get up and black the boots for me of the coldest winter mornings. She did when we was in humbler life, she did.

Enter MARY.

You have a good heart, Mary!

MARY. — Have I, dear John? [*sadly.*]

JOHN. — Yes, child — yes. I think a better never beat in woman's bosom. You're good to everybody — good to your parents whom you send half your wages to: good to your employers whom you never robbed of a halfpenny.

MARY [*whimpering*]. — Yes, I did, John. I took the jelly when you were in bed with the influenza; and brought you the pork-wine negus.

JOHN. — Port, not pork, child. Pork is the hanimal which Jews ab'or. Port is from Oporto in Portugal.

MARY [*still crying*]. — Yes, John; you know every thing a'most, John.

JOHN. — And you, poor child, but little! It's not your heart you want, you little trump, it's education, Mary: it's information: it's head, head, head! You can't learn. You never can learn. Your ideers ain't no good. You never can hinterchange 'em with mine. Conversation between us is impossible. It's not your fault. Some people are born clever; some are born tall, I ain't tall.

MARY. — Ho! you're big enough for me, John. [*Offers to take his hand.*]

JOHN. — Let go my 'and — my a-hand, Mary! I say, some people are born with brains, and some with big figures. Look at that great ass, Bulkeley, Lady K.'s man — the besotted, stupid beast! He's as big as a life-guardsman, but he ain't no more education nor ideers than the ox he feeds on.

MARY. — Law, John, whathever do you mean?

JOHN. — Hm! you know not, little one! you never can know. Have *you* ever felt the pangs of imprisoned genius? have *you* ever felt what 'tis to be a slave?

MARY. — Not in a free country, I should hope, John Howell — no such a thing. A place is a place, and I know mine, and am content with the spear of life in which it pleases heaven to place me, John: and I wish you were, and remembered what we learned from our parson when we went to school together in dear old Pigeoncot, John — when you used to help little Mary with her lessons, John, and fought Bob Brown, the big butcher's boy, because he was rude to me, John, and he gave you that black hi.

JOHN. — Say eye, Mary, not heye [*gently*].

MARY. — Eye; and I thought you never looked better in all your life than you did then: and we both took service at Squire Milliken's — me as dairy-girl, and you as knife-boy; and good masters have they been to us from our youth hup: both old Squire Milliken and Mr. Charles as is master now, and poor Mrs. as is dead, though she had her tantrums — and I thought we should save up and take "The Milliken Arms" — and now we have saved up — and now, now, now — oh, you are a stone, a stone, a stone! and I wish you were hung round my neck, and I were put down the well! There's the hup-stairs bell. [*She starts, changing her manner as she hears the bell, and exit.*]

JOHN [*looking after her*]. — It's all true. Gospel-true. We were children in the same village — sat on the same form at school. And it was for her sake that Bob Brown the butcher's boy whopped me. A black eye! I'm not handsome. But if I were ugly as the Saracen's 'Ead, ugly as that beast Bulkeley, I know it would be all the same to Mary. *She* has never forgot the boy she loved, that brought birds'-nests for her, and spent his halfpenny on cherries, and bought a fairing with his first half-crown — a brooch it was, I remember, of two billing doves a-hopping on one twig, and brought it home for little yellow-haired, blue-eyed, red-cheeked Mary. Lord, Lord! I don't like to think how I've kissed 'em, the pretty cheeks! they've got quite pale now with crying — and she has never once reproached me, not once, the trump, the little tr-rump!

Is it my fault [*stamping*] that Fate has separated us? Why did my young master take me up to Oxford, and give me the run of his libery and the society of the best scouts in the University? Why did he take me abroad? Why have I been to Italy, France, Jummany with him — their manners noted and their realms surveyed, by jingo! I've improved myself, and Mary has remained as you was. I try a conversation, and she can't respond. She's never got a word of poetry beyond Watt's Ims, and if I talk of Byron or Moore to her, I'm blest if she knows any thing more about 'em than the cook, who is as hignorant as a pig, or that beast Bulkeley, Lady Kick's footman. Above all, why, why did I see the woman upon whom my wretched heart is fixed forever, and who carries away my soul with her — prostrate, I say, prostrate, through the mud at the skirts of her gownd! Enslaver! why did I ever come near you? O enchantress Kelipso! how you have got hold of me! It was Fate, Fate, Fate. When Mrs. Milliken fell ill of scarlet fever at Naples, Milliken was away at Petersborough, Rooshia, looking after his property. Her foring woman fled. Me and the governess remained and nursed her and the children. We nursed the little ones out of the fever. We buried their mother. We brought the children home over Halp and Happenine. I nursed 'em all three. I tended 'em all three, the orphans, and the lovely gu-gu-governess. At Rome, where she took ill, I waited on her; as we went to Florence, had we been attacked by twenty thousand brigands, this little arm had courage for them all! And if I loved thee, Julia, was I wrong? and if I basked in thy beauty day and night, Julia, am I not man? and if, before this Peri, this enchantress, this gazelle, I forgot poor little Mary Barlow, how could I help it? I say, how the doose could I help it?

Enter Lady KICKLEBURY, BULKELEY *following with parcels and a spaniel.*

LADY K. — Are the children and the governess come home?

JOHN. — Yes, my lady [*in a perfectly altered tone*].

LADY K. — Bulkeley, take those parcels to my sitting-room.

JOHN. — Get up, old stoopid. Push along, old daddylonglegs [*aside to* BULKELEY].

LADY K. — Does any one dine here to-day, Howell?

JOHN. — Captain Touchit, my lady.

LADY K. — He's always dining here.

JOHN. — My master's oldest friend.

LADY K. — Don't tell me. He comes from his club. He smells of smoke; he is a low, vulgar person. Send Pinhorn up to me when you go down stairs. [*Exit* Lady *K.*]

JOHN. — I know. Send Pinhorn to me, means, Send my bonny brown hair, and send my beautiful complexion, and send my figure — and, O Lord! O Lord! what an old tigress that is! What an old Hector! How she do twist Milliken round her thumb! He's born to be bullied by women: and I remember him henpecked — let's see, ever since — ever since the time of that little gloveress at Woodstock, whose picter poor Mrs. M. made such a noise about when she found it in the lumber-room. Heh! *her* picture will be going into the lumber-room some day. M. must marry to get rid of his mother-in-law and mother over him: no man can stand it, not M. himself, who's a Job of a man. Isn't he, look at him! [*As he has been speaking, the bell has rung, the* Page *has run to the garden-door, and* MILLIKEN *enters through the garden, laden with a hamper, bandbox, and cricket-bat*].

MILLIKEN. — Why was the carriage not sent for me, Howell? There was no cab at the station, and I have had to toil all the way up the hill with these confounded parcels of my lady's.

JOHN. — I suppose the shower took off all the cabs, sir. When *did* a man ever git a cab in a shower? — or a policeman at a pinch — or a friend when you wanted him — or any thing at the right time, sir?

MILLIKEN. — But, sir, why didn't the carriage come, I say?

JOHN. — *You* know.

MILLIKEN.— How do you mean I know? confound your impudence!

JOHN. — Lady Kicklebury took it — your mother-in-law took it — went out a visiting — Ham Common, Petersham, Twick'nam — doose knows where. She, and her footman, and her span'l dog.

MILLIKEN. — Well, sir, suppose her ladyship *did* take the carriage? Hasn't she a perfect right? And if the carriage was gone, I want to know, John, why the devil the pony-chaise wasn't sent with the groom? Am I to bring a bonnet-box and a hamper of fish in my own hands, I should like to know?

JOHN. — Heh! [*laughs*].

MILLIKEN. — Why do you grin, you Cheshire cat?

JOHN. — Your mother-in-law had the carriage; and your mother sent for the pony-chaise. Your Pa wanted to go and see the Wicar of Putney. Mr. Bonnington don't like walking when he can ride.

MILLIKEN. — And why shouldn't Mr. Bonnington ride, sir, as long as there's a carriage in my stable? Mr. Bonnington has had the gout, sir! Mr. Bonnington is a clergyman, and married to my mother. He has *every* title to my respect.

JOHN. — And to your pony-chaise — yes, sir.

MILLIKEN. — And to every thing he likes in this house, sir.

JOHN. — What a good fellow you are, sir! You'd give your head off your shoulders, that you would. Is the fish for dinner to-day? Band-box for my lady, I suppose, sir? [*Looks in*] — Turban, feathers, bugles, marabouts, spangles — doose knows what. Yes, it's for her ladyship. [*To* Page.] Charles, take this band-box to her ladyship's maid. [*To his master.*] What sauce would you like with the turbot? Lobster sauce or Hollandaise? Hollandaise is best — most wholesome for you. Anybody besides Captain Touchit coming to dinner?

MILLIKEN. — No one that I know of.

JOHN. — Very good. Bring up a bottle of the brown hock? He likes the brown hock, Touchit does. [*Exit* JOHN.]

Enter Children. *They run to* MILLIKEN.

BOTH. — How d'you do, Papa! How do you do, papa!

MILLIKEN. — Kiss your old father, Arabella. Come here, George — What?

GEORGE. — Don't care for kissing — kissing's for gals. Have you brought me that bat from London?

MILLIKEN. — Yes. Here's the bat; and here's the ball [*takes one from pocket*] — and —

GEORGE. — Where's the wickets, Papa. O-o-o — where's the wickets? [*howls.*]

MILLIKEN. — My dear, darling boy! I left them at the office. What a silly papa I was to forget them! Parkins forgot them.

GEORGE. — Then turn him away, I say! Turn him away! [*He stamps.*]

MILLIKEN. — What! an old, faithful clerk and servant of your father and grandfather for thirty years past? An old man who loves us all, and has nothing but our pay to live on?

ARABELLA. — Oh, you naughty boy!

GEORGE. — I ain't a naughty boy.

ARABELLA. — You *are* a naughty boy.

GEORGE. — He! he! he! he! [*Grins at her.*]

MILLIKEN.—Hush, children! Here,

Arabella darling, here is a book for you. Look — aren't they pretty pictures?

ARABELLA. — Is it a story, Papa? I don't care for stories in general. I like something instructive and serious. Grandmamma Bonnington and grandpapa say —

GEORGE. — He's *not* your grandpapa.

ARABELLA. — He *is* my grandpapa.

GEORGE. — Oh, you great story! Look! look! there's a cab. [*Runs out. The head of a Hansom cab is seen over the garden-gate. Bell rings.* Page *comes. Altercation between* Cabman *and* Captain TOUCHIT *appears to go on, during which*]

MILLIKEN. — Come and kiss your old father, Arabella. He's hungry for kisses.

ARABELLA. — Don't. I want to go and look at the cab; and to tell Captain Touchit that he mustn't use naughty words. [*Runs towards garden.* Page *is seen carrying a carpet-bag.*]

Enter TOUCHIT *through the open window smoking a cigar.*

TOUCHIT. — How d'ye do, Milliken? How are tallows, hey, my noble merchant? I have brought my bag, and intend to sleep —

GEORGE. — I say, godpapa —

TOUCHIT. — Well, godson!

GEORGE. — Give us a cigar!

TOUCHIT. — Oh, you enfant terrible!

MILLIKEN [*wheezily*]. — Ah — ahem — George Touchit! you wouldn't mind — a — smoking that cigar in the garden, would you? Ah — ah!

TOUCHIT. — Hullo! What's in the wind now? You used to be a most inveterate smoker, Horace.

MILLIKEN. — The fact is — my mother-in-law — Lady Kicklebury — doesn't like it, and while she's with us, you know —

TOUCHIT. — Of course, of course [*throws away cigar*]. I beg her ladyship's pardon. I remember when you were courting her daughter she used not to mind it.

MILLIKEN. — Don't — don't allude to those times. [*He looks at his wife's picture.*]

GEORGE. — My mamma was a Kicklebury. The Kickleburys are the oldest family in the world. My name is George Kicklebury Milliken, of Pigeoncot, Hants; the Grove, Richmond, Surrey; and Portland Place, London, Esquire — my name is.

TOUCHIT. — You have forgotten Billiter Street, hemp and tallow merchant.

GEORGE. — Oh, bother! I don't care about that. I shall leave that when I'm a man: when I'm a man and come into my property.

MILLIKEN. — You come into your property?

GEORGE. — I shall, you know, when you're dead, papa. I shall have this house, and Pigeoncot; and the house in town — no, I don't mind about the house in town — and I shan't let Bella live with me — no, I won't.

BELLA. — No; *I* won't live with *you*. And *I'll* have Pigeoncot.

GEORGE. — You shan't have Pigeoncot. I'll have it: and the ponies: and I won't let you ride them — and the dogs, and you shan't have even a puppy to play with — and the dairy — and won't I have as much cream as I like — that's all!

TOUCHIT. — What a darling boy! Your children are brought up beautifully, Milliken. It is quite delightful to see them together.

GEORGE. — And I shall sink the name of Milliken, I shall.

MILLIKEN. — Sink the name? why, George?

GEORGE. — Because the Millikens are nobodies. Grandmamma says they are nobodies. The Kickleburys are gentlemen, and came over with William the Conqueror.

BELLA. — I know when that was. One thousand one hundred and one thousand one hundred and onety-one!

GEORGE. — Bother when they came

over! But I know this, when I come into the property I shall sink the name of Milliken.

MILLIKEN. — So you are ashamed of your father's name, are you, George, my boy?

GEORGE. — Ashamed! No, I ain't ashamed. Only Kicklebury is sweller I know it is. Grandmamma says so.

BELLA. — *My* grandmamma does not say so. *My* dear grandmamma says that family pride is sinful, and all belongs to this wicked world; and that in a very few years what our names are will not matter.

GEORGE. — Yes, she says so because her father kept a shop; and so did Pa's father keep a sort of shop — only Pa's a gentleman now.

TOUCHIT. — Darling child! How I wish I were married! If I had such a dear boy as you, George, do you know what I would give him?

GEORGE [*quite pleased*]. — What would you give him, godpapa?

TOUCHIT. — I would give him as sound a flogging as ever boy had, my darling. I would whip this nonsense out of him. I would send him to school, where I would pray that he might be well thrashed: and if when he came home he was still ashamed of his father, I would put him apprentice to a chimney-sweep — that's what I would do.

GEORGE. — I'm glad you're not my father, that's all.

BELLA. — And *I'm* glad you're not my father, because you are a wicked man!

MILLIKEN. — Arabella!

BELLA. — Grandmamma says so. He is a worldly man, and the world is wicked. And he goes to the play: and he smokes, and he says —

TOUCHIT. — Bella, what do I say?

BELLA. — Oh, something dreadful! You know you do! I heard you say it to the cabman.

TOUCHIT. — So I did, so I did! He asked me fifteen shillings from Piccadilly, and I told him to go to —— to somebody whose name begins with a D.

CHILDREN. — Here's another carriage passing.

BELLA. — The Lady Rumble's carriage.

GEORGE. — No, it ain't: it's Captain Boxer's carriage [*they run into the garden*].

TOUCHIT. — And this is the pass to which you have brought yourself, Horace Milliken! Why, in your wife's time, it was better than this, my poor fellow!

MILLIKEN. — Don't speak of her in *that* way, George Touchit!

TOUCHIT. — What have I said? I am only regretting her loss for your sake. She tyrannized over you; turned your friends out of doors; took your name out of your clubs; dragged you about from party to party, though you can no more dance than a bear, and from opera to opera, though you don't know "God Save the Queen" from "Rule Britannia." You don't, sir; you know you don't. But Arabella was better than her mother, who has taken possession of you since your widowhood.

MILLIKEN. — My dear fellow! no, she hasn't. There's *my* mother.

TOUCHIT. — Yes, to be sure, there's Mrs. Bonnington, and they quarrel over you like the two ladies over the baby before King Solomon.

MILLIKEN. — Play the satirist, my good friend! laugh at my weakness!

TOUCHIT. — I know you to be as plucky a fellow as ever stepped, Milliken, when a man's in the case. I know you and I stood up to each other for an hour and a half at Westminster.

MILLIKEN. — Thank you! We were both dragons of war! tremendous champions! Perhaps *I am* a little soft as regards women. I know my weakness well enough; but in my case what is my remedy? Put yourself in my position. Be a widower with two young children. What is more natural than that the mother of my poor wife should come and superintend my family? My own mother can't. She has a half-dozen of little half brothers and sisters, and a husband of her own to attend to. I dare say Mr. Bonnington and my mother will come to dinner to-day.

TOUCHIT. — Of course they will, my poor old Milliken, you don't dare to dine without them.

MILLIKEN. — Don't go on in that manner, George Touchit! Why should not my stepfather and my mother dine with me? I can afford it. I am a domestic man, and like to see my relations about me. I am in the city all day.

TOUCHIT. — Luckily for you.

MILLIKEN. — And my pleasure of an evening is to sit under my own vine and under my own fig-tree with my own olive-branches round about me; to sit by my fire with my children at my knees; to coze over a snug bottle of claret after dinner with a friend like you to share it; to see the young folks at the breakfast-table of a morning, and to kiss them and so off to business with a cheerful heart. This was my scheme in marrying, had it pleased heaven to prosper my plan. When I was a boy, and came from school and college, I used to see Mr. Bonnington, my father-in-law, with *his* young ones clustering round about him, so happy to be with him! so eager to wait on him! all down on their little knees round my mother before breakfast, or jumping up on his after dinner. It was who should reach his hat, and who should bring his coat, and who should fetch his umbrella, and who should get the last kiss.

TOUCHIT. — What? didn't he kiss *you?* Oh the hard-hearted old ogre!

MILLIKEN.—*Don't,* Touchit! Don't laugh at Mr. Bonnington! He is as good a fellow as ever breathed. Between you and me, as my half brothers and sisters increased and multiplied year after year, I used to feel rather lonely, rather bowled out, you understand. But I saw them so happy that I longed to have a home of my own. When my mother proposed Arabella for me (for she and Lady Kicklebury were immense friends at one time), I was glad enough to give up clubs and bachelorhood, and to settle down as a married man. My mother acted for the best. My poor wife's character, my mother used to say, changed after marriage. I was not as happy as I hoped to be; but I tried for it. George, I am not so comfortable now as I might be. A house without a mistress, with two mothers-in-law reigning over it — one worldly and aristocratic, another what you call serious, though she don't mind a rubber of whist: I give you my honor my mother plays a game at whist, and an uncommonly good game too — each woman dragging over a child to her side: of course such a family cannot be comfortable. [*Bell rings.*] There's the first dinner-bell. Go and dress, for heaven's sake.

TOUCHIT. — Why dress? There is no company!

MILLIKEN. — Why? ah! her ladyship likes it, you see. And it costs nothing to humor her. Quick, for she don't like to be kept waiting.

TOUCHIT. — Horace Milliken! what a pity it is the law declares a widower shall not marry his wife's mother! She would marry you else, — she would, on my word.

Enter JOHN.

JOHN. — I have took the Captain's things in the blue room, sir. [*Exeunt gentlemen,* JOHN *arranges tables, &c.*]

Ha! Mrs. Prior! I ain't partial to Mrs. Prior. I think she's an artful old dodger, Mrs. Prior. I think there's mystery in her unfathomable pockets, and schemes in the folds of her umbrella. But — but she's Julia's mother, and for the beloved one's sake I am civil to her.

MRS. PRIOR. —Thank you, Charles [*to the* Page, *who has been seen to let her in at the garden-gate*], I am so much obliged to you! Good-afternoon, Mr. Howell. Is my daughter — are the darling children well? Oh, I am quite tired and weary! Three horrid omnibuses were full, and I have had to walk the whole weary long way. Ah! times are changed with me, Mr. Howell. Once when I was young and strong, I had my husband's carriage to ride in.

JOHN [*aside*]. — His carriage! his coal-wagon! I know well enough who old Prior was. A merchant? yes, a pretty merchant! kep' a lodging-house, share in a barge, touting for orders, and at last a snug little place in "The Gazette."

MRS. PRIOR. — How is your cough, Mr. Howell? I have brought you some lozenges for it [*takes numberless articles from her pocket*], and if you would take them of a night and morning — oh, indeed, you would get better! The late Sir Henry Halford recommended them to Mr. Prior. He was his late Majesty's physician and ours. You know we have seen happier times, Mr. Howell. Oh, I am quite tired and faint.

JOHN. — Will you take any thing before the school-room tea, ma'am? You will stop to tea, I hope, with Miss Prior, and our young folks?

MRS. PRIOR. — Thank you: a little glass of wine when one is so faint — a little crumb of biscuit when one is so old and tired! I have not been accustomed to want, you know; and in my poor dear Mr. Prior's time —

JOHN. — I'll fetch some wine, ma'am. [*Exit to the dining-room.*]

MRS. PRIOR. — Bless the man, how abrupt he is in his manner! He quite shocks a poor lady who has been used to better days. What's here? Invitations — ho! Bills for Lady Kicklebury! *They* are not paid. Where is Mr. M. going to dine, I wonder? Captain and Mrs. Hopkinson, Sir John and Lady Tomkinson, request the pleasure. Request the pleasure! Of course they do. They are always asking Mr. M. to dinner. They have daughters to marry, and Mr. M. is a widower with three thousand a year, every shilling of it. I must tell Lady Kicklebury. He must never go to these places — never, never — mustn't be allowed. [*While talking, she opens all the letters on the table, rummages the portfolio and writing-box, looks at cards on mantelpiece, work in work-basket, tries tea-box, and shows the greatest activity and curiosity.*]

Re-enter JOHN, *bearing a tray with cakes, a decanter, &c.*

Thank you, thank you, Mr. Howell! Oh, oh, dear me, not so much as that! Half a glass, and *one* biscuit, please. What elegant sherry! [*Sips a little, and puts down glass on tray.*] Do you know, I remember in better days, Mr. Howell, when my poor dear husband? —

JOHN. — Beg your pardon. There's Milliken's bell going like mad. [*Exit* JOHN.]

MRS. PRIOR. — What an abrupt person! Oh, but it's comfortable, this wine is! And — and I think how my poor Charlotte would like a little — she so weak, and ordered wine by the medical man! And when dear Adolphus comes home from Christ's Hospital, quite tired, poor boy, and hungry, wouldn't a bit of nice cake do him good! Adolphus is so fond of plum-cake, the darling child! And so is Frederick, little saucy rogue; and I'll give them *my* piece, and keep my glass of wine for my dear delicate angel Shatty! [*Takes bottle and paper out of her pocket, cuts off a great slice of cake, and pours wine from wine-glass and decanter into bottle.*]

Enter PAGE.

PAGE. — Master George and Miss Bella is going to have their teas down here with Miss Prior, Mrs. Prior, and she's up in the school-room, and my lady says you may stay to tea.

MRS. PRIOR. — Thank you, Charles! How tall you grow! Those trousers would fit my darling Frederick to a nicety. Thank you, Charles. I know the way to the nursery. [*Exit* MRS. P.]

PAGE. — Know the way! I believe she *do* know the way. Been

a having cake and wine. Howell always gives her cake and wine — jolly cake, ain't it! and wine, oh, my!

Re-enter John.

John. — You young gormandizing cormorant! What! five meals a day ain't enough for you! What? beer ain't good enough for you, hey? [*Pulls boy's ears.*]

Page [*crying*]. — Oh, oh, do-o-n't, Mr. Howell. I only took half a glass, upon my honor.

John. — Your a-honor, you lying young vagabond! I wonder the ground don't open and swallow you. Half a glass! [*Holds up decanter.*] You've took half a bottle, you young Ananias! Mark this, sir! When I was a boy, a boy on my promotion, a child kindly took in from charity-school, a horphan in buttons like you, I never lied; no, nor never stole, and you've done both, you little scoundrel. Don't tell *me*, sir! there's plums on your coat, crumbs on your cheek, and you smell sherry, sir! I ain't time to whop you now, but come to my pantry to-night after you've took the tray down. Come *without your jacket on*, sir, and *then* I'll teach you what it is to lie and steal. There's the outer bell. Scud, you vagabond!

Enter Lady K.

Lady K. — What was that noise, pray?

John. — A difference between me and young Page, my lady. I was instructing him to keep his hands from picking and stealing. I was learning him his lesson, my lady, and he was a-crying it out.

Lady K. — It seems to me you are most unkind to that boy, Howell. He is my boy, sir. He comes from my estate. I will not have him ill used. I think you presume on your long services. I shall speak to my son-in-law about you. ["Yes, my lady; no, my lady; very good, my lady." *John has answered each sentence as she is speaking, and exit, gravely bowing.*] That man must quit the house. Horace says he can't do without him, but he *must* do without him. My poor dear Arabella was fond of him, but he presumes on that defunct angel's partiality. Horace says this person keeps all his accounts, sorts all his letters, manages all his affairs, may be trusted with untold gold, and rescued little George out of the fire. Now I have come to live with my son-in-law, *I* will keep his accounts, sort his letters, and take charge of his money: and if little Georgy gets into the grate, *I* will take him out of the fire. What is here? Invitation from Captain and Mrs. Hopkinson. Invitation from Sir John and Lady Tomkinson, who don't even ask *me!* Monstrous! he never shall go — he shall not go! [Mrs. Prior *has re-entered, she drops a very low courtesy to* Lady K., *as the latter, perceiving her, lays the cards down.*]

Mrs. Prior. — Ah, dear madam! how kind your ladyship's message was to the poor lonely widow-woman! Oh, how thoughtful it was of your ladyship to ask me to stay to tea!

Lady K. — With your daughter and the children? Indeed, my good Mrs. Prior, you are very welcome!

Mrs. Prior. — Ah! but isn't it a cause of thankfulness to be *made* welcome? Oughtn't I to be grateful for these blessings? — yes, I say *blessings*. And I am — I am, Lady Kicklebury — to the mother — of — that angel who is gone [*points to the picture*]. It was your sainted daughter left us — left my child to the care of Mr. Milliken, and — and you, who are now his guardian angel I may say. You *are*, Lady Kicklebury — you are. I say to my girl, Julia, Lady Kicklebury is Mr. Milliken's guardian angel, is *your* guardian angel — for without you could she keep her place as governess to these darling children? It would tear her heart in two to leave them, and yet she would be forced to do so. You know that some one — shall I hesitate to say whom *I mean?* — that Mr.

Milliken's mother, excellent lady though she is, does not love my child because *you* love her. You *do* love her, Lady Kicklebury, and oh! a mother's fond heart pays you back! but for you, my poor Julia must go — go, and leave the children whom a dying angel confided to her!

LADY K. — Go! no, never! not whilst *I* am in this house, Mrs. Prior. Your daughter is a well-behaved young woman: you have confided to me her long engagement to Lieutenant — Lieutenant What-d'you-call-'im, in the Indian service. She has been very, very good to my grandchildren — she brought them over from Naples when my — my angel of an Arabella died there, and I will protect Miss Prior.

MRS. PRIOR. — Bless you, bless you, noble, admirable woman! Don't take it away! I must, I *will* kiss your dear, generous hand! Take a mother's, a widow's blessings, Lady Kicklebury — the blessings of one who has known misfortune and seen better days, and thanks heaven — yes, heaven! — for the protectors she has found!

LADY K. — You said — you had — several children, I think, my good Mrs. Prior?

MRS. PRIOR. — Three boys — one, my eldest blessing, is in a wine-merchant's office — ah, if Mr. Milliken *would* but give him an order! an order from *this* house! an order from Lady Kicklebury's son-in-law! —

LADY K. — It shall be done, my good Prior — we will see.

MRS. PRIOR. — Another, Adolphus, dear fellow! is in Christ's Hospital. It was dear, good Mr. Milliken's nomination. Frederick is at Merchant Taylor's: my darling Julia pays his schooling. Besides, I have two girls — Amelia, quite a little toddles, just the size, though not so beautiful — but in a mother's eyes all children are lovely, dear Lady Kicklebury — just the size of your dear granddaughter, whose clothes would fit her, I am sure. And my second, Charlotte, a girl as tall as your ladyship, though not with so fine a figure. "Ah, no, Shatty!" I say to her, "you are as tall as our dear patroness, Lady Kicklebury, whom you long so to see; but you have not got her ladyship's carriage and figure, child." Five children have I, left fatherless and penniless by my poor dear husband — but heaven takes care of the widow and orphan, madam — and heaven's *best creatures* feed them! — *you* know whom I mean.

LADY K. — Should you not like, would you object to take — a frock or two of little Arabella's to your child? and if Pinhorn, my maid, will let me, Mrs. Prior, I will see if I cannot find something against winter for your second daughter, as you say we are of a size.

MRS. PRIOR. — The widow's and orphans' blessings upon you! I said my Charlotte was as tall, but I never said she had such a figure as yours — who has?

CHARLES *announces* —

CHARLES. — Mrs. Bonnington! [*Enter* MRS. BONNINGTON.]

MRS. B. — How do you do, Lady Kicklebury?

LADY K. — My dear Mrs. Bonnington! and you come to dinner of course?

MRS. B. — To dine with my own son, I may take the liberty. How are my grandchildren? my darling little Emily, is she well, Mrs. Prior?

LADY K. [*aside*]. — Emily? why does she not call the child by her blessed mother's name of Arabella? [*To* Mrs. B.] *Arabella* is quite well, Mrs. Bonnington. Mr. Squillings said it was nothing; only her grandmamma Bonnington spoiling her, as usual. Mr. Bonnington and all your numerous young folk are well, I hope?

MRS. B. — My family are all in perfect health, I thank you. Is Horace come home from the city?

LADY K. — Goodness! there's the dinner-bell, — I must run to dress.

Mrs. Prior. — Shall I come with you, dear Lady Kicklebury?

Lady K. — Not for worlds, my good Mrs. Prior. [*Exit* Lady K.]

Mrs. Prior. — How do you do, my *dear* madam? Is dear Mr. Bonnington *quite* well? What a sweet, sweet sermon he gave us last Sunday! I often say to my girl, I must not go to hear Mr. Bonnington, I really must not, he makes me cry so. Oh! he is a great and gifted man, and shall I not have one glimpse of him?

Mrs. B. — Saturday evening, my good Mrs. Prior. Don't you know that my husband never goes out on Saturday, having his sermon to compose?

Mrs. P. — Oh, those dear, dear sermons! Do you know, madam, that my little Adolphus, for whom your son's bounty procured his place at Christ's Hospital, was very much touched indeed, the dear child, with Mr. Bonnington's discourse last Sunday three weeks, and refused to play marbles afterwards at school? The wicked, naughty boys beat the poor child; but Adolphus has his consolation! Is Master Edward well, ma'am, and Master Robert, and Master Frederick, and dear little funny Master William?

Mrs. B. — Thank you, Mrs. Prior; you have a good heart, indeed!

Mrs. P. — Ah, what blessings those dears are to you! I wish your dearest little *grandson* —

Mrs. B. — The little naughty wretch! Do you know, Mrs. Prior, my grandson, George Milliken, spilt the ink over my dear husband's bands, which he keeps in his great dictionary; and fought with my child, Frederick, who is three years older than George — actually beat his own uncle!

Mrs. P. — Gracious mercy! Master Frederick was not hurt, I hope?

Mrs. B. — No; he cried a great deal; and then Robert came up, and that graceless little George took a stick; and then my husband came out, and do you know George Milliken actually kicked Mr. Bonnington on his shins, and butted him like a little naughty ram?

Mrs. P. — Mercy, mercy! what a little rebel! He is spoiled, dear madam, and you know by *whom*.

Mrs. B. — By his grandmamma Kicklebury. I know it. I want my son to whip that child, but he refuses. He will come to no good, that child.

Mrs. P. — Ah, madam! don't say so! Let us hope for the best. Master George's high temper will subside when certain persons who pet him are gone away.

Mrs. B. — Gone away! they never will go away! No, mark my words, Mrs. Prior, that woman will never go away. She has made the house her own: she commands every thing and everybody in it. She has driven me — me — Mr. Milliken's own mother — almost out of it. She has so annoyed my dear husband, that Mr. Bonnington will scarcely come here. Is she not always sneering at private tutors, because Mr. Bonnington was my son's private tutor, and greatly valued by the late Mr. Milliken? Is she not making constant allusions to old women marrying young men, because Mr. Bonnington happens to be younger than me? I have no words to express my indignation respecting Lady Kicklebury. She never pays any one, and runs up debts in the whole town. Her man Bulkeley's conduct in the neighborhood is quite — quite —

Mrs. B. — Gracious goodness, ma'am, you don't say so! And then what an appetite the gormandizing monster has! Mary tells me that what he eats in the servants' hall is something perfectly frightful.

Mrs. B. — Everybody feeds on my poor son! You are looking at my cap, Mrs. Prior? [*During this time* Mrs. Prior, *has been peering into a parcel which* Mrs. Bonnington *brought in her hand.*] I brought it with me across the Park. I could not walk through the Park in my cap. Isn't it a pretty ribbon, Mrs. Prior?

MRS. P. — Beautiful! beautiful! How blue becomes you! Who would think you were the mother of Mr. Milliken and seven other darling children? You can afford what Lady Kicklebury cannot.

MRS. B. — And what is that, Prior? A poor clergyman's wife, with a large family, cannot afford much.

MRS. P. — He! he! You can afford to be seen as you are, which Lady K. cannot. Did you not remark how afraid she seemed lest I should enter her dressing-room? Only Pinhorn, her maid, goes there, to arrange the roses, and the lilies, and the figure — he! he! Oh, what a sweet, sweet cap-ribbon! When you have worn it, and are tired of it, you will give it me, won't you? It will be good enough for poor old Martha Prior!

MRS. B. — Do you really like it? Call at Greenwood Place, Mrs. Prior, the next time you pay Richmond a visit, and bring your little girl with you, and we will see.

MRS. P. — Oh, thank you! thank you! Nay, don't be offended! I must! I must! [*Kisses* MRS. BONNINGTON.]

MRS. B. — There, there! We must not stay chattering! The bell has rung. I must go and put the cap on, Mrs. Prior.

MRS. P. — And I may come, too? *You* are not afraid of my seeing your hair, dear Mrs. Bonnington! Mr. Bonnington too young for *you!* Why, you don't look twenty!

MRS. B.— Oh, Mrs. Prior!

MRS. P. — Well, five and twenty, upon my word — not more than five and twenty — and that is the very prime of life! [*Exeunt* MRS. B. *and* MRS. P. *hand in hand. As* Captain TOUCHIT *enters, dressed for dinner, he bows and passes on.*]

TOUCHIT. — So, we are to wear our white cravats, and our varnished boots, and dine in ceremony. What is the use of a man being a widower, if he can't dine in his shooting-jacket? Poor Mill! He has the slavery now without the wife. [*He speaks sarcastically to the picture.*] Well, well! Mrs. Milliken! *You,* at any rate, are gone; and, with the utmost respect for you, I like your picture even better than the original. Miss Prior!

Enter MISS PRIOR.

MISS PRIOR.— I beg pardon. I thought you were gone to dinner. I heard the second bell some time since. [*She is drawing back.*]

TOUCHIT. — Stop! I say, Julia! [*She returns, he looks at her, takes her hand.*] Why do you dress yourself in this odd poky way? You used to be a very smartly dressed girl. Why do you hide your hair, and wear such a dowdy, high gown, Julia?

JULIA. — You mustn't call me Julia, Captain Touchit.

TOUCHIT. — Why? when I lived in your mother's lodging, I called you Julia. When you brought up the tea, you didn't mind being called Julia. When we used to go to the play with the tickets the Editor gave us, who lived on the second floor —

JULIA. — The wretch! — don't speak of him!

TOUCHIT. — Ah! I am afraid he was a sad deceiver, that Editor. He was a very clever fellow. What droll songs he used to sing! What a heap of play-tickets, diorama-tickets, concert-tickets, he used to give you! Did he touch your heart, Julia?

JULIA. — Fiddlededee! No man ever touched my heart, Captain Touchit.

TOUCHIT. — What! not even Tom Flight, who had the second floor after the Editor left it — and who cried so bitterly at the idea of going out to India without you? You had a *tendre* for him — a little passion — you know you had. Why, even the ladies here know it. Mrs. Bonnington told me that you were waiting for a sweetheart in India, to whom you were engaged; and Lady Kicklebury thinks you are dying in love for the absent swain.

JULIA. — I hope — I hope — you did not contradict them, Captain Touchit.

TOUCHIT. — Why not, my dear?

JULIA. — May I be frank with you? You were a kind, very kind friend to us—to me, in my youth.

TOUCHIT. — I paid my lodgings regularly, and my bills without asking questions. I never weighed the tea in the caddy, or counted the lumps of sugar, or heeded the rapid consumption of my *liqueur*—

JULIA. — Hush, hush! I know they were taken. I know you were very good to us. You helped my poor papa out of many a difficulty.

TOUCHIT [*aside*].—Tipsy old coal-merchant! I did, and he helped himself too.

JULIA. — And you were always our best friend, Captain Touchit. When our misfortunes came, you got me this situation with Mrs. Milliken —and, and—don't you see?—

TOUCHIT.—Well—what?

JULIA [*laughing*]. — I think it is best, under the circumstances, that the ladies here should suppose I am engaged to be married — or — or, they might be — might be jealous, you understand. Women are sometimes jealous of others, — especially mothers and mothers-in-law.

TOUCHIT. — Oh, you arch-schemer! And it is for that you cover up that beautiful hair of yours, and wear that demure cap?

JULIA [*slyly*]. — I am subject to rheumatism in the head, Captain Touchit.

TOUCHIT. — It is for that you put on the spectacles, and make yourself look a hundred years old?

JULIA. — My eyes are weak, Captain Touchit.

TOUCHIT. — Weak with weeping for Tom Flight. You hypocrite! Show me your eyes?

MISS P. — Nonsense!

TOUCHIT. — Show me your eyes, I say, or I'll tell about Tom Flight, and that he has been married at Madras these two years.

MISS P. — Oh, you horrid man! [*Takes glasses off.*] There.

TOUCHIT. — Translucent orbs! beams of flashing light! lovely lashes veiling celestial brightness! No, they haven't cried much for Tom Flight, that faithless captain! nor for Lawrence O'Reilly, that killing Editor. It is lucky you keep the glasses on them, or they would transfix Horace Milliken, my friend the widower here. *Do* you always wear them when you are alone with him?

MISS P. — I never *am* alone with him. Bless me! If Lady Kicklebury thought my eyes were—well, well—you know what I mean, — if she thought her son-in-law looked at me, I should be turned out of doors the next day, I am sure I should. And then, poor Mr. Milliken! he never looks at *me* — heaven help him! Why, he can't see me for her Ladyship's nose and awful caps and ribbons! He sits and looks at the portrait yonder, and sighs so. He thinks that he is lost in grief for his wife at this very moment.

TOUCHIT. — What a woman that was — eh, Julia — that departed angel! What a temper she had before her departure!

MISS P.—But the wind was tempered to the lamb. If she was angry — the lamb was so very lamblike and meek and fleecy.

TOUCHIT. — And what a desperate flirt the departed angel was! I knew half a dozen fellows, before her marriage, whom she threw over, because Milliken was so rich.

MISS P. — She was consistent at least, and did not change after marriage, as some ladies do; but flirted, as you call it, just as much as before. At Paris, young Mr. Verney, the attaché, was never out of the house: at Rome, Mr. Beard, the artist, was always drawing pictures of her: at Naples, when poor Mr. M. went away to look after his affairs at St. Petersburg, little Count Posilippo was forever coming to learn English and practise duets. She scarcely ever saw the poor children — [*changing her manner as* Lady KICKLEBURY *enters*] Hush — my lady!

TOUCHIT. — You may well say, "poor children," deprived of such a woman! Miss Prior, whom I knew in very early days — as your ladyship knows — was speaking — was speaking of the loss our poor friend sustained.

LADY K. — Ah, sir, what a loss! [*looking at the picture.*]

TOUCHIT. — What a woman she was — what a superior creature!

LADY K. — A creature — an angel!

TOUCHIT. — Mercy upon us! how she and my lady used to quarrel! [*aside.*] What a temper!

LADY K. — Hm — oh, yes — what a temper [*rather doubtfully at first*].

TOUCHIT. — What a loss to Milliken and the darling children!

MISS PRIOR. — Luckily they have *you* with them, madam.

LADY K. — And I will stay with them, Miss Prior; I will stay with them! I will never part from Horace, I am determined.

MISS P. — Ah! I am very glad you stay, for if I had not *you* for a protector I think you know I must go, Lady Kicklebury. I think you know there are those who would forget my attachment to these darling children, my services to — to her — and dismiss the poor governess. But while you stay I can stay, dear Lady Kicklebury! With you to defend me from jealousy I need not *quite* be afraid.

LADY K. — Of Mrs. Bonnington? Of Mr. Milliken's mother; of the parson's wife who writes out his stupid sermons, and has half a dozen children of her own? I should think *not* indeed! *I* am the natural protector of these children. *I* am their mother. *I* have no husband! You *stay* in this house, Miss Prior. You are a faithful, attached creature — though you were sent in by somebody I don't like very much [*pointing to* TOUCHIT, *who went off laughing when* JULIA *began her speech, and is now looking at prints, &c., in next room*].

MISS P. — Captain Touchit may not be in all things what one could wish. But his kindness has formed the happiness of my life in making me acquainted with *you*, ma'am: and I am sure you would not have me be ungrateful to him.

LADY K. — A most highly principled young woman. [*Goes out in garden and walks up and down with* Captain TOUCHIT.]

Enter MRS. BONNINGTON.

MISS P. — Oh, how glad I am you are come, Mrs. Bonnington. Have you brought me that pretty hymn you promised me? You always keep your promises, even to poor governesses. I read dear Mr. Bonnington's sermon! It was so interesting that I really could not think of going to sleep until I had read it all through; it was delightful, but oh! it's still better when he preaches it! I hope I did not do wrong in copying a part of it? I wish to impress it on the children. There are some worldly influences at work with them, dear madam [*looking at* Lady K. *in the garden*], which I do my feeble effort to — to modify. I wish *you* could come oftener.

MRS. B. — I will try, my dear — I will try. Emily has sweet dispositions.

MRS. P. — Ah, she takes after her grandmamma Bonnington!

MRS. B. — But George was sadly fractious just now in the school-room because I tried him with a tract.

MISS P. — Let us hope for better times! Do be with your children, dear Mrs. Bonnington, as constantly as ever you can, for *my* sake as well as theirs! *I* want protection and advice as well as they do. The *governess*, dear lady, looks up to you as well as the pupils; *she* wants the teaching which you and dear Mr. Bonnington can give her! Ah, why could not Mr. and Mrs. Bonnington come and live here, I often think?

The children would have companions in their dear young uncles and aunts; so pleasant it would be. The house is quite large enough; that is, if her ladyship did not occupy the three south rooms in the left wing. Ah, why, *why* couldn't you come?

MRS. B. — You are a kind, affectionate creature, Miss Prior. I do not very much like the gentleman who recommended you to Arabella, you know. But I do think he sent my son a good governess for his children.

Two Ladies walk up and down in front garden.

TOUCHIT *enters.*

TOUCHIT. — Miss Julia Prior, you are a wonder! I watch you with respect and surprise.

MISS. P. — Me! what have I done? a poor, friendless governess — respect *me*?

TOUCHIT. — I have a mind to tell those two ladies what I think of Miss Julia Prior. If they knew you as I know you, O Julia Prior, what a short reign yours would be!

MISS P. — I have to manage them a little. Each separately it is not so difficult. But when they are together, oh, it is very hard sometimes.

Enter MILLIKEN, *dressed, shakes hands with* MISS P.

MILLIKEN. — Miss Prior! are you well? Have the children been good? and learned all their lessons?

MISS P. — The children are pretty good, sir.

MILLIKEN. — Well, that's a great deal as times go. Do not bother them with too much learning, Miss Prior. Let them have an easy life. Time enough for trouble when age comes.

Enter JOHN.

JOHN. — Dinner, sir. [*And exit.*]

MILLIKEN. — Dinner, ladies. My Lady Kicklebury [*gives arm to* Lady K].

LADY K. — My dear Horace, you *shouldn't* shake hands with Miss Prior. You should keep people of that class at a distance, my dear creature. [*They go in to dinner,* Captain TOUCHIT *following with* Mrs. BONNINGTON. *As they go out, enter* MARY, *with children's tea-tray, &c., children following, and after them* Mrs. PRIOR. MARY *gives her tea.*]

MRS. PRIOR. — Thank you, Mary! You are so very kind! Oh, what delicious tea!

GEORGY. — I say, Mrs. Prior, I dare say you would like to dine best, wouldn't you?

MRS. P. — Bless you, my darling love, I had my dinner at one o'clock with my children at home.

GEORGY. — So had we: but we go in to dessert very often; and then don't we have cakes and oranges and candied-peel and macaroons and things! We are not to go in to-day; because Bella ate so many strawberries she made herself ill.

BELLA. — So did you.

GEORGY. — I'm a man, and men eat more than women, twice as much as women. When I'm a man, I'll eat as much cake as ever I like. I say, Mary, give us the marmalade.

MRS. P. — Oh, what nice marmalade! *I* know of some poor children —

MISS P. — Mamma! don't, mamma [*in an imploring tone*].

MRS. P. — I know of two poor children at home, who have very seldom nice marmalade and cake, young people.

GEORGE. — You mean Adolphus and Frederick and Amelia, your children. Well, they shall have marmalade and cake.

BELLA. — Oh, yes! I'll give them mine.

MRS. P. — Darling, dearest child!

GEORGE [*his mouth full*]. — I won't give 'em mine: but they can have another pot, you know. You have always got a basket with you, Mrs. Prior, I know you have. You had it that day you took the cold fowl.

MRS. P. — For the poor blind, black man! oh, how thankful he was!

GEORGE. — I don't know whether it was for a black man. Mary, get us another pot of marmalade.

MARY. — I don't know, Master George.

GEORGE. — I *will* have another pot of marmalade. If you don't, I'll — I'll smash every thing — I will.

BELLA. — Oh, you naughty, rude boy!

GEORGE. — Hold *your* tongue! I *will* have it. Mary shall go and get it.

MRS. P. — Do humor him, Mary; and I'm sure my poor children at home will be the better for it.

GEORGE. — There's your basket! now put this cake in, and this pat of butter, and this sugar. Hurray, hurray! Oh, what jolly fun! Tell Adolphus and Amelia I sent it to them — tell 'em they shall never want for any thing as long as George Kicklebury Milliken, Esq., can give it 'em. Did Adolphus like my gray coat that I didn't want?

MISS P. — You did not give him your new gray coat?

GEORGE. — Don't you speak to me; I'm going to school — I'm not going to have no more governesses soon.

MRS. P. — Oh, my dear Master George, what a nice coat it is, and how well my poor boy looked in it!

MISS P. — Don't, mamma! I pray and entreat you not to take the things!

Enter JOHN *from dining-room with a tray.*

JOHN. — Some cream, some jelly, a little champagne, Miss Prior; I thought you might like some.

GEORGE. — Oh, jolly! give us hold of the jelly! give us a glass of champagne.

JOHN. — I will not give you any.

GEORGE. — I'll smash every glass in the room if you don't; I'll cut my fingers; I'll poison myself — there! I'll eat all this sealing-wax if you don't, and it's rank poison, you know it is.

MRS. P. — My dear Master George! [*Exit* JOHN.]

GEORGE. — Ha, ha! I knew you'd give it me; another boy taught me that.

BELLA. — And a very naughty, rude boy.

GEORGE. — He, he, he! hold your tongue, Miss! And said he always got wine so; and so I used to do it to my poor mamma, Mrs. Prior. Usedn't to like mamma much.

BELLA. — Oh, you wicked boy!

GEORGY. — She usedn't to see us much. She used to say I tried her nerves: what's nerves, Mrs. Prior? Give us some more champagne! Will have it. Ha, ha, ha! ain't it jolly? Now I'll go out and have a run in the garden. [*Runs into garden.*]

MRS. P. — And you, my dear?

BELLA. — I shall go and resume the perusal of "The Pilgrim's Progress," which my grandpapa, Mr. Bonnington, sent me. [*Exit* ARABELLA.]

MISS P. — How those children are spoilt! Goodness, what can I do? If I correct one, he flies to grandmamma Kicklebury; if I speak to another, she appeals to grandmamma Bonnington. When I was alone with them, I had them in something like order. Now, between the one grandmother and the other, the children are going to ruin, and so would the house too, but that Howell — that odd, rude, but honest and intelligent creature, I must say — keeps it up. It is wonderful how a person in his rank of life should have instructed himself so. He really knows — I really think he knows more than I do myself.

MRS. P. — Julia, dear!

MISS P. — What is it, mamma?

MRS. P. — Your little sister wants some under-clothing sadly, Julia dear, and poor Adolphus's shoes are quite worn out.

MISS P. — I thought so: I have given you all I could, mamma.

MRS. P. — Yes, my love! you are

a good love, and generous, heaven knows, to your poor old mother who has seen better days. If we had not wanted, would I have ever allowed you to be a governess — a poor degraded governess? If that brute O'Reilly who lived on our second floor had not behaved so shamefully wicked to you, and married Miss Flack, the singer, might you not have been Editress of "The Champion of Liberty" at this very moment, and had your Opera box every night? [*She drinks champagne while talking, and excites herself.*]

Miss P. — Don't take that, mamma.

Mrs. P. — Don't take it? why, it costs nothing; Milliken can afford it. Do you suppose I get champagne every day? I might have had it as a girl when I first married your father, and we kep' our gig and horse, and lived at Clapham, and had the best of every thing. But the coal-trade is not what it was, Julia. We met with misfortunes, Julia, and we went into poverty: and your poor father went into the Bench for twenty-three months — two year all but a month he did — and my poor girl was obliged to dance at "The Coburg Theatre" — yes, you were, at ten shillings a week, in the Oriental ballet of "The Bulbul and the Rose:" you were, my poor darling child.

Miss P. — Hush, hush, mamma!

Mrs. P. — And we kep' a lodging-house in Bury Street, St. James's, which your father's brother furnished for us, who was an extensive oil-merchant. He brought you up; and afterwards he quarrelled with my poor James, Robert Prior did, and he died, not leaving us a shilling. And my dear eldest boy went into a wine-merchant's office: and my poor darling Julia became a governess, when you had had the best of education at Clapham; you had, Julia. And to think that you were obliged, my blessed thing, to go on in the Oriental ballet of "The Rose and the Bul" —

Miss P. — Mamma, hush, hush! forget that story.

Enter Page *from dining-room.*

Page. — Miss Prior! please, the ladies are coming from the dining-room. Mrs. B. have had her two glasses of port, and her ladyship is now a-telling the story about the Prince of Wales when she danced with him at Carlton House. [*Exit* Page.]

Miss P. — Quick, quick! There, take your basket! Put on your bonnet, and good-night, mamma. Here, here is a half-sovereign and three shillings; it is all the money I have in the world; take it, and buy the shoes for Adolphus.

Mrs. P. — And the under-clothing, my love — little Amelia's under-clothing?

Miss P. — We will see about it. Good-night [*kisses her*]. Don't be seen here, — Lady K. doesn't like it.

Enter Gentlemen *and* Ladies *from dining-room.*

Lady K. — We follow the Continental fashion. We don't sit after dinner, Captain Touchit.

Captain T. — Confound the Continental fashion! I like to sit a little while after dinner [*aside*].

Mrs. B. — So does my dear Mr. Bonnington, Captain Touchit. He likes a little port-wine after dinner.

Touchit. — I'm not surprised at it, ma'am.

Mrs. B. — When did you say your son was coming, Lady Kicklebury?

Lady K. — My Clarence! He will be here immediately, I hope, the dear boy. You know my Clarence?

Touchit. — Yes, ma'am.

Lady K. — And like him, I'm sure, Captain Touchit! Everybody does like Clarence Kicklebury.

Touchit. — The confounded young scamp! I say, Horace, do you like your brother-in-law?

Milliken. — Well — I — I can't say — I — like him — in fact, I don't. But that's no reason why his mother shouldn't. [*During this,* Howell *preceded by* BULKELEY, *hands round coffee. The garden without has darkened, as if evening.* BULKELEY *is going away without offering coffee to* Miss PRIOR. JOHN *stamps on his foot, and points to her.* Captain TOUCHIT, *laughing, goes up and talks to her now the servants are gone.*]

MRS. B. — Horace! I must tell you that the waste at your table is shocking. What is the need of opening all this wine? You and Lady Kicklebury were the only persons who took champagne.

TOUCHIT. — I never drink it — never touch the rubbish! Too old a stager!

LADY K. — Port, I think, is your favorite, Mrs. Bonnington?

MRS. B. — My dear lady, I do not mean that you should not have champagne, if you like. Pray, pray, don't be angry! But why on earth, for you, who take so little, and Horace, who only drinks it to keep you company, should not Howell open a pint instead of a great large bottle?

LADY K. — Oh, Howell! Howell! We must not mention Howell, my dear Mrs. Bonnington. Howell is faultless! Howell has the keys of every thing! Howell is not to be controlled in any thing! Howell is to be at liberty to be rude to my servant!

MILLIKEN. — Is that all? I am sure I should have thought your man was big enough to resent any rudeness from poor little Howell.

LADY K. — Horace! Excuse me for saying that you don't know — the — the class of servant to whom Bulkeley belongs. I had him, as a great favor, from Lord Toddleby. That class of servant is accustomed generally not to go out single.

MILLIKEN. — Unless they are two behind a carriage-perch they pine away, as one love-bird does without his mate!

LADY K. — No doubt! no doubt! I only say you are not accustomed here — in this kind of establishment, you understand — to that class of —

MRS. B. — Lady Kicklebury! is my son's establishment not good enough for any powdered monster in England? Is the house of a British merchant? —

LADY K. — My dear creature! my dear creature! it *is* the house of a British merchant, and a very comfortable house.

MRS. B.—Yes, as you find it.

LADY K. — Yes, as I find it, when I come to take care of my departed angel's children, Mrs. Bonnington — [*pointing to picture*] — of *that* dear seraph's orphans, Mrs. Bonnington. *You* cannot. You have other duties — other children — a husband at home in delicate health, who —

MRS. B. — Lady Kicklebury, no one shall say I don't take care of my dear husband!

MILLIKEN. — My dear mother! My dear Lady Kicklebury! [*To* T., *who has come forward.*] They spar so every night they meet, Touchit. Ain't it hard?

LADY K. — I say you *do* take care of Mr. Bonnington, Mrs. Bonnington, my dear creature! and that is why you can't attend to Horace. And as he is of a very easy temper — except sometimes with his poor Arabella's mother — he allows all his tradesmen to cheat him, all his servants to cheat him, Howell to be rude to everybody — to me amongst other people, and why not to my servant Bulkeley, with whom Lord Toddleby's groom of the chambers gave me the very highest character.

MRS. B. — I'm surprised that noblemen *have* grooms in their chambers. I should think they were much better in the stables. I am sure I always think so when we dine with Doctor Clinker. His man does bring such a smell of the stable with him.

LADY K. — He! he! you mistake, my dearest creature! Your poor mother mistakes, my good Horace. You have lived in a quiet and most respectable sphere — but not — not —

MRS. B. — Not what, Lady Kicklebury? We have lived at Richmond twenty years — in my late husband's time — when we saw a great deal of company, and when this dear Horace was a dear boy at Westminster School. And we have *paid* for every thing we have had for twenty years, and we have owed not a penny to any *tradesman*, though we mayn't have had *powdered footmen six feet high*, who were impertinent to all the maids in the place — don't! I *will* speak, Horace — but servants who loved us, and who lived in our families.

MILLIKEN. — Mamma, now, my dear, good old mother! I am sure Lady Kicklebury meant no harm.

LADY K. — Me! my dear Horace! harm! What harm could I mean?

MILLIKEN. — Come! let us have a game at whist. Touchit, will you make a fourth? They go on so every night almost. Ain't it a pity, now?

TOUCHIT. — Miss Prior generally plays, doesn't she?

MILLIKEN. — And a very good player, too. But I thought you might like it.

TOUCHIT. — Well, not exactly. I don't like sixpenny points, Horace, or quarrelling with old dragons about the odd trick. I will go and smoke a cigar on the terrace, and contemplate the silver Thames, the darkling woods, the starry hosts of heaven. I — I like smoking better than playing whist. [MILLIKEN *rings bell.*]

MILLIKEN. — Ah, George! you're not fit for domestic felicity.

TOUCHIT. — No, not exactly.

HOWELL *enters.*

MILLIKEN. — Lights and a whist-table. Oh, I see you bring 'em. You know every thing I want. He knows every thing I want, Howell does. Let us cut. Miss Prior, you and I are partners!

ACT II.

SCENE. — *As before.*

LADY K. — Don't smoke, you naughty boy. I don't like it. Besides, it will encourage your brother-in-law to smoke.

CLARENCE K. — Any thing to oblige you, I'm sure. But can't do without it, mother; it's good for my health. When I was in the Plungers, our doctor used to say, "You ought never to smoke more than eight cigars a day" — an order, you know, to do it — don't you see?

LADY K. — Ah, my child! I am very glad you are not with those unfortunate people in the East.

K. — So am I. Sold out just in time. Much better fun being here, than having the cholera at Scutari. Nice house, Milliken's. Snob, but good fellow — good cellar, doosid good cook. Really, that salmi yesterday, — couldn't have it better done at "The Rag" now. You have got into good quarters here, mother.

LADY K. — The meals are very good, and the house is very good; the manners are not of the first order. But what can you expect of city people? I always told your poor dear sister, when she married Mr. Milliken, that she might look for every thing substantial, — but not manners. Poor dear Arabella *would* marry him.

K. — Would! that is a good one, mamma! Why, you made her! It's a dozen years ago. But I recollect, when I came home from Eton, seeing her crying because Charley Tufton —

LADY K. — Mr. Tufton had not a shilling to bless himself with. The marriage was absurd and impossible.

K. — He hadn't a shilling then. I guess he has plenty now. Elder brother killed, out hunting. Father dead. Tuf a baronet, with four thousand a year if he's a shilling.

LADY K. — Not so much.

K. — Four thousand if it's a shilling. Why, the property adjoins Kicklebury's — I ought to know. I've shot over it a thousand times

Heh! *I* remember, when I was quite a young 'un, how Arabella used to go out into Tufton Park to meet Charley — and he is a doosid good fellow, and a gentlemanlike fellow, and a doosid deal better than this city fellow.

Lady K. — If you don't like this city fellow, Clarence, why do you come here? why didn't you stop with your elder brother at Kicklebury?

K. — Why didn't I? Why didn't *you* stop at Kicklebury, mamma? Because you had notice to quit. Serious daughter-in-law, quarrels about management of the house — row in the building. My brother interferes, and politely requests mamma to shorten her visit. So it is with your other two daughters; so it was with Arabella when she was alive. What shindies you used to have with her, Lady Kicklebury! Heh! I had a row with my brother and sister about a confounded little nursery-maid.

Lady K. — Clarence!

K. — And so I had notice to quit too. And I'm in very good quarters here, and I intend to stay in 'em, mamma. I say —

Lady K. — What do you say?

K. — Since I sold out, you know, and the regiment went abroad, confound me, the brutes at "The Rag" will hardly speak to me! I was so ill, I couldn't go. Who the doose can live the life I've led, and keep health enough for that infernal Crimea? Besides, how could I help it? I was so cursedly in debt that I was *obliged* to have the money, you know. *You* hadn't got any.

Lady K. — Not a halfpenny, my darling. I am dreadfully in debt myself.

K. — I know you are. So am I. My brother wouldn't give me any, not a dump. Hang him! Said he had his children to look to. Milliken wouldn't advance me any more — said I did him in that horse transaction. He! he! he! so I did! What had I to do but to sell out? And the fellows cut me, by Jove. Ain't it too bad? I'll take my name off "The Rag," I will, though.

Lady K. — We must sow our wild oats, and we must sober down; and we must live here, where the living is very good and very cheap, Clarence, you naughty boy! And we must get you a rich wife. Did you see at church yesterday that young woman in light green, with rather red hair and a pink bonnet?

K. — I was asleep, ma'am, most of the time, or I was bookin' up the odds for the Chester Cup. When I'm bookin' up, I think of nothin' else, ma'am,— nothin'.

Lady K. — That was Miss Brocksopp — Briggs, Brown and Brocksopp, the great sugar-bakers. They say she will have eighty thousand pound. We will ask her to dinner here.

K. — I say — why the doose do you have such old women to dinner here? Why don't you get some pretty girls? Such a set of confounded old frumps as eat Milliken's mutton I never saw. There's you, and his old mother Mrs. Bonnington, and old Mrs. Fogram, and old Miss What's-her-name, the woman with the squint eye, and that immense Mrs. Crowder. It's so stoopid, that if it weren't for Touchit coming down sometimes, and the billiards and boatin', I should die here — expire, by gad! Why don't you have some pretty women into the house, Lady Kicklebury?

Lady K. — Why! Do you think I want that picture taken down: and another Mrs. Milliken? Wisehead! If Horace married again, would he be your banker, and keep this house, now that ungrateful son of mine has turned me out of his? No pretty women shall come into the house whilst I am here.

K. — Governess seems a pretty woman: weak eyes, bad figure, poky, badly dressed, but doosid pretty woman.

Lady K. — Bah! There is no danger from *her*. She is a most

faithful creature, attached to me beyond every thing. And her eyes — her eyes are weak with crying for some young man who is in India. She has his miniature in her room, locked up in one of her drawers.

K. — Then how the doose did you come to see it?

LADY K. — We see a number of things, Clarence. Will you drive with me?

K. — Not as I knows on, thank you. No, Ma; drivin's *too* slow: and you're goin' to call on two or three old dowagers in the Park? Thank your ladyship for the delightful offer.

Enter JOHN.

JOHN. — Please, sir, here's the man with the bill for the boats; two pound three.

K. — Damn it, pay it — don't bother *me!*

JOHN. — Haven't got the money, sir.

LADY K. — Howell! I saw Mr. Milliken give you a check for twenty-five pounds before he went into town this morning. Look, sir [*runs, opens drawer, takes out check-book*]. There it is, marked, "Howell, 25*l.*"

JOHN. — Would your ladyship like to step down into my pantry and see what I've paid with the twenty-five pounds? Did my master leave any orders that your ladyship was to inspect my accounts?

LADY K. — Step down into the pantry! inspect your accounts? I never heard such impertinence. What do you mean, sir?

K. — Dammy, sir, what do you mean?

JOHN. — I thought, as her ladyship kept a heye over my master's private book, she might like to look at mine too.

LADY K. — Upon my word, this insolence is too much.

JOHN. — I beg your ladyship's pardon. I am sure I have said nothing.

K. — Said, sir! your manner is mutinous, by Jove, sir! if I had you in the regiment! —

JOHN. — I understood that you had left the regiment, sir, just before it went on the campaign, sir.

K. — Confound you, sir! [*Starts up.*]

LADY K. — Clarence, my child, my child!

JOHN. — Your ladyship needn't be alarmed; I'm a little man, my lady, but I don't think Mr. Clarence was a-goin' for to hit me, my lady; not before a lady, I'm sure. I suppose, sir, that you *won't* pay the boatman?

K. — No, sir, I won't pay him, nor any man who uses this sort of damned impertinence!

JOHN. — I told Rullocks, sir, I thought it was *jest* possible you wouldn't. [*Exit.*]

K. — That's a nice man, that is — an impudent villain!

LADY K. — Ruined by Horace's weakness. He ruins everybody, poor good-natured Horace!

K. — Why don't you get rid of the blackguard?

LADY K. — There is a time for all things, my dear. This man is very convenient to Horace. Mr. Milliken is exceedingly lazy, and Howell spares him a great deal of trouble. Some day or other I shall take all this domestic trouble off his hands. But not yet: your poor brother-in-law is restive, like many weak men. He is subjected to other influences: his odious mother thwarts me a great deal.

K. — Why, you used to be the dearest friends in the world. I recollect when I was at Eton —

LADY K. — Were; but friendship don't last forever. Mrs. Bonnington and I have had serious differences since I came to live here: she has a natural jealousy, perhaps, at my superintending her son's affairs. When she ceases to visit at the house, as she very possibly will, things will go more easily; and Mr. Howell will go too, you may depend upon it. I am always sorry when my temper breaks out, as it will sometimes.

K. — Won't it, that's all!

Lady K. — At his insolence, my temper is high; so is yours, my dear. Calm it for the present, especially as regards Howell.

K. — Gad! d'you know I was very nearly pitching into him? But once, one night in the Haymarket, at a lobster-shop, where I was with some fellows, we chaffed some other fellows, and there was one fellah — quite a little fellah — and I pitched into him, and he gave me the most confounded lickin' I ever had in my life, since my brother Kicklebury licked me when we were at Eton; and that, you see, was a lesson to me, ma'am. Never trust those little fellows, never chaff 'em: dammy, they may be boxers.

Lady K. — You quarrelsome boy! I remember you coming home with your naughty head *so* bruised. [*Looks at watch.*] I must go now to take my drive. [*Exit* Lady K.]

K. — I owe a doose of a tick at that billiard-room; I shall have that boatman dunnin' me. Why hasn't Milliken got any horses to ride? Hang him! suppose he can't ride — suppose he's a tailor. He ain't *my* tailor though, though I owe him a doosid deal of money. There goes mamma with that darling nephew and niece of mine. [*Enter* Bulkeley.] Why haven't you gone with my lady, you, sir? [*To* Bulkeley.]

Bulkeley. — My lady have a-took the pony-carriage, sir; Mrs. Bonnington have a-took the hopen carriage and 'orses, sir, this mornin', which the Bishop of London is 'olding a confirmation at Teddington, sir, and Mr. Bonnington is attending the serimony. And I have told Mr. 'Owell, sir, that my lady would prefer the hopen carriage, sir, which I like the hexercise myself, sir, and that the pony-carriage was good enough for Mrs. Bonnington, sir; and Mr. 'Owell was very hinsolent to me, sir; and I don't think I can stay in the 'ouse with him.

K. — Hold your jaw, sir.

Bulkeley. — Yes, sir. [*Exit* Bulkeley.]

K. — I wonder who that governess is? — sang rather prettily last night — wish she'd come and sing now — wish she'd come and amuse me — I've seen her face before — where have I seen her face? — it ain't at all a bad one. What shall I do? dammy, I'll read a book: I've not read a book this ever so long. What's here? [*looks amongst books, selects one, sinks down in easy-chair so as quite to be lost*].

Enter Miss Prior.

Miss Prior. — There's peace in the house! those noisy children are away with their grandmamma. The weather is beautiful, and I hope they will take a long drive. Now I can have a quiet half-hour, and finish that dear pretty "Ruth" — oh, how it makes me cry, that pretty story. *Lays down her bonnet on table — goes to glass — takes off cap and spectacles — arranges her hair — Clarence has got on chair looking at her.*)

K. — By Jove! I know who it is now! Remember her as well as possible. Four years ago, when little Foxbury used to dance in the ballet over the water. *Don't* I remember her! She boxed my ears behind the scenes, by jingo. [*Coming forwards.*] Miss Pemberton! Star of the ballet! Light of the harem! Don't you remember the grand Oriental ballet of "The Bulbul and the Peri"?

Miss P. — Oh! [*Screams.*] No, n — no, sir. You are mistaken: my name is Prior. I — never was at "The Coburg Theatre." I —

K. — [*seizing her hand.*] — No, you don't, though! What! don't you remember well that little hand slapping this face? which nature hadn't then adorned with whiskers, by gad! You pretend you have forgotten little Foxbury, whom Charley Calverley used to come after, and who used to drive to "The Coburg" every night in her brougham? How did you know it was "The Coburg"? That *is* a good one! *Had* you there, I think.

MISS P. — Sir, in the name of heaven, pity me! I have to keep my mother and my sisters and my brothers. When — when you saw me, we were in great poverty; and almost all the wretched earnings I made at that time were given to my poor father then lying in the Queen's Bench hard by. You know there was nothing against my character — you know there was not. Ask Captain Touchit whether I was not a good girl. It was he who brought me to this house.

K. — Touchit! the old villain!

MISS P. — I had your sister's confidence. I tended her abroad on her death-bed. I have brought up your nephew and niece. Ask any one if I have not been honest? As a man, as a gentleman, I entreat you to keep my secret! I implore you for the sake of my poor mother and her children! [*kneeling.*]

K. — by Jove! how handsome you are! How crying becomes your eyes! Get up, get up! Of course I'll keep your secret, but —

MISS P. — Ah! ah! [*She screams as he tries to embrace her.* HOWELL *rushes in.*]

HOWELL. — Hands off, you little villain! Stir a step and I'll kill you, if you were a regiment of captains! What! insult this lady who kept watch at your sister's death-bed and has took charge of her children! Don't be frightened, Miss Prior. Julia — dear, dear Julia — I'm by you. If the scoundrel touches you, I'll kill him. I — I love you — there — it's here — love you madly — with all my 'art — my a-heart!

MISS P. — Howell — for heaven's sake, Howell!

K. — Pooh — ooh! [*bursting with laughter*]. Here's a novel, by jingo! Here's John in love with the governess. Fond of plush, Miss Pemberton — ey? Gad, it's the best thing I ever knew. Saved a good bit, ey, Jeames? Take a public house? By Jove! I'll buy my beer there.

JOHN. — Owe for it, you mean. I don't think your tradesmen profit much by your custom, ex-Cornet Kicklebury.

K. — By Jove! I'll do for you, you villain!

JOHN. — No, not that way, Captain. [*Struggles with and throws him.*]

K. [*screams*]. — Hallo, Bulkeley! [BULKELEY *is seen strolling in the garden.*]

Enter BULKELEY.

BULKELEY. — What is it, sir?

K. — Take this confounded villain off me, and pitch him into the Thames — do you hear?

JOHN. — Come here, and I'll break every bone in your hulking body. [*To* BULKELEY.]

BULKELEY. — Come, come! what hever his hall this year row about?

MISS P. — For heaven's sake, don't strike that poor man.

BULKELEY. — *You* be quiet. What's he a hittin' about my master for?

JOHN. — Take off your hat, sir, when you speak to a lady. [*Takes up a poker.*] And now come on both of you, cowards! [*Rushes at* BULKELEY *and knocks his hat off his head.*]

BULKELEY [*stepping back*]. — If you'll put down that there poker, you know, then I'll pitch into you fast enough. But that there poker ain't fair, you know.

K. — You villain! Of course you will leave this house. And, Miss Prior, I think you understand that you will go too. I don't think my niece wants to learn *dancin'*, you understand. Good-by. Here, Bulkeley! [*Gets behind footman, and exit.*]

MISS P. — Do you know the meaning of that threat, Mr. Howell?

JOHN. — Yes, Miss Prior.

MISS P. — I was a dancer once, for three months, four years ago, when my poor father was in prison.

JOHN. — Yes, Miss Prior, I knew it. And I saw you a many times.

MISS P. — And you kept my secret?

JOHN. — Yes, Ju — Jul — Miss Prior.

MISS P. — Thank you, and God bless you, John Howell. There, there, you mustn't! indeed, you mustn't!

JOHN. — You don't remember the printer's boy who used to come to Mr. O'Reilly, and sit in your 'all in Bury Street, Miss Prior? I was that boy. I was a country-bred boy — that is if you call Putney country, and Wimbledon Common, and that. I served the Milliken family seven year. I went with Master Horace to college, and then I revolted against service, and I thought I'd be a man and turn printer like Dr. Frankling. And I got in an office; and I went with proofs to Mr. O'Reilly, and I saw you. And though I might have been in love with somebody else before I did — yet it was all hup when I saw you.

MISS P. [*kindly*]. — You must not talk to me in that way, John Howell.

JOHN. — Let's tell the tale out. I couldn't stand the newspaper night-work. I had a mother and brothers and sisters to keep, as you had. I went back to Horace Milliken, and said, "Sir, I've lost my work. I and mine want bread. Will you take me back again?" And he did. He's a kind, kind soul is my master.

MISS P. — He *is* a kind, kind soul.

JOHN. — He's good to all the poor. His hand's in his pocket for everybody. Everybody takes advantage of him. His mother-in-lor rides over him. So does his Ma. So do I, I may say; but that's over now; and you and I have had our notice to quit, Miss, I should say.

MISS P. — Yes.

JOHN. — I have saved a bit of money — not much — a hundred pound. Miss Prior — Julia — here I am — look — I'm a poor feller — a poor servant — but I've the heart of a man — and — I love you — oh! I love you!

MARY. — Oh — ho — ho! [MARY *has entered from garden, and bursts out crying.*]

MISS P. — It can't be, John Howell — my dear, brave, kind John Howell. It can't be. I have watched this for some time past, and poor Mary's despair here. [*Kisses* MARY, *who cries plentifully.*] You have the heart of a true, brave man, and must show it and prove it now. I am not — am not of your — pardon me for saying so — of your class in life. I was bred by my uncle, away from my poor parents, though I came back to them after his sudden death; and to poverty, and to this dependent life I am now leading. I am a servant like you, John, but in another sphere — have to seek another place now; and heaven knows if I shall procure one, now that that unlucky passage in my life is known. Oh the coward to recall it! the coward!

MARY. — But John whopped him, Miss! that he did. He gave it him well, John did. [*Crying.*]

MISS P. — You can't — you ought not to forego an attachment like that, John Howell. A more honest and true-hearted creature never breathed than Mary Barlow.

JOHN. — No, indeed.

MISS P. — She has loved you since she was a little child. And you loved her once, and do now, John.

MARY. — Oh, Miss! you hare a hangel, — I hallways said you were a hangel.

MISS P. — You are better than I am, my dear — much, much better than I am, John. The curse of my poverty has been that I have had to flatter and to dissemble, and hide the faults of those I wanted to help, and to smile when I was hurt, and laugh when I was sad, and to coax, and to tack, and to bide my time, — not with Mr. Milliken: he is all honor, and kindness, and simplicity. Who did *he* ever injure, or what unkind word did *he* ever say? But do you think, with the jealousy of those poor ladies over his house, I could have staid here without being a hypocrite to both of them? Go, John. My good, dear friend, John Howell, marry Mary. You'll be happier with her than with me. There! there! [*They embrace.*]

MARY. — O — o — o — ! I think I'll go and hiron hout Miss Harabella's frocks now [*Exit* MARY.]

Enter MILLIKEN *with* CLARENCE — *who is explaining things to him.*

CLARENCE. — Here they are, I give you my word of honor. Ask 'em, damn 'em.

MILLIKEN. — What is this I hear? You, John Howell, have dared to strike a gentleman under my roof! Your master's brother-in-law?

JOHN. — Yes, by Jove! and I'd do it again.

MILLIKEN. — Are you drunk or mad, Howell?

JOHN. — I'm as sober and as sensible as ever I was in my life, sir — I not only struck the master, but I struck the man, who's twice as big, only not quite as big a coward, I think.

MILLIKEN. — Hold your scurrilous tongue, sir! My good nature ruins everybody about me. Make up your accounts. Pack your trunks — and never let me see your face again.

JOHN. — Very good, sir.

MILLIKEN. — I suppose, Miss Prior, you will also be disposed to — to follow Mr. Howell?

MISS P. — To quit you, now you know what has passed? I never supposed it could be otherwise — I deceived you, Mr. Milliken — as I kept a secret from you, and must pay the penalty. It is a relief to me, the sword has been hanging over me. I wish I had told your poor wife, as I was often minded to do.

MILLIKEN. — Oh, you were minded to do it in Italy, were you?

MISS P. — Captain Touchit knew it, sir, all along: and that my motives, and, thank God, my life were honorable.

MILLIKEN. — Oh, Touchit knew it, did he? and thought it honorable — honorable. Ha! ha! to marry a footman — and keep a public-house? I — I beg your pardon, John Howell — I mean nothing against you, you know. You're an honorable man enough, except that you have been damned insolent to my brother-in-law.

JOHN. — Oh, heaven! [JOHN *strikes his forehead, and walks away.*]

MISS P. — You mistake me, sir. What I wished to speak of was the fact which this gentleman has no doubt communicated to you — that I danced on the stage for three months.

MILLIKEN. — Oh, yes. Oh, damme, yes. I forgot. I wasn't thinking of that.

KICKLEBURY. — You see she owns it.

MISS P. — We were in the depths of poverty. Our furniture and lodging-house under execution — from which Captain Touchit, when he came to know of our difficulties, nobly afterwards released us. My father was in prison, and wanted shillings for medicine, and I — I went and danced on the stage.

MILLIKEN. — Well?

MISS P. — And I kept the secret afterwards; knowing that I could never hope as governess to obtain a place after having been a stage-dancer.

MILLIKEN. — Of course you couldn't, — it's out of the question; and may I ask, are you going to resume that delightful profession when you enter the married state with Mr. Howell?

MISS P. — Poor John! it is not I who am going to — that is, it's Mary, the school-room maid.

MILLIKEN. — Eternal blazes! Have you turned Mormon, John Howell, and are you going to marry the whole house?

JOHN. — I made a hass of myself about Miss Prior. I couldn't help her being l — l — lovely.

KICK. — Gad, he proposed to her in my presence.

JOHN. — What I proposed to her, Cornet Clarence Kicklebury, was my heart, and my honor, and my best, and my every thing — and you — you wanted to take advantage of her secret, and you offered her indignities, and you laid a cowardly hand on her — a cowardly hand! — and I struck you, and I'd do it again.

MILLIKEN. — What? Is this true? [*Turning round very fiercely to K.*]

KICK. — Gad! Well — I only —

MILLIKEN. — You only what? You only insulted a lady under my roof — the friend and nurse of your dead sister — the guardian of my children. You only took advantage of a defenceless girl, and would have extorted your infernal pay out of her fear. You miserable sneak and coward!

KICK. — Hallo! Come, come! I say I won't stand this sort of chaff. Dammy, I'll send a friend to you!

MILLIKEN. — Go out of that window, sir. March! or I will tell my servant, John Howell, to kick you out, you wretched little scamp! Tell that big brute, — what's-his-name? — Lady Kicklebury's man, to pack this young man's portmanteau and bear's-grease pots; and if ever you enter these doors again, Clarence Kicklebury, by the heaven that made me! — by your sister who is dead! — I will cane your life out of your bones. Angel in heaven! Shade of my Arabella — to think that your brother in your house should be found to insult the guardian of your children!

JOHN. — By jingo, you're a good-plucked one! I knew he was, Miss, — I told you he was. [*Exit, shaking hands with his master, and with* Miss P., *and dancing for joy. Exit,* CLARENCE, *scared, out of window.*]

JOHN [*without*]. — Bulkeley, pack up the Capting's luggage!

MILLIKEN. — How can I ask your pardon, Miss Prior? In my wife's name I ask it — in the name of that angel whose dying-bed you watched and soothed — of the innocent children whom you have faithfully tended since.

MISS P. — Ah, sir! it is granted when you speak so to me.

MILLIKEN. — Eh, eh — d — don't call me sir!

MISS P. — It is for me to ask pardon for hiding what you know now: but if I had told you — you — you never would have taken me into your house — your wife never would.

MILLIKEN. — No, no. [*Weeping.*]

MISS P. — My dear, kind Captain Touchit knows it all. It was by his counsel I acted. He it was who relieved our distress. Ask him whether my conduct was not honorable — ask him whether my life was not devoted to my parents — ask him when — when I am gone.

MILLIKEN. — When you are gone, Julia! Why are you going? Why should you go, my love — that is — why need you go, in the devil's name?

MISS P. — Because, when your mother — when your mother-in-law comes to hear that your children's governess has been a dancer on the stage, they will send me away, and you will not have the power to resist them. They ought to send me away, sir; but I have acted honestly by the children and their poor mother, and you'll think of me kindly when — I — am — gone?

MILLIKEN. — Julia, my dearest — dear — noble — dar — the devil! here's old Kicklebury.

Enter LADY K., CHILDREN, *and* CLARENCE.

LADY K. — So, Miss Prior! this is what I hear, is it? A dancer in my house! a serpent in my bosom — poisoning — yes, poisoning those blessed children! — occasioning quarrels between my own son and my dearest son-in-law; flirting with the footman! When do you intend to leave, madam, the house which you have po — poll — luted?

MISS P. — I need no hard language, Lady Kicklebury: and I will reply to none. I have signified to Mr. Milliken my wish to leave his house.

MILLIKEN. — Not, not, if you will stay. [*To* Miss P.]

LADY K. — Stay, Horace! she

shall *never* stay as governess in this house!

MILLIKEN. — Julia! will you stay as mistress? You have known me for a year alone — before, not so well — when the house had a mistress that is gone. You know what my temper is, and that my tastes are simple, and my heart not unkind. I have watched you, and have never seen you out of temper, though you have been tried. I have long thought you good and beautiful, but I never thought to ask the question which I put to you now: — come in, sir! [*to* CLARENCE *at door*]: — now that you have been persecuted by those who ought to have upheld you, and insulted by those who owed you gratitude and respect. I am tired of their domination, and as weary of a man's cowardly impertinence [*to* CLARENCE] as of a woman's jealous tyranny. They have made what was my Arabella's home miserable by their oppression and their quarrels. Julia! my wife's friend, my children's friend! be mine, and make me happy! Don't leave me, Julia! say you won't — say you won't — dearest — dearest girl!

MISS P. — I won't — leave — you.

GEORGE [*without*]. — Oh, I say! Arabella, look here: here's papa a-kissing Miss Prior!

LADY K. — Horace — Clarence my son! Shade of my Arabella! can you behold this horrible scene, and not shudder in heaven! Bulkeley! Clarence! go for a doctor — go to Doctor Straitwaist at the Asylum — Horace Milliken, who has married the descendant of the Kickleburys of the Conqueror, marry a dancing-girl off the stage! Horace Milliken! do you wish to see me die in convulsions at your feet? I writhe there, I grovel there. Look! look at me on my knees! your own mother-in-law! drive away this fiend!

MILLIKEN. — Hem! I ought to thank you, Lady Kicklebury, for it is you that have given her to me.

LADY K. — He won't listen! he turns away and kisses her horrible hand. This will never do: help me up, Clarence, I must go and fetch his mother. Ah, ah! there she is, there she is! [Lady K. *rushes out, as the top of a barouche, with* Mr. *and* Mrs. BONNINGTON *and* Coachman, *is seen over the gate.*]

MRS. B. — What is this I hear, my son, my son? You are going to marry a — a stage-dancer? you are driving me mad, Horace!

MILLIKEN. — Give me my second chance, mother, to be happy. You have had yourself two chances.

MRS. B. — Speak to him, Mr. Bonnington. [BONNINGTON *makes dumb show.*]

LADY K. — Implore him, Mr. Bonnington.

MRS. B. — Pray, pray for him, Mr. Bonnington, my love — my lost, abandoned boy!

LADY K. — Oh, my poor dear Mrs. Bonnington!

MRS. B. — Oh, my poor dear Lady Kicklebury! [*They embrace each other.*]

LADY K. — I have been down on my knees to him, dearest Mrs. Bonnington.

MRS. B. — Let us both — both go down on our knees — I *will* [*to her husband*]. Edward, I will! [*Both ladies on their knees.* BONNINGTON *with outstretched hands behind them.*] Look, unhappy boy! look, Horace! two mothers on their wretched knees before you, imploring you to send away this monster! Speak to him, Mr. Bonnington. Edward! use authority with him, if he will not listen to his mother —

LADY K. — To his mothers!

Enter TOUCHIT.

TOUCHIT. — What is this comedy going on, ladies and gentlemen? The ladies on their elderly knees — Miss Prior with her hair down her back. Is it tragedy or comedy — is it a rehearsal for a charade, or are we acting for Horace's birthday? or, oh! — I beg your Reverence's pardon — you were perhaps going to a professional duty?

Mrs. B. — It's *we* who are praying this child, Touchit. This child, with whom you used to come home from Westminster when you were boys. You have influence with him; he listens to you. Entreat him to pause in his madness.

Touchit. — What madness?

Mrs. B. — That — that woman — that serpent yonder — that — that dancing-woman, whom you introduced to Arabella Milliken, — ah! and I rue the day: — Horace is going to mum — mum — marry her!

Touchit. — Well! I always thought he would. Ever since I saw him and her playing at whist together, when I came down here a month ago, I thought he would do it.

Mrs. B. — Oh, it's the whist, the whist! Why did I ever play at whist, Edward? My poor Mr. Milliken used to like his rubber.

Touchit. — Since he has been a widower —

Lady K. — A widower of that angel! [*Points to picture.*]

Touchit. — Pooh, pooh, angel! You two ladies have never given the poor fellow any peace. You were always quarrelling over him. You took possession of his house, bullied his servants, spoiled his children; you did, Lady Kicklebury.

Lady K. — Sir, you are a rude, low, presuming, vulgar man. Clarence! beat this rude man!

Touchit. — From what I have heard of your amiable son, he is not in the warlike line, I think. My dear Julia, I am delighted with all my heart that my old friend should have found a woman of sense, good conduct, good temper — a woman who has had many trials, and borne them with great patience — to take charge of him and make him happy. Horace, give me your hand! I knew Miss Prior in great poverty. I am sure she will bear as nobly her present good fortune; for good fortune it is to any woman to become the wife of such a loyal, honest, kindly gentleman as you are!

Enter John.

John. — If you please, my lady — if you please, sir — Bulkeley —

Lady K. — What of Bulkeley, sir?

John. — He has packed his things, and Cornet Kicklebury's things, my lady.

Milliken. — Let the fellow go.

John. — He won't go, sir, till my lady have paid him his book and wages. Here's the book, sir.

Lady K. — Insolence! quit my presence! And I, Mr. Milliken, will quit a house —

John. — Shall I call your ladyship a carriage?

Lady K. — Where I have met with rudeness, cruelty, and fiendish [*to* Miss P., *who smiles and courtesies*] — yes, fiendish ingratitude. I will go, I say, as soon as I have made arrangements for taking other lodgings. You cannot expect a lady of fashion to turn out like a servant.

John. — Hire "The Star and Garter" for her, sir. Send down to "The Castle;" any thing to get rid of her. I'll tell her maid to pack her traps. Pinhorn! [*Beckons maid and gives orders.*]

Touchit. — You had better go at once, my dear Lady Kicklebury.

Lady K. — Sir!

Touchit. — *The other mother-in-law is coming!* I met her on the road with all her family. He! he! he! [*Screams.*]

Enter Mrs. Prior *and* Children.

Mrs. P. — My lady! I hope your ladyship is quite well! Dear, kind Mrs. Bonnington! I came to pay my duty to you, ma'am. This is Charlotte, my lady — the great girl whom your ladyship so kindly promised the gown for; and this is my little girl, Mrs. Bonnington, ma'am, please; and this is my Bluecoat boy. Go and speak to dear, kind Mr. Milliken — our best friend and protector — the son and son-in-law of these dear ladies. Look, sir! He has brought his copy to show you. [Boy *shows copy.*] Ain't it creditable to a boy of his age, Captain Touchit? And my best and most grateful services to you, sir. Julia, Julia, my dear, where's your cap and spectacles, you stupid thing? You've let your hair drop down. What! what! — [*Begins to be puzzled.*]

MRS. B. — Is this collusion, madam?

MRS. P. — Collusion, dear Mrs. Bonnington!

LADY K. — Or insolence, Mrs. Prior?

MRS. P. — Insolence, your ladyship! What — what is it? what has happened? What's Julia's hair down for? Ah! you've not sent the poor girl away? the poor, poor child, and the poor, poor children!

TOUCHIT. — That dancing at the "Coburg" has come out, Mrs. Prior.

MRS. P. — Not the darling's fault. It was to help her poor father in prison. It was I who forced her to do it. Oh! don't, don't, dear Lady Kicklebury, take the bread out of the mouths of these poor orphans! [*Crying.*]

MILLIKEN. — Enough of this, Mrs. Prior: your daughter is not going away. Julia has promised to stay with me — and — never to leave me — as governess no longer, but as wife to me.

MRS. P. — Is it — is it true, Julia?

MISS P. — Yes, mamma.

MRS. P. — Oh! oh! oh! [*Flings down her umbrella, kisses* JULIA, *and running to* MILLIKEN,] My son, my son! Come here, children. Come, Adolphus, Amelia, Charlotte — kiss your dear brother, children. What my dears! How do you do, dears? [*to* MILLIKEN'S *children.*] Have they heard the news? And do you know that my daughter is going to be your mamma? There — there — go and play with your little uncles and aunts, that's good children! [*She motions off the* Children, *who retire towards garden. Her manner changes to one of great patronage and intense satisfaction.*] Most hot weather, your ladyship, I'm sure. Mr. Bonnington, you must find it hot weather for preachin'! Lor'! there's that little wretch beatin' Adolphus! George, sir! have done, sir! [*Runs to separate them.*] How ever shall we make those children agree, Julia?

MISS P. — They have been a little spoiled, and I think Mr. Milliken will send George and Arabella to school, mamma: will you not, Horace?

MR. MILLIKEN. — I think school will be the very best thing for them.

MRS. P. — And [Mrs. P. *whispers, pointing to her own children*] the blue room, the green room, the rooms old Lady Kick has — plenty of room for us, my dear!

MISS P. — No, mamma, I think it will be too large a party, — Mr. Milliken has often said that he would like to go abroad, and I hope that now he will be able to make his tour.

MRS. P. — Oh, then! we can live in the house, you know: what's the use of payin' lodgin', my dear?

MISS P. — The house is going to be painted. You had best live in your own house, mamma; and if you want any thing, Horace, Mr. Milliken, I am sure, will make it comfortable for you. He has had too many visitors of late, and will like a more quiet life, I think. Will you not?

MILLIKEN. — I shall like a life with *you*, Julia.

JOHN. — Cab, sir, for her ladyship!

LADY K. — This instant let me go! Call my people. Clarence, your arm! Bulkeley, Pinhorn! Mrs. Bonnington, I wish you good-morning! Arabella, angel! [*looks at picture*] I leave you. I shall come to you erelong. [*Exit, refusing* MILLIKEN'S *hand, passes up garden, with her servants following her.* MARY *and other servants of the house are collected together, whom* Lady K. *waves off.* Bluecoat boy *on wall, eating plums.* Page, *as she goes, cries, Hurray, hurray!* Bluecoat boy *cries, Hurray! When* Lady K. *is gone,* JOHN *advances.*]

JOHN. — I think I heard you say, sir, that it was your intention to go abroad?

MILLIKEN. — Yes; oh, yes! Are we going abroad, my Julia?

MISS P. — To settle matters, to have the house painted, and clear [*pointing to children, mother, &c.*] Don't you think it is the best thing that we can do?

MILLIKEN. — Surely, surely: we are going abroad. Howell, you will come with us of course, and with your experiences you will make a capital courier. Won't Howell make a capital courier, Julia? Good, honest fellow, John Howell. Beg your pardon for being so rude to you just now. But my temper is very hot, very!

JOHN [*laughing*]. — You are a Tartar, sir. Such a tyrant! isn't he, ma'am?

MISS P. — Well, no; I don't think you have a very bad temper, Mr. Milliken, a — Horace.

JOHN. — You must — take care of him — alone, Miss Prior — Julia — I mean Mrs. Milliken. Man and boy I've waited on him this fifteen year: with the exception of that trial at the printing-office, which — which I won't talk of *now*, madam. I never knew him angry; though many a time I have known him provoked. I never knew him say a hard word, though sometimes perhaps we've deserved it. Not often — such a good master as that is pretty sure of getting a good servant — that is, if a man has a heart in his bosom; and these things are found both in and out of livery. Yes, I have been a honest servant to him, — haven't I, Mr. Milliken?

MILLIKEN. — Indeed, yes, John.

JOHN. — And so has Mary Barlow. Mary, my dear! [MARY *comes forward.*] Will you allow me to introduce you, sir, to the futur' Mrs. Howell? — if Mr. Bonnington does *your* little business for you, as I dare say [*turning to* Mr. B.], hold gov'nor, you will! — Make it up with your poor son, Mrs. Bonnington, ma'am. You have took a second 'elpmate, why shouldn't Master Horace? [*to* Mrs. B.] He — he wants somebody to help him, and take care of him, more than you do.

TOUCHIT. — You never spoke a truer word in your life, Howell.

JOHN. — It's my general 'abit, Capting, to indulge in them sort of statements. A true friend I have been to my master, and a true friend I'll remain when he's my master no more.

MILLIKEN. — Why, John, you are not going to leave me?

JOHN. — It's best, sir, I should go. I — I'm not fit to be a servant in this house any longer. I wish to sit in my own little home, with my own little wife by my side. Poor dear! you've no conversation, Mary; but you're a good little soul. We've saved a hundred pound apiece, and if we want more, I know who won't grudge it us, a good feller — a good master — for whom I've saved many a hundred pound myself, and will take "The Milliken Arms" at old Pigeoncot — and once a year or so, at this hanniversary, we will pay our respects to you, sir, and madam. Perhaps we will bring some children with us, perhaps we will find some more in this villa. Bless 'em beforehand! Good-by, sir, and madam — come away, Mary! [*going*].

MRS. P. [*entering with clothes, &c.*] — She has not left a single thing in her room. Amelia, come here! this cloak will do capital for you, and this — this garment is the very thing for Adolphus. Oh, John! eh, Howell! will you please to see that my children have something to eat immediately! The Milliken children, I suppose, have dined already?

JOHN. — Yes, ma'am; certainly, ma'am.

MRS. P. — I see he is inclined to be civil to me *now!*

MISS P. — John Howell is about to leave us, mamma. He is engaged to Mary Barlow, and when we go away, he is going to set up housekeeping for himself. Good-by, and thank you, John Howell [*gives her hand to* JOHN, *but with great reserve of manner*]. You have been a kind and true friend to us — if ever we can serve you, count upon us — may he not, Mr. Milliken?

MILLIKEN. — Always, always.

MISS P. — But you will still wait upon us — upon Mr. Milliken, for a day or two, won't you, John? until we — until Mr. Milliken has found some one to replace you. He will never find any one more honest than you, and good, kind, little Mary. Thank you, Mary, for your goodness to the poor governess.

MARY. — Oh, miss! oh, mum! [MISS P. *kisses* MARY *patronizingly*.]

MISS P. [*to* JOHN]. — And after they have had some refreshment, get a cab for my brother and sisters, if you please, John. Don't you think that will be best, my — my dear?

MILLIKEN. — Of course, of course, dear Julia!

MISS P. — And, Captain Touchit, you will stay, I hope, and dine with Mr. Milliken? And, Mrs. Bonnington, if you will receive as a daughter one who has always had a sincere regard for you, I think you will aid in making your son happy, as I promise you with all my heart and all my life to endeavor to do. [MISS P. *and* M. *go up to* MRS. BONNINGTON.]

MRS. BONNINGTON. — Well, there then, since it must be so, bless you, my children.

TOUCHIT. — Spoken like a sensible woman! And now, as I do not wish to interrupt this felicity, I will go and dine at "The Star and Garter."

MISS P. — My dear Captain Touchit, not for worlds! Don't you know I mustn't be alone with Mr. Milliken until — until? —

MILLIKEN. — Until I am made the happiest man alive! And you will come down and see us often, Touchit, won't you? And we hope to see our friends here often. And we will have a little life and spirit and gayety in the place. Oh, mother! oh, George! oh, Julia! what a comfort it is to me to think that I am released from the tyranny of that terrible mother-in-law!

MRS. PRIOR. — Come in to your teas, children. Come this moment, I say. [*The* Children *pass, quarrelling, behind the characters,* MRS. PRIOR *summoning them;* JOHN *and* MARY *standing on each side of the dining-room door, as the curtain falls.*]

THE END.